Marcello La Rosa
Pnina Soffer (Eds.)

Business Process Management Workshops

BPM 2012 International Workshops
Tallinn, Estonia, September 3, 2012
Revised Papers

 Springer

Volume Editors

Marcello La Rosa
Queensland University of Technology
Brisbane, QLD, Australia
E-mail: m.larosa@qut.edu.au

Pnina Soffer
University of Haifa
Haifa, Israel
E-mail: spnina@is.haifa.ac.il

ISSN 1865-1348   e-ISSN 1865-1356
ISBN 978-3-642-36284-2   e-ISBN 978-3-642-36285-9
DOI 10.1007/978-3-642-36285-9
Springer Heidelberg Dordrecht London New York

Library of Congress Control Number: 2012956059

ACM Computing Classification (1998): J.1, H.4, D.2, J.3

Typesetting: Camera-ready by author, data conversion by Scientific Publishing Services, Chennai, India

Printed on acid-free paper

Springer is part of Springer Science+Business Media (www.springer.com)

Lecture Notes
in Business Information Processing   132

Foreword

This volume collects the proceedings of the workshops held on September 3, 2012, in conjunction with the 10th International Conference on Business Process Management (BPM 2012), which took place in Tallinn, Estonia. The proceedings are so-called post-workshop proceedings, in that the authors were allowed to revise and improve their papers after the workshops, so as to take into account the feedback obtained from the audience during their presentations.

The BPM conference is considered the leading research conference in this area, whose practicality appeals to researchers and practitioners alike. As such, BPM is perceived as a premium event to co-locate a workshop with – both by academia and by industry. The 2012 edition of the conference attracted 15 workshop proposals with topics ranging from well-established BPM areas, such as process design and process mining, to recent areas that are gaining growing interest from the research and industry communities, such as adaptive case management, artifact-centric BPM, process model collections, and more. Given the high quality of the submissions, selecting candidate workshops and assembling the best mix of workshops was not an easy task. Eventually, the following 13 workshops were selected for co-location with BPM 2012:

First International Workshop on Adaptive Case Management and Other Non-workflow Approaches to BPM (ACM 2012) – organized by Irina Rychkova, Ilia Bider, and Keith Swenson.

The goal of ACM 2012 was to bring together researchers and practitioners to discuss theoretical and practical problems and solutions in the area of non-workflow-based approaches to BPM in general, and adaptive case management (as a leading movement) in particular. This workshop aimed to promote new, non-traditional ways of modeling and controlling business processes, the ones that suit better the dynamic environment in which contemporary enterprises and public organizations function.

8th International Workshop on Business Process Design (BPD 2012) – organized by Marta Indulska, Michael Rosemann, and Michael zur Muehlen.

The BPD 2012 workshop was dedicated to improving the understanding, reliability, and quality of process design. The event was exclusively focused on the design, innovation, evaluation, and comparison of process improvement methods, tools, and techniques. In particular, the workshop sought papers that propose innovative approaches toward the design of processes and complementary artifacts (e.g., organizational design).

8th International Workshop on Business Process Intelligence (BPI 2012) – organized by Boudewijn van Dongen, Diogo Ferreira, and Barbara Weber.

BPI 2012 aimed to bring together practitioners and researchers from different communities such as BPM, information systems research, business administration, software engineering, artificial intelligence, process and data mining with the goal of providing a better understanding of techniques and algorithms to support a company's processes at build-time and the way they are handled at run-time.

5th International Workshop on Business Process Management and Social Software (BPMS2 2012) – organized by Selmin Nurcan and Rainer Schmidt.

The objective of BPMS2 2012 was to explore (1) how social software interacts with business process management; (2) how business process management has to change to comply with social software and business processes may profit from social software and social media; and (3) how those new opportunities offered by social software impact the design, development, software support, and continuous improvement of business processes.

First International Workshop on Data- and Artifact-Centric BPM (DAB 2012) – organized by Lior Limonad, Boudewijn van Dongen, Jianwen Su, and Roman Vaculin.

DAB 2012 was the first workshop aimed at bringing together researchers and practitioners whose common interests are in study and development of data- and artifact-centric approaches to BPM. Recently, various approaches such as case-management and artifact-centric BPM have emerged, emphasizing the integration of data and control as key aspects of flexible and rich business-process specification. Consequently, studying the fundamental relationships and properties of the integrated perspective where data and process are considered together was set as the focal point of DAB.

6th International Workshop on Event-Driven Business Process Management (edBPM 2012) – organized by Nenad Stojanovic, Opher Etzion, Adrian Paschke, and Christian Janiesch.

edBPM 2012 was focused on applying methods and techniques from the real-time data/stream processing in the BPM domain, enabling more agile, flexible, and responsive business processes. The idea was to enable a smooth integration of the processing of real-time information, sensed in the process as well as from the business environment, in the business logic. The topics covered new concepts for designing, realizing, and managing such systems, including the presentation and analysis of existing solutions. The main goal was to enable of sharing the new ideas and defining of new challenges for this emerging research and application domain.

Third International Workshop on Empirical Research in Business Process Management (ER-BPM 2012) – organized by Bela Mutschler, Jan Recker, and Roel Wieringa.

ER-BPM 2012 stimulated empirical research that can contribute to a better understanding of the problems, challenges, and existing solutions in the BPM field. The workshop provided an interdisciplinary forum for both researchers and practitioners to improve the understanding of BPM-specific requirements, methods and theories, as well as tools and techniques.

Second International Workshop on Process Model Collections (PMC 2012) – organized by Hajo Reijers, Mathias Weske, and Remco Dijkman.

PMC 2012 aimed to discuss novel research in the area of managing business process model collections. Currently, organizations, reaching higher levels of business process management maturity, tend to collect large numbers of business process models, which may amount to hundreds of models. The workshop discussed challenges related to management and utilization of such model collections.

Second International Workshop on Process-Aware Logistics Systems (PALS 2011) – organized by Kamel Barkaoui, Virginia Dignum, Huib Aldewereld, Walid Gaaloul, Cherif Sadfi, and Ichiro Satoh.

PALS 2012 dealt with problems related to the design and optimization of global logistics systems, from a business process management perspective. It was dedicated to exploring and mastering the tools needed for operating, reconfiguring, and in general making decisions within logistics-based systems, in order to provide the customers and system users with the greatest possible value. PALS provided the participants with a perspective on the tools that are now available for modeling and solving logistics-oriented problems on a large-scale, and with an emphasis on the business process and information technology perspectives.

Joint Workshop on Process-Oriented Information Systems in Healthcare (Pro-Health) and Knowledge Representation for Health Care (KRH4C) – organized by Richard Lenz, Silvia Miksch, Mor Peleg, Manfred Reichert, David Riaño, and Annette ten Teije.

This workshop brought together researchers from two communities facing similar challenges to improve the understanding of domain-specific requirements, theories, methods, and tools. Both communities have been addressing the unique characteristics of healthcare processes and clinical-guideline-based decision-support systems, including their high degree of flexibility, the integration with electronic medical records and shared semantics of healthcare domain concepts, and the need for tight cooperation and communication among medical care teams.

The papers of this workshop appeared in separate proceedings and are thus not included in this volume.

Third International Workshop on Reuse in Business Process Management (rBPM 2012) – organized by Marcelo Fantinato, Maria Beatriz Felgar de Toledo, Itana Maria de Souza Gimenes, Lucineia Heloisa Thom, and Cirano Iochpe.

rBPM 2011 focused on exploring any type of reuse in the BPM domain at its various levels: the basic service-oriented foundation composition level; the management and monitoring upper level; and the quality of service and semantics orthogonal level.

First Joint International Workshop on Security in Business Processes (SBP 2012) – organized by Peter Karpati, Marco Montali, Rafael Accorsi, and Raimundas Matulevicius.

SBP 2012 aimed to bring together researchers and practitioners working toward the reliable security management of business process models in process-aware information systems. SBP 2012 encouraged innovative methods for business process security audit and control along the entire business process life cycle, welcoming contributions beyond the strictly technical character, considering economic, legal, and standardization issues.

First International Workshop on Theory and Applications of Process Visualization (TAProViz 2012) – organized by Ross Brown, Simone Kriglstein, and Stefanie Rinderle-Ma.

TAProViz 2012 intended to promote and nurture the development of process visualization topics as continuing research areas. To date, many process model representations have not developed beyond minimally interactive 2D representations of directed graphs. In the workshop, research in computer–human interaction, games, and interactive entertainment was extended toward BPM to engage, provide insight, and to promote collaboration.

With these 13 workshops, the BPM 2012 workshop program was rich and stimulating with a variety of topics, and formed an extraordinary and balanced program of high-quality events. BPM 2012 had more than 250 participants including both researchers and practitioners. In total, 141 papers were submitted to the various workshops, from which 80 were selected for presentation. The papers that were presented in the workshops report innovative and state-of-the-art advancements in the BPM area, spanning from formal to conceptual and empirical research. We are confident the reader will enjoy this volume as much as we enjoyed organizing this outstanding program and assembling its proceedings.

Finally, we did not organize everything on our own. Many people of the BPM 2012 Organizing Committee contributed to the success of the workshop program. We would particularly like to thank the General Chair, Marlon Dumas, for involving us in this unique event, the Local Organization Chairs, Raimundas Matulevicius, Laura Kalda, and Georg Singer, for the smooth management of all on-site issues, and the workshop organizers for managing their workshops and diligently answering the wealth of emails we sent around. Last but not least, we would like to thank the authors of the various workshop papers for making all this possible.

September 2012

Marcello La Rosa
Pnina Soffer

Preface

The following preface is a collection of the prefaces of the post-workshop proceedings of the individual workshops. The workshop papers, grouped by event, form the body of the volume.

First International Workshop on Adaptive Case Management and Other Non-Workflow Approaches to BPM (ACM 2012)

Organizers: Irina Rychkova, Ilia Bider, Keith D. Swenson

Introduction

The sign of our times is the amazing speed with which changes in the business world happen. This requires from the enterprises of today, and even more of the future, to become agile, i.e., capable of adjusting themselves to changes in the surrounding world. At the same time, current process thinking is mostly preoccupied with the issue of optimizing performance through standardization, specialization, and automation. A focus on optimization has resulted in the workflow view (in which a process is considered as a flow of operations) emerging as predominant in the field of business process management (BPM). An optimized workflow constitutes a completely prescriptive definition of the process execution rules. Besides requiring a long time to develop, such execution rules can reduce the creativity of people participating in the process and thereby result in poor performance.

A focus on agility requires a paradigm shift in BPM that promotes process execution rules being less prescriptive to give people the opportunity to creatively use their knowledge and experience in volatile environments. Here, we need to move from workflow-based process management to constraint-based process management. The constraint-based process management should focus on more declarative definition of execution rules, i.e., a combination of guidelines and restrictions.

The needs for the paradigm shift have already been identified by practitioners. This shift can also be seen in a strong practical movement appearing called adaptive case management (ACM), which "[...] is information technology that exposes structured and unstructured business information (business data and content) and allows structured (business) and unstructured (social) organizations to execute work (routine and emergent processes) in a secure but transparent manner" (http://www.xpdl.org/ nugen/p/adaptive-case-management/public.htm).

Goal

While practitioners are trying to overcome the restrictions of workflow thinking, the research on the topic is somewhat lagging. The goal of this workshop is to bring together researchers and practitioners to discuss theoretical and practical problems and solutions in the area of unpredictable processes. This workshop aims to promote new, non-traditional ways of supporting volatile work that better suit the dynamic environment in which contemporary enterprises and public organizations function.

Submissions, Organization, and Attendees

For this first edition of the workshop we received 13 submissions. After the reviewing process, six full papers and three short papers were accepted. The workshop was attended by 22 participants, including eight speakers. Exactly half of the participants were from universities, while the other half represented industry or industrial research. The papers were presented in three sections:

1st section: Idea papers reporting on university research
2st section: Experience reports on case management solutions
3rd section: Critics on the conventional BPM approaches.

Ilia Bider opened the workshop with a keynote talk and Keith Swenson and Sandy Kemsley closed the event driving a wrap-up panel discussion. The objective of this discussion was to outline the roadmap of the future research in the area of ACM. The following sections present a summary of the workshop presentations.

Idea Papers Reporting on University Research

Ilia Bider started with a keynote talk "Towards a Non-workflow Theory of Business Processes." He models enterprises as complex multilevel adaptable systems using systems theory. According to this theory, process instances are represented as moving through state space, and the process model is represented as a set of formal rules describing the valid paths of the possible trajectories.

Lars Taxén presented his idea paper "Adaptive Case Management from the Activity Modality Perspective." He proposes to use six activity modalities in order to model any situation where people are accomplishing goals. These modalities are: objectivation, contextualization, spatialization, temporalization, stabilization, and transition. Defined by neural science, these modalities represent a – natural to a human brain – framework for capturing and understanding the activities. Traditional workflow style BPM has focused primarily on the temporalization modality; but highly volatile unpredictable work requires other modalities to be considered.

Nicolas Mundbrod presented "Toward a System Support of Collaborative Knowledge Work." Much of the ACM literature has focused on knowledge workers coordinating work. The paper discusses collaboration on knowledge work tasks and aspects of uncertainty, goal orientation, emergence of work, and growing knowledge base. The authors measure collaborative knowledge work using nine dimensions: knowledge action types, methodology, interdisciplinary, organizational frame, spatial proximity, involved knowledge workers, temporary constraints, information interdependency, and number of repetitions.

Irina Rychkova presented "Toward Automated Support for Case Management Processes with Declarative Configurable Specifications" covering her attempt to model a mortgage application process with BPMN and finding a number of challenges. Among her findings is that the problem is not with the BPMN language itself, but with the imperative modeling style – traditionally associated with BPMN – that consists of putting tasks in a specific order. Instead we need a declarative style where tasks can be defined without explicit ordering, but with rules that allow tasks to be dynamically enabled and disabled based on conditions.

Experience Reports on Case Management Solutions

Helle Frisak Sem presented "On Two Approaches to ACM" that details the system — in production at the Norwegian Food Safety Authority (NFSA) — for food safety inspections, information and investigations. There are two approaches built into this system: one for controlling and scheduling more regular tasks, and another for handling emergencies in a much more flexible manner.

Rüdiger Pryss presented "Mobile Task Management for Medical Ward Rounds — The MEDo Approach." He describes a mobile task management system for medical ward rounds that is currently adopted by several medical hospitals in Germany. After finding that a traditional workflow approach did not match the needs of the doctors, they switched to more flexible tasklist-oriented approach. Collaborative design with medical personnel and subsequent work on improving usability of the system represented the major issues.

"Data Centric BPM and the Emerging Case Management Standard: A Short Survey" covers the current state of the evolving case management model and notation effort at the OMG.

Critics on the Conventional BPM Approaches

Keith Swenson asked whether "BPMN Is Incompatible with ACM." According to Keith, not BPMN per se, but any two-dimensional graphical language is questioned on the basis of usability and practicality for a knowledge worker. He outlines three key design requirements that must be met: the knowledge worker must be able to design quickly, must not require training that detracts from focusing on their profession, and the resulting notation must not have hidden dependencies. These criteria were never considered in the design of traditional BPM graphical languages.

Ilia Bider asked "Do Workflow-Based Systems Satisfy the Demands of the Agile Enterprise of the Future?" According to Ilia, business agility will become one of the most important properties of the next-generation enterprises. He shows that designing and putting into operation workflowable processes may neither be possible nor desirable in the enterprise of the future. This conclusion should have an impact on the software tools, systems, and services aimed at supporting business processes.

Conclusion

This workshop paves the way for a line of reasoning and research into the areas of unpredictable (knowledge-driven) work that is hard to support with traditional workflow-oriented BPM approaches. As a conclusion of the event, we outlined the roadmap for future research asking the following questions: What really constitutes knowledge work? How much technical training should be necessary to draw a workflow diagram? Is modeling in the traditional sense needed at all? How many different ACM approaches exist today, and how are they compared? What is the proper level of detail? How much data modeling is required? What are the adoption rates for case management solutions and what affects this rate? What role does usability play in adoption of ACM? And ultimately, what is the return on investment of supporting knowledge work in a case management environment? It is the sincere desire of the Program Committee and all attendees that this work can continue to answer some of these open questions.

September 2012

Irina Rychkova
Ilia Bider
Keith D. Swenson

Program Committee

Birger Andersson	DSV SU, Stockholm, Sweden
Ilia Bider	DSV SU/Ibissoft , Stockholm, Sweden
Karsten Böhm	FH KufsteinTirol, University of Applied Sciences, Austria
Paul Johannesson	DSV SU, Stockholm, Sweden
Erik Perjons	DSV SU, Stockholm, Sweden
Gil Regev	Ecole Polytechnique Fédérale de Lausanne, Switzerland
Colette Rolland	University of Paris 1 Pantheon Sorbonne, France
Irina Rychkova	University of Paris 1 Pantheon Sorbonne, France
Gregor Scheithauer	Siemens AG
Keith Swenson	Fujitsu America, USA
Lars Taxén	Linköping University, Linköping, Sweden

Alain Wegmann	Ecole Polytechnique Fédérale de Lausanne, Switzerland
Judith Barrios Albornoz	University of Los Andes, Systems Engineering School, Venezuela
Rebecca Deneckere	Centre de Recherches en Informatique, University of Paris 1 Pantheon-Sorbonne
Elena Kornyshova	Centre de Recherches en Informatique, University of Paris 1 Pantheon-Sorbonne
Rainer Schmidt	Aalen University, Germany
Jelena Zdravkovic	Stockholm University, Sweden

8th International Workshop on Business Process Design (BPD 2012)

Organizers: Marta Indulska, Michael zur Muehlen, Michael Rosemann

This year marked the 8th consecutive year of the International Workshop on Business Process Design (BPD), which was organized in conjunction with the 10th International Conference on Business Process Management, in Tallinn, Estonia. The workshop was initiated on the recognition that the act of designing processes is a challenging task and requires an understanding of organizational strategies, goals, constraints, and IT capabilities, to name just a few. This task is the most value-adding, and likely the most exciting step in the process life cycle, yet it has attracted limited academic contributions. Accordingly, the BPD workshop continues to provide a forum for researchers interested in all aspects of design, innovation, evaluation, and comparison of process improvement techniques and tools.

The opening of BPD2012 was a keynote presentation on the topic of "Design Is How We Change the World." In this talk, Michael zur Muehlen distinguished process design as a creative activity from process engineering as a goal-seeking activity. He highlighted the need to separate the concept of a design space, which encompasses possible process solutions, from the concept of an evaluation space, which ranks these solutions along multiple evaluation dimensions.

This year, five research papers were accepted for publication at BPD2012. The paper selection was based on a rigorous review process, which resulted in a 50% acceptance rate. The five papers included in this volume cover the quality of process models; improving the assignment of resources to activities; representing knowledge-intensive processes; managing business process management systems; and the organizational adoption of business process management. As Organizing Chairs of the BPD workshop, we would like to sincerely thank the members of the Program Committee for their thorough reviews of the submissions. We would like to extend our thanks to the authors for their presentations, and to all participants of the workshop for their comments on the presented papers.

September 2012   Marta Indulska
                                                          Michael zur Muehlen
                                                           Michael Rosemann

Program Committee

8th International Workshop on Business Process Intelligence (BPI 2012)

Organizers: Boudewijn van Dongen, Diogo R. Ferreira, Barbara Weber

Business process intelligence (BPI) is an area that is quickly gaining interest and importance in industry and research. BPI refers to the application of various measurement and analysis techniques in the area of business process management. In practice, BPI is embodied in tools for managing process execution quality by offering several features such as analysis, prediction, monitoring, control, and optimization.

The goal of this workshop is to promote a better understanding of the techniques and algorithms to support business processes at design-time and the way they are handled at runtime. We aim to bring together practitioners and researchers from different communities, e.g., business process management, information systems, database systems, business administration, software engineering, artificial intelligence, and data mining, who share an interest in the analysis and optimization of business processes and process-aware information systems. The workshop aims at discussing the current state of ongoing research and sharing practical experiences, exchanging ideas, and setting up future research directions that better respond to real needs. In a nutshell, it serves as a forum for shaping the BPI area.

The 8th edition of this workshop attracted 17 international submissions. Each paper was reviewed by at least three members of the Program Committee. From these submissions, the top five were accepted as full papers and, in addition, another three interesting submissions were accepted as short papers for presentation at the workshop.

The papers presented at the workshop provide a mix of novel research ideas, evaluations of existing process mining techniques, as well as new tool support. The paper by Adriansyah, Munoz-Gama, Carmona, and van Dongen is motivated by the need to measure the conformance of an event log with respect to a predefined process model and presents a method for measuring precision based on the alignment between the event log and the process model. Ferreira, Szimanski, and Ralha propose a method for discovering the relationships between micro-level events recorded in an event log and the macro-level activities in a business process. Goel, Bhat, and Weber describe a non-intrusive technique to discover end-to-end processes from process-unaware systems. Suriadi, Ouyang, van der Aalst, and ter Hofstede address the use of event logs for root cause analysis and propose a systematic technique for enriching and transforming event logs with attributes required for such analysis. Claes and Poels present the results of an exploratory survey on the adoption of process mining tools and the usage of the process mining framework ProM. Esposito, Vaz, Rodrigues, and Souza present the MANA tool for mining unstructured business processes. Verbeek and van der Aalst provide an experimental evaluation of a process mining technique based on integer liner programming enhanced with passage-based discovery. Finally, Pika, van der Aalst, Fidge, ter Hofstede, and Wynn introduce an approach to predict the risk of deadline transgressions in business processes based on indicators that can be obtained from event logs.

For the second time, the workshop was accompanied by the BPI challenge, a process mining contest based on a real-world event log. In this year's challenge, an event log from a Dutch financial institute was made available and participants were asked to extract as much information as possible from this log. We invited the jury to comment on the submissions and our sponsors – Perceptive Software and Fluxicon – provided prizes for the best submission and for all other participants.

In total, six submissions were received, all of which were of very high quality. The jury selected the submission by A.D. Bautista, L. Wangikar, and S.M. Kumail Akbar from CKM Advisors, New York. According to the jury, "their submission shows a very results-driven method of analyzing, where every analysis seemed to be driven by the motivation to prove/disprove a specific hypothesis, related to a concrete and actionable improvement potential in the client company. This results in a successful conversion of analysis to digestible business-level results and recommendations."

The winner received a new iPad, combined with a license for Disco Enterprise, a process mining tool from Fluxicon, and all other participants received licenses for Disco Professional. A two-page abstract of five of the submissions is included in these proceedings.

As with previous editions of the workshop, we hope that the reader will find this selection of papers useful to keep track of the latest advances in the area of business process intelligence, and we look forward to keep bringing new advances in future editions of the BPI workshop.

September 2012

Boudewijn van Dongen
Diogo R. Ferreira
Barbara Weber

Program Committee

Wil van der Aalst	Eindhoven University of Technology, The Netherlands
Boualem Benatallah	University of New South Wales, Australia
Jagadeesh Chandra Bose	Eindhoven University of Technology, The Netherlands
Peter Dadam	University of Ulm, Germany
Walid Gaaloul	Insitut Telecom, France
Gianluigi Greco	University of Calabria, Italy
Daniela Grigori	University of Versailles St-Quentin an Yvelines, France
Antonella Guzzo	University of Calabria, Italy

Michael Leyer	Frankfurt School of Finance and Management, Germany
Jan Mendling	Wirtschafts Universität Wien, Austria
Oscar Pastor	University of Valencia, Spain
Viara Popova	Tallinn University of Technology, Estonia
Manfred Reichert	University of Ulm, Germany
Michael Rosemann	Queensland University of Technology, Australia
Anne Rozinat	Fluxicon, The Netherlands
Phina Soffer	University of Haita, Israel
Alessandro Sperduti	Padua University, Italy
Hans Weigand	University of Tilburg, The Netherlands
Ton Weijters	Eindhoven University of Technology, The Netherlands
Mathias Weske	Hasso Plattner Institute at University of Potsdam, Germany

5th International Workshop on Business Process Management and Social Software (BPMS2 2012)

Organizers: Selmin Nurcan, Rainer Schmidt

Social software[1] is a new paradigm that is spreading quickly in society, organizations, and economics. Social software has created a multitude of success stories such as wikipedia.org. Therefore, more and more enterprises regard social software as a means for further improvement of their business processes and business models. For example, they integrate their customers into product development by using blogs to capture ideas for new products and features. Thus, business processes have to be adapted to new communication patterns between customers and the enterprise: for example, the communication with the customer is increasingly a bi-directional communication with the customer and among the customers. Social software also offers new possibilities to enhance business processes by improving the exchange of knowledge and information, to speed up decisions, etc.

Social software is based on four principles: weak ties, social production, egalitarianism, and mutual service provisioning.

Weak Ties[2]: Weak-ties are spontaneously established contacts between individuals that create new views and allow combining of competencies. Social software supports the creation of weak ties by helping to create contacts in impulse between non-predetermined individuals

Social Production[3,4]: Social Production is the creation of artifacts, by combining the input from independent contributors without predetermining the way to do this. By this means it is possible to integrate new and innovative contributions not identified or planned in advance. Social mechanisms such as reputation assure quality in social production in an a posteriori approach by enabling a collective evaluation by all participants.

Egalitarianism: Egalitarianism is the notion of handling individuals equally. Social software highly relies on egalitarianism and therefore strives to give all participants the same rights to contribute. This is done with the intention of encouraging a maximum of contributors and getting the best solution fusing a high number of contributions, thus enabling the wisdom of the crowds. Social software realizes egalitarianism by abolishing hierarchical structures, merging the roles of contributors and consumers and introducing a culture of trust.

Mutual Service Provisioning: Social software abolishes the separation of service provider and consumer by introducing the idea that service provisioning

---

[1] R. Schmidt and S. Nurcan, "BPM and Social Software," Business Process Management Workshops, 2009, pp. 649-658.

[2] M.S. Granovetter, "The Strength of Weak Ties," American Journal of Sociology, vol. 78, 1973, S. 1360.

[3] Y. Benkler, The Wealth of Networks: How Social Production Transforms Markets and Freedom, Yale University Press, 2006.

[4] J. Surowiecki, The Wisdom of Crowds, Anchor, 2005.

is a mutual process of service exchange. Thus both service provider and consumer (or better prosumer) provide services to one another in order co-create value. This mutual service provisioning contrasts the idea of industrial service provisioning, where services are produced in separation from the customer to achieve scaling effects.

To date, the interaction of social software and its underlying paradigms with business processes have not been investigated in depth. Therefore, the objective of the workshop is to explore how social software interacts with business process management, how business process management has to change to comply with weak ties, social production, egalitarianism, and mutual service, and how business processes may profit from these principles.

The workshop discussed three topics:

1. New opportunities provided by social software for BPM
2. Engineering next generation of business processes: BPM 2.0?
3. Business process implementation support by social software

Based on the successful BPMS2 2008, BPMS2 2009, BPMS2 2010, BPMS2 2011 workshops, the goal of the workshop is to promote the integration of business process management with social software and to enlarge the community pursuing the theme.

Six papers were accepted for presentation. In his paper "Application and Simplification of BPM Techniques for Personal Process Management," Marco Brambilla identified the socialization of task management as an important issue. Therefore, his paper gives a vision toward the application of BPM techniques and tools to personal task management. By this means, the interactions, dependencies, and constraints between tasks can be handled in a structured way.

Rainer Schmidt shows in his paper how data created within social software, called social data, can be used to support product innovation, marketing, and customer relations. Social data are created by the core mechanisms of social software: social production, weak ties, and collective decisions. They allow for the innovation of products more thoroughly and rapidly than before. Customer requirements can be identified better than before when using social data. Also, relevant events in the relationship between customer and enterprise can be detected earlier and more reliably.

In the paper "A Conceptual Approach to Characterize Dynamic Communities in Social Networks: Application to Business Process Management" from Cassio Melo, Bénédicte Le Grand, and Marie-Aude Aufaure, measures based on formal concept analysis are used to determine the conceptual proximity between people. Significant insights into trends and market behavior can be obtained from analyzing the evolution of this proximity measure. A case study on Twitter exemplifies the research.

There are still many tasks that require human intelligence instead of digital-based computation. The paper from Pavel Kucherbaev, Stefano Tranquillini,

Florian Daniel, Fabio Casati, Maurizio Marchese, Marco Brambilla, and Piero Fraternali, "Business Processes for the Crowd Computer," introduces the idea of a crowd computer. The authors describe both the architecture and a crowd programming interface. Furthermore, they show how such a crowd computer can be programmed and identify patterns for crowdsourcing.

Seyed Alireza Hajimirsadeghi, Hye-Young Paik, and John Andrew Shepherd introduce processbooks as means for social network-based personal process management. They start from the observation that many individual processes are codified via websites. Users have to discover and integrate these processes in order to accomplish their personal goals. The authors introduce so-called processbooks to extract personal process models from online sources. The extracted processes can be customized, maintained, and shared with other users. Process books also support the execution of personal processes.

Ralf Laue and Michael Becker introduce a new approach for comparing business process models in their paper "Evaluating Social Tagging for Business Process Models." Social tagging enriches models with words or short phrases describing the content of the models. Social tagging creates a new way for comparing and searching for business process models. Furthermore, the authors compare social tagging with established approaches that use named elements and model structure.

We wish to thank all authors for having shared their work with us, as well as the members of the BPMS2 2012 Program Committee and the workshop organizers of BPM 2012 for their help with the organization of the workshop.

September 2012   Selmin Nurcan
                                                              Rainer Schmidt

Program Committee

Ilia Bider	IbisSoft, Sweden
Arndt Borgmeier	Aalen University, Germany
Jan Bosch	Intuit, Mountain View, California, USA
Marco Brambilla	Politecnico di Milano, Italy
Piero Fraternali	Politecnico di Milano, Italy
Dragan Gasevic	School of Computing and Information Systems, Athabasca University, Canada
Chihab Hanachi	University of Toulouse 1, France
Monique Janneck	Lübeck University of Applied Sciences, Germany
Rania Khalaf	IBM T.J. Watson Research Center, USA
Ralf Klamma	Informatik 5, RWTH Aachen, Germany
Agnes Koschmider	Karlsruhe Institute of Technology, Germany
Sai Peck Lee	University of Malaya, Kuala Lumpur, Malaysia

Myriam Lewkowicz	UTT, France
Claudia Loebbecke	University of Cologne, Germany
Walid Maalej	TU München, Germany
Gustaf Neumann	Vienna University of Economics and Business Administration, Vienna, Austria
Selmin Nurcan	University of Paris 1 Pantheon Sorbonne, France
Andreas Oberweis	Karlsruhe Institute of Technology, Germany
Erik Proper	Public Research Centre, Henri Tudor, Luxembourg
Gil Regev	EPFL and Itecor, Switzerland
Sebastian Richly	Technical University of Dresden, Germany
Michael Rosemann	Faculty of Information Technology Queensland University of Technology, Australia
Rainer Schmidt	University of Applied Sciences, Aalen, Germany
Miguel-Ángel Sicilia	University of Alcalá, Madrid, Spain
Pnina Soffer	University of Haifa, Israel
Markus Strohmaier	Graz University of Technology, Austria
Karsten Wendland	University of Applied Sciences, Aalen, Germany
Christian Zirpins	Seeberger AG, Germany

First International Workshop on Data- and Artifact-Centric BPM (DAB 2012)

Organizers: Lior Limonad, Boudewijn van Dongen, Jianwen Su, and Roman Vaculin

Traditionally the management of business operations caters around two key issues: control flow and data. As a result, each of the two has attracted over the past years people both in academia and industry, manifesting itself into a plethora of methods and tools that have been designed to assist with the management of these two concerns. However, the natural and yet independent evolution in both areas has led to a reality in which in many cases the handling of one concern is treated as an afterthought with respect to the other.

Recently, however, we have seen the emergence of paradigms that aim to blend the two concerns, seeking for new approaches that may naturally and seamlessly unify the two in order to better streamline the overall complexity in BPM. Contemporary examples include artifact-centric BPM, Petri nets, and case management. Therefore, the DAB workshop is aimed at bringing together researchers and practitioners whose common interest and experience is the study and development of new foundations, models, methods, and technologies that are intended to uniformly and holistically align data and control flow.

The first DAB 2012 workshop took place in Tallinn, Estonia, coinciding with the BPM 2012 conference. A total of 12 papers were submitted, out of which six were accepted for presentation. It was also our great pleasure to include two invited talks in the DAB 2012 program: "On the Convergence of Data and Process Engineering," by Marlon Dumas (University of Tartu), and "Verification of Artifact-Centric Business Processes" by Alin Deutsch (University of California). We would like to thank all the authors for submitting their papers, the Program Committee members, and the reviewers. We hope this DAB workshop was the first in an ongoing series.

September 2012   Lior Limonad
                                                          Boudewijn van Dongen
                                                                   Jianwen Su
                                                               Roman Vaculin

Invited Talk: On the Convergence of Data and Process Engineering

Marlon Dumas, Institute of Computer Science, University of Tartu, Estonia

Data engineering is a well-trodden field with established methods and tools that allow engineers to capture complex data requirements and to refine these requirements down to the level of database schemas in a seamless and largely standardized manner. Concomitantly, database systems and associated middleware enable the development of robust and scalable data-driven applications to support a wide spectrum of business functions. Eventually though, individual business functions supported by database applications need to be integrated in order to automate end-to-end business processes. This facet of information systems engineering falls under the realm of business process engineering.

Business process engineering on the other hand is also an established discipline, with its own methods and tools. Process analysis and design methods typically start with process models that capture how tasks, events, and decision points are inter-connected, and what data objects are consumed and produced throughout a process. These models are first captured at a high level of abstraction and then refined down to executable process models that can be deployed in business process management systems. The division between data and process engineering is driven by various factors, including the fact that data are shared across multiple processes, that data and processes evolve at different rates and according to different requirements. Notwithstanding these reasons, the divide between data and processes leads to redundancies in large-scale information systems that, in the long run, hinder on their coherence and maintainability. This talk gives an overview of emerging approaches that aim at bridging the traditional divide between data and processes. In particular, the talk discusses the emerging "artifact-centric" process management paradigm, and how this paradigm in conjunction with service-oriented architectures and platforms, enable higher levels of integration and responsiveness to process change.

Marlon Dumas is the Swedbank Professor of Software Engineering at the University of Tartu, Estonia. He is also Strategic Area Leader at the Software Technology and Applications Competence Centre — a collaborative research center that gathers ten IT companies and two universities with the goal of conducting industry-driven research in software service engineering and data mining. From 2000 to 2007, he worked in the Business Process Management Research Group at Queensland University of Technology (Australia), where he held a Queensland State Fellowship between 2004 and 2007. He has also been visiting professor at the University of Grenoble (France), the University of Nancy (France), the University of Macau, and Visiting Researcher at SAP Research. Professor Dumas has been the recipient of best paper awards at ETAPS 2006 and BPM 2010 and the recipient of the 10-year most influential paper award at MODELS 2011. He is coinventor of three granted patents in the field of business process technologies and co-editor of a textbook on *Process-Aware Information Systems*.

Invited Talk: Verification of Artifact-Centric Business Processes

Alin Deutsch, Department of Computer Science and Engineering, University of California, San Diego, USA

Business process specification frameworks have recently evolved from the traditional process-centric approach toward data-awareness. Process-centric formalisms focus on control flow while under-specifying the underlying data and their manipulations by the process tasks, often abstracting them away completely. In contrast, data-aware formalisms treat data as first-class citizens.

The holistic view of data and processes together promises to avoid the notorious discrepancy between data modeling and process modeling of more traditional approaches that consider these two aspects separately. In particular, this separation precludes the development of data-aware automatic tools for formal verification, i.e., static analysis and run-time monitoring. Such tools are needed to tackle the complexity of modern business processes, much of which is due to subtle interactions between business process tasks and data.

Data-aware processes deeply challenge formal verification by requiring simultaneous attention to both data and process: indeed, on the one hand they deal with full-edged processes and require analysis in terms of sophisticated temporal properties; on the other hand, the presence of possibly unbounded data makes the usual analysis based on model checking of finite-state systems impossible in general, since, when data evolution is taken into account, the whole system becomes infinite-state. A notable exponent of the data-aware class of specification frameworks is the artifact-centric model, recently deployed by IBM in commercial products and consulting services, and studied in an increasing line of research papers. Business artifacts (or simply "artifacts") model key business-relevant entities, which are updated by a set of business process tasks. In this talk we survey results on data-aware static verification, selecting the artifact-centric model as a natural vehicle for our investigation owing to its practical relevance.

Alin Deutsch is a professor of computer science at the University of California, San Diego, USA. His research is motivated by the data management challenges raised by applications that are powered by underlying databases (viewed in a broad sense that includes traditional database management systems but also collections of semi- and un-structured data providing a query interface, however rudimentary). Prominent examples he focuses on are the World-Wide Web and business processes. Alin's education includes a PhD degree from the University of Pennsylvania, an MSc degree from the Technical University of Darmstadt (Germany), and a BSc degree from the Polytechnic University Bucharest (Romania).

He is the recipient of a Sloan fellowship and an NSF CAREER award, and has served as PC Chair of the ICDT-2012 International Conference on Database Theory, the PLANX-2009 Workshop on Programming Language Techniques for XML, and the WebDB-2006 International Workshop on the Web and Databases.

Program Committee

Wil van der Aalst	Eindhoven University of Technology, Eindhoven, The Netherlands
Diego Calvanese	Free University of Bozen-Bolzano, Bolzano, Italy
Alessio Lomuscio	Imperial College London, UK
Richard Hull	IBM T.J. Watson Research Center, USA
Mathias Weske	Hasso Plattner University of Potsdam, Germany
Barbara Weber	University of Innsbruck, Austria
Victor Vianu	U.C. San Diego, CA, USA
Manfred Reichert	Institute of Databases and Information Systems, Ulm University, Germany
Giuseppe De Giacomo	Sapienza University of Rome, Italy
Karsten Wolf	Universität Rostock, Germany
Eric Badouel	INRIA/IRISA Rennes, France
Theresa Pardo	University at Albany, New York
Viara Popova	University of Tartu, Estonia
Fabio Patrizi	Sapienza University of Rome, Italy

6th International Workshop on Event-Driven Business Process Management (edBPM 2012)

Organizers: Opher Etzion, Adrian Paschke, Christian Janiesch, Nenad Stojanovic

Event-driven computing is gaining ever increasing attention by the industry and research communities and this workshop shows its importance in the business process management domain. We had seven submissions from industry and academia. Topics ranged from modeling data-intensive processes, to various types of monitoring business processes. Events have become first-class citizens in BPM, enabling novel real-time applications on top of business process execution. However, there still is a lot to be done, especially in the context of a unified terminology and conceptualization (e.g., what is an event in the BPM).

We selected five papers for presentation, although almost every submission contained very interesting material for this kind of workshop and we would like to thank to all authors for their great job.

We also thank the members of the Program Committee for very constructive reviews, which will hopefully help authors in improving their work.

September 2012

Opher Etzion
Adrian Paschke
Christian Janiesch
Nenad Stojanovic

Program Committee

Alexandre Alves	Oracle Co, USA
Dimitris Apostolou	National and Technical University of Athens, Greece
Opher Etzion	IBM Research Lab Haifa, Israel
Christian Janiesch	Karlsruhe Institute of Technology, Germany
Guido Governatori	QRL, Australia
Dimka Karastoyanova	Stuttgart, Germany
Adrian Paschke	Free University Berlin, Germany and RuleML Inc., Canada
Guy Sharon	IBM Research Lab Haifa, Israel
Ljiljana Stojanovic	FZI Research Center for Information Technologies Karlsruhe, Germany
Nenad Stojanovic	FZI Research Center for Information Technologies Karlsruhe, Germany
Erwin Zinser	University of Applied Sciences, Graz, Austria

Third International Workshop on
Empirical Research in Business Process Management
(ER-BPM 2012)

Organizers: Bela Mutschler, Jan Recker, Roel Wieringa

Introduction

Empirical research in business process management(BPM) is coming of age. In 2009, when the inaugural ER-BPM workshop was held, the field of BPM research was characterized by a strong emphasis on solution development, but also by an increasing demand for insights or evaluations of BPM technology based on dedicated empirical research strategies. The ER-BPM workshop series was created to provide an international forum for researchers to discuss and present such research.

In 2012, empirical research in BPM is now firmly established as an important strand of research around the use of BPM. Several of the key journals in the information systems discipline have run and published special issues or special sections on BPM research, either with a dedicated emphasis on empirical issues and empirical findings .[3] or with a focus on research that mixes both design and empirical work ..[1, 5]. Further special issues are in the pipeline .[4].

Aside from empirical BPM research finding a dedicated space in the academic journals, an increasing number of empirical research papers are also being published as identified by Houy et al. .[2] and Shown in Fig. 1.

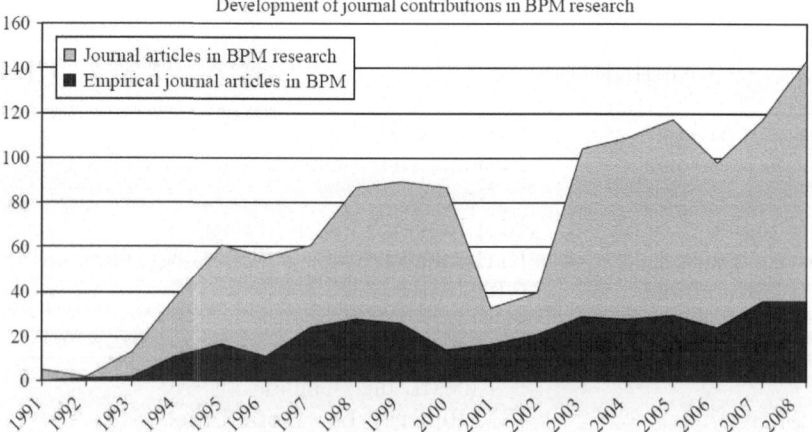

Fig. 1: Published BPM research articles over time .[2].

The benefits of empirical research include improved understanding of the problems that can be solved by BPM and improved insight into the performance of techniques in practice. While these benefits are now increasingly being demonstrated in the field of BPM, the field is still growing and maturing. The

ER-BPM workshop thus continues to be an important forum in which to discuss ongoing work, challenges, and outcomes.

The ER-BPM 2012 Workshop

Our ER-BPM 2012 workshop continued to address the demand for empirical research in BPM, and set out to stimulate empirical research that can contribute to a better understanding of the problems, challenges, and existing solutions in the BPM field.

In particular, we envisage the workshop to provide an *interdisciplinary* forum for researchers as well as interested practitioners to improve the understanding of BPM-specific requirements, methods and theories, tools and techniques. Accordingly, we defined the following (not exhaustive) list of topics as relevant to the current state of empirical research in BPM:

- Empirical research on BPM methods, BPM technologies, BPM tools
- Empirical research on process-aware information systems
- BPM-related (software) experiments
- BPM-related action research
- BPM-related surveys
- BPM-related case studies
- BPM-related modeling and simulation studies
- BPM-related experience reports
- Critical success factor analyses of BPM methods, technologies, tools
- Evaluations and comparisons of BPM tools, platforms, and standards
- Frameworks for quantitatively analyzing BPM methods, technologies, tools
- Frameworks for qualitatively evaluating BPM methods, technologies, tools
- Requirements on empirical and experimental BPM research
- Usability and ease-of-use of BPM technologies and BPM tools
- User acceptance of BPM projects
- BPM success, failure, and contingency models
- Studies on the role of standards in practical BPM projects
- Comparative studies of BPM technology
- Empirical studies of cross-organizational BPM coordination and settings
- Costs, benefits, and risks of applying BPM methods, technologies, and tools
- Evaluation approaches for BPM methods, BPM technologies, and BPM tools
- Practice-driven challenges for future BPM research
- Reflections on the use of empirical methods in the BPM field
- Advances in empirical methods for BPM research

We invited papers that outline research in progress as well as completed research papers. Submitted papers were reviewed by at least three members of the Program Committee, and were evaluated on the basis of significance, originality, technical quality, and exposition.

The Workshop Papers

In 2012, we accepted three papers for presentation in a dedicated ER-BPM session. These articles provide a snapshot of current examples of how empirical research in BPM can be conducted, and what insights such research can uncover.

The paper "Exploring Workaround Situations in Business Processes" by Nesi Outmazgin reports on a multiple case study on types and reasons of workarounds in business process. This is a relevant topic that has not yet been extensively researched, which in turn makes it a perfect fit to the workshop.

The paper "Investigating the Process of Process Modeling with Eye Movement Analysis" by Jakob Pinggera, Marco Furtner, Markus Martini, Pierre Sachse, Katharina Reiter, Stefan Zugal, and Barbara Weber examines a new data collection and analysis technique – eye movement analysis – and its application to a study of the process of process modeling. The paper was selected because it addresses an important topic with a refreshingly new approach to research.

The third paper, "Business Process Orientation: An Empirical Study of Its Impact on Employees' Innovativeness," by Jing Tang, L.G. Pee, and Junichi Iijima, explores the role of process orientation as an organizational mindset in an effort toward organizational innovation. Interestingly, this paper considers data from a survey of Japanese organizations, thereby adding insights into cultural and national BPM practices that have been under-represented.

We hope you find these papers stimulating and interesting. We would like to thank the authors for their efforts, and also the Program Committee for dedicating their time to evaluating and selecting these papers.

September 2012

Bela Mutschler
Jan Recker
Roel Wieringa

References

1. Dumas, M., Recker, J., Weske, M.: Management and Engineering of Process-aware Information Systems: Introduction to the Special Issue. Information Systems 37, 77–79 (2012)
2. Houy, C., Fettke, P., Loos, P.: Empirical Research in Business Process Management – Analysis of an Emerging Field of Research. Business Process Management Journal 16, 619–661 (2010)
3. Recker, J., Mutschler, B., Wieringa, R.: Empirical Research in Business Process Management: Introduction to the Special Issue. Information Systems and e-Business Management 9, 303–306 (2011)
4. Rosemann, M., Zur Muehlen, M., Becker, J., Röglinger, M.: BISE – Call for Papers Issue 5/2012 Business Process Management. Business & Information Systems Engineering 3, 183–184 (2011)
5. Rothenberger, M.A.: Editorial: Design Artifacts for Organizational Processes. Journal of Information Technology Theory and Application 12, 1–4 (2011)

Program Committee

Second International Workshop on Process Model Collections (PMC 2012)

Organizers: Hajo Reijers, Mathias Weske, Remco Dijkman

Nowadays, as organizations reach higher levels of business process management maturity, they tend to possess and actively use large numbers of business process models. It is quite common that such collections of industry-strength business process models include thousands of activities and related business objects such as data, applications, risks, etc. These models are used to solve a variety of modeling challenges, and they are increasingly published to a large number of stakeholders with varying skills and responsibilities. In that sense, it may not come as a surprise that many organizations struggle to manage such high volumes of complex process models. The problem is exacerbated by overlapping content across models, poor version management, process models that are used simultaneously for different purposes, the use of various modeling notations such as EPCs, BPMN, etc.

Against this backdrop, the aim of the workshop is to discuss novel research in the area of business process model collections. To this end, four papers were selected for presentation, from a total of eight submissions. In addition a keynote speaker was invited.

September 2012   Hajo Reijers
                                                                    Mathias Weske
                                                                    Remco Dijkman

Invited Talk: Managing Large Process Model Collections: Challenges and Expectations from Practice

Marcello La Rosa, Queensland University of Technology, Australia

The last decade has experienced a growing interest of researchers in the problem of managing large process model collections. A plethora of approaches, techniques, and tools have been proposed that investigate this problem and provide solutions to it from different perspectives and degrees of depth. For example, work has been done to query a repository of process models for similarities or exact matches; to consolidate a set of similar process models into a merged model or via shared sub-processes; to simplify a repository based on various refactoring opportunities; and to visualize relations between process models or variants thereof.

There are at least two independent reasons behind this increased research focus in managing large process model collections. On the one hand, as research in business process management matures, it becomes natural to explore relationships between process models rather than looking at a single process model at a time. For instance, new challenges arise when an existing technique has to scale up to a whole collection of process models. On the other hand, process model collections from practice are emerging with the broad application of process modeling initiatives within various industries, offering ideal testbeds to evaluate the research outcomes. For example, Suncorp—one of the largest Australian insurers—offers more than 30 products for personal, motor vehicle, and commercial insurance by controlling over 15 insurance brands, which are the result of a series of mergers and acquisitions the company has recently gone through. This has led to more than 3,000 process models that are managed on a daily basis by various teams of process analysts.

Clearly, managing these large process model collections comes with various "concrete issues" that practitioners must face (the so-called modeling in the large challenge). For example, the high variability in Suncorp's process models repository yields high costs for the development and maintenance of the IT infrastructure implementing such processes, which the company is no longer willing to tolerate (the sole process modeling initiative is estimated to have cost the company more than $4 million).

Against this backdrop, it is opportune to reflect on which practical questions have been answered by the research community so far, and what still remains open. This talk first profiles, the emerging research area of "managing large process model collections" through an overview and classification of its state of the art. Based on this, and taking the case of Suncorp as an example, it illustrates some typical challenges practitioners are facing in this context, and to what extent these challenges have indeed been solved by research. The talk concludes by exploring some ideas for bringing research supply in this area closer to industry demand.

Marcello La Rosa is an associate professor and the IS School Academic Director for Corporate Engagements at Queensland University of Technology (QUT) in Brisbane, Australia. He is also a researcher at the National ICT Australia. Marcello obtained his MSc in Computer Engineering from Politecnico di Torino in 2005, and his PhD in Computer Science from QUT in 2009. His research interests focus on process consolidation, configuration, and automation. Marcello has published more than 60 refereed papers on these topics including papers in journals like *ACM TOSEM, Formal Aspects of Computing,* and *Information Systems.* He leads the Apromore initiative (www.apromore.org) – a strategic collaboration between various universities for the development of an advanced process model repository. Marcello has taught process management to students and practitioners in Australia for over five years. Based on this experience, he recently co-authored *Fundamentals of Business Process Management* (Springer 2013) – the first, comprehensive textbook on business process management for graduate students. More information on him can be found at www.marcellolarosa.com.

Program Committee

Wil van der Aalst	Eindhoven University of Technology, The Netherlands
Ahmed Awad	Cairo University, Egypt
Boudewijn van Dongen	Eindhoven University of Technology, The Netherlands
Peter Fettke	German Research Center for Artificial Intelligence, Germany
Luciano Garcia-Banuelos	University of Tartu, Estonia
Paul Johannesson	Stockholm University, Sweden
Agnes Koschmider	University of Karlsruhe, Germany
Akhil Kumar	Penn State University, USA
Peter Loos	Universität des Saarlandes, Germany
Jan Mendling	Wirtschafts Universität Wien, Austria
Manfred Reichert	University of Ulm, Germany
Stefanie Rinderle-Ma	University of Vienna, Austria
Michael Rosemann	Queensland University of Technology, Australia
Sergey Smirnov	SAP Research, Germany
Jianmin Wang	Tsinghua University, China
Barbara Weber	University of Innsbruck, Austria
Matthias Weidlich	Technion, Israel
Petia Wohed	Stockholm University, Sweden

Second International Workshop on Process-Aware Logistics Systems (PALS 2012)

Organizers: Kamel Barkaoui, Virginia Dignum, Huib Aldewereld, Walid Gaaloul, Cherif Sadfi, Ichiro Satoh

The PALS workshop deals with problems related to the design and optimization of global logistics systems, from a business process management perspective. It is dedicated to exploring and mastering the tools needed for operating, reconfiguring and, in general, making decisions within logistics-based systems, in order to provide the customers and system users with the greatest possible value.

Our vision is that the business process models, which are used on a daily basis for making the decisions needed for operate and reconfigure the logistics systems, can naturally serve as the starting point for the problem formulations needed to optimize these logistics systems.

Topics and Papers

The workshop attracted nine paper submissions. Each of these submissions was reviewed by at least three Program Committee members. After receiving the reviews, from these submissions, the top four were accepted as full papers and, in addition, another interesting submission was accepted as a short paper. A keynote speaker was also invited.

The first long paper proposes a high-level logistic process modeling environment supporting logistic services according to the business document choreography defined for these services. This approach allows an end-user to orchestrate a business process based on commercial decisions for service delivery by hiding details of the choreography, especially cancellation rules.

The second long paper is interested in modeling and managing capabilities as standalone entities, presented via an action verb and a set of domain-related attributes/features. In order to illustrate their conceptual model benefits, the authors apply it in describing logistics capabilities.

In the third long paper the authors argue that the mobility of an agent is a basic issue to express interactions of flow actions, consequently modeling migration process is a crucial issue. Therefore they propose to integrate Ferber and Müller's influence/reaction model in agent Petri nets to model migration mobile agents. This model clarifies the migration process of an agent from one environment to another and enhances its capacity for formal verification.

The fourth long paper presents a novel approach to carbon credit trading with pervasive computing technologies, particularly RFID (or barcode) technology. It introduces RFID tags as certificates for the rights to claim carbon credits in carbon offsetting and trading. The approach was constructed and evaluated with real customers and real carbon credits in a real supply chain. It can also be used to encourage industries and homes to reduce greenhouse gas emissions.

Finally, the short paper shows the necessity of the formal the verification of Web services properties to ensure a dynamic service composition. A logistics-based process was used as a use case in order to validate their approach.

September 2012

Kamel Barkaoui
Virginia Dignum
Huib Aldewereld
Walid Gaaloul
Cherif Sadfi
Ichiro Satoh

Committees

General Co-chairs

| Kamel Barkaoui | CNAM, France |
| Virginia Dignum | Delft University of Technology, The Netherlands |

Program Committee Co-chairs

Huib Aldewereld	Delft University of Technology, The Netherland
Walid Gaaloul	Telecom SudParis, France
Cherif Sadfi	National Engineering School of Tunis, Tunisia
Ichiro Satoh	National Institute of Informatics, Japan

Steering Committee

Nejib Ben Hadj-Alouane	Manouba University, Tunisia
Samir Tata	Institut Telecom, Telecom SudParis, France
Moez Yeddes	Manouba University, Tunisia

Program Committee

Nejib Ben Hadj-Alouane	Manouba University, Tunisia
Chihab Hanachi	Toulouse 1 University, IRIT Laboratory, France
Hans Weigand	University of Tilburg, The Netherlands
Samir Tata	Institut Telecom, Telecom SudParis, France
Moez Yeddes	Manouba University, Tunisia
Yao-hua Tan	TU Delft, The Netherlands
Wout Hofman	TNO, The Netherlands
Bram Klievink	TU Delft, The Netherlands

Christian Mueller	DFKI, Germany
Mustafa Çagri Gürbüz	ZLC, Spain
Mario M. Monsreal Barrera	ZLC, Spain
Karim Baïna	ENSIAS of Rab, Morrocco
Mohamed Sellami	Institut Telecom, Telecom SudParis, France
Inge Lucassen	ITNO, The Netherlands
Mohamed Sellami	Institut TELECOM, France
Mohamed Graiet	ISMIM-Monastir, Tunisia
Khaled Gaaloul	CRP Henri Tudor, Luxembourg
Imed Kacem	Université de Lorraine, France
Nguyen Ngoc Chan	TELECOM SudParis, France
Dimka Karastoyanova	University of Stuttgart, Germany
Mohamed Jmaiel	ReDCAD ENIS, Tunisia
Zhangbing Zhou	University of Geosciences, China
Tammo van Lessen	Taval, Germany
Kais Klai	Université Paris 13, France
Adnene Guabtni	NICTA, Australia
François Charoy	University Henri Poincaré Nancy 1 - LORIA, France
Sami Bhiri	National University of Ireland, Galway, Ireland
Malika Boukala-Ioualalen	USTHB, Algeria
Feng Chu	Université d'Evry Val d'Essonne, France
Maria Di Mascolo	University of Grenoble, France

Third International Workshop on Reuse in Business Process Management (rBPM 2012)

Organizers: Marcelo Fantinato, Maria Beatriz Felgar de Toledo, Itana Maria de Souza Gimenes, Lucin'eia Heloisa Thom, Cirano Iochpe

Aims and Scope: Academia and Industry

The current complexity of the corporative world demands dynamic and flexible IT infrastructure to provide technical solutions for conducting business. Business process management (BPM) has been providing important technological support to improve organization competitiveness. In order to increase dynamism and competitiveness, BPM can benefit from reuse techniques and tools at several stages of the business process life cycle.

The Third International Workshop on Reuse in Business Process Management was dedicated to exploring any type of reuse in the BPM domain, taking into account both the results of research in academia and the results of applications in industry. It was a forum in which to discuss systematic reuse applied to BPM at its various levels and different life cycle stages, including:

1. Basic service-oriented foundation level: including service development, description, publication, discovery, selection, negotiation, and aggregation
2. Management and monitoring upper level: including business process modeling, execution, monitoring, administration, and optimization

Moreover, the impact of reuse on business- and service-oriented engineering as well as analyzing how it can help in the design of higher-quality process models were very important topics for discussion. Different existing reuse approaches and techniques can be extended to be applied to this fairly new domain, including: software product line or software product families; variability descriptors; design patterns such as feature modeling; aspect-orientation; and component-based development. In addition, completely novel approaches and techniques can be proposed. Their application should also be discussed, preferably under experimentation as well as analysis of the results.

September 2012

Marcelo Fantinato
Maria Beatriz Felgar de Toledo
Itana Maria de Souza Gimenes
Lucin'eia Heloisa Thom
Cirano Iochpe

Invited Talk: Overcoming Challenges of Reuse in Large Collections of Process Models

Barbara Weber, University of Innsbruck, Austria

The increasing adoption of process-aware information systems (PAIS), together with the reuse of process knowledge, has resulted in process model repositories with large collections of process models. Understandability and maintainability of the process models in the repository are preconditions for their successful reuse. However, industrial process models display a wide range of quality problems impeding their comprehensibility and consequently hampering their maintainability and reuse. The literature reports, for example, error rates between 10% and 20% in industrial process model collections. Moreover, non-intention-revealing or inconsistent naming, redundant process fragments, and overly large and unnecessarily complex process models are typical quality problems that can be observed in existing process model collections.

These problems have resulted in abundant research with the goal of obtaining a better understanding of factors influencing the quality of process models as well as techniques fostering their understandability and maintainability. For obtaining high-quality models it is essential to understand the factors that are influencing the quality of process models, but also the way process models are created. This challenge can be approached by taking a cognitive perspective and by analyzing the process of creating and maintaining process models (in addition to the modeling artifacts created). In part I of the talk I report on some of the findings obtained so far, discuss their implications for the reuse of process models, and outline future research directions. Part II of this keynote covers different techniques for fostering understandability as well as maintainability of process models that were developed in our group such as test-driven modeling, literate process modeling, but also techniques for the refactoring of large collections of process models. Again, implications for the reuse of process models are discussed.

Barbara Weber obtained her PhD in Economics at the Institute of Information Systems. Since 2004, she has been a researcher at the Department of Computer Science at the University of Innsbruck where she holds an Associate Professor position. She is a member of the quality engineering (QE) research group and head of the research cluster on business processes and workflows at QE. Her research areas include business process management, process flexibility, process modeling, integrated process lifecycle support and process mining. She has published more than 80 papers and articles in, among others, *Data & Knowledge Engineering, Computers in Industry, Science of Computer Programming,*

Software Evolution and Maintenance, Requirements Engineering, and Enterprise Systems. Together with Manfred Reichert she has co-authored the book *Enabling Flexibility in Process-aware Information Systems.* She has been Co-chair of the successful BPI (business process intelligence) workshop series since 2007, is a member of the IEEE Task Force on Process Mining, and will be PC Chair of next year's BPM conference.

Program Committee

Akhil Kumar	Penn State University, USA
Ana Karla A. de Medeiros	Capgemini Consulting, The Netherlands
Antonio Ruiz-Cortés	University of Seville, Spain
Arnon Sturm	Ben-Gurion University of the Negev, Israel
Barbara Weber	University of Innsbruck, Austria
Bertram Ludäscher	University of California at Davis, USA
Christoph Bussler	Saba Software, Inc., USA
Claudia Cappelli	Federal University of Rio de Janeiro State, Brazil
Claudia Roncancio	University of Grenoble, France
Eduardo S. de Almeida	Federal University of Bahia, Brazil
Fernanda A. Baiao	Federal University of Rio de Janeiro State, Brazil
Flavia M. Santoro	Federal University of Rio de Janeiro State, Brazil
Gustavo Rossi	National University of La Plata, Argentina
Hajo Reijers	Eindhoven University of Technology, The Netherlands
Heiko Ludwig	IBM T.J. Watson Research Center, USA
Jaejoon Lee	Lancaster University, UK
Jan Mendling	Wirtschafts Universität Wien, Austria
Joao Porto de Albuquerque	University of Sao Paulo, Brazil
Luciano A. Digiampietri	University of Sao Paulo, Brazil
Manfred Reichert	University of Ulm, Germany
Mathias Weske	University of Potsdam, Germany
Miriam A. M. Capretz	The University of Western Ontario, Canada
Paulo F. Pires	Federal University of Rio Grande do Norte, Brazil
Renata de M. Galante	Federal University of Rio Grande do Sul, Brazil
Renata M. de Araujo	Federal University of Rio de Janeiro State, Brazil
Sergiu Dascalu	University of Nevada, USA

Joint Workshop on Security in Business Processes (SBP 2012)

Organizers: Rafael Accorsi, Raimundas Matulevicius

Workshop Goal

The automation of business processes by means of business process management systems enables the flexible adjustment of enterprise systems to the current demand. This is highly appreciated at managerial level. Automation also provides for a systematic separation of processes and IT architectures, allowing, for example the seamless outsourcing of process fragments to a cloud or the selection of different services for process execution.

Despite these immediate advantages, enterprises are still reluctant in fully relying on automated business processes. On the one hand, there are various concerns regarding the deployment of architectures and the correct modeling, enactment, monitoring, and audit of processes with regard to security, privacy, and compliance demands. On the other hand, there is the imminent danger of insider threats and attacks, which are facilitated by a flexible service architecture.

While research, methodologies, and corresponding tool-support lying at the intersection of business process management, security and privacy, and (formal) analysis could provide an appropriate basis for tackling these issues, the current state of the art fails to be carried over to practitioners. Certification to provably attest and control business process adherence to compliance requirements and auditing so as to detect violations are essential instruments for achieving reliably secure process-aware information systems. The SBP workshop series on Security in Business Processes brings together researchers and practitioners investigating and applying preventive and detective analyses to check security and compliance requirements for business process models and the corresponding management systems.

Scientific Program

The program of SBP included two invited speakers, five long papers, and four short papers. The balance of academia and industry authors and the high attendance indicate that the topics addressed by the SBP workshop are of relevance to both communities, suggesting a high potential to transfer research techniques into commercial tools.

The workshop was divided into four sessions. The first session was dedicated to the perspectives of secure business processes. The keynote speech by Opdahl gave the audience a coherent view on identification and visualization of dependability concerns, especially focusing on the application to business process management. The second session paper by Goldstein and Frank introduced objectives and requirements of the language for multi-perspective modeling of IT security.

In the second workshop session the emphasis was placed on security and compliance. Knuplesch et al. provided insight into compliance of cross-organizational processes and their changes. The discussion was continued by Brucker and Hang, who were analyzed how to implement secure and compliant business-driven systems. The session was completed by Depaire et al., who reported on the process deviation analysis framework.

The third workshop session dedicated to security and Internet services was started by the second keynote speech. Heiberg presented the industrial experience on the new technologies for democratic elections. This talk was followed by a presentation on storage and execution of business processes in the cloud. Martinho and Ferreira argued that these activities should be carried out securely. In the last session talk, Fonda et al. presented an advanced protection technique called SEWebSessions to secure workflow sessions.

The fourth session of the workshop was dedicated to engineering of secure business processes. Lehmann and Lohmann presented a modeling wizard for confidential business processes. In another talk, Soomro and Ahmed introduced extensions to the misuse case diagrams to deal with security risk management. The final workshop presentation given by Leitner et al. introduced a method to produce the current-state RBAC model. The authors reported on the case study where process mining suitability is considered.

We wish to thank all those who contributed to making SBP a success: the authors who submitted papers, members of the Program Committee who carefully reviewed and discussed the submissions, and the speakers who presented their work at the workshop. In particular, we thank the keynote speakers for their enthusiastic and insightful keynotes. We also express our gratitude to the BPM 2012 Workshop Chairs for their support in preparing the workshop. Finally, we thank our colleagues from the Steering Committee – Wil van der Aalst and Guttorm Sindre – and from the Organizing Committee – Peter Karpati and Marco Montali – for their support and contribution to the SBP 2012 workshop.

September 2012

Rafael Accorsi
Raimundas Matulevicius

Program Committee

Federico Chesani	University of Bologna, Italy
Jason Crampton	Royal Holloway University of London, UK
Chiara Difrancescomarino	Fundazione Bruno Kessler, Italy
Eduardo B. Fernández	Florida Atlantic University, USA
Khaled Gaaloul	Center Henri Tudor, Luxembourg
Aditya Ghose	University of Wollongong, Australia
Paolo Giorgini	University of Trento, Italy
Michael Huth	Imperial College, UK

Dieter Hutter   German Research Center for Artificial
                                 Intelligence GmbH, Germany
Mieke Jans   Hasselt University, Belgium
Jan Jürjens   Technical University of Dortmund, Germany
Seok-Won Lee   Ajou University, Korea
Niels Lohmann   University of Rostock, Germany
Heiko Ludwig   IBM Almaden, USA
Fabrizio M. Maggi   Technical University of Eindhoven,
                                 The Netherlands
Per H. Meland   SINTEF, Norway
Haralambos Mouratidis   University of East London, UK
Andreas L. Opdahl   University of Bergen, Norway
Günther Pernul   University of Regensburg, Germany
Silvio Ranise   Fundazione Bruno Kessler, Italy
Stefanie Rinderle-Ma   University of Vienna, Austria
David G. Rosado   University of Castilla-La Mancha, Spain
Shazia Sadiq   University of Queensland, Australia
Mark Strembeck   Vienna University of Economics and Business,
                                 Austria
Uldis Sukovskis   Riga Technical University, Latvia
Jan M. van der Werf   Technical University of Eindhoven,
                                 The Netherlands
Barbara Weber   University of Innsbruck, Austria

First International Workshop on
Theory and Applications of Process Visualization
(TAProViz 2012)

Organizers: Ross Brown, Simone Kriglstein, Stefanie Rinderle-Ma

Introduction

The representation of business process models has been a continuing research topic for many years now. However, many process model representations have not developed beyond minimally interactive 2D icon-based representations of directed graphs and networks, with little or no annotation for information overlays. With the rise of desktop computers and commodity mobile devices capable of supporting rich interactive 3D environments, we believe that much of the research performed in computer-human interaction, virtual reality, games, and interactive entertainment has much potential in areas of BPM; to engage, provide insight, and to promote collaboration among analysts and stakeholders alike. This initial visualization workshop sought to initiate the development of a high-quality international forum to present and discuss research in this field. Via this workshop, we intend to create a community to unify and nurture the development of process visualization topics as a continuing research area.

Topics and Papers

The workshop attracted 11 paper submissions. Each of these submissions was reviewed by at least three Program Committee members. After receiving the reviews, three full papers and one tool report paper were accepted for presentation at the workshop. In addition, we invited a keynote speaker, Manfred Reichert, from the University of Ulm.

The papers address a number of topics in the area of process model visualization, in particular:

- 3D process model representations
- Visualizing the process of process modeling
- Visual analysis of large-scale activity data
- Visualization of process hierarchies in large collections

The keynote on "Visualizing Large Business Process Models — Challenges, Techniques, Applications" by Manfred Reichert, presented examples of large process models to discuss the challenges to be tackled when visualizing and abstracting such models. The keynote also includes the presentation of a comprehensive framework that allows for personalized process model visualizations, which can be tailored to the specific needs of different user groups.

Philip Effinger presented his tool report, "A 3D Navigator for Business Process Models" describing Flight Navigator, an approach to inspecting and presenting business process models in 3D. Flight Navigator supports numerous interaction paradigms that enable the user to easily present, inspect, and analyze a process model in a 3D environment.

Jan Claes, Irene Vanderfeesten, Jakob Pinggera, Hajo Reijers, Barbara Weber, and Geert Poels presented their full paper, "Visualizing the Process of Process Modeling with PPMCharts." This paper reports on efforts to visualize the process modeling process, in such a way that relevant characteristics of the modeling process can be observed graphically. The graphical representation that this process mining tool plug-in generates allows for the discovery of different patterns of process modeling.

Kazuo Misue and Seiya Yazaki presented their full paper, "Panoramic View for Visual Analysis of Large-scale Activity Data," which describes a representation technique to provide a panoramic view of activities in large-scale organizations. The representation embeds charts expressing activities into cells of a treemap. By using this representation, both quantitative and temporal aspects of activities can be seen simultaneously.

Finally, Andreas Seyfang, Katharina Kaiser, Theresia Gschwandtner, and Silvia Miksch, presented their full paper "Visualizing Complex Process Hierarchies During the Modeling Process" detailing a novel visualization, Plan Strips, which represents the hierarchy of plans, i.e., processes, as a set of nested strips. It represents the synchronization of the plans by color coding and ordering these strips, thus saving considerable display space compared to typical graph representations.

September 2012

Ross Brown
Simone Kriglstein
Stefanie Rinderle-Ma

Program Committee

Ralph Bobrik	University of Ulm, Germany
Michael Burch	University of Stuttgart, Germany
Massimiliano De Leoni	Eindhoven University of Technology, The Netherland
Philip Effinger	University of Tübingen, Germany
Hans Georg-Fill	University of Vienna, Austria
Sonja Kabicher-Fuchs	University of Vienna, Austria
Florian Mansmann	University of Konstanz, Germany
Silvia Miksch	Technical University of Vienna, Austria

Table of Contents

8th International Workshop on Business Process Intelligence (BPI 2012)

5th International Workshop on Business Process Management and Social Software (BPMS2 2012)

1st International Workshop on Data- and Artifact-Centric BPM (DAB 2012)

6th International Workshop on Event-Driven Business Process Management (edBPM 2012)

3rd International Workshop on Empirical Research in Business Process Management (ER-BPM 2012)

2nd International Workshop on Process Model Collections (PMC 2012)

2nd International Workshop on Process-Aware Logistics Systems (PALS 2012)

3rd International Workshop on Reuse in Business Process Management (rBPM 2012)

Joint Workshop on Security in Business Processes (SBP 2012)

1st International Workshop on Theory and Applications of Process Visualization (TAProViz 2012)

Towards a Non-workflow Theory of Business Processes

Ilia Bider

DSV, Stockholm University/IbisSoft, Stockholm, Sweden
ilia@{dsv.su,ibissoft}.se

Extended abstract of keynote at ACM 2012, Tallinn, Estonia, 3 September 2012

The keynote overviews the efforts of a group of researchers and practitioners to build and test a theory of business processes (BP) that could be of use for building non-workflow based business processes support (BPS) systems. The background for these efforts lies in two scientific disciplines outside the domain of *Business Process Management*, namely: *Systems Thinking* and *Mathematical System Theory*.

Systems Thinking served as an inspiration of regarding a BP instance/case as a temporal (sub)system created as a reaction on changes in the enterprise's external or/and internal environment and discarded after the goal set for the subsystem has been reached. This view can be explained with the help of system-coupling diagrams from [1] as illustrated in Fig. 1. The diagram describes a general case when a particular situation in the environment, on the left-hand side of the diagram, causes a larger system, e.g., an enterprise, to create a respondent system, e.g., a project, to handle the situation. The respondent system is built from the assets that the larger system already has. Some of these assets are people, or other actors (e.g., robots). Other assets are control elements, e.g. policy documents, that define the behavior of the respondent system. The latter are denoted as black dots in Fig. 1.

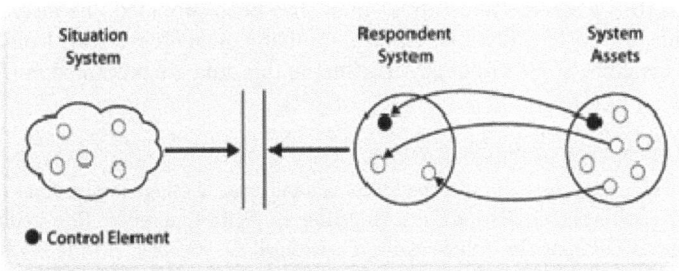

Fig. 1. System coupling diagrams from [1] (Courtesy of Harold Lawson)

Based on the above interpretation, we have drafted a dynamic model of enterprise as a system the behavior of which is defined by interactions between three types of elements: assets, sensors, and business process instances (BPI) [2]. Sensors "watch" the enterprise's environment and starts BPI's when needed. Both sensors and assets are regarded as (sub)systems that are "manned" by assets. Some of these assets are control elements that guide the work of sensors and assets. Sensors and BPI's can be complex and decompose in the same way as the larger system. Assets on their own do

M. La Rosa and P. Soffer (Eds.): BPM 2012 Workshops, LNBIP 132, pp. 1–2, 2013.

not produce any changes inside or outside the enterprise; all changes are introduced via BPI's (respondent systems (in terms of Fig. 1) "manned" by assets.

Mathematical system theory [3] deals with the dynamical systems/processes in the physical world. This theory gave an inspiration to consider a BPI as a point moving in a multi-dimensional state-space. A BPI is defined as a trajectory in the space-time, and business process model - as a set of formal rules describing all "valid" trajectories. Different formalisms can be used for describing valid trajectories; the choice of the most appropriate one depends on the nature of the business process in question. When valid trajectories are grouped together so that deviations between them are insignificant, a prescriptive way, e.g. workflow, can be of use. When deviations between the instances are significant some constraint-based rules are to be preferred. One of the non-prescriptive ways of defining rules, operationalized via dynamic distributed planning, was suggested in [4,5].

From the state-oriented point of view, a BPS system is a system that assists a BPI's participants to follow one of the valid trajectories. When the workflow model is appropriate for describing the process, a system based on a workflow engine can suite well the task. However, when deviations between the trajectories are substantial, such a system will hinder the participant to find the right "road" through the state space instead of helping them. When the "territory" is shifting like on Iceland, a road that was good yesterday might become impassable the next day. In such circumstances, the minimum a BPS system can do is to provide a BPI's participants with a common interactive "map" where they can together try to find their path towards the BPI's goal despite the "roadblocks" appearing where they are not expected. As the space is multidimensional, the "map" should allow participants to move the instance independently in different sub-spaces where appropriate, and coordinate their efforts where the movement in several dimensions should be done simultaneously. Such a map could be provided in a form of a shared space available to all BPI's participants. Some of our experiments on different ways of structuring and using such maps are presented in [6]. When the interactive "map" has been provided, the next step would be to provide a kind of a flexible "navigator" that can suggest a path from any given position to the goal. Some of our experiments in this area are presented in [5].

References

[1] Lawson, H.: A Journey Through the Systems Landscape. College Publications (2010)
[2] Bider, I., Bellinger, G., Perjons, E.: Modeling an Agile Enterprise: Reconciling Systems and Process Thinking. In: Johannesson, P., Krogstie, J., Opdahl, A.L. (eds.) PoEM 2011. LNBIP, vol. 92, pp. 238–252. Springer, Heidelberg (2011)
[3] Kalman, R.E., Falb, P.L., Arbib, M.A.: Topics in Mathematical System Theory. McGraw-Hill (1969)
[4] Khomyakov, M., Bider, I.: Achieving Workflow Flexibility through Taming the Chaos. In: Proceedings of 6th OOIS, pp. 85–92. Springer (2000)
[5] Bider, I., Striy, A.: Controlling business process instance flexibility via rules of planning. IJBPIM 3(1), 15–25 (2008)
[6] Bider, I., Johannesson, P., Perjons, E.: In Search of the Holy Grail: Integrating Social Software with BPM Experience Report. In: Bider, I., Halpin, T., Krogstie, J., Nurcan, S., Proper, E., Schmidt, R., Ukor, R. (eds.) BPMDS 2010 and EMMSAD 2010. LNBIP, vol. 50, pp. 1–13. Springer, Heidelberg (2010)

Analysis and Documentation
of Knowledge-Intensive Processes

Gregor Scheithauer and Sven Hellmann

OPITZ CONSULTING GmbH
Weltenburger Str. 4, 81677 Munich
scheithauer@acm.org

Abstract. Business Process Management is a prevailing topic that addresses value-added activities in a company. Processes are modeled, realized, executed, and continuously improved. While this approach proves itself appropriate for routine work, it is not applicable for knowledge-intensive processes. Adaptive Case Management (ACM) defines this as knowledge work that is not or is rarely repeated, unable to be foreseen, occurs spontaneously, and depends on context. This paper pinpoints the differences between routine and knowledge work, and introduces ACM as a concept.

Keywords: Adaptive Case Management (ACM), Business Process Management (BPM), Knowledge Management.

1   Introduction

In recent years, knowledge work has gained significance importance in many companies. At the same time novel strategies are sought for providing ideal support to end users as well as for optimizing mainly unstructured and knowledge-intensive processes.

Davenport, on this basis, deals in his article "Rethinking knowledge work: A strategic approach" [1] with the question of how the productivity of knowledge workers can be enhanced, as they play a key role in companies' success according to his point of view. Knowledge workers either act in defined procedures and processes or totally independently and based on their own preferences. In practice, the first approach often reaches its limits, as in general the processes are complex in a way that it is difficult to express within a normative process flow with a given notation. In these cases, it is therefore often too expensive to model and technically implement all process variants. Furthermore, especially in knowledge-intensive processes process descriptions need to be adapted while carrying out the actual work, demonstrating why the topic of ACM has a lot of potential in this context. Examples of processes' diversity and adaptability can be found as part of patient's medical records, insurance cases, law suits, or complaint handling.

In all of the examples above, however, it is obvious that these processes cannot be handled without human participation. The scope of the manual interactions depends

M. La Rosa and P. Soffer (Eds.): BPM 2012 Workshops, LNBIP 132, pp. 3–11, 2013.

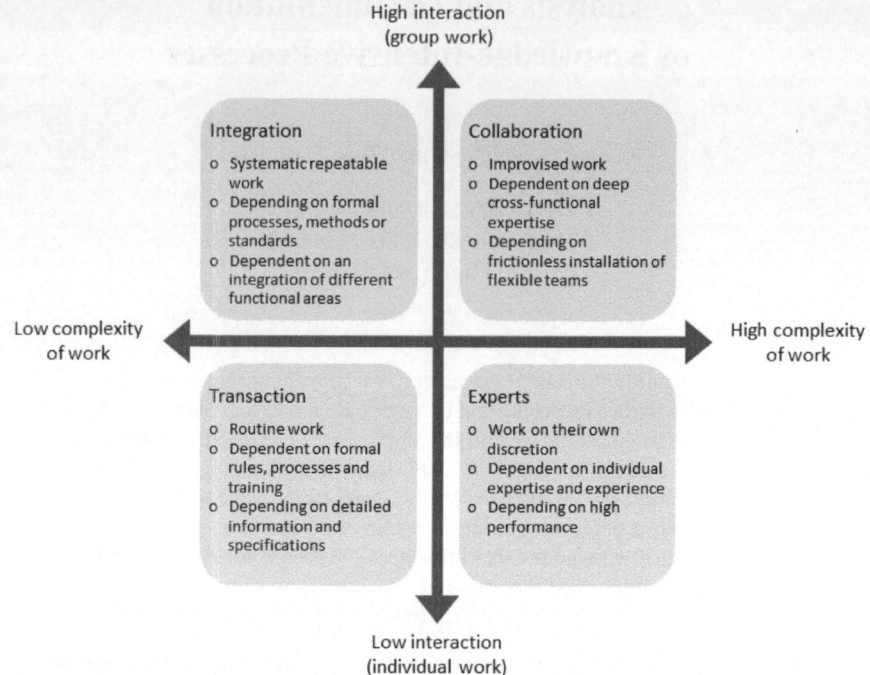

Fig. 1. Structure of different types of work according to Davenport [3]

on the respective case and can be different for each execution. In spite of the high integration of persons within a process, ACM should not be confused with expert systems. The difference between them is the addressing of different target groups. Expert systems are IT-based systems to identify possible solutions for tasks. For this purpose, expert systems include a knowledge base and algorithms to derive new knowledge. The knowledge of the system originates from experts and is represented by a model, enabling non-experts to solve knowledge-intensive tasks. ACM, on the other hand, does not try to map the knowledge of experts but to assist experts in knowledge tasks through IT systems.

This article is structured as follows: chapter 2 elaborates the differences between routine and knowledge work. Chapter 3 introduces concepts of Adaptive Case Management. Chapter 4 summarizes this work and provides an outlook for future work.

2   Routine and Knowledge Work

An essential concept of ACM is the distinction between routine work and knowledge work. The following paragraphs present different approaches for the differentiation of labor.

According to Swenson and Ukelson[2], routine work is understood and able to be planned by all parties concerned, and thus it is possible to describe it with structured

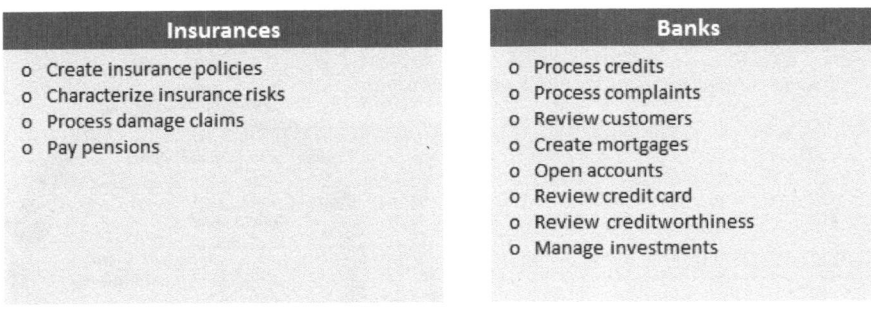

Fig. 2. Examples of knowledge-intensive work in the services sector [4]

business processes and objects. Knowledge work, however, is not repeatable. It is unpredictable and unfolds unexpectedly and robustly in different circumstances.

Knowledge-intensive work is not repeated or if so only rarely. This is the case in situations that occur sporadically, such as the merger of two companies. Work that occurs repeatedly can be documented and thus transferred into routine work. Furthermore, knowledge work is characterized by the fact that the sequence of steps is not predictable and varies depending on the situation. Swenson goes on to argue that knowledge work is iterative [2] and expands itself. This refers to the fact that not all possible tasks can be seen at the beginning of a process, but rather more options for action are revealed after each iteration, whichlead to a desired result. An additional feature of knowledge work is that it can also be carried out under different and changing circumstances.

Davenportpresents a further classification of work in [3]. Figure 1 shows four different types of work that differ in their complexity and the required interaction between workers. Transactional and integration work can be categorized under routine work. They require a specification as well as compliance with operational procedures, such as processes, which usually do not allow deviations. The types of experts and collaboration can be allocated in the category knowledge work. In order to asses and address complex tasks, knowledge and experience are required. In addition, unexpected work cannot be defined in advance, which leads to deviations, for example through improvisation.

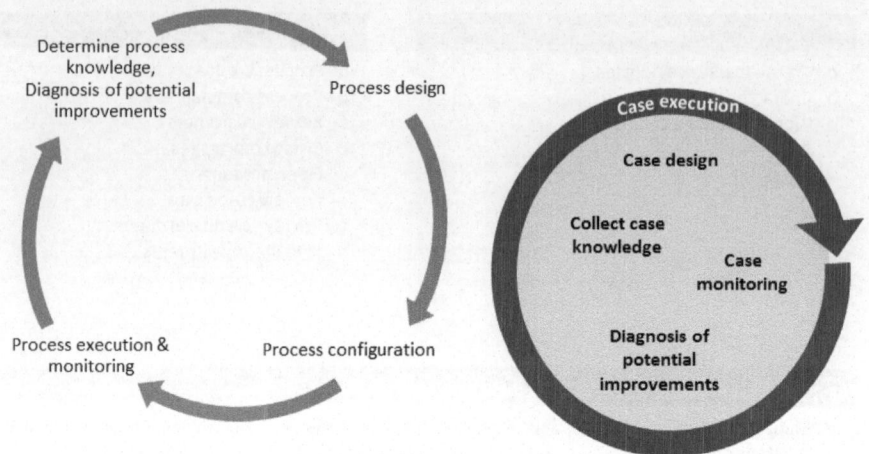

Fig. 3. Procedure of the classical process and case management

Economic sectors offer another way to distinguish routine work from knowledge work [4]: insurances, banks, healthcare, public authorities, and providers are characterized by the fact that they can be assigned to the service sector and imply a high level of customer interactions. In addition, experts are needed to perform the respective tasks.

Figure 2 shows examples of knowledge-intensive work according to the aforementioned economic sectors. The listed criteria for knowledge-intensive work can also be applied here. According to Zhu [4], use-cases for knowledge-intensive work, such as customer complaints, customer conflict management and fraud investigation, can be found in every economic sector.

3   Adaptive Case Management

After providing details about knowledge-intensive work and routine work, this chapter focuses on ACM as a business process management discipline. First, it is explained how documentation of adaptive processes differs from classical process modeling. A model is then presented that supports the identification of knowledge-intensive processes. Lastly, possibilities for eliciting and documentingadaptive processes are shown.

3.1   Differences between knowledge and Normative Processes

ZurMuehlen and Ho [5] define processes as a sequence of necessary activities in order to manipulate business objects in a goal-oriented fashion. Business process management, on the other hand, is described as the application of planning, control, and organization activities. Aalst et al. [6] define business process management as a discipline to be able to analyze, define, establish, and control processes. Both definitions are based on the fact that management of processes is a sequence of discrete functions. The left side in Figure 3 shows the sequence of these functions. On the one hand, discrete in this case means that following functions can only be addressed if a function is completed, for example that a process can only be defined if the corresponding process knowledge was determined. On the other hand, the discrete sequence also implies that the processing of the individual functions is performed by various persons in different roles.

In the first step, a process analysis is performed to determine actual business processes in companies. This can be done through structured interviews, workshops or examination of documents in collaboration with process owners, process participants and analysts. In the next step, the processes with a normative character are defined by analysts. The process will then be implemented organizationally and technically by appropriate experts. The fourth step is the execution of processes by process participants. At the same time, the execution will be measured according to predefined criteria or KPI. This is particularly important for the subsequent step of diagnosing potential improvements for the observed processes.

The literature provides a narrow number of definitions for ACM. The Object Management Group (OMG) [7] defines case management as a goal-oriented discipline for holistic treatment of cases. A case in turn refers to a situation or a circumstance that requires a number of actions for an acceptable outcome.

Pucher describes ACM [2] from three perspectives: (1) ACM is a system that includes organization and processes which are transparent and freely modifiable, (2) employees are always in a position to define new processes or adapt existing ones on the basis of business objects, user interfaces, business rules, and social interactions, and (3) the collection and documentation of knowledge does not happen during a phase of discrete analysis but is shifted to the phase of the process execution (see right side in Figure 3).

Zhu et al. [4] describe ACM as the handling of cases. A case contains a collection of information and coordinated tasks which are performed by knowledge workers in order to achieve a desired goal.

It is evident that all definitions have something in common. Situations to which an organization is able to react are treated as individual cases. In addition, a case is not defined by a process or the stringent sequence of tasks, but rather a definition is made by one or more results and the possible optional execution of tasks. The decision as to which tasks result in a desired outcome is up to knowledge workers of an organization. Furthermore, it can be seen that functions relating to the management of cases are comparable with those of the traditional process management. Unlike process management, the functions are not performed discretely but rather continuously. The right side in Figure 3 showsthat functions are performed continuously during case executions. Another difference is that the functions are primarily executed by participants (experts). The focus is thereby on the case processing or execution. Gained knowledge is continuously collected, analyzed and added to the case definition.

Characteristics	Routine work	Knowledge-intensive work
Quantity of repetition	High	Low
Determined unit	High	Low
Communication intensity	Low	High
Process complexity	Low	High
Number of persons	High	High
Qualification of persons	Low	Low
Degree of technology	High	Low
Relevant time	High	Moderate
Relevant quality	Moderate	High
Relevant costs	High	Low
Relevant risk	Moderate	Low

Fig. 4. Process types, Fischermanns [8]

3.2   Knowledge Processes

After distinguishing knowledge-intensive work from routine work, and the motivation of ACM as a solution for knowledge-intensive work, this chapter characterizes knowledge-intensive processes. The analysis of process types is important, since it may lead to different approaches towards how to elicit, analyze, and document business processes.

Fischermanns [8] distinguishes between three process types: (1) routine processes, (2) control processes, and (3) ad-hoc processes. According to him, routine processes can be treated with established process notations, but this does not apply to ad-hoc processesAt the same time Fischermanns offers characteristics for a distinction of ad-hoc processes (see Figure 4).

A similar approach is allowed byKimsley[9]. She distinguishes between four process types: structured processes, structured processes with ad-hoc exceptions, adaptive processes with partially structures sub-processes and adaptive processes.

3.3   Documentation of Knowledge-Intensive Processes

After presenting definitions for ACM and demonstrating possibilities as to how knowledge-intensive processes can be identified, this chapter shows what means are

	Ukelson	Shepherd	Khoyi and Swenson	Zhu et al.
Goal	X			
Result document	X		X	X
Deadline	X			
Mandatory rules		X		
Optional rules		X		
Business object			X	X
Tasks			X	X
Roles				X

Fig. 5. Case conceptions

available for documenting such processes. As a running example, a process for vehicle damage report will be introduced. According to Ukelson[2], the goal-oriented processing of a case always includes staff and has a result document as an outcome at a specified deadline. In connection with the example, the case is defined as follows: the goal is to record the damage and to provide this damage report as a result document for an insurance company. A valid deadline has to deal with the reported damage within 6 hours.

Unlike Ukelson, Shepherd [2] additionally takes guidelines as part of a case into account. As well as providing assistance for employees while processing the case, guidelines can also map dependencies between tasks that must be adhered due to legal reasons or reasons of quality assurance. Shepherd describes guidelines as rules which either must be met (mandatory rules) or can be met (optional rules). Mandatory rules have a legal background, such as data protection. In case of the damage report, a mandatory rule can state that any damage notification has to be evaluated before it is processed.

Unlike the mandatory rule, an optional rule describes best practices or solutions. Such rules tend to encodethe knowledge and experience of other knowledge workers who may be involved in current case handlings. In the case of the damage report, an optional rule can state that in event of a light collision the damage does not have to be reported to the insurance company but has to be paid by the company itself, since this is cheaper in medium-term.

Another definition of a case is provided by Khoyi and Swenson [2]. They describe the basis for the definition of cases with business objects (data) and their relationships among each other as well as with tasks to manipulate business objects and related documents. On this basis it is then possible to define cases as a logical connection of business objects, tasks and documents. In the context of a damage report, business objects include the accident data, damage type and customer data. Tasks corresponding to the customer data of the business object may include creating a customer, searching lease contracts by customer ID or printing customer data. These business objects und tasks can be gathered together in a case damage report. The employee can manipulate objects through tasks, if he or she wishes to do so.

Similar to Khoyi and Swenson, Zhu et al. [4] define a case via over business objects, documents and tasks. In addition, Zhu et al. distinguish roles. This allows the determination of specific, competent and responsible employees for business objects or tasks. In connection with the example introduced above, different roles are responsible for processing a damage report: while an employee records the damage report, the head of department is responsible for assessing the damage report.

The definitions above illustrate the granted degree of freedom for knowledge workers. Figure 5 compares the different definitions. It shows that cases are described with different states and how these should be achieved to finish a case. The requirement of a sequential process is completely omitted, as is otherwise usual in the classical process modeling. An already mentioned possibility to structure the processing of a case is the usage of guidelines, which can be described by means of rules. Furthermore, it should be noted that business data and tasks assume a function in the framework of case management, although established processes are avoided.

4 Summary

Knowledge-intensive processes as well as Adaptive Case Management are often discussed in the scientific community. This article examines the differences between routine and knowledge work, and subsequently introduces the ACM concept as a discipline in business process management. As well as differentiating between classical approaches, it also analyses the various characteristics for identifying knowledge-intensive processes.

This paper presents possibilities for analyzing and documenting knowledge-intensive processes. On the basis of relevant literature, it shows how to define a case with the help of the example of the damage report process. It is particularly striking that the users and not the process determine the run time and which task is performed when. Adaptive processes enable the modeling of technical relevant aspects without being bound by notation rules or similar artificial determinations. Between the poles of standardization and individual freedom, this is an important prerequisite, since the optimal utilization of human resources, in this case the knowledge worker,takes priority.

References

[1] Davenport, T.H.: Rethinking knowledge work: A strategic approach. McKinsey Quarterly (2011),
http://www.mckinseyquarterly.com/
Rethinking_knowledge_work_A_strategic_approach_2739

[2] Swenson, K.D.: Mastering the Unpredictable: How Adaptive Case Management Will Revolutionize the Way That Knowledge Workers Get Things Done. Meghan-Kiffer Press, Tampa (2010)

[3] Davenport, T.H.: Thinking for a Living: How to Get Better Performance and Results from Knowledge Workers. Harvard Business School Press, Boston (2005)

[4] Zhu, W.-D., Becker, B., Boudreaux, J., Braman, S., Do, T., Gomez, D., Marin, M., Vaughan, A.: Advanced Case Management with IBM Case Manager (2011), http://ibm.com/redbooks (lastly visited November 22, 2011)

[5] zur Mühlen, M., Ho, D.T.-Y.: Risk Management in the BPM Lifecycle. In: Bussler, C.J., Haller, A. (eds.) BPM 2005. LNCS, vol. 3812, pp. 454–466. Springer, Heidelberg (2006)

[6] van der Aalst, W.M.P., ter Hofstede, A.H.M., Weske, M.: Business Process Management: A Survey. In: van der Aalst, W.M.P., ter Hofstede, A.H.M., Weske, M. (eds.) BPM 2003. LNCS, vol. 2678, pp. 1–12. Springer, Heidelberg (2003)

[7] Object Management Group (OMG), Case Management Process Modeling (CMPM) Request For Proposal (2009) (lastly visited November 22, 2011)

[8] Fischermanns, G.: Prozesstypen anhand des Prozessprofils (2011), http://prozessfenster-blog.de/2011/02/28/prozesstyp/ (lastly visited November 22, 2011)

[9] Kemsley, S.: Case Management and BPM (2011), http://www.softwareag.com/corporate/images/sec_SAG_WP_Case-Mgmt-&-BPM_May11-web_tcm16-86062.pdf (lastly visited November 22, 2011)

On Two Approaches to ACM

Helle Frisak Sem, Steinar Carlsen, and Gunnar John Coll

Computas AS, Lysaker torg 45,
N-1327 Lysaker, Norway
{Helle.Frisak.Sem,Steinar.Carlsen,Gunnar.John.Coll}@computas.com

Abstract. MATS is an operational system in use by The Norwegian Food Safety Authority. This paper demonstrates how ACM can support time critical emergency action as well as planned case work, in one unified system. A brief account is given of these two different approaches to ACM, and the interaction between them in MATS, providing a basis for discussion. On the one hand, we have an ACM approach with task support, structured domain data and flexible work support for known bits and pieces of the tasks at hand. On the other hand, we have an extremely flexible ACM approach with functionality to keep control of who is to do what and to document the incident handling. The paper concludes with a discussion on domain specific and domain neutral ACM systems.

Keywords: Adaptive Case Management (ACM), Domain Specific ACM, Domain Neutral ACM, Activity support, Task support, Work folder.

1 Introduction

The Norwegian Food Safety Authority's (NFSA) overall objective is to ensure safe food and animal welfare. Since 2009, about 1000 of NFSA's knowledge workers (veterinarians, biologists, engineers, other professionals) use the control activity module of MATS actively as a decision support system for the main bulk of their professional work; to plan, conduct and register audits and inspections, to consider applications and issue certificates and licenses. MATS also includes an emergency response module used for collaboration and logging of work related to incident handling.

The control activity module and the emergency response module both support ACM, albeit in very different ways. This paper explains and contrasts the two different approaches, and outlines some questions for further work. In particular, we argue that we can distinguish between domain specific ACMs and domain neutral ACMs which apply different mechanisms for providing adaptable work support. A domain specific ACM focuses on encoded knowledge in a rich domain model, whereas a domain neutral ACM primarily offers collaboration support.

MATS is the Public Sector Gold Winner in the 2012 Global Awards for Excellence in Adaptive Case Management [3], [4].

M. La Rosa and P. Soffer (Eds.): BPM 2012 Workshops, LNBIP 132, pp. 12–23, 2013.
© Springer-Verlag Berlin Heidelberg 2013

The control activity module of MATS is based on the FrameSolutions™ ACM framework by Computas AS [1]. FrameSolutions provides focus on task support rather than workflow support [5], [6], [7], [8]. FrameSolutions is a complete framework for developing process-centric business systems. A rich solution platform is configured in the customer environment. On top of this, the desired business systems for the customer's business are implemented, with shared access to the underlying services.

FrameSolutions is available in Java and .NET as a set of well-defined and documented modules and interfaces for development of process-centric business systems, including: process module with task definitions and process / task engine, organization module with role definitions for functional roles, rule module with rule engine and a rich language for representing rules and codes, task list/inbox for users / user groups / projects, work folders for organizing information and tasks, and support features such as document creation, mail merge and report generation. Process centered case management solutions built on FrameSolutions have more than 100 000 users, and handle an annual cash flow of around 50 billion NOK – equivalent to 6 billion EUR.

2   ACM Example 1: The Control Activity of NFSA

MATS is an active task support system also providing decision support for NFSA's operational *control activities*; inspection, audit, sampling and document control. The system is the kernel of NFSA's quality system for the control activities process.

Every establishment or person controlled by NFSA is viewed as a case, having a corresponding case folder in MATS. Each case is followed by NFSA over a possible time span of many years, subjected to both planned and event driven control activities (inspection, audit, sampling and document control).

The application and control activity modules of MATS focus on task support rather than workflow. Work definitions (processes, tasks, activities) share a rich domain model, and work folders can be offered as active case folders - embedding worklists, documents, and domain data. These work folders are contextual views towards the shared domain model. The folders give knowledge workers active and dynamic task support, ensuring consistent high-quality NFSA control activities.

2.1   Activity and Task Support

Traditional BPM is based on modeling the workflow from A to Z with description of all alternative paths that may occur in the process. This is ill suited to the needs of highly qualified knowledge work, as the alternatives are so numerous and hard to foresee that the BPM charts will often turn out both unintelligible (to humans), and unfinished – or even incorrect.

We started out with models of the NFSA business processes at a high level of abstraction. At this level, the specialists in the different fields of NFSA were able to agree. As we went deeper into the matter, however, disagreements surfaced.

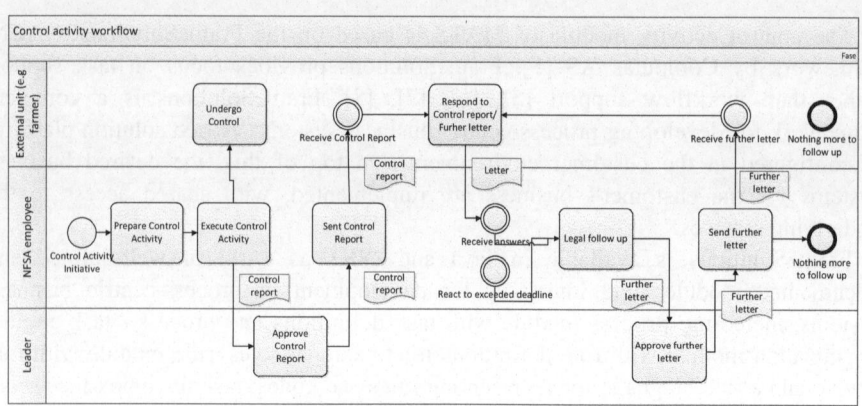

Fig. 1. Sketch of the NFSA control activity process, at a high level of abstraction

The general structure of a control activity such as inspection or auditing is fairly well agreed upon at the level illustrated in Figure 1. The legal actions available to NFSA personnel and principles of the Public Administrations Act (Forvaltningsloven) also apply throughout NFSA's fields of responsibility. The inspectors are subject specialists, without legal expertise. The quality of their legal decisions and selected measures is guaranteed by the task templates, the structured registration and the generation of letters to the controlled party.

Instead of completing the analysis top-down, we switched to the user perspective, focusing on work performance of smaller segments, e.g. "Prepare inspection", leaving the overall workflow to the direct or indirect choices of the user, or to the state of the context. Thus, the way ahead is only partly defined, while the workflow up to the current step will be fully traceable in each particular case.

We have defined support for each activity, as a detailed and stepwise work definition with executable functionality. The resulting tasks constitute recipes for how to perform the activity and provides the functionality to get it done, allowing for flexibility on the part of the user as well as control by the system where appropriate.

In the general task template, each step may have an include condition determining when the step shall be included in the use of the template in performing a particular task. These include conditions may depend on context data including the connected case, environmental variables like the current user or task history.

Each step may also be enhanced with conditions deciding whether it is mandatory, repeatable or presupposes the fulfillment of other steps. Thus the sequence of performance is only partially determined, and the case worker may choose whether to perform any non-mandatory step, and how many times to apply steps that are repeatable. Steps may appear or disappear as a consequence of changes made by the user or other users, or due to environmental factors.

Each available system service can be invoked from a step. Conditions and actions in the step definitions also have access to all available system functionality. By allowing a step to create new tasks, adaptive workflow can be accomplished.

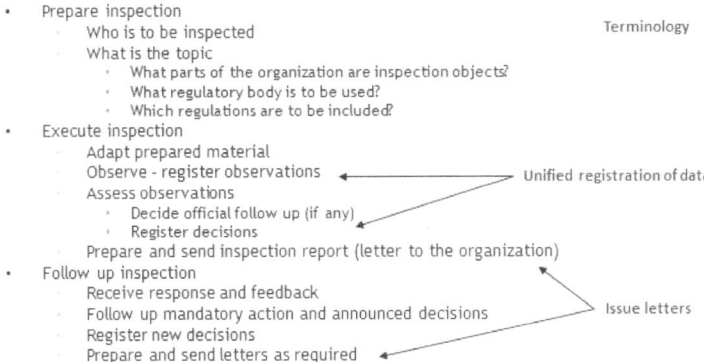

Fig. 2. Disagreements emerge when going deeper into the matter

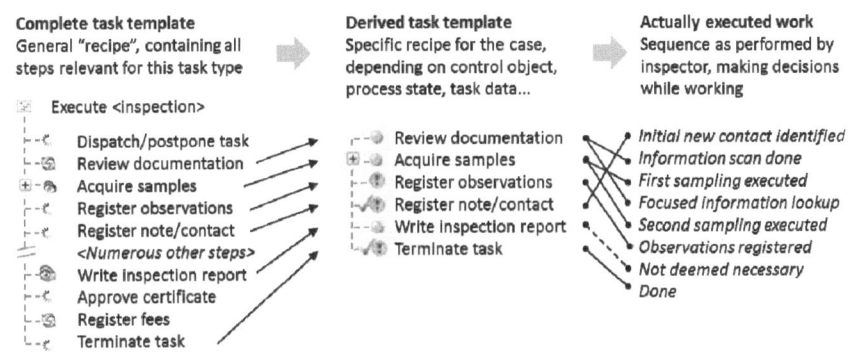

Fig. 3. Activity work definition and appearance in a particular context

2.2 Task Library Enhances Flexibility

Tasks may be created and assigned to worklists as a result of an event, for instance the arrival of a new document in the document archive system, or the submission of an application in the self-service web client, or as a consequence of performing steps in a derived task template.

Complementing event-driven task creation, a task library is available in connection with the worklists. The inspector may opt to start any of the tasks available to him in the library, start to perform them or send them to someone else. Access to the tasks is controlled by permissions linked to actively managed user roles. Tasks with a user supplied textual description but without task template, may be started and sent.

The case manager, e.g. an inspector, may thus start a control activity task, a general task for an informal letter, a registration task or any other task defined in the system, whenever he wants.

As activity work definitions are conceived at a sufficiently high level of abstraction for the different field experts to agree, we have been able to make few and general work definitions supporting uniform work practices, rather than numerous specific work definitions for each field.

The work definitions (task templates and task library) are managed in a separate editor, generating xml files. These work definitions are thus declarative and not implemented as part of the program code. It is in principle possible for expert users to define activity work support themselves, and to deploy these definitions in the system at runtime.

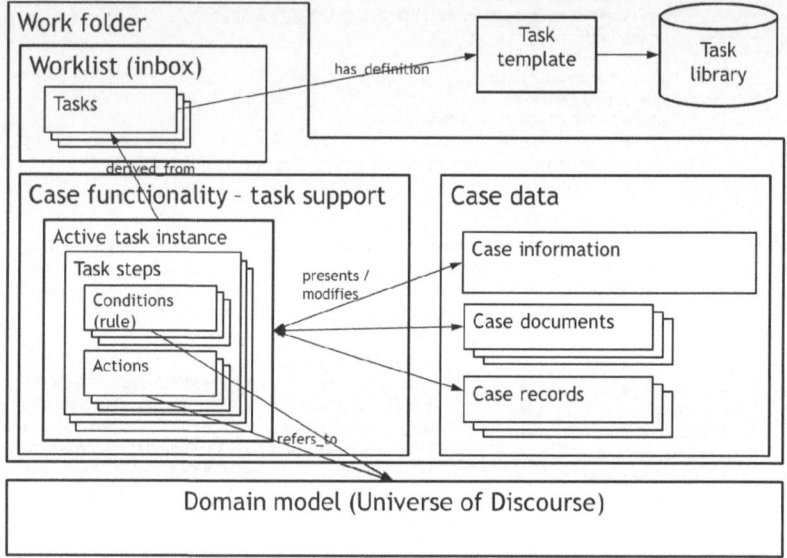

Fig. 4. Work folders providing task support

2.3   A Brief Walk-Through of a Regular Control Case

When an NFSA inspector starts a control activity in MATS, he must decide which control activity object(s) of a case folder that will be subject to control. MATS presents the acts relevant for the chosen control objects, and the inspector decides the legal foundation for this particular control. He then selects a list of corresponding requirements from the requirement base, created and maintained by central experts responsible for each field.

The inspector proceeds to the actual control activity, registering each observation with respect to the selected requirements. Every observation must be connected to a requirement, and thus to a point in the legislation. He can add requirements when needed. Based on observations, he may make a decision e.g. to close a restaurant. MATS ensures that he specifies the precise legal basis for the decision, explains how the observations constitute non-conformities, specifies what measures are to be enforced, and states the reason for selecting the measures in question. In the future, field inspections will be supported by smartphone or pad.

Based on the registered data and a structured document template, the system generates a letter, containing correctly presented inspection results as well as required elements such as information about the right to complain. The inspector may add text in specified slots to complete the letter.

If necessary, he can go back and revise the registered data, and regenerate the letter, keeping his own added text. Only when he performs the step confirming that the letter has been sent, the system archives the letter as a journaled document, and the data and documents are then locked for editing. All documents are filed in a separate system for document handling, conforming to the Norwegian archives Act. The archiving process and journaling is performed by MATS.

All information and documents registered for an NFSA client are collected and presented in the context of the relevant case folder. External identification keys for the different types of control activity objects ensure that the system is also able to present information from external sources. Control activity objects can also be connected through external sources, such as the Norwegian Land Registry (Eiendomsregisteret).

Every NFSA employee has a personal worklist. Organizational units have one or several common worklists for handling requests that are not yet allocated to a particular inspector. Any one task may appear in several worklists, and will normally be found both in the worklist of an inspector and in the worklist of the case folder connected to the task. The case folder provides an overview of the tasks pertaining to the case at hand, indicating to whom each task has been allocated.

3   ACM Example 2: Emergency Response Support for NFSA

NFSA are faced with a plethora of external events that they must handle. Many such events lead to control activities, but some are considered so potentially harmful that NFSA treat them as emergencies. Whether an event or situation is to be treated as an emergency, is up to the judgment of the NFSA worker. There is no formal requirement to start an incident log in the emergency response module. In principle, the same external event (e.g. a dead cow) may lead to control activity with inspection and sampling, or it may trigger an emergency response.

In an emergency, NFSA workers must fill multiple roles handling media requests, organizing the NFSA effort to solve the problem, serve the government and if necessary alert international systems. The incident log keeps track of all these events, and gives all involved personnel a shared overall picture. It also documents all activities in retrospect.

When the incident is closed, log information is exported to an excel work book automatically deposited in the document archive system. Since the emergency module is an integral part of MATS, all involved personnel have access to the full MATS functionality, including all control activity objects and control activity results.

3.1   A Loosely Structured Incident Log

An emergency situation is a highly unstructured incident and every case is a new case. Each emergency must be handled to meet the unique requirements of the situation.

The MATS emergency response module does not provide task- or workflow support for emergencies.

As soon as a situation is identified as a possible emergency, an incident log is created to keep track of, and document, the handling of the incident. This log can be viewed as a case folder for the emergency incident.

Incident log elements can be of three different types; action, media request or decision. The types are used only for categorization, and all elements have identical functionality.

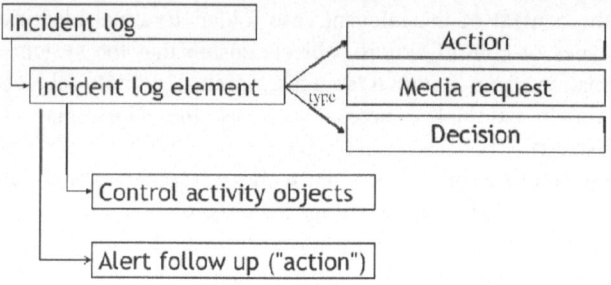

Fig. 5. Incident log structure

Each log element is presented using:

- A main page with details and
  - A description field where each new addition is marked with author and date.
  - A list of comments where each comment gets marked with time and who made it.
  - A tool to assign duties to organizational entities (persons or departments) in MATS
  - A set of useful web links
  - A history for the element
- A page for relevant control activity objects
- A page to handle distribution and follow-up of alerts. The organizational entities registered as having duties will automatically be added as recipients for alerts. It is possible to add further recipients for alerts and send alerts several times to different recipients.

3.2   Connected Control Activity Objects

An emergency in the NFSA domain can be connected to any number of establishments or persons subjected to control activities by NFSA. An example is the discovery of an animal disease, such as an outbreak of BSE. It is important to keep track of the control activity objects, here farms, that may be involved. The page for connected control activity objects serves this purpose. A control activity object is connected to the log element either directly by using the functionality on the page, or from actual inspections involving a disease that requires emergency logging. This may either be an emergency case discovered during control activity or additional information added to an existing case.

From the page in the log element, regular work folders of the related control activity objects and disease cases in MATS can be accessed.

3.3   Sending Alerts

Alerts about proposed incident actions are sent as tasks, with rudimentary task support to acknowledge the proposed action. Each department already has an inbox – a monitored MATS worklist – and the employees engaged in control activities use their inboxes daily for ordinary control activity work.

The incident worker can make a list of organizational units to alert. The system will automatically suggest those organizational units that have been assigned duties on the main page.

4   Interaction between the ACM modules

The fact that the emergency response module is an integral part of MATS, gives several advantages:

- The emergency response module may use MATS directly, for instance in the search of control activity objects, geographically close control activity objects, displaying the control activities in maps, and in sending tasks alerting the organization.
- The emergency situation worker may use the functionality of MATS, searching in the registers of MATS for control activities, disease cases, restrictions, control activity history etc.
- The inspectors of NFSA can see the emergency log elements that an establishment or person has been connected to, via a control activity object.
- The inspectors of NFSA can contribute to the emergency situation log

Since the emergency response module is a part of MATS, the incident worker can make full use of MATS for searching and overviewing different kinds of objects, including viewing located objects in maps. Objects viewable in maps are control activity objects of a certain activity type or subjected to a specific type of restriction by the NFSA, and disease cases. The map view of control objects is integrated in the emergency log module itself.

The integration between the control activity work support and the emergency response module maximizes availability of relevant information in the chosen context.

5   Questions for Discussion

We have described two versions of case management systems. On the one hand, the incident log is an extremely flexible version of case management with minimally structured functionality to document the case handling, to manage alerts and to keep track of actions and responsibilities - its purpose is to support time-critical collaboration. The limitations in structured functionality remain even if we add other general functionality, such as search engines, social software and mobile technology. We therefore propose to call this a *domain neutral* ACM system. It lacks the activity- and domain models for the types of cases that it supports in a particular use. The mark of such an ACM system is that it may be used across domains.

On the other hand, we presented the control activity system, an example of ACM with structured domain data and flexible work support for known bits and pieces of the tasks of the knowledge worker. This version is flexible within the limits of control activities and covers a vast subject matter domain, including specific legislation. The control activity worker will confront ever changing situations that need to be solved in a suitable way. Even with predefined work support such as described above, the control activity worker must be able to adapt to such different situations. It may be possible to "transplant" the system to a different area of control activity, but this would require a good deal of work, changing to the legislation in question, defining other control activity types and so on. We therefore propose to call this a *domain specific* ACM system. The mark of such an ACM system is that it inherently belongs inside its native domain.

The ability to adapt to the context at hand is central to ACM. In the emergency response module, adaptivity is provided by a general purpose workspace with no specific work support. Loosely-structured logs serve as case folders, enabling collaborative work. This produces a set of proposed and mutually agreed mitigating actions for dealing with the incident.

In the control activity module, adaptivity is provided by offering a rich and flexible domain model with a repertory of activity elements. These are dynamically assembled into active task support under the control of the user.

Written plans and procedures exist for handling various aspects of incidents. This suggests that active task support may be within reach for emergency response as well. This can be provided as a supplement to the existing solution, both to reach qualitatively better actions and to have mitigating actions proposed more quickly.

The existing interaction between the emergency response module and the control activity module demonstrates that specific domain elements may be a useful augmentation to the domain neutral ACM.

Below, we raise and elaborate on some important questions regarding domain specific and domain neutral ACMs.

5.1   Is Domain Specificity by Necessity Something That Restrains Flexibility?

Work support designed for the area of expertise and integrated with a rich domain model increase the possible impact and effectiveness of a system. It can enable and enforce the collection and building up of highly structured, searchable and reportable data, as well as provide the means for directed guidance and even control of how tasks may be performed.

In one sense, all structuring, guidance and control will decrease flexibility. In most cases, however, the structuring, guidance and control are highly desirable, even required properties. The challenge is to provide the desired flexibility in combination with structure and control.

5.2   Is it Useful to Include Domain Neutral Systems in the ACM-Family?

A general purpose system without domain knowledge beyond what is necessary for the collaboration on 'whatever', may be very useful. Systems like Outlook and Facebook may be viewed as such systems. They may even be viewed as ACM-systems, since they gather information in folders that may be seen as case folders.

We think, however, that there is reason to discuss whether or not some domain representation and specific work support ought to be required to include a system in the ACM-family.

5.3   How Adaptive Must a Case Management System Be to Be Called an ACM?

A Production Case Management system (PCM) [9] has been described as similar to an ACM in dealing with unpredictability, but with less adaptability. Any case management solution, whether an ACM or a PCM, needs access to domain data. A CM may utilize hot-deployable work definitions, codes and parts of its domain model or even have tools to build or change these on the fly. Can we draw the line between ACMs and PCMs by distinguishing between how knowledge is represented in the system, and how knowledge assets dynamically may be recombined under the guidance of an expert user during use?

5.4   Is the Control Activity Module of MATS a Good Example of a Domain Specific ACM System?

Our answer to the need for flexibility together with structure has been to have a rich domain model together with a library of snippets of work support highly integrated with the domain model. This gives the user flexibility on many levels, and we argue that case folders in the form of work folders as described meet the ACM criteria even though it is not possible for end users to create and change work definitions on the fly.

5.5   When Is It Useful to Extend a Domain Neutral ACM with Domain Knowledge?

We believe that generally, a domain specific system is preferable to a domain neutral one to support experts in their work. Mostly, the experts will benefit from structured data being collected and from using some level of formal procedure or approach to their problems. In many cases, however, the area of expertise is only partly covered with standard procedures or plans. A transformation from domain neutral to domain specific may be done incrementally, and in particular in an ACM context, we think that such an approach will be valuable. We believe that the choice of a domain neutral system rather than a domain specific one often is made for reasons of time, cost and lack of knowledge, rather than because of some intrinsic property of the area in question.

6   Lessons Learned

Most of our experience with operational ACM solutions is with domain specific ACMs which include a shared domain model for all snippets of work support. We have tried to summarize some best practices and key learning points [4] from MATS and other projects based on the FrameSolutions ACM framework:

- Provide work folders instead of document folders: Work folders can offer a particular perspective on a case, with access to worklists, task support and domain data as an enhancement to traditional documents.

- Work performance support can be provided through customized task support templates with loosely ordered task steps with associated actions and conditions for ensuring correct case handling.

- Offer the users a high degree of freedom in choosing, starting and forwarding tasks. Such freedom may reduce the needs for very detailed "exception handling" processes.

- Maximize declarative representations for covering business logic: processes and task definitions, business rules, codes and code sets, document templates can all be separated from the programming code; they can be maintained in their own lifecycles and subject to hot-deployment.

- Engage subject matter experts in the system development effort – in the development phases as many "experts" as "system developers" should contribute.

- Use stepwise delivery in order to reduce risk and engage users.

- Do not get preoccupied with ACM. Starting a new project, you will discover together with the customers subject matter experts what kind of work performance support shall be offered.

References

1. Computas AS, http://www.computas.com/
2. Norwegian Food Safety Authority (Mattilsynet), http://mattilsynet.no/
3. 2012 Winners Announced in Global Awards for Excellence in Adaptive Case Management, http://adaptivecasemanagement.org/awards_2012_winners.html

4. Sem, H.F., Carlsen, S., Coll, G.J.: Norwegian Food Safety Authority, Nominated by Computas AS, Norway. In: Fischer, L. (ed.) How Knowledge Workers Get Things Done - Real-world Adaptive Case Management. Future Strategies Inc., Florida (2012)
5. Johansson, S.E., Kallåk, B.H., Pettersen, T.B., Ressem, J.E.: Expert Workflow: Building Knowledge Based Workflow Systems with Object Technology. In: OOPSLA 1997 - Conference on Object Oriented Programming Systems Languages and Applications (1997)
6. Dehli, E., Kallåk, B.H., Pettersen, T.B., Ressem, J.E., Sørli, A., Waagbø, G.: SARA - A Software Reuse Architechture for Building Expert Workflow Systems. In: AAAI 1998, Workshop on Using AI for Knowledge Management and Business Process Reengineering (1998)
7. Kallåk, B.H., Pettersen, T.B., Ressem, J.E.: Object-Oriented Workflow Management: Intelligence, flexibility, and real support for business processes. In: OOPSLA 1998, Workshop on Implementation and Application of Object-Oriented Workflow Management Systems (1998)
8. Sørli, A., Coll, G.J., Dehli, E., Tangen, K.: Knowledge sharing in distributed organisations. In: IJCAI 1999, Workshop on Knowledge Management and Organizational Memories Systems (1999)
9. Production Case Management vs. Adaptive Case Management, http://social-biz.org/2012/05/14/production-case-management-vs-adaptive-case-management/

Data Centric BPM and the Emerging Case Management Standard: A Short Survey

Mike Marin[1,2], Richard Hull[3,*], and Roman Vaculín[3]

[1] IBM Software Group, 1540 Scenic Ave., Costa Mesa, CA 92626 USA
mikemarin@us.ibm.com
[2] University of South Africa, Pretoria
49097040@mylife.unisa.ac.za
[3] IBM T.J. Watson Research Center, Hawthorne, NY 10532 USA
{hull,vaculin}@us.ibm.com

Abstract. Case Management, with its emphasis on the case folder as the anchor for managing business processes, is emerging as a way to provide rich flexibility for knowledge workers while retaining key advantages of BPM systems. This has introduced new challenges in connection with modeling case processes. This short survey traces the history of key modeling ideas and constructs that are being incorporated into the emerging "Case Management Model and Notation (CMMN)" response to the Object Management Group (OMG) request for proposals for a Case Management Process Modeling standard.

Keywords: Case handling systems, Case Management, Case Folder, Business Artifact, Guard-Stage-Milestone, CMMN, Modeling notation.

1 Introduction

Case Management (e.g., [1]) is emerging as a way to support knowledge workers in applications that require a level of flexibility beyond the process flows of classical Business Process Management (BPM). Case Management provides this flexibility through the use of a case folder, which holds a collection of business documents and other information, as the primary building block for managing business processes. In 2010 the Object Management Group (OMG) published a request for proposals [2] for a Case Management Process Model standard, and a response entitled "Case Management Model and Notation (CMMN)" [3] is now under development by a consortium of 10 companies. Although CMMN is still a work in progress, agreement has been reached on the core model and notation. This short survey traces the history of key modeling constructs and ideas that have helped to form the model of CMMN.

Case management (see Sect. 2) is fundamentally data-centric, and draws from a stream of research on data-centric approaches to BPM. One of the most important

---

* This author supported in part by NSF grant IIS-0812578, and by the European Community's Seventh Framework Programme FP7/2007-2013 under grant agreement number 257593 (ACSI).

M. La Rosa and P. Soffer (Eds.): BPM 2012 Workshops, LNBIP 132, pp. 24–30, 2013.
© Springer-Verlag Berlin Heidelberg 2013

influences on CMMN is the notion of *business artifacts* (also known as "business entities with lifecycles"), introduced in 2003 [4,5] (Sect. 3). A business artifact provides a tight marriage of data and process, incorporating both an *information model* and a *lifecycle model*. Early work on business artifacts, and also some work on business objects (e.g., [6,7]), focused on procedural lifecycle models (Sect. 4). Declarative approaches to data-centric BPM (Sect. 5) have roots in the Event-Condition-Action (ECA) rules paradigm, and began with Vortex [8] and the Case Handling system of [9]. The declarative Guard-Stage-Milestone (GSM) model for business artifacts [10,11,12] draws from that work. Commercial Case Management systems (Sect. 6) are adopting declarative approaches. GSM provides the basis for one of the systems [13], and also provides the foundation for the CMMN core model (Sect. 7).

2   Case Management

Case management or case handling was originally developed to help manage social work and related application areas. It was introduced in the BPM literature by van der Aalst and Weske in 2005 [9] who describe it as "a new paradigm for supporting flexible and knowledge intensive business processes. It is strongly based on data as the typical product of these processes." Market analysts at Forrester define case management as "a highly structured, but also collaborative, dynamic, and information-intensive process that is driven by outside events and requires incremental and progressive responses from the business domain handling the case. Examples of case folders include a patient record, a lawsuit, an insurance claim, or a contract, and the case folder would include all the documents, data, collaboration artifacts, policies, rules, analytics, and other information needed to process and manage the case." [14].

The definitions concur that case management is strongly based on data [9] and is information & knowledge intensive [14]. Although business artifacts were originally developed for traditional BPM domains, they have emerged as a good fit for case management. That premise was analyzed by de Man [15] in 2009, where he found that procedurally-based business artifacts provided useful aspects applicable to case management, but not enough to cover all uses. The introduction of Guard-Stage-Milestone [10] in 2010 enhanced business artifacts to the point that the group of companies working on CMMN [3] has found it a good foundation.

3   Introduction of Business Artifacts

Business artifacts were first introduced in the literature by Nigam and Caswell [4]. In the same year Kumaran et. al. [5] introduced the closely related "Adaptive Documents (ADocs)" model. Both models look at process from the perspective of the information represented in the business artifact (or ADoc) as it evolves over time. Both distinguish business artifacts from business objects; historically the latter are based on a more abstract object-oriented concept that does not explicitly model the lifecycle aspect.

Nigam and Caswell [4] were concerned with "a notation and a methodology useful for business process design at the business operational level". Their operational specification (OpS) tries to achieve a balance between being understandable by business users, and a formal characterization useful for verification. An OpS model specifies the information models and lifecycle models for a family of related business artifact types, and there is no distinction between control flow and data flow.

Document engineering [16] is also related to business artifacts. For example, the document-driven workflows of Wang and Kumar [17] model the process as a flow with *business documents* and *activities* connected by and-forks, or-forks and joins. Each activity produces a distinct document; this contrasts with business artifacts, for which multiple activities may interact with documents over a long period of time.

4   Finite-State Machine Based Lifecycles

In the second half of the decade 2000-2010 the business artifact community and groups extending business objects gravitated towards the use of finite state machines to represent the lifecycles. The notion of associating a state machine with an artifact lifecycle appears in the original ADocs [5]. Kumaran et. al. [18] proposes this association much more explicitly and in particular incorporates activities directly into the state machine, as annotations on the transitions between states. In contrast with OpS, in [18] the interaction between artifacts is limited to activities of one artifact being able to send a message to a different artifact. CMMN also makes this assumption.

In the Business Entity Lifecycle Analytics (BELA) method [19] the states are thought of as *milestones*, i.e., business-relevant operational objectives that an artifact may achieve. Over time the notion of milestone has matured in BELA, and now includes specification of *achieving conditions*, based on which attributes have been assigned values. A related, less formal notion of *milestones with deadlines* is discussed in [20].

Similar to business artifacts, PHILharmonicFlows [7], enable a strong integration of process and data, supporting business objects with finite-state machine based lifecycles. Another finite-state machine based approach for business objects is FlexConnect [6]. In contrast with the artifact approach and with [7], states in FlexConnect represent activities, and the transition between states corresponds implicitly to achievement of a business goal.

5   Declarative Lifecycles

A key ingredient in enabling rich flexibility in data-centric workflow and BPM systems is the shift from procedural to declarative lifecycle models. The prominent work in this area has been rule-based (rather than using, e.g., Linear Temporal Logic).

Perhaps the first publication describing a declarative, data-centric process framework is on Vortex [8], introduced in 1999. Vortex supports highly flexible workflows, especially automated ones for personalization applications in call routing and web store fronts. In Vortex, condition-based *guards* control if/when modules are launched, providing more flexibility than typical flow-based approaches. However, the core Vortex constructs have limitations that prevent their use for general-purpose BPM.

The first publication describing a declarative case management model is [9]. The Case Handling model there is quite rich. The model provides for a collection of *data object definitions* (essentially a case folder) and a collection of *activity definitions*. Each activity has a finite-state machine based lifecycle, and activities are arranged into a directed acyclic graph. The control of activities is formally specified by Event-Condition-Action (ECA) rules derived from the concept of activity pre-conditions.

The GSM approach for specifying declarative artifact lifecycles was introduced in [10] and further refined in [11,12]. GSM can be viewed as a substantial generalization of Vortex that permits multiple artifact types and removes many of the restrictions required in Vortex. Figure 1 shows a sketch of the Requisition

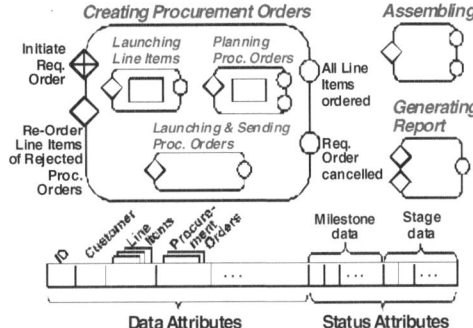

Fig. 1. Requisition Order artifact of "Make to Order" application (adapted from [11])

Order artifact from a "Make to Order" application [11]. In the figure, rounded rectangles represent *stages*, which model clusters of work performed for the artifact. Stages are hierarchical and may run in parallel. The circles represent *milestones*, corresponding to business-relevant operational objectives that an artifact may achieve. Diamonds correspond to *guards*, which control stage opening. If a stage is open and one of its milestones becomes true, the stage closes (intuitively, because the purpose of a stage is to achieve one of its milestones).

Guards and milestones are controlled by *sentries*, i.e. expressions of the form **on** <event> **if** <condition> (the **on** or **if** part might be empty). Events may come from the external environment, or be internal, corresponding to a change in stage or milestone status. Sentries are mapped to ECA-like rules, similar to [9]. The operational semantics is based on the notion of *Business Step* (*B-step*), which corresponds intuitively to having the system respond to a single incoming event, including the firing of all applicable ECA rules until stability is achieved.

6   Commercial Products

There are at least three products that have been influential on CMMN development.

FLOWer*:* The Case Handling model described in [9] is a formalization of the model used by the commercial system FLOWer, offered by the company Pallas Athena. As mentioned in Section 5, the Case Handling model assumes that the case processing activities will be executed based on a pre-designed acyclic graph. Activities might be omitted because of pre-designed rules or by case worker choice.

IBM Case Manager: This product [13] was developed based on the GSM ideas. It uses a content management repository for the information model, which consist of a case folder hierarchy and document classes. Placing, removing, or modifying documents in those directories trigger events; these and other kinds of events can be used in guard conditions to launch stages as in GSM.

Cordys Case Management: This product [21] is event driven, and uses the concept of case file with properties for the informational model. The basic building block of the behavioral model is *activity cluster*, which may hold tasks and/or other activity clusters. At the outermost level activity clusters are organized into a state machine. *Dynamic planning* allows users to do instance level planning and adding new tasks.

7   OMG Case Management Process Modeling

The emerging Case Management Model and Notation (CMMN) combines a variety of capabilities, many of which can be traced back to the literature and products described in preceding sections. As with any case-based approach, there is a clear separation in CMMN between the case folder (information model) and the case behavioral model (lifecycle). Since IBM and Cordys are active participants of the team developing CMMN, their products [13,21] have had an influence on the proposal.

The core behavioral model of CMMN comes from GSM. In particular, the behavioral model is composed of tasks, hierarchical stages, milestones and events. These are essentially the same constructs as in GSM, generalized to support finite-state machine based lifecycles (cf. [9]). The GSM operational semantics is generalized for the CMMN model. In GSM milestones are tightly linked to stages, whereas in CMMN the milestones may stand separately from stages (although they can occur nested inside stages).

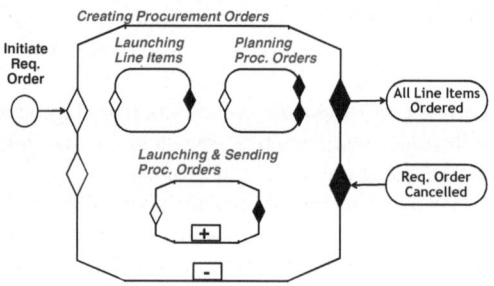

An important influence of the Cordys model [21] on CMMN is the ability for case workers to alter the runtime plan. This feature is not present in any of the published business artifact models.

Fig. 2. One stage of Requisition Order of Figure 1, modeled using CMMN notation

Although the current version of the CMMN proposal [3] does not include examples or a definitive indication on how the notation should be used, we have attempted to model the behavioral aspect of one stage of the "Make to Order" application from Figure 1 in the CMMN notation, shown in Figure 2. (Key – task: rounded rectangle; stage: cut-corner rectangle; milestone: elongated circle; event (listener): circle; guard: white diamond; terminating criteria: black diamond. Arrows are used as a shorthand indicating a triggering relationship.)

8   Conclusions

This survey has traced the history of key concepts that contribute into the draft Case Management Model and Notation (CMMN) standards proposal, with an emphasis on the core modeling constructs. CMMN is just the first step in the establishment of a Case Management standard; we can anticipate refinements and extensions as the community starts to use CMMN in practical settings.

References

1. Swenson, K.D. (ed.): Mastering the Unpredictable: How Adaptive Case Management will Revolutionize the Way that Knowledge Workers Get Things Done. Meghan-Kiffer Press, Tampa (2010)
2. Object Management Group. Case Management Process Modeling (CMPM) Request for Proposal. Document bmi/2009-09-23 (October 2009)
3. BizAgi, Cordys, IBM, Oracle, SAP AG, Singularity (OMG Submitters), Agile Enterprise Design, Stiftelsen SINTEF, TIBCO, Trisotech (Co-Authors). Proposal for: Case Management Modeling and Notation (CMMN) Specification 1.0. (OMG Document bmi/2012-07-10). In response to: Case Management Process Modeling (CMPM) RFP (OMG Document bmi/2009-09-04). Object Management Group (July 2012)
4. Nigam, A., Caswell, N.S.: Business artifacts: An approach to operational specification. IBM Systems Journal 42(3), 428–445 (2003)
5. Kumaran, S., Nandi, P., Heath, T., Bhaskaran, K., Das, R.: ADoc-oriented programming. In: Symp. on Applications and the Internet, SAINT, pp. 334–343 (2003)
6. Redding, G., Dumas, M., ter Hofstede, A.H.M., Iordachescu, A.: Modelling flexible processes with business objects. In: Proc. 11th IEEE Intl. Conf. on Commerce and Enterprise Computing, pp. 41–48 (2009)
7. Künzle, V., Reichert, M.: PHILharmonicFlows: Towards a framework for object-aware process management. Journal of Software Maintenance 23(4), 205–244 (2011)
8. Hull, R., Llirbat, F., Siman, E., Su, J., Dong, G., Kumar, B., Zhou, G.: Declarative workflows that support easy modification and dynamic browsing. In: Proceedings of the International Joint Conference on Work Activities Coordination and Collaboration, WACC, pp. 69–78 (1999)
9. van der Aalst, W.M.P., Weske, M.: Case Handling: a new paradigm for business process support. Data & Knowledge Engineering 53(2), 129–162 (2005)
10. Hull, R., Damaggio, E., Fournier, F., Gupta, M., Heath III, F(T.), Hobson, S., Linehan, M., Maradugu, S., Nigam, A., Sukaviriya, P., Vaculin, R.: Introducing the Guard-Stage-Milestone Approach for Specifying Business Entity Lifecycles. In: Bravetti, M. (ed.) WS-FM 2010. LNCS, vol. 6551, pp. 1–24. Springer, Heidelberg (2011)
11. Hull, R., Damaggio, E., De Masellis, R., Fournier, F., Gupta, M., Heath, T., Hobson, S., Linehan, M., Maradugu, S., Nigam, A., Sukaviriya, P., Vaculín, R.: Business Artifacts with Guard-Stage-Milestone Lifecycles: Managing Artifact Interactions with Conditions and Events. In: Proc. ACM Intl. Conf. Distributed Event-Based Systems, DEBS (2011)
12. Damaggio, E., Hull, R., Vaculín, R.: On the Equivalence of Incremental and Fixpoint Semantics for Business Artifacts with Guard-Stage-Milestone Lifecycles. In: Rinderle-Ma, S., Toumani, F., Wolf, K. (eds.) BPM 2011. LNCS, vol. 6896, pp. 396–412. Springer, Heidelberg (2011)
13. Zhu, W., Becker, B., Boudreaux, J., Braman, S., Do, T., Gomez, D., Marin, M., Vaughan, A.: Advanced Case Management with IBM Case Manager. IBM Redbooks, New York (2011)
14. Moore, C., Le Clair, C., Vitti, R.: Dynamic Case Management - An Old Idea Catches New Fire. Forrester (December 2009)
15. de Man, H.: Case Management: A Review of Modeling Approaches. BPTrends (January 2009)
16. Glushko, R.J., McGrath, T.: Document Engineering: Analyzing and Designing Documents for Business Informatics and Web Services. MIT Press, Cambridge (2005)

17. Wang, J., Kumar, A.: A Framework for Document-Driven Workflow Systems. In: van der Aalst, W.M.P., Benatallah, B., Casati, F., Curbera, F. (eds.) BPM 2005. LNCS, vol. 3649, pp. 285–301. Springer, Heidelberg (2005)
18. Kumaran, S., Liu, R., Wu, F.Y.: On the Duality of Information-Centric and Activity-Centric Models of Business Processes. In: Bellahsène, Z., Léonard, M. (eds.) CAiSE 2008. LNCS, vol. 5074, pp. 32–47. Springer, Heidelberg (2008)
19. Strosnider, J.K., Nandi, P., Kumaran, S., Ghosh, S., Arsanjani, A.: Model-driven synthesis of SOA solutions. IBM Systems Journal 47(3), 415–432 (2008)
20. Rooze, E.J., Paapst, M., Sombekke, J.: eCase Management: An international study in judicial organization. Report sponsored by the Netherlands Council for the Judiciary (2007)
21. de Man, H.: Case Management: Cordys Approach. BPTrends (February 2009)

Towards a System Support
of Collaborative Knowledge Work

Nicolas Mundbrod, Jens Kolb, and Manfred Reichert

Institute of Databases and Information Systems
Ulm University, Germany
{nicolas.mundbrod,jens.kolb,manfred.reichert}@uni-ulm.de
http://www.uni-ulm.de/dbis

Abstract. Knowledge work is becoming the predominant type of work in developed countries. Leveraging their expertise, skills, and experiences, knowledge workers daily deal with demanding situations. Therefore, they widely work autonomously, but usually collaborate in multiple contexts. Further, their work is influenced by dynamic factors like time constraints, costs, and available resources, and thereby it cannot be pre-specified like routine work. The lack of an appropriate context and process support, in turn, reduces their productivity and hinders the reuse as well as the continuous improvement of elaborated solutions. This paper structures collaborative knowledge work and presents its characteristics and dimensions. Moreover, we introduce a lifecycle methodology to support collaborative knowledge workers holistically.

Keywords: knowledge work, knowledge workers, collaboration, lifecycle support, CSCW.

1 Introduction

A change from an industrial towards a knowledge-based society is taking place in developed countries: *knowledge work* is becoming the predominant type of work [1]. Utilizing their distinguished skills, gained experiences, and expertise, knowledge workers (e.g., doctors, engineers, or researchers) daily solve demanding and sophisticated tasks. Hence, knowledge work represents an important part of today's corporate business processes. Contemporary process-aware information systems (PAISs) are not able to support knowledge workers adequately as pre-specified business process models are required. These models cannot be provided since knowledge work's tasks and their order are not predictable in detail. Instead, knowledge workers have to manually interrelate process-related information encapsulated in a variety of heterogeneous software systems (e.g., social and special-purpose software). Hence, there is no knowledge work assistance comparable to the support a PAIS can provide for routine work.

Based on [2], this paper discussed how *collaborative knowledge work* (CKW) can be supported by an adaptive information system (CKW system) (*objective I*). For this purpose, a sound definitional framework of CKW is established and

M. La Rosa and P. Soffer (Eds.): BPM 2012 Workshops, LNBIP 132, pp. 31–42, 2013.

CKW characteristics and dimensions are presented based on a case study (*objective II*). The remainder of this paper is structured as follows: Section 2 introduces the fundamentals of CKW. Subsequently, Section 3 presents representative CKW use cases. Section 4 provides CKW characteristics and dimensions. Section 5 introduces a lifecycle methodology for CKW. Finally, Section 6 summarizes the results and gives insights into future research.

2   Fundamentals of Collaborative Knowledge Work

2.1   Knowledge

Generally, the term of *knowledge* does not obtain a unique definition [3]. However, from the perspective of computer science, it is desirable to classify the terms of *data*, *information* and *knowledge* as those are often used synonymously by mistake. *Data* represents syntactic entities comprising a set of symbols (with no meaning), whereas *information* represents the output from data interpretation and hence data with meaning (i.e., semantics) [4]. Finally, *knowledge* is learned information, incorporated in an agent's reasoning resources (cf. Definition 1).

Definition 1. *Knowledge is a fluid mix of framed experiences, values, contextual information, and expert insights that provides a framework for evaluating and incorporating new experiences and information. It originates and is applied in the minds of knowers. In organizations, it often becomes embedded, not only in documents or repositories, but also in organizational routines, processes, practices, and norms. [5]*

For every collaboration, it is crucial that knowledge is communicable, enabling knowledge workers to easily share it. Already implied in Definition 1, epistemological scientist Polanyi shaped a distinction between *tacit* and *explicit knowledge* through the phrase *"We can know more than we can tell"* [6]. One can hold *tacit knowledge* without having the capability to explicitly express the quintessence, e.g., the capability to hold the balance on a bicycle. In contrast, *explicit knowledge* is expressible in a formal, systematic language and therefore it can be regarded as communicable knowledge (i.e., information). The differentiation provides the basis for Nonaka's and Takeuchi's theory of (corporate) *knowledge creation* [7]. Four different conversion modes between tacit and explicit knowledge are described: *socialization* (i.e., from tacit to tacit knowledge), *externalization* (i.e., tacit to explicit), *combination* (i.e., explicit), and *internalization* (i.e., explicit to tacit). A constant repetition of the different conversions provides the basis of the individual and organizational knowledge generation process: knowledge is spirally advanced and transferred from being individually obtained to organizationally or even inter-organizationally shared (cf. Figure 1).

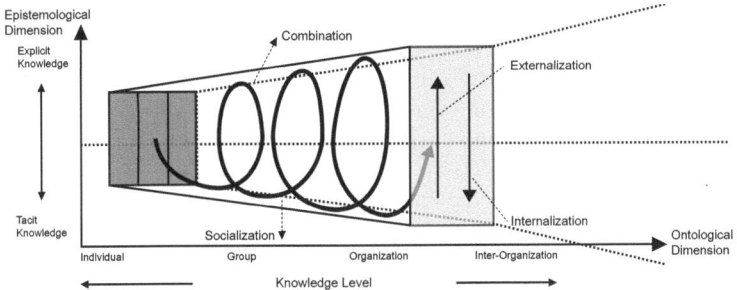

Fig. 1. Organizational Knowledge Creation Spiral [7]

2.2   Knowledge Work

Hube assessed 16 definitions of knowledge work in relation to four self-established criteria: *applicability, process description, context relation*, and *distinction* [8]. He suggests Definition 2 as the most appropriate one for *knowledge work*[1] [8].

Definition 2. *Knowledge work is comprised of objectifying intellectual activities, addressing novel and complex processes and (work) results, which require external means of control and a dual field of action.*

Hube separates the term of knowledge work from the related term of *intellectual work*. While intellectual work generally contains *mental work*, knowledge work comprises only activities addressing novel and complex processes as well as work results. Hence, routine mental work is excluded. Based on the *theory of action regulation*, an individual performing knowledge work is supposed to use a *referential* and an *actual field of action* [9]. In the *referential field of action*, one merely deals with a problem theoretically. Thereby, one can deliberately act and test different approaches, not causing any impact on the assignment. In comparison, necessary instruments, actions and resources are used in the *actual field of action* to properly manage the complex processes. Further, the results of the referential field of action are transferred to finally achieve the work's objective.

2.3   Knowledge Work Process

Due to knowledge work's focus on novelty and complexity, obviously, there is no pre-specified process an individual can perform. However, a generic and ideal-typical *knowledge work process* is described as shown in Figure 2. Note that each of the process steps can be executed multiple times and might be skipped as well. First, an individual performing knowledge work deducts an assignment from an ambition and available information (Step 1). Subsequently, orientation (2) and planning (3) in the actual field of action take place, the assignment is concretized, and possible resources are evaluated. Then, theoretical solutions are

---
[1] Definition 2 is translated from German.

reviewed (4) and a solution strategy is designed (5). Consequently, the plan is put into operation (6), and the intermediate work result is constantly assessed. On the one hand the result is evaluated considering its formal quality (7), on the other hand the original plan might be adapted (8). Additionally, it is even possible that the whole assignment has to be re-evaluated (9).

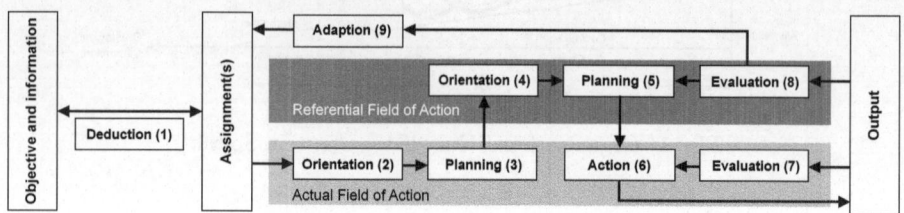

Fig. 2. Generic Knowledge Work Process [8]

2.4   Knowledge Workers

Naturally, a knowledge work process highly depends on the knowledge of the individuals who perform knowledge work. There are various definitions addressing the question who exactly is a knowledge worker or not (cf. [8,10,11]). Concluding, Definition 3 introduces the term of a *knowledge worker* [12].

Definition 3. *Knowledge workers* *have high degrees of expertise, education, or experience, and the primary purpose of their jobs involves the process and accomplishment of knowledge work.*

Obviously, whether an individual rates a task to be routine or rather novel and challenging, depends on his personal degree of foreknowledge. Knowledge workers exposing high degrees of expertise, education, and experience usually deal better with novel and complex situations as others without respective foreknowledge. This coherence rounds out the connection between Definitions 2 and 3. Generally, knowledge workers comprise various professions: A manager of literally any company is supposed to perform knowledge work in order to successfully manage and improve a company's business [12]. Further, Definition 3 underlines that knowledge workers hold responsible positions, i.e., their productivity is a crucial concern for any company.

Usually, the processing of novel and complex problems is split into manageable parts, which are assigned to knowledge workers who feature the needed expertise and experiences [8]. However, based on their expertise and experiences, knowledge workers are concurrently requested in multiple contexts, where they need to adopt different roles. This exposes the main issues knowledge workers face these days: they have to manually filter, classify and manage context-related information to project their thoughts into the corresponding context. Furthermore, they must cope with the related issue of attention fragmentation, while trying to keep track of any progress being made in different context. In order to adequately inspect the properties of CKW, Definition 4 defines it formally.

Definition 4. *Collaborative knowledge work (CKW) is described as knowledge work jointly performed by two or more knowledge workers in order to achieve a common business goal.*

3 Collaborative Knowledge Work Use Cases

To validate the definitions, three different CKW use cases are introduced.[2] Based on these, CKW characteristics and dimensions are derived in Section 4.

UC1: Development Project. This use case is based on a *development project* for an embedded system in the automotive sector. It features multidisciplinary collaboration of knowledge workers, e.g., vehicles require complex mechatronic systems developed by engineers of various professions. Typically, a best practice (e.g., a V-model) is used to systematically synchronize results of concurrent development teams (i.e., qualitative development course) and to provide an understandable overview whereby knowledge workers can orientate. Moreover, a virtual system prototype is created and gradually enhanced. Development, research, and implementation projects can be generally considered to deal with the well-organized creation of solutions (i.e., explicit knowledge) considering a pre-defined problem. Complex problems are extensively studied, analyzed, and evaluated up-front to collaboratively develop a solution based on a deployed project methodology (e.g., a domain-related best practice).

UC2: Criminal Investigations. *Criminal investigations* are addressed in this use case: *"an investigation is the examination, study, tracking, and gathering of factual information that answers questions or solves problems"* [13]. Investigative work often contains several concurrently emerging angles with dedicated investigative staff members ascertaining. While there are standardized investigative actions (e.g., securing of evidence), investigators in charge have to individually determine which of the standard procedures need to be applied. Comparably, the work of attorneys, judges and researchers is naturally connected to the work of public investigation authorities. Moreover, companies are increasingly obliged to provide information on requests of customers, citizens, regulators, or board members (e.g., audit requests or fraud detection).

UC3: Complex Financial Service Request. Business processes in the financial service sector are highly standardized today. However, there are still exceptional situations which have to be handled individually. Presumably, a financial service company receives a request for a large-scale combination of financial products from a key customer. Therefore, financial experts, who are specialized to specific products, are involved on demand by the responsible key account manager to meet the customer's needs. In this case, related use cases are insurance claim handling, product change requests, loan origination, customer onboarding, and intensive patient care. All these have in common that they are

---

[2] Detailed descriptions of the use cases are available in [2].

dependent on human assessment and decisions based on expertise and experiences, continuously gained information and the proper handling of unexpected events and occurring problems.

4 Characteristics and Dimensions

Based on the use cases (cf. Section 3), characteristics (cf. Section 4.1) and dimensions (cf. Section 4.2) are presented. Figure 3 gives an overview of the CKW characteristics and their coherence.

4.1 Characteristics

C1: Uncertainty. The notion of complexity, implicitly addressed by knowledge work, refers to problems or situations comprising an unmanageable set of *influencing factors* intertwined via dynamic correlations [8]. Consequently, the generic knowledge work process (cf. Section 2.3) includes three feedback loops that are motivated by the need to continuously assess the planned and finally conducted actions. The course of actions is dynamically determined by the involved knowledge workers and based on their expertise and experiences. Considering the collaboration of knowledge workers, obviously, labor division comprises *interdependencies* and mutual *interference* between involved knowledge workers which further increase the general dynamics.

C2: Goal Orientation. A *common goal*, e.g., to meet customer's needs (cf. UC3), can be considered as the integrative factor for knowledge workers. In relation, Drucker stated that the crucial question in a knowledge worker's productivity is *"what is the task?"* [14]. In UC2, investigators collaborate to solve a crime and thereby derive the required tasks. Ideally, knowledge workers' individual goals are well integrated into the scope of a common goal. To adequately cope with complex and unpredictable CKW, sub-goals[3] are derived that are achievable in a shorter period of time. While a common goal in CKW should remain rather stable, sub-goals can be modified or even removed.

C3: Emergence. While pursuing a common goal and addressing uncertainty, knowledge workers continually adapt activities to successfully achieve their sub-goals. As a result of C1, knowledge workers have to focus on the planning of activities conducted any time soon (proximity of time). Activities scheduled later on might be brought up in principle, but not defined in detail yet. This agile planning and working implicates that CKW processes gradually emerge: knowledge workers constantly evaluate possible activities on the basis of their current state and in consideration of influencing factors. At every point, they have the choice between several performable actions to achieve further states and to further approach their common goal (cf. Figure 3).

---

[3] Also commonly known as milestones.

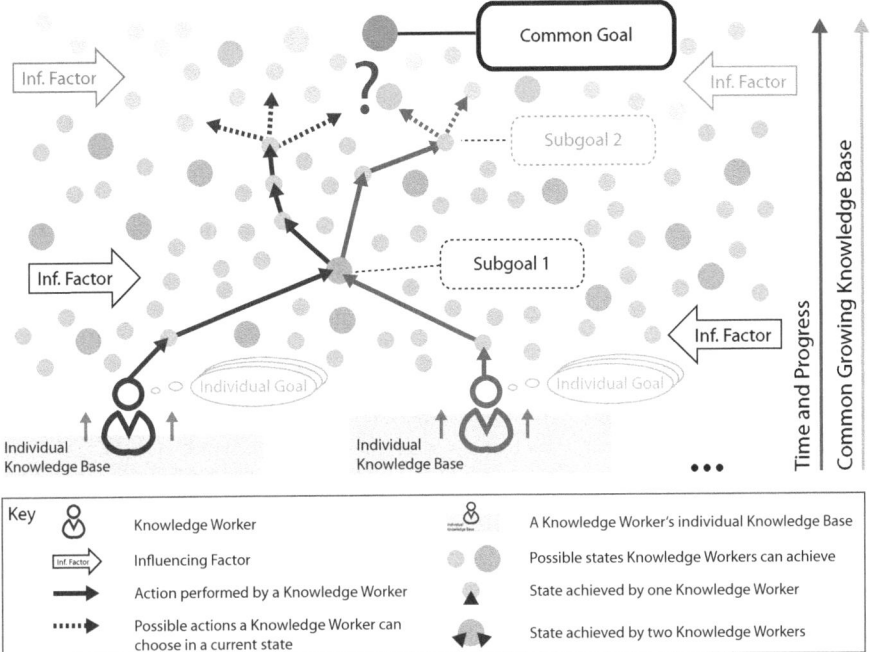

Fig. 3. CKW Characteristics and their Coherence

C4: Growing Knowledge Base. Externalization of knowledge in the shape of communicable information is crucially needed to achieve organizationally shared knowledge—a prerequisite for collaboration (cf. Section 2.1). CKW's explicit *knowledge base* usually comprises heterogeneous information, which has to be managed properly (e.g., office documents, e-mails, and handwritten notes). In general, the progress of a use case towards its goal is strongly connected to the advancement of the tacit and explicit knowledge base. For instance, information like schedules, responsibilities and methodologies is stepwise created to organize the project at the beginning of UC1. Afterwards, a prototype or developed components can represent the current state of development.

4.2   Dimensions

Naturally, countless dimensions can be considered by which CKW scenarios could be differentiated. Hence, this section focuses on dimensions clearly exposing significant implications for the system support of CKW.

D1: Knowledge Action Type. CKW can be differentiated by the predominant way the knowledge workers deal with knowledge and information. In relation, Davenport distinguishes between the knowledge actions *acquisition, application, creation, dissemination, documentation,* and *packaging of knowledge* [15].

Further types are presented in [16,17]. Although there are different approaches, pragmatic analyses of the main knowledge actions can yield benefits as the support of CKW can be adjusted accordingly.

D2: Methodology. The degree of adherence to a common methodology discernibly varies in UC1-UC3. The automotive development team (UC1), for example, decides to apply a V-model to organize CKW and to ensure a qualitative development progress. While individual activities are still subject to the different knowledge workers, an overall defined methodology is given. Methodologies do not have to be explicitly illustrated, renowned or even described to be successfully applied: a team can follow a tacit methodology, known and accepted by all knowledge workers as well as robust in the face of varying conditions.

D3: Interdisciplinarity. The use cases UC1-UC3 additionally unveiled that CKW varies from *domain-specific* to *interdisciplinary* work. CKW involving different domains can lead to misunderstandings, discords (e.g., about common procedures), or even severe inconsistencies. In this context, synonyms and homonyms can result in high effort to synchronize contributions. However, especially interdisciplinary work is highly promising for novel and complex issues.

D4: Organizational Frame. CKW is not compulsorily bound to organizational units or hierarchical structures. It can be distinguished by the surrounding *organizational frame* as well. In general, knowledge workers usually collaborate either spontaneously (i.e., without a dedicated organizational frame), or based on organizational frames like a *case* or *project*. Especially coordination aspects (i.e., responsibilities, organizational models, work allocations, and synchronizations) are influenced by the surrounding organizational frame.

D5: Spatial Proximity. Apart from preferred knowledge actions and organizational frames, CKW depends on the fact whether knowledge workers can directly communicate with each other, or not. Physical closeness empowers knowledge workers to directly communicate face to face, whereas physically separated knowledge workers obviously have to rely on communication and collaboration tools to virtually bridge a spatial gap. Hence, CKW can be distinguished by the degree of *spatial proximity* the knowledge workers have during their collaboration.

D6: Involved Knowledge Workers. The number of involved knowledge workers can vary between CKW projects as well. The complexity of CKW is a driver of the knowledge workers' headcount. Moreover, the corporate importance of CKW may be another reason to include more knowledge workers. In general, the number of involved knowledge workers results in an increased demand for appropriate support, especially for the systematic allocation and synchronization of work (coordination).

D7: Temporal Constraints. *Time constraints* [18] may also distinguish CKW projects. For example, fixed deadlines can be initially connected with objectives (i.e., fixed time frames). Considering UC2, there are sometime only relative or even no fixed deadlines, but investigators still suffer from a time pressure to solve the crime. In general, some CKW projects may be scheduled for months or even years whereas others have to be finished within hours or days.

D8: Information Interdependency. The acquisition of information to detect causal relationships can be regarded as the main purpose of investigative activities (cf. use case UC2). Closely related to dimension D1 and characteristic C4, CKW can also be distinguished by the complexity and importance of *information interdependencies*. Apart from internal information interdependencies in a company, CKW projects can also feature coordinative and information interdependencies between each other. Furthermore, the degree of interdependencies also raises coordination efforts.

D9: Number of Repetitions. The number of repetitive occurrences provides another dimension to distinguish CKW. As CKW is characterized to be emergent and rather unique, the dimension might sound curious. However, when common goals are considered in detail, a repetitive occurrence of CKW can be observed. Apart from a common goal, the presented dimensions D1-D8 can also be utilized to determine whether CKW projects share common properties. In general, the provision of a specific support for CKW depends on the possibility to determine the level of similarity an ongoing collaboration shares with already finished CKW. Thereby, it has to be assessed which parts of past scenarios can be leveraged for the support of the ongoing collaboration (i.e., sustainable support).

5   Collaborative Knowledge Work Lifecycle

In order to systematically support CKW by a dedicated information system (*CKW system*), the availability, advancement and communication of knowledge have to be ensured. If knowledge workers are empowered to quickly retrieve context-relevant information as well as experiential knowledge in the right shape and at the right point of time, their efficiency and effectiveness can be increased [8]. To establish a context- and process-aware support, the BPM lifecycle [19] can be leveraged: the *Collaborative Knowledge Work Lifecycle (CKWL)* (cf. Figure 4) describes integral phases, a CKW system has to provide.

The lifecycle consistently draws on the generic knowledge work process (cf. Section 2.3) as it features the phases *Orientation*[4], *Template Design*, *Collaboration Run Time*, and *Records Evaluation*. Further, it includes *action regulation* (cf. Section 2.2) implemented by a feedback loop (i.e., knowledge retrieval). The subsequent sections discuss the different lifecycle phases in detail.

Orientation Phase. Information about how knowledge workers usually collaborate in a certain context has to be gathered in the *orientation phase*. Dimension

---

[4] The CKWL is entered in the orientation phase.

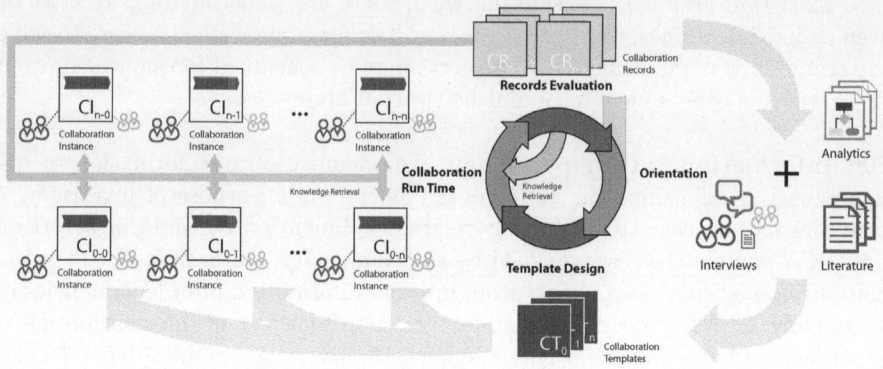

Fig. 4. The Collaborative Knowledge Work Lifecycle

D9 implies that CKW can be regarded to occur multiple times and hence be aggregated to a dedicated *collaboration type*. To perform a sound aggregation, dimensions D1-D8 can be utilized. Moreover, records of finalized collaborations are leveraged, involved knowledge workers systematically interviewed, or subject-related literature and expert experiences taken into consideration. In general, while the flow of activities is the main subject in the design phase of the BPM lifecycle, the orientation phase focuses on the *knowledge workers' information flow*. So, data sources and relevant information systems need to be explicitly documented and integrated [20]. Besides identifying information sources, the main *knowledge actions* of knowledge workers have to be considered as well (cf. D1). Further, their communication structure has to be addressed, especially in case that knowledge workers are distributed and need to communicate remotely (cf. D5). Coordination aspects also have to be taken into account: for instance, commonly used methodologies, organizational frames and frequently arising tasks must be documented. Finally, awareness information knowledge workers require to initiate, perform and manage communication and coordination has to be covered, as well.

Template Design Phase. Based on a thorough examination of collaboration types and their implicit information flows, *collaboration templates (CT)* need to be created. Thereby, a CT is comparable to a process model supporting standardizable work. A certain CT is then leveraged as a blueprint for a range of *collaboration instances (CIs)*. A CI refers to a virtual unit supporting CKW, e.g., a specific development project. The involved knowledge workers are initially supported by providing access to the content they likely require when performing their work. However, in comparison to a process model, a CT neither prescribes a set of activities nor their ordering. Predominantly, it is supposed to provide information access, communication, and coordination support embedded in an adaptable and growing CKW system. Further, a CT features a goal for the optimal collaboration between knowledge workers in relation to their current context. Logically, a CT has to be highly adaptable and carefully designed in order to support knowledge workers without obtruding or even restraining them.

Collaboration Run Time Phase. Knowledge workers can instantiate a CT according to their preferences and within their current CKW context. If there is no adequate CT available, knowledge workers can choose a rather generic CT. Moreover, CTs have to be highly adaptive to empower knowledge workers to conduct a wide range of changes without being overstrained by technical details and issues. Knowledge workers are supposed to fully utilize the defined CT to collaborate towards the achievement of their common goal in CKW. On the basis of available information, knowledge workers can communicate and coordinate using communication and coordination features of a supportive system, or additionally available, context-related integrated systems. Finally, the effectiveness and efficiency of knowledge workers' collaboration depends on the provision of experiential knowledge as well. Knowledge workers need to be able to access *collaboration records* (*CR*; i.e., finalized CIs) in order to retrieve important information, i.e., knowledge that can substantially facilitate and speed up the achievement of a common goal.

Records Evaluation Phase. CRs can be considered as an important common knowledge base for CIs and knowledge workers involved. Knowledge workers can look up details about past CKW and benefit from documentations. Furthermore, information and their interdependencies from a particular CI can be compared with information and connections available in the archived CRs. In addition, CRs can be used for advancing existing CTs as well as for developing new ones. Moreover, a finished and archived CI can also be used as starting point for a succeeding CI, drawing upon the achieved results and established knowledge base. Naturally, a CKW system should check which parts of a specific CT have been adapted during run time or not been used. Moreover, involved knowledge workers may be interviewed to rate the importance and relevance of information for future endeavors.

6   Conclusion

This paper provides sound definitions in terms of *knowledge work, knowledge worker* and *CKW* for future use in the scope of BPM (objective II). The definitions are validated by assessing representative use cases, resulting in CKW characteristics and dimensions that can be leveraged to underpin future CKW support. For the latter, a generic CKW methodology is introduced by the CKWL (objective I) aiming at significant improvement of knowledge workers' productivity.

As a conclusion, the holistic and process-oriented support for collaborative knowledge workers is a challenge in the literal sense. Although there is a broad range of available technologies targeting single aspects, the integration of those into a utilizable support implies high efforts and distinguished concepts for the interplay of these technologies. However, the provided aspects may be used as a vision to gradually extend and interconnect concepts and technologies towards an intended holistic support according to the CKWL.

References

1. Pfiffner, M., Stadelmann, P.: Wissen wirksam machen. Haupt Verlag, Bern (1998)
2. Mundbrod, N.: Business Process Support for Collaborative Knowledge Workers. Master thesis, Ulm University (2012)
3. Alavi, M., Leidner, D.E.: Review: Knowledge Management and Knowledge Management Systems: Conceptual Foundations and Research Issues. MIS Quarterly 25(1), 107–136 (2001)
4. Aamodt, A., Nygard, M.: Different Roles and Mutual Dependencies of Data, Information, and Knowledge - An AI Perspective on their Integration. Data and Knowledge Engineering 16(3), 191–222 (1995)
5. Davenport, T.H., Prusak, L.: Working Knowledge. Harvard Business School Press, Boston (2000)
6. Polanyi, M.: Tacit Dimension. Peter Smith Publisher Inc., Gloucester (1983)
7. Nonaka, I., Takeuchi, H.: The Knowledge-Creating Company. Oxford University Press, New York (1995)
8. Hube, G.: Beitrag zur Beschreibung und Analyse von Wissensarbeit. PhD thesis, University of Stuttgart, Stuttgart (2005)
9. Resch, M.: Die Handlungsregulation geistiger Arbeit. Huber, Bern (1988)
10. Tiemann, M.: Wissensintensive Berufe. Bundesinstitut für Berufsbildung, Bonn (2010)
11. Swenson, K.D.: The Nature of Knowledge Work. In: Swenson, K.D. (ed.) Mastering the Unpredictable. How Adaptive Case Management Will Revolutionize the Way That Knowledge Workers Get Things Done, pp. 5–28. Meghan-Kiffer-Press (2010)
12. Davenport, T.H.: Thinking for a Living: How to Get Better Performance and Results from Knowledge Workers. Harvard Business School Press (2005)
13. Sennewald, C.A., Tsukayama, J.K.: The Process of Investigation. Butterworth-Heinemann ET - 3 TS - WorldCat, Burlington (2006)
14. Drucker, P.F.: Management Challenges for the 21st Century. Elsevier Science & Technology, Oxford (2007)
15. Davenport, T.O.: Human Capital. Jossey-Bass, San Francisco (1999)
16. Holsapple, C.W., Jones, K.: Exploring Primary Activities of the Knowledge Chain. Knowledge and Process Management 11(3), 155–174 (2004)
17. Reinhardt, W., Schmidt, B., Sloep, P., Drachsler, H.: Knowledge Worker Roles and Actions-Results of Two Empirical Studies. Knowledge and Process Management 18(3), 150–174 (2011)
18. Lanz, A., Weber, B., Reichert, M.: Workflow Time Patterns for Process-Aware Information Systems. In: Bider, I., Halpin, T., Krogstie, J., Nurcan, S., Proper, E., Schmidt, R., Ukor, R. (eds.) BPMDS 2010 and EMMSAD 2010. LNBIP, vol. 50, pp. 94–107. Springer, Heidelberg (2010)
19. Reichert, M., Weber, B.: Enabling Flexibility in Process-Aware Information Systems: Challenges, Methods, Technologies. Springer, Heidelberg (2012)
20. Michelberger, B., Mutschler, B., Reichert, M.: A Context Framework for Process-Oriented Information Logistics. In: Abramowicz, W., Kriksciuniene, D., Sakalauskas, V. (eds.) BIS 2012. LNBIP, vol. 117, pp. 260–271. Springer, Heidelberg (2012)

Mobile Task Management for Medical Ward Rounds – The MEDo Approach

Rüdiger Pryss, David Langer, Manfred Reichert, and Alena Hallerbach

Institute of Databases and Information Systems, Ulm University, Germany
{ruediger.pryss,manfred.reichert}@uni-ulm.de,
mail@davidlanger.de, alena.h@llerba.ch

Abstract. In hospitals, ward rounds are crucial for decision-making in the context of patient treatment processes. In the course of a ward round, new tasks are defined and allocated to physicians and nurses. In clinical practice, however, these tasks are not systematically managed. During ward rounds, they are jotted down using pen and paper, and their later processing is prone to errors. Furthermore, medical staff must keep track of the processing status of its tasks (e.g., medical orders). To relieve staff members from such a manual task management, the MEDo approach supports ward rounds by transforming the pen and paper worksheet to a mobile user interface on a tablet integrating process support, mobile task management, and access to the electronic patient record. Interviews we conducted have confirmed that medical staff craves for mobile task and process support on wards. Furthermore, in several user experiments, we have proven that MEDo puts task acquisition on a level comparable to that of pen and paper. Overall, with MEDo, physicians can create, monitor and share tasks using a mobile and user-friendly platform.

Keywords: Mobility, Healthcare, Mobile Task Management.

1 Introduction

In the context of clincial ward rounds, there is a high demand for improving interactions and communication among healthcare professionals. Problems of ward inpatients become more and more complex and managing patient data directly at the bedside is a must. Although existing technology tailored to clinical demands has reached a mature level, still there is a lack of digital task support during ward rounds. To better understand how such a support can be smoothly provided, we attended numerous ward rounds, interviewed medical staff, and considered existing solutions established in clinical practice. Our findings have raised two major issues clinicians sorely need. First of all, the paper-based task worksheet shall be transferred to a mobile and digital variant. Clinicians use such worksheets as their personal information system to organize their tasks. In turn, data gathered with this sheet is not related to the one of the hospital information system. For example, for adding a new task to his sheet during a ward round, a physician will make a note like *"Mrs.Richards: X-ray request arranged, monitor*

M. La Rosa and P. Soffer (Eds.): BPM 2012 Workshops, LNBIP 132, pp. 43–54, 2013.
© Springer-Verlag Berlin Heidelberg 2013

status and check images today". In the pen and paper version, basically, each task description solely consists of the patient's name and free text. Therefore, another demand posed by clinicians is to enhance task management with both workflow support (e.g., to keep track of medical orders) and integrated access to patient data. With MEDo[1] (MedicalDo), we target at a process-aware, mobile task support of the medical staff during ward rounds. This paper reports on the experiences we gathered with MEDo during a number of clinical ward rounds.

The remainder of this paper is organized as follows: Section 2 describes the method we applied to understand the requirements of medical ward rounds. In Section 3, we share the experiences we gathered with MEDo and discuss our lessons learned. Section 4 discusses related work and Section 5 concludes with an outlook.

2   MEDo Pre-Phase: Ward Round Investigation

We started our clinical investigations with a survey. In particular, we evaluated how physicians perceive the current management of ward rounds when using pen and paper. First, we revealed how physicians perceive task acquisition. Second, we asked them how they currently manage ward rounds in general, i.e., the communication with other healthcare professionals or the access to patient information provided by any hospital information system. Fig. 1 depicts the results of this survey. Later, we will compare the use of pen and paper in the context of a ward round with the one of MEDo.

Question	Mean Value	Standard Deviation
Task Definition	2.22	1.30
Ward Round Management	2.50	1.12
	Scale from 1 to 6 | 1: Best Value | 6: Worst Value |	

Fig. 1. MEDo Pre-Phase Evaluation

To identify and capture relevant requirements issues and to understand how they are currently addressed, we analyzed several ward rounds. More precisely, we participated in four wards rounds at different clinical departments. The basic facts related to these ward rounds are summarized in Fig. 2. Interestingly, only one clinical department already provides IT support for accessing patient information during ward rounds; i.e., imaging data and laboratory results can be accessed during the ward round using a tablet PC. As can be further seen, the ward rounds we analyzed vary significantly in respect to their characteristics (cf. Fig. 2).

Based on these insights, we extracted procedures performed or triggered in the context of a ward round. In particular, we were interested in how they can

---

[1] MEDo video under `http://apps.dbis.info/medo/medo.mov`

	Internal Medicine Ward	Emergency Ward	Orthopaedics Ward (Paraplegic Patients)	Trauma Surgery Ward
Hospital	University hospital Ulm	University hospital Ulm	University and Rehabilitation Hospital Ulm (RKU)	University hospital Ulm
Number of Beds	25	12	35	>100
Average Period of Hospitalisation	Days, Weeks	Hours	Weeks, Months	A couple of days up to one month
Frequency of Ward Round	Twice a day	Three times a day	Once a day	Once a week
Aim of Ward Round	Daily overview	Sharing information with the team responsible for the next shift	Daily overview	Overview for head physician
Involved Parties	Two ward physicians, Two nurses	6-8 ward physicians, One senior physician Additionally needed experts	3 Ward physicians, 1-3 nurses Multiple therapists	Head physician of surgery, Proxy of head physician, Respective ward physicians
Treatment Time per Patient	7 + 3.5 Minutes (Preparation + Treatment)	4 Minutes	4 Minutes	3 Minutes
Clinical Information System	SAP, ERP Software	SAP, ERP Software	MCC, Meierhofer AG	SAP, ERP Software
Mobile accessible Data				
Vital Data	✓ (Nursing documentation)	✓ (Nursing documentation)	✓ (Nursing documentation)	✓ (Nursing documentation)
Medication	✓ (Nursing documentation)	✓ (Nursing documentation)	✓ (Nursing documentation)	✓ (Nursing documentation)
Imaging Diagnostics	✗	✗	✓ (Tablet)	✓ (Printout)
Laboratory Findings	✗	✗	✓ (Tablet)	✓ (Printout)
		(✓) : available | (✗) : not available		

Fig. 2. Basic Facts Characterizing the Investigated Ward Rounds

be smoothly integrated with mobile task assistance. Additionally, we identified the patient data physicians want to access in the context of their task lists.

In order to identify required procedures and needed patient information, we attended the four different ward rounds several times and then transfered the insights we gained to a more formal IT representation. In particular, explicitly modeling the identified procedures in terms of BPMN has proven to be useful; i.e., BPMN models provided a good basis for discussing the procedures in the context of a ward round with physicians. Relevant patient information, medical staff quickly wants to access is depicted in Fig. 3a. Additionally, Fig. 3b shows the data privileges required by physicians and nurses in this context. It is noteworthy that physicians want to share their task sheets with nurses and colleagues in order to improve communication.

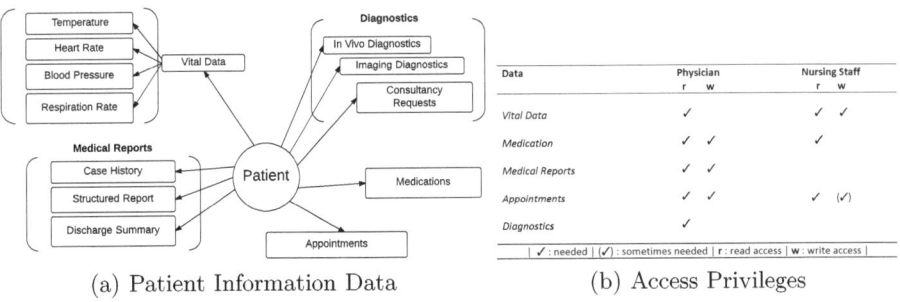

(a) Patient Information Data   (b) Access Privileges

Fig. 3. Patient Information and Access Privileges

We present two wards rounds in detail.

2.1 Ward Rounds in Internal Medicine

Fig. 4 shows the process for coordinating the steps of a ward round in a department of internal medicine. This type of ward round is common to many hospitals and encompasses two stages. In the first stage, the physician analyzes the cases of all inpatients without seeing the patients. For this purpose, he accesses the hospital information system to retrieve information about the inpatients. Further, he is assisted by a nurse and receives information from her. Finally, relevant issues and alternatives regarding patient treatment are discussed in this first phase. In the second phase, the physician visits the inpatients, makes notes using pen and paper, and verifies his decisions. If new tasks (e.g., medical orders) emerge, he makes a note on his worksheet and adopts this change in the hospital information systems afterwards. Examples of tasks and workflows, respectively, emerging in the context of the second phase include requests for X-ray examinations, laboratory tests, consultancy requests, and changes in patient medication. Making appointments with external hospital departments constitutes another kind of task emerging in the context of a ward round. In summary, task worksheets based on pen and paper are crucial for ward rounds in internal medicine.

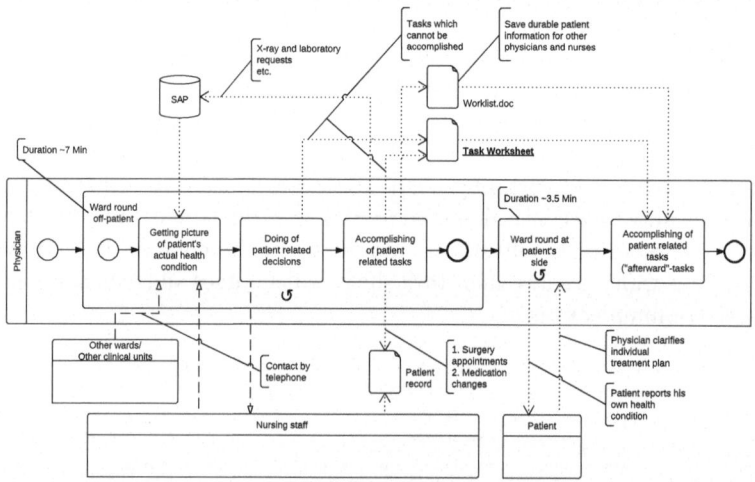

Fig. 4. Two-phased Process Related to Ward Rounds in Internal Medicine

2.2 Ward Rounds in Orthopaedic Medicine

Fig. 5 shows the basic procedure of the ward round in orthopaedic medicine we accompanied. In particular, no mobile access to the complete electronic patient record is provided. However, the preparation of certain patient-related tasks can be accomplished by using a tablet PC, which provides mobile access to selected parts of the hospital information system (HIS). Although, the functions provided by this HIS are not adequately mapped to the tablet, physicians may order certain examinations based on this mobile user interface. Still, most orders are processed in a paper-based fashion afterwards. Interestingly, physicians considered this mobile way of acquiring tasks and making medical orders as useful, and emphasized that it contributes to reduce error rates (e.g., ommissions). Again, the paper-based task worksheet constitutes the most prevalent instrument for memorizing and communicating upcoming tasks. During a ward round, physicians make notes about upcoming tasks and after the ward round they start processing them. For this scenario, we identified more or less the same workflows as for the other two ward rounds depicted in Fig. 2. However, requests for external appointments are not required due to the crucial health status of the patients.

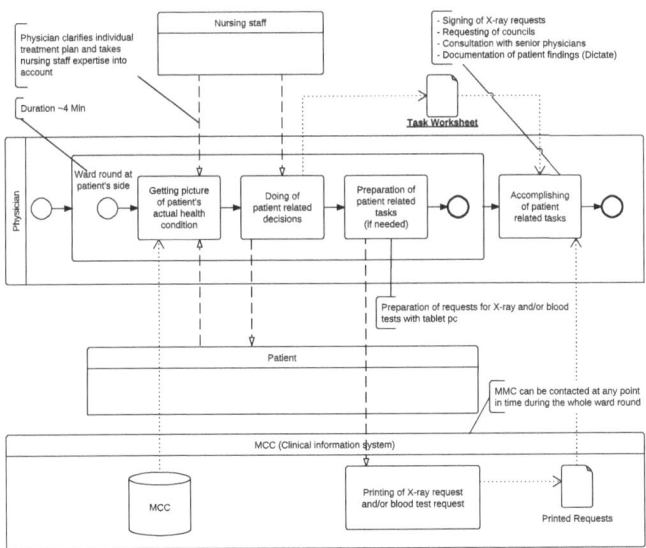

Fig. 5. Process for Ward Rounds in Orthopaedic Medicine

When analyzing the other two ward round types depicted in Fig. 2, basically, we identified the same or similar workflows for implementing core tasks. Based on the overall experiences gathered during the analysis of the different ward round scenarios, we are able to define fundamental requirements to be met by any mobile task support during a ward round. We considered these requirements when designing the MEDo prototype.

3   MEDo Findings

Before designing and implementing MEDo, we evaluated existing mobile tablet frameworks to select the one meeting our requirements best. In this context, aspects like size, weight, display resolution, viewing angle dependency, and input sensibility were considered. Based on these properties, we deciced to develop the MEDo proof-of-concept for mobile task management on the iPad. Our findings with MEDo are presented along three dimensions. First, we discuss findings related to digital task creation and management. Second, we give insights related to the workflows supporting respective tasks. Third, we discusss findings related to the information architecture (i.e., the user interface and control flow structure) we realized in MEDo.

3.1   Task Creation and Management

We first summarize the requirements raised by physicians with respect to worksheets enabling mobile task management. We derived these requirements by attending ward rounds and interviewing medical staff. Usually, physicians and nurses organize their pending and daily tasks based on paper worksheets. Thereby, task definition is always accomplished the same way. For example, physicians make handwritten notes on their worksheet, whereas each note consists of a patient name and descriptive free text. Creating and managing tasks this way means being quick and flexible. Thus, tasks can be acquired in different context and task acquisition can be interrupted at any time. Exactly these two aspects have been mentioned by physicians as major reasons for still using pen and paper. Hence, when transferring task management to a mobile IT application, one must ensure that its use is time-efficient and intuitive, offering the same flexibility as pen and paper. In particular, usability can be improved using results from cognitive science and design techniques from usability engineering, like choosing the right colours or realizing a comprehensible and useful segmentation of the application screen. Interviews and usability tests with medical staff helped us to figure out what elements are intuitive for them. Fig. 6 summarizes major requirements for mobile task creation and management.

	Task Requirements	Description
R₁	Manage the task digitally with mobile assistance	Provide patient's name and free text to physicians in order to manage their digital task entries (todo-items) comparable to that of pen and paper.
R₂	Access patient information contextually linked to tasks	Provide quick access to patient information, e.g., vital data, medical reports, external appointments, medications, and diagnostics.
R₃	Ensure a high input speed for task acquisition	Provide high input speed for the task definition.
	R₃₁ Provide text templates for the task creation	Provide pre-defined text templates to physicians for creating tasks quickly.
	R₃₂ Enable voice recording for the task creation	Provide voice recording feature to physicians for executing tasks comfortably.
	R₃₃ Enable the creation of new text templates	Enable physicians to create new or personally tailored text templates.
R₄	Enable barcode scanning for medications, plasters, bandages, etc.	Provide nurses with a barcode feature to scan medications, plasters, bandages, or to dress material used for patients.
R₅	Provide filter functions for tasks	Provide a filter function to physicians to save time while managing task entries.
R₆	Organize tasks according to their importance	Provide physicians with a feature to organize tasks according to their importance.

Fig. 6. Requirements for Mobile Task Creation and Management

Overall, when meeting these requirements, tasks can be created quickly and smoothly integrated with patient information. However, regarding our first prototype it has turned out that task acquisition was perceived as not being fast enough. To reach a level of usability comparable to that of pen and paper, therefore, further improvements became necessary (cf. R_{31}-R_{33} in Fig. 6). Among others, we realized a collection of text templates that may be used when creating tasks. Our user tests have shown that these text templates have increased task acquisition speed significantly. Furthermore, tasks may be acquired and created using the voice recording feature we integrated with MEDo.

3.2 Workflow Management

Flexible workflow support [1] is another key requirement raised by physicians. By integrating mobile task assistance with workflows, it shall become possible for physicians to easily keep track of their tasks (e.g., medical orders), get aggregated overview lists, or be immediatly notified whenever any problems occurs. For example, the state of an X-ray examination, requested during a ward round, can be easily monitored based on the corresponding workflow. Fig. 7 depicts an example of such a workflow.

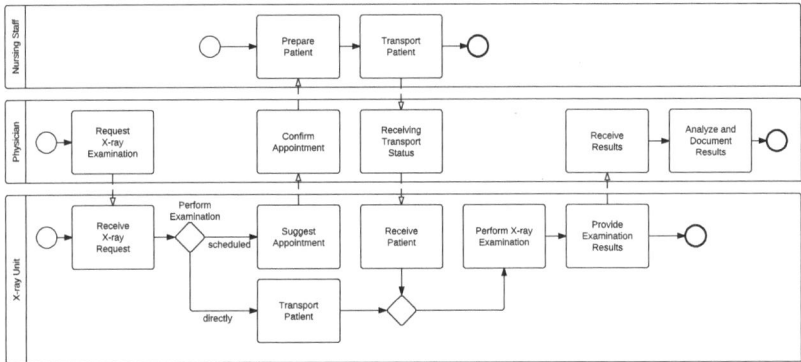

Fig. 7. Process for Handling X-ray Examinations

Concerning workflow-based task support, we gathered three major requirements from physicians. First, they asked for a quick overview of tasks and related workflows (cf. R_9). Second, these workflows shall be automatically triggered and coordinated by a process-aware HIS when defining tasks (cf. R_7). Third, the current state of a task and its underlying workflow, respectively, shall be accessible and changeable based on different user views (cf. R_8, R_9). For example, if the results of a laboratory order arrive, the physician will get immediate access to them. Afterwards, he may change the state of this task and its related workflow to "seen". In particular, this user interaction is possible from different views in MEDo. For example, the physician may change the status of her task by using the task overview or laboratory view. Fig. 8 summarizes the requirements related to workflow-based task support in MEDo.

	Workflow Requirements	Description
R₇	Use workflows to keep track of the status of tasks	Support workflows for handling and processing tasks and integrate these workflows smoothly with the hospital information system.
R₈	Interrupt tasks and continue them later	Workflows as well as user interfaces must enable healthcare professionals to interrupt their current work at any point in time and to continue it later.
R₉	Provide personalized views on workflows to users	The workflows must be intuitively presented to healthcare professionals.

Fig. 8. Workflow Requirements

3.3   Information Architecture

Another fundamental aspect of any digital task worksheet is to identify how the information architecture (i.e., the fundamental control flow structure of the user interface) shall look like. For example, it is compelling to allow users to interrupt a task at any point in time and to continue it later. In practice, this means that users must be able to switch between different views within the mobile application. To identify which views and context switches are actually needed, we identified scenarios covering task acquisition and execution, characteristic types of tasks, and situations requiring context switches. Fig. 9 exemplarily depicts three task creating scenarios.

Scenario	Description
Scenario I	After a ward round, the physician wants to see all upcoming tasks of the day at a glance. He then uses this overview for planning his work day (cf. Fig. 11a).
Scenario II	During a ward round, the physician wants to know whether an X-ray examination has already been requested and what status the examination currently has. Fig. 11b shows that the X-ray has arrived and the physicians can finish the workflow by setting the state to *Mark as seen*.
Scenario III	During a ward round, a set of tasks shall be created. Often, a particular physician makes orders, while another one is collecting them. Fig. 12a shows the creation of a task using text templates, whereas Fig. 12b shows the creation of a laboratory request using a specialized laboratory creation view.

Fig. 9. Example Scenarios

The information architecture realized in MEDo is depicted in Fig. 10. Most important, tasks constitute the predominant paradigm for user interaction. In particular, the physician does not need to switch her current view if she wants to create a new task. For example, a request for an X-ray examination may be entered using the task view or alternatively within every other view (e.g., the laboratory view). Due to lack of space, we only present selected features of the MEDo information architecture. In particular, we want to give some impressions related to the scenarios described in Fig. 9 and discuss how they are realized in MEDo. Fig. 11a shows the MEDo entry view. *Marking 1* refers to the list of all patients. In MEDo, patients may either be listed alphabetically or according to the rooms they are assigned to.

Marking 2 refers to both upcoming and recently completed tasks. In turn, *Marking 3* shows the processing state of a selected task (X-ray request). For example, when the X-ray images arrive, a symbol change notifies the physician about this status change. To study the results obtained, in turn, she may switch to the imaging view depicted in Fig. 11b. *Marking 4* refers to an element allowing the physician to change the state of the X-ray request to "finished". Finally, the corresponding workflow is completed. *Marking 5* in Fig. 12a shows the predefined text templates the physician can use when defining a task. This feature

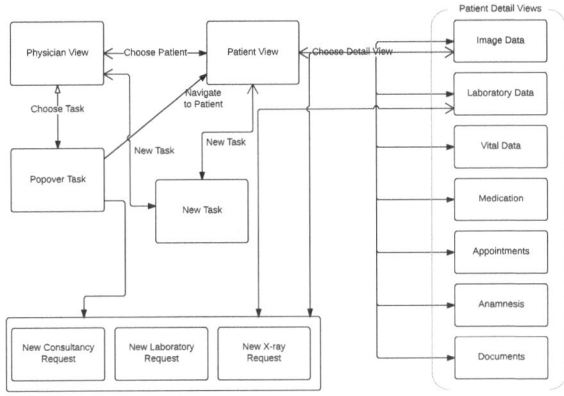

Fig. 10. MEDo Information Architecture

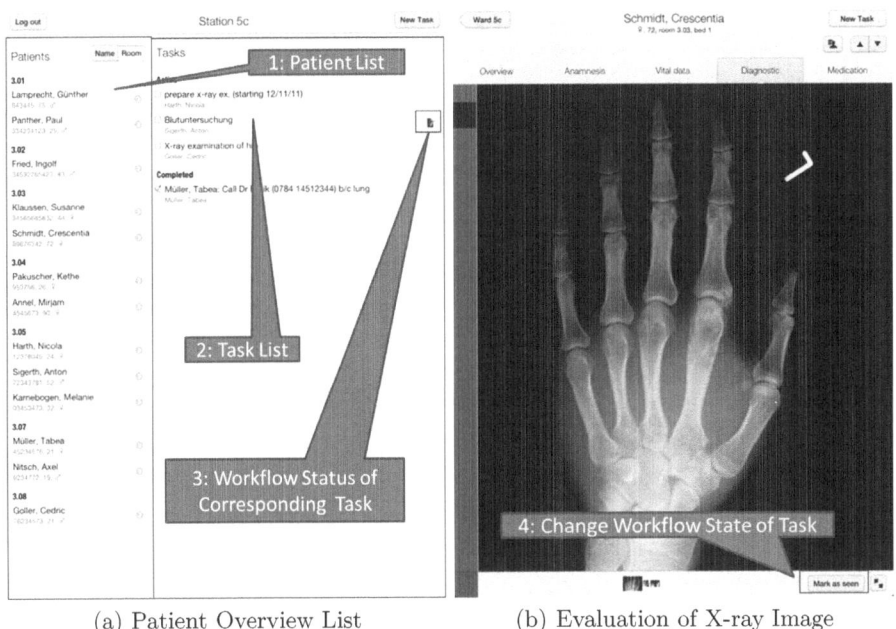

(a) Patient Overview List   (b) Evaluation of X-ray Image

Fig. 11. Patient Overview List and X-ray Diagnostic View

has turned out to increase task acquisition speed significantly. In addition, related workflows can be automatically derived from task definitions based on these text templates. For example, if a physician uses text template *Request Council* when defining a task, a corresponding workflow will be started in the background. In addition to text templates, we integrated a voice feature (cf. Marking 6), i.e., the physician may use her voice for recording a task. What is missing at this point, is to derive respective workflows directly from these voice recordings.

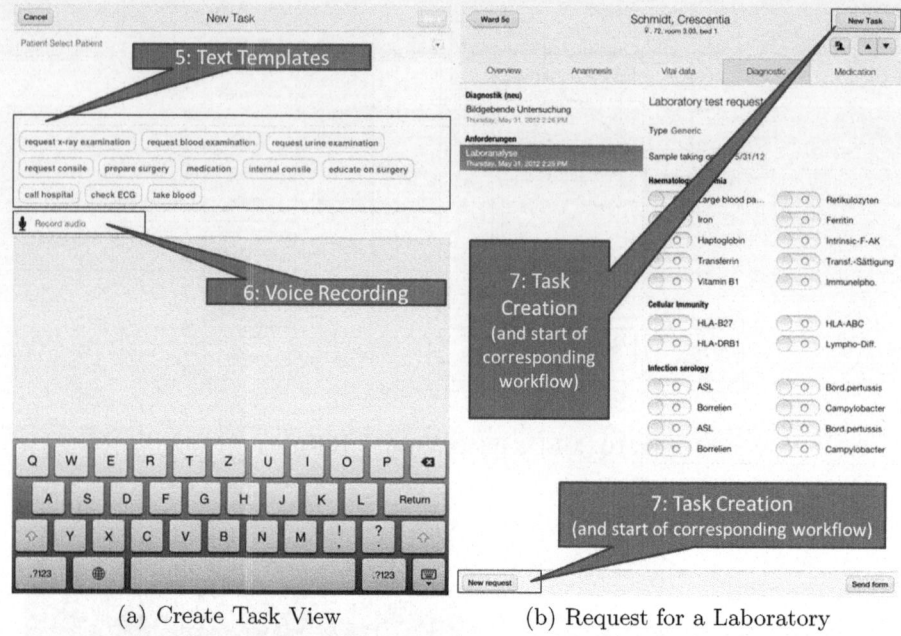

(a) Create Task View   (b) Request for a Laboratory

Fig. 12. MEDo Task Creation and Laboratory Diagnostic View

Fig. 12b shows the form of a laboratory request. *Marking 7* exemplarily shows
different ways of creating tasks for the laboratory view. In interviews with physicians and nurses, for every MEDo view we revealed how many creation buttons
for tasks are useful and in what way they should be positioned on the screen. The
user interface was optimised in several cycles based on the feedback provided by
medical members. Finally, after working with MEDo, we interviewed physicians
whether they feel comfortable with the MEDo information architecture (see Fig.
13 for results).

Question	Mean Value	Standard Deviation
View Navigation	2.00	0.47
Patient Communication	3.67	1.66
Overall Impression	1.90	0.50
Scale from 1 to 6 | 1: Best Value | 6: Worst Value		

Fig. 13. MEDo Information Architecture Evaluation

Fig. 14 summarizes all basic requirements for our MEDo information architecture. Requirements R_{10}-R_{12} refer to collaboration among medical staff in
connection with their tasks. Obviously, collaboration is crucial in the context of
ward rounds and hence must be smoothly integrated with task management.

	Information Architecture Requirements	Description
R$_{10}$	Share the task list with other physicians and nurses	Share tasks with other physicians and nurses.
R$_{11}$	Provide a multi-user mode for tasks	Provide different views for physicians and nurses.
R$_{12}$	Enable an easy shift management for task lists	Electronic worksheets have to be easily handed over between the staff of a shift.
R$_{13}$	Provide the user with special views on upcoming tasks	Handling upcoming tasks shall be eased. Access to them must be quick and easy.
R$_{14}$	Provide the user with views on examination results	A fast and adequate access to examination results is very important.

Fig. 14. Information Architecture Requirements

3.4 Lessons Learned

When interviewing the physicians, we learned that patient communication suffers from using MEDo; i.e., an intense pursuit with the mobile application distracts physicians from inpatients. Hence, further research is needed to deal with this issue. We further learned that the status of workflows should be presented more intuitively to clinicians. Most of them demand a status notification similiar to traffic lights (i.e., using three colours for presenting status information). Furthermore, physicians missed sub-categories for the pre-defined text templates. Another demand was to integrate more patient information in MEDo (e.g, practitioner information or surgery appointments.). Finally, MEDo must be smoothly integrated into existing hospital information systems.

3.5 Overall Conclusion

After using MEDo over a period of four weeks we evaluated it again the same way as described in Section 2. Corresponding results are depicted in Fig. 15.

Question	Mean Value	Standard Deviation
Task Definition	1.90	0.50
Ward Round Management	1.80	0.53
	Scale from 1 to 6 | 1: Best Value | 6: Worst Value |	

Fig. 15. MEDo Evaluation

First, physicians conceived the task creation with MEDo on the same level as that of pen and paper (cf. Section 3.1). Second, physicians considered MEDo during wards rounds as useful. More precisely, physicians considered the integration of patient information and workflows as the major issues for using MEDo (cf. Section 3.2). Third, regarding the information architecture, only few issues have been criticised (cf. Section 3.3). For example, the shapes of certain buttons were not intuitively enough in some views. Overall, physicians were satisfied using MEDo when comparing the evaluation results from Figs. 15 and 1.

4   Related Work

In [2,3,4], approaches adopting mobile information technology to ward rounds are described. However, none of these approaches is centered around mobile task

assistance as supported in MEDo. Similar concerns hold for approaches supporting ward rounds by using workflow technology [5,6,7] as well as for approaches
transferring information technology to ward rounds [8,9,10]. Furthermore, commercial solutions have to be considered, like the one from the orthopaedic ward
round (cf. Fig. 2). Finally, much research effort has been spent on the measuring
of ward rounds [11,12]. Overall, none of these approaches centers the solution
around a suitable mobile task assistance.

5   Summary and Outlook

Existing information technology does not consider requirements of hospital ward
rounds adequately. To cope with this drawback, we suggest mobile task management as designed in MEDo as a first approach towards this direction. In further
research, we will extend MEDo considering the demands discussed in Section 3.

References

1. Reichert, M., Weber, B.: Enabling Flexibility in Process-Aware Information Systems: Challenges, Methods, Technologies. Springer, Heidelberg (2012)
2. Carlsson, V., Klug, T., Ziegert, T., Zinnen, A.: Wearable Computers in Clinical
   Ward Rounds, Berlin/Offenbach, Germany (2006)
3. Lamber, P., Ludwig, B., Ricci, F., Zini, F., Mitterer, M.: Message-based patient
   guidance in day-hospital. In: Proc. IEEE 12th Int'l Conf. on. MDM 2011, pp.
   162–167. IEEE Computer Society (2011)
4. Kofod-Petersen, A.: Challenges in case-based reasoning for context awareness in
   ambient intelligent systems. In: 8th European Conf. on CaseBased Reasoning, Ölü-
   deniz, p. 287 (2006)
5. Ali Fareedi, A., Tarasov, V.: Modelling of the Ward Round Process in a Healthcare
   Unit. In: Johannesson, P., Krogstie, J., Opdahl, A.L. (eds.) PoEM 2011. LNBIP,
   vol. 92, pp. 223–237. Springer, Heidelberg (2011)
6. Reichert, M.: What BPM Technology Can Do for Healthcare Process Support. In:
   Peleg, M., Lavrač, N., Combi, C. (eds.) AIME 2011. LNCS (LNAI), vol. 6747, pp.
   2–13. Springer, Heidelberg (2011)
7. Wang, L.: An Agent-based Simulation for Workflow in Emergency Department. In:
   Proc. 2009 IEEE Systems and Information, pp. 19–23. IEEE (2009)
8. Bardram, J.E., Bossen, C.: A web of coordinative artifacts: collaborative work at
   a hospital ward. In: Proc. GROUP 2005, pp. 168–176. ACM (2005)
9. Ammenwerth, E., Buchauer, A., Bludau, B., Haux, R.: Mobile information and
   communication tools in the hospital. Int'l Journal of Medical Informatics 57, 21–
   40 (2000)
10. Pryss, R., Tiedeken, J., Kreher, U., Reichert, M.: Towards Flexible Process Support
    on Mobile Devices. In: Soffer, P., Proper, E. (eds.) CAiSE Forum 2010. LNBIP,
    vol. 72, pp. 150–165. Springer, Heidelberg (2011)
11. Alvarez, G., Coiera, E.W.: Interruptive communication patterns in the intensive
    care unit ward round. I. J. Medical Informatics 74, 791–796 (2005)
12. Weber, H., Stöckli, M., Nübling, M., Langewitz, W.A.: Communication during
    ward rounds in internal medicine. an analysis of patient-nurse-physician interac-
    tions using rias. Patient Education and Counseling 67, 343–348 (2007)

Position: BPMN Is Incompatible with ACM

Keith D. Swenson

Fujitsu America, 1250 E Arques Ave, Sunnyvale, California
kswenson@us.fujitsu.com

Abstract. The role of two-dimensional process graphing in Adaptive Case Management (ACM) is examined. Three design criteria are identified for ACM that were never considered for BPMN. The question for discussion is whether these requirements eliminate all kinds of flow-chart type languages from consideration for use as a process modeling language for users of ACM.

1   Introduction

Within our current technology setting, essentially all discussions of business process make the implicit assumption that Business Process Modeling Notation (BPMN) will be the graphical language for expressing the business process. For the purpose of discussion, consider this decidedly radical proposition: "Any work support system that depends upon processes designed with BPMN (or BPMN-like languages) cannot be considered an ACM system."

This statement is intentionally bold in order to question our basic assumptions about process modeling for ACM where all modeling is done by the end user: the knowledge worker. Is it reasonable to expect case managers to ever have the skills to use a two dimensional BPMN-like process language? If not, does this lack of skill in itself become a barrier to effective use? The question is not how BPMN might have to be changed to suit case managers. What this is proposing is that whenever a system depends upon a two-dimensional design format for describing the processes, that dependence itself makes it unsuited for use as an ACM System (ACMS). The proposition is that an ACMS absolutely must not have BPMN, in order to be considered an ACMS where planning must be performed by end users while working.

2   Setting

In the early days of business processes management – we called it business process *reengineering* back then – I published a number of papers about graphical business process definition languages which were designed to be used by business people directly[1,2]. This visual language is surprisingly similar to BPMN with some superficial differences. The main elements were tasks, represented as ellipses instead of the rounded rectangles that BPMN uses today. Transitions between activities were arrows. Specific nodes performed branching and joining. Start and end nodes were hexagons instead of circles in BPMN. Most notably, events were represented as small

M. La Rosa and P. Soffer (Eds.): BPM 2012 Workshops, LNBIP 132, pp. 55–58, 2013.

circle on the edge of an activity. Those diagrams can be isomorphically translated into a BPMN diagram today, with equivalent readability / expressibility.

At Fujitsu, I was able to produce a system that supported the graphical definition of business processes, and the enactment of them.[3] The most important aspect of that system was the ability to change the process at any time by anybody. Any business user of the system can retrieve and edit a business process at any point in time. Simply point the browser at the server, to retrieve your task list, and if desired you can also edit any process as well.

We found over 15 years that business users essentially *never* design a graphical business process. Processes are always designed by some sort of developer. Those process enthusiasts who train themselves on process technology do not represent the typical knowledge worker. Even managers who design detailed interaction patterns for their team, will rarely actually draw a picture of the process themselves. Instead they hire process specialists who will draw the diagrams for them. Even office workers who are comfortable reading a process diagrams and who use them for training about a given process will rarely actually draw the process.

My conclusions (given here without any evidence) are that:

- Drawing a diagram requires a kind of abstract thinking about the process that a business user is not comfortable with. Instead, they want to define activities in terms of responsibilities on people, and not in terms of a flow of a token through a series of tasks.
- Drawing a diagram actually involves some programmer-like skills. For example, a branch node requires variables, which need to be set up in advance so that the branch condition can test those values. Separating the information into discrete units in a format that can be tested is a developer skill unfamiliar to business users.
- Modifying someone else's diagram is particularly difficult because all of the assumptions that went into drawing the diagram are not present in the diagram. A simple example is that one node may initialize a variable, and another may use that variable, so switching the order of these nodes would break the functioning of the diagram. There is no way to indicate in the diagram might or might not be safe. Like most programming languages, it is designed to embody a set of assumptions, and not to necessarily express those assumptions. We can say that the original rules and assumptions are *hidden* by the resulting process diagram.

3   Relevance to ACM

A graphical process definition plays different roles in different styles of process technology. For example, in Process Driven Server Integration (PDSI) – a name for the kind of BPM which is commonly associated with a Service Oriented Architecture (SOA) environment – the process diagram is part of the programming process, or it may simply be in the design spec and completely replaced by the implementation. This programming and designing of the server integration is done by programmers, and not business users, so use of BPMN is not impeded.

For Human Process Management (HPM) – a type of BPM targeted at modeling routine human activities – it is a process specialist, or possibly a programmer, who designs a process which is used by the process participants. Typically in HPM the end user does not have to design processes.

The same is true for Production Case Management (PCM) where once again you have specialists who define the interaction patterns, which are developed and deployed as a finished application to the production users.

ACM however is different from these all of these because there is no distinct design phase. Designing and performing the work are done at the same time by the end user. There is no distinction between the users and the developers. The business users themselves must design the process. Even professionally designed templates must be modifiable by the case managers to fit the needs of each case, and so must not have hidden assumptions.

4   Use of the Language

BPMN-like languages were originally designed for an expert to express something very precisely. The expression will take into account many understood rules, but may not express those rules directly. The developer says *what* to do, and not *why* to do it.

This can be a large investment of time. If the process is executed many times, then a large up-front cost of developing a process can be compensated by a modest increased efficiency of the process. The investment that most styles of process technology (PDSI, HPM, PCM) require is not a particular problem.

For ACM the process is designed by the case manager as they do the work, and usually just for the benefit of that one case. If things work out well, that process may become a template and reused many times, but each case manager must justify the effort of creating the diagram in terms of the case they are currently working on. From this see criteria 1:

- Ability to design a basic process quickly with very little investment by the user is far more important than the ability to define a precise process which uses more time an attention from the business user.

In ACM, process change is an everyday activity. If the ACMS were to require skill in BPMN to change the process, then the case managers without that skill will be prevented from using ACMS as intended. This brings us to design criteria 2:

- Process design must not require a skill beyond what business users possess.

Even if the business user is an expert in BPMN, they still may find it difficult to change the process because of the hidden assumptions problem. BPMN-like languages are designed to express a final process, and not all the steps and decisions along the way to develop the process. This brings us to the design criteria 3:

- For a process definition to be modified by business users there must be no hidden assumptions.

The third criteria deserves means either that the process diagram must include a lot of additional information to express all the decisions behind the way the process is designed, or it means that there is a limitation on how complicated the process can be.

5   A Process Language Designed for Change

A case manager needs to be able to change a process quickly and effectively every time without error. This means that all possible changes need to be valid changes. If the case manager needs to switch the order of two activities for a good reason, there should be no possibility that such a switch can cause a failure of the process to execute. A language that is designed for change will allow (almost) any change, and will prompt for the resolution of any problems that arise because of the change.

Gödel's Theorem might imply that it is impossible for a developer to express all of the reasons for designing a process in a particular way. Even if it is possible, we can be certain that it is tedious and far beyond the skills of a business user.

For this reason, I think that the right process definition language for ACM will be one that appears, compared to BPMN, to be very simple. It will appear to be very loose, flexible, and unstructured. However, it will be such that every business user can read and understand without special skills, and it will be one that can be changed in any way, without causing inconsistency. Some will question the utility of such an approach, but this is a case of "less is more".

6   Summary

The goal here is not to state any conclusions in this paper, only to raise questions for discussion. I hope that the results of the discussion can produce a set of actions items that can resolve the issue. What experiment or measurement is necessary to determine if flowcharts can be effectively used by business users? What experiment would show that checklists function more effectively? How can we determine the likelihood that business users will learn enough formal process modeling skills to be effective at ACM?

References

1. Swenson, K.D.: A Visual Language to Describe Collaborative Work. In: Proceedings of the International Workshop for Visual Languages (1993)
2. Swenson, K.D.: Visual Support for Reengineering Work Processes. In: Proceedings of the Conference on Organizational Computing Systems (1993)
3. Swenson, K.D., et al.: A business process environment supporting collaborative planning. Journal of Collaborative Computing (1994)
4. Swenson, K.D.: Workflow for the Information Worker. In: Fisher(ed, L. (ed.) Workflow Handbook 2001. Future Strategies (2001)

Do Workflow-Based Systems Satisfy the Demands of the Agile Enterprise of the Future?

Ilia Bider, Paul Johannesson, and Erik Perjons

Department of computer and systems science, Stockholm University
{ilia,pajo,perjons}@dsv.su.se

Abstract. Workflow-based systems dominate the theory and practice of Business Process Management (BPM) leaving little space to other directions, including Adaptive Case Management. While there are reasons for such dominance in today's enterprise environment, it is time the BPM community studied this dominance in the light of the requirements of the enterprises of the future. This paper analyzes whether workflow-based systems will be able to satisfy business needs in the future based on the assumption that the essential property of the enterprise of the future is agility. The paper identifies properties that a business process should possess in order to be suitable for employing a workflow-based system to support it. Then, it analyzes whether these properties are compatible with the needs of the enterprise of the future and shows why workflow-based systems may become obsolete in the future.

Keywords: Workflow, Enterprise agility, BPM, non-workflow.

1   Motivation

Workflow-based systems comprise the major paradigm in today's Business Process Management (BPM) practice. There are several reasons for this state of affairs:

1. The paradigm is connected to the wide-spread operational view on business processes, where a process is considered to be a sequence of operations (activities) for reaching a goal, alternatively for transforming inputs into outputs.
2. The paradigm is imbedded in industry standards, like UML, BPMN.
3. The paradigm, because of 1 and 2, is being realized in modeling tools, workflow engines, and BPM suites, which are enthusiastically marketed by both small and large vendor, including IBM and Oracle.

As the result of 1-3, very little space is left to BPM approaches that are based on other views than workflow. The latter encompass Adaptive Case Management (ACM). To expand the area where ACM and other non-workflow methods are applied, argumentation is required where and why workflow-based systems are not suitable. This argumentation need to be understandable and convincible for practitioners, and it is the responsibility of researchers, at least, to prepare some ground for such argumentation.

M. La Rosa and P. Soffer (Eds.): BPM 2012 Workshops, LNBIP 132, pp. 59–64, 2013.

We envision three ways of expanding the non-workflow BPM, and defending it against the mainstream:

1. Expand in the areas traditionally working in a case-based manner, such as law, healthcare, government.
2. Show examples where the workflow-paradigm has failed.
3. Assess future developments and analyze whether the workflow-based systems can still be applied for the new generation of enterprises.

Choosing only one direction from the above list might not be sufficient. If we concentrate only on the first direction, non-workflow BPM will still be considered as a niched direction and will continue to be vulnerable against the mainstream marketing efforts. The second direction is difficult to pursue, as people are hesitant to openly report on their failures. Except [1], we have not come across actual experience reports about the failures of the workflow paradigm. Besides, learning from failures of others, rather than own, does not always work. In this paper, we focus on the third line of argumentation and analyze the suitability of the workflow-based BPM for the enterprises of the future.

When developing our argumentation, we assume the following:

1. The main reason for the dominance of the workflow paradigm is that BPM is considered as a tool for optimizing the usage of enterprise resources by using standardization, specialization, and automation. For such purposes, the workflow paradigm is indeed suitable.
2. Business agility will become one of the most important properties of the next generation of the enterprises. We consider enterprise/business agility [2] as a property of an enterprise to function in a highly dynamic world. The agility concerns both being able to adjust the enterprise to changes in the surrounding environment, and discovering new opportunities constantly appearing in the dynamic world for launching completely new products/services.

To build our argumentation, we first define the properties of a business process that make it suitable to be supported by a workflow based system. Then we try to answer the following three questions: "Whether it makes sense to design workflowable processes in a highly dynamic business environment?", "Whether it will really be optimal for such an environment (Section 4)?", "Whether separate optimization of processes is beneficial for the enterprise as a whole?". The summary of the finding is than presented in Conclusion.

2   Properties of a Workflowable Process

The workflow-based systems are built upon the operational view on business processes. The most widespread definition of a workflow is being "a sequence of operations, declared as work of a person, a group of persons" (from Wikipedia [3][1]).

---

[1] We intentionally refer to Wikipedia as this is a place where a practitioner will go for information.

Term workflowability has been introduced in [4] as a characteristic of business processes that are "ideal" to be supported by workflow-based software systems. Below, we list properties of a business process that can be fully represented as a workflow chart, e.g., a UML activity diagram, Petri Net, or in BPMN notation. The list is based on analysis from [4,5], and includes the following properties:

1. The process can be split into well-defined steps or operations common for all instances/cases of the given process (type).
2. For each step, inputs and outputs are fully formalized (e.g., a document, an application form, a drawing).
3. It is fully determined what outputs serve as inputs for other steps.

In this paper, we will use a simplified example of a systems development process the main steps and input/outputs of which are presented in Fig. 1.

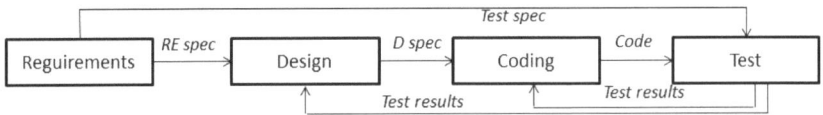

Fig. 1. Steps in the software development processes that is used as an example in this paper

4. Execution of each step does not require any other information than the one included in its formalized inputs.
5. Two steps are not allowed to be executed simultaneously (in parallel) if outputs from one of them serve as inputs for another. Besides this rule, parallel execution is encouraged. Loops are also allowed.
6. Each step is executed by a special group or one person. From the optimization point of view the latter alternative is more preferable. If in addition, each such group or person is responsible only for one step, an even greater degree of optimal usage of human resources can be achieved (via full specialization).

The set of properties above can serve as a checklist to ensure that a process is suitable for employing a workflow-based BPM system. If the above properties are confirmed, the process can run as on a conveyor belt, allowing optimization of the usage of human resources.

3   Is There Time to Optimize a Process in an Agile Enterprise?

As follows from the previous section, designing a workflowable process requires full formalization of all inputs and outputs, and decomposing the process into relatively small steps. Each step is entrusted to a particular role, and as many steps as possible are made independent of each other so that they can run in parallel. It is unrealistic to expect that a workflowable process can be designed in one go and without several rounds of unsuccessful trials.

Creating a worflowable process can constitute a valid approach to getting a process optimized only in a situation when the needs for radical change are infrequent. In the highly dynamic business environment that is expected in the future, there might not be much time to make the process workflowable before discovering that it is time to drastically change it or to remove it altogether. The agile organization of the future needs to be content with non-workflowable processes, as long as it is easy to set them into operation and introduce radical changes in them. It should also find another way of providing technological support for its business processes than employing a workflow-based BPM system, e.g., by employing ACM.

4   Does Workflowability Always Produce an Optimal Process?

The list of properties of a workflowable process introduced in section 2 sets some limitations on how a process instance/case could be conducted. For example, if the process in Fig. 1 is considered to be workflowable, it would not be allowed to start the design phase before the full set of requirements has been established. It also means that all requirements should be explicitly defined, and designers should not informally communicate with requirements engineers to clarify the meaning of the requirements, as the latter might not be available for questioning.

From the point of view of optimizing of usage of human resources, the above limitation sounds like an adequate solution. Starting the design phase before the requirements have been established means taking a risk that requirements discovered later may force redoing parts or all of the already done design.

Suppose, however, that the workflowable system development process is used for creating a new product for the market in a highly competitive dynamic environment. Then avoiding the risk of starting design before finishing the requirements engineering means taking the risk of coming with the new product too late. To minimize the risks of being too late and redoing too much of the design, the agile enterprise needs to find a solution different from workflowability, for example:

1. Dependent steps are allowed to run in parallel.
2. Inputs/outputs for the steps are less formalized and partly rely on on-going personal communication between requirements engineers and product designers.
3. The same people are allowed to be engaged in different step (less specialization), especially if they run in parallel. This will facilitate tacit transfer of the outputs from one step as inputs into another.

Implementing a process from Fig. 1 according to the above, more or less, equals to introducing agile system development, which can hardly be regarded as workfloable.

5   Is Optimization of a Process Beneficial for the Whole Enterprise?

Let us consider another aspect of the system development process aimed at producing a product for the market. Suppose we have created a high-quality set of requirements that would ensure that a new product will satisfy the needs existing in the market. Suppose also that the new system is fairly complex, and it takes a long time, say a year, to develop it. While the developers design, code and test, the needs in the highly dynamic market would continue to evolve creating a risk that the new system will be outdated when it hits the market. In this situation, there is a need to provide the development team with information on the changes in the market demands so that they can adjust the product to the evolving needs even when the process is in the design and coding phases.

The information on the changes in the market that is needed for the development team is easier to obtain by people who spend most of their time outside the enterprise. To the latter, for example, belong people engaged in what we call boundary processes, like sales and field services. These people normally belong to another department than Engineering and they, usually, are not engaged in the development process. There are two options to arrange knowledge transfer from the "boundary" processes to the "internal" ones. One is to arrange additional internal processes for transferring the knowledge on changes in the outer world. The other solution is cross-manning of business processes [6] as depicted in Fig. 2. As the first solution requires extra overhead, we believe that the second one is more attractive for the agile enterprise of the future.

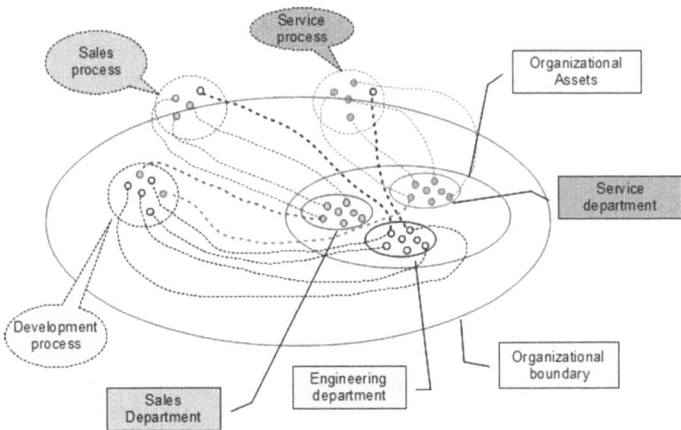

Fig. 2. Cross-manning of business processes

Cross-manning means that people participating in the development process participate also in the boundary processes (e.g., sales and/or field services). It can be sales people, or service engineers, that participate in the development process, and/or the developers that participate in the sales and/or field services processes. The advantage of cross-manning is that the development team gets the knowledge directly (without much overhead) through participating in the boundary processes. The disadvantages are that business processes need to be adjusted to allow participation of the "foreigners". This might lead to each process becoming less "optimal" on its own. However, this loss might be a small penalty for ensuring the shortest time to market for the product that will also be "right" for the market. Effective transfer of knowledge on the current needs and problems to the development team is not the only effect of cross-manning. The sales, or field service team that possesses the knowledge on the products under development may start transferring this knowledge to existing and future customers far in advance of the product reaching the market. This will create expectations and ensure smoother transferring of knowledge on how to use the new product in practice.

Cross-manning of business processes have serious implications on the way the processes are to be developed, maintained, and supported by IT tools. The two most important implications are:

1. Each cross-manned process has multiple goals to achieve.
2. The process team becomes heterogeneous, i.e., it includes people with different backgrounds, experiences and goals.

The above implications mean that the idea of a process as a conveyor belt that could be optimized for one particular goal no longer applies.

6   Conclusion

Our analysis shows that designing and putting into operation workflowable processes may neither be possible (Section 3) nor desirable (Sections 4 and 5) in the enterprise of the future. This conclusion should have an impact on the software tools, systems, and services aimed at supporting business processes. The focus needs to be shifted to facilitating coordination and collaboration rather than optimizing processes. This is especially important for heterogeneous, cross-manned processes, where the system should support process participants in fully understanding each other's goals, and tracking the progress of their achievement in run-time. This is where ACM and other non-workflow based systems can be of help; see, for example, our suggestions in [7] based on using specially formatted shared spaces to represent the progress achieved in each process instance, as well as facilitate collaboration.

References

[1] Kleiner, N.: The Focus of Requirements Engineering in Workflow Application Development. CEUR workshops proceedings, vol. 75, pp. 372–377 (2003)
[2] Sherehiy, B., Karwowski, W., Layer, J.K.: A review of enterprise agility: Concepts, frameworks, and attributes. International Journal of Industrial Ergonomics 37, 445–460 (2007)
[3] Wikepedia (May 2012), http://en.wikipedia.org/wiki/Workflow
[4] Baresi, L., et al.: Workflow design methodology. In: Grefen, Pernici, Sanchez (eds.) Database Support for Workflow Management: The WIDE Project, pp. 47–94. Kluwer (1999)
[5] Bider, I., Perjons, E.: Preparing for the Era of Cloud Computing: Towards a Framework for Selecting Business Process Support Services. In: Bider, I., Halpin, T., Krogstie, J., Nurcan, S., Proper, E., Schmidt, R., Soffer, P., Wrycza, S. (eds.) EMMSAD 2012 and BPMDS 2012. LNBIP, vol. 113, pp. 16–30. Springer, Heidelberg (2012)
[6] Bider, I., Bellinger, G., Perjons, E.: Modeling an Agile Enterprise: Reconciling Systems and Process Thinking. In: Johannesson, P., Krogstie, J., Opdahl, A.L. (eds.) PoEM 2011. LNBIP, vol. 92, pp. 238–252. Springer, Heidelberg (2011)
[7] Bider, I., Johannesson, P., Perjons, E.: A Strategy for Merging Social Software with Business Process Support. In: zur Muehlen, M., Su, J. (eds.) BPM 2010 Workshops. LNBIP, vol. 66, pp. 372–383. Springer, Heidelberg (2011)

Towards Automated Support for Case Management Processes with Declarative Configurable Specifications

Irina Rychkova

Centre de Recherches en Informatique, University Paris 1 Pantheon-Sorbonne,
90, rue Tolbiac, 75013 Paris, France
Irina.Rychkova@univ-paris1.fr

Abstract. Until recently, efficiency gained through process automation and control was the main preoccupation of BPM practitioners. As a result, the majority of mainstream process modeling standards today is characterized by the imperative modeling style. This style encourages a modeler to commit to a well-determined process execution scenario already at the early design stages. For *case management processes*, however, a strict commitment to a predefined control flow is considered by organizations as a serious handicap. This is the main reason why case management as well as other knowledge-intensive processes in the organizations mostly remain "pen and paper". In this article we demonstrate how *configurable data objects and context-based configuration rules* can be integrated into a process model in order to improve the process post-design adaptability and to pave the road for case management automated support. These concepts are defined as a part of DeCo (the Declarative Configurable process specification language). DeCo is a declarative modeling approach that is currently under development. We illustrate our results on the example.

Keywords: Business process modeling, BPMN, declarative modeling, configurability.

1 Introduction

During the last decades, business process management (BPM) became an imperative for efficient functioning and evolution of organizations and gave a rise to the third wave of research interest in business process modeling and analysis [1]. Since then, the main efforts of researchers have been focused on development of process modeling languages that would be easy to understand by both technical and business users and that would provide better control over processes. As a result, the majority of the process modeling methodologies widely used today (e.g. BPMN, UML, EPC) is characterized by a powerful graphical notation, a rich design environment, and by the *imperative* style of their models.

Imperative modeling largely contributes to the process control [2]. Modeling approaches based, for example, on coupling a graphical language such as BPMN and an operational language such as BPEL infinitely attract BPM practitioners giving them a toolbox to design, execute, test and eventually instantiate and deploy the process models.

M. La Rosa and P. Soffer (Eds.): BPM 2012 Workshops, LNBIP 132, pp. 65–76, 2012.
© Springer-Verlag Berlin Heidelberg 2012

Requiring large upfront investments into a process scenario definition, such approaches still pay off very well for deterministic, repetitive processes (such as automated production lines). Assuming that execution scenarios are changing rarely, once the process is automated, an organization will quickly benefit from the economy of scales.

Latest publications show the increasing interest of BPM practitioners in unstructured, knowledge-driven processes. The term "knowledge-driven" or "knowledge-intensive" refers to the fact that a process execution scenario significantly depends on knowledge of a human expert rather then on the predefined process model. Such process can vary from one execution to another demonstrating large unpredictability [3][4][5]. One of the examples of knowledge-driven processes is case management (CMP). OMG defines case management as *"A coordinative and goal-oriented discipline, to handle cases from opening to closure, interactively between persons involved with the subject of the case and a case manager or case team"*.

Seeking to increase their efficiency by process automation, organizations also admit that for the knowledge-driven processes such as CMP, the ability to adapt the process scenario according to a situation (we call it post-design adaptability) is the most essential. This makes automation of case management processes following an imperative approach too expensive: a number of modifications to initial process model will quickly outweigh any automation benefits [6].

In the CMPM request for proposal released in November 2009 [4], OMG formulates in detail the problem of case management process modeling and support, illustrating the need for another paradigm.

Declarative Configurable specification language (DeCo) was first introduced in [7]. With DeCo, we exploit an idea that an activity of "scenario definition" for a business process is not limited to a process design time (as imperative BPM requires) but it makes an integrated part of process deployment and even execution. In this paper, we define configurable process elements (namely, configurable data objects) and context-based configuration rules for DeCo. These modeling concepts allow one to continuously adapt the process along its lifecycle and, consequently, they pave the road for the automated decision-making support of knowledge workers. We illustrate our ideas on the example of a mortgage approval process.

The reminder of this article is organized as follows: in Section 2 we discuss the related works. In Section 3 we introduce the mortgage approval process (a CMP example), present our motivations in creating DeCo and relate this work with our previous research. In Section 4 we discuss the modeling principles of DeCo and introduce the configurable data object and context-based configuration rules concepts. In Section 5 we present conclusions and discuss our future work.

2   Related Works

Today, the majority of de-facto modeling standards including UML, EPC, BPMN exploit the *imperative* modeling style. Imperative process models are suitable for simulation [9], thus they can be highly advantageous for practitioners helping them to control the process and to exclude incorrect or undesirable scenarios already at design. BPEL[10] is a standard executable language for process models documented in BPMN. Operational semantics for process model execution based on Petri Nets and Pi calculus is considered in [11][12]. The research reported in [13] proposes a formal semantics of BPMN defined using Petri nets. In [14], the technique for simulation and analysis of process specified with DEMO [15] is presented.

Yet providing the means for simulation and control, imperative process models are proven to be restrictive [16]: specification of numerous options and variations for the sake of process adaptability becomes difficult if at all possible in such models [17][5]. Alternatively, a process can be specified *declaratively*: this modeling style supports non-determinism and allows modeler to postpone the decision making about the process execution scenario until its deployment or even execution. In [18], the detailed comparison of imperative and declarative modeling styles is provided. In [19][20], SEAM (for Systemic Enterprise Architecture Methodology) is presented. In SEAM, processes in an organization can be modeled as *joint actions* with implicit (nondeterministic) execution scenarios. Modeler refines SEAM models selecting an appropriate level of details. Thus the detailed specification of the process flow can be postponed. In the similar way, the MAP methodology [21][22] addresses the process specifications using the notions of *intentions* and *strategies*. Each intention in MAP can be realized following one or multiple alternative strategies, leaving the process execution largely nondeterministic and, therefore, adaptable for a given context. MAP notation was used to address process variability and to model process lines in [37].

Whereas some researchers decide to develop their modeling notations from scratch, others extend the existing standards providing them with the desired properties. In [23] both the EPC (Event Process Chain) and the BPMN metamodels are extended with elements for modeling process goals and process performance measures. In [24] the BPMN notation is extended to provide the concepts for querying the business process definitions and extracting the business process patterns. In [25][26] the (imperative) EPC notation is extended with the concepts for process configurability along the control-flow, data, and resource perspectives.

While supporting process adaptability, declarative models encompass a significant ambiguity and, as a consequence, are not suitable for simulation. Numerous efforts to achieve adaptability and control under the roof of the same process modeling approaches have been reported in the literature. The underlying semantics is ranged from LTL (linear temporal logic) and FOL (first-order logic) to Petri nets enabling automated modelchecking and theorem proving techniques for model validation and analysis known from the software engineering. In [27], DecSerFlow language for Declarative modeling of service flows is presented. In [28] the same authors present the DECLARE system for supporting declarative (loosely-structured) process models. The formal semantics of DECLARE and DecSerFlow is based on LTL. The formal semantics for the Configurable Integrated EPC (C-iEPC) modeling notation presented in [25] is based on FOL and serves to validate the process model correctness.

3   DeCo: Motivation and Relation to Our Previous Research

In [29][30] the declarative semantics for a graphical modeling notation for enterprise modeling called SEAM is discussed. In [29] we consider the variability aspects of business process modeling and propose declarative modeling approach and semantics based on Alloy [31]. Alloy specification language allows one to validate the conformance between a high-level declarative design specification of a process with its low level imperative implementation specification.

In [32][7], we put the research of the previous years together in order to develop an approach offering to a modeler an extensive configurability opportunities while implementing the principles of declarative modeling and supporting automated model analysis and step-wise refinement [33]. We called this approach DeCo – for Declarative Configurable process specifications.

In [36] we introduce a configurable roles and add this concept to MAP notation.

This work introduces another two modeling concepts of DeCo: configurable data objects and contextual configuration rules. We illustrate the use of these concepts on the example of mortgage approval process.

3.1   Motivating Example: Mortgage Approval Process

Mortgage approval process is a typical example of a case management process. In this paper, we provide a generic mortgage approval process description as defined by different financial institutions in the USA. The information provided below represents a compilation of guidelines and descriptions of mortgage approval process, provided by different loan consulting firms, financial advisors, and banks and available on the web (e.g. http://www.homebuyinginstitute.com/, http://www.mortgage-resource-center.com/, http://homebuyereducation.bankofamerica.com/, etc.)

A mortgage is a loan for buying a house. The mortgage approval process can be divided into the following sub processes: Pre-qualification, Formal Application, Document Review, Pre-approval, Property Appraisal, Final Approval, Closing. Whereas the order of these main sub processes varies rarely, the documents required, the sequences of tasks, the participants of each sub process can be different depending on the place, the financial institution's policies, and the applicant's situation and requirements. In this paper, we focus only on the Formal Application sub process:

Formal Application
0 An applicant can request the application package by e-mail or by post. Alternatively, all the forms can be downloaded from the web site of a prospective lender.
1 A mortgage application can be submitted electronically or during a personal meeting with the mortgage lender.
2 The exact set of documents may vary depending on the financial institution and the particular situation of an applicant. These documents may include: the social security card, record for past two years for residence address, employer data, various Internal Revenue Service (IRS) forms, recent pay-stubs, etc.
3-5 During the formal application, in some states, the mortgage lender provides the applicant with a Good Faith Estimate (GFE) of costs of loan closing; the applicant can be also asked to make a final decision on the type of mortgage loan and to lock in an interest rate.

6 Usually during the formal application submission an applicant has to pay the application fee and the appraisal fee. For some agencies, however, the appraisal will be charged later, whereas the application procedure can be free of charge.

Though substantially simplified, the description above illustrates the variability of activities, actors, and information involved into the process. The process scenario can also differ substantially depending on the execution context (e.g. the country, state, agency). For a financial organization operating globally and dealing with multiple environments definition of a single process model becomes a challenging task.

In our previous work reported in [32] we modeled this Formal Application sub process using BPMN and formulated *five* modeling challenges common for imperative modeling approaches in general:

1. Need to specify task inputs/outputs while distinguishing obligatory and optional data objects, alternatives (possible replacements), and synonyms (identical artifacts called differently).
2. Need to specify role hierarchy, alternative roles and synonyms.
3. Need to specify optional, obligatory, alternative task and synonyms.
4. Need to specify multiple control flow possibilities.
5. Need to specify an impact of data on different tasks and the task flow.

4   Improving Adaptability of Mortgage Approval Process Model with DeCo

4.1   Replacing Imperative Scenario with Declarative Specification

The graphical notation of DeCo is based on BPMN [34] whose modeling concepts are widely used and recognized by practitioners. But similarities terminate here since, compared to BPMN, DeCo implements the declarative modeling principles. These principles allow one to postpone the decision making about the eventual process scenario until its deployment or even execution.

Declarative approach to process modeling represents an alternative to continuous exception definition, use of "if-then-else" or "switch" constructions within a traditional, workflow-based process model [31]. Instead of modeling a flow of process activities, in DeCo, we focus on modeling individual activities (or clusters of activities). Each activity is associated with its *contract* that specifies (i) a conditions or a situation when this activity can be executed (ii) a situation that will result from this execution. As a result, instead of a flow of preordered tasks, DeCo specification describes:

- a set of tasks (with no explicit ordering) that must, should, or could be executed during the process;
- a set of rules allowing a dynamic task selection at a given process state from the list of tasks enabled at this state [7].

In a general case, the resulting process scenario is highly nondeterministic as each of the enabled task, if selected, will result in a different case development. Strictly speaking, the concrete scenario of how a given case has been managed can be known only upon the process termination. We call it an execution trace.

4.2   The Role of Context

Dey in [35] defines a context as "*.. any information that can be used to characterize the situation of an entity. An entity is a person, place or object that is considered relevant to the interaction between a user and an application, including the user and applications themselves.*"

As our example shows, mortgage approval process can vary strongly from country to country, agency to agency, and even from one mortgage application to another. These entities make a part of the process context and should be taken into consideration while configuring a concrete process scenario. More specifically, the context relevant to our process should encompass the characteristics of a mortgage lender and an applicant. The mortgage lender (a financial institution) can be characterized by its internal policies and adopted standards in customer services, risk management etc. For any concrete agency, also its resources available for process execution should be taken into consideration: number of employees, their roles, expertise, and responsibilities. Moreover, any financial institution should comply with some external regulations (e.g. federal law, etc.) that are defined by its country or state of residence. Thus, a geographical situation of a mortgage lender is also a context for mortgage approval process. The information about a mortgage applicant is explicitly handled by the process – it is a mortgage application file itself.

At design time, usually little is known about a process context: a CMP should comply with an industry standard, other external regulations and, if known, internal policies of an organization implementing it.

At deployment, the context is getting more explicit: agency type, its location, local resources and other specific facts about the process context allow designer to configure the process accordingly.

The final and the most specific part of the process context (or case context) is an application file – it appears and fills in during the mortgage approval execution. It allows configuring the process scenario in all details.

According to DeCo modeling approach, all the emerging context information should be constantly transformed into process configuration rules (at design, and deployment) or used to check the task compliance with such rules (at deployment and execution). Thus, the DeCo specification of mortgage approval process can be seen as a repository of tasks where each task can be instantiated for a given country, agency and even application case by answering the following questions:

-what resources (data, people, etc) are required for the task execution?
-what will be produced/modified upon termination of this task?
-what other constraints (e.g. functional, temporary, legacy, etc) must be fulfilled for the task execution?

DeCo does not provide means for modeling process context but rely strongly on the availability of context information. Coupling of DeCo with some context modeling approach will be explored in our future research.

4.3   Configurability at Multiple Perspectives

In the literature, several major perspectives of the process models are specified [8]: *the control flow perspective* that captures the temporal ordering of process tasks, events, and decision points; *the data perspective* that captures the lifecycle of data objects (creation, usage, modification, deletion) within the process; *the resource perspective* that describes how the process is carried out within the organization and deals with roles and resource assignments; *the operational perspective* that addresses the technical aspects of process execution and specifies the elementary process tasks and their assignment to concrete applications or application components of the organizations; *the context perspective* that describes the attributes related to the process execution context; *the performance perspective*, addressing the process cost effectiveness.

DeCo defines the concepts and semantics addressing process model configurability (i) on the *control flow* perspective by supporting *declarative style* and allowing non-deterministic execution scenarios; (ii) on the *data, operational,* and *resource* perspectives, providing the modeling notation for *configurable data objects, tasks, and roles* respectively; (iii) on the *context* perspective, providing *contextual configuration rules*.

Configurable roles in DeCo was already addressed in [36]. In this paper, we introduce the notation and semantics for configurable data objects and context-based configuration rules in DeCo. The other concepts will be addressed in detail in our future publications.

4.4   Configurable Data Objects and Their Semantics

A case of a foreign applicant recently arrived to the US following a new job assignment can become extremely difficult for a potential mortgage lender. The main problem with this case is that the applicant cannot provide the documents *required* by the standard process; instead, she is submitting *other* documents issued by a bank, an employer, or authority of her previous country of residence. Not matching the standards, such application can launch a long investigation process or can be simply rejected.

DeCo defines configuration mechanisms for data objects that include *optional* and *obligatory* data objects, specifies if a certain data artifact is *consumed, produced,* or *modified* by a given task and defines *synonym* and *alternative* relations between data objects as illustrated in Fig.1. These mechanisms help knowledge worker to anticipate the situation that she never met before, to process the data artifacts not "previewed" by a standard process scenario (if one exists) and to use them for more efficient decision-making.

Data object configuration in DeCo corresponds to configurability along the data perspective according to the taxonomy defined in [8].

Figure 1 illustrates the data object configuration diagram for *Tax forms* and *Tax return forms* required for formal mortgage application in the USA. A rectangle with thick outline and "C" in the right corner refers to a data object that can be further **configured** in the process model based on the situation or context.

By *alternatives* we specify the data objects that can replace the data object originally required by the task; *synonyms* are completely identical data objects used under different names by organizations or departments of one organization. A dashed line with a tag "syn" depicts the synonym relation. A solid line with a tag "alt" depicts the alternative relation. More formally, these relations can be specified as follows:

Let $T\{d_{1},...,d_{n}\}$ be a task where $d_1,...,d_n$ are the data objects consumed, produced, or modified by T.

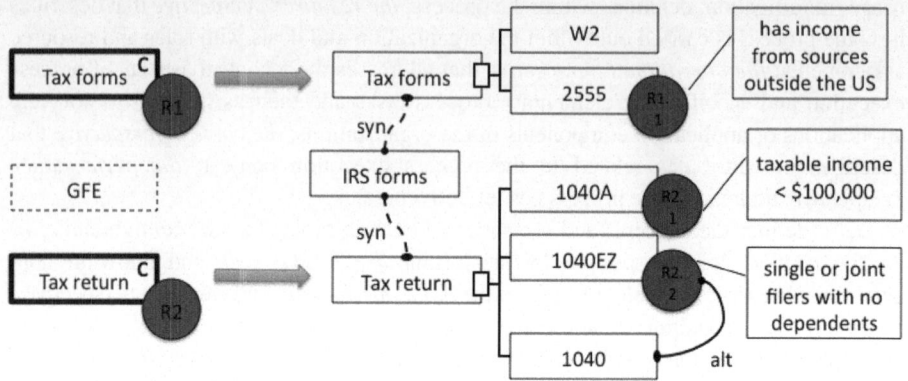

Fig. 1. Data object configuration in DeCo

Definition 1: Data object x is a *synonym* of d_i for a given process π iff it can replace d_i in T with no impact on π:

$$x = Syn_{\pi}(d_i) \sim T(...,x,..) \Leftrightarrow T(...,d_i,...)$$

In Fig. 1 both tax forms and tax return forms can be called Internal Revenue Service (IRS) forms [source: wikipedia]. This is expressed using a synonym relation.

Definition 2: The fact that for a given process   and task T the data object y is an *alternative* for d_i under a certain condition R implies that: If R holds then y can be accepted by T instead of d_i:

$$y = Alt_{x}(d_i,T,R) \sim R \rightarrow T(...,y,..)$$

In Fig.2, the form 1040EZ is a simplified form that can be applicable to single and joint filers with no dependents [source: wikipedia]. It can be considered as an alternative of the obligatory 1040 form. The rule 2.2 in this diagram explicitly specifies the condition where this alternative is applicable.

A data object d is *optional* for a given task T if it can be omitted in the contract of T. For example, the GFE certificate is optional for some countries and can be omitted in *Register Application* task. In DeCo, optional data objects are depicted with dashed borders.

Using the data object configuration, we can separate the management of data objects from the process scenario management.

Let us now come back to the foreign applicant example. Considering that the bank is willing to satisfy the foreign applicant's request, the main trouble for a loan officer would be to identify the relations between the standard forms provided by this applicant but unknown for the current bank and the standard forms required by the mortgage approval process of this bank. Such investigation terminates with conclusions like the following:

- The form X provided by the applicant is an analogy of the form Y required by the process;
- The form X provided by the applicant can be accepted in place of the form Y required by the process under certain condition C;
- The form X provided by the applicant is irrelevant to the process.

This information can be expressed in terms of synonym, alternative relations or optional/obligatory property in DeCo:

- The form X provided by the applicant is an analogy of the form Y required by the process → *X is a synonym of Y within this process;*
- The form X provided by the applicant can be accepted in place of the form Y required by the process under certain condition C → *if condition C is met, then X is an alternative to Y within this process;*
- The form X provided by the applicant is irrelevant to the process → *X is optional within this process.*

The more synonym or alternative relations are determined, the more process model evolves, and the better decision-making support for the loan officer is provided.

4.5   Modeling Contextual Configuration Rules

One process often needs to be customized in order to meet the requirements of its deployment environment (e.g. country, state, corporate division) and/or to anticipate the concrete case circumstances [7]. Therefore, the possibility to enable/disable synonym and alternative relations and optional/obligatory properties of an element has to be provided not only at process design but also at customization and instantiation. For this purpose, DeCo defines context configuration rules (*context rules* for short).

In DeCo diagrams, context rules are depicted with dark circles labeled with a name of the rule. In the current version of DeCo, these rules are formulated as predicate expressions. If, based on the context, such predicate evaluates to *True,* then the corresponding configuration mechanism is enabled.

This concept can be illustrated on the following example: According to the banking regulations in the US, in certain cases the mortgage applicant may be asked to provide the lender with one or several supplementary tax forms and tax return forms. The diagram in Fig.1 illustrates the context rules implementing these regulations. Here the form W2 (Wage and Tax Statement) is an obligatory data object for the mortgage application; the form 2555 (Foreign Earned Income) should be provided by taxpayers who have earned income from sources outside the United States (a context rule 1.1). The form 1040A is limited to taxpayers with taxable income below $100,000 (this is expressed by the rule 2.1.). The form 1040EZ is a simplified form that can be applicable to single and joint filers with no dependents [source: wikipedia]. Under this condition, which can be expressed as a contextual rule 2.2, this form can be considered as an alternative of the obligatory 1040 form.

Context configuration rules can be defined based on (a) external regulations imposed by a concrete location (country, state, city) of the organization implementing the process, (b) internal policies specified at a company level (its country division, local branch or agency), (c) particular case conditions (e.g. a foreign applicant, sub-prime, first-time buyer, etc). Other context rules for the mortgage approval process may include: *isAvailable(InternalAppraisalAgent) = true; agencyLocation = North Carolina;* etc. The context rules should be specified for a process at design, refined at deployment and then controlled at execution.

5   Conclusion and Future Work

In this work the Declarative Configurable process specification language has been presented. The graphical notation of DeCo is based on BPMN, but similarities terminate here since, compared to BPMN, DeCo implements the declarative modeling principles. DeCo language is in its infancy. Validation of its modeling concepts and development of a modeling tool are the main milestones for our future research.

In this paper, we specified configurable data objects and contextual configuration rules. These concepts are integrated into DeCo process models. Other concepts defined in DeCo will be presented in our next publications.

Using the Mortgage approval process as an example, we illustrated how declarative modeling principles and configurability mechanisms can be used in order to improve the post-design process model adaptability - the characteristic utterly desired for knowledge-driven processes. Since the execution scenario of such processes cannot be predefined at design, *non-deterministic* declarative specifications become a natural solution.

Though encompassing a significant ambiguity and not suitable for simulation, declarative process specifications may serve a useful tool for process validation and verification – the techniques known from software engineering [31]. As soon as new context information emerges, the declarative process specification evolves and ideally becomes more and more deterministic. This evolution can be compared to a *step-wise refinement* of software specifications [33]; the notion of refinement for graphical specifications is presented in [30]. The step-wise process refinement and its validation in DeCo will be addressed in our future publications.

Context rules play an important role in process configuration. Providing that an organization can be exposed to various sources of regulations, thousand context rules will emerge in a process model. This increases a risk of conflicting rules leading to the process model inconsistency. DeCo provides a FOL-based semantics for the context rules. The next step of our research will be focused on modeling, validation and verification of context rules.

The modeling method presented in this work is in its infancy. The modeling notation still requires major improvement in order to be adopted by practitioners. However the most important issue for us is scalability and validity of the DeCo process specifications. Modeling more elaborated (real life) case management process with DeCo and validation of results is a critical milestone in our research.

References

1. Smith, H., Fingar, P.: Business Process Management: The Third Wave. Meghan-Kiffer Press (2003)
2. Barjis, J.: The Importance of Business Process Modeling in Software Systems Design. Journal of the Science of Computer Programming 71(1), 73–875 (2008)
3. Hill, J.B., Lheureux, B.J., Olding, E., Plummer, D.C., Rosser, B., Sinur, J.: Predicts 2010: Business Process Management Will Expand Beyond Traditional Boundaries, http://www.gartner.com/resId=1231219
4. OMG, Case Management Process Modeling (CMPM) Request For Proposal: Bmi/2009-09-23
5. Swenson, K.D.: Mastering the Unpredictable. How adaptive case management will revolutionize the way the knowledge workers get things done. Meghan-Kiffer Press (2010)
6. de Man, H.: Case Management: A Review of Modeling Approaches, BPTrends (January 2009)
7. Rychkova, I., Nurcan, S.: Towards Adaptability and Control for Knowledge-Intensive Business Processes: Declarative Configurable Process Specifications. In: Proc. 44th Annual Hawaii International Conference on System Sciences, HICSS, pp. 1–10. IEEE (2011)
8. Jablonski, S., Bussler, C.: Workflow Management: Modeling Concepts, Architecture, and Implementation. International Thomson Computer Press (1996)
9. Barjis, J., Rychkova, I., Yilmaz, L.: Modeling and Simulation Driven Software Development. In: Chinni, M.J., Weed, D. (eds.) Spring Simulation Multi Conference, pp. 4–10 (2011)
10. OASIS Web Services Business Process Execution Language, WSBPEL (2006)
11. van der Aalst, W.M.P.: Pi calculus versus Petri nets: Let us eat "humble pie" rather than further inflate the "Pi hype". BP Trends 3(5), 1–11 (2005)
12. van der Aalst, W.M.P.: Making Work Flow: On the Application of Petri Nets to Business Process Management. In: Esparza, J., Lakos, C. (eds.) ICATPN 2002. LNCS, vol. 2360, pp. 1–22. Springer, Heidelberg (2002)
13. Dijkman, R.M., Dumas, M., Ouyang, C.: Semantics and analysis of business process models in BPMN. Information and Software Technology 50, 1281–1294 (2008)
14. Barjis, J.: Automatic Business Process Analysis and Simulation Based on DEMO. J. Enterprise Information Systems 1(4), 365–381 (2007)
15. Dietz, J.L.G.: Enterprise Ontology –Theory and Methodology. Springer, New York (2006)
16. van der Aalst, W.M.P., Pesic, M., Schonenberg, H.: Declarative workflows: Balancing between flexibility and support. Computer Science – Research and Development 23(2), 99–113 (2009)
17. Yu, E.S.K., Mylopoulos, J.: Understanding "why" in software process modeling, analysis, and design. In: The Proceedings of ICSE 1994, pp. 159–168 (1994)
18. Fahland, D., Lübke, D., Mendling, J., Reijers, H., Weber, B., Weidlich, M., Zugal, S.: Declarative versus Imperative Process Modeling Languages: The Issue of Understandability. In: Halpin, T., Krogstie, J., Nurcan, S., Proper, E., Schmidt, R., Soffer, P., Ukor, R. (eds.) BPMDS 2009 and EMMSAD 2009. LNBIP, vol. 29, pp. 353–366. Springer, Heidelberg (2009)
19. Wegmann, A.: On the Systemic Enterprise Architecture Methodology (SEAM). In: Proc. 5th International Conference on Enterprise Information Systems, pp. 483–490 (2003)

20. Wegmann, A., Lê, L.-S., Regev, G., Woods, B.: Enterprise Modeling Using the Foundation Concepts of the RM-ODP ISO/ITU. Standard Information Systems and E-Business Management, vol. 5, pp. 397–413 (2007)
21. Rolland, C., Prakash, N., Benjamen, A.: A Multi-Model View of Process Modeling. In: Requirements Engineering, vol. 4(4). Springer, London (1999)
22. Nurcan, S., Etien, A., Kaabi, A., Zoukar, I., Rolland, C.: A Strategy Driven Business Process Modelling Approach. Special issue of the Business Process Management Journal on Goal-Oriented Business Process Modeling (2005)
23. Korherr, B., List, B.: Extending the EPC and the BPMN with Business Process Goals and Performance Measures. In: ICEIS, vol. (3), pp. 287–294 (2007)
24. Awad, A.: BPMN-Q: A Language to Query Business Processes. In: EMISA, pp. 115–128 (2007)
25. La Rosa, M., Dumas, M., ter Hofstede, A.H.M., Mendling, J.: Configurable multi-perspective business process models. Journal Information Systems 36(2) (2011)
26. La Rosa, M., Dumas, M., ter Hofstede, A.H.M., Mendling, J., Gottschalk, F.: Beyond Control-Flow: Extending Business Process Configuration to Roles and Objects. In: Li, Q., Spaccapietra, S., Yu, E., Olivé, A. (eds.) ER 2008. LNCS, vol. 5231, pp. 199–215. Springer, Heidelberg (2008)
27. van der Aalst, W.M.P., Pesic, M.: DecSerFlow: Towards a Truly Declarative Service Flow Language. In: Bravetti, M., Núñez, M., Zavattaro, G. (eds.) WS-FM 2006. LNCS, vol. 4184, pp. 1–23. Springer, Heidelberg (2006)
28. Pesic, M., Schonenberg, H., van der Aalst, W.M.P.: DECLARE: Full Support for Loosely-Structured Processes. In: Spies, M., Blake, M.B. (eds.) Proc.11th IEEE International Enterprise Distributed Object Computing Conference (EDOC), pp. 287–298. IEEE (2007)
29. Rychkova, I., Regev, G., Wegmann, A.: Using Declarative Specification. In: Business Process Design. International Journal of Computer Science & Applications (2008)
30. Rychkova, I.: Formal semantics for refinement verification of entreprise models. Dir.: Alain Wegmann. Thèse EPFL, no 4210 (2008),
    http://library.epfl.ch/theses/?nr=4210
31. Jackson, D.: Software Abstractions: Logic, Language, and Analysis. The MIT Press (2006)
32. Rychkova, I., Nurcan, S.: The Old Therapy for the New Problem: Declarative Configurable Process Specifications for the Adaptive Case Management Support. In: zur Muehlen, M., Su, J. (eds.) BPM 2010 Workshops. LNBIP, vol. 66, pp. 420–432. Springer, Heidelberg (2011)
33. Wirth, N.: Program development by stepwise refinement. Communications of the ACM (1971)
34. BPMI/OMG, Inc. Business Process Modeling Notation. Version 1.0 (February 6, 2006),
    http://www.bpmn.org/
35. Dey, A.: Understanding and Using Context. Personal and Ubiquitous Computing 5, 4–7 (2001)
36. Denekere, R., Rychkova, I., Nurcan, S.: Modeling the role variability in the MAP process model. In: Proc. RCIS (2011)
37. Rolland, C., Nurcan, S.: Business Process Lines to deal with the Variability. In: Hawaii International Conference on System Sciences (HICSS), Hawaii, USA (January 2010)

A Qualitative Research Perspective on BPM Adoption and the Pitfalls of Business Process Modeling

Monika Malinova and Jan Mendling

Institute for Information Business, Wirtschaftsuniversität Wien, Austria
{monika.malinova,jan.mendling}@wu.ac.at

Abstract. Business Process Management (BPM) is used by organizations as a method to increase awareness and knowledge of business processes. Although many companies adopt BPM, there is still a notable insecurity of how to set it up in the most effective way. A considerate amount of research concerning partial aspects of BPM adoption has been done, such as the pitfalls of business process modeling. However, up until now hardly any empirical research has been conducted that aims at validating them. In this paper we address this research gap by conducting eleven in-depth interviews with BPM experts from various companies. We use the Grounded Theory approach to qualitatively analyze the data. Our contribution is twofold. First, we derive a conceptual framework showing the insights of BPM adoption by organizations. Second, we use the evidence from the interviews to discuss the pitfalls of business process modeling and show the countermeasures that are taken by companies.

Keywords: BPM Adoption, Business Process Modeling Pitfalls.

1 Introduction

Business process management (BPM) is adopted by an increasing number of companies for achieving different goals, from business-oriented ones such as performance improvement to system-oriented ones like process automation. Although BPM as a discipline has been established already in the 1990s, there is still a notable insecurity of how to set up BPM in a company in the most effective way. Partially, this fact is explained with the diversity of scenarios in which BPM is introduced. Furthermore, the intertwining of BPM with various strategic and operational parts of the company makes BPM adoption a complex topic to study.

Up until now, there have been different contributions to research focusing on partial aspects of BPM adoption. Business process redesign is one important perspective of BPM adoption, being summarized in Kettinger et al. [1] and supported by best practice [2]. Also success factors of business process modeling have been identified with a focus on individual projects [3]. There is also a list of business process modeling pitfalls, which address a set of important issues of general BPM adoption. While a subset of these pitfalls directly relate to the adoption question, there is currently hardly any empirical research reported that aims at validating them.

M. La Rosa and P. Soffer (Eds.): BPM 2012 Workshops, LNBIP 132, pp. 77–88, 2013.

In this paper, we approach the gap of dedicated empirical research on BPM adoption as a starting point. We took a Grounded Theory approach and conducted a set of interviews with BPM experts from adopting companies. Our contribution is a conceptual model that helps to understand BPM adoption in more detail. Specifically, we use the evidence from the interviews to discuss the pitfalls of business process modeling. Our discussion shows the validity of the pitfalls and illustrates counter-measures that are taken by companies.

The paper is structured as follows. Section 2 discusses the background of our research. It introduces the essential concepts of BPM and the pitfalls being identified by Rosemann. Section 3 describes our research design based on Grounded Theory accompanied with demographics on the interview partners. Section 4 presents our findings. First, the conceptual model is discussed. Second, its relationship to the pitfalls is investigated. Section 5 concludes and gives an outlook on future research.

2   Background

There are many studies focusing on the success factors concerning enterprise information systems [4]. Some of them found that for an organization to ensure a successful enterprise system implementation, they must pay sufficient attention to BPM [5]. To achieve BPM success, it is important to understand the organizational context [6]. Indulska et al. suggests that while academics mainly research on the issues related to the development and evaluation of artifacts, practitioners are interested in the purpose and adoption of BPM [7]. However, this latter issue is not getting enough research coverage though being of great importance for practitioners.

Several studies attempt to identify the capabilities organizations should adopt in order to support their BPM initiative. For instance, Bandara binds the concept of success to its context of BPM adoption [8]. The study illustrates that a process modeling project is successful if it is effective, i.e. fulfilling its objectives, and efficient, i.e. the process modeling activities are completed with the allocated resources [8]. According to Trkman, BPM should translate a firm's strategy into specific requirements and enable the execution of the strategy [9]. Hence, success could be defined as the resulting status of when the intended goals of the BPM initiative are met to a satisfactory level [10].

However, BPM by itself is not trivial to implement, as there are various aspects that need to be considered for it to bring beneficial outcomes. As much as the business process modeling success factors have been studied, there are also studies illustrating the most common pitfalls for organizations, potentially leading to BPM failure altogether. The lack of alignment between strategy and BPM projects is one of the identified failure causes when adopting BPM [9]. Beyond that, organizations tend to spend a lot of time on modeling their processes in terms of scope and depth [11], neglecting issues like selecting the right processes to model, deciding on the required level of detail, or choosing an appropriate framework. In addition it has been argued that companies often underestimate understanding issues of elaborated modeling techniques [11]. For that reason, BPM is criticized as being time-consuming and not delivering sufficient value [11]. Therefore, it is important to scope the role of BPM in an organization appropriately [11].

The purpose of the pitfalls suggested by Rosemann was to increase the awareness of the most common mistakes organizations can make when implementing a BPM initiative [11, 12]. However, up until now, hardly any attempt has been made to evaluate them systematically. It is important for such to be based on empirical research, rather than on review of literature. For that reason, we not only focus on reasons and consequences of BPM adoption, but also on how organizations are dealing with potential pitfalls.

3   Methodology

For this paper, we utilized a qualitative research approach. This approach is advised for emerging research topics in which a small amount of previous studies has been conducted [13, 14]. It involves a purposeful description, explanation, and inter-pretation of collected data [15] and permits an in-depth investigation of the subject matter [16].

3.1   Data Collection

We conducted eleven semi-structured in-depth interviews with BPM experts from organizations from various industries. The BPM experts are employees involved in all stages of the BPM implementation. First, an interview guideline was developed, with questions relating to the BPM initiative. All interviews followed the same structure and were conducted in German. The interviews took place between September 2011 and February 2012. Because of the open nature of semi-structured interviews, the interviews ended up in an open discussion on perceived drivers and consequences of BPM. The amount of time for each interview ranged from 30-120 minutes, depending on the availability of the BPM expert from the respective organization.

Table 1. Interview Participants

ID	Industry	Company Size	Years of BPM	Number of Processes	Documented Processes
I1	Service/Retail	93	Not known	~1000	~20
I2	Service/Retail	740	Not known	400	Not known
I3	Service/Medical	~21000	Not known	Not known	Not known
I4	Insurance	881	Not known	Not known	242
I5	Service/Energy	313	1	Not known	Not known
I6	Consulting	~4300	1	>150	~80
I7	Service/Retail	~100	3	~100	~50
I8	Service/Retail	~1000	3	Not known	120
I9	Insurance	~5900	8	Not known	~350
I10	Consulting	75	Not known	Not known	Not known
I11	Consulting	~160	Not known	Not known	Not known

The questions were classified into the following three different categories: Process documentation (e.g. How do you document your processes?), Process identification (e.g. How do you decide what processes need to be modeled?) and Modeling guidelines (e.g. What does the modeling guideline contain?). We encountered organizations that find themselves in any of the phases of the BPM lifecycle.

3.2   Data Analysis

The qualitative analysis of the interviews was done using Grounded Theory as defined by Glaser and Strauss in 1967. This method supports inductive discovery of a theory grounded in the data [18]. The initial theory has been divided into two, namely Glaserian and Straussian approach. For this study we chose to follow the Straussian approach as it enables systematic analysis of the data collected from the interviews to unveil the essential relationships, consequently building a theory [18].

The data analysis was done in three steps consisting of three types of coding: open, axial and selective, respectively. *Open coding* is the process of examining, conceptualizing, and categorizing the data [18]. Conceptualizing is the first step we did. This was done by going through the interview data, giving each sentence or paragraph a discrete name representing the phenomenon. Next, we grouped the derived concepts that we found to point to the same phenomenon. To keep track of the concepts, categories, and the relationships, we used the specialized qualitative analysis software *ATLAS.ti. Axial coding* is a set of procedures where connections between the categories are derived [18]. This is done by utilizing a coding paradigm involving Causal Conditions, Phenomenon, Actions and Strategies, and Consequences (see Figure 1). This stage of analysis assigns accordingly the concepts derived from the open coding to each category offered by the coding paradigm [18]. Thus, if a category identifies the reasons for BPM adoption, this category turns into a subcategory of the main category Causal Conditions. *Selective coding* is the process of selecting and focusing on a core category, where a core category is the central phenomenon around which all other categories are integrated [18]. This phase is aligned around the conceptualization of a descriptive story about the central phenomenon of this study [18]. As a result we derived a conceptual framework explaining the phenomenon of BPM adoption.

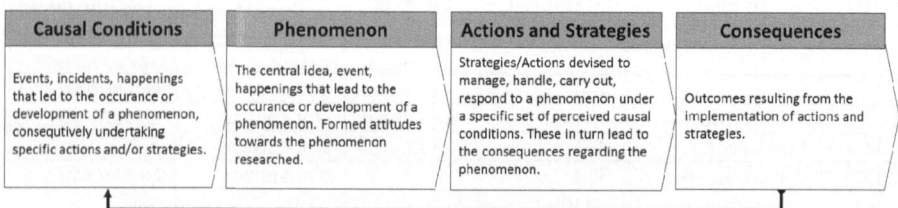

Fig. 1. Coding paradigm (adopted from [8])

4   Research Findings

The findings of our research are twofold. First, based on the concepts and categories obtained from the qualitative data analysis with Grounded Theory a conceptual framework was created. The framework provides insights into the reasons for BPM adoption, the actions organizations carry out for its implementation, as well as the subsequent consequences. Second, we use the concepts and categories from the framework along with some insights from our interview material and reference them accordingly to discuss some of the pitfalls suggested by Rosemann [11, 12]. As a result we reveal the perceptions of organizations about the underlying meaning of the respective pitfalls and the manner they avoid or resolve them.

4.1   Conceptual Framework for BPM Adoption

The BPM adoption conceptual framework as shown in Figure 2 has been aligned with the coding paradigm suggested by the Straussian Grounded Theory approach. Thus, the concepts were organized in the four predefined categories, each tied to the next in a sequence. During the coding of the interview material we identified the reasons that trigger organizations to adopt BPM. In addition, these reasons contribute to the organizations forming their own view about the phenomenon or an aspect thereof i.e. BPM adoption as means of a modeling language. This successively triggers the actions and strategies they undertake for the BPM implementation. As a result of the BPM adoption, organizations are faced with a set of consequences which could in turn generate further reasons for BPM adoption.

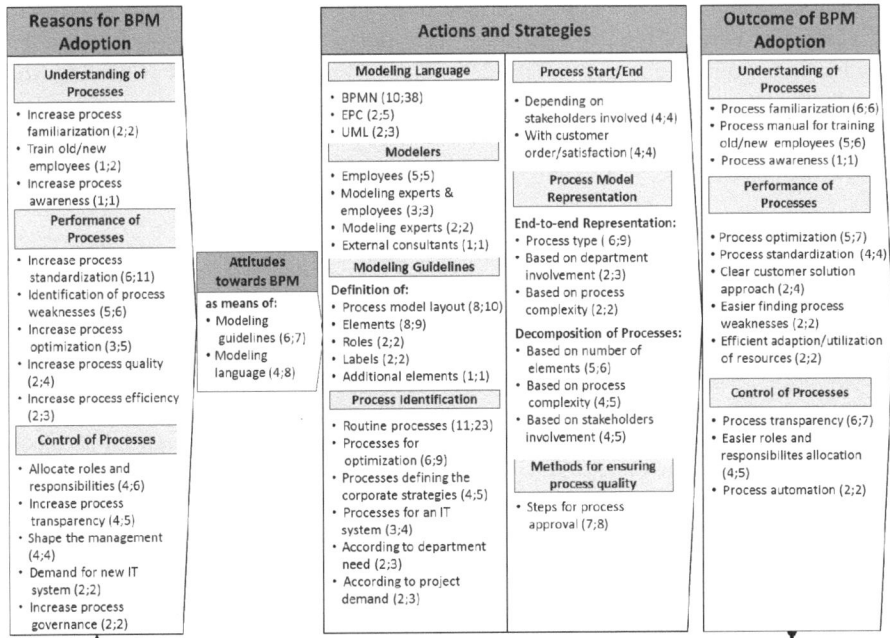

Fig. 2. BPM Adoption Conceptual Framework

The relative importance of each concept in the framework can be assessed by the number of companies that mentioned them, as well as the number of times each interviewee mentioned them. Therefore, they could be used as a preliminary indicator for relevance. This number is shown in brackets next to each concept (e.g. Category: *Reasons for BPM Adoption*; Subcategory: *Performance of Processes*; concept: *Identification of process weaknesses (5;6)*). The first number reflects the number of interviews the respective concept was mentioned in, whereas the second number indicates the number of occurrences this concept had in all interviews.

4.1.1 Reasons for BPM Adoption

Each organization has particular motives for undertaking a BPM initiative. Our analysis unveiled a list of reasons for organizations to start modeling their processes. The reasons for BPM adoption presented in Figure 2 reflect the expectations upon the results BPM will yield. These can be classified into three categories: reasons concerned with understanding of processes, performance of processes and control of processes.

More than half of our interviewees pointed out the importance of standardizing their current processes. This need is *"because we have a large amount of people employed and more departments...therefore we wanted to standardize the processes so that every employee applies the process the same way as the others"*(I7). Moreover, five companies indicated the necessity of identifying process weaknesses, arguing that without BPM the course of doing that would have been more difficult or even impossible: *"...it is much simpler to find the cutting points"*(I6).

Whereas understanding and performance of processes has proved to be important, the issue of control was also mentioned as a potential driver. Almost half of the organizations pointed out that a clear definition of responsibilities is critical for the overall effectiveness of the company. This was particularly important when a number of employees or departments are involved with one process: *"... we model the process flow of the processes which are influenced by many organizational units..."*(I9).

4.1.2 Phenomenon

A central event leads to the occurrence or development of the phenomenon, which is here the formed attitude of an organization towards BPM [18]. Besides the general attitude towards BPM, we identified two additional specific attitudes, namely, attitude towards modeling languages and modeling guidelines. Organizations believed that *"Without a goal and purpose for the modeling initiative everything is difficult"*(I10), implying that most often difficulties would arise with redundancy, overhead and lack of organizational improvement.

We found that almost all of the interviewed organizations tend to put strong emphasis on the process modeling language. Almost all chose or are planning to transfer to BPMN. The key reasons are either to be able to model the processes with high level of granularity, to transition to process automation or for easier identification of the process weaknesses *"We use BPMN when we want to discuss the cutting points of the processes"*(I9). This is usually practiced when a process goes through more than one department. What is more is that organizations of our interview partners put relevance on having clear modeling guidelines that each modeler will follow for later consistent process modeling, thus making the process models comprehensible for all *"...because by having guidelines it is easier for the employees to read and understand the processes"*(I8).

4.1.3 Actions and Strategies

Actions and Strategies are devised to manage, handle, carry out and respond to a phenomenon under a specific set of predefined causal conditions [18]. We categorized the actions and strategies we found organizations to be carrying out into seven subcategories: Modeling language, Modelers, Modeling guidelines, Process identification, Process start and end, Process model representation and Methods for ensuring process quality.

Compliant to the attitude towards modeling languages, we found that our interviewed organizations started modeling their processes with BPMN or planned to transition to it; *"We moved from UML to BPMN"*(I2). In addition, most of our interviewees compelled their employees to model the processes they are involved with, *"Everybody in the company has to model"*(I2). However, training in the respective modeling language is provided beforehand. Alternatively, when a process modeling expert is employed, we observed an interaction between the modelers and the employees, *"The modeler who is responsible for the sales processes interacts with the employees of the sales department regularly in order to get to know the processes in detail"*(I8).

Being confronted with complex processes, organizations need to decide in advance on a set of modeling guidelines in order to control potential process model complexity. Our data suggests that companies typically developed specific guidelines which need to be considered in this context. These guidelines define the range of elements modelers are allowed to use when modeling their business processes, *"We have elements which are allowed to be used"*(I6). Additionally, they defined the maximum number of elements one process model should not exceed, the model layout, the roles of each process, and their parts.

Moreover, we discovered a list of processes companies' model first. All eleven companies concentrated on modeling the processes they use on daily bases. Also, more than half started modeling the processes which needed improvement, *"At the beginning, the processes which we knew needed an improvement, we tried to model them..."*(I6). Some organizations started modeling those processes that reflect the company's strategy *"What is important are the processes contributing to the company's strategy, goals, ..."*(I10). In addition, we observed that organizations put emphasis on the start and end of one process. For most of our interviewees, this was based on the departments or employees involved. Hence, when more than one stakeholder is involved in the execution of a single process, they decomposed it accordingly, *"Process ends when one department did its job, and another department needs to continue"*(I11). Others do this depending on a customer perspective.

According to Indulska et al., the definition of an appropriate level of detail is ranked fifth on the scale of ten process modeling issues [7]. Other studies consider an end-to-end representation of processes imperative for better understanding among the stakeholders [19]. Our findings outlined that some companies tried to capture all details of the routine processes, *"An end-to-end representation of the process is used when the process is a simple service that is used on daily basis, like customer orders"*(I11). While others preferred a process model not to be decomposed if only one department is involved in its execution, *"...so we don't decompose it* [the process] *if it is the same department that deals with the process, but model it until the end no matter how big and complex the process gets"*(I9). In general, our data indicated the usefulness of decomposing a process model. It is considered as a more comprehensible way of representation when a process model has been decomposed in case the number of elements exceeds the specified number of elements allowed, *"However, if the process gets too big, more than 15 elements, we try to decompose it"*(I8). We also observed that most organizations ensured the accuracy of the process models by either using predefined steps for process approval, or depending on the decision of the process manager, *"When the process model has been modeled by the two expert modelers, the process manager ensures the process is correct and decides on its approval"*(I7).

4.1.4   Outcome of BPM Adoption

The consequences followed by the choice of actions lead to a set of various outcomes. Consistent with the reasons for adopting BPM, these outcomes can be classified into three categories: understanding of processes, performance of processes and control of processes. Ordinarily these should all be expected outcomes, mirrored to each initial reason for BPM adoption. However, we also observed some that were not anticipated by the organizations.

Our data showed that five organizations used the process models to train their employees, *"This process is used as a manual of how the process works and what needs to be done"*(I10), compared to only one stating this as a reason. Similarly, more organizations than those with clear expectations yielded process improvements, *"We used them* [the process models] *mainly for faster processing of events, shortening of waiting periods in the processes..."*(I4). BPM also appears to contribute to an easier definition of roles and responsibilities, *"[The process models are used] to define what stakeholders each of the processes have"*(I5). Moreover, we found that some organizations used the process models as a tool for easier approaching their customer demands in order to *"avoid ignorance when new projects arrive, but go directly to solving"*(I6).

4.2   Business Process Modeling Pitfalls

Based on the conceptual framework as well as some additional insights from our interview material, we were able to reference some of the pitfalls that Rosemann suggested as challenging for practitioners [11, 12].

Lack of Strategic Connection. The first pitfall implies the lack of demonstrable connection to one or more critical business issues [11]. According to Rosemann if an organization does not consider such connections, the initiative is considered as a form of "waste" and should be stopped [11]. We observed that organizations appear to be aware of their reasons for pursuing business process modeling. Almost half of our interviewees pointed out the importance of identifying the processes that define the company's strategy, *"We first started to model the processes which we consider core, the most important for the company's strategy. So these 5-7 processes are our priority"*(I7). Accordingly, they use BPM to better execute their corporate strategy.

Lack of Governance. A good governance system is necessary, as it aims towards effective communication and collaboration in an organization. There are few studies that proposed a set of principles for effective process governance, one of which points out the relevance of process prioritization [3,20,21]. It is suggested that a company should have an appointed BPM expert who makes the key decisions about the BPM implementation. These range from the decision of who will model the processes, the selection of the processes to be modeled, the level of granularity for each process model, etc. Our interviewees, being BPM experts themselves, clearly stated the emphasis they put on identification of the processes to be modeled first. This is done by prioritizing the processes the company considers as most important which sequentially leads to the commencement of a framework where the process models will be stored. Having established process governance is also important when the organization is planning to undertake some change. In line with that, we found that there are a number of companies that first modeled the processes they plan to automate, *"...we are also starting to consider automation of the processes, so we are preparing the process models for future implementation as a workflow"*(I9). In this way they aim to assure that the processes will be standardized and quality proved before they are transitioned to automation.

Additionally, Rosemann pointed out the lack of knowledge concerning the success of BPM adoption and how it is measured [11]. In order to address this point, we found that organizations formulated expectations of certain outcomes from the BPM adoption, compliant with their initial reasons. However, the frequencies of reasons and consequences in the conceptual framework reveal that organizations experienced certain expected outcomes, but also some unexpected beneficial outcomes, such as using the process models to clearly approach their customer demands, *"Avoid ignorance when new projects arrive, but go directly to solving"*(I6).

Lack of Synergies. Our data illustrated various reasons acting as triggers for BPM adoption. In addition, Rosemann argues that different departments within one organization are triggered by different purposes, consequently modeling the same process independently from each other [11]. Yet, our data suggests that some organizations were aware of this particular problem occurring. Accordingly, they applied specific strategies in order to avoid it. For instance, there are companies that get requests from their departments as to what processes they need to be modeled, *"The processes which we identified to be modeled are those that the different departments need, processes in which we want to find the cutting points, which need optimization, and so on"*(I5). Moreover, there are service providers integrating process modeling competence where appropriate, *"We have an internal service* *provider ... and when the departments approach the provider with some problem, task, project, we consult them that it would be a good idea to do this or that."*(I9).

Lack of Qualified Modelers. A business process analyst must be able to translate process documentation into structured process models [11]. According to Rosemann, practitioners mainly focus on explaining the modeling tool rather than training the modelers [11]. Our data suggested that the employees were trained in the respective modeling language in order to model the processes they are involved in. Some organizations employed process modeling experts or external consultants. This appeared to happen when a process needed to be modeled with a higher level of granularity because of a specific reason. Nonetheless, they usually collaborated with the employees involved with the processes, *"...so the modeler who is responsible for modeling the sales processes interacts with the employees of the sales department regularly"(I8)*. This in turn helped capturing the correct flow of the processes. In addition, organizations used specified set of modeling guidelines. In this way, those companies that compelled their employees to model aimed to reduce the complexity of the modeling tool, *"*[Following the modeling guidelines] *because it is easier for the employees who are beginners with BPMN to learn how to use it"*(I2). Furthermore, acknowledging quality assurance as a part of the modeling process [11], we found that organizations used various steps to assure model quality, *"After the processes have been modeled, we* [the modelers] *show the process models again to the employees from the different departments to verify them"*(I9).

Lack of Realism. Our interview data emphasizes the importance of selecting the processes to be modeled first. The initial reasons for adopting BPM appear to be used as guidance for identifying the most relevant processes that will lead to the realization of their expected outcome. Besides that, we also found that companies did not allow loosing themselves in the vast amount of process models. Rather, they modeled only those processes they require for specific purpose, *"We concentrate mainly on customer demands. So we don't just sit there and say 'ok, we have like 1000 processes so which ones do we model'"* (I9).

Lack of Details. Rosemann discusses the limitations existing modeling languages offer and that they hardly satisfy the range of application areas the process models are used for [12]. Thus, organizations need to be aware of the language they choose for modeling their processes, as this language should be able to capture the required level of detail. Two things should be considered. First, modeling languages and tool functionality has advanced in the recent years. Second, it was emphasized that modeling languages were selected to best serve the purpose of the process models, *"We used EPC because of staff requirement evaluation."*(I9). In addition, many used BPMN to capture the technical process models *"We started using BPMN 2.0 to direct ourselves to automation of the processes"*(I5). Moreover, companies also decided on BPMN in order to be able to represent the processes with high level of granularity, *"...companies transfer to BPMN 2.0 because they want to capture all details of the process"*(I11).

L'Art pour l'Art. It is important to be clear of the purpose the process models have. This is primarily because the purpose of the model determines how detailed the process should be modeled. Rosemann argues that process models do not necessarily need to be complete, however they have to be relevant [12]. In line with that, we found that the modeling guidelines are used as a barrier for creating process models of inappropriate detail. This is based either on the relevance the organization puts on specific processes, or the requirements from the respective department. Thus, whereas one organization modeled those processes that go through more than one department detailed, others captured the entire process flow depending on the process type, *"Customer processes are modeled almost 100%"*(I7).

5   Conclusion

In this paper we investigated BPM adoption and its relation to business process modeling pitfalls. We conducted eleven in-depth interviews with companies from various industries and qualitatively analyzed the data using Grounded Theory. We derived a conceptual framework integrating reasons for BPM adoption, the actions and strategies undertaken for its implementation, as well as the subsequent consequences. We found that organizations commence on the BPM initiative for better understanding, performance and control of processes. One of the main expected outcomes was that process models can be used to clearly allocate roles and responsibilities, especially when more departments are involved with a single process. Additionally, unanticipated outputs were discovered, one of which was that the process model helps to approach customer demands in a clearer way. Beyond that, we used the framework along with insights from our interview material to discuss some of the business process modeling pitfalls suggested by Rosemann [11, 12]. As a result we founded that organizations were aware of the BPM consequences, thus they selected the actions appropriately, based on their initial reasons for BPM adoption.

We identify as a limitation the small number of interviews made. At this stage, we did not ensure a conceptual saturation. Therefore, in future research we plan to increase the number of interviews by finding interview partners from various industries. Furthermore, we plan to broaden our interview guideline, aiming towards more insights of how oranizations are dealing with the pitfalls of business process modeling.

References

1. Kettinger, W., Teng, J., Guha, S.: Business process change: A Study of methodologies, techniques, and tools. MIS Quarterly 1(21), 55–80 (1997)
2. Reijers, H.A., Liman Mansar, S.: Best practices in business process redesign: an overview and qualitaive evaluation of successful redesign heuristics, pp. 283–306 (2005)
3. Bandara, W., Gable, G., Rosemann, M.: Factors and measures of business process modeling: model building through a multiple case study. European Journal of Information Systems, 347–360 (2005)
4. Petter, S., DeLone, W., McLean, E.: The Past, Present, and Future of "IS Success". Journal of the AIS, 341–362 (2012)

5. Al-Mudimigh, A.: The role and impact of business process management in enterprise systems implementation. Business Process Management Journal 13, 866–874 (2007)
6. Reijers, H.A., van Wijk, S., Mutschler, B., Leurs, M.: BPM in Practice: Who Is Doing What? In: Hull, R., Mendling, J., Tai, S. (eds.) BPM 2010. LNCS, vol. 6336, pp. 45–60. Springer, Heidelberg (2010)
7. Indulska, M., Recker, J., Rosemann, M., Green, P.: Business Process Modeling: Current Issues and Future Challenges. In: van Eck, P., Gordijn, J., Wieringa, R. (eds.) CAiSE 2009. LNCS, vol. 5565, pp. 501–514. Springer, Heidelberg (2009)
8. Bandara, W., Guy, G., Rosemann, M.: Business Process Modeling Success: An Empirically Tested Measurement Model. In: Proc. Int. Conf. on Information Systems, pp.1–20 (2006)
9. Trkman, P.: The Critical Success Factors of Business Process Management. International Journal of Information Management, 125–134 (2010)
10. Bandara, W., Alibabaei, A., Aghdasi, M.: Means of achieving Business Process Management success factors. In: Proc. Mediterranean Conf. on Information Systems (2009)
11. Rosemann, M.: Potential pitfalls of process modeling: part A. Business Process Management Journal, 249–254 (2006)
12. Rosemann, M.: Potential pitfalls of process modeling: part B. Business Process Management Journal 12(3), 377–384 (2006)
13. Lee, A.: A scientific methodology for MIS case studies. Management Information Systems Quarterly, 32–50 (1989)
14. Yan, R.: Case study research methods, California (1994)
15. Williams, C.: Research Methods. J. of Business & Economic Research 5(3), 65–72 (2007)
16. Creswell, J.: Research Design: Qualitative, Quantitative and Mixed Methods Approaches, 2nd edn. SAGE Publications, Thousand Oaks (2003)
17. Benbasat, I., Goldstein, D., Mead, M.: The Case Research Strategy in Studies of Information Systems. MIS Quarterly 11(3), 369–385 (1987)
18. Strauss, A., Corbin, J.: Basics of Qualitative Research: Grounded Theory Procedures and Techniques. SAGE Publications (1998)
19. Spanyi, A.: More for less: the power of process management. Meghan-Kiffer Press (2006)
20. de Bruin, T., Doebeli, G.: Progressing an Organizational Approach to BPM: Integrating Experience from Industry and Research. In: Proper, E., Harmsen, F., Dietz, J.L.G. (eds.) PRET 2009. LNBIP, vol. 28, pp. 34–49. Springer, Heidelberg (2009)
21. Richardson, C.: Process Governance Best Practices: Building a BPM Center of Excellence. BPTrends (2006)

How Good Is an AS-IS Model Really?

I. Guven Arkilic[1], Hajo A. Reijers[2], and Roy R.H.M.J. Goverde[1]

[1] Precedence B.V., The Netherlands
{Guven.Arkilic,Roy.Goverde}@precedence.nl
[2] Eindhoven University of Technology, The Netherlands
H.A.Reijers@tue.nl

Abstract. Redesign projects for business processes usually start with analysing and mapping an actual situation within an organization. This step is called "developing an AS-IS business process model". However, many contemporary organizations have invested in developing and sustaining process models of their existing operations, which are often created by domain experts themselves. In case a new redesign project is to be initiated, a dilemma occurs. Is it safe to use a model from the existing collection or should the AS-IS model be developed all over by a BPM specialist? Clearly, an important consideration here is whether AS-IS models developed by domain experts rather than BPM experts is of sufficient quality to drive a redesign effort. To empirically investigate this issue, we examined a business process within a multinational high-tech organization. Unlike most of the studies focused on one specific aspect of quality (e.g. control flow), we used a framework from the literature that covers three quality aspects. The framework was applied to determine the potential problems in the AS-IS model.

Keywords: Business process analysis, Business process reengineering, Business process redesign, Business process improvement, Business process modeling, AS-IS models, Business process case study.

Classification of the topic. Case studies and experiments.

1   Introduction

Companies and organizations are struggling to improve their performance to gain a competitive advantage over their rivals in their competitive industries. Business Process Reengineering (i.e. Business Process Redesign, or in a short form, BPR) can be a way for companies and organizations to achieve their goals by enabling them to redesign business processes within their companies or organizations to improve performance metrics.

Different approaches can be followed before starting to redesign business processes. The first one proposes a "clean sheet" approach in which processes should be created from scratch without considering the current situation of a process. However, the second one proposes to take a current situation as a starting point to redesign it. It was revealed that most of redesign projects follow the second approach

M. La Rosa and P. Soffer (Eds.): BPM 2012 Workshops, LNBIP 132, pp. 89–100, 2013.
© Springer-Verlag Berlin Heidelberg 2013

[1][2]. Since most of these projects build on the correct understanding of a current situation, the importance of mapping AS-IS models within organizations is evident. Yet, it is not always the case that AS-IS models within organizations are modeled by Business Process Management (BPM) practitioners who have a deep understanding of BPM and process-thinking. Sometimes these models are, instead, modeled by employees whose expertise is not directly related to BPM. If such is the case, related steps may be necessary to analyze AS-IS models and detect potential problems. A redesigned model is achieved based on the analysis of the weaknesses and strengths of a current situation [3]. Moreover, it is also important that correctness of a model is ensured since incorrect models can cause wrong decisions and may result with unsatisfactory implementations of information systems [4].

Due to the fact that the analysis and correctness of AS-IS models are quite important in the BPM domain, it is worthwhile to discuss the problems involved in AS-IS models which are developed by domain experts themselves and its potential impact on organizational efforts like redesign projects. By doing so, the impact caused by the problems of AS-IS models can be understood better and mitigated.

Although some research has been devoted to the quality and reliability of AS-IS models, the main focus is on the control-flow aspect (e.g. problems related with deadlock, dangling references, synchronization issues etc.). Other important aspects that contribute to the quality of a process are not covered to the same degree. For instance, it has been shown several times that control-flow errors can be checked in an automated way. However, checking if a model reflects *reality* is not such an easy task, since it builds on other validation mechanisms (e.g. discussions with stakeholders). We believe that a process model should not be just evaluated from a specific aspect, but should be assessed from several aspects to come up with a "complete" assessment. Therefore, the study in this paper offers a wider analysis of the quality of processes and applies it on a group of business processes as mapped within a high-tech company to determine their reliability and quality.

Against this background, the rest of the paper is organized as follows. In Section 2, related work is summarized and our motivation to conduct our study is described in more detail. In Section 3, the profile of the involved company is presented, along with information about the business processes under investigation. In Section 4, the quality aspects used to analyze the business processes and the methodology followed in this analysis are discussed. In Section 5, problems and limitations of the existing AS-IS models are discussed and the results of the analysis are presented to see how good the models as developed within the company actually are. Finally in Section 6 the conclusion of the research and the future work were presented.

2   Motivation and Related Work

There are two baselines for the motivation in this study. The first one is related to the importance of AS-IS models and their usage in redesign projects. Business process redesign projects mainly build on and aim to evolve a current situation. Some of them can be exemplified as follows. In [5], an actual process model was discovered by using process mining techniques. Based on the performance problem (i.e. bottlenecks), a redesign was made to shorten the throughput time. In [6], the problem of inconsistent and incomplete information caused by an isolated information system in a healthcare enterprise was fixed by deploying a workflow system. In [7], a checklist of redesign heuristics was used to redesign the "intake" process in a healthcare case, which enabled the authors to follow a structured approach. Similar to other redesign projects in the literature, these projects also made use of the current situations within their contexts (unlike the "clean sheet" approach as originally proposed by Michael Hammer in [8]). It is also important to stress that the models in the aforementioned projects were mapped by the people who have a deep experience with BPM and BPR; the mapped AS-IS models were directly usable for improvement purposes. Therefore, this gives rise to the expectation that modeling expertise may play a role in the quality of AS-IS models.

The second motivation for this study is closely related with the first one, since it relates to the quality of AS-IS process models developed within organizations. A number of studies have been done to evaluate business process models. In [9], 735 industrial business processes from finance, telecommunications, and other domains were checked by using different tools in terms of control-flow aspect. The models were checked for soundness (i.e. deadlock and synchronization issues). These 735 process models were grouped into five libraries in which three of them are overlapping. It was found that 54% of the process models do not comply with the rules. The automated way of checking the business processes showed that business processes can be checked in a few milliseconds. In [10], a study was conducted to analyze the connection between formal errors (e.g. deadlock) and a set of metrics in EPC models. EPC soundness was selected as a criterion. Validation aspects such as content, understandability, modeling pragmatics were not considered. Overall ratio of 10.7% was found among 2003 EPC models.

Apart from these two studies that just focused on control-flow aspect, another study was conducted that extended the analysis to object flow and role assignment, which was called Integrated EPCs (iEPCs). The idea in [4] was to combine these three perspectives in a comprehensive verification approach for object existence and role availability. Three theorems were defined that allowed a systematic verification for control-flow problems, object-flow problems and suitable role subsets, respectively. The authors aimed a better identification for correctness of models.

To summarize this section, the first group of studies in the literature showed that AS-IS models are important means for projects to gain an understanding of the contexts of the improvement project better, to locate problems in existing situations, and finally offer improvement scenarios. The second group of studies showed that analyzing the quality of models continues to be an important and challenging issue in BPM domain, whereas, most of the studies focus on a specific aspect, notably control-flow.

Therefore, the motivation behind the study in this paper is to balance both the verification and validation aspects of the analysis of business process models and show that both of the aspects are important for the reliability and quality of models. By doing so, instead of developing AS-IS models completely from scratch, they can potentially be checked for problems and updated to become useful for redesign purposes.

3   Company Profile and Case Study Description

The business processes analyzed in this study were developed within a high-tech company in the Veldhoven region in the Netherlands (because of confidential issues, the name of the company is hidden). The processes are valuable for this study because they were mapped by the employees (domain experts) of the company. These employees had developed the model as side tasks to their main job and they typically had very little experience with BPM (process modeling, redesign, simulation, etc). Therefore, these models represented an important source for us to analyze the issues and problems as a real-life case.

Although these processes were modeled to show the way of working to employees and assure a structured manner of work, they are considered as means for a redesign approach in this study. These models were analyzed from different aspects (see Methodology section) to see if they can be a sufficient basis to initiate a redesign project. We asked ourselves whether it would be possible, like in most of the redesign and improvement projects derived in the literature, to follow a similar approach by taking the current situation into account in this study. Because there already exist mapped processes within the organization, it would be highly efficient to make use of these models. However, due to the fact that the quality of the AS-IS models obviously affects the quality of the analysis of the existing situation and that of the redesign scenarios, additional required efforts may be required in the analysis step.

The goals of the business processes which are under investigation are represented below and business processes themselves can be found here[1] (because of confidential issues, details in the processes such as activity names and roles are hidden).

- "Manage Skill & Learning" process is used to secure the availability of defined skills within ML (Manufacturing & Logistics).

This process gives insight into actual and target skill level based on pre-defined skill frameworks. A role is assigned to an employee and based on this role, short and long term goals of an employee are set. To achieve a goal, a training or trainings should be followed by an employee. To do this, offered trainings are searched and booked based on the goals and availability of an employee. At the end, a training is followed and based on the result of this training, the result is recorded in the learning history and the employee moves (or does not move) from actual to target skill level.

- "Manage Carousel" subprocess is to secure the effective execution of the "Manage Skill & Learning" process by controlling / managing the actual versus new skill targets of the employees.

This subprocess is used to update skill and learning status reports of employees. Deviations in the current skill level of employees with respect to targets are analyzed. Based on this analysis, required skill framework changes are determined and actual

---

[1] https://www.dropbox.com/s/3ent4Orsy7oxgtk/AS-IS%20Processes.pdf

versus new skill targets are controlled. If required, the masterdata is adopted according to the results.

- "Manage Forecast" subprocess is to manage and control the identification and anticipation on current and future training needs within ML.

This subprocess analyzes actual training needs and availability of training materials and resources such as trainers, rooms and equipments based on individual learning plans and requests. The goal in this subprocess is to match the training materials and resources with the requests made by employees. Manufacturing & Logistics (ML) and Customer Support (CS) are the departments that conduct training forecast; however, ML department is responsible to approve / disapprove the CS training proposal and also its own training proposal. At the end of this subprocess, when the matching between demands of employees and offerings of departments is ensured, the data about training forecast is registered into the learning management system.

For these processes, there are 10 different roles and 255 people are responsible within the organization. Around 675 cases are handled in a year.

The reason why this research analyzes the skill and learning management process and the related subprocesses is as follows. The related processes are quite important for the organization since trainings (along with the materials and resources) are scheduled, new hires are trained, and the defined skills are managed based on these processes. Moreover, since the industry of the organization is quite fluctuant in terms of the customer demand, the organization dismisses many people from employment and also employs many people at once. When many people are hired by the organization at once, the organization does not want to spend too much time to train these people because there may be a downturn in the industry soon and all the efforts may be wasted. As our investigation revealed, the duration and also quality of these processes are vital for the company that is in a highly fluctuant field and therefore, the characteristic of industry makes these processes more important than ever. As a result, BPR was selected by the organization to utilize these business processes. Finally, mentioned business processes can be found here.

4   Methodology

As it was mentioned before, the goal of this paper is to analyze and also understand the problems exist in the existing business processes of a company. It was seen in the Motivation and Related Work section that most of the studies focused on the control-flow analysis, which is a syntactic quality, to evaluate business processes. Due to the fact that this study aims to extend this analysis, the SIQ Framework described in [11] was used as a guideline for analyzing the business process models of the organization. The SIQ Framework is about process model quality and it is based on three types of quality [11]:

1. *Syntactic Quality:* This quality aspect assures that a business process complies with the rules of the modeling technique used to model the business process and therefore, vocabulary and syntax of the modeling language play an important role [11]. To give an example for this quality aspect in the modeled processes, a decision entity cannot have just one outgoing route because it is against its usage. Another example can be that the process should end without any problem such as a deadlock or dangling references.

2. *Semantic Quality:* This quality aspect assures that process models should make true statements about the real world [11]. It indicates that models should be related and correct to the problem and also contain all related statements [11]. An example of this aspect in the modeled processes can be that if a trainer executes a specific task regarding trainings in the real life, this must be reflected in the model.

3. *Pragmatic Quality:* This quality aspect assures that business process models should be understandable by people [11]. The order of the building blocks and the flow between the elements might be a good example for the modeled processes.

Based on the quality aspects above, the AS-IS models were analyzed. While evaluating these quality aspects, different methods were used due to the different characteristics of the various quality aspects. For example, as a first step, the syntactic quality of the models was analyzed. Because this aspect concerns the rules of the modeling technique, no or very limited contact with the stakeholders was needed. Tools that offer verification and checking the models manually were sufficient to analyze this particular quality aspect. Secondly, the semantic quality of the models was established. This quality aspect was more complicated to analyze, because there was a need to understand the models in detail to see if they reflected the reality. Therefore, meetings with the stakeholders (there were 10 different roles) were organized and questions were asked to reveal the actual way of working within the organization. Last but not least, pragmatic quality was questioned. This was done in cooperation with the stakeholders and the experience of the researchers played an important role for this aspect.

The results associated with these three quality aspects can be found in the next Section.

5   Results

In this section, the outcome of the analysis of the AS-IS models was discussed. Based on the quality aspects, the results were presented under three categories, namely Syntactic, Semantic and Pragmatic quality problems.

5.1   Syntactic Quality Problems

Finding -1-
A workflow is called "sound" when it terminates properly (e.g. when no deadlock, livelock, dangling references exists in the model) [12]. In the AS-IS model, a

deadlock occurs when "Task 4" and then "Task 5" are executed successively. As it is seen, a parallelism starts after "Decision1" and it is merged before executing "Task6". When the result of "Decision2" becomes "No" and a case is routed to "Task4" and then "Task5", the Parallel Merge gateway waits for a token from the other parallel branch that will never receive. Therefore, the deadlock occurs because of the parallelism here. In reality, the model does not require a parallelism (or in other words does not require one of the parallel branches) because one of the parallel branches does not have any activities to be executed. That branch is just an arc in the model that starts from the Parallel Split gateway and finishes at the Parallel Merge gateway without any activities on it.

5.2   Semantic Quality Problems

Finding -2-
The mapping of a resource to the activities exposes an inconsistency. Exactly the same resources were used with different names for different tasks which introduced confusion. To make this clear, think about a resource named "Resource1". Although exactly the same resource was responsible for other tasks, the name of the resource was renamed such as "Resource2". This problem made the process harder to understand who should execute which activity.

Finding -3-
Before following a training, an employee has to search all training offerings (see "Task6") and then book one of them (see "Task7") according to a date the employee is available. As another case in the existing situation, when an employee cannot pass a training (this is decided with "Decision4"), s/he has to go back and book another training. However, booking a training is not logical without searching all other training offerings because training dates / places might be updated. Therefore, the next step after an unsuccessful training was missed.

Finding -4-
The status of a training is stored when the outcome of a training of an employee is considered successful. However, in reality, the status is updated even if an outcome of a training is unsuccessful. This detail was missing in the existing model (see "Decision4" and "Task9"). "Decision4" was used to decide if a training is successful or not. If it is considered as successful, "Task9" is executed to store the result of the training. This action should also be reflected when "Decision4" considers a training unsuccessful.

Finding -5-
Managing the masterdata task seems to be executed for all incoming cases in the model (see "Subprocess1" which does not have any time trigger attached to it). In reality, it is an extensive task that is executed semi-annually (once in every six months). The reason why there is a need to separate managing the masterdata and the remaining process flow is that masterdata is managed for correct and complete

information available in the learning management system that provides employees to make use of the remaining process flow. This is why the masterdata is managed semi-annually unlike the remaining process flow that is executed for all the incoming cases. This situation is same for other two tasks where time triggers were neglected (see "Task8" and "Task10").

Finding -6-
There are two types of trainings. One of them is a training in a classroom environment ("Normal training") and the other is on a computer ("Computer-based training (CBT)"). If a new hire / employee takes a "CBT", s/he does not have to follow all the steps required for a normal training (e.g. searching training offerings, booking training offerings) because "CBTs" can be immediately taken. Therefore, there are two different types of trainings and each of these trainings should have its own control flow. In the existing model, no distinction was made to handle these different types of trainings and therefore, different control flows were not captured.

Finding -7-
The training forecast is performed for Manufacturing & Logistics (ML) and Customer Support (CS) departments. It may be the case that a training forecast is initiated just for ML, just for CS or both of them at the same time. In the existing model, Exclusive OR (XOR) decision gateway (see "Decision11") was used to route the cases to either ML department or CS department. Due to the structure of the XOR decision gateway, one of the outgoing paths is selected and a case is routed to this path. The XOR decision gateway is not capable of routing a case to both of the outgoing routes and therefore it does not allow all the options specified above (instead of XOR decision gateway, OR decision gateway is capable of such options).

5.3   Pragmatic Quality Problems

Finding -8-
This finding concerns the abstraction level (hierarchical structure) of tasks. Subprocesses are supposed to be used as entities that encapsulate related tasks. They represent a group of tasks and therefore it becomes easier to understand the scope of a process. In the existing model, some of the tasks were depicted as subprocesses although they just represent the single activities of the resources (see "Task16", "Subprocess3" and "Subprocess5").

Finding -9-
The name of the tasks / activities should ideally be in a verb-noun form [13]. An example may be "Send an invoice". This kind of naming gives a good insight to stakeholders about the goal of a task. This naming convention was also mentioned as one of the seven process modeling guidelines that are used to model a quality process [14]. In the AS-IS model, it was revealed that 24.24% of the tasks and subprocesses (8 out of 33) were not compliant with this rule.

Finding -10-

The last finding represents a limitation about the modeling notation. At the beginning of "Manage Carousel" subprocess, three tasks are executed in parallel. There is another occurrence of parallelism in "Manage Skill & Learning" process where two routes are executed in parallel. However, the existing model had a difficulty in capturing and presenting these structures well. For instance; "Task11", "Task14" and "Task15" are executed in parallel but since no Parallel Split gateway was used to initiate the parallelism, it is hard to realize the parallelism. Another example can be the parallelism after "Decision1". The parallelism starts after "Decision1" and ends before "Task6". However, because of spaghetti-like modeling in that part, it is hard to see the two parallel branches.

Swimlane diagrams were specifically selected by the mentioned organization as a modeling language to make the responsibilities clear for employees who are executing the activities in the processes. Since there is no Workflow Management System (WfMS) within the organization, task executors are using the AS-IS models to see the tasks they should execute in Swimlane diagrams easily. However, the modeling notation has been used in a way that tracking the tasks and data became complicated to understand. To show this complexity, process fragment modeled within the company in Swimlane notation and modeled by the authors in Petri-net notation are presented here[2]. The original process fragment was placed on the left side where no alteration took place (Swimlane notation). On the right side, exactly the same process fragment was remodeled (Petri-net notation). It is important to note that resources (task / activity executors) were removed from this model and the locations of the tasks were moved to more appropriate places to make the flow easier.

The process fragment, which is on the left side, was modeled in the Swimlane notation. In this fragment, the parallelism, which also introduces a deadlock, was modeled by a domain expert within the company. The domain expert tried to model the way of working but while doing this, introduced a deadlock and also used the parallelism in a wrong way (see one of the parallel paths that does not have any activities on it). The disorder in the notation provoked the domain expert to model the way of working in a worse and harder way. Furthermore, the employees whose responsibility is to carry out the process were also confused how to follow the activities in the business process (this was revealed by asking questions to employees about how they follow the activities).

On the other hand, the process fragment, which is on the right side and modeled in the Petri-net notation, made the flow more explicit to track the task and information flow due to the remodeling approach. For instance, the parallelism and deadlock became clearer. This was revealed by showing the original process fragment and the remodeled process fragment to employees and asking them to compare them. The remodeled fragment was the one easier to understand. This finding showed how the modeling notation can make a model harder / easier to understand (in the original process model it was harder for the stakeholders to understand the model).

---

[2] https://www.dropbox.com/s/1kj2ihaa03ng3ps/Finding10.pdf

6   Discussion and Conclusion

AS-IS models can be regarded as valuable resources to understand the existing operations within an organization. In the context of redesign projects, they are used to show the way of working and help to locate problems in business processes.

A well managed process model collection is an extremely valuable asset for an organization due to its other advantages also. These are as follows.

-   It enables organizations to perform what-if scenario testing whenever needed at low cost. This increases the quality of decision making.
-   A correct process administration enables organizations to resolve incidents faster. By knowing how processes interact with each other, IT as well as organizational errors can be explained and solved faster.
-   A correct process administration enables organizations to train personnel and to optimize internal communication and understanding, since there is one accepted truth.

Moreover, it becomes an important decision that when AS-IS models can be used or cannot be used within the scope of a project. For example, they are advised to be used in the following circumstances.

-   If process models have been made by experts (to ensure that the three quality aspects covered in the SIQ Framework are applied).
-   If process models are well-maintained and updated regularly regarding changes within an organization.
-   If process models are not modeled for one specific purpose (e.g. SOX Compliance or a specific goal). These "views" are sufficient for the purpose they were modeled for, however not a solid base for reusability in a companywide perspective.

When business experts develop such models themselves, there is a probability that they display problems. If the question arises whether such models are to be used as the basis for a redesign project, it becomes crucial to ensure that those models are reliable enough to make use of them.

In this study, an assessment of AS-IS models of an organization by using a quality framework from the literature was presented. It was shown that, if AS-IS models developed by inexperienced people are used; relevant revisions and fixes have to be applied. To show this, the AS-IS models of a real life organization have been analyzed. However, besides just focusing on the verification aspect, other aspects mentioned in the SIQ Framework (Syntactic, Semantic and Pragmatic) were also analyzed. The results revealed that the business processes under investigation contain one syntactic problem, six semantic problems and three pragmatic problems. It became clear that it is not enough to use a specific aspect to assess the reliability of business processes. For instance, a process model can be free of syntactic problems. However, because of semantic or pragmatic problems, the same process model becomes ineffective or even unusable.

In this study, processes related with the training management of an organization and skill development of employees have been checked from different perspectives to see how reliable they were developed. Although the research gave good insights about the reliability of the AS-IS models developed within an organization, only specific processes have been used. In the future, this project can be extended to cover other AS-IS models within different departments of the organization or other organizations to get an idea about the reliability of AS-IS models developed by the industry. Furthermore, our research may provide input for a method to transfer existing AS-IS models into more usable ones.

References

1. Reijers, H.A.: Design and Control of Workflow Processes. LNCS, vol. 2617. Springer, Heidelberg (2003)
2. O'Neill, P., Soha, A.S.: Business Process Reengineering A review of recent literature. Technovation 19, 571–581 (1999)
3. van Vliet, H.: Software Engineering: Principles and Practice. John Wiley & Sons (2008)
4. Mendling, J., La Rosa, M., ter Hofstede, A.H.M.: Correctness of Business Process Models with Roles and Objects. QUT ePrints Technical Report #13172, Queensland University of Technology (2008)
5. Maruster, L., van Beest, N.R.T.P.: Redesigning business processes: a methodology based on simulation and process mining techniques. Knowledge and Information Systems 21, 267–297 (2009)
6. Becker, J., Fischer, R., Janiesch, C., Scherpbier, H.J.: Optimizing US Health Care Processes-A Case Study in Business Process Management. In: 13th Americas Conference on Information Systems, pp. 1–9 (2007)
7. Jansen-Vullers, M.H., Reijers, H.A.: Business Process Redesign in Healthcare: Towards a Structured Approach. INFOR: Information Systems and Operational Research 43, 321–339 (2005)
8. Hammer, M.: Reengineering Work: Don't Automate, Obliterate. Harvard Business Review 68, 104–112 (1990)
9. Fahland, D., Favre, C., Jobstmann, B., Koehler, J., Lohmann, N., Völzer, H., Wolf, K.: Analysis on Demand: Instantaneous Soundness Checking of Industrial Business Process Models. Data & Knowledge Engineering 70, 448–466 (2011)
10. Mendling, J., Neumann, G., van der Aalst, W.M.P.: Understanding the Occurrence of Errors in Process Models Based on Metrics. In: Meersman, R., Tari, Z. (eds.) OTM 2007, Part I. LNCS, vol. 4803, pp. 113–130. Springer, Heidelberg (2007)
11. Reijers, H.A., Mendling, J., Recker, J.: Business Process Quality Management. In: Handbook on Business Process Management 1, International Handbooks on Information Systems, Part II, pp. 167–185 (2010)
12. van der Aalst, W.M.P.: Workflow Verification: Finding Control-Flow Errors Using Petri-Net-Based Techniques. In: van der Aalst, W.M.P., Desel, J., Oberweis, A. (eds.) Business Process Management. LNCS, vol. 1806, pp. 161–183. Springer, Heidelberg (2000)
13. Sharp, A., McDermott, P.: Workflow Modeling: Tools for Process Improvement and Applications Development. Artech House, Norwood (2009)
14. Mendling, J., Reijers, H.A., van der Aalst, W.M.P.: Seven Process Modeling Guidelines (7PMG). Information and Software Technology 52, 127–136 (2010)

APPENDIX

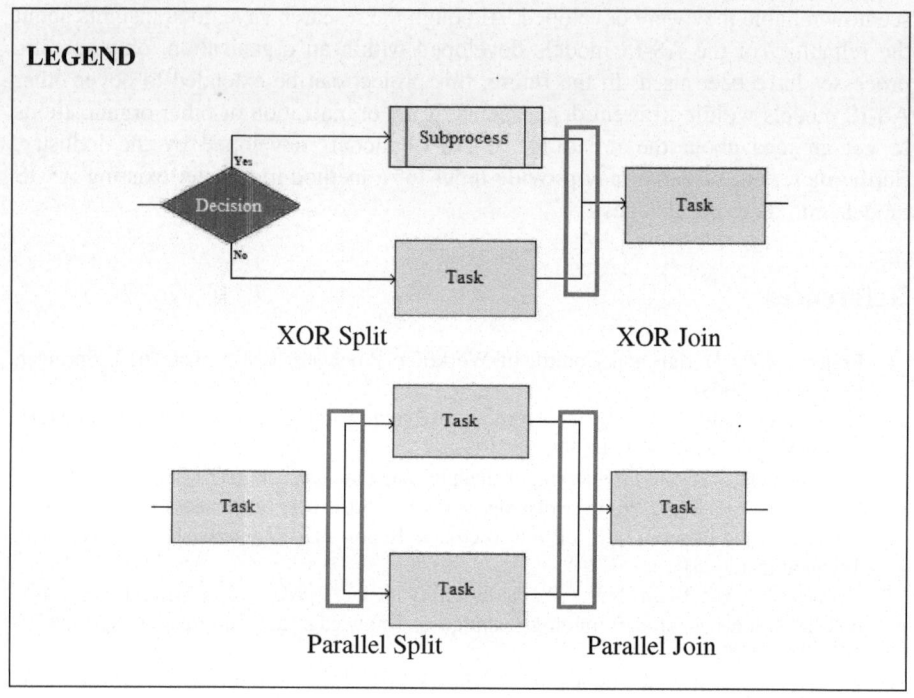

Designing Business Processes with History-Aware Resource Assignments*

Cristina Cabanillas, Manuel Resinas, and Antonio Ruiz-Cortés

Universidad de Sevilla, Spain
{cristinacabanillas,resinas,aruiz}@us.es

Abstract. Human resources are actively involved in business process management (BPM), due to their participation in the execution of the work developed within business process (BP) activities. They, thus, constitute a crucial aspect in BP design. Different approaches have been recently introduced aiming at extending existing BP modelling notations to improve their capabilities for human resource management. However, the scope of the proposals is usually quite limited, and most of them provide ad-hoc solutions for specific scenarios. Resource Assignment Language (RAL) was developed just to overcome such shortcomings, being independent of the modelling notation in which it is used, and providing interesting resource analysis mechanisms. Still, RAL is currently focused on a single BP instance and, thus, resource assignments cannot contain constraints between two process instances. In this paper, we introduce a complete (i.e. syntactical and semantical) extension for RAL to provide it with history-aware expressions. These expressions will, in turn, be able to be automatically resolved and analysed along with the other RAL expressions, thanks to RAL's semantics based on Description Logics (DLs).

Keywords: Human resource management, history-based distribution, RAL, resource-aware business process design, design-time business process analysis.

1 Introduction

Human resource management is one of the key aspects to consider when designing a BP, since the participation of people drives the execution of the processes carried out in an organization. Therefore, if we want everything to work properly and efficiently at run time, the design of an appropriate distribution of the work among the members of an organization is crucial.

As a proof of that, lots of approaches dealing with issues related to human resource management have been introduced in the recent years, and current Business Process Management Systems (BPMSs) are increasingly concerned about improving the support they provide for that purpose. Several proposals address

---

* This work has been partially supported by the European Commission (FEDER), Spanish Government under project SETI (TIN2009-07366); and projects THEOS (TIC-5906) and ISABEL (TIC-2533) funded by the Andalusian Local Government.

M. La Rosa and P. Soffer (Eds.): BPM 2012 Workshops, LNBIP 132, pp. 101–112, 2013.

the extension of Business Process Modelling Notation (BPMN) to enhance the resource perspective [1,2]; others extend Unified Modelling Language (UML) to specify and check well-known rules such as Segregation of Duties (SoD) and Binding of Duties (BoD) [3]. New resource assignment languages that can be used in combination with different process modelling notations have also been introduced [4,5]. However, in spite of the large amount of solutions, most of them are ad-hoc, their scope is quite limited, or they are just incomplete, meaning that they focus on specific aspects and leave others aside.

From the existing approaches, we are going to focus on RAL, a Domain Specific Language (DSL) to define resource assignment expressions in BP activities, aimed at exceeding the scope of similar approaches [5]. It has notable advantages, to be named: (i) it offers a wide collection of resource assignment expressions, (ii) it is not designed for a concrete BP modelling notation, and (iii) it provides automated analysis capabilities derived from its formal semantics based on DLs. Section 2 contains background on RAL. Nonetheless, the current scope of the language is restricted to a single BP instance, without considering past information in the resource assignments. In particular, RAL covers ten out the eleven Creation Patterns belonging to the Workflow Resource Patterns (WRPs) described by Russell et al. [6], but support for the following pattern referred to history information is currently missing:

History-Based Distribution: The ability to distribute work items to resources on the basis of their previous execution history.

We consider this an important limitation of the language, since this pattern is already supported by some other proposals, and there are constraints such as the aforementioned SoD and BoD that sometimes need information from previous BP executions (e.g. static SoD [3]). RAL's specification and semantics should, thus, be extended to include this pattern. In this paper, we introduce such an extension. As a result, we provide RAL with the required elements to specify that: (i) an activity has to be performed by the person that executed a certain activity in a previous instance of the BP; and (ii) an activity cannot be undertaken by somebody that has participated in the process in instances run during the last week. We wanted to keep RAL expressive enough to enable the specification of assignments that are likely to be used in organizations, so we have introduced history-aware assignment expressions both at activity level and at process level (cf. Section 3 for details). Besides that, in Section 4 we describe the DL-based semantics of the new RAL expressions, as well as the mechanism to automatically resolve such expressions to obtain the set of potential performers of an activity. Only one of the candidates might be later allocated to the task at run time. Finally, some related work is briefly introduced in Section 5, and the paper ends up with some conclusions and future work in Section 6.

2   Background

The work we present in this paper is the continuation of previous work on the improvement of resource management in BPs. A study we carried out about the features provided by BPMN (and other BP modelling notations) as for resource management, revealed that the capabilities offered by current notations are not sufficient to cater for all the resource management needs of an organization. This impelled us to develop a language that allowed an easier definition of resource assignments in BP models, while keeping expressiveness in the collection of assignments that could be specified [5]. The result was RAL, a DSL specifically developed to express resource assignments in BP activities overcoming some drawbacks present in other existing approaches [1,2,3]. RAL expressions cover from simple assignments of activities to specific individuals of the company, to complex assignments containing (access-control) constraints between activities, as well as compound expressions. RAL's syntax, quite similar to natural language, increases its understandability, as shown in the following examples:

RAL 1: IS Samuel
RAL 2: NOT (IS PERSON WHO DID ACTIVITY CreateResolutionProposal)
RAL 3:(HAS ROLE DocumentWriter) OR (HAS POSITION ACDocumentSigner)

Besides, the language was equipped with formal semantics based on DLs, which enabled the design-time analysis of resource assignment expressions by using DL reasoners existing in the market [7]. This allowed us to infer information automatically from *RAL-aware BP models*, i.e. models with RAL expressions associated with the BP activities, such as (i) the potential performers of each activity; or (ii) the potential set of activities each person of an organization can be allocated at run time. As a proof of concept, we developed RAL Solver, a plug-in for Oryx [8] that emerged both to test the use of RAL expressions in BP models, and the benefits of its DL-based semantics to analyse RAL-aware BP models at design-time [7,9].

Some benefits of design-time resource-related analysis are that it informs the company about the possible workload of its employees, and warns about potential allocation problems that may arise at run time. Furthermore, it eases the detection of inconsistencies between the resource assignments associated to the activities of a BP model and the structure of the organization where it is used, e.g. non-existent roles or persons.

In the rest of this paper, we introduce an extension for RAL to deal with history information in resource assignment expressions. In particular, we have added some new expressions to the specification of the language, and we have mapped them into DLs in order to be able to automatically resolve them, and so take them into consideration along with the rest of RAL expressions.

3   Extending RAL's Specification to Support History-Based Distribution

We have extended RAL expression IS PERSON WHO DID ACTIVITY activityName (line 11 in Language 1), which stated that an activity had to be allocated to the same person that had performed another activity (assuming the same instance

---

Language 1. EBNF specification for RAL's new expressions

```
1    Expression := IS PersonConstraint
2       | HAS GroupResourceType GroupResourceConstraint
3       | SHARES Amount GroupResourceType WITH PersonConstraint
4       | HAS CAPABILITY CapabilityConstraint
5       | IS ASSIGNMENT IN ACTIVITY activityName
6       | RelationshipExpression
7       | CompoundExpression
8
9    PersonConstraint := personName
10      | PERSON IN DATA FIELD dataObject.fieldName
11      | PERSON WHO DID ACTIVITY activityName [HistoryExpression]
12      | PERSON WHO HAS PARTICIPATED IN BPHistoryExpression
13
14   HistoryExpression := IN CURRENT INSTANCE
15      | IN ANY INSTANCE
16      | IN ANOTHER INSTANCE
17      | FROM startDate TO endDate
18
19   BPHistoryExpression := CURRENT PROCESS INSTANCE
20      | ANY PROCESS INSTANCE
21      | ANOTHER PROCESS INSTANCE
22      | A PROCESS INSTANCE BETWEEN startDate AND endDate
```

---

of the BP), to deal with the history-based distribution pattern (lines 14 to 17). The extension consists of spreading the scope to other BP instances, allowing the definition of constraints about the instance in which the referenced activity was executed, specifically:

- *Line 14.* The same process instance currently running. This is the option selected by default in case no *HistoryExpression* is specified.
- *Line 15.* Any instance of the process (including the ongoing one).
- *Line 16.* Any previous process instance (excluding the ongoing one).
- *Line 17.* Those process instances in which the activity has been completed between two given dates (regardless of whether the process instance itself is over or not).

Furthermore, based on the same constraints, we have introduced a new expression in the language (line 12). In it, we do not specify the activity whose performer is referenced, but the BP instance in which he/she has participated, i.e. he/she has undertaken some activity in that process instance. It is a more generic expression but can be useful not to limit so much the scope of the constraint. This way, lines 12 and 19-22 state that an activity has to be performed by somebody that executed *some* activity in (i) the ongoing process instance, (ii) any process instance, (iii) a previous process instance, and (iv) any process instance, provided that the activity was completed between two given dates (similarly to expression in line 17, it is not required the whole process instance being over by that moment).

Besides, we remind that RAL has a negation operator (NOT) we could use to define the opposite expressions, e.g. to state that an activity cannot be performed by the person that undertook another activity at any time in the past.

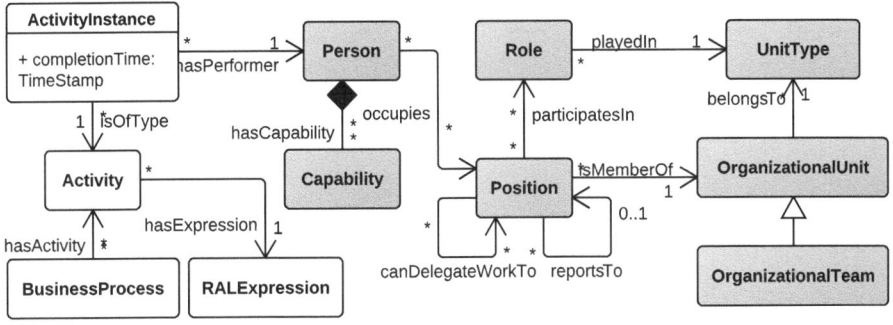

Fig. 1. Meta model with the required elements for history-aware RAL expressions

The organizational meta model on which RAL is based does not need to be modified in order to apply this extension. However, we have to provide a way to store the information required for the history-aware expressions. In Figure 1, classes related to organizational aspects are shown in gray. They correspond to the excerpt of the organizational meta model described by Russell et al. [10] RAL has always used. New elements to deal with history information are introduced in white. These elements contain the execution information necessary to resolve the new expressions. Specifically, a *BusinessProcess* has a set of *Activities*, which have associated a *RALExpression* indicating the resources allowed to perform the task at run time (i.e. potential performers of the activity). For each BP instance, zero, one or more instances of its activities can be executed. Each *ActivityInstance* (a.k.a. *work item*) can have a different *actual performer*, as long as that person meets the conditions stated by the resource assignment expression. The completion time of each activity instance is recorded, so that RAL expressions in lines 17 and 22 can be resolved. The set of work items undertaken by a single person constitute his/her execution history. The meta model shown in Figure 1, thus, contains all the information required to use the previous version of RAL and the new history-aware expressions.

3.1 Application Example

We are going to use the same use case we used when we first introduced RAL to exemplify the use of the new expressions [5].

The BP represented by the BPMN model in Figure 2 illustrates a simplified version of the process to manage the trip a conference (according to the rules of the University of Seville). It starts with the submission of the Camera Ready version of a paper accepted for publication at the conference. Then, one of the authors fills in a form requesting for authorization both to travel to the venue place and to take the funds from some funding source. This document must be approved by some person allowed to authorize the applicant to attend the conference and take funds from the project specified in the authorization form, e.g. the project coordinator. The signed document is sent for revision to an

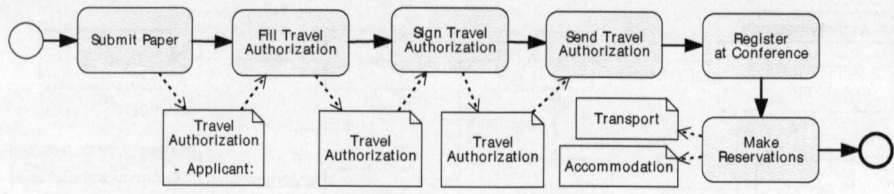

Fig. 2. Business process for conference trip management

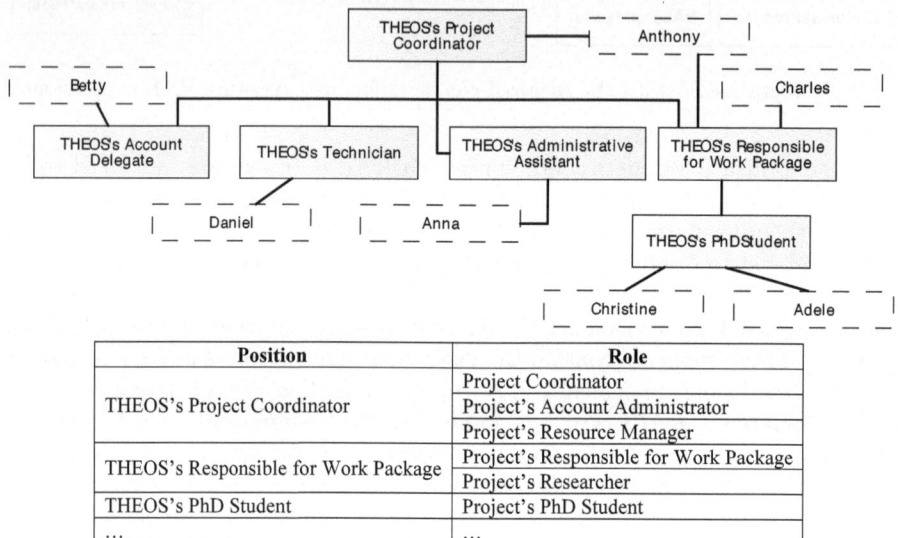

Position	Role
THEOS's Project Coordinator	Project Coordinator
	Project's Account Administrator
	Project's Resource Manager
THEOS's Responsible for Work Package	Project's Responsible for Work Package
	Project's Researcher
THEOS's PhD Student	Project's PhD Student
...	...

Fig. 3. Excerpt of the organizational model of ISA Group for project THEOS

external entity, where someone evaluates the request. If it is approved, one author of the paper must register at the conference and make the reservations required.

Imagine that the previous BP is used in an organization with the structure shown in Figure 3. It is actually an excerpt of the structure of the ISA research group of the University of Seville with regard to a research project called *THEOS* (class *OrganizationalUnit* of the meta model in Figure 1). It has six positions and seven persons occupying them. Each position of the model can delegate work to any inferior position and report work to its immediately upper position. The relationship *participatesIn* of the organizational meta model is summarized in the table attached to the figure.

Figure 4 shows possible RAL assignments for some activities of the process in Figure 2. The DL definitions of the expressions necessary to automate their resolution can also be seen in the figure (cf. Section 4.4 for details about the mapping to DLs).

Submit Paper: A *Project's PhD Student* is in charge of submitting the paper.
RAL: HAS ROLE ProjectsPhDStudent
DL: $RALSubmitPaper \equiv \exists occupies.(\exists participatesIn.\{ProjectsPhDStudent\})$

Fill Travel Authorization: The performer of task *Submit Paper* in the ongoing instance must fill in the authorization form.
RAL: IS PERSON WHO DID ACTIVITY SubmitPaper IN CURRENT INSTANCE
DL: $RALFillTA \equiv \exists hasPerformer^-.(\exists hasActivity^-.\{tm_1\} \sqcap SubmitPaper)$

Make Reservations: Anybody but the performer of task *Sign Travel Authorization* can make the reservations required.
RAL: NOT (IS PERSON WHO DID ACTIVITY SignTA IN ANY INSTANCE)
DL: $RALMakeReservations \equiv Person \sqcap \neg(\exists hasPerformer^-.(\exists hasActivity^-.$
$((\exists hasBPexecution^-.\{hist\} \sqcap TripManagement)) \sqcap SignTA))$

Fig. 4. Resource assignments to activities of the process in Figure 2

4   Extending RAL's Semantics to Support History-Based Distribution

As explained in [7], RAL's semantics is defined in DLs [11], which provides the language with analysis capabilities that can be exploited with operations implemented in current DL reasoners, e.g. Pellet and HermiT. The goal now is to define formal semantics for the history-aware RAL expressions. For them to be accurate, it is necessary to store run-time information that is necessary to know the actual performer of any activity already executed. Therefore, ontological elements relating to the performers of the activities of each instance of a BP have to be added to the previous Web Ontology Language (OWL) ontology defined for RAL as detailed in the following sections.

4.1   New OWL Upper Ontology

Previous RAL's semantics was provided from design-time perspective for a single instance of the BP. Only organizational aspects were thus considered in the OWL ontology generated to resolve the assignments. However, in order to store and use information about who has performed each activity of a BP in the different execution instances, new *classes* and *properties* have to added to the TBox of the OWL upper ontology. In particular, we have added one OWL class for *some* of the classes related to BPs (white boxes in the meta model of Figure 1), specifically for *Activity*, and *BusinessProcess*. Class *RALExpression* can be considered equivalent to current class *Person*, since a RAL expression represents a sub-set of the members of an organization [5]. Therefore, it is not inserted as a new OWL class in the upper ontology, using *Person* for the same purpose. In addition, although class *ActivityInstance* has been added to the meta model in Figure 1 to show the real link between the organizational meta model and the BP meta model, it actually represents an *instance* of an activity, so it is

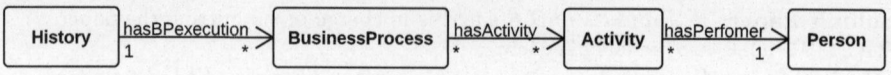

Fig. 5. OWL upper ontology extension to deal with history information

not part of the upper ontology, either. However, we have had to add some extra information required to deal with the negation form (i.e. operator NOT) of the history-aware RAL expressions. Specifically, class *History* has been created to represent the overall history of the executions of the BPs of the organization.

Object properties *hasBPexecution, hasActivity* and *hasPerformer* have been added respectively to associate *History* with *BusinessProcess, BusinessProcess* with *Activity*, and *Activity* with *Person*, as depicted in Figure 5. Inverse properties have been created to ease the use of the ontology[1]. Furthermore, class *Activity* has a *data property* called *wasCompleted* of standard type *xsd:dateTime*, to save the completion date of the activity.

4.2 Refining the Ontology for Each Business Process

The upper ontology in the TBox will be refined for each BP used in the organization, by introducing sub-classes of the classes previously defined, together with specific configuration necessary to make it work properly. We are taking as example activity *Submit Paper* of the BP in Figure 2 to show this refinement.

First of all, a sub-class of *BusinessProcess* has to be defined to represent the BP for conference trip management. Then, a new sub-class of *Activity* is introduced for each activity *type* of the process. Similarly, classes representing the RAL expressions of the activities (e.g. *RALSubmitPaper*) are added, together with one axiom for each activity to indicate that it has *exactly* one performer that belongs to the subset of *Person* defined by the RAL expression. Finally, two axioms are added to state that the process is composed of all of its activities and to indicate that all activities are disjoint. The definition in DL is done as follows:

$TripManagement \sqsubseteq BusinessProcess$
$SubmitPaper \sqsubseteq Activity$
$SubmitPaper \sqsubseteq= 1hasPerformer.RALSubmitPaper$
$TripManagement \sqsubseteq \exists hasActivity.(SubmitPaper \sqcup ... \sqcup MakeReservations)$
$SubmitPaper \sqsubseteq \neg\{FillTravelAuthorization, ..., MakeReservations\}$

4.3 Instantiation of the BP-related Elements

Regarding instantiation of the classes, we will have one and only one instance of class *History*, which will be related to the specific elements stored in the ontology. Then, every time a new process instance is started, OWL instances (or individuals) of the corresponding classes have to be added to the ontology, and the appropriate property associations have to be configured also at this level.

---

[1] For the sake of understanding, we will use syntax *property⁻* to refer to them.

$History(hist)$
$TripManagement(tm_1)$
$hasBPexecution(hist, tm_1)$
$SubmitPaper(sp_{tm_1}^1)$
$hasActivity(tm_1, sp_{tm_1}^1)$

Once a person is selected from the set of potential performers (i.e. the activity might be allocated to that person at run time), the individual must be added as performer of *that* instance of the activity. Similarly, when the activity instance is complete, the completion time is set on the activity.

$hasPerformer(sp_{tm_1}^1, person_X)$
$wasCompleted(sp_{tm_1}^1, timestamp_1)$

Finally, some technical details are required to complete the ontology. First, all instances are set as different from each other, since DL does not assume it. Second, to avoid unintuitive effects of the open world assumption in DL [11], each time a new execution is added to the ontology (e.g. a new activity $sp_{tm_j}^i$ of type *SubmitPaper* is started in process tm_j), the instance tm_j is updated to indicate that it has exactly i activities of type *SubmitPaper*. The same applies to new processes and the history instance:

$tm_1 \neq tm_2 \neq ... \neq tm_n, sp_{tm_1}^1 \neq sp_{tm_2}^1, \neq ... \neq, sp_{tm_n}^1$
$tm_j \in= ihasActivity.SubmitPaper$
$hist \in= jhasBPexecution.TripManagement$

4.4   Mapping History-Aware RAL Expressions into DLs

Finally, we have to map every RAL expression of the BP into DLs, e.g. the assignment defined in class *RALSubmitPaper*. In order to do so, each kind of RAL expression must have an accurate and well-defined semantics. In Table 1, we present the DL definition of the history-aware RAL expressions. As execution information is sometimes needed, to be able to provide accurate semantics we assume we are running the process and, thus, we know the identifier of the current process instance (in this case tm_1). Activity *Submit Paper* is once again used as example. If operator NOT is used, e.g. NOT (IS PERSON WHO DID ACTIVITY SubmitPaper IN ANOTHER INSTANCE), the mapping of such expressions is $Person \sqcap \neg(map_p(expr))$, where $map_p(expr)$ is the corresponding DL expression in Table 1.

Notice that the semantics we have defined implies that the expressions are resolved at run time, since they require run-time information. To enable design-time analysis, design-time semantics of the history-aware RAL expressions is provided in Table 2. As for the negation, all the expressions in the table are mapped to *Person*. Obviously, this mapping just provides an approximation of the real semantics (cf. Table 1), useful to work at design-time, when run-time data is missing.

4.5   Automated Resolution of History-Based RAL Expressions

As explained in [7], as RAL's semantics is defined in DLs, we can use operations already implemented in existing DL reasoners to perform analysis operations

Table 1. Accurate mapping of history-aware RAL expressions into DL *concepts*

History-Based RAL Expression (*expr*)	DL Mapping ($map_p(expr)$)
IS PERSON WHO DID ACTIVITY SubmitPaper	
IN CURRENT INSTANCE	$\exists hasPerformer^{-}.(\exists hasActivity^{-}.\{tm_1\}\sqcap SubmitPaper)$
IN ANY INSTANCE	$\exists hasPerformer^{-}.(\exists hasActivity^{-}.((\exists hasBPexecution^{-}.\{hist\} \sqcap TripManagement)\sqcap SubmitPaper))$
IN ANOTHER INSTANCE	$\exists hasPerformer^{-}.(\exists hasActivity^{-}.((\exists hasBPexecution^{-}.\{hist\} \sqcap TripManagement)\sqcap\neg\{tm_1\}) \sqcap SubmitPaper)$
FROM startDate TO endDate	$\exists hasPerformer^{-}.(\exists hasActivity^{-}.((\exists hasBPexecution^{-}.\{hist\} \sqcap TripManagement)\sqcap SubmitPaper \sqcap \exists(wasCompleted \geq startDate)\sqcap\exists(wasCompleted \leq endDate)))$
IS PERSON WHO HAS PARTICIPATED IN	
CURRENT INSTANCE INSTANCE	$\exists hasPerformer^{-}.(\exists hasActivity^{-}.\{tm_1\})$
ANY PROCESS INSTANCE	$\exists hasPerformer^{-}.(\exists hasActivity^{-}.(\exists hasBPexecution^{-}.\{hist\} \sqcap TripManagement))$
ANOTHER PROCESS INSTANCE	$\exists hasPerformer^{-}.(\exists hasActivity^{-}.((\exists hasBPexecution^{-}.\{hist\} \sqcap TripManagement)\sqcap\neg\{tm_1\})$
A PROCESS INSTANCE BETWEEN startDate AND endDate	$\exists hasPerformer^{-}.(\exists hasActivity^{-}.((\exists hasBPexecution^{-}.\{hist\} \sqcap TripManagement)\sqcap\exists(wasCompleted \geq startDate)\sqcap\exists(wasCompleted \leq endDate)))$

Table 2. Approximate mapping of history-aware RAL expressions into DL *concepts*. The mappings missing are done exactly like in Table 1.

History-Based RAL Expression (*expr*)	DL Mapping ($map_p(expr)$)
IS PERSON WHO DID ACTIVITY SubmitPaper	
IN CURRENT INSTANCE	
IN ANY INSTANCE	$\exists hasPerformer^{-}.SubmitPaper$
IN ANOTHER INSTANCE	
IS PERSON WHO HAS PARTICIPATED IN	
CURRENT INSTANCE INSTANCE	
ANY PROCESS INSTANCE	$\exists hasPerformer^{-}.(\exists hasActivity^{-}.TripManagement)$
ANOTHER PROCESS INSTANCE	

over the RAL expressions of a BP and, so, infer information about how resources are being managed in the process. Specifically, to obtain the potential performers of an activity we must execute the operation *individuals* on the RAL expression, e.g. for activity *Submit Paper* it is $individuals(\exists hasPerformer^{-}.SubmitPaper)$.

5 Related Work

The importance of considering resources as part of BPM is a well-known concern [12]. Approaches have typically focused on one single process instance, disregarding what has happened in the past [13]. However, more and more history-based allocation is coming on stage, and we can find several proposals dealing with the introduction of this pattern in BP models.

Bertino et al. presented a language for defining Role-Based Access Control (RBAC) constraints to tasks in a workflow (WF) [4]. The approach is similar to RAL in the sense that it is also built on a formal basis and is also aimed at checking constraint consistency. Besides, algorithms for planning resource assignments to the various tasks were also introduced. However, the language was considerably difficult to use, as it was not user-oriented.

Wolter and Schaad assigned specific semantics to BPMN swimlanes in order to represent role hierarchies, introduced Manual Tasks and extended some BPMN artifacts to define assignments [1]. Only four creation patterns were supported by this approach, History-Based Distribution among them.

Russell and van der Aalst examined BPEL4People and WS-HumanTask[2] using the WRPs as evaluation framework [14]. Compared to RAL, these standards provide less support for the creation patterns, but past information is maintained as history task events.

Awad et al. used the WRPs again as a reference framework to study resource management in BPMN 1.2, and proposed a meta model extension for the notation [2]. The meta model used to capture history information is very similar to ours (cf. Figure 1) and the approach was quite expressive, but the solution is ad-hoc for BPMN and there is not a unified formalism to assign and analyse resources. Different techniques are utilised for each pattern instead.

Recently, Strembeck and Mendling have introduced *Business Activities*, a UML extension that enables the definition of process-related RBAC models [3]. The history of a process instance is recorded in what they call Business Activity RBAC Model (BRM). However, unlike RAL, it is constrained to UML, and other types of resource assignments are not considered in their proposal.

6 Conclusions and Future Work

In this paper, we have described how to add history execution information of a BP to RAL, extending so the scope of the language. The result is a resource assignment language that can be used in different BP notations, supports all the creation patterns [10] and can be used with other WRPs (visit

---

[2] http://www.oasis-open.org/committees/bpel4people/

`www.isa.us.es/cristal` for further information about RAL and the WRPs), and has analysis capabilities to automatically resolve RAL expressions and infer interesting information from a RAL-aware BP model, now considering past executions as well. The next improvement step is to provide RAL with accurate *execution* semantics, integrate it into a BPMS, and undertake performance tests to optimize it. Part of this work is currently being performed.

References

1. Wolter, C., Schaad, A.: Modeling of Task-Based Authorization Constraints in BPMN. In: Alonso, G., Dadam, P., Rosemann, M. (eds.) BPM 2007. LNCS, vol. 4714, pp. 64–79. Springer, Heidelberg (2007)
2. Awad, A., Grosskopf, A., Meyer, A., Weske, M.: Enabling Resource Assignment Constraints in BPMN. tech. rep., BPT (2009)
3. Strembeck, M., Mendling, J.: Modeling process-related RBAC models with extended UML activity models. Inf. Softw. Technol. 53, 456–483 (2011)
4. Bertino, E., Ferrari, E., Atluri, V.: The specification and enforcement of authorization constraints in workflow management systems. ACM Trans. Inf. Syst. Secur. 2, 65–104 (1999)
5. Cabanillas, C., Resinas, M., Ruiz-Cortés, A.: RAL: A High-Level User-Oriented Resource Assignment Language for Business Processes. In: Daniel, F., Barkaoui, K., Dustdar, S. (eds.) BPM Workshops 2011, Part I. LNBIP, vol. 99, pp. 50–61. Springer, Heidelberg (2012)
6. Russell, N., van der Aalst, W.M.P., ter Hofstede, A.H.M., Edmond, D.: Workflow Resource Patterns: Identification, Representation and Tool Support. In: Pastor, Ó., Falcão e Cunha, J. (eds.) CAiSE 2005. LNCS, vol. 3520, pp. 216–232. Springer, Heidelberg (2005)
7. Cabanillas, C., Resinas, M., Ruiz-Cortés, A.: Defining and Analysing Resource Assignments in Business Processes with RAL. In: Kappel, G., Maamar, Z., Motahari-Nezhad, H.R. (eds.) ICSOC 2011. LNCS, vol. 7084, pp. 477–486. Springer, Heidelberg (2011)
8. Decker, G., Overdick, H., Weske, M.: Oryx – An Open Modeling Platform for the BPM Community. In: Dumas, M., Reichert, M., Shan, M.-C. (eds.) BPM 2008. LNCS, vol. 5240, pp. 382–385. Springer, Heidelberg (2008)
9. Cabanillas, C., del-Río-Ortega, A., Resinas, M., Ruiz-Cortés, A.: CRISTAL: Collection of Resource-centrIc Supporting Tools And Languages. In: Lohmann, N., Moser, S. (eds.) BPM 2012 Demos, vol. 940, pp. 51–56. CEUR-WS (2012)
10. Russell, N., ter Hofstede, A., Edmond, D., van der Aalst, W.: Workflow Resource Patterns. tech. rep., BETA Working Paper Series, WP 127, Eindhoven University of Technology, Eindhoven (2004)
11. Baader, F., Calvanese, D., McGuinness, D., Nardi, D., Patel-Schneider, P.: The Description Logics Handbook: Theory, Implementations, and Applications. Cambridge University Press (2003)
12. Künzle, V., Reichert, M.: Integrating Users in Object-Aware Process Management Systems: Issues and Challenges. In: Rinderle-Ma, S., Sadiq, S., Leymann, F. (eds.) BPM 2009. LNBIP, vol. 43, pp. 29–41. Springer, Heidelberg (2010)
13. Grosskopf, A.: An Extended Resource Information Layer for BPMN. Tech. rep., BPT (2007)
14. Russell, N., van der Aalst, W.M.P.: Work Distribution and Resource Management in BPEL4People: Capabilities and Opportunities. In: Bellahsène, Z., Léonard, M. (eds.) CAiSE 2008. LNCS, vol. 5074, pp. 94–108. Springer, Heidelberg (2008)

Supervisory Control for Business Process Management Systems

Mohamed Karim Aroua and Belhassen Zouari

University of Tunis El Manar, Faculty of Sciences of Tunis, LIP2 Laboratory, Tunisia
Mohamed.karim.aroua@gmail.com, Belhassen.zouari@fst.rnu.tn

Abstract. The behavior of a business process often needs to be constrained according to a given control specification, that comes to cope with new business requirements. Such a control, called supervisory control, is applied to an existing business process specification without having to re-design the running procedures. Hence, there is no need to create a new complete business process model every time the control parameters change. The objective of supervisory control is to limit the behavior of the initial business process to only desired situations. In this paper, a controller synthesis method for business processes is proposed by adapting the supervisory control theory initiated by Ramadge and Wonham. Business process models are specified by using a variant of Workflow nets, which introduces colors in order to represent different process instances and the related data. An algorithm allowing automatic generation of a controller described by a colored Petri net is provided in this paper.

Keywords: Business process management, supervisory control, workflow nets, colored Petri nets, controller synthesis, active controller.

1 Introduction

A theoretical framework, called supervisory control, for controlling discrete event systems (DESs) has been introduced by Ramadge and Wonham [1]. The objective of the supervisory control is to issue, for an existing system, a controller (or a supervisor) that guarantees that the system behaves in conformity to a given control specification. The supervisory control can be seen as a predictive measure to avoid undesirable behaviors of a system. Such behaviors vary from deadlocks, livelocks, and security breaches to abnormal terminations. The supervisory control theory was studied in the context of automaton based models. Besides, Petri net models have been used for supervisory control methodologies but only for automated-oriented systems [2], [3], [4], since they represent a good trade-off between modeling power and analysis capabilities [5]. The use of supervisory control in business process management is almost absent in existing works although it appears useful for numerous types of systems [6]. In this paper, we propose a supervisory control method in the business process management context using a class of colored Petri nets. [7] defines a business process management system as "a generic software system that is driven by explicit process representations to coordinate the enactment of business

M. La Rosa and P. Soffer (Eds.): BPM 2012 Workshops, LNBIP 132, pp. 113–125, 2013.

processes." Then, in a business process management system, a process instance has a set of attributes such as process identifier, involved data, beginning and termination dates... Observed attributes can be recorded. The analysis of these attributes may be used to monitor the behavior of the process instances. Then the diagnosis of a current state of running instances is feasible in order to predict their probable issues [8]. This is how monitoring systems operate. Among the goals of process monitoring is fault detection of infrequent process patterns as compared with the normal or frequent pattern [9]. Besides, supervisory control does not look for predicting probable issues of business processes but aims at avoiding forbidden situations.

This paper addresses the control of business processes modeled with workflow colored nets (WFC-nets), a variant of workflow nets (WF-nets) [10], [11]. WFC-nets are WF-nets extended by the notion of Petri net colors [12]. Introducing colors in WFC-nets is especially interesting to express multiple instances of a business process. The use of Petri nets in business process modeling is intensive, unlike that of colored Petri nets (CP-net) which is lacking [11], [13]. We chose to use CP-nets because they afford a concise description which is engineer oriented. In addition, the verification of interesting model properties can be parametric in the actual color definitions, thus yielding results that are valid for classes of models instead of a single model as stated in [19]. WF-nets are suitable for the representation, validation and verification of workflow procedures [10]. Similarly to [10], we make abstraction of resource handling in WFC-nets in this paper. We provide a WFC-net approach that allows the generation of controllers for business process management systems. We consider the problem of forbidden states under the hypothesis of existence of uncontrollable transitions. The proposed method is based on the dynamic properties of the WFC-net representing the initial business process model by exploring its occurrence graph. We assume that control constraints are specified through a set of forbidden states. The proposed approach is based on two steps: the admissibility computation and the controller synthesis. The generated controller, that we call active controller, consists in a fixed number of places and transitions that we connect to the initial WFC-net.

The remainder of this paper is organized as follows: section 2 presents the supervisory control framework. In section 3, we show how we specify business processes through WFC-nets and the way we generate a description of an admissible behavior of the WFC-net from the reachability graph. A method of constructing a controller for existing process model is described in section 4. Section 5 proves that the behavior of the controlled system is equivalent to the admissible behavior and section 6 concludes the paper.

2   Supervisory Control Framework

The Supervisory Control Theory [14] was developed to extend control theory concepts for continuous systems to the Discrete Event Systems. When applied to an existing system, supervisory control allows to design and generate a controller (or a supervisor) that interacts with the original model such that the overall system satisfies a given control specification. From a methodological point of view, supervisory control theory separates the control level of a system from the design and implementation levels in order to better suit the evolving of control requirements over a running system. Supervisory control is particularly well adapted to business process management as it concerns discrete event systems and where control is not only a relevant issue but also would frequently change over an available running system. The specification of control may be in terms of non-desired situations or in terms of non-desired action sequences. The solution consists in generating a controller, in the case of non-desired states, or a supervisor in the case of non-desired actions. Some hypothesis imposed by the real system, as the uncontrollability of some actions, may complicate the problem resolution. Supervisory control aims at generating solutions that have some interesting properties. It generally requires the controlled system to be no blocking, and to be maximally permissive while taking into account the situations to be avoided (forbidden states). Supervisory control was mainly studied in the context of automaton based models and language theory. Then, Petri-net-based approaches to supervisory control design have been considered [4], [5], [15]. State specifications are less general than language specifications but more frequently used to deal with a set of forbidden states (markings) that a controller should avoid [16]. Most of Petri net approaches used in supervisory control were based on ordinary Petri nets. For example, the approach used in [3] is based on the dynamic properties of ordinary Petri nets. It focuses on a class of Petri net called elementary composed state machines, and defines the set of reachable markings. Besides, High-level Petri nets, especially Colored Petri nets (CP-nets) [12], provide a great improvement over the ordinary Petri nets. Notably, the high expressiveness of CP-nets allows obtaining compact models even for large systems, while keeping the same formal analysis capabilities. However, few works have addressed the supervisory control problem with CP-nets. [17] considers a class of CP-nets with a finite color set and with a symmetry specification. In the framework, a set of forbidden markings expresses a control specification in order to deal with the forbidden state control problem. Admissible markings are computed and a controller is embodied with the plant model. The behavior of the controller is modeled through an automaton. Our approach is more homogenous, we synthesize a Coloured Petri-net model for the supervisor of a business process instead of an automaton. Moreover, in business process management, process models define restrictions on process instances. Thus, process instances should be properly handled and controlled in the concurrency context [18]. In this paper, we use a CP-net based approach to control business processes. Our methodology allows the automatic synthesis of a generic controller called Active Controller. We consider the problem of forbidden states under the hypothesis of existence of uncontrollable transitions [14].

3   Representation of the Behavior of Business Processes

3.1   Specification of the Business Processes

Business processes may be modeled by using workflow nets (WF-nets). A WF-net is a Petri net with one start place and one end place. All tasks have to be on a path from the start place to the end place. WF-nets form a subclass of Petri nets for which the analysis of desirable properties, for example, whether process instances of a workflow can always terminate, is feasible.

In order to express process instance concurrency and to represent the coloring of tokens explicitly, we propose a slight extension of WF-nets called Workflow Colored nets (WFC-nets). WFC-nets are particular CP-nets. We formally define WFC-nets on the basis of the CP-net model defined in [19] which obeys to some structural and syntactic rules.

Definition 1. A Workflow Colored net (WFC-net) is a 6-tuple $N= (P, T, C,W^+,W^-, M_0)$ where P is a set of places, T is a set of finite transitions, C is the color function, defined from P∪T into a set of finite non-empty sets called color domains, W^+,W^- are the input and output functions, defined on $P \times T$ such that $W^-(p,t)$ and $W^+(p,t)$ belong to the set of linear application mapping $Bag(C(t))$ onto $Bag(C(p))$ for all $(p,t) \in P \times T$, M_0 the initial marking is a function defined on P, such that : $M_0(p) \in Bag(C(p))$, for all $p \in P$; and :

- There is a distinguished place $i \in P$ (initial place) that has no incoming edge, i.e., •i $= \emptyset$
- There is a distinguished place $o \in P$ (final place) that has no outgoing edge, i.e., o• $= \emptyset$
  - Every place and every transition is located on a path from the initial place to the final place

Due to the specificities of business process behaviors, the color functions labeling arcs in the initial model (before adding control) are limited to the identity functions. A particular color class C_{Pr} made up of process instance identities is initially defined. Hence, the initial marking of start place is $M_0(i)= C_{Pr}$.

Like CP-nets, WFC-nets focus on the control flow behavior of a process. Places represent progression states and colored tokens represent identified process instances. Activities of a business process are represented by transitions in the WFC-nets. The process instances handling is achieved by the multiple token markings and appropriate color functions labeling arcs. This allows concurrent running of tokens over the WFC-net. Furthermore, tokens hold application data including data classification and access rights granted to user roles, but this is out of the scope of this paper and will be presented in a further work. In order to consider the concept of controllability of supervisory control theory, we assume T, the set of transitions, partitioned into two subsets T_u and T_c, of controllable and uncontrollable transitions respectively. Intuitively, an uncontrollable transition is a transition that cannot be, by hypothesis, inhibited or blocked by the controller. Initially, an engineer has to determine which transitions are uncontrollable according to its application specificities. Fig.1 shows an online transaction management process in which, initially, the request is recorded and, concurrently, the availability of the requested item and the customer credit are checked. After the results have been gathered, an assessment of the request is performed. In the case of a positive assessment, the product is shipped. In the case of a negative assessment, the transaction is rejected. Finally the process completes.

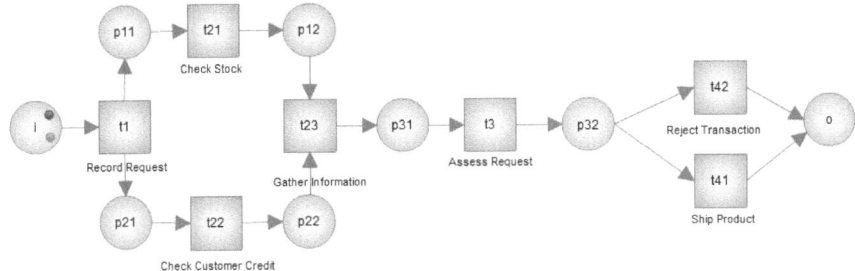

Fig. 1. Online transaction WFC-net

The maximum number of process instances MaxInst in the WFC-net can be defined by the process manager. The number of running instances is not known in advance, it can vary between 1 and MaxInst. In order to simplify the online transaction example, we deal with two process instances pr1 and pr2.

We have: $P=\{i, p11, p21, p12, p22, p31, p32, o\}$;
$T=\{t1, t21, t22, t23, t3, t41, t42\}$ with $T= T_c$ and $T_u= \emptyset$
$C_{Pr} = \{pr1, pr2 \}$ the class of process instances ; $M_0(i)= C_{Pr}$;

In some cases, while a process instance pr1 is in place p31 or p32 and the quantity of product requested empties the stock, another process pr2 can be in place p11. In this situation, the product has not yet been issued, so the stock is not yet empty at the information system. The firing of t21 leads to an inconsistent situation. We call this kind of situations forbidden situations. That's why t21 should be controlled by blocking it when there are tokens in p31 and p32. The generated controller will block t21 whenever its firing will lead to the forbidden marking. In the next section, we show how to compute the admissible behavior according to the control specification. It is the first step to achieve the generation of a controller. In our case, it consists in removing forbidden markings from reachability graph. This graph can be reduced using symbolic reachability graph in order to avoid considering the actual state space of the model [19]. Reduction of the reachability graph will be dealt with in a separate paper.

3.2   Admissible Behavior of Business Processes

The admissible behavior of a business process is an accessible behavior of the corresponding WFC-nets respecting the control specification. In order to compute the admissible behavior, we suppose that we have the reachability graph of the initial WFC-nets and the finite set of specified forbidden states. These states can be either blocking markings or any other undesirable markings. The specification of forbidden states can be made using a language close to practitioners and transformed in a set of forbidden markings. This transformation is out of the scope of this paper. It is worth to note that a general forbidden situation, such as interlocking situations, can be automatically derived in many forbidden markings. We start by going all over the reachability graph

G and determine information about some reachability markings (called dangerous markings "DM") from which control has to be applied in order to avoid reaching one forbidden state. A dangerous marking (or dangerous state) is defined as a node of G, from which there exists at least one transition that inevitably leads (when fired) to a forbidden state. Moreover, it is important to handle, with every dangerous state, information about transitions that must not be fired because each of them leads to a forbidden marking. Let d be a dangerous state, then the set FT(d) of forbidden transitions related to d is the set of transitions enabled from d according to the reachability graph G and which inevitably lead to a forbidden or inadmissible state. Given a reachability graph G and a specification of forbidden states FS, the first output of this stage is the set DS of dangerous markings and the associated sets FT(d) for all d∈ DS. FT may be viewed as an application from DS to the set of subsets of T. Its second output is the graph Rc, which is called admissibility graph, obtained when all forbidden states (specified and calculated) are removed from G and representing the desirable behavior for the controlled system. The computation of the admissibility graph Rc and the set Ω is given by Algorithm 1 which is inspired from a previous work [20]. The algorithm considers the reachability graph R of the plant model, the set FM of specified forbidden markings, the set MS of final markings and the set T_u of uncontrollable transitions. In each iteration of the main loop, we identify forbidden markings. These markings and their input/output arcs are then removed from the graph. After that, we qualify as forbidden the markings which are not reachable from the initial marking. Further, non coreachable nodes are qualified as forbidden. The loop terminates when all forbidden markings (those initially declared and those newly identified) are processed.

input :   R reachability graph; FM is the set of initially specified forbidden markings;
        MS is the set of final markings; T_u is the set of uncontrollable transitions
output: Rc the admissibility graph; Ω the set of state-transitions
DM ← ∅; TE ← ∅; Ω ← ∅; Rc ← R
repeat
    Take a non colored element f from FM; Color f in FM
    for every input arc (x,(t, c), f) of f *do*
        if t ∈ T_u *then*   FM ← FM ∪ {x} *else*   DM ← DM ∪ {x} ;
                                        TE ← TE ∪ {(x,(t, c))}
    Remove f, the input and output arcs of f from Rc
    for every node M of Rc *do*
        if M is not reachable from M0 or M is not coreachable or (M has no output arcs and M ∉ MS) *then* FM ← FM ∪ {M}
    if M_0 ∈ FM *then* exit //*there is no solution*
until all elements of FM are colored;
DM = DM \ FM
for every element y of DM *do*
    for any element (x,(t, c)) of TE *do*
        if y = x *then* Ω ← Ω ∪ {(x,(t, c))}

Algorithm 1: Computing the admissibility graph

One can easily verify that the algorithm terminates correctly. As we deal with finite reachability graph, FM is finite, and the main loop of the algorithm will necessarily stop thanks to the graph coloring technique. Let us apply the algorithm on the graph of Fig. 2 representing a part of the reachability graph of the example presented in Fig. 1. The part is selected as a sample showing how some sequences leading to some forbidden states.

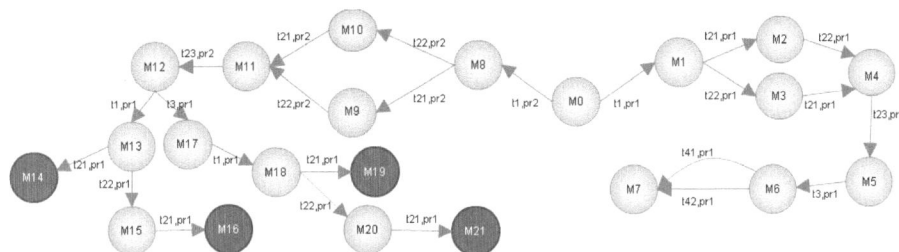

Fig. 2. A part of the reachability graph

If the specified forbidden states are "M14", "M16", "M19", and "M21" (representing forbidden markings), then the algorithm gives : DM={M13, M15, M18, M20}, FT(M13)={t21}, FT(M15)={t21}, FT(M18)={t21}, FT(M20)={t21} and Ω={(((0, pr1,0, pr1, 0, pr2,0,0),t21) ; ((0, pr1, 0, 0, pr1, pr2, 0, 0),t21); ((0, pr1, 0, pr1, 0, 0, pr2,0),t21) }. ((0, pr1, 0, 0, pr1, 0, pr2, 0),t21)}. Rc is obtained by deleting forbidden states and transitions from the reachability graph.

4   Controller Generation Method

After computing the set of forbidden state transitions, we describe in this section the generation of the CP-net controller and its connection to the initial system. In the end of this section, an example facilitates the understanding of the method.

At this stage, we have two kinds of specifications: the control specification as described in the previous section. More precisely, the set DS of dangerous markings and the application FT, that determines the associated forbidden transitions. The second specification describes the initial business process represented by a WFC-net N = (P, T, C,W^+,W^-, M_0) and the associated information as defined in Definition 1.

Our method will result in a new WFC-net obtained on the basis of the previous specification and which functioning automatically satisfies the control. The key idea is to handle enough information by the controller to detect reaching dangerous states, and from which, remove appropriate authorizations in order to disable the firing of forbidden transitions. This method relies on the following points. We introduce a new place holding information on dangerous states and associated forbidden transitions. Its marking is defined by Ω. We handle the current state (marking) of the WFC-net in a special added place. The information is modeled by a composed token (tuple of colors) in accordance with WFC-net semantics. We add a place that manages authorizations of firing forbidden transitions. We add two transitions: one is fired when a dangerous marking is detected, and the other is fired when it is quitted. These two controller transitions have special high priority over all the other transitions and are fired immediately when enabled. Priority of transitions is used to control the execution of Petri net models [21]. We define the necessary additional WFC-net components (color functions, synchronization arcs, markings, etc.) to ensure the desired management by the controller.

Let us formally define this method. The system under control is a WFC-nets N^* obtained from N so that $N^* = (P^*, T^*, C^*, W^{*+}, W^{*-}, M^*_0)$ where $P^* = P \cup \{CM, DM, AT, AS\}$, with CM representing the Current Marking, DM the Dangerous Markings, AT the Authorizations for forbidden Transitions, AS the Alert State of the controller; and $T^* = T \cup \{A\_In, A\_Out\}$, with A_In representing entering the alert state, A_Out quitting the alert state, A_In and A_Out have the highest priority. If one or many transitions are enabled at the same time as A_In (or A_Out), then A_In (or A_Out) will fire first.

Now, we define the following additional color classes: C_{FT} is a class representing all forbidden transitions. $C_{num} = \{0, 1, 2, ..., MaxInt\}$ is a class representing a set of finite positive integers. Its elements will model the instances of business processes represented in the WFC-nets by tokens. We assume MaxInt large enough to be greater than the bound of the maximum occurrences of any token in a reachable marking. As we deal with bounded WFC-nets, this property holds.

In the following, and for simplicity reasons, we may denote N^* by N. Now, we determine the color domain of the additional places as well as their initial marking. Place CM has a color domain defined on C_{num} on the basis of the number of places in the process. The role of CM is to handle information about the current marking. CM is always mono-marked and its initial marking $M_0(CM)$ is performed on the basis of initial markings of the whole WFC-net. The token marking CM is a tuple made up of counters where each one holds the information about the occurrence of tokens in a given place (according to a lexical order) among process places. $M_0(CM)$ may be algorithmically determined. Besides, linking the active controller to each transition may reduce the readability of the process model. A solution is to draw these special transitions in the white color (color of the background). Place DM has the color domain: $C(DM) = C(CM) \times C_{FT}$. Its initial marking contains tokens that represent dangerous markings with the associated forbidden transitions. The initial marking does not change since this place is only read accessed. The number of tokens in DM is given by: $\Sigma_{d \in DS}\ card(FT(d))$.

The color domain and initial marking of AT are: $C(AT) = C_{FT}$, and $M_0(AT) = C_{FT}$; Initially, all forbidden transitions are authorized. The color domain and initial marking of place AS are: $C(AS) = C(DM)$; $M_0(AS) = 0$ (empty marking).

Finally, we have to determine the additional arcs of transitions by defining the associated color functions:

- Input and output arcs of place CM: as its role is to hold the current marking of N, it is associated with every transition of T, an input arc (reading marking) and an output arc (updating marking).

$$\forall t \in T,\ W^-(CM, t) = <X_1, ..., X_k> = <X>$$

where X_j is a variable (representing the identity function) defined on C_{num} allowing reading the marking of place j in the process ; and
$W^+(CM,t)= <X'_1, ..., X'_k > =<X'>$ where X'_j are variables defined on C_{num} determined as follows: $X'_j = X_j - \chi$, with $\chi= W^+(p_j,t)-W^-(p_j,t)$,

To every forbidden transition, are added one input arc and one output arc associated with place AT labeled by the same variable Xt in order to check the presence of firing authorization: $\forall t \in C_{FT}, W^-(AT,t)= W^+(AT,t)= <Xt>$,
   where Xt is defined on C_{FT} and represent the identity of the transition.
- The place DM acts like a database of dangerous markings which is accessed in read-only mode. Then, a double arc (loop) is added to transition A_In with the following functions:
   $W^-(DM, A\_In)= W^+(DM, A\_In)=<X, Xt >$, where $X \in C(CM)$ (i.e. X is a tuple of variables)
- Transitions A_In and A_out require the additional following arcs :
   $W^-(CM, A\_In) = W^+(CM, A\_In)= <X>$;
   $W^-(AT, A\_In) = < Xt>$; $W^+(AS, A\_In)= <X, Xt >$;
   $W^-(AS, A\_Out)= <X, Xt >$; $W^-(CM, A\_Out) = <Y>$;
   $W^+(AT, A\_Out) = < Xt>$;
Transition A_Out is associated with the predicate: $[X \neq Y]$

As shown in Fig. 3, the controller is connected to the initial WFC-net specification through the places AT and CM as it was previously defined. [22] gives a method to prove that a controller is maximum permissive.

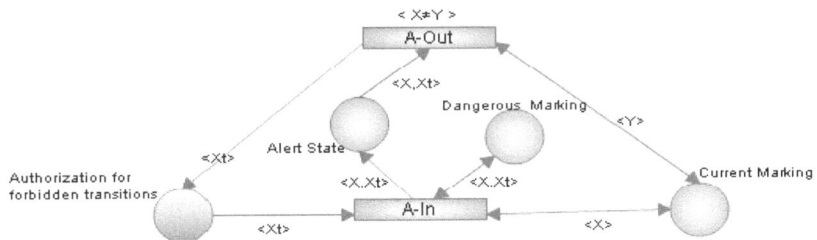

Fig. 3. Controller subnet

Example
Let us consider the example of Fig. 1.   As the initial model is made up of 8 places, we have: $C(CM)= (C_{num})^8$; a token marking CM is a tuple $<x_1, ..., x_8>$ where x_1 is the value of token counter representing place i, x_2 is the value of token counter representing p_{11}, x_3 is the value of token counter representing p_{12},..., and x_8 is the value of token counter representing o.

   $-M_0(CM)=<2,0,0,0,0,0,0,0>$ (current marking place)
   $-C(DM)= C(CM) \times C_{FT}$; (dangerous markings place)

$-M_0$ (DM)= <<0, 1, 0, 1, 0, 1, 0, 0>, t21> +<<0, 1, 0, 0, 1, 1, 0, 0>, t21> +
  <<0, 1, 0, 1, 0, 0, 1,0>, t21>   + <<0, pr1, 0, 0, pr1, 0, pr2,
0>, t21>
$-M_0$ (AT)= {t21}; (authorizations place)

Through the example of Fig.4, we show how the controller subnet is connected to some transitions of the initial business process management system specification.

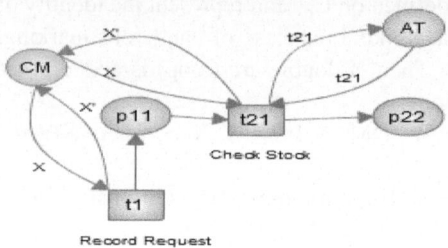

Fig. 4. Controller connection

An implementation of the approach is already done in our laboratory, and a new CPN Tools module is in the test phase.

5   Equivalence between the Admissible and the Controlled Behaviors

In this section, we prove that the behavior of the controlled system is equivalent to the computed admissible behavior represented by Rc.

Proof: First we prove that all information about the current state are stored in CM. Second, we verify that, at any state, we have in AT only the authorizations of the forbidden transition which could be fired at the current state. Finally, we prove that only admissible markings are reachable.

STEP 1: A current state is defined when we have the information about each place marking of the process. For this reason, we associate a counter with each place in order to save current state. This hypothesis justifies the color domain of CM. But let us prove that the structure of the CM's token permits to represent any accessible state. The initial marking of the WFC-net can be modeled using the specified structure. Indeed, the initial marking of the WFC-net places indicates the finite number of available processes. Now, let us prove that all accessible states from the initial marking could be modeled using the structure of the CM's token. Suppose M' such that M[t(c))M'. M is modeled using a specified structure. When t(c) is fired, the token handled in CM will be modified. Indeed, we add (respectively take off) 1 to each counter associated with successors (respectively predecessors) process places. As a result, we have in CM a new token modeling the new state of the system. Then the token handled in CM place specifies, at any time, the current state of the system.

STEP 2: We prove, using proof by contradiction, that any forbidden state is reachable. Suppose that the system has reached a forbidden state. So, there exists a sequence of events which permits to access this state from an admissible one. We will consider the last controllable transition "t". According to the algorithm computing Rc, this transition will be determined as forbidden. For this reason it must find authorization in AT when it will be fired. Besides, the place AT is joined to the transition A_In, which will be validated when the system reaches the dangerous state associated with "t". As A_In has a high priority, it will be fired immediately and removes all forbidden transitions authorizations. All removed authorizations will be replaced in AT only when A_Out is fired. This transition will be fired only when the system exits the dangerous state. According to the last results, "t" will never find its authorization in AT when the current state of the system corresponds to its associated dangerous state. For this reason a forbidden state cannot be reached.

STEP 3: The admissibility graph Rc is connected, and according to algorithm "Computing the admissibility graph", if a node is declared as a forbidden state, all its related nodes will be declared forbidden if these nodes are not reached at least from an admissible one. Finally, all forbidden nodes will be removed from Rc, and the resulting graph is a connected one. Indeed, any admissible node could be reached from another and all nodes could be reached from the initial node. Under control there are two types of nodes: non-dangerous states: here all transitions are authorized and consequently all successor nodes could be reached, and dangerous states: as we have previously proved, only transition permitting to reach forbidden states will be removed from AT; consequently all admissible successors states could be reached. Then, under control all admissible states are reachable.

6   Conclusion

We have presented in this paper a way of representing and controlling business processes by using a class of colored Petri nets, called WFC-nets. WFC-nets are an extension of WF-nets. They allow to deal with different types of process instances and their related data. Our main contribution is to propose a supervisory control approach for business process management systems based on WFC-nets. The presented method does not extend or abbreviate the original model. It transforms the reachability graph into an admissibility one in order to generate a controller that, when connected to the original WFC-net, excludes forbidden situations. The present work is under implementation within the well-known environment CPN-Tools [23] in order to use the available verification tools and to go further in analysis of business processes. The use of WFC-nets in modeling business process management, provides a concise description of business processes and an efficient way to verify interesting model properties, thus giving results that are valid for classes of models instead of a single model. Moreover, a future work will aim at using this method in order to avoid violation of security requirements of business processes such as unauthorized access and separation of duties.

References

1. Ramadge, P.J., Wonham, W.M.: Supervisory control of a class of discrete event processes. SIAM Journal on Control and Optimization 25(1), 206–230 (1987)
2. Zouari, B., Zairi, S.: Synthesis of Active Controller for Resources Allocation Systems. In: 6th Workshop and Tutorial on Practical Use of Coloured Petri Nets and the CPN Tool, CPN 2005 (2005)
3. Giua, A., DiCesare, F.: Petri net structural analysis for supervisory control. IEEE Transactions on Robotics and Automation 10(2), 185–195 (1994)
4. Sreenivas, S., Sreenivas, R.S.: On the existence of supervisory policies that enforce liveness in discrete event dynamic systems modeled by controlled petri nets. IEEE Transactions on Automatic Control 42, 94–95 (1997)
5. Abid, C.A., Zairi, S., Zouari, B.: Petri Nets: Applications. In: Pawlewski, P. (ed.) Supervisory Control and High-level Petri Nets, ch. 14, pp. 281–306 (2010)
6. Santos, E.A.P., Francisco, R., Vieira, A.D., de F.R. Loures, E., Busetti, M.A.: Modeling Business Rules for Supervisory Control of Process-Aware Information Systems. In: Daniel, F., Barkaoui, K., Dustdar, S. (eds.) BPM Workshops 2011, Part II. LNBIP, vol. 100, pp. 447–458. Springer, Heidelberg (2012)
7. Weske, M.: Business Process: Management Concepts, Languages, Architectures. Springer, Heidelberg (2007)
8. Wang, D., Romagnoli, J.A.: Robust multi-scale principal components analysis with applications to process monitoring. Journal of Process Control 15(8), 869–882 (2005)
9. Kang, B., Kim, D., Kang, S.H.: Real-time business process monitoring method for prediction of abnormal termination using KNNI-based LOF prediction. Expert Systems with Applications 39, 6061–6068 (2012)
10. van der Aalst, W.M.P.: Verification of Workflow Nets. In: Azéma, P., Balbo, G. (eds.) ICATPN 1997. LNCS, vol. 1248, pp. 407–426. Springer, Heidelberg (1997)
11. van der Aalst, W.M.P., Jørgensen, J.B., Lassen, K.B.: Let's Go All the Way: From Requirements Via Colored Workflow Nets to a BPEL Implementation of a New Bank System. In: Meersman, R. (ed.) OTM 2005. LNCS, vol. 3760, pp. 22–39. Springer, Heidelberg (2005)
12. Jensen, K., Rozenberg, G.: High-Level Petri Nets. Theory and application. S. Verlag (1991)
13. Liu, D., Wang, J., Chan, S.C.F., Sun, J., Zhang, L.: Modeling workflow processes with colored Petri nets. Computers in Industry 49(3), 267–281 (2002)
14. Ramadge, P.J., Wonham, W.M.: The control of discrete event systems. Proceedings of the IEEE 77(1), 81–98 (1989)
15. Giua, A., DiCesare, F.: Supervisory design using Petri nets. In: Proceedings of the 30th Conference on Decision and Control, pp. 92–97 (1991)
16. Iordache, M.V., Antsaklis, P.J.: Supervisory Control of Concurrent Systems: A Petri Net Structural Approach. Birkhäuser (2006)
17. Makungu, M., Barbeau, M., St-Denis, R.: Synthesis of controllers of process modeled as coloured petri nets. Journal Discrete Event Dynamic Systems Theory Applications 9(2), 147–169 (1999)
18. Li, L., Wonham, W.M.: Control of vector discrete-event systems I—The base model. IEEE Transactions on Automatic Control 38(8), 1214–1227 (1993)
19. Chiola, G., Dutheillet, C., Franceschinis, G., Haddad, S.: A Symbolic Reachability Graph for Coloured Petri Nets. Theoretical Computer Science 176(1-2), 39–65 (1997)

20. Zouari, B., Ghedira, K.: Synthesis of controllers using coloured petri nets and theory of regions. In: Proc. of IFAC Workshop on Discrete Event Systems (WODES 2004), pp. 231–236 (2004)
21. van der Aalst, W.M.P.: Petri net based scheduling. Computing Science Reports 95/23, Eindhoven University of Technology, Eindhoven (1995)
22. Ghaffari, A., Rezg, N., Xie, X.: Design of a live and maximally permissive Petri net controller using the theory of regions. IEEE Transactions on Robotics 19(1), 137–141 (2003)
23. Jensen, K., Christensen, S., Huber, P., Holla, M.: "CPNtools" Reference Manual. Computer Science Department, University of Aarhus, Denmark (2003), http://cpntools.org/

Towards Knowledge-Intensive Processes Representation

Juliana Baptista dos Santos França, Joanne Manhães Netto,
Rafael Gomes Barradas, Flávia Santoro, and Fernanda Araujo Baião

Research and Practice Group in Information Architecture (NP2Tec)
Department of Applied Informatics
Federal University of the State of Rio de Janeiro (UNIRIO) - Brazil
{juliana.franca,joanne.netto,rafael.barradas,flavia.santoro,
fernanda.baiao}@uniriotec.br

Abstract. An organization that aligns Knowledge Management (KM) to its business processes is able to identify gaps, to correct mistakes and to keep updated more quickly. The need to identify and represent the dynamic generation and use of existing knowledge embedded into a business process, especially into a Knowledge-Intensive Process (KIP), has proved increasingly relevant. In this context, one important issue is to come up with adequate models and notations to represent KIPs. This paper presents an evaluation of current widely-used modeling languages, such as UML, EPC and BPMN, and also two others specifically proposed to deal with KIPs. The results point out which KIP characteristics could be adequately represented by using notational elements that are inherent to those modeling approaches.

Topics Covered: Process improvement techniques and tools, Process design in collaborative environments, Linking process design to organizational strategy and goals.

1 Introduction

Our Society has been characterized by highly dynamic and knowledge-intensive actions, which typically demand a variety of procedures for capturing, storing, controlling and giving secure access to the pieces of information involved in their execution. This information has been acknowledged by organizations as the main asset for achieving economic benefits and goals. According to Drucker [6], Organizations are currently focusing on the activities that produce and distribute information and knowledge, which has been named the Knowledge Age. An important issue, however, is to establish mechanisms to avoid that the produced knowledge be restricted to few people or that it be lost along the time; in this context, the relationship with business processes are fundamental for generating competitive advantage for the Organization [26].

An organization that aligns Knowledge Management (KM) to its business process is able to identify gaps, correct mistakes and to keep updated more quickly. For this reason, the main goal of the so called "Business Process-Oriented Knowledge Management" is to discover and represent the dynamic conversion of existing knowledge

M. La Rosa and P. Soffer (Eds.): BPM 2012 Workshops, LNBIP 132, pp. 126–136, 2013.

among the participants involved in the execution of business processes. As a result, it makes Knowledge and Business Processes interconnected directly [12].

For the Business Process-Oriented Knowledge Management, Knowledge-Intensive Processes (KIPs) are considered a primary approach [14]. A KIP is characterized by being highly dependent on the knowledge embedded in the participants´ minds, and in the tasks and activities that compose it [12]. Moreover, they are typically an unstructured or semi-structured proceeding, encompasses a highly dynamic complexity [16].

Although it manipulates critical information within an Organization, a KIP typically lacks a description and a representation that would allow its executors to enhance it, external participants to perfectly understand it, and information systems to adequately support it [8]. The specification of a precise conceptualization, together with a subjacent representation notation, that precisely describes the dynamics with which knowledge is created and manipulated during a KIP, is still an open issue.

Business process modeling approaches that are widely-followed in current research and practice scenarios (BPMN [19], EPC [24], UML [20]) were not meant for KIPs, since they assume a process as a deterministic machine, composed by a well-structured control flow among its activities, low uncertainty and complexity (that is, the existence of few and pre-defined exceptions). Other approaches addressing the representation of KIPs, such as the Business Process Knowledge (BPK) [21], DECOR [1], CommonKADS [25] and the one from Donadel [5] did not experience a wide adoption among organizations and are very incipient, comprising only a subset of all KIP characteristics, as discussed in [8] and [9]. In order to improve a KIP representation, França et al. [8] proposed KIPO (Knowledge-Intensive Process Ontology), which intends to explicit and organize the concepts and relationships that constitute a KIP.

The present work carries out an evaluation of which KIPO elements are potentially supported by the above-mentioned language metamodels. Besides, it presents an example using the best evaluated approach. Furthermore, it points alternatives for representing elements that not adequately addressed yet.

The paper is organized as follows. Section 2 presents the concepts that describe Knowledge-Intensive Business Process. Section 3 presents the main characteristics of traditional approaches for business process modeling, evaluates how well they support the representation of all relevant KIP elements, and presents a practical example. Section 4 concludes this paper.

2   Describing Knowledge-Intensive Process

According to Gronau et al. [11], a KIP commonly presents a diversity of information sources. Its execution involves many participants and the assistance of many experts, who carry out actions that are highly creative and innovative. In addition, KIP are typically unstructured or semi-structured, in the sense that they present a very dynamic and unstable control-flow, comprising very complex activities that frequently change over time and at runtime [16].

Due to those characteristics, building a process model for a KIP is not an easy task, especially when applying traditional approaches that focus on the representation of deterministic process. Thus, some authors have attempted to develop approaches for the representation of KIP, such as the Business Process Knowledge (BPK) [21], DECOR [1], CommonKADS [25] and the work from Donadel [5]. The DECOR approach [1] aims to structure the business process, the dynamic context, contextual information and the representations of memories embedded in the production process. The BPK [21] provides a methodological guidance for the implementation of business process-oriented knowledge management (BPOKM). This approach has two distinct tasks that are the conventional ones, which represent the working structure of the business process and the knowledge management, describing the work tasks associated with the generation, storage, application and distribution of knowledge in the represented business process. CommonKADS [25] supports the construction of knowledge systems in a large-scale, structured, controllable and repeatable way. It proposes the use of computer generated models to represent how the tasks are performed, which agents and experiences are involved. Donadel [5] aims to support the management of knowledge resources related to business processes.

Although the aforesaid approaches have advanced in order to register and manage processes with high knowledge intensity, they focus on activities and tasks inherent to the processes, leaving important issues – such as the intentions behind each action, the decisions taken at runtime, collaboration among stakeholders –unexplored or not registered. Franca et al. ([8], [9]) point the strengths and weaknesses of KIP representation approaches and highlight the lack of clarity in the representation of important KIP features (agents that influences the actions; dynamic aspects; collaboration; communication and interaction among actors while they produce knowledge; decision making rationale based on experience and creativity; and rules that might interfere on agents decisions).

In order to propose a solution that is capable of explaining a KIP, considering both the knowledge within their actions and other relevant elements (such as interaction among agents, decisions and specific working rules), França et al. [8] proposed the Knowledge-Intensive Process Ontology (KIPO) that precisely represents the concepts of this domain, providing a common understanding about what exactly is a knowledge-intensive process.

KIPO is based on the Unified Foundational Ontology (UFO) [10], and is composed by five sub-Ontologies that cover different perspectives within a KIP: Collaborative Ontology (CO) [18], Business Process Ontology (BPO) [19], Business Rules Ontology (BRO) [15], Decision Ontology (DO) [22], and Knowledge-Intensive Process Core Ontology (KIPCO). Figure 1 presents an extended version of KIPO, exploring the collaboration concepts and participants characteristics in greater detail.

In its current version, a KIPO *Agent* is someone that executes a *Knowledge-Intensive Activity* based on some *Intention*. An *Intention* may be motivated by the *Desire* or the *Belief* of an *Agent*. An *Agent* is also characterized by its *Experiences*.

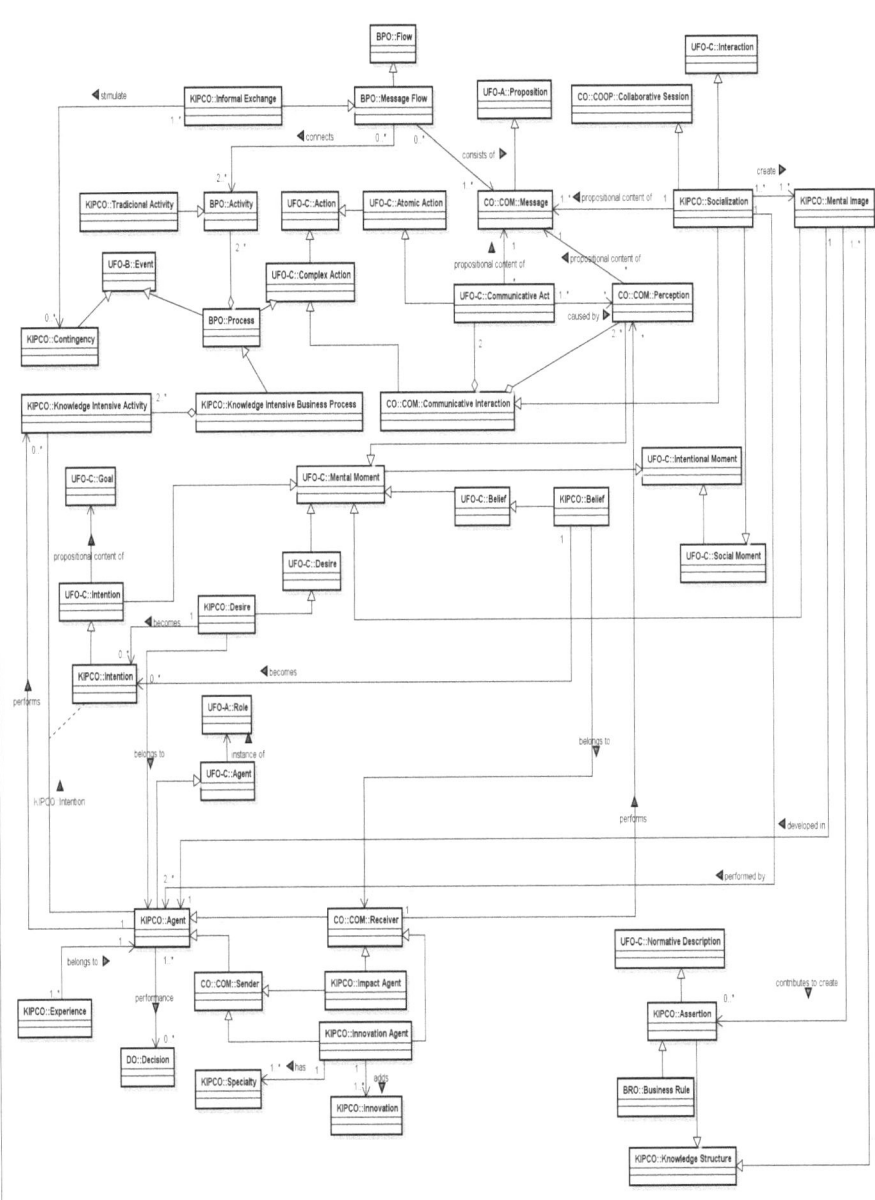

Fig. 1. Knowledge-Intensive Process Ontology – KIPO

An *Experience* is a previous situation in which the *Agent* has participated in. Two special subtypes of *Agent* are the *Innovation Agent*, who applies its known *Specialties* to execute an Activity, and the *Impact Agent*, who performs many tasks at once. *Knowledge-IntensiveAgents* participate in a *Socialization* with KIP stakeholders. A *Socialization* is a subtype of *Communicative Interaction* that involves exchanging messages. A *Mental Image* is developed by an *Agent* from the messages he/she exchanged. A *Socialization* contributes to the creation of *Assertions*. A special type of *Assertion* is the definition of a *Business Rule*. *Assertions* and *Mental Images* may be used as inputs by *Agents* when performing a process *Activity*.

Table 1 presents the definition of core KIPO concepts, grouped according to the questions that led to their identification. Most of these concepts compose KIPCO. The concepts originated from other sub-Ontologies are further described in [18], [19], [15] and [22].

Table 1. Core KIPO Concepts Definitions

Group	Concepts	Definition
What types of agents must interact during a KIP?	Agent	Process participant that can be: Impact Agent and Innovation Agent
	Impact Agent	A process participant that executes many actions simultaneously. He/she applies tacit knowledge to execute a KIP action, typically based on his/her previous experiences.
	Innovation Agent	A process participant that is responsible for executing actions with innovation and creativity.
How the interactions occur in a KIP?	Informal Exchange	Knowledge Exchange that occurs informally (either face-to-face between agents, or by means of a documentation).
	Socialization	Action during which the agents interact and exchange information through messages. During the execution of a Socialization, issues and possible alternatives for decision making are discussed and mental images are created. A Socialization also contributes to the creation of assertions.
Which elements are abstractions of the real world?	Knowledge-Intensive Activity	A special type of process activity that is not enough specified to be systematically executed. Its execution is based on previous experiences and tacit knowledge from its executor, may require specialty, may comprise innovation, or may involve making decisions. This activity is unpredictable and defined at runtime
	Knowledge-Intensive Process	A process with a high degree of dynamism in the objectives' change associated to it, high complexity, and dependent on the explicit and tacit knowledge of people involved in the process and the activities that compose it.
	Contingency	An external and unpredictable event that influences the process execution. It is responsible for determining the execution of unforeseen activities.
	Decision	A solution taken by an agent during the execution of a process.
	Knowledge Structure	The structure in which knowledge is organized.
	Mental Image	Organization of knowledge acquired from the message exchanges occurring in socialization. It shows the knowledge acquired by the agent.
	Assertion	A representation of sense completely abstracted, capable of verbal expression. Present the formalism of knowledge built in process explained.
	Intention	The deliberative state of agent, the exact choice made by an agent. What the agent has committed to perform.
	Belief	What someone thinks about the world In a certain point of time
	Desire	The "will" of an agent towards a specific goal, although he/she might never actually pursue these goals.
	Experience	A set of past situations lived by an agent, acquired by the previous execution of actions.
	Innovation	Unpublished elements that are incorporated into knowledge-intensive activities by an innovation agent.
	Specialty	Competence in the execution of an action. A field of study and work to which the agent is dedicated in a particular way. The specialty gives the agent that possesses ability to perform specific actions and related to the domain.

As a meta-model, KIPO defines the concepts and relationships in a KIP; it does not provide a graphical notation for them. However, Moody [17] argues that visual notations are effective because they provide powerful resources for the human visual system and are transmitted in a more concise and precise manner than ordinary text-based language. The representation of a domain has as its main goal the understanding of its underlying concepts, and of how these concepts are interrelated. Although KIPO does not address the problem of representing this kind of process graphically, it opens a way to explore the potential of traditional business process modeling approaches for it, as well as the usage of the specific KIP approaches with their unique features. In this section, we discuss the usage of KIPO concepts as a basis to model KIP processes graphically.

3   Investigating Graphical Representations for KIP

According to OMG [19], a standard notation for business modeling can provide organizations with the ability to understand their internal business procedures in a graphical form and give them the ability to communicate these procedures in a uniform way.

Based on this, organizations have focused efforts on the representation of their business processes. With the dissemination of Business Process Management (BPM) practices, they began to appreciate process modeling and an entire universe of related assets. According to Schreiber et al. [24], process modeling then became essential for the systematization and management of organizational knowledge artifacts.

However, an integrated and effective knowledge management approach goes beyond the static mapping of knowledge artifacts, also requiring the coordination of process activities and an efficient knowledge flow among stakeholders [11]. França et al. [8] proposed KIPO, a formal metamodel that highlights the key concepts and relationships characterizing knowledge-intensive business processes. Korherr et al. [14] points to some process modeling languages that are already consolidated in both academia and industry, and others that are yet restricted to research literature.

For discussion purposes, in this paper we take the constructs from KIPO as a complete set of elements that are required to precisely represent a KIP, and evaluated some existing languages to verify how well they were able to adequately represent each concept. The evaluated representation languages were UML, BPMN and EPC (which are adopted by many available modeling tools in current organizations), KMDL [12] and Oliveira's methodology [18].

The goal of the Unified Modeling Language (UML) [20] is mainly and originally for modeling IT systems. It comprises a set of diagrams for different stages of an IT application development lifecycle. One of these diagrams is the Activity diagram, which describes the sequence of activities and control flows of software systems. Event Process Chain (EPC) [24] was developed for modeling business processes in order to be easily understood, used by business people and focused on the customer's perspective. The Business Process Modeling Notation (BPMN) [19] provides a representation of business processes with the objective of being a simple notation to facilitate understanding of the process being modeled, and powerful enough to provide the ability to model complex business processes. The Knowledge Modeling Description Language (KMDL) [11] represents both tacit and explicit knowledge of the process. Thus, the different possibilities of knowledge conversion can be modeled and the flow of knowledge between actors is depicted. Oliveira's methodology [18] is an extension of Ericsson et al. [7] for business process modeling, which composed of diagrams and sub-models e uses constructs adapted from KMDL to model business processes, considering Knowledge Management aspects.

The evaluation of the modeling languages was performed by three analysts, who were responsible for observing how well the KIPO concepts could be represented in each language. The analysts individually evaluated the correlation between language elements and ontology concepts, considering its definitions and relationships. Table 2 consolidates the results of these evaluateons, where an "X" indicates the possibility of representing a concept using that language.

Table 2 shows an overview on the applicability of traditional modeling languages for representing a KIP. The *Agent, Communicative Interaction, Decision, Informal Exchange, Knowledge-Intensive Process, Knowledge Structure, Message, Receiver, Sender, Socialization* and *Specialty* concepts may be represented in all languages. The *Belief, Collaborative Section, Contingency, Desire, Innovation, Mental Image* and *Perception* concepts are not addressed at all, in any of the languages.

Table 2. Verification of KIPO concepts representation by modeling approaches

Concepts	UML	EPC	BPMN	KMDL	Oliveira
Agent	X	X	X	X	X
Assertion		X	X	X	X
Belief					
Business Rule	X	X	X		X
Collaborative Session					
Communicative interaction	X	X	X	X	X
Contingency					
Decision	X	X	X		
Desire					
Experience	X		X	X	X
Impact Agent					X
Informal Exchange	X	X	X	X	X
Innovation					
Innovation Agent					X
Intention		X			
Knowledge-Intensive Business Activity	X	X	X	X	
Knowledge-Intensive Business Process	X	X	X	X	X
Knowledge Structure	X	X	X	X	X
Mental Image					
Message	X	X	X	X	
Perception					
Receiver	X	X	X	X	X
Sender	X	X	X	X	X
Socialization	X	X	X	X	X
Speciality	X	X	X	X	X

As shown in Section 2, a KIP has special features that differ from traditional processes. Process models that do not highlight such characteristics or that incorporate them in an ambiguous form incur in loss of information. Our evaluation showed that the resulting KIP models presented low information representation quality, according to the principles discussed by Cabral et al. [3], as explained in the following examples.

Most languages present a construct overload problem [17], since there is no representation distinction between ordinary and knowledge-intensive activities. This problem reduces the understandability of a knowledge-intensive activity by stakeholders.

The fact that *Belief*, *Desire* and *Perception* concepts could not be represented by any of the approaches impacts on the understanding of which are the real intentions and objectives to be achieved by the process, as discussed in [4] and [23]. The explicit representation of these concepts would allow a stakeholder to understand what motivated a change in the control flow or the execution of an unexpected activity, which frequently occur in KIPs.

Other KIPO concepts, although addressed by some (or all) evaluated languages, were not adequately represented. First, a *Socialization* between agents could only be represented as a relationship of various actors with the same activity; however, the environment in which socialization was practiced (namely a *Collaborative Session* in KIPO) was not well detailed, that is, it did not mention important things such as the conditions under which the socialization occurred, what triggered it, which *communication acts* – *message sending* and *message receipt* – took place, and which roles were involved. Second, *Decisions* made during a KIP appeared into the UML, EPC and BPMN models; however, human emotions involved in this step could not be explicit, although it is notorious that they do interfere in the rationale of a decision and therefore are important knowledge to be considered. We also observe that elements such as *Business Rules* and *Decision* were not represented by KMDL approach. This approach does not allow integration with business process context.

In general, the evaluation results also showed that, even when a concept could be represented, some of its relationships were not, thus meaning that its conceptualization differed from the KIPO definition. This was the case, for example, with *Socialization* and *Message* concepts in Oliveira's approach. One of the features of this approach is to represent knowledge conversions among process participants, but we could not represent the messages exchanged. A peculiarity of this approach is the lack of representation for *Knowledge-Intensive Business Activity*. *Knowledge-Intensive Business Processes* are represented and its composing activities are arranged and described; however, there is no graphical representation for them and their relationships.

Finally, *Agents* specializations (*Impact Agent* and *Innovation Agent*) were only addressed in the Oliveira's approach. The lack of these specific elements in the KIP model prevents the organization from mapping *experiences*, *innovations* and *expertise* that influence the actions and decisions of process participants.

A KIP Modeling Representation

Our evaluation results showed an important loss of information in KIP representations, either because relevant concepts were not addressed by existing approaches or because these concepts were represented in a very high abstraction level. This may lead to ambiguous and unclear knowledge-intensive process models. BPMN was the modeling language that presented the broadest coverage of the set of KIPO concepts.

Therefore, this Section illustrates a KIP model using BPMN, on top of the ARIS express tool [2]. The chosen process for this example reflects a real Data Management process in a software development company (Figure 2). The process is highly dynamic and some of its activities are very dependent on the participants experience, expertise and creativity.

The process starts when the manager of the data modeling department receives a request of a data model for a system or module. Then, the manager allocates a Data Analyst (DA) for the activity and he/she starts the interaction with the client area. Depending on the required detail level, the DA schedules meetings with stakeholders for specification and modeling purposes. When those meeting are finished, the business data analysis and modeling phase begin. In this phase, the DA verifies information and data sources and analyzes the current corporate data model. If needed, the DA negotiates with other systems/business data modelers to perform integration, which may require additional meetings with stakeholders to assess how the integration will take place, that is, which objects should be integrated, reused or created. When the integration specification is finished, the Business Analyst, Project Leader, DA and Database Analyst (DBA) conduct an internal evaluation. If there are restrictions or corrections to me made, the document keeps being refined until it correctly addresses the original request, according to the DA, the project leader and the DBA. A validation meeting is conducted with stakeholders and, ultimately, the entire process is documented following standards for analysis of its performance indicators.

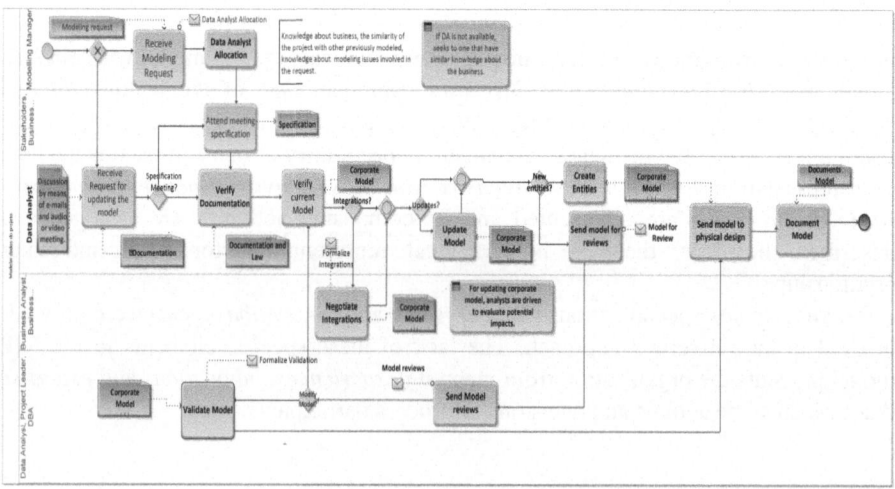

Fig. 2. A KIP model in BPMN

Although the process contains semi-ordered activities, relevant tacit aspects could not be represented, such as the perception of the data analyst about what is being modeled, the criteria used to obtain relevant information and their innovation and creativity strategies introduced by the process. Another point to note is that the agents are represented by the 'lanes', but it is not clear the model if the modeling manager, for example, assumes the responsibilities of an innovation or impact agent. Also, aspects related to the contingency of the process were not possible to be represented (for example, the impact of changing the schedule and project costs and the availability of resources for its execution).

4   Conclusions

This paper presented an evaluation of modeling languages to represent a KIP, taking the conceptualization defined by KIPO [8] as a baseline. This evaluation concluded that current process modeling representation languages are not adequate for the representation of KIPs, since relevant information about the KIP dynamics is lost.

In order to observe the practical applicability of the evaluated approaches, a process model of a real Data Management process in a software development company (Figure 2) was illustrated using BPMN. The conclusions confirm the above discussions, since important KIP characteristics details could not be observed. All approaches were very similar in the number of concepts represented, with EPC and BPMN with the highest representation coverage.

A further evaluation should consider the representation of the KIP elements making use of adaptations and extensions of traditional modeling approaches. A deeper analysis of each approach and the involvement of professionals will also be addressed. Finally, we are working on the development of a graphical notation for KIPs that is able to embrace all relevant concepts and dynamics proposed by KIPO.

References

1. Abecker, A.: DECOR Consortium: DECOR – Delivery of context-sensitive organizational knowledge. E-Work and E-Commerce. IOS Press (2001)
2. ARIS Express, http://www.ariscommunity.com/aris-express/download (accessed in: December 04, 2011)
3. Cabral, L., Norton, B., Domingue, J.: The Business Process Modelling Ontology. In: 4th International Workshop on Semantic Business Process Management (SBPM 2009), Workshop at ESWC 2009, Crete (June 2009)
4. Cardoso, E.C.S., Santos Jr., P.S., Almeida, J.P.A., Guizzardi, R.S.S., Guizzardi, G.: Semantic Integration of Goal and Business Process Modeling. In: Anais da International Conference on Research and Practical Issues of Enterprise Information Systems (CONFENIS 2010), Natal/RN, Brasil (2010)
5. Donadel, A.C.: A method for representing knowledge-intensive processes. MSc Dissertation. Programa de Pós-Graduação em Engenharia e Gestão do Conhecimento, Universidade Federal de Santa Catarina, Brazil (2007) (in Portuguese)
6. Drucker, P.: Sociedade Pós Capitalista. São Paulo, Pioneira (1993)
7. Eriksson, H.-E., Penker, M.: Business Modeling with UML: Business patterns at work. E.U.A.: John Wiley and Sons (2000)

8. França, J.B.S., Santoro, F.M., Baião, F.A.: Towards Characterizing Knowledge-Intensive Processes. In: IEEE International Conference on Computer-Supported Cooperative Work in Design (CSCWD 2012), Wuhan, China (2012)
9. França, J.B.S., Netto, J.M., Carvalho, J.E.S., Santoro, F.M., Baião, F.A., Pimentel, M.: An Exploratory Study on Collaboratively Conceptualizing Knowledge-Intensive Processes. In: International Series of Working Conferences on Business Process Modeling, Development and Support (BPMDS 2012), Gdansk, Poland (accepted for publication, 2012)
10. Guizzardi, G.: Ontological Foundations for Structural Conceptual Models. Universal Press, The Netherlands (2005) ISBN 90-75176-81-3
11. Gronau, N., Weber, E.: Defining an infrastructure for knowledge-intensive business process. In: I-KNOW, Graz, Austria, vol. 4. Proceedings..., Graz (2004)
12. Gronau, N., Muller, C., Korf, R.: KMDL – Capturing, analyzing and improving Knowledge-intensive business process. Journal of Universal Computer Science 11(4), 452–472 (2005)
13. Hagen, C.R., Ratz, D., Povalej, R.: Towards self-organizing knowledge-intensive processes. Journal of Universal Knowledge Management (2), 148–169 (2005)
14. Korherr, B., List, B.: Extending the epc and the bpmn with business goals and performance measures,
    http://www.wit.at/people/korherr/publications/iceis2007.pdf
    (accessed in: June 26, 2011)
15. Lopes, M., Baião, F., Siqueira, S.: Expressing Business Rules in a Foundational-based Domain Ontology: Towards Higher-quality Conceptual Models. In: International Conference on Information Integration and Web-Based Applications & Services, Paris (2010)
16. Maldonado, M.U.: Analysis the impact of policy creation and transfer of knowledge in knowledge-intensive processes: A model of system dynamics. MSc Dissertation. 138f. Programa de Pós-Graduação em Engenharia e Gestão do Conhecimento, Universidade Federal de Santa Catarina, Florianópolis, Brazil (2008) (in Portuguese)
17. Moody, D.L.: The physics of notations: Towards a scientific basis for constructing visual notations in software engineering. IEEE Transactions on Software Engineering 35(5), 756–779 (2009)
18. Oliveira, F.F.: Ontology Collaboration and its Applications. MSc Dissertation. Programa de Pós-Graduação em Informática, Universidade Federal do Espírito Santo, Vitória, Brazil (2009) (in Portuguese)
19. OMG: Business Process Modeling and Notation (BPMN). Version 2.0, (2011),
    http://www.bpmn.org/ (accessed in: June 26, 2011)
20. OMG: Unified Modeling Language (UML). Version 2.0 (2011),
    http://www.uml.org/
21. Papavassiliou, G., Ntioudis, S., Abecker, A., Mentzas, G.: Business Process Knowledge Modeling: method tool. In: Database and Expert Systems Applications (2003)
22. Pereira, A., Santoro, F.: Cognitive Decision Making Process as Context Information. In: The 15th IFIP WG8.3 International Conference on Decision Support Systems (DSS 2010), Lisboa, Portugal (2010)
23. Rao, A.S., Georgeff, M.P.: BDI Agents: From Theory to Practice. In: Proceedings of the First International Conference on Multiagent Systems, ICMAS 1995 (1995)
24. Scheer, A.W.: ARIS – Business Process Modeling. Springer (1999)
25. Schreiber, G., Akkermans, H., Anjewierden, A., Hoog, R., Shadbolt, N., De Velde, W.V., Wielinga, B.: Knowledge Engineering and Management: The Common KADS Methodology. MIT Press, Cambridge (2002)
26. Steels, L.: Corporate knowledge management. In: Proceedings of ISMICK 1993 Conference, Compiégne, France, pp. 9–30 (1993)

Alignment Based Precision Checking

Arya Adriansyah[1], Jorge Munoz-Gama[2], Josep Carmona[2],
Boudewijn F. van Dongen[1], and Wil M.P. van der Aalst[1]

[1] Department of Mathematics and Computer Science
Eindhoven University of Technology
P.O. Box 513, 5600 MB Eindhoven, The Netherlands
{a.adriansyah,b.f.v.dongen,w.m.p.v.d.aalst}@tue.nl
[2] Universitat Politecnica de Catalunya
Barcelona, Spain
{jmunoz,jcarmona}@lsi.upc.edu

Abstract. Most organizations have process models describing how cases
need to be handled. In fact, legislation and standardization (cf. the
Sarbanes-Oxley Act, the Basel II Accord, and the ISO 9000 family of
standards) are forcing organizations to document their processes. These
processes are often not enforced by information systems. However, tor-
rents of event data are recorded by today's information systems. These
recorded events reflect how processes are really executed. Often reality
deviates from the modeled behavior. Therefore, measuring the extent
process executions *conform* to a predefined process model is increasingly
important. In this paper, we propose an approach to measure the *precision* of a process model with respect to an event log. Unlike earlier
approaches, we first *align* model and log thus making our approach more
robust, even in case of deviations. The approach has been implemented
in the ProM 6 tool and evaluated using both artificial and real life cases.

Keywords: Precision measurement, Log-model alignment, Conformance
checking, Process mining.

1 Introduction

Process models are the starting point for most Business Process Management
(BPM) activities, as they provide insights into possible scenarios [10]. Process
models are used for analysis (e.g. simulation), enactment, redesign, and process
improvement. Therefore, they should reflect the dominant behavior accurately.
The increasing availability of event data enables the application of *conformance
checking* [9, 12, 13]. Conformance checking techniques compare *event logs* with
process models such that deviations can be diagnosed and quantified.

Conformance can be viewed along multiple orthogonal dimensions: (1) Fitness,
(2) Simplicity, (3) Precision, and (4) Generalization [12]. In this paper, we focus
on the *precision* dimension. Precision penalizes a process model for allowing
behavior that is unlikely given the observed behavior in the event log. Take for
example the two models and the event log in Figure 1. All traces in the log can
be reproduced by both models, i.e. the traces perfectly *fit* the models. However,

M. La Rosa and P. Soffer (Eds.): BPM 2012 Workshops, LNBIP 132, pp. 137–149, 2013.
© Springer-Verlag Berlin Heidelberg 2013

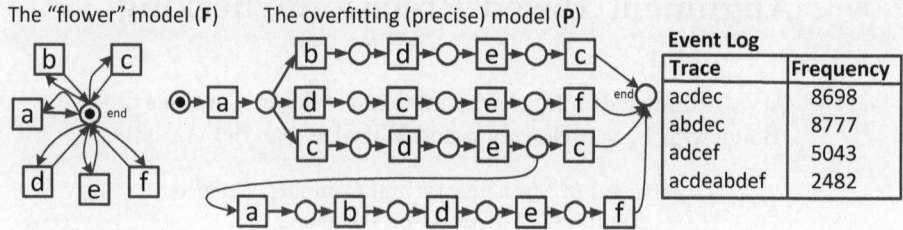

Fig. 1. Example of an extremely precise (overfitting) and imprecise model (underfitting) for a given log

notice that the "flower" model (**F**) may provide misleading insights, as it also allows for much more behavior not appearing in the log. In contrast, the other model (**P**) only allows traces that occur in the log. Hence, the *precision* of model **P** is better than model **F** with respect to the log.

Many existing precision metrics (e.g. [4,7,9]) assume that the event log perfectly fits the model, while many case studies show that this assumption does not hold (e.g. [5,8,14]). In this paper, we do not use such assumptions and propose a robust approach to measure the *precision* between an event log and a model. This way we combine our earlier work on *precision* [6,7] and *alignments* [1,2].

The paper is organized as follows: Section 2 shows the notations and preliminary concepts that are used throughout this paper. Alignment between event logs and models is explained in Section 3. Alignment-based precision measurements are presented in Section 4. Experimental results are given in Section 5. Section 6 concludes the paper.

2   Preliminaries

Conformance checking requires as input both a process model and an event log. Therefore, we first formalize process models and logs.

2.1   Sequence and Multiset

Let W be a set. For (finite) *sequences* of elements over a set W, we use ϵ to denote an empty sequence. A concatenation of sequences σ_1 and σ_2 is denoted with $\sigma_1 \cdot \sigma_2$. W^* denotes the set of all finite sequences over W. We refer to the i-th element of a sequence σ as $\sigma[i]$ and we use $|\sigma|$ to represent the length of sequence σ. We say that any $x \in (W \times W)$ is a *pair*. We use $sel_1(x)$ and $sel_2(x)$ to refer to the first and the second element of pair x respectively. We generalize this notation to sequences: $sel_i(\sigma) = \langle sel_i(\sigma[1]), ..., sel_i(\sigma[|\sigma|]) \rangle$. For all $Q \subseteq W$, $\sigma_{\downarrow Q}$ denotes the projection of $\sigma \in W^*$ on Q, e.g., $\langle a, a, b, c \rangle_{\downarrow \{a,c\}} = \langle a, a, c \rangle$. For simplicity, we omit brackets for sequences whenever their elements are clearly distinguishable, e.g. we write aac instead of $\langle a, a, c \rangle$.

A *multiset* m over W is a mapping $m : W \to I\!N$. We overload the set notation, using $\emptyset$ for the empty multiset and $\in$ for the element inclusion. We write e.g.

$m = [p^2, q]$ or $m = [p, p, q]$ for a multiset m with $m(p) = 2$, $m(q) = 1$, and $m(x) = 0$ for all $x \notin \{p, q\}$. We use $|m|$ to indicate the total number of elements in multiset m (e.g. $|[p^2, q]| = 3$). When we iterate over m, we refer to each unique element in m, e.g. for all function $f : W \to I\!N$, $\sum\limits_{x \in m} f(x) = \sum\limits_{x \in W} m(x) \cdot f(x)$.

2.2 Event Log and Process Model

The starting point for conformance checking is an *event log*. An event log records the execution of all cases (i.e. process instances). Each case is described by a *trace*, i.e., an activity sequence. Different cases may have exactly the same trace. In reality, not all activities performed in a process are logged. We define the set of all logged activities from the universe of activities A as $A_L \subseteq A$. An event log over A_L is a multiset $L : A_L{}^* \to I\!N$. For example, the log in Figure 1 is formalized as $L = [acdec^{8698}, abdec^{8777}, adcef^{5043}, acdeabdef^{2482}]$.

Similarly, a *process model* defines a set of sequences of activities that leads to proper termination of the process. Furthermore, some activities in a process may not appear in its model. Thus, we define a set of modeled activities over the set of all activities A as $A_M \subseteq A$. A process model is a set of complete activity sequences $M \subseteq A_M{}^*$, i.e., executions from the initial state to some final state. Consider for example the precise model (**P**) in Figure 1. Assuming that the end state is reached when the "end" place contains exactly one token, the model are formalized by the set $\{acdec, abdec, adcef, acdeabdef\}$. Note that the set of modeled activities and the set of logged activities may be disjoint, i.e. $A_M \cap A_L$ can be an empty set.

3   Cost-Optimal Alignment

An alignment between an event log and a process model relates occurrences of activities in the log to execution steps of the model. As the execution of a case is often performed independently of the execution of another case, aligning is performed on the basis of traces.

For each trace in an event log that fits a process model, each "move" in the trace, i.e., an event observed in the log, can be mimicked by a "move" in the model, i.e., an action executed in the model. However, this is not the case if the trace does not fit the model perfectly. We use the symbol $\bot$ to denote "no move" in either the log or the model. Hence, we introduce the set $A_L^\bot = A_L \cup \{\bot\}$ where any $x \in A_L^\bot$ refers to a "move in log" and the set $A_M^\bot = A_M \cup \{\bot\}$ where any $y \in A_M^\bot$ refers to a "move in model". Formally, a *move* is represented by a pair $(x, y) \in A_L^\bot \times A_M^\bot$ such that:

- (x, y) is a *move in log* if $x \in A_L$ and $y = \bot$,
- (x, y) is a *move in model* if $x = \bot$ and $y \in A_M$,
- (x, y) is a *synchronous move/move in both* if $x \in A_L$, $y \in A_M$, and $x = y$,
- (x, y) is a *illegal move* in all other cases.

We use A_{LM} to denote the set of all pairs of *legal moves*, i.e. all possible pairs of move in log, move in model, and move in both.

Along this section, let L be a log over A_L, let $\sigma_L \in L$ be a trace, and let $\sigma_M \in M$ be a complete execution of the model. An *alignment* between σ_L and σ_M is a sequence $\gamma \in A_{LM}^*$ where the projection of the first element (ignoring $\perp$) yields σ_L (i.e. $sel_1(\gamma)_{\downarrow A_L} = \sigma_L$) and projection of the second element yields σ_M (i.e. $sel_2(\gamma)_{\downarrow A_M} = \sigma_M$).

Take for example a trace $\sigma_L = aacef$ and an activity sequence $adcef$ allowed by model **P** in Figure 1. Some possible alignments between the two are:

$$\gamma_1 = \begin{array}{|c|c|c|c|c|c|} \hline a & a & \perp & c & e & f \\ \hline a & \perp & d & c & e & f \\ \hline \end{array} \quad \gamma_2 = \begin{array}{|c|c|c|c|c|c|} \hline a & a & \perp & c & e & f \\ \hline \perp & a & d & c & e & f \\ \hline \end{array} \quad \gamma_3 = \begin{array}{|c|c|c|c|c|c|} \hline a & \perp & a & c & e & f \\ \hline a & d & \perp & c & e & f \\ \hline \end{array} \quad \gamma_4 = \begin{array}{|c|c|c|c|c|c|} \hline a & a & c & \perp & \perp & e & f \\ \hline \perp & a & \perp & d & c & e & f \\ \hline \end{array}$$

The moves are represented vertically, e.g., the first move of γ_2 is $(a, \perp)$, indicating that the log moves a while the model does not make any move. Note that the projections of all moves in model in all alignments are by definition complete activity sequences allowed by the model. This property is not always guaranteed in some other approaches that also relates occurrences of observed activities in the logs to execution steps in process models (e.g. [9]).

To measure the cost of an alignment, we define a *distance function* δ : $A_{LM} \to I\!N$ where for all $(a_L, a_M) \in A_{LM}, \delta((a_L, a_M)) = 0$ if $a_L = a_M$ and $\delta(a_L, a_M) = 1$ otherwise[1]. The distance function can be generalized to alignments $\gamma \in A_{LM}^*$ by taking the sum of the costs of all individual moves: $\delta(\gamma) = \sum_{(a_L, a_M) \in \gamma} \delta((a_L, a_M))$. Using this function, the cost of alignment γ_1 is $\delta(\gamma_1) = \delta((a, a)) + \delta((a, \perp)) + \delta((\perp, d)) + \delta((c, c)) + \delta((e, e)) + \delta((f, f)) = 0 + 1 + 1 + 0 + 0 + 0 = 2$. Note that the function returns the number of mismatches in the alignment.

Given a trace from an event log and a process model, we are interested in an activity sequence from the model that is similar to the trace. Therefore, we define the set of *alignments* $\Gamma_{\sigma_L, M} = \{\gamma \in A_{LM}^* \mid \exists_{\sigma_M \in M} : \gamma$ is an alignment between σ_L and $\sigma_M\}$ to be all possible alignments between σ_L and complete activity sequences of M. Accordingly, we define the set of *optimal alignments* as the set of all alignments with minimum cost, i.e. $\Gamma_{\sigma_L, M}^o = \{\gamma \in \Gamma_{\sigma_L, M} \mid \forall_{\gamma' \in \Gamma_{\sigma_L, M}} \delta(\gamma) \le \delta(\gamma')\}$. It is easy to see that there can be more than one optimal alignment between a trace and a model. For example, $\{\gamma_1, \gamma_2, \gamma_3\}$ is the set of optimal alignments between the trace $\sigma_L = aacef$ and model **P** in Figure 1.

Given a log and a model, one can measure precision based on all optimal alignments between traces in the log and the model or take just one representative element for each trace. In this paper, we investigate both approaches. We define a function $\lambda_M \in A_L^* \to A_{LM}^*$ that maps each trace in the log to an optimal alignment, i.e. for any $\sigma_L \in L$, $\lambda_M(\sigma_L) = \gamma$, where $\gamma \in \Gamma_{\sigma_L, M}^o$. If there are multiple optimal alignments, λ_M chooses one of them according to other external criteria. With our previous example, suppose that λ_M selects an alignment that has the earliest occurrence of non-synchronous moves, $\lambda_M(\sigma_L) = \gamma_2$.

---

[1] The distance function can be user-defined, but for simplicity we use a default distance function that assigns unit costs to moves in log/model only.

We define a function $\overline{\lambda}_M \in A_L{}^* \to M$ based on λ_M such that for any trace σ_L in log L and a model M, $\overline{\lambda}_M(\sigma_L) = sel_2(\lambda_M(\sigma_L))_{\downarrow A_M}$. Function $\overline{\lambda}_M$ provides an "oracle" that produces one complete activity sequence allowed by models. In [1,2] various approaches to obtain an optimal alignment with respect to different cost function are investigated. For any given trace and model, we can always obtain an activity sequence that both perfectly fits the model and closest to the trace.

Note that in cases where process model has duplicate tasks (more than one task to represent an activity) or unlogged tasks (tasks whose execution are not logged), approaches to construct alignments (e.g. [1,2]) keep the mapping from all model moves to the tasks they correspond to. Hence, given an alignment of a trace and such models, we know exactly which task is executed for each model move. Due to space constraints, we refer to [1,2] for further details on how such mapping is constructed.

4   Alignment-Aware Precision

Given an event log and a model, the technique described in the previous section provides one optimal alignment (through the λ_M function) or all optimal alignments (through the $\Gamma^o_{\sigma_L,M}$ set) for each trace in the log. This section presents a technique to compute *precision* based on the use of these optimal alignments. The technique is grounded on the methods described in [6,7]. However, there is a fundamental difference: whereas in [6,7] traces in the log are simply replayed in the model, our new approach is based on alignments.

The advantages of the approach presented in this paper are manifold. First of all, traces in the log do not need to be completely fitting. In [6,7] the non-fitting parts are simply ignored. For most real-life logs this implies that only a fraction of the event log can be used for computing precision. Second, the existence of indeterminism in the model poses no problems when using the alignments. In [6,7], ad-hoc heuristics were used to deal with non-determinism. Finally, the use of alignments instead of log-based model replay improves the robustness of conformance checking (as will be demonstrated later when we present the experimental results). The remainder of this section is devoted to explain how precision can be calculated.

Precision is estimated by confronting model and log behaviors: *imprecisions* between the model and the log (i.e., situations where the model allows more behavior than the one reflected in the log) are detected and analyzed. For instance, there are 5 clear cases of imprecision (b, c, d, e, f) in the initial state of the **F** model in Figure 1, where a, b, c, d, e, f are possible activities according to the model but only a occurs in the initial state according to the log.

First, log behavior must be determined in terms of model perspective, i.e., we consider the optimal alignments of each trace for this purpose. In particular, the projection of the second element of each optimal alignment, i.e., $sel_2(\gamma)_{\downarrow A_M}$. These sequences are used to build the *alignment automaton*, i.e., a prefix automaton that includes information of all log traces. Depending on whether all the possible optimal alignments are used to build the automaton (i.e., $\Gamma^o_{\sigma_L,M}$) or just one (i.e., λ_M), we will refer to the instantiation of the automaton as $\mathcal{A}$ or $\mathcal{A}^1$ respectively. Clearly, $\mathcal{A}$ provides more information than $\mathcal{A}^1$, and hence the precision value will be closer to the reality. But for large logs it may be difficult to compute all optimal alignments. Apart from providing individual precision metrics for each one of these two automata, the experiments demonstrate that using $\mathcal{A}^1$ in the precision metric is a good approximation to the value provided by using $\mathcal{A}$.

Take for example the model and the log $L = [\sigma_1, \sigma_1, \sigma_2, \sigma_2]$ in Figure 2, where $\sigma_1 = abcde$ and $\sigma_2 = acbde$. The set of optimal alignments for the two possible traces consists of:

$$\gamma_5 = \begin{array}{|c|c|c|c|c|c|} a & b & c & d & e & \bot \\ \hline \bot & b & \bot & d & e & c \end{array} \quad \gamma_6 = \begin{array}{|c|c|c|c|c|} a & b & c & d & e \\ \hline \bot & b & c & \bot & \bot \end{array} \quad \gamma_7 = \begin{array}{|c|c|c|c|c|c|} a & b & c & d & e & \bot \\ \hline \bot & b & \bot & d & e & a \end{array}$$

$$\gamma_8 = \begin{array}{|c|c|c|c|c|c|} a & c & b & d & e & \bot \\ \hline \bot & \bot & b & d & e & a \end{array} \quad \gamma_9 = \begin{array}{|c|c|c|c|c|c|} a & c & b & d & e & \bot \\ \hline \bot & \bot & b & d & e & c \end{array}$$

In the first part of this section we consider the case where only one optimal alignment per trace is used, i.e., we use function $\lambda_M(\sigma_L)$ rather than $\Gamma^o_{\sigma_L, M}$ to construct the automaton $\mathcal{A}^1$ (the case where all the optimal alignments are considered is detailed at the end of the section). Considering the distance function and an external criteria, the optimal alignments selected for the traces in the log could be, for instance, $\lambda_M(\sigma_1) = \gamma_5$ and $\lambda_M(\sigma_2) = \gamma_8$. The projection of the second element of each optimal alignment (e.g., $\overline{\lambda}_M(\sigma_1) = bdec$ and $\overline{\lambda}_M(\sigma_2) = bdea$) is used to build the automaton $\mathcal{A}^1$, where the states of that automaton are determined by complete set of all the prefixes of the alignment projections (e.g., $\{\epsilon, b, bd, bde, bdea, bdec\}$ on this example).

Formally, the alignment automaton is defined such that:

- The set of *states* corresponds to all prefixes.
- The set of *labels* corresponds to the activities.
- The *arcs* define the concatenation between prefixes and activities, e.g., states bd and bde are connected by arc labeled e.
- The state corresponding with the empty sequence ϵ is the initial state.
- The function ω determines the weight of each state according to its importance for the precision computation. Graphically it is shown as a number inside the state.

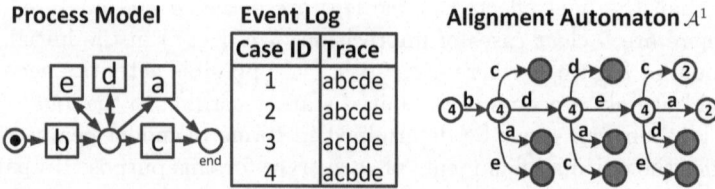

Fig. 2. Example of a model with an unfitting log and its alignment automaton (appended with available actions, colored grey), considering one optimal alignment per trace ($\mathcal{A}^1$)

Function ω is used to determine the importance of the states based on frequencies. In this example, where only one alignment per trace is considered, value of ω for a state is the number of occurrences of the state in the multiset of all visited states when replaying the log, e.g. using the example in Figure 2, $\omega(b) = 4$ because b is a prefix of both $\overline{\lambda}_M(\sigma_1)$ and $\overline{\lambda}_M(\sigma_2)$ and $L(\sigma_1) + L(\sigma_2) = 2 + 2 = 4$. $\omega(bdea) = 2$ because $bdea$ is only a prefix of $\overline{\lambda}_M(\sigma_2)$ and $L(\sigma_2) = 2$.

Note that the alignment automaton is similar to the *prefix automaton* presented in [6]. However, the alignment automaton is built from proper firing sequences, i.e., the projections of the alignments. Therefore, any sequence of activities corresponding with a prefix of the automaton can be replayed unambiguously on the model. This also ensures that occurrences of activities that are modeled but not logged (i.e. unlogged tasks) and duplicate tasks (i.e. which task an event is mapped to) are identified correctly. This is not the case on the construction of the prefix automaton in [6].

Once the log behavior has been determined in terms of the model's perspective, the confrontation with the actual model behavior is required in order to determine the precision of the system. For each state of the automaton, we compute its set of *available actions*, i.e. possible direct successor activities according to the model ($a_v(\sigma)$), and then compare it with the set of *executed actions*, i.e. activities really executed in the log ($e_x(\sigma)$). Take for example the alignment automaton and process model in Figure 2. $e_x(bde) = \{a, c\}$ as after the state bde in the alignment automaton, only a and c occur in the log. $a_v(bde) = \{a, c, d, e\}$ because after firing transitions bde, the model allows to fire $a, c, d,$ or e. Note that, by construction $e_x(\sigma) \subseteq a_v(\sigma)$, i.e., the set of executed actions of a given state is always a subset of all available actions according to the model.

The actions available in a state but never observed in the log are used to collect the *imprecision* of the system, i.e., an activity that escapes from the log behavior. These imprecisions are represented in gray in the automaton of Figure 2. For example, the imprecisions of the state bde are $\{a, c, d, e\} \setminus \{a, c\} = \{d, e\}$. The computation and analysis of these imprecisions are the cornerstone of the precision checking presented in this paper. All identified imprecisions can be analyzed and further used to correct the model and make it more precise. Furthermore, in order to globally estimate precision, these imprecisions in turn are pondered by their weight within the process.

The *align-based precision* (a_p^1) of a system, where only one alignment per trace is considered (hence, using automaton $\mathcal{A}^1$), is determined by the formula:

$$a_p^1(\mathcal{A}^1) = \frac{\sum\limits_{\sigma \in S} \omega(\sigma) \cdot |e_x(\sigma)|}{\sum\limits_{\sigma \in S} \omega(\sigma) \cdot |a_v(\sigma)|}$$

where S is the set of states of the alignment automaton $\mathcal{A}^1$, i.e. S is the set of all prefixes of all constructed optimal alignments.

The metric compares the number of available actions and executed actions for each state in an alignment automaton, weighted with their importance. For example, given the automaton, appended with available actions in Figure 2, precision is computed as:

$$\frac{1\cdot 4+1\cdot 4+1\cdot 4+2\cdot 4+0\cdot 2+0\cdot 2}{1\cdot 4+4\cdot 4+4\cdot 4+4\cdot 4+0\cdot 2+0\cdot 2}=0.38$$

where each $s\cdot w$ summand refers to a state on the automaton, i.e., s is the number of available/executed actions of the state and w is the number of occurrence of the prefix represented by the state in the log.

In order to focus on the important parts of the process and to mitigate the effects produced by rarely occuring traces or incomplete traces, the precision defined above could be restricted to consider only such states with a weight greater than a given pruning threshold (called τ). In the remainder, we assume no pruning (i.e., $\tau = 0$), unless it is stated otherwise. The effects of the pruning can be seen in [7]. Additionally, it is also possible to consider the precision with a severity factor associated to the activity that escapes from the log behavior.

The case considered so far is the one where only one optimal alignment per trace is used to build the automaton ($\mathcal{A}^1$). The same idea can be used to propose a metric for the general case (denoted a_p) where all the best alignments of a trace are used to build the alignment automaton ($\mathcal{A}$). For instance, following the running example, there are three optimal alignments for the trace σ_1 (γ_5,γ_6 and γ_7), and two for the trace σ_2 (γ_8 and γ_9). The process of building the alignment automaton $\mathcal{A}$ (see Figure 3) and computing the metric a_p is the same as computing a_p^1, except the definition of the function ω.

Unlike the case with one alignment, in this case the importance of each state does not depend exclusively on the frequency, but must also be equally balanced among all its alignments. Consider for instance the state corresponding with the prefix b. This prefix appears in all the optimal alignments of all the traces in the log (σ_1 and σ_2). So, the weight of this state is 4 (1 for each trace and both traces occur twice in the log), as shown in Figure 3. However, this is not the case for the state bc. This state only appears in the set of optimal alignments of only one trace (σ_1) that occurs twice in the log. The first naive attempt would be then assign to this state a weight of 2 (1 for each occurrence). However, note that, there are cases where the number of optimal alignments of one trace may not coincide with another trace, e.g. σ_1 has 3 alignments and σ_2 has 2. In order to eliminate the bias produced by traces with many optimal alignments, this value needs to be normalized, i.e., we consider also the number of optimal alignments

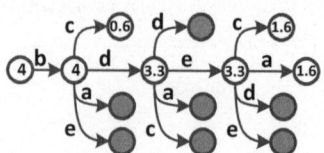

Fig. 3. Alignment automaton $\mathcal{A}$ of model and log in Figure 2, considering all optimal alignments per trace (appended with available actions, colored grey)

of the trace and also in how many of them the prefix appears. For example, the weight of state bc in Figure 3 is $1/3$ (it appears only in one of the 3 optimal alignments of the trace σ_1) times 2 (σ_1 occurs twice in the log), i.e., $1/3 \cdot 2 \approx 0.6$.

Let L be a log over A_L, let $M \subseteq A_M{}^*$ be a model, and let $\mathcal{A}$ be the alignment automaton constructed from all best alignments of all traces in L with M, the function ω for all states s of $\mathcal{A}$ is defined as:

$$\omega(s) = \sum_{\sigma_L \in L} \frac{|\{\gamma \in \Gamma^o_{\sigma_L, M} \mid sel_2(\gamma)_{\downarrow A_M} = s \cdot \sigma' \wedge \sigma' \in A_M{}^*\}|}{|\Gamma^o_{\sigma_L, M}|}$$

Note that there are theoretical differences concerning the imprecisions of $\mathcal{A}^1$ and $\mathcal{A}$. For instance, in the running example, bc is an imprecision in $\mathcal{A}^1$ but not in $\mathcal{A}$. This difference is reflected in the values of a_p and a_p^1 (0.47 and 0.38 respectively). Since all the optimal alignments are taken into account, a more complete characterization of log behavior is considered in $\mathcal{A}$. However, the experiments show that, the use of a_p^1 is a good approximation of a_p, in such cases where complexity is an issue (see Sec. 5).

The metrics presented in this section coincide with the intuition for precision presented in the introduction of this paper. This is illustrated by the the results of the a_p^1 and a_p metrics for the example log and model in Figure 1. As expected, the precision for models **P** is high (1.00 for both a_p and a_p^1) while the precision for model **F** is low (0.20 for both a_p and a_p^1).

5   Experiments

We have implemented the proposed precision calculation as a ProM 6 plugin, publicly available from www.processmining.org. We used it to perform a range of experiments to test the robustness of our proposed approach using both synthetic and real-life models and logs.

5.1   Artificial Cases

The first set of experiments was performed to evaluate the values provided by the proposed metrics. We measured precision between various logs and models whose expected values are known and compare them against etc_P [7] precision as benchmark for existing precision metrics. We created new models whose expected precision values are between the two extremes by combining the models and log in Figure 1 (**P** and **F**) in different orders. Two models are combined by merging the end place of one with the initially marked place of another. Merged models are named according to the their original models, e.g. **PF** model is the result of merging the end place of **P** with the initially marked place of **F**. The activity names in the merged models and logs are renamed such that splitting the logs and models into two parts yields back the original logs and models. Precision values were measured 10 times for event logs consisting of 5,000 traces, generated by simulating the precise model (i.e. **PP**). The results are shown in Fig. 4(i).

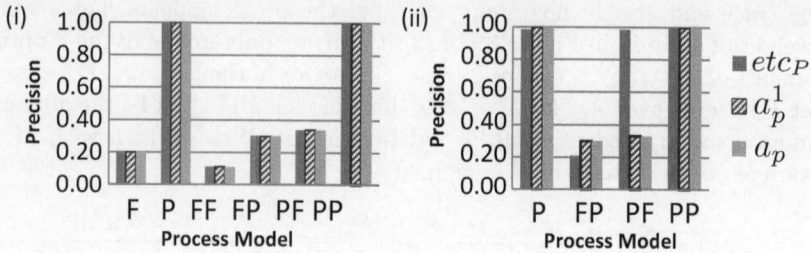

Fig. 4. Precision values for (i) perfectly fitting logs, and (ii) unfitting logs where 4 events are removed from each trace in the logs

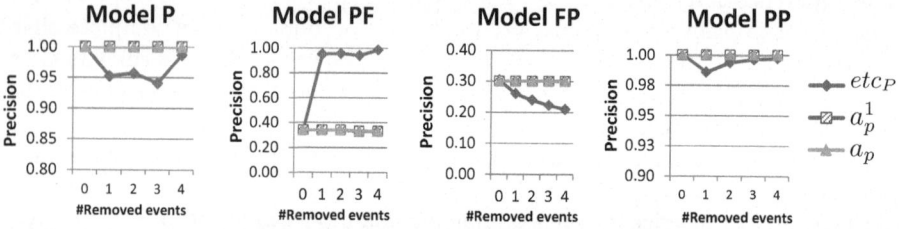

Fig. 5. Robustness of Precision to Unfitting Logs

As shown in Figure 4(i), both a_p and a_p^1 give the same values as etc_P. In cases where logs are perfectly fit to models and activity execution can be mapped unambiguously to tasks in the models, values of both a_p, a_p^1, and etc_P are the same as there is only one optimal alignment per trace.

The second set of experiments were conducted to evaluate the robustness of the proposed metric against non-fitting logs. We took the models and log from the previous experiment and create unfitting logs by removing n number of events randomly per trace from the fitting log. To ensure that the created logs are unfitting, only events that belong to the precise part (i.e. mapped to **P** part) are removed. Figure 4(ii) and Figure 5 show the results.

As it is shown in Figure 4(ii) and Figure 5, our metrics are more robust to noise than etc_P. Even in cases where almost half of the events in all traces are removed, both metrics provide the same value as the ones given for perfectly fitting traces. In contrast, the etc_P value may change significantly because for all non-fitting traces, it ignores the rest of the traces after the first non-fitting event occur. In the experiment with model **PF**, etc_P value changes significantly even when only one event is removed per trace as the remaining events that belong to the imprecise model are ignored. In the experiment with model **FP**, etc_P values gets closer to the precision value of the **F** model as the number of removed events increases, because non fitting events always occur in the precise part of the model (i.e. **P**). Figure 5 also shows that a_p^1 values are good approximation to a_p values because the aggregation of all selected optimal alignments for each trace in the logs cover all traces allowed by the **P** part of all four models.

Table 1. Precision values from experiments on real-life logs and models

Log	#Cases	#Events	Process model		#Not sync. moves/case	a_p^1	time (sec)	a_p	time (sec)	etc_P	a_b'
			#place	#trans.							
MLog1	3181	20491	15	12	5.33	0.92	11.3	1.00	321.1	0.97	0.82
MLog2	1861	15708	16	19	1.45	0.93	3.7	0.93	53.5	0.97	0.92
MLog4	4852	29737	16	27	2.09	0.96	4.1	0.99	15.7	0.86	0.75
Bouw-1	139	3364	33	34	9.46	0.82	0.7	n/a	n/a	0.85	0.95
Bouw-4	109	2331	31	31	6.18	0.44	2.4	n/a	n/a	0.34	n/a

* n/a : not found in 6 hours.

5.2 Real-Life Logs and Models

To evaluate the applicability of the approach to handle real life logs, we use 5 pairs of process models and logs from the CoSeLoG project [3, 11]. The models and logs were obtained from participating municipalities in the Netherlands. We consider processes related to five types of building permission applications. All processes have unlogged tasks, and two of the models allow loops. We have compared the proposed precision measurements with related metrics such as the etc_P metric [7] and the advanced behavioral appropriateness a_b' [9]. The results are shown in Table 1.

An important conclusion that can be drawn from Table 1 is that the computation time of a_p takes much longer than a_p^1. From all evaluated precision metrics, a_p^1 managed to provide precision values for all logs and models under 12 seconds, while a_p calculation takes much longer. Similarity between states optimation technique to find one optimal alignment is not applicable to find all alignments. However, this is not a problem because a_p^1 provides a close estimation to a_p. Table 1 also shows that in reality, the observed traces are not perfectly fitting the corresponding models (see #not synchronous moves/case) and hence justifies the need of having precision measurements that are robust to non-fitting logs. Other than a_p^1, etc_P metric is the only precision metric that could be computed in a timely manner in our set of experiments. However, as shown in subsection 5.1, it is very sensitive to non-fitting traces.

6 Conclusion

In literature, conformance checking has been mainly focusing on fitness, i.e., quantifying the proportion of the event log that is possible according to a given model. However, it is also important to analyze precision. A process model that allows for behavior unrelated to the example behavior seen in the log is too general. Existing approaches for quantifying precision are time consuming and have problems dealing with non-fitting traces. This results in unreliable precision measurements as shown in this paper. Therefore, we developed an approach that first aligns event log and model. The pre-alignment of log and model makes it possible to measure precision more accurately. In this work we presented two metrics (a_p^1 and a_p) to measure the precision, considering just one or all possible optimal alignments respectively. The results show experimentally the usefulness and the robustness of the approach proposed. Since the metrics only measure the precision dimension, they should be used together with other metrics that measure other dimension of conformance to provide a comprehensive evaluation on how "good" is a model, given its executions [9].

Acknowledgments. This work is supported by NWO (proj. 612.063.919), the projects TIN2011-22484 and TIN2007-66523, and by the Spanish Ministerio de Educación (AP2009-4959).

References

1. Adriansyah, A., Sidorova, N., van Dongen, B.F.: Cost-Based Fitness in Conformance Checking. In: International Conference on Application of Concurrency to System Design, pp. 57–66 (2011)
2. Adriansyah, A., van Dongen, B.F., van der Aalst, W.M.P.: Conformance Checking Using Cost-Based Fitness Analysis. In: IEEE International Enterprise Distributed Object Computing Conference, pp. 55–64 (2011)
3. Buijs, J.C.A.M., van Dongen, B.F., van der Aalst, W.M.P.: Towards Cross-Organizational Process Mining in Collections of Process Models and Their Executions. In: Daniel, F., Barkaoui, K., Dustdar, S. (eds.) BPM Workshops 2011, Part II. LNBIP, vol. 100, pp. 2–13. Springer, Heidelberg (2012)
4. Calders, T., Günther, C.W., Pechenizkiy, M., Rozinat, A.: Using Minimum Description Length for Process Mining. In: Proceedings of the 2009 ACM Symposium on Applied Computing, SAC 2009, pp. 1451–1455. ACM, New York (2009)
5. Gerke, K., Cardoso, J., Claus, A.: Measuring the Compliance of Processes with Reference Models. In: Meersman, R., Dillon, T., Herrero, P. (eds.) OTM 2009, Part I. LNCS, vol. 5870, pp. 76–93. Springer, Heidelberg (2009)
6. Muñoz-Gama, J., Carmona, J.: A Fresh Look at Precision in Process Conformance. In: Hull, R., Mendling, J., Tai, S. (eds.) BPM 2010. LNCS, vol. 6336, pp. 211–226. Springer, Heidelberg (2010)
7. Munoz-Gama, J., Carmona, J.: Enhancing precision in process conformance: Stability, confidence and severity. In: IEEE Symposium on Computational Intelligence and Data Mining, CIDM 2011, pp. 184–191. IEEE (April 2011)
8. Rozinat, A., de Jong, I.S.M., Günther, C.W., van der Aalst, W.M.P.: Process Mining Applied to the Test Process of Wafer Steppers in ASML. IEEE Transactions on Systems, Man and Cybernetics - Part C: Applications and Reviews 39, 474–479 (2009)
9. Rozinat, A., van der Aalst, W.M.P.: Conformance Checking of Processes Based on Monitoring Real Behavior. Information Systems 33(1), 64–95 (2008)
10. ter Hofstede, A.H.M., van der Aalst, W.M.P., Adams, M., Russell, N.: Modern Business Process Automation. Springer (2010)
11. van der Aalst, W.M.P.: Business Process Configuration in the Cloud: How to Support and Analyze Multi-Tenant Processes? In: Zavattaro, G., Schreier, U., Pautasso, C. (eds.) Proceedings of the 9th IEEE European Conference on Web Services (ECOWS 2011), pp. 3–10. IEEE Computer Society Press (2011)
12. van der Aalst, W.M.P.: Process Mining: Discovery, Conformance and Enhancement of Business Processes. Springer, Berlin (2011)

13. van der Aalst, W.M.P., Adriansyah, A., van Dongen, B.: Replaying History on Process Models for Conformance Checking and Performance Analysis. Wiley Interdisciplinary Reviews: Data Mining and Knowledge Discovery 2(2), 182–192 (2012)
14. Weidlich, M., Polyvyanyy, A., Desai, N., Mendling, J.: Process Compliance Measurement Based on Behavioural Profiles. In: Pernici, B. (ed.) CAiSE 2010. LNCS, vol. 6051, pp. 499–514. Springer, Heidelberg (2010)

A Hierarchical Markov Model to Understand the Behaviour of Agents in Business Processes

Diogo R. Ferreira[1], Fernando Szimanski[2], and Célia Ghedini Ralha[2]

[1] IST – Technical University of Lisbon, Portugal
diogo.ferreira@ist.utl.pt
[2] Universidade de Brasília (UnB), Brazil
fszimanski@gmail.com, ghedini@cic.unb.br

Abstract. Process mining techniques are able to discover process models from event logs but there is a gap between the low-level nature of events and the high-level abstraction of business activities. In this work we present a hierarchical Markov model together with mining techniques to discover the relationship between low-level events and a high-level description of the business process. This can be used to understand how agents perform activities at run-time. In a case study experiment using an agent-based simulation platform (AOR), we show how the proposed approach is able to discover the behaviour of agents in each activity of a business process for which a high-level model is known.

Keywords: Process Mining, Agent-Based Simulation, Markov Models, Expectation-Maximization, Agent-Object-Relationship (AOR).

1 Introduction

If one would try to understand a business process by observing people at work in an organization, the apparently chaotic nature of events would be quite confusing. However, if a high-level description of the business process is provided (for example, one that partitions the process into two or three main stages) then it becomes much easier to understand the sequence of events.

Using process mining techniques [1], it is possible to analyse the low-level events that are recorded in information systems as people carry out their work. However, there is often a gap between the granularity of the recorded low-level events and the high level of abstraction at which processes are understood, documented and communicated throughout an organisation. Process mining techniques are able to capture and analyse behaviour at the level of the recorded events, whereas business analysts describe the process in terms of high-level activities, where each activity may correspond to several low-level events.

Some techniques have already been proposed to address this gap by producing more abstract models from an event log. Basically, existing approaches can be divided into two main groups:

(a) Those techniques that work on the basis of models, by producing a mined model from the event log and then trying to create more abstract representations of that model. Examples are [2] and [3].

M. La Rosa and P. Soffer (Eds.): BPM 2012 Workshops, LNBIP 132, pp. 150–161, 2013.

(b) Those techniques that work on the basis of events, by translating the event log into a more abstract sequence of events, and then producing a mined model from that translated event log. Examples are [4] and [5].

In this work, we consider that the event log is produced by a number of agents who collaborate when performing the activities in a business process. Here, an agent is understood in the sense of intelligent agent [6], and it is used to represent a human actor in agent-based simulations. Each activity may involve several agents, and every time an agent performs some action, a new event is recorded. Therefore, each activity in the process may be the origin of several events in the event log. The way in which agents collaborate is assumed to be non-deterministic, and process execution is assumed to be non-deterministic as well. While the business process is described in terms of high-level activities that are familiar to business users, the collaboration of agents at run-time is recorded in the event log as a sequence of low-level events.

In general, both the macro-level description of the business process and the micro-level sequence of events can be obtained: the first is provided by business analysts or process documentation, and the second can be found in event logs. However, the way in which micro-level events can be mapped to macro-level activities is unknown, and this is precisely what we want to find out. Given a micro-level event log and a macro-level model of the business process, our goal is to discover: (1) a micro-level model for the behaviour of agents and also (2) how this micro-level model fits into the macro-level description of the business process. For this purpose, we develop a hierarchical Markov model that is able to capture the macro-behaviour of the business process, the micro-behaviour of agents as they work in each activity, and the relationship between the two.

2   An Example

Consider a business process that can be described on a high level as comprising the three main activities A, B, and C. Also, consider that three agents X, Y and Z collaborate in order to perform each activity. In particular, activity A leads to a sequence of actions by the three agents that can be represented by the sequence of events XYZ. In a similar way, activity B leads to a sequence of events in the form YZZ(Z)..., where there may be multiple actions of agent Z until a certain condition holds. Finally, activity C leads to a sequence of events in the form ZXY. This process is represented in Figure 1.

Executing this simple process corresponds to performing the sequence of activities ABC. However, in the event log we find traces such as XYZYZZZXY without having any idea of how this sequence of events can be mapped to the sequence of activities ABC. The sequence ABC will be called the *macro-sequence* and the high-level model for the business process is referred to as the *macro-model*. On the other hand, the sequence of events XYZYZZZXY will be called the *micro-sequence* and the behaviour of agents during each high-level activity is referred to as a *micro-model*. The problem addressed in this work is *how to discover*

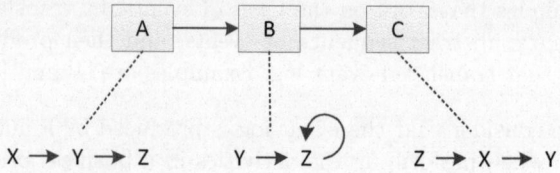

Fig. 1. A simple example of a hierarchical process model

the macro-sequence and the micro-models from a given macro-model and micro-sequence, where these models (both macro and micro) are represented as Markov chains.

3 Definitions

Let $\mathbf{S}$ be the set of possible states in a Markov chain, and let i and j be any two such states. Then $\mathbb{P}(j \mid i)$ is the transition probability from the current state i to a subsequent state j. In this work, as in [7], we extend the set $\mathbf{S}$ with two special states – a start state ($\circ$) and an end state ($\bullet$) – in order to include the probability of the Markov chain starting and ending in certain states. We represent this augmented set of states as $\overline{\mathbf{S}} = \mathbf{S} \cup \{\circ, \bullet\}$. For example, $\mathbb{P}(i \mid \circ)$ is the probability of the Markov chain starting in state i. Similarly, $\mathbb{P}(\bullet \mid i)$ is the probability of the Markov chain ending in state i.

By definition, $\mathbb{P}(\circ \mid i) \triangleq 0, \forall_{i \in \overline{\mathbf{S}}}$ since nothing can come before the start state. In the same way, $\mathbb{P}(i \mid \bullet) \triangleq 0, \forall_{i \in \overline{\mathbf{S}}}$ since nothing can come after the end state. Also, $\mathbb{P}(\bullet \mid \circ) \triangleq 0$ since the Markov chain cannot start and end immediately without going through an observable state.

A Markov chain is represented by a matrix $\mathbf{T} = \{p_{ij}\}$ of transition probabilities, where $p_{ij} = \mathbb{P}(j \mid i), \forall_{i,j \in \overline{\mathbf{S}}}$. More formally, a Markov chain $\mathcal{M} = \langle \overline{\mathbf{S}}, \mathbf{T} \rangle$ is defined as a tuple where $\overline{\mathbf{S}}$ is the augmented set of states and $\mathbf{T}$ is the transition matrix between those states. The nature of the Markov chain is such that $\sum_{j \in \overline{\mathbf{S}}} \mathbb{P}(j \mid i) = 1$ for all states $i \in \overline{\mathbf{S}} \setminus \{\bullet\}$. In other words, there is always some subsequent state to the current state i, except when the end state has been reached; in this case, we have $\sum_{j \in \overline{\mathbf{S}}} \mathbb{P}(j \mid \bullet) = 0$.

The fact that $\forall_{j \in \overline{\mathbf{S}}} : \mathbb{P}(j \mid \bullet) = 0$ means that the last row in matrix $\mathbf{T}$ is zero. Also, the fact that $\forall_{i \in \overline{\mathbf{S}}} : \mathbb{P}(\circ \mid i) = 0$ means that the first column in matrix $\mathbf{T}$ is zero. Finally, the fact that $\mathbb{P}(\bullet \mid \circ) = 0$ means that the last element in the first row of the matrix is zero. These facts are illustrated in Figure 2.

In a hierarchical Markov model, there is a Markov chain to describe the macro-model (upper level in Figure 1), and there is a set of Markov chains to describe the micro-model for each activity (lower level in Figure 1).

The macro-model is defined as a Markov chain $\mathcal{M}' = \langle \overline{\mathbf{S}'}, \mathbf{T}' \rangle$ where $\mathbf{S}'$ is the set of states that represent the activities in the high-level description of the business process. On the other hand, the micro-model is defined as a set of

$$\mathbf{T} = \begin{array}{c|cccccc} & \circ & 1 & 2 & \ldots & n & \bullet \\ \hline \circ & 0 & p_{01} & p_{02} & \ldots & p_{0n} & 0 \\ 1 & 0 & p_{11} & p_{12} & \ldots & p_{1n} & p_{1(n+1)} \\ 2 & 0 & p_{21} & p_{22} & \ldots & p_{2n} & p_{2(n+1)} \\ \ldots & \ldots & \ldots & \ldots & \ldots & \ldots & \ldots \\ n & 0 & p_{n1} & p_{n2} & \ldots & p_{nn} & p_{n(n+1)} \\ \bullet & 0 & 0 & 0 & \ldots & 0 & 0 \end{array} \qquad \begin{array}{l} (\sum_j p_{0j} = 1) \\ (\sum_j p_{1j} = 1) \\ (\sum_j p_{2j} = 1) \\ \ldots \\ (\sum_j p_{nj} = 1) \\ (\sum_j p_{(n+1)j} = 0) \end{array}$$

Fig. 2. General form of a transition matrix

$$\mathcal{M}' = \langle \overline{\mathbf{S}'}, \mathbf{T}' \rangle \qquad \overline{\mathbf{S}'} = \{\circ, A, B, C, \bullet\} \qquad \mathbf{T}' = \begin{array}{c|ccccc} & \circ & A & B & C & \bullet \\ \hline \circ & 0 & 1 & 0 & 0 & 0 \\ A & 0 & 0 & 1 & 0 & 0 \\ B & 0 & 0 & 0 & 1 & 0 \\ C & 0 & 0 & 0 & 0 & 1 \\ \bullet & 0 & 0 & 0 & 0 & 0 \end{array}$$

$$\mathcal{M}''_A = \langle \overline{\mathbf{S}''_A}, \mathbf{T}''_A \rangle \qquad \mathcal{M}''_B = \langle \overline{\mathbf{S}''_B}, \mathbf{T}''_B \rangle \qquad \mathcal{M}''_C = \langle \overline{\mathbf{S}''_C}, \mathbf{T}''_C \rangle$$

$$\overline{\mathbf{S}''_A} = \{\circ, X, Y, Z, \bullet\} \qquad \overline{\mathbf{S}''_B} = \{\circ, Y, Z, \bullet\} \qquad \overline{\mathbf{S}''_C} = \{\circ, X, Y, Z, \bullet\}$$

$$\mathbf{T}''_A = \begin{array}{c|ccccc} & \circ & X & Y & Z & \bullet \\ \hline \circ & 0 & 1 & 0 & 0 & 0 \\ X & 0 & 0 & 1 & 0 & 0 \\ Y & 0 & 0 & 0 & 1 & 0 \\ Z & 0 & 0 & 0 & 0 & 1 \\ \bullet & 0 & 0 & 0 & 0 & 0 \end{array} \qquad \mathbf{T}''_B = \begin{array}{c|cccc} & \circ & Y & Z & \bullet \\ \hline \circ & 0 & 1 & 0 & 0 \\ Y & 0 & 0 & 1 & 0 \\ Z & 0 & 0 & .5 & .5 \\ \bullet & 0 & 0 & 0 & 0 \end{array} \qquad \mathbf{T}''_C = \begin{array}{c|ccccc} & \circ & X & Y & Z & \bullet \\ \hline \circ & 0 & 0 & 0 & 1 & 0 \\ X & 0 & 0 & 1 & 0 & 0 \\ Y & 0 & 0 & 0 & 0 & 1 \\ Z & 0 & 1 & 0 & 0 & 0 \\ \bullet & 0 & 0 & 0 & 0 & 0 \end{array}$$

Fig. 3. An example of a hierarchical Markov model

Markov chains $\{\mathcal{M}''_i : i \in \mathbf{S}'\}$ where $\mathcal{M}''_i = \langle \overline{\mathbf{S}''_i}, \mathbf{T}''_i \rangle$ is a Markov chain that describes the behaviour of agents when performing activity $i \in \mathbf{S}'$.

For the example in Figure 1, one possible model is shown in Figure 3. In $\mathbf{T}''_B$ it is assumed that the probability of going from state Z to the same state Z is equal to the probability of terminating the Markov chain in that state. The execution semantics for a hierarchical Markov model can be described as follows:

(a) Run the macro-model $\mathcal{M}' = \langle \overline{\mathbf{S}'}, \mathbf{T}' \rangle$ as Markov chain, beginning with the start state ($\circ$) and generating a number of transitions according to the transition probabilities in $\mathbf{T}'$, until the end state ($\bullet$) is reached.

(b) For each macro-state i that the macro-model $\mathcal{M}'$ goes into, run the corresponding micro-model $\mathcal{M}''_i$ as a Markov chain, again beginning with the start state ($\circ$) and generating a number of transitions according to the transition probabilities in $\mathbf{T}''_i$, until the end state ($\bullet$) is reached.

(c) The *micro-sequence* $\mathbf{s}''$ is obtained by concatenating every state observed at the micro-level. The *macro-sequence* $\mathbf{s}'$ is the sequence of states that the macro-model was in at the time when each micro-state was observed. In the previous example, we had $s'' = $ XYZYZZZXY and $s' = $ AAABBBCCC.

Our goal is to find the macro-sequence s' and the micro-model $\mathcal{M}_i''$ for every state $i \in S'$. For this purpose, only the micro-sequence s'' and the macro-model $\mathcal{M}'$ are known. Note that, without knowing s' nor $\{\mathcal{M}_i''\}$ to start with, there is no idea about how an observed micro-sequence such as $s'' = $ XYZYZZZXY can be partitioned into a set of activities. An algorithm to find an estimate for both s' and $\{\mathcal{M}_i''\}$ is developed in the next section.

4   Algorithms

The problem above is equivalent to that of finding the unknown parameters $\{\mathcal{M}_i''\}$ for a model that produces both observed data (s'') and unobserved data (s'). Such type of problem fits well into the framework of Expectation-Maximization [8,9]. If the missing data s' were known, then it would be possible to calculate $\{\mathcal{M}_i''\}$ directly from s' and s''. On the other hand, if the model parameters $\{\mathcal{M}_i''\}$ were known, then it would be possible to determine the missing data s'. What makes the problem especially difficult is the fact that both $\{\mathcal{M}_i''\}$ and s' are unavailable.

For this kind of problem, it is possible to devise an Expectation-Maximization procedure along the following lines:

(a) Obtain, by some means, an initial estimate for the missing data.
(b) With the current estimate for the missing data, obtain an improved estimated for the unknown model parameters.
(c) With the current estimate for the model parameters, obtain an improved estimate for the missing data.
(d) Repeat the sequence of steps (b) and (c) above until the missing data and the model parameters converge.

Algorithm 1 describes an adaptation of the above procedure to solve our problem. We start by randomizing the macro-sequence s' (step 1) and then use this sequence to obtain an estimate for the micro-models $\{\mathcal{M}_i''\}$ (step 2). After that, we use the current estimate of $\{\mathcal{M}_i''\}$ to obtain a better estimate for s' (step 3), and then use this s' to obtain a better estimate for $\{\mathcal{M}_i''\}$ (step 2), and so on, until both estimates converge. The problem now is how to perform steps 2 and 3 in Algorithm 1. A solution to these sub-problems is described in Sections 4.1 and 4.2, respectively.

4.1   Finding $\{\mathcal{M}_i''\}$ When s' Is Known

In this section we suppose that the macro-sequence s' is known, for example $s' = $ AAABBBCCC. Then, what is left to find out is $\mathcal{M}_i''$ for all states $i \in S'$. This is described in Algorithm 2. Basically, one considers the transitions that occur in the micro-sequence s'' within each state in macro-sequence s'. For $s'' = $ XYZYZZZXY

Algorithm 1. Estimate the micro-models $\{\mathcal{M}_i''\}$ and the macro-sequence $\mathbf{s}'$ from the macro-model $\mathcal{M}'$ and the micro-sequence $\mathbf{s}''$

---

1. Draw a random sequence $\tilde{\mathbf{s}}$ from the Markov chain $\mathcal{M}'$ and use this sequence as the basis to build a macro-sequence $\mathbf{s}'$ with the same length as $\mathbf{s}''$ (for example, if $\tilde{\mathbf{s}} =$ ABC and $\mathbf{s}'' =$ XYZYZZZXY then $\mathbf{s}' =$ AAABBBCCC)
2. From the micro-sequence $\mathbf{s}''$, the macro-model $\mathcal{M}'$ and the current estimate for $\mathbf{s}'$ find an estimate for $\{\mathcal{M}_i''\}$ (see Algorithm 2 in Section 4.1)
3. From the micro-sequence $\mathbf{s}''$, the macro-model $\mathcal{M}'$ and the current estimate for $\{\mathcal{M}_i''\}$ find an estimate for $\mathbf{s}'$ (see Algorithm 3 in Section 4.2)
4. Go back to step 2 and repeat until the estimates for $\mathbf{s}'$ and $\{\mathcal{M}_i''\}$ converge.

---

and $\mathbf{s}' =$ AAABBBCCC, the substring for state A is ∘XYZ•, the substring for state B is ∘YZZ•, and the substring for state C is ∘ZXY•. (Note that if state A would appear again in $\mathbf{s}'$ then a second substring would be associated with A, and similarly for other states.) From the set of substrings associated with each state i (step 1), one counts the number of transitions (step 2b) and, after normalization (step 2c), the result yields $\mathcal{M}_i''$.

4.2 Finding $\mathbf{s}'$ When $\{\mathcal{M}_i''\}$ Are Known

In this section, we suppose that the micro-model $\mathcal{M}_i''$ for each state $i \in \mathbf{S}'$ is available, but the macro-sequence $\mathbf{s}'$ is unknown, so we want to determine $\mathbf{s}'$ from $\mathbf{s}''$, $\{\mathcal{M}_i''\}$ and $\mathcal{M}'$. Note that the macro-sequence $\mathbf{s}'$ is produced by the macro-model $\mathcal{M}'$, which is a Markov chain, so there may be several possibilities for $\mathbf{s}'$. In general, we will be interested in finding the most likely solution for $\mathbf{s}'$.

The most likely $\mathbf{s}'$ is given by the sequence of macro-states that is able to produce $\mathbf{s}''$ with highest probability. In the example above, we had $\mathbf{s}'' =$ XYZYZZZXY. We know that $\mathbf{s}''$ begins with X and therefore the macro-sequence $\mathbf{s}'$ must be initiated by a macro-state whose micro-model can begin with X. As it happens, there is a single such macro-state in Figure 3, and it is A. So now that we have begun with A, we try to parse the following symbols in $\mathbf{s}''$ with the micro-model $\mathcal{M}_A''$. We find that this micro-model can account for the substring XYZ, after which it ends, so a new macro-state must be chosen to account for the second Y in $\mathbf{s}''$.

In Figure 3, the only micro-model that begins with Y is $\mathcal{M}_B''$. Therefore, the second macro-state is B. We now use $\mathcal{M}_B''$ to parse the following symbols of $\mathbf{s}''$, taking us all the way through YZZZ, when $\mathcal{M}_B''$ cannot parse the following X. A third macro-state is needed to parse the final XY but no suitable solution can be found, because the micro-model $\mathcal{M}_A''$ begins with X but does not end in Y. The problem is that the parsing of micro-model $\mathcal{M}_B''$ went too far. It should have stopped on YZZ and let the final ZXY be parsed by micro-model $\mathcal{M}_C''$. In this case we would have $\mathbf{s}' =$ AAABBBCCC.

This simple example is enough to realize that there may be the need to backtrack and there may be several possible solutions for $\mathbf{s}'$. With both $\mathbf{s}'$ and $\mathbf{s}''$,

Algorithm 2. Estimate the micro-models $\{\mathcal{M}_i''\}$ from the micro-sequence $\mathbf{s}''$ and the macro-sequence $\mathbf{s}'$

1. Separate the micro-sequence $\mathbf{s}''$ into a set of substrings corresponding to the different macro-states in $\mathbf{s}'$. Let $\mathbf{s}''[n_1 : n_2]$ denote a substring of $\mathbf{s}''$ from position n_1 to position n_2. Then, for $\mathbf{s}'$ in the form,

$$\mathbf{s}' = \underbrace{aa...a}_{n_a}\underbrace{bb...b}_{n_b}...\underbrace{cc...c}_{n_c}$$

   pick the first n_a elements in the micro-sequence $\mathbf{s}''$ and create a substring $(\mathbf{s}''[1: n_a])$ associated with state a, pick the following n_b elements of $\mathbf{s}''$ and create a substring $(\mathbf{s}''[n_a+1: n_a+n_b])$ associated with state b, and so on. Each substring should include the start ($\circ$) and end ($\bullet$) states. In the next step, $subs(i)$ is used to denote the set of substrings associated with state i.

2. For each distinct state i found in $\mathbf{s}'$, do the following:
   (a) Initialize the corresponding micro-model $\mathcal{M}_i'' = (\overline{\mathbf{S}}_i'', \mathbf{T}_i'')$ where $\overline{\mathbf{S}}_i''$ is the set of distinct states found in the substrings of $subs(i)$ and $\mathbf{T}_i''$ is a transition matrix initialized with zeros.
   (b) For every consecutive pair of micro-states $\mathbf{s}''[k: k+1]$ in each substring in $subs(i)$, count the transition from micro-state $\mathbf{s}''[k]$ to micro-state $\mathbf{s}''[k+1]$ by incrementing the corresponding position in matrix $\mathbf{T}_i''$. Such counting includes the start ($\circ$) and end ($\bullet$) states as well.
   (c) Normalize each row of the transition matrix $\mathbf{T}_i''$ such that the sum of values in each row is equal to 1.0, except for the last row which represents the end state and therefore its sum should be zero as in Figure 2.

---

together with $\mathcal{M}'$ and $\{\mathcal{M}_i''\}$, it is possible to calculate the probability of observing a particular micro-sequence $\mathbf{s}''$. This is the product of all transition probabilities in the macro- and micro-models. Let $\mathbf{T}(i,j)$ denote the transition probability from state i to state j in a transition matrix $\mathbf{T}$. Then, in the example above, we have:

$s'[1] = \mathsf{A}$	$s''[1] = \mathsf{X}$	$\mathbf{T}'(\circ, \mathsf{A}) \times \mathbf{T}_\mathsf{A}''(\circ, \mathsf{X})$	$= 1.0 \times 1.0$
$s'[2] = \mathsf{A}$	$s''[2] = \mathsf{Y}$	$\mathbf{T}_\mathsf{A}''(\mathsf{X}, \mathsf{Y})$	$= 1.0$
$s'[3] = \mathsf{A}$	$s''[3] = \mathsf{Z}$	$\mathbf{T}_\mathsf{A}''(\mathsf{Y}, \mathsf{Z})$	$= 1.0$
$s'[4] = \mathsf{B}$	$s''[4] = \mathsf{Y}$	$\mathbf{T}_\mathsf{A}''(\mathsf{Z}, \bullet) \times \mathbf{T}'(\mathsf{A}, \mathsf{B}) \times \mathbf{T}_\mathsf{B}''(\circ, \mathsf{Y})$	$= 1.0 \times 1.0 \times 1.0$
$s'[5] = \mathsf{B}$	$s''[5] = \mathsf{Z}$	$\mathbf{T}_\mathsf{B}''(\mathsf{Y}, \mathsf{Z})$	$= 1.0$
$s'[6] = \mathsf{B}$	$s''[6] = \mathsf{Z}$	$\mathbf{T}_\mathsf{B}''(\mathsf{Z}, \mathsf{Z})$	$= 0.5$
$s'[7] = \mathsf{C}$	$s''[7] = \mathsf{Z}$	$\mathbf{T}_\mathsf{B}''(\mathsf{Z}, \bullet) \times \mathbf{T}'(\mathsf{B}, \mathsf{C}) \times \mathbf{T}_\mathsf{C}''(\circ, \mathsf{Z})$	$= 0.5 \times 1.0 \times 1.0$
$s'[8] = \mathsf{C}$	$s''[8] = \mathsf{X}$	$\mathbf{T}_\mathsf{C}''(\mathsf{Z}, \mathsf{X})$	$= 1.0$
$s'[9] = \mathsf{C}$	$s''[9] = \mathsf{Y}$	$\mathbf{T}_\mathsf{C}''(\mathsf{X}, \mathsf{Y}) \times \mathbf{T}_\mathsf{C}''(\mathsf{Y}, \bullet) \times \mathbf{T}'(\mathsf{C}, \bullet)$	$= 1.0 \times 1.0 \times 1.0$

The product of all these probabilities is $p = 0.25$. For computational reasons, we use the log probability $log(p)$ instead. In general, we choose the solution for $\mathbf{s}'$ which yields the highest value for the log probability. The procedure is described in Algorithm 3. In particular, step 2 in Algorithm 3 is a recursive function that explores all possibilities for $\mathbf{s}'$ with non-zero probability. Such recursive

Algorithm 3. Determine the most likely macro-sequence $\mathbf{s}'$ for a given micro-sequence $\mathbf{s}''$ when both $\mathcal{M}'$ and $\{\mathcal{M}_i''\}$ are known

1. Let $\mathbf{s}''[k]$ be the micro-state at position k in the micro-sequence $\mathbf{s}''$ and let $\mathbf{s}'[k]$ be the corresponding macro-state which is to be determined. Both sequences start at $k = 1$ and end at $k = n$. Run step 2 recursively, starting from $k = 1$.
2. Consider the following possibilities for $\mathbf{s}'[k]$:
   (a) If $k = 1$ then $\mathbf{s}'[k]$ can be any macro-state i such that $\mathbf{T}'(\circ, i) > 0$ and $\mathbf{T}_i''(\circ, \mathbf{s}''[k]) > 0$. For every such macro-state i, set $\mathbf{s}'[k] := i$ and run step 2 for $k := k+1$.
   (b) If $1 < k \leq n$ then consider the following cases:
      i. if both $\mathbf{s}''[k-1]$ and $\mathbf{s}''[k]$ come from the same micro-model $\mathcal{M}_i''$ then $\mathbf{s}'[k-1] = \mathbf{s}'[k] = i$. Consider this case only if $\mathbf{T}_i''(\mathbf{s}''[k-1], \mathbf{s}''[k]) > 0$. If so, set $\mathbf{s}'[k] := i$ and run step 2 for $k := k+1$.
      ii. if $\mathbf{s}''[k-1]$ comes from $\mathcal{M}_i''$ and $\mathbf{s}''[k]$ comes from $\mathcal{M}_j''$ (with $i \neq j$) then $\mathbf{s}'[k-1] = i$ and $\mathbf{s}'[k] = j$. Consider every possible macro-state j for which $\mathbf{T}_i''(\mathbf{s}''[k-1], \bullet) \times \mathbf{T}'(i, j) \times \mathbf{T}_j''(\circ, \mathbf{s}''[k]) > 0$. For every such macro-state j, set $\mathbf{s}'[k] := j$ and run step 2 for $k := k+1$.
   (c) If $k = n$ then we have reached the end of $\mathbf{s}''$ and now have a complete candidate for $\mathbf{s}'$. Accept this candidate only if it terminates correctly, i.e. only if $\mathbf{T}_i''(\mathbf{s}''[n], \bullet) \times \mathbf{T}'(i, \bullet) > 0$ where $i = \mathbf{s}'[n]$.
3. From all candidates for $\mathbf{s}'$ collected in step 2, return the candidate which provides the highest log probability for $\mathbf{s}''$.

exploration has the form of a tree, since the possibilities for $\mathbf{s}'[k+1]$ are built upon the possibilities for $\mathbf{s}'[k]$. The complete path from root $(k = 1)$ to every leaf $(k = n)$ represents a different candidate for $\mathbf{s}'$. In step 3, the algorithm returns the candidate with highest log probability, where this log probability is the sum of the log probabilities along the path in the tree.

5 Case Study

Agent-based simulation [10,11] is an effective means to study the behaviour of systems involving the actions and interactions of autonomous agents. Although there are several platforms for agent-based simulation [12], here we turn our attention to the Agent-Object-Relationship approach (AOR) introduced by [13] and which can be used to model and simulate business processes [14].

The AOR system is a simulation platform where agents respond to events in their environment by executing actions and interacting with each other, which in turn generates new events. There are basically two different kinds of events. An *exogenous* event is an external event (such as the arrival of a new customer) which does not depend on the actions of agents. Usually, the occurrence of an exogenous event is what triggers a simulation run. To run multiple instances of a business process, the AOR system schedules the occurrence of exogenous events to trigger the whole process at different points in time.

The second kind of event is a *message* and it is the basis of simulation in the AOR system. Agents send messages to one another, which in turn generates new messages. For example, if agent X sends a message M1 to agent Y, then this may result in a new message M2 being sent from Y to Z. Such chaining of messages keeps the simulation running until there are no more messages to be exchanged. At that point, a new exogenous event is required to trigger a new simulation run. In this work, we represent the exchange of a message M being sent from agent X to agent Y as: X $\xrightarrow{\text{M}}$ Y.

Our case study is based on the implementation of a purchasing scenario in the AOR system. On a high (macro) level, the process can be represented as in Figure 4 and can be described as follows. In a company, an employee needs a certain commodity (e.g. a printer cartridge). If the product is available at the warehouse, then the warehouse dispatches the product to the employee. Otherwise, the product must be purchased from an external supplier. All purchases must be previously approved by the purchasing department. If the purchase is not approved, the process ends immediately. If the purchase is approved, the process proceeds with the purchasing department ordering and paying for the product from the supplier. The supplier delivers the product to the warehouse, and the warehouse dispatches the product to the employee.

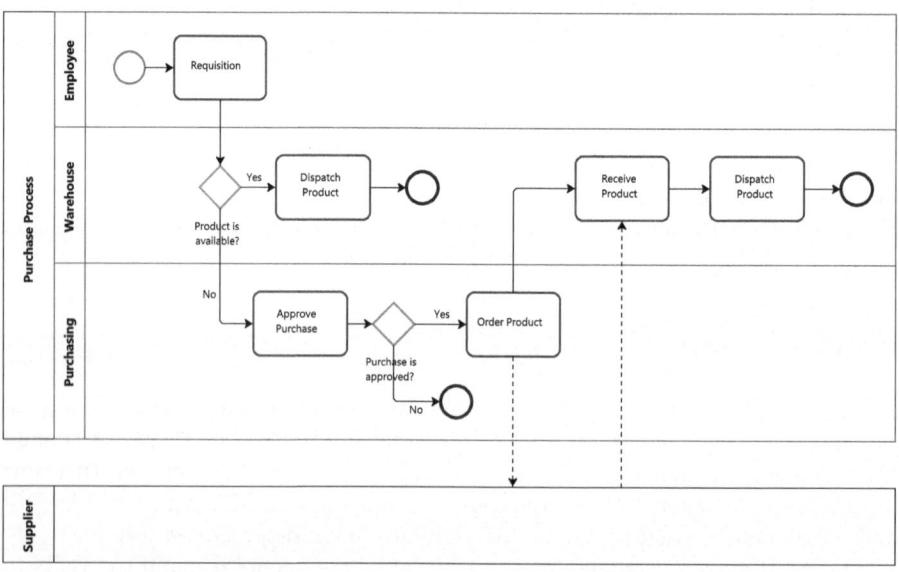

Fig. 4. Macro-level description of a purchase process

This process was implemented in the AOR system using the AOR Simulation Language (AORSL) [15] to specify the message exchanges between agents. There are four types of agent: Employee, Warehouse, Purchasing, and Supplier. There is one instance of the Warehouse agent and one instance of the Purchasing agent. However, there are multiple instances of the Employee agent (each instance exists during a simulation run; it is created at the start of the run and destroyed when the run finishes). We could have done the same for the Supplier agent, but for simplicity we considered only one instance of Supplier.

The process includes the following message exchanges:

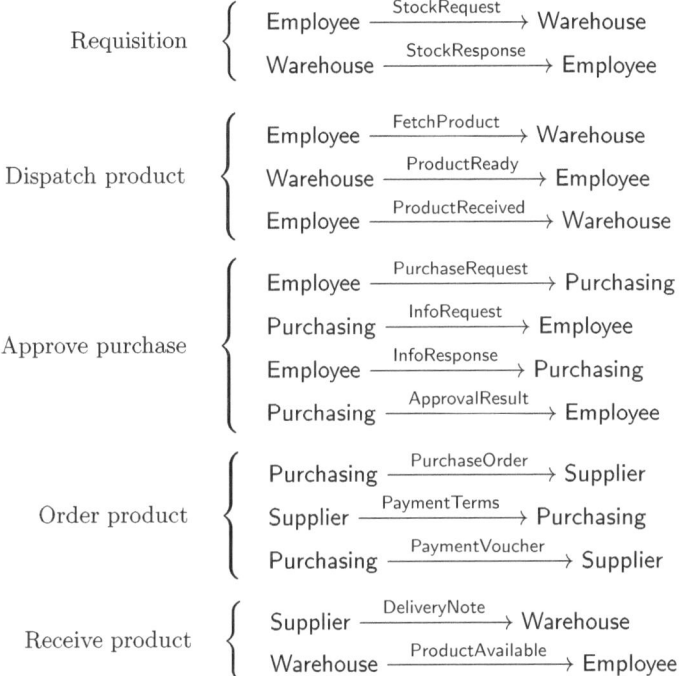

It should be noted that the AOR system has no knowledge about the macro-level activities on the left-hand side. Instead, the agents have rules to implement the message exchanges on the right-hand side. In addition, we suppose that:

- For the purchase request to be approved, the purchasing department may enquire the employee an arbitrary number of times to obtain further info about the purchase request. This means that the exchanges InfoRequest and InfoResponse may occur multiple times (or even not occur at all).
- The purchasing department may not be satisfied with the payment terms requested by a particular supplier, and may choose to negotiate those terms or get in contact with another supplier. This means that PurchaseOrder and PaymentTerms may occur multiple times (but they must occur at least once).

Simulating this process in AOR produces an event log with an AOR-specific XML structure. From this event log, it is possible to recognize each new instance of the Employee agent as a different instance of the process. Therefore, we collected the sequence of events for each Employee agent; these represent our traces, i.e. the micro-sequences. The process in Figure 4 represents the macro-model, and it was converted to a Markov chain representation. Feeding the micro-sequences

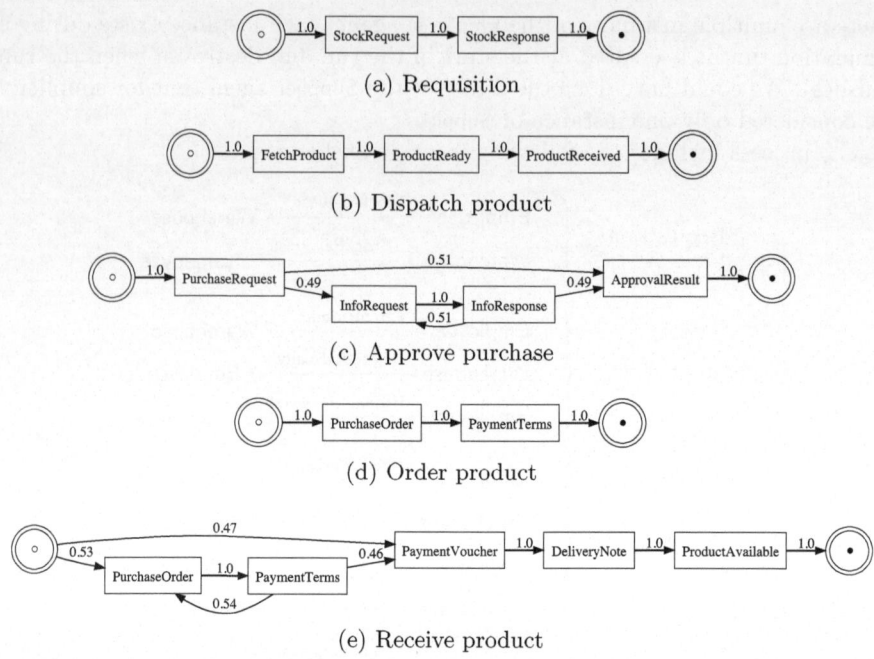

(a) Requisition

(b) Dispatch product

(c) Approve purchase

(d) Order product

(e) Receive product

Fig. 5. Results obtained for an AOR simulation with 10.000 simulation steps

and the macro-model to Algorithm 1, we obtained the micro-models shown in Figure 5, in graphical form.

The results in Figure 5 represent the correct behaviour, except for the fact that PurchaseOrder, PaymentTerms and, PaymentVoucher also appear in the "Receive product" activity rather than only in the "Order product" activity. Since these two activities always occur together and sequentially in the model of Figure 4, there is no way to determine that those events belong to the first activity and not to the second. In the random initialization step in Algorithm 1, some of these events are attributed to "Order product" and others are attributed to "Receive product". Also, when the loop between PurchaseOrder and PaymentTerms repeats, the micro-sequence is longer and therefore it becomes more likely that some of these events are captured by "Receive product".

6   Conclusion

In this work we have described a hierarchical Markov model and an Expectation-Maximization procedure to discover the relationship between the micro-level events recorded in an event log and the macro-level activities in a business process model. We have shown that the proposed approach is able to perform a correct discovery, at least in an experimental setting where we used an agent simulation platform. Except for a couple of events, the algorithm was able to associate the micro-events with the correct macro-activity, while also providing a micro-model for the behaviour of agents in each of those activities. In future work, we will be looking into the problems that arise when applying the approach to real-world event logs with noise. The approach can be applied in scenarios where a macro-level description of the business process is available.

References

1. van der Aalst, W.M.P.: Process Mining: Discovery, Conformance and Enhancement of Business Processes. Springer (2011)
2. Greco, G., Guzzo, A., Pontieri, L.: Mining Hierarchies of Models: From Abstract Views to Concrete Specifications. In: van der Aalst, W.M.P., Benatallah, B., Casati, F., Curbera, F. (eds.) BPM 2005. LNCS, vol. 3649, pp. 32–47. Springer, Heidelberg (2005)
3. Günther, C.W., van der Aalst, W.M.P.: Fuzzy Mining – Adaptive Process Simplification Based on Multi-perspective Metrics. In: Alonso, G., Dadam, P., Rosemann, M. (eds.) BPM 2007. LNCS, vol. 4714, pp. 328–343. Springer, Heidelberg (2007)
4. Günther, C.W., Rozinat, A., van der Aalst, W.M.P.: Activity Mining by Global Trace Segmentation. In: Rinderle-Ma, S., Sadiq, S., Leymann, F. (eds.) BPM 2009. LNBIP, vol. 43, pp. 128–139. Springer, Heidelberg (2010)
5. Bose, R.P.J.C., Verbeek, E.H.M.W., van der Aalst, W.M.P.: Discovering Hierarchical Process Models Using ProM. In: Nurcan, S. (ed.) CAiSE Forum 2011. LNBIP, vol. 107, pp. 33–48. Springer, Heidelberg (2012)
6. Wooldridge, M., Jennings, N.R.: Intelligent agents: Theory and practice. Knowledge Engineering Review 10(2), 115–152 (1995)
7. Veiga, G.M., Ferreira, D.R.: Understanding Spaghetti Models with Sequence Clustering for ProM. In: Rinderle-Ma, S., Sadiq, S., Leymann, F. (eds.) BPM 2009 Workshops. LNBIP, vol. 43, pp. 92–103. Springer, Heidelberg (2010)
8. Dempster, A.P., Laird, N.M., Rubin, D.B.: Maximum likelihood from incomplete data via the EM algorithm. Journal of the Royal Statistical Society 39(1), 1–38 (1977)
9. McLachlan, G.J., Krishnan, T.: The EM Algorithm and Extensions. Wiley Series in Probability and Statistics. Wiley-Interscience (2008)
10. Bonabeau, E.: Agent-based modeling: Methods and techniques for simulating human systems. PNAS 99(suppl. 3), 7280–7287 (2002)
11. Davidsson, P., Holmgren, J., Kyhlbäck, H., Mengistu, D., Persson, M.: Applications of Agent Based Simulation. In: Antunes, L., Takadama, K. (eds.) MABS 2006. LNCS (LNAI), vol. 4442, pp. 15–27. Springer, Heidelberg (2007)
12. Railsback, S.F., Lytinen, S.L., Jackson, S.K.: Agent-based simulation platforms: Review and development recommendations. Simulation 82(9), 609–623 (2006)
13. Wagner, G.: AOR Modelling and Simulation: Towards a General Architecture for Agent-Based Discrete Event Simulation. In: Giorgini, P., Henderson-Sellers, B., Winikoff, M. (eds.) AOIS 2003. LNCS (LNAI), vol. 3030, pp. 174–188. Springer, Heidelberg (2004)
14. Wagner, G., Nicolae, O., Werner, J.: Extending discrete event simulation by adding an activity concept for business process modeling and simulation. In: Proceedings of the 2009 Winter Simulation Conference, pp. 2951–2962 (2009)
15. Nicolae, O., Wagner, G., Werner, J.: Towards an Executable Semantics for Activities Using Discrete Event Simulation. In: Rinderle-Ma, S., Sadiq, S., Leymann, F. (eds.) BPM 2009 Workshops. LNBIP, vol. 43, pp. 369–380. Springer, Heidelberg (2010)

End-to-End Process Extraction in Process Unaware Systems

Sukriti Goel[1], Jyoti M. Bhat[2], and Barbara Weber[3]

[1] BPM Research Group, Infosys Labs, Infosys Limited, India
Sukriti_goel@infosys.com
[2] Information Systems, Indian Institute of Management, Bangalore, India
Jyoti.bhat@iimb.ernet.in
[3] Department of Computer Science, University of Innsbruck, Innsbruck, Austria
Barbara.Weber@uibk.ac.at

Abstract. Knowledge of current business processes is a critical requirement for organizational initiatives like compliance management, regulatory reporting, process optimization, reengineering the IT systems and outsourcing. Existing process discovery techniques expect process execution information or event logs while organization's business processes are often executed on heterogeneous systems across different departments, by integration and data hand-offs between systems. Traditional information systems, however, are designed for storing and processing transaction data which persists in databases and other data storage mechanisms. In this paper we identify the challenges and propose a solution for extracting end-to-end processes from persistent process execution data available in multiple heterogeneous applications. The approach consists of analyzing persistent system data to identify and obtain events in a non-intrusive manner. The approach to get the end-to-end process involves a combination of data and process mining.

1 Introduction

Global customers and multi-location presence of enterprises implies that organizational processes are executed leveraging technologies like the internet, web services and cloud computing, yet safeguarding the existing investments in legacy applications, enterprise packages and products. The business process logic and rules are coded in algorithms, batch jobs, database constraints, etc.; and the process flow is not explicit as it is achieved by integration of multiple applications. A single end-to-end business process is implemented across several applications many of them being process unaware systems [1]. Over time applications are modified due to business requirements of various stakeholders, technology enhancements and regular system maintenance. But existing process documentation is usually not updated with the systems' changes. As a consequence the process documentation and the business process supported by the organization's information systems (ISs) run out of synch. Process stakeholders, however, need to know the As-Is processes executed in the systems for controlling and improving business process performance [19]. In addition to the process flow, varying

M. La Rosa and P. Soffer (Eds.): BPM 2012 Workshops, LNBIP 132, pp. 162–173, 2013.

level of process details are needed, For e.g., average cycle time of execution, process measures and SLAs based on the nature of the business process initiative.

Common approaches to discover or extract business processes like process elicitation by interviewing different stakeholders, code study and study of existing system documents and manuals can be used to elicit the process flows. However, these approaches are insufficient to obtain other details like process performance measures, cycle times and queue times. Moreover, they are costly, time consuming, and heavily dependent on business knowledge of the stakeholders [2]. Process mining addresses this problem by extracting the business process from the information systems supporting them at an operational level. Process mining uses event logs where each event refers to a case and is totally ordered [6]. While multiple automated process mining tools [3] are available, they expect event logs provided in a certain format as available in a process aware information system (PAIS). In traditional information systems event logs are not available since logging mechanisms are typically missing and the processes often execute across multiple applications. To address this problem of unavailability of event logs in traditional information systems, static analysis of code followed by instrumentation and dynamic analysis has been used to generate the log files [4, 20, 21]. However, making modifications to production systems is risky and involves many stakeholders. Moreover, many organizations do not allow modifications to the existing systems in any form.

We propose a process extraction method which can extract multiple end-to-end processes executed in various heterogeneous systems in a non-intrusive manner. In this paper we will list the challenges for end-to-end process extraction from the process execution data of process unaware information systems (cf. Sect. 2), provide an overview of related work (cf. Sect. 3). We will present the proposed method for extracting the end-to-end process by tracking the process execution data (cf. Sect. 4) along with a case study (cf. Sect. 5). Finally, we provide conclusions and discuss future work (cf. Sect. 6).

2   Process Extraction: Challenges

C1 - Missing process awareness: The concept of a business activity is missing in traditional ISs as the process flow is implicit and implemented by invoking methods, procedures and programs (callable units). This creates a challenge of not knowing what business activities are executed [20, 21]. PAISs have explicit process definitions and execute the process as sequences of activities and maintain the status of execution [8]. Often traditional ISs are viewed as a graph where nodes are the different callable units and propose an approach to map each callable unit to a business activity for process mining [20, 21]. Using this information for discovering a process requires instrumentation of code.

C2 - Systems Landscape: As an end-to-end business process may span multiple applications and technologies, the challenge is to identify all the systems involved in the process. For example, the order to remittance process of a software service provider spans across 30 applications like CRM, project allocation and delivery, time sheet management, and finance applications.

C3 - Granularity: The difference in granularity of business activities and data traces pose another challenge as it is difficult to decide which data traces are to be considered for processing. Business activity 'interest calculation' is of interest to process stakeholders, but the details of how interest is calculated (e.g., 'get interest rate', 'get account details') are too fine-grained to be included in a process model. Additionally, different data storage systems record execution data at different levels of granularity. The data traces in log files and audit logs are typically fine-grained (e.g., event for entering data for one particular attribute), while one entry in a transaction table in DBMS might be related to multiple activities which occurred on the business entity.

C4 - Unstructured data: Even in automated business processes, certain parts of the process information may be in an unstructured form like scanned documents or e-mails. It is difficult to interpret and associate unstructured data with the business process and its activities. It is an even bigger challenge to interpret data from scanned documents without indexing information and emails written in natural language.

C5 - Multiple process identifiers: Traditional ISs do not have a unique identifier for a process instance. The multiple entities involved in process execution are stored with different identifiers in the process execution data and hence there may not be a single identifier that flows across the systems which can be used to identify an individual case [11]. For example, in an order management system, the entities involved are *order, item, invoice* and *shipment,* thus, multiple identifiers such as *order id, item id, invoice id* and *shipment id* exist. The challenge is to correlate the various entities and the conditions on which correlation can be done.

C6 - Overwritten data: Depending on the design of the data structures, data gets overwritten in some transaction data sources such as DBMS and indexed files. For example, the status of an order may be maintained using a *status* field in the *order_details* table which gets updated during system execution with values 'created', 'invoice created' 'payment received' or 'shipment sent'. In some cases the time stamp of the event gets overwritten each time a change is made in the tuple (e.g., column "last_modification_date' is updated each time a change occurs in the row and the modification date of previous events is lost).

C7 - Missing timestamps: Process extraction from persistent data has another challenge related to timestamps. Typically, data traces are logged at the completion of an event, thus, the timestamps available are usually completion times. The start times of the activities are usually not available. In addition, there may be some activities which are recorded in the persistent data sources with no information of date of execution. Such actions may be listed in the process model but order of execution cannot be known.

3   Related Work

Process discovery and documentation is of interest for many organizational initiatives like process improvements, systems reengineering, process performance monitoring, system maintenance and outsourcing. Various approaches and tools are used to understand and document the business process executed in ISs. Process elicitation by interviewing business users and conducting workshops with the process stakeholders is a popular method for process discovery. The drawback of process elicitation is its dependence on business users who narrate the process and the consultants who understand and document the process. In addition to being costly and time consuming, this method depends on the process knowledge with the people and is vulnerable to human interpretations and political influences [2].

There are other manual techniques where the task execution data is collected while users are working on the tasks. These methods expect either the process user or the external observer to note execution data like instance id, task name, task start and end times for each of the task while working on it [16, 17]. These methods reduce the overhead on the business user, but introduce extra cost by demanding extra work from process workers or by introducing the role of observers. Though time consuming, this method is usually used for analyzing processes in the context of process improvement initiatives (e.g., six-sigma).

Business provenance technology [9] helps identify end-to-end business processes, especially unstructured processes, across heterogeneous systems by collecting, co-relating and analyzing operational data. This approach involves creating a provenance graph for the specific application needs like compliance monitoring. The provenance data generated depends on the information about the business operations that is to be extracted from the applications. Moreover, the provenance data is generated by accessing application events from event reporting middleware or by processing the application data and identifying the events. This approach expects the applications to generate the provenance data in a pre-defined format; otherwise the applications need to be instrumented.

Process Mining has been around for more than a decade [10]. Existing process mining techniques assume the presence of event logs [12], which is however not always that easy. Though process mining techniques have the drawback of not being able to discover the manual part of the process, they are gaining popularity for the processes which are automated.

ProMImport [8] is a framework for converting logs in any format into event logs as required by many of the process mining techniques. Though the framework is extensible to add more input formats, it does not provide suggestions on generating the event logs for processes executed in process unaware systems and processes executed across multiple heterogeneous systems.

To handle the challenge of generating event logs for traditional ISs and process unaware systems with instrumentation a combination of static and dynamic analysis of source code has been proposed [20, 21]. The code needs to be modified in the production environment to generate the event logs while the process is executed. Hence, for long running processes, the process would need to be executed for a long time to get enough information (i.e., certain processes have a periodicity of months, with annual events and seasonal differences).

Process spaceship [11] is a tool for semi-automatic definition of a process space over heterogeneous IT systems in an enterprise. In particular, it allows analyzing the information items in an enterprise, correlating them into process instances and generating process views. This work addresses process discovery in heterogeneous systems using multiple data sources, though it does not specifically refer to IT systems. The approach is based on systems using web services with message exchanges between them. Moreover, the process spaceship approach does not deal with heterogeneity of the enterprise events and data sources, but is dependent on Extract, Transform and Load (ETL) tools. Another observation is that this work considers each tuple as one event which may not be true. In many practical settings, a tuple may contain information of multiple events

Existing Business Activity Monitoring (BAM) tools like ARIS Process Performance Manager (PPM) [4] can reconstruct the execution of each transaction from start to finish by combining the process-relevant data from multiple IT systems (e.g., ERP, workflow, legacy systems, etc.). Organizations can obtain a comprehensive performance overview of their business workflows using process indicators and a graphical visualization of the actual structure of their transactions. ARIS PPM collects information related to the transactions during execution and hence does not have to correlate the transactions. But to discover the process, sufficient number of transactions needs to be captured by ARIS PPM over a period of time. This poses a problem specifically for long running process.

Other methods have been proposed for mining business processes from event logs when there are missing case ids [22, 23]. But these approaches do not handle traditional IS where the process execution data resides across multiple heterogeneous systems. The method of process extraction described in this paper complements to existing methods of process mining.

4   Process Extraction (PE) Approach Overview

As multiple robust process mining algorithms are already available [6, 11-16], the proposed method concentrates on the generation of event logs in a non-intrusive manner using persistent process execution data, for e.g. transaction data. The approach does not intrude the system either by adding code or introducing probes. Additionally, as historical data in systems are archived due to business and regulatory requirements, generating a sufficiently large event log to address long running processes is not a problem. The event logs can be then used to extract the process flow and apply business intelligence techniques [19] to generate the process models. Figure 1 provides an overview of the proposed technique.

A. Identify Activities

The first step in order to identify activities is to know the data relevant to the end-to-end process. The information about the business entities and systems involved in the process is acquired from business users and IT staff respectively. Once the systems are identified, all data storage mechanisms, where the process execution data is stored are identified such as DBMS, system log files, middleware log files or flat files. Then

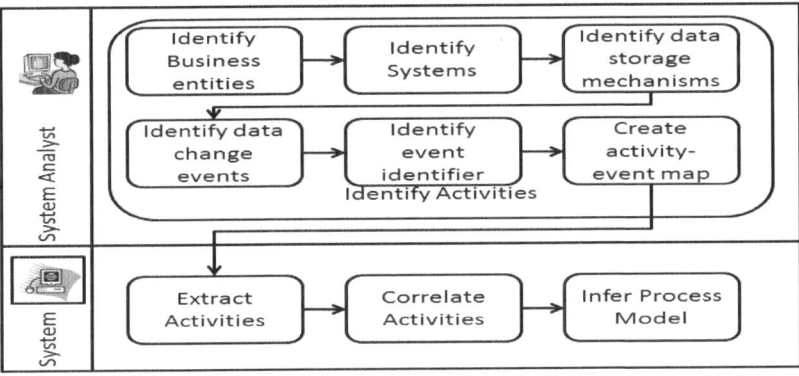

Fig. 1. Process discovery approach

we analyze the data sources and identify the data change events related to *create* and *update* operations in the data sources. It may not be possible to identify some *update* operations and any of the *read* and *delete* operations from the data sources in the absence of audit logs. Typical data traces left by process execution are - insert row in a DB table, update a row in DB table, create new file, add a new log entry in a file, send a mail or receive a mail. Each of these data operations corresponds to at least one event. We ignore the data operation performed on master tables and any data operation with no time stamp.

The granularity of identified data events varies from one data source to another. Coarse grained data events from transaction database tables may be clubbed with data events from other data sources, e.g., web logs or application log files. Also, if the identified events are too fine grained then some of the events can be ignored either while mapping them to activities or during the process model inference using mining algorithms.

Next, the correlation identifiers for each data event are marked. Applications store entity id and time stamps in one form or another to distinguish the instances from each other for future processing [7]. The applications store this information in various forms like transaction tables in database, audit logs or flat files. Usually, the correlation identifier is the tuple identifier which includes composite identifiers. Data change events in DBMS and indexed files can be represented by 1) the table name, 2) an id (i.e., correlation id), 3) a condition which helps mapping multiple events from the same tuple to different business activities and 4) a date (i.e., timestamp). Table 1 provides several examples. Table *invoice_details* has both order_id and invoice_id columns which help in correlating events captured from two different table. Presence of foreign keys in the database schema makes it easy to correlate events read from different database tables. Each of the events is mapped to an activity as mentioned in the last column.

B. Extract and Correlate Activities

Once the activities are identified, the data sources are parsed and the events extracted in an automated manner. Each event is mapped to a business activity based on the

Table 1. Representing Events and Activity Mapping

Table	Id	Condition	Date	Activity
order_details	*order_id*	*null*	*create_date*	*Create Order*
order_details	*order_id*	*Status='cancel'*	*cancellation_da te*	*Cancel Order*
order_details	*order_id*	*cancellation_da te !=null*	*cancellation_da te*	*Cancel Order*
invoice_detai ls	*order_id+ invoice_id*	*null*	*create_date*	*Create Invoice*

mapping rules defined in the previous step. This creates a cloud of unrelated activities.

As the objective of correlating the activities is to generate an event log comprising of process instances of the business process, the events are sorted by timestamp. The events are correlated using composite disjunctive conditions [11]. There is no prior knowledge of relations between the events as conversations and time constraints do not exist in the data sources considered. The process instance identifier or correlation identifier is progressively built using the event identifiers based on the events which match the existing correlation identifier. If correlation identifier of the activity matches with any of the correlation identifier of the existing process instances, the activity is added to that instance. If the activity has more than one identifier (i.e., a composite identifier), all the correlation identifiers are added to the process instance identifier. If the activity identifier does not match with any of the existing process instances, a new process instance is created and the correlation identifier of the process instance is set as the event identifier of the activity. In some cases, one activity can correlate with multiple activities of same type, e.g. *create order* activity can correlate with multiple *create invoice* activities as one order can have multiple invoices created.

We explain our approach for activity correlation using an example process with two entities: order and invoice. The time sorted activities of the process are shown in table 2.

Table 2. Activity Cloud

Activity	Id	Time stamp
create order	*order_id = 1*	*t1*
create invoice	*order_id=1,invoice_id=100*	*t2*
create order	*order_id=2*	*t3*
receive payment	*invoice id=100*	*t4*

When 'create order' is processed by the correlation algorithm, there is no process instance with correlation identifier "order_id=1", thus, a new process instance is created with correlation identifier "order_id=1". When activity 'create invoice' with identifier "order_id=1, invoice_id=100" is considered, it matches the process instance with identifier "order_id=1". The correlation identifier of that process instance is updated to "order_id=1, invoice_id=100". Again 'create order' with order_id=2 does not match any existing process instance so a new one is created with correlation identifier "order_id=2". When activity 'received payment' with identifier "invoice_id=100" is encountered, the event identifier matches with the process instance identifier "order_id=1, invoice_id=100" (using disjunctive correlation conditions). The event is added to the process instance, but the process instance identifier is not updated.

The process instances can be built from the extracted activities in the event cloud in an automated manner.

C. Infer Process Model

The process instances obtained by correlating the activities are used to obtain the process model. Most of the existing process mining algorithms can be applied to obtain the end-to-end process model [3, 6, 12]. The process model is refined using various methods available in process mining tool, which we refer to as discovered process. The discovered process is reviewed with the process stakeholders and the final process signed off after making the required changes in the process. Rozinat et. al. [5] define fitness and appropriateness metrics to compare the discovered process and the existing process model documented. But here we use the discovered process and extend it to create the final process model, as existing process models and documents are absent. The metrics, fitness and behavioral appropriateness are not relevant here, as the process model is discovered using execution logs. Rather the process stakeholders may want to add paths to the process model which were not discovered using the given method. In such cases, we recommend to using persistent data of a longer period to actually validate the additions made by process stakeholders. There may be some undesired activities in the process model which can be removed by the stakeholders at the time of review. Currently we manually convert the process model obtained in petri net or heuristic net into BPMN. Hence structural issues are handled manually and hence assessing the structural appropriateness of discovered model is not of concern.

There is a need to measure completeness of discovered process model as compared to final process model. Completeness can be measured for activities and transitions. For calculating completeness of activities C_A and completeness of transitions C_T we use following:

$$C_A = \frac{N_d}{N}$$
$$C_T = \frac{T_d}{T}$$

where:

N_d is the number of activities in discovered process
N is the number of activities in final process
T_d is the number of transitions in discovered process
T is the number of transitions in final process

We can get a weighted average of C_A and C_T to arrive at single measure of completeness of process as follows:

$$C = 0.5\, C_A + 0.5\, C_T$$

5   Case study: Purchase Order Process

We applied the process extraction approach to discover a real-life end-to-end process spanning three heterogeneous systems. In the case study we aimed at the discovery of the purchase order process from the process execution data of a large services organization. Goal of the case study was to evaluate our technique by measuring the completeness of the discovered process vis-à-vis the final process signed off by the process stakeholders.

Obtaining Event Logs

With inputs of process stakeholders and system owners, we identified that the purchase order process executes across two departments (i.e., purchase and finance department) using the following systems and data sources:

1. Purchase Request (PR) System - used by the employees of the organization, uses a RDBMS and partly mail based for approvals
2. Purchase Order (PO) System – used by the back office of the organization, uses a RDBMS for storing data
3. Accounts receivable (AR) system – uses RDBMS for storing data with detailed audit logs

We found that when a new request is created, a new row is inserted in the *Purchase_Requisition* table in the PR system. When a new purchase order is created, a new row is inserted in the *Purchase_Order* table in the PO system. For obtaining senior management approval, a mail is sent to the approver in controlled natural language and the approver replies to the mail with approve or reject along with comments, leading to challenge C4.

When identifying the *insert* and *update* operations in the data sources, we detected that some important data gets overwritten. The *status* column of table *Purchase_Requisition* gets overwritten each time the status of a request is changed (i.e., the value changes from *created*, *PO generated*, to *approved* to *completed or cancelled*) as discussed in challenge C6. In some cases the data gets overwritten in one table, but at the same time a new data record is created in another table. For example, when the *status* field is updated to *PO generated*, a new row is inserted into *Purchase_order* table in PO system and is captured as *create purchase order* activity. Therefore, the challenge of overwriting data could be overcome in our case to some extent by considering multiple systems and data sources.

In our case study, we found the same data change events available both in transaction tables and audit logs. Audit logs and audit tables due to their fundamental purpose, capture all events of importance in the system for reporting, compliance monitoring and future analysis and data is not overwritten or deleted. Whereas, in transaction tables, data is sometimes overwritten and the tables only store information that is needed for further processing of the process instance. In the AR system, for the same process we identified 24 distinct data events using the audit logs and 10 events with transaction tables leading to different granularity of extracted process as discussed in challenge C3. Using audit logs, more fine grained process can be obtained as compared to using transactions tables. One important finding of our case study is that audit logs should be used wherever possible to identify data events.

We used the keyword search on the email sent and received by the PR system as controlled natural language is used. We could identify the name of the approver, date of approval requested and action taken by the approver along with the date.

We found the unique identifiers of the tuples were sufficient to identify the events. We used the primary keys of the tables (e.g., *purchase_request_id*, *purchase_order_id*) as correlation ids. As approval request and response mails had the *purchase_request_id*, the same could be used to correlate the events across email and PR system. Rules for mapping individual data events to business activities were defined. The events were then extracted by reading the data sources and correlated to generate the event logs or process instances in a fully automated manner using the correlation algorithm.

Discovering the End-to-End Process

We used the Heuristic miner plug-in of ProM to discover the end-to-end processes from the event log generated. Our event log was for a 6 months period and it contained 6700 instances and 51200 events. The maximum number of events per instance was 26, while the minimum was 1. The extracted process was then reviewed with the stakeholders and system owners to evaluate the completeness and correctness of the process.

We measured the completeness by comparing the process as signed off by process stakeholders with the process discovered by ProM. We could discover the process with a completeness CA of 0.75 and CT of 0.65. The process completeness was not 100% as some of the process execution data was lost as the data was overwritten in the transaction tables with no corresponding entries in audit logs or other data sources.

It took us a manual effort of 3 days to go through the systems, identify the data sources, tables, unique identifiers, etc. Manual effort was also spent in converting the heuristic-net model into a BPMN model, which was around 2 days.

Based on our experience of applying the proposed method to extract multiple different processes, we find that the results depend on the availability of the persistent data. We could achieve completeness of 50% to 95% based on the data available. In presence of audit logs or multiple sources of inputs for the same system, e.g. database transactions, system logs, etc., the completeness is much higher as compared to using transactional data only. The completeness also depends on whether the transaction logs contain all possible paths which the process can take like exception handling and infrequent events. This to some extent is handled by collecting the transaction logs for a significantly large period.

6 Conclusions and Further Work

Automation-assisted process extraction holds a lot of promise today. It offers the capability of discovering the process as executed in non-process aware systems. Automated process extraction does not interfere with the execution of processes as it uses available historical data to discover the process. The process is extracted from persistent process execution data available in various data sources. Business transaction data is usually logged during execution for further processing. A limitation of our current approach is that business activities that do not leave a trace in the persistent data cannot be extracted; manual activities and the processing done in system/program memory fall under this category. Transaction data getting overwritten can be handled to a certain extent by identifying another data source of the system where the data event may persist.

The challenges related to identifying the system landscape and granularity of the process can be resolved with the help of domain experts. The proposed approach takes care of multiple process identifiers of the process across systems by using the disjunctive correlation method. Though we have not used text mining on the emails in the case study, there exist techniques to identify data events from unstructured data [9], which can be applied to further improve the effectiveness of our method.

The availability of process information required for Business Process Intelligence (BPI) and process optimization depends on the quality of data traces. Usually, the data traces do not store data at the start of an activity, so it may be difficult to generate information like average time to complete an activity. Also the currently available mining algorithms do not mine the process flow rules along with the extracted process.

Future research can explore mining the business flow rules along with process discovery using the data traces available in the systems. Another area of work is to improve the quality of event logs to generate enough process information as required by process optimization and BPR initiative.

References

[1] Leymann, F., Reisig, W., Thatte, S.R., van der Aalst, W.M.P.: The Role of Business Processes in Service Oriented Architectures, number 6291, Dagstuhl Seminar Proceedings. Internationales Begegnungs- und Forschungszentrum fuer Informatik (IBFI), Schloss Dagstuhl, Germany (July 2006)

[2] Verner, L.: The Challenge of Process Discovery, BP Trends (May 2004)

[3] van Dongen, B.F., de Medeiros, A.K.A., Verbeek, H.M.W., Weijters, A.J.M.M., van der Aalst, W.M.P.: The ProM Framework: A New Era in Process Mining Tool Support. In: Ciardo, G., Darondeau, P. (eds.) ICATPN 2005. LNCS, vol. 3536, pp. 444–454. Springer, Heidelberg (2005)

[4] Blickle, T., Hess, H.: Automatic Process Discovery with ARIS Process Performance Manager (ARIS PPM), Expert Paper, IDS Scheer

[5] Rozinat, A., van der Aalst, W.M.P.: Conformance Checking of Processes Based on Monitoring Real Behavior. Information Systems 33(1), 64–95 (2008)

[6] van der Aalst, W.M.P., Weijters, A., Maruster, L.: Workflow Mining: Discovering Process Models from Event Logs. IEEE Transactions on Knowledge and Data Engineering 16(9), 1128–1142 (2004)

[7] Woodfill, J., Stonebraker, M.: An Implementation of Hypothetical Relations. In: Schkolnick, M., Thanos, C. (eds.) 9th International Conference on Very Large Data Bases Very Large Data Bases, pp. 157–166. Morgan Kaufmann Publishers, San Francisco (1983)

[8] Dumas, M., van der Aalst, W.M.P., Hofstede, T.: Process-aware information systems: Bridging people and software through process technology. John Wiley & Sons, Inc. (2005)

[9] Curbera, F., Doganata, Y., Martens, A., Mukhi, N.K., Slominski, A.: Business Provenance – A Technology to Increase Traceability of End-to-End Operations. In: Meersman, R., Tari, Z. (eds.) OTM 2008, Part I. LNCS, vol. 5331, pp. 100–119. Springer, Heidelberg (2008)

[10] Cook, J.E., Wolf, A.L.: Discovering Models of Software Processes from Event-Based Data. ACM Transactions on Software Engineering and Methodology 7(3), 215–249 (1998)

[11] Motahari-Nezhad, H.R., Saint-Paul, R., Benatallah, B., Casati, F., Andritsos, P.: Process Spaceship: Discovering Process views in Process Spaces, Technical Report, UNSW-CSE-TR-0721, The School of Computer Science and Engineering, Australia (December 2007)

[12] Alves, A.K.: Using Genetic Algorithms to Mine Process Models: Representation, Operators and Results (2003)

[13] van Dongen, B.F., van der Aalst, W.M.P.: Multi-phase Process Mining: Building Instance Graphs. In: Atzeni, P., Chu, W., Lu, H., Zhou, S., Ling, T.-W. (eds.) ER 2004. LNCS, vol. 3288, pp. 362–376. Springer, Heidelberg (2004)

[14] Agrawal, R., Gunopulos, D., Leymann, F.: Mining Process Models from Workflow Logs. In: Schek, H.-J., Saltor, F., Ramos, I., Alonso, G. (eds.) EDBT 1998. LNCS, vol. 1377, pp. 469–483. Springer, Heidelberg (1998)

[15] Goedertier, S., Martens, D., Vanthienen, J., Baesens, B.: Robust Process Discovery with Artificial Negative Events. The Journal of Machine Learning Research 10 (December 2009)

[16] Basili, V.R., Weiss, D.M.: A methodology for collecting valid software engineering data. IEEE Transactions on Software Engineering, SE-10(6), 728–738 (1984)

[17] Wolf, A.L., Rosenblum, D.S.: A Study in Software Process Capture and Analysis. In: 2nd International Conference on the Software Process, Berlin, Germany (February 1993)

[18] van der Aalst, W.M.P.: Process Mining and Monitoring Processes and Services: Workshop Report. In: Leymann, F., Reisig, W., Thatte, S.R., van der Aalst, W.M.P. (eds.) The Role of Business Processes in Service Oriented Architectures. Dagstuhl Seminar Proceedings, vol. 6291, Internationales Begegnungs- und Forschungszentrum fuer Informatik (IBFI), Schloss Dagstuhl, Germany (July 2006)

[19] Castellanos, M., Alves de Medeiros, K., Mendling, J., Weber, B., Weitjers, A.J.M.M.: Business Process Intelligence. In: Cardoso, J., van der Aalst, W.M.P. (eds.) Handbook of Research on Business Process Modeling, pp. 456–480. Idea Group Inc. (2009)

[20] Pérez-Castillo, R., Weber, B., de Guzmán, I.G.R., Piattini, M.: Process mining through dynamic analysis for modernising legacy systems. IET Software 5(3), 304–319 (2011)

[21] Pérez-Castillo, R., Weber, B., Pinggera, J., Zugal, S., de Guzmán, I.G.R., Piattini, M.: Generating event logs from non-process-aware systems enabling business process mining. Enterprise IS 5(3), 301–335 (2011)

[22] Ferreira, D.R., Gillblad, D.: Discovering Process Models from Unlabelled Event Logs. In: Dayal, U., Eder, J., Koehler, J., Reijers, H.A. (eds.) BPM 2009. LNCS, vol. 5701, pp. 143–158. Springer, Heidelberg (2009)

[23] Burattin, A., Vigo, R.: A framework for semi-automated process instance discovery from decorative attributes. In: CIDM, pp. 176–183 (2011)

Root Cause Analysis with Enriched Process Logs

Suriadi Suriadi[1], Chun Ouyang[1], Wil M.P. van der Aalst[1,2],
and Arthur H.M. ter Hofstede[1,2]

[1] Queensland University of Technology, Australia
{s.suriadi,c.ouyang,a.terhofstede}@qut.edu.au
[2] Eindhoven University of Technology, The Netherlands
{w.m.p.v.d.aalst,a.h.m.ter.hofstede}@tue.nl

Abstract. In the field of process mining, the use of event logs for the
purpose of root cause analysis is increasingly studied. In such an analysis,
the availability of attributes/features that may explain the root cause
of some phenomena is crucial. Currently, the process of obtaining these
attributes from raw event logs is performed more or less on a case-by-case
basis: there is still a lack of generalized systematic approach that captures
this process. This paper proposes a systematic approach to enrich and
transform event logs in order to obtain the required attributes for root
cause analysis using classical data mining techniques, the *classification*
techniques. This approach is formalized and its applicability has been
validated using both self-generated and publicly-available logs.

Keywords: process mining, root cause analysis, event logs.

1 Introduction

A recent survey by Gartner shows that risk management is one of the top strategic business priorities for CEOs and senior executives [4]. A common way to
mitigate risks is to remove or minimize the presence of key factors which are
known to contribute to the occurrence of unwanted risk events. For example,
it is well-established that pilot fatigue is one of the key factors contributing to
airline safety issues [5]. Thus, measures to mitigate the chance of pilots being
fatigued during working hours have routinely been implemented.

Root cause analysis (RCA) has been applied widely in organisations. Many
techniques have been developed, including flow charts, brainstorming, and others [1]. Through RCA, one aims to find an explanation of risk incidents, preferably an explanation involving a minimal number of factors. As many events are
recorded in logs nowadays (e.g. by devices or software applications) one can exploit this data for the purpose of RCA with the added advantage that the data
reflects reality and not a perception (e.g. in the form of a model) of reality. As we
focus on operational processes in this paper, one can take post-execution event
data as a starting point and compare features, recorded as attributes, of cases
(i.e. process instances) that were classified as successful with those features of
cases that were classified as unsuccessful. This way we can define a *classification*
problem whose results provide valuable input for RCA.

M. La Rosa and P. Soffer (Eds.): BPM 2012 Workshops, LNBIP 132, pp. 174–186, 2013.
© Springer-Verlag Berlin Heidelberg 2013

The features which may be the root cause(s) of risk incidents may come from various contexts, including instance context, process contexts, social context, and environmental context [21]. However, raw data from post-execution logs (commonly known as event logs), may not readily contain the needed features/attributes that can be used to explain the possible root cause(s) of risk incidents. Currently, the process of manipulating raw data to obtain these attributes is more or less conducted on a case-by-case basis: there is a lack of generic systematic approach in the derivation of these attributes.

In this paper, we propose a systematic RCA approach that starts with an existing event log and enriches it with relevant contextual information for explaining possible root cause(s) of risk incidents. This enriched log can then be manipulated further such that it can be analyzed using established *classification* techniques. In other words, we transform a process mining problem, i.e. RCA based on event logs, into a standard *classification* problem. In this paper, we focus on the approach and not on the selection of variables/features (which is commonly addressed in classical data mining study). In fact, in order to illustrate our approach and also to scope our paper, we investigate the effect of workload on 'overtime' (long-running) cases. This approach is formalized and applied to RCA with workload-*enriched* logs, and its applicability is validated using both self-generated and publicly-available logs.

2   Approach

In this section, we describe our approach to mining the root cause of risk incidents (such as overtime cases) through the *transformation* of a process mining problem into a standard *classification* problem. Our approach starts with determining relevant information needed to explain the root cause of a risk incident, followed by the enrichment of the event log with the required information to facilitate an RCA is captured. Through the application of aggregation functions and other refinement procedures, we transform this enriched event log into a form that is suitable to be analysed by *classification* techniques (see Fig. 1).

RCA Data Requirements. As a requirement from *classification* techniques, RCA uses a *response* variable for the labelling of 'successful/unsuccessful' cases. An example of a response variable can be seen as a feature in a log which states the outcome of a case as either being 'on-time' or 'overtime'. The features which may influence the occurrence of 'successful/unsuccessful' cases are labelled as *predictor* variables. An example of a predictor variable can be specified by workload which may have impact on the occurrence of long-running (over-time) cases.

Thus, the first step of our approach is to determine the *response* variable capturing the risk incident we want to analyze, and the set of *predictor* variables which may contribute to the occurrence of the incident. The determination of these attributes can be informed by established management theories, studies, and/or a company's risk registries. In process mining, these variables may be taken from various contexts, including instance context (e.g. size of an insurance

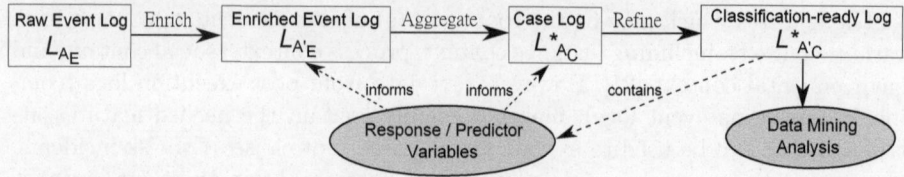

Fig. 1. Approach Diagram

claim), process context (e.g. total number of resources involved), social context (e.g. stress level), and external context (e.g. weather) [21].

Enrich Raw Event Log. Once the *predictor* and *response* variables are determined, we need to verify if our raw event log contains sufficient information to captures those variables. Sometimes, the information may not be readily available in the raw event log, but can be derived from the data in the log. There are also situations when the required information needs to be obtained from external sources and be correlated to the raw event log. Once the above information is determined to be obtainable, we can then extend the raw event log with such information thus resulting in an enriched event log).

Definition 1 (Event log). An *event log* consists of a set of events. Events are characterised by various attributes, e.g., an event may have a timestamp, correspond to an activity, etc. Let $A_E = \{a_1, ..., a_n\}$ be a set of event attributes. For each attribute $a_i \in A_E$ $(1 \leqslant i \leqslant n)$, $D(a_i)$ is the domain of a_i, e.g., the domain of attribute *timestamp* is the set of all possible time values. $L_{A_E} \subseteq 2^{D(a_1) \times ... \times D(a_n)}$ is an *event log* based on the set of attributes A_E. For any event $e \in L_{A_E}$ and attribute $a \in A_E$: $\#_a(e)$ is the value of attribute a for event e.

Definition 2 (Event log enrichment). Let L_{A_E} be an event log based on the set of attributes A_E. Let A_D be a set of derivable attributes whose value can be calculated from A_E, i.e. for each attribute $d \in A_D$, $L_{A_E \cup \{d\}} = \delta_d(L_{A_E})$ where δ_d is a derivative function that computes the value of attribute d for all events in L_{A_E}. Let A_K be a set of correlatable attributes whose value can be obtained from external sources based on some key attributes in A_E, i.e. for each attribute $k \in A_E$, $L_{A_E \cup \{k\}} = \omega_k(L_{A_E})$ where ω_k is a correlative function that retrieves the value of attribute k for all events in L_{A_E}. $L_{A'_E}$ where $A'_E = A_E \cup A_D \cup A_K$, is an *enriched* event log with a set of extended (derivable and correlatable) attributes.

From Event Log to Case Log. The next step is to transform the event log into a case log. This is necessary because RCA is normally performed at case level.

Definition 3 (Case log). A *case log* comprises of a set of cases. Cases, like events, have attributes, e.g., a case has a case identifier, corresponds to a trace (i.e. a sequence of events), etc. Let $A_C = \{s_1, ..., s_m\}$ be a set of case attributes, including a mandatory attribute named *case_id* which uniquely identifies a case. For each $s_i \in A_C$ $(1 \leqslant i \leqslant m)$, $D(s_i)$ is the domain of s_i. Let $\mathcal{C}$ be the set of all possible case identifiers. $L^*_{A_C} \subseteq 2^{D(s_1) \times ... \mathcal{C} \times ... D(s_m)}$ is a case log based on the set of attributes A_C. For any case $c \in L^*_{A_C}$ and attribute $s \in A_C$: $\#_s(c)$ is the value of attribute s for case c. For any $c_1, c_2 \in L^*_{A_C}$, $\#_{case\_id}(c_1) \neq \#_{case\_id}(c_2)$.

Definition 4 (Aggregation of event log to case log). Let L_{A_E} be an event log based on the set of event attributes A_E where $case\_id \in A_E$. A corresponding case log $L^*_{A_C}$ based on the set of attributes A_C can be generated from L_{A_E} as: (1) the set of case identifiers $\bigcup_{c \in L^*_{A_C}} \#_{case\_id}(c) = \bigcup_{e \in L_{A_E}} \#_{case\_id}(e)$; and (2) for each case $c \in L^*_{A_C}$ and attribute $s \in A_C \setminus \{case\_id\}$, $\#_s(c) = \alpha_s(L_{A_E}, \#_{case\_id}(c))$ where α_s is an *aggregation function* that calculates the value of attribute s in case c from the relevant events in L_{A_E}.

Get Case Log Ready for Classification. For *classification* techniques to work, most *classification* techniques require the value of each *response* variable to be presented in a categorial (nominal) form. For a *predictor* variable its value *may* be categorical (but not mandatory). If our data is not already in the correct format, we need to further transform the attributes in a case log accordingly.

Definition 5 (Classification-ready case log). Let $L^*_{A_C}$ be a case log based on the set of case attributes A_C. Let $A_C^\diamond$ be a set of classification attributes whose value is of categorical form and can be computed from the set of case attributes A_C. $L^*_{A'_C}$ where $A'_C = A_C \cup A_C^\diamond$, is a *classification-ready case log*. For each case $c \in L^*_{A'_C}$ and attribute $q \in A_C^\diamond$: $\#_q(c) = \chi_q(L^*_{A_C}, c)$ where χ_q is a classification function that derives the value of attribute q in case c based on the corresponding case data in $L^*_{A_C}$.

RCA with Classification Techniques. Through the process detailed so far, we have now transformed a raw event log into a case log in a format that is suitable for classification analysis. The enriched case log now has the values of both the *response* and *predictor* variables of interest. One can feed these data into various data mining algorithms to find the root cause(s) of a risk incident.

3   RCA with Workload-Enriched Logs

We apply our approach to the analysis of *overtime cases* using event logs enriched with *workload* information. In business processes, workload has been defined in different ways (e.g. [14]). In this paper, we consider *workload as a list of work items that have been assigned to and/or started by a resource in a specified time period*. Note that only passively assigned work items to resources are considered as their workload in this regard.

Workload is usually not recorded directly in a raw event log but can be derived from a set of basic event attributes that capture the information about resource, activity, timestamp, and transaction type (which refers to the life-cycle of activities, e.g. start, complete) associated with each event. Below, we precisely define workload based on the information in a given event log of any process.

Definition 6 (Workload). Let L be an event log based on the set of event attributes including $\{case\_id, resource, activity, time, trans\}$, where $D(trans) = \{assign, start, complete\}$. For any resource r in L, the workload of r in time period (t_s, t_e) as derived from event log L is $WL_L(r, t_s, t_e) = WL_L^{t_s}(r) \cup WL_L^{(t_s, t_e)}(r)$.

- first of all, assume three short notations:
  - $L^{r, t_s} = \{e \in L \mid \#_{resource}(e) = r \wedge \#_{time}(e) < t_s\}$
  - $L^{r, t_s, t_e} = \{e \in L \mid \#_{resource}(e) = r \wedge t_s \leqslant \#_{time}(e) \leqslant t_e\}$
  - $\forall e \in L, wi(e) = (\#_{activity}(e), \#_{case\_id}(e))$. Then:
- $WL_L^{t_s}(r) = \{wi(e) \mid e \in L^{r, t_s} \wedge \#_{trans}(e) \in \{assign, start\}\} \setminus \{wi(e) \mid e \in L^{r, t_s} \wedge \#_{trans}(e) = complete\}$, i.e. the set of work items that have been assigned to and/or started but not yet completed by resource r at time t_s; and
- $WL_L^{(t_s, t_e)}(r) = \{wi(e) \mid e \in L^{r, t_s, t_e} \wedge \#_{trans}(e) \in \{assign, start\}\} \setminus WL_L^{t_s}(r)$, i.e. the set of *additional* work items that are assigned to and/or started by resource r within time period (t_s, t_e).

Following the approach in Sect. 2, we enrich a raw event log L_{A_E} with workload information. A derivable attribute *res_workload* is defined to capture the workload of all resources in the log within certain time periods. A time period is specified by referencing the timestamp of an individual event in L_{A_E} and using the process' *average activity duration* (AAD) as time duration. We assume an existing function *AvgActDuration* which takes an event log and returns the corresponding AAD[1]. Let R be the set of resources in L_{A_E} and d_h shortly represent half of L_{A_E}'s AAD, then for every event $e \in L_{A_E}$, $\#_{res\_workload}(e) = \{(r, WL_{L_{A_E}}(r, t_s, t_e)) \mid r \in R \wedge t_s = \#_{time}(e) - d_h \wedge t_s = \#_{time}(e) + d_h\}$.

Algorithm 1 defines the computaton of *res_workload* based on L_{A_E}. First, a relation $R_{WL} \subseteq 2^{D(time) \times D(res\_workload)}$ is derived capturing the workload of all resources each time an event is recorded in L_{A_E}. By definition, an event log can be treated as a relation where the set of event attributes specify its relation scheme. Hence, in Algorithm 1 three relational algebra operators [12] are used to define certain log operations: the *selection* (σ) of a set of events that satifies specific conditions in the log; the *projection* (π) of all events in the log restricted to a set of attributes; and finally the *natural join* ($\bowtie$) for combining all events in L_{A_E} and all tuples in R_{WL} on their common attribute *time* to yield the workload-enriched log $L_{A_E \cup \{res\_workload\}}$.

Now consider the set of event attributes $A_C = \{case\_id, time\_start, time\_end, avg\_workload, resources\}$ that are required for deriving the value of predictor and response variables in the next step. We generate case log $L^*_{A_C}$ from (the above enriched) event log $L_{A_E \cup \{res\_workload\}}$. For each case $c \in L^*_{A_C}$, we calculate:

- $\#_{time\_start}(c) = Min(\pi_{\{time\}}(\sigma_{case\_id = \#_{case\_id}(c)}(L_{A_E})))$
- $\#_{time\_end}(c) = Max(\pi_{\{time\}}(\sigma_{case\_id = \#_{case\_id}(c)}(L_{A_E})))$
- $\#_{resources}(c) = \{\#_{resource}(e) \mid e \in \sigma_{case\_id = \#_{case\_id}(c)}(L_{A_E})\}$
- $\#_{avg\_workload}(c) = \{(r, (\sum_{e_i \in L^c_{A_E}} |workload(r, e_i)|) / |L^c_{A_E}|) \mid r \in R\}$ where

---

[1] The underlying computation for such function is already supported by a number of log pre-processing tools, such as Nitro (see http://www.fluxicon.com/nitro/).

Algorithm 1. Generation of workload-enriched event log.

Input: an event log L_{A_E} and a derivable attribute *res_workload*
Output: a workload-enriched event log $L_{A_E \cup \{res\_workload\}}$
begin

> $R_{WL} := \emptyset$; /* R_{WL} is a relation of $\{time, res\_workload\}$ */
> $R := \{\#_{resource}(e) \mid e \in L_{A_E}\}$;
> $T := \{\#_{time}(e) \mid e \in L_{A_E}\}$;
> $d_h := AvgActDuration(L_{A_E})/2$;
> **for** $t \in T$ **do**
>
>> $rwl := \emptyset$;
>> $t_s := t - d_h$;
>> $t_e := t + d_h$;
>> **for** $r \in R$ **do**
>>
>>> $L^r := \sigma_{resource=r}(L_{A_E})$;
>>> /* calculate assigned/started but not completed work items at time t_s */
>>> $L^{r,t_s} := \sigma_{time<t_s}(L^r)$;
>>> **for** $tr \in \{assign, start, complete\}$ **do**
>>>
>>>> $L^{tr}_{WI} := \pi_{\{case\_id, activity\}}(\sigma_{trans=tr}(L^{r,t_s}))$;
>>>
>>> $rwl := rwl \cup \{(r, (L^{assign}_{WI} \cup L^{start}_{WI}) \setminus L^{complete}_{WI})\}$;
>>> /* calculate assigned/started work items within time period (t_s, t_e) */
>>> $L^{r,t_s,t_e}_M := \sigma_{t_s \leqslant time \leqslant t_e}(L^r)$;
>>> **for** $tr \in \{assign, start\}$ **do**
>>>
>>>> $L^{tr}_{WI} := \pi_{\{case\_id, activity\}}(\sigma_{trans=tr}(L^{r,t_s,t_e}))$;
>>>
>>> $rwl := rwl \cup \{(r, (L^{assign}_{WI} \cup L^{start}_{WI}))\}$
>>
>> $R_{WL} := R_{WL} \cup \{(t, rwl)\}$
>
> $L_{A_E \cup \{res\_workload\}} = \bowtie_{\{time\}} (L_{A_E}, R_{WL})$

- $R = \{\#_{resource}(e) \mid e \in L_{A_E}\}$ is the set of resources recorded in L_{A_E},
- $L^c_{A_E} = \sigma_{\#_{time\_start}(c) \leqslant time \leqslant \#_{time\_end}(c)}(L_{A_E})$ is the set of all events in L_{A_E} that occurred between the start and the end of case c,
- $workload(r, e_i)$ is the workload of resource r at the time of event e_i, which is specified in $\#_{res\_workload}(e_i)$.

Finally, given classification-ready attributes $A^\diamond_C = \{isOvertime, isRxInvolved\}$, *isOvertime* signals if a case duration exceeds a specific *threshold* value, and *isRxInvolved* indicates if resource Rx is involved in a case. Both return a boolean value (valid categorical form). Let $A'_C = A_C \cup A^\diamond_C$, for each case $c \in L^*_{A'_C}$: $\#_{isOvertime}(c) = ((\#_{time\_end}(c) - \#_{time\_start}(c) > threshold)$ and $\#_{isRxInvolved}(c) = (Rx \in \#_{resources}(c))$.

4   Validation of Approach

Two rounds of approach validation were conducted. The first validation round (Sect. 4.1) was based on a self-generated synthetic log. It was conducted during the development of our approach to facilitate step-by-step validation and refinement of our approach. The second validation round (Sect. 4.2) was conducted to demonstrate the *general applicability* of our approach by applying it to a log whose generation was beyond our control.

Log Quality. To derive workload information, we assume the existence of an event log of certain quality: (1) a minimum of 3-star log quality (as defined in the process mining manifesto [20]), (2) the existence of a number of open XES-equivalent attributes: (a) `concept:name` (at trace and event level), (b) `lifecycle:transition`, `org:resource`, `time:timestamp` (at event level), and (3) the recording of `start` (or `assign`) and `complete` transition of each activity.

4.1   Validation with Synthetic Log

The first validation round was conducted on a synthetic log generated from a Coloured Petri Net (CPN) [10] model of a purchase order process using the MXML-log-generator plug-in [13]. This log records the `assign`, `start`, and `complete` transitions for each activity. The log file was imported to a MySQL database for relational algebra manipulations. The workload derivation function and case log aggregation functions (as defined in Sect. 3) were implemented as a Java program which interacted with the database. The final *classification-ready* case log was successfully fed into the WEKA data mining tool such that the root cause of 'overtime' cases can be analyzed by the application of various *classification* algorithms (e.g. J48 [15] and JRip [6]). The *classification* analysis result from this log showed that average resources' workload was a key factor in the occurence of 'overtime' cases. This validation round confirms the applicability of our approach in performing an RCA through the enrichment and transformation of a process log (see the extended version of this paper [18] for details).

4.2   Validation with Public Log

While the first validation round was necessary to confirm the applicability of our approach, it was weak as it was based on self-generated log. To demonstrate the general applicability of our approach, we conducted a second validation round using an event log that was generated by other people (available from the process mining website).[2] Equally important, while further refinement is still needed, the second validation round confirms the generalizability of the Java program developed in enriching and transforming event log with resources' workload and involvement information. Thus, the steps described in the remainder of this section can be automated and streamlined, independent of the event log used, as long as the log meets the minimum quality standard explained earlier.

The log used in this validation round was generated from a telephone repair process. This log contains the necessary attributes as defined in M. There are four activities in this log: 'Analyze Defects', 'Repair (Complex)', 'Repair

---

[2] http://www.processmining.org/_media/tutorial/repairexample.zip

(Simple)', and 'Test Repair'. There are 12 resources in the log: SolverC1, SolverC2, SolverC3, SolverS1, SolverS2, SolverS3, Tester1, Tester2, ..., Tester6. There are more than 1100 cases (mostly completed cases).

Log Enrichment with Workload. The log used in this validation round meets the minimum log quality as stated earlier. Thus, we can proceed to enrich the log with workload information. This log was imported to a MySQL database table (called eventlog table) for relational algebra manipulations (see Table 1).

Table 1. A snippet of the eventlog database table

caseID	Activity	eventType	timestamp	resource
18	Analyze Defect	start	1970-01-01 15:36:00	Tester6
18	Analyze Defect	complete	1970-01-01 15:44:00	Tester6
15	Repair (Complex)	start	1970-01-01 19:29:00	SolverC3
....	...	...	...	...

The workload derivation function (Algorithm 1) was implemented in a Java program (which interacted with the eventlog through SQL queries). This program outputs a table called workloadstarted as a realization of R_{WL}). The AAD used is 450 seconds. The log used in our validation only contains the start and complete transition, thus, workloadstarted only reflects the work items that were still being executed by a particular resource at a point in time when an event was recorded in the log (see Table 2 for a snippet of the table). The content of each field named after each resource identifier (e.g. SolverC1 and SolverC3) represents the workload of the resource at the corresponding timestamp. For example, using 1970-01-03 00:37:00 as a reference time, resource SolverC1 had no work items being executed (or assigned to) between the period of 1970-01-03 00:33:15 and 1970-01-03 00:40:45, while resource SolverS3 had two work items (the activity 'Repair (Simple)' for case number 70 and 34) over the same period. The *workload-enriched* event log (i.e. $L_{A'_E}$) is obtained by *joining* Table 2 and Table 1 *on* timestamp field.

Table 2. A snippet of the workloadstarted table (R_{WL})

timestamp	Workload$_{SolverC1}$	...	Workload$_{SolverC3}$	Workload$_{SolverS3}$	...
1970-01-03 00:37:00	(empty)	...	(empty)	(70:Repair (Simple)), (34:Repair (Simple))	...
1970-01-03 14:10:00	(36:Repair (Complex))	...	(60:Repair (Complex))	(empty)	...
...	...	...	...	...	...

Aggregation to Case Log. The *workload-enriched* event log obtained so far contains the workload information of each resource at every timestamp in the log. Since a case may consist of more than one event, we need to aggregate the workload information among all relevant events for one case in the log. We have implemented the necessary functions to obtain $\#_{time\_start}(c)$, $\#_{time\_end}(c)$, $\#_{resources}(c)$, and $\#_{avg\_workload}(c)$ (case attributes defined in Sect. 3). In our implementation, the average workload for each resource (quantified as the number of work items) is stored in a separate field, each named in format avgWL_{r_x}, where r_x is a resource's identifier (see Table 3). The results of these aggregation functions were stored in another table caseLog (manifestation of $L^*_{A_C}$).

Classification-ready Case Log. Finally, we transformed caseLog into a form that is ready for classification analysis. Currently, caseLog does not contain a proper *response* variable. With the start and end time of each case, we can obtain the duration of that case and categorize the case as 'on-time' or 'overtime'. In other words, we need to implement a function to obtain the $\#_{isOvertime(c)}$ attribute (defined in Sect. 3). In our implementation, 'on-time' cases were labeled with a '0' value, while 'overtime' cases were labelled with a '1' value. The threshold value which determines if a case is overdue or not is set to 1 hour, resulting in $\approx 60\%/40\%$ distribution between 'on-time'/'overtime' classes. In practice, the setting of threshold relies on domain knowledge, and is not the main concern of this paper.

We have also implemented a function to obtain $\#_{isRxInvolved(c)}$ (defined in Sect. 3). For n-number of resources, this function creates n new fields, namely isInvolved_{r_x} (where r_x is a resource's identifier). Each of these fields can now be labelled individually as a distinct *predictor* variable. The caseLog table was then extended with the results of these functions. A snippet of the final *classification-ready* case log table is shown in Table 3 (manifestation of $L^*_{A'_C}$).

Table 3. A snippet of a *classifier-ready* case log ($L^*_{A'_C}$)

caseID	start	end	isOverdue	avgWL$_{SolverC1}$	...	avgWL$_{Tester6}$	isInvolved$_{SolverC1}$	...
1070	1970-01-23 20:58:00	...	1	1.36364	...	0	false	...
1075	1970-01-24 13:22:00	...	0	0.782609	...	1.6087	false	...

RCA with Classification Techniques. We fed the *classification-ready* case log into WEKA [23] for RCA. Domain knowledge can be applied to exclude/include certain attributes in the analysis (not all attributes *must* be used). WEKA supports *classification* algorithms, such as J.48 [15] and JRip [6]. We started the analysis with the average workload of all resources as *predictor* variables. A snippet of decision tree from applying the J.48 algorithm under 10-fold cross validation mode [19, Chapter 3] is shown in Fig. 2 (top part).[3] Line 3 in Fig. 2 shows that if the average workload of resource SolverS1 is equal or less than 0.66667 and that of SolverC3 is equal to or less than 0.117647 (line 4), then the rule generated by the algorithm states that all 177 cases which fulfill these criteria should be classified as 'on-time' (represented as '0'). While the records in the log show that this rule misclassified 14 cases, this rule is correct in the majority of cases (163 cases out of 177).

---

[3] Our aim is to show that the *classification-ready* log can be used by typical *classification* algorithms. Thus, the trade-off between various algorithms, or the reasons behind the selection of a certain algorithm, is beyond the scope of our paper.

```
 1   J.48 Classification Tree - Predictor Variables: average workload for all resources
 2   =====================================================================================
 3   avgWL_s1 <= 0.066667
 4   |    avgWL_c3 <= 0.117647: 0 (177.0/14.0)
 5   |    avgWL_c3 > 0.117647
 6   |    |    avgWL_c1 <= 0.44
 7   (...further details not shown - space limitation .......)
 8
 9   JRip Algorithm - Predictor Variables: resources' average workload and involvement
10   =====================================================================================
11   (isInvolved_SolverC3 = 1) => isOverdue=1 (201.0/6.0)
12   (isInvolved_SolverS1 = 1) => isOverdue=1 (206.0/41.0)
13   (isInvolved_SolverC2 = 1) and (isInvolved_SolverC1 = 1) => isOverdue=1 (22.0/3.0)
14   => isOverdue=0 (675.0/64.0)
```

Fig. 2. J.48 and JRip Analysis Results

However, the accuracy of the classification result is rather low. For 'on-time' class, the true positive (TP) rate (that is, the proportion of all 'on-time' cases which were correctly classified as 'on-time') is $\approx 70\%$; however, the false positive (FP) rate (that is, the proportion of all 'overtime' cases which were incorrectly classified as 'on-time') is close to 40%. For 'overtime' class, the TP rate (that is, the percentage of 'overtime' cases which were correctly classified as 'overtime') is only $\approx 60\%$, while the FP rate is as high as 25%. This analysis result suggests that the average workload for a number of resources seem to have an influence the occurrence of long-running cases, however, the correlation is weak (full accuracy metrics available in the extended version of this paper [18]).

It may be argued that the workload of resources which were not involved in a case will have no effect whatsoever on the duration of the case. However, it is possible for the workload of a resource which was not involved in a case to *indirectly* affect the duration of the case. For example, due to the high workload of a resource R_1 (an expert), a task that could have been completed in a much shorter time by R_1 was instead assigned to another resource R_2 (an amateur) who took longer to complete, thus prolonging the duration of the case. We have performed a corresponding *classification* analysis using the combined average workload of only those resources involved in a particular case as the *predictor* variable. The analysis does not show any significant improvement in our anaysis by using the average workload of only those resources involved in a given case as a *predictor* variable (details available in the extended version of this paper [18]).

The low accuracy of our result simply demonstrates the weak correlation between resources' workload and performance. It does not reflect the inefficacy of our approach: features selection is part of classical data mining study which is beyond the scope of our approach.

Beyond Workload. We included another predictor variable isInvolved$_{R_x}$ (see Sect. 3) in our analysis. The same J.48 algorithm was executed, except that this time, we used the average workload of all resources and resource involvement information as *predictor* variables. The result obtained was more accurate: 89% TP rate/ 18% FP rate (for 'on-time' cases), and 81% TP rate/10% FP rate (for overtime cases). Both predictor variables were used in the generated classification tree; however, the complexity of the generated classification tree is high - this may suggest an overfitting model (the decision tree is not shown in this paper). The full accuracy metrics are available in the extended version of this paper [18].

We also applied a rule-based classification algorithm (JRip) to the same data set. The result obtained was much simpler (only 4 rules - see Fig. 2 bottom part). For example, the rule in line 15 states that all 201 cases in which SolverC3 is involved will run 'overtime' (in reality, this rule only misclassifies 6 cases). More interestingly, however, is that the generated rules do not include resources' workload as a factor in lovertime cases (although they were included in the analysis). The accuracy of the result was also comparable: $\approx 92\%/16\%$ (TP/FP rate) for 'on-time' cases, and $\approx 83\%/7\%$ (TP/FP rate) for 'overtime' cases. The full accuracy metrics are available in the extended version of this paper [18].

By comparing these results, we may say that both workload and resource involvement may be the root causes of overtime cases in our log; however, the nature of resource involvement alone may already be sufficient to explain the occurrence of 'overtime' cases in most instances.

5   Related Work

Traditional RCA techniques have been frequently applied in the domain of business and risk management (e.g. Andersen and Fagerhaug [1] and Wilson et al. [22]), as well as manufacturing industries (e.g. Horev [9]). Similarly, the use of data mining techniques in business domain has also been heavily studied and applied (e.g. Cao et al. [7]). The use of data mining techniques to systematically perform an RCA of process-related issues is gaining popularity in the field of process mining (and business process management in general) as evidence by literature in this area. For example, Heravizadeh et al [8] proposed a root cause analysis approach based on business process models and augmented it with concepts from requirement engineering - this is in contrast with our approach which is based on post-execution data.

Rozinat and van der Aalst [17] proposed the use of *classification* technique to find the correlation between data attributes and the routing choices made in business processes. This approach is different from ours in that our approach focuses on the enrichment and transformation of event logs to classification-ready log for the purpose of RCA. The classification-ready log can be used to find the 'root cause' of various routing decisions, but not limited to such cases only.

In the work by Nakatumba and van der Aalst [14], a form of RCA focusing on the correlation between resources' workload and their performance was performed using process mining and data mining techniques (linear regression). Using *classification* techniques, Liu [11] and Bose [2] explore the predictive power of *feature sets* of traces in a log in explaining the root cause(s) of hardware faults. A more elaborate application of data mining techniques for RCA has also been conducted by Cakir [3]. Finally, in the work by Rozinat et al. [16], results obtained from a process mining exercise were used to explain the root cause of the occurence of idle times in a manufacturing test process. The focus of their approaches was on the RCA itself rather than the general *approach* to facilitate such an analysis as proposed in this paper.

6   Conclusions

We have presented and formalized an approach to enrich and transform event log into a form that allows an RCA based on *classification* techniques. The applicability of our approach to facilitate RCA of risk incidents has been validated using both self-generated synthetic log and publicly available log. Future work include the validation of our approach using real-life log and a richer set of derivable/correlatable attributes. The packaging of our approach as a plug-in to the process mining tool (ProM) will also be pursued. While *predictor* variables selection is not the main focus of this work, it is a critical element in RCA. Thus, future work also includes the extension of our approach with a feedback loop from the results of data mining analysis back to the log enrichment step in order to refine the selection of *predictor* variables.

References

1. Andersen, B., Fagerhaug, T.: Root Cause Analysis: Simplified Tools and Techniques, 2nd edn. ASQ Quality Press (2006) ISBN-12 978-0-87389-692-4
2. R.P. Jagadeesh Chandra Bose. Process Mining in the Large: Preprocessing, Discovery, and Diagnostic. PhD thesis, TUE, Eindhoven, The Netherlands (2012)
3. Cakir, G.S.: Development of a condition based maintenance decision model by data mining. Master's thesis, TUE, Eindhoven, The Netherlands (2011)
4. Caldwell, F.: CEO survey 2012: CIOs must link risk management and compliance to business priorities. Gartner (G00226165) (March 2012)
5. Chen, S.: Pilot fatigue is like 'having too much to drink'. CNN News (May 2009)
6. Cohen, W.W.: Fast effective rule induction. In: Proceedings of 12th International Conference on Machine Learning, pp. 115–123. Morgan Kaufmann (1995)
7. Cao, L., et al. (eds.): Data Mining for Business Applications. Springer (2009)
8. Heravizadeh, M., et al.: Root cause analysis in business processes. Technical report, Queensland University of Technology (2008)
9. Horev, M.: Root Cause Analysis in Process-Based Industries. Trafford Publishing (2008)
10. Jensen, K., Kristensen, L.M.: Coloured Petri Nets - Modelling and Validation of Concurrent Systems. Springer (2009)
11. Liu, F.: Fault diagnosis using process mining. Master's thesis, TUE, Eindhoven, The Netherlands (2010)
12. Maier, D.: The Theory of Relational Databases. Computer Science Press (1983)
13. De Medeiros, A.K.A., Günther, C.W.: Process mining: Using CPN tools to create test logs for mining algorithms. In: 6th Workshop and Tutorial on Practical Use of Coloured Petri Nets and the CPN Tools, pp. 177–190 (2005)
14. Nakatumba, J., van der Aalst, W.M.P.: Analyzing Resource Behavior Using Process Mining. In: Rinderle-Ma, S., Sadiq, S., Leymann, F. (eds.) BPM 2009. LNBIP, vol. 43, pp. 69–80. Springer, Heidelberg (2010)

15. Quinlan, J.R.: C4.5: programs for machine learning. Morgan Kaufmann Publishers Inc., San Francisco (1993)
16. Rozinat, A., et al.: Process mining applied to the test process of wafer scanners in ASML. IEEE Transactions on Systems, Man, and Cybernetics, Part C: Applications and Reviews 39(4), 474–479 (2009)
17. Rozinat, A., van der Aalst, W.M.P.: Decision Mining in ProM. In: Dustdar, S., Fiadeiro, J.L., Sheth, A.P. (eds.) BPM 2006. LNCS, vol. 4102, pp. 420–425. Springer, Heidelberg (2006)
18. Suriadi, S., Ouyang, C., van der Aalst, W.M.P., ter Hofstede, A.: Root cause analysis with enriched process logs. Technical Report 50748, Queensland University of Technology (2012), http://eprints.qut.edu.au/50748/
19. van der Aalst, W.M.P.: Process Mining - Discovery, Conformance and Enhancement of Business Processes. Springer (2011)
20. van der Aalst, W., Adriansyah, A., de Medeiros, A.K.A., Arcieri, F., Baier, T., Blickle, T., Bose, J.C., van den Brand, P., Brandtjen, R., Buijs, J., Burattin, A., Carmona, J., Castellanos, M., Claes, J., Cook, J., Costantini, N., Curbera, F., Damiani, E., de Leoni, M., Delias, P., van Dongen, B.F., Dumas, M., Dustdar, S., Fahland, D., Ferreira, D.R., Gaaloul, W., van Geffen, F., Goel, S., Günther, C., Guzzo, A., Harmon, P., ter Hofstede, A., Hoogland, J., Ingvaldsen, J.E., Kato, K., Kuhn, R., Kumar, A., La Rosa, M., Maggi, F., Malerba, D., Mans, R.S., Manuel, A., McCreesh, M., Mello, P., Mendling, J., Montali, M., Motahari-Nezhad, H.R., zur Muehlen, M., Munoz-Gama, J., Pontieri, L., Ribeiro, J., Rozinat, A., Seguel Pérez, H., Seguel Pérez, R., Sepúlveda, M., Sinur, J., Soffer, P., Song, M., Sperduti, A., Stilo, G., Stoel, C., Swenson, K., Talamo, M., Tan, W., Turner, C., Vanthienen, J., Varvaressos, G., Verbeek, E., Verdonk, M., Vigo, R., Wang, J., Weber, B., Weidlich, M., Weijters, T., Wen, L., Westergaard, M., Wynn, M.: Process Mining Manifesto. In: Daniel, F., Barkaoui, K., Dustdar, S. (eds.) BPM Workshops 2011, Part I. LNBIP, vol. 99, pp. 169–194. Springer, Heidelberg (2012)
21. van der Aalst, W.M.P., Dustdar, S.: Process mining put into context. IEEE Internet Computing 16, 82–86 (2012)
22. Wilson, P.F., et al.: Root Cause Analysis: A Tool for Total Quality Management. ASQ Quality Press (1993)
23. Witten, I.H., et al.: Weka: Practical machine learning tools and techniques with java implementations (1999)

Process Mining and the ProM Framework: An Exploratory Survey

Jan Claes and Geert Poels

Department of Management Information Science and Operations Management,
Faculty of Economics and Business Administration
Ghent University, Belgium
{jan.claes,geert.poels}@ugent.be

Abstract. In the last decade the field of process mining gained attention from research and practice. There is, however, not much known about the use and the appreciation of the involved techniques and tools, many of which are integrated into the well-known ProM framework. Therefore a questionnaire was sent out to ask people's opinions about process mining and the ProM framework. This paper reports on the answers and tries to link them to existing knowledge from academic literature and popular articles. It must be seen as a first, exploratory attempt to reveal the adoption of process mining and the actual use of the ProM framework.

Keywords: Process Mining, ProM Framework, Survey Research.

1   Introduction

In the recently published Process Mining Manifesto [1] 11 challenges and 6 guidelines for future development of the process mining field are listed. The paper was authored by 77 researchers and practitioners in the context of the IEEE Task Force on Process Mining[1] and is therefore assumed to reflect the opinion of the process mining community. This provided the inspiration to compose a questionnaire[2] to be able to ask the community for their opinion on related topics. The survey comprised 5 questions about process mining and 5 questions about the most popular process mining framework ProM[3]. Another 5 questions covered the demographical background of the respondents.

This is how the paper is structured: Section 2 explains the methodology. Section 3 provides an overview of the main results of the questionnaire. Section 4 discusses the impact on research and practice.

---

[1] For more information we refer to http://www.win.tue.nl/ieeetfpm
[2] The questions can be consulted at http://processmining.ugent.be/survey.php
[3] For information and download we refer to http://www.promtools.org

M. La Rosa and P. Soffer (Eds.): BPM 2012 Workshops, LNBIP 132, pp. 187–198, 2013.
© Springer-Verlag Berlin Heidelberg 2013

2   Methodology

The intention of the research was to perform an *exploratory* study to reveal *perceptions* of process mining in general (i.e., the concept, its techniques and tools) and the ProM framework in particular. Therefore, we decided to not derive hypotheses from theory, but to formulate open, optional questions that we deemed relevant. In our opinion, this approach would result in getting more respondents. In total 90 people completed all 15 survey questions (43 more than a recent survey about process mining use cases [2]). Another advantage of open questions is that participants are less influenced to give certain predefined answers than in a multiple choice questionnaire. Getting more respondents and less influenced answers provides a certain degree of face validity to what can be learned from the survey.

The questionnaire was put online at 2012-3-18 and was closed at 2012-5-1. We approached possible respondents by mail and by social media (i.e., LinkedIn and Twitter). 90 respondents completed all questions. The survey had a maximum of 119 answers, a minimum of 28 answers, and an average of 97 answers per question. At 2012-4-7 we added 3 additional questions about the most popular plug-ins according to the results so far (see Section 3.6 and 3.8), for which we counted 48 respondents.

We refer to http://www.janclaes.info/papers/PMSurvey for an extended report. The dataset with the provided answers can be downloaded via the same link.

3   Results

3.1   Demographics

The collected demographical data shows that the respondents form a heterogeneous group (see Fig. 1).

- Almost half of the respondents *study* process mining (researchers and students), and half of them *use* the techniques for practical, commercial purposes (other categories).
- The age of respondents varies between 21 and 60 year, but has a high concentration between 25 to 35 year. It is possible that this correctly reflects the process mining community if mainly novice (younger) researchers and practitioners joined the community, because the field only exists for some 15 years.
- There were almost as much respondents that indicated having good and excellent knowledge as the number that indicated having intermediate and bad knowledge about process mining.
- Respondents use process mining techniques mainly for analyzing process quality and performance and for performing process audits.
- The survey attracted respondents from 26 countries with a high concentration in the Netherlands and Belgium. This high concentration can be explained by the fact that the authors are located in Belgium, but can also be a consequence of the community having a high concentration of members in these areas.

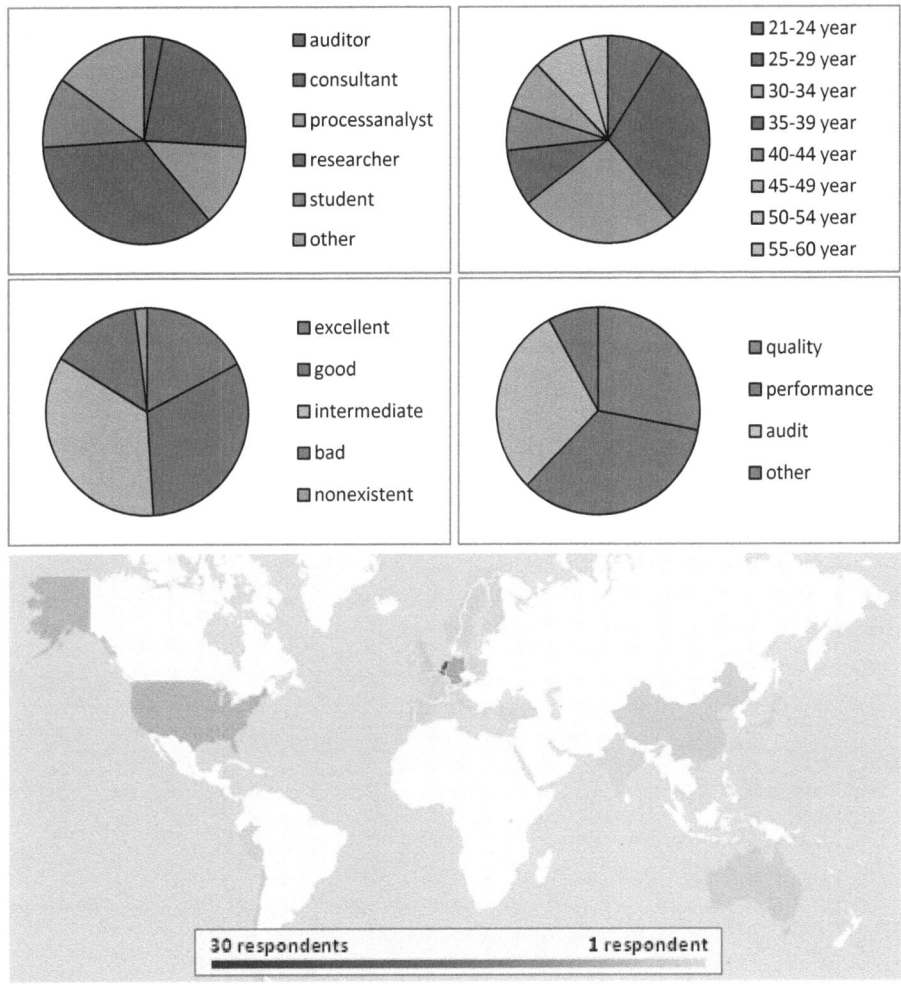

Fig. 1. Demographics of the respondents (question 11 (98), 12 (87), 13 (98), 14 (90), 15 (90 respondents) [2], map by ammap.com)

3.2   Benefits and Drawbacks of Process Mining Techniques

Results

The chart in Fig. 2 shows the indicated *benefits* of process mining techniques. We grouped similar answers in clusters and picked a term from within the group of answers to define the cluster. The clear main perceived benefit is *objectivity* (the use of real process data assures a certain degree of objectivity of analyses). Some respondents focused on the application of the techniques and highlighted *conformance checking* and the possibility to *find causes* of certain characteristics of the process models as the most appreciated applications.

Discussion

A recent survey [2] asked the same question ("What do you think is the biggest benefit of process mining"). Apart from functional qualities, that study concluded that the main benefits are related to objectivity, accuracy, speed, and transparency. Our survey seems to confirm these answers.

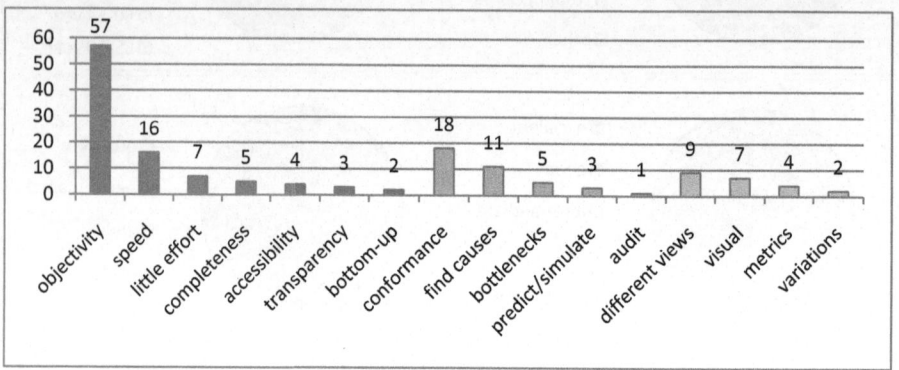

Fig. 2. Benefits of process mining techniques (question 4 [2], 94 respondents) (blue: characteristic, green: application, orange: representation)

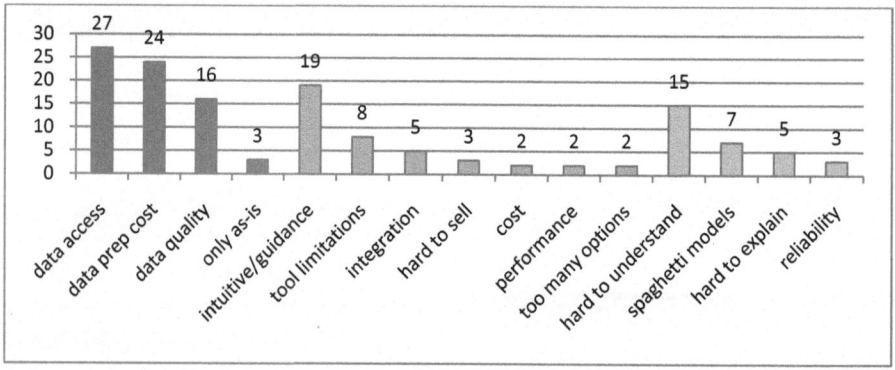

Fig. 3. Drawbacks of process mining techniques (question 5 [2], 90 respondents) (blue: input, green: techniques, orange: output)

Results

Perhaps more interesting for further research are the perceived *drawbacks* of process mining techniques (see Fig. 3). Most indicated drawbacks relate to data properties. It seems to be problematic to *find* and *prepare* the *right* data for process mining. The existing tools for process mining form another important indicated problem: They provide too little guidance and suffer from severe limitations. The current process mining tools also need to be (more) integrated with other tools and techniques. The output of process mining techniques (mostly discovered process models) is hard to understand (e.g., spaghetti models) and hard to explain.

Discussion

These main drawbacks are also addressed by the process mining manifesto [1]. Challenge 1 reports on the difficulties in finding, merging, and cleaning event data. Challenges 8 and 9 indicate that techniques and tools need to be more integrated with other analysis approaches. Challenges 10 and 11 concern the difficulty for non-experts to use and understand the techniques.

3.3 Tools for Process Mining

Results

The most popular process mining tool for research and practice is the ProM framework (see Fig. 4). Notice that the next three tools in the ranking are tools that help prepare event logs for the ProM framework. Another remarkable conclusion to draw is that the Disco tool - that was not officially released and only available to beta testers at the time of the survey - completes the top 5.

Discussion

We found three documented case studies in academic papers [3–5], they mentioned only ProM as a tool used in the study.

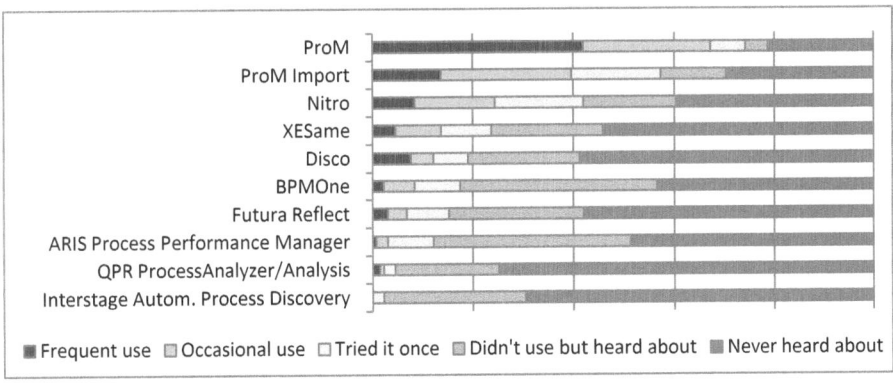

Fig. 4. Tools for process mining (question 2 [2], 119 respondents)

3.4 Benefits and Drawbacks of ProM

Results

The main indicated benefit of the ProM framework is that it comes with many plug-ins (see Fig. 5). Also the fact that it is open source is perceived as a main benefit (whether this relates to the possibility to change or extend the software or to the fact it is a free tool is not clear). Another suggested benefit is the clear interface of the framework. The limited ease of use of the software is the main indicated drawback.

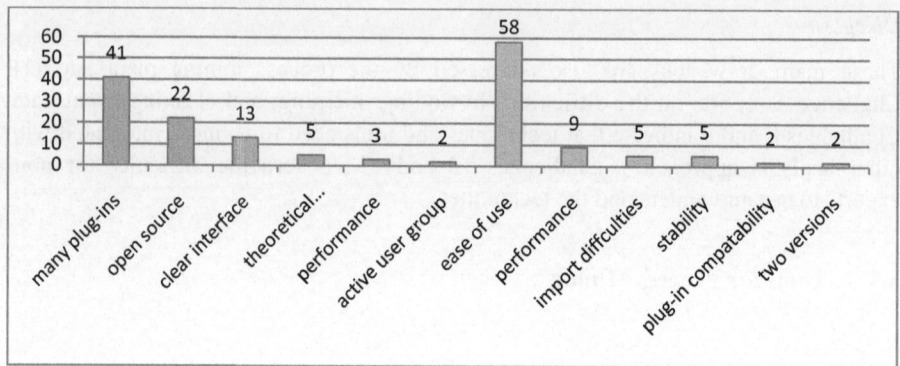

Fig. 5. Benefits and drawbacks of ProM (question 9 [2], 78 respondents) (green: benefits, orange: drawbacks)

3.5   Used Versions of ProM

Results

Fig. 6 shows information about the usage of the latest major ProM versions ProM 5 and ProM 6. Observe that for research (researchers and students) both tools are almost equally used, but 10% (5 out of 50 researchers) indicated to have never heard of ProM 6. For practice (consultants, process analysts and others) ProM 5 is still more used than ProM 6. A blog post from Fluxicon might reveal the reasons for practitioners to not switch to the newest version of ProM [6, 7]: "bugs are still found and fixed" and "a lot of plugins from ProM 5.2, (…), are missing at this point" in ProM 6 (see also Section 3.10).

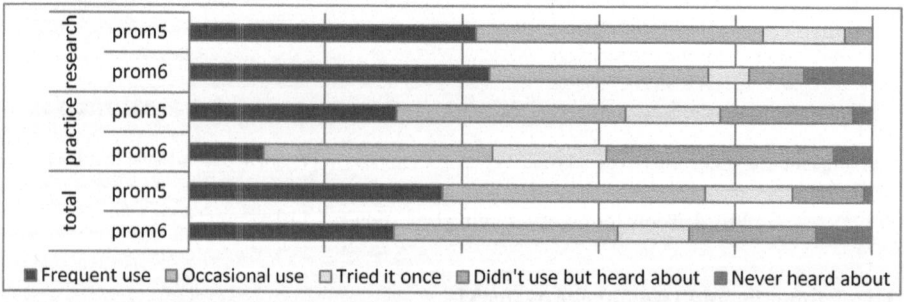

Fig. 6. Used versions of ProM (question 6 [2], 114 respondents)

3.6   Used Process Mining Techniques in ProM 5

Results

A list of the most used plug-ins of ProM 5.2 is provided in Fig. 7. The most popular plug-ins are Fuzzy Miner [8], Heuristics Miner [9], Social Network Miner [10], Dotted Chart Analysis [11] and Alpha algorithm plugin [12].

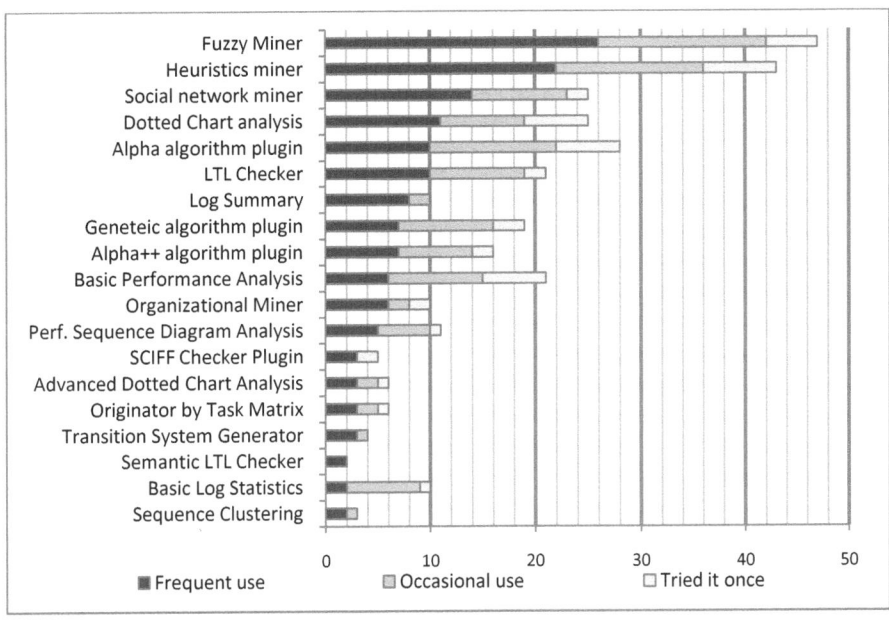

Fig. 7. Used process mining techniques in ProM 5.2 (question 7 [2], 115 respondents)

3.7 Evaluation of Most Used Process Mining Techniques in ProM 5

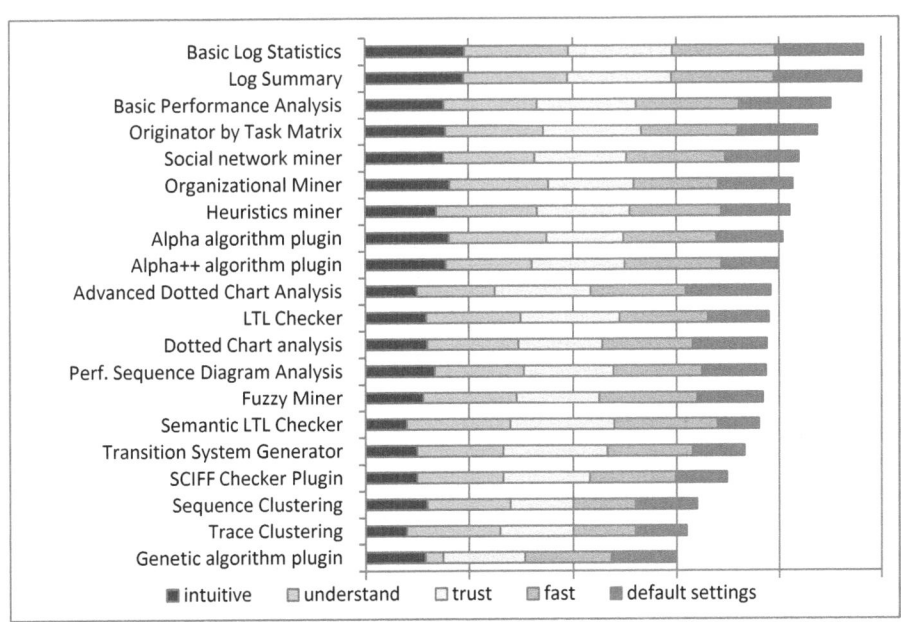

Fig. 8. Evaluation of most used process mining techniques in ProM 5.2 (question 16 & 17 [2], 48 respondents)

Results

Fig. 8 shows the perception of the respondents concerning 5 (possible) characteristics: intuitiveness of the technique, understandability of the results, trust in the result, speed of the technique and whether users adapt parameter settings. Each colored bar in Fig. 8 represents how many percent of the respondents classified the technique as belonging to the category that corresponds to the color of the bar. Notice that there seems to be no clear relation between the usage of a technique (Fig. 7) and its perceived characteristics (that, perhaps except for using default parameter settings, might be seen as quality indicators).

Discussion

In [13] strong indications are found that Heuristics Miner is "*the most appropriate and robust technique in a real-life context in terms of accuracy, comprehensibility, and scalability*" from a set of 8 investigated miners (see [13]). It scores better than Alpha miner and Genetic miner, which is also the case for our survey, although there are 6 miners that score even better than Heuristics Miner in our survey (see Fig. 8).

3.8   Used Process Mining Techniques in ProM 6

Results

Also in ProM 6.1 Heuristics Miner, Fuzzy Miner and Dotted Chart analysis are the most popular techniques. Furthermore, we observe a lot of popular plug-ins of ProM 5.2 (Fig. 7) are not in the list of ProM 6.1 (e.g., Genetic algorithm plug-in [14], Basic Performance Analysis). For some of them the reason is simply because they do not exist in ProM 6.1 (e.g., Basic Performance Analysis, see Section 3.10). For the others (e.g., Genetic algorithm plug-in) it is not clear why they are not popular in ProM 6.1.

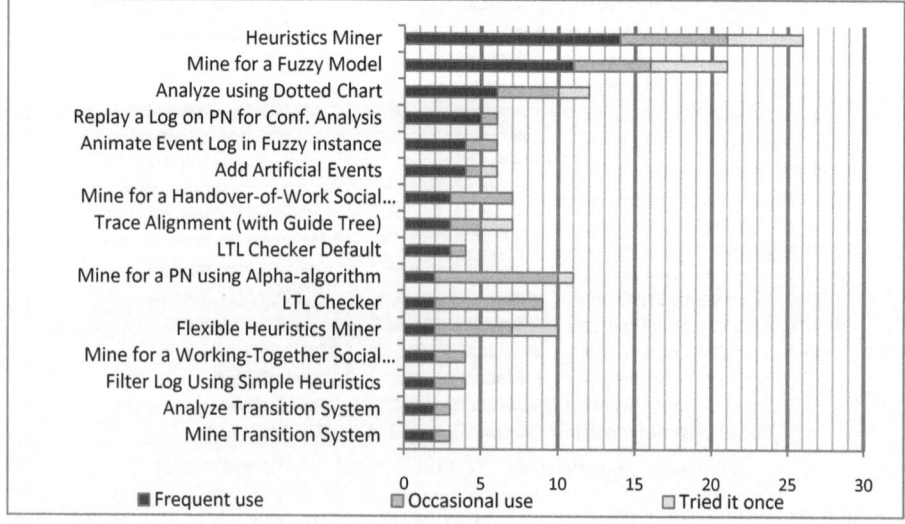

Fig. 9. Used process mining techniques in ProM 6.1 (question 8 [2], 115 respondents)

3.9   Evaluation of Most Used Process Mining Techniques in ProM 6

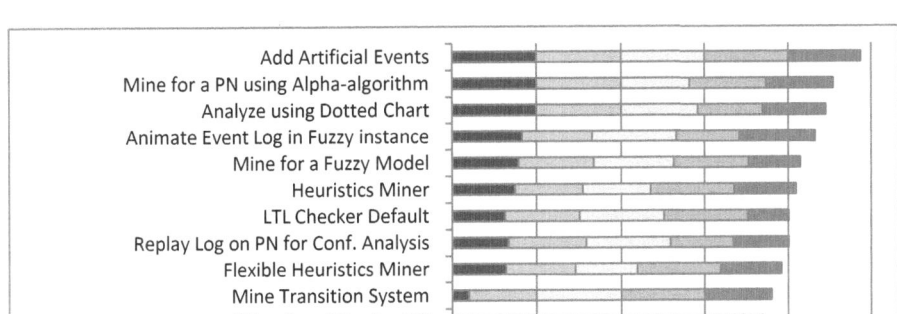

Fig. 9. Evaluation of most used process mining techniques in ProM 6.1 (question 18 [2], 48 respondents)

Results

Equally as for ProM 5.2 respondents were asked to indicate for ProM 6.1 if they feel the techniques and results are (i) intuitive, (ii) easy to understand, (iii) trustworthy, (iv) fast, and (v) if default options can be used. Next to the (subjective) perceived *trust* in the correctness of results, it is also important to investigate the (objective) theoretical correctness of the results. The need for a process mining evaluation framework for research and practice is discussed in [16].

Discussion

In Fig. 10 each colored bar shows how many percent of the respondents classified a plug-in in the category as indicated by its color. Add Artificial Events scored best, but this is only a very simple plug-in that adds an artificial start and/or end event in each trace. Trace Alignment (with Guide Tree) [15] scores poorly on all 5 categories. We recommend that involved developers take a closer look at the data in the extended report[4] to find out how their plug-in is evaluated and what can be improved.

3.10   Missing Process Mining Techniques in ProM 6

Results

The question about which plug-ins are missing in ProM 6.1 suggested that this could be existing plug-ins from ProM 5.2 that are not included in ProM 6.1 or new plug-ins that never existed in the ProM framework. Table 1 summarizes the answers. Notice that only 28 respondents answered this question. Some specific plug-ins of ProM 5.2 (see left column of Table 1) are missed in ProM 6.1 (e.g., advanced filters and performance plug-

---

[4] See http://www.janclaes.info/papers/PMSurvey/

ins). Respondents also would like to have better versions of some techniques (e.g., performance and discovery plug-ins) and a log or model editor is requested.

Table 1. Plug-ins that are missed in ProM 6.1 (question 10 [2], 28 respondents)

Existing plug-ins from ProM 5.2	New or enhanced plug-ins
Advanced filters (5x)	Robust performance analysis (2x)
Conformance Checker (3x)	Log/Model editor (2x)
Basic Performance Analysis (3x)	Security analysis (2x)
Performance Sequence Diagram Analysis (2x)	*Better* process discovery techniques
Alpha Algorithm(s)	*Better* performance analysis plugin
Trace Clustering	Medical analysis plug-in
Region Miner	Self organising maps
Pattern Sequence Analyser	Export to image option in *all* plugins

4   Discussion

This paper presents the results of a survey that was conducted as an exploratory study of the perceptions of process mining in general and the ProM framework in particular that are held by the process mining community of researchers and practitioners. The focus is clearly on relevance rather than rigor. "*Overemphasis on rigor in behavioral IS research has often resulted in a corresponding lowering of relevance*" [17]. We think the relevance of this work is proven (i) by the number of visits to the web page (336 different browser sessions were registered between 18 March and 30 April), (ii) by the number of respondents (there was no incentive to participate, yet 90 respondents completed the whole questionnaire) and (iii) by the number of people that indicated they like to receive a report on the results (87 respondents). Especially the data on which plug-ins are used seems to be most interesting (115 respondents).

However, there is still a need to focus on a number of methodological issues that should be taken into account when this exploratory study is replicated in a more rigorous way. First, the questions were formulated without specific hypotheses in mind. Most questions are formulated as open question with the risk of misinterpretation of individual answers. We argue that in a multiple choice setting, the interpretation is done by the respondent and therefore the risk of misinterpretation exists on the side of the respondent.

Second, all questions were optional. The result is that some questions were answered by many respondents (a maximum of 119) and others had few answers (a minimum of 28). This means that not all questions offer the same confidence in their results. This also causes difficulties when linking the answers of different questions to each other. For example, in section 3.5 the answers were divided in two groups according to the indicated profession of the respondent (research and practice). For this question only 86 of the 93 answers of respondents could be included, because the other 7 respondents did not indicate their profession.

Third, some anomalies were determined. We discovered that at least two respondents filled in some questions more than once. Because no personal information was collected, only the respondents that used the same browser session to complete the survey could be detected, so in reality there might be more than two duplicate sets of answers.

The results of the survey have several important implications. For *research*, it provides preliminary insights in the perception of the process mining domain and the ProM framework. Researchers can derive hypotheses from the results of this survey that have to be examined by other, more rigorous research. At least two very relevant research questions emerge from this study. Section 3.4 shows the need for a better, faster and cheaper support of the preparation phase of a process mining effort (i.e., finding and structuring the necessary data). The comparison of the results described in Section 3.6 and 3.8 and the results described in Section 3.7 and 3.8 indicates that popular process mining techniques are not considered to be better and vice versa. Is this correct? Why is this so?

For *practice*, this study can help users of the ProM framework to find their way in the long list of available plug-ins. Fig. 7 and Fig. 9 summarize which plug-ins are most used and Fig. 8 and Fig. 10 provide insight in which plug-ins are most appreciated.

In particular for *developers*, the survey points to a number of very specific shortcomings of the currently available ProM plug-ins. First, Table 1 contains a list of programming updates that are desired by the respondents. Second, from the chart of indicated benefits and drawbacks of the ProM framework in Fig. 5 it is clear the ease of use of the plug-ins should be improved. Also Section 3.2 points to the lack of intuitivism and guidance. We suggest more effort can be made to create a user friendly user interface (e.g., tooltip help for each parameter setting) and to provide (better) documentation.

To conclude, we would like to stress that this survey must be seen in the right context. Although we admit that we cannot guarantee full reliability of the data, we are convinced that this paper offers an interesting novel view on the community's perception of process mining and the ProM framework. This exploratory study forms the base to formulate hypotheses to be rigorously corroborated by future research.

Acknowledgements. We would like to thank Joel Ribeiro for his help with the selection of questions for this survey.

References

1. van der Aalst, W., Adriansyah, A., de Medeiros, A.K.A., Arcieri, F., Baier, T., Blickle, T., Bose, J.C., van den Brand, P., Brandtjen, R., Buijs, J., Burattin, A., Carmona, J., Castellanos, M., Claes, J., Cook, J., Costantini, N., Curbera, F., Damiani, E., de Leoni, M., Delias, P., van Dongen, B.F., Dumas, M., Dustdar, S., Fahland, D., Ferreira, D.R., Gaaloul, W., van Geffen, F., Goel, S., Günther, C., Guzzo, A., Harmon, P., ter Hofstede, A., Hoogland, J., Ingvaldsen, J.E., Kato, K., Kuhn, R., Kumar, A., La Rosa, M., Maggi, F., Malerba, D., Mans, R.S., Manuel, A., McCreesh, M., Mello, P., Mendling, J., Montali, M., Motahari-Nezhad, H.R., zur Muehlen, M., Munoz-Gama, J., Pontieri, L., Ribeiro, J., Rozinat, A., Seguel Pérez, H., Seguel Pérez, R., Sepúlveda, M., Sinur, J., Soffer, P., Song, M., Sperduti, A., Stilo, G., Stoel, C., Swenson, K., Talamo, M., Tan, W., Turner, C., Vanthienen, J., Varvaressos, G., Verbeek, E., Verdonk, M., Vigo, R., Wang, J., Weber, B., Weidlich, M., Weijters, T., Wen, L., Westergaard, M., Wynn, M.: Process Mining Manifesto. In: Daniel, F., Barkaoui, K., Dustdar, S. (eds.) BPM Workshops 2011, Part I. LNBIP, vol. 99, pp. 169–194. Springer, Heidelberg (2012)

2. Ailenei, I., Rozinat, A., Eckert, A., van der Aalst, W.M.P.: Definition and Validation of Process Mining Use Cases. In: Daniel, F., Barkaoui, K., Dustdar, S. (eds.) BPM Workshops 2011, Part I. LNBIP, vol. 99, pp. 75–86. Springer, Heidelberg (2012)

3. Mans, R., Schonenberg, M., Song, M., Van der Aalst, W.M.P., Bakker, P.J.M.: Process mining in healthcare: a case study. In: Proc. BIOSTEC 2008, pp. 425–438. Springer (2008)

4. Van der Aalst, W.M.P., Reijers, H.A., Weijters, A.J.M.M., Van Dongen, B.F., de Medeiros, A.K.A., Song, M., Verbeek, H.M.W.: Business process mining: An industrial application. Information Systems 32(5), 713–732 (2007)

5. Rozinat, A., De Jong, I., Günther, C.W., Van der Aalst, W.M.P.: Process mining applied to the test process of wafer scanners in ASML. IEEE Transactions on Systems, Man, and Cybernetics, Part C: Applications and Reviews 39(4), 474–479 (2009)

6. Rozinat, A., Günther, C.W.: Why We Hate ProM 6,
http://fluxicon.com/blog/2010/11/why-we-hate-prom-6

7. Rozinat, A., Günther, C.W.: Why We Love ProM 6,
http://fluxicon.com/blog/2010/11/why-we-love-prom-6

8. Günther, C.W., van der Aalst, W.M.P.: Fuzzy Mining – Adaptive Process Simplification Based on Multi-perspective Metrics. In: Alonso, G., Dadam, P., Rosemann, M. (eds.) BPM 2007. LNCS, vol. 4714, pp. 328–343. Springer, Heidelberg (2007)

9. Weijters, A.J.M.M., Van der Aalst, W.M.P.: Process mining with the heuristics miner-algorithm. Technische Universiteit Eindhoven, Tech. Rep. WP 166, 1–34 (2006)

10. van der Aalst, W.M.P., Song, M.S.: Mining Social Networks: Uncovering Interaction Patterns in Business Processes. In: Desel, J., Pernici, B., Weske, M. (eds.) BPM 2004. LNCS, vol. 3080, pp. 244–260. Springer, Heidelberg (2004)

11. Song, M., Van der Aalst, W.M.P.: Supporting process mining by showing events at a glance. In: Proc. WITS 2007, pp. 139–145 (2007)

12. Li, J., Liu, D., Yang, B.: Process Mining: Extending α-Algorithm to Mine Duplicate Tasks in Process Logs. In: Chang, K.C.-C., Wang, W., Chen, L., Ellis, C.A., Hsu, C.-H., Tsoi, A.C., Wang, H. (eds.) APWeb/WAIM 2007. LNCS, vol. 4537, pp. 396–407. Springer, Heidelberg (2007)

13. De Weerdt, J., De Backer, M., Vanthienen, J.: A multi-dimensional quality assessment of state-of-the-art process discovery algorithms using real-life event logs. Information Systems 37(7), 654–676 (2012)

14. de Medeiros, A.K.A., Weijters, A.J.M.M.: Genetic process mining: an experimental evaluation. Data Mining and Knowledge Discovery 14(2), 245–304 (2007)

15. Bose, J.C., Van der Aalst, W.M.P.: Process diagnostics using trace alignment: opportunities, issues, and challenges. Information Systems 37(2), 117–141 (2011)

16. Rozinat, A., de Medeiros, A.K.A., Günther, C.W., Weijters, A.J.M.M., van der Aalst, W.M.P.: The Need for a Process Mining Evaluation Framework in Research and Practice Position Paper. In: ter Hofstede, A.H.M., Benatallah, B., Paik, H.-Y. (eds.) BPM 2007 Workshops. LNCS, vol. 4928, pp. 84–89. Springer, Heidelberg (2008)

17. Hevner, A.R., March, S.T., Park, J., Ram, S.: Design science in information systems research. Mis Quarterly 28(1), 75–105 (2004)

MANA: Identifying and Mining Unstructured Business Processes

Pedro M. Esposito, Marco A.A. Vaz, Sérgio A. Rodrigues, and Jano M. de Souza

Federal University of Rio de Janeiro, Brazil
{pmesposito,mvaz,sergio,jano}@cos.ufrj.br

Abstract. The process mining field supports the discovery of process models using audit trails logged by information systems. Several mining techniques are able to deal with unstructured processes, mainly through cluster analysis. However, they assume the previous extraction of an event log containing related instances. This task is not trivial when the source system doesn't provide a reliable separation of its processes and allows the input of data through free text fields. The identification of related instances should, in this case, be explorative and integrated into the process mining tool used in later stages of the analyst's workflow. To this goal, the MANA approach was developed, allowing the explorative selection and grouping of instances through a canonical database.

Keywords: Process Mining, Process Discovery, Business Process Management, Unstructured Processes.

1 Introduction

Process discovery, one of the main branches of process mining, involves the discovery of process models from event logs extracted from information systems. This approach can avoid the modeling of biased and too broad views of the process [1] and allows the reduction of modeling costs. However, despite their success in the discovery of models from event logs, these algorithms fail in some real world situations. Several information systems don't impose a task flow on the user, allowing him to adapt the execution of a process in a case-by-case manner. If there are no specific guidelines, users may improvise. When these unstructured processes are processed through traditional mining techniques, the result is a *spaghetti process model*. These models are extremely complex, and are of little use for the understanding of the business. Spaghetti models aren't incorrect, but they show that the underlying process is highly unstructured [2]. They may reflect a serious lack of internal organization, and their visual impact can be a great motivation for the inception of process reengineering projects. Several techniques have been proposed to deal with unstructured processes, mainly based on clustering, such as the trace clustering algorithm [3]. They aim to transform a complex problem into a smaller one. The fuzzy miner [2] uses a different approach, with a map abstraction, grouping tasks from a single process model into subprocesses.

M. La Rosa and P. Soffer (Eds.): BPM 2012 Workshops, LNBIP 132, pp. 199–204, 2013.
© Springer-Verlag Berlin Heidelberg 2013

Current process mining tools, even when dealing with unstructured processes, assume there is a previously processed event log containing related process instances. The ProM framework [4] is the main existing process mining tool, implementing the state of the art in process mining techniques and covering a vast range of solutions. It works through the input of XML files including instances, events and their attributes, such as task names and originators. External tools facilitate the conversion of data to event logs; however, they don't allow the identification of similar instances.

However, when dealing with information systems supporting unstructured processes, mainly when the user is allowed to input data through free text fields, is it often hard to previously identify which instances should be part of an event log. Even if there is a *subject* field recorded for each instance, it may not be reliable, being too broad, too specific, biased by personal preferences or contain incorrect data. Related instances may be registered with close but not equal information. These nuances are usually not explicit in the database, and knowledge about the correct separation of processes may be hard to obtain, inexistent or hidden. Thus, the discovery of process models should be done in an explorative manner [2]. Extracting an entire database of instances and importing it into the ProM framework, however, is impracticable, and useful data would be lost. Reloading an event log for each mining attempt is also counterproductive.

To deal with this issue, the MANA approach was developed, integrating identification and process mining tasks into the same tool. Instead of importing event log files, it works with a canonical database, containing all process instances extracted from an information system. Instances are selected through sets of filters that define a *process query*. This filtering step allows the user to explore the database and identify relevant processes and tightly related instances, gaining knowledge about the organization. A query can then be processed through existing process mining and analysis techniques.

2   The MANA Approach

The MANA approach was developed to deal with the problem of selecting related process instances when the source information system is not aware of recommended task flows (allowing any task sequence to be recorded) and reasonable process types are not predefined. It is centered in a canonical database containing all instances extracted from an information system, recording data such as subject, description, origin, status, stakeholder, timestamps, tasks executed and their originators. This database allows the exploration of semantically relevant data, enabling users to enhance their knowledge about the processes under analysis. A tool was built to support this approach. It is worth noting that the Aris Process Performance Manager tool [5] also includes process mining functionality using an instance database. However, it assumes that all processes are structured, using process types as the basis for its analysis. The MANA tool was also designed to have a small learning curve for process analysts who are not experts in process mining. The ProM framework, although being the reference in the field, requires a great understanding of its techniques to achieve useful results [1].

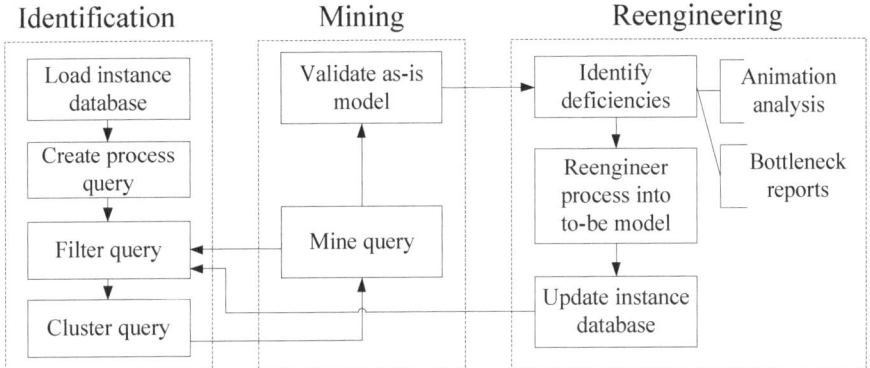

Fig. 1. Workflow supported by the MANA approach

The proposed workflow, shown in figure 1, is split into three phases: *identification*, *mining* and *reengineering*. The *identification* phase involves the selection of related instances. Initially, data from an information system containing process instances and events should be loaded into the canonical database. This can be done, for instance, through ETL (Extract, Transform and Load) tasks. The next step is the creation of a new *process query*. It is defined by a group of filters over the instance database. A query should contain related instances, which can be used for later tasks. While it begins contemplating the entire instance database, this cluster is incrementally narrowed with each added filter. Manual filters, for database exploration, and automatic clustering are supported. The following attributes are currently available for manual filtering: *subject, description, status, stakeholder, year, source, task, first unit, last unit and participating unit*. Filters are selected through searches over the current query's instances. The returned values are sorted by the number of instances that match each result, since the user may be searching for the most relevant processes to model. For example, a search for the value *contract* in the attribute *subject* may return a list of the following subjects: *insurance contract* (298 instances), *acquisition contract* (88 instances), *acq. contract* (10 instances). The user may then choose to commit a filter including or excluding each resulting value from the current query. For example, he may choose to consider all acquisition contracts, resulting in the filters shown in (1). Filters differing only in their value are joined by the disjunction operator (OR), while each group of filters are joined by the conjunction operator (AND), resulting in an expression in conjunctive normal form.

$$(\text{subject} = \text{Acquisition Contract OR subject} = \text{Aqu. Contract}) \tag{1}$$

Once a process query is built, it can be used on the *mining* phase. Its goal is the discovery of as-is process models from previously selected. Currently, the tool supports the Heuristics Miner [6], using the ProM framework's implementation. This algorithm was chosen because it deals well with noisy logs. This process model may then be validated and enhanced through meetings with its stakeholders. To support this, the tool integrates a BPMN modeler. This phase also supports the discovery of the flow between units (instead of tasks), since several process control systems emphasize more the *where* than the *what* during the recording of a process event. Each unit in the model can later be replaced by the task (or tasks) it executes through careful analysis. Since BPMN's swimlanes (the default notation for process participants) would not satisfy this use case, *organizational unit* nodes were added to the modeler, having the same behavior as task nodes. This approach will be exemplified later by the case study.

The *reengineering* phase allows the identification of deficiencies, which can be optimized in a to-be version of the model. Specifically, visual tools allow an intuitive impact of the current status of the process, allowing an easy identification of bottlenecks. The animation analysis, shown later in this paper, exemplifies this. It was inspired by the animation supported by the fuzzy miner. The animation is built considering the names of the tasks executed by each instance. Each dependency relation is animated. Each instance is shown as a circle, moving from its current place to the next task. In the MANA tool's implementation, if the progress is paused, and an instance is selected, its full data and flow are exhibited. This case-by-case analysis assists in the detection of issues affecting specific instances. Node colors are also coded in a scale between red and green, based on their delays, which enhances the visual analysis.

Besides the process animation, the tool also allows the analysis of task and unit performance through the generation of reports for each process query. For each task, the minimum, average and maximum delay is calculated. Although this approach does not aspire to support a highly complex process analysis, it allows the user to easily obtain insights into the current status of the process. The reporting module also allows the visualization of charts containing all events related to the task under analysis, with scatter plots indicating each task's delay and timelines similar to the approach proposed in [1]. Finally, updated instances can be loaded to the canonical database. Further filtering may be needed to clean the new data. Date filters can be used to compare an outdated process and its current version, ideally including optimizations that correct selected deficiencies. The reevaluation of the source information system is also predicted, but it will not be studied in further details in this paper.

3 Case Study

The following case study exemplifies the use of the developed tool to mine and analyze unstructured processes. The data was extracted from a process control information system from a public organization in Brazil. It handles the registration of processes and their progress between units. Available data includes process subjects, descriptions, stakeholders, origins and status. For each event, the system records a timestamp and its source and destination units. No task names are recorded for the events, so organizational units were used for process discovery. Due to confidentiality concerns, data such as unit names were replaced by letters. The main goal of the study was to analyze important processes from the Information Technology department.

The workflow begins by the creation of a process query. Since the focus is the IT department, instances that went through it or any of its subunits were searched. Subunits are marked by a slash after its parent unit's name. So, all results from the search

IT/% were added to the query, resulting in filters such as the ones exemplified in (2). The % symbol can match any substring.

$$\text{unit} = \text{IT OR unit} = \text{IT/A OR unit}=\text{IT/B OR unit}=\text{IT/C/D} (\ldots) \tag{2}$$

Although predefined process subjects are available, this field is blank for roughly 2/3 of all instances. They are also too generic (e.g. management and operations), reducing their usefulness for process identification tasks. Instance descriptions were used instead. However, since this data is input through free text fields, it should be handled with care. First, by searching all descriptions, the frequent value *disposal of computer equipment* was selected for further analysis. To allow the inclusion of related instance descriptions, the search *disposing%comp%* was used. All returned descriptions were added as filters to the query, totalizing about one thousand instances. The most frequent results include: *disposal of computer equipment*, *disposal of computer material*, *disposal of computer materials*. (sic) and *disposal of computer goods*. Note that the ProM framework would not allow this kind of exploration and filtering.

The next preprocessing step was the removal of rare exceptions, chosen as instances containing units present in less than 1% of all instances. Although these cases are important for exception detection, they would add unnecessary complexities considering the goal of this analysis. This filtering step removed 19 units from the process query, removing only 27 instances from the query. After the data preprocessing, the query was mined using the Heuristics Miner with its default parameters. Since a reasonable process model was achieved, no further clustering was needed. The resulting process model is shown in figure 2. This model can be further enriched through the addition of BPMN gateways and events. Since units were used instead of tasks during the mining phase, further analysis may be needed to deal with units that execute more than one task.

Figure 2 also depicts the animation of the filtered instances over the process model. The color and the slow flow of instances from units E and G provided a visual cue indicating that they should be closely inspected. Through the generation of a report for each unit's delay, it was verified that unit E took the maximum of 476 and the average of 97 days to execute its task. Unit G took the maximum of 1206 days and the average of 108 days. These values are much higher than those from other units participating in the process. The identification of the exact causes for these delays requires a deeper organizational analysis involving the process' stakeholders.

4   Conclusions and Future Work

The modeling of unstructured processes using process mining techniques is a challenging task. This paper presented an explorative approach that allows a process analyst to incrementally identify related process instances and gain knowledge about the organization. A tool was developed to support this through the construction of process queries, filtering instances from a canonical database. It also aims at providing visual tools and an intuitive workflow. Our case study shows that this approach is successful and can be used when there is no clear separation between process types in the source database. Future work includes the addition of further filtering attributes and techniques. The support for extra process mining and clustering algorithms is also important for advanced users, allowing further improvement and customization of their results. Note that the tool already allows the exportation of queries to XES files if techniques implemented in the ProM framework are needed. Finally, support for a deeper process analysis is planned, through the use data warehousing technology.

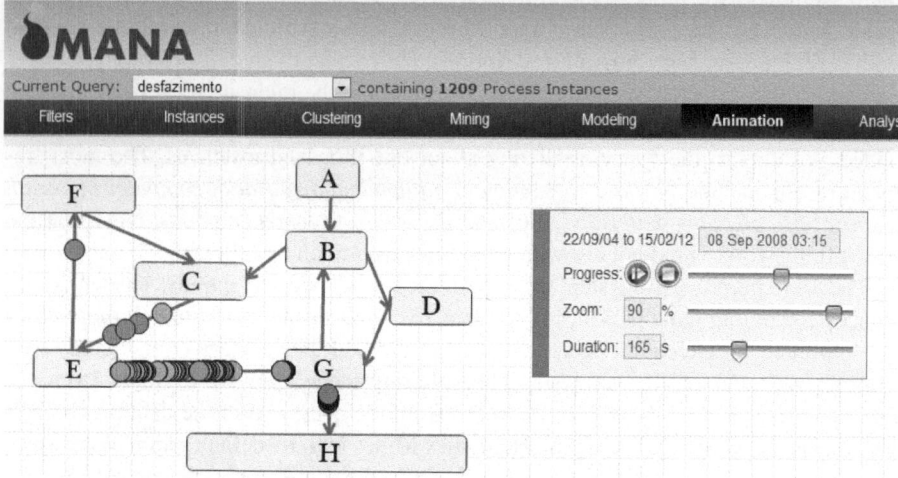

Fig. 2. Animation of the mined process model

References

1. van der Aalst, W.M.P.: Process Mining: Discovery, Conformance and Enhancement of Business Processes. Springer (2011)
2. van der Aalst, W.M.P., Gunther, C.W.: Finding Structure in Unstructured Processes: The Case for Process Mining. In: Proceedings of the Seventh International Conference on Application of Concurrency to System Design, pp. 3–12. IEEE Computer Society, Washington, DC (2007)
3. Song, M., Günther, C.W., van der Aalst, W.M.P.: Trace Clustering in Process Mining. In: Ardagna, D., Mecella, M., Yang, J. (eds.) BPM 2008 Workshops. LNBIP, vol. 17, pp. 109–120. Springer, Heidelberg (2009)
4. van Dongen, B.F., de Medeiros, A.K.A., Verbeek, H.M.W., Weijters, A.J.M.M., van der Aalst, W.M.P.: The ProM Framework: A New Era in Process Mining Tool Support. In: Ciardo, G., Darondeau, P. (eds.) ICATPN 2005. LNCS, vol. 3536, pp. 444–454. Springer, Heidelberg (2005)
5. Blickle, T., Hess, H.: Automatic Process Discovery with ARIS Process Performance Manager (white paper). Software AG (2010)
6. Weijters, A.J.M.M., van der Aalst, W.M.P., De Medeiros, A.K.A.: Process Mining with the HeuristicsMiner Algorithm. BETA Working Paper Series, WP 166, Eindhoven University of Technology, Eindhoven (2006)

An Experimental Evaluation of Passage-Based Process Discovery

H.M.W. (Eric) Verbeek and Wil M.P. van der Aalst

Technische Universiteit Eindhoven
Department of Mathematics and Computer Science
P.O. Box 513, 5600 MB Eindhoven, The Netherlands
{h.m.w.verbeek,w.m.p.v.d.aalst}@tue.nl

Abstract. In the area of process mining, the ILP Miner is known for the fact that it always returns a Petri net that perfectly fits a given event log. Like for most process discovery algorithms, its complexity is linear in the size of the event log and exponential in the number of event classes (i.e., distinct activities). As a result, the potential gain by partitioning the event classes is much higher than the potential gain by partitioning the traces in the event log over multiple event logs. This paper proposes to use the so-called passages to split up the event classes over multiple event logs, and shows the results are for seven large real-life event logs and one artificial event log: The use of passages indeed alleviates the complexity, but much hinges on the size of the largest passage detected.

Keywords: Process Discovery, Fitness, Petri nets, Passages.

1 Introduction

Process discovery, i.e., learning a process model from an event log, remains the most challenging process mining task [1]. The best-known process discovery algorithm is the α-algorithm [2]. Under some assumptions, this algorithm results in a Petri net that fits the original event log. However, if these assumptions do not hold, this Petri net may not even be free of deadlocks.

An example of a process discovery algorithm that always discovers a perfectly fitting Petri net is the so-called ILP Miner [3]. This algorithm uses Integer Linear Programming (ILP) techniques to check whether or not adding a place would harm perfect fitness. However, the downside of this algorithm is that lots of places need to be checked, as we have to check all combinations of possible inputs and outputs. As a result, the ILP Miner works fine for event logs that contain only a few event classes, but it may require excessive computation time in case the number of event classes is even moderate (say, 20 or more).

Recently, the notion of *passages* was introduced to decompose process mining problems [4]. Instead of having to mine the entire log for a perfectly fitting Petri net, we can partition the log into several smaller passage logs and mine every passage log for a Petri net. At the end, we can simply combine the resulting passage Petri nets into a single Petri net for which we know that it perfectly fits

M. La Rosa and P. Soffer (Eds.): BPM 2012 Workshops, LNBIP 132, pp. 205–210, 2013.

the entire log. As a result, passage-based decomposition may help to address the complexity problem of the ILP Miner.

This paper aims at evaluating the passage technique introduced in [4] using a number of large real-life logs with many event classes. For details on the passages, we refer to [4]. For a more detailed version of this paper, please see [5]. Here, it suffices to mention that the passage technique requires the addition of a unique start event and a unique end event, and that it allows for two abstract algorithms γ_c and γ_p, where γ_c is used to detect causal relations (which underly the different passage logs) between event classes, and γ_p is used to mine a Petri net from a single passage log.

The remainder of this paper is organized as follows. First, Section 2 describes the experimental setup and Section 3 presents the experimental evaluation. The latter shows that although the passages alleviate performance problems to a large extent, there may still be large passages that are to big for the ILP Miner to handle. Section 4 presents a possible solution to the problem of big passages, which allows the user of the ILP Miner to focus on the most obvious places and to simply ignore the less obvious ones. Finally, Section 5 concludes the paper by wrapping up the results and offering hints for future work.

2   Experimental Setup

The initial experimental setup contains 7 real-life event logs (A to G). Table 1 shows the characteristics of these logs. A contains test events for the deployment of high-tech equipment, which contains both in-factory tests and on-site test events. B is the BPI Challenge 2012 event log [6]. C contains diagnostic and treatment events from a hospital department. D and E contain events from a municipality, where D contains events that correspond to citizens objecting to the valuation of their houses, and E contains events that correspond to citizens that request for building permits. F contains events from a web server. Finally, G contains events related to invoices at a provincial office of the Dutch national public works.

Each of these logs will be mined using both the standard ILP Miner[1] and the passage-enhanced ILP Miner[2] as they are implemented in ProM 6.2[3].

Table 2 shows the characteristics of the system we used to run both miners on.

3   Experimental Evaluation

Table 3 shows the run times we obtained from the standard ILP Miner. For sake of completeness, we mention that the run times have been rounded to the nearest

---

[1] The ILP Miner plug-in from the ILPMiner package with default settings.

[2] The Mine Petri net using Passages plug-in from the Passage package with γ_c set to Heuristics Miner (Relative-to-best set to 0 and Dependency set to 100) and γ_p set to ILP Miner.

[3] ProM 6.2 can be downloaded from www.processmining.org

number containing only two relevant digits. For example, the run time for B is rounded from 4620.97 to 4600. The standard ILP Miner ran out of memory for A and F and ran out of time (more than a week) for C.

In contrast, Table 5 shows (among other things) the run times for the passage-enhanced ILP Miner. For example, it shows that the run time for B has decreased from 4600 to 290 seconds, that 16 passages were detected, that the largest passage contains 13 event classes, and that it took the ILP Miner 92 seconds to mine the Petri net for the largest passage. The run times for the largest passages show that we do not gain much by running the ILP Miner on different computers for different passages, as the overall run time mainly depends on the run time for the largest passage. Only if several other passages are about as large as the largest passage, then using different computers might help. Finally, note that this miner also cannot handle F: It simply contains too many event classes to be kept in memory.

These results show that splitting up the event log into many event logs using passages typically helps in reducing the run times, while still resulting in a Petri net that perfectly replays the original event log. It also shows, that the better the distribution among the passages is, the better the reduction will be: If some passage is still large in size, the run time will still be large as well. Finally, G shows that the passage-enhanced ILP Miner comes with a little overhead (the additional start and end event classes), which may result in worse run times in case the log cannot really be split up into passages.

Of course, one could argue that the passage-enhanced ILP Miner takes less run time because it produces different results, i.e., different Petri nets. Therefore, we also conducted experiments where we used the *proper completion* ILP Miner as both the γ_c algorithm and the γ_p algorithm[4]: If we split up the net as obtained from the proper completion ILP Miner into passages, run the same miner on every passage, and glue the resulting net into a single Petri net, then we expect that the end result is identical to the result of the initial ILP Miner. However, this requires that the event log at hand contains almost no noise, as the ILP Miner translates noise into causal dependencies, which typically results in a net that contains only a single passage.

Therefore, we created a model for a paper review system and used the model to create a noise-free event log, called H, which contains 54 event classes, 71,800 events, and 2500 traces. We ran the miner as mentioned above on this event log, and we compared both the resulting Petri nets (both the end result as the result of the γ_c algorithm) and the execution times.

The γ_c ILP Miner took 1300 seconds. From the resulting Petri net, 30 passages were derived of which the largest passage contains 7 event classes. In total, filtering the log for every passage, running the γ_p ILP Miner for every resulting sublog, and synthesizing all 30 subnets into a single Petri net took 140 seconds, and resulted in the same Petri net. This clearly shows that the passage-enhanced

---

[4] The `Mine Petri net using Passages` plug-in from the `Passage` package with γ_c set to `Flower and ILP Miner with Proper Completion` and γ_p set to `ILP Miner with Proper Completion`.

Table 1. Characteristics for the different event logs

Event log	Event classes	Events	Traces
A	720	154,966	24
B	36	262,200	13,087
C	615	53,874	2713
D	96	124,862	130
E	255	67,271	2076
F	5415	612,340	2246
G	15	119,021	14,279

Table 2. Basic information on the system used

Key	Value
Computer	Dell Precision T5400
Processor	Intel® Xeon® CPU, E5430 @ 2.66Ghz (2 processors)
Installed memory (RAM)	16.0 GB
System type	64-bit Windows 7 Enterprise SP 1
JRE	64-bit jdk1.6.0_24
VM arguments	-ea -Xmx4G

Table 3. Run times obtained for the standard ILP Miner

Event log	Run time in seconds
A	-
B	4600
C	-
D	45,000
E	110,000
F	-
G	56

Table 4. Run times obtained for the passage-enhanced ILP Miner, restricted to 20 event classes

Event log	Run time in seconds
A	11,000
B	320
C	650
D	420
E	650
F	-
G	85

Table 5. Run times (and other characteristics) obtained for the passage-enhanced ILP Miner

Event log	Run time in seconds	Passages #	Largest passage in event classes	Run time largest passage in seconds
A	220,000	382	641	210,000
B	290	16	13	92
C	300,000	113	337	230,000
D	15,000	36	45	14,000
E	16,000	94	83	15,000
F	-	-	-	-
G	84	2	16	72

ILP Miner can produce the same Petri net as the standard ILP Miner, but using only a fraction of the time.

4   A Possible Relaxation

Obviously, large passages can pose as much as a problem as a large collection of event classes in a log can. However, we could use the fact that we know how many event classes there will be before we start the ILP Miner on a passage. In case we think that the collection of event classes is still too large (641 for A), we can simply decide not to use the ILP Miner for such a passage, but just to return a Petri net that contains a transition for every event class. This means that we overgeneralize the behavior of large passages, as we allow for any combination of the transitions present in large passage. Intuitively, one could argue that these large passages correspond to difficult causal structures that are hard to comprehend in the first place, so why would the user want to see these complex structures? Instead, it just might be better for the user to see the more simple structures, which can be easily obtained by running the ILP Miner only on those passages that are small enough.

Please note that the standard ILP Miner does not offer this possibility: Either the collection of event classes in the event log is small enough and we will get a connected Petri net, or the collection is too big and we will get a Petri net containing only transitions. The fact that the passage-enhanced ILP Miner can check the number of event classes per passage is obviously useful here.

For this reason, we have extended the experiment with a maximum passage size of 20: A passage-enhanced ILP Miner that only uses the ILP Miner in case the passage at hand contains less than 20 event classes (based on the earlier experiments, 20 seems to be still reasonable)[5]. Possibly, this miner results in a Petri net that is disconnected, but it is very likely that it will also contain connected parts, and it will still fit the original event log perfectly. Table 4 shows the results. F still contains too many event classes to be handled, while A contains a trace that results in more than 10,0000 events for some passages, which explains the exceptional long run time for this log. The other run times are quite acceptable: in a matter of minutes, the process is discovered.

5   Conclusions

In this paper, we showed that passages can help the ILP Miner in finding a Petri net that perfectly fits a given event log. For two logs (A and C), the passage-enhanced ILP Miner finds a Petri net, where the standard ILP Miner did not. For three logs (B, D, and E), the passage-enhanced ILP Miner performed way better than the standard ILP Miner. For one log (F), both the passage-enhanced ILP Miner and the standard ILP Miner ran out of memory because

---

[5] The Mine Petri net using Passages plug-in from the Passage package with γ_c set to Heuristics Miner (Relative-to-best set to 0 and Dependency set to 100), γ_p set to ILP Miner, and max size set to 20.

of the huge number of event classes. For one log (G), the passage-enhanced ILP Miner performed worse than the standard ILP Miner. This is explained by the fact that size of the largest passage exceeds the size of the original net, which is possible as the passage technique requires the addition of a unique start event and a unique end event.

We also showed that by adding a restriction on the size of the passages, the run times of the passage-enhanced ILP Miner can even be reduced further, although his typically results in disconnected Petri nets. In some cases, this can be regarded as positive, as the disconnected parts might offer the domain expert the information he needs. As a result, there seems to be a possible trade-off between run time and precision, while keeping the fitness at a perfect level: The further we restrict the number of event classes in passages (which means that passages that exceed this restriction will not be mined for a Petri net), the more disconnected (and the less precise) the resulting Petri net will be, but the faster the ILP Miner will finish. We could even think of extending the passage-enhanced ILP Miner with a certain time limit: It will only consider the smallest passages, and while the time limit still permits, it will also consider the smallest of the unconsidered passages as well.

Another option for future research is to remove causal relations while turning the causal structure into passages. For example, if the removal of a single, infrequent, causal relation would cause the largest passage to break apart into multiple passages, then it might be worthwhile to indeed remove this relation. To do so, we can consider the causal structure produced by the Heuristics Miner, which provides such frequencies.

References

1. van der Aalst, W.M.P.: Process Mining: Discovery, Conformance and Enhancement of Business Processes. Springer (2011)
2. van der Aalst, W.M.P., Weijters, A.J.M.M., Maruster, L.: Workflow Mining: Discovering Process Models from Event Logs. IEEE Transactions on Knowledge and Data Engineering 16(9), 1128–1142 (2004)
3. van der Werf, J.M.E.M., van Dongen, B.F., Hurkens, C.A.J., Serebrenik, A.: Process discovery using integer linear programming. Fundam. Inform. 94(3-4), 387–412 (2009)
4. van der Aalst, W.M.P.: Decomposing Process Mining Problems Using Passages. In: Haddad, S., Pomello, L. (eds.) PETRI NETS 2012. LNCS, vol. 7347, pp. 72–91. Springer, Heidelberg (2012)
5. Verbeek, H.M.W., van der Aalst, W.M.P.: An experimental evaluation of passage-based process discovery. BPM Center Report BPM-12-14, BPMcenter.org (2012)
6. van Dongen, B.F.: BPI challenge 2012. Dataset (2012),
   http://dx.doi.org/10.4121/uuid:3926db30-f712-4394-aebc-75976070e91f

Predicting Deadline Transgressions Using Event Logs

Anastasiia Pika[1], Wil M.P. van der Aalst[2,1], Colin J. Fidge[1],
Arthur H.M. ter Hofstede[1,2], and Moe T. Wynn[1]

[1] Queensland University of Technology, Brisbane, Australia
{a.pika,c.fidge,a.terhofstede,m.wynn}@qut.edu.au
[2] Eindhoven University of Technology, Eindhoven, The Netherlands
{w.m.p.v.d.aalst}@tue.nl

Abstract. Effective risk management is crucial for any organisation. One of its key steps is risk identification, but few tools exist to support this process. Here we present a method for the automatic discovery of a particular type of process-related risk, the danger of deadline transgressions or overruns, based on the analysis of event logs. We define a set of time-related process risk indicators, i.e., patterns observable in event logs that highlight the likelihood of an overrun, and then show how instances of these patterns can be identified automatically using statistical principles. To demonstrate its feasibility, the approach has been implemented as a plug-in module to the process mining framework ProM and tested using an event log from a Dutch financial institution.

1 Introduction

Effective risk management is crucial for organisations. ISO Guide 73:2009 defines risk as the "effect of uncertainty on objectives" where effect is "a deviation from the expected — positive and/or negative" [3]. One of the most important aspects of risk management is *risk identification* [7]. Traditional risk management approaches offer only high-level guidance about risk identification methods and rely on the knowledge of domain experts [7]. Accordingly, our goal is to show how the data recorded in event logs by contemporary workflow management systems can be exploited for the purpose of risk identification.

Various approaches for predicting timeliness have been proposed in the literature [8,9] and serve as a starting point for our work. Van der Aalst et al.'s approach [8] builds an annotated transition system and remaining process time is then predicted based on the average of earlier cases visiting the same state. Van Dongen et al.'s approach [9] predicts the remaining cycle time of a case by using non-parametric regression based on case-related data as the predictor variables. A framework for identification and analysis of the operational risks associated with single business process activities, as well as a whole process, was proposed by Jallow et al. [4]. Wickboldt et al. proposed a framework that makes use of a process model and process execution data from historical records for risk prediction [10]. The use of process mining for the identification of transactional

M. La Rosa and P. Soffer (Eds.): BPM 2012 Workshops, LNBIP 132, pp. 211–216, 2013.

fraud risk was proposed by Jans et al. [5]. Overall, our approach differs from previous work in that: it does not require as an input risk indicators defined by experts or pre-classified data [4,10]; it is not restricted to transactional fraud risk [5]; and it focuses on identifying the risk of not meeting a deadline rather than estimating the remaining cycle time of a case [8,9].

Since our approach is based on actual data in event logs, it focuses on *process-related* risks only. We refer to a risk as *process-related* if its root cause is any combination of process behaviour (notably the activities performed and their sequence), resource behaviour (e.g., resource availability, capabilities and inter-action patterns) or case-related data. Process-related risks can jeopardise the achievement of process goals in terms of cost, timeliness or the quality of out-puts [4]. In this paper we consider only one type of risk, the likelihood that cases do not meet their deadline, however our general strategy is not restricted to time-related risks. Our approach consists of three steps: 1) definition of Process Risk Indicators (PRIs); 2) devising a way to identify instances of risk patterns in a log; and 3) defining a predictor function that characterises the risk of a case failing (from its local characteristics only).

2   Risk Identification Method

Before introducing our Process Risk Indicators (PRIs), we first introduce some notations. Let α denote a *run* of a *process model*. Random variable X_α denotes a case's outcome in terms of timeliness per run α. In this paper, we assume that X_α takes one of two possible values: *1* if a case is delayed and *0* if it is completed in time. Per run α there is *cumulative distribution function* F_α such that $F_\alpha(x) = P(X_\alpha \leq x)$ for X_α. In this way the risk of case delay can be quantified. Function F_α captures both impact and likelihood. Assuming that a process is in a steady state there exists such a function F_α for all runs. Our goal is to define a function G that predicts the value of X_α, i.e., we would like to minimize the expected value of the difference $|X_\alpha - G_\alpha|$. Function G_α is based on a few local characteristics of α. Let $\mathcal{E}$ denote the set of all possible *events*. A *trace* is a sequence of events $\delta \in \mathcal{E}^*$. An *event log* L is a set of traces. We assume that each event has the following attributes: an *activity name*, a *time stamp*, a *resource* and a *transaction type* (including *start* and *complete*). Each case is described by a *trace* $\delta \in L$ which can be related to a process model *run*.

Using indicators for risk monitoring is a common practice in areas such as safety and fraud detection, so we use "risk indicators" for identification of process-related risks. We define a *Process Risk Indicator* as a pattern observable in an event log whose presence indicates a higher likelihood of some process-related risk. In this paper we consider only the risk of a case overrun. Our aim is to identify domain-independent indicators that can be identified by analysing event logs and do not require any additional information, e.g. a process model. We have defined five time-related PRIs.

- **PRI 1: Abnormal activity execution time.** A case contains an activity whose duration is significantly higher than its normal duration.

- **PRI 2: Abnormal waiting time.** Activity execution is not started for an abnormally long period of time after it has been enabled.
- **PRI 3: Multiple activity repetitions.** An activity is repeated multiple times in a case.
- **PRI 4: Atypical activities.** A case contains an activity that has not been performed often previously.
- **PRI 5: Multiple resource involvement.** The number of resources involved in a case significantly exceeds the norm.

Our method for PRI discovery is based on unsupervised statistical techniques for outlier identification. They have the advantage of not requiring pre-classified data samples for learning. We use the "sample standard deviations" approach for outlier detection which assumes that the sampled values follow a normal distribution. A cut-off threshold for a normally distributed population is usually defined as $\mu \pm 2\sigma$ (for a 95% confidence interval). Observations whose values are outside this range are considered outliers. If a sample contains extreme outliers a cut-off threshold defined by the mean $\bar{x}$ and standard deviation s is often unnecessarily biased, so for a normally distributed population the median $\tilde{x}$ is a robust estimator for $\bar{x}$ and a robust estimator for s is 1.483MAD [6]. Our method for PRI identification consists of two steps: (1) Identify a cut-off threshold by analysing the given event log; and (2) For a given case (represented by a trace) identify outliers using the learned threshold. For each trace $\delta \in L$ we introduce attributes for each risk indicator n, denoted PRI_n. These attributes are used by the risk identification method to store information about the indicators found in a trace. Attribute PRI_n is 1 if indicator n is found, and 0 otherwise.

Following Zhang et al. [11], we assume that activity durations follow a log-normal distribution, therefore logarithms of activity durations approximately follow a normal distribution. To identify the presence of PRI_1 in a trace belonging to a run α of the process model, the following procedure is followed. For every activity a occurring in at least one trace corresponding to α: create a sample x of logarithms of the durations of all occurrences of a in traces corresponding to α (difference between *complete* and *start* events); calculate a cut-off threshold $t = \bar{x} + 2s$; for a given activity instance compare logarithm of its duration with the threshold t and if it exceeds the threshold set the value of the corresponding case's attribute $PRI_1 = 1$. A similar procedure is followed for other PRIs. For PRI_2 we also assume that waiting times follow a log-normal distribution [11]. The waiting time is calculated as the difference between the end time and the start time of two consecutive activities in a log. Importantly, this assumption may not always be true. For PRI_3 and PRI_5 we assume that the number of activity executions in a case and the number of resources involved in a case follow a normal distribution. An activity is considered atypical (PRI_4) if it has been executed in fewer than a certain number of cases in the log. The threshold t is an input parameter that represents the fraction of cases where a particular activity has been executed.

We define a predictor function G that estimates the risk level of a case based on the risk indicators it exhibits. Thus binary function G predicts a delay if *any* of the indicators is found in a case. We have also defined a function *Score* that returns a "suspicion score" based on the number of identified indicators for each case. A high suspicion score means that many indicators were found in a case, and can be used to calibrate risk alert levels. Let δ be a trace that represents a given case, $\delta(PRI_n)$ denote the value of attribute PRI_n of trace δ, $\{PRI_1, \ldots, PRI_k\}$ be a set of k PRIs, and w_i denote the weight chosen for indicator PRI_i:

$$G(\delta) = \bigvee_{i=1}^{k} \delta(PRI_i); \; Score(\delta) = \sum_{i=1}^{k} w_i * \delta(PRI_i)$$

In our current implementation once a risk indicator is identified we update the corresponding attribute of a trace. Functions G and *Score* are calculated for each complete trace and the values are compared with actual case durations to evaluate the performance of the functions.

3   Experimental Results

Our approach has been implemented as a plug-in of the process mining framework ProM 6. Its main functionality is to identify occurrences of our five PRIs in a given log and to thus predict the likelihood of a case being delayed. Predicted values are then compared with the actual outcome of a case to evaluate the performance of the predictor functions. In order to isolate traces corresponding to different process model runs the plug-in uses either the existing ProM 6 "replay" plug-in [1] or the trace clustering plug-in [2] (if the process model is not available). We evaluated our approach using an event log which represents the application process for a personal loan or overdraft from a Dutch financial institution given for the BPI Challenge 2012.[1] The log contains 13,087 traces in total and we first filtered this log to produce 934 traces suited to our experimental purposes. The plug-in that uses the trace clustering was applied. The filtered log was grouped into 12 clusters with the total number of traces in each cluster ranging from 20 to 206. After clustering, the traces in each cluster were put into either a training set (used to learn cut-off thresholds) or a test set. For each cluster within the training set we estimated the normal case duration as $\tilde{x} + 2 * 1.483 * MAD$. Cases whose durations exceeded this value were considered to be delayed.

Table 1 shows the experimental results for the test set of 462 traces. To evaluate the quality of predictions we used the mean absolute error (MAE). This is calculated as $\frac{1}{n} \sum_{i=1}^{n} |p_i - r_i|$ for both delayed cases (yielding the MAE for false negatives) and for cases that are in time (yielding the MAE for false positives), where n is the number of cases in each category and p_i and r_i denote predicted and real values respectively. We calculated the MAE separately for delayed cases and cases that are on time, because it is often important to distinguish between different types of errors, both false-negatives and false-positives,

---

[1] BPI Challenge 2012. doi:10.4121/uuid:3926db30-f712-4394-aebc-75976070e91f.

Table 1. Experimental results showcasing the predictive value of five process risk indicators (PRIs) on the test set of the BPI Challenge event log

	5 PRIs				PRI 1		PRI 2		PRI 3		PRI 4		PRI 5	
	Delayed		In Time											
	TN	FN	FP	TP	TN	FP	TN	FP	TN	FP	TN	FP	TN	FP
Traces	22	7	221	212	8	115	0	19	19	121	0	2	3	25
%	76%	24%	51%	49%	28%	27%	0%	4%	66%	28%	0%	0.5%	10%	6%

Legend: TN—True Negatives; FN—False Negatives; FP—False Positives; TP—True Positives

as their impact on business performance can be very different. We can observe that the MAE for delayed cases with 5 PRIs is 0.24, i.e., the predictor function estimated correctly the outcome of 76% of delayed cases ("True Negatives" in Table 1). On the other hand, the MAE for the cases that are not delayed is 0.51 ("False Positives" in Table 1). From further analysis, we observed that 74% of the 221 cases that were falsely predicted as delayed have durations that are very close to the cut-off threshold (the difference is lower than 5% of assumed normal case duration). From the individual PRI results, we can see that for this particular log almost all predicted problems ("True Negatives" in Table 1) are based on observations of PRIs 1, 3 and 5. We have also analysed the ability of PRIs to provide operational support. For this particular event log, we were able to identify the presence of PRIs 1, 3 and 4 early during a case's execution, while PRIs 2 and 5 for most of the cases could only be discovered after half of the normal case duration for the run corresponding to that case had passed.

Table 1 focussed on the results from our first predictor function, G. We also tested the weighted *Score* function (with $w_i = 1$ for all PRIs) and found that for most of the cases predicted as delayed just one of the indicators was discovered (64% of correctly predicted cases and 76% of falsely predicted cases). This reveals that the "suspicion" attached to these poor results of G was actually very low.

After examining the BPI Challenge event log we noted certain log characteristics that may have influenced the presented results and discovered opportunities for the improvement of the risk identification method. The durations of the cases assigned to a cluster did not significantly deviate from the cut-off thresholds, thus there were very few outlier cases. Also, the number of traces in some clusters were too small to get statistically significant results. Many activities have very small durations compared to the total case duration. Discarding durations whose values are lower than some predefined threshold may help to filter out false positive predictions. The event log used does not contain *start* events recorded for all activities. To be able to work with the event logs that do not contain *start* events we can use an indicator "PRI 6: Abnormal sub-process duration" that considers both activity service and waiting time (sub-process durations are calculated as the time difference between two consecutive *complete* events). Applying PRI 6 and PRI 3 v.2 (that considers the absolute values of repetition durations) we were able to correctly estimate the outcome of 86% of delayed cases and 30% of cases in time were falsely predicted as delayed.

4 Conclusions

We have presented a new approach for predicting whether or not a case will meet its deadline. We first defined relevant "Process Risk Indicators" and then used statistical methods to identify their presence in event logs. Our initial results indicate that further work is needed to properly calibrate the analysis, perhaps on a process-specific basis, to minimise the annoyance of false-positive warnings and the more serious threat of false-negative alert failures. (As noted above, the data set available to us for experimentation was not well-suited to our purposes. We have recently obtained a larger data set from an Insurance Company and will use it for experiments.) Although we only focused on the risk of case overruns in this paper, we believe that the overall strategy is suitable for any quantifiable type of risk, such as financial losses or low-quality outputs.

Acknowledgement. This research is funded by the ARC Discovery Project "Risk-aware Business Process Management" (DP110100091).

References

1. Adriansyah, A., van Dongen, B.F., van der Aalst, W.M.P.: Conformance checking using cost-based fitness analysis. In: 2011 15th IEEE International Enterprise Distributed Object Computing Conference (EDOC), pp. 55–64. IEEE (2011)
2. Bose, R., van der Aalst, W.M.P.: Context aware trace clustering: Towards improving process mining results. In: Proceedings of the SIAM International Conference on Data Mining, SDM, pp. 401–412 (2009)
3. International Organization for Standardization. Risk management: vocabulary = Management du risque: vocabulaire (ISO guide 73), Geneva (2009)
4. Jallow, A.K., Majeed, B., Vergidis, K., Tiwari, A., Roy, R.: Operational risk analysis in business processes. BT Technology Journal 25(1), 168–177 (2007)
5. Jans, M., Lybaert, N., Vanhoof, K., van der Werf, J.M.: A business process mining application for internal transaction fraud mitigation. Expert Systems with Applications 38(10), 13351–13359 (2011)
6. Rousseeuw, P.J.: Robust estimation and identifying outliers. In: Handbook of Statistical Methods for Engineers and Scientists, ch. 16. McGraw-Hill, New York (1990)
7. Standards Australia and Standards New Zealand. Risk management: principles and guidelines (AS/NZS ISO 31000:2009), 3rd edn., Sydney, NSW, Wellington, NZ (2009)
8. van der Aalst, W.M.P., Schonenberg, M.H., Song, M.: Time prediction based on process mining. Information Systems 36(2), 450–475 (2011)
9. Dongen, B.v., Crooy, R., van der Aalst, W.M.P.: Cycle time prediction: When will this case finally be finished? In: On the Move to Meaningful Internet Systems: OTM 2008, pp. 319–336 (2008)
10. Wickboldt, J.A., Bianchin, L.A., Lunardi, R.C., Granville, L.Z., Gaspary, L.P., Bartolini, C.: A framework for risk assessment based on analysis of historical information of workflow execution in it systems. Computer Networks 55(13), 2954–2975 (2011)
11. Zhang, P., Serban, N.: Discovery, visualization and performance analysis of enterprise workflow. Computational Statistics & Data Analysis 51(5), 2670–2687 (2007)

Mining Process Performance from Event Logs

Arya Adriansyah and Joos C.A.M Buijs

Department of Mathematics and Computer Science
Eindhoven University of Technology
P.O. Box 513, 5600 MB Eindhoven, The Netherlands
{a.adriansyah,j.c.a.m.buijs}@tue.nl

Abstract. In systems where process executions are not strictly enforced by a predefined process model, obtaining reliable performance information is not trivial. In this paper, we analyzed an event log of a real-life process, taken from a Dutch financial institute, using process mining techniques. In particular, we exploited the *alignment* technique [2] to gain insights into the control flow and performance of the process execution. We showed that alignments between event logs and discovered process models from process discovery algorithms reveal insights into frequently occurring deviations and how such insights can be exploited to repair the original process models to better reflect reality. Furthermore, we showed that the alignments can be further exploited to obtain performance information. All analysis in this paper is performed using plug-ins within the open-source process mining toolkit ProM.

1 Process Discovery

Performance analysis require process models that describe process executions as they are executed in reality. For more complex processes such as the one under investigation, applying process discovery algorithms is not sufficient to obtain good process models. For this challenge, we performed the following 4 steps to obtain good process models: (1) **Log filtering**, (2) **Process model discovery** using existing process discovery algorithms, (3) **Evaluate quality of discovered models**, taking into account the *fitness, precision*, and *simplicity* quality dimensions, and (4) **Manually improve process model**.

In step (1), the log was preprocessed and then split into homogeneous clusters that can be treated independently. The steps (2)-(4) were performed iteratively. The α-algorithm, heuristics miner, and the ILP-Miner were used to perform step (2). Alignments [2] between traces in the log and model were used to measure the model quality in step (3). Step (4) was performed manually, after taking into account diagnostics information provided by various visualizations of alignments. Several alignment visualizations are used, each of them highlights deviations from a specific perspective and therefore being complementary to each other. For example, projection of alignments onto a process model visualizes frequently visited paths, points of deviation, and the type of deviation (see Fig. 1a). Visualization of alignments using trace alignment shows the context

M. La Rosa and P. Soffer (Eds.): BPM 2012 Workshops, LNBIP 132, pp. 217–218, 2013.
© Springer-Verlag Berlin Heidelberg 2013

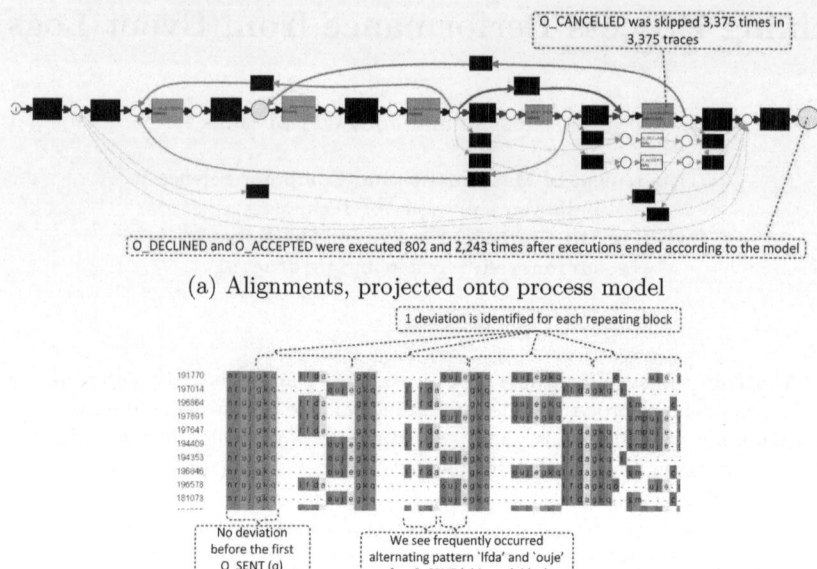

(a) Alignments, projected onto process model

(b) Alignments, visualized using trace alignment technique

Fig. 1. Examples of different visualizations of alignments

where deviations occur (see Fig. 1b). We use the plugin *Replay a Log on Petri Net for Conformance Analysis* to obtain alignments and visualize them.

2   Performance Analysis

Various visualizations of alignments were used to extract performance-related information from pairs of process models and logs. The projection of alignments onto process models explicitly reveals the activities in each process that cause bottlenecks, even in cases where an activity is associated with more than one tasks (i.e. duplicate tasks). Furthermore, we proposed a matrix visualization of the elapsed time between all pairs of synchronous activities to identify automated activities in the process. The reader is referred to [1] for a comprehensive report on the approach, analysis, and results.

References

1. Adriansyah, A., Buijs, J.C.A.M.: Mining Process Performance from Event Logs: The BPI Challenge, Case Study. Technical report, BPMcenter.org, BPM Center Report BPM-12-15 (2012)
2. van der Aalst, W.M.P., Adriansyah, A., van Dongen, B.F.: Replaying history on process models for conformance checking and performance analysis. Wiley Interdisciplinary Reviews: Data Mining and Knowledge Discovery 2(2), 182–192 (2012)

Process Mining-Driven Optimization of a Consumer Loan Approvals Process
The BPIC 2012 Challenge Case Study

Arjel D. Bautista, Lalit Wangikar, and Syed M. Kumail Akbar

CKM Advisors, 711 Third Avenue, Suite 1806, New York, NY, USA
{abautista,lwangikar,sakbar}@ckmadvisors.com

Abstract. A real life event log of the loan and overdraft approvals process from a bank in the Netherlands is analyzed using process mining and other analytical techniques. The log consists of 262,200 events and 13,087 cases. Using a combination of traditional spreadsheet-based approaches, process-mining capabilities available in Disco and exploratory analytics using Classification and Regression Trees (CART). We examined the data in great detail and at multiple levels of granularity. In this report, we present our findings on how we developed a deep understanding of the process using the event log data, assessed potential areas of efficiency improvement within the institution's operations and identified opportunities to use knowledge gathered during process execution to make predictions about likely eventual outcome of a loan application. We also discuss unique challenges of working with such data, and opportunities for enhancing the impact of such analyses by incorporating additional data elements that should be available internally to the bank.

1   Introduction and Analysis Plan

The situation depicted in BPIC 2012 focuses on the loan and overdraft approvals process of a real-world financial institution in the Netherlands. In our analysis of this information, we sought to understand the underlying business processes in detail and at multiple levels of granularity. In doing so, we combined the use of dedicated process mining technologies with traditional spreadsheet modeling techniques to identify crucial steps and discover important correlations in the data.[1]We began by determining the standard case flow for a successful application (Figure 1) and used this baseline to examine the data in great detail. Our combination of techniques uncovered a number of interesting insights about the approvals process (Figure 2).

2   Conclusions

Through comprehensive analysis of the BPIC 2012 event log, we managed to convert a data set containing 262,200 events and 13,087 cases into a clearly interpretable, end-to-end workflow for a loan and overdraft approvals process. We examined the data at multiple levels of granularity and discovered interesting insights at the event, resource,

M. La Rosa and P. Soffer (Eds.): BPM 2012 Workshops, LNBIP 132, pp. 219–220, 2013.
© Springer-Verlag Berlin Heidelberg 2013

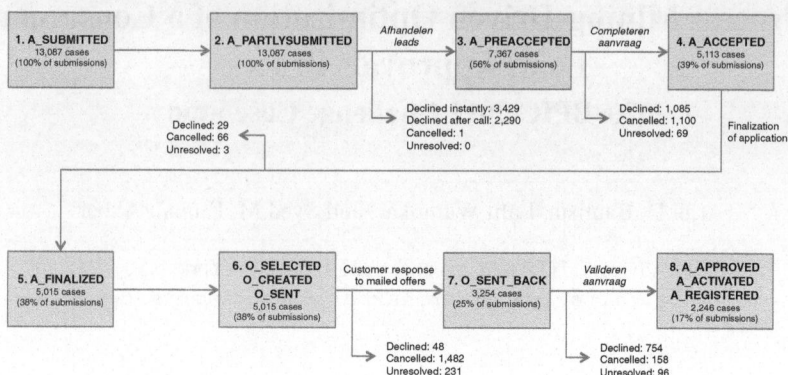

Fig. 1. Key Process Steps and Application Volume Flow

and case levels. Through our work we also uncovered potential improvements at all three levels, including revision of automated processes, restructuring of key resources, and evaluation of current case handling procedures.

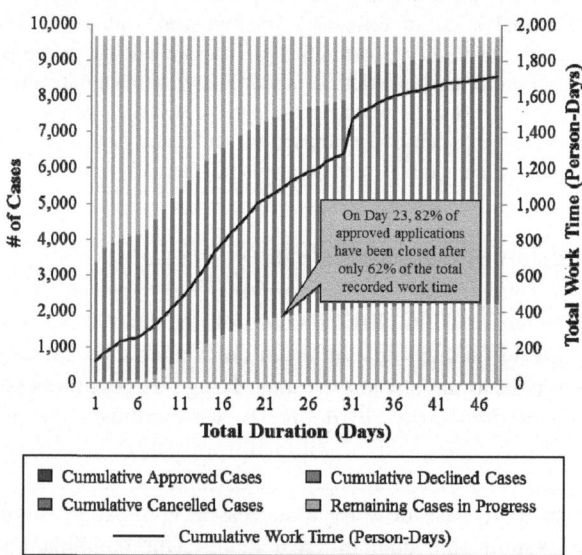

Fig. 2. Distribution of Cases by Eventual Outcome and Duration, with Cumulative Work Effort Overlaid (Excludes 3,472 Instantly Declined Cases)

Reference

1. Bautista, A.D., Wangikar, L., Akbar, S.M.K.: Process Mining-Driven Optimization of a Consumer Loan Approvals Process. Technical Report BPM 2012, ckmadvisors.com (2012), http://www.ckmadvisors.com/pages/BPIC_2012_CKM_Advisors.pdf

Process Mining Applied to the BPI Challenge 2012: Divide and Conquer While Discerning Resources

R.P. Jagadeesh Chandra Bose and Wil M.P. van der Aalst

Eindhoven University of Technology, The Netherlands
{j.c.b.rantham.prabhakara,w.m.p.v.d.aalst}@tue.nl

Abstract. A real-life event log, taken from a Dutch financial institute, is analyzed using state-of-the-art process mining techniques. The log contains events related to loan/overdraft applications of customers. We propose a hierarchical decomposition of the log into homogenous subsets of cases based on characteristics such as the final decision, offer, and suspicion of fraud. These subsets are used to uncover interesting insights. The event log in its entirety and the homogeneous subsets are analyzed using various process mining techniques. More specifically, we analyze the event log (a) on the resource perspective and the influence of resources on execution/turnaround times of activities, (b) on the control-flow perspective, and (c) for process diagnostics. A dedicated ProM[1] plug-in developed for this challenge allows for a comprehensive analysis of the resource perspective. For the analysis of control-flow and process diagnostics, we use recent, but pre-existing, ProM plug-ins. As the evaluation shows, our mix of techniques is able to uncover many interesting findings and could be used to improve the underlying loan/overdraft application handling process.

1 Analysis

The event log provided for the challenge pertains to the application process for a personal loan or overdraft within a Dutch financial institute. We analyze the event log on three different aspects:

– *Resource perspective:* Understanding the correlations between resources, workloads, and processing speeds of cases is gaining attention in recent years in process mining. We focus on the resource perspective and analyze whether there are remarkable differences between resources in their way of handling applications and the final outcome, in their execution and turnaround times on different activities and their influence on cycle times of cases. We have developed a dedicated plug-in called **Resource Work Analysis** in ProM for this analysis.

---

[1] ProM is an extensible framework that provides a comprehensive set of tools/plug-ins for the discovery and analysis of process models from event logs. See http://www. processmining.org for more information and to download ProM.

M. La Rosa and P. Soffer (Eds.): BPM 2012 Workshops, LNBIP 132, pp. 221–222, 2013.

- *Control-flow perspective:* Control-flow discovery is one of the crucial steps in understanding the real process execution behavior. The event log provided for the challenge is characterized by (i) *heterogeneity of cases* and (ii) *concurrency within the process.* Traditional process discovery algorithms have difficulties in dealing with these issues and generate spaghetti-like process models. We propose a hierarchical decomposition of the log based on homogeneity in cases and apply the two-phase approach to process discovery [1] to mine comprehensible process maps.
- *Process diagnostics:* Our third analysis is focussed on uncovering deviations and other non-conforming behavior. We analyze the event log using trace alignment [2], which has been proposed as a powerful technique for process diagnostics. Trace alignment can be used to explore the process in the early stages of analysis and to answer specific questions in later stages of analysis.

2   Results and Conclusions

Our analysis of the event log reveals that several resources perform multi-tasking, i.e., work on simultaneous cases. Such resources exhibit a negative influence on the execution times of activities leading to high turnaround times. Furthermore, several resources are often idle although an activity is available for execution. This impacts the cycle time of cases. Obviously, these are undesirable for customers and the organization. From a control-flow perspective, at first glance, the event log may seem complex due to the heterogeneity in the log. However, a hierarchical classification of the log based on the characteristics of the loan/overdraft applications (e.g., final decision, offer, suspicion of fraud, etc.) helps to simplify analysis significantly. Analyzing homogenous subsets of cases in the event log based on the classification reveals that the process is in fact rather simple. Comprehensible process models and interesting diagnostic insights can be uncovered using such a classification. For example, we uncovered several outliers in the event log such as the approval of loan applications by automated resource and execution of activities even after the cancellation and/or approval of loan applications. The reader is referred to [3] for a comprehensive report on the approach, analysis, and results.

References

1. Li, J., Bose, R.P.J.C., van der Aalst, W.M.P.: Mining Context-Dependent and Interactive Business Process Maps Using Execution Patterns. In: zur Muehlen, M., Su, J. (eds.) BPM 2010 Workshops. LNBIP, vol. 66, pp. 109–121. Springer, Heidelberg (2011)
2. Bose, R.P.J.C., van der Aalst, W.M.P.: Process Diagnostics Using Trace Alignment: Opportunities, Issues, and Challenges. Information Systems 37(2), 117–141 (2012)
3. Bose, R.P.J.C., van der Aalst, W.M.P.: Process Mining Applied to the BPI Challenge 2012: Divide and Conquer While Discerning Resources. Technical Report BPM-12-16, BPMCenter.org (2012),
   http://bpmcenter.org/wp-content/uploads/reports/2012/BPM-12-16.pdf

Dotted Chart and Control-Flow Analysis
for a Loan Application Process

Thomas Molka[1,2], Wasif Gilani[1], and Xiao-Jun Zeng[2]

Business Intelligence Practice, SAP Research, Belfast, UK
The University of Manchester, School of Computer Science, Manchester, UK
{thomas.molka,wasif.gilani}@sap.com, x.zeng@manchester.ac.uk

Abstract. We summarise our approach and results of analysing a real-life event log taken from a loan application process in a Dutch financial institute. We mine the control-flow model and analyse different variants of the process statistically and with dotted charts. This allows us to conclude performance properties of the historic execution of the process. Furthermore we examine the resources assigned to different process steps.

1 Control Flow Analysis

The process describes the flow of customers applying for a loan/overdraft at a financial institute. It starts with creating the application which is done by the customer, followed by several tasks for processing it automatically by systems and manually by employees and finishing with an approval or rejection of the application. The process consists of 3 sub-processes. One focuses on work that involves human interaction spanning across a longer period of time (e.g. checking for fraud, calling the customer, assessing the application) while the other two describe results of an action or a decision about the application (e.g. declined, cancelled, accepted, approved, sent back, finalised, etc.). A submitted application can be declined immediately by the system, which is the most common way of handling applications (happens in 26% of the cases). If the application is not automatically declined, it can either be examined for fraud (and based on that declined or further processed), or further processed by employees. If the application is not declined, it is either pre-accepted by the system or an employee examines it manually (activity "fixing incoming lead"). After that the application is initially accepted and an employee starts filling in information for it. An offer is created and sent to the customer, then the customer is called once or more, in order to discuss the offer. Finally the customer sends the offer back, so it can be assessed. Phone calls with the customer to clarify issues about missing documents constitute the most frequent and time consuming activity in that phase of the process. Based on the assessment the offer can then still be declined or approved (in which case it is also always registered and activated). An approval of the applications happens only 2,246 out of 13,087 times. We used different methods for mining the control flow. The fuzzy miner in the software *Disco* allowed for the best understanding of the process on different levels of abstraction from infrequent behaviour.

M. La Rosa and P. Soffer (Eds.): BPM 2012 Workshops, LNBIP 132, pp. 223–224, 2013.
© Springer-Verlag Berlin Heidelberg 2013

2   Dotted Chart Analysis

For getting an overview of the log from different perspectives of the process we performed a dotted chart analysis, i.e. the event log is plotted in a chart. The chart puts various properties of the events (e.g. the activity, resource and trace the event belongs to or the time of its occurrence) into relation. An example of such a chart can be seen in Figure 1. Every dot in the chart represents an event

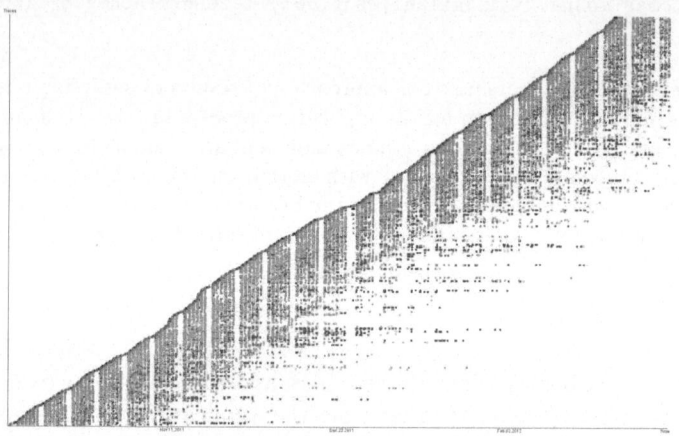

Fig. 1. Dotted Chart of the Event Log

in the log. The coordinates of the dots (time, trace) describe the time the event occurred and the process instance it belongs to. The colour of the dot represents the corresponding business process activity. Process instances (traces) in the chart are sorted by the time of their instantiation. Zooming into the chart and filtering different properties, one can easily see how long the process instances are running, how many and which activities are involved and whether there are repetitions, which days are of low or high workload, etc. Patterns in the chart become obvious (e.g. many applications are cancelled automatically after 31 days) and can then be further analysed. Looking at charts from a resource perspective, we learned more about the performance of the resources and which roles they take in the process (which sets of activities they are assigned to). Six of the resources have rights for approving loans while a single resource is doing most of the fraud checks (78%). More observations and a more detailed description of the process and used methods are given in the full report [1].

Reference

1. Molka, T., Gilani, W., Zeng, X.-J.: Dotted Chart and Control-Flow Analysis for a Loan Application Process, Report for BPI Challenge 2012 (2012), http://www.win.tue.nl/bpi2012/lib/exe/fetch.php?media=molka.pdf

BPI Challenge 2012: The Transition System Case

H.M.W. (Eric) Verbeek

Technische Universiteit Eindhoven
Department of Mathematics and Computer Science
P.O. Box 513, 5600 MB Eindhoven, The Netherlands
h.m.w.verbeek@tue.nl

1 Abstract

Using the Transition System Miner as available in ProM 6 [1], we have investigated the control-flow perspective, the data perspective, and the resource perspective of the process that underlies the event log provided for the BPI Challenge 2012 [2].

For the control-flow perspective, we discovered several transition systems that explain the underlying process, which seems to be nicely structured. For the Application events, we concluded that they occur in a certain order (see Fig. 1), that the events A_ACTIVATED, A_APPROVED, and A_REGISTERED occur in parallel, and that the most time is spend in the A_FINALIZED state.

For the Offer events, we concluded that they also occur in a certain order (see Fig. 2), and that the successor of the O_CANCELLED state depends on its predecessor: If the predecessor was O_SELECTED, then the successor will be O_CREATED, else the successor will be O_SELECTED. For the combination of Application and Offer events, we concluded that the A_ACTIVATED events occur in parallel with the O_ACCEPTED events, and that the A_FINALIZED events occur in parallel with the O_SELECTED events, which link both Figures nicely together.

For the Work Item events, we concluded that, except for W_BEOORDELEN FRAUDE which can occur at almost any moment, they also occur in a certain order (see Fig. 3). For the combination of Application and Work Item events, we concluded that W_AFHANDELEN LEADS is typically preceded by A_SUBMITTED and typically followed by either A_PREACCEPTED or A_DECLINED, that W_COMPLETEREN AANVRAAG is typically preceded by A_PREACCEPTED and typically followed by either A_ACCEPTED or A_DECLINED, and that the other W_ events are typically preceded by A_FINALIZED and followed by either A_ACTIVATED, A_DECLINED, or A_CANCELLED.

For the data perspective, we have obtained transition systems for the Application events and have extended these with 5 buckets for the two trace attributes that were provided: AMOUNT_REQ (the requested amount for the application) and REG_DATA (the registration date for the application). Based on the minimal and maximal values as found for these attributes in the log, the entire range (from minimal to maximal) was split up into these 5 buckets, where bucket 20 corresponds to the lowest 20% in this range, 40 to the next 20%, etc. For the requested amounts, we concluded that the vast majority of the applications were for small amounts, and that only exceptionally a very high amount was requested. We could not conclude that more time was spend on applications that involved a higher requested amount, but we did note that the buckets 40 and 60 contained a relatively high number of activated cases (1 out of 4, 1 out of 5), whereas the 80 and

M. La Rosa and P. Soffer (Eds.): BPM 2012 Workshops, LNBIP 132, pp. 225–226, 2013.
© Springer-Verlag Berlin Heidelberg 2013

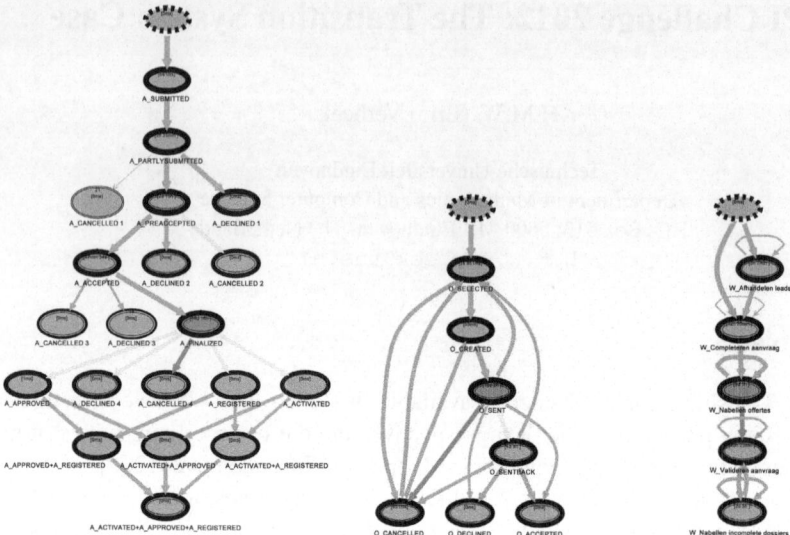

Fig. 1. Application states   **Fig. 2.** Offer states   **Fig. 3.** Work Item states

100 buckets contained a relatively small number of activated cases (1 out of 10, 1 out of 15). For the registration date, we concluded that the time to handle an application was especially low in the 100 bucket, that is, at the end of the logged period.

For the resource perspective, we have obtained transition systems from the Work Item events (as these were assumed to be related to resources), and have investigated behavior of the 5 most-frequent resources related to the W_NABELLEN OFFERTES Work Item. From this, we concluded that no case manager is associated to an application in the geven process, and that the 5 selected resources all handover work (possibly through a number of unselected resources) to each other. We also concluded that for some of the Work Item events no resource was specified, and that this EMPTY resource was actually the most-frequent resource. Finally, we concluded that the selected resources all could redo the completion of the Work item without restarting it, and that the applications in which this redoing occur typically take more time than the applications in which this does not occur.

To get to these conclusions, we mainly used the Simple Log Filter, the Transition System Miner, and the Transition System Analyzer plug-ins as they are implemented in ProM 6. This shows that this set of plug-ins is very versatile, and that many different types of results can be obtained using them. The Simple Log Filter was used to obtain a log that contains the events one is interested in. The Transition System Miner was used to create a transition system from an event log, where basically any combination of attributes present in the log can be used to identify the states in the transition system. The Transition System Analyzer was used to extend the mined transition system with timing and frequency data as aggregated from the event log.

References

1. Verbeek, H.M.W., Buijs, J.C.A.M., van Dongen, B.F., van der Aalst, W.M.P.: Prom 6: The process mining toolkit. In: Rosa, M.L. (ed.) Proc. of BPM Demonstration Track 2010, Hoboken, USA. CEUR Workshop Proceedings, vol. 615, pp. 34–39, CEUR-WS.org (September 2010)
2. van Dongen, B.F.: BPI challenge 2012. Dataset (2012), http://dx.doi.org/10.4121/uuid:3926db30-f712-4394-aebc-75976070e91f

Application and Simplification of BPM Techniques for Personal Process Management

Marco Brambilla

Politecnico di Milano, Dipartimento di Elettronica e Informazione, Milano, Italy
marco.brambilla@polimi.it
http://home.dei.polimi.it/mbrambil

Abstract. With the advent of Web 2.0 and online social interactions, people started sharing thoughts, contents and tasks online. This evolved to cover also socialization of task management, which is currently supported by a plethora of online services directed to the final user. However, all these tools share a common weakness: they don't provide any way for structuring the interactions, dependencies or constraints between tasks. This paper discusses a vision towards the application of BPM techniques and tools to personal task management. The challenge of this roadmap is finding the appropriate level of complexity of processes: the language for modeling such processes should be complete enough for describing basic processes but also simple enough to let people understand, accept and use them in their everyday life. Therefore, our proposal describes how to strip off some of the expressive power of enterprise business processes, so as to accommodate end user needs and acceptance.

Keywords: Business process management, personal process management, social BPM, BPM, social network, personal productivity.

1 Introduction

With the advent of Web 2.0 and online social interactions, people started sharing thoughts, contents and tasks online. This started as means for producing content, then evolved to a means for building and maintaining social connections, and finally ended with a way for sharing experiences on the go, with systems such as Foursquare, Twitter, and others.

As one of the last trends, the move towards online social sharing evolved to cover also socialization of task management, which is currently supported by a plethora of online services directed to the final user, such as RememberTheMilk and many others.

These tools are extremely user friendly, allow to manage personal tasks, social interactions, and even assignment of tasks to fiends. However, all these tools share a common weakness: they don't provide any way for structuring the interactions, dependencies or constraints between tasks. In technical terms, these tools do not embrace the practices of BPM at all and do not consider the advancements of BPM towards the integration of social aspects. In a sense, despite

M. La Rosa and P. Soffer (Eds.): BPM 2012 Workshops, LNBIP 132, pp. 227–233, 2013.

being the integration of the enterprise practice of BPM and the end user trend towards social networking, Social BPM remains an approach which is studied only in the academic and industrial setting, leaving out all the possible interesting exploitation scenarios for the end users.

This paper discusses a vision towards the application of BPM and Social BPM techniques and tools to personal task management, with the purpose of introducing the concept of process and execution flow in personal, everyday life tasks. We call this Personal Process Management (PPM).

The challenge of this objective is finding the appropriate level of complexity of processes, methods and tools that can be accepted by end users: the language for modeling such processes should be complete enough for describing basic processes but also simple enough to let people understand, accept and use them in their everyday life.

The paper is organized as follows: Section 2 discusses the state of the art of PPM and Personal Task Management Tools; Section 3 presents and motivates the simplified modeling language we propose; Section 4 shows our implementation of a prototype online tool that supports our approach; and Section 5 concludes.

2   Related Work

Despite being a more and more important issue, personal task planning has received limited attention from academic research so far. Just a few visionary statements can be found on this, e.g., the reader can have a look at the blog posts by prof. Michael Rosemann [2] and by Armin Sander [3] which lay the basic principles of Personal Process Management. The only structured research that can be found is reported in a Technical Report of UNSW [4]. The report discusses a possible implementation of personal process management, in a similar manner to what we will propose. However, our approach differentiates on some fundamental aspects. First, the choice of control flow patterns to be covered is different: while [4] mainly focuses on sequential and conditional (alternative) constraints, our proposal is centered on parallel executions. Furthermore, their proposal is intended primarily for personal use, without prominent attention to the ability to share and assign tasks to other users, while our challenge is to build a social process planning system in the first place. Notice that the two decisions are connected: parallel executions would not be so crucial in case of a single executor, while they are paramount for shared processes. The report [4] also proposed a formal grammar for the design of personal processes and based the approach on that notation. While formally precise, this solution is not going to be so attractive to the end user, who expect user-friendly and convenient ways for defining his processes.

On the other side, a large number of commercial online tools exist for personal tasks management. A short list of them is reported in Table 1. These tools are explicitly oriented to end users and provide a plethora of convenient features, as summarized in Table 2, including task creation, editing, tracking and sharing;

social network integration; importing and exporting; notification and synchronization. They also support some kind of project management, in the sense of managing pools of tasks altogether. However, none of them allow structuring sets of tasks into process models.

Table 1. List and URLs of Online Personal Task Management Tools

Tool	Url
Remember The Milk	http://www.rememberthemilk.com
Online Task List	http://www.onlinetasklist.com/
Hi Task	http://hitask.com/
Todoist	http://todoist.com/
Toodledo	http://www.toodledo.com/
Tadalist	http://tadalist.com/
Voo2do	http://voo2do.com/
Astrid	http://astrid.com/
Cozi	http://www.cozi.com/
Blablalist	http://blablalist.com/
CCtodo	http://cctodo.com/
Tasktoy	http://www.tasktoy.com/
GTDagenda	http://www.gtdagenda.com/
Manymoon	https://manymoon.com/
Producteev	http://www.producteev.com/
Workhack	http://workhack.com/
Webtodo	http://webtodo.wndmll.com/
Theonlineceo	http://roughunderbelly.com/user/login
Nozbe	http://www.nozbe.com/
Tedium	http://www.mcqn.com/tedium/account/login
Checkvist	http://checkvist.com/
Hiveminder	http://hiveminder.com/splash/
Stayuseful	http://stayuseful.com/
Nutshell	http://www.gonutshell.com/

3 BPM Approach to Personal Processes

To support users in adopting BPM in their everyday life, we propose three features of PPM that aim at increasing the adoption and acceptance of the approach:

1. First, we propose to reduce the expressive power, and thereby the complexity, of business process modeling semantics.
2. Second, we define social interactions, social sharing and gamification (i.e., the possibility of increasing engagement of users through mechanisms that are typical of games, such as points, badges and so on) as first class citizens in the approach.
3. Third, we propose to embrace the ease of use, flexibility and productivity of the personal task management tools presented in Section 2.

In this section we address the former two points, while in Section 4 we cover our implementation experience that tries to convey the latter.

Table 2. Summary of the features of Online Personal Task Management Tools

Feature \ Online Task Mgmt Platform	Remember the milk	Onlinetasklist	Hitask	Todoist	Toodledo	Tadalist	Voo2do	Astrid	Cozi	Blablalist	Cctodo	Theonlineceo	Taskboy	Workhach	Webtodo	GTDagenda	Manuymoon	Producteev
Social network integration	Y			Y			Y									Y	Y	Y
Creation of tasks via email	Y		Y			Y										Y		Y
Quick submission	Y		Y		Y		Y	Y	Y			Y	Y	Y	Y		Y	Y
Tagging / Categories	Y	Y	Y	Y	Y		Y	Y			Y		Y			Y	Y	Y
Localization	Y				Y													
Contacts management	Y	Y	Y			Y	Y	Y	Y							Y	Y	
Development API	Y																	
Export	Y	Y	Y	Y	Y		Y							Y		Y		
Import		Y			Y		Y									Y		Y
Feed	Y		Y			Y				Y			Y	Y				
Search	Y		Y	Y							Y					Y		Y
Notifications	Y	Y					Y											Y
Synchronization	Y																	Y
Keyboard shortcuts	Y	Y		Y			Y											
Project management	Y	Y	Y				Y						Y			Y	Y	
Permissions		Y															Y	
Task assignment	Y	Y					Y	Y	Y	Y	Y							Y
Public sharing	Y	Y				Y	Y	Y		Y			Y	Y				
Reports / Stats	Y	Y					Y	Y										Y
Drag&Drop		Y	Y		Y	Y					Y		Y	Y			Y	
File upload	Y	Y		Y													Y	
Time tracking		Y			Y		Y											
Multiple insertion		Y	Y															
Backup/Restore		Y	Y		Y													
Booklet printing		Y	Y															
Periodic checklist																Y		

3.1   Expressive Power Reduction and Notation Simplification

Simplification of expressive power has been carried out based on the observation that end users have rather simple needs and usually aim at describing collaborative activities performed together with their acquaintances.

In our informal investigation with users, by asking them to design some typical personal workflows, we noticed that:

- Users don't need personal process management in the sense of structuring their own workplans, because for that purpose they are happy enough with plain tasklists (possibly based on temporal deadlines) with no particular structure.

- Users want to easily specify task assignment to friends.
- Users want to describe simple sequential constraints between tasks or the possibility of performing actions altogether.
- Users don't want to deal with complex decision points, involving definition of conditional expressions, complex event management, or exceedingly complex process structures.

Based on this, we propose a PPM model that is based on BPM practices but actually covers a fairly reduced expressive power. In particular, our execution model covers only the design of process types that comprise: **atomic tasks, sequential task dependency, and parallel execution**. Assignment of one task is allowed to one and only one person. The design consists of task types, assigned to actual people (not roles). Therefore, the reuse of process models (in the sense of having several executions of them) is possible but not really frequent.

This being said, also the visual notation that one can apply for representing this kind of processes can be a stripped down version of well-known standardized tasks. In particular, we propose to start from a notation that only includes two elements:

1. Atomic tasks, represented by white boxes, which can be assigned to one person.
2. Sequential dependencies, represented by directed arcs between boxes.
3. Parallel execution, represented by two or more arrows exiting one box (split point) and merging into another (merge point).

Notice that no gateways, events or any other complex element is shown. No cycles are allowed in the task dependencies. Therefore, the proposed notation is straightforward. A typical example of personal process model is shown in Figure 1.

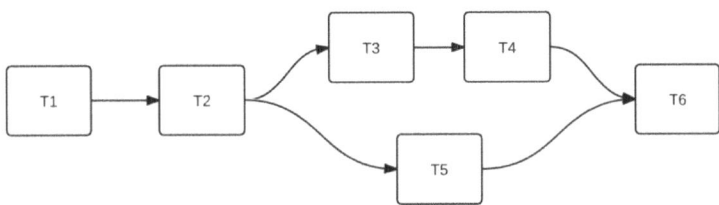

Fig. 1. Example showing the PPM notation, with sequential and parallel executions

3.2 Socialization

From the socialization perspective, the user needs are quite basic: they need the possibility of inviting users from social networks or mailing lists, they want them to see their tasks appear in the todo list in the right moment, and they want to award them somehow for the work done, e.g., through gamification mechanism.

4   PPM Tool and Experience

To validate our approach, we implemented a prototype online tool for personal and social task management. A demonstration video of the tool is available at [1]. The tool covers the expressive power of a PPM language as described in Section 3.1 and allows to make processes and tasks social according to the vision outlined in Section 3.2. On the other hand, the tool adopts the ease of use, mobility and flexibility aspects of task management tools described in Section 2. The tool is implemented as a completely online service where users can focus on their process planning and sharing with friends. The application is integrated with Facebook for sharing the task invitations and also for posting task outcomes. Figure 2(a) shows a snapshot of the modeling tool, where users can drag and drop tasks and friends (taken from Facebook) on the editing panel. The advancement of the process is also shown through different colors of the boxes. Figure 2(b) shows an example of invitation message posted on the Facebook wall of users invited to perform a task. The invitation is sent out only when the preceding task(s) are completed. A similar message notifies users about the end of a task. One interesting feature is that processes can be changed even while in execution already, for the part that has not been completed yet. The execution control is in charge of a tiny ad hoc process engine that covers only the simple control flow cases supported by the method.

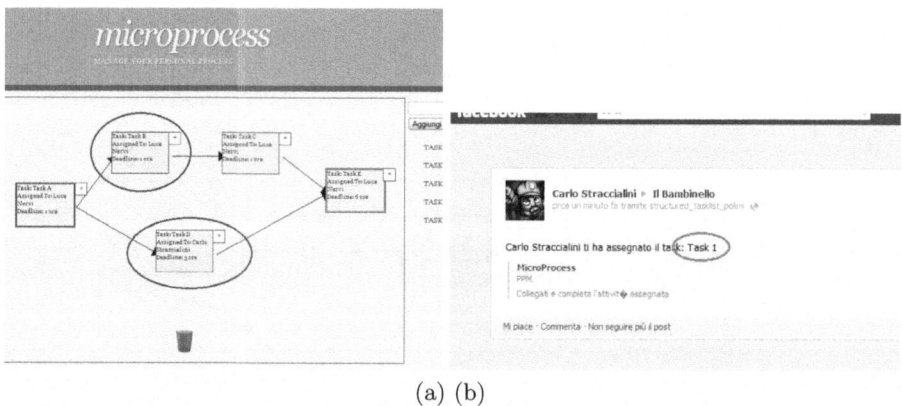

(a) (b)

Fig. 2. (a)The personal process editing panel, showing the advancement of the process (red tasks are late, green ones are done and on time, black ones are still to be executed). (b) Invitation messages posted on Facebook walls of users invited to perform a task.

5   Conclusions

This paper presented a vision and a concrete tool implementation that demonstrate the validity of personal process management as a solution to everyday task organization. Future work will address refinement of the tool implementation (especially with respect to gamification and utility features such as allowing attachment of forms, documents, maps, etc to tasks), formalization of the approach and thorough comparison of different reduced sets of business process modeling constructs in terms of acceptability and convenience for end users.

Acknowledgements. This work is partially supported by the BPM4People project, funded by the European Commission under the SME Capacities program of the 7th Framework Programme. More details at: `http://www.bpm4people.org`. I wish to thank Carlo Straccialini for his work on the tool implementation.

References

1. Brambilla, M., Straccialini, C.: Microprocess tool description and demonstration video, `http://dbgroup.como.polimi.it/brambilla/personal-processes`
2. Rosemann, M.: Personal Process Management. Rosemann's blog, `http://www.michaelrosemann.com/uncategorized/113/`
3. Sander, A.: Personal Process Management. Armin's blog, `http://www.replicator.org/content/personal-process-management`
4. Weber, I., Paik, H.-Y., Benatallah, B., Vorwerk, C., Zheng, L., Kim, S.: Personal Process Management: Design and Execution for End-Users. Technical Report UNSW-CSE-TR-1018, School of Computer Science and Engineering, the University of New South Wales, Sydney, NSW 2052, Australia (2010)

Social Data for Product Innovation, Marketing and Customer Relations

Rainer Schmidt

Aalen University
Beethovenstraße 1
73430 Aalen
Germany
Rainer.Schmidt@htw-aalen.de

Abstract. Social data are created by the core mechanisms of social software: social production, weak ties and collective decisions. They contain graph-oriented information about content items and their links, relations between people and the statistical information from collective decision mechanisms. Social data can be used to support many business activities. Product innovation, marketing, customer relations can benefit from social data. Products can be improved quicker and more thoroughly as before by analyzing social data. Marketing identifies individual customer requirements from social data. Important events in customer relations can be detected more reliably and earlier if social data are surveyed.

1 Introduction

Business process management and social software [1] cooperate in two directions. First social software can be used to support the design of business processes. Requirements for the business process or suggestions for improving the business process may be elicited using social software. Thus, social software acts upon business process (models). Second business process management may use social software for enhancing business processes. Social software is used in business processes to better interact with the customer e.g. a blog is used to collect suggestions for product improvements etc.

Social software has become an vital means for doing business. Many organizations use social software to enable social business [2]. Social software is embedded into business processes. By this means, tasks shall be   accomplished not feasible with existing technologies. By using mechanisms of social software such as blog, wikis etc. the information exchange with the customer can be improved. Examples for the successful use of social software with in companies are documented in [3].

Social networks created using social software are quickly gaining members [4] and have become a significant part of the marketing strategy. Most enterprises regard social software as beneficial for managing customer relationships [2]. Social software

M. La Rosa and P. Soffer (Eds.): BPM 2012 Workshops, LNBIP 132, pp. 234–245, 2013.

is especially valuable for several externally facing areas [2] such as marketing, the management of the company's reputation, and customer service. New products can be cocreated by social software. Social software is also useful to create contacts with prospective talents. Furthermore, supplier relationships can be improved by using social software.

Up to now, social software has been used in business processes from a functional perspective. That means social software has been used to support certain functions in business processes. However, using social software in business processes creates a large amount of data, called social data. Social data are data collected in applications of social software. Research shows that using data for decision making is beneficial for enterprises[5]. Therefore, this paper analyzes how social data can leverage benefits for business. It analyzes which social data can be obtained by using social software and which business processes may profit from social data.

The paper proceeds as follows. First, social software and applications of social software such as social media and social networks are defined and differentiated. Then, the sources for social data are identified in the basic mechanisms of social software: social production, weak ties and collective decisions. In the following section, business activities are identified that profit the social data. However, there are also risks from using social data. Therefore, the risks are discussed in the following section. Then related work is discussed. Finally, a summary is given.

2   Applications of Social Software

Social software [1] is defined as software that supports social production, the creation of weak ties and egalitarian and collective decisions. Social production [6] is the – at least partial – bottom-up organization of production enabling the integration of customer-initiated features. Social software replaces the Taylorism [7] and Fordism [8], [9] -oriented production of goods and provisioning of services by a co-creation oriented one. Goods are produced and services are provisioned together with the customer by collecting suggestions, evaluations and comments of the customer. Weak ties [10] facilitate the exploitation of new ideas and knowledge by creating connection between persons across organizational structures. Social software also supports collective decision approaches often subsumed as wisdom of the crowds [11]. It says that the collective decisions of many, independent, persons yields better results as those of single specialists. Although there may be specialists that yield better results as the collective decision, it is not possible to identify those specialists in advance.

Social media, social networks and social business are applications of social software, as shown in figure 1. Social media are media created and edited using a social production approach supported by social software. In [2] social software is differentiated from social media as set for tools supporting the participants of a social network. Social media are the virtual encounter of people using social software. Social networks are networks created by weak ties. Often collective decisions are a key element of social networks.

Social business [12] is the application of social software to business processes[1]. Social business is based on three ideas: First, there is no in- or outside; instead, anyone can participate. Second, value is created in a shared manner. Content is shared within the network, e.g. Third, social business is organized bottom-up and in a self-organizing manner. It contains both an external and internal perspective. The external perspective embraces the integration of social media and social networks for business process support. The internal perspective, also called Enterprise 2.0 [14] strives for optimizing the internal business processes by the use of social software.

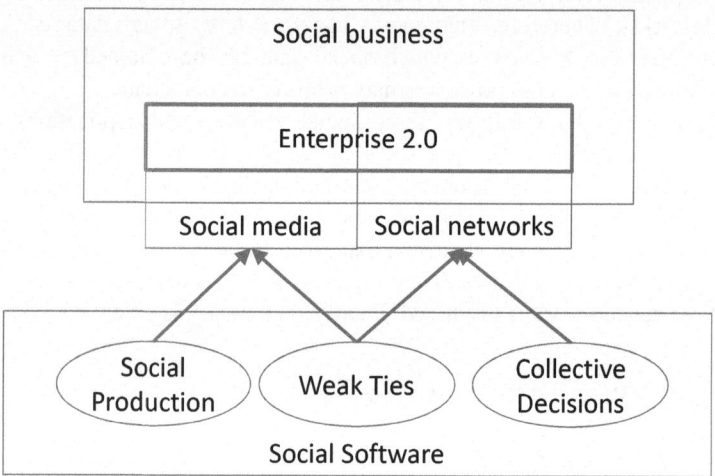

Fig. 1. Applications of social software

The mechanisms provided by social software have changed the architecture of e-commerce web-sites and many other business information systems significantly. In the beginning, e-commerce web sites provided only a one-way communication from the seller to the buyer. There had been no possibilities for the buyer to give feedback to the seller. Nowadays, many e-commerce web-sites offer to evaluate the product or service offered. By this means an important source of feedback information is created.

3   Sources of Social Data

Social data are created by the three core mechanisms of social software: social production, weak ties and collective decisions. It may be created directly or indirectly by analyzing the log files of social software systems. Social data may be enriched by two other kinds of data, spatial data and sensor data.

---

[1] Social business used in the context here should not be confused with other concepts such as [13].

3.1   Social Data from Social Production

Social production in social software can be abstracted as the peer-production [12], association or aggregation of content following a bottom-up approach. The user of social software creates content items such as blog and wiki entries and associates or aggregates them with other content items. The association of content items creates links between them and the content items remain independent entities. In blogs the entries are the content items and are associated with other blog entries. Contrary to the association of content items, the aggregation of content items does not preserve the individual content items. Wikis are important examples for aggregation. Although the content items originate from different authors, they are merged into a new one.

Content can be differentiated into primary and secondary content. Primary content is content created directly for a certain purpose such as the description of a product etc. Secondary content is created to annotate primary content in the form of comments, suggestions, etc.

Important information can be found analyzing which persons have created which content items and how this content is related to other content items and persons. By analyzing the links between content items, it is possible to detect, which persons have cooperated with whom in order to create content. So called indirect ties are created by annotating the content of other persons. Examples are comments to the entries of other persons. Transitive ties are created by the visibility of content to other persons. The content may influence the opinion of persons about products and services.

3.2   Data from Weak Ties

Social data from weak ties are graph oriented. First there are direct weak ties. These ties are indicated by establishing a "friend" relationship in Facebook, a follower relationship in twitter etc. Second there are transitive weak ties created by concatenating "friend"-relationships. The structure of weak ties can be used in two ways. First it tells about probable flows of information and opinion between people. Second by analyzing with whom a person is tied with, information about the person itself may be gained. A person that has many ties to persons with a certain interest is probable to share these interests, even if this is not directly stated.

3.3   Data from Collective Decisions

Many applications of social software use collective decisions in different forms. Products and services are evaluated from customers by assigning points, stars etc. Another example is the "like-button" in Facebook or the "+-button" in Google+. Collective decisions may evaluate both primary and secondary content. An example for collective decisions concerning primary content is the evaluation of products. Customers evaluate a product by giving marks, points etc. Secondary content such as textual evaluations of products may be the object of collective decisions too. Often it is possible to evaluate the value of a comment. This information is introduced with sentences such as "5 Customers liked this comment ..".

Both the average evaluation and the distribution of evaluation are presented to possible customers. In many cases, the data from collective decisions can be extracted easily, because it is already available in a numerical format.

3.4   Indirect Social Data from Log Files

The content created by social productions, weak ties and collective decision represent the current status of the social software system. Sometime also the log files of social software systems may contain valuable information. They provide information about the history of the creation of content, weak ties and collective decisions and thus allow a deeper insight. An example is the order of creation of weak ties. In this way, older ties – and probably tighter ties - can be differentiated from newer ties.

3.5   Spatial Data

Spatial data are increasingly crucial for gaining social data, due to the increasing use of smartphones and tablets. Spatial data provide the location of a user of social software when entering or modifying content, creating ties or participating in decisions. The value of social data may be increased if combined with spatial data. First, information provided to users of social software can be tailored according to their actual location. Second, the trustworthiness of content provided can be assessed when using spatial data. The evaluation of a hotel can be assessed based on the location of the user providing the evaluation, e.g. In this way, fake evaluations can be detected.

3.6   Sensor Data

A rather new approach is the combination of sensor data with social data. Many smartphones contain sensors that allow knowing what the user is doing. The velocity information can be used to decide whether the user is driving by car or by train, e.g.. As same as spatial data, this information can be used to tailor information provided to the user. Furthermore, the profile by the user can be completed. For example, the preferred means for transport of the user can be identified.

4   Using Social Data

Porter's value chain approach [15] is used to enumerate social data in enterprises systematically. It differentiates primary activities and supporting activities. Primary activities participate directly in the value creating process. The first activity is inbound logistics. Products and services from suppliers are brought into the company. Operations is the creation of products or the rendering of services. The activity "outgoing logistics" embraces all necessary steps to deliver the fabricated goods or rendered services. The activity marketing and sales is responsible for selling products and services. After delivery of the product or services, the service activity is responsible for handling complaints or requests for maintenance.

The supporting activities support the primary activities in the delivery of products or services. The "human resources" activity assures that enough personnel is available for operations. Research & Development creates new products and services. Procurement is necessary to buy goods or services that are not built in the enterprise itself. Finally, infrastructure provides services that enable all other activities.

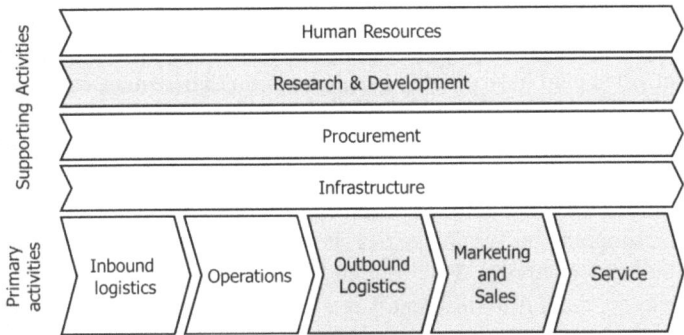

Fig. 2. Porter's value chain

There are four areas in Porter's value chain that are in direct contact with the customer. They are research and development, marketing and sales, outbound logistics and service.

4.1 Research and Development

Research and development may profit from social data in several ways, consumers have been identified as an important source for innovation [16]. First, analyzing a company's blogs and wikis may provide valuable ideas and insights for the development of new products and the improvement of existing ones. Thus, research and development directly profits from the social production taking place in social software systems. This need to integrate the innovations provided by consumers has been identified in [16]. Second the collective decision processes may help to evaluate new technologies and products in a more thorough way. The data provided by analyzing the weak ties of social software may help to assess the importance of opinions appropriately.

4.2 Marketing and Sales

The marketing and sales activity contains three phases: investigation, intention and agreement. In the investigation phase, the customer collects information. In the intention phase, the customer selects a concrete product and develops a concrete configuration of the product. Often, the intention phase is associated with a shopping basket. The agreement phase embraces the decision of the customer to buy the product and the confirmation of the company to deliver the product.

In the investigation phase, the potential customer collects information about the product or service offered. Before the rise of social software, only the actions on the company's website could be used to collect information about the potential customer's requirements. Now, further activities of the customer can be used to create a complete picture of the customer's requirements. The relations of the potential customer with other people interested in the product or service, existing customers and former customers can be analyzed. A potential customer that is in relation with many other potential customers is of high interest for the company. Therefore, significant effort should be applied in persuading him to become a customer.

In the intention phase, the potential customer starts to select and / or to configure a concrete product or service. Social data can provide unprecedented possibilities to personalize the offerings. It is possible to identify requirements not explicitly told by the customer. Similarities with other users in the social network can be identified by analyzing the shopping basket. Weak ties show if there are already other customers of the same product or service. This relation of the potential customer with existing customers may be helpful in different ways. If the existing customers have a positive attitude towards the product or service, this may help to convince the customer. If the existing customers in relation with the potential customer have a negative attitude, significant effort may be necessary. If the existing customers expressed their negative opinion in a blog etc, their argument should be refuted. Of particular interest are potential customers in relation with former customers. Probably, there will be a negative bias; however, the connections with former customers can also be used to regain the former customers.

At the end of the intention phase, the customer has a fully configured product or service and a contract ready for signing. However, until signing the customer may still decide otherwise not finalize the contract. Therefore, both the actions of the customer in social networks and actions of persons tied to him have to be analyzed for potential events causing a defect.

In the agreement phase, behavior of the customer should be analyzed for indications that he is not satisfied with his decision. Indications may be activities in social networks, which question his decision. Examples are questions about the product bought and contacts with a person already owning the product.

4.3   Outbound Logistics and Fulfillment

In outbound logistics and fulfillment, the product is delivered to the customer or the service rendered. The strength of the customer has increased significantly due to social software. If a hotel does not fulfill the expectations of the customer, he has the possibility to put his complaint into public and deter potential customers, e.g.. Before, the customer could only complain at the hotel directly or perhaps the travel agency.

Potential negative statements of the customer have to be handled carefully. Special attention has to be paid to valued customers. A company's best customers are the most likely ones for becoming worse enemies [17]. On the other hand, such relationship focused customers react in the most positive way to recovery efforts [17].

4.4 Service

After the product is delivered or service is rendered, the services phase start. It is particularly beneficial to analyze thoroughly social data in this phase, because escalated online complaints of disappointed customers can be devastating for the reputation of a company. Social media not only creates an additional channel of interaction between customer and company, but also a large audience for disappointed customers. Product and service failures can be made known to a broad public using social media. An example is described in in [18]: A musician whose guitar had been broken during a flight and who did not get a compensation published his complaint in a YouTube video regarded by several million people.

Many online complaints are caused by customers feeling betrayed by the company, because the problem with the product or service is not resolved. This leads to extremely strong negative feelings including the desire for revenge. Fortunately, by quickly reacting the customers's desire for revenge can be reduced significantly [20]. Therefore, hotel companies monitor social media such as twitter for negative entries [19]. In [21], so called „double deviations", are identified as a main cause for online public complaining. Double deviations are the coincidence of a product or service failure with an inappropriate handling of the failure by the company. The product and service failure is so severe that it cannot be ignored by the customer [21].

In some countries of the European Union, there are remarkably generous laws allowing sending back a product to the seller without cost for the buyer. Therefore, customers should be carefully tracked to identify those who think about sending back a product. Possible indicators may be negative evaluations or comments on the company's web site.

4.5 Other Activities

For most other activities, the importance of social data diminishes because only few or none customer contacts take place. An exception is human resource management. For many human resource departments, social data are an indispensable source of insight into the personality and capability of possible employees. Therefore, the activities of applicants in social networks are analyzed. Also, operations may profit from social data. Improvements of the production process can be identified by analyzing the social data.

5 Risks from the Use of Social Data

Although there are many opportunities from the use of social data, there are also significant risks, which have to be considered. The huge amount of data collected may cause a loss of personal privacy. Also, fraud using social data is already happening.

Furthermore, the quantity of data may provide an apparent exactness, not existing in practice.

A far-reaching access on personal information is necessary, to profit fully from the information contained in social networks. However, this broad use of social data implies a enormous loss of privacy. Events that stayed in the private sphere before, are now visible to the public and are processed by companies.

One of the many risks by the use of social data is the misuse in health care. Health insurances may use indications of dangerous behavior obtained from social networks, such as certain kinds of sport, consummation of alcoholic beverages etc.. This data allow to identify consumers with higher risks for certain diseases. In this way, the information given away in social networks would harm the consumer by higher health insurance fees. Another potential harmful usage of personal data published in social networks may be employers who get informed about real or assumed inappropriate behavior.

Surprisingly, up to now, many people do not mind that they give personal information away when creating content in social networks. However, this attitude may change over time, if the information from social networks is not used for co-creation but to damage the customer. Especially in Europe there is a growing criticism in the wide spread use of personal data.

Up to now, it is assumed that the content provided to social software systems is created in a benevolent way. However, there are first examples showing that enterprises try to influence the public image of their products and services by faked content and evaluations. One could even think about attacks on competitors by inserting negative information into social software systems.

The large quantity of data provided by social software systems misleads to the assumption easily that these data provide a perfect reflection of the world. However, it has to be taken into account, that social data often need interpretation to be useful [22]. This interpretation is an significant source of errors and misconceptions.

6   Related Work

There are a number of approaches to leverage social software for business. In [12] the informal steps for developing a social business strategy are developed. The analysis of social data is done in social (media) analytics [23], [24]. Concepts for the analysis of social data from a mathematical point of view are discussed in [25]. A general view on the potential usages of social data in companies can be found in [26]. Technical means for the analysis of social data using a cloud infrastructure are described in [27]. Unfortunately, a classical data-warehouse architecture is chosen.

A Business Intelligence approach analyzing only internal data sources is not adequate to the quickly changing environment created by social software and media. Social data often arrives as stream [28]. That means, data is created by users asynchronously to the business processes and arriving continuously. To assure that relevant facts are detected and handled properly, the data stream has to be processed immediately. The analysis has to happen close to real time because social software and media create a steady stream of data containing valuable information. A batch-like processing of data is no longer feasible. Speed is the most crucial criterion for analyzing data. Furthermore, when processing social data not only the present data may are of relevance but also datasets which have arrived before or may arrive in the future. Technologies such as Big Data [29], [30] are specialized in the analysis of data arriving continuously in high volumes, with high variety and velocity. To cope with the high volume of data cloud-based solution [31] are chosen.

The use of social data is only one possibility for combining social software and business process management. In [32] the changes to BPM introduced by social software are analyzed. Social BPM enables business processes containing one-to-many and many-to-many interaction patterns. These interaction patterns may be ad-hoc. Furthermore, social software enables many asynchronous interaction patterns. Social software is also able to support an agile BPM life cycle by improving responsiveness, organizational and semantic integration [33]. Three prerequisites for an agile BPM lifecycle exist: The capability of the BPM lifecycle to adapt in reaction to external events is called responsiveness. The capability to receive input from all stakeholders of the business process is called organizational integration. The ability to merge the different views of the stakeholders to a common body of knowledge is called semantic integration.

In [34] 7 elements of social data are identified: demographic, product, psychographic, behavioral, referral, location and intention data. Demographic data are data about the customer itself. The matching of products as found on many e-commerce web-sites is enabled by product data. The pains and aspirations of consumers are represented in psychographic data. Behavioral data contain information about interactions of the consumer with web sites. Ratings, reviews, recommendations etc. are called referral data. Location data are collected of particular interest, if the consumer uses mobile devices. Intention data are the most difficult to collect but particularly helpful to predict future actions of the consumer. These 7 elements of social data partially overlap with the kind of data defined in this paper.

7   Summary

Social data are data that are created by the three core mechanisms of social software: social production, weak ties and collective decisions. Social data created by social production is data about content items and their associations and aggregations. Weak ties in their direct and indirect form are also important social data. The results of collective decisions provide valuable social data too. The combination of social data with spatial and sensor data makes those even more valuable.

Social data contain information not available up to now, because it does not fit to predefined schemata or exists only in an implicit form. Social data are particularly valuable for supporting business processes in a number of areas. Customer-facing activities such as marketing and sales, research & development, outbound logistics and service profit the most from the use of social data. Offers can be tailored better to the customer requirements, because not only internal data but also external data from social media and network can be used to identify requirements. In this way, also requirements not explicitly expressed by the customer can be taken into account. Research and development may profit from the co-creation of value with the customer by seizing ideas and suggestion made in blogs and wikis. Also, fulfillment and service may profit from the usage of social data. A possible negative attitude of the customer can be detected. Thus, negative actions such as sending back bought products or public complaints can be avoided or at least reduced.

References

[1] Schmidt, R., Nurcan, S.: BPM and Social Software. In: Ardagna, D., Mecella, M., Yang, J. (eds.) BPM 2008 Workshops. LNBIP, vol. 17, pp. 649–658. Springer, Heidelberg (2009)

[2] Kiron, D., Palmer, D., Phillips, A.N., Kruschwitz, N.: Social Business: What are Companies Really Doing

[3] Online business Network connect.basf, http://www.slideshare.net/basf/socialconnectbasf (accessed June 09, 2012)

[4] The Adoption Rates of E-Mail Social Networks and E2.0

[5] Brynjolfsson, E., Hitt, L.M., Kim, H.H.: Strength in Numbers: How Does Data-Driven Decisionmaking Affect Firm Performance? SSRN eLibrary (April 2011)

[6] Benkler, Y.: The Wealth of Networks: How Social Production Transforms Markets and Freedom. Yale University Press (2006)

[7] Taylor, F.W.: The Principles of Scientific Management. General Books LLC (2010)

[8] Shiomi, H., Wada, K.: Fordism transformed: the development of production methods in the automobile industry. Oxford University Press, USA (1995)

[9] Fordismus – Wikipedia, http://de.wikipedia.org/wiki/Fordismus (accessed April 26, 2011)

[10] Granovetter, M.: strength of weak ties

[11] Surowiecki, J.: The Wisdom of Crowds. Anchor (2005)

[12] Hinchcliffe, D., Kim, P.: Social Business By Design: Transformative Social Media Strategies for the Connected Company. Jossey-Bass (2012)

[13] Yunus, M., Weber, K.: Creating a world without poverty: Social business and the future of capitalism. Public Affairs (2007)

[14] McAfee, A.P.: Enterprise 2.0: The Dawn of Emergent Collaboration. MIT Sloan Management Review 47, 21–28 (2006)

[15] Porter, M.E., Millar, V.E.: How information gives you competitive advantage. Harvard Business Review 63(4), 149–160 (1985)

[16] Hippel, E., Ogawa, S., Jong, J.P.J.: The age of the consumer-innovator. MIT Sloan Management Review: MIT's Journal of Management Research and Ideas 53(1), 27–35 (2011)

[17] Grégoire, Y., Fisher, R.J.: Customer betrayal and retaliation: when your best customers become your worst enemies. Journal of the Academy of Marketing Science 36(2), 247–261 (2008)

[18] United Breaks Guitars - YouTube, http://www.youtube.com/watch?v=5YGc4zOqozo (accessed May 30, 2012)

[19] Grégoire, Y., Tripp, T.M., Legoux, R.: When customer love turns into lasting hate: the effects of relationship strength and time on customer revenge and avoidance. Journal of Marketing 73(6), 18–32 (2009)

[20] How Twitter and Facebook Can Get You Better Service At Hotels - WSJ.com, http://online.wsj.com/article/SB100014240527487042563045753207309771161348.html#printMode (accessed May 30, 2012)

[21] Tripp, T.M., Grégoire, Y.: When Unhappy Customers Strike Back on the Internet. MIT Sloan Management Review 52(3), 37–44 (2011)

[22] What data can and cannot do | News | guardian.co.uk, http://www.guardian.co.uk/news/datablog/2012/may/31/data-journalism-focused-critical (accessed May 31, 2012)

[23] Zeng, D., Chen, H., Lusch, R., Li, S.H.: Social media analytics and intelligence. IEEE Intelligent Systems 25(6), 13–16 (2010)

[24] Franks, B.: Taming The Big Data Tidal Wave: Finding Opportunities in Huge Data Streams with Advanced Analytics, 1st edn. Wiley (2012)

[25] Social Network Data Analytics - Charu C. Aggarwal - Google Books, http://books.google.de/books?hl=de&lr=&id=SE2iRgeYYwcC&oi=fnd&pg=PR5&dq=social+data&ots=lHgQLkS_Ou&sig=HRj_Cspw3zSKJXccaS5neD3K_hA#v=onepage&q=social%20data&f=false (accessed: June 13, 2012)

[26] Palmer, D.: Making Sense of Social Data (2011)

[27] Ting, I., Lin, C.H., Wang, C.S.: Constructing A Cloud Computing Based Social Networks Data Warehousing and Analyzing System. In: 2011 International Conference on Advances in Social Networks Analysis and Mining (ASONAM), pp. 735–740 (2011)

[28] Park, J., Shin, Y., Kim, K., Chung, B.S.: Searching social media streams on the web. IEEE Intelligent Systems 25(6), 24–31 (2010)

[29] Big data: The next frontier for innovation, competition, and productivity, McKinsey Global Institute

[30] Zikopoulos, P.C., Eaton, C., Zikopoulos, P.: Understanding Big Data: Analytics for Enterprise Class Hadoop and Streaming Data. Mcgraw-Hill Professional (2012)

[31] Make Your Business a Social Enterprise with Salesforce Social Hub - Radian6.com, http://www.radian6.com/what-we-sell/social-enterprise/ (accessed: May 31, 2012)

[32] Schmidt, R.: A Framework for the Support of Value Co-creation by Social Software. In: Daniel, F., Barkaoui, K., Dustdar, S. (eds.) BPM 2011 Workshops, Part I. LNBIP, vol. 99, pp. 242–252. Springer, Heidelberg (2012)

[33] Bruno, G., Dengler, F., Jennings, B., Khalaf, R., Nurcan, S., Prilla, M., Sarini, M., Schmidt, R., Silva, R.: Key challenges for enabling agile BPM with social software. J. Softw. Maint. Evol.: Res. Pract., n/a–n/a (2011)

[34] To Understand Your Market, Harness The 7 Elements of Customer and Social Data | Web Strategy by Jeremiah Owyang | Social Media, Web Marketing, http://www.web-strategist.com/blog/2011/02/08/seve_elements_of_social_data/ (accessed: July 29, 2012)

A Conceptual Approach to Characterize Dynamic Communities in Social Networks: Application to Business Process Management

Cassio Melo[1], Bénédicte Le Grand[2], and Marie-Aude Aufaure[1]

[1] MAS - École Centrale Paris, Châtenay-Malabry, France
{cassio.melo,marie-aude.aufaure}@ecp.fr
[2] Université Pierre et Marie Curie, LIP6-CNRS France
benedicte.le-grand@lip6.fr

Abstract. In the enterprise decision making process, specifically product design and CRM, the analysis of all the available and relevant customer information is a major task. In this paper we propose measures based on Formal Concept Analysis to determine conceptual proximity between people. We explain how FCA can support market analysts in their task of CRM marketing and management, with the automatic discovery of knowledge in large amounts of enterprise information (e.g. document collections). The temporal evolution of this proximity measure may be analyzed, and provides significant insights on trends and market behavior. This approach has been exemplified with a case study on Twitter with an emphasis on content dynamics within user communities.

1 Introduction

There is a growing interest for the use of social software in Business Process Management (BPM) as it allows the mutual collaboration of users, artifacts sharing, quick access to resources and people, empowerment of individuals in the sense-making process, to name a few.

The social assets from a company can be seen as networks: individuals and groups are connected by shared interests (e.g. people who bought the same product), people involved in the same process, or co-location. These networks are often dynamic in the sense that nodes join or leave communities, new interactions are created, information flows through connected peers, among many others events [1][2][3]. In this context, a challenge is to tackle with the heterogeneity of data and discover patterns that can be valuable in a business context.

Formal Concept Analysis (FCA) emerged in the early 80's as a mathematical framework to reveal co-occurrence patterns between sets of objects and sets of attributes, in a partial-ordering fashion. FCA is able to discover hitherto implicit information considering multiples sources and has been succesfully applied in a variety of domains such as information retrieval [4][5]; genes expression [6]; machine learning [7] (for a survey see [8]). However only few studies are related to BPM [9] [10].

We argue that FCA is well suited in the BPM context, in particular to observe evolving networks in the case of marketing analysis, taking into account at the same time

M. La Rosa and P. Soffer (Eds.): BPM 2012 Workshops, LNBIP 132, pp. 246–255, 2013.

topological features, semantics and context of customers and potential buyers. In order to do so, we propose to leverage FCA as a similarity criterion where nodes (i.e. people) are characterized by their conceptual distance to other users in the network. We applied the proposed approach to the Twitter network and preliminar results revealed many interesting insights about trends and social behavior.

This paper is organized as follows: Section 2 summarizes the motivation of this work; we explain why the conceptual approach we propose to characterize communities may be of particular interest in the context of agile Business Process Management. Section 3 introduces our conceptual measures for the analysis of evolving communities, followed by the proposed approach in Section 4; Section 5 presents a case study on the Twitter network and Section 6 outlines the conclusions and future directions of this work.

2 Conceptual Community Detection and Business Process Management

2.1 FCA-Based Community Detection in Social Networks

The conceptual approach we propose for user community detection in social networks is based on Formal Concept analysis and exploits at the same time the network's topological features, semantics and context. We illustrate our methodology on a popular online social network: Twitter. Identifying user communities on Twitter is challenging, considering the number of users and the number of tweets generated daily.

We have already used FCA in earlier works for social network analysis [11], but this approach suffers from scalability issues [12]. The approach we propose in this paper therefore combines a very efficient community detection algorithm based on modularity optimization [13] and FCA measures based on Galois lattices.

The community detection algorithm based on modularity optimization identifies clusters of densely-connected users (who are not much connected to users in others clusters). Users are linked in the network through the 'follower'' relationship. We use the resulting community structure relying on the social network topology as a basis of our work. In the following, these topological communities are reflected by the colour of nodes in the various representations (see Section 5).

Formal Concept Analysis is then used, through the computation of a Galois lattice, to study the evolution of these communities, based on the content of users tweets. Instead of using traditional data analysis approaches, we use a FCA approach as we know from our previous work that is takes into account an implicit context which is not captured with traditional approaches.

We then compute, for all users, a conceptual similarity value with other users, based on the generated Galois lattice. The similarity matrix, containing all similarity values between users, allows us to draw 2D maps, usind MDS projections.

The evolution of these maps over time shows how users get closer to one another within their own community, and how they may get closer to other communities.

2.2   Interest of Conceptual Community Detection and Analysis for Business Process Management

Several works have recently investigated the interest of social software in the context of Business Process Management [14]. In particular, they have shown how the specific features of social software (weak ties, social production, egalitarianism and mutual service provisioning) can be exploited to make BPM more agile [15]. In this section, we explain how our methodology for social networks community analysis allows to further exploit these social software features for BPM.

Wide Range of Social Software. Earlier work on social software-based BPM have shown the interest of tools such as wikis to create a 'community spirit'" and therefore enhance collaborative process design. The approach we propose for community detection and analysis also enables the inference of communities from online social networks, which are not as structured as wikis or forums.

Exploitation of Weak Ties. Our conceptual approach is extremely adapted in this context as it allows the identification of implicit ties between users (which would be missed with traditional data analysis approaches). The strong ties among users are expressed by the "follower" relationship, when users explicitly state their interest in specific people's opinion. We take these strong links into account for the initial (topological) community structure we build from collected data. However the conceptual approach we follow to study the evolution of communities no longer considers these strong ties. Galois lattices cluster users in an overlapping conceptual structure, according to similar content in their tweets. Users which have no explicit connection in the social network may therefore appear in the same concepts from the lattice, thus being implicitly (weakly) tied. The FCA-based approach goes further than traditional approaches because the generated clusters are overlapping and reflect any common content (even minor) among users.

Egalitarianism. As stated in [16], social software allows all users to contribute with the same status, abolishing hierarchy. In the example we use in this paper, there is no restriction in users contributions: any person may write a tweet. The community detection and analysis methodology we present respects this egalitarism as all users and all content are considered of equal importance during the creation of a concept lattice. The un-hierarchical feature of social software is therefore preserved throughout our data processing.

Social Production. Our approach allows to identify a concrete social production which would be rather scattered if we only considered Twitter as it is (as opposed to a forum or a wiki). So we may say that our approach allows us to infer a better-defined social production in online social networks.

Among the primary activities of a firm identified by Porter [17], the one we more specifically target with our methodology for dynamic communities analysis in social networks is Marketing and sales. Indeed, being able to identify communities of potential customers for specific products, and to follow the evolution of this community, is a very precious asset for a company.

Moreover, the approach we propose may integrate structured and unstructured data, typically database content and information coming from social networks. This allows us to exploit simultaneaously explicit corporate knowledge, e.g. logs of clients' past orders, and implicit knowledge learnt from social networks, e.g. customers' comments about specific products. In this paper, we illustrate our methodology on unstructured data, consisting of messages (called tweets) from the Twitter online social network. We show how we manage, from this unstructured data, to identify communities and study the evolution of what we call the conceptual distance between the users. In the context of avdertising, these communities could be used as specific target groups.

3   Conceptual Measures for Community Analysis

A FCA-based similarity method is proposed. It takes into account tweets published by users, generates a concept lattice and measures the conceptual distance among concepts, in order to compute conceptual similarity values among users.

We define a terminology for network and conceptual structure and the implied operations. Let $N = \{G, E\}$, where $G = \{g_1, g_2, \ldots, g_n\}$ is the set of users, and $E \subseteq G \times G$ is the set of directed links between users. Each directed link $e_{ij} = (g_i, g_j) \in E$ indicates that user g_i follows user g_j. Now given a (formal) context $K = (G, M, I)$, where G is called a set of users or *extent*, M is called a set of terms or *intent*, and the binary relation $I \subseteq G \times M$ specifies which users have which terms, the *derivation operators* $(\cdot)\prime$ are defined for $A \subseteq G$ and $B \subseteq M$:

$$A\prime = \{m \in M | \forall g \in A : gIm\} \quad \text{and} \quad B\prime = \{g \in G | \forall m \in B : gIm\} \tag{1}$$

Finally, let $S(u)$ be the set of all concepts in the context K containing user u and $u \subseteq G$ with a support μ and stability β. Conversely, let $F(u)$ be the set of all concepts in the context K containing all friends of user u and $u \in G$ with a support μ and stability β. Stability (*intent*) is a measure of how likely a concept is to change if one or more of its attributes are removed. Support (*extent*) measures the frequency of an object in concepts in relation to the total set of objects.

We recall the FCA-based similarity measure proposed by Boutari *et al.* [18]:

Concept similarity. It is a coefficient for calculating the ratio of shared attributes between concepts. We define concept similarity as:

$$CSim(p,q) = \frac{|m_p' \cap m_q'|}{|m_p'| + |m_q'|} + \frac{|m_p'' \cap m_q''|}{|m_p''| + |m_q''|} \tag{2}$$

Proximity. Let L be the concept lattice of context G. Conceptual proximity is the topological distance between concepts p and q in the lattice L.

$$prox(p,q) = 1 - \frac{shortestDistance(p,q)}{diameter(L)} \tag{3}$$

Strength. It is the average concept similarity value (CSim) along the shortest path be-tween a pair of concepts.

Average conceptual similarity. We extended the previous measures in order to com-pute the similarity for each pair of users $u, v \in G$ based on $S(u)$:

$$avgSimUser(u,v) = \sum_{p}\sum_{q} \frac{\alpha Prox(p,q) + (1-\alpha)Str(p,q)}{|S(u) \cup S(v)|} \tag{4}$$

where p and q are formal concepts, $p \in S(u)$ and $q \in S(v)$, α is the ratio between proximity and strength measures.

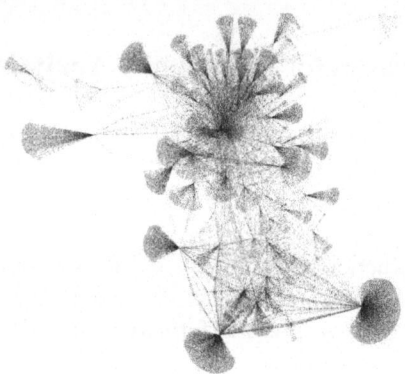

Fig. 1. Users from three communities on Twitter. Community 1 (red nodes, at the top of the figure - 4,630 users), community 2 (purple nodes, at the bottom - 4,550) and community 3 (green nodes, in the middle - 1,640).

4   FCA Approach for Community Content Analysis

There is a growing number of studies on the evolutionary properties of communities in social networks, in particular the identification of overlapping of communities over time. Ovelapping and nesting of communities are two important aspects to be consid-ered because of their analogy with the real world: people usually belong to more than one community at the same time, e.g. familly, class, school, neighbourhood, etc. No-tably, the Clique Percolation Method (CPM) [19] is able to identify overlapping com-munities by the union of cliques that can be reached from each other clique. In [20] Palla et al. described an algorithm based on clique-percolation method for character-izing the lifetime of communities: merge, split, creation and dispersal of a community over time. Changes in the network can also take a proactive role in the community de-tection method, as demostrated in [21]. Unlike those approaches, however, the present work aims at investigating the evolution of "conceptual communities" in complement to their connections.

The methodology for our FCA-based community content analysis is composed of three phases: Pre-processing; Concept lattice generation and similarity computation; Community dynamics analysis. The following sections will detail each of them.

4.1 Pre-processing

The first step consists in creating a formal context from the content produced by users. Instead of extracting keywords from text, we used an "automatic tagging" of text provided by the *Concept Tagging* service from *AlchemyAPI* [22]. This yielded a particular level of generalization for the terms (in our case, from tweets) that increased the efficiency of the algorithm by 17%[1]. For example, the tweet "mens usa volleyball Olympic MVP Clay Stanley on knee surgery and will be watching in London " yields "2012 Summer Olympics", "USA volleyball team". Once the *user × term* matrix is defined, a filter is applied to remove attributes with low support. We then obtain the formal context used for the computation of the Galois lattice.

4.2 Concept Lattice Generation and Similarity Computation

A concept lattice is generated from the previous formal context. A formal concept in this case contains in its *intent* a set of terms and its *extent* is a set of users whose tweets contain such terms. For each user in the concept lattice, we use (4) to calculate distances between every pair of users in the concept lattice. Next, we project the distance matrix on a Multidimensional Scaling (MDS) map which gives an intuitive view of how conceptually close users are.

4.3 Community Dynamic Analysis

Association rules are patterns of attributes co-occurences in a concept lattice. They can be derived from the relationships between concepts and provide a set of implications. For example, by accounting terms that appear frequently together it is possible to obtain a collection of related terms. We used association rules to highlight related content from users tweets.

5 Case Study: Twitter Community Dynamics

5.1 Data Collection and Community Identification

We randomly collected data produced by 51,006 users on Twitter using a snowball approach from followers of the popular band "Coldplay". The network data on Twitter can be seen as a directed graph of who "follows" who. The content data refers to the last 200 published tweets of each user. Both network and content data collected were split in monthly timespans containing changes in the network such as new connections and published tweets.

---

[1] The average attribute support increased about 17% in comparison to the keyword extraction method, resulting in fewer concepts overall.

We first applied a community detection algorithm based on modularity [13]. From the 125 communities identified we selected the three largest, a connected graph containing 10,820 users, 14,598 links and 1,238,667 tweets in total (Figure 1).

5.2   Community Content Analysis

We investigated the relation between the topology of communities and their content. The intuition is that connected people are more likely to share the same interests with their counterparts than with others outside the community.

This can be illustrated by analyzing the most popular concepts published by the green community, where presumably, most users are from South Africa (Figure 2).

Fig. 2. Popular concepts from community 3 and community 1 respectively

Community Characterization. The association rules among concepts provided valuable insights on community characterization and content inference. For instance, for community 3, 1,106 association rules were generated, among them, "2003 Cricket World Cup" ⇒ "South Africa" (92% of confidence) or more sophisticated: "African National Congress" ∧ "Jacob Zuma" ⇒ "Thabo Mbeki" (83% of confidence).

Content Evolution. The evolution of content can be traced by snapshots of MDS map for conceptual similarity as illustrated in Figures 3 and 4.

The sequence of snapshots illustrates the "conceptual movement" of users, approaching and moving away from each other, eventually to form clusters around a "buzz" (Figure 3 *A* and *C*). Figure 3 *A* corresponds to a small group of people in the same topological community publishing topics related to "parties" such as "saturday night", "disco", "dj", etc. Figure 3 *C* is an interesting region of the map where people from three communities are conceptually similar but belong to different communities. Such event may indicate future collaboration between communities, with nodes switching from one community to the other. These users are not necessary following each other, which may be interesting for link prediction models. A more accurate analysis of similar conceptual groups and of network linking will remain as a future work.

A subsequent timespan is illustrated by Figure 4 showing a unusual mutual gathering of users from all communities. This happened to be October 2011 where people were moved by the death of Steve Jobs hence becoming a common subject of discussion.

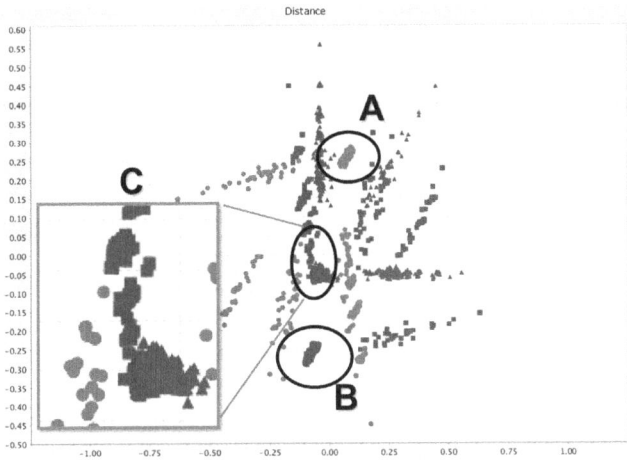

Fig. 3. MDS map for the conceptual similarity between users from each community in timespan t_n

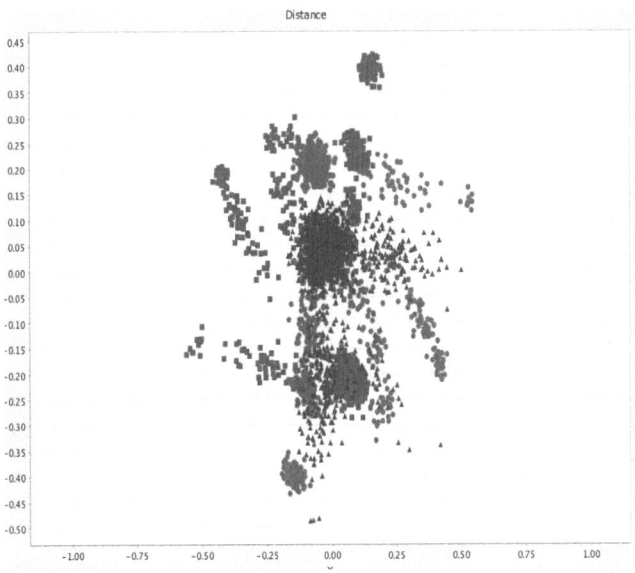

Fig. 4. MDS map for the conceptual similarity between users from each community in timespan t_{n+m}

6   Conclusions and Perspectives

In this article, we presented ongoing work on a FCA-based approach for dynamic content analysis in communities in social networks. FCA provides a hierarchical and overlapping classification of content from people of the same community and highlights co-occurence patterns. In a BPM context, our approach provides a more valuable analysis of customers' profiles when some properties change over time, such as posts, interests, location, etc. In other words, the characterization of social networks by sets of concepts brings a complementary view compared to the pure topological one. Zones of conceptual proximity may indicate potential beneficial interactions and conceptual links establishes implications among those properties. In a practical example, when the methodology is applied to observe the evolution of customers interests, it allows the identification of specific niches that the enterprise can approach with pertinent marketing strategies and eventually attract customers from one niche to another.

Another sector which could benefit from this work is the Human Resource Management support activity [17]. In this case, knowledge about employees' profiles and skills could be used in conjunction with information gathered from internal wiki in order to identify optimal teams for a given project. Taking into account communities dynamics would moreover allow to add new people to the team as distances within people evolve over time.

As future work we envision a link prediction model based on patterns of content dynamics. We will also apply this methodology to a dataset relevant to market analyis.

References

1. Ma, P.C.H., Chan, K.C.C., Yao, X., Chiu, D.K.Y.: An evolutionary clustering algorithm for gene expression microarray data analysis. IEEE Transactions on Evolutionary Computation 10, 296–314 (2006)
2. Chakrabarti, D., Kumar, R., Tomkins, A.: Evolutionary clustering. In: KDD 2006: Proceedings of the 12th ACM SIGKDD International Conference on Knowledge Discovery and Data Mining, pp. 554–560. ACM, New York (2006)
3. Zheleva, E., Sharara, H., Getoor, L.: Co-evolution of social and affiliation networks. In: 15th ACM SIGKDD Conference on Knowledge Discovery and Data Mining, KDD (June 2009)
4. Carpineto, C., Romano, G.: Using Concept Lattices for Text Retrieval and Mining. In: Ganter, B., Stumme, G., Wille, R. (eds.) Formal Concept Analysis. LNCS (LNAI), vol. 3626, pp. 161–179. Springer, Heidelberg (2005)
5. Cheung, K.S., Vogel, D.: Complexity reduction in lattice-based information retrieval. Inf. Retr. 8(2), 285–299 (2005), http://dx.doi.org/10.1007/s10791-005-5663-y
6. Akand, E., Bain, M., Temple, M.: A visual analytics approach to augmenting formal concepts with relational background knowledge in a biological domain. In: Meyer, T., Orgun, M., Taylor, K, eds. (December 2010)
7. Kuznetsov, S.O.: Machine Learning and Formal Concept Analysis. In: Eklund, P. (ed.) ICFCA 2004. LNCS (LNAI), vol. 2961, pp. 287–312. Springer, Heidelberg (2004)
8. Poelmans, J., Elzinga, P., Viaene, S., Dedene, G.: Formal Concept Analysis in Knowledge Discovery: A Survey. In: Croitoru, M., Ferré, S., Lukose, D. (eds.) ICCS 2010. LNCS, vol. 6208, pp. 139–153. Springer, Heidelberg (2010), http://dl.acm.org/citation.cfm?id=1881168.1881185

9. Kang, B., Jung, J.-Y., Cho, N.W., Kang, S.-H.: Real-time business process monitoring using formal concept analysis. Industrial Management and Data Systems 111(5), 652–674 (2011), http://www.ingentaconnect.com/content/mcb/029/2011/00000111/00000005/art00001

10. Laukaitis, A., Vasilecas, O.: Formal concept analysis and information systems modeling. In: Proceedings of the 2007 International Conference on Computer Systems and Technologies, Ser. CompSysTech 2007, pp. 1–17. ACM, New York (2007), http://doi.acm.org/10.1145/1330598.1330618

11. Riadh, T.M., Le Grand, B., Aufaure, M.-A., Soto, M.: Conceptual and statistical foot-prints for social networks' characterization. In: Proceedings of the 3rd Workshop on Social Network Mining and Analysis, Ser. SNA-KDD 2009, pp. 1–8. ACM, New York (2009), http://doi.acm.org/10.1145/1731011.1731019

12. Trad, M.R., Grand, B.L., Aufaure, M.-A., Soto, M.: Powerconcept: Conceptual metrics' distributed computation. In: 8th International Conference on Formal Concept Analysis, ICFCA (2010)

13. Good, B., Montjoye, Y.D., Clauset, A.: Performance of modularity maximization in practical contexts. Physical Review E 81(4), 046106 (2010)

14. Erol, S., Granitzer, M., Happ, S., Jantunen, S., Jennings, B., Johannesson, P., Koschmider, A., Nurcan, S., Rossi, D., Schmidt, R.: Combining bpm and social software: contradiction or chance? J. Softw. Maint. Evol. 22(6&7), 449–476 (2010), http://dx.doi.org/10.1002/smr.v22:6/7

15. Bruno, G., Dengler, F., Jennings, B., Khalaf, R., Nurcan, S., Prilla, M., Sarini, M., Schmidt, R., Silva, R.: Key challenges for enabling agile bpm with social software. J. Softw. Maint. Evol. 23(4), 297–326 (2011), http://dx.doi.org/10.1002/smr.523

16. Granovetter, M.: The Strength of Weak Ties. The American Journal of Sociology 78(6), 1360–1380 (1973)

17. Porter, M.E.: The Value Chain and Competitive Advantage. In: Barnes, D. (ed.) Understanding Business Processes, 1st edn. Routledge (November 2000)

18. Boutari, A.M., Carpineto, C., Nicolussi, R.: Evaluating term concept association measures for short text expansion: two case studies of classification and clustering. In: Proceedings of the Seventh International Conference on Concept Lattices and their Applications, CLA 2010 (2010)

19. Palla, G., Derényi, I., Farkas, I., Vicsek, T.: Uncovering the overlapping community structure of complex networks in nature and society. Nature 435(7043), 814–818 (2005), http://dx.doi.org/10.1038/nature03607

20. Palla, G., László Barabási, A., Vicsek, T., Hungary, B.: Quantifying social group evolution. Nature 446, 2007 (2007)

21. Cazabet, R., Amblard, F., Hanachi, C.: Detection of overlapping communities in dynamical social networks. In: 2010 IEEE Second International Conference on Social Computing (SocialCom), pp. 309–314 (August 2010)

22. Alchemy, Alchemyapi - a web service for text processing

Business Processes for the Crowd Computer

Pavel Kucherbaev[1], Stefano Tranquillini[1], Florian Daniel[1], Fabio Casati[1],
Maurizio Marchese[1], Marco Brambilla[2], and Piero Fraternali[2]

[1] University of Trento, Via Sommarive 5, 38123 Povo (TN), Italy
surname@disi.unitn.it
[2] Politecnico di Milano, Piazza L. da Vinci 32, 20133 Milano, Italy
name.surname@polimi.it

Abstract. Social networks and crowdsourcing platforms provide powerful means to execute tasks that require human intelligence instead of just machine computation power. Especially crowdsourcing has demonstrated its applicability in many fields, and a variety of platforms have been created for delegating small tasks to human solvers on the Web. However, creating applications that are structured, thus applications that combine more than a single task, is a complex and typically manual endeavor that requires many different interactions with crowdsourcing platforms. In this paper, we introduce the idea of a *crowd computer*, discuss its properties, and propose a programming paradigm for the development of crowdsourcing applications. In particular, we argue in favor of business processes as formalism to program the crowd computer and show how they enable the reuse of intricate crowdsourcing practices.

1 Introduction

The ability to connect a large number of people and to lower the effort barrier to collecting input from them in all sorts of contexts - while in the office, home, or while waiting in line at the grocery store - facilitates the involvement of humans in computations and information sourcing and processing tasks. The process of involving humans in computations is typically referred to as *crowdsourcing*, *social computing*, or variations thereof based on the aspect of human information processing one wants to emphasize. As common in a relatively novel area of research, there are a number of variations of the interpretation of these terms, but, in general, they refer to the process of outsourcing task solving to a possibly unknown and large number of people - the crowd [5], thereby harvesting the collective intelligence to realize greater value from the interaction between users and information [11].

Many social computing systems are already available on the market, some of them born before the term "social computing" became widely known and used. If we consider them based on the kind of computations they support, we can notice that there are essentially two kinds of platforms: horizontal platforms, allowing people to post different kinds of computing problems, and applications, tailored at a specific kind of crowdsourcing task. An example of the former is Amazon

M. La Rosa and P. Soffer (Eds.): BPM 2012 Workshops, LNBIP 132, pp. 256–267, 2013.
© Springer-Verlag Berlin Heidelberg 2013

Mechanical Turk (MTurk), that gives the ability to post generic tasks to users and collects results. In a way, MTurk– together with its user base – resembles the notion of a traditional computer, that is, something we can program to execute a task. An example of crowdsourcing application is Wikipedia, where the information is indeed crowdsourced but the task is restricted to that of providing and managing information for an encyclopedia. In IT terms, this is indeed more similar to a packaged application more than a computer.

Despite the early success of some of these platforms and applications, creating a crowdsourcing application – or even a task on platforms such as MTurk – is still an art, and in practice it is unfeasible to leverage a (social) *computing platform* such as MTurk to create an *application* such as Wikipedia or others. Indeed, MTurk is mostly used for very simple tasks, many of which oriented to research studies on people's behavior [10]. Indeed, social computing is still in its infancy as a scientific discipline. The crowd can be a terrific source of information and of "computing power", able to execute some "computations" that a computer (or a crowd of computers – the cloud) cannot do (or cannot do as effectively and efficiently). However, there is no consensus or understanding of what a social computer is, which its fundamental concepts, components and functionality are, and how it can be "programmed".

In this paper we discuss the characteristics of a particular instance of social computer, a *crowd computer*, that is, a platform that can be programmed, with a flexibility conceptually comparable to that of a traditional computer, to create crowdsourcing applications. We propose and sketch-out a separation between what are the basic functions of a crowd computer (conceptually analogous to the instruction set of a microprocessor) and what should be instead specified by programs that leverage these functions to generate applications. We then identify programming language templates, expressed as process skeletons, that can be reused by programmers to develop their applications. The goal is to capture practices for the various aspects of business logic commonly needed in crowdsourcing applications, simplifying the programming of the crowd computer and laying a foundation the actual social computer.

This is a preliminary study based on our earlier analysis of what can be achieved by social/crowd platforms and derived from some recent work (e.g., the work on CrowdSearch [2] and the work appearing at BPM2012 [12]).

Notice that this vision, while opening up a plethora of new application scenarios and implementation possibilities, also implies addressing a wide set of related problems, spanning from ethical issues related to using human brains as "components" of a computation platforms, to security, trust and performance of this new platforms. In this paper we don't address these issues directly, but we design our solution also considering the need of addressing them in the future.

2   Scenario

For demonstration and explanation purposes, let's imagine we want to organize and manage a photo contest for a given thematic area, e.g., crowdsourcing. The

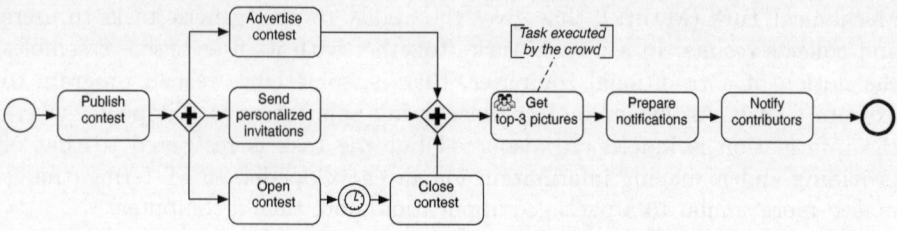

Fig. 1. A simple photo contest crowdsourcing the selection of the top-3 contributions

idea is to publish a simple website for the submission of photos and to adver-
tise the contest via journals, magazines, and newspapers related to photography,
as well as via direct contacts (e.g., emails, Facebook contacts, Google+ circles,
etc.) to potentially interested photographers. The submission system is to be
kept open for one month, in parallel to all advertising activities. Upon the closure of the submission system, we simply want to crowdsource the selection of
the best three contributions, that is, we do not want to create an internal jury for
the selection of the best three photographs and instead delegate the task to the
crowd. Once the three best photos have been determined by the crowd, we prepare and send out the notifications to photographers. The process is illustrated
in Figure 1.

While the overall process is a traditional BPM problem, the crowdsourcing of
the selection of the top-3 contributions is not. There are many possible crowdsourcing platforms we can use and many different ways we can use them to
obtain the ranking of photos. For instance, if we use Amazon Mechanical Turk
(MTurk) we must split the task into smaller chunks, in order to have tasks of
reasonable size (asking for a ranking of all submissions in one single task would
be too complex for a single worker). For example, a set of 10 photos could be
big enough to provide a reasonable choice to the worker and small enough to
allow fast decisions. We ask each worker for a ranking of the best three photos
out of their set, then we aggregate all results into one global ranking and select
the best three. Of course, we could also have another intermediate selection step
before the global ranking, split the photos differently, ask workers to order *all*
of their photos, etc. Specifying a good logic can be a complex, iterative task.

Whatever logic we adopt, the above idea of splitting the ranking into sub-tasks
is relatively naive, in that it does not consider possible quality issues regarding
the feedback that can be obtained from crowsourcing platforms like MTurk (and
others). In order to grant a better quality of the final result, we could for instance
assign each chunk to two different workers and then average their rankings, or we
could have chunks that partially overlap, or we could ask to workers to agree on a
common ranking, and so on. Instead of focusing on the quality of the feedbacks,
we could also try to select only workers that we trust are able to judge photos,
e.g., because they are photographers themselves. Doing so would require us to
set up a suitable qualification test and to admit to the "crowdsourced jury" only
those that pass the test. We could get this information either by looking at their

profiles or by simply asking them. But, again, there are many possibilities. In summary, several options are at hand and it is not trivial to understand which solution suits best which task.

3   The Crowd Computer: Architecture and Instruction Set

In the following, we present and discuss a conceptual architecture of a *crowd computer*, an information collection and processing system that can be programmed to execute crowd computing applications.

3.1   Architecture

The crowd computer can be described based on an analogy and comparison with a traditional computer or a cloud computing cluster. In both cases we have computing systems: the main difference being that in the crowd computer the "hardware" also includes the crowd, in addition to the traditional elements of a computer (CPU, memory, etc.). This means that the information sources, sinks, and processors can be humans, and therefore each processor operates at will and in a rather non-deterministic fashion. Correspondingly, the *instruction set* of a crowd computer also needs to be extended to interact with this new type of processing entities, for example to distribute the work (possibly in a redundant fashion), accept or reject it, remind workers, maintain profile and rating information, and the like. These instructions are conceptually analogous to an API for accessing the crowd (or, in other words, they represent a *crowd programming interface*, or CPI).

Figure 2 shows the main components of the ***crowd computer***, namely:

- two kinds of *computing components*: i) a traditional computer (in Von Neumann's terms, the arithmetic logic unit) and ii), the crowd;
- the *crowdsourcing engine*, that is, in terms of the Von Neumann machine, the control unit that coordinates the execution of social computing programs. These programs are in turn composed of the instructions within the instruction set, executed either by a CPU or by the crowd;
- a *storage* which, besides memory for data and instructions, includes data on the crowd (members, their execution performance and history, ratings, payment information, etc.);
- the *crowd interaction component* (a Graphical User Interface – GUI) that connects the engine with the crowd. Because the crowd is made of humans, interactions always occur through some (typically graphical) interface, which can be a traditional desktop UI, a mobile UI, sensor-based, and the like. For instance, in the case of Amazon Mechanical Turk, the GUI is the directly the website mturk.com. In the general case, the GUI would adapt and provide the needed human-computer interaction for the specific social application.

In this conceptual architecture we focus on the crowd aspect, assuming that applications will obviously require traditional functionalities too. We also observe

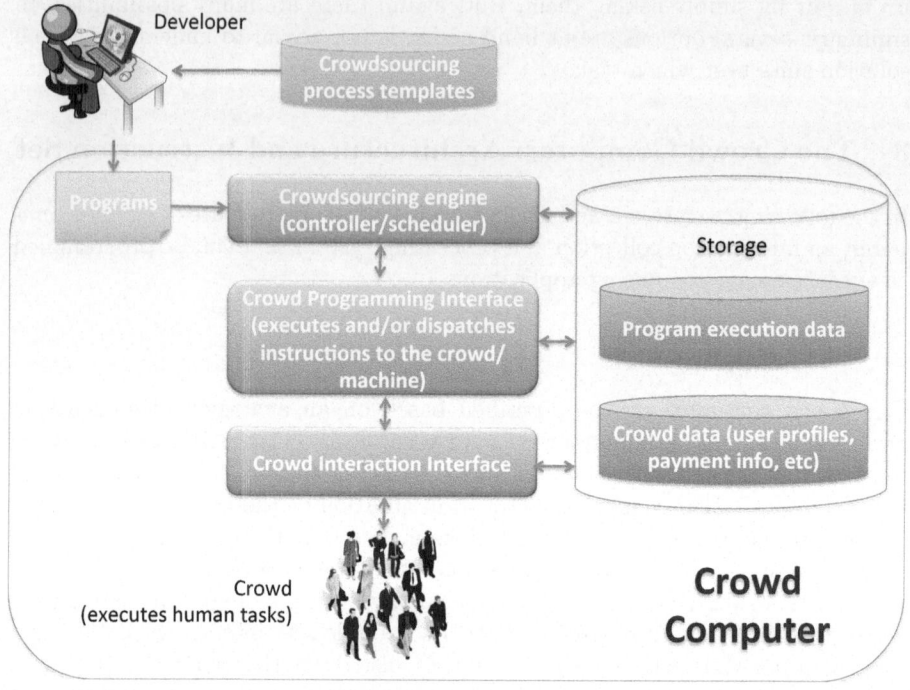

Fig. 2. Conceptual architecture of the crowd computer

that a crowd computer is naturally more open and dynamic than a traditional one in that: the members and the profile of the crowd can change over time; the specification of the tasks assigned to the crowd and the way they are executed are more flexible; and and even the UI to communicate with the crowd may be programmable as each application may want or need to have its own mechanisms for communicating or collecting information from the crowd.

3.2   The Crowd Programming Interface (CPI)

When designing a crowd computer, a key decision lies in identifying the instruction set that it should have to support a reasonably large class of programs while keeping the instruction set simple, manageable, and efficient. Our approach starts from providing a minimal instruction set, which is then extended once we get an understanding of the most commonly used patterns of invocation. A program combines the instructions to implement specific behaviors or policies. We take a similar stand here, briefly listing below which are the operations that should be provided to the crowd programmer to implement crowd computing behaviors. We then present process templates that can combine these instructions to define behaviors and policies. In the following we will use the terms crowd instructions, CPI (Crowd Programming Interface) or API interchangeably. The definition of these functions stays at a high level of abstraction, trying to emphasize the needed functionality of API. As the reader will notice, a crowd computer with the proposed instruction set will be more flexible (or less "hardcoded") than current crowdsourcing applications and even of current crowdsourcing platforms that tend to hardcode some of the behaviors, which we instead see as being specified at the programming (process) level. The crowd computer design relies on the following definitions:

Human Task. This set of operations (and of corresponding data, stored as part of the crowd computer storage) manages the human tasks lifecycle, essentially submitting tasks to users and collecting replies. It provides several functions like: *create task* - function that creates a new task with metadata about it; *read task* - returns data and metadata about the task; *update task* - updates task parameters (like deadline, maximum executors per task); *delete task* - deletes information about the task; *activate task* - makes the task visible for crowd workers; *cancel task* - makes task invisible for crowd workers; *assign task* - assigns task with a list of crowd workers to be performed; *connect task* - connects task with another task, making possible creation of processes; *get list of tasks* - returns a list of tasks filtered by parameters; *perform task* - executor saves results of solving task; *submit task* - executor submits results of solving task; *confirm task* - requester confirms submitted results.

Profile. This CPI block stores and manages personal and skills information of crowd workers. It contains a list of functions like: *register profile* - creates a new profile of a crowdworker or a requester; *authorize profile* - authorization of user profile by login and password; *update profile* - changes personal information in profile or user skills information; *delete profile*; *read profile information*; *get list of profiles* - returns a list of user profiles filtered by some parameters (age, skills, education, experience); *connect profiles* - connects one profile with others for creating groups, teams or substitutable crowd workers; *update workers' experience.*

Qualification. This CPI block takes care of qualification tests in the crowd-sourcing process to make sure crowd workers have enough expertise to solve a given task. Here the list of core functions: *create test* - create a new qualification test to check crowd worker experience; *update test*; *delete test*; *connect test with task*; *validate test*; *create experience parameter.*

Payment. This block holds the payment basic functions, like: *create reward* - creates an information in the payment system about an account of the requester and the reward amount; *propose reward* - connects the proposed reward with the task; *pay reward* - after results are confirmed the requester pays the executor.

In addition, a crowd computer would offer management operations that provide runtime and statistical information on task completion status, performances, and the like. Notice that the strategy on how to design and monitor the crowd computing behaviour (starting from the definition of which tasks are performed by humans and which ones by actual machines) lays in the hand of a human designer. In this first version of the work we don't address the problem of dynamic or collaborative design of the crowd computer.

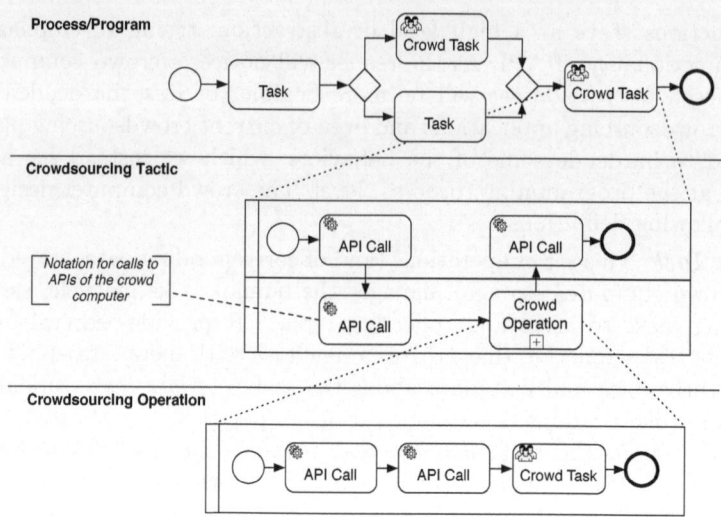

Fig. 3. A three-layered approach to assisted programming of the crowd computer

4   Programming the Crowd Computer

What does it now mean to *program* a crowd computer? In essence, we need to program the APIs exposed by the underlying crowdsourcing platform in such a way that the resulting "program" (the set of API invocations) solves the task we would like to crowdsource. In our reference scenario, this task is the ranking of the top-3 photographs. We have seen that crowdsourcing that task requires spitting the problem into sub-tasks, deciding on the order in which to execute sub-tasks, aggregate feedbacks, control quality, possibly pre-select workers, etc. As a matter of fact, this is like programming.

In fact, we envision a *process-driven paradigm* to "programming" the crowd computer, as such seems a natural fit for structuring and managing both work and people. In line with this design choice, as crowdsourcing engine (see Figure 2) we envision a business process engine with suitable crowdsourcing extensions.

We have also seen that integrating crowd tasks into a common business process logic is not trivial at all. For this integration, we identify three conceptual layers of abstraction that help understand, modularize, and program crowdsourcing applications (see Figure 3):

- At the top-most level, we have the ***process/program*** layer. This is the place where we model the actual process logic, such as the one illustrated in Figure 1. We use the BPMN to express processes plus add a new construct to it, i.e., the crowd task (labeled with a crowd icon), to tell which tasks are to be delegated to the crowd. This layer talks about tasks and crowd tasks.
- Next, we have the ***crowdsourcing tactic*** layer. This is where we decide how to approach the crowd and how to manage the overall crowdsourcing

process of each individual crowd task. For instance, MTurk implements a so-called *marketplace* tactic. If we used other platforms, we could have, for instance, organized a *contest* tactic (like in Prizes.org), or similar. The tactic decides how work is assigned, how workers are motivated, and how they are remunerated. This layer shows API invocations and uses sub-processes exposed by the lower layer.

– At the lower-most level, we have the ***crowdsourcing operations***. This is where we concretely decide about how to pre-select workers, how to control quality, how to aggregate feedback, how to split input data, and similar. For each aspect (e.g., pre-selection) there are typically several options for how to implement it. This is the lowest level of detail and shows how to operatively enact the different choices in terms of API calls or crowd tasks.

The three layers are tightly integrated with each other, yet they provide for the necessary abstractions and flexibility to configure each crowd task according to its very own characteristics and goals. The use of tactics on top of a crowd computer allows us to abstract away from individual platform specifics (today, each platform typically implements one tactic) and instead to focus on what is best for each individual crowd task. Modular crowdsourcing operations enable the flexible configuration of the different tactics and foster reuse.

In the following, we specifically look into the details of these latter two layers, leaving the details of the process/program layer to future work. Specifically, we express the two layers in terms of reusable BPMN patterns (sub-processes), which assist the developer in programming the crowd computer. We choose BPMN as a design notation because of its widespread adoption and rather solid semantics (also considering that our patterns are quite simple and do not make use of the most controversial aspects of the BPMN notation).

5   Crowdsourcing Patterns

We start by explaining the logic of the tactics, focusing on two of the most used approaches, i.e., *marketplace* and *contest*, then we show the operations that are needed to turn the tactics into concrete API calls and crowd tasks.

5.1   Crowdsourcing Tactics

In the general case, a crowd task is not an atomic action that can be executed by one single worker, but rather a combination of steps and multiple workers. The tactic tells which steps to use and which and how many workers to involve. Yet, in current crowdsourcing platforms these tactics are typically applied at the level of the individual task executed by a crowd worker. Therefore, before applying a tactic to a given simple task, we split the complex crowd task into smaller tasks. Only then we apply a tactic to each of the small tasks, and finally merge all results into a final result for the crowd task. This logic is illustrated in Figure 4(a). Different tactics to crowdsourced work exist; for space reasons, we only illustrate the two most common ones, the *market* and the *contest*.

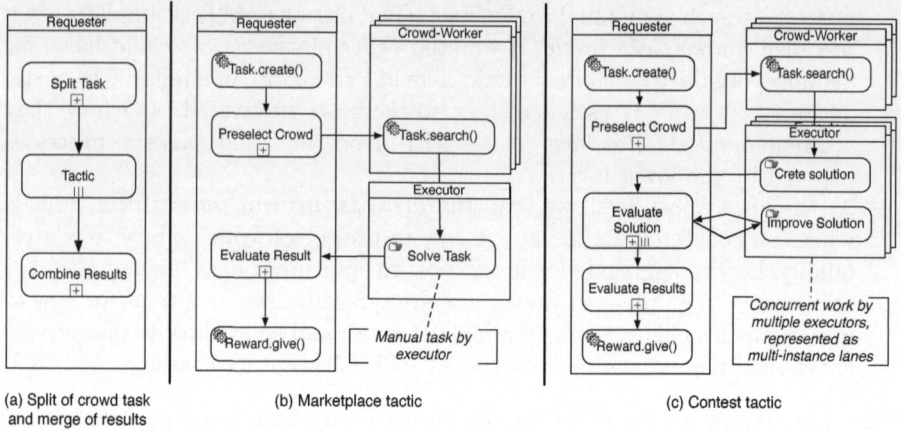

(a) Split of crowd task and merge of results

(b) Marketplace tactic

(c) Contest tactic

Fig. 4. Splitting a crowd task, choosing a tactic, and merging the results

In Figure 4(b) we model the *marketplace* tactic. The marketplace is based on the idea of a shared place where multiple requesters offer work for a given reward, and workers can choose among the offers the one they like most. The crowd worker who executes a task is called executor. Once the task is taken by an executor it is removed from the platform. The executor is paid when he submits his answer and when the answer is accepted by the requester.

Figure 4(c) models the *contest* tactic. The marketplace and the contest share common parts, the beginning, where there is the creation and pre-selection, and the end, where there is the validation and reward. Yet, in the contest, a task is made available for a given amount of time, and many different executors may perform it and submit answers. They are aware that they are in competition with each other and that in the end only one (or some) will get the reward. Executors can improve their solution as long as the task is active by taking into account comments from the requester or by looking at the solutions by others.

Typically, the difference of these two tactics manifests itself also in the reward. In the marketplace, solving a task is generally rewarded only with some cents, and an executor is almost sure to receive this small amount. In the contest, the reward is higher (up to hundreds or thousands of dollars), but only one or few executors receive the reward.

5.2   Crowdsourcing Operations

The tactics described in Figure 4 require the expansion of four sub-processes for the splitting of the crowd task, the pre-selection of crowd workers, quality control, and the final merge of feedbacks. Again, for each of these we may have different typical solutions. We exemplify the most interesting ones here.

Preselection. Worker selection is one of the crucial steps in creating a crowd task. Pre-selecting workers means defining minimum requirements to be eligible

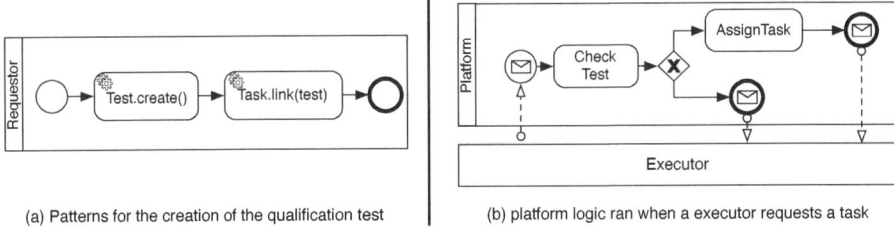

(a) Patterns for the creation of the qualification test   (b) platform logic ran when a executor requests a task

Fig. 5. Qualification test pre-selection pattern with requester and platform concerns

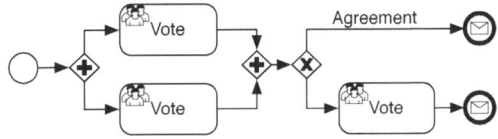

Fig. 6. The agreement operation for quality control

to perform a task. This operation is fundamental, since pre-selecting the right crowd may increase the quality of results. We have different pre-selection options:

- *Implicit by platform choice.* Each crowdsourcing platform available today is different, with different workers, having different skills, expecting different behaviors, etc. Choosing which platform to use implicitly limits the worker basis to the audience of that platform only.
- *User profile and performance data.* We can inspect the workers' profile and pre-select the characteristics of the desired workers by specifying constraints, e.g., on nationality, age, and the like. In addition to user profile data, also the historical performance of workers can be taken into account.
- *Qualification tests.* We can also ask workers to pass a task-specific qualification test before being able to take and solve a task. We depict this pattern in Figure 5, which creates the test and links the test with the corresponding task. Part (b) of the figure shows how the platform internally implements and manages the test: if the worker has passed the test, the system assigns the task, otherwise the worker is notified with a message.

Quality Control. Quality control is the evaluation of the executors' results. It decides about the acceptance or rejection of performed work and about the payment. We again can implement this operation in multiple ways:

- *Requester evaluation.* This is the base case. The requester evaluates by himself the work deciding if it is acceptable or not.
- *Expert evaluation.* Similar to the previous case, only one person evaluates the work, but an expert is selected from the crowd via a suitable pre-selection. The expert evaluation is a crowd-task.

- *Top-k.* This patterns asks a set of executors to vote and rank results, accepting only the best k results. The top-k patterns is a combination of crowd tasks for collecting votes from the crowd.
- *Agreement.* The agreement pattern involves two judges, chosen from the crowd, which evaluate the solution. If the two judges are in an agreement, their answer is taken as the official one. If they disagree, a third judge gets involved. The third judge basically decides. The pattern can be modeled by asking directly to three judges, while the model in Figure 6 is cheaper in case of immediate agreement. The pattern requires three crowd tasks.
- *Automatic.* This practice injects control questions into the response form. Control questions are questions whose answer is known a priori. Based on the quality of the answers to the control questions, the system can automatically assess the quality of the actual work.
- *Average.* Following the idea of *wisdom of the crowd* [4], we can also compute the average of all collected answers (in case of numeric answers), assuming that the average (or any other aggregation) represents the best result.

Sensibly using reusable crowdsourcing operations to instantiate a crowdsourcing tactic means "programming" the crowd in an easy and effective way and allows the developer to leverage on common crowdsourcing practice.

6   Related Work

Complex crowd tasks are generally dealt with by **splitting** them into smaller tasks, combining their solutions, and constructing the integrated solution, as in the MapReduce algorithm know from distributed computing [3]. MapReduce applied to crowdsourcing has been proposed by Kittur et al. [6] and Kulkarni et al. [7]. The authors propose two similar systems, allowing a crowd worker to decide whether to solve a task as is or to split it into smaller chunks for other workers. The worker who splits a task has the duty of recomposing the solutions of the smaller tasks, practically providing an aggregated solution to the task he spitted. Little et al. [9] use iterative and parallel tasks to structure complex crowd tasks, which however does still not provide enough flexibility.

Programming the crowd like a computer is a research trend that is growing fast. A set of purpose-built languages and solutions to program the crowd have been proposed so far. For instance, Turkit [8] is a scripting language that allows one to create applications for solving tasks with the help of the crowd. The approach conciliates human labor of Amazon Mechanical Turk and computations performed by a machine. The language is equipped with an execution engine able to run crowdsourcing applications. In order to achieve a deterministic behavior (like applications on a regular computers), the system provides the possibility to store the results of the executors' works for later reuse. e.g. to restart after a crash.This crash-and-rerun approach can save time and money and guarantees re-produceable results in case of interruptions. Jabberwocky [1] is another interesting approach. In this work, Ahmad et al. introduce a social computing stack that consists of a platform (Dormouse) that interacts with the crowd, a method for splitting and aggregating tasks called ManReduce, inspired by [6], and a scripting language (Dog) to specify the crowdsourcing logic and also the graphical interface of the application. These scripting languages indeed allow one to implement crowdsourcing applications from scratch. However they do not come with reusable patterns and are not suitable for integration with business process management practices, feasible through BPMN instead.

7   Conclusions

We leverage on the intrinsic process nature of crowdsourcing and propose a *process-based programming paradigm* for what we call the *crowd computer*, i.e., an information collection and processing system for crowd computing applications. The core of the proposal is an extensible set of reusable crowdsourcing practices, which we group into *tactics* (telling how to approach the crowd) and *operations* (telling how to manage the crowd). The work is in an early stage, and we still have to formalize a varied set of crowdsourcing patterns and to implement an own crowd computer.

Acknowledgements. This work is partially funded by the BPM4People project (http://www.bpm4people.org) of the EU FP7 SME Capacities program.

References

1. Ahmad, S., Battle, A., Malkani, Z., Kamvar, S.: The jabberwocky programming environment for structured social computing. In: UIST 2011, pp. 53–64 (2011)
2. Bozzon, A., Brambilla, M., Ceri, S.: Answering search queries with crowdsearcher. In: World Wide Web Conference 2012, WWW, Lyon, France, pp. 1009–1018. ACM (2012)
3. Dean, J., Ghemawat, S.: Mapreduce: simplified data processing on large clusters. Commun. ACM 51(1), 107–113 (2008)
4. Galton, F.: Vox populi (the wisdom of crowds). Nature 75 (1907)
5. Howe, J.: The rise of crowdsourcing. 14(14), 1–7 (October 2006)
6. Kittur, A., Smus, B., Khamkar, S., Kraut, R.E.: Crowdforge: crowdsourcing complex work. In: UIST 2011, pp. 43–52 (2011)
7. Kulkarni, A.P., Can, M., Hartmann, B.: Turkomatic: automatic recursive task and workflow design for mechanical turk. In: CHI EA 2011, pp. 2053–2058 (2011)
8. Little, G., Chilton, L.B., Goldman, M., Miller, R.C.: Turkit: tools for iterative tasks on mechanical turk. In: HCOMP 2009, pp. 29–30 (2009)
9. Little, G., Chilton, L.B., Goldman, M., Miller, R.C.: Exploring iterative and parallel human computation processes. In: CHI EA 2010, p. 4309 (2010)
10. Ross, J., Tomlinson, B.: Who are the crowdworkers? shifting demographics in mechanical turk. In: CHI 2010, pp. 2863–2872 (2010)
11. Surowiecki, J.: The Wisdom of Crowds: Why the Many Are Smarter Than the Few and How Collective Wisdom Shapes Business, Economies, Societies and Nations, p. 320. Doubleday (2004), http://www.amazon.ca/gp/product/0385503865
12. Tranquillini, S., Spieß, P., Daniel, F., Karnouskos, S., Casati, F., Oertel, N., Mottola, L., Oppermann, F.J., Picco, G.P., Römer, K., Voigt, T.: Process-Based Design and Integration of Wireless Sensor Network Applications. In: Barros, A., Gal, A., Kindler, E. (eds.) BPM 2012. LNCS, vol. 7481, pp. 134–149. Springer, Heidelberg (2012)

Processbook: Towards Social Network-Based Personal Process Management

Seyed Alireza Hajimirsadeghi, Hye-Young Paik, and John Shepherd

University of New South Wales, Sydney, NSW 2052, Australia
{seyedh,hpaik,jas}@cse.unsw.edu.au

Abstract. In modern society, we are frequently required to perform administrative processes to achieve our personal goals. While the last decade has seen many of these individual processes codified via Web sites, there remain significant problems in discovering and integrating the sets of tasks needed to accomplish these personal goals. This paper introduces *Processbook*, a social-network-based framework for managing personal processes. *Processbook* allows users to extract personal process models from online sources, to customise and maintain these models and to share them with other users. It also supports the execution of personal processes, allowing the underlying process model to be adjusted as circumstances change. The paper discusses the rationale for *Processbook*, describes its overall architecture, and defines the structure of process models.

Keywords: Personal Process Management, Social Networks, Process Modelling Support, Process Model Recommendation.

1 Introduction

In modern society, we are frequently required to perform administrative or business processes in order to achieve our goals. While the last decade has seen many of these individual processes codified via Web sites, there remain significant problems in discovering and integrating the sets of tasks that are typically required in order to achieve many useful outcomes. One important aspect of the problem is that tasks frequently span organisational boundaries and there are few mechanisms to carry information and outcomes from the processes in one organisation to those in the next organisation. Another major factor is that it is sometimes difficult even to identify precisely which organisations and which processes within those organisations are required to accomplish a stated goal.

Discovering which business processes are relevant is frequently achieved either by searching on the Web or by being given information from friends who have previously accomplished these tasks. One aim of social software is for people to share information among their social circle. It seems natural that one could consider the use of social software as a way of sharing information about business processes, but doing this as effectively as possible is a more challenging task.

This paper introduces an approach to using a specialised social software framework named *Processbook* as a basis for managing a repository of business process

M. La Rosa and P. Soffer (Eds.): BPM 2012 Workshops, LNBIP 132, pp. 268–279, 2013.

descriptions, assisting in the discovery of these descriptions, and using these descriptions to assist users in carrying out the corresponding processes. Under this framework, users can construct descriptions of processes that span multiple organisations and which describe processes from a goal-oriented perspective. Since these processes are focussed on the aims of an individual, and since their details are typically discovered by an individual attempting to accomplish some personal goal, we call them *personal processes.*

The specific goals of *Processbook* are:

- to allow users to describe, refine and share personal process models
- to allow users with similar goals to make use of each other's experience
- to allow users to feed back information (e.g. problems, better approaches, etc.)
- to keep users informed of changes in processes which may affect them

The ultimate goal is that *Processbook* users should be able to find processes to achieve their current goals, be assisted in performing the required tasks, and be able to achieve their goals with significantly less effort than is currently required. However this paper mainly discusses the rational for *Processbook* and gives a conceptual overview of the system's architecture without going deep into implementation details.

In section 2, we describe the problem area with examples. Section 3 describes related work in the space of social software and personal processes. Section 4 presents an overview of the system. Sections 5 and 6 explain the personal process model and specifications that underpin *Processbook*. We conclude the paper in section 7 with future work.

2   The Problem

In this section, we elaborate on the problem of carrying out personal processes by considering a not uncommon example of such a process: a student from a non English-speaking country who wishes to study for a PhD in an English-speaking country. This student would typically have two primary goals: find a university that would accept them; maximise the amount of funding to assist their study. These goals could be augmented by additional constraints such as: must be a good University (e.g. ranked in top 100); must be in a country where there is the opportunity to work after graduation, etc. etc.

The above task would generally be accomplished by first identifying potential universities that satisfy the constraints. This would often be done by asking friends or by searching on the Web. Once universities are identified, information about the entry requirements and scholarship availability for each university would be collected and collated. The requirements might identify further subgoals and the process might identify documents that need to be provided, timelines for applications, etc.

In carrying out the above, questions would arise at each stage. For example, the web site at some university might specify that a student needs to provide an undergraduate transcript and English proficiency test results, but might not mention the kind of visa that the student requires or how to obtain such a visa. In the best case, the University web site would link to a government visa web-site, but that leads to a whole new process and potentially a new set of questions.

If we consider the above approach at a more abstract level, we can map many common tasks into this approach, regardless of the specific domain of the goal. Typical questions that might arise during this process are: what step should I take next, what do I do at each step, which organisation should I deal with, etc. Several strategies that are used to deal with such questions and with the encompassing process: ask friends or consultants, visit organisation websites, ask questions in online forums, or search for the answers in online "how-to" lists.

In solving the above, getting advice from someone experienced with the specific process would be extremely useful, but finding such an expert might be difficult. Experts bring domain and process knowledge, but also need to have your personal circumstances communicated to them. A more effective approach might be to have the process information available online, and have a system that understands both the process information and your personal situation (in terms of progress through the process), and can offer sufficient information that you can determine how to proceed.

In practice, a number of difficult issues need to be dealt with before such a system can be realised:

Invalid data. We may be faced with untrusted sources of information, or conflicting items of information, or may be given out-of-date information. For example, a university may change its entry requirements and may require additional information which had not previously been thought necessary.

Incomplete data. Sometimes, we simply do not know certain parts of the process. In other cases, there may be hidden (or ignored) pieces of information. For example, Middle Eastern students may face a wait of up to six months in applying for a US student visa.

Inability to predict task effects. Sometimes it is difficult to know what kind of effect accomplishing a specific task will have on the process as a whole. For example, while either of the IELTS and TOEFL English competency tests are accepted world wide, it is better to have IELTS scores if applying for Australian universities because they are better regarded.

Difficulty in monitoring task flow. Personal processes typically span multiple organisations and need to combine several workflows into a single process. Organisations may impose constraints, change their processes or policies. Keeping track of all of these, and maintaining a useful notion of each user's state within their overall process is challenging.

Difficulty in detecting data flow. Similar to task flow, tracking flows of data across multiple organisations, each with their own internal workflow, is difficult. Additional complications may arise from data dependencies between documents and forms in different organisations.

In section 3 we will examine previous works in the area of social software and business process modelling which may provide input into our design.

3   Related Work

The need to remain competitive in today's fast-changing business environment has made enterprises introduce flexibility into their process models. [1] investigates four distinct approaches to gain flexibility within a Process-Aware Information System (PAIS): flexibility by design, by deviation, by underspecification and by change. All of these approaches trade off user support for flexibility. Moreover PAIS suffers from lacking a systematic approach for reusing and sharing knowledge. [2] also expresses the need of a new management system for personal processes - business processes as experienced and described by a single person.

The most notable defect of classical BPM is the model-reality divide, the distance between abstract process models and the processes executed in practice. [3] even states that agile BPM not only requires changes to the BPM life cycle, but also a paradigmatic change. [4] argues that more realistic models can be designed by applying social software features such as self identification, transparency, signing, logging, discussion and banning to the mechanism of process modelling. [5] contrasts the work management style in social software and business process modelling system(BPMS) and then proposes a set of guidelines suggesting how to use both in organisations. portrays an ideal modelling framework which eliminates the conventional hierarchic views of the world, includes more people in designing models and removes *a priori* decisions on process modelling.

Others attempted to combine social software and process modelling tools. [6] targets the problem of "one person modelling tools" which has brought a general dissatisfaction among business users. As a solution, it proposes a social-based recommendation system for business process modelling tools in which formalisation dialogue of creating process models has been improved. [7] embeds social software features, such as collaboration and wiki-like features, in the modelling and execution tools of business processes with the aim of encouraging people participate in the bottom-up design and execution of business processes. On the other hand [8] concerns of participation of end users in modelling processes, thus presenting an ad-hoc workflow system that focuses on non-intrusive capturing of human interactions.

[9] takes another perspective focusing on the execution of business processes in the context of Web 2.0 and social software in a self-managed and decentralised environment. It examines the use of status feeds for supporting the execution of non-predictable business processes. [10] presents a process design methodology for addressing the extension of business processes with social features. In particular they extend BPMN 2.0 with social roles, present a gallery of design patterns and finally propose WebRatio BPM as a technical framework for generating Social BPM applications from specifications encoded in Social BPMN.

While most of the existing works in the area focus on adding social features to an existing BPM framework, our proposal intends to create a flexible BPM environment within a social network structure. We inspire from how we manage our personal processes, e.g., the way we consult friends, looking for ready-to-use information on the web and sharing information with others. In our proposed system we adjust the typical features of a social network like collaboration, knowledge sharing, item recommendation and notification messages to help individuals manage their personal processes.

4   *Processbook* Overview

Processbook aims to provide a goal-oriented social network whose users actively participate in the managing and sharing of personal processes. More specifically, (i) it supports users to, collaboratively, create and carry out personal processes, (ii) it allows users to utilise various data sources from the web to create *process fragments* as constituents of a personal process, (iii) it encourages users to share the intermediate results with others and receive feedback from them, and (iv) it creates links between people with similar goals so that each other's experiences are shared.

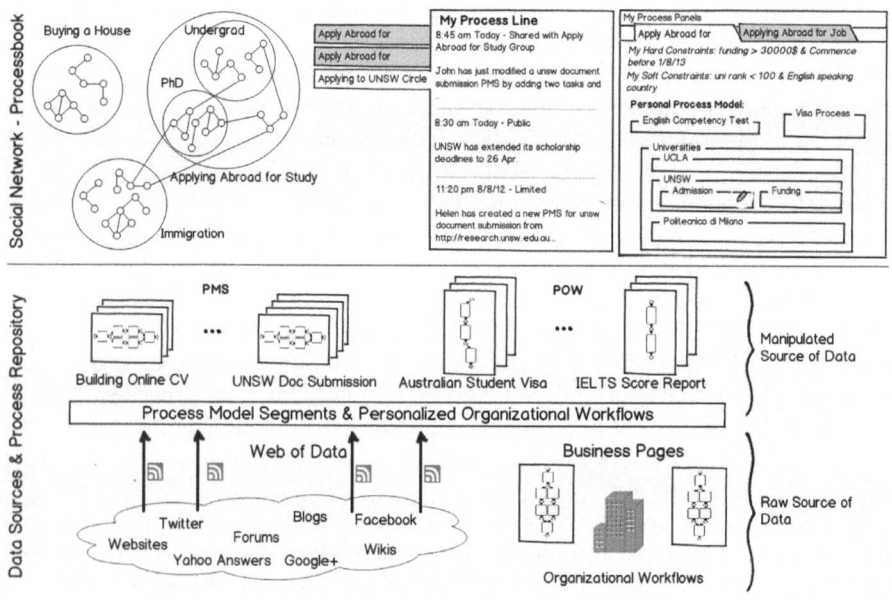

Fig. 1. *Processbook* Conceptual Overview

Figure 1 gives a conceptual overview of the *Processbook* system. It shows the different sections of the system and suggests how the social network module (top left) is integrated with the process modelling and process execution modules. Upon registration in *Processbook*, users will be given a personal workspace called a *process panel* where they have the facilities to create processes and execute them. Once the user defines the goal/purpose of the process she wants to engage in, and any constraints (e.g., "the amount of funding needed to study PhD abroad"), she will be offered the option to join groups of people working on similar goals. She can now "follow" or "be followed by" other people, forming links and groups.

After that, the *Processbook* process modelling task (i.e., defining a personal process) continues with the user receiving a recommendation package consisting of business pages, web feeds and personal processes of her group mates. The recommendations are based on the goal and constraints specified, and the three components in the package are the main data sources from which the user may derive her own *Processbook* process.

The bottom half of Figure 1 shows the data sources. *Processbook* users may use a combination of them to create their own personal process:

- **Business pages**: Organisations, institutions and business owners upload their business process and workflow models in special pages called business pages. These models can be downloaded and brought to the user's process panel to form part of her own personal process.
- **Web feeds**: Data spread over the web in blogs, forums, news pages, web sites provide a useful source of information for the descriptions of personal processes (e.g., a discussion forum on PhD applications, a university's scholarship application page). *Processbook* makes the data accessible for users in the form of *web feeds*. Users can search the feeds, subscribe to them and, importantly, can extract process fragments out of them and share them with others.
- **Other users' processes**: Instead of searching in raw data in feeds and business pages, users can rely on their followers or the groups they belong to, and follow the work of others. If they discover a useful process model developed by another user, they can extract the whole model or some parts of it and customise it to fit their own constraints. They can also integrate process models from two or more users.

Through the process panel (shown top right in Figure 1) a user can search through recommended items to find any process fragments that might be useful to complete her model. She is also able to browse her *process line*[1] to figure out what actions other users have taken to manage their processes. The social network section in the figure illustrates circles of people in *Processbook* grouped based on their goal. Lines between users indicate that they are also following each other's work. By following a user, recommended items from that user will be prioritised and their actions could also be tracked in the process line.

5 Personal Process Model

Now we define the structure of a *personal process model* which underpins *Processbook*. The proposed social network in Section 4 allows users to build personal processes in terms of this structure and then execute *personal process instances*

---

[1] The idea of process line is similar to Facebook Timeline or Google+ Stream.

based on these models. In the remainder of this paper, we generally refer to personal process instances simply as *processes*. Note that the term *process fragment* used in Section 4 refers to process models that have been stored in *Process-book* with the intention of being used to drive process instances and re-used in building larger-scale process models.

A **personal process model** *ppm* is defined as a six-tuple (G, C, D, T, M, A), where:

- G is the goal of the process,
- C is a set of constraints,
- D is a set of inputs and outputs (data),
- T is a set of tasks,
- M is a mapping that describes how tasks are connected,
- A is a set of annotations associated with the tasks.

Each task in T is either a simple activity or is a nested personal process model, thus models may be re-used in the construction of other larger models.

The goal G describes the intended outcome of the process and is used by *Pro-cessbook* to classify models. The goal in the example illustrated in Section 2 is "Going abroad to study for PhD in computer science". The set of constraints C specifies requirements to be satisfied in achieving the goal. C contains two kinds of elements: soft constraints (SC) and hard constraints (HC). Soft constraints are user preferences; satisfying them adds value to the process, but violating them does not prevent the process from reaching the goal. For example, being admitted to a university not far from ones hometown may be defined as a preference, but is not a pre-requisite, Hard constraints, are critical requirements; violating them may lead to the failure of the whole process. In our example, securing at least $30,000 of annual funding may be essential.

Individuals decide whether a constraint is soft or hard in the domain of each process model. The set of constraints may be updated several times during the life of the process. Such updates are inevitable, due to the complexity and longevity of personal processes, which makes it difficult to foresee every aspect. For instance, receiving a low score in a language test may introduce a new hard constraint which limits the user's choices to those universities which accept students with equal or lower scores. Users may also add constraints later to take account of particular conditions which were unknown or not considered when the process commenced. For example, "applying for universities in countries which their student visa allows working beside studying" could become a constraint for users who were not thinking of such a visa condition initially.

The set D describes the inputs and outputs to the process; it identifies what data is required in order to commence the process and what data will be produced when the process completes. Data flow between the tasks in the process model is given by the mapping function M. A is a set of annotations, where each annotation is added to a task to help possible automation of the task (e.g for sending documents by email, adding the email address helps automate this task).

As noted above, tasks in T are of two types: simple activities and nested process models. Simple activities are the basic unit of activity in process models.

Each simple activity has inputs and outputs (the source and destination of these is defined in M). Any process model can be treated as a task and included in some other process model. This allows us, for example, to integrate known organisational processes as a component of our own personal processes.

In practice, tasks are drawn from several different sources in *Processbook*. Based on this, we can partition tasks into three sets: $T = POW \cup PMS \cup GFT$.

POW contains *personalised organisational workflows*. Each task in *POW* is derived from a standard business process model from one organisation in the *Business Pages*. Personal processes may involve multiple workflows from several organisations thus have to be gathered to shape the whole personal process model. As organisations usually include all variations of paths and conditions in their workflows, it is desirable for individuals to have their own personalised views of those workflows e.g. by pruning extra paths and omitting unnecessary tasks. In our example scenario, the "visa application" workflow could be personalised to "postgraduate student visa application subclass 574".

PMS contains *process model segments*. Each task in *PMS* is derived from a source outside any organisational workflow, typically from a description of a process on a web site. Such tasks are typically found by users searching the *Web Feeds*. In our scenario, tasks such as submitting documents to a university scholarship office, or registering for an English language test would typically be process model segments.

GFT, gap-filler tasks, are any other tasks that are necessary to guarantee the completeness of the process model, but are not included in *POW* or *PMS*. Such tasks are generally not present in organisational workflows or model segments for the following reasons:

- The task exists outside any organisation or institution and is also out of the scope of texts discussing related issues.
- The task is assumed too trivial to be modelled in business workflows or be mentioned in texts.
- The task may be handled in so many different ways that it makes the modelling too complicated or the texts too lengthy.

All tasks, no matter how small, should be considered in the final model. Even an apparently trivial task such as *going to the post office to send documents to the destination university* in the "apply abroad for PhD" process consumes time and budget and may even introduce new constraints.

6   *Processbook* Specification

Linking users to the Web Feeds and Business Pages (i.e., organisational workflows) and providing them with a process modelling and execution tool will not guarantee the success of their personal process. The inconsistent and untrusted nature of web-based data, combined with the complexity and dynamism of personal processes pose the kinds of problems discussed previously in Section 2. To overcome these issues, We have customised some of the conventional concepts used in social networking sites and applied them to the process management cycle in *Processbook*. In the following, the four main capabilities of our proposed social network are explained.

6.1 Collaborative Process Modelling

Once a user starts to create a process model, it is associated with their profile and can be shared with others. Sharing is controlled by the user and could be: public, a group they belong to, or friendship circles. Users who have been granted a permission to view other user's process model may:

- `like` the model
- `flag` the model as a faulty or incomplete
- `comment` on the model
- `copy` the model or its components to their process panel
- `modify` the model by adding, deleting, renaming, annotating tasks or changing the task or data flow

Modification of a process model will result in a new version of that model. A set of different versions of process models which describe a single sub-goal are kept in a pool and ranked based on the feedback given from users. Feedback is quantified using the factors such as number of likes and flags a model received, number of times copied, etc. Storing all versions of a model helps new users expedite their modelling process by reusing a model from the pool. Figure 2 illustrates such collaboration between Helen and John in extracting a PMS for "document submission to UNSW for research degree application". It shows the real excerpt from the website on the right and process panels on the left. The order of actions are shown on the figures; the dotted boxes indicates annotations for tasks. John refines an existing annotation, adds a branch to PMS and enriches it by adding more annotations. He then flags Helen's work to inform other possible visitors of her seemingly incorrect PMS.

Once a user is given permission on a model, they can see all of its components, including constraints, tasks and annotations. *Processbook* also provides users with a view on the execution of models belonging to friends and group members, or users they are following, via their *process line*. The process line is a place where users can observe other's activities sorted by time. It serves as an area from which users can obtain ideas on how to manage their own personal processes.

6.2 Knowledge Capturing and Sharing

Processbook aims to enhance the process management life-cycle by improving knowledge and information exchange, which in turns speeds up modelling and execution decisions. The key point in information exchange is to find a method that automatically and non-intrusively captures users' modelling and execution experiences and then shares the captured data appropriately. Since users' actions are all performed in a web based social network framework, a web monitoring component in conjunction with a log analyser could provide users with the

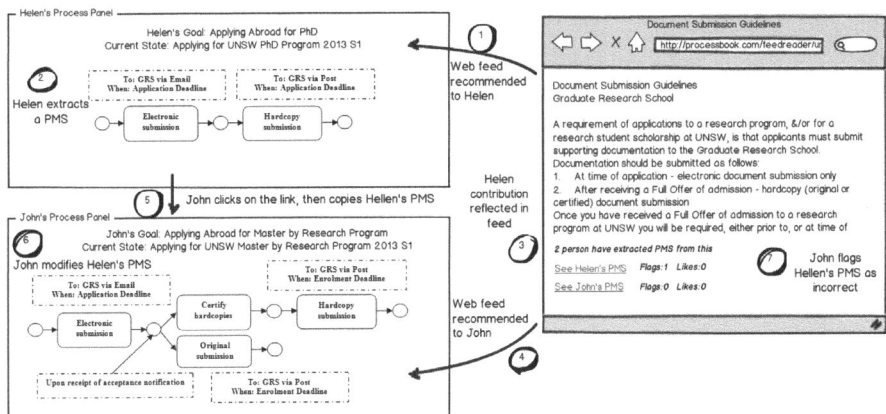

Fig. 2. *PMS* Extraction and Collaborative Process Modelling in *Processbook*

needed information. The extracted information could then be posted by a user and shared according to their preferences. A post consists of following elements:

- topic: the type of action
- timestamp: time of the action
- group_access: the group of people for whom the post is visible
- auto_desc: an automatically generated description of the user's action
- action_param: a set of action parameters
- meta: meta data part containing the user's goal, satisfied and broken constraints, and a progress plan in terms of completed and planned tasks

Table 1 summarizes the most important action types. The parameters of each action type are given in brackets.

Table 1. Action types in *Processbook* posts

Type	Description
Extract a process model segment	I have just extracted a process model out of [web feed W] which I have earlier found by searching [Terms a set of terms T] or which was recommended to me. I created the process model to reach [Sub-goal SG] on the way to accomplishing [Ultimate-goal UG].
Personalise an organisational workflow	I have just personalised [organisational workflow OW] from [business page BP] to reach [Sub-goal g] on the way to accomplishing [Ultimate-goal G].
Modify a process model segment	I have just modified [process model segment PMS] by [set of modelling activities MA]
Create a task	I have just created a gap filler task to integrate [PMS/POW/GFT] with [PMS/POW/GFT] to reach [Sub-goal SG] on the way to accomplishing [Ultimate-goal UG].
Execute a task	I just did [Action A] to reach [Sub-goal g] on the way to accomplishing [Ultimate-goal G]. This action has satisfied [Constraint C_1] while breaking [Constraint C_2].
Undo a task	I just did undo [Action A]. This will also restore my broken [Constraint C].

6.3 Social Network-Based Recommendation

Processbook's built-in recommender system filters the process knowledge repository for each user based on the user's goal, preferences and status. An *intelligent query processor* module will implicitly and non-intrusively build a query from the user's goal, soft and hard constraints, past actions - recorded as described in section 6.2 - and the process execution state of the user's personal process model. When users choose to get *PMS* or *POW* suggestions, a query of their request is built and executed over the process knowledge repository where the users' posts and a link to related *PMS*, *POW*, web feeds, business pages and other action parameters are stored. Users would specify whether to search all the repository or limit the search to items shared by the group they belong to or by their friend circles. In addition to recommending process model elements, the *Processbook* recommender system may also suggest a user to follow other users' process panels or to subscribe to a web feed or a business page.

Here is a sample of an automatically generated query for a user of the "apply abroad for PhD" process, wanting more than $30,000 funding per year. The query states that she has already taken an English competency exam and also prepared her undergrad transcripts, and returns the set of *PMS* and *POW* needed to complete the remaining tasks.

```
SELECT PMS, POW
FROM GROUP ''Apply abroad for PhD''
WHERE CONSTRAINT IN
(country="Australia" & annual-funding >= 30,000 & major="computer science")
HAVING COMPLETED TASKS
{getting transcripts from undergrad universities, taken English test}
ORDER BY POST DATE;
```

6.4 Notification-Based Management of the Dynamic Environment

Processbook makes use of a notification mechanism to reflect both regular changes in user-defined process models and policy changes in business environments. When an institution obsoletes a workflow, changes its policies or adds new criteria to one of its old workflows, *Processbook* will send notification alarms to those who either have created *POW* from that workflow themselves or copied an existing *POW* associated with that workflow. Similarly when a new *PMS* is extracted from a web feed or when an existing *PMS* is flagged as inappropriate, a notification message will be sent to those directly involved in creating that *PMS* and those who copied it to their process panels. Moreover when the top ranked *PMS* in a pool of *PMS*s - depicting the same goal - changes based on the users' feedback, it will be announced to users working on that pool to be aware of the new best practice *PMS*. It is also possible to get notification messages directly from one of the group or circle members stating new updates from her personal model.

7 Conclusion and Future Work

We have presented a conceptual framework for *Processbook*, a specialised social network for managing personal processes. While many focus on adding social features to an existing BPM framework, our proposal intends to create a BPM environment within a social network structure. Ultimately, the system aims to realise an environment where users can find relevant processes, be assisted to perform the required tasks by other users and the system, and to have their experiences recorded and shared. Our immediate future work includes more detailed work on the model and specifications, assisted process model extraction methods, process model/fragment recommendation methods (including an intelligent personal process query language), and approaches to resolving data conflict arising from integrating multiple data sources for a process model.

References

1. Schonenberg, H., Mans, R., Russell, N., Mulyar, N., van der Aalst, W.M.P.: Process Flexibility: A Survey of Contemporary Approaches. In: EOMAS, pp. 16–30 (2008)
2. Weber, I., Paik, H.Y., Benatallah, B., Vorwerk, C., Zheng, L., Kim, S.: Personal Process Management: Design and Execution for End-Users. Technical report, UNSW-CSE-TR-1018 (2010)
3. Bruno, G., Dengler, F., Jennings, B., Khalaf, R., Nurcan, S., Prilla, M., Sarini, M., Schmidt, R., Silva, R.: Key Challenges for Enabling Agile BPM with Social Software. Journal of Software Maintenance 23(4), 297–326 (2011)
4. Erol, S., Granitzer, M., Happ, S., Jantunen, S., Jennings, B., Johannesson, P., Koschmider, A., Nurcan, S., Rossi, D., Schmidt, R.: Combining BPM and Social Software: Contradiction or Chance? Journal of Software Maintenance 22(6-7), 449–476 (2010)
5. Johannesson, P., Andersson, B., Wohed, P.: Business Process Management with Social Software Systems – A New Paradigm for Work Organisation. In: Ardagna, D., Mecella, M., Yang, J. (eds.) BPM 2008 Workshops. LNBIP, vol. 17, pp. 659–665. Springer, Heidelberg (2009)
6. Koschmider, A., Song, M., Reijers, H.A.: Social Software for Modeling Business Processes. In: Ardagna, D., Mecella, M., Yang, J. (eds.) Business 2009 Workshops. LNBIP, vol. 17, pp. 666–677. Springer, Heidelberg (2009)
7. Silva, A.R., Meziani, R., Magalhães, R., Martinho, D., Aguiar, A., Flores, N.: AGILIPO: Embedding Social Software Features into Business Process Tools. In: Rinderle-Ma, S., Sadiq, S., Leymann, F. (eds.) BPM 2009 Workshops. LNBIP, vol. 43, pp. 219–230. Springer, Heidelberg (2010)
8. Martinho, D., Rito Silva, A.: Non-intrusive Capture of Business Processes Using Social Software - Capturing the End Users' Tacit Knowledge. In: Daniel, F., Barkaoui, K., Dustdar, S. (eds.) BPM 2011 Workshops, Part I. LNBIP, vol. 99, pp. 207–218. Springer, Heidelberg (2012)
9. Vogt, S., Fink, A.: Using Status Feeds for Peer Production by Coordinating Non-predictable Business Processes. In: Daniel, F., Barkaoui, K., Dustdar, S. (eds.) BPM Workshops 2011, Part I. LNBIP, vol. 99, pp. 253–265. Springer, Heidelberg (2012)
10. Brambilla, M., Fraternali, P., Vaca, C.: BPMN and Design Patterns for Engineering Social BPM Solutions. In: Daniel, F., Barkaoui, K., Dustdar, S. (eds.) BPM 2011 Workshops, Part I. LNBIP, vol. 99, pp. 219–230. Springer, Heidelberg (2012)

Evaluating Social Tagging for Business Process Models

Ralf Laue[1] and Michael Becker[2]

[1] University of Applied Sciences of Zwickau, Germany
ralf.laue@fh-zwickau.de
[2] Department of Business Information Systems, University of Leipzig, Germany
michael.becker@uni-leipzig.de

Abstract. Finding business process models in a model repository is a challenge that needs to be tackled for efficient business process management. Existing process model similarity measures compare models based on named elements and model structure. Social tagging enriches models with so-called tags – words or short phrases describing the content of the model. The tags given to models offer another possibility to judge about the similarity between models. In this paper we compare both approaches based on a study conducted with students. We discuss first insights and perspectives for tag-based search for process models.

Keywords: New opportunities provided by social software for BPM, process model, similarity, tagging.

1 Introduction

Due to the vast amount of existing process models in organisations, it is necessary to support users in developing, finding, and reusing models [1]. One approach for finding models in a repository is using an existing process model similarity measure. In [2] we presented a selection and comparison of different such measures.

One of the main success factors of social software, the *wisdom of the crowds*, can be seen as an inspiration for an alternative way to judge about the similarity between models. So-called tags – words or short phrases that describe the content of the model – can be assigned to the models in a repository by its users. Models are regarded as similar to each other if similar tags have been assigned to them. Social tagging for the purpose of finding models in a repository has been suggested by various authors such as Nigel et al. [3], Prilla [4] and Vanderhaeghen et al. [5].

Tools such as *Oryx* [6] and process model repositories[1] already offer possibilities for tagging and tag-based searching. However, we are not aware of any study that researches the suitability of social tagging for business process models. With our paper, we want to compare a similarity measure based on social tagging (obtained from an experiment) with eight existing approaches for calculating the

---

[1] see for example www.businessprocessincubator.com

M. La Rosa and P. Soffer (Eds.): BPM 2012 Workshops, LNBIP 132, pp. 280–291, 2013.
© Springer-Verlag Berlin Heidelberg 2013

similarity between business process models. In doing so, a first evaluation of the suitability can be established and used as groundwork for further research.

The remainder of this paper is structured as follows. Sect. 2 presents the experimental setup for assigning tags to models. Following, in Sect. 3 we describe the models used for comparison. Sect. 4 and 5 present the similarity of models based on similarity measures and on tag similarity. In Sect. 6 we compare the two approaches for calculating similarity. Finally, Sect. 7 presents conclusions and further research directions.

2   Experimental Setup

After giving a lecture on BPMN to a group of 23 bachelor students of information science at the University of Applied Sciences of Zwickau, we presented 15 BPMN models on paper to the students. We asked them to add tags describing the models such that those tags can be used by someone who searches for a model in a repository. Deliberately, the students did not get training in selecting "good" tags. The tasks had to be carried out as a pen-and-paper exercise, and no time limit was given. The labels were in German language which was the native language of all participating students.

Two of the students clearly misunderstood the nature of the tagging exercise and described the model in whole sentences. Their answers had to be disregarded, i.e. we collected the tags given by 21 students.

When compiling the machine-readable tag lists from the filled papers, we applied some simple sanity checks. For example, we corrected some spelling errors and used the same form for tags that appeared in different versions (for example both "check in" and "checkin" were transformed to "check-in"). All those sanity checks could easily be made by a computer system.

3   Models

To compare the different approaches for calculating similarity between process models, we selected 15 BPMN models. As booking of a flight or travel is a frequently used example in the BPMN literature, we selected several such models from different sources. This way, we tried to emulate a situation typically occurring in an organisation: Different modellers create models for the same kind of process with different granularity, different vocabulary and emphasis on different aspects.

For the purpose of this paper we named the models such that the model name clearly shows which activity is described by the model. The suffix ONLINE shows that the modelled process is performed using a web portal. Due to space limitations we only give a brief overview about the models. However, the entire collection of models is publicly available[2].

---

[2] http://bis.informatik.uni-leipzig.de/MichaelBecker/files?get=bpms2.zip

Table 1 shows the models we use in this paper. For every model, a unique name and a short description of the model is shown as well as the source. Many models marked as "created for the purpose of this paper" are adapted examples taken from [7]. For each model, we provide the number of nodes (activities and gateways) and edges.

4   Calculating Model Similarity

Several approaches for calculating similarity between process models have been introduced in the academic literature. In [2] we analysed a variety of these approaches and compared them according to several properties. We have identified three distinct types of measures: The first group (group A) contains measures based on activity labels only, not taking into account the control flow in a process model. The second group (group B) contains measures based on graph edit distance, i.e. the amount of steps necessary to transform one process model represented as a direct graph into another one. The third group (group C) considers causal dependencies between activities. These similarity measures analyse predecessor and successor relations between activities or compare sets of execution logs with each other.

To automate similarity calculation we have developed a plug-in for the process mining framework *ProM* [12]. This plug-in is publicly available as open source[3] and can be used as a standalone application, too. We used the *ProM* plug-in and an adaption of the measures as described in [2] for calculating several similarity measures for the models described in Sect. 3. Using the tool *Gephi* [13], the results of the calculations have been visualised as graphs in Fig. 1. The models are depicted as nodes. Similarity between nodes that exceeds a certain limit is depicted as an edge. The thickness of the vertices corresponds to the calculated similarity, i.e. the nodes depicting models that have been ranked as very similar to each other are connected by a thick edge. In addition, the Force Atlas algorithm built in in *Gephi* was used to visualise the similarity between models by the position of their corresponding nodes in the graph. It uses the principle of force-based graph layout algorithms [14]: similar nodes attract each other while non-similar ones are pushed apart.

The following measures were used to calculate similarity between process models:

(A1) *Similarity score based on common activity names*: Akkiraju and Ivan [15] propose a similarity measure based on the number of identically labelled activities. In order to calculate similarity, they use Dice's coefficient [16] for activity names.

(A2) *Label matching similarity*: The approach proposed by Dijkman et al. [1] is similar to measure A1 described above. However, Dijkman et al. introduce a threshold, i.e. the similarity of two activities is set to 0 if it is below a specific threshold.

---

[3] https://sourceforge.net/projects/prom-similarity

Table 1. Models for similarity calculation

BOOKING-FLIGHT1 (7 activities, 4 gateways, 12 edges, source: [8])
Passengers check and reserve seats and book flights. If booking takes too long, there is a timeout.

BOOKING-FLIGHT2 (4 activities, 8 gateways, 15 edges, source: [9])
Passengers catch information on flight plans and delays, choose on-board catering, and process travel card.

BOOKING-FLIGHT3 (3 activities, 4 gateways, 8 edges, source: [9])
Passengers catch information on flight plans and delays and book a flight.

BOOKING-TRAVEL1 (source: [10])
This model of a travel booking process involves more than one swimlane and messages between actors. See Sect. 6 for details.

BOOKING-FLIGHT-ONLINE1 (12 activities, 4 gateways, 19 edges, created for the purpose of this paper)
Passengers log in to a website and book a flight.

BOOKING-TRAVEL-ONLINE (16 activities, 7 gateways, 27 edges, created for the purpose of this paper)
Passengers log in to a website and book a flight. Furthermore, they can book a hotel, reserve a rental car, and buy travel cancellation insurance.

BOOKING-TRAVEL2 (8 activities, 6 gateways, 17 edges, source: [11])
Passengers book a flight at a travel agency including hotel and rental car reservation.

BOARDING1 (4 activities, 2 gateways, created for the purpose of this paper)
The boarding pass of travelers is checked during boarding.

BOARDING2 (4 activities, 2 gateways, 6 edges, created for the purpose of this paper)
Essentially the same model as BOARDING1 with renamed activities.

MILES-ONLINE (7 activities, 4 gateways, 12 edges, created for the purpose of this paper)
Passengers log in to a website and can spend their frequent flyer miles by ordering products.

UPGRADE-ONLINE (10 activities, 8 gateways, 21 edges, created for the purpose of this paper)
Passengers log in to a website and select an upgrade for their flight.

CANCEL-ONLINE (6 activities, 2 gateways, 9 edges, source: created for the purpose of this paper)
Passengers log in to a website and cancel their booking by entering a booking code.

BAGGAGE (7 activities, 4 gateways, 12 edges, source: created for the purpose of this paper)
Luggage is weighted. If it is too heavy or too big, the passengers have to pay fees for excess luggage. Luggage is registered and a luggage security control is conducted.

CHECK-IN (7 activities, 4 gateways, 13 edges, source: created for the purpose of this paper)
Passengers need to proof their identity using a pass, a frequent flyer card, or an ID card. Following, their ticket is scanned, a seat is selected, and the boarding pass is printed.

SHOP-ONLINE (10 activities, 8 gateways, 22 edges, source: created for the purpose of this paper)
Process for an online bookshop: Customers log in or register, browse book offers, and order books. Payment can be done using a credit card, direct debit, or a by using their frequent flyer card.

(A3) *Feature-based similarity estimation*: Yan et al. [17] compare models by taking into account the similarity of activity names in conjunction with similarity based of the amount of incoming and outgoing edges of an activity node.

(A4) *Percentage of common nodes and edges in the graph*: Minor et al. [18] transform process models into their graph representation and calculate similarity according to the amount of identically labelled activity nodes and coinciding edges between these nodes.

(A5) *Node- and link-based similarity*: In [19] Huang et al. present a similarity measure that works on common nodes and edges, too. However, they weight edges according to their relevance in the process model, e.g. outgoing edges of an XOR-split with n exits get a weight of $\frac{1}{n}$.

(B1) *Graph edit distance similarity*: Dijkman et al. [1] use a graph edit distance consisting of the amount of necessary elementary operations to transform one process model graph into another one. Examples for such elementary operations are adding and deleting nodes and edges.

(C1) *Dependency graph comparison by hierarchical clustering*: Jung et al. [20] analyse similarity based on dependencies between activities introduced due to control flow connections. Furthermore, they assign so-called execution probabilities to activities. The execution probability is governed by preceding control flow splits, e.g. exclusive choices or parallelisation. Similarity is then calculated by comparing dependencies and execution probabilities of two process models.

(C2) *TAR-similarity*: Similar to the dependency graph established by Jung et al., Zha et al. [21] introduce a TAR set containing activities that are in direct predecessor-successor-relation. The similarity of two process models is established by comparing their TAR sets with each other.

Before it is possible to calculate similarity between process models, a mapping between elements of these models is necessary. This means that for each node (in particular for each activity node) in a model it has to be analysed whether there is a node in the other model that corresponds to this node. Approaches for finding such a mapping are discussed in [1,22]. For the purpose of our paper, we established a mapping manually (which is most likely superior to computer-based algorithms). Due to the nature of the models every node in one model corresponds to exactly one node in the model to compare with. This is especially worth mentioning when a similarity measure takes the edges of a graph into account - which is done by most similarity measures used in this paper, with A1 and A2 being the only exceptions.

5   Calculating Tag Similarity

In our experiment, a total of 1637 tags were given to the models, detailed statistics are shown in Tab. 2.

We regarded the tags given to a model M as the elements of a multiset T (where an element can be contained more than once). For calculating the

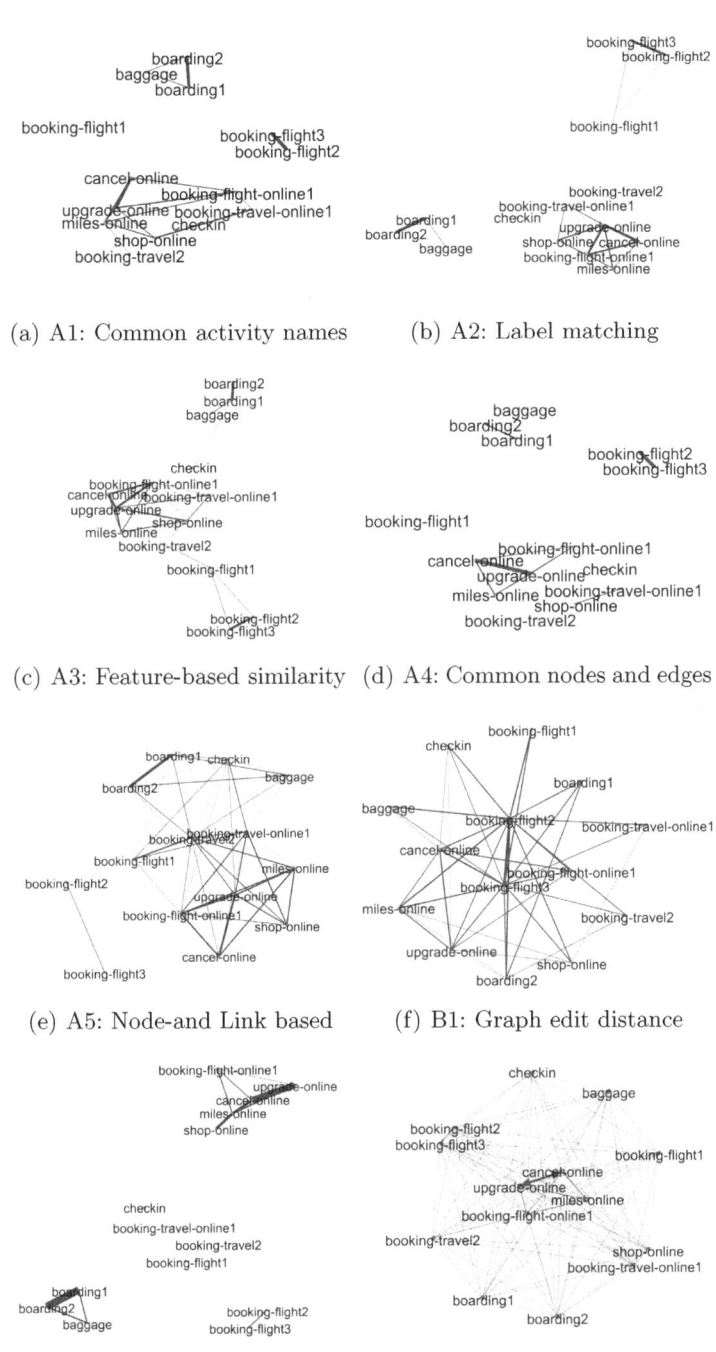

(a) A1: Common activity names   (b) A2: Label matching

(c) A3: Feature-based similarity   (d) A4: Common nodes and edges

(e) A5: Node-and Link based   (f) B1: Graph edit distance

(g) C1: Dependency graph   (h) C2: TAR sets

Fig. 1. Visualisation of the similarity, calculated by different measures

Table 2. Number of tags collected from the 21 participants

Model	Tags	Different tags	Tags given by at least 2 persons
BAGGAGE	117	60	22
BOARDING1	82	45	17
BOARDING2	78	39	17
BOOKING-FLIGHT-ONLINE1	153	66	32
BOOKING-FLIGHT1	92	35	14
BOOKING-FLIGHT2	81	37	10
BOOKING-FLIGHT3	68	30	10
BOOKING-TRAVEL-ONLINE1	184	88	38
BOOKING-TRAVEL1	145	60	21
BOOKING-TRAVEL2	92	38	14
CANCEL-ONLINE	94	41	17
CHECK-IN	96	44	17
MILES-ONLINE	94	50	14
SHOP-ONLINE	156	68	27
UPGRADE-ONLINE	105	50	20

similarity between a model M_1 with the multiset of tags T_1 and a model M_2 with the multiset of tags T_2, we used Dice's coefficient [16], which is defined as $similarity(M_1, M_2) = \frac{2|T_1 \cap T_2|}{|T_1| + |T_2|}$, where $|T_i|$ denotes the number of elements in the tag list T_i (if the multiset contains an element more than once, each occurrence is counted.) This resulted in the similarity measures given in Table 3.

Fig. 2. Visualisation of Tag-based similarity

6   Comparing Similarity Based on Tags to Other Approaches

The similarity measure calculated from the tag lists turned out to have some desirable properties: The largest similarity value (0.52) has been given to the

Table 3. Tag similarity (percentage of tags occurring in both models)

Model	BAGGAGE	BOARDING1	BOARDING2	BOOKING-FLIGHT-ONLINE1	BOOKING-FLIGHT1	BOOKING-FLIGHT2	BOOKING-FLIGHT3	BOOKING-TRAVEL-ONLINE-1	BOOKING-TRAVEL1	BOOKING-TRAVEL2	CANCEL-ONLINE	CHECK-IN	MILES-ONLINE	SHOP-ONLINE	UPGRADE-ONLINE
BAGGAGE	100	17	10	7	2	3	3	5	3	1	3	11	2	4	3
BOARDING1	17	100	30	5	10	4	5	3	4	5	3	21	6	1	3
BOARDING2	10	30	100	3	3	2	2	2	2	3	2	11	2	2	2
BOOKING-FLIGHT-ONLINE1	5	5	3	100	15	2	16	33	15	8	36	6	29	27	43
BOOKING-FLIGHT1	2	10	3	15	100	5	21	10	21	16	21	12	9	1	9
BOOKING-FLIGHT2	3	4	2	2	5	100	52	3	4	1	3	5	4	0	3
BOOKING-FLIGHT3	3	5	2	16	21	52	100	10	18	3	11	6	6	0	12
BOOKING-TRAVEL-ONLINE1	5	3	2	33	10	3	10	100	17	18	16	3	11	25	26
BOOKING-TRAVEL1	3	4	2	15	21	4	18	17	100	15	10	4	15	11	16
BOOKING-TRAVEL2	1	5	3	8	16	1	3	18	15	100	2	2	3	12	11
CANCEL-ONLINE	3	3	2	36	21	3	11	16	10	2	100	4	27	14	42
CHECK-IN	11	21	11	6	12	5	6	3	4	2	4	100	5	2	4
MILES-ONLINE	2	6	2	29	9	4	6	11	15	3	27	5	100	29	33
SHOP-ONLINE	4	1	2	27	1	0	0	25	11	12	14	2	29	100	29
UPGRADE-ONLINE	3	3	2	43	9	3	12	26	16	11	42	4	33	29	100

two models BOOKING-FLIGHT2 and BOOKING-FLIGHT3, the models that have been published as examples for variants of the same base model in [9]. The second largest similarity value (0.43) has been calculated between UPGRADE-ONLINE and BOOKING-FLIGHT-ONLINE which also seems to be quite reasonable.

The models BOARDING1 and BOARDING2 (in fact identical models, due to activity renaming) have 30% of the tags in common. On the other hand, the model SHOP-ONLINE (for which the only link to the airline domain is that it is possible to pay using frequent flyer miles) received the lowest similarity scores when being compared with non-online processes. The most similar model to SHOP-ONLINE is MILES-ONLINE - in fact both represent a possibility to spend frequent flyer miles using a web site.

If we compare Fig. 2 with the graphs in Fig. 1, we can see that the tag-based similarity measure has some commonalities with the results obtained by measures A1, A2, and A3. Measures that calculate similarity based on direct predecessor-successor-relations like B1 and C2 cannot find similarities between models that do not share edges. For example, models BOOKING-FLIGHT-ONLINE1 and BOOKING-TRAVEL-ONLINE1 share several activities that occur in a sequence. However, due to different ordering of sequences, measure B1 results in a large number of edit operations necessary to modify the edges. Measure C2 on the other hand does not find common sequences of activities. Both facts result in a rather low similarity score in comparison to tag similarity for these two models. Therefore, we conclude that similarity search based social tagging is at least a useful alternative to the established algorithms for detecting similar models.

An interesting observation was that some tags were given not based on the information directly available in the model but based on the domain knowledge of the users. Examples for such tags were "terminal" (where baggage check and check-in take place) and "complete vacation package" (for booking hotel, flight and rental car together). Finding such connections is really hard to achieve by computer-based similarity detection - even by using ontology-based approaches. This is the major difference between a tag-based similarity measure and measures that compare activity names only (such as measure A1 and A2). However, as Koschmider et al. [23] pointed out, it is reasonable to combine both approaches by using activity names as candidates for tags.

Two other advantages of tag-based search are worth mentioning as well. First, all currently known algorithms for calculating model similarity (see [2]) only consider the most basic notational elements of a modelling language such as BPMN. None of these algorithms take model elements like data-flow, swimlanes, exceptions, etc. into account. This is the reason why the model BOOKING-TRAVEL1 which makes use of swimlanes and data-flow arcs could not be compared to the other models using the traditional algorithms. Second, tag-based search can be used in a more flexible way than similarity-based search. While the latter requires constructing a model before searching for similar ones, it would be sufficient to type in a few tags in order to make use of tag-based search in a model repository.

Besides differences in the results, there are also some technical differences between tag similarity and existing similarity measures. A great advantage of tag based similarity is that it is not necessary to establish a mapping between elements of the process models. Furthermore, the similarity between tags can be calculated relatively efficiently. Both facts reduce the complexity and increase the efficiency of calculating tag similarity in comparison to the other approaches. However, it is necessary to note that tag bases similarity cannot take the structure of models into account, i.e. structural differences between models are not identified if the models are tagged with similar words. Homonyms (words which have more than one meaning) add to the relevance of this problem.

7   Conclusion

In this paper we presented two different approaches for calculating similarity between process models. First, similarity can be calculated using an established measure from literature based on process models as direct input. Second, we presented a measure calculating the similarity between tags that have been manually assigned to the models. We compared the results of these measures and pointed out some observations worth mentioning.

For comparing tags we used a rather simple similarity measure based on Dice's coefficient. In real-world applications, better results can be expected when this measure is tuned for dealing with flawed tags and imprecise use of language. For example, using synonyms and preprocessing homonyms as shown in [24] is a reasonable approach to increase the precision of tag similarity. Furthermore, users of tagging systems might be supported by spell checkers and corporate taxonomies.

The study described in this paper was accomplished using tags given by bachelor students. The students are process model novices and we did not restrict their creativity during tagging. This might seem as a limitation of the experiment. Anyway, we think that we were able to obtain promising results (based on the comparison to model similarity) in this experimental setting. These findings should encourage future research to repeat the experiment with both students trained in process modelling as well as practitioners having better domain knowledge.

The results of this paper can be seen as a first evaluation of searching process models based on tag similarity. Using this evaluation as a basis, it was possible to identify advantages and disadvantages of this approach. However, due to our experimental setup, we cannot state whether the results of a tag-based search for similar models meet the expectations of users. In future research, it is necessary to empirically evaluate the results. This can be achieved by comparing the tag similarity with a manually established ranking of models similar to the evaluation in [1].

Acknowledgement. The German Federal Ministry of Education and Research (Bundesministerium für Bildung und Forschung, BMBF) partially supported this work in the context of the DLR project "Concept and Implementation of an Information Production System (IPS) for Precision Farming" ("Konzept und Implementierung eines Informations-Produktionssystems (IPS) im Precision Farming", support code 01IS12013B). Additional information on this project can be found online at http://ips.uni-leipzig.de.

References

1. Dijkman, R., Dumas, M., van Dongen, B., Kaarik, R., Mendling, J.: Similarity of business process models: Metrics and evaluation. Information Systems 36(2), 498–516 (2011)
2. Becker, M., Laue, R.: A comparative survey of business process similarity measures. Computers in Industry 63(2), 148–167 (2012)
3. Fengel, J., Rebstock, M., Nüttgens, M.: Modell-Tagging zur semantischen Verlinkung heterogener Modelle. In: EMISA 2008, Sankt Augustin, Germany, Gesellschaft für Informatik, pp. 53–69 (September 2008)

4. Prilla, M.: Models, Social Tagging and Knowledge Management – A fruitful Combination for Process Improvement. In: Rinderle-Ma, S., Sadiq, S., Leymann, F. (eds.) BPM 2009 Workshops. LNBIP, vol. 43, pp. 266–277. Springer, Heidelberg (2010)

5. Vanderhaeghen, D., Fettke, P., Loos, P.: Organizational and technological options for business process management from the perspective of web 2.0. Business & Information Systems Engineering 2(1), 15–28 (2010)

6. Decker, G., Overdick, H., Weske, M.: Oryx – An Open Modeling Platform for the BPM Community. In: Dumas, M., Reichert, M., Shan, M.-C. (eds.) BPM 2008. LNCS, vol. 5240, pp. 382–385. Springer, Heidelberg (2008)

7. Störrle, H.: UML 2 erfolgreich einsetzen. Addison-Wesley, Munich (2005)

8. Wong, P.Y.H., Gibbons, J.: A Process Semantics for BPMN. In: Liu, S., Araki, K. (eds.) ICFEM 2008. LNCS, vol. 5256, pp. 355–374. Springer, Heidelberg (2008)

9. Montero, I., Na, J.P., Ruiz-Cortés, A.: ATL transformation: Feature models for representing runtime variability in BIS to business process model notation (2008), http://www.isa.us.es/uploads/tools/fm2bpmn/doc/draft.pdf

10. Gravesande, K., Kim, S., Mowla, R., Resptrepo, A., Thomas, C., Weaver, S.: The essentials of BPEL (2008), http://csis.pace.edu/~ctappert/dps/d861-08/team1.pdf

11. White, S.A.: Using BPMN to model a BPEL process. BP Trends (March 2005)

12. van Dongen, B.F., de Medeiros, A.K.A., Verbeek, H.M.W., Weijters, A.J.M.M., van der Aalst, W.M.P.: The ProM Framework: A New Era in Process Mining Tool Support. In: Ciardo, G., Darondeau, P. (eds.) ICATPN 2005. LNCS, vol. 3536, pp. 444–454. Springer, Heidelberg (2005)

13. Bastian, M., Heymann, S., Jacomy, M.: Gephi: An open source software for exploring and manipulating networks. In: Adar, E., Hurst, M., Finin, T., Glance, N.S., Nicolov, N., Tseng, B.L. (eds.) ICWSM. The AAAI Press (2009)

14. Fruchterman, T.M.J., Reingold, E.M.: Graph drawing by force-directed placement. Software: Practice and Experience 21(11), 1129–1164 (1991)

15. Akkiraju, R., Ivan, A.: Discovering Business Process Similarities: An Empirical Study with SAP Best Practice Business Processes. In: Maglio, P.P., Weske, M., Yang, J., Fantinato, M. (eds.) ICSOC 2010. LNCS, vol. 6470, pp. 515–526. Springer, Heidelberg (2010)

16. Dice, L.R.: Measures of the amount of ecologic association between species. Ecology 26(3), 297–302 (1945)

17. Yan, Z., Dijkman, R., Grefen, P.: Fast Business Process Similarity Search with Feature-Based Similarity Estimation. In: Meersman, R., Dillon, T.S., Herrero, P. (eds.) OTM 2010. LNCS, vol. 6426, pp. 60–77. Springer, Heidelberg (2010)

18. Minor, M., Tartakovski, A., Bergmann, R.: Representation and Structure-Based Similarity Assessment for Agile Workflows. In: Weber, R.O., Richter, M.M. (eds.) ICCBR 2007. LNCS (LNAI), vol. 4626, pp. 224–238. Springer, Heidelberg (2007)

19. Huang, K., Zhou, Z., Han, Y., Li, G., Wang, J.: An Algorithm for Calculating Process Similarity to Cluster Open-Source Process Designs. In: Jin, H., Pan, Y., Xiao, N., Sun, J. (eds.) GCC 2004 Workshops. LNCS, vol. 3252, pp. 107–114. Springer, Heidelberg (2004)

20. Jung, J.Y., Bae, J., Liu, L.: Hierarchical clustering of business process models. International Journal of Innovative Computing, Information and Control 5(12), 1349–4198 (2009)

21. Zha, H., Wang, J., Wen, L., Wang, C., Sun, J.: A workflow net similarity measure based on transition adjacency relations. Computers in Industry 61(5), 463–471 (2010)
22. Weidlich, M., Dijkman, R., Mendling, J.: The ICoP Framework: Identification of Correspondences between Process Models. In: Pernici, B. (ed.) CAiSE 2010. LNCS, vol. 6051, pp. 483–498. Springer, Heidelberg (2010)
23. Koschmider, A., Hornung, T., Oberweis, A.: Recommendation-based editor for business process modeling. Data & Knowledge Engineering 70(6), 483–503 (2011)
24. Ehrig, M., Koschmider, A., Oberweis, A.: Measuring similarity between semantic business process models. In: APCCM 2007: Proceedings of the Fourth Asia-Pacific Conference on Comceptual Modelling, pp. 71–80. Australian Computer Society, Inc., Darlinghurst (2007)

Artifact-Centric Business Process Models in UML

Montserrat Estañol[1], Anna Queralt[2],
Maria Ribera Sancho[1], and Ernest Teniente[1]

[1] Universitat Politècnica de Catalunya
Departament d'Enginyeria de Serveis i Sistemes d'Informació
Jordi Girona 1-3, 08034 Barcelona
{estanyol,ribera,teniente}@essi.upc.edu
[2] Barcelona Supercomputing Center
Jordi Girona 31, 08034 Barcelona
anna.queralt@bsc.es

Abstract. Business process modeling using an artifact-centric approach has raised a significant interest over the last few years. This approach is usually stated in terms of the BALSA framework which defines the four "dimensions" of an artifact-centric business process model: Business Artifacts, Lifecycles, Services and Associations. One of the research challenges in this area is looking for different diagrams to represent these dimensions. Bearing this in mind, the present paper shows how all the elements in BALSA can be represented by using the UML language. The advantages of using UML are many. First of all, it is a formal language with a precise semantics. Secondly, it is widely used and understandable by both business people and software developers. And, last but not least, UML allows us to provide an artifact-centric specification for BALSA which incorporates also some aspects of process-awareness.

Keywords: business artifacts, BALSA framework, business process modeling, UML.

1 Introduction

Business process design is one of the most critical tasks in current organizations since they rely on the services they offer, i.e. on the business they perform. Business process models have been traditionally based on an activity-centric perspective and thus specified by means of diagrams which define how a business process or workflow is supposed to operate, but giving little importance (or none at all) to the information produced as a consequence of the process execution. Therefore, this approach under-specifies the data underlying the service and the way it is manipulated by the process tasks [1].

Nearly a decade ago, a new information-centric approach to business process modeling emerged [2] and it is still used today. It relies on the assumption that any business needs to record details of what it produces in terms of concrete

M. La Rosa and P. Soffer (Eds.): BPM 2012 Workshops, LNBIP 132, pp. 292–303, 2013.

information. Business artifacts, or simply artifacts, are proposed as a means to record this information. They model key business-relevant entities which are updated by a set of services (specified by pre and postconditions) that implement business process tasks. This approach has been successfully applied in practice [3] and it provides a simple and robust structure for workflow modeling.

The artifact-centric approach to business process specification has been shown to have a great intuitive appeal to business managers. However, further research is needed with regards to the "best" artifact-centric model since none of the existing models can adequately handle the broad requirements of business process modeling [4]. The chosen formalization should be based on a formal structure suitable for use in rigorous development and design analysis [2]. Moreover, it should support flexibility both at the level of the individual enactment of the workflow and by enabling rich evolution of the workflow schema.

Our work in this paper represents a step forward in this direction since we propose to specify artifact-centric business process models by means of well-known UML diagrams, from a high-level, technology-independent, perspective. The advantages of using UML are many. First of all, it is an OMG and ISO/IEC standard [5]. Secondly, it is used to represent both the static structure and the dynamic behavior of the elements that are part of a system using a graphical notation; thus it is possible to use diagrams to represent most of BALSA's components. In addition, these diagrams are understandable by people involved in the business process, both from the business and from the system development perspectives. Finally, UML provides extensibility mechanisms that permit more flexibility in its use without losing its formality.

The diagrams we have chosen to use for business process specification allow recording what information is produced by the business and how it is produced, thus achieving the advantages of artifact-centric modeling. Moreover, these diagrams and the way we specify them make our proposal artifact-centric but incorporating also some notions of process-awareness. In this way, we may also explicitly capture the control flow of the business process, aspect which is usually lacking in previous artifact-centric proposals.

The rest of the paper is structured in the following way. Section 2 provides the details of our proposal for artifact-centric business process models in UML and shows its application to an example. Section 3 compares our proposal with related work. Finally, section 4 summarizes our conclusions and points out further work.

2   Artifact-Centric Business Process Models in UML

Traditional process-centric business process models are essentially uni-dimensional in the sense that they focus almost entirely on the process model, its constructs and its patterns, and provide little or no support for understanding the structure or the lifecycle of the data that underlies and tracks the history of most workflows [4].

In contrast, the artifact-centric approach provides four explicit, inter-related but "separable" dimensions in the specification of the business process [4,6].

This four-dimensional framework is referred to as "BALSA" - Business Artifacts, Lifecycles, Services and Associations. By varying the model and constructs used in each of the four dimensions one can obtain different artifact-centric business process models with different characteristics [4]. By showing the UML diagram which is more appropriate to define each one of these four dimensions we will be able to construct our proposal for the specification of artifact-centric business process models in this language.

Usually, UML diagrams make use of some textual notation to precisely specify those aspects that cannot be graphically represented. Currently, OCL (Object Constraint Language) [7] is probably the most popular of these notations and an ISO/IEC standard. OCL supplements UML by providing expressions that have neither the ambiguities of natural language nor the inherent difficulty of using complex mathematics. It was initially developed by IBM and now it is part of the UML standard. Therefore, we will also use it in our proposal.

In the following subsections, we give a brief explanation of the four BALSA dimensions and we detail how we propose to specify them in UML. We also illustrate our proposal by showing some examples drawn from its application to a well-known and widely used case study: EU-Rent, which summarizes a generic process for renting a car within a car rental company. The whole specification of EU-Rent as an artifact-centric business process model in UML can be found in [8].

2.1   Business Artifacts as a Class Diagram

The conceptual schema of business artifacts is intended to hold all of the information needed to complete business process execution. A business artifact has an *identity*, which makes it distinguishable from any other artifact, and can be tracked as it progresses through the workflow of the business process execution. It will usually also have a set of *attributes* to store the data needed for the workflow execution. The relationship of a business artifact with other artifacts must also be shown when this information is relevant for the business being defined. In business terms, an artifact represents the explicit knowledge concerning progress toward a business operational goal at any instant. Therefore, at any time of the execution, the information contained in the set of artifacts records all the information about the business operation.

There is a strong parallelism between the notion of business artifact and that of "domain concept" in conceptual modeling [9]. Domain concepts are represented in UML by means of class diagrams. A UML class diagram shows the business entities and how they are related to each other, represented as classes and associations respectively. Each class (or business artifact) may have a series of attributes that represent relevant information for the business. Moreover, they can be externally identified by specific attributes or by the relationships they take part in. A class diagram may also require a list of integrity constraints that, as their name implies, establish a series of restrictions over the class diagram. Constraints can be specified either graphically in the UML class diagram or textually by means of the OCL language.

Furthermore, UML allows representing class hierarchies graphically. We will benefit from this by representing the different states in an artifact's lifecycle as subclasses of a superclass, as long as these subclasses hold relevant information or are in relevant relationships. The advantage of having different subclasses for a particular artifact is that it allows having exactly those attributes and relationships that are needed according to its state, preserving at the same time the artifact's original ID and the characteristics that are independent of the artifact's state which are represented in the superclass.

In our example, the diagram in Figure 1 shows the relevant EU-Rent business artifacts and how they relate to each other. Integrity constraints are defined in natural language instead of OCL for the sake of readability.

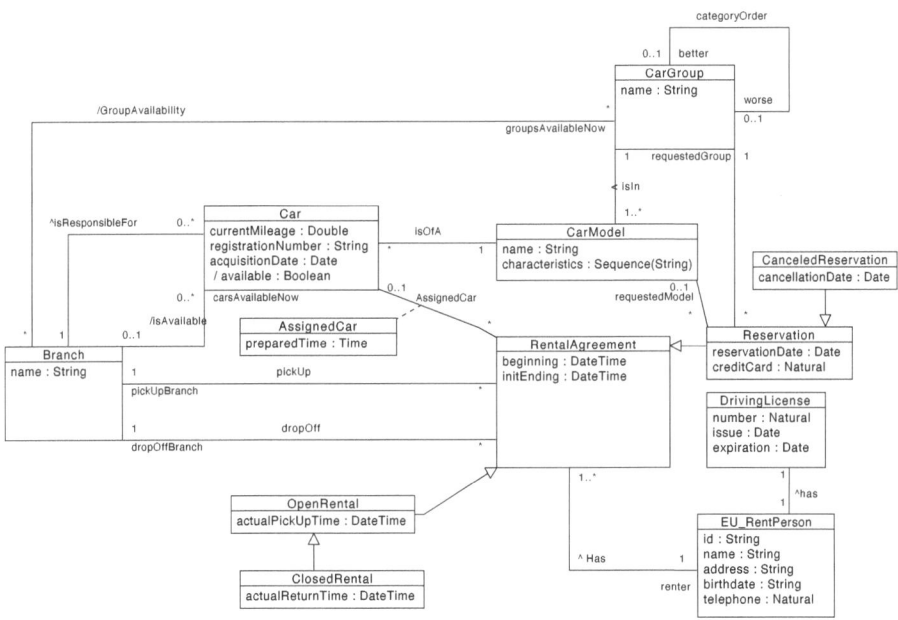

Fig. 1. Class diagram showing the business artifacts as classes

The integrity constraints for Figure 1 are the following:

- *EU_RentPerson* is identified by its *id*.
- *DrivingLicense* is identified by *number*.
- *Branch*, *CarModel* and *CarGroup* are identified by their *name*.
- *Car* is identified by *registrationNumber*.
- *RentalAgreement* is identified by *beginning* and its *renter*.
- An *EU_RentPerson* cannot have overlapping *RentalAgreements*.
- An *EU_RentPerson* must have a valid (i.e not expired) *DrivingLicense* for the *RentalAgreement* duration.

- The *initEnding* of a *RentalAgreement* must be later than its *beginning*. The *actualPickUpTime* of an *OpenRental* must be later or equal to its *beginning*. The *actualReturnTime* of a *ClosedRental* must also be later than its *actualPickUpTime*.
- Relationship *categoryOrder* of *CarGroup* cannot have any cycles.
- A *Car* is available if all the rentals that it is assigned to are closed or canceled. Otherwise it is not available.
- Relationship *IsAvailable*: *Cars* that a *Branch* is responsible for and that are available.
- Relationship *GroupAvailability*: *CarGroups* available for a particular *Branch*, obtained through the available *Cars*.

In Figure 1, *RentalAgreement* is the key business artifact in the car rental process. A *RentalAgreement* is the result of an *EU-RentPerson* wanting to rent a car for a particular period of time. It is identified by its attribute *beginning* and a business artifact it is related to, *EU_RentPerson*. Notice that it is related to many of the other classes in the diagram. It has a pick-up and drop-off *Branch*, and may have a car assigned. A *RentalAgreement* may also be of several subtypes. It will be of the *Reservation* subtype if the client has made a reservation in advance. A *Reservation* is linked to a *CarGroup* for the rental, and may also be linked to a particular *CarModel* if the client has expressed his/her preferences for a particular brand and model of car. *Reservations* can be canceled, so there is also a *CanceledReservation* subtype. A *RentalAgreement* will become of the *OpenRental* subtype when a car is successfully handed over to the customer, and will be of the *ClosedRental* subtype when the client returns the car to the branch.

2.2   Business Artifacts Lifecycles as State Machine Diagrams

The lifecycle of a business artifact states the key, business-relevant, *stages* in the possible evolution of the artifact, from inception to final disposal and archiving. It is natural to represent it by using a variant of state machines, where each state of the machine corresponds to a possible stage in the lifecycle of an artifact from the class diagram [4].

We propose representing the states an artifact may go through in a UML state machine diagram, in a similar way to the one proposed in [6]. However, in contrast to this work, our state machine diagram includes a representation of the events and the conditions about them that trigger the transitions between consecutive states of the business artifact.

We distinguish two different kinds of events: *external events* (named call or signal events in [9]) and *internal events* (named temporal or condition events in [9]). External events are explicitly requested by the customer of the business process and their behavior is specified by means of a set of associated services. Internal events correspond to conditions stated over the content of the business artifacts and cause the execution of services without requiring the customer intervention. Services will be defined in the next section.

In Figure 2 we can see the corresponding state machine diagram for the business artifact *RentalAgreement*. Initially, the *RentalAgreement* can be a *Reservation* or an *OpenRental*, depending on whether the client makes a reservation to pick up the car on a later date (*Make Reservation* event) or he wishes to rent a car immediately (*Make Walk-In Rental* event). If the user picks up the car after having made a reservation (*Pick Up Car* event), the *RentalAgreement* becomes an *OpenRental*. On the other hand, if the customer does not pick up the car on the scheduled day or he decides to cancel the *Reservation* (*Cancel Reservation by Customer Demand* event), the *RentalAgreement* becomes a *CanceledReservation*. Finally, from *OpenRental* we will reach state *ClosedRental* after the user returns the car (*Return Car* event). All the events are external, except the one that takes place when the customer does not pick up the car. In this case, the transition is triggered by comparing the current date with the beginning of the rental agreement, when the beginning of the rental agreement has already gone by. In this case, *Cancel Reservation* is executed. Finally, we should note that there is a condition between square brackets in some of the events, *success*, that indicates that the event should finish successfully in order for the business artifact to change state.

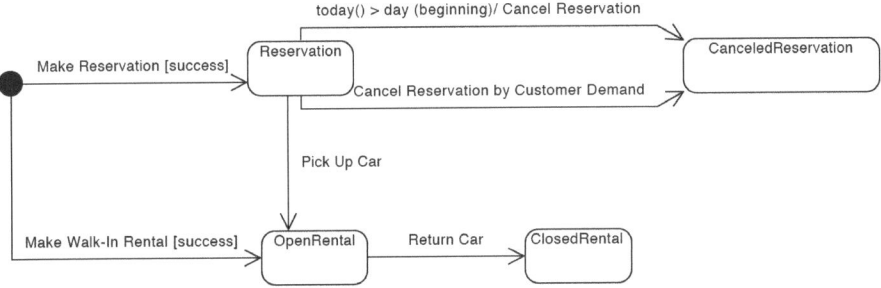

Fig. 2. State machine diagram that represents the lifecycle of RentalAgreement

It is worth noting that this diagram does not follow exactly the standard described in [5]. For instance, we have more than one outgoing transition from the start node. This is necessary because the *RentalAgreement* can be created in different ways (e.g. by making a walk-in rental or a reservation).

2.3   Services as Operation Contracts in OCL

A service (or "task") in a business process encapsulates a unit of work meaningful to the whole business process. The action of services makes business artifacts evolve, e.g. they may cause modifications on the information stored by the artifacts or they may make artifacts to evolve to a new stage, relevant from the business perspective.

Existing approaches usually specify services by means of *preconditions* and *postconditions*. We follow in this line by using OCL operation contracts. As we have mentioned before, OCL is a formal language that avoids ambiguities. Moreover, it is declarative, which means that it does not indicate *how* things should be done, but rather *what* should be done. The advantage of using OCL is that it is a part of the UML specification, which is an OMG standard and also a ISO/IEC standard [5]. Moreover, it can be automatically translated into first-order logic [10] or description logics [11], for instance, thus permitting to perform automatic reasoning on the UML/OCL specification.

Operation contracts consist of a set of input parameters and output parameters, a precondition and a postcondition. Both input and output parameters can be classes (i.e. business artifacts) or simple types (e.g. integers, strings, etc.). A precondition states the conditions that must be true before invoking the operation and refers to the values of artifact attributes at the time when the service is called. The postcondition indicates the state of the business artifacts after the execution of the operation. It may refer to the values of artifact attributes at the time when the service is called (appending operator *@pre*) *and* to their values after the service has finished execution (no operator or appending operator *@post*). Those artifacts that do not appear in the postcondition keep their state from before the execution of the operation.

Returning to the example, we will focus on the process of making a walk-in rental. A walk-in rental can be defined as the process whereby a client goes to a branch of the company and rents a car on the spot without any previous reservation, as long as there are available cars. Therefore, we need a service or operation that obtains all the data necessary for the rental. We have named it *Obtain-RentalData* and its code can be seen in Listing 1. Given an *EU_RentPerson*, the pick-up and drop-off *Branches* of the car, a *CarGroup* and/or a *CarModel*, and the end date, the operation creates a new *RentalAgreement*. Note that we do not check, for example, that this new *RentalAgremeent* does not overlap with other *RentalAgreements* that the *EU_RentPerson* may have. This is because we want to avoid redundancy and therefore we do not check conditions which are guaranteed somewhere else in the artifacts' specification, such as the class diagram, as described in [12]. The non-overlapping rental condition is already guaranteed by the class diagram and its integrity constraints.

Listing 1. OCL code for *ObtainRentalData*

```
action ObtainRentalData(endDate: Date, dropOffBranch: String, carG:
    String, carM: String, p: EU_RentPerson): RentalAgreement

localPre availableCarModel: carM<>'' implies
    currentBranch().carsAvailableNow.carModel.name->includes(carM)
localPre availableCarGroup: carG<>'' implies
    currentBranch().groupsAvailableNow.name->includes(carG)

localPost:

-- Create Rental Agreement --
RentalAgreement.allInstances() -> exists(ra.oclIsNew() and ra.renter=p
    and ra.beginning=now() and ra.initEnding=endDate and
    ra.pickUpBranch=currentBranch() and
    ra.dropOffBranch=Branch.allInstances()->select(dob |
    dob.name=dropOffBranch) and
-- We assign the car model with the least mileage --
```

```
(if (carM <> '') then
    ra.car = currentBranch().carsAvailableNow -> select(c |
        c.carModel.name=carM)->sortedBy(currentMileage) -> first()
else
    (if (carG = '') then
        ra.car = currentBranch().carsAvailableNow ->
            sortedBy(currentMileage) -> first()
    else
        ra.car = currentBranch().carsAvailableNow -> select(c |
            c.carModel.carGroup.name=carG) -> sortedBy(currentMileage)
            -> first()
    endif)
endif)
and
-- We return the Rental Agreement --
result = ra)
```

As it can be seen in Listing 1, the service requires an *EU_RentPerson* as a parameter; therefore, we need to obtain this business artifact in some way before its invocation. To do so, we need to check if the person is already registered and, in case he/she is not, insert him/her into the system. As it will be seen in the next section, we have split this job into two different services. We do not show their details here due to space limitations.

2.4 Associations as Activity Diagrams

Having the services as detailed above is not enough. We also need a way to establish the conditions under which services can be executed since, in a business process, they make changes to artifacts in a manner that is restricted by a family of constraints. These conditions/constraints might either be defined through a procedural specification or through a declarative one. Most of the existing proposals follow the second approach and define associations by means of Condition-Action rules (as done in [13,14,15]) or by encoding them into the *service* definition itself (see for instance [1]).

We propose to follow a procedural specification and to use UML activity diagrams for specifying associations since they are aimed at defining the right sequencing of service execution. In particular, we will have an activity diagram for each external event in our state machine diagrams. In this way, each service in which the event is decomposed is represented as an action (a rounded rectangle) in the activity diagram. Arrows show the order in which actions (i.e. services) have to be executed. Swimlanes indicate the main business artifact involved in each action, and the notes stereotyped as *Participant* indicate who is responsible for carrying out that action.

By modeling associations in this way we achieve our purpose of incorporating some notions of process awareness, despite the intrinsic artifact-centric nature of our proposal. Therefore, our proposal shows a way to explicitly and graphically capture the control flow of the business process; in contrast to many proposals such as [15] or [13] where they are represented textually.

The corresponding activity diagram for the external event *Make Walk-In Rental* from our example is detailed in Figure 3.

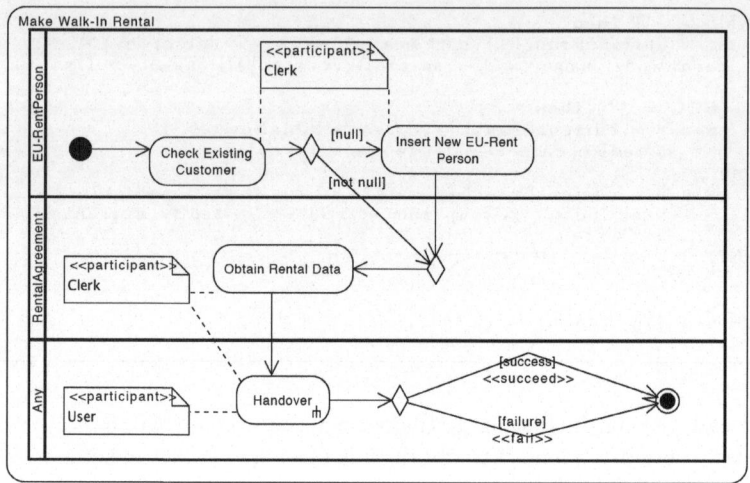

Fig. 3. Correspoding activity diagram for *Make Walk-In Rental*

As it can be seen in the diagram, we need to execute the service *CheckExisting-Customer* first. Depending on its output, which will indicate whether the person is registered in the system or not, we may insert a new customer (*InsertNewEU-RentPerson*). In the end, we obtain the data for the rental (*ObtainRentalData*) and we create a new *RentalAgreement*.

Notice that, apart from the services described above, there is an additional action, *Handover*, with a rake-like symbol. This indicates an action that is further defined in another activity diagram. The transition leading out of this action takes us to a decision node. Depending on the result of the Handover action, indicated between square brackets, *Make Walk-In Rental* will end successfully (stereotyped as *succeed*) or not (stereotyped as *fail*). Although the process ends in the same way regardless of its success or failure, it is important to make this distinction, as the next stage in the lifecycle of the artifact *RentalAgreement* depends on this outcome (see Figure 2).

Due to space limitations, we do not show the activity diagram of Handover nor the details of the services/actions that make it up. They can be found on [8].

3   Related Work

This section will look at the different alternatives used to represent the four elements in the BALSA framework, i.e. business artifacts, lifecycles, services and associations. Although most papers do not specifically state which form of representation is used for each element, it is not difficult to establish a correspondence between the representation in the different papers and the BALSA elements.

Business artifacts, sometimes referred to as business entities, are represented in different ways in the literature. Various authors use database schemas [13,14,16]. A similar representation is proposed in [1,15,17,2] where artifacts consist of a set of attributes or variables. [18] represents the business artifact and its lifecycle in one model that includes the artifact's attributes. Another possibility for representing them is using using an Entity-Relationship model as it is done in [6]. [19] represents the data model of their example by means of an UML class diagram. This differs from our proposal in that we propose using the UML class diagram for representing the business artifacts themselves. [20] chooses to represent artifacts as state machines defined by Petri nets.

Regarding the lifecycle of business artifacts, there are two main alternatives: they either offer an explicit representation of the evolution of the artifact or it is implicit. The explicit representations are normally based on a state machine diagram. Examples are [6,13]. A more formal approach is the one used in [19,20], where lifecycles are represented in variants of Petri nets. A similar alternative is proposed in [21], where ArtiNets (similar to Petri nets) and DecSerFlow, a declarative language, are used to represent the lifecycle of an artifact and its constraints. Sometimes there is a variable in the artifact which stores its state [1,15]. [18] uses GSM to represent the artifacts' lifecycles. The notation shares some characteristics with ours, such as the ability to represent graphically guards and stages. However, it adds the concept of milestone to represent conditions that determine the closing of a state. On the other hand, the sequencing of stages is determined by guard conditions instead of edges connecting the stages (although it is possible to use edges as a *macro*). In other cases, the lifecycle is implicitly represented by dynamic constraints expressed in logic [13] or the actions that act upon artifacts [16,14].

Services are also referred to as tasks or actions. Despite the different terminology, in general they are described by using pre and postconditions (also called effects). [13,1,15,17,16] use different variants of logic for this purpose. [14] follows the same idea but omitting the preconditions. [6] uses natural language to specify pre and postconditions.

Associations are represented in different ways depending on the approach of the paper. Some authors opt for using condition-action rules defined in logic [13,14]. [15] calls these conditions business rules; they should not be confused with business rules in [1], which are conditions that are superimposed in the already existing ones. In [1], preconditions determine the execution of the actions; therefore, they act as associations. [6] also uses event-condition-action rules, but they are defined in natural language. [19] uses what they call *channels* to define the connections between *proclets*. A proclet is a labeled Petri net with ports that describes the internal lifecycle of an artifact. Another alternative is DecSerFlow, that allows specifying restrictions on the sequencing of services, and it is used in [21]. It is a language grounded on temporal logic but also includes a graphical representation. On the other hand, [2,3] opt for a graphical representation using flowcharts. However, unlike our proposal, they do not use a particular language and little attention is given to the way of creating the flowchart.

4   Conclusions

There is no consensus on the best way to represent an information-centric model and, in all probability, there will never be, due to the great variety of uses of data-centric models. However, as [4] points out, it is important to experiment with different models, in order to examine the different possibilities that each one offers. Therefore, one contribution of this paper is identifying the UML diagrams that can be used to represent a process from an artifact-centric perspective following the BALSA framework.

To our knowledge, ours is the first proposal that suggests the use of UML diagrams for representing all the elements in this framework. We have shown that business artifacts can be represented in a class diagram, each artifact's lifecycle can be shown in a UML state machine diagram, services can be represented by using OCL operation contracts, and a possible way of defining associations is by means of a UML activity diagram. The use of an activity diagram for representing the associations between services brings it closer to process-centric methodologies and, at the same time, makes it easier to understand than just having textual restrictions in the form of condition-action rules represented in logic.

The importance of our contribution lies in the fact that UML is a standard in the world of conceptual modeling, and OCL, as a complement to UML, is used to represent those elements that cannot be graphically specified in UML. Moreover, both languages can be automatically translated into logic and the translation can be used for reasoning purposes. Therefore, our proposal offers the advantages of a graphical representation, understandable by the users, without losing the capacity of being used for reasoning.

As further work, we intend to define a way to perform automatic reasoning on the definition of a process using our diagrams in order to be able to validate its correctness, appropriateness and its quality before it is implemented.

Acknowledgments. This work has been partially supported by the Ministerio de Ciencia e Innovación under projects TIN2011-24747 and TIN2008-00444, Grupo Consolidado, the FEDER funds and Universitat Politècnica de Catalunya.

References

1. Damaggio, E., Deutsch, A., Hull, R., Vianu, V.: Automatic Verification of Data-Centric Business Processes. In: Rinderle-Ma, S., Toumani, F., Wolf, K. (eds.) BPM 2011. LNCS, vol. 6896, pp. 3–16. Springer, Heidelberg (2011)
2. Nigam, A., Caswell, N.S.: Business artifacts: an approach to operational specification. IBM Syst. J. 42(3), 428–445 (2003)
3. Bhattacharya, K., Caswell, N.S., Kumaran, S., Nigam, A., Wu, F.Y.: Artifact-centered operational modeling: lessons from customer engagements. IBM Syst. J. 46(4), 703–721 (2007)
4. Hull, R.: Artifact-Centric Business Process Models: Brief Survey of Research Results and Challenges. In: Meersman, R., Tari, Z. (eds.) OTM 2008, Part II. LNCS, vol. 5332, pp. 1152–1163. Springer, Heidelberg (2008)

5. ISO: ISO/IEC 19505-2:2012 - OMG UML superstructure 2.4.1 (2012),
http://www.iso.org/iso/iso_catalogue/catalogue_tc/
catalogue_detail.htm?csnumber=52854
6. Bhattacharya, K., Hull, R., Su, J.: A Data-Centric Design Methodology for Business Processes. In: Handbook of Research on Business Process Management, pp. 1–28 (2009)
7. ISO: ISO/IEC 19507:2012 - OMG OCL version 2.3.1 (2012),
http://www.iso.org/iso/iso_catalogue/catalogue_tc/
catalogue_detail.htm?csnumber=57306
8. Estañol, M., Queralt, A., Sancho, M.R., Teniente, E.: EU-Rent as an artifact-centric business process model (2012),
http://www.essi.upc.edu/~estanyol/docs/artifacts_eu_rent.pdf
9. Olivé, A.: Conceptual Modeling of Information Systems. Springer (2007)
10. Queralt, A., Teniente, E.: Verification and validation of UML conceptual schemas with OCL constraints. ACM Trans. Softw. Eng. Methodol. 21(2), 13 (2012)
11. Queralt, A., Artale, A., Calvanese, D., Teniente, E.: OCL-Lite: Finite reasoning on UML/OCL conceptual schemas. Data & Knowledge Engineering 73, 1–22 (2012)
12. Queralt, A., Teniente, E.: Specifying the Semantics of Operation Contracts in Conceptual Modeling. In: Spaccapietra, S. (ed.) Journal on Data Semantics VII. LNCS, vol. 4244, pp. 33–56. Springer, Heidelberg (2006)
13. Bagheri Hariri, B., Calvanese, D., De Giacomo, G., De Masellis, R., Felli, P.: Foundations of Relational Artifacts Verification. In: Rinderle-Ma, S., Toumani, F., Wolf, K. (eds.) BPM 2011. LNCS, vol. 6896, pp. 379–395. Springer, Heidelberg (2011)
14. Cangialosi, P., De Giacomo, G., De Masellis, R., Rosati, R.: Conjunctive Artifact-Centric Services. In: Maglio, P.P., Weske, M., Yang, J., Fantinato, M. (eds.) ICSOC 2010. LNCS, vol. 6470, pp. 318–333. Springer, Heidelberg (2010)
15. Bhattacharya, K., Gerede, C.E., Hull, R., Liu, R., Su, J.: Towards Formal Analysis of Artifact-Centric Business Process Models. In: Alonso, G., Dadam, P., Rosemann, M. (eds.) BPM 2007. LNCS, vol. 4714, pp. 288–304. Springer, Heidelberg (2007)
16. Belardinelli, F., Lomuscio, A., Patrizi, F.: Verification of Deployed Artifact Systems via Data Abstraction. In: Kappel, G., Maamar, Z., Motahari-Nezhad, H.R. (eds.) ICSOC 2011. LNCS, vol. 7084, pp. 142–156. Springer, Heidelberg (2011)
17. Fritz, C., Hull, R., Su, J.: Automatic construction of simple artifact-based business processes. In: Fagin, R. (ed.) ICDT 2009, vol. 361, pp. 225–238. ACM (2009)
18. Hull, R., Damaggio, E., Fournier, F., Gupta, M., Heath III, F(T.), Hobson, S., Linehan, M., Maradugu, S., Nigam, A., Sukaviriya, P., Vaculin, R.: Introducing the Guard-Stage-Milestone Approach for Specifying Business Entity Lifecycles. In: Bravetti, M., Bultan, T. (eds.) WS-FM 2010. LNCS, vol. 6551, pp. 1–24. Springer, Heidelberg (2011)
19. Fahland, D., de Leoni, M., van Dongen, B.F., van der Aalst, W.M.P.: Behavioral Conformance of Artifact-Centric Process Models. In: Abramowicz, W. (ed.) BIS 2011. LNBIP, vol. 87, pp. 37–49. Springer, Heidelberg (2011)
20. Lohmann, N., Wolf, K.: Artifact-Centric Choreographies. In: Maglio, P.P., Weske, M., Yang, J., Fantinato, M. (eds.) ICSOC 2010. LNCS, vol. 6470, pp. 32–46. Springer, Heidelberg (2010)
21. Kucukoguz, E., Su, J.: On Lifecycle Constraints of Artifact-Centric Workflows. In: Bravetti, M. (ed.) WS-FM 2010. LNCS, vol. 6551, pp. 71–85. Springer, Heidelberg (2011)

Multilevel Business Artifacts

Christoph Schütz[1,*], Lois M.L. Delcambre[2,**], and Michael Schrefl[1]

[1] Johannes Kepler University, Department of Business Informatics –
Data & Knowledge Engineering, Altenberger Str. 69, 4040 Linz, Austria
{schuetz,schrefl}@dke.uni-linz.ac.at
[2] Portland State University, Computer Science Department,
1900 Southwest 4th Avenue, Portland, OR 97201, USA
lmd@cs.pdx.edu

Abstract. The representation of many real-world scenarios in conceptual models benefits from the use of multilevel abstraction hierarchies. Product models, for example, are typically grouped into product categories which, in turn, constitute the company's range of products. Multilevel abstraction hierarchies often reflect the organizational structure of a company and the different information needs of the various departments. Current modeling techniques, however, lack extensive support for the representation of multilevel abstraction hierarchies in business process models. The explicit consideration of multilevel abstraction hierarchies in business process models might improve the alignment of processes across different organizational entities. In this paper, we introduce the concept of the multilevel business artifact (MBA) for representing multilevel abstraction hierarchies of both data and process models. An MBA encapsulates in a single object the data and process models of various levels, thereby expanding consequently the idea of business artifacts to the realm of multilevel abstraction hierarchies.

Keywords: Conceptual Modeling, Multilevel Abstraction, Metamodeling, Object Life Cycles.

1 Introduction

In many modeling situations, data objects are arranged in multilevel abstraction hierarchies. In such hierarchies, data objects at lower levels of abstraction are collected into more abstract, higher-level objects. These higher-level objects provide an alternative view of the represented problem domain, carrying information that is not present in, yet related to, the lower-level objects. Product models, for example, are typically grouped into product categories which, in turn, constitute the company's range of products. A product model typically has a list price. The actual selling price, however, might be influenced by the tax rate attached to the corresponding product category.

---

* This work was supported by a Marshall Plan Scholarship granted by the Austrian Marshall Plan Foundation for a research stay at Portland State University.
** This work was supported by the U.S. National Science Foundation (No. 0840668).

M. La Rosa and P. Soffer (Eds.): BPM 2012 Workshops, LNBIP 132, pp. 304–315, 2013.

Multilevel abstraction hierarchies can support differing information needs within a company. Different departments process data objects at different levels of abstraction but the processes dealing with these data objects are interdependent. For example, top management decides which product categories the company should offer whereas the marketing and production departments are concerned with individual products. The decisions of top management, although they concern data on a different level of abstraction, affect the marketing and production departments. If top management decides to focus, for example, luxury goods rather than budget products, marketing may adjust its pricing strategy for individual products and production may shift priorities to rigorous quality management rather than low-cost production.

The explicit consideration of multilevel abstraction hierarchies in process models might improve the alignment of processes across different organizational entities. Current modeling techniques lack extensive support for the representation of multilevel abstraction hierarchies in business process models. Note that the use of multilevel abstraction hierarchies in business process models as presented in this paper differs from other approaches with abstraction which represent the same process at varying levels of detail.

In this paper, we introduce the multilevel business artifact (MBA) for representing multilevel abstraction hierarchies of both data and process models. We base the MBA approach on multilevel objects (m-objects) which offer a compact and flexible formalism in conceptual models for the representation of multilevel abstraction hierarchies with possibly heterogeneous levels [1,2]. M-objects, however, focus mainly on the static aspects of the conceptual model, lacking any information about the execution order of methods. An MBA, on the other hand, encapsulates in a single object the data and process models of various levels, thereby expanding the idea of a business artifact – a "chunk of information that can be used to run a business" [3] – to multilevel abstraction hierarchies.

The remainder of this paper is organized as follows. In Section 2, we introduce the MBA approach for a compact representation of interdependent processes at various levels of abstraction. In Section 3, we present multilevel concretization for increased modeling flexibility. In Section 4, we formally define the MBA metamodel and its semantics in terms of UML. In Section 5, we discuss the potential benefits of the MBA approach in relation to existing work. In Section 6, we conclude with a summary and outline future research on multilevel business process modeling.

2 Multilevel Business Artifact

In multilevel abstraction hierarchies, data objects at higher levels of abstraction are considered aggregates of more concrete, lower-level objects. Nevertheless, the data objects at each level have their own distinct features. Consider, for example, the data model of a fictitious travel agency with a wide range of guided tours. Within various categories, the company offers several tour packages. A tour package represents a proposed set of travel activities over a number of days.

Based on these tour packages, the travel agency organizes particular trips with a specific start and end date.

Besides their static features, data objects at different levels of abstraction have interdependent life cycles. For example, a travel company's range of guided tours is constantly being reassessed, resulting in the addition of new tour categories. Likewise, within each tour category, the development of new packages is regularly initiated. And each tour package undergoes a development phase before the launch puts the package on offer. A tour package may be selected for organizing a trip only when the package is on offer. Note that attributes of higher-level data objects can constrain the processes at lower levels of abstraction. For example, a trip's start and end date are constrained by the corresponding package's number of days.

Multilevel objects (m-objects), as introduced by Neumayr et al. [1,2], encapsulate in a single object information about an entire abstraction hierarchy. An m-object defines a number of abstraction levels and their hierarchical order as well as a class for each of these levels. The different classes are associated by aggregation relationships along the abstraction level hierarchy. M-objects, however, omit the dynamic aspects of the represented information.

A multilevel business artifact (MBA) accounts for the dynamic aspects of multilevel abstraction hierarchies. Basically, an MBA is an m-object extended with life cycle models where each abstraction level has a single life cycle model that defines the legal execution order of the methods of the class.

Figure 1 illustrates MBA *Tour* (and MBA *CityTour*) for the management of tour data. Each box on the left-hand side represents a class. Within each box, the top compartment contains, in arrow brackets, the name of the level the class is associated with. MBA *Tour* defines classes, connected by dotted lines, for levels *range*, *category*, *package*, and *trip*, where *range* is the most abstract and *trip* is the most concrete level. The other compartments contain attribute and method definitions, respectively.

We use UML state machine diagrams [4] for modeling object life cycles. A state machine consists of states and transitions between these states. Transitions are triggered by events. For an MBA, the triggering events are *call events* raised by the invocation of a method. Thus, the state machine models the legal execution order of methods.

In Figure 1, for example, the state machine diagram at the *package* level of MBA *Tour* restricts changes in the number of days (*nrOfDays*) to the development phase. Consequently, method *setNrOfDays* may be invoked only on objects in the *Developing* state. The invocation of method *launch* puts an object in state *On Offer*. In this state, only method *requestTrip* may be invoked. Note that this method cannot be invoked when the object is in the development phase.

For each transition in a state machine, pre- and post-conditions may be specified. These pre- and post-conditions relate the life cycle models of different abstraction levels. For example, at the *range* level, the post-condition of the recursive transition of the *Analyzing* state relates levels *range* and *category* by requiring that, after the execution of method *addCategory*, the set of objects

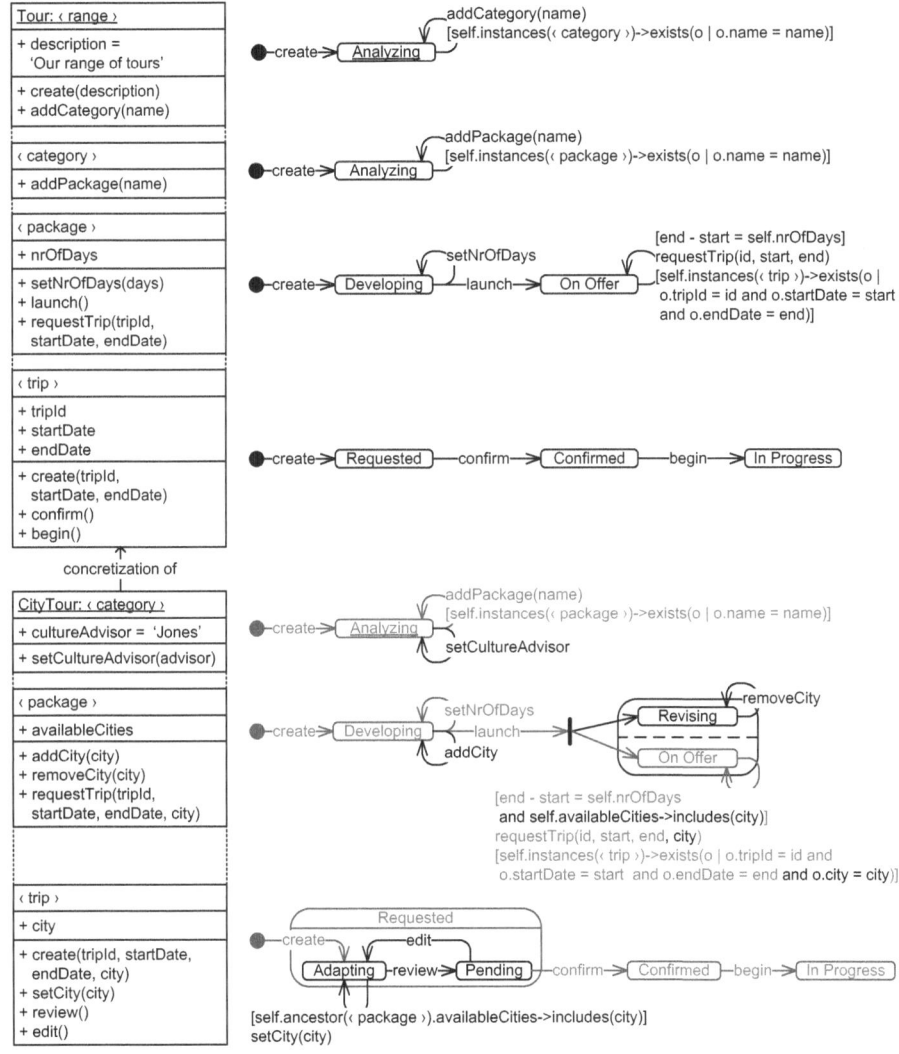

Fig. 1. An MBA and one of its concretizations for the management of tour data

instantiating the class associated with level *category* must contain an object with the specified name. An attribute *name* is implicitly defined for every MBA and is assumed to be unique. Similar conditions relate levels *category* and *package* as well as levels *package* and *trip*. Pre- and post-conditions may also be used to relate different levels by defining invariants. For example, the number of days at the *package* level constrains the selection of the dates at the *trip* level.

An MBA instantiates the class at the single most abstract level. An MBA therefore assigns values to attributes associated with the top level and executes the corresponding life cycle model. MBA *Tour* in Figure 1 instantiates the class at the *range* level, assigning a value to attribute *description*, and sets the current state in the life cycle to *Analyzing*. MBA *CityTour*, on the other hand, instantiates the class at the *category* level.

3   Multilevel Concretization

An MBA presents characteristics of both class and object. An MBA defines classes which are arranged in an aggregation hierarchy according to their levels of abstraction. The instances of these classes are again MBAs. Therefore, an MBA describes the schema of a (sub-)hierarchy. An MBA, however, is also part of the abstraction hierarchy. Given this duality of class and object, a special type of relationship is needed to describe an abstraction hierarchy with MBAs. This relationship type is multilevel concretization, adapted from m-objects [1].

Through concretization, MBAs are collected into aggregates. For example, in Figure 1, MBA *CityTour* is a concretization of MBA *Tour*. The single most abstract level of *CityTour* is *category*, which is the second level of MBA *Tour*. MBA *CityTour* instantiates the class at its top level, *category*, and becomes part of the range of guided tours represented by MBA *Tour*. MBA *CityTour* is among the instances of the class defined by MBA *Tour* at the *category* level.

The concretizing MBA must instantiate the class associated with the second level of its abstraction, the concretized MBA. Consequently, the concretizing MBA becomes part of the set of all instances of this class, and is thus part of the aggregate object represented by its abstraction. In this sense, multilevel concretization presents semantics of both instantiation and aggregation.

Multilevel concretization, however, is not merely a mechanism for instantiation and aggregation. The main purpose of concretization is to support modeling flexibility through specialization. For each level an MBA shares with its parent, the concretizing MBA specializes the class that the parent MBA associates with this level. For example, in Figure 1, MBA *CityTour* specializes the classes defined by its parent, MBA *Tour*, by adding attributes and methods. Note that the inherited features are not shown in this diagram.

Concretization does not restrict specialization to the static aspects of an MBA. Life cycle models may also be specialized. A concretizing MBA may add additional transitions and states or refine existing states in an inherited life cycle model. The semantics of life cycle specialization is based on existing work which has extensively studied behavior-consistent specialization of life cycle models [5,6]. For example, the state machine diagram at the *category* level of MBA *CityTour* has an additional transition with respect to the inherited life cycle model. The state machine diagram at the *package* level, on the other hand, has an additional state, *Revising*, parallel to *On Offer*. At the *trip* level, the state machine diagram presents a refined state *Requested*. Note that gray color marks inherited states and transitions throughout this paper.

An MBA describes the common, global schema of a hierarchy which, through concretization, may be specialized for a particular sub-hierarchy. The concretizing MBA describes a specialized schema that is valid only for a sub-hierarchy.

For this sub-hierarchy, the specialized schema of the concretizing MBA becomes the common schema which, again, may be further specialized by other MBAs through concretization. An employee can select the appropriate MBA which best fits the information demands of a particular task, without the overhead of unnecessary information.

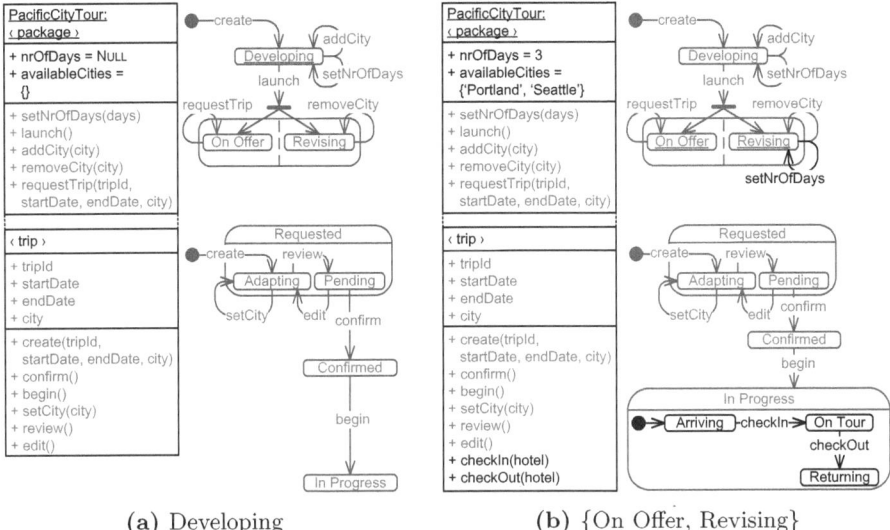

(a) Developing   (b) {On Offer, Revising}

Fig. 2. A concretization of MBA *CityTour* in different life cycle states

Concretization is not a one-shot activity. Rather, concretization itself is an incremental process. Consider, for example, MBA *PacificCityTour*, a concretization of *CityTour*, in Figure 2. Initially, MBA *PacificCityTour* has only the inherited class and life cycle models, is in the *Developing* state, and has NULL values assigned to the top-level attributes (Figure 2a). During the development phase, values are assigned to attributes *nrOfDays* and *availableCities* and the inherited class and life cycle models are specialized. The invocation of method *launch* terminates the *Developing* phase and puts MBA *PacificCityTour* simultaneously in the states *On Offer* and *Revising* (Figure 2b). In this state, the attributes at the *package* level already have values assigned and the class and life cycle models differ from the inherited models. For the *PacificCityTour* package, the number of days can now also be altered after the product launch. At the *trip* level, the process of what happens after beginning the trip has been further clarified. Note that inherited pre- and postconditions have been omitted in Figure 2.

Since concretization itself is a process, an MBA may also account for meta-process activities in order to control local changes made to the imposed business process models. Every MBA implicitly has pre-defined reflective methods which enable changes of class and life cycle models at runtime. By default, the reflective

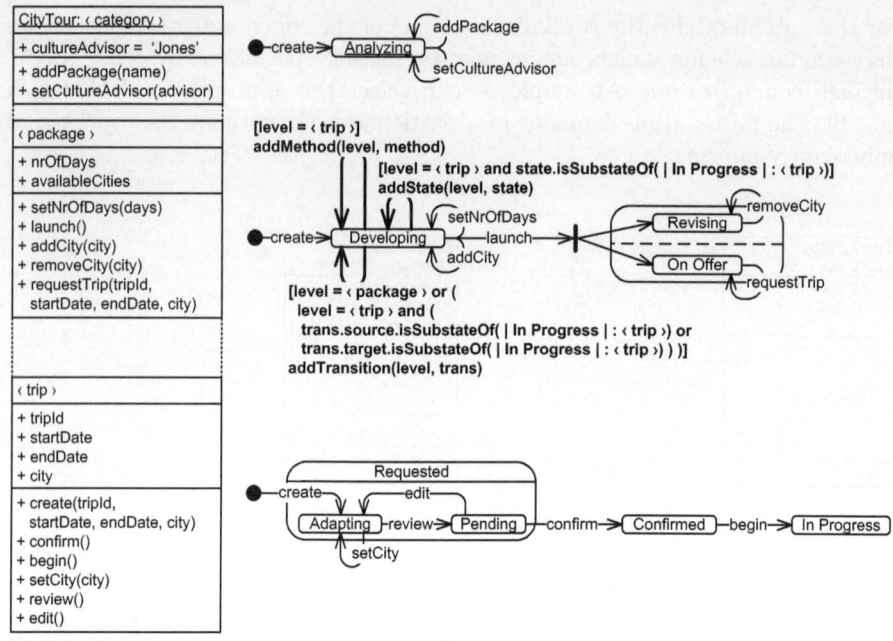

Fig. 3. MBA *CityTour* with meta-process model elements (in boldface)

methods of an MBA can be invoked in any state. In this case, classes and life cycle models can be extended as long as the semantics of class and life cycle specialization are obeyed. The explicit mention of reflective methods in the life cycle model, however, allows the modeler to further restrict specialization and thus deliberately limit flexibility.

Figure 3 shows an alternative version of MBA *CityTour* with reflective methods in one of its life cycle models. Inherited pre- and postconditions have been omitted. According to the life cycle model for the *package* level, methods, states, and transitions can be added only in the *Developing* state. Using pre-conditions, flexibility can be constrained even further. In this example, new methods may only be added to the model associated with the *trip* level. Likewise, new states may only be added for the *trip* level and only as sub-states of *In Progress*. Transitions may be added for levels *package* and *trip*. For the *trip* level, transitions may only be added if they come from or lead to a sub-state of *In Progress*.

4   Metamodel and UML Semantics

The Meta-Object Facility [7] and the Unified Modeling Language (UML) [4] provide the framework for the formal definition of the MBA approach. The Object Constraint Language (OCL) [8], in turn, allows for the specification of additional consistency criteria. Figure 4 illustrates the MBA metamodel. Figure 5 describes adapted consistency criteria from m-objects [1] using OCL constraints.

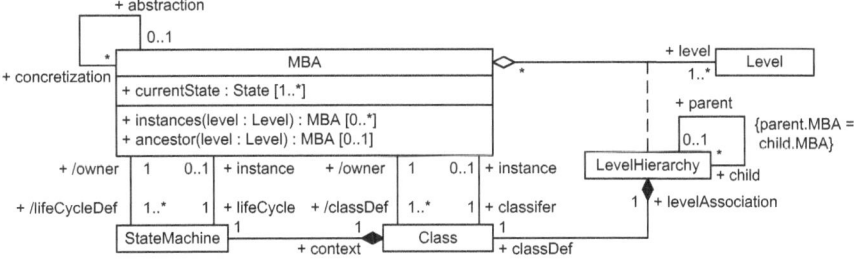

Fig. 4. The MBA metamodel

Fig. 5. Consistency criteria for the MBA metamodel

An MBA references several levels which exist independently from an MBA. Attached to each link between an MBA and a level is a reference to a parent level. Note that the same level may have different parent levels, depending on the MBA. The links between an MBA and its levels together with the records of the parent levels constitute a level hierarchy. In this hierarchy, a level cannot be its own ancestor (Constraint 1). Furthermore, an MBA has a single most abstract level, the top level, which has no parent level within the MBA (Constraint 2).

An MBA defines classes, one for each associated level. Each link between an MBA and a level references a class. Each class, in turn, has a UML state machine as life cycle model. For convenience, an MBA directly references each class and life cycle model. Therefore, the associations between *MBA* and *Class* as well as between *MBA* and *StateMachine* are derived from the level hierarchy (as indicated by a slash before the role names in Figure 4).

The classes associated with the levels of an MBA are instantiated by MBAs. For this reason, class *MBA* is a specialization of *InstanceSpecification* from the UML Kernel [4]. From this class, *MBA* inherits its association to *Classifer*, referenced by the role name *classifier*, which *MBA* restricts to *Class*. This *classifier* references the class that is associated with the MBA's top level (Constraint 3). Similarly, *lifeCycle* references the top-level life cycle model. The *instances* method of an MBA retrieves all instances of a class associated with a particular level using the pre-defined *allInstances* operation (Constraint 4). The result of this query includes instances of sub-classes.

The recursive one-to-many association of class *MBA* represents concretization. Besides its immediate parent, an MBA will frequently access ancestors at more abstract levels. Method *ancestor* of class *MBA* retrieves the ancestor having a particular top level (Constraint 5).

Constraints 6-10 must be satisfied in order for an MBA to be a consistent concretization of its parent. First, the top level of the concretizing MBA must be a child of the top level of the parent MBA (Constraint 6). Second, the concretizing MBA contains every level of the parent MBA from the concretizing MBA's top level downwards (Constraint 7). Third, the relative order of the levels is the same in both the concretizing MBA and its parent MBA (Constraint 8). Fourth, the class and life cycle models defined by the concretizing MBA are specializations of the corresponding models in the parent MBA (Constraints 9 and 10).

In this paper, we do not formally define the notions of class and life cycle specialization. Specialization of classes is extensively described by the UML standard. The notion of life cycle specialization, on the other hand, depends largely on the modeling formalism employed. In general, a specialized process model may refine states by adding sub-states; it may also add parallel paths. We refer to Stumptner and Schrefl [5] for a formal definition of behavior-consistent specialization in UML state machine diagrams. These authors [6] also provide a more in-depth analysis of behavior-consistent specialization of life cycle models, including rules for consistency checking. We refer to Grossmann et al. [9] for an analysis of the complexity of checking behavior-consistent specialization.

Finally, Figure 6 illustrates the UML semantics of the running example used throughout this paper. This UML diagram consists of several aggregation hierarchies of classes. The topmost class of each hierarchy is a singleton class with one instance. The other classes are specialized, and thus relate the different aggregation hierarchies. Together with the instances on the right-hand side, each of these aggregation hierarchies corresponds to an MBA. Note that instances are shown with their name followed by their type, separated by a colon and both underlined.

The leftmost aggregation hierarchy in Figure 6 consists of classes *TourRange*, *TourCategory*, *TourPackage*, and *TourTrip*. Each of these classes is associated

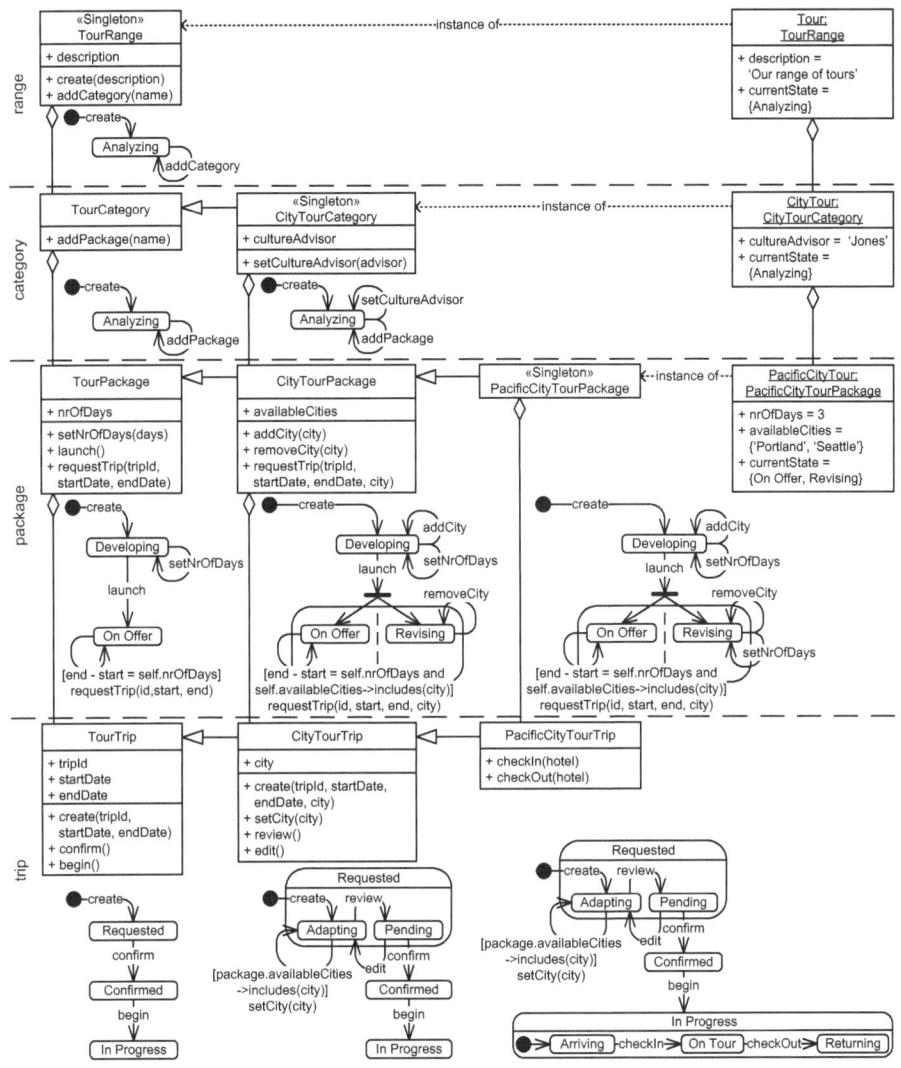

Fig. 6. UML class and state machine diagrams for the management of tour data

with a life cycle model. This aggregation hierarchy corresponds to the class and life cycle definitions of MBA *Tour*.

The aggregation hierarchy in the middle consists of classes *CityTourCategory*, *CityTourPackage*, and *CityTourTrip*. These classes are specializations of classes *TourCategory*, *TourPackage*, and *TourTrip*, respectively. This aggregation hierarchy corresponds to the class and life cycle definitions of MBA *CityTour*, which is a concretization of MBA *Tour*.

The rightmost aggregation hierarchy consists of classes *PacificCityTourPackage* and *PacificCityTourTrip*. These classes are specializations of classes

TourPackage and *TourTrip*, respectively. This aggregation hierarchy corresponds to the class and life cycle definitions of MBA *PacificCityTour*, which is a concretization of MBA *CityTour*.

5   Related Work

An early predecessor of current data-centric approaches to business process modeling are object/behavior diagrams [10]. The principle of describing the structure and dynamics of data in a single object has been successfully advanced by the business artifact approach [3]. The MBA approach as presented in this paper adopts this idea and expands it to multiple levels of abstraction. Instead of describing only a single abstraction level, an MBA combines structure and dynamics of multilevel data in a single object. This view on business process model abstraction differs from other approaches, for example by Smirnov et al. [11] or the guard-stage-milestone modeling approach for business artifacts [12]. These approaches describe the same process at different levels of detail. The MBA approach, on the other hand, considers interdependent processes of objects at various levels of abstraction.

In recent years, the interest in flexibility and dynamic change in data-centric business process models has been increasing. Flexible process models allow a company to adapt to the changing business environment [13]. In order to better suit a particular business situation, process models should be allowed to change [14], especially when dealing with less-structured processes [15]. Similarly, Weidlich et al. [16] stress the importance of managing variants of process models which exist in a company due to differing requirements across departments. Furthermore, in order to support flexibility in business process modeling, process models should be allowed to adapt dynamically during their execution [17]. The MBA approach offers these kinds of flexibility through the concretization mechanism. Moreover, through its reflective capabilities, the MBA approach allows the modeler to explicitly represent and constrain dynamic change in the model.

6   Summary and Future Work

This paper is a first introduction to multilevel business process modeling. We introduced the concept of the MBA which, in the spirit of the business artifact approach, encapsulates in a single object data and life cycle models of an abstraction hierarchy. Through concretization, these data and life cycle models can be specialized for particular sub-hierarchies. Future work will address several issues. First, in order to enable message passing between MBAs that are not in a concretization relationship, a new relationship type should be introduced. Second, actors should be incorporated explicitly within the model. Third, an implementation of the MBA approach should support modelers in creating a central repository of multilevel business process models.

References

1. Neumayr, B., Grün, K., Schrefl, M.: Multi-level domain modeling with m-objects and m-relationships. In: 6th Asia-Pacific Conference on Conceptual Modeling, pp. 61–70. Australian Computer Society, Darlinghurst (2009)
2. Neumayr, B., Schrefl, M., Thalheim, B.: Modeling Techniques for Multi-level Abstraction. In: Kaschek, R., Delcambre, L. (eds.) The Evolution of Conceptual Modeling. LNCS, vol. 6520, pp. 68–92. Springer, Heidelberg (2011)
3. Nigam, A., Caswell, N.S.: Business artifacts: An approach to operational specification. IBM Systems Journal 42(3), 428–445 (2003)
4. Object Management Group: OMG Unified Modeling Language (OMG UML), Superstructure, version 2.4.1, http://www.omg.org/spec/UML/2.4.1/
5. Stumptner, M., Schrefl, M.: Behavior Consistent Inheritance in UML. In: Laender, A.H.F., Liddle, S.W., Storey, V.C. (eds.) ER 2000. LNCS, vol. 1920, pp. 527–542. Springer, Heidelberg (2000)
6. Schrefl, M., Stumptner, M.: Behavior-consistent specialization of object life cycles. ACM Transactions on Software Engineering and Methodology 11(1), 92–148 (2002)
7. Object Management Group: OMG Meta Object Facility (MOF), Superstructure, version 2.4.1, http://www.omg.org/spec/MOF/2.4.1/
8. Object Management Group: OMG Object Constraint Language (OCL), version 2.3.1, http://www.omg.org/spec/OCL/2.3.1/
9. Grossmann, G., Schrefl, M., Stumptner, M.: Design for service compatibility – behavioural compatibility checking and diagnosis. Software and Systems Modeling (2012), http://dx.doi.org/10.1007/s10270-012-0229-0
10. Kappel, G., Schrefl, M.: Object/behavior diagrams. In: 7th International Conference on Data Engineering, pp. 530–539. IEEE, New York (1991)
11. Smirnov, S., Reijers, H.A., Weske, M.: A Semantic Approach for Business Process Model Abstraction. In: Mouratidis, H., Rolland, C. (eds.) CAiSE 2011. LNCS, vol. 6741, pp. 497–511. Springer, Heidelberg (2011)
12. Hull, R., Damaggio, E., De Masellis, R., Fournier, F., Gupta, M., Heath, F.T., Hobson, S., Linehan, M.H., Maradugu, S., Nigam, A., Sukaviriya, P.N., Vaculín, R.: Business artifacts with guard-stage-milestone lifecycles: Managing artifact interactions with conditions and events. In: 5th ACM International Conference on Distributed Event-Based Systems, pp. 51–62. ACM, New York (2011)
13. Reichert, M., Rinderle-Ma, S., Dadam, P.: Flexibility in Process-Aware Information Systems. In: Jensen, K., van der Aalst, W.M.P. (eds.) ToPNoc II. LNCS, vol. 5460, pp. 115–135. Springer, Heidelberg (2009)
14. Weber, B., Reichert, M., Rinderle-Ma, S.: Change patterns and change support features - enhancing flexibility in process-aware information systems. Data & Knowledge Engineering 66(3), 438–466 (2008)
15. Künzle, V., Weber, B., Reichert, M.: Object-aware business processes: Fundamental requirements and their support in existing approaches. International Journal of Information System Modeling and Design 2(2), 19–46 (2011)
16. Weidlich, M., Mendling, J., Weske, M.: A Foundational Approach for Managing Process Variability. In: Mouratidis, H., Rolland, C. (eds.) CAiSE 2011. LNCS, vol. 6741, pp. 267–282. Springer, Heidelberg (2011)
17. Rinderle, S., Reichert, M., Dadam, P.: Correctness criteria for dynamic changes in workflow systems – a survey. Data & Knowledge Engineering 50(1), 9–34 (2004)

Automatic Discovery of Data-Centric and Artifact-Centric Processes

Erik H.J. Nooijen, Boudewijn F. van Dongen, and Dirk Fahland

Eindhoven University of Technology
Eindhoven, The Netherlands
enooijen@gmail.com, {b.f.v.dongen,d.fahland}@tue.nl

Abstract. Process discovery is a technique that allows for automatically discovering a process model from recorded executions of a process as it happens in reality. This technique has successfully been applied for classical processes where one process execution is constituted by a single case with a unique case identifier. Data-centric and artifact-centric systems such as ERP systems violate this assumption. Here a process execution is driven by process data having various notions of interrelated identifiers that distinguish the various interrelated data objects of the process. Classical process mining techniques fail in this setting. This paper presents an automatic technique for discovering for each notion of data object in the process a separate process model that describes the evolution of this object, also known as artifact life-cycle model. Given a relational database that stores process execution information of a data-centric system, the technique extracts event information, case identifiers and their interrelations, discovers the central process data objects and their associated events, and decomposes the data source into multiple logs, each describing the cases of a separate data object. Then classical process discovery techniques can be applied to obtain a process model for each object. The technique is implemented and has been evaluated on the production ERP system of a large retailer.

Keywords: artifact, process discovery, ERP system, event log.

1 Introduction

Process discovery is a technique for automatically discovering a process model from recorded executions of the process. The technique is successfully applied for classical processes where each process execution is recorded as a *case* (the sequence of its events) in an *event log*. Each event of the process is related to exactly one *case* by a *case id*. [1]

However, when looking at the data models of ERP products such as SAP Business Suite, Microsoft Dynamics AX, Oracle E-Business Suite, Exact Globe, Infor ERP, and Oracle JD Edwards EnterpriseOne, one can easily see that this assumption is *not* valid for real-life processes, which are *data-centric*. There are one-to-many and many-to-many relationships between data *objects*, such as customers, orderlines, orders, deliveries, payments, etc., and a single event can relate to and update several objects. Such systems do not have a unique notion of a *process instance* by which we can trace and isolate its executions, and process discovery fails.

M. La Rosa and P. Soffer (Eds.): BPM 2012 Workshops, LNBIP 132, pp. 316–327, 2013.

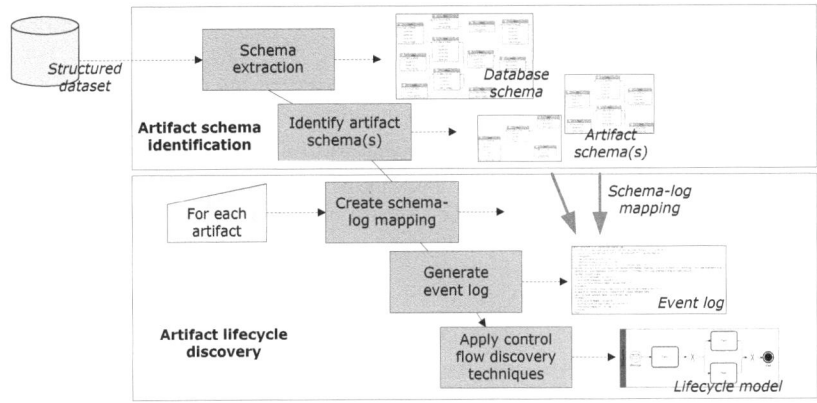

Fig. 1. Approach to Artifact Discovery

Previous approaches to use this data for process discovery particularly failed to separate events related to various objects; in particular analyzing what was part of the process was hard and time consuming [11, 15, 16]. The *artifact-centric approach* [7] provides an appropriate conceptual lense: the entire process is seen as a set of interacting business entities called *artifacts*. Each of these artifacts can be described by an information schema (called an artifact schema) and a non-trivial lifecycle describing how the artifact evolves through a process execution [9, 10].

Process discovery for artifact-centric processes is an unsolved problem. The problem reads as follow. We assume a structured data source R to be given that contains information about the events that have occurred in past process executions, usually in the form of *timestamps* written in the records of R. For example, we found production databases of ERP systems to satisfy this assumption. From this data source, we want to discover (1) the artifacts (i.e., business entities) of the process, (2) their information model (i.e., artifact schema), and (3) the life-cycle model of each artifact.

In this paper we present a first automatic technique for discovering artifact-centric processes from a structured data source R. Our technique, illustrated in Fig. 1 reuses a number of existing techniques and fills in a crucial missing gap to solve the problem. For the given structured data source R, first the schema S_R including column types and primary and foreign keys is rediscovered (this may be necessary as the documented schema of R can be incomplete regarding its actual contents, e.g., non-documented foreign key relations). Then the schema S_R is partitioned into artifact schemas $A_1, \ldots, A_k$ using weighted k-means clustering, where k is a parameter chosen by the user. Each artifact schema A_i describes the information model of one artifact and consists of all tables that contain relevant information about A_i. We then extract from R a log that describes all instances of A_i and their evolution over time. For this, we extract from artifact schema A_i automatically an event specification (called *schema-log mapping*) in terms of attributes of A_i. This event type specification is then used to construct database queries which extract from R all events with their attributes, group them into cases, order them by time stamp, and write the result into a classical log L_i of A_i. Each case of L_i is a sequence of events related to the same case id of A_i, which satisfies the assumptions for classical processes. Then a classical process discovery algorithm can be used to obtain a life-cycle model for artifact A_i.

In the following, we first discuss related work to extracting event information from data sources in Sect. 2. Sect. 3 presents the techniques to discover artifact schemas from a relational data source. Sect. 4 presents the main technical contribution of this paper: to extract event specifications from artifact schemas which is then used for actual log extraction and life-cycle discovery. We report on experimental results in Sect. 5, and conclude and discuss open problems in Sect. 6.

2   Related Work

In principle, an artifact-centric model of a running system could be obtained through interviews of process stakeholders [5], by first looking at what data is important and then investigating how the process operates on the data [12]. Besides being time-consuming, this approach suffers from the fact that interviews will reveal how people think the process should run rather than how it is actually run [1]. Thus, an automated approach to discovering artifact models from process data sources is preferable.

Over 40 algorithms were developed for control flow discovery given an event log [17]. The authors of [17] provide an overview of these algorithms and describe when each algorithm can be applied successfully. The process analysis approach described in [6] explains how these techniques should be applied and which points of attentions should be taken into account to improve the quality of the results.

All process discovery techniques assume an *event log* to be given as input which consists of a set of *cases* being sequences of *events*; events of one case relate to the same *case identifiers* [1].

Related work on event log extraction can be separated into support for event log extraction in general and case studies on event log extraction from specific ERP systems. The most recent generic approach to event log extraction is XESame [18]. In this, as in all known generic approaches, first a mapping between source data and event log needs to be defined *manually*. Then an algorithm extracts events, sorts them into traces, and writes traces into a log. In case of XESame the mapping is translated to SQL queries on a database which returns the events of the log.

The only ERP systems for which event log extraction was studied were SAP [11,15] and PeopleSoft [16]. A variety of approaches were tested to extract event logs from these systems. The underlying assumption of these approaches was the existence of a unique case identifier. As ERP systems in general provide multiple case identifiers, the majority of these approaches failed; success could only be reported when database tables were carefully selected by hand. The artifact-centric approach of multiple inter-related artifacts [7] sheds a better view on data in ERP systems which we exploit in the following.

3   Discovering Artifact Schemas

In this paper we want to solve the problem of discovering an artifact-centric process model from a structured data source, i.e., a relational database R. In light of existing work discussed in Sect. 2, we need (1) a technique to *automatically* identify the relevant case identifiers in R, each case identifier then gives rise to an artifact (a business object with a life-cycle); (2) a technique to *automatically* extract from R an event log for each artifact, preferably by leveraging a generic approach to event log extraction; (3) discover artifact life-cycle models for each log.

We solve the first problem in this section by applying a number of existing data mining techniques. We solve log extraction by leveraging the generic approach of [18] in Sect. 4. Finally, artifact life-cycle discovery is solved by applying any classical process discovery algorithm [1, 17] on the extracted log. Fig. 1 shows the overall approach that was already outlined in the introduction; in the following we present the details.

3.1 Assumed Input and Schema Extraction

We assume a relational database R (e.g., an ERP system's database) to be given as input for the discovery. We assume that R recorded its state evolved over time in *timestamp attributes*, for instance, important updates of a record were logged in a separate attribute. We found this to be a feasible assumption for many ERP systems in practice. If R has no historic information, then process discovery is infeasible, however, one could use trigger mechanisms of active databases to log updates of R in a generic way.

To identify the relevant case identifers in R and corresponding artifact schemas, the schema information of R needs to be *complete*: each column has to have *type*, each table needs a *primary key* and functional dependencies between tables need to be documented as *foreign key* relations. However in reality, schema information in ERP system databases is often incomplete [15, 16]; typically due to data dependencies created at the application layer that are not documented in R. Thus, *schema extraction* techniques may be required to reconstruct the database schema. Various techniques exist to group columns into a number of attributes with the same domain [3, 22], to rediscover primary keys of a table [2] and to rediscover foreign keys between tables [4, 13, 21]. A particular focus has to be put on identifying *timestamp* attributes of R as these document events of the process. A detailed comparison is given in [14].

The result of schema extraction is a relational schema $S = (T, F, D, dom)$ of the database with a set T of table schemas and a set F of foreign keys. Each table schema $T = (C_T, C_p) \in T$ contains a set C_T of columns and a primary key $C_p \subseteq C_T$; let C denote all columns of S. Each $F = (T_p, C_p, T_c, C_c) \in F$ is a foreign key from parent table T_p with primary key C_p to child table T_c with referencing columns C_c. Function $dom : C \to D$ assigns each column a domain from the set D of domains.

Note that schema extraction techniques discover data dependencies of the application that are not documented in the database [15, 16]. For instance when a column C in R is used as a unique index by the application, but not declared as primary key in R, schema extraction will identify C as primary key. Correspondingly, undocumented foreign key relations (used in the application, but not declared as such) are identified.

3.2 Discovering Artifact Schemas

Database R and its schema S contain all process data as a whole. The idea of artifacts is to decompose this data into the business objects, or *artifacts*, of the process. Each artifact instance has a unique identifier and follows a *life-cycle* describing how attributes of the artifact change as the process evolves. An *artifact schema* describes the data model of an artifact in terms of R. Technically, an artifact schema $A = (T, F, D, dom, T^m)$ is a relational schema (T, F, D, dom) that distinguishes a main table $T^m \in T$ of the artifact, the primary key of the main table is the identifier of the artifact. All other tables in A define additional attributes of the artifact.

In principle, one could identify artifact schemas from S through interviews [12]. In the following, we identify artifact schemas $A_1, \ldots, A_k$ from S *automatically* through *clustering*. The idea is that business objects (and in particular their identifiers) materialize in R as somehow "important" tables. Attributes of these artifacts are materialized in "auxiliary" tables related to the "important" tables, thus, the tables that constitute an artifact form a cluster of corresponding tables. Such clusters of tables can be identified using standard *schema summarization techniques* [19, 20].

Schema summarization first defines a *distance* between any two tables in S (based on the actual records in the tables of R). The distance function between tables incorporate two factors: importance and foreign key relations.

1. Importance of a table is defined by its entropy (the more unique records a table has, the more important it is). The higher the importance of two tables is, the farther they are away (each important table defines a business object, two business objects should be represented separately).
2. Foreign key relations between tables associate auxiliary tables to important tables. Here, a child table is closer to a parent table if there are more records in the parent table relating to the child table. Various definitions are possible [14].

The concrete definition of the distance function between two tables based on their records is omitted here for space limitations, see [14] for details. Based on this distance function the tables of S are clustered into k clusters (for a user-chosen number k) using *weighted k-means clustering*. In the clusters, all tables of one cluster are closer to each other than to any table in another cluster. Experience has shown that in each cluster, a unique *main table* T^m with the least distance to all other tables in the cluster exists [19, 20]. Thus, the clustering returns a set $\{A_1, ..., A_k\}$ of artifact schemas which solves the first problem: to automatically discover artifact schemas from a structured datasource.

The parameter k determines how many artifacts shall be returned. If k is chosen wrongly, say $k = 1$, the artifacts will have an unnatural shape. We found an iterative approach of gradually increasing k until the rightly shaped artifacts appear, to be feasible. Finding the right number k based on R alone might require domain knowledge or more sophisticated technique, which we consider as further work.

4   Extracting Logs and Discovering Life-Cycles

Having discovered artifact schemas $A_1, ..., A_k$ from R, the next step is to extract for each artifact A_i a log L_i describing the life-cycle of A_i. The artifact schema A_i contains all structural information of this artifact, including timestamp attributes that record when an instance of A_i changed its state. The actual information is stored in R and has to be extracted.

For this we define a *schema-log mapping* that defines (1) a set of *event types* identified in A_i, and (2) a mapping from the attributes and tables of A_i to these event types. This mapping can then be used to construct database queries which extract the actual events from R. In the following, we first present a *automatic* approach to *discover* a schema-log mapping from A_i, and then discuss the log extraction based on this mapping.

4.1 Automatically Discovering a Schema-Log Mapping

Schema-to-log mappings can be identified automatically by a four-step approach based on timestamps and foreign key relations, which are available by the techniques of Sect. 3. The first step of the approach is to identify event (type) columns based on their domain: Exactly one event should be created for each value in one of these columns. The remaining columns are then assigned as attributes to either the artifact instances or to one or more event types. The event type and attribute information is used to create event mappings. Finally these event mappings and artifact instance attribute information are combined to create a trace mapping. The result of the algorithm is an event log trace mapping $TM = (C_{\text{TID}}, T_{\text{from}}, F_{link}, EM, AM_{\text{T}}, LA_{\text{T}})$ with:

- columns C_{TID} identify the different traces,
- main table T_{from}, links to other tables of the artifact in the form of foreign keys F_{link},
- a set of event mappings EM, a set of attribute mappings AM_{T} of the trace, and set of list attributes LA_{T} of the trace.

Each event mapping $EM = (event\_comlumn\_name, C_{\text{EID}}, C_e, T_{\text{from}}, F_{\text{link}}, AM_{\text{E}}, LA_{\text{E}}) \in EM$ defines one event type of the artifact with:

- event $event\_column\_name$,
- columns C_{EID} defining the eventID,
- event column C_e defining the time stamp of the event,
- main table T_{from}, links to other tables in the form of foreign keys F_{link}, and
- attribute mappings AM_{E} and list attributes LA_{E} of the event type.

A list attribute (of a trace or of an event) is an attribute with multiple values and defined by the list attribute mapping $LA = (key, C_{\text{AID}}, T_{\text{from}}, F_{fink}, AM_{\text{L}}, LA_{\text{L}})$ with:

- the given key,
- attributeID columns C_{AID},
- main table T_{from}, links to other tables in the form of foreign keys F_{link}, and
- attribute mappings AM_{L} and list attributes LA_{L}.

Finally each attribute mapping defines an attribute with a single value, i.e., $AM = (name, type, C_a) \in AM$ has a given $name, type$ and attribute column C_a. Note that a list attribute can recursively contain further list attributes.

Algorithm 1 shows the CREATETRACEMAPPING algorithm which creates a mapping from a schema to an event log. First all event types in the artifact schema are identified automatically (line 1). Then columns are assigned as attributes to traces (lines 2 to 4) and events (lines 7 and 8). Next mappings are created for event types (lines 9 and 10) and the trace (lines 13 and 14) using the CREATEMAPPING algorithm shown in

---

Algorithm 1. CreateTraceMapping(S)

Require: An artifact schema $S = (T, F, D, dom, T^m)$
1: $ET \leftarrow IdentifyEventTypes(S)$
2: $T_{instance} \leftarrow \{T^m\} \cup AllParents(\{T^m\}, S)$
3: $T_{instance} \leftarrow T_{instance} \cup SelectInstanceChildTables(T^m, T_{instance}, S)$
4: $C_A \leftarrow GetNonEventColumns(T_{instance})$
5: $EM \leftarrow \emptyset$
6: **for all** $ET = (T_{ET}, C_e) \in ET$ **do**
7:     $T_{event} \leftarrow \{T_{ET}\} \cup SelectEventAttributeTables(T_{ET}, \{T_{ET}\} \cup T_{instance}, S)$
8:     $C_a \leftarrow GetNonEventColumns(T_{event} \setminus T_{instance})$
9:     $(C_{EID}, T_{from}, F_{link}, AM_E, LA_E) \leftarrow CreateMapping(T^m, T_{ET}, T_{event}, C_a, S)$
10:     $EM \leftarrow (event\_column\_name, C_{EID}, C_e, T_{from}, F_{link}, AM_E, LA_E)$
11:     $EM \leftarrow EM \cup \{EM\}$
12: **end for**
13: $(C_{TID}, T_{from}, F_{link}, AM_T, LA_T) \leftarrow CreateMapping(T^m, T^m, T_{instance}, C_A, S)$
14: $TM \leftarrow (C_{TID}, T_{from}, F_{link}, EM, AM_T, LA_T)$
15: **return** A TraceMapping TM for the artifact

Algorithm 2. The steps in the algorithms are briefly described below. Further details of the algorithms can be found in [14].

Event types are identified by selecting all columns with a timestamp domain as event columns, except for columns that are part of a parent table of the main table. The latter columns are excluded since they are identical for several instances and therefore less likely to be events. For each event column an event type ET is constructed with event

---

Algorithm 2. CreateMapping($T^m, T_0, T_{attr}, C_{attr}, S$)

Require: A main artifact table T^m, base table T_0 (with primary key C_{ID}), a set of attribute tables T_{attr}, a set of attribute columns C_{attr} and an artifact schema S
1: $T_{from} \leftarrow T^m$
2: $F_{link} \leftarrow Path(T^m, T_0)$
3: $AM \leftarrow \emptyset$
4: $LA \leftarrow \emptyset$
5: $(T_{one2one}, T_{one2many}) \leftarrow SplitOneAndMany(T_0, S)$
6: **for all** $T \in (T_{one2one} \cap T_{attr}) \cup \{T_0\}$ **do**
7:     $F_{link} \leftarrow F_{link} \cup Path(T_0, T)$
8:     **for all** $C \in C_T \cap C_{attr}$ **do**
9:         $AM \leftarrow CreateAttributeMapping(C)$
10:         $AM \leftarrow AM \cup \{AM\}$
11:     **end for**
12: **end for**
13: $T_{attr} \leftarrow T_{attr} \setminus T_{one2one}$
14: **for all** $T \in T_{one2many}$ **do**
15:     **if** $T \in T_{attr} \vee (T_{attr} \cap AllChildren(T, S)) \neq \emptyset$ **then**
16:         $LA \leftarrow CreateMapping(T^m, T, T_{attr}, C_{attr}, S)$
17:         $LA \leftarrow LA \cup \{LA\}$
18:     **end if**
19: **end for**
20: **return** general mapping item ($C_{ID}, T_{from}, F_{link}, AM, LA$)

table T_{ET}, event column C_e and an initially empty set of event attribute columns C_a. T_{ET} is the table that contains C_e.

All columns that are not considered to be events are considered to be attributes. These attribute columns are assigned to the most specific event possible or as instance attributes if it is not possible to assign them to a specific event. For example: If an attribute column is part of a table without event columns, then it will be assigned to event columns in the parent table (assuming they exist). If there are event columns in the same table, the attribute columns will be assigned to those event columns. The assignment is done based on the table that contains the column as following.

Columns in the set of artifact instance tables T_{instance} are assigned as instance attributes. The set of artifact instance tables consists of the main artifact table, all of its parents and all children that do not have another parent table with event columns (the instance child tables).

For each event type, all columns in the corresponding set of event attribute tables T_{event} are assigned as event attributes. For event columns in the main artifact table there are no separate event attributes, thus then the set is empty. Otherwise the set consists of (1) the event table T_{ET}, (2) all child tables for which there is a foreign key path from the event table to the child table that does not contain another event table and (3) all parent tables of the child tables that are not part of the set of instance tables T_{instance} and do not have another event table as one of their parents. Note that the second subset may contain tables that are also assigned to other event types.

The *CreateMapping* algorithm creates a tuple $(C_{\mathrm{ID}}, T_{\mathrm{from}}, F_{\mathrm{link}}, AM, LA)$ called a "general mapping item" that serves as the basis for a trace mapping, event mapping or list attribute mapping. The basic idea is that each created mapping consists of a set of tables for which only one record exists for each record in the chosen base table T_0, thus ensuring that multiple values do not occur. The algorithm starts by splitting the given attribute tables T_{attr} into a set for which this condition holds T_{one2one} and a set of attribute tables for which this condition does not hold T_{one2many} as explained below. One mapping is then created for the base table and all tables in T_{one2one}. This mapping contains a number of submappings (the list attributes LA) as required for the tables in T_{one2many}. Note that to create an event mapping the event column C_e and an event name are added to the resulting general mapping item (as shown on line 10 of Algorithm 1), and to create a trace mapping the set of event mappings EM is added (as shown on line 14 of Algorithm 1).

The split of tables into the T_{one2one} and T_{one2many} sets is done by recursively verifying foreign keys in the child direction and the parent direction. In the parent direction there will always be only one record for each record in the base table. In the child direction it has to be checked if more records exist in the child table for each record in the base table. A repeated part of the algorithm is the path between two tables which consists of the sequence of foreign keys connecting those tables; it can be calculated using e.g. Dijkstra's algorithm [8].

4.2   Extracting Logs and Discovering Life-Cycles

Extracting logs. The extracted event log-trace mapping TM defines for a given artifact schema S how to shape the event information contained in the database R into events (with attributes), and how to group events into different traces (distinguished by their trace ids and having further attributes). This information is sufficient to automatically extract a classical log (sequences of events) from R. For the extraction, we employ (and slightly adapt) the log extraction technique of XESame [18]. XESame is a technique and tool that extracts classical logs in XES format from a database in 4 steps: (1) specify an event-log to trace mapping, (2) construct database queries to extract data, (3) execute the queries to populate a cache database and (4) create a XES event log from the cache database.

The first step in XESame is manual: the user manually specifies an event log-trace mapping based on the given database tables, columns and keys. Algorithm 1 does the same, but fully automatically. Thus, by handing the event log-trace mapping to the second step of XESame, XESame automatically generates the database queries needed to extract the log. Technically, XESame then extracts for each given event mapping an event and finally groups events to traces based on the trace mapping.

The events of an event mapping $(name, C_{\mathrm{EID}}, C_e, T_{\mathrm{from}}, F_{\mathrm{link}}, AM_{\mathrm{E}}, LA_{\mathrm{E}}) \in EM$ are extracted by first joining the tables containing the time stamp attribute C_e and the event id attribute C_{EID} with the main table T_{from} (this may require to include further tables in the join based on the foreign key relations in F_{link}). Each record in the joined table defines an event with the given name, that occurred at the time-stamp written in column C_e. Note that the joined table also contains the trace id columns C_{TID} of T_{from}, thus associating each event with exactly one trace. Attributes of this event are obtained from AM_{E} and LA_{E} in a similar way by joining the table containing C_{EID} with the tables of the id columns of the respective attribute.

All events of all traces are extracted in this way, then grouped by the values on the trace id columns C_{TID} of T_{from}, and finally ordered by their time-stamp attribute values. Each group defines a trace which gets additional attributes; again by joining the main table T_{from} with the attribute identifying tables as specified in the attribute and list attribute mappings. The resulting traces of events are written in XES format. We slightly adopted the approach of [18] for our purposes by defining explicit event ids and attribute ids in the schema-log mapping; details can be found in [14].

Discovering artifact life-cycles. This technique allows to extract logs $L_1, \ldots, L_k$ for artifacts $A_1, \ldots, A_k$ from R. This effectively reduces the problem of discovering artifact life-cycles in R to the problem of discovering a process model from each log $L_1, \ldots, L_k$. For this problem a large number of existing process discovery algorithms can be applied [1, 17].

5   Empirical Evaluation

The approach described in the previous sections was evaluated using a prototype implementation. We evaluated the technique on an artificial data-set R_A of an order-to-cash process, and on a real-life dataset R_R obtained from the production ERP system of a large food wholesale and retail company. R_R comprised > 300 tables containing > 40GiB of data. Details on the datasets and the prototype implementation can be found in [14].

The reallife dataset showed that different steps in our approach are differently hard to solve. During schema extraction, finding attribute types required >15hrs to discover all

Table 1. Results on schema-logmapping

	$|T|$	$|C|$	$|ET|$	$|LA|$	$|AM|$	time
A1	3	10	0	0	5	<0.5 s
A2	6	23	9	2	8	<0.5 s
A3	10	35	11	3	13	<0.5 s
R1	1	195	23	0	171	<0.1 s
R2	47	869	127	0	841	1.4 s

Fig. 2. Discovered life-cycle of R2

timestamped attribute types. Key discovery is an $\mathcal{NP}$-complete problem; we observed runtimes of 4.5hrs to find all primary keys in the reallife dataset. Foreign key discovery took 5hrs to find all single column foreign keys and 6days to find all double column foreign keys. Finally, artifact schema discovery required approx. 17hrs to compute table entropies and approx. 5hrs to compute table distances for clustering; clustering itself succeeded in less than a second. This allows to try various numbers k of clusters to identify without computational penalty. See [14] for details.

For R_A we could identify 3 reasonable artifacts (A1-A3). For R_R analysis of the right number of artifacts was more involved. In an iterative approach, we could identify around 20 different artifacts. The largest one comprised 47 tables over 869 columns see Tab. 1 which shows the numbers for A1-A3 and two artifacts R1 and R2 of R_R. We then discovered schema-log mappings using the technique of Sect. 4 requiring less then 2 seconds in all cases. Artifacts A2 and A3 follow a life-cycle whereas A1 has no event associated; a closer analysis revealed that A1 is a static data object that relates instances of A2 to instances of A3. For R1 and R2 we identified 23 and 127 event types and 171 and 841 attributes, respectively.

Log extraction with XESame took more time as the entire dataset has to be processed. For artifacts A1-A3 logs of 100-200 traces and approx. 10 events per trace could be extracted within a few seconds; for R1 and R2 extraction required several hours where serializing logs files takes the lion share of the time. For validation, we sampled the data

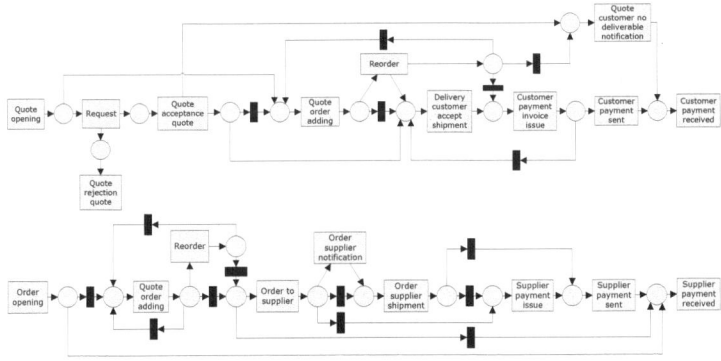

Fig. 3. Discovered life-cycle models of A2 and A3 of an order-to-cash process

source of R2 to 1000 traces of >246,000 events which required approx. 1hr to execute the query and approx. 32hrs to write the log file.

Using the Heuristics Miner [1] we obtained the life-cycle model of R2 shown in Fig. 2. Despite its complex structure it was validated as correct by the process owner. For A2 and A3 we had expected lifecycle models available; to validate precision of our technique we checked fitness of the expected models of A2 and A3 to the extracted logs (i.e., whether the models can replay the log) [1], and obtained high fitness values of 0.99 and 0.95. The lifecycle models discovered from these logs using a genetic miner [1] are shown in Fig. 3. Note that both life-cycle models share some activities, for instance *reorder*, indicating that instances of these artifacts synchronize occasionally through a process execution on the same event.

6   Conclusion

This paper addressed the problem of automatically discovering a process model of a data-centric process. Such processes lack a unique notion of a case, but rather provide multiple notions of cases related to the business objects of the process. Following the artifact-centric approach [7], we provided a technique to automatically extract artifact schemas $A_1, \ldots, A_k$ and corresponding artifact life-cycle logs $L_1, \ldots, L_k$ which describe how each of the artifacts evolved during past process executions. From these logs life-cycle models can be discovered with classical techniques.

Our approach is conceptually similar to the manual interviewing approach of [12] by first identifying objects and then processes. However, our approach is fully automatic up to picking the number k of artifacts to be discovered. The complete approach combines a number of non-trivial, existing techniques for schema discovery, schema summarization, log extraction, and life-cycle discovery. Technically, we contributed a new and first automatic discovery of schema-log mapping needed for log extraction. Our technique is general as it has no restrictions on the input apart from it being a relational database in which an event's timestamp is recorded in a separate database column. This assumption is backed by practice: most ERP systems such as SAP and PeopleSoft record events in that form. The approach is implemented in a prototype tool and was validated on actual data from an ERP production system of a large retailer.

However, some open problems remain. Currently, the user has to pick the number k of artifacts to be discovered. While an iterative approach to find the right k yielding the "right" artifacts has proven feasible, a more automatic approach to identify the relevant artifacts of the process is needed. Generally, it could be desirable to include domain information when discovering artifact schemas. The same remark applies for discovering the schema-log mapping. The identified definition of event types and their attributes could improve in quality if domain knowledge is included or the mapping is manually refined afterwards. Finally, our technique currently focuses on discovering artifact life-cycles, but ignores artifact interactions as they are documented by object relations in the original data source; more research is required here.

Acknowledgements. The research leading to these results has received funding from the European Community's Seventh Framework Programme FP7/2007-2013 under grant agreement no. 257593 (ACSI).

References

1. van der Aalst, W.M.P.: Process Mining: Discovery, Conformance and Enhancement of Business Processes. Springer (2011)
2. Abedjan, Z., Naumann, F.: Advancing the Discovery of Unique Column Combinations. In: CIKM 2011, pp. 1565–1570. ACM (2011)
3. Ahmadi, B., Hadjieleftheriou, M., Seidl, T., Srivastava, D., Venkatasubramanian, S.: Type-Based Categorization of Relational Attributes. In: EDBT 2009, pp. 84–95. ACM (2009)
4. Bauckmann, J., Leser, U., Naumann, F., Tietz, V.: Efficiently Detecting Inclusion Dependencies, pp. 1448–1450. IEEE (April 2007)
5. Bhattacharya, K., Guttman, R., Lyman, K., Heath, I.I.I., Kumaran, S., Nandi, P., Wu, F., Athma, P., Freiberg, C., Johannsen, L., et al.: A model-driven approach to industrializing discovery processes in pharmaceutical research. IBM Systems Journal 44(1), 145–162 (2005)
6. Bozkaya, M., Gabriels, J., Werf, J.: Process Diagnostics: A Method Based on Process Mining, pp. 22–27. IEEE (February 2009)
7. Cohn, D., Hull, R.: Business artifacts: A data-centric approach to modeling business operations and processes. IEEE Data Eng. Bull. 32(3), 3–9 (2009)
8. Dijkstra, E.W.: A note on two problems in connexion with graphs. Numerische Mathematik 1(1), 269–271 (1959)
9. Dumas, M.: On the Convergence of Data and Process Engineering. In: Eder, J., Bielikova, M., Tjoa, A.M. (eds.) ADBIS 2011. LNCS, vol. 6909, pp. 19–26. Springer, Heidelberg (2011)
10. Heath, T.: Siena: a tool for modeling and executing artifact-centric business processes (December 2009)
11. Ingvaldsen, J.E., Gulla, J.A.: Preprocessing Support for Large Scale Process Mining of SAP Transactions. In: ter Hofstede, A.H.M., Benatallah, B., Paik, H.-Y. (eds.) BPM 2007 Workshops. LNCS, vol. 4928, pp. 30–41. Springer, Heidelberg (2008)
12. Liu, R., Bhattacharya, K., Wu, F.Y.: Modeling Business Contexture and Behavior Using Business Artifacts. In: Krogstie, J., Opdahl, A.L., Sindre, G. (eds.) CAiSE 2007. LNCS, vol. 4495, pp. 324–339. Springer, Heidelberg (2007)
13. Marchi, F.D., Lopes, S., Petit, J.M.: Unary and n-ary inclusion dependency discovery in relational databases. J. Intell. Inf. Syst. 32(1), 53–73 (2009)
14. Nooijen, E.: Artifact-Centric Process Analysis: Process Discovery in ERP Systems (April 2012)
15. Piessens, D.: Event Log Extraction from SAP ECC 6.0 (April 2011)
16. Ramesh, A.: Process mining in PeopleSoft (2006)
17. Tiwari, A., Turner, C., Majeed, B.: A review of business process mining: State-of-the-art and future trends. Business Process Management Journal 14(1), 5–22 (2008)
18. Verbeek, H.M.W., Buijs, J.C.A.M., van Dongen, B.F., van der Aalst, W.M.P.: XES, XESame, and ProM 6. In: Soffer, P., Proper, E. (eds.) CAiSE Forum 2010. LNBIP, vol. 72, pp. 60–75. Springer, Heidelberg (2011)
19. Wu, W., Reinwald, B., Sismanis, Y., Manjrekar, R.: Discovering Topical Structures of Databases. In: SIGMOD 2008, pp. 1019–1030. ACM (2008)
20. Yang, X., Procopiuc, C.M., Srivastava, D.: Summarizing relational databases. Proc. VLDB Endow. 2, 634–645 (2009)
21. Zhang, M., Hadjieleftheriou, M., Ooi, B.C., Procopiuc, C.M., Srivastava, D.: On multi-column foreign key discovery. Proc. VLDB Endow. 3, 805–814 (2010)
22. Zhang, M., Hadjieleftheriou, M., Ooi, B.C., Procopiuc, C.M., Srivastava, D.: Automatic discovery of attributes in relational databases. In: SIGMOD 2011, pp. 109–120. ACM (2011)

Schema Evolution in Object and Process-Aware Information Systems: Issues and Challenges

Carolina Ming Chiao, Vera Künzle, and Manfred Reichert

Institute of Databases and Information Systems, Ulm University, Germany
{carolina.chiao,vera.kuenzle,manfred.reichert}@uni-ulm.de

Abstract. Enabling process flexibility is crucial for any process-aware information system (PAIS). In particular, implemented processes may have to be frequently adapted to accommodate to changing environments and evolving needs. When evolving a PAIS, corresponding process schemas have to be changed in a controlled manner. In the context of object-aware processes, which are characterized by a tight integration of process and data, PAIS evolution not only requires process schema evolution, but the evolution of data and user authorization schemas as well. Since the different schemas of an object-aware PAIS are tightly integrated, modifying one of them usually requires concomitant changes of the other schemas. This paper presents a framework for object-aware process support and discusses major requirements and challenges for enabling schema evolution in object-aware PAIS.

1 Introduction

Contemporary PAISs are usually *activity-driven*; i.e., processes are modeled in terms of "black-box" activities and their control flow, defining the order and constraints for executing these activities. Business data, in turn, is treated as a second-class citizen [4,1] and is usually stored in external databases. Hence, activity-centric PAISs are unable to provide immediate access to process-related information at any point of time. Moreover, many PAIS limitations (e.g., application data only being accessible in the context of an activity) can be traced back to the missing integration of process and data [5,6,7,8]. To address these drawbacks, we have developed the PHILharmonicFlows framework, which allows for the operational support of *object-aware* processes at two levels of granularity: *object behavior* and *object interaction* [7,9]. In addition, data-driven process execution as well as integrated access to process and application data become possible. One aspect neglected so far PHILharmonicFlows concerns the evolution of object-aware processes and their components (i.e., the schemas defining object behavior and interactions, data structures, and user authorization). In this context, one does not only have to deal with changes of process schemas (including their propagation to running instances), but of other components of the object-aware PAIS as well (e.g., changes of the data model might affect object behavior and object interactions). Generally, when evolving one particular component of an object-aware PAIS, this might necessitate changes of dependent

M. La Rosa and P. Soffer (Eds.): BPM 2012 Workshops, LNBIP 132, pp. 328–339, 2013.
© Springer-Verlag Berlin Heidelberg 2013

components as well (with potentially cascading effects). This paper discusses some of the fundamental challenges to be tackled when targeting at schema evolution in object-aware PAISs. These challenges were derived from case studies as well as a comprehensive literature study.

Section 2 gives an overview of the PHILharmonicFlows framework. The challenges emerging in the context of schema evolution in an object-aware PAIS are presented in Section 3. Section 4 discusses related work, and Section 5 concludes the paper.

2 Object-Aware Process Support

We first present a simple process scenario along which we introduce basic concepts related to object-aware processes. This scenario deals with proposing extension courses at a university; i.e., courses for professionals that aim at refreshing and updating their knowledge in a certain area of expertise. To propose an extension course, the course coordinator must create a project describing it. The latter must be approved by the faculty coordinator as well as the extension course committee.

Example 1 (Extension course proposal): The course coordinator creates an extension course project using a form. In this context, he must provide details about the course, like name, start date, duration, and description. Following this, professors may start creating the lectures for the extension course. Each lecture, in turn, must have detailed study plan items, which describe the activities of the lecture. To each lecture, (external) invited speakers may be assigned. The latter either may accept or reject the invitation.
After receiving the responses for these invitations and creating the lectures, the coordinator may request an approval for the extension course project. First, it must be approved by the faculty director. If he wants to reject it, he must provide a reason for his decision and the course must not take place. Otherwise, the project is sent to the extension course committee, which will evaluate it. If there are more rejections than approvals, the extension course project is rejected. Otherwise, it is approved and hence may take place.

Our PHILharmonicFlows framework allows for the comprehensive support of such scenarios. In particular, it overcomes many limitations of existing PAISs by enabling a tight integration of process and data [7,8]. The framework supports object-aware processes focusing on the processing of business data and business objects respectively. In this context, *object-awareness* means that the overall process model is structured and divided according to the *object types* involved. These object types are organized in a data model and may refer to other object types or be referenced by them. Moreover, for each object type, a separate process type, defining the corresponding *object behavior*, exists. At runtime, each object type then may comprise a varying number of object instances. Since the creation of an object instance is directly coupled with the creation of a corresponding process instance, a complex *process structure* emerges. Thereby, process instances referring to object instances of the same type are executed asynchronously to each other as well as asynchronously to process instances related to object instances of different types. However, their execution may have to be synchronized at certain points in time. Overall, we differentiate between *micro* and *macro processes* to capture *object behavior* as well as *object interactions*.

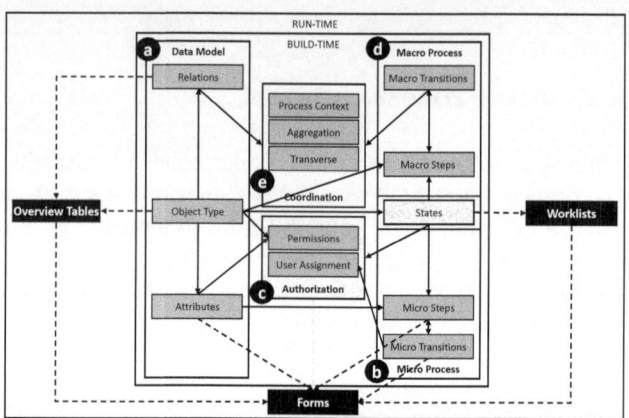

Fig. 1. Overview of the PHILharmonicFlows Framework

Data model (cf. Fig. 1a): A *data model* defines the object types as well as their attributes and relations (including cardinalities).

Example 2 (Data structure): Fig. 2a illustrates the data model relating to Example 1. Object types lecture and decision committee refer to object type extension course project. In turn, object types invitation and study plan item refer to lecture. At run-time, these relations allow for a varying number of interrelated object instances whose processing must be coordinated. Additionally, cardinality constraints restrict the minimum and maximum number of instances of an object type that may reference the same higher-level object instance. Fig. 2b shows a corresponding run-time data structure.

Micro Process Level (cf. Fig. 1b): To express object behavior, for each object type of a data model, a *micro process type* must be defined. At run-time, the creation of an object instance is directly coupled with the creation of a corresponding *micro process instance*. The latter coordinates the processing of the object instance among different users and specifies the order in which object attributes may be written. For this purpose, a micro process type comprises a number of *micro step types* (cf. Fig 1b), of which each refers to one specific object attribute and describes an atomic action for writing it. At run-time, a micro step is reached if a value is set for the corresponding attribute; i.e., a *data-driven execution* is enabled. Further, micro step types may be inter-connected

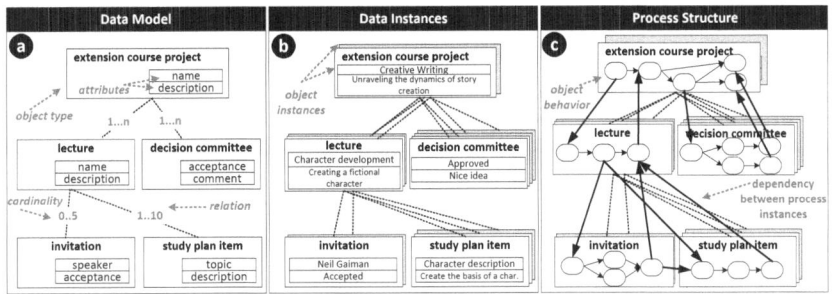

Fig. 2. Data Structure (Data Model and Instances) and Process Structure

using *micro transition types* in order to express their default execution order. When using form-based activities, these transition types define the order in which input fields shall be filled (i.e., the internal logic of forms).

To coordinate the processing of individual object instances among different users, micro step types can be aggregated to *state types*. At the instance level, a state may only be left if the values for all attributes associated with the micro steps of the respective state type are set.

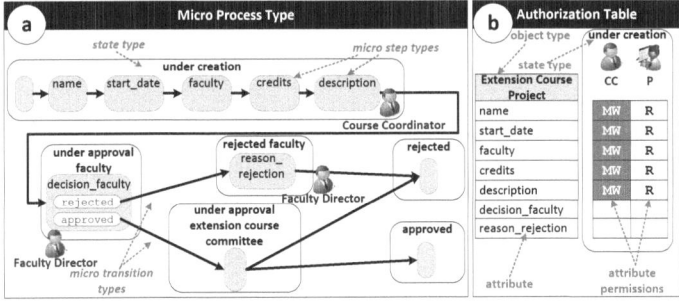

Fig. 3. Micro Process Type and Authorization Table for State "under creation"

Example 3 (Micro process type): Fig. 3a shows the micro process type related to object type `extension course project`. While the extension course project is in state `under creation`, the `course coordinator` may set the attributes to which the corresponding micro step types refer (e.g., `name`, `start_date`, or `description`). Following this, a user decision is made in state `under approval faculty`; i.e., the `faculty director` either approves or rejects the extension course project. If the value of attribute `decision_faculty` corresponds to `rejected`, a value for attribute `reason_rejection` is required.

User authorization (Fig. 1c): User roles are associated with the different states of a micro process type. At run-time, corresponding users must assign required attribute values, as indicated by the micro steps related to the respective state; i.e., a mandatory activity (i.e., a user form) is created and assigned to the user's worklist. To allow for optional activities, for each object type, PHIL-harmonicFlows additionally generates an *authorization table*. More precisely, it allows granting different permissions to user roles for reading and writing attribute values as well as for creating and deleting object instances (cf. Fig. 1d). Furthermore, permissions may vary depending on the state of an object instance. The framework ensures that each user, who must execute a mandatory activity, owns corresponding write permissions; i.e., data and process authorization are compliant with each other. The initially generated authorization table may be further adjusted by assigning optional permissions to other users. In this context, we differentiate between *mandatory* and *optional write* permissions. Attributes, permissions, and the described micro process logic together provide the foundation for automatically generating *user forms* at run-time. In particular, when taking the currently activated state of the micro process instance into account, the authorization table specifies which input fields can be read or written by the respective user in this state. Opposed to existing PAISs, any alteration directly affecting the forms becomes transparent to the end-user; i.e., the forms do not need to be manually updated.

Example 4 (Authorization Table): In Fig. 3b, in state under creation of micro process type extension course project, the course coordinator (CC) has mandatory write (MW) permission for attributes name, start_date, faculty, credits, and description. A professor (P), in turn, has read permission (R) to these attributes in the respective state.

Macro process level (cf. Fig. 1d): At run-time, object instances of the same or different types may be created or deleted at arbitrary points in time; i.e., the data structure dynamically evolves depending on the number of created object instances and the types. In particular, whether subsequent states of micro process instances can be reached may depend on other micro process instances as well; i.e., the processing of an object instance may depend on the processing of a varying number of instances of a related object type. Taking these dependencies among objects into account, a complex *process structure* results (Fig. 2c). To enable proper interaction among the micro process instances, a *coordination* mechanism is required to specify the interaction points of the processes involved. For this purpose, PHILharmonicFlows automatically derives a state-based view for each micro process type. This view is then used for modeling *macro process types* defining the respective *object interactions*. The latter hides most of the complexity of the emerging process structure from users. Each *macro process type* (Fig. 4) consists of *macro step types* and *macro transitions types* connecting them. As opposed to traditional process modeling approaches, where process steps are defined in terms of black-box activities, a macro step type always refers to an object type together with a corresponding state type; i.e., the latter serve as interface between micro and macro process types.

The activation of a particular macro state might depend on instances of different micro process types. To express this, for each macro step type, a respective *macro input type* has to be defined. The latter can be connected to several incoming macro transitions. At run-time, a macro step is enabled if at least one of its macro inputs becomes activated.

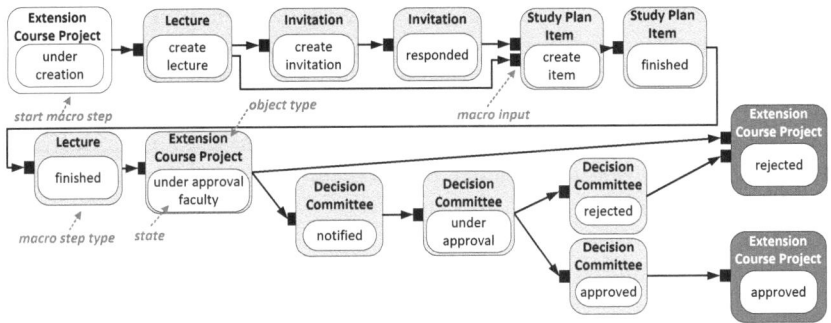

Fig. 4. Example of a Macro Process Type

Coordination (cf. Fig. 1e): To take the dynamically evolving number of object instances as well as the asynchronous execution of corresponding micro process instances into account, for each macro transition, a corresponding *coordination component* needs to be defined. For this purpose, PHILharmonicFlows utilizes object relations from the data model. More details about the coordination components can be found in [7].

3   Challenges

As shown, data structures as well as fine-grained authorization mechanisms are incorporated into the PAIS. Regarding PHILharmonicFlows, not only the schemas of micro and macro process are required to evolve, but the data schemas and authorization settings as well. Another challenge stems from the interdependences among the different components of an object-aware PAIS (i.e., object types, micro process types, macro process type, authorization table, etc.) (cf. Fig. 1). More precisely, changing one of these components might necessitate changes of dependent components. In turn, the latter might trigger cascading changes. This section discusses challenges related to schema evolution in object-aware PAISs. Thereby, both type and instance levels are presented in a single as well as a cross-perspective. In the former perspective, we discuss which requirements are needed to evolve a particular component. The cross-perspective, in turn, focuses on the challenges regarding secondary changes due to the dependencies among components.

3.1 Schema Evolution at Type Level

Evolution in Single Perspective. First, a set of primitive change operations with precise semantics is required for accomplishing changes of each perspective. Such a set must be *complete*, i.e., the change operations comprising this set must allow transforming a valid schema S to any other valid schema S' [15]. Compared to activity-centric PAISs (Fig. 5a), in which a process model comprises activities, events, gateways, and connectors (edges), defining a complete set of change operations for object-aware PAISs causes more efforts due to the vast number of components (Fig. 5b). In particular, we must define change operations for each schema (e.g., data schema, micro process schema, macro process schema, and user authorization) (cf. Fig. 6). Particularly, for each component, at least one operation for *adding* and *deleting* it must be defined. Note that similar concerns hold for other proposals related to data-centric processes (e.g., artifact-centric [4,13] or product-based processes [16]).

Moreover, when applying a change to a schema, schema *correctness* must not be affected; i.e., the changed schema must confirm with a set of correctness constraints. For example, when adding a micro step type in a state type, the latter must not refer to an attribute, if this attribute is already referred by another micro step type having same state type [9].

Example 5 (Change scenario I: add attribute): When the faculty director approves the extension course project, he may add comments on the extension course in question.

Example 5 refers to object type extension course project (cf. Fig. 3b). To be more precise, a new attribute is needed; i.e., the change operation add attribute should be applied. However, this change must be in accordance with the correctness constraints set out by PHILharmonicFlows. For example, the attribute must have a unique name (e.g., approval_remarks). Besides, only adding a new attribute to the object type is not sufficient. To make the attribute accessible

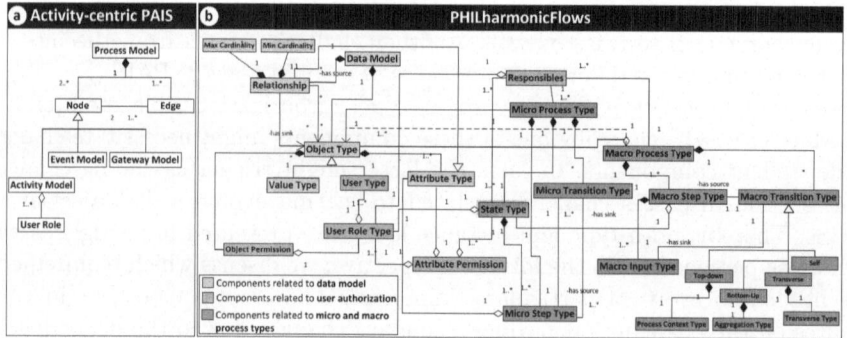

Fig. 5. Metamodel of a) Activity-centric PAIS and b) PHILharmonicFlows

Data Model	Micro Process Type	Macro Process Type	User Authorization
add object type delete object type add attribute delete attribute add relation delete relation	add micro process type delete micro process type add micro step type delete micro step type add micro transition type (...)	add macro step type delete macro step type add macro transition type delete macro transition type (...)	add attribute permission delete attribute permission add object permission delete object permission (...)

Fig. 6. Set of Primitive Change Operations

at run-time, a respective attribute permission must be created as well; e.g., the `faculty director` must obtain an *optional write* permission for this attribute.

Evolution in cross-perspective. As shown in Example 5, focusing only on the component, which is primarily changed, is insufficient. Instead, the change of one component may trigger secondary (i.e., cascading) changes in other components.

Example 6 (Change scenario II: delete attribute): The `start date` of the course will not be specified in the `extension course project` anymore.

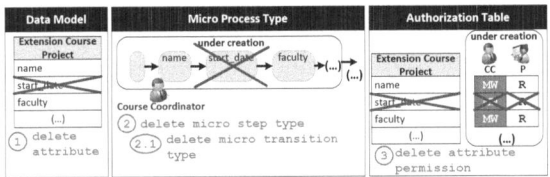

Fig. 7. Change Scenario II - Delete Attribute

In Example 6, operation `delete attribute` is applied to attribute `start_date`. However, to maintain correctness of the data schema, micro and macro process schemas, and user authorization settings, cascading changes are required as well. Fig. 7 illustrates the effects of this attribute deletion. At the micro process type, the micro step type associated with the deleted attribute must be deleted as well. Again, only deleting the micro step type might not be sufficient. In the given example, for instance, the user must be informed about the inconsistency of the micro process type due to the "gap" left between micro step types `name` and `faculty`. In addition, attribute permissions in the authorization table must be deleted as well.

Example 7 (Change scenario III - add object type): When approving the `extension course project` by the `extension course committee`, the members of the committee may ask questions to the `course coordinator`. These questions must be answered, before committee members make their decision.

In Example 7, a new object type `question committee` is added to the data model. Accompanying to this, a micro process type needs to be added as well

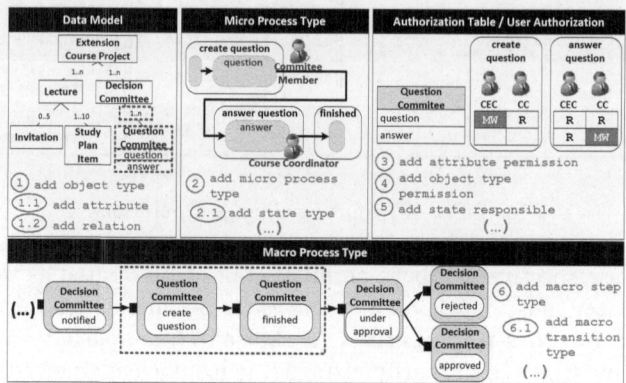

Fig. 8. Change Scenario III - Add Object Type

as respective attributes and user permissions (cf. Fig. 8). In this particular case, new instances of object type `question committee` may only be created when an instance of object type decision committee is initialized; i.e., when the `extension course project` is approved by the `committee` members. Additionally, the micro process instance related to object instance `decision committee` might continue its execution only after finishing all micro process instances of object type `question committee` (i.e., all questions of a committee member are answered). Therefore, new synchronization points must be added to enable the interaction between the two object types; i.e., new macro step types must be created in the macro process type as well. However, the addition of new macro step types is a design choice in the given context; i.e., the engineer may decide to change the macro process type, but this is not essential to maintain correctness of all schemas in the given scenario.

As shown, there are two categories of secondary changes: *mandatory* and *optional* ones. A mandatory secondary change must be applied to maintain correctness of all related schemas. For example, when deleting an attribute, the micro step types referring to it as well as corresponding attribute permissions must be deleted as well. In turn, optional secondary changes refer to design choices made by the user when changing a schema. Hence, mechanisms identifying the impact caused by any schema change become necessary. In particular, these must identify and inform the user about required (i.e., mandatory) secondary changes. To modify the schemas in a controlled manner, an input from the user confirming the schema modification is needed. Therefore, an interface assisting the user with decision making is required. In addition, such an interface must assist users by displaying optional secondary changes to them. In Example 7, adding new macro step types contribute on examples of optional secondary changes. In turn, the addition of new macro transition types to connect the macro step types are mandatory secondary changes, once they are necessary to avoid inconsistencies at the macro process type.

3.2   Schema Evolution at Instance Level

Evolution in Single Perspective. When evolving schemas in an object-aware PAIS, we must ensure that no error occurs concerning object instances and corresponding micro and macro process instances. Hence, for each schema (e.g., data schema, micro and macro process schemas, and user authorization settings), different issues arise. For example, when modifying a data schema, the risk of data loss must be taken into account, since missing data might cause several inconsistencies for running processes. For example, when deleting an attribute from an object type, some object instances or micro process instances related to the object type in question may still depend on data related to this attribute, causing inconsistencies at run-time. To avoid respective problems, data relating to the deleted attribute must still be accessible for reading or writing; i.e., even if in the new schema this attribute does not exist, it must be possible that old object and micro process instances refer to a schema where this attribute (and its respective data) still exists. For this, mechanisms for *data schema versioning* must be provided. With them, different versions of the same data schema may co-exist, letting instances that were created before modifying the data schema refer to older schema versions.

A similar problem arises when evolving a micro process schema. If a micro step type or a state type is deleted, there might be inconsistencies in running micro process instances, since they now refer to inexistent micro steps or states. To avoid such inconsistencies, these instances must be able to reach such states or micro steps by referring to the old schema version, but not the new one. However, only maintaining different versions of the schema is not sufficient. The engineer may decide that running micro process instances should be executed according to the new schema, if possible. Therefore, a mechanism permitting the *migration* of micro process instances to the a new schema version is needed. However, not all micro process instances can be migrated to the new schema. For example, when deleting a state type, micro process instances for which this state is currently activated must not migrate to the new version. If micro steps relating to the deleted state were already executed, migrating these micro process instances might create inconsistencies regarding their execution. Hence, precise migration and correctness criteria must be established.

Evolution in Cross-Perspective. As shown in Section 3.1, changing a component triggers a set of secondary changes. These secondary changes must be also taken into account at the instance level. When managing schema versions, for each schema, it becomes necessary that all involved instances (object instances, micro process instances and macro process instances) refer to consistent schema versions; i.e., the different schema versions must not have inconsistencies like micro process instances referring to missing attributes or macro processes referring to missing micro process states. Regarding Example 6, for instance, when object instances refer to a new data schema version, for which attribute start_date no longer exists, the respective micro process instances must refer to that micro process schema version, for which the respective micro step does not exist as well. Otherwise, there will be a schema inconsistency.

4   Related Work

PHILharmonicFlows provides a comprehensive framework for object-aware processes, enabling advanced support for object behavior, object interactions, and data-driven process execution. In [8], we have already shown that traditional approaches (i.e., imperative and declarative process paradigms) do not meet these properties. In literature, a number of approaches enabling data-centric processes are discussed, but they do not consider the aforementioned properties in a comprehensive and integrated way [8,7]. Moreover, although approaches like artifact-based processes [4,13] and product-based workflows [16] provide rich capabilities for process modeling, they do not explicitly take runtime issues into account.

Schema evolution in object-oriented databases (OODB) might trigger consistency problems in respect to external applications as well. Frameworks like ORION [2], OTGen [11], and GemStone [14] provide mechanisms for automated database reorganization. Concerning business process evolution, [17] defines a set of change patterns as well as change support features to adequately cope with business process changes. In [15], a formal framework for comprehensive support of process type and process instance changes is defined.

In the context of data-driven processes, [12] describes strategies for adapting data-driven process structures both at design- and run-time. However, changes in the definition of a single data object type (e.g., adding or deleting object attributes) are not considered. Regarding artifact-centric workflows, an approach focusing on dynamically modifiable workflow models is presented in [18]. However, this approach does not focus on artifact modifications.

5   Outlook

Our overall vision is to develop a mechanism enabling schema evolution in object-aware PAIS; i.e., a generic component enabling evolutionary changes in object-aware processes. However, this is a non-trivial task, since object-aware PAISs not only comprise process schemas, but also data and user authorization schemas. These different schemas are tightly integrated, and modifying one of them might require concomitant changes of other schemas. In this paper, we discussed some of the major challenges to be tackled in order to enable schema evolution in object-aware PAISs at both type and instance level. The main challenge is to cope with concomitant changes of the different schemas; i.e., a schema change of any component might require secondary changes of related schemas to preserve consistency. In future work, we will provide comprehensive solutions to cope with these challenges.

References

1. van der Aalst, W.M.P., Weske, M., Grünbauer, D.: Case Handling: A New Paradigm for Business Process Support. Data & Know. Eng. 53(2), 129–162 (2005)
2. Banerjee, J., Kim, W., Kim, H., Korth, H.F.: Semantics and Implementation of Schema Evolution in Object-oriented Databases. In: Proc. SIGMOD 1987, pp. 331–322 (1987)

3. Casati, F., Ceri, S., Pernici, B., Pozzi, G.: Workflow Evolution. In: Thalheim, B. (ed.) ER 1996. LNCS, vol. 1157, pp. 438–455. Springer, Heidelberg (1996)
4. Cohn, D., Hull, R.: Business Artifacts: A Data-centric Approach to Modeling Business Operations and Processes. IEEE Data Engineering Bull. 32(3), 3–9 (2009)
5. Künzle, V., Reichert, M.: Towards Object-Aware Process Management Systems: Issues, Challenges, Benefits. In: Halpin, T., Krogstie, J., Nurcan, S., Proper, E., Schmidt, R., Soffer, P., Ukor, R. (eds.) BPMDS 2009 and EMMSAD 2009. LNBIP, vol. 29, pp. 197–210. Springer, Heidelberg (2009)
6. Künzle, V., Reichert, M.: Integrating Users in Object-Aware Process Management Systems: Issues and Challenges. In: Rinderle-Ma, S., Sadiq, S., Leymann, F. (eds.) BPM 2009 Workshops. LNBIP, vol. 43, pp. 29–41. Springer, Heidelberg (2010)
7. Künzle, V., Reichert, M.: PHILharmonicFlows: Towards a Framework for Object-aware Process Management. Journal of Software Maintenance and Evolution: Research and Practice 23(4), 205–244 (2011)
8. Künzle, V., Weber, B., Reichert, M.: Object-aware Business Processes: Fundamental Requirements and their Support in Existing Approaches. Int'l Journal of Information System Modeling and Design 2(2), 19–46 (2011)
9. Künzle, V., Reichert, M.: A Modeling Paradigm for Integrating Processes and Data at the Micro Level. In: Halpin, T., Nurcan, S., Krogstie, J., Soffer, P., Proper, E., Schmidt, R., Bider, I. (eds.) BPMDS 2011 and EMMSAD 2011. LNBIP, vol. 81, pp. 201–215. Springer, Heidelberg (2011)
10. Künzle, V., Reichert, M.: Striving for Object-Aware Process Support: How Existing Approaches Fit Together. In: Aberer, K., Damiani, E., Dillon, T. (eds.) SIMPDA 2011. LNBIP, vol. 116, pp. 169–188. Springer, Heidelberg (2012)
11. Lerner, B.S., Habbermann, A.N.: Beyond Schema Evolution to Database Reorganization. In: Proc. OOPSLA/ECOOP 1990, pp. 67–76 (1990)
12. Müller, D., Reichert, M., Herbst, J.: A New Paradigm for the Enactment and Dynamic Adaptation of Data-Driven Process Structures. In: Bellahsène, Z., Léonard, M. (eds.) CAiSE 2008. LNCS, vol. 5074, pp. 48–63. Springer, Heidelberg (2008)
13. Nigam, A., Caswell, N.S.: Business artifacts: An Approach to Operational Specification. IBM Systems Journal 42(3), 428–445 (2003)
14. Penney, D.J., Stein, J.: Class Modification in the GemStone Object-oriented DBMS. In: Proc. OOPSLA 1987, pp. 111–117 (1987)
15. Rinderle, S., Reichert, M., Dadam, P.: Flexible Support of Team Processes by Adaptive Workflow Systems. Distr. and Par. Databases 16(1), 91–116 (2004)
16. Vanderfeesten, I.T.P., Reijers, H.A., van der Aalst, W.M.P.: Product Based Workflow Support: Dynamic Workflow Execution. In: Bellahsène, Z., Léonard, M. (eds.) CAiSE 2008. LNCS, vol. 5074, pp. 571–574. Springer, Heidelberg (2008)
17. Weber, B., Reichert, M., Rinderle-Ma, S.: Change Patterns and Change Support Features - Enhancing Flexibility in Process-Aware Information Systems. Data & Know. Eng. 66(3), 438–466 (2008)
18. Xu, W., Su, J., Yan, Z., Yang, J., Zhang, L.: An Artifact-Centric Approach to Dynamic Modification of Workflow Execution. In: Meersman, R., Dillon, T., Herrero, P., Kumar, A., Reichert, M., Qing, L., Ooi, B.-C., Damiani, E., Schmidt, D.C., White, J., Hauswirth, M., Hitzler, P., Mohania, M. (eds.) OTM 2011, Part I. LNCS, vol. 7044, pp. 256–273. Springer, Heidelberg (2011)

From Petri Nets to Guard-Stage-Milestone Models

Viara Popova and Marlon Dumas

Institute of Computer Science,
University of Tartu, J. Liivi 2,
Tartu 50409, Estonia
{viara.popova,marlon.dumas}@ut.ee

Abstract. Artifact-centric modeling is an approach for modeling business processes based on business artifacts, i.e., entities that are central for the company's operations. Existing process mining methods usually focus on traditional process-centric rather than artifact-centric models. Furthermore, currently no methods exist for discovering models in Guard-Stage-Milestone (GSM) notation from event logs. To bridge this gap, we propose a method for translating Petri Net models into GSM which gives the possibility to use the numerous existing algorithms for mining Petri Nets for discovering the life cycles of single artifacts and then generating GSM models.

Keywords: Artifact-Centric Modeling, Guard-Stage-Milestone, Petri Nets, Process Mining.

1 Introduction

Artifact-centric modeling is a new promising approach for modeling business processes based on the so-called business artifacts [2,9] - key entities driving the company's operations and whose life cycles define the overall business process. An artifact type contains an information model with all data relevant for the entities of that type as well as a life cycle model which specifies how the entity can progress responding to events and undergoing transformations from its creation until it is archived.

Most existing work on business artifacts has focused on the use of life cycle models based on variants of finite state machines. Recently, a new approach was introduced - the Guard-Stage-Milestone (GSM) meta-model [5,6] for artifact life cycles which is more declarative than the finite state machine variants, and supports hierarchy and parallelism within a single artifact instance.

Some of the advantages of GSM [5,6] are in the intuitive nature of the used constructs which reflect the way stakeholders think about their business. Furthermore, its hierarchical structure allows for a high-level, abstract view on the operations while still being executable. It supports a wide range of process types,

M. La Rosa and P. Soffer (Eds.): BPM 2012 Workshops, LNBIP 132, pp. 340–351, 2013.

from the highly prescriptive to the highly descriptive. It also provides a natural, modular structuring for specifying the overall behavior and constraints of a model of business operations in terms of ECA-like rules.

Currently, GSM models are created manually which can require a lot of effort and domain knowledge. The area of Process Mining focuses on developing methods for automatic discovery and analysis of process models such as conformance checking, repair and so on. Most existing methods consider only process-centric models, most often Petri Nets (PN) and no methods have been developed that are applicable to GSM models. In order to bridge the gap, this paper proposes a method for translating PN models to models in GSM. As a result, existing methods can be applied for discovering the life cycles of the separate artifacts which can then be represented as GSM models. Furthermore, manually created PN can be translated to GSM which allows to explore and reuse existing model libraries, case studies and domain knowledge.

The method presented in this paper is implemented as a software plug-in for ProM, a generic open-source framework and architecture for implementing process mining tools in a standard environment [13] which is the *de facto* industry standard in process mining. The implementation is part of the ArtifactModeling package which is available from www.processmining.org.

The paper is organized as follows. Section 2 introduces the case study used for illustration. Section 3 gives a brief overview of the modeling approaches needed for the presentation of the contribution of the paper. Sections 4, 5 and 6 introduce the method for translating PN models to GSM proposed in this paper. Finally, section 7 concludes the paper.

2   Case Study

As a case study we consider a model of an order-to-cash process as follows. The process starts when the manufacturer receives a purchase order from a customer for a product that needs to be manufactured. This product typically requires multiple components or materials which need to be sourced from suppliers. To keep track of this process, the manufacturer first creates the so-called work order which includes multiple line items - one for each required component. Multiple suppliers can supply the same materials thus the manufacturer needs to select suppliers first then place a number of material orders to the selected ones.

Suppliers can accept or reject the orders. If an order is rejected by the supplier then a new supplier is found for these components. If accepted, the order is assembled and delivered and, in parallel, an invoice is sent to the manufacturer. When all material orders for the same purchase order are received, the product is assembled and delivered to the customer and an invoice is sent for it.

The customer can cancel a purchase order. The request for cancellation is forwarded to the suppliers and assessed. If accepted, cancellation fee is determined, otherwise the order is delivered and invoiced in full.

Figure 1 shows one way of modeling the order-to-cash example using Proclet notation as will be described in the next section.

3   Background

We first give the necessary background in order to present the PN to GSM translation method by a very brief introduction to both modeling approaches.

Petri nets [8] are an established tool for modeling and analyzing workflow processes. They have been used in a wide variety of contexts and a great number of the developed process mining techniques assume or generate Petri Nets.

A PN is a directed bipartite graph with two types of nodes called *places* (represented by circles) and *transitions* (represented by rectangles) connected with arcs. Intuitively, the transitions correspond to activities while the places are conditions necessary for the activity to be executed. Transitions which correspond to business-relevant activities observable in the actual execution of the process will be called visible transitions, otherwise they are invisible transitions. A labeled PN is a net with a labeling function that assigns a label (name) for each place and transition. Invisible transitions are assigned a special label τ.

An arc can only connect a place to a transition or a transition to a place. A place p is called a pre-place of a transition t iff there exists a directed arc from p to t. A place p is called a post-place of transition t iff there exists a directed arc from t to p. Similarly we define a pre-transition and a post-transition to a place.

At any time a place contains zero of more tokens. The current state of the PN is the distribution of tokens over the places of the net. A transition t is enabled iff each pre-place p of t contains at least one token. An enabled transition may fire. If transition t fires, then t consumes one token from each pre-place p of t and produces one token in each post-place p of t.

In order to use the PN notation for modeling artifact-centric systems, we need a generalization of PN which reflects the artifact structure and interactions. For this, **Proclets** [12] can be used as discussed in the following paragraphs.

A *proclet* $P = (N, ports)$ is a labeled PN, which describes the internal life cycle of one artifact, and a set of ports, through which P can communicate with other proclets. Relations between several proclets are described in a *proclet system* $\mathcal{P} = (\{P_1, \ldots, P_n\}, C)$ consisting of a set of proclets $\{P_1, \ldots, P_n\}$ and a set C of *channels*. Each channel $(p, q) \in C$ connects two ports p and q of two proclets of $\mathcal{P}$ which send and receive messages along these channels. The channels also reflects the relations between entity types: annotations at the ports define how many instances of a proclet interact with how many instances of another proclet. Each half-round shape represents a port: the bow indicates the direction of communication. A dashed line between 2 ports denotes a channel of the system. Creation and termination of an artifact instance is expressed by a respective transition, drawn in bold lines.

Fig. 1 shows one way of modeling the order-to-cash example as a proclet system of two proclets that model artifacts PurchaseOrder and MaterialOrder.

Proclets are suitable for describing multi-artifact systems due to the annotations $1, ?, +$ in the ports [12]. The first annotation, called *cardinality*, specifies how many messages one proclet instance sends to (receives from) other instances when the attached transition occurs. The second annotation,

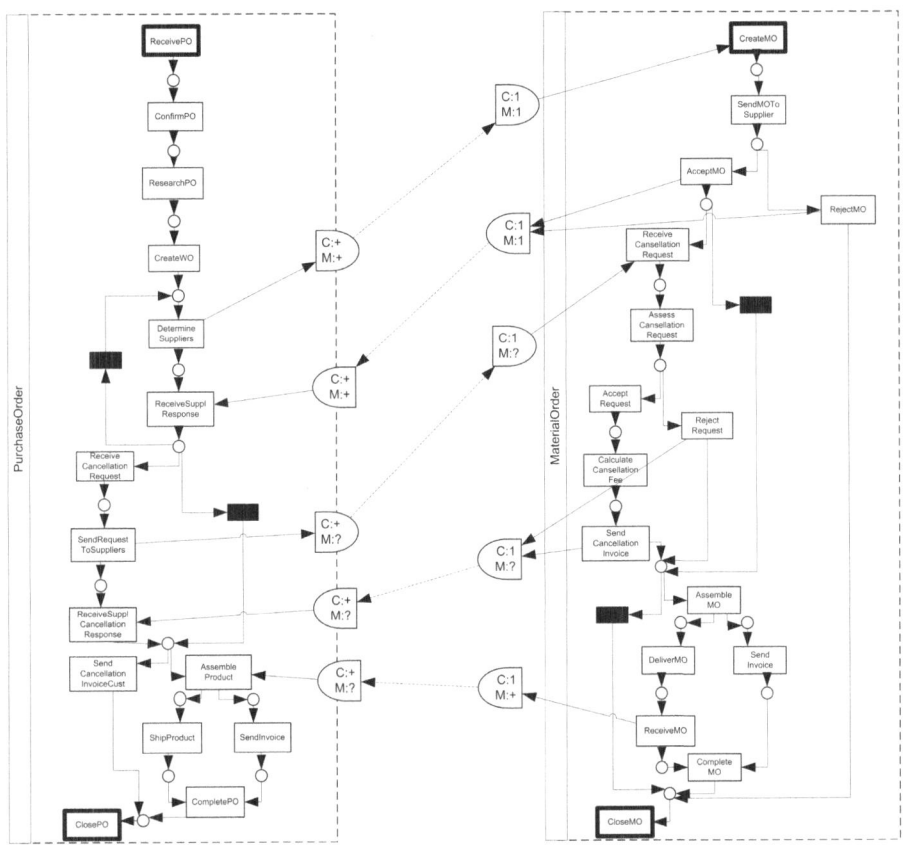

Fig. 1. The Proclet model of the Order-to-Cash example

multiplicity, specifies how often this port is used in the lifetime of a proclet instance. For example, the port of DetermineSuppliers has cardinality + and multiplicity + denoting that a PurchaseOrder instance sends out one or more messages with ordered items to multiple MaterialOrders and this can happen once or multiple times in the lifetime of the PurchaseOrder instance.

In this paper we concentrate on the artifact life cycle rather than the communication between artifacts. Therefore we only consider single proclets which are in fact Petri nets. In the rest of this paper we talk about translating Petri net models to GSM models. All the results are in fact applicable for proclets and thus for single artifact life cycle models.

The **Guard-Stage-Milestone meta-model** [5,6] provides a more declarative approach for modeling artifact life cycles which allows a natural way for representing hierarchy and parallelism within the same instance of an artifact and between instances of different artifacts.

The key GSM elements for representing the artifact life cycle are stages, guards and milestones which are defined as follows.

Milestones correspond to business-relevant operational objectives, and are achieved (and possibly invalidated) based on triggering events and/or conditions over the information models of active artifact instances. Stages correspond to clusters of activity preformed for, with or by an artifact instance intended to achieve one of the milestones belonging to the stage. Guards control when stages are activated, and, as with milestones, are based on triggering events and/or conditions. A stage can have one or more guards and one or more milestones. It becomes active (or open) when a guard becomes true and inactive (or closed) when a milestone becomes true.

Furthermore, sentries are used in guards and milestones, to control when stages open and when milestones are achieved or invalidated. Sentries represent the triggering event type and/or a condition of the guards and milestones. The events may be external or internal, and both the internal events and the conditions may refer to the artifact instance under consideration, and to other artifact instances in the artifact system.

4   Petri Nets to GSM Models - The General Approach

A straightforward approach to translating PNs to GSM models would proceed as follows. The visible transitions of the PN represent activities which are part of the business process. Therefore it is logical to represent them as atomic stages where the activity corresponds to the task associated with the stage. The control flow of the PN can then be encoded using the guards and milestones of these stages.

It is possible to use an explicit representation of the places of the PN using a collection of variables which will be part of the information model of the GSM component. These variables will be assigned true or false simulating the presence or absence of tokens in the places. This will be a relatively intuitive approach for designers skilled in the PN notation. However we argue that this would make the model less intuitive to the user and the relations between the tasks and stages become implicit and not easy to trace. Here we take a different approach which will be discussed in this section at a more general level and in the next sections in more detail.

The intuition behind this approach is that the immediate ordering relations between transitions in the PN are extracted, translated into conditions and combined using appropriate logical operators (for AND- and OR-splits and joins) into sentries which are then assigned to the guards. The milestones are assigned sentries that depend on the execution of the task associated with the stage - a milestone is achieved as soon as the task is executed and is invalidated when the stage is re-opened.

As an example, consider the transition ResearchPO from the order-to-cash model in Fig. 1. It can only be executed after the transition ConfirmPO has been executed and there is a token in the connecting place. This can be represented as a part of a GSM model in the following way. Both transitions are represented by atomic stages. The guard of the stage ResearchPO has a sentry with expression (given here informally) "on ConfirmPOMilestone.achieved()" and will become true when the event of achieving the milestone of stage ConfirmPO occurs. The milestone of stage ResearchPO has a sentry "on ResearchPOTask.executed()" and will become true when the associated task is executed. Similarly the milestone of ConfirmPO has a sentry "on ConfirmPOTask.executed()".

While this example is very straightforward, a number of factors can complicate the sentries. Most importantly, we need to consider the possibility of revisiting a stage multiple times - this can be the case when the corresponding transition in the PN is part of a loop. Furthermore the transition might depend on the execution of multiple pre-transitions together and this cannot be represented using events - conditions need to be used instead. The conditions should express the fact that new executions of the pre-transitions have occurred. This means that the last execution of each relevant pre-transition occurred after the last execution of the transition in focus but also after every "alternative" transition, i.e., transition that is an alternative choice.

For example consider the transition CompletePO in Fig. 1 which can only fire if both ShipProduct and SendInvoice have fired. While this is not part of the model, imagine the hypothetical situation that CompletePO, ShipProduct and SendInvoice were part of a loop and could be executed multiple times. Since a sentry cannot contain multiple events, the guard of CompletePO has to be expressed by conditions instead. The naïve solution "if ShipProductTask.hasBeenExecuted() and SendInvoiceTask.hasBeenExecuted()" which checks if the two tasks have been executed in the past is not correct, since it becomes true the first time the activities ShipProduct and SendInvoice were executed and cannot reflect any new execution after that. We need a different expression to represent that new executions have occurred that have not yet triggered an execution of ConfirmPO. This will be discussed in detail later in the next section.

Another factor that needs to be considered is the presence of invisible transitions, i.e., transitions without associated activity in the real world. For such invisible transitions no stage will be generated. Therefore, in order to compose the guard sentries, only visible pre-transitions should be considered. Thus we need to backtrack in the PN until we reach a visible transition and "collect" the relevant conditions of the branches we traverse. As an example, consider the transition DetermineSuppliers in Fig. 1. It can fire multiple times - at first when CreateWO has been executed and then every time the invisible pre-transition represented by a black rectangle fires. We backtrack to find the pre-places of the invisible transition and their pre-transitions. Here we determine that the only such pre-transition is ReceiveSupplResponse and this branch has an associated condition - we can only take this branch if the supplier rejects an order and a new supplier has to be determined.

With all these considerations in mind, the resulting guard sentry can become more complex and partly lose its advantage of being able to give intuition about how the execution of one task influences the execution of others. In order to solve this problem, we apply methods for decomposing the expression into multiple simpler sentries which are then assigned to separate guards of the same stage. The composition and decomposition of guard sentries will be described more precisely in the next section.

Let t_o be the "origin", i.e., the (visible) transition for which we compose a guard. At a more abstract level the proposed method for generating guard sentries for the stage of t_o proceeds as follows:

Step 1: Find the relevant branch conditions and the pre-transitions whose execution will (help) trigger the execution of t_o.

Step 2: Decompose into groups that can be represented by separate guards.

Step 3: For each group, determine the appropriate format of the sentry and generate its expression.

5   Guard Sentries Generation

Our approach for achieving step 1 is inspired by the research presented in [10] for translating BPMN models and UML activity Diagrams into BPEL. It generates so-called precondition sets for all activities which encode possible ways of enabling an activity. Next, all the precondition sets with their associated activities, are transformed into a set of Event-Condition-Action (ECA) rules.

Before giving the precise definitions of the approach proposed here, we first illustrate the intuition behind it by a couple of examples. Consider the transition CompletePO in Fig. 1. In order for it to be enabled and subsequently fire, there need to be tokens in both of its pre-places. Therefore the precondition for enabling CompletePO is a conjunction of two expressions, each of which related to one pre-place and representing the fact that there is a token in this pre-place. This token could come from exactly one of the pre-transitions of this place. Consider for example the transition AssembleProduct. It has one pre-place which has two pre-transitions. Therefore the precondition here is a disjunction of two expressions each related to the firing of one pre-transition.

Thus the general form of the composed expression is a conjunction of disjunctions of expressions. These expressions, however, can themselves be conjunctions of disjunctions. This happens when a pre-transition is invisible (not observable in reality) and we need to consider recursively its pre-places and pre-transitions. The building blocks of the composed expression are expressions each of which corresponds to the firing of one visible transition t that can (help) trigger the firing of the transition in focus t_o (the "origin"). We denote each of these building blocks by $prcExpression(t, t_o)$ for a transition t with respect to t_o and they will be discussed in the next section.

Furthermore, the presence of a token in a pre-place is not a guarantee that a transition will fire. In the case of AssembleProduct, a token in its pre-place enables two transitions, AssembleProduct and SendCancellationInvoiceCust, but only one will fire. Which one is determined by conditions associated with each outgoing arc of the place. These conditions are domain-specific and, in the following, we assume that these conditions are given - they can be provided by the user or mined from the logs using existing tools such as the decision miner from [11]. Therefore, the general form of the composed expression should have these conditions added to the conjunction.

The following more precise definitions reflect these intuitions on the general form of the expression and its recursive nature. By $prc(t_o)$ we denote the composed expression (of "pre-conditions") of the guard sentry for a stage/transition t_o. Let $IA(t_o)$ be the set of incoming arcs in t_o and let $cond_a$ be a condition associated with the arc a if the connected pre-place is a decision point (i.e., a place with multiple outgoing arcs) or $true$ if it is not a decision point (no condition). Also, $init$ denotes the specific expression of the event of the creation of the artifact instance, e.g. "onCreate()", $PT(a)$ is the set of pre-transitions t_p connected to the pre-place of the arc a.

We can then define $prc(t_o)$ using a recursive definition as follows:

$$prc(t_o) = \bigwedge_{a \in IA(t_o)} P_a \wedge cond_a$$

where P_a is defined as:

$$P_a = \begin{cases} init & \text{if } P_a \text{ is the initial place,} \\ \bigvee_{p \in PT(a)} T_p & \text{otherwise.} \end{cases}$$

T_p, in turn, is defined as follows:

$$T_p = \begin{cases} prcExpression(t_p, t_o) & \text{if } t_p \text{ is a visible transition,} \\ prc(t_p) & \text{if } t_p \text{ is an invisible transition.} \end{cases}$$

Here, as mentioned earlier, $prcExpression(t_p, t_o)$ is the specific expression that will be added to the sentry condition for each relevant visible transition t_p with respect to the "origin" t_o. Their format will be discussed in the next section.

The expression for $prc(t_o)$ can be represented in a tree structure in a straightforward way. The internal nodes of the tree represent logical operators ("and" or "or") with are applied on their child branches. The leaves represent either transitions that need to fire (which will be represented in the guard sentry by an expression $prcExpression(t_p, t_o)$ for the specific transition t_p in the leaf) or decision point conditions that need to be true in order the "origin" transition t_o to be able to fire. In the following we use the words tree and expression interchangeably since, in this context, they represent the same information.

An example of such a tree is given in Figure 2 constructed for the transition AssembleProduct. Looking at the model in Figure 1 we can see that AssembleProduct can only fire if there is a token in its pre-place and the condition associated with the connecting arc is true. We denote this condition here as Condition 1. The token can arrive from two possible transitions - ReceiveSupplCancellationResponse or the invisible transition represented as a black rectangle. We need to traverse back from the invisible transition and find out that it can only fire if the transition ReceiveSupplResponse fires and the condition associated with the connecting arc is true (we denote this condition by

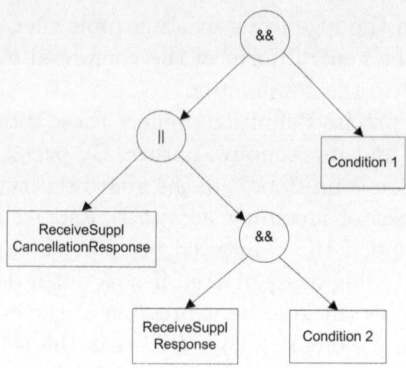

Fig. 2. An example of an expression tree which will be used to generate the guard(s) for stage AssembleProduct

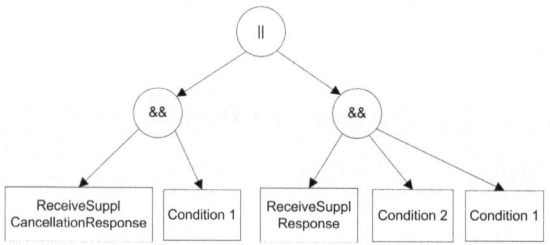

Fig. 3. The expression tree for stage AssembleProduct in DNF

Condition 2). This analysis results in the tree in Figure 2. The leaves of the tree are named by the corresponding transition or condition and, in fact, represent the specific expression for that transition/condition. However we delay the exact formulation of the expressions until the tree is built and analyzed, as will be described in the next section.

As mentioned earlier, an intermediate step of the algorithms decomposes $prc(t_o)$ into several expressions which then are used to generate separate guards of the stage. Since $prc(t_o)$ is a logical formula, we can convert it into Disjunctive Normal Form and assign each conjunction to a separate guard sentry.

After converting the example tree from Figure 2 into DNF, we now have the tree in Figure 3. Each child of the root node will generate one separate guard - here we have two guards. Intuitively the first guard tells us that the stage will open if task ReceiveSupplCancellationResponse was executed and Condition 1 is true. Similarly, the second guard tells us that the stage will open if task ReceiveSupplResponse was executed and both Condition 1 and Condition 2 are true.

As a final step, the $prcExpression(t_p, t_o)$ for the leaves of the tree are assigned as discussed in the next section.

6 Formats for Pre-condition Expressions

In this section we look into the expressions $prcExpression(t_p, t_o)$ in more details and define their format. Their assignment is delayed until the end, after $prc(t_o)$ is composed and, if needed, decomposed into separate sentries. Only then it can be decided which format each expression should take. We consider two possible formats for the expression of $prcExpression(t_p, t_o)$ depending on the context as discussed below.

The most simple case is when $prc(t_o)$ contains only one transition t_p with its expression $prcExpression(t_p, t_o)$ and $init$ is not present in $prc(t_o)$. Then $prcExpression(t_p, t_o)$ can be replaced by the event corresponding to the finished execution of the activity of t_p, we denote this by "on t_p executed". It can be expressed using the event of achieving the milestone of the stage of t_p or, alternatively, the closing of that stage among other options.

For example, for t_o = ReceiveSupplCancellationResponse the expression tree contains only one leaf corresponding to the transition t_p = SendRequestToSuppliers, i.e., the only way to enable t_o is by a token produced by t_p and this token cannot be consumed by another transition. Then the expression for t_p and t_o will be $prc(t_o) = prcExpression(t_p, t_o) =$ "on t_p executed".

If this is not the case, i.e., multiple transitions are present, then a more complex version of the expression needs to be included since we cannot use more than one event in the sentry. This form of the expression is discussed in the following paragraphs.

We introduce the following notation: for transitions t_1 and t_2, $t_1 \xrightarrow{\tau} t_2$ iff there exists a directed path in the graph of the net from t_1 to t_2 containing no visible transitions other than t_1 and t_2.

We now define the following set of "alternative" transitions to t_o, i.e., visible transitions that are connected to a place on the path from t_p to t_o:

$$Alt(t_p, t_o) = \{t \mid \exists \text{ place } p : t_p \xrightarrow{\tau} p \xrightarrow{\tau} t_o \wedge p \xrightarrow{\tau} t\}.$$

$Alt(t_p, t_o)$ are the set of transitions that "compete" with t_o for the token produced by t_p. Therefore in order to represent the situation when a token is present in the pre-place of t_o and the stage t_o should be opened we need to consider whether any of the "alternative" transitions have occurred (and "stolen" the token). Note that, according to this definition, t_o will also belong to the set.

Let us consider again the stage t_o = AssembleProduct and the expression tree in Fig. 3. Here we can use the simple format of the expressions for each leaf since in each branch there is only one transition. However for illustration purposes we assume that more that one transition was present in each branch and we need to use the more complex format for the expressions as follows. For the leaf t_p = ReceiveSupplCancellationResponse, $Alt(t_p, t_o) =$ {SendCancellationInvoiceCust, AssembleProduct}. Looking at Fig. 1, we can see that the transition SendCancellationInvoiceCust is indeed an "alternative" to AssembleProduct in the sense that is can "steal" the token produced by the transition ReceiveSupplCancellationResponse in the connecting place. Similarly, for $t_p = $ ReceiveSupplResponse, $Alt(t_p, t_o) = \{$ReceiveCancellationRequest, SendCancellationInvoiceCust, AssembleProduct$\}$.

Then we define the expression as follows:

$$prcExpression(t_p, t_o) = \bigwedge_{t_s \in Alt(t_p, t_o)} executedAfter(t_p, t_s).$$

Here $executedAfter(t_p, t_s)$ expresses the situation when there is a new execution of t_p which occurs after the last execution of t_s, meaning that it is relevant for triggering the opening of the stage of t_o. How this will be expressed in the specific implementation can vary. Here we show how this can be done using the state of a milestone (achieved or not) and the time a milestone was last toggled. In that case:

$$executedAfter(t_p, t_s) = m_p.achieved \ \wedge \ m_p.lastToggled > m_s.lastToggled.$$

In other words, the milestone m_p of t_p is achieved and it was last toggled after the milestone m_s of t_s. Here we rely on the fact that the milestone of a stage will be invalidated as soon as the stage is reopened. This is ensured by including an invalidating sentry for each milestone.

For example, for $t_o = $ AssembleProduct, $t_p = $ ReceiveSupplCancellationResponse and $t_s = $ SendCancellationInvoiceCust,

$$prcExpression(t_p, t_o) = executedAfter(t_p, t_s) \ \wedge \ executedAfter(t_p, t_o) =$$
$$= m_p.achieved \ \wedge \ m_p.lastToggled > m_s.lastToggled \ \wedge$$
$$\wedge \ m_p.lastToggled > m_o.lastToggled,$$

in other words, ReceiveSupplCancellationResponse was executed after the last execution of SendCancellationInvoiceCust and after the last execution of Assemble Product, i.e., the token in the connecting place has not been consumed yet.

7   Conclusions and Future Work

This paper proposed a method for translating PNs to GSM models which allows to use existing process mining algorithms for discovering PNs from event logs and generating GSM models from them. This contributes significantly to solving the problem of mining artifact-centric models from event logs by generating the life cycles of artifacts.

Additionally, the information model can be built by considering the logs as well and extracting the data attributes for each event type of the artifact. Existing tools such as [11] can be used to mine data-dependent conditions for the guards based on the discovered information model.

Future work will also develop methods that allow to discover the interactions between artifacts and thus multi-artifact GSM models can be generated.

The method in this paper generates a flat model where no hierarchy of stages is used. Future work will also consider methods for stage aggregation. One possible solution is to use existing algorithms for process abstraction (e.g. [1,3]) for business process models and translate the discovered process hierarchy to GSM stage hierarchy. For example the Refined Process Structure Tree [7] can be a first step to discovering such a hierarchy.

Acknowledgment. The research leading to these results has received funding from the European Community's Seventh Framework Programme FP7/2007-2013 under grant agreement no 257593 (ACSI).

References

1. Bose, R.P.J.C., Verbeek, H.M.W., van der Aalst, W.M.P.: Discovering Hierarchical Process Models using ProM. In: Proc. of CAiSE Forum, CEUR Workshop Proc., vol. 734, pp. 33–40 (2011)
2. Cohn, D., Hull, R.: Business artifacts: A data-centric approach to modeling business operations and processes. IEEE Data Eng. Bull. 32, 3–9 (2009)
3. Günther, C., van der Aalst, W.: Mining activity clusters from low-level event logs, BETA Working Paper Series, WP 165, TU/e (2006)
4. Hein, J.L.: Discrete Structures, Logic, and Computability. Jones and Bartlett Publishers (2010)
5. Hull, R., Damaggio, E., Fournier, F., Gupta, M., Heath III, F(T.), Hobson, S., Linehan, M., Maradugu, S., Nigam, A., Sukaviriya, P., Vaculin, R.: Introducing the Guard-Stage-Milestone Approach for Specifying Business Entity Lifecycles. In: Bravetti, M. (ed.) WS-FM 2010. LNCS, vol. 6551, pp. 1–24. Springer, Heidelberg (2011)
6. Hull, R., et al.: Business Artifacts with Guard-Stage-Milestone Lifecycles: Managing Artifact Interactions with Conditions and Events. In: DEBS 2011, pp. 51–62 (2011)
7. Johnson, R., Pearson, D., Pingali, K.: The Program Structure Tree: Computing Control Regions in Linear Time. In: Proc. of the ACM SIGPLAN 1994 Conference on Programming Language Design and Implementation, pp. 171–185. ACM (1994)
8. Murata, T.: Petri nets: Properties, Analysis and Applications. In: Proc. of the IEEE, pp. 541–580 (1989)
9. Nigam, A., Caswell, N.S.: Business artifacts: An approach to operational specification. IBM Systems Journal 42(3), 428–445 (2003)
10. Ouyang, C., Dumas, M., Breutel, S., ter Hofstede, A.H.M.: Translating Standard Process Models to BPEL. In: Martinez, F.H., Pohl, K. (eds.) CAiSE 2006. LNCS, vol. 4001, pp. 417–432. Springer, Heidelberg (2006)
11. Rozinat, A., van der Aalst, W.M.P.: Decision Mining in ProM. In: Dustdar, S., Fiadeiro, J.L., Sheth, A.P. (eds.) BPM 2006. LNCS, vol. 4102, pp. 420–425. Springer, Heidelberg (2006)
12. van der Aalst, W., Barthelmess, P., Ellis, C., Wainer, J.: Proclets: A Framework for Lightweight Interacting Workflow Processes. Int. J. Cooperative Inf. Syst. 10(4), 443–481 (2001)
13. Verbeek, H., Buijs, J.C., van Dongen, B.F., van der Aalst, W.M.P.: Prom: The process mining toolkit. In: Proc. of BPM Demonstration Track. CEUR Workshop Proc., vol. 615 (2010)
14. Wilson, J.: Algorithms for obtaining normal forms of logical expressions. International Journal of Computer Mathematics 27(2), 85–90 (1989)

On Decidability of Simulation in Data-Centric Business Protocols

L. Akroun[1], B. Benatallah[2], L. Nourine[1], and Farouk Toumani[1]

[1] LIMOS, CNRS, Blaise Pascal University, Clermont-Ferrand, France
{akroun,nourine,ftoumani}@isima.fr
[2] CSE, UNSW, Sydney
boualem.benatallah@gmail.com

Abstract. We consider the problem of analyzing specifications of data-centric services. Specifications of such services incorporate data in business protocols. We focus our study on the decidability of the problem of checking the simulation preorder in the framework of the Colombo model. Colombo is a data-centric service that appears, at a first glance, to have a limited expressivity. Our first result, presented in this paper, shows that even in this restricted framework, both simulation and state reachability problems are already undecidable. Even worse, these problems remain undecidable in the case of non-communicating, read-only services.

Keywords: Data-centric services, artifact-centric business processes, simulation preorder.

1 Introduction

We consider the problem of analyzing specifications of data-centric services. Specifications of such services incorporate data in service business protocols (i.e., descriptions of external behaviors of a service). Formal models (e.g., [2,13,5,1]) used to describe such specifications are essentially communicating guarded transitions systems in which transitions are used to model either messages exchanges between a service and its environment (i.e. a *client*), or actions (i.e., read, write) on a global database shared among existing services. The incorporation of data turns out to be very challenging since it makes service specifications infinite which leads, in most cases, to the undecidability of many verification problems. The two sources of difficulties that lead to the infiniteness of the specifications are: (i) services act as value-passing processes, where the values come from an infinite data-space (i.e., value domains are infinite), and (ii) an infinite number of possible initial databases for a given service which makes service specification an infinite state machine.

In this paper we investigate the decidability issue of service simulation in the framework of the Colombo model. We focus our study on the problem of checking the simulation preorder since simulation is recognized as an appropriate means for comparing the structures of state-transitions systems. It enables to formalize

M. La Rosa and P. Soffer (Eds.): BPM 2012 Workshops, LNBIP 132, pp. 352–363, 2013.
© Springer-Verlag Berlin Heidelberg 2013

the idea that a given service is able to faithfully reproduce the external visible behavior of another service. In the context of web services, simulation has been shown to be a fundamental notion to study business protocol compatibility and substitution [4] as well as composition [11,8,6]. We consider this problem in the framework of the Colombo model. Colombo [5] is a pioneer data-centric service model that has been used to investigate the service composition problem. At first glance, the Colombo model appears to have a limited expressivity since: (i) it restricts accesses to the database only through atomic processes, and (ii) it supports a very limited database 'query' language which consists in simple key-based access functions. We show that even in this restricted framework, the simulation problem is already undecidable. Our proof is based on a reduction from the halting problem of a two counter machine (a Minsky machine) into the state reachability problem in Colombo services, knowing that this later problem can be recast as a simulation problem. Even worse, the way the proof is constructed enables to deduce that the reachability and simulation problems remain undecidable even in the case of non-communicating Colombo services with read-only accesses to the database (i.e., services that are not able to modify the world database or communicate with other services).

The main source of undecidability comes from the ability of a Colombo service to perform an unbounded number of read-accesses to the database. This is a decidability border since, although not presented here for space reasons, we can show that simulation is decidable in Colombo services with bounded accesses to the database. This later result is not surprising since bounded Colombo services are 'essentially' finite state systems, usually obtained by partitioning the original infinite state space into a finite number of equivalence classes and then using a symbolic procedure that manipulates (finite) sets of states (i.e., the equivalence classes) instead of (infinite) individual states.

The rest of this paper is organized as follows: Section 2 presents the *Colombo* model and defines the associated simulation problem. Section 3 describes our first results regarding undecidability of unbounded Colombo. Section 4 briefly discusses related works and draw future research directions.

2   Overview on the Colombo Model

We present below a simplified version of the Colombo model which is sufficient to present our results[1]. A detailed description of the Colombo model is given in [5]. We assume some familiarity with relational database theory (e.g., see [3]). A *world* database schema, denoted $\mathcal{W}$, is a finite set of relation schemas having the form $R_k(A_1, \ldots, A_k; B_1, \ldots, B_n)$, where the A_is form a key for R_k. A world database is an instance over the schema $\mathcal{W}$. Let $R(A_1, \ldots, A_k; B_1, \ldots, B_n)$ be a relation schema in $\mathcal{W}$, then $f_j^R(A_1, \ldots, A_k)$ is an access function that returns the j-th element of the tuple t in R identified by the key $(A_1, \ldots, A_k)$. Given a set of constants C and variables V, the set of accessible terms over C and V is

---

[1] In particular, we omit notions like *QStore*, linkage, ..., which are not relevant for our purposes.

defined recursively to include all the terms constructed using C, V and the f_j^R functions.

Example 1. Figure 1(c) depicts an example of a world database. For example, access to the relation Inventory(code, available, warehouse, price) is only possible through the access function $f_j^{Inventory}(code)$ with $j \in [1,3]$. For example, the function $f_2^{Inventory}("HP15")$ returns the value "NGW", corresponding to the value of the second attribute (i.e., the attribute warehouse) of the tuple identified by the code "$HP15$" in the relation Inventory.

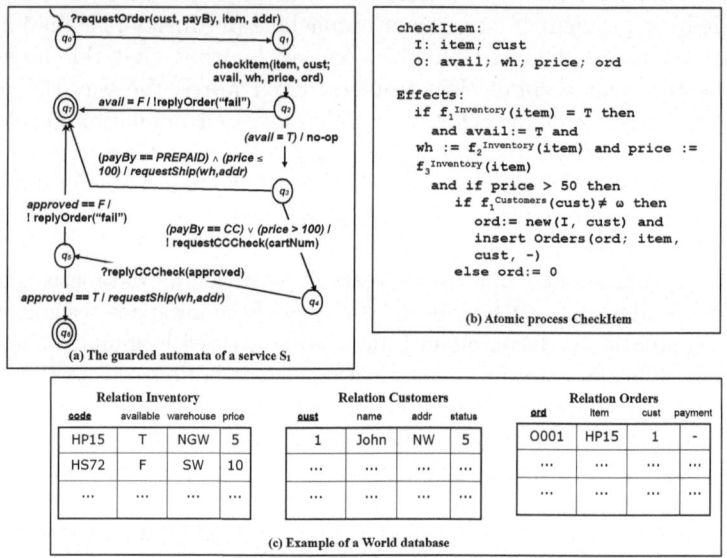

Fig. 1. Example of Colombo service (from [5])

In the Colombo model, services *actions* are achieved using the notion of atomic processes. An atomic process is a triplet $p = (I, O, CE)$ where: I and O are respectively input and output signatures (i.e., sets of typed variables) and $CE = \{(\theta, E)\}$, is a set of conditional effects, with:

- Condition θ is a boolean expression over atoms over accessible terms over some family of constants[2] and the input variables $u_1, \ldots, u_n$ in I,
- A set of effects E where each effect $e \in E$ is a pair (es, ev) with:
    - es, effect on world state, is a set of modifications on the global database (i.e., expressions of the form insert, delete or modify),
    - ev, effects on output variables, is a set of expressions of the forms: $v_j := t$, $\forall v_j \in O$ such that either $t = \omega$ or t is an accessible term over some set of constants and over the input variables $u_1, \ldots, u_n$.

---

[2] The symbol ω is used to denote an *undefined* (or null) value.

Example 2. Figure 1(b) shows an example of a specification of an atomic process (the atomic process CheckItem). This process takes as input an item code and returns the warehouse the item is available in and the price. Otherwise, if the item is not available, the CheckItem process simply returns output parameter $avail = F$.

A message type has the form $m(p_1, \ldots, p_n)$ where m is the message name and $p_1, \ldots, p_n$ are message parameters. Each parameter p_i is defined over a domain $\mathcal{D}$ (w.l.o.g., we assume that all the messages parameters are defined over the same values domain $\mathcal{D}$). The behavior of a Colombo service is given by the notion of *guarded automata* as defined below.

Definition 1. *A **guarded automaton** (GA) of a service S is a tuple $GA(S) = \langle Q, \delta, q_0, F, LStore(S) \rangle$, where :*

- *Q is a finite set of control states with $q_0 \in Q$ the initial state,*
- *$F \subseteq Q$ is a set of final states,*
- *$LStore(S)$ is a finite set of typed variables,*
- *the transition function δ contains tuples (q, θ, μ, q') where $q, q' \in Q$, θ is a condition over $LStore$ (no access to world instance), and μ has one of the following forms:*
    - *(incoming message) $\mu = ?m(v_1, \ldots, v_n)$ where m is a message having as signature $m(p_1, \ldots, p_n)$, and $v_i \in LStore(S), \forall i \in [1, n]$, or*
    - *(send message) $\mu = !m(b_1, \ldots, b_n)$ where m is a message having as signature $m(p_1, \ldots, p_n)$, and $\forall i \in [1, n]$, each b_i is either a variable of $LStore(S)$ or a constant, or*
    - *(atomic process invocation) $\mu = p(u_1, \ldots, u_n; v_1, \ldots, v_m, CE)$ with p an atomic process having n inputs, m outputs and CE as conditional effects, and $\forall i \in [1, n]$, each u_i (respectively, v_i) is either a variable of $LStore(S)$ or a constant.*

$LStore(S)$ can be viewed as a working area of a service. The variables of $LStore(S)$ are used to (i) capture the values of incoming messages, (ii) capture the output values of atomic processes, (iii) populate the parameters of outgoing messages, and (iv) populate the input parameters of atomic processes.

Example 3. Figure 1(a), borrowed from [5], shows the guarded automata of a Warehouse service. The states of the automata represent the different phases that the service may go through during its execution. Transitions are associated with a send or a receive message or with an atomic process. The Warehouse service is initially at its initial state (i.e., the state indicated in the figure by an unlabeled entering arrow). The service starts its execution upon receiving a requestOrder message. Then, depending on the requested payment mode and the price, respectively given by the values of the received message parameters payBy and price, the service can make two possible moves: (i) if the payment mode is CC (credit card) or the price > 100, the service sends a requestCCCheck message, for example to a bank, in order the check whether the credit card can be used to make the payment, or (ii) if the payment mode is $PREPAID$ and the price ≤ 100, the service will execute the atomic process **charge** in order to achieve the payement. The service ends its execution at a final state, depicted in the figure by double-circled states.

If a given guarded automaton $GA(S)$ uses only transitions of the form (q, θ, μ, q') with μ is an atomic process, in this case the corresponding service S is called a *non-communicating* service (since S cannot exchange messages with its environment). Moreover, if all the atomic processes used in a guarded automaton $GA(S)$ have no effects on world states (i.e., the set es of each atomic process is empty), in this case the service S is called a *read-only* Colombo service.

Semantics. We use the notion of an extended automaton to define the semantics of a Colombo service. At every point in time, the behavior of an instance of a Colombo service S is determined by its *instantaneous configuration (or simply, configuration)*. A configuration of a service is given by a triplet $id = (l, \mathcal{I}, \alpha)$ where l is its current control state, $\mathcal{I}$ a world database instance and α is a valuation over the variables of $LStore$.

Definition 2. *(service runs)*

Let $GA(S) = \langle Q, \delta, l_0, F, LStore(S) \rangle$ *be a guarded automata of a service S. A run σ of S is a finite sequence* $\sigma = id_0 \xrightarrow{\mu_0} id_1 \xrightarrow{\mu_1} \dots \xrightarrow{\mu_{n-1}} id_n$ *wich satisfy the following conditions:*

- *(Initiation) $id_0 = (l_0, \mathcal{I}_0, \alpha_0)$ is an initial configuration of the run with $\mathcal{I}_0$ is an arbitrary database over $\mathcal{W}$ and $\alpha_0(x) = \omega, \forall x \in LStore(S)$.*
- *(Consecution) $\forall i \in [1, n]$, $id_i = (l_i, \mathcal{I}_i, \alpha_i)$ and there is a transition $(l_i, \theta, \mu, l_{i+1}) \in \delta$ such that $\alpha_i(\theta) \equiv$ true and one of the following conditions holds:*
    - $\mu =?m(v_1, \dots, v_n)$ *and $\mu_i =?m(c_1, \dots, c_n)$, with c_j a constant $\forall j \in [1, n]$, then $\mathcal{I}_{i+1} = \mathcal{I}_i$ and $\alpha_{i+1}(v_j) = c_j$ and $\forall v \in LStore(S) \setminus \{v_1, \dots, v_n\}, \alpha_{i+1}(v) = \alpha_i(v)$,*
    - $\mu =!m(b_1, \dots, b_n)$ *and $\mu_i =!m(\alpha_i(b_1), \dots, (\alpha_i(b_n))$ then $\mathcal{I}_{i+1} = \mathcal{I}_i$ and $\forall v \in LStore(S), \alpha_{i+1}(v) = \alpha_i(v)$, and*
    - $\mu = p(u_1, \dots, u_n; v_1, \dots, v_m, CE)$ *and $\mu_i = p(\alpha_i(u_1), \dots, \alpha_i(u_n); \alpha_{i+1}(v_1), \dots, \alpha_{i+1}(v_m), CE)$ then*
        - *if there is no $(c, E) \in CE$ s.t. $\alpha_i(c) \equiv$ true (or there is more than one such (c, E)) then $\mathcal{I}_{i+1} = \mathcal{I}_i$ and $\forall v \in LStore(S), \alpha_{i+1}(v) = \alpha_i(v)$, or*
        - *let (c, E) be the unique conditional effects in CE s.t. $\alpha_i(c) \equiv$ true, and let (es, ev) be a non-deterministicall chosen element of E, then:*
            - *for each statement insert $R(t_1, \dots, t_k, s_1, \dots, s_l)$, delete $R(t_1, \dots, t_k)$, or modify $R(t_1, \dots, t_k, s_1, \dots, s_l)$ in es, apply the corresponding modification obtained by replacing t_i (respectively, s_i) by $\alpha_i(t_i)$ (respectively, $\alpha_i(s_i)$ on the instance $\mathcal{I}_i$. The obtained instance is the database $\mathcal{I}_{i+1}$.*
            - $\forall v_j := t \in ev$, $\alpha_{i+1}(v_j) = \alpha_i(t)$ *and $\alpha_{i+1}(v) = \alpha_i(v)$ for all the other variables v of $LStore(S)$.*

An execution of a service S starts at an initial configuration $id_0 = (l_0, \mathcal{I}_0, \alpha_0)$, with l_0 the initial control state of $GA(S)$, $\mathcal{I}_0$ an arbitrary database over $\mathcal{W}$ and $\alpha_0(x) = \omega$, $\forall x \in LStore(S)$. Then, a service moves from an id_i to id_j according to the mechanics defined by the set of transitions of $GA(S)$. If $id_i \xrightarrow{\mu_0} id_j$ satisfies the consecution condition above, we say that μ_0 is allowed from id_i.

The semantics of a Colombo service can be captured by the following notion of an extended infinite state machine.

Definition 3. *(extended state machine) Let $GA(S) = \langle Q, \delta, l_0, F, LStore(S) \rangle$ be a guarded automata of a service S. The associated infinite state machine, noted $E(S)$, is a tuple $E(S) = (\mathbb{Q}, \mathbb{Q}_0, \mathbb{F}, \Delta)$ where:*

- $\mathbb{Q} = \{(l, \mathcal{I}, \alpha)\}$ *with $l \in Q$, $\mathcal{I}$ a database over $\mathcal{W}$ and α a valuation over the variables of $LStore$. The set $\mathbb{Q}$ contains all the possible configurations of $E(S)$.*
- $\mathbb{Q}_0 = \{(l_0, \mathcal{I}_0, \alpha_0)\}$, *with $\mathcal{I}_0$ an arbitrary database over $\mathcal{W}$ and $\alpha_0(x) = \omega$, $\forall x \in LStore(S)$. $\mathbb{Q}_0$ is the infinite set of initial configurations of $E(S)$.*
- $\mathbb{F} = \{(l_f, \mathcal{I}, \alpha) \mid l_f \in F\}$. *$F$ is the set of final configurations of $E(S)$.*
- Δ *is an (infinite) set of transitions of the form $\tau = (l_i, \mathcal{I}_i, \alpha_i) \xrightarrow{\mu_i} (l_j, \mathcal{I}_j, \alpha_j)$ such that μ_i is allowed from $(l_i, \mathcal{I}_i, \alpha_i)$ (i.e., τ satisfies the consecution condition of definition 2).*

A run of $E(S)$ is any finite path from an initial configuration of $E(S)$ to one of its final configurations. Given an initial configuration id_0 of $E(S)$, all the possible runs of $E(S)$ starting from id_0 form an (infinite) execution tree having id_0 as its root. Hence, due to the infinite number of initial databases, all the runs of service S are captured in an (infinite) forest, that contains all possible execution trees of $E(S)$ (i.e., the set of trees having as a root an initial configuration id with $id \in \mathbb{Q}_0$).

We define now the notion of simulation between two Colombo services.

Definition 4. *(Simulation) Let S and S' be two Colombo services and let $E(S) = (\mathbb{Q}, \mathbb{Q}_0, \mathbb{F}, \Delta)$ and $E(S') = (\mathbb{Q}', \mathbb{Q}'_0, \mathbb{F}', \Delta')$ be respectively their associated extended state machines.*

- *Let $(id, id') \in \mathbb{Q} \times \mathbb{Q}'$. The configuration $id = (l, \mathcal{I}, \alpha)$ is simulated by $id' = (l', \mathcal{I}', \alpha')$, noted $id \preceq id'$, iff:*
  - $\mathcal{I} = \mathcal{I}'$, *and*
  - $\forall id \xrightarrow{\mu} id_j \in \Delta$, *there exists $id' \xrightarrow{\mu'} id'_l \in \Delta'$ such that $\mu = \mu'$ and $id_j \preceq id'_l$*
- *The extended state machine $E(S)$ is simulated by the extended state machine $E(S')$, noted $E(S) \preceq E(S')$, iff $\forall id_0 \in \mathbb{Q}_0, \exists id'_0 \in \mathbb{Q}'_0$ such that $id_0 \preceq id'_0$*

- *A Colombo service S is simulated by a Colombo service S', noted $S \preceq S'$, iff $E(S) \preceq E(S')$.*

Informally, if $S \preceq S'$, this means that S' is able to faithfully reproduce the external visible behavior of S. The external visible behavior of a service is defined here with respect to the content of the world database as well as the exchanged *concrete* messages (i.e., message name together with the values of the message parameters). The existence of a simulation relation ensures that each execution tree of S is also an execution tree of S' (in fact, a subtree of S'), modulo a relabeling of control states.

3   Undecidability of Simulation in Unbounded Colombo

We shall show that the simulation problem is undecidable for Colombo services.

Problem 1. Let S and S' be two Colombo services. The simulation problem, noted CheckSim(S, S'), is the problem of deciding whether $S \preceq S'$.

We start by establishing a connection between the problems of *state reacheability* and checking simulation between services. We exploit then this connection to establish undecidability of simulation.

Let us first define the state reachability problem for *Colombo* services.

Problem 2. Let S be a Colombo service and $E(S) = (\mathbb{Q}, \mathbb{Q}_0, \mathbb{F}, \Delta)$ its extended state machine. Let $l \in Q$ be a control state in $GA(S)$. A reachability problem, noted reach($E(S), l$), is the following: Is there a database $\mathcal{J}$ over the scheme $\mathcal{W}$ and a valuation α over $LStore(S)$ such that the configuration $(l, \mathcal{J}, \alpha)$ appears in a run of $E(S)$?

We exhibit the following straightforward link between composition and reachability.

Theorem 1. *If the reachability problem for a given class of Colombo service is undecidable so is simulation in that class.*

Proof. (sketch)

Let S be a Colombo service and l be a state in $GA(S)$. W.l.o.g., we assume that for any transition (l', c, μ, l) of $GA(S)$, the label μ is unique (i.e., μ do not appear in any another transition of $GA(S)$). Then, given a reachability problem reach($E(S), l$), we build a new service S', such that $GA(S')$ is obtained from $GA(S)$ by deleting the state l. Consider now the simulation problem $CheckSim(S, S')$. Hence in this case, it is easy to prove that $S \preceq S'$ iff l is not reachable in $E(S)$.

Let us consider now the reachability problem in Colombo.

Lemma 1. *The reachability problem in Colombo is undecidable.*

The proof of this lemma is achieved by a reduction from halting problem of a Minsky machine with counters initialized to zero [10]. A Minsky machine M

consists of two nonnegative *counters*, cpt_1 and cpt_2, and a sequence of labelled instructions:

$$L_0 : instr_0; \; L_1 : instr_1; \ldots L_{n-1} : instr_{n-1}; \; L_n : halt$$

where each of the first n instructions has one of the following forms:

1. $L_i : cpt_k := cpt_k + 1$; goto L_j, or
2. $L_i :$ if $cpt_k = 0$ then goto L_j else $cpt_k := cpt_k-1$; goto L_l.
   with $k \in \{1,2\}$, $i \in [0,n\text{-}1]$ and $j,l \in [0,n]$.

A machine M starts its execution with counters $cpt_1 = cpt_2 = 0$ and the control at label L_0. Then, when the control is at a label $L_i, i \in [0,n\text{-}1]$, the machine executes the instruction $instr_i$ and jumps to the appropriate label as specified in this instruction. The machine M halts if the control reaches the halt instruction at label L_n. It is known that the halting problem of Minsky machines, i.e., whether the execution of a given machine halts, is undecidable even in the case when the two counters are initialized to zero [10].

Given a Minsky machine M, we construct a Colombo service S_M that captures the execution of M. S_M uses a world database schema containing a single binary relation schema (i.e., $\mathcal{W} = \{R(A;B)\}$). The main idea to simulate a machine M is to make S_M working only on parts of instances of R that form a *chain* having the constant 0 as a root. A chain of length k is any set $\Upsilon_k = \{(c_0, c_1), \ldots, (c_{k-1}, c_k) \mid \forall i \in [0, k\text{-}1], c_i \text{ is a constant}\}$. The constant c_0 is called the root of Υ_k. For a pair $(c_l, c_{l+1}) \in \Upsilon_k$, we note by $d(c_l) = l$ the *distance* of c_l with respect to the root c_0 in the chain Υ_k. An instance I of R is said k-standard if there exists a chain Υ_k such that $\Upsilon_k \subseteq I$ and $c_0 = 0$. Hence, a k-standard instance contains a chain of length k that starts with pair $(0, c_1)$. To simulate the counters cpt_1 and cpt_2 during an execution of M, S_M uses respectively two variables, namely x_1 and x_2 (hereafter called counter variables), of its LStore. The variables x_1 and x_2 are initially set to 0. Intuitively, a value of a counter cpt_j, with $j \in \{1,2\}$, is captured by the *distance* between the current value of the variable x_j w.r.t. to the root 0 of the chain (i.e., $cpt_j = d(x_j)$). Hence, a given counter cpt_j of a minsky machine M is equal to 0 iff its corresponding counter variable x_j is equal to 0 (with $j \in \{1,2\}$). Incrementing a counter cpt_j is captured in S_M by moving forward the corresponding variable x_j in the chain Υ_k while decreasing a counter amounts to moving x_k backward in the chain. Moreover, to be able to simulate correctly an execution of a Minsky machine M, a service S_M requires an input database which is at least k_{max}-standard where k_{max} is the maximum value reached by the counters cpt_1 and cpt_2 of M in the considered execution. Hence, during its execution a service S_M needs to continuously check that the current database is k_{max}-standard. Due to the limited expressivity of the Colombo model, the implementation of such verification operations as well as the incrementation and decrementation of the counter variables x_1 and x_2 are not straightforward. We explain below in more details how the service S_M is constructed.

Let M be a Minsky machine defined as above. We associate to M, a Colombo service S_M, called the corresponding service of M, with the guarded automata $GA(S_M) = \langle Q, \delta, q_{start}, F, LStore(S) \rangle$. The set of states Q contains among other states, a state q_{L_i} for each label L_i in M, with $i \in [1, n\text{-}1]$, the initial state q_{start} and two final states q_{fail} and q_{halt}. The state q_{halt} corresponds to the label L_n of the halt instruction of M. An execution of S_M ends at the final state q_{halt} if the corresponding Minsky machine execution halts. An execution of S_M reaches the final state q_{fail} every time it is given as input an initial database which is not k_{max}-standard. To achieve this task, the service S_M uses a boolean variable noted x_{flag} to control the conformity of the current database: x_{flag} is initialized to true and then it is set to false if during a given execution the service finds out that the current database is not k_{max}-standard. Setting the boolean variable x_{flag} to false, will make the execution moving to the final state q_{fail}.

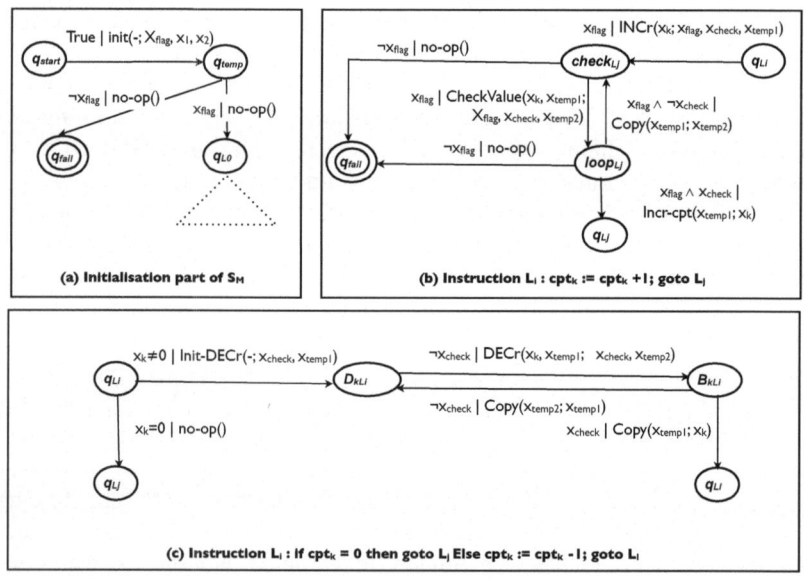

Fig. 2. Sub-processes of S_M

Figure 2 shows fragments of a Colombo service used to model the two kinds of instructions used by Minsky machines while figure 3 describes the associated atomic processes. Figure 2 (a) depicts the initialisation of a service S_M. An execution of such a service starts by executing the atomic process init and moves to the state q_{temp}. The init process checks that the initial database is 1-standard (i.e., it contains a tuple $(0, c_1)$) and in this case sets the counter variables to 0 and the boolean variable x_{flag} to true. In case the initial database is not 1-standard, the variable x_{flag} is set to false which will make the execution moving from state q_{temp} to the final state q_{fail}.

Init
> Input : -
> Output: V_{flag}, V_{temp1}, V_{temp2}
> Effects:
>> If $f_1{}^R(0) \neq \omega$ Then $V_{temp1} := 0$; $V_{temp1} := 0$; $V_{flag} := true$;
>> Else $V_{flag} := false$;

INCr
> Input : V_1
> Output: V_{flag}, V_{check}, V_{temp1}
> Effects:
>> If $f_1{}^R(V_1) \neq \omega \wedge f_1{}^R(V_1) \neq 0$ Then $V_{temp1} := 0$;
>> $V_{check} := false$;
>> Else $V_{flag} := false$;

CheckValue
> Input : V_1, V_{temp1}
> Output: V_{flag}, V_{check}, V_{temp2}
> Effects:
>> If $V_{temp1} = V_1$ Then $V_{check} := true$;
>> Else IF $f_1{}^R(V_1) = f_1{}^R(V_{temp1})$ then $V_{flag} := false$;
>> Else $V_{temp2} = f_1{}^R(V_{temp1})$;

Init-Decr
> Input: -
> Output: V_{check}, V_{temp1}
> Effects: $V_{check} := false$; $V_{temp1} := 0$;

DECr
> Input: V_1, V_{temp1}
> Output: V_{check}, V_{temp2}
> Effects:
>> If $V_1 = f_1{}^R(V_{temp1})$ Then $V_{check} := true$;
>> Else $V_{temp2} := V_{temp1}$;

Copy
> Input: V_{temp3}
> Output: V_{temp2}
> Effects: $V_{temp2} := V_{temp3}$;

Incr-cpt
> Input: V_{temp1}
> Output: V_1
> Effects: $V_1 := f_1{}^R(V_{temp1})$;

Fig. 3. Atomic processes of the Colombo service S_M

The figure 2(b) depicts part of a service that implements Minsky machine instructions of type 1: $L_i : cpt_k := cpt_k + 1$; goto L_j (i.e., incrementation of a counter cpt_k, with $k \in \{1, 2\}$). As explained above, incrementation amounts to moving forward in the chain the corresponding counter variable x_k. Assume that the current value of the variable x_k is $x_k = c_l$, with c_l a constant. The incrementation of x_k requires to: (i) first check that $f_1^R(x_k) \neq \omega$ (i.e., the chain is long enough to handle the new value of the counter), and (ii) check that $f_1^R(c_l)$ is a new value which has not already appeared in the chain. These two conditions ensure that the considered database is k-standard (with $k = d(c_l)+1$). The first condition is easy to check (c.f., atomic process INCr) while the second one is handled by reading the chain starting from the root until the tuple (c_{l-1}, c_l) and checking at each step whether the value $f_1^R(c_l)$ has already appeared or not. To achieve this task, an execution of S_M enters the state $check_{L_j}$ and then recursively calls the atomic process CheckValue starting from the root $(0, c_1)$ of the chain (c.f., loop between the states $Check_{L_j}$ and $Loop_{L_j}$ in figure 2(b)). The execution exits from the loop in two cases: (i) either it reaches to tuple (c_{l-1}, c_l), which means that the current database is k-standard (with $k = d(c_l)+1$) and hence the service moves to the state q_{L_j} and continue the execution, or (ii) it reaches a tuple $(c_i, f_1^R(c_l))$ in the chain which means that the database is not k-standard (with $k = d(c_l)+1$) and hence the service moves to the final state q_{fail}.

We consider now the implementation of instructions of type 2: L_i : if $cpt_k = 0$ then goto L_j else $cpt_k := cpt_k\text{-}1$ then goto L_l (c.f., figure 2(c)). The main difficulty here lies in the implementation of the decrementation operation (which amounts to moving back the counter x_k in the chain). Assume that the current value of x_k is c_l. Decrementing x_k amounts to assigning to x_k the constant c such that $f_1^R(c) = c_l$. To find the constant c one needs to read again the chain starting from the root. In the service S_M this is implemented by first entering the state D_{kL_i}, by executing the Init-Decr process, and then recursively calling the atomic process DECRr (c.f., loop between the states D_{kL_i} and B_{kL_l} of figure 2(c)) to explore the chain starting from the root and stopping at the tuple (c, c_l) (we are sure that such a tuple exist because during the incrementation step to reach the value c_l, the database has been checked to be at least $d(c_l)$-standard).

We give now the main property of the proposed construction that enables to prove lemma 1.

Lemma 2. *Let M be a Minsky machine and S_M the corresponding Colombo service, then: M halts iff* reach$(E(S_M), q_{halt})$

This result is obtained from the connection that exists between executions of M and the executions of S_M that use as input a k-standard databases. In particular, the different values taken by the counter cpt_1 and cpt_2 during an execution of M are captured by the distances of the counter variables x_1 and x_2 during the execution of S_M. Hence, it is possible to map any execution of M into an execution of S_M on a k-standard database and conversely. Moreover, it is easy to show that if there exists an execution of M that halts and in which k_{max} is the maximum value reached by the counters of M, then the execution of the corresponding service S_M using a k_{max}-standard initial database terminates at the final state q_{halt}. On the other side, by construction, S_M terminates at the final state q_{halt} iff it takes as initial database a k-standard database (which hence can be mapped into an execution of M that halts).

From theorem 1 and lemma 1, we obtain the following main result regarding simulation in the Colombo model.

Theorem 2. *Let S and S' be two Colombo services, then* CheckSim(S, S') *is undecidable.*

Finally, the following theorem can be straightforwardly derived from the previous proof since the constructed service S_M is a non-communicating read-only Colombo service.

Theorem 3. *Let S and S' be two non-communicating services with read-only accesses to the world database and let l be a control state in $GA(S)$, then both* CheckSim(S, S') *and* reach$(E(S), l)$ *are undecidable.*

4   Discussion

Dealing with data in state-based systems (web services, artifact-centered business processes) is not an easy task. Many recent works addressed different problems in the context of such systems. [5] investigates the service composition problem using a very constrained class of Colombo, called $Colombo^{k,b}$, which poses several restrictions on the type and number of accesses to the database and bounds both the communication of services with clients as well as the size of the mediators. As a consequence of these restrictions, $Colombo^{k,b}$ can be represented as a (symbolic) finite state machine, which makes exhaustive exploration of the search space possible. The main result of [5] is to show that service composition is 2-$EXPTIME$ in $Colombo^{k,b}$. In [12], the authors study the composition problem for data-centric services using an approach based on the simulation relation. [12] considers also a very restrictive model with, for example, non-communicating services and bounded databases. The authors show that, in this restricted context, service composition can be reduced into a simulation test between finite state machines. The decidability of the composition problem in a less restrictive model is left open both in [5] and [12].

Verification of data-centric services and artifact-centric business processes attracted a lot of attention from the research community these recent years [9,7]. In this context also the verification problem is undecidable in the general case. Existing works focus on identification of specific models and restrictions in which the verification problem can be solved.

Our future work will be devoted to the investigation of decidability and complexity of verification and composition of data-centric service in order to provide tight results regarding different restrictions on such models.

References

1. Vianu, V., Deutsch, A., Sui, L.: Specification and verification of data-driven web applications. J. Comput. Syst. Sci., 442–474 (2007)
2. Caswell, N., Nigam, A.: Business artifacts: An approach to operational specification. IBM Systems Journal 3(42), 428–445 (2003)
3. Abiteboul, S., Hull, R., Vianu, V.: Foundations of Databases. Addison-Wesley (1995)
4. Benatallah, B., Casati, F., Toumani, F.: Representing, analysing and managing web service protocols. DKE 58(3), 327–357 (2006)
5. Berardi, D., Calvanese, D., De Giacomo, G., Hull, R., Mecella, M.: Automatic composition of transition-based semantic web services with messaging. In: VLDB, pp. 613–624 (2005)
6. Berardi, D., Cheikh, F., De Giacomo, G., Patrizi, F.: Automatic service composition via simulation. IJFCS 19(2), 429–451 (2008)
7. Deutsch, A., Hull, R., Patrizi, F., Vianu, V.: Automatic verification of data-centric business processes. In: ICDT, pp. 252–267 (2009)
8. Ragab Hassen, R., Nourine, L., Toumani, F.: Protocol-Based Web Service Composition. In: Bouguettaya, A., Krueger, I., Margaria, T. (eds.) ICSOC 2008. LNCS, vol. 5364, pp. 38–53. Springer, Heidelberg (2008)
9. Hull, R.: Artifact-Centric Business Process Models: Brief Survey of Research Results and Challenges. In: Meersman, R., Tari, Z. (eds.) OTM 2008, Part II. LNCS, vol. 5332, pp. 1152–1163. Springer, Heidelberg (2008)
10. Minsky, M.: Computation Finite and Infinite Machines. Prentice-Hall (1967)
11. Muscholl, A., Walukiewicz, I.: A Lower Bound on Web Services Composition. In: Seidl, H. (ed.) FOSSACS 2007. LNCS, vol. 4423, pp. 274–286. Springer, Heidelberg (2007)
12. Patrizi, F., De Giacomo, G.: Composition of services that share an infinite-state blackboard (extended abstract). In: IIWEB (2009)
13. Spielmann, M.: Verification of relational transducers for electronic commerce. J. Comput. Syst. Sci. 66(1), 40–65 (2003)

Nondeterministic Events in Business Processes

Albert Fleischmann[1], Werner Schmidt[2], Christian Stary[3], and Florian Strecker[1]

[1] Metasonic AG, Münchner Str. 29, 85276 Hettenshausen, Germany
{Albert.Fleischmann,Florian.Strecker}@metasonic.de
[2] Ingolstadt University of Applied Sciences, Esplanade 10, 85049 Ingolstadt, Germany
werner.schmidt@haw-ingolstadt.de
[3] Johannes Kepler University Linz, Freistädterstraße 315, 4040 Linz, Austria
Christian.stary@jku.at

Abstract. In this article we describe how Complex Event Processing (CEP) can be smoothly integrated into Subject-oriented Business Process Management (S-BPM). This approach is grounded on communication patterns between acting systems (i.e. subjects), such as people and software systems. The integration is done twofold. Firstly, complex event processing units can be seen as one way to instantiate a process. Secondly, CEP units can be integrated into subjects as internal functions. Based on evaluating various data patterns the subject containing the CEP function can inform other subjects by sending corresponding messages. In this way, nondeterministic (since not predictable) events can be dealt with at runtime. An informed subject may actively influence further system behavior by delegating further observation tasks to the subject containing the complex event processing unit. Based on the introduced concepts and their straightforward implementation actual business operations can not only be represented, but also processed more accurately.

Keywords: events, message guard, implementation, CEP, S-BPM.

1   Introduction

In this paper we describe how the specification of business processes and event processing can be combined in order to handle deterministic and non deterministic business situations. Additionally we will show how such specifications with non deterministic events can be implemented in a straight forward way.

Business processes are the behavioral parts of organizations. Business process specifications describe which event causes the instantiation of a business process, which parties in a process execute which activities, using which tools and which communication acts they perform in order to synchronize work in a world with a high degree of division of work. Business processes can be instantiated for various reasons and must be able to handle deterministic and nondeterministic events during its execution. Deterministic events are those which occurrence in time can be specified accurately, i.e. it is known that they will occur and when they will occur. In case of nondeterministic events it is not known whether they occur at all and in case of occurrence when they actually occur.

M. La Rosa and P. Soffer (Eds.): BPM 2012 Workshops, LNBIP 132, pp. 364–377, 2013.
© Springer-Verlag Berlin Heidelberg 2013

In this paper events are considered to be messages sent from a sender to a receiver. Messages may transport some data from the sender to the receiver. In Business Process Management (BPM) we distinguish between events which cause the creation of a process instance and events which are created during the execution of a process instance.

Events Which Cause Process Instances

Depending on the source of an event which causes a new process instance we distinguish we four types:

- Human actor interference
  A human initiates the execution of a process. For example somebody calls a service center because he/she has problems with a certain device. The service center creates a process instance of a process which handles such incident calls.

- Time
  An instance of a process must be created regularly in order to produce certain results which are required by various people. Every day in the evening a process is executed which collects data from several service organizations, creates a report and distributes that report to several employees interested in that report.

- Other business processes
  An instance of a business processes triggers the instantiation of another business process. A sales process causes the instantiation of a corresponding production process if a customer accepts an order.

- Data state
  If certain conditions become valid in some data storage a process instance is instantiated. An observer realizes that a defined condition becomes true and creates an instance of a process which handles that situation. Data changes can be caused by human interactions or software programs like complex event filters. A complex event processing unit discovers a certain constellation in the external event stream which has to be handled by a business process. The filter triggers the instantiation of the corresponding business process (see [4]).

Events Which Are Created during Process Instance Execution

Process instances created for certain reasons are executed according to the process specification. During process execution several deterministic and nondeterministic communications (events) can occur. For deterministic communication it is defined when and by whom they are sent and how the receiver reacts. Non deterministic events are messages randomly sent from parties in a process. We call these types of messages process instance execution events or, for short, internal process events. An example of such an internal event can be a cancelation message. A customer informs the service center that he could solve the problem by his own and the incident ticket can be closed.

During the execution for those events it is unclear whether they occur at all, and if so, when they occur. Reactions differ depending on the state the process instance is in by the time the event occurs.

Process models are templates for creating and executing process instances. Thus a model not only needs to describe the sequence of activities being executed and the messages being sent and received with regard to deterministic events. The challenge is to also include internal events into the model and have them handled at runtime.

In this article we show how internal events can be easily integrated in subject-oriented business process models. After this introduction we shed some light on related work regarding event handling in business process management. After that we briefly introduce Subject-oriented Business Process Management (S-BPM) and discuss the integration of Complex Event Processing (CEP) into S-BPM. Complex events are built out of lots of simple events which as a group serve as an element in a specific situation for a particular purpose [17]. We will show how complex event processing units can be integrated into subject-oriented process specifications. Our goal is to integrate complex event processing at process instance execution rather than on the process instance creation level. This approach better matches actual business operation which is characterized by nondeterministic events, e.g. the change of an order or purchases stocks if certain prices are reached. Chapter 4 presents the concept and a prototype implementation of the message guard concept in S-BPM, suitable to handle process instance execution events. We end with the conclusion in chapter 5.

2   Challenges to Capture Nondeterministic Events in BPM

Being able to flexibly react on unforeseen events when executing business processes is both a constraint and a valuable asset for an agile organization. We look at the way how state-of-the-art approaches to business process modeling and execution cope with the representation and execution of event-driven actions.

2.1   Event-Driven Process Chains (EPC)

The flow-oriented EPCs are the major model type of the control view in the ARIS methodology of business process modeling. Per definition, events drive the control flow, but the possibility to model events is limited to deterministic ones. The method does not offer concepts to handle asynchronous, nondeterministic events as mentioned in section 1. As a consequence those events are not considered when EPCs are transferred to executable code during IT implementation.

2.2   Business Process Model and Notation (BPMN)

BPMN 2.0 includes 'catching events' (trigger has fired) and 'throwing events' (event fires) as flow elements in the description of a process. Those events can be of various type (e.g. message event, timer event, signal event, terminate event, cancel event), each represented by a dedicated symbol [13, 14, 19].

Nondeterministic events can be modeled as so-called exceptions. They can be used to interrupt a running sub process. The overall process is then continued on the higher level of the calling process. It is not clearly defined who can be the source of such an exception and it is difficult to describe the way back to the interrupted process after the exception was handled.

If, for example, a customer changes an order the change request message (e.g. increasing the number of products ordered) can arrive in any execution state on the seller side of the order process. This means the seller must be able to react to it at many different points in a suitable way. If the message arrives before picking and packing the goods the reaction can just be changing the number and continuing the process instance in the state where the change request had arrived. In case delivery has already been started the reaction might be to create a new instance with the missing number of goods causing a second delivery. BPMN 2.0 falls short in clear semantics to precisely express such situations as well as the message exchange [18]. It is limited in its expressiveness for conditional event-driven reaction logic [20] and does not offer possibilities to integrate facilities which are able to handle process external event patterns (see p. 376 in [4]). In order to generally tackle BPMN 2.0 shortcomings, some additional definitions beyond the standard are necessary, like proposed by Silver [19].

2.3   Event-Driven Business Process Management (ED-BPM)

Event-Driven Business Process Management (ED-BPM) combines two different disciplines: Business Process Management (BPM) and Complex Event Processing (CEP) [4, 5, 17]. Basic idea is that single events occurring in an event cloud are processed (mainly filtered) by an event processing platform and thus aggregated into a complex event [14, 15], which can be modeled in a process execution language of a BPMS triggering changes in the runtime behavior of a process. This view brings together the abstract description of processes at design time with unforeseen events (i.e. nondeterministic) affecting the execution of process instances during runtime.

Von Ammon et al. suggest a general framework for ED-BPM and discuss how business process execution can be enhanced on the basis of ED-BPM, e.g. by enhancing WS-BPEL, which in its "standard form cannot execute event-driven processes" [4].

Paschke also mentions the limits of pure syntactic BPM languages like BPEL and BPMN in the context of 'complex decision logic and conditional event-driven reaction logic' [20]. For orchestration of business processes he proposes a declarative middleware based on rules and events and combining CEP technologies with those for declarative rule-based programming [22].

The CEVICHE framework presented by Hermosillo et al. [23] combines an XML-based Standard Business Process Language (SBPL) with an aspect-oriented extension to BPEL (AO4BPEL). The first allows to translate process information to different CEP engines, the ladder makes it possible to adapt the process behavior at runtime without redeploying the whole model before.

3   Subject-Oriented Business Process Management

3.1   Fundamentals

The S-BPM approach roots in the observation that humans usually use standard semantics of natural language with subject, predicate, and object when they describe what they are doing in a business process. Consequently the S-BPM modeling language allows for representing these building blocks of a complete sentence in natural language, where the subject is the starting point for describing a situation or a sequence of events, the activities are denoted by predicates and an object is the target of an activity. Resulting models describe structural properties and behavioral alternatives, including the message-based interaction occurring in the technical and/or organizational environment. Thus S-BPM enriches flow concepts of function-driven BPM approaches by active entities sending and receiving messages [1, 6, 8]. These active entities are called subjects. In order to keep a process specification independent from a special organizational and technical environment subjects are a more abstract view on active entities than actors or agents. A subject abstractly models an agent which executes some specified behavior; for example a subject can stand for a person acting in a given situation (process) or for a thread in an IT system (software agent). A concrete agent (when acting) instantiates (the behavior of) a subject. Thus one agent may be able to execute the behavior of different subjects and vice versa different agents may execute the same behavior, as defined by one subject. These different executions are independent of each other. Assigning an actor or agent to a subject is part of the implementation of a subject.

The graphical notation of the S-BPM modeling language with only a few symbols is based on process algebra with a clear formal semantic allowing automated code generation. This makes subject-oriented process descriptions executable and supports seamless round-trip engineering [1, 8].

Using the Abstract State Machine (ASM) method Egon Börger [16] developed a precise formulation for the semantics of the S-BPM constructs in form of a high-level subject-oriented interpreter model and gave proof both of ground model and refinement correctness of the interpreter (for details see [2] and pp. 346-395 in [1]).

3.2   Modeling

In order to demonstrate the mapping of a language-based representation to a subject-oriented model we use the application for a business trip as a simple example. Figure 1 shows the natural language description of this process.

An employee applies for a business trip. His manager checks the request and informs the employee whether he approves or rejects the request. The approved request is forwarded to the travel office which does all the travel arrangements.

Fig. 1. Natural language description of the business trip application process

The subject-oriented description of the process starts with the identification of process-specific roles involved in the process, the subjects, and the messages exchanged between them. When sending messages, the required data is transmitted from the sender to the receiver via simple parameters or more complex business objects if necessary. Thus, with the message 'business trip request' sent by the employee to the supervisor, among other things, the start and end date are transmitted.

Figure 2 depicts the interaction structure of the process, the so-called Subject Interaction Diagram.

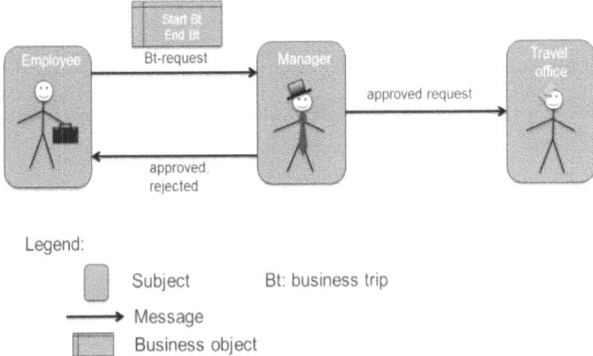

Fig. 2. The business trip application process with the involved subjects and their interactions

In a further refinement step, the modeler describes which activities and interactions the subjects have to perform in which order during the execution of the process, i.e., he defines the behavior of individual subjects.

The so-called Subject Behavior Diagram in figure 3 shows the order in which the employee sends and receives messages, or executes internal actions, and the states he is in during his business trip application.

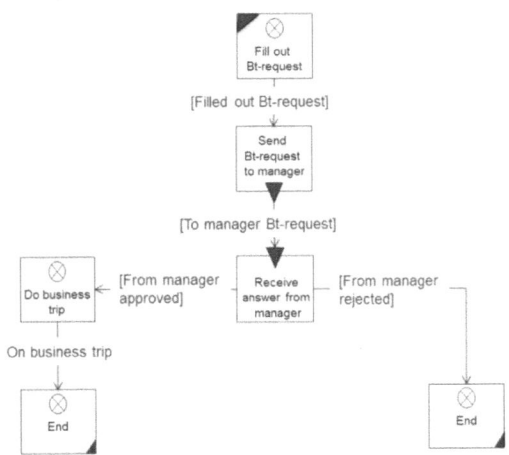

Fig. 3. Graphical representation of employee behavior when applying for a business trip

The initial state is marked by a triangle in the upper left corner. It is a function state in which the employees complete their business trip request. The state transition 'filled out Bt-request' leads to a send state in which they send the application to the manager, before entering the receive state, in which an answer is received from the manager. Here, the applicants wait for the response of the manager. In case they receive a rejection message from the manager, the process comes to an end. In case the employees receive the approval message from the manager, they go on the trip on the agreed date and the business trip application process is completed.

The behavior of the manager is complementary to that of the employee (see figure 4). Messages sent by the employee are received by the manager, and vice versa. The manager therefore first waits in a receiving state for a business trip request from the employee. After receiving the application, he goes to a state of checking which leads either to the approval or rejection of the request. In the second case, a send state follows to send the refusal to the employee. In the first case, the manager first moves to a send state for transmitting the approval to the applicant, and then proceeds to a state of informing the travel office about the approved business trip request.

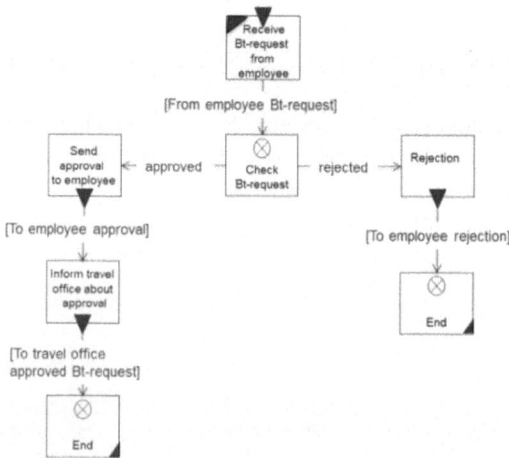

Fig. 4. Graphical representation of the manager's behavior when handling a business trip request

The behavior of the travel office can be described analogous. This short example illustrates the essential elements of a subject-oriented model as there are:

- The subjects involved in the process,
- The interactions taking place between them,
- The messages they send or receive during each interaction, and
- The behavior of the individual subjects

3.3   Integrating Complex Event Processing (CEP) in S-BPM

In the CEP context an event processing agent (EPA) denotes a unit processing complex events [15, 17]. As in S-BPM we distinguish between abstract subjects and actors/agents (see section 3.1) we need a term for a more abstract view on complex event processing in the subject-oriented context. We introduce the event processing functionality (EPF), which becomes an event processing agent as defined in [15] and [17] once the functions are assigned to an entity (software, people etc.) able to perform them. This means we want to consider event processing functionality independent from the executing 'technology'.

Complex Event Processing can be easily integrated in S-BPM in a twofold manner:

Complex event functionality triggers process instances. It observes the incoming events in the event cloud. When it discovers a defined constellation a corresponding business process instance is created to handle that constellation.

Complex event processing is part of processes. Event processing functionality can be considered as functions in the behavior of a subject and if the subject is assigned to an agent we have an EPA. As soon as a process is instantiated this agent is also instantiated and can start working. When a predefined event pattern is discovered the internal function of the related exit transition is executed. Due to the fact that the modeler can define several exits for each internal function, this function can search for different patterns. The following figure shows a subject with event processing functionality.

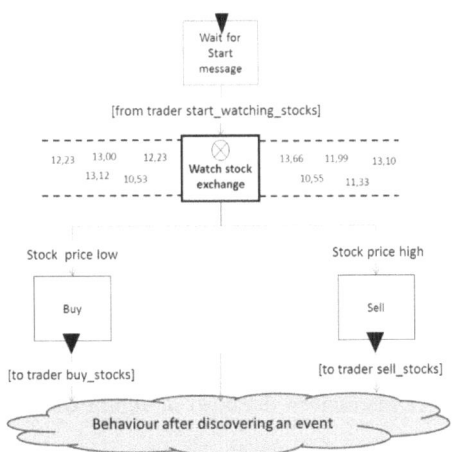

Fig. 5. A subject with event processing functionality

The subject receives a message 'start_watching_stocks'. After accepting that message the subject is in state 'watch_stock_exchange'. If 'Stock price low' is discovered the corresponding transition is executed and in the following send state the message 'buy_stocks' is sent to the subject 'trader'. If the result 'stock price high' is discovered the corresponding message is sent. With these messages the corresponding buy or sell processes are started. After that the subject can do some other work depending on the behavior specification.

As the function discovers events it passes the information on to other subjects in the process which handle the activities to be accomplished because of an event. This type of events (i.e. messages) is nondeterministic. It is unclear whether the message is sent and when it will be sent. Other subjects can also send messages to the event processor subject containing information which constellations should be observed (in our example in the message 'start event processing') in order to make the complex event function change its observation conditions. This means subjects must be able to handle nondeterministic messages.

In the following chapter we present the Message Guard concept which details the aforementioned possibilities S-BPM provides to handle asynchronous, nondeterministic events.

4   Message Guard Concept in S-BPM

4.1   Specification

We use the term Message Guard as a synonym for handling an exception. It is a behavioral description for a subject that is relevant when a specific, exceptional situation occurs along executing a subject behavior specification. It is activated when a corresponding message is received, and the subject is in a state being able to respond to exception handling (see p. 147 ff. in [1]). In such a case, the transition to exception handling has the highest priority and will be enforced.

Exception handling can occur in a process in many behavior states of subjects. The receipt of certain messages, e.g., to abort the process, always results in the same processing pattern. This pattern should also be modeled for each state in which it is relevant. Exception handlings cause high modeling effort and lead to complex process models, since from each affected state a corresponding transition has to be specified. In order to prevent this situation, we introduce a concept similar to exception handling in programming languages or interrupt handling in operating systems.

To illustrate the compact description of exception handlings, we enhance our business trip example by introducing an additional subject 'Service desk'. This subject identifies a need for a business trip in the context of solving a customer problem - an employee needs to visit the customer to provide a service locally. According to the subject interaction diagram in figure 6 the subject 'Service desk'

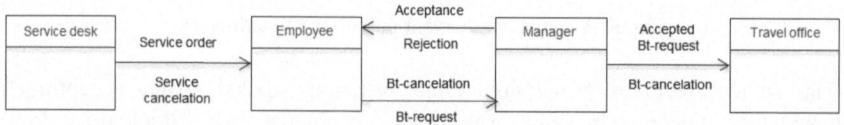

Fig. 6. Subject interaction diagram of the business trip application process including cancelation messages

passes on a service order to an employee. Hence, the employee issues a business trip request. The service order may be canceled up to its completion in principle at each stage of processing. The cancelation message is passed on to all affected subjects to bring the process towards a defined end.

As for the behavior we first describe what the model would look like without applying the message guard concept of exception handling. A cancelation message can be received by the employee either while filling in the application, or while waiting for the approval or rejection message from the manager. With respect to the behavior of the subject 'employee', the state 'response received from manager' needs to be enriched with the possible input message containing the cancelation and the associated consequences, too. The verification whether filling in the request is followed by a cancelation is modeled through a receive state with a timeout. In case the timeout is zero, there is no cancelation message in the input pool and the business trip request is sent to the manager (for details of the input pool and timeout concept (see p. 96 ff. in [1]). In the other case, the manager is informed of the cancelation and the process terminates for the subject 'employee'. A corresponding adjustment of the behavior needs to be made for each subject, which can receive a cancelation message, including the manager and the travel office.

This relatively simple example already shows that paying attention to such exception messages can quickly make behavior descriptions extensive and confusing to understand. The concept of exception handling, therefore, should enable supplementing exceptions to the default behavior of subjects in a structured and compact form. Figure 7 shows how such a concept affects the behavior of the employee.

Instead of modeling receive states with a time-out zero and corresponding state transitions, the behavioral description is enriched with the exception handling 'service

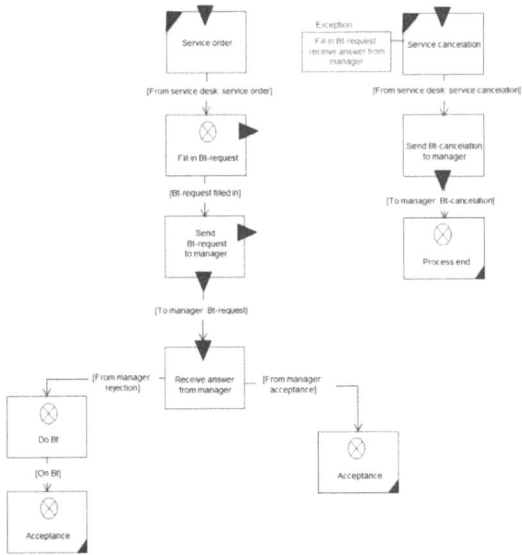

Fig. 7. Behavior of subject 'employee' with exception handling

cancelation'. Its initial state is labeled with the states from which is branched to, once the message 'service cancelation' is received. In the example, these are the states 'business trip application complete' and 'receive answer from manager'. Each of them is marked by a triangle on the right edge of the state symbol. The exception behavior leads to an exit of the subject, after the message 'service cancelation' has been sent to the subject 'manager'.

Basically, a subject behavior does not need to stop here; it may be continued from there as specified in some default behavior. Exception handling behavior in a subject may vary, depending from which state or by what type of message (cancelation, temporary stopping of the process, etc.) it is called. The initial state of exception handling can be a receive state or a function state.

Messages that, like 'service cancelation', lead to exception handling always have higher priority than other messages. Thus, modelers express that specific messages are read in a preferred way. For instance, when the approval message from the manager and shortly thereafter the cancelation message are received in the input pool of the employee, the latter is read first. It causes corresponding abort consequences.

4.2   Implementation

Sections 3.2 and 4.1 demonstrated the concepts S-BPM offers to model nondeterministic events in a transparent and efficient way. To have functions based on these concepts available in a Business Process Management System (BPMS), extensions are necessary in the design part and in the execution part of a tool suite supporting the S-BPM approach.

Strecker presents a prototype solution enhancing the Metasonic Suite as a BPMS by functionality allowing to model exception handling according to the message guard concept and to perform the modeled behavior at runtime [3].

4.2.1   Extension for Modeling and Execution

Although Metasonic's modeling environment 'Metasonic Build' is Eclipse-based and can therefore easily being adapted or extended, Strecker did not alter the core of the BPMS, but used out-of-the-box possibilities like modeling conventions (e.g. different, multi-colored symbols) and existing custom modeling parameters [10] for his quick and easy prototype implementation.

Figure 8 depicts how a message guard behavior is modeled with the mentioned means:

- The message guard behavior is placed to the right of the standard behavior.
- The complete message guard behavior is shimmed with a light-blue box and marked as "message guard behavior" with a text box.
- The start of the message guard behavior is a receive state; therefore, it is possible to distinguish different messages there.
- The start of the message guard behavior is marked with a blue triangle on its top.
- In the standard behavior, all states which can be left to access the message guard behavior, are marked with a dark-blue triangle on their upper right corner.

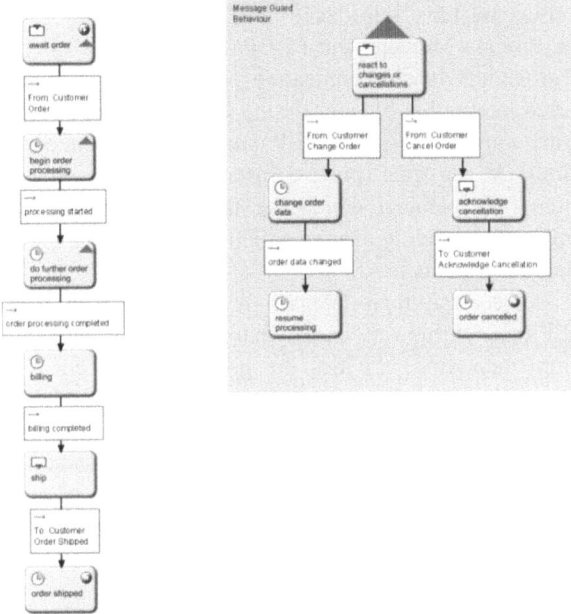

Fig. 8. A subject behavior employing a message guard behavior

The process engine 'Flow' as a part of the Metasonic Suite allows creating custom extensions to enhance the runtime environment via so-called engine add-ons [10]. These extensions can react to certain, well-defined events, and are implemented using the so-called observer pattern [11].

As we defined events as incoming messages an InputpoolObserver is needed to react to message entries in the subject's input pool. The StateChangeObserver is applied for handling the message guard behavior. It checks the process model for custom modeling parameters described in the previous section and reacts on the parameter values as events. A certain parameter constellation for example can make the observer switch a subject state and thus altering the subject behavior at runtime.

The implementation including some examples can be downloaded at [12].

5   Conclusion and Future Work

Business Process Management (BPM) recognizing complex events requires corresponding representation and execution schemes, as those events reflect in situ business settings and organizational behavior patterns. In particular, events that are uncertain with respect to their occurrence and their time of occurrence, so called nondeterministic events, require proper management at runtime. Approaches to embed Complex Event Processing (CEP) into BPM neither support specification of handling nondeterministic events, e.g., BPMN, nor reflect dynamic handling of those events, e.g., EPC.

In this contribution we have introduced how CEP can be integrated into Subject-oriented Business Process Management (S-BPM). In contrast to existing functional approaches it is grounded on communication patterns between acting systems (i.e. subjects). We started integration by considering CEP units as one way to instantiate a process, i.e. creating a process instance. CEP units can then be integrated into subjects as internal functions. At run time (process instance execution), based on evaluating various data patterns the subject containing the CEP function can inform other subjects by sending corresponding messages. This represents the basic concept for the handling of nondeterministic events.

The informed subjects may then delegate further observation tasks to the subject containing the CEP unit. In this way they dynamically influence the system behavior. The prototype implementation provides the proof of concept. We have used the message guard concept for straightforward implementation.

Future work should include detailing and evaluating the concept as well as the prototype implementation, e.g. in terms of relating it to the standard event processing architecture introduced by [17] or in terms of interaction with existing CEP solutions. Questions still to be answered also refer to performance, limitations and a comparison with existing approaches like mentioned in section 2.3.

References

1. Fleischmann, A., Schmidt, W., Stary, C., Obermeier, S., Börger, E.: Subjektorientiertes Prozessmanagement, Hanser, München (2011), To appear in English at Springer, Berlin, Heidelberg (October 2012)
2. Börger, E.: The Subject-Oriented Approach to Software Design and the Abstract State Machines Method. In: Düsterhöft, A., Klettke, M., Schewe, K.-D. (eds.) Conceptual Modelling and Its Theoretical Foundations. LNCS, vol. 7260, pp. 52–72. Springer, Heidelberg (2012)
3. Strecker, F.: New Modeling Concepts in S-BPM: The First Implementation of the "Message Guard" and "Macro" Behavior Extensions. In: Oppl, S., Fleischmann, A. (eds.) S-BPM ONE 2012. CCIS, vol. 284, pp. 121–134. Springer, Heidelberg (2012)
4. von Ammon, R., Ertlmaier, T., Etzion, O., Kofman, A., Paulus, T.: Integrating Complex Events for Collaborating and Dynamically Changing Business Processes. In: Dan, A., Gittler, F., Toumani, F. (eds.) ICSOC/ServiceWave 2009. LNCS, vol. 6275, pp. 370–384. Springer, Heidelberg (2010)
5. von Ammon, R., Etzion, O., Paschke, A., Stojanovic, N.: Event-Driven Business Process Management. In: ED-BPM Workshop, ServiceWave 2008, Madrid (2008), http://www.nessi-europe.com/Nessi/adminP/ArchivedPages/ServiceWave2008WorkshopBPM/tabid/468/Default.aspx (last access April 16, 2011)
6. Fleischmann, A., Stary, C.: Whom to talk to? A stakeholder perspective on business process development, Universal Access in the Information Society (2011), doi: 10.1007/s10209-011-0236-x
7. Weber, J.E., Schmidt, W., Weber, P.S.: Using Social Network Analysis and Derivatives to Develop the S-BPM Approach and Community of Practice. In: Stary, C. (ed.) S-BPM ONE 2012. LNBIP, vol. 104, pp. 205–217. Springer, Heidelberg (2012)

8. Fleischmann, A., Schmidt, W., Stary, C.: A Primer to Subject-Oriented Business Process Modeling. In: Stary, C. (ed.) S-BPM ONE 2012. LNBIP, vol. 104, pp. 218–240. Springer, Heidelberg (2012)

9. Fleischmann, A., Stary, C.: Key Features of Subject-Oriented Modeling and Organizational Deployment Tools. In: Stephanidis, C. (ed.) HCII 2011 and UAHCI 2011, Part IV. LNCS, vol. 6768, pp. 205–214. Springer, Heidelberg (2011)

10. Metasonic, A.G.: Metasonic Suite Developer Documentation 4.4. Pfaffenhofen (2011), http://www.metasonic.de

11. Metasonic   AG: ExecutionOrderWithinRefinementsAndObservers   (com.jcom1. documentation.refinements.ExecutionOrderWithinRefinementsAndObservers).   In: Metasonic AG: Metasonic Suite Developer Documentation 4.4. Pfaffenhofen (2011), http://www.metasonic.de

12. Strecker, Florian: http://www.floooooo.de/s-bpm/#sbpmone2012

13. OMG, Business Process Management Initiative, BPMN, http://www.omg.org/spec/BPMN/2.0/PDF/ (last access May 26, 2012)

14. Freund, J., Rücker, B.: Praxishandbuch BPMN 2.0. Hanser, München (2010)

15. Luckham, D., Schulte, R. (Hrsg.): Event Processing Glossary Version 2.0/2011, Event Processing Technical Society, http://www.complexevents.com/2011/08/23/ event-processing-glossary-version-2-0/ (last access May 30, 2012)

16. Börger, E., Stärk, R.: Abstract State Machines: A Method for High-Level System Design and Analysis. Springer, Heidelberg (2003)

17. Etzion, O., Niblett, P.: Event Processing in Action. Manning Publications, Stamford (2011)

18. Börger, E.: Approaches to Modeling Business Processes. A Critical Analysis of BPMN, Workflow Patterns and YAWL. Software & Systems Modeling 11(3), 305–318 (2012)

19. Silver, B.: BPMN Method and Style, 2nd edn., with BPMN Implementer's Guide: A Structured Approach for Business Process Modeling and Implementation Using BPMN. Cody-Cassidy Press (2011)

20. Paschke, A.: A Semantic Rule and Event Driven Approach for Agile Decision-Centric Business Process Management. In: Abramowicz, W., Llorente, I.M., Surridge, M., Zisman, A., Vayssière, J. (eds.) ServiceWave 2011. LNCS, vol. 6994, pp. 254–267. Springer, Heidelberg (2011)

21. Janiesch, C., Matzner, M., Müller, O.: A Blueprint for Event-Driven Business Activity Management. In: Rinderle-Ma, S., Toumani, F., Wolf, K. (eds.) BPM 2011. LNCS, vol. 6896, pp. 17–28. Springer, Heidelberg (2011)

22. Paschke, A., Kozlenkov, A.: A Rule-based Middleware for Business Process Execution. In: Bichler, M., Hess, T., et al. (eds.) Proceedings of Multikonferenz Wirtschaftsinformatik (MKWI 2008), pp. 1409–1420. GITO, Berlin (2008)

23. Hermosillo, G., Seinturier, L., Duchien, L.: Using Complex Event Processing for Dynamic Business Process Adaptation. In: Proceedings of the 7th IEEE International Conference on Service Computing (SCC), Miami, pp. 466–473 (2010)

A Model-Driven Approach for Event-Based Business Process Monitoring

Falko Koetter[1] and Monika Kochanowski[2]

[1] University of Stuttgart IAT, Germany
`falko.koetter@iao.fraunhofer.de`
[2] Fraunhofer IAO, Germany
`monika.kochanowski@iao.fraunhofer.de`

Abstract. Today event-driven business process management has matured from a scientific vision to a realizable methodology for companies of all sizes and shapes. However, leveraging the power of complex event processing for supporting business process monitoring is cumbersome because of the complicated modeling of rules and alerts as well as key performance indicators in machine readable format using the event languages. However, using a model-driven approach for generating a monitoring infrastructure based on events like the aPro architecture is one possibility to enable companies with various infrastructures to leverage the advantages of business process monitoring. This paper describes how KPIs are modeled and transferred into event rules by a model-driven approach.

Keywords: business process management, process monitoring, business process goals, complex event processing, business intelligence.

1 Introduction

Today many companies work at improving their business processes and spend lots of time and effort on this [8]. However apart from the business process management strategies like CMMI [8] or the concepts of automated workflow execution [19][3], the transparency and monitoring [3] of the business processes is a major point for reacting fast on market changes [7]. One method for leveraging transparency is the introduction of complex event processing [13] (CEP) techniques in service processes [18][5]. CEP allows extracting information from business processes based on events for example from distributed service systems.

However, creating a CEP infrastructure is a cumbersome task. Apart from setting up the CEP engine, the business rules in business processes need to be transferred into an event language, the monitoring infrastructure including event collection has to be created, and the events need to be generated within the business processes or legacy systems supporting the business processes. In order to simplify these steps various approaches are possible. For example, one could use a graphical modeling language for simplifying the rule generation [18][5]. However, this only supports one task - the task of modeling rules - in the manifold

M. La Rosa and P. Soffer (Eds.): BPM 2012 Workshops, LNBIP 132, pp. 378–389, 2013.

challenges. Another way is to use built-in monitoring technology in a workflow engine [3]. These approaches are usually limited to one workflow technology and are therefore not applicable for distributed systems with different system environments. Therefore, we developed a model-driven approach in order to generate the complete monitoring infrastructure in an overall methodology called architecture for business process optimization (aPro) [12], which uses a format called ProGoalML as a basis. In this paper we will extend the architecture by automatic creation of CEP rules, formal definitions of the transformation algorithm, as well as description of the challenges in creating rules for certain process patterns.

This paper is organized as follows. In Section 2 we describe the aPro architecture. Based on this, we analyze additional needs for monitoring business processes and derive new ProGoalML elements fulfilling these needs in Section 2.1. In Section 2.2, we will describe the creation of CEP rules based on ProGoalML. In Section 2.3, we will describe challenges including exclusive gateways, parallelization in business processes, as well as iteration in detail. Section 3 shows how the concept is applied to a real-world use case of support request processing. We compare our approach to related work in Section 4. Finally, in Section 5 a conclusion and an outlook on future work are given.

2   Concept

In this section we give a short overview of the aPro approach (see Figure 1) [12]. In order to monitor a process, aPro uses four components: (1) *Monitoring stubs and web services* are used to collect measurements from application systems, (2) a *CEP engine* processes these measurements and calculate key performance indicators (KPIs) and goals, the resulting data is stored in a (3) *data warehouse*. A (4) *dashboard* displays real-time as well as long-time monitoring data and alerts

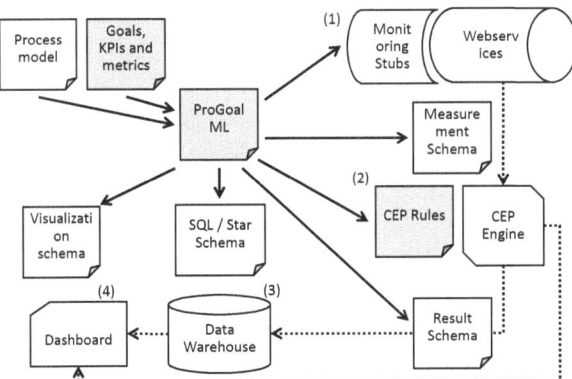

Fig. 1. Overview of documents created with ProGoalML. Dotted lines indicate flow of monitoring data between components. Grey parts highlight focus of this work.

the user in case a goal is violated. Configuration of aPro begins with modeling a process model in BPMN 2.0. In order to define what is to be monitored within the process, we extended BPMN 2.0 with modeling elements for metrics, KPIs, and goals for allowing the user to add a *goal model* to the process. Process and goal model are stored in ProGoalML, the *Process Goal Markup Language*, which serves as a central interchange format from which all other configuration files are generated. This file is used to generate the complete monitoring infrastructure automatically for standard monitoring problems and only needs human intervention for complex cases as well as additional requirements, like fine-tuning the dashboard.

2.1   Extended aPro Notation and Additional ProGoalML Elements

The aPro notation has been introduced in [11]. However, for allowing a purely model-driven approach for event-driven business process monitoring, it has to be possible to model two novel elements: (1) *aggregated KPIs*, which allow KPIs to be filtered aggregated over certain time periods, and (2) *timing goals*, which allow alerting the user based on non-conducted measurements (missing event). An overview of all elements is shown in Figure 2.

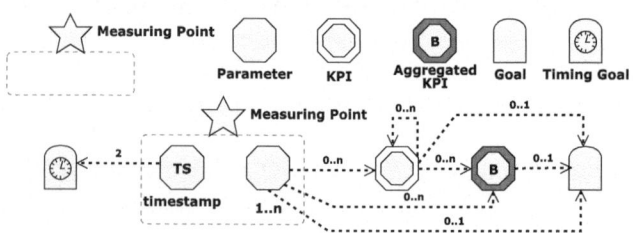

Fig. 2. ProGoalML modeling elements

A single measured value is called a *Parameter*; these are grouped in *measuring points*. A measuring point may be attached to any BPMN element at which a measurement shall occur. Whenever this element is reached during execution, the values of all parameters of the attached measuring point are included in a data set called a *measurement*.

A single *Parameter* p is a tuple
$$p \in P = (n, t, E_p)$$
where P is the set of all parameters, n is the name and $t \in T$ is the type. If $t = Enumeration$, then E_p is the set of possible values of p, else $E_p = \emptyset$.

$T = \{$Boolean, Enumeration, Integer, Double, String, ID, Long, Timestamp$\}$

is the set of types, determining the possible values. The type *Timestamp* is used for measuring points in time. As each measurement occurs at a specific time, each measuring point has to have a parameter *timestamp* of type Timestamp, which is either modeled explicitly or added to the generated ProGoalML automatically.

A *measuring point* m is defined as a tuple

$m \in M = (e, P_m)$

where M is the set of all measuring points, e is the BPMN element the measuring point is attached to and P_m is the set of parameters belonging to m. A parameter may only belong to a single measuring point. However, names of parameters have to be unique only within the measuring point:

$\forall p_1, p_2 \in P : (\exists m \in M : p_1, p_2 \in P_m) \rightarrow n_{p_1} \neq n_{p_2}$

Each measuring point has to contain the timestamp of the measurement:

$\forall m \in M : ('timestamp', Timestamp, \emptyset) \in P_m$

A *Key Performance Indicators* (KPI) is seen "as a key process metric, which is evaluated in a certain analysis period and has a target value which should be reached or preserved within the analysis period indicating the achievement of predefined business goals" [20] and in our approach is calculated from the gathered measurements, and the target value to be reached is called *goal* here (see below). In aPro two kinds of KPIs are distinguished: (1) a *regular KPI* is calculated once for each process instance from the measurements and other KPIs of the process instance and is defined as follows:

$k \in K = (n, f, V_k)$

where K is the set of all regular KPIs, n is the Name of the KPI, f is the function to calculate the KPI and $V_k \subset P \cup K$ is the set of input variables.

In comparison, an (2) *aggregated KPI* is calculated from the measurements of multiple process instances, e.g. to get an average:

$a \in A = (n, f, V_k, w, c)$

where A is the set of all aggregated KPIs, and n is the name. f is the aggregating function like average, sum, count, etc. w is the window used for aggregation. It may either specify a length (number of measurements) or a time window (measurements in a timespan). c is a filter condition for measurements to be used in the aggregation (e.g. successful process instances). Aggregated KPIs may not serve as input variables for other KPIs as their windows might be different and correct calculations might not be possible.

Goals define desired results of the process. A goal is defined as follows:

$g \in G = (n, f, v)$

where G is the set of all goals, f is the function to determine if the goal is fulfilled and $v \in P \cup K \cup A$ is the input variable. Goals are calculated from a single input. A special goal type is the *timing goal tg*, which imposes a timing restriction between two measurements and is defined as follows:

$tg \in TG = (t, p_s, p_e)$

with TG as the set of all timing goals, p_s as the parameter timestamp of the first measurement, p_e as the parameter timestamp of the second measurement and t as the maximum acceptable time between both measurements. The timing goal is fulfilled iff $p_e - p_s \leq t$. Differentiating timing goals from regular goals is necessary in order to detect a timing violation in absence of the second measurement as soon as more time than t has passed.

2.2 Generic Approach for Rule Generation

For model-driven automated monitoring *CEP rules* have to be created automatically from the ProGoalML, providing following functionality:

1. Correlate all measurements of a single process instance
2. Calculate regular KPIs and goals after the instance has finished
3. Calculate aggregated KPIs and goals every time an instance has finished
4. Raise an alert if a goal or timing goal is violated

On 1.: Parameters of type *ID* are used to identify process instances and thus to correlate measurements within instances. If two measurements contain an ID parameter with the same name and the same value, both measurements are assumed to stem from the same process instance and can be correlated. In case of multiple IDs within one instance it might be necessary to match these similarly to a join in a relational database [11]. If measurements within one instance cannot be correlated with each other, the process is divided in multiple *coverage classes* cc, for each of which a separate rule set is generated:

$cc \in CC = (M_{cc}, K_{cc}, A_{cc}, G_{cc})$

$M_{cc} = \{m \in M | \forall m_a \in M_{cc} \exists m_0, ..., m_n \in M : m_0 = m_a \wedge m_n = m \wedge \forall i \in [0, n) : \exists p_1 \in P_{m_i}, p_2 \in P_{m_{i+1}} : n_{p_1} = n_{p_2} \wedge t_{p_1} = t_{p_2} = ID\}$

$K_{cc} = \{k \in K | V_k \subseteq P_{cc} \cup K_{cc}\}$

$A_{cc} = \{a \in A | V_a \subseteq P_{cc} \cup K_{cc}\}$

$G_{cc} = \{g \in G | v_g \in P_{cc} \cup K_{cc} \cup A_{cc}\}$

with the set of parameters $P_{cc} = \{p | p \in P_m \wedge m \in M_{cc}\}$. Each coverage class thus contains all measurement points which may be correlated as well as all calculated KPIs and goals. If a KPI is calculated from multiple parameters, these parameters have to be in the same coverage class, because otherwise the set of input variables cannot be determined:

$\forall k \in K : \forall v_1, v_2 \in V_k : \exists cc \in CC : v_1, v_2 \in P_{cc} \cup K_{cc}$

The rules generated in the first step gather all measurements for each coverage class using the IDs and a pattern. All parameters p and their measured values v of a process instance are written in a single complex event e_0:

$e_0 = \{(p, v) | \exists m \in M_{cc} : p \in P_m \wedge v = measurement(p)\}$

On 2.: The next step is to calculate the values of all regular KPIs and goals. As KPIs and goals may use other KPIs as input variables, an order of calculation has to be found. In order to calculate a KPI, all its input variables have to available beforehand. Using the relation of input variables, we can define a graph of calculation dependencies as follows:

$G_{cc} = (V_{cc}, E_{cc})$

$V_{cc} = P_{cc} \cup K_{cc} \cup \{g | g \in G_{cc} \wedge v_g \notin A\}$

$E_{cc} = \{(s, k) | k \in K_{cc} \wedge s \in V_k\} \cup \{(s, g) | g \in G_{cc} \wedge s = v_g\}$

Cycles may not be modeled, as calculation of KPIs in the cycle would be impossible. The dependency graph is thus a directed acyclic graph, where the calculation order can be obtained using a modified algorithm for topological ordering [9]:

Algorithm for calculation order

$Rest := V_{cc} \setminus P_{cc}$
$Calculated := P_{cc}$
$i := 0$
while $(Rest \neq \emptyset)$
    $i := i + 1$
    $Step_i := \{k \in Rest | k \in K_{cc} \wedge V_k \subseteq Calculated\}$
        $\cup \{g \in Rest | g \in G_{cc} \wedge v_g \in Calculated\}$
    $Calculated := Calculated \cup Step_i$
    $Rest := Rest \setminus Step_i$
endwhile

For each $Step_i$ calculated by the algorithm a rule has to be generated which calculates the KPIs and goals in $Step_i$ using the results of the previous step $i - 1$ and adding the result to the complex event:

$e_i = e_{i-1} \cup \{(x,v) | x \in Step_i \wedge v = f_x(e_{i-1})\}$

On 3.: The result of the last step is an event e containing the values of all regular KPIs, goals, and parameters for a single process instance. These events serve as input for the calculation of aggregated KPIs, which use separate rules as they rely on a context beyond a single instance. A rule is generated for each aggregated KPI a calculating the result of its function f_a for all applicable events:

$e_a = (n_a, f_a(\{e | e \in w_a \wedge c(e) = true\}))$

Applicable events are the events which occur within the specified window at time of rule evaluation and fulfill the filter condition.

On 4.: For each goal g an alert rule is defined, which generates an alert event e_g whenever the goal is not fulfilled. Depending on the KPI or parameter the goal is defined on, the appropriate events have to be used as input variables. As goals and regular KPIs of a process are only calculated after an instance is finished, timing goals use separate rules to alert in case of missing or late measurements. For each timing goal tg a pattern is used which generates an alert event e_g if after receiving a measurement containing p_s the time t passes without receiving a measurement containing p_e.

2.3 Challenges in Rule Generation

An *event pattern* is a sequence of specific events which triggers the generation of a complex event [13]. In a sequential process, generating these patterns is straightforward as the pattern only has to account for all measurements arriving in sequential order. However, dealing with complex, non-linear process structures generating these patterns poses some challenges. This includes basically three types of problems: (a) conditional branches, (b) parallel execution of tasks, and (c) loops (see Figure 3).

For conditional branches in process models several problems appear. First of all, in scenario (a.1) in Figure 3 on the left side it is impossible to detect if

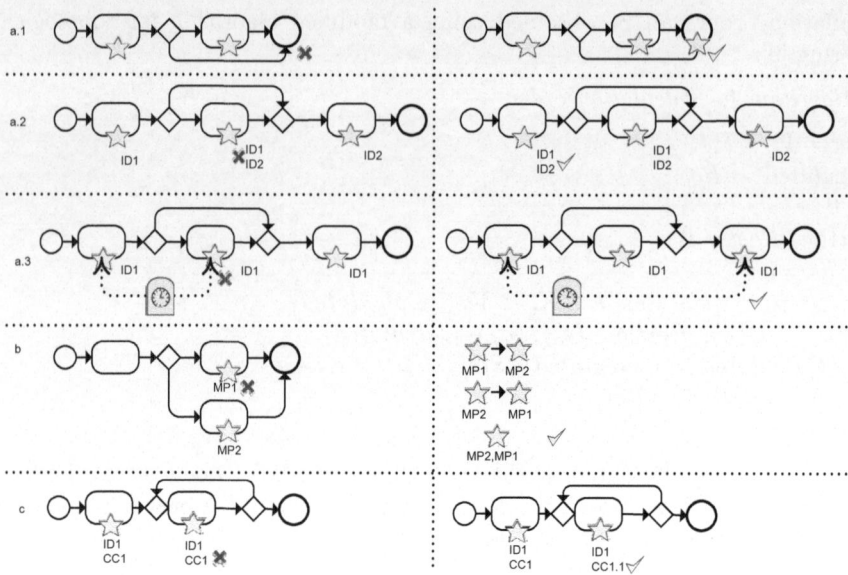

Fig. 3. Challenges in modeling goals, KPIs, and parameters in complex situations

a process has finished. Using the first measuring point marked by a star, the process start is detected, and a measurement for the second measuring point is anticipated. However, using the empty process branch, there will never be a second measurement. As this is a variant of the halting problem [17], it is undecidable. To resolve this issue, a third measuring point at the end of the process needs to be inserted (see right side).

A different scenario (a.2) in Figure 3 deals with the detection of coverage classes for measuring points [12]. On the first glance, all measuring points belong to the same coverage class. However, the second measuring point which is needed to correlate $ID1$ and $ID2$ is conditional and thus some process instances will not contain the measurement, making it impossible to correlate measurements and calculate KPIs. Therefore, it shall not be allowed to merge coverage classes using conditional measuring points (resolution on the right).

In scenario (a.3) it is shown that timing goals cannot be positioned in and outside of a certain conditional branch. Depending on the process instance, the second measuring point might not be traversed at all, resulting in (invalid) alerts as the measurement is never taken. If regular KPIs are calculated across conditional measurements, the KPI value is defined as *null* if one measurement with an input variable is missing; a null value is neglected for aggregated KPIs.

When dealing with parallel measurements, each measurement may be taken first (b). Thus, the pattern must be able to recognize all possible combinations.

In loop scenarios (c) it is difficult to detect how many loop executions are performed. Otherwise, similarly to (a.1) it is impossible to wait for an infinite number of loops, making it impossible to determine when the process instance has finished. Additionally, the semantics of a measuring point within a loop are unclear considering what the results of measuring have to be. Consider for example a KPI between both measuring points in (c). If multiple measurements of the second point occur, it is unclear which is to be used as an input variable for KPI calculation. Therefore, steps within a loop are regarded as their own coverage class, which is not merged with measuring points outside the loop even if the same IDs are used. This allows for example calculations of aggregated KPIs outside the loop and inside the loop, but not merged.

These basic cases may occur multiple times or nested within each other, thus resulting in further challenges for pattern creation. Currently, our approach has two steps. In the first step the BPMN process is converted into a Petri net[6]. A petri net is chosen in order to reduce the cases to be handled in pattern detection and in order to leave open the possibility for extending aPro to other modeling languages. This Petri net is then used to find the coverage classes and a pattern for each coverage class. Currently, the scenarios (a.1), (a.2), (a.3) are excluded, whereas (b) and (c) are resolved as described.

3   Use Case and Evaluation

The use case shows a two level support process (see Figure 4). First, the support request is opened and the request is given a *RequestID*, a parameter of type ID, measured in a measuring point called *MP1*. Additionally MP1 contains the registered timestamp of the measurement, indicated by the reserved word *timestamp*. In the first level support process, the parameter *Resolved* marks if the request has been resolved at this stage. The total cost *TotalCost* of the process is also available at MP2. Second level support only is called if an issue is not resolved in first level, containing basically the same parameters. Finally, the support request is closed, monitoring when and at what level the support request was resolved.

From the described parameters, various KPIs and aggregated KPIs are derived. First of all, the duration of the second level is measured as *Duration_second-_level*. This is derived from MP3.timestamp - MP2.timestamp, aggregated over a certain time. Measuring the cost is slightly more complicated, as the cost in our example is not available at every process step, but only at MP2 and MP4. This is possible by calculating the cost of the process at the end, subtracting the cost of the first level support (MP5.TotalCost - MP2.TotalCost), filtering the non-resolved support requests using MP2.Resolved. Finally we use a timing goal called *Duration_below_5_days* in order to ensure that all support requests are closed within this timespan. Additionally there is a goal for the average duration *Duration_average* to be below 2 days *Duration_average_below_2_days*. However in contrast to the timing goal, in this measurement only completed measurements are included, causing the necessity of timing goals for possible alerts of non-submitted events. Finally, the non-aggregated KPI *Resolved_Level* is measured, which shows in which level a certain issue has been resolved. Possible values therefore indicate first level, second level, and other. An exemplary subset of the generated CEP rules follows, starting with the correlation of all measurements

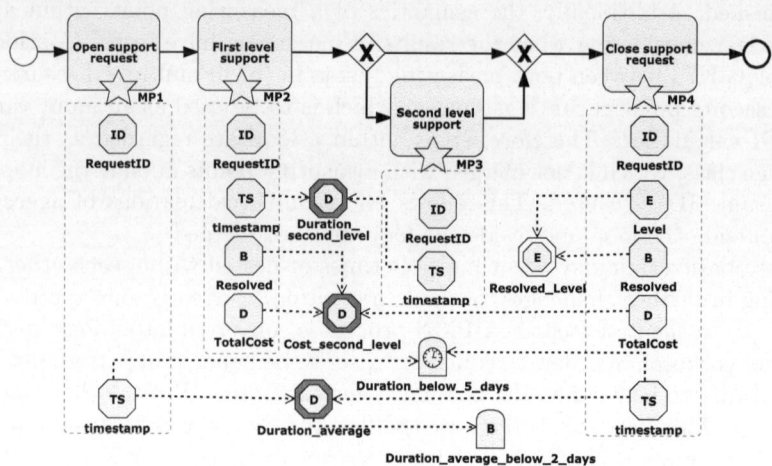

Fig. 4. Use case of two level support request processing

as described in Section 2.1 in step 1 and as described in step 2 calculating the KPIs and goals with only parameters as input variables. *IN* is the prefix used for incoming event streams for the measuring points, while *OUT* is the prefix used for outgoing event streams.

```
INSERT INTO 'OUTUseCase' SELECT MP4.RequestID AS RequestID,
MP4.Resolved AS MP4___Resolved, [..]
CASE WHEN (MP4.Level="1") THEN "1" WHEN (MP4.Resolved)
THEN "2" ELSE "Other" END AS Resolved_Level,
MP4.timestamp.after(MP1.timestamp, 0 sec, 5 day) AS
Duration_below_5_days FROM PATTERN
[(EVERY MP1 = INMP1 -> MP2 = INMP2(RequestID = MP1.RequestID) ->
MP4 = INMP4(RequestID = MP1.RequestID AND RequestID
NOT IN (select INMP3.RequestID FROM INMP3.win:keepall())))) OR
(EVERY MP1 = INMP1 -> MP2 = INMP2(RequestID = MP1.RequestID) ->
MP3 = INMP3(RequestID = MP1.RequestID) ->
MP4 = INMP4(RequestID = MP1.RequestID))]
```

The calculation of aggregated KPIs follows as described in step 3. Note that the output events of the first rule are used as input for aggregated KPIs.

```
INSERT INTO 'OUTDuration_average'
SELECT (AVG(MP4___timestamp - MP1___timestamp))/3600000
AS Duration_average FROM 'OUTUseCase'.win:length(100)

INSERT INTO 'OUTDuration_average_below_2_days'
SELECT OUTDuration_average.Duration_average<(2*24) AS
```

```
Duration_average_below_2_days FROM
PATTERN [EVERY OUTDuration_average = OUTDuration_average]

INSERT INTO 'OUTCost_second_level'
SELECT AVG(MP4___TotalCost - MP2___TotalCost) AS
Cost_second_level FROM
'OUTUseCase'.win:length(100) WHERE NOT(MP2___Resolved)
```

Finally an example of an alert rule as described in step 4 is shown.

```
INSERT INTO 'OUTDuration_below_5_daysAlerts'
SELECT MP1.RequestID AS RequestID FROM PATTERN
[EVERY MP1 = INMP1 -> (timer:interval(5 day) AND NOT
MP4 = INMP4(RequestID = MP1.RequestID))]
```

To evaluate the approach, a prototype has been created which generates the above rules automatically. Additionally, an automatic deployment of the rules has been implemented in the open source CEP engine Esper [1]. The modeling tool is based on an open modeling framework, whereas the monitoring web services are based on Java REST-calls. Current work aims at implementing a dashboard automatically using a semantic dashboard description language [10].

4 Related Work

The related work to this paper is structured in two main topics: (1) approaches to modeling KPIs and (2) approaches for modeling CEP rules for monitoring.

For modeling KPIs a semantic approach is presented in [15]. Although most constructs of ProGoalML are described similarly, to our knowledge the approach does not tackle the generation of CEP rules based on a model. Another way to model metrics in a BPEL process is presented in [19]. These are then transformed for the use in Business Activity Monitoring. In [2] not only instance, but also aggregate performance metrics are considered. However, these approaches have not been used for defining CEP rules for event-driven platform-independent business process monitoring. A model-driven approach for KPIs in a BPEL process is [14], in which a monitoring model is derived across multiple abstraction levels. The complexity of the underlying platform is hidden as in aPro, but only specific systems can be monitored.

For modeling CEP rules (2) several approaches exist as well. One possibility to define complex events in a BPMN process is called BEMN [5]. However, this focuses on defining CEP rules instead of showing the business perspective of KPIs and goals. Business users are more used to thinking in KPIs, aggregating information, and specifying views on information, than in event processing language constructs. For finding service level violations [4] defines hierarchical organized Service Level Objects. Monitoring data is correlated using event logs. However, the approach we present here focuses on different event sources, not only considering logs, and the event organization is directly extracted from the

ProGoalML. In [16] events are polled from the process execution. For preparation, a process model and event descriptions and requirements are described to configure the non-intrusive monitoring. However, the creation of a monitoring policy is not performed automatically. WS-BPEL processes are validated in run-time in [3]. Similarly to ProGoalML goals compliance is checked. However, the rules are not automatically generated from a graphical or xml notation. The same accounts for [2], which extends the runtime engine, submitting events for monitoring. The rules for monitors have also to be specified manually, requiring a process engine. Similarly to CEP rules[13] they deliver numeric or Boolean values, but have to be specified separately from the process.

5   Conclusion and Outlook

In this paper we showed how the aPro approach can be used to automatically generate CEP based on the ProGoalML format. This allows for a model-driven generation of the complete monitoring infrastructure, which we have implemented in a prototype. This is a large simplification for setting up monitoring in non-workflow environments distributed over several legacy systems, allowing the involvement of business users in the modeling of their monitoring needs and allowing changes by using the model-driven approach.

However, the shortcomings of this approach include a limited complexity of possible rule patterns. Although it is possible to aggregate KPIs, it is not possible to correlate aggregated KPIs to each other, like for example having a distribution over averages over a certain enumeration, which exceeds the power of the graphical representation. In the future we will show how to integrate fully automated dashboard generation for displaying the monitored data in a user-centric way based on [10]. Finally additional work on the topics of patterns for conditional branches and loops is planned.

Altogether this paper shows a large step towards the vision of event-based model-driven business process monitoring. However, in context of the larger aPro architecture and the goal of event-driven BPM, generated rules need to provide KPIs and goals as soon as possible so adaptation is possible within the same process instance. We will further tackle this challenge when detailing adaptation.

References

1. Esper - Complex Event Processing, http://esper.codehaus.org/
2. Barbon, F., Traverso, P., Pistore, M., Trainotti, M.: Run-Time Monitoring of Instances and Classes of Web Service Compositions. In: International Conference on Web Services, ICWS 2006, pp. 63–71 (2006)
3. Baresi, L., Guinea, S.: Towards Dynamic Monitoring of WS-BPEL Processes. In: Benatallah, B., Casati, F., Traverso, P. (eds.) ICSOC 2005. LNCS, vol. 3826, pp. 269–282. Springer, Heidelberg (2005)

4. Bodenstaff, L., Wombacher, A., Reichert, M., Jaeger, M.C.: Monitoring Dependencies for SLAs: The MoDe4SLA Approach. In: IEEE 5th Int'l. Conference on Services Computing, pp. 21–29. IEEE Computer Society Press (2008)
5. Decker, G., Grosskopf, A., Barros, A.: A Graphical Notation for Modeling Complex Events in Business Processes. In: 11th IEEE International Enterprise Distributed Object Computing Conference, EDOC 2007, p. 27 (2007)
6. Dijkman, R.M., Dumas, M., Ouyang, C.: Formal Semantics and Analysis of BPMN Process Models using Petri Nets
7. Gartner: Gartner Reveals Five Business Process Management Predictions for 2010, and Beyond (2010), http://www.gartner.com/it/page.jsp?id=1278415
8. Goldenson, D., Gibson, D.: Demonstrating the Impact and Benefits of CMMI: an Update and Preliminary Results. Tech. rep. (2003)
9. Kahn, A.B.: Topological Sorting of Large Networks. Commun. ACM 5, 558–562 (1962)
10. Kintz, M.: A Semantic Dashboard Description Language for a Process-oriented Dashboard Design Methodology. In: Proceedings of 2nd International Workshop on Model-based Interactive Ubiquitous Systems (MODIQUITOUS 2012), Copenhagen, Denmark (to appear, 2012)
11. Koetter, F., Kochanowski, M.: Goal-Oriented Model-Driven Business Process Monitoring Using ProGoalML. In: Abramowicz, W., Kriksciuniene, D., Sakalauskas, V. (eds.) BIS 2012. LNBIP, vol. 117, pp. 72–83. Springer, Heidelberg (2012)
12. Koetter, F., Weisbecker, A., Renner, T.: Business Process Optimization in Cross-Company Service Networks - Architecture and Maturity Model. In: Proceedings of the 2012 Annual SRII Global Conference (SRII 2012) (to be published, 2012)
13. Luckham, D.C.: The Power of Events: An Introduction to Complex Event Processing in Distributed Enterprise Systems. Addison-Wesley, Boston (2001)
14. Momm, C., Gebhart, M., Abeck, S.: A Model-Driven Approach for Monitoring Business Performance in Web Service Compositions. In: Proceedings of the 2009 Fourth International Conference on Internet and Web Applications and Services, pp. 343–350. IEEE Computer Society, Washington, DC (2009)
15. del-Río-Ortega, A., Resinas, M., Ruiz-Cortés, A.: Defining Process Performance Indicators: An Ontological Approach. In: Meersman, R., Dillon, T.S., Herrero, P. (eds.) OTM 2010. LNCS, vol. 6426, pp. 555–572. Springer, Heidelberg (2010)
16. Spanoudakis, G.: Non Intrusive Monitoring of Service Based Systems. International Journal of Cooperative Information Systems 15, 325–358 (2006)
17. Turing, A.M.: On Computable Numbers, with an Application to the Entscheidungsproblem. Proceedings of the London Mathematical Society 42, 230–265 (1936)
18. Vidačković, K., Weiner, N., Kett, H., Renner, T.: Towards Business-Oriented Monitoring and Adaptation of Distributed Service-Based Applications from a Process Owner's Viewpoint. In: Dan, A., Gittler, F., Toumani, F. (eds.) ICSOC/ServiceWave 2009. LNCS, vol. 6275, pp. 385–394. Springer, Heidelberg (2010)
19. Wetzstein, B., Strauch, S., Leymann, F.: Measuring Performance Metrics of WS-BPEL Service Compositions. In: Fifth International Conference on Networking and Services, ICNS 2009, pp. 49–56 (2009)
20. Wetzstein, B., Ma, Z., Leymann, F.: Towards Measuring Key Performance Indicators of Semantic Business Processes. In: Abramowicz, W., Fensel, D. (eds.) BIS 2008. LNBIP, pp. 227–238. Springer, Heidelberg (2008)

Event-Driven Scientific Workflow Execution

Zhili Zhao and Adrian Paschke

Institute of Computer Science,
Freie Universität Berlin,
Corporate Semantic Web Work Group
Königin-Luise-Str. 24/26, 14195 Berlin, Germany
{zhili,paschke}@inf.fu-berlin.de
http://www.corporate-semantic-web.de/

Abstract. Scientific workflows streamline large-scale, complex scientific processes and enable different parts of a process to be systematically and efficiently executed on distributed resources. In this paper, we propose an event-driven framework for scientific workflows, which goes beyond the typical paradigm of global ECA (Event-Condition-Action) rules and executes scientific processes in terms of event message-driven conversations between rule agents. The behavioral reaction logic implemented by messaging reaction rules in combination with derivation rules used to represent complicated scientific conditional logic provides a highly expressive, scalable and flexible way to define complex scientific workflow patterns. Finally, a prototype system based on a Web rule engine Prova and a tool for rule-based collaboration Rule Responder is demonstrated.

Keywords: Reaction rules, Derivation Rules, Scientific Workflows.

1 Introduction

Scientific workflows have attracted more and more interest in the recent years, as science becomes increasingly reliant on the analysis of massive data sets and the use of distributed resources [13]. A scientific workflow enables scientists to represent and manage large-scale and complex scientific processes and accelerates the pace of scientific progress in different disciplines. However, compared to the traditional business workflows, scientific workflows still haven't been widely used in research activities.

Scientific experiments usually involve many complicated processes to prove a goal or gain meaningful result. For example, a bag-of-task[1] is usually time-intensive work, which requires to be divided and assigned to separate processes in a distributed system (e.g. genome alternative splicing analysis in bioinformatics, virtual screening in drug discovery, etc.). Traditional business processes usually focus on the common workflow constructs and cannot describe these kinds of ad hoc scientific processes. Moreover, scientific workflows are often exploratory in nature, with new analysis methods being rapidly evolved from some some initial

---

[1] http://www.cs.odu.edu/~fmccown/research/remoting_taskbag/about.html

M. La Rosa and P. Soffer (Eds.): BPM 2012 Workshops, LNBIP 132, pp. 390–401, 2013.

ideas and preliminary workflow designs [9]. This means scientific workflows need to be easily reused and modified. On the contrary, business workflows undergo far fewer changes and are executed frequently with newly acquired datasets or varying parameter settings and are expected to run reliably and efficiently [6]. For example, the OSASIS Web Serivces Business Process Execution Language (BPEL, also known as BPEL4WS or WSBPEL) that completely specifies computation as a set of connected statements (i.e. every possible behavior must be explicitly specified) and is limited to a flexible design.

Scientific workflows enable different parts of a process to be systematically and efficiently executed in an environment, which is characterized by the large volumes of data and events generated and by the distributed and heterogeneous nature of the involved resources [7]. Currently, there are many industrial-strength Business Process Management (BPM) workflow tools available. However, when they come to the weakly-structured knowledge-intensive scientific workflows, practice experiences have shown that the modelled scientific process representations are often not enacted correctly, consistently and homogeneously [12]. For the purpose of improving the adaptability and flexibility, many prominent approaches have been proposed to deal with dynamic changes during the execution of scientific workflows. Among them the most suited one is Event-Condition-Action (ECA)-based languages [4]. The ECA rules allow a system to react to occurrences in its environment and are the key factor in upcoming agile and flexible IT infrastructures and distributed loosely coupled service oriented environments [11]. However, traditional ECA rules are usually global rules and strictly follow the form *On* Event *If* Condition *Do* Action to detect and react to events. When they come to the scientific workflow domain, they are still limited to describing complicated scientific conditional procedures and scientific rules.

In this paper, we present an event-driven framework for scientific workflows, which goes beyond the typical paradigm of global ECA (Event-Condition-Action) rules and executes scientific processes in terms of the order of sending and receiving event messages between distributed rule agents. Event-driven architecture not only allows to detect and respond to events generated during the execution immediately, but also supports to form a scalable choreography style workflow execution environment via distributed agents. Moreover, with the combination the derivation rules to represent complicated scientific conditional logic and the messaging reaction rules to describe conversation-based process flows between distributed agents, we present a declarative and expressive rule-based way to describe complicated scientific processes. As a whole, our solution is characterized by the following advantages:

- Abstraction via a distributed multi-agent model for distributed choreography style workflow execution.
- Decoupled via event messages enabling asynchronous communication and parallel processing of problem solving tasks in distributed agents.
- Situation-awareness and behavioural dynamic reactions via reaction rules leading to dynamic and agile workflow reaction patterns.

- Complex decision logic via derivation rules and logical inference deductions beyond the typical restricted expressiveness of simple gateways in process execution models.
- Semantic workflow execution via domain models and information models represented as ontologies which are integrated into semantically typed rules.

The rest of the paper is structured as follows: in Section 2 we describe several key requirements of event-driven scientific workflows. In Section 3, we introduce the event-driven framework for scientific workflows. After that, we present a prototype system based on a Web rule engine Prova and a tool for rule-based collaboration Rule Resdponder used to seamlessly connect distributed rule agents in Section 4. We give the related work in Section 5 and close the paper with some concluding remarks and future research directions in Section 6.

2   The Key Requirements of Event-Driven Scientific Workflows

Besides the common requirements of scientific workflows, such as service composition and reuse, reliability, reproducibility, etc., in this section we put our view on the requirements of executing scientific workflows in terms of events generated at runtime.

2.1   Event-Driven Architecture

The infrastructure of scientific workflows is comprised of inter-connected research instruments, computing facilities, data sources, etc., which are autonomous and may come or disappear at any time. In order to detect and react to these changes immediately, it is necessary to employ event-based reaction rules to drive the enactment of scientific workflows. In addition, other benefits may also bring along, such as: flexibility, agility, etc.

2.2   Global Events Messaging

Scientific workflows involve geographically distributed resources which are managed by different domains or organizations. An agent not only has to deal with internal events, but also the events from external counterparts. Therefore, an event messaging mechanism is required to define global reaction logic via sending and receiving event messages between distributed rule agents.

2.3   High Expressiveness

Scientific workflows often describe complicated scientific processes and involve many knowledge-intensive decision-centric activities. Although event-based architecture brings flexibility with global behavioral and reactive logic, it is still necessary to provide a high expressiveness to describe complicated scientific decision logic and rules.

2.4   Complex Event Processing

Events in scientific workflows are typically not atomic but complex, consisting of several atomic events occurred in the defined order and quantity, such as: conjunction, disjunction, sequence, etc. In order to support sophisticated behavioural dynamic reactions, the complex event processing operators which model and define complex event types are desired.

2.5   External Ontologies Integration

To cope with dynamic changes at runtime, it is necessary for workflow engines to understand operations, events and their context, especially in knowledge-intensive scientific workflows. To do so, integrating existing domain specific glossaries, taxonomies and Semantic Web ontologies is helpful.

3   Event-Driven Framework for Scientific Workflows

Figure 1 gives our event-driven framework for scientific workflows. We provide a declarative rule-based approach, which describes complicated scientific processes via the combination of messaging reaction rules and derivation rules. The reaction rules follow the typical ECA (Event-Condition-Action) paradigm but go beyond it by defining complex behavioural reaction logic and are capable of detecting complex events and responding with flexible sub-branches (e.g. actions). The derivation rules, on the other hand, express complicated scientific decision logic and provide a higher expressiveness than typical boolean expressions or simple rules in traditional business workflow languages. For the purpose of dynamically selecting available services to perform each individual step at runtime, we define them with users' capability requirements, instead of concrete their execution details and name these abstract services *tasks* in our work to make a difference.

The execution environment consists of distributed *rule agents*, which act as proxies or stubs of existing *services*, but complement them with additional semantics-based knowledge for service discovery, selection, invocation and composition. The knowledge could be the information about available services represented as ontologies or scientific rules used to evaluate the precondition before service invocation or postcondition, etc. As a basic unit of workflow, each *task* is performed by a *rule agent* with one or more concrete *services*. To represent their organizations, an Agent-Task ontology describes the relationships between *agents* and *tasks*, and a Task/Service ontology, which describes the relationship between *tasks* and their required *services* are used.

The execution of scientific workflows is driven by the order of sending and receiving event messages. To support the interaction, an Enterprise Service Bus (ESB) is employed to seamlessly connect these distributed *rule agents*. The architecture inherently combines the strength of both orchestration and choreography, which represent a centralized and decentralized service composition respectively:

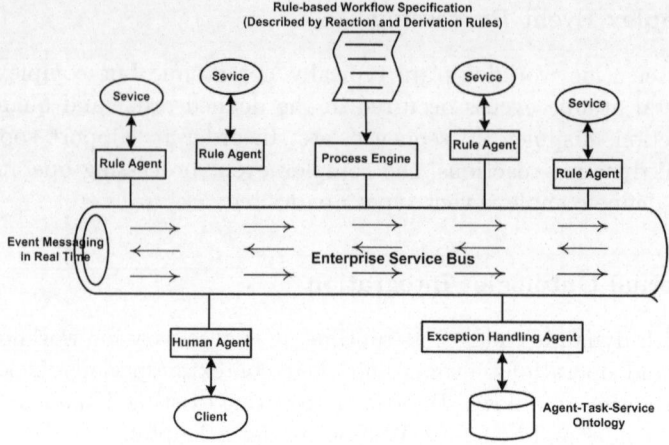

Fig. 1. Event-Driven Framework for Scientific Workflows

a centralized process engine (rule agent) takes control a scientific workflow involving a group of *tasks*, and completes it via the coordination between distributed *rule agents*, which are not aware of the whole complex workflow (orchestration). For each individual *task*, the appointed *agent* attempts to finish the *task*, and other *agents* may be involved once the appointed agent cannot fulfil it. That means, an *agent* may form a local collaborative environment to complete a single *task* without notifying the central process engine and provides a scalable execution at runtime (choreography).

Additionally, our framework supports both automatic exception handling and human involved decision making. The runtime exceptions in our work are also represented as event messages and transferring across the ESB. Once an *exception* occurs, an Exception Handling Agent is usually employed to receive the *exception* and query the public Agent-Task-Service ontology to find the alternative counterparts with the same effect and replace the failed sub-process dynamically. Once the *exception* cannot be handled by the Exception Handling Agent, a Human Agent is involved to ask users to make a decision or complement with the required resources. More details about exception handling see Section 4.4.

4   Event-Driven Scientific Workflow Execution

Based on aforementioned event-driven framework, we develop a prototype system, which executes scientific processes in terms of event message-driven conversations between rule agents. We employ Prova[2], which is both a Semantic Web rule language and a highly expressive rule engine to define and execute complicated scientific processes. In order to connect and manage the distributed rule

---

[2] http://www.prova.ws/

agents, a tool for rule-based collaboration Rule Responder is used. Moreover, we build the Agent-Task ontology and the Task-Service ontology to organize underlying resources.

4.1 Rule-Based Workflow Formalism and Complex Event Processing

As a highly expressive rule language, Prova draws on backward-reasoning logic programming concepts to formalize decision logic in terms of derivation rules and combines them with forward-directed messaging reaction rules for distributed event and action processing in order to exploit the benefits of both worlds. Prova supports declarative decision rules, complex reaction rule-based workflows, rule-based complex event processing, dynamic access to external data sources (e.g. databases, Semantic Web ontologies) and enables users to define complicated scientific processes.

The following example exemplifies the policies of screening the snow depth data (samples) measured by local meteorological stations in the experiment of building a snow depth model based on AMSR-E[3] brightness temperature and local measured meteorological data. In the experiment of building a snow depth model in the pastoral area of Northern Xinjiang (in China) [15], the depth of the valid samples must be more than 3.0 centimeters and got from the location, where must be at an elevation lower than 2000 meters and has a temperature less than 6 °C. The screening policies are implemented by a derivation rule named "checkObservationData", and this rule will be proved if all its subgoals, which are used to check the elevation, depth, and temperature of the samples are proved. The critical values of the criteria are represented as facts, such as the fact "depth(3.0, centimeter).". Since the observed data may have different metrics (e.g. the snow depth is usually measured in centimeter, decimeter or meter), the conversions between different metrics are also implemented via derivation rules.

Screening Observation Data of Snowfall with Derivation Rules

```
depth(3.0, centimeter).
depth(D, decimeter) :-
   depth(D1, centimeter),
   math_mult(D1,10,D).

depth(D, meter) :-
   depth(D1, centimeter),
   math_mult(D1,100,D).

temperature(6, celsius).
temperature(T, fahrenheit):-
   temperature(T1, celsius),
   math_mult(T1,1.8,T2),
   math_add(T2,32,T).

elevation(2000, meter).
elevation(E,kilometer) :-
   elevation(E1, meter),
   math_div(E1,1000,E).
```

---

[3] http://www.ghcc.msfc.nasa.gov/AMSR/

```
checkObservationData(depth(Dep, DM), elevation(Ele, EM),temperature(Tem, TM)) :-
    checkDepth(Dep, DM),
    checkElevation(Ele,EM),
    checkTemperature(Tem,TM).

checkElevation(Ele, EM) :-
    elevation(E, EM),
    less(Ele, E).

checkTemperature(Tem, TM) :-
    temperature(T,TM)
    less(Tem,T).

checkDepth(Dep, DM) :-
    depth(D, DM),
    moreequ(Dep, D).
```

Reactive messaging is the foundation of the event message-based communication and is used to coordinate distributed rule agents to complete scientific goals. Prova provides the following constructs to send and receive one or more context-dependent multiple outbound or inbound event messages:

```
sendMsg(XID, Protocol, Agent, Performative, Payload|Context)
rcvMsg(XID, Protocol, From, Performative, Payload|Context)
rcvMult(XID, Protocol, From, Performative, Payload|Context)
```

where *XID* is the conversation identifier of a message. *Protocol* defines the communication protocol. *Agent* and *From* denote the destination and source of the message respectively. *Performative* describes the pragmatic context in which the message is sent. And *Payload—Context* denotes the actual content of the event message. It is worth noticing that *rcvMsg* can be both a *global reaction rule*, which has a rule base lifetime scope, and an *inline reaction rule*, whose scope can be controlled by other reactions. This means that it is possible for users to describe the complicated scientific logic via the arbitrary combination of sending and receiving event messages.

For the purpose of detecting and reacting complex events, Prova employs the *reaction group*, which implements the event algebra to specify complicated events constraints. Based on the primitive reactive constructs *rcvMsg* and *rcvMult*, Prova is capable of grouping more than one *inline reaction* using a logical operator and allowing detected composite events to be used in further processing. In other words, an exit channel intercepts the internal message sent by multiple event channels when an event pattern is successfully detected. In Prova 3.0, it supports two logical grouping: @and, which requires *all* the event channels to be successfully proved, and @or, which requires *either* of the event channels to be successfully proved. Around them, Prova 3.0 includes a great number of group annotations (see [5]) to define much more expressive and sophisticated complex event processing patterns, such as: @count, @size, @timeout, @not, @paused, @resume, @stop, etc.

The following example shows how reaction rules are used to detect the follow-up sequences of a "logout" followed by a "login" from another "IP". The principle is that, when the Prova engine finds the *AND* group, the special event of the message type *AND* is sent internally after all the conjuncted reactions are successfully detected and its payload, captured in the variable "Events", which contains the full history of events. The @timeout annotation in the example is used to wait for the follow-up event ("login") for a limited amount of time.

Example of Complex Event Processing

```
server() :-
    % Start detection on each new login
    rcvMult(XID,Protocol,From,request,login(User,IP)),
    server_1(XID).

server_1(XID) :-
    @group(g1) % reaction group "g1"
    rcvMsg(XID,Protocol,From,request,logout(User,IP)),
    println(["Got 1"]),

    % logout followed by login from different IP within 1 second
    @group(g1) @timeout(1000) % reaction group "g1"
    rcvMsg(XID,Protocol,From,request,login(User,IP2)) [IP2!=IP],
    println(["Got 2"]).

server_1(XID) :-
    @and(g1) @timeout(2000) % "and" event correlation in reaction group "g1"
    rcvMsg(XID,Protocol,From,and,Events),
    println(["Suspicious Login Pattern detected: ",Events]," ").
```

4.2   Rule Responder as Communication Middleware

To seamlessly connect distributed rule agents together quickly and easily, enabling them to exchange data, a tool for rule-based collaboration Rule Responder[4] is used as communication middleware. Rule Responder is built on top of the enterprise service bus Mule[5] for specifying virtual organizations and allows deploying the rule agents as Web-based endpoints in the Mule object broker. The broker object follows the Staged Event Driven Architecture (SEDA) pattern [14], which decomposes a complex, event-driven application into a set of stages connected by queues and avoids the high overhead associated with thread-based currency models. In addition, the de-facto standard Reaction RuleML[6] is used as a platform independent rule interchange format and a translator framework is provided to translate from Prova execution syntax into Reaction RuleML and vice versa.

4.3   The Agent-Task and Task-Service Ontology

As we mentioned before, the tasks in our workflow specifications are abstract ones and represent users' capability requirements that are used by distributed rule agents to find available concrete services at runtime. Our Agent-Task and Task-Service ontologies are the basis for the dynamic agent and service discovery at runtime. In the prototype system, we use an OWL DL[7] ontology to represent the relationship between agents and their capabilities (i.e. the tasks it can

---

[4] http://responder.ruleml.org/
[5] http://www.mulesoft.org
[6] http://ruleml.org/reaction/
[7] http://www.w3.org/TR/owl-ref/

perform). To improve the flexibility of the system, each task can be executed by one or more agents, and each agent may be responsible for more than one task, as shown in the following syntax of OWL.

```
<owl:ObjectProperty rdf:ID="isResponsibleFor">
    <rdfs:domain rdf:resource="#Agent"/>
    <rdfs:range rdf:resource="#Task"/>
    <owl:inverseOf rdf:resource="#isExecutedBy"/>
</owl:ObjectProperty>
<owl:ObjectProperty rdf:ID="isExecutedBy"/>
```

To tie together a set of tasks with the same functionality, the identity is indicated by the "sameAs" object property of OWL. For instance, the task "sub" and "minus" in following example are identical.

```
<service:Task rdf:ID="sub">
  <owl:sameAs rdf:resource="#minus" />
</service:Task>
```

Besides the Agent-Task ontology, we build a Task-Service ontology based on OWL-S[8], but tailor it by only reusing its atomic process description since an OWL composite process specifies the steps interacting with a single Web service implementation [1]. In terms of OWL-S, our current efforts focus on the functional description of each service by its input, output, precondition, the task it performs and the details of how an agent can access it. Similar with OWL-S, we describe the precondition expressions of a service with SWRL[9], which is an expressive OWL-based rule language.

4.4   Event-Driven Exception Handling

Rule-based specification and event-driven execution of scientific workflows bring a lot of superiorities, such as flexibility, adaptation, exception handling, etc. by detecting and reacting to runtime events and reasoning internal and external knowledge. In our prototype system, a scientific workflow is executed by the coordination of distributed Prova agents in an implicit hierarchical way, i.e. the

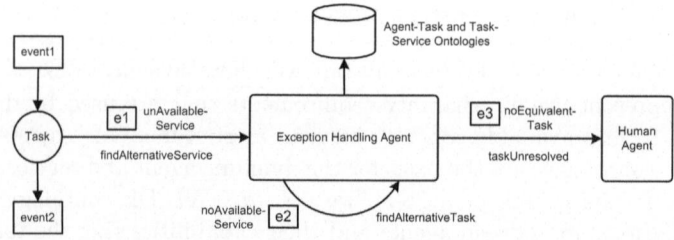

Fig. 2. Exception Handling in Event-Driven Scientific Workflows

---

[8] http://www.w3.org/Submission/OWL-S/
[9] http://www.w3.org/Submission/SWRL/

workflow execution is controlled by a centralized Prova engine, and the abstract tasks describing with users' capability requirements are allocated to distributed Prova agents and performed with concrete services. As we mentioned in Section 4.1, each Prova agent is endowed with the ability to reason external knowledge. That means, when an exception occurs, the involved Prova agents can query the Agent-Task and Task-Service ontologies to find alternative counterparts to deal with the exception. Figure 2 gives an example of handling a unavailable service exception. In case a service for a task is unavailable, an exception event message *e1* (unAvailableService) will be generated and sent to the Exception Handling Agent to find an alternative service via reasoning the Task-Service ontology. The failed service will be replaced once the alternative one is found. If there is no alternative service available, an exception event message *e2* (noAvailableService) will be generated to check if any alternative task exists via consulting the Agent-Task ontology. The workflow engine will reallocate the alternative task to a new agent once it is found. An exception event message *e3* (noEquivalentTask) will be sent to the Human Agent to ask scientists to intervene if the previous exception still cannot be resolved by the Exception Handling Agent. The scientists then will be involved to check the context information contained in the exception (*e3*), and make a decision on possible operations, such as: modify the task specification or update the knowledge base, etc.

5   Related Work and Discussion

There are quite a few efforts related to event-driven workflow execution have been made to deal with the dynamic changes in business and scientific environments. The paper [3] introduces an approach of using ECA rules to realize the workflow modeling and service composition. For the purpose of validating service composition at design time, an automatic event composition algorithm is developed. However, the approach focuses on the typical ECA rules and is limited to describing complicated process logic and complex event processing. Our previous work [11] elaborates a homogeneous integration approach, which combines derivation rules, reaction rules and other rule types such as integrity constraints into a general framework of logical programming. The approach exploits the advantages of different logic and rule-based approaches, and establishes a foundation for our event-driven framework for scientific workflows. The papers [2,10] introduce Rule Responder, which is a framework for specifying virtual organizations as semantic multi-agent to support collaborative teams. Human members of an organization are assisted by autonomous rule-based agents, which use Semantic Web rules to describe aspects of their owner's derivation and reaction logic. The solution provides a flexible and scalable framework to achieve complex goals and is the skeleton of our effort to scientific workflows.

In addition, the paper [7] proposes an event-driven publish/subscribe platform to serve as a runtime environment for the decentralized execution and avoids a single point of failure and the potential performance bottleneck in a centralized approach. The paper [8] proposes an inteorganizational workflow execution framework based on process agents and ECA rules. The whole interorganizational workflow is modeled as a multi-agent system with a process agent in each organization. Each local workflow is described by the ECA rules to control internal state transition and the process agent is used to control the external state transition of tasks by interaction protocols.

Compared to our rule-based approach, although both approaches mentioned above support event-driven workflow execution and provide the scalability at runtime, they are less expressive and flexible than our solution, which is capable of describing arbitrary scientific logic by combining reaction rules and derivation rules and logical inference deductions. Prova has a tight integration with Java, Semantic Web technologies and enterprise service-oriented computing and complex event processing technologies, it offers a syntactically economic and compact way of specifying agents' behaviour while allowing for efficient Java-based extensions to improve performance of critical operations. Moreover, the automatic exception handling based on the integration of Semantic Web ontologies and human involved decision making are also supported in our work.

6   Conclusions and Future Work

Many rigorous scientific workflow architectures and tools have been proposed since the workflow technology was applied to automate complex scientific processes. Typically these architectures support process languages, which are prescriptive and limited to a flexible design and processing dynamic runtime changes. In this paper, we propose an event-driven framework for scientific workflows, which supports the situation awareness via detecting internal and external events, reasoning the context information and triggering the following actions. With the combination the derivation rules to represent complicated scientific decision logic and the messaging reaction rules to describe behavioral reaction logic, it is possible to support workflow execution in terms of the event-driven conversations between distributed agents. Based on the prototype system implemented by Prova and Rule Responder, we have shown that our solution is not only a highly expressive declarative way of describing complicated scientific processes, but also is capable of integrating external knowledge bases to handle runtime exceptions and modify workflow structures dynamically.

Although the event-driven execution of scientific workflows improves the flexibility and scalability, it still faces the challenge of reproducibility, which requires the logging of the specific details of creating a derived data product and is very helpful for scientists to repeat workflows or validate their assumptions. In the future, we will focus on how to record and manage provenance data during the execution of scientific workflows driven by event messages across distributed rule agents.

References

1. Matskanis, N., Surridge, M., Silvestri, F., Cantalupo, B., Giammarino, L.: Semantic Workflow Representation and Samples. Technical report, University of Southampton IT Innovation Centre (2005)
2. Boley, H., Paschke, A.: Rule Responder Agents Framework and Instantiations. In: Elçi, A., Koné, M.T., Orgun, M.A. (eds.) Semantic Agent Systems. SCI, vol. 344, pp. 3–23. Springer, Heidelberg (2011)
3. Chen, L., Li, M., Cao, J.: A Rule-Based Workflow Approach for Service Composition. In: Pan, Y., Chen, D., Guo, M., Cao, J., Dongarra, J. (eds.) ISPA 2005. LNCS, vol. 3758, pp. 1036–1046. Springer, Heidelberg (2005)
4. Frincu, M., Craciun, C.: Dynamic and Adaptive Rule-Based Workflow Engine for Scientific Problems in Distributed Environments, ch. 10, pp. 227–251. CRC Press (2010)
5. Kozlenkov, A.: Prova Rule Language Version 3.0 User's Guide. Technical report (2010)
6. Leymann, F., Roller, D.: Production Workflow: Concepts and Techniques. Prentice Hall PTR, Upper Saddle River (2000)
7. Li, G., Muthusamy, V., Jacobsen, H.-A., Mankovski, S.: Decentralized Execution of Event-Driven Scientific Workflows. In: Proceedings of the IEEE Services Computing Workshops, SCW 2006, pp. 73–82. IEEE Computer Society, Washington, DC (2006)
8. Lin, D., Sheng, H., Ishida, T.: Interorganizational Workflow Execution Based on Process Agents and ECA Rules. IEICE - Trans. Inf. Syst. E90-D(9), 1335–1342 (2007)
9. Ludäscher, B., Weske, M., McPhillips, T., Bowers, S.: Scientific Workflows: Business as Usual? In: Dayal, U., Eder, J., Koehler, J., Reijers, H.A. (eds.) BPM 2009. LNCS, vol. 5701, pp. 31–47. Springer, Heidelberg (2009)
10. Paschke, A.: Rule Responder HCLS eScience Infrastructure. In: Proceedings of the 3rd International Conference on the Pragmatic Web: Innovating the Interactive Society, ICPW 2008, pp. 59–67. ACM, New York (2008)
11. Paschke, A., Kozlenkov, A., Boley, H.: A Homogenous Reaction Rules Language for Complex Event Processing. In: International Workshop on Event Drive Architecture for Complex Event Process (2007)
12. Paschke, A., Zhao, Z.: Process Makna - A Semantic Wiki for Scientific Workflows. In: Proceedings of the 3rd International Workshop on Semantic Web Applications and Tools for the Life Sciences (2010)
13. Taylor, I.J., Deelman, E., Gannon, D.B., Shields, M.: Workflows for e-Science: Scientific Workflows for Grids. Springer-Verlag New York, Inc., Secaucus (2006)
14. Welsh, M., Culler, D.E., Brewer, E.A.: SEDA: An Architecture for Well-Conditioned, Scalable Internet Services. In: SOSP, pp. 230–243 (2001)
15. Yu, H., Feng, Q., Zhang, X., Huang, X., Liang, T.: An Approach for Monitoring Snow Depth Based on AMSR-E Data in The Pastoral Area of Northern Xinjiang. Acta Prataculturae Sinica, 210–216 (2009)

An Event-Driven System for Business Awareness Management in the Logistics Domain

Babis Magoutas[1], Dominik Riemer[2], Dimitris Apostolou[1], Jun Ma[2], Gregoris Mentzas[1], and Nenad Stojanovic[2]

[1] Information Management Unit,National Technical University of Athens, 9 Iroon Polytechniou str., 157 80 Zografou, Athens, Greece
{elbabmag,dapost,gmentzas}@mail.ntua.gr
[2] FZI Research Center for Information Technologies, Haid-und-Neu-Str. 10-14, 76131 Karlsruhe, Germany
{riemer,ma,nstojano}@fzi.de

Abstract. Modern organizations need real-time awareness about the current business conditions and the various events that occur from multiple and heterogeneous environments and influence their business operations. Moreover, based on real-time awareness they need a mechanism that allows them to respond quickly to the changing business conditions, in order to either avoid problematic situations or exploit opportunities that may arise in their business environment. In this paper we present an event-driven system that enables awareness about the situations happening in business environments and increases organizations' responsiveness to them. We illustrate how the proposed system increases the awareness of stakeholders about the running business processes, as well as their flexibility by presenting a practical application of the system in the logistics domain.

Keywords: Business Awareness Management, Logistics, Situation-Action-Network.

1 Introduction

To thrive in today's competitive market, organizations need to be agile, responding quickly to changing market conditions and exceeding customers' demands. Achieving business flexibility is a necessary condition for the business development of organizations, especially nowadays due to the global market downstream. Business flexibility, however, implies flexibility in the underlying ICT infrastructure and business processes.

A major challenge of current business process management solutions is to continuously monitor on-going activities in a business environment [1] and to respond to business events with minimal latency. Recent advancements in event-based systems and complex event processing [2] enable faster response to critical business events by efficiently processing many events occurring across all the layers of an organization and identifying the most meaningful ones within heterogeneous business environments.

M. La Rosa and P. Soffer (Eds.): BPM 2012 Workshops, LNBIP 132, pp. 402–413, 2013.
© Springer-Verlag Berlin Heidelberg 2013

A recent research stream focuses on monitoring and responding to business situations detected through event patterns. For example SARI [3] provides an event-based rule management framework, which allows modeling business situations and exceptions with sense and respond rules. To wholly realize the potential of this research stream, it is essential to allow business users to model and intuitively comprehend the appropriate responses to business situations by using concepts that are familiar to them, like milestones and goals. Goal-orientation is based on separating the declarative statements defining desired system behavior from the various ways to achieve that behavior, thus hiding from business users the details about low-level events.

Hence, there is a clear need for an event-driven goal-oriented system, which would provide recommendations for reacting to interesting or critical business situations, while it would increase the awareness of business users regarding the running business processes.

In this paper, we focus on the challenges of enabling awareness about the business situations happening in business environments and increasing organizations' responsiveness to them. We present an event-driven framework for business awareness management, which aims to manage, i.e. monitor and control over time business situations and business systems that support the execution of business processes.

2   Motivating Scenario

Our presented scenario is based in the business area of large, end-customer oriented logistic companies like parcel deliverers. Usually, those companies operate a fleet of delivery vehicles that transport parcels, starting from a central repository, to the customer. Today, it is widely accepted that a predefined, optimized (in terms of time) routing plan leads to remarkable reductions of expenses in terms of fuel consumption and time savings. However, previously computed optimizations also imply less flexibility in the execution of business processes. Even in the case that routes can be changed during the business day, this is often a manually triggered, exceptional process that does not fully exploit new business opportunities that may appear.

From now on, we consider the case of a pickup service, which is the pickup of parcels directly at the customer's location. A pickup request is usually triggered by a customer via phone and entered in a CRM system by the call center agent. After that, one of the two situations applies: a) For important customers ("gold customers"), the agent might try to find a vehicle nearby to the customer and call the driver to pickup the parcel or b) the pickup is scheduled for the next business day.

Taking into account the real-time movement of vehicles (gathered by GPS devices) and external conditions like traffic, it is possible to automatically determine and inform the involved parties if it makes sense to pickup parcels immediately at the same day. We argue that adding more flexibility to this process can be beneficial for both customers and deliverers. Customers might profit from such an "express pickup" service in terms of the earlier pickup of parcels itself, while deliverers profit from increased customer satisfaction and less opportunity costs.

In the following sections, we provide a solution for this scenario by making use of advanced event processing capabilities and a contextual decision framework.

3   System Architecture

This section provides an overview of the major components our system is comprised of. Technically, the system is implemented as an event-driven architecture that connects several external services via a publish/subscribe broker using events in order to communicate between those components in a loosely-coupled fashion. Fig.1 shows the overall architecture of the proposed system.

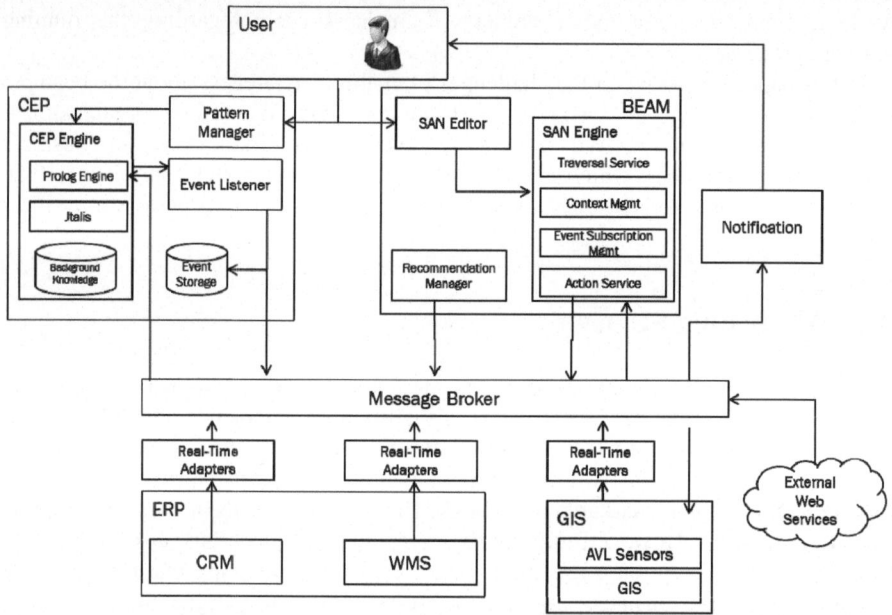

Fig. 1. Overall Architecture of the System

In general, we distinguish between event producers, software systems that provide the data needed for the presented use case, and event consumers, that subscribe to events in order to detect and trigger situations in real-time. As follows, we will describe the single components of the system architecture in more detail with an emphasis in the Complex Event Processing (CEP) and BusinEss Awareness Management (BEAM) components:

ERP. The ERP systems provide information about customers, orders and warehouse status. The systems have been extended with real-time adapters in order to directly capture status changes in the underlying systems. CRM produces events in case that new customers or orders have been created. Additionally, an adapter to a warehouse management system provides information about changes in a company's stock.

GIS. The Geographical Information System (GIS) consists of two parts. Vehicles are equipped with sensors that send information about the current position and fuel level to the system. The second part of the GIS is a service to provide information about routes.

CEP. Events in our scenario will come from multiple services as described above. These events are also known as atomic events, and they are instantaneous. Notifications about these occurred events together with their timestamps and possibly further associated data (such as involved entities, numerical parameters of the event, or provenance data) enter the event processing engine in the order of their occurrence.

Our engine is based on the logic-based ETALIS framework, which allows stream reasoning based on predefined background knowledge (e.g. duration of a working day). ETALIS correlates simple events in order to create complex (derived) events. The correlation is based on temporal, causal and semantic relations that can be established between events and possible background knowledge. An event query or pattern is a complex event description by means of which complex events can be specified as temporal constellations of atomic events. The complex events, thus defined, can in turn be used to compose even more complex events i.e., they can be turned back as input events. As opposed to atomic events, those complex events are not considered instantaneous but are endowed with a time interval denoting when the event started and when it ended. Event patterns in ETALIS are specified by a language for event processing [4]. Additionally, we provide a graphical editor for generating event patterns which abstracts from the technical prolog-based pattern language in order to allow a more user-friendly way of pattern definition as described in [5].

Finally – when detecting complex events – ETALIS may consult domain knowledge. This knowledge can be used to interpret events, data carried by events, as well as relations in which events and data are defined (e.g., subclass relationships etc.). ETALIS can evaluate the background knowledge on the fly, possibly inferring complex events that involve new implicit knowledge. This knowledge is derived as a logical consequence from event driven deductive rules, thereby providing the Stream Reasoning capability.

ETALIS internally comprises of three components. ETALIS Core engine is written in Prolog language, hence it requires a Prolog system to run (e.g., SWI, YAP, XSB etc.). Still to interface ETALIS Core engine with the message broker we provide a Java interface called jtalis. Event queries (patterns) are written in ETALIS Language for Events. ETALIS compiles these patterns into executable rules (written in Prolog). These rules may be accompanied with background knowledge to describe the domain of interest (as discussed above). Domain knowledge is expected to be expressed either in Prolog or as an RDFS ontology. Currently, we support usage of static domain knowledge defined in Prolog, more potential advantages of using domain knowledge within event processing that are planned to be integrated in the future are described in section 6. A backing store provides a log service for events. It records log data about current and past event interactions. This includes atomic and complex events as well as intermediate events that were generated during the detection of complex events. Providing a persistent storage for atomic, complex and intermediate events will be used to analyze an existing set of event patterns and to automate process of creation of new patterns.

BEAM. BEAM is based on the assumption that there exist specific goals that a business process and system should fulfill and proposes the adoption of a goal-directed model able to track the fulfillment of goals at run time. We utilize goal-directed modeling in which we follow a hierarchical goal decomposition model we have developed as part of our previous work, called Situation-Action-Network (SAN) [6]. In SANs, goals are related to situations that trigger their activation and reactions that should be performed towards achieving goals if certain conditions are met; for details about the SAN models the reader is referred to [7].

In BEAM, the detection of critical and/or interesting situations is performed by employing CEP capabilities. BEAM exploits the complex event patterns identified by the CEP engine in order to sense critical/interesting situations. Then, by taking into account the current business context, BEAM recommends appropriate responses with the aim to cope with problematic situations or exploit opportunities that may arise in the business environment. More details about our approach for context management can be found in [8].

The BEAM layer consists of several sub-components allowing the definition of goal-oriented situation-aware recommendations, the modeling of desired, meaningful reactions to interesting situations and the execution of the related SAN models. The SAN Editor is a graphical design tool developed in Adobe Flash/Flex. It is used for the development of SAN models represented in RDF (Resource Description Framework). SAN Engine undertakes the traversing of SAN trees stored in SAN Repository (implemented using Sesame 2.6.2) through the Traversal Service, as well as the subscription/unsubscription of complex event patterns in the Pub/Sub through the Subscriptions Management subcomponent. The Context Management subcomponent updates the current context and evaluates the necessary contextual conditions based on detected situations. Context changes are stored into a Context Repository. Action Service triggers actions in external systems and recommends actions to human actors by transmitting events through the message broker. Finally, the SAN engine is responsible for recommending actions which include notifications to users, subscriptions to other simple or complex events, and adaptations to running business processes.

Notification. A notification module receives recommendations from BEAM and informs participants of results, e.g. the driver to pickup some parcels or the customer about the time of pickup.

External Web Services. To enable the usage of external data like traffic information, our system provides adapters to integrate such services.

4   System Walkthrough

In the section we present a practical application of the proposed event-driven system for business awareness management in the logistics domain and more specifically in a Courier company. In order to understand how the proposed system can increase the awareness of managers about the running business processes, as well as their flexibility we discuss in the following an indicative pilot scenario. The pilot scenario is used for describing the practical role and use of the proposed system framework.

Consider the situation where a gold customer requests a pickup and provides his/her availability in terms of a time window. Information about the pickup including the location of the customer is incorporated into a pickup event generated by the CRM system. In ETALIS, a pickup event would be defined as follows:

```
pickupRequest(EventId, Timestamp, OrderId, CustomerId,
Latitude, Longitude)
```

Latitude and longitude have been calculated in advance by geocoding the address of the customer from the underlying CRM system. In the same time window that the customer has indicated his/her availability, one or more of the company's trucks are moving into a geographical area which is rather close to the customer. The following ETALIS pattern describes this situation (by looking for a vehicle that is within a range of 10km of the customer's location):

```
rule 1: nearbyVehicle(EventId, VehicleId, OrderId,
Distance, Latitude, Longitude) <- gpsEvent(EventId,
VehicleId, Latitude, Longitude, Speed) AND
pickupRequest(EventId, Timestamp, OrderId, CustomerId,
Loclat, Loclng) where getDistance(Latitude, Longitude,
Loclat, Loclng, Distance), Distance < 10
```

The getDistance function is a mathematical function that calculates the distance between two latitude/longitude pairs. After a nearbyVehicle event has been produced by ETALIS, it should be checked whether the specific vehicle actually moves to the right direction of the target location. Therefore, the following pattern is deployed:

```
rule 2: vehicleRecommendation(EventId, VehicleId,
OrderId, H, I) <- (nearbyVehicle(A, VehicleId, orderId,
D, E, F) SEQ nearbyVehicle(B, VehicleId, orderId, G, H,
I) where G<D)
```

Other rules that need to be added in order to ensure delivery within a certain time window or to avoid multiple recommendations of the same vehicle are not shown in these examples.

The aforementioned situation may be an opportunity for the company, as it may be beneficial to add dynamically an additional stop to the routing plan of one of its trucks, in order to allow it to pickup immediately the package. In this scenario the proposed software framework identifies interesting business situations like the one described above, investigates the feasibility and benefits of the various alternative actions and recommends the best one, while it also informs the employees of the company about the detected situation(s).

More specifically, BEAM starts the execution of the underlying SAN model (see Fig.2) when the aforementioned situation is detected by the CEP engine, i.e. when a truck is nearby the customer during the given time window (see point 1 of Fig.2), while it triggers a GIS query to compute a new route for the truck and an estimation of the time needed to get there (see point 2). It should be noted that traffic services are available for the GPS devices embedded in the company's trucks that provide them through FM signals with information about the traffic conditions. In this scenario, GIS generates a new event containing an estimation of the time needed for the truck to get to the customer and pick up the product, as well as the information that there is currently a traffic jam nearby the customer (see point 3).

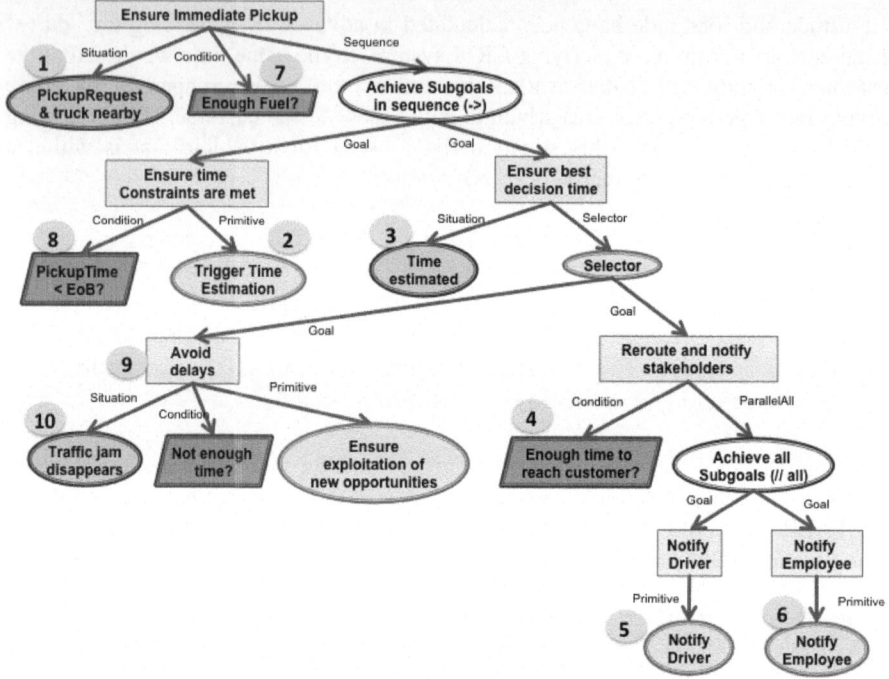

Fig. 2. Underlying SAN model of the Scenario

In case that the truck is close to the customer or it is estimated that the truck will be able to get to the customer in a rather short time (see point 4), while on the same time additional contextual parameters of the business environment allow it, BEAM decides to recommend the addition of an extra stop to the truck's route by triggering GIS through an appropriate event (see point 5) and notify the employee about that (see point 6). Regarding contextual parameters, these include specific business contexts of the Courier company for which it makes no sense to even investigate the possibility of recommending the addition of the extra stop to the planned route. Examples include the case that the truck has not enough fuel (see point 7), the case that the pick up request occurs close to the end of the company's business day (see point 8 - EoB stands for End of Business Day), the case that the truck is failing to execute the deliveries according to the specified time schedule (see point 4) and so on. So, in all of the above cases BEAM makes no recommendation.

On the other hand, in case that the business context allows it and the estimated time is above a predefined threshold (e.g. one hour), BEAM decides to "decide later", in the sense that it defines a new situation to be monitored by the CEP engine in terms of a complex event pattern (CEPAT), in which a decision about the package pickup can be made (point 9). The CEP engine monitors events from an online traffic service, as well as the GPS trails of the company's trucks and figures out - by detecting a CEPAT previously deployed by BEAM - that the traffic jam nearby the customer disappears (point 10) and another vehicle is approaching the customer, so it informs BEAM about the new opportunity. BEAM enters again the decision loop and this time recommends to the new truck to pickup the package from the customer, while it informs the customers about the estimated pickup time based on the calculations of GIS. As real time information is taken into account for estimating pickup time, the estimation is much better than the current state. Finally, BEAM generates an event that informs the business users about the successful pickup of the package.

5   Related Work

To enable Business Awareness Management, we examined and reviewed technologies that can enable awareness about changing circumstances that may require reactions as well as mechanisms for monitoring business activities. In this context, we consider relevant for our work approaches from the research fields of Situation Awareness, Business Activity Monitoring (BAM), goal-orientation and Complex Event Processing (CEP).

Situation awareness was introduced by Mica Endsley whose definition of the term is a generally accepted one: "Situation Awareness is the perception of the elements in the environment within a volume of time and space, the comprehension of their meaning, and the projection of their status in the near future" [9]. Since this original work, a lot of situation-related research has been carried out and has become a critical issue in domains in which there is the need to automatically and continuously identify and act on complex, often incomplete and unpredictable, dynamic situations; as a result, effective methods of situation recognition, prediction, reasoning, and control are required — operations collectively identifiable as situation management (SM) [10].

BAM describes the processes and technologies that provide real-time situation awareness, along with access to, and analysis of, the critical business performance indicators, based on the event-driven sources of data [11]. BAM is used to improve the speed and effectiveness of business operations by keeping track of what is happening now, and raising awareness of issues as soon as they can be detected. BAM applications may emit alerts about a business opportunity or problem, drive a dashboard with metrics or status, make use of predictive and historical information, display an event log, and offer drill-down features [12].

In principle, goal-orientation is based on separating the declarative statements defining desired system behaviour from the various ways to achieve that behaviour [13]. Rimassa and Burmeister [14] propose GO-BPMN, a visual modelling language for the specification of business processes, which is an extension of the OMG standard BPMN. This notation helps to add goals, activity plans, and their relationships to process models. The Tibco's approach for goal-driven BPM [15], [16] follows a process of sense-and-response incremental improvements, making possible the creation of the most dynamic, agile, and responsive processes. For the "sense" part of the aforementioned process, the approach exploits CEP in order to identify important business-worthy events and respond to them; i.e. the response is event-driven.

CEP is a very active field of research and is being approached from many angles. A multitude of languages are proposed to formulate complex event patterns and different event processing paradigms are proposed to match these patterns over events [2], [17].

The framework proposed in the context of this paper enhances existing BAM applications by incorporating concepts and technologies from the research areas of CEP, situation awareness and goal-oriented business modeling. According to [18], most key performance indicators (KPIs) in business activity monitoring and performance management scenarios are complex events (although not all complex events are KPIs). Although most process monitors implement a basic form of CEP in the sense that they apply rules and perform computations on multiple event objects to calculate what is happening in a business process, they are not general-purpose CEP engines, and they don't "listen" to events from outside the managed business process. The proposed approach links CEP with business process monitoring, allowing the provision of a broad, robust situation awareness capability that encompasses both internal process events and external business events. BAM on the basis of CEP shall improve the existing, often complained IT blindness, which is caused by thousands of low-level events per second without any semantics [19].

BAM usually sets up target values for each performance indicator. These target values are not the goals of the business processes, but the goals of the performance indicators. They usually lack meaning or purpose and are just values to be reached. They exist separately without relationships and hence it is hard to share a united vision of the monitored business processes. Therefore, there is a need to align the business processes with strategic goal architectures, which requires a change in emphasis from process to goal-oriented monitoring [20]. The proposed BEAM layer enables goal-oriented monitoring by using a process description oriented toward goals related to interesting situations, instead of using BPMN (or similar) process descriptions; for an example of the later approach please see [21], where the authors present a general framework for edBPM as well as a use case in the context of a large logistic company. Further, our approach incorporates a rule model that enables dynamic parsing of rules. Parsing or rules is dynamic because rules are hierarchically nested; rules lower in the hierarchy are activated only when a parent rule is fired. Finally, goal orientation of our approach enables users to effortlessly conceptualize critical business situations as well as to define and group hierarchically pertinent rules for monitoring critical situations.

6   Concluding Remarks and Further Work

Modern organizations need real-time awareness about the current business conditions and the various events that occur from multiple and heterogeneous environments. Moreover, the need for flexible processes is big in today's competitive environment as a lost customer, or a missed opportunity to recruit a new customer, may never be recouped. In this paper we presented a software framework dealing with such a need and an application of the framework in the logistics domain.

The adoption of the proposed approach would bring added value to all stakeholders compared to the current situation. For example, currently there are several problems in the case that the courier company utilizes predefined routing plans that cannot be changed during the business day. The customer has to wait until the next routing plan in order to have his/her package picked up. Moreover, while several drivers of the company having available space in their trucks may pass nearby the customer, both the drivers and the employees lack the necessary knowledge to take the right decision. These problems result in delays, additional costs for the courier companies in terms of personnel and transportation, unsatisfied customers and even lost customers in the very competitive courier industry.

Even in the case that the Courier company is using some sort of dynamic planning for specific customer categories (e.g. gold customers), the adoption of the proposed approach would bring additional added value as information is communicated to the interested stakeholders by following a "push" rather than a "pull" communication paradigm. For example, in the as-is situation employees of the Courier company take the initiative to get information (information pull paradigm) about the location of trucks when they receive a pickup request, in order to identify possible opportunities for immediate pickups. On the other hand, the proposed system identifies automatically and "pushes" to them information about the various opportunities, making the whole process less laborious and time-consuming. Moreover, currently dynamic planning is performed on a per employee basis, in the sense that each employee of the company is responsible to take a decision about planning based on subjective criteria when a pickup request arrives; therefore it is very difficult for the company to enforce a common strategy per customer segment.

In addition to enabling an "express pickup" service as discussed in the context of this paper, our vision for the proposed software framework is that it can facilitate the transition to a new business model of pickup and delivery services in the courier industry, where the price of the service varies in real-time depending on the market conditions and the user requirements (e.g. urgency of delivery). Today, most of the courier companies simply use flat rates for entire cities (depending on the size of the package, of course) for next-day or same day courier services. However, customers are demanding more from their courier partners. A shift where, more and more customers prefer to use the services of companies who are able to provide more flexibility and levels of service is being witnessed [22]. Therefore, some customers may be willing to pay more for getting specific features of a courier service like immediate pickup in less than one hour or exact estimation of the pickup time.

The proposed framework is able to support such features, which constitute a real advancement compared to what is possible today. In the new real-time pricing model the customer satisfaction will be given more importance as the customer himself will be able to track the order, get the perfect details of where his parcel is and when it will be delivered and at what time and cost. On the other hand the courier companies will be able to exploit the business opportunities in an ad-hoc manner, reduce inventory to a minimum, save substantial money while at the same time increasing their revenues.

To better support this new model we plan several extensions of the proposed system such as making use of static data, namely historical events as well as integration of existing ERP databases. By combining knowledge from the courier's database, (static) information about parcel sizes (that have been loaded into the vehicle as well as the size about already delivered parcels) and the current space left in a vehicle, pickup recommendations can be improved. Additionally, by using historical events processed by the system, it becomes possible to make predictions [23], e.g., if it makes sense to pickup a parcel, when a specific traffic situation exists. This requires the computation of partial patterns as proposed in [24] and historical events, in order to compute the degree that an event pattern has been fulfilled. If a pattern has been fulfilled by a certain degree, it is possible to estimate the probability of its complete fulfillment in the near future.

Finally, regarding the evaluation of the proposed system, we are currently deploying it into a logistics company in the context of an FP7 project, while its complete and thorough evaluation is expected until the end of the year. The evaluation will concern issues like the usability, scalability and technical performance of the system, while its added value will be examined by assessing the satisfaction of all stakeholders. Finally, in the context of the evaluation we will empirically calibrate some predefined parameters of our model (e.g. time thresholds)in order to increase the anticipated benefits for all involved stakeholders.

Acknowledgements. This work is partly funded by the European Commission projects FP7 SME ReFLEX(262305) and FP7 ICT PLAY (258659).

References

1. Sayal, M., Casati, F., Dayal, U., Shan, M.-C.: Business Process Cockpit. In: Proceedings of the 28th VLDB Conference, HP (2002)
2. Luckham, D.: The Power of Events: An Introduction to Complex Event Processing in Distributed Enterprise Systems. Addison-Wesley, Reading (2005)
3. Schiefer, J., Rozsnyai, S., Rauscher, C., Saurer, G.: Event-driven rules for sensing and responding to business situations. In: Proceedings of DEBS 2007, pp. 198–205. ACM, New York (2007)
4. Anicic, D., Fodor, P., Rudolph, S., Stühmer, R., Stojanovic, N., Studer, R.: A Rule-Based Language for Complex Event Processing and Reasoning. In: Hitzler, P., Lukasiewicz, T. (eds.) RR 2010. LNCS, vol. 6333, pp. 42–57. Springer, Heidelberg (2010)
5. Sen, S., Stojanovic, N.: GRUVe: A Methodology for Complex Event Pattern Life Cycle Management. In: Pernici, B. (ed.) CAiSE 2010. LNCS, vol. 6051, pp. 209–223. Springer, Heidelberg (2010)
6. Patiniotiakis, I., Papageorgiou, N., Verginadis, Y., Apostolou, D., Mentzas, G.: A Framework for Situation-Aware Adaptation of Service-Based Applications. In: 1st International Workshop on Adaptive Services for the Future Internet (WAS4FI), in Conjuction with ServiceWave, Poland (2011)
7. Verginadis, Y., Papageorgiou, N., Patiniotakis, I., Apostolou, D., Mentzas, G.: A goal driven dynamic event subscription approach. In: 6th ACM International Conference on Distributed Event-Based Systems, DEBS 2012, pp. 81–84. ACM, New York (2012)
8. Verginadis, Y., Patiniotakis, I., Papageorgiou, N., Apostolou, D., Mentzas, G., Stojanovic, N.: Context Management in Event Marketplaces. In: 7th International Workshop on Semantic Business Process Management, Heraklion, Greece (2012)

9. Endsley, R.: Toward a theory of situation awareness in dynamic systems: Situation awareness. Human factors 37, 32–64 (1995)
10. Jakobson, G., Buford, J., Lewis, L.: Situation management: Basic concepts and approaches. Information Fusion and Geographic Information Systems, 18–33 (2007)
11. McCoy, D.: Business Activity Monitoring: Calm before the storm (2002), http://www.gartner.com/DisplayDocument?doc_cd=105562
12. McCoy, D., Cantara, M.: Hype Cycle for Business Process Management (2010), http://www.gartner.com/DisplayDocument?doc_cd=200990   (accessed October 26, 2011)
13. Greenwood, D., Rimassa, G.: Autonomic Goal-Oriented Business Process Management. In: Proceedings of the Third International Conference on Autonomic and Autonomous Systems, p. 43. IEEE Computer Society (2007)
14. Rimassa, G., Burmeister, B.: Achieving Business Process Agility in Engineering Change Management with Agent Technology. Whitestein Technologies AG & DaimlerChrysler AG, Group Research (2007), Retrieved from http://citeseerx.ist.psu.edu/viewdoc/summary?doi=10.1.1.145.4626
15. Tibco: Goal-driven business process management: Creating agile business processes for an unpredictable environment. Tibco Whitepaper (2006)
16. Tibco, Software, and Inc.: Tibco iprocess conductor (2007)
17. Etzion, O., Niblett, P.: Event Processing in Action, 1st edn. Manning Publications Co., Greenwich (2010)
18. Schulte, W.R., Sinur, J.: Use of Event Processing Increases Success of BPM Projects (2009), http://www.gartner.com/DisplayDocument?id=993012
19. Ammon, R.V., Silberbauer, C., Wolff, C.: Domain Specific Reference Models for Event Patterns – for Faster Developing of Business Activity Monitoring Applications. In: VIPSI 2007, Lake Bled, Slovenia, October 8-11 (2007)
20. Chen, P.: Goal-oriented business process monitoring: an approach based on user requirement notation combined with business intelligence and Web services. Carleton University Dissertation, Ottawa (2007)
21. Ammon, R.V., Emmersberger, C., Springer, F., Wolff, C.: Event-Driven Business Process Management and its Practical Application Taking the Example of DHL. In: 1st International Workshop on Complex Event Processing for Future Internet - Realizing Reactive Future Internet, FIS 2008, Vienna, Austria, September 28-30 (2008)
22. Scruz, A.: Study of the supply chain in courier industry. Dissertation Thesis, Christ University Institute of Management (2011)
23. Engel, Y., Etzion, O.: Towards proactive event-driven computing. In: Proceedings of the 5th ACM International Conference on Distributed Event-Based System, DEBS 2011, pp. 125–136. ACM, New York (2011)
24. Stojanovic, L., Ortega, F., Canas, L., Duenas, S.: ALERT: Active Support and Real-Time Coordination Based on Event Processing in Open Source Software Development. In: 15th European Conference on Software Maintenance and Reengineering, pp. 359–362 (2011)

An Aspect Oriented Approach for Implementing Situational Driven Adaptation of BPMN2.0 Workflows

Ioannis Patiniotakis[1], Nikos Papageorgiou[1], Yiannis Verginadis[1],
Dimitris Apostolou[2], and Gregoris Mentzas[1]

[1] Institute of Communications and Computer Systems,
National Technical University of Athens
{ipatini,npapag,dapost,jverg,gmentzas}@mail.ntua.gr
[2] Univeristy of Piraeus
dapost@unipi.gr

Abstract. To address the issue of business process adaptation, we focus on handling adaptation needs as cross-cutting concerns because they rely or must affect many parts of a business process. Our research objective is to enhance aspect-oriented business process management with event-driven capabilities for discovering situations requiring adaptations. To this end, we develop an aspect-oriented extension to BPMN2.0 and we couple it with an event-driven approach for detecting and reasoning about situations that require adaptation of business processes. We use event processing in order to monitor the process execution environment and, when execution violates some quality "threshold" or a problem arises, to detect it and trigger lookup for a suitable process adaptation, using a reasoning mechanism. We demonstrate that our approach is able to address simultaneously adaptation on process model and execution level.

Keywords: Workflow Adaptation, BPMN2.0, Situation-Action-Networks.

1 Introduction

Today's business environments are challenged by the need for continuously adapting business processes in order to meet certain standards of performance and maintain competitive quality of process. Existing Web service-based process automation approaches such as BPEL often lead to business process definitions which need to be redeployed in order to be adapted. Process re-deployment is costly and generates downtime for systems and possible loss of information about on-going transactions [1]. The only changes possible at runtime are the bindings to partner links, but they have to be previously defined at deploy-time [2]. Moreover, in the context of composite Web services several kinds of changes and faults may arise e.g., partner services may go down, services may be updated to require new policies, etc. after service deployment. Most available process orchestration engines do not provide automated support for detecting and reacting to such situations and handling them can only be done through manual human intervention. Manual intervention approaches are inappropriate because the operation of the process is discontinued, certain

M. La Rosa and P. Soffer (Eds.): BPM 2012 Workshops, LNBIP 132, pp. 414–425, 2013.

processes may be interrupted in the middle of a business transaction, and also because of the large administrative overhead.

To address business process adaptation, we focus on handling adaptation needs as cross-cutting concerns because they rely or must affect many parts of a business process. Aspect-oriented workflow languages have been introduced [3] to address the problems of crosscutting concern modularity in workflow languages. These languages provide concepts that are geared toward the modularization of crosscutting concerns such as aspect, pointcut, and advice. Existing work on AOP workflow languages have focused both on crosscutting concerns at the process execution level [4] and on process modeling level [5]. The later work introduced AO4BPMN [5], which is an aspect-oriented extension to BPMN supporting the modularization of crosscutting concerns.

Our research objective is to enhance AO4BPMN with event-driven capabilities for discovering situations requiring adaptations. To this end, we extend AO4BPMN and couple it with an event-driven approach for detecting and reasoning about situations that require adaptation of business processes. Events generated by software components including workflow engines can provide the means to discover situations requiring adaptations. Event processing, a paradigm of choice in many monitoring and reactive applications, enables events to be propagated, filtered aggregated and composed into complex events enabling detection of situations [6]. In our case, event processing will be utilized in order to monitor the process execution environment and, when execution violates some quality "threshold" or a problem arises, to detect it and trigger lookup for a suitable process adaptation, using a reasoning mechanism.

2   Motivating Scenario

The notion of adaptation has been extensively studied in the computer science domain as it is considered as one of the most desired functionalities of today's highly dynamic, distributed and ubiquitous environments in the service-oriented setting [7]. Adaptation, the process of modifying a system or application in order to satisfy new requirements and to fit new situations, can be performed either because monitoring has revealed a problem or because the application identifies possible optimizations or because its execution context has changed.

We consider a crisis management scenario, related to a nuclear accident. This scenario is used as one case study within the PLAY FP7 ICT project (www.play-project.eu). A large quantity of radioactive substance is accidentally released in the atmosphere, due to a critical accident in a nuclear plant. To resolve this crisis, a lot of heterogeneous actors, may be involved along with a number of associated services. This heterogeneity is considered to be one of the main reasons that such crisis situations are so difficult to be managed. In the case of such an accident, a number of mitigating actions should have been predefined, in the form of workflows, involving several different actors, authorities and services (e.g. police, military, fire brigade, National Institute for Radioprotection and Nuclear Safety, Representatives of National Authority etc.). However situations may appear where the standard actions should be modified and in most of the cases this cannot be captured in a workflow model at design time. Considering the specific example the appropriate authorities should have access to real time meteorological data, field reporting data and information coming from grids of radiation sensors that monitor radiation levels in the area around the nuclear plant. Based on such information and alerts, authorities can take the proper decisions in order to minimize the consequences from the accident. Such a process is described in the workflow depicted in figure 1.

One of the hundreds different processes that are carried out during the management of a nuclear accident is described in figure 1. The specific process is called "situation management process" and is composed of 9 activities under the responsibility of the actor "Representative of the national authority", who is responsible for assessing the current situation and deciding the nature of operations (e.g. evacuate, distribute iodine capsules etc.). This process receives events from a distributed event middleware platform that provides intelligent publish/subscribe and event storing capabilities called PLAY platform (www.play-project.eu). This platform undertakes the task of forwarding and storing all events coming from all the actors and services involved in our nuclear crisis management scenario.

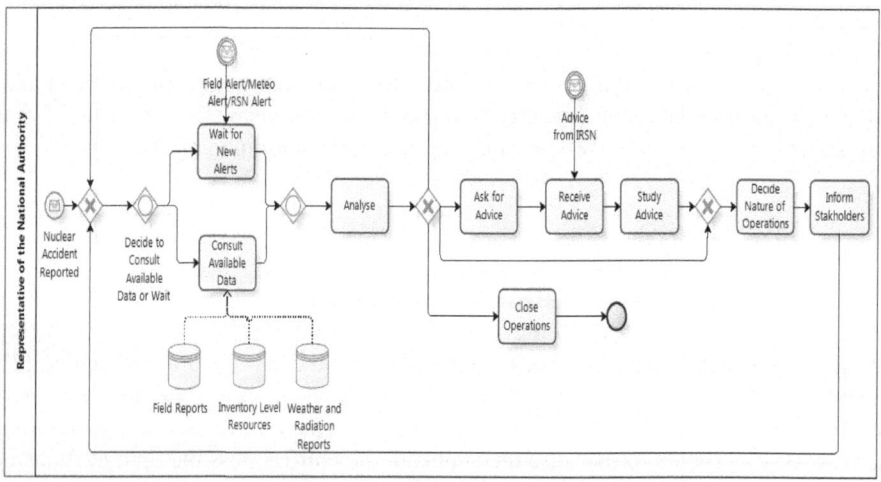

Fig. 1. Situation Management Process

In this process, the actor can consult all the available past data (e.g. field reports, inventory level resources and previous weather and radiation reports) in order to analyze the criticality of a given situation, but it is also important to take into account real time data and alerts from the radiation survey network (RSN), the meteo service (MS) and from the field of operations. Such data should be accounted for before or after any given task of a crisis management process (e.g. before asking an advice from the Institute for Radioprotection and Nuclear Safety (IRSN), the actor should forward a summary of such alerts to the scientists in case these have been detected).

It is obvious that such dynamic behavior it is difficult to be described in advance (before and after any given task) and captured inside a workflow model. A mechanism for detecting situations which require for adaptation and implementing them at run time is needed. In this work, we present our approach where Situation-Action-Networks (SAN) are used to detect situations that dictate for adaptation actions and an aspect oriented extension to BPMN2.0 workflow engines (called AO4BPMN2.0) is discussed for implementing this dynamic behavior at run time.

3   Aspect Oriented Approach for BPMN2.0 Workflow Adaptation

3.1   AO4BPMN2.0 Approach

We adopt the modeling notation of AO4BPMN [4] for business process aspects and we transfer it to BPMN2.0. Since the most recent version of BPMN (i.e. BPMN2.0) is executable in dedicated workflow engines, we use the already introduced AO4BPMN, which has been proposed only as a modeling notation and hence could be used only for design-time process transformation and adaptation, and extend it in order to map and implement adaptation actions to the executable xml representations of BPMN2.0 process models. In addition, we aim to deal with the approach of aspect composition that was not possible with AO4BPMN and the runtime weaving of aspects, by implementing aspect-oriented extensions in a BPMN2.0 engine.

Core concepts of both AO4BPMN and AO4BPMN2.0 are: *Aspects*, *Pointcuts*, *Join Points* and *Advices*. *Aspects* are placeholders that consist of one or more pointcuts and one advice. *Pointcuts* are the constructs (i.e. queries or annotations) that allow the selection of the desired join-points of the process model in which the adaptation should occur. *Join points* are points in the process model, where an adaptation can be introduced. In AO4BPMN2.0 join points can be the flow objects i.e. activities or events. An *advice* is a business process which implements the crosscutting adaptation logic of the aspect. An advice may include a special activity named "Proceed". The semantics of the advice is to replace the joint-points (i.e. activities or events) of the process with the adaptation sub-process. The use of "Proceed" activity in an advice denotes that in that particular point the original join-point (activity or event) should be executed. In that way an advice can implement before, after, around and replace types of weaving or even more complicated adaptations which for example could put the join-point activity in parallel with other activities.

In our approach, we introduce the notion of dynamic, situation-aware pointcuts by combing aspects with Situation-Action-Networks (SANs) [8], [9]. SAN is a modeling framework that can be used for defining systems' reactions to significant situations with the purpose of fulfilling or satisfying a goal. SANs are hierarchical goal-directed, tree-like models that comprise nodes with specific semantics in order to decompose goals into subgoals and recommend at run time reactions to detected situations. SANs are traversed (i.e. executed) by a dedicated software component named SAN Engine [9]. In this approach we propose the use of SANs as a monitoring layer on top of the business process execution one.

BPMN2.0 processes are comprised of activities/tasks, sub- processes, event nodes and gateways, connected sequentially, in parallel or in mixed ways. The actionable entities however, are the activities, which carry out a specific piece of work, and the event nodes, which send or receive messages to other process instances or to the environment. Therefore, every time the execution reaches an activity or an event node (just before its execution) the BPMN2.0 engine can exchange notifications with the SAN engine through a bridging component that manages the adaptation process (i.e. Adaptation Manager, see section 3.2) in order to check whether the specific node is a join-point. This decision will take place based on the pointcut definitions of the active aspects. This bridging component should be able to suspend the execution of that particular process instance and find the advice (using SANs) that should be weaved in the business process, in case that SAN engine denoted it as join-point. After the successful adaptation the normal process execution resumes just after the join-point.

The combination of SANs with aspects can lead to a variety of adaptation modes depending on the level of SAN's involvement to the adaptation process. We distinguish the following adaptation modes:

- Aspects are modeled at design time and captured in suitable definition files or in an adaptation repository. The situation logic which is executed in the SAN engine adds/removes or enables/disables aspects at runtime (i.e. process execution time). The weaving of advices is done by the aspect-oriented extension of the BPMN2.0 engine.
- Aspects are generated (or modified) by SAN engine and deployed at runtime to the BPMN2.0 engine.
- The SAN engine determines at runtime whether a join-point is a pointcut and thus if an advice should be weaved. This can be achieved by querying a SAN before any action that is scheduled to be executed in BPMN2.0 engine. The SAN engine maintains all knowledge about aspects and states and directs workflow adaptation accordingly.
- The SAN engine executes the advice instead of the BPMN2.0 engine. This mode overlaps and extends previous mode. The SAN engine executes all adaptation related tasks, based on the workflow events emitted by the BPMN2.0 engine.

All these different adaptation modes will be implemented based on some of the following adaptation strategies:

- QoS-Driven vs. Functional-Driven: This distinction refers to the reason of the adaptation based on whether it is related to QoS-driven issue (e.g. web-service that violates a SLA) or to a functional one (e.g. Radiation Survey network unable to reply due an earthquake that completely destroyed it).
- Global vs. Local: This categorization refers to the width of the adaptation effect. So the adaptation strategy can be named as "Global" in case the adaptation advices affect all workflow instances, "Glocal" in case they affect all workflow instances of a specific model and "Local" when they affect only one specific workflow instance.

There are five elementary adaptation types (Table 1) that can be applied on a joint point regardless the adaptation strategy selected. Specifically, adaptation tasks can be inserted before, after or both before and after a joint point. It is also possible that the adaptation task replaces the joint point. An extreme case is omitting the joint point (bypassing it). These basic adaptation types are depicted in the following BPMN diagrams. The task marked as PROCEED represents the joint point of the original process.

Table 1. Adaptation Types

	BEFORE adaptation type
	AFTER adaptation type
	AROUND adaptation type
	REPLACE adaptation type
	BYPASS adaptation type

Each adaptation task in the diagrams (indicated as BEFORE, AFTER, REPLACE) can be in fact whole process fragments rather than atomic activities. Moreover, it is possible to mix the basic adaptation types into more complex adaptations (Table 2).

Table 2. Complex Adaptation Types

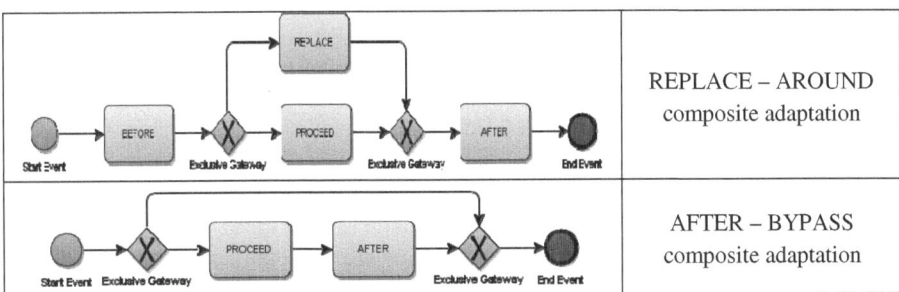

	REPLACE – AROUND composite adaptation
	AFTER – BYPASS composite adaptation

3.2   AO4BPMN2.0 Framework Architecture

The conceptual architecture of the proposed aspect-oriented approach, which provides the necessary framework for implementing situational–driven adaptation of BPMN2.0 workflows, is presented in figure 2. The architecture components are: SAN Engine, Adaptation Manager, Aspect Repository and an aspect-oriented extended BPMN2.0 Engine that are described below.

SAN Engine. It is an engine that handles the execution of Situation-Action-Networks and is comprised of the SAN repository, SAN execution component, Event management component and Context component. For more information see [8], [9].

Adaptation Manager. This component acts as bridge between BPMN2.0 engine and SAN engine. Its primary role is to closely monitor the execution of process instances, detect whether execution comes to an active joint point, check the associated pointcuts and activate the corresponding advices. When required, Adaptation Manager communicates with SAN engine to complete the required adaptation tasks. Interaction with SAN engine can be achieved either:

- by sending to and receiving events from SAN engine through a common event bus, or
- by implementing a dedicated BPMN2.0 Engine-to-SAN connection. This option is more efficient since it avoids the use of event bus, event processing and parsing, which might incur a significant overhead and delay.

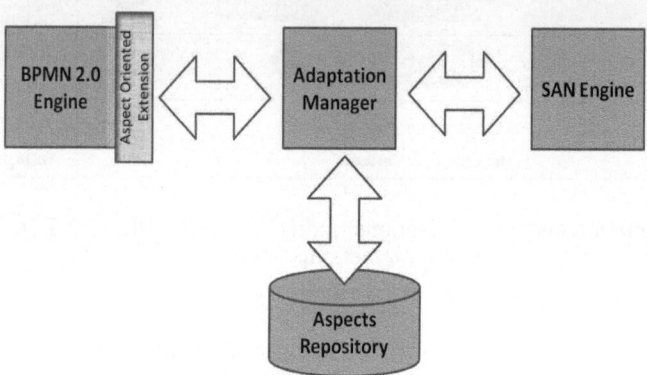

Fig. 2. Situation Management Process

Aspects Repository. Stores the definitions of aspects along with their comprising parts. It can be a collection of files (containing the aspect definitions), or a database or any other persistent storage system. Aspects Repository can be omitted when SAN engine directly monitors and controls (through Adaptation Manager API) the workflow execution and check pointcuts and adaptation implementation.

BPMN 2.0 engine. It is a workflow engine capable to execute BPMN 2.0 process definitions. Its internal structure and operation should enable the implementation of features such as control and modification of workflows with respect to individual process instances, all active process instances, or even to the process definition itself (modification applies to all present/future process instances).

In order to be able to properly use and adapt workflows executed on this BPMN2.0 engine, *an aspect-oriented extension* is needed. We have already implemented such an extension on the WorkToken engine, constituting the specific engine capable of applying dynamic adaptations during the processes execution. WorkToken is an open source, light-weight, BPMN 2.0 engine that does not introduce any BPMN2.0 extensions nor does it require property editors, connectors, data mappers or property dialog boxes and code written in a scripting language. It rather requires the programmer to provide annotated java classes as implementations of the tasks and event nodes used in BPMN2.0 processes. The engine is responsible for instantiation of these objects, persistence and token routing. In our application, we have created default implementations for various tasks; for instance User Tasks display popup dialogs asking for user's input or interaction, Service Tasks call external web services and Script Tasks execute system commands or Java classes.

3.3   Walkthrough

Based on our motivating scenario described in section 2 and the capabilities offered by our approach, the following exemplary adaptation actions can be implemented.

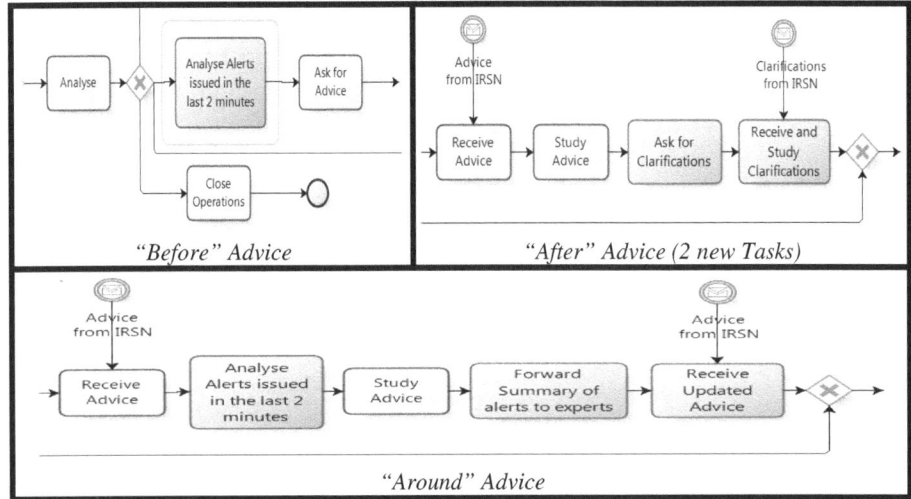

Fig. 3. "Before", After" and "Around Advices", Implemented for the Situation Management Process

These possible adaptation actions are (see figure 3):

− Insert before any workflow task the task "Analyse Alerts issued in the last 2 minutes", in case that new alerts have been detected and have not been forwarded (through workflow) to the appropriate actor − "Before" adaptation advice (Advice 1).
− Insert after any task that involves the study of advices given by experts the tasks in the following sequence: "Ask for clarifications", "Receive and study clarifications", in case that the "study advice" task takes more than 30 minutes − "After" adaptation advice (Advice 2).
− Insert around any task that involves the study of advices given by experts firstly the task "Analyse Alerts issued in the last 2 minutes" and secondly (i.e. after the normal execution of the workflow task), the tasks "forward summary of alerts to experts" and "Study their advice", in case that new alerts have been detected and have not been forwarded (through workflow) to the appropriate actor − "Around" adaptation advice (Advice 3).

In order to implement the aforementioned adaptation advices at run time we have deployed the SAN that is depicted in Figure 4. Based on this SAN, the SAN engine is able to monitor the "Situation Management Process", detect situations where an adaptation action should take place (i.e. pointcuts), decide which the most appropriate advice is and implement it using the AO4BPMN2.0 extension of Work Token engine. Specifically, for every instance of the specific workflow our system will detect the need for further clarifications of the received by the experts' advice and implement the advice 2 (i.e. Goal: Adapt based on the content of task being executed). In addition two different kinds of adaptations will be implemented based on the received alerts. This refers to the case in which a new alert is detected but it will not be considered by the representative of the national authority since the dedicated modeled task for this action (i.e. Wait for new alerts) has already been executed. So, advice 1 is implemented if the actor has not asked for any advice from the experts yet (i.e. Goal: Implement adaptation) or advice 3 is implemented if the actor has already received the expert's advice but has started to study it yet (i.e. Goal: Implement adaptation based on the point of Workflow execution).

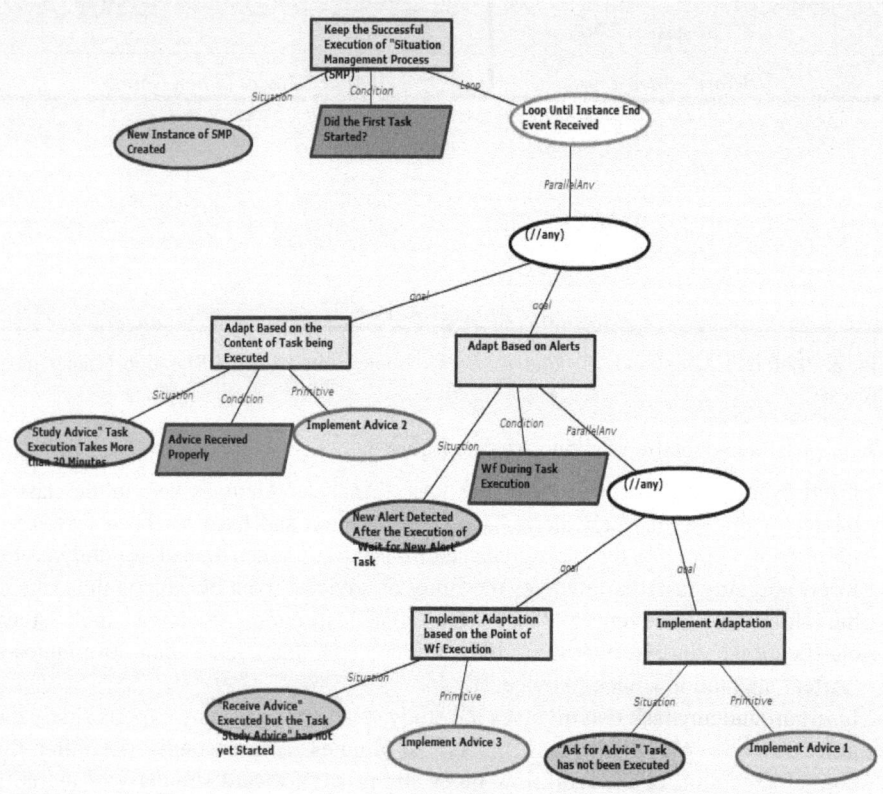

Fig. 4. SAN deployed for implementing adaptations on the Situation Management Process

4   Related Work

Charfi and Mezini [4] introduced AO4BPEL, an XML-based language that creates a wrapper around the BPEL and has the ability to weave aspects at runtime to business processes. Aspects consist of one or several pointcuts and advices. AO4BPEL is based on XPath , which is used to select activity join points (i.e., points corresponding to the execution of activities) and internal join points (i.e., points inside the execution of activities such as the point where the outgoing message of an invoke activity is generated). An advice is the new behaviour to be included at a join point and contains the new code to be executed. Special constructs may be used inside the advice to access the input/output data of the join points, the respective SOAP messages, as well as reflective information. The advantage of using AO4BPEL is that the business process specifications can change at runtime without the need to redeploy them and lose all the on-going transactions.

Charfi et al. [10] have extended AO4BPEL that initially supported only the manual activation and deactivation of aspects via the administrator interface with special support for dynamic plug-ins through generating, activating, and deactivating aspects at runtime. Their proposed architecture includes an orchestration engine, extended by special self-adaptation plug-ins using two kinds of extension points: implicit and explicit. Every process activity is an implicit extension point where the plug-in can execute adaptation logic. At the explicit extension points, the architecture may be extended with Web services that are provided by the self-adaptation plug-in (e.g., for monitoring or for diagnosis so that the plug-in can decide if adaptation is needed). Each plug-in follows a well-defined objective (e.g., self-healing). It consists of several aspects and infrastructural services and is developed by domain experts, e.g., an administrator and deployed to the orchestration engine at runtime through an administrator console. Inside the plug-ins, two types of aspects are used: monitoring aspects, which collect information and decide based on it whether adaptation is needed and adaptation aspects, which handle the erroneous situations and events detected by the monitoring aspects. The monitoring aspects are able to activate and deactivate the adaptation aspects at runtime.

Another approach which considers aspects in BPEL is the work of [11]. The BPEL'n'Aspects approach is not restricted to only BPEL code for the advice implementations, but rather allows for the use of any Web services (WS). Additionally, they avoid extending BPEL in order to claim reuse of legacy BPEL processes. In their approach, they combine standard BPEL, with the publish/subscribe paradigm and WS-Policy so that WS operations play the role of aspects with respect to BPEL processes. Morin et al. [12], proposed an approach that leverages Aspect-Oriented Modelling (AOM) and Model Driven Engineering (MDE) in order to manage variability and adaptation on the architecture of running systems. Their work relies on the notion of aspect models that can be woven into an explicit model of the runtime configuration seating on top of the running system. In [13] they extended their initial work, in order to show how aspects can help designers determine interactions between dynamic variants and how runtime models can be used to validate new configurations on the fly, before actually adapting the running system. They focus on variation points and variants, represented by aspects, instead of focusing on whole configurations.

Another aspect-oriented implementation can be found in the work [14], who proposed an adaptable ECA centric architecture and implementation mechanism based on service-oriented computing and aspect-oriented programming for rule-based enterprise information systems. They use contracts to assign Web services to instances of execution calls. Baresi et al., [15] introduced a design process model for the definition of supervised BPEL processes, in which supervision rules are automatically generated starting from the policies that characterize external services. These policies exploit WSCoL as a language for describing constraints on the messages exchanged with the business process. WS-Policy policies are specified in a deployment descriptor and transformed to supervision rules that are automatically enforced by an AOP-based framework implemented with AspectJ on top of ActiveBPEL. Adaptation at runtime is not supported as AspectJ uses static weaving. Finally, Moser et al., [16] presented the VieDAME environment, which is an extension to the ActiveBPEL engine that allows the monitoring of BPEL processes according to Quality of Service (QoS) attributes and replacement of existing partner services based on various replacement strategies.

All of the above research approaches although they use the AOP paradigm to enforce adaptation they don't take advantage of the EDA paradigm that can amplify the dynamicity of such systems and ensure that adaptations will take place at appropriate times.

Hermosillo et al. [1] proposed the CEVICHE framework aiming to support context-aware business processes that are able to adapt dynamically in order to respond to different scenarios. The main focus of CEVICHE is to provide a mechanism for automatic adaptations in order to maintain high QoS, in terms of service performance and service availability, of business processes. CEVICHE relies on the BPEL extension AO4BPEL [4] and on the use of CEP engines for detecting situations that need adaptation. For that, they defined a language called the Standard Business Process Language (SBPL), which gathers in an XML file, all the information about the processes, contextual environment, business rules, and adaptation conditions. We consider the specific approach as complementary to our AO4BPMN approach as it follows both the AOP and EDA paradigms. Differentiations consist of considering more generic situations (than just QoS issues) that dictate for adaptation while implementing these adaptations on BPMN 2.0 processes instead of BPEL processes.

5   Conclusions

To address the issue of business process adaptation, we combined an aspect-oriented business process management approach with event-driven capabilities for discovering situations requiring adaptations. We developed an aspect-oriented extension to the BPMN2.0 Work Token engine which we coupled with an event-driven approach for detecting and reasoning about situations that pose the need for business processes adaptation. The application is capable of executing BPMN 2.0 processes and applying dynamic adaptations during their execution. Our approach can effectively address simultaneous adaptation on process model and execution level, by focusing on aspect oriented extensions of BPMN2.0. We demonstrated how event processing can be utilized in order to monitor the process execution environment and, when execution violates some quality "threshold" or a problem arises, to detect it and trigger lookup for a suitable process adaptation, using a reasoning mechanism.

Acknowledgments. This work has been partially funded by the European Commission under project PLAY (Grant FP7-258659). The authors would like to thank the project partners for their advices and comments regarding this work.

References

1. Hermosillo, G., Seinturier, L., Duchien, L.: Using Complex Event Processing for Dynamic Business Process Adaptation. In: Proceedings of the IEEE SCC 2010, pp. 466–473 (2010)
2. Juric, M.B.: Business Process Execution Language for Web Services BPEL and BPEL4WS, 2nd edn. Packt Publishing (2006)
3. Charfi, A., Mezini, M.: Aspect-Oriented Workflow Languages. In: Meersman, R., Tari, Z. (eds.) OTM 2006. LNCS, vol. 4275, pp. 183–200. Springer, Heidelberg (2006)
4. Charfi, A., Mezini, M.: AO4BPEL: An Aspect-Oriented Extension to BPEL. World Wide Web Journal: Recent Advances on Web Services (2007) (special issue)
5. Charfi, A., Müller, H., Mezini, M.: Aspect-Oriented Business Process Modeling with AO4BPMN. In: Kühne, T., Selic, B., Gervais, M.-P., Terrier, F. (eds.) ECMFA 2010. LNCS, vol. 6138, pp. 48–61. Springer, Heidelberg (2010)
6. Hinze, A., Sachs, K., Buchmann, A.: Event-Based Applications and Enabling Technologies. In: DEBS 2009, Nashville, USA, July 6-9 (2009)
7. Kazhamiakin, R., Benbernou, S., Baresi, L., Plebani, P., Uhlig, M., Barais, O.: Adaptation of Service-Based Systems. In: Papazoglou, M., Pohl, K., Parkin, M., Metzger, A. (eds.) Service Research Challenges and Solutions for the Future Internet. LNCS, vol. 6500, pp. 117–156. Springer, Heidelberg (2010)
8. Patiniotiakis, I., Papageorgiou, N., Verginadis, Y., Apostolou, D., Mentzas, G.: A Framework for Situation-Aware Adaptation of Service-Based Applications. In: 1st International Workshop on Adaptive Services for the Future Internet (WAS4FI), in Conjuction with ServiceWave, Poland (2011)
9. Verginadis, Y., Patiniotakis, I., Papageorgiou, N., Apostolou, D., Mentzas, G.: A Goal Driven Dynamic Event Subscription Approach. In: The 6th ACM International Conference on Distributed Event-Based Systems (DEBS 2012), Berlin, Germany (2012)
10. Charfi, A., Dinkelaker, T., Mezini, M.: A plug-in architecture for self-adaptive web service compositions. In: Proceedings of the 2009 IEEE International Conference on Web Services (ICWS 2009), pp. 35–42. IEEE Computer Society (2009)
11. Karastoyanova, D., Leymann, F.: BPEL'n'Aspects: Adapting Service Orchestration Logic. In: Proceedings of the IEEE International Conference on Web Services, ICWS 2009, pp. 222–229 (2009)
12. Morin, B., Fleurey, F., Bencomo, N., Jézéquel, J.-M., Solberg, A., Dehlen, V., Blair, G.S.: An Aspect-Oriented and Model-Driven Approach for Managing Dynamic Variability. In: Czarnecki, K., Ober, I., Bruel, J.-M., Uhl, A., Völter, M. (eds.) MoDELS 2008. LNCS, vol. 5301, pp. 782–796. Springer, Heidelberg (2008)
13. Morin, B., Barais, O., Nain, G., Jézequel, J.M.: Taming dynamically adaptive systems using models and aspects. In: Proceedings of the 31st International Conference on Software Engineering, Vancouver, Canada, pp. 122–132 (2009)
14. Rahman, S.S., Aoumeur, N., Saake, G.: An adaptive eca-centric architecture for agile service-based business processes with compliant aspectual.net environment. In: Proceedings of the 10th International Conference on Information Integration and Web-based Applications & Services, pp. 240–247. ACM (2008)
15. Baresi, L., Guinea, S., Plebani, P.: Policies and Aspects for the Supervision of BPEL Processes. In: Krogstie, J., Opdahl, A.L., Sindre, G. (eds.) CAiSE 2007. LNCS, vol. 4495, pp. 340–354. Springer, Heidelberg (2007)
16. Moser, O., Rosenberg, F., Dustdar, S.: Non-Intrusive Monitoring and Service Adaptation for WS-BPEL. In: Proceedings of the International Conference on World Wide Web, pp. 815–824 (2008)

Exploring Workaround Situations in Business Processes

Nesi Outmazgin

Department of Information Systems, University of Haifa, Israel, 31905
nesi@zefat.ac.il

Abstract. Business process management (BPM) systems are implemented by organizations in order to gain a full control of processes and ensure their efficient and effective performance according to specified procedures. However, a common phenomenon found in organizations is that processes are bypassed and worked around by their participants. The premise underlying this paper is that workarounds are performed for reasons. Understanding these reasons may reveal flaws in process design or in the implementation of BPM systems. The paper reports an exploratory multiple-case study, performed in three organizations, intended to gain an understanding of business process workarounds and the situations in which they are performed. The study identified six workaround types and 24 situational factors related to them.

Keywords: Business Process design, BPM implementation, Workaround, Case studies.

1 Introduction

Technological developments, competitive markets, and the need to streamline processes and information management motivate more and more organizations to adopt Business Process Management (BPM) systems [1].

BPM systems allow managing the organization's business processes in an orderly fashion, including both manual and computerized steps, as well as transition conditions between them. A proper implementation of business processes could lead to increased effectiveness and efficiency of the processes and of further organizational aspects [2]. Numerous studies have addressed the practical aspect of BPM systems in different organizations. Some focus on uncovering the critical success factors (CSFs) for successful implementation of these systems, while others also offer valid frameworks for implementing the systems and address a variety of aspects in the implementation process [3]. A failed or improper implementation of a BPM systems in general and an improper business process design in particular, could lead to a situation where the organization's employees do not use the process properly, bypass and work around the system [4]. However, even a successful implementation does not necessarily guarantee that the organization's different processes will work well, efficiently and effectively as desired. BPM performance in an organization needs to continuously be examined from the operational perspective, and if necessary, improvements should be made and suggested [5].

M. La Rosa and P. Soffer (Eds.): BPM 2012 Workshops, LNBIP 132, pp. 426–437, 2013.
© Springer-Verlag Berlin Heidelberg 2013

One of the issues to be monitored is compliance to the specified process. This can be done using appropriate process mining techniques [6]. However, these can only detect part of the workarounds, not the ones that manually bypass the process. Furthermore, while indicating the existence of workarounds or poor conformance, these techniques are not helpful in considering human or other factors which could also affect the actual process. Therefore, more about the actual process behavior and less about the factors affecting this behavior can be learnt through them.

The premise underlying this paper is that workarounds are performed for reasons. Understanding these reasons may reveal flaws in the process design or in the implementation of BPM systems. While these reasons can also be related to organizational and managerial culture, we do not focus on these aspects. Our aim is to understand situational factors that can be associated with workarounds performed in business processes. We focus on design, implementation, and technology aspects, attempting to understand what causes employees and managers of different organizations to bypass, work around and report business process parts retroactively. We do that by examining and gaining an in-depth understanding of the actual process, how it is implemented, types of deviations from the specified process, and the situations in which they occur. We consider this study as a first step towards understanding reasons for workarounds in business processes on a general level. Such understanding would facilitate the design and implementation of business processes to be more effective and applicable in practice.

The research methodology is of multiple case studies in several different organizations. Initially, each case was studied separately and afterwards an attempt was made to combine all the studies to try and understand the phenomenon and expose the different workaround factors. The next section presents the methodology and research procedure. In section 3, the research findings, including workaround types and associated situational factors, are presented. In section 4, a discussion of the various findings and their contribution is presented. In section 5, the relevant related work is reviewed, and the last section provides conclusions and outlines future research directions.

2   Research Methods

This is a qualitative exploratory study, using multiple case studies and applying several different research tools to gather information from the field and analyze it. The central research tool is a semi-structured interview with which the findings may be revealed. Interviews are the main and most common tool used in qualitative IS research and can be structured, semi-structured, open, or questionnaire-like [7]. Throughout this study, the data collection and analysis focused on two central research questions: 1) What types of workarounds are performed in business processes? 2) What situational factors characterize business processes where these workarounds are performed?

Below is a breakdown of the research procedure and information gathering from the different research tools.

2.1   Research Procedure and Tools

1. Planned semi-structured interview - we have planned the interviews based on an in-depth literary review. The interviews comprised several open questions. Some were designed to examine the organizational culture and BPM implementation method, some focused on an in-depth understanding of the business process from both the IT and business aspects, while others focused on exposing workarounds in the business process. The interviews were semi-structured to allow expanding and gathering information also on issues not built into it.
2. Selected three case studies for the research - we have selected three case studies and obtained the organizations' approval, promising confidentiality and anonymity and explaining the possible contribution of this research to them.
3. Collected documents from the organization and their websites - relevant documents such as design documents, ISO work procedures or all business process and work method documentation, reports, diagrams, etc. These gave us a more formal and detailed view of the processes and enabled us to understand their core activities and examine several key processes for the research.
4. Selected business processes from the organizations - we selected the processes of purchase requisition management, purchase order management, student intake, and employee intake as representative complicated core processes of these organizations, which can commonly be found in different organizations.
5. Conducted the interviews in the organizations - 16 interviews were conducted in the three organizations. Ten of the interviewees were managers, stakeholders and decision-makers, and six were employees who participated in implementing the processes in the organization, and were familiar with these processes as part of their daily duties. The work experience of the interviewees was 3-15 years, the average being 8 years. The interviews lasted 45-90 minutes each, and took place in various offices in the researched environment. All the interviews were recorded and transcribed.
6. Gathered information from the information systems - relevant information was gathered from the information systems, including existing models and event log files of the process, in order to compare the prescribed processes with the actual ones and to understand the process from the technological aspect e.g., understanding the rules, statuses, transition conditions, etc.
7. Process modeling - representing several processes in BPMN [8], to (a) gain a full understanding of the process and its workarounds, (b) get approval of this understanding from the interviewees, and (c) prompt further information from the study participants. Each model was sent or shown to the relevant participants for feedback and verification.
8. Analyzed process models – first, we analyzed each model from each case study to identify recurrent workaround types and second, we generalized from all cases.
9. Performed text analysis - we performed text analysis and interpretation of the transcribed interviews to identify categories of workaround situational factors.
10. Questionnaires - we prepared and distributed a questionnaire examining the level of agreement about the most common factors exposed during the study, using a five-level Likert scale. The questionnaire was sent to the relevant interviewees from all case studies for validation of the different factors and findings. The

Questionnaires were used as a last step, after analyzing the data obtained by the previous research tools.

2.2   Research Population and Case Studies

Three medium to large organizations from different lines of business were selected:

Organization 1. In case study 1, an organization in the academic field was studied. This organization focuses on developing and promoting academic study programs to grant graduates academic degrees. It has over 500 employees and a range of computerized business processes assimilated in two central information systems, one that manages the academic processes and the other is an ERP. The processes studied use both systems, and are both departmental and cross-organizational.

Organization 2. Case study 2 addressed a large global organization in the IS and IT field with 430,000 employees in hundreds of brunches over the world. This organization focuses on selling technological equipment, providing comprehensive solutions for enterprises, and performing extensive projects worldwide. The study focused on one branch with over 1000 employees, while examining global regulations which are also applicable to all other branches. The organization has a variety of information systems, supporting specific as well as general functions. The studied processes span several information systems; one of the processes is cross-organizational, cross-system and cross-branches.

Organization 3. In case study 3, a medium-size organization in the field of control and monitoring systems and satellite communication was studied. This organization focuses on selling comprehensive solutions in various markets, as well as providing long term service. It has two branches overseas, a staff of approximately 300 employees, and one central information management system. All the processes addressed use this system, and are primarily cross-organizational.

2.3   Data Analysis and Interpretation

The data analysis and display process comprised several stages:

Initial analysis. This stage has a relatively open nature. All the material collected from all the different sources was arranged and re-read in depth, while repeated interaction took place between the data collection and the analysis. This was performed to prepare the ground for the official, more advanced analysis [9]. In this stage, open coding was performed, identifying recurring categories in the text and starting to piece the puzzle together. The stage continued until a clear understanding of the material collected, including the process model and all the associated workarounds, was obtained and validated with the interviewees.

Maps analysis. In this stage, the categories uncovered in the previous stage were mapped and examined, while checking for any relationship between them, and if necessary, also dividing them into sub-categories. The end result of this stage should be a tree structure containing all the categories that have been examined, coded and adapted for their location on the tree in relation to others [10]. In our case, the top-level was workaround types, while groups and individual situational factors were in the lower levels. Initially, this process was performed for each case study separately and at a more advanced summarization stage on all the different cases in an attempt to compare and match categories with different names and coding in every case or in part, but with a similar significance to the rest.

Focused analysis. This stage is based on the previous stage and its primary purpose is to arrange all the categories by a certain division and order based on several leading key categories [10]. Specifically, we grouped the identified factors into four categories, to obtain some higher level classification of factors.

3   Research Finding

After organizing all the findings uncovered following the above procedure and integrating all the interactions and business process models of every case separately and comparatively across the case studies, 24 different factors associated with workarounds of different processes were uncovered. These factors are associated to 6 types of workarounds, as shown in table 1. Attributing each workaround factor to a workaround type was done according to the number of occurrences in the same context, so it is possible that a certain factor could also relate to another workaround type, but in a different context or less frequently. Below we discuss each of the workaround types and its associated factors.

Type A – Full or Partial Bypass of the Process

Example. In a purchasing process, certain participants order equipment and services from different suppliers by email or phone, and only afterwards initiate the formal approval process. The workaround can be full (bypassing the entire process) or partial. From the findings: "Using the process is cumbersome and delays getting the work done. It takes a long time to obtain full approval for a purchase request..."

Explanation. In these workarounds, the process is partially or fully bypassed, reporting in retrospect to the system. This workaround type has been repeatedly mentioned in the interviews, and is associated with many factors. Some factors are related to system problems, like poor user friendliness and lack of integration among systems. Some other factors relate to process design, which can be complicated and cumbersome, hard to understand, involving many different roles, or not in line with the actual needs and the way the process is actually practiced. Some of the participants even consider the system-managed process as disconnected from the actual process that is performed manually. Consequently, they perform their work "outside" the BPM system, e.g. phone or email purchase orders, employee intake using manual forms, etc. One interviewee said: "The impression is that the computerized system is "supposedly" what interferes in performing the ongoing work, so reporting to the BPM system is separate from the actual work". It was also found that these workarounds are common in situations where parts of the process are not computerized, e.g. manual signing of documents, sending or waiting for paper-based material, etc. As in the findings: "Manual work is performed when sending the student file to the different faculties, and it is unknown whether it is received there or not. There is a lack of communication between us".

Table 1. Summary of the process-level workaround types and factors

Workaround type		Process-level workaround factors
A	Full or partial bypass of the process	1. Complicated process or with unclear rules and transition conditions. 2. Unfriendly, complicated BPM system. 3. The process requires several systems that are not integrated. 4. The process takes a long time or certain stages in the process are delayed beyond what is desired. 5. Dependence on external entities, like committees, overseas companies, etc. to continue the process. 6. The process includes initial steps whose output is needed much later in the process. 7. Lack of feedback for the process participants concerning its progress. Only at the end of the process are updates received. 8. The process definition does not match the actual needs expressed by its participants. 9. Part of the process depends on manual operations or non-computerized material.
B	Selecting an entity instance that fits a preferable path	10. Inflexible transition conditions which seem redundant to some participants. 11. Lack of a suitable solution in the process for extraordinary or urgent cases.
C	Post factum Information changes	12. Overabundance of authorizations and lack of business rules and control. 13. Multiple statuses whose transitions are not governed. 14. Loose access control of data updates after the control steps.
D	Performance of operations not in one's responsibility	15. Unclear responsibility boundaries between holders of different positions. 16. Differences or a lack of know-how to perform the process steps in a certain area of responsibility. 17. Participants with overlapping areas of responsibility. 18. Identical transition conditions and unnecessary duplicate rules.
E	Creation of fictitious entity instances in the process	19. Incomplete process definition, with missing entity types or life-cycle phases that require monitoring and documentation. 20. Missing links to other related processes.
F	Separation of the actual process from the managed one	21. The sequence of operations moves back and forth between organizational units. 22. A certain part of the process serves as a "rubber stamp" and cannot actually affect reaching the goal of the process. 23. Bottleneck situations in certain parts of the process. 24. Process definition does not cover all the lifecycle of the handled entity.

Type B – Selecting an Entity Instance that Fits a Preferable Path

Example. In a purchasing process, purchase requests or orders are split so that instead of entering one purchase request or order (as is correct and desired), several purchase requests or orders are created, each at a relatively small price, not requiring a long approval trail. "In certain cases there's no option but to split the purchase request, otherwise it is delayed a long time…"

Explanation. This type of workaround relates to situations where a "legitimate" process execution is performed, but the entity instance that is used does not represent the actual one. Rather, it is chosen in order to comply with the transition conditions of the process. Usually, the process participants who perform this type of workaround are considered those who are familiar with the 'rules of the game'. Consequently, the workarounds are performed systematically and sophisticatedly. The participants invest thought before performing such workaround, to the point of developing skills and expertise in performing them. The findings show that these workarounds are mainly associated with complicated and inflexible transition conditions. Fig.1 shows an example process fragment, specifying diverse transition condition rules (based on ordered amounts and order type) to approve an order. At this point, participants who are familiar with the rules, might act and enter information so as to work around this part, particularly in urgent cases.

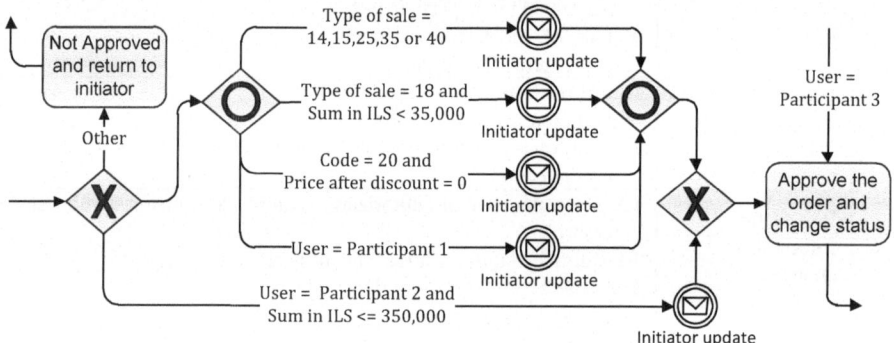

Fig. 1. Transition conditions of a purchasing process at the order approval stage

Type C – Post Factum Information Changes

Example. In a purchasing process, participants give false information (amounts, purchase items, suppliers, quantities, etc.) which allows the process to move "smoothly" and quickly, and only once the approval steps are completed do they change the information to reflect the real needs. Entering the correct information from the initial stage would have required a different path of approvals and control. Quoting one interview: "Sometimes in order to promote the process, I enter purchase items which do not require approval of the deputy CEO, and once the purchase is approved, I change the type of items required".

Explanation. As with workaround type B, and following the example shown in Fig. 1, this workaround type is also intentional and sophisticated, requiring expertise of the participants. In this case, some of the participants exploit situations of over-flexibility, excess authorizations and loose access control. In particular, some processes employ multiple statuses denoting transitions among different process phases. These transitions can be controlled by business and access control rules. Fig. 2 illustrates the status transitions in one of the processes that were studied, differentiating controlled and uncontrolled transitions. Process participants exploit this lack of control to manipulate information after the process passes certain stages (e.g., using the uncontrolled transition from Approved to Reopened). This type of workaround can also stem from a lack of knowledge of the process and the implications of incorrect use of the different status transitions. One participant said: "It is unclear which status to use in each stage, and what this actually means is that anyone can change statuses". Last, this workaround can also be used when the needs change during the process (e.g., it is suddenly realized that the needed amount is larger than asked for). Rather than re-initiating the process with the correct amount, participants simply change the already approved amount.

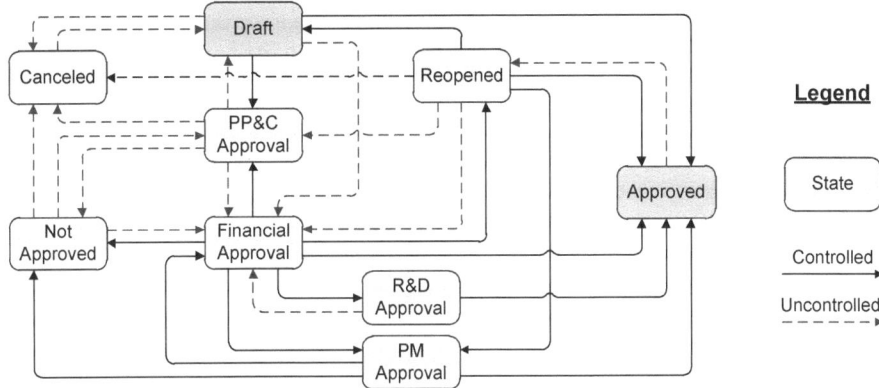

Fig. 2. Example of multiple transition statuses and duplicate rules from one case study

Type D – Performance of Operations Not under One's Responsibility

Example. In a purchasing process, the initiating participant should only create a purchase request, which should then be handled by the purchasing department, for obtaining price quotations and selecting a supplier. The workaround is when the initiating participant directly contacts suppliers and selects one, rather than leaving this to the purchasing department.

Explanation. In this type of workaround, participants perform operations in the process which are not under their responsibility. The findings show that these workarounds arise mainly from a lack of clear definitions of responsibility assignment at different parts of the process, and complicated transition conditions, In particular, responsibility assignment might not match the knowledge required for certain tasks (e.g., a purchase clerk might not have sufficient technical knowledge to evaluate the available product configurations). Some interviewees noted that in their opinion the responsibility assignment in the process creates delays and problems in performing their ongoing roles. "In my opinion, separating roles at this point is most problematic and irrelevant...". In addition, from the process models it appears that when several users in different areas of responsibility are involved in identical or overlapping transition conditions, there are more frequent workarounds at that point (see Fig. 2).

Type E – Creation of Fictitious Entity Instances in the Process

Example. In a student intake process, it is impossible to perform an acceptance interview with a candidate before he registers (and has a record). The workaround is creating a fictitious registration in order to continue the process and invite the candidate for an interview. "I set interviews and simultaneously attribute all students to a fictitious room (to mark that they are awaiting an interview) until they complete the process. It's faster and easier".

Explanation. The findings show that this type of workaround is taken due to incomplete definition of the process. When certain steps or cases actually exist although they are not considered and supported as part of the process, to gain possibility of documentation and monitoring, fictitious entity instances are created (e.g., StudentID 99999). This is also common in purchasing processes, when purchase requests are made for items before they exist in the system. To promote the process, fictitious item codes are used.

Type F – Separation of the Actual Process from the Managed Process

Example. In a purchasing process, when the chance that the purchase will not be approved is extremely low to non-existent, process participants might not wait for the desired approval and move forward with the actual process. "Sometimes purchase requests are delayed unnecessarily. In any case, there has never been a case when the chairman refused to sign..."

Explanation. This type of workaround was found to be very common (following type A). In this type, at a certain stage the process participants complete the process manually, working around all the remaining process parts until it is completed. In parallel, the steps which should be performed as defined in the BPM system (mainly administrative steps) are continued in an orderly manner only for the purpose of documentation and reporting. As opposed to workarounds of type A, where the process flow can go "backwards", here the prescribed order is kept after bypassing a certain step. The findings show that this type of workaround arises in situations that include a high number of administrative steps that do not make real contribution or promote the achievement of the process goal, especially if these steps are likely to cause a delay and entail a long waiting time. "From my viewpoint, the moment the status has been changed to faculty X handling, I continue the intake process..." It also appears that workarounds of this type are common when the process moves from one organizational unit to another and then back to the first one, or when the actual process includes many manual steps, not reflected in the BPM system.

4   Discussion

As noted, many studies address the implementation of business processes and BPM systems in different organizations. While it cannot be assumed that all workarounds are a direct or indirect result of unsuccessful process design or BPM implementation, it is reasonable to believe that a large portion can be attributed to them. Hence, this paper attempts to uncover situational process-level factors that can be associated with different workaround types. We note that workarounds could also be caused by various factors not necessarily connected to BPM or its implementation, such as human, cultural, and managerial factors, and may also materialize later on as a result of certain changes in the organization and in the work methods.

The research findings indicate 24 workaround situational factors related to the different workaround types. These can be grouped according to different aspects of the process in the organization: (1) Problems arising from process design – these include over-complicated transition rules, incomplete coverage of all the lifecycle phases of the handled entities, creation of over-dependencies among organizational units, and gaps between the process design and the needs expressed by its participants. Note that role and responsibility assignment of specific process parts can be a major contributor to workarounds. Sometimes role responsibility can be assigned independently of the designed control-flow, and sometimes the inclusion of certain activities implies who should perform them (e.g., vice-president approval). In addition, bottlenecks in the process which might hold the process for a long time can also be viewed as a problem of process design or of resource allocation. (2) Problems related to the information flow in the process. These include a lack of feedback as well as the use of manual work (whose status cannot be monitored), and auxiliary systems. (3) Access control, permissions and business rules – both an overabundance of rules and over-permissiveness might lead to workarounds. (4) The technological implementation of the system in the organization, including the work environment user-friendliness and flexibility levels given to the different participants.

The research has two main limitations. First, it was conducted in three organizations located only in Israel. Hence, the findings might not be generalizable to other countries. It should be noted that two of the studied organizations have branches in other countries, and one of these two is a global organization with hundreds of branches worldwide. Also note that the processes that were studied in this organization are on a comprehensive global organizational level. Still, the processes were mainly addressed from a local view.

Second, this is a multiple case study research, based primarily on interviews. An inherent weakness is a limited external validity and generalizability. To increase the validity of the findings, we selected medium to large organizations in different industries. We have also performed the qualitative analysis systematically, including gathering material from the field as well as modeling and studying the processes.

5   Related Work

Little attention has been given to understanding the workaround phenomena in business processes. Most studies in this area focus more on attempting to uncover the various Critical Success Factors (CSF) in the BPM and BPMS implementation processes in organizations [4][11]. Frameworks for successful implementation are offered [12] as well as on-line diagnostic tools for the actual processes, such as Business Process Analysis (BPA), Business Activity Monitoring (BAM), addressing performance enhancement, exposure of bottlenecks, etc. [13][14]. Diagnosing and learning the process can also take place off-line, e.g., by Process Mining [15][16]. Some of the factors uncovered in this study, such as performance times, bottlenecks and the information flow in the process, may be identified by diagnostic methods of the processes indicated [17]. Process mining techniques enable uncovering and diagnosing the process performance on the basis of event logs, and thereby can support the identification and understanding of performance-related factors [18].

Other factors that can be indicated by process mining, and particularly organization and social network mining [19], relate to complicated task assignment patterns. Conformance testing compares the actual process as recorded in the system logs with a prescribed or "normative" process, and can indicate deviations related to workarounds [6]. However, this does not shed light on the situational factors that lead to these workarounds. Hence, these efforts have not really reached and examined the root of the problem, the causes of performing workarounds. Furthermore, not all workaround types identified in our findings can be detected by conformance testing methods, since they are not reflected in the logs.

One initial attempt to understand the workaround phenomenon is reported in [20], who studied workarounds connected to system implementation. They proposed a method and tools for identifying possible workarounds. However, this work remains at the starting point, building on one case study, not continued to provide some general-level understanding. In summary, this study takes a step in the direction of understanding problems in process design as well as BPM implementation by investigating workarounds and their situational factors at the process level.

6   Conclusions

In this study, BPM workaround phenomena in various organizations were explored with emphasis on the detailed, in-depth process view, including examination of various aspects faced by the different process participants who work with these processes daily. Nevertheless, it is important to note that other broader aspects cannot be overlooked. These are connected to the organizational level and to cultural and managerial aspects, which can strengthen or reduce the occurrence of workarounds.

The contributions of this study to research is in highlighting the workaround phenomenon as an indication of process design and BPM implementation problems and in take a first step towards understanding problems that leads to workarounds in BPM. The paper reports initial findings, characterizing workaround types and situational factors. This line of research can continue and serve as a basis for process design and BPM implementation guidelines. The contributions of the study to practice are (1) it can raise the level of awareness and understanding of workarounds, and thereby promote attempts to reduce them from a managerial perspective, (2) The situational factors and workaround types indicated here, can be considered by organizations in the course of process design and BPM implementation to avoid situations where workarounds are likely to be taken, and (3) Organizations can analyze workarounds in existing processes and improve the processes accordingly.

This study is part of a larger study, investigating additional organizations and workaround aspects, such as organizational and human aspects. The larger study employs qualitative as well as quantitative methods, in order to strengthen the internal and external validity of the research findings.

Future work will extend the research population to organizations in other countries in a cross-cultural study. This is expected to lead to more universal findings that can serve as a general basis for process design and BPM implementation guidelines.

References

1. Zabjek, D., Kovacic, A., Stemberger, M.I.: The influence of business process management and some other CSFs on successful ERP implementation. Business Process Management Journal 15(4), 588 (2009)
2. Bandara, W., Indulska, M., Chong, S., Sadiq, S.: Major issues in business process management: An expert perspective. In: 15th European Conference on Information Systems, St Gallen, Switzerland, June 7-9, pp. 1240–1251 (2007)
3. Ko, R.K.L., Lee, S.S.G., Lee, E.W.: Business process management (BPM) standards: A survey. Business Process Management Journal 15(5), 744–791 (2009)
4. Ravesteyn, J.P.P., Batenburg, R.S.: Surveying the Critical Success Factors of BPM-systems Implementation. In: Business Process Management Journal, pp. 492–507 (2010)
5. Siha, S., Saad, H.: Business Process Improvement: Empirical Assessment and Extensions. Business Process Management Journal 14(6), 778–802 (2008)
6. Rozinat, A., van der Aalst, W.M.P.: Conformance checking of processes based on monitoring real behavior. Inf. Syst. 33(1), 64–95 (2008)
7. Myers, M.D., Newman, M.: The Qualitative Interview in IS Research: Examining the Craft. Information and Organization 17, 2–26 (2007)
8. Wohed, P., van der Aalst, W.M.P., Dumas, M., ter Hofstede, A.H.M., Russell, N.: On the Suitability of BPMN for Business Process Modelling. In: Dustdar, S., Fiadeiro, J.L., Sheth, A.P. (eds.) BPM 2006. LNCS, vol. 4102, pp. 161–176. Springer, Heidelberg (2006)
9. Strauss, A., Corbin, J.: Basics of Qualitative Research: Grounded Theory Procedures and Techniques. Sage Publications, London (1990)
10. Shekedi, A.: Words that try to touch: Qualitative Research - Theory and Implementation. Ramot Publications, Tel-Aviv (2003)
11. Ravesteyn, J.P.P., Versendaal, J.: Success factors of business process management systems implementation. paper presented at Australasian Conference on Information Systems, Toowoomba (December 2007)
12. Ravesteyn, J.P.P.: Business process management systems: hype or new paradigm. paper presented at International Information Management Association, Beijing (October 2007)
13. Kim, H., Lee, Y.-H., Yim, H., Cho, N.W.: Design and Implementation of a Personalized Business Activity Monitoring System. In: Jacko, J.A. (ed.) HCI 2007. LNCS, vol. 4553, pp. 581–590. Springer, Heidelberg (2007)
14. Kang, J.G., Han, K.H.: A business activity monitoring system supporting real-time business performance management. In: Third International Conference on Convergence and Hybrid Information Technology, ICCIT 2008, vol. 1, pp. 473–478 (November 2008)
15. Van der Aalst, W.M.P., Rubin, V., van Dongen, B.F., Kindler, E., Gunther, C.W.: Process Mining: A Two-Step Approach to Balance between under fitting and over fitting. Software and Systems Modeling 9(1), 87–111 (2010)
16. Van der Aalst, W.M.P., de Beer, H.T., van Dongen, B.F.: Process Mining and Verification of Properties: An Approach Based on Temporal Logic. Springer, New York (2005)
17. Weske, M., van der Aalst, W.M.P., Verbeek, H.M.W.: Advances in business process management. Data & Knowledge Engineering 50, 1–8 (2004)
18. van der Aalst, W.M.P., van Dongen, B.F.: Discovering Workflow Performance Models from Timed Logs. In: Han, Y., Tai, S., Wikarski, D. (eds.) EDCIS 2002. LNCS, vol. 2480, pp. 45–63. Springer, Heidelberg (2002)
19. Song, M., van der Aalst, W.M.P.: Towards comprehensive support for organizational mining. Decision Support Systems 46(1), 300–317 (2008)
20. Christopher, M., Philip, K.: Representing User Workarounds as a Component of System Dependability. In: PRDC 2004, pp. 353–362 (2004)

Investigating the Process of Process Modeling with Eye Movement Analysis

(Full Paper)

Jakob Pinggera[1], Marco Furtner[2], Markus Martini[2], Pierre Sachse[2],
Katharina Reiter[2], Stefan Zugal[1], and Barbara Weber[1]

[1] Department of Computer Science, University of Innsbruck, Austria
{jakob.pinggera,stefan.zugal,barbara.weber}@uibk.ac.at
[2] Department of Psychology, University of Innsbruck, Austria
{marco.furtner,markus.martini,pierre.sachse}@uibk.ac.at,
{katharina.reiter}@student.uibk.ac.at

Abstract. Research on quality issues of business process models has recently begun to explore the process of creating process models by analyzing the modeler's interactions with the modeling environment. In this paper we aim to complement previous insights on the modeler's modeling behavior with data gathered by tracking the modeler's eye movements when engaged in the act of modeling. We present preliminary results and outline directions for future research to triangulate toward a more comprehensive understanding of the process of process modeling. We believe that combining different views on the process of process modeling constitutes another building block in understanding this process that will ultimately enable us to support modelers in creating better process models.

Keywords: business process modeling, process of process modeling, modeling phase diagrams, eye movement analysis, empirical research.

1 Introduction

Considering the heavy usage of business process modeling in all types of business contexts, it is important to acknowledge both the relevance of process models and their associated quality issues. On the one hand, it has been shown that a good understanding of a process model has a positive impact on the success of a modeling initiative [1]. On the other hand, actual process models display a wide range of problems that impede their understandability [2]. Clearly, an in-depth understanding of factors influencing process model quality is in demand.

Most research in this area puts a strong emphasis on the *product* of the process modeling act, i.e., the process model, (e.g., [3]). Other works—instead of dealing with the quality of individual models—focus on the characteristics of modeling languages (e.g., [4]). Recently, research has begun to explore another dimension presumably affecting the quality of business process models by looking into the *process of creating a process model* (e.g., [5,6,7,8]). Thereby, the focus has

M. La Rosa and P. Soffer (Eds.): BPM 2012 Workshops, LNBIP 132, pp. 438–450, 2013.

been put on the *formalization phase*, in which a process modeler is facing the challenge of constructing a syntactically correct model reflecting a given domain description [9]. Our research can be attributed to the latter stream of research.

This paper contributes to our understanding of the process of process modeling (PPM) by combining modeling phase diagrams [6] with data collected by analysing the modeler's eye movements. We demonstrate the feasibility of using eye movement analysis to complement existing analysis techniques for the PPM by presenting preliminary results and outline directions for future work. We postulate that by analysing the PPM from different viewpoints, a more comprehensive understanding of the process underlying the creation of process models can be obtained, facilitating the creation of modeling environments that support modelers in creating high quality models. Similarly, improved knowledge about the PPM can be exploited for teaching students in the craft of modeling.

The paper is structured as follows. Section 2 presents backgrounds on the PPM. Section 3 introduces eye movement analysis. Section 4 describes the conducted modeling sessions, whereas Section 5 presents preliminary results. The paper is concluded with related work in Section 6 and a summary in Section 7.

2   Background

This section describes backgrounds of the PPM and illustrates how the PPM can be visualized using modeling phase diagrams.

2.1   The Process of Process Modeling

During the formalization phase process modelers are creating a formal process model reflecting a given textual domain description by interacting with the process modeling environment [9]. At an operational level, the modeler's interactions with the tool would typically consist of a cycle of the three successive phases of (1) comprehension (i.e., the modeler forms a mental model of domain behavior), (2) modeling (i.e., the modeler maps the mental model to modeling constructs), and (3) reconciliation (i.e., the modeler reorganizes the process model) [5,6].

Comprehension. According to [10], when facing a task, the problem solver first formulates a mental representation of the problem, and then uses it for reasoning about the solution and which methods to apply for solving the problem. In process modeling, the task is to create a model which represents the behavior of a domain. The process of forming mental models and applying methods for achieving the task is not done in one step applied to the entire problem. Rather, due to the limited capacity of working memory, the problem is broken down to pieces that are addressed sequentially, chunk by chunk [5,6].

Modeling. The modeler uses the problem and solution developed in working memory during the previous comprehension phase to materialize the solution in a process model (by creating or changing it) [5,6]. The modeler's utilization of working memory influences the number of modeling steps executed during the

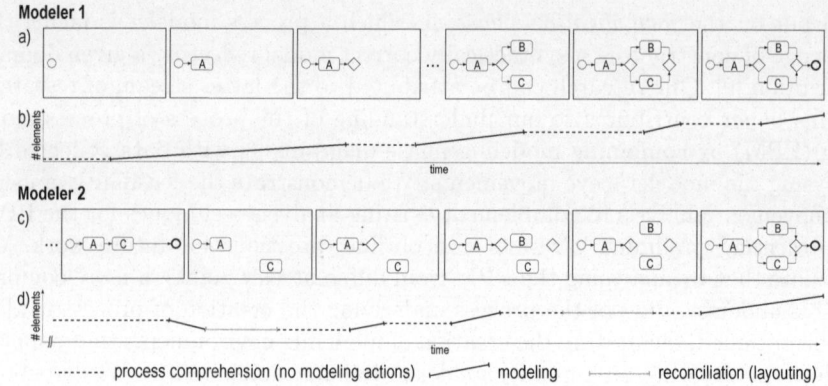

Fig. 1. Two different PPM instances creating the same process model [6]

modeling phase before forcing the modeler to revisit the textual description for acquiring more information [6].

Reconciliation. After modeling, modelers typically reorganize the process model (e.g., renaming of activities) and utilize the process model's *secondary notation* (e.g., notation of layout, typographic cues) to enhance the process model's understandability [11]. However, the number of reconciliation phases in the PPM is influenced by a modeler's ability of placing elements correctly when creating them, alleviating the need for additional layouting [6].

Modeling Phase Diagrams (MPD). In order to facilitate the systematic investigation of the PPM, Cheetah Experimental Platform (CEP) has been developed [12]. In particular, a basic process modeling editor is instrumented to record each user's interactions in an event log, describing the creation of the process model step by step. When modeling in a process modeling environment, process modeling consists of adding nodes and edges to the process model, naming or renaming activities, and adding conditions to edges. In addition to these interactions, a modeler can influence the process model's secondary notation, e.g., by laying out the process model using move operations for nodes or by utilizing bendpoints to influence the routing of edges, see [6] for details. By capturing all of the described interactions with the modeling tool, we are able to *replay* a recorded modeling process at any point in time[1] [6].

In [6] a technique for visualizing the PPM is proposed by mapping the modeler's interactions with the modeling environment to the phases described above. Fig. 1a shows several states of a typical modeling process as it can be observed during replay. Fig. 1c shows the states of a different modeling process that nonetheless results in the *same* model.

To obtain a better understanding of the modeling process and its phases, we supplement model replay with a *modeling phase diagram*, quantitatively highlighting the three phases of modeling, comprehension, and reconciliation. It de-

---

[1] A replay demo is available at http://cheetahplatform.org

picts how the size of the model (vertical axis) evolves over time (horizontal axis), as can be seen in Fig. 1b and Fig. 1d for the modeling processes in Fig. 1a and Fig. 1c, respectively. A *modeling phase* consists of a sequence of interactions to create or delete model elements such as activities or edges. A modeler usually does not create a model in a continuous sequence of interactions, but rather pauses after several interactions to inspect the intermediate result and to plan the next steps. Syntactically, this manifests in reduced modeling activity or even inactivity, i.e, a *comprehension phase*. Besides, modelers need to *reorganize* the model. Reconciliation interactions manifest in moving or renaming model elements to prepare the next modeling interactions or to support their comprehension of the model. A sequence of such interactions is a *reconciliation phase*.

3 Eye Movement Analysis

Even though MPDs provide valuable insights into the PPM, the modeler's cognitive processes are left in the realm of speculation. More specifically, in a MPD the various phases are detected by classifying the modeler's interactions with the modeling environment and aggregating them to the various phases of the PPM [6]. Comprehension phases in a MPD are assessed by measuring the duration not interacting with the modeling tool [6]. Thresholds are utilized for differentiating between an actual comprehension phase and the usual inactivity between creating model elements, i.e., the time it takes the modeler to select a different tool and create the next model element [6]. This draws a rather coarse grained picture of the PPM, i.e., shorter comprehension phases are not detected. Similarly, the authors in [6] claim that there are diverse reasons for comprehension phases. On the one hand, the modeler might create an internal representation of the modeling task presented as an informal description. On the other hand, the modeler might be understanding the process model or inspecting it for potential errors. In order to develop a more fine grained understanding of the PPM, we propose the combination of different views on the PPM. Subsequently, we introduce eye movement analysis, which is combined with the corresponding MPD to triangulate toward a more comprehensive understanding of the PPM.

Eye Movements. When creating a formal process model from an informal specification, a modeler relies on his visual perception for reading the task description and creating the process model using the modeling environment. In this context, high-resolution visual information input is of special interest, which is necessary for reading a word or seeing an element of the process model. High-resolution visual information input can only occur during so-called *fixations*, i.e., the modeler fixates the area of interest on the screen with the fovea, the central point of highest visual acuity [13]. Fixations can be detected when the velocity of eye movements is below a certain threshold for a pre-defined duration [14]. Using eye fixations, we can identify areas on the screen the modeler is focusing attention on [15], e.g., the task description, features of the modeling environment or modeling constructs.

In order to perform a detailed analysis, the modeler's eye movements need to be quantified. For this purpose, several different parameters exist [16]. In this study we focus on two of the most widely used eye movement parameters [14].

Number of Fixations. The number of fixations is calculated by counting the number of fixations in a pre-specified timeframe on a certain area on the screen. This allows researchers to compare the number of fixations on certain areas on the computer screen, e.g., the task description versus the process model.

Mean Fixation Duration. The mean duration of fixations is calculated by measuring the durations of fixations on a certain area on the screen in a pre-defined timeframe and calculating the average duration. Longer durations could be interpreted toward deeper processing of information [16], but might indicate inactivity of the participant if fixation durations become too long compared to the participants usual fixation durations [17].

4   Data Collection

In order to test the feasibility of combining eye movement analysis with existing research on the PPM, i.e., MPD, we designed modeling sessions with students of computer science and information systems. Participants were recorded using an eye tracker when translating an informal description into formal process model.

4.1   Definition and Planning

This section describes the definition and planning of the modeling sessions.

Subjects. The targeted subjects should be familiar with business process management and imperative process modeling notations. More specifically, they should have prior experience in creating process models using BPMN. We are not targeting modelers who are not familiar with BPMN at all to avoid measuring their learning instead of the modeling behavior.

Objects. The modeling session was designed to collect PPM instances of students creating a formal process model in BPMN from an informal description. The informal description was formulated in German since all participants were native German speakers, avoiding potential translation problems. The object that was to be modeled is a process describing the handling of mortgage request by a bank[2]. The process model consists of 19 activities and contains the basic control flow pattern: sequence, parallel split, synchronization, exclusive choice, simple merge and structured loop [18].

Response Variables. As already mentioned in the previous section, we recorded the number of fixations and the duration of fixations. The PPM instances were cut into several parts as detailed in Section 5 and subsequently analysed. CEP

---

[2] Material download: http://pinggera.info/experiment/EyeMovementAnalysis

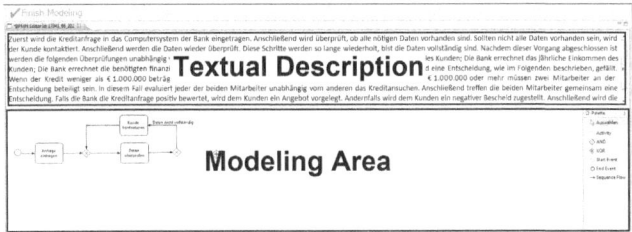

Fig. 2. The BPMN Modeling Editor

recorded the PPM instances on an operational level permitting the generation of a MPD for each PPM instance.

Instrumentation and Data Collection. CEP was utilized for recording the participants' PPM instances. To mitigate the risk that PPM instances were impacted by complicated tools or notations [19], we decided to use a subset of BPMN. In order to investigate the modeler's eye movements in the process model, but also in the textual description we juxtapose the task description with the modeling area (cf. Fig. 2). Several pre-tests were conducted to ensure the usability of the tool and the understandability of the task description.

For performing the eye movement analysis we utilized a table mounted eye tracker, i.e., Eyegaze Analysis System[3], recording eye movements using two binocular cameras positioned beneath a 17" computer display with a frequency of 60 Hz each. Data recording is carried out with the pupil center corneal reflection method [20]. Data collection and analysis is performed using NYAN 2.0[4]. The eye tracker is calibrated for each participant individually; calibrations are accepted if the fixation accuracy shows an average drifting error of at most 0.25 inches. Two observation monitors allow watching both eyes separately while in the process of eye-tracking to correct the sitting posture of participants to recalibrate during recording if necessary.

4.2   Performing the Modeling Session

This section describes the modeling sessions' execution.

Experimental Execution. Since we have only access to a single eye tracker, each modeler has to be recorded individually. 25 students of computer science or information systems participated in the study. Each participant has taken classes on business process management including the creation of business process models in BPMN. Modeling sessions were conducted between February 2012 and May 2012 at the University of Innsbruck. The experiment was guided by CEP's experimental workflow engine [12], leading students through the modeling task, a concluding questionnaire and a feedback questionnaire. Participation was voluntary; data collection was performed anonymously.

---

[3] http://www.eyegaze.com

[4] http://www.interactive-minds.com

Data Validation. Similar to [21] we screened the subjects for familiarity with BPMN by asking them whether they would consider them to be very familiar with BPMN, using a Likert scale with values ranging from *Strongly disagree* (1) over *Neutral* (4) to *Strongly agree* (7). The computed mean for familiarity with BPMN is 4.84 (slightly below *Somewhat Agree*). For confidence in understanding BPMN models, a mean value of 5.76 was reached (slightly below *Agree*). Finally, for perceived competence in creating BPMN models, a mean value of 5.4 (between *Somewhat Agree* and *Agree*) could be computed. Since all values range above average, we conclude that the participating subjects fit the targeted profile.

5   Combining MPD and Eye Movement Analysis

In this section we demonstrate the feasibility of combining eye movement analysis with existing research on the PPM. Based on the data analysis procedure described in Section 5.1 two PPM instances are presented and briefly discussed in Section 5.2. Preliminary results from combining eye movement analysis with the corresponding MPD are discussed in Section 5.3.

5.1   Data Analysis

In this preliminary study, our focus was put on evaluating the feasibility of combining eye movement analysis with existing research on the PPM, e.g., [6,7,8], and to investigate potential benefits of such a combined analysis. For this purpose, we select two PPM instances for further analysis. Similar to [6], we use CEP to generate the MPD for each modeler. In combination with CEP's replay feature we are able to gain an inital understanding of the modeler's behavior. In order to validate and extend our insights, we perform the eye movement analysis of the PPM. Since there are several interesting timeframes exhibiting different characteristics in the PPM, we manually separate the PPM into several, so-called, timeframes of interest (TOI). TOIs are identified based on changes in the modeling behavior of the participant, e.g., the modeler switches from adding model elements to resolving problems. Please note that TOIs are identified for each modeler individually and cannot be compared to TOIs of other modelers.

For each TOI in the PPM we distinguish between fixations on the textual description and fixations on the modeling area (cf. Fig. 2). The relationship between fixations on the textual description and fixations on the process model is expressed by calculating the percentage of fixations on the textual description out of the total number of fixation (textual description and process model). Additionally, we calculate the mean fixation duration for fixations on the textual description and the mean fixation duration for fixations on the process model.

5.2   PPM Examples

In this section we present the MPDs selected for further analysis.

Modeler M1. Fig. 3 illustrates the PPM of M1. In general, M1 produces the process model in a straight forward manner, presumably with a clear conception of the resulting process model in mind. The MPD shows several iterations of comprehension phases followed by long modeling phases. TOI V constitutes an exception in the rather straight forward modeling approach since an error is introduced, i.e., the modeler forgets

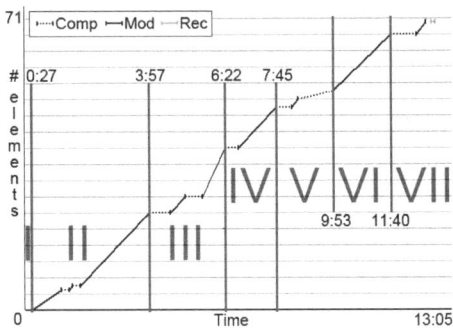

Fig. 3. MPD of M1 with 7 TOIs

about an activity. The modeler immediately detects the problem and resolves it. The MPD shows two comprehension phases which are only briefly interrupted by a modeling phase[5]. The PPM is concluded by a brief reconciliation phase (the only one in this PPM).

Modeler M2. In contrast to M1, the MPD of M2 shows a very long PPM (cf. Fig. 4). After a fast start, M2 experiences first difficulties in TOI III, where M2 seems to struggle with introducing a loop in the process model. After resolving this issues, the modeler returns to a fast modeling style before experiencing problems toward the end of the PPM. In TOI V, M2 adds parts of the process model just to remove them immediately on a trial and error basis. This behavior changes in TOI VI when several long comprehension phases and less delete operations can be observed. After achieving a complete model at the end of TOI VI M2 checks the model for inconsistencies in TOI VII to make occasional improvements.

5.3 Preliminary Results

Table 1 and Table 2 show the various eye movement parameters for each TOI of M1 and M2 respectively. Subsequently, we present preliminary results deduced from combining eye movement analysis with the corresponding MPD.

Shorter Fixations when Reading. When comparing mean fixation durations it can be observed that mean durations are lower for fixations on the task description compared to fixations on the process model. This finding is consistent with results reported in literature indicating shorter fixations when reading [22].

Fast and Focused Modeling. In our previous research we observed phases in the PPM when modelers created large chunks of their process models in relatively short periods of time. We had the impression that modelers had a clear picture of the PPM in mind, often alleviating them from subsequent reconciliation phases

---

[5] The number of elements in the process model can also change during a comprehension phase in a MPD since several comprehension phases can be merged when interrupted by brief modeling actions [6].

Table 1. Eye Movement Analysis of M1

| TOI | Textual Description | | Process Model | | Fix. on |
	Nr. of Fix.	Mean Dur.[ms]	Nr. of Fix.	Mean Dur.[ms]	Text[%]
I	12	154	15	387	44.4%
II	174	164	442	199	28.2%
III	306	179	386	205	44.2%
IV	147	169	154	220	48.8%
V	228	204	215	237	51.5%
VI	19	156	415	192	4.4%
VII	31	188	194	249	13.8%

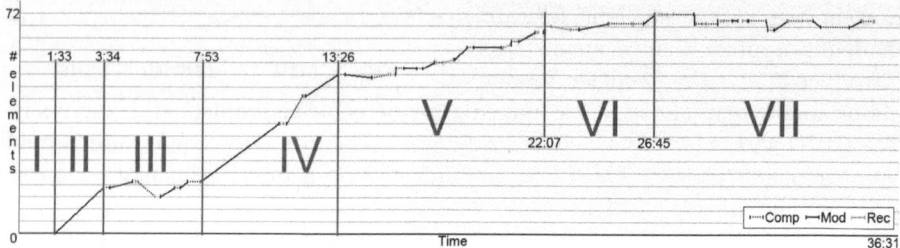

Fig. 4. MPD of M2 with 7 TOIs

since they placed model elements at strategic places right from the beginning [6]. In a MPD, those periods are mostly indicated by long and steep modeling phases. Also M1 and M2 exhibit such phases. M1 starts with long modeling phases in TOI II and has another long modeling phase in TOI VI. M2 has similar phases in TOI II and TOI IV. All TOIs have low mean fixation durations, indicating a lower perceived complexity of the situation at hand compared to other TOIs [23]. The lower perceived complexity, in turn, allows modelers to consider additional model characteristics like the process model's secondary notation right from the beginning. This finding corroborates our impression of phases in the PPM where modelers have a good understanding of the current task.

Challenging Situations. During the creation of process models, the two modelers were facing situations they perceived to be more challenging. This is underpinned by the recorded mean fixation durations. When only considering the fixations on the process model, TOI V and TOI VII are the most challenging for M1, since the mean fixation duration is increased, pointing toward higher attention and a deeper processing of information [16]. This seems reasonable when considering the MPD and CEP's replay. M1 detects an error in the process model in TOI V. In TOI VII, the mean duration of fixations on the process model is increased by more than 50ms, i.e., an increase of 29.7% compared to TOI VI. In fact, M1 is working on arguably the most challenging part of the process model, i.e., a long back edge to an earlier part of the process model [24]. For M2, a similar increase in fixation durations in TOI III can be observed. The modeler interrupts their modeling endeavour for additional comprehension and removes some elements from the process model. In TOI VI of M2, the mean fixation duration is also increased. Notably, M2 is also working on the challenging part of the process model. Long mean durations of fixations, however, observed

Table 2. Eye Movement Analysis of M2

	Textual Description		Process Model		Fix. on
TOI	Nr. of Fix.	Mean Dur.[ms]	Nr. of Fix.	Mean Dur.[ms]	Text[%]
I	297	203	54	223	84.6%
II	88	165	368	204	19.3%
III	79	162	882	221	8.2%
IV	430	158	947	205	31.2%
V	491	173	1,710	209	22.3%
VI	95	177	921	233	9.4%
VII	319	149	1,760	211	15.3%

on their own do not necessarily imply challenging situations. For example, when considering TOI I of M1, the combination of very long mean duration of fixations on the process model and the absence of interactions with the modeling environment point toward inactivity [17].

Causes for Comprehension. Modelers interrupt their modeling endeavor for comprehension phases. In a MPD the reason for such a comprehension phases so far remains in the realm of speculation. On the one hand, modeler might create the internal representation of the task description [6]. On the other hand, they might have a perfect understanding of the task, but struggle to convert it into the formal process model [6]. We claim that inspecting the ratio of fixations on the task description can provide valuable insights. For instance, M2 has several comprehension phases in TOI III, but the ratio of fixation on the task description is only 8.2%. Therefore, we conclude that M2 was rather struggling with the modeling notation. On the contrary, M1 detects an error in his process model in TOI V. Similar to M2, several comprehension phases can be identified in the MPD, but the ratio of fixations on the task description points toward a different problem. 51.5% of the fixations are on the task description, the highest percentage of all TOIs. Therefore, we conclude that M1 had a problem with the task description instead of the modeling notation.

5.4   Outlook

Insights presented in the previous section raise the question whether there are certain situations in the PPM that are perceived to be more challenging by the majority of process modelers (with a certain level of experience). This might be an interesting aspect for future work, since a better understanding of factors influencing the PPM could be helpful for teaching students in the craft of modeling. Additionally, we should aim for supporting modelers in challenging phases of the PPM by providing them specialized tool support rather than supporting them in phases of fast and focused modeling.

In the near future, we are planning a more detailed eye movement analysis. On the one hand, we work on separating each PPM instance into phases based on the part of the process model that is currently edited. This allows us to compare eye movements of several modelers for a specific part of the process model. Additionally, a more detailed analysis than comparing fixations on the textual description and fixations on the process model is in demand. One interesting aspect might be how often modelers look back to previously created parts of the process model. Reasons for this might be the validation of previously created parts, but they could also be looking for similarities to the current problem to facilitate their problem solving.

6   Related Work

Our work is essentially related to model quality frameworks, research on the PPM and usage of eye movement analysis in conceptual modeling.

Regarding model quality frameworks, there are different frameworks and guidelines available that define quality for process models. Among others, the SE-QUAL framework uses semiotic theory for identifying various aspects of process model quality [25], the Guidelines of Process Modeling describe quality considerations for process models [26], and the Seven Process Modeling Guidelines define desirable characteristics of a process model [27]. While each of these frameworks has been validated empirically, they rather take a static view by focusing on the resulting process model, but not on the act of modeling itself. Our research takes another approach by investigating the process followed to create the process model.

Research on the process of modeling typically focuses on interactions between different parties. In a classical setting, a system analyst directs a domain expert through a structured discussion subdivided into the stages elicitation, modeling, verification, and validation [9]. The procedure of developing process models in a team is analyzed in [28]. Interpretation tasks and classification tasks are identified on the semantic level of modeling. These works build on observation of modeling practice and distill normative procedures for steering the process of modeling toward a good completion. Our work, in turn, focuses on the formalization of process models, i.e., the modeler's interactions with the modeling environment when creating the formal process model.

In the context of conceptual modeling several experiments have been conducted investigating the comprehension of UML models, e.g., [29] and the interpretation of data models, e.g., [30] using eye movement analysis. In business process management a research agenda has been proposed in [31] for investigating user satisfaction. Our research, focuses on the process of translating an informal textual description into a formal conceptual model instead of investigating the comprehension of existing models.

7   Summary

This paper demonstrates the feasibility of combining eye movement analysis with existing research on the PPM to triangulate toward a more comprehensive understanding of the PPM. Modeling sessions were conducted to collect PPM instances from students while tracking their eye movements. Based on their MPDs we selected two examples to illustrate the combination of existing analysis techniques with eye movement analysis. This combination helps to shed light on parts of this hardly understood process. Preliminary results revealed insights into the PPM that could not be obtained by using one analysis technique on its own. For future work we plan more detailed evaluations with a higher number of participants to perform quantitative analysis on their PPM instances. We believe that a better understanding regarding the PPM will be beneficial for future process modeling environments and will support teachers in mentoring their students on their way to professional process modelers.

Acknowledgements. This research was funded by the Austrian Science Fund (FWF): P23699-N23.

References

1. Kock, N., Verville, J., Danesh-Pajou, A., DeLuca, D.: Communication flow orientation in business process modeling and its effect on redesign success: results from a field study. DSS 46(2), 562–575 (2009)
2. Mendling, J.: Metrics for Process Models: Empirical Foundations of Verification, Error Prediction, and Guidelines for Correctness. Springer (2008)
3. Van der Aalst, W., Ter Hofstede, A.: Verification of workflow task structures: A petri-net-baset approach. IS 25, 43–69 (2000)
4. Moody, D.L.: The "Physics" of Notations: Toward a Scientific Basis for Constructing Visual Notations in Software Engineering. IEEE Trans. Software Eng. 35, 756–779 (2009)
5. Soffer, P., Kaner, M., Wand, Y.: Towards Understanding the Process of Process Modeling: Theoretical and Empirical Considerations. In: Daniel, F., Barkaoui, K., Dustdar, S. (eds.) BPM 2011 Workshops, Part I. LNBIP, vol. 99, pp. 357–369. Springer, Heidelberg (2012)
6. Pinggera, J., Zugal, S., Weidlich, M., Fahland, D., Weber, B., Mendling, J., Reijers, H.A.: Tracing the Process of Process Modeling with Modeling Phase Diagrams. In: Daniel, F., Barkaoui, K., Dustdar, S. (eds.) BPM 2011 Workshops, Part I. LNBIP, vol. 99, pp. 370–382. Springer, Heidelberg (2012)
7. Pinggera, J., Soffer, P., Zugal, S., Weber, B., Weidlich, M., Fahland, D., Reijers, H.A., Mendling, J.: Modeling Styles in Business Process Modeling. In: Bider, I., Halpin, T., Krogstie, J., Nurcan, S., Proper, E., Schmidt, R., Soffer, P., Wrycza, S. (eds.) BPMDS 2012 and EMMSAD 2012. LNBIP, vol. 113, pp. 151–166. Springer, Heidelberg (2012)
8. Claes, J., Vanderfeesten, I., Reijers, H.A., Pinggera, J., Weidlich, M., Zugal, S., Fahland, D., Weber, B., Mendling, J., Poels, G.: Tying Process Model Quality to the Modeling Process: The Impact of Structuring, Movement, and Speed. In: Barros, A., Gal, A., Kindler, E. (eds.) BPM 2012. LNCS, vol. 7481, pp. 33–48. Springer, Heidelberg (2012)
9. Hoppenbrouwers, S.J.B.A., Proper, H.A(E.), van der Weide, T.P.: A Fundamental View on the Process of Conceptual Modeling. In: Delcambre, L.M.L., Kop, C., Mayr, H.C., Mylopoulos, J., Pastor, Ó. (eds.) ER 2005. LNCS, vol. 3716, pp. 128–143. Springer, Heidelberg (2005)
10. Newell, A., Simon, H.: Human problem Solving. Prentice Hall (1972)
11. Petre, M.: Why Looking Isn't Always Seeing: Readership Skills and Graphical Programming. Commun. ACM, 33–44 (1995)
12. Pinggera, J., Zugal, S., Weber, B.: Investigating the process of process modeling with cheetah experimental platform. In: Proc. ER-POIS 2010, pp. 13–18 (2010)

13. Posner, M.I.: Attention in cognitive neuroscience. In: The Cognitive Neurosciences, pp. 615–624. MIT Press (1995)
14. Jacob, R.J.K., Karn, K.S.: Eye Tracking in Human-Computer Interaction and Usability Research: Ready to Deliver the Promises. In: The Mind's Eye. Cognitive and Applied Aspects of Eye Movement Research, pp. 573–603. Elsevier (2003)
15. Furtner, M., Sachse, P.: The psychology of eye-hand coordination in human computer interaction. In: Proc. HCI 2008, pp. 144–149 (2008)
16. Rauthmann, J.F., Seubert, C.T., Sachse, P., Furtner, M.: Eyes as windows to the soul: Gazing behavior is related to personality. Journal of Research in Personality 46, 147–156 (2012)
17. Wolfseher, T., Furtner, M., Sachse, P.: Die Auswirkung auditiver Ablenkung auf die visuelle Informationsverarbeitung. In: Reflexionen und Visionen der Mensch-Maschine-Interaktion - Aus der Vergangenheit lernen, Zukunft gestalten, pp. 393–396. VDI Verlag (2011)
18. van der Aalst, W., ter Hofstede, A., Kiepuszewski, B., Barros, A.: Workflow patterns. Distributed and Parallel Databases 14, 5–51 (2003)
19. Crapo, A.W., Waisel, L.B., Wallace, W.A., Willemain, T.R.: Visualization and the process of modeling: a cognitive-theoretic view. In: Proc. KDD 2000, pp. 218–226 (2000)
20. Ohno, T., Mukawa, N., Yoshikawa, A.: Freegaze: A gaze tracking system for everyday gaze interaction. In: Proc. ETRA 2002, pp. 125–132 (2002)
21. Mendling, J., Reijers, H.A., Cardoso, J.: What Makes Process Models Understandable? In: Alonso, G., Dadam, P., Rosemann, M. (eds.) BPM 2007. LNCS, vol. 4714, pp. 48–63. Springer, Heidelberg (2007)
22. Furtner, M., Rauthmann, J.F., Sachse, P.: Investigating word class effects in first and second languages. Perceptual and Motor Skills 113, 87–97 (2011)
23. Unema, P., Rötting, M.: Differences in eye movements and mental workload between experienced and inexperienced drivers. In: Visual Search, pp. 193–202. Taylor & Francis (1990)
24. Reijers, H.A., Mendling, J.: A Study into the Factors that Influence the Understandability of Business Process Models. SMCA Part A 41, 449–462 (2011)
25. Krogstie, J., Sindre, G., Jørgensen, H.: Process models representing knowledge for action: a revised quality framework. EJIS 15, 91–102 (2006)
26. Becker, J., Rosemann, M., von Uthmann, C.: Guidelines of Business Process Modeling. In: van der Aalst, W.M.P., Desel, J., Oberweis, A. (eds.) Business Process Management. LNCS, vol. 1806, pp. 30–49. Springer, Heidelberg (2000)
27. Mendling, J., Reijers, H.A., van der Aalst, W.M.P.: Seven process modeling guidelines (7pmg). Information & Software Technology 52, 127–136 (2010)
28. Rittgen, P.: Negotiating Models. In: Krogstie, J., Opdahl, A.L., Sindre, G. (eds.) CAiSE 2007. LNCS, vol. 4495, pp. 561–573. Springer, Heidelberg (2007)
29. Cepeda Porras, G., Guéhéneuc, Y.G.: An empirical study on the efficiency of different design pattern representations in uml class diagrams. Empirical Software Engineering 15, 493–522 (2010)
30. Nordbotten, J.C., Crosby, M.E.: The effect of graphic style on data model interpretation. Information Systems Journal 9, 139–155 (1999)
31. Hogrebe, F., Gehrke, N., Nüttgens, M.: Eye Tracking Experiments in Business Process Modeling: Agenda Setting and Proof of Concept. In: Proc. EMISA 2011, pp. 183–188 (2011)

Business Process Orientation: An Empirical Study of Its Impact on Employees' Innovativeness

Jing Tang, L.G. Pee, and Junichi Iijima

Tokyo Institute of Technology
2-12-1, Ookayama, Meguro-ku, Tokyo, 152-8552, Japan
{tang.j.aa,peelg.aa,iijima.j.aa}@m.titech.ac.jp

Abstract. Under the competitive environment, innovation becomes a destination of many companies. Business process orientation (BPO) represents "a state of mind" of organizations to rethink and redesign the business. This study considers BPO can get the "innovation" ball rolling within organizations through fostering an organizational flow of information and communication. Results from a survey of Japanese companies designate that BPO improves cross-functional integration and customer orientation, which, in turn, motivate employees to innovate. This paper contributes to research by proposing a path model from BPO to employees' innovativeness, which empirically substantiates the effectiveness of business process management towards innovation. The findings suggest managers to cultivate BPO as a key organizational resource and support the process-based interaction internally and externally.

Keywords: Business Process Orientation, Cross-Functional Integration, Customer Orientation, Employees' Innovativeness.

1   Introduction

In this information- and knowledge-intensive era, intense competitions require firms to establish hard-to-duplicate capabilities that distinguish themselves from competitors in the market. Innovation is considered as the firm's "core competency" to offer superior customer value by innovating or renovating products/services [18]. It is characterized by the degree of newness, which implies innovation as a complex, unstructured, and uncertain interactive process, involving many shareholders. As a result, efficient innovation management challenges researchers and managers nowadays.

From the resource-based view [2], the employees' innovativeness can be considered as the company's potential key resource towards sustained competitive advantage, according to the properties of valuable, rare, in-imitable, and non-substitutable. Xerri and Brunetto [38] suggest innovative behavior of employees to be an important factor for organizations to improve the overall efficiency and effectiveness of organizational processes. At present, the importance of developing the innovative behavior of employees has become important not only for large companies, but also SMEs [38]. Employees' innovativeness is possible to be influenced by various factors such as knowledge, interpersonal relation, and task specification, etc. [1, 3, 25, 31].

M. La Rosa and P. Soffer (Eds.): BPM 2012 Workshops, LNBIP 132, pp. 451–464, 2013.
© Springer-Verlag Berlin Heidelberg 2013

As a new trend of business process management, business process orientation (BPO) places special emphasis on the effectiveness and efficiency of the horizontal "end-to-end" processes for both internal and external customers [27]. BPO refers to "a state of mind" of organization to evolutionarily reconsider and reengineer its business processes, together with IT transformation, according to customer needs [12, 22]. BPO consists of a multi-perspective change in a company, which in turn can help firms yield extraordinary performance improvements such as quality increase, satisfaction enhancement, procedures optimization, and, especially, cross-functional connectedness increment [12, 23]. This study considers BPO can get the "innovation" ball rolling within organizations through fostering cross-functional integration and customer orientation. The research question is: How does Business Process Orientation initiate employees' innovativeness?

Through a questionnaire survey of 127 Japanese companies, we tested whether BPO has significant effects on cross-functional integration and customer orientation, and then to employees' innovativeness sequentially. The main contribution is the deeper understanding of the link between BPO and employees' innovativeness.

2   Conceptual Background

2.1   Business Process Orientation (BPO)

A business process is a "specific group of activities and subordinate tasks which results in the performance of a service that is of value" [23], focusing on the core business processes rather than functions [12]. It is a shift from vertical system to horizontal system [27], which aims to the better-satisfied customers, more efficiently, less costly, and eventually achieve better firm performance. That is why we can consider BPO as an important ingredient for successful reengineering and redesign efforts.

BPO includes three aspects: process view, process jobs, and process management and measurement [22, 33]. Process view is a way how a company functions, and emphasizes the value of process defining and process thinking. Process job refers to jobs that are assigned basing main business processes. It requires frontline employees or teams to take full responsibility to processes. In other words, process-oriented jobs are usually multidimensional, dynamic and learning-based. Process management and measurement refer to the shift of management focusing from products or functions to processes and outcomes. To be precise, a firm with high BPO degree does not just focus on the outcomes of business process, but also the effectiveness of weaving related organizational resources, especially human capital, into key business processes.

When a strict organization exhibits very outstanding characteristics: limitation in problem solving; inability to innovate; limitation in experiment; and screening out new knowledge, it might cause the result of extreme insularity [19]. It is necessary to break these insularity islands of knowledge. By applying BPO, we can create the ties between them by establishing the flow of information. As BPO captures the continuous changing, the company can move forward with the increase of performance. As the process of innovation is both creation and synthesis [19], establishing the intra- and extra-organization interaction and communication seems to shine the benefit to employees' innovativeness, we should understand the effect of both cross-functional integration (intra-organizational) and customer orientation (extra-organizational).

2.2   Cross-Functional Integration (CFI)

Good innovation requests knowledge from various fields boundaries. Cross-functional integration is considered by the organizational aspect as the "incorporation of the different functions in the organizational structure" [4]. The definitions of cross-functional integration are summarized in Table 1. In this study, cross-functional integration refers to the degree of cooperation at daily practices between functional units for organizational benefits. Building a team with people from diverse professional domains seems important for the success of innovation project due to the recognized advantages of cross-functional integration as the increasing of information flow in the organization via communication and interaction, flexibility in workforce and capital resources, and enhancement of utilization of organizational resources [36].

Table 1. Summary of Cross-functional Integration Definition

Author(s)	Definition of Cross-functional Integration
Kahn [17]	Cross-functional integration is "a multidimensional process of interaction and collaboration between functions, where interaction refers to the structured nature of cross-functional activities, such as the use and exchange of communication among functions, and collaboration if the unstructured."
Song et al. [34]	Cross-functional integration is "the magnitude of interaction and communication, the level of information sharing, the degree of coordination, and the extent of joint involvement across functions in specific new product development tasks."
Joshi [16]	Cross-functional integration is "the establishment of mechanisms and links that facilitate the needed coordination of the activities of different functions to ensure that these functions work together effectively to achieve the overall objectives of the organization."
Botzenhardt et al. [4]	"Cross-functional integration is a well-established practice in product development", whose success factors of product management and product design consist of (1) organizational setup; (2) communication; (3) collaboration; and (4) decision-making.

Table 2. Summary of Customer Orientation Definition

Author(s)	Definition of Customer Orientation
Narver and Slater [24]	Customer orientation is "the organizational culture that most effectively and efficiently creates the necessary behaviors for the creation of superior value for buyers."
Ruekert [29]	Customer orientation is as "the degree to which the organization obtains and uses information from customers, develops a strategy which will meet customer needs, and implements that strategy by being responsive to customers' needs and wants."

Table 2. *(Continued)*

Deshpande et al. [6]	Customer orientation is "the set of beliefs that puts the customer's interest first, while not excluding those of all other stakeholders such as owners, managers, employees, in order to develop a long term profitable enterprise."
Pelham and Wilson [26]	Customer orientation is a concept that consists of customer understanding orientation and customer satisfaction focus.

2.3   Customer Orientation (CO)

The general goal of innovation is to create new products and services to meet or exceed customer's needs. Many sustainable innovative ideas are originated by the customers, especially the leading customers [7]. Table 2 shows the summary of definition of customer orientation. In this study, customer orientation is classified as the organizational culture that keeps a closed communication to their customers, collects the customer's needs and response for creation of valuable information. We can consider customers as the "co-creators of values" because they are a source of competence [10]. Despite the incorporation of resources from customers into processes of a company in open processes is able to generate a tremendous value, it is a company's tough work and risk for understanding their customers precisely and completely, and challenging the inherent risks of customer involvement. Enkel et al. [8] found that the business models need to be interpreted and adapted for each scenario. Thereby, companies need not only redesign of their business models and practices, but also a shift to customer-oriented mind-set.

2.4   Employees' Innovativeness (EI)

Enhancing the creativity and innovation among employees is one imperative step to generate hard-to-imitate competitive advantage [35]. Many practitioners and scholars have investigated the potential simulation of innovative behaviors, and identified many individual and organizational antecedents from different perspectives, such as proactivity, self-confidence, problem-solving style, leadership, work group relationship, job autonomy, organizational knowledge structure, and organizational support [5, 31]. Table 3 shows the definitions of employees' innovativeness, including the enabler that affects employees' innovativeness. In this study, employees' innovativeness is defined as employees' engagement in innovation "directly towards the initiation and intentional introduction (within a work role, group, or organization) of new and useful ideas, processes, products, or procedures" [5].

Table 3. Summary of Employees' Innovativeness Definition and related terms

Author(s)	Definition of Employees' Innovativeness	Enabler(s)
Barron and Harrington [3]	Creativity of employees is "an ability manifested by performance in critical trials in which one individual can be compared with another on a precisely defined scale."	Abilities; Task-specific; Knowledge

Table 3. *(Continued)*

Scott and Bruce [31]	Innovative behavior is related to the ability to recognize problem, generate ideas and solutions, together with the willingness and skill to work with the generated ideas.	Leadership; Team-member change; Problem-solving sty Support for innovation; Res supply
Amabile et al. [1]	Innovative behavior starts when "employees use new idea and different ways in their work, and is induced by both organization and manager's support and encouragement."	Learning orientation
Paulus [25]	Employees' creativity means "divergent thinking in groups as reflected in ideational fluency."	Diversity in skills and knowledge
De Jong and Den Hartog [5]	Innovation behavior is "employees' behavior directed towards the initiation and intentional introduction (within a work role, group, or organization) of new and useful ideas, processes, products, or procedures."	Leadership

3   Research Model and Hypotheses

The research model and hypotheses are shown in Fig.1. Currently, organizational attention changes from products and markets to daily practices and processes. Organizations need to rethink the business orientation from internal and external customers, which initiates many cross-functional processes within companies, even without structural transformation. The process-based cooperation at daily work is likely to support a cooperative culture and trust for non-routine events or projects. Moreover, McCormack and Johnson's research [23] demonstrates BPO can decrease cross-functional conflict (caused by incompatible goals), increase internal coordination, and develop a feeling of "being in it together" within organizations through process redesigning and process-based view, which is not relied on specific type of leadership or a leader. Interestingly, literature about change management also stresses the importance of giving attention to processes and procedures as a mean to ensure employees' cooperation during the change [37]. In other words, BPO integrates separated staffs, teams, functions, and units together as a whole for the better performance. Thus, we consider BPO makes organizations become integrative via the following hypothesis:

> *H1: Business process orientation is positively associated with cross-functional integration.*

The term of BPO emphasizes customer's satisfaction during successful business reengineering. Main principles here are external/internal customer's needs and customer-supplier relationships. An "end-to-end" process view of organization can stretch the focus of a single process to an organizational-wide perspective, and in turn towards core customer value-adding activities. Being process-oriented, process owners and staffs have to keep looking at external customers, and process improvements

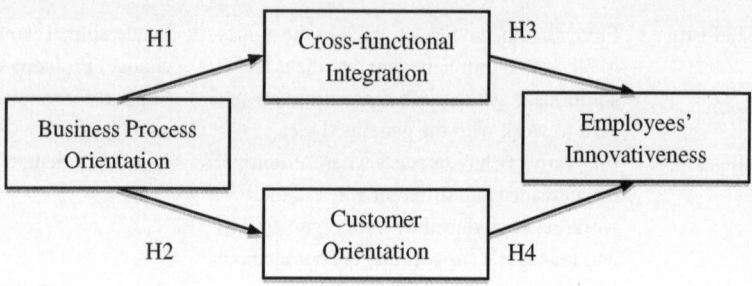

Fig. 1. Research Model and Hypotheses

and innovations are often initiated by unsatisfied and latent customer's needs. As a result, along with evolution of customer needs, concentration, interaction with customers, the tight relationship with customer stemmed from BPO should be able to help organizations capturing the real customer needs, wants, and desires, and then lead to more profitable outcomes sequentially. We, therefore, propose this hypothesis:

H2: Business process orientation is positively associated with customer orientation.

Innovation is not simple as a new idea, but successful implementation of the idea in the market. So, rather than the talent of specialists, currently, innovation asks for the diverse knowledge and cooperation [35]. It is obvious that organization's ability to exploit, transfer, and combine knowledge affects the performance of innovation. As knowledge is basically personal, cross-functional integration is likely to increase the potential for creativity by breaking the boundary of functional units and facilitating employees to share their daily experience and knowledge [32]. It helps gathering individual tacit knowledge to be team's collective knowledge in the new product development [15]. In the firm with high cross-functional integration, employees can more efficiently absorb knowledge from and donate knowledge to other colleagues to innovate. As a result, the next hypothesis is expected:

H3: Cross-functional integration is positively associated with employees' innovativeness.

Because innovation aims to provide new values to customer, latent customer's need is strongly related to innovation initiatives and outcomes. As the rapid evolution of customer's needs, many practitioners and researchers increase addressing that it needs to pay more attention to customers, as a partner integrated in the innovation process. Han et al. [13] found that the level of customer orientation can effect number of innovations implemented. Moreover, according to the idea of open innovation, customers are also the key innovation contributor to propose original innovation ideas. In addition, customer orientation also "helps organization to integrate the internal resources", and encourages innovation according to unsatisfied needs [21]. In the high customer-oriented firm, employees are more likely to innovate, together with a closed and efficient interaction with customers. Thus, we pose the following hypothesis:

H4: Customer orientation is positively associated with employees' innovativeness.

4   Research Method

4.1   Survey Instrument Development

The list of the questionnaire items is in the Appendix. For the measurement of business process orientation, we use the 12 questions developed by McCormack [22]. Among them, four questions are related to process view (e.g., "Business is viewed as a series of linked processes."), three questions are related to process jobs (e.g., "Jobs are usually multidimensional and not just simple tasks."), and five questions are related to process management and measurement (e.g., "Process performance (e.g., process outcomes, customer satisfaction) is measured."). As reported by McCormack [22], the result of his component factor analysis showed problems with several measures along with the components of process-matched flat structures, and process values and beliefs specifically. Along these lines, we decided to exclude those factors, and apply three-factor model, which is also used by other studies [11, 33].

Based on professors and experts from the Innovation Management College of Japan, which is the Japanese institute doing research, providing information, and developing programs to support innovation, the cross-functional integration was measured by three items related to cross-functional human resource development, cross-functional project management, and cross-functional products/services development. Due to the increasing interdependence among constituents at all levels, the human resources department should focus on cross-functional human resource development. It consists of "cross-departmental representatives" [20]. Cross-functional project management processes are commonplace today as well as being seen in the well-known Japanese auto-sector examples which have developed efficient practices for new product development [14]. Cross-functional product development team as the group of members from different departments is brought together under one manager who is in charge of development decisions. The examples of the survey questions are "My company has a formal system for cross-functional human resource development" and "My company has formal cross-functional collaborative processes in new product/services development".

Customer orientation was measured, based also on the Innovation Management College of Japan, with four questions related to customer communication: customer needs analysis; customer satisfaction analysis; and corresponding information sharing system. The examples of the survey questions consist of "For continuous innovation, my company keeps a closed communication with customers" and "My company has information systems to capture and analyze the purchasing behavior of customer."

The questions related to employees' innovativeness were adapted from prior studies applying the theory of planned behavior, which is well-conceived and has been used to understand a wide range of behaviors [9]. Employees' innovativeness was measured with four questions related to frequency of innovation, time spent on innovation, activeness in innovation, and participation in innovation projects. Examples include "In general, employees in my company innovate actively" and "In general, employees in my company spend significant time innovating at work."

All survey questions were measured by five-point Likert scales anchored by "strongly disagree" (1) and "strongly agree" (5). Many prior studies suggested firm size as an important factor to influence company's innovation performance. Large firms, with advantages of stronger cash flow, higher economy of scale, and wider knowledge base is considered to be more innovative [28]. However, some SMEs with higher flexibility are also very innovative, especially in high technology [28]. In this research, firm size and industry were control variables. Firm size was measured by the number of employees. Industry was measured as a categorical variable indicated by respondents as either from manufacturing or non-manufacturing sectors.

4.2   Data Collection

A survey was conducted in Japan with the support of the Innovation Management College of Japan in early 2011. The firms are listed in the database of NTT DATA Corporation. 127 completed responses were received. Response rate is around 10%. Most of responses were from large companies with more than 1,000 employees (64.6 percent). The industries spanned to service, finance, and transportation. The majority of them came from the manufacturing sector (70 percent). With regard of department, more than half of respondents (74.8 percent) were from the corporate development department, which is in charge of business planning and innovation. In job position, 48.8 percent were section heads, and 32.3 percent were core staffs that are manager candidates.

5   Data Analysis

5.1   Test of Measurement Model

The proposed model was assessed with the data of 127 samples. It was tested by structural equation modeling (SEM), using Smart PLS (Partial Least Square) version 2.0, the Bootstrap resampling method with 100 resamples, and IBM SPSS Statistics version 19. Assessment of measurement model includes reliability, convergent validity, and discriminant validity.

Cronbach's alpha coefficient, composite reliability (CR), and significance of item loading (see Table 4) were used to assess the reliability and internal consistency of constructs. For our samples, all Cronbach's alphas estimate for BPO, cross-functional integration, customer orientation, and employees' innovativeness were greater than the recommended threshold of 0.70. All CRs of reflective constructs were also above 0.86 (0.70 is the suggested benchmark of CR). In addition, the loadings of each item to corresponded constructs were significant at 0.01 level.

Convergent validity was assessed by average variance extracted (AVE) and factor analysis. In Table 4, all AVEs were above the recommended acceptable value of 0.50. The principal component factor analysis with Equamax rotation in SPSS supported our proposed evaluation of constructs. Six corresponding variables were extracted. BPO consisted of three of them: process view, process jobs, and process management and measurement. Next, an acceptable individual reliability of items was shown by the item loadings to their corresponded constructs being above 0.70. In our study, all loadings of each item to corresponded constructs in the sample achieved the recommended benchmark of 0.70.

The discriminant validity demonstrates the difference of construct measures in the research model. Results of comparing square root of AVEs and constructs correlation coefficients confirmed the adequate discriminant validity of our questionnaire. All of constructs correlation coefficients (off-diagonal entries in the construct correlation part), excluding the column of BPO, were bigger than the corresponding square roots of AVE (bold diagonal entries in the construct correlation part), which means all these constructs were more correlated with their own measuring items than with any other constructs.

Table 4. Psychometric Properties of Constructs and Construct Correlations

Construct	Cronbach's Alpha	AVE	CR	Construct Correlation						
				BPO	PV	PJ	PM	CFI	CO	EI
Business Process Orientation (BPO)	.90	.51	.92	**.71**						
Process View (PV)	.82	.64	.88	.84	**.80**					
Process Jobs (PJ)	.86	.78	.91	.61	.36	**.88**				
Process Management and Measurement (PM)	.94	.80	.95	.91	.66	.36	**.89**			
Cross-functional Integration (CFI)	.82	.67	.86	.47	.36	.31	.41	**.82**		
Customer Orientation (CO)	.80	.63	.87	.51	.36	.29	.50	.67	**.81**	
Employees' Innovativeness (EI)	.89	.75	.92	.54	.43	.38	.50	.54	.55	**.87**

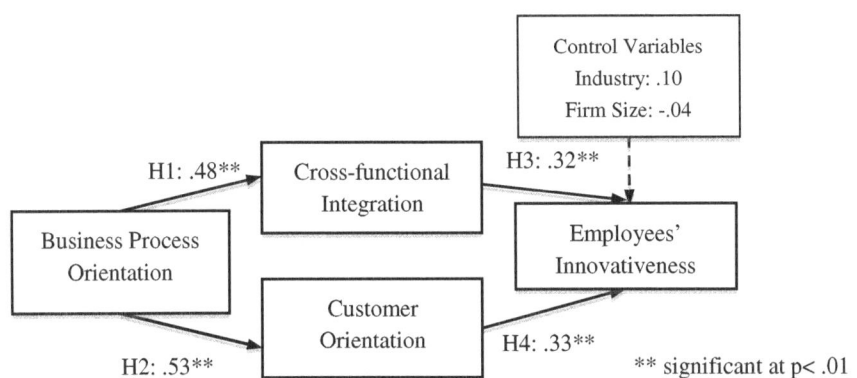

Fig. 2. Test of Structural Model

5.2   Test of Structural Model

Fig. 2 shows the results of our structural model analysis. First, according to R-squared values, about 22 percent of the cross-functional integration, 29 percent of the customer orientation, and 35 percent of the total variability of employees' innovativeness were explained by the constructs used in our model. All of them were above the recommended benchmark of 0.10, so the nomological validity was adequate [30]. Second, we verified whether the signs of hypothesized paths show the same direction as our hypotheses. At this point, all hypotheses were confirmed by the data. Third, we checked the significance of path coefficients. Referring to the corresponding t-value obtained from Bootstrap procedure in Smart PLS, the path coefficients related all hypotheses were statistically significant at 0.01 level. Considering the above two aspects, we can accept all of them. Therefore, there is a path model from BPO to employees' innovativeness, through cross-functional integration and customer orientation.

6   Discussion and Implications

Because innovation is in need of new ideas coming from people, employees' innovativeness is a critical human perspective resource with competitive advantage to innovate. BPO refers to a change of organizational mind-set to be process oriented, fundamental rethinking and reengineering business processes, and gradual improvement of these reengineered processes during implementation. BPO implies both discontinuous and continuous changes in a continuum. The results of PLS analysis supported all hypotheses in our research model. BPO can support a cross-functional integration and customer orientation, which benefit employees' innovativeness as expected. This finding revealed a path model from being BPO to employees' innovativeness empirically. Key characteristics of BPO, which differ from other methods, are continually taking into account the dynamics of external environment (especially customer's needs), integrating isolated units, and building an innovation habit at work.

With the movement of knowledge in the cross-functional units via the information sharing, interaction, collaboration, and communication, the different types of know-how can be integrated, transformed, and increasingly espoused for enhancing knowledge creation and innovation. Through this movement, the innovativeness inside the employees' competence will be promoted.

Next is customer orientation during daily activities. Nowadays, as the customer is gradually treated as a value-adder of business, customer cooperation and integration in new products and services development become a commonplace of efficient innovation management. However, to understand customers clearly is costly, and strongly depends on the selected methods and tools. Different from previous researches considering fundamental information gathering of customers solely on a product or service, this study focuses on continuously looking at customer's needs. In order to create superior customer's value, customer orientation should not simply be a marketing concept, but it should be emphasized in the entire business processes. It helps employees changing to be more forward looking, and creating a shared experience with customers which benefits customer cooperation during the complex innovation processes.

This study potentially contributes to research and practice in several ways. We firstly proposed and verified a potential link between BPO and employees' innovativeness, which exposes a positive effect of BPO towards innovation empirically. Next, focusing on the effects of cross-functional integration and customer orientation helps us to point out considering client needs and integration of diverse disciplines are the key components or engines to innovate. Thirdly, this paper is one among the limited number of innovation researches conducted in Japan.

This research also provides some implementations. Firstly, managers should cultivate BPO within organizations according to the shifting environment, which is able to not only increase effectiveness of processes, but also initiate an innovative behavior among employees in organizations. In order to strength the effect of BPO on innovativeness, managers should also support this change to launch in companies with corresponding innovation reward system and training system. Next, as employees' innovativeness calls for effective integration of cross-functional boundary, it is necessary to enhance the flexibility in workforce, capital resources, organizational system, and information flow. One of the popular practical approaches is applying knowledge management system (KMS) inside the company to provide the useful information resource for all departments to get the knowledge in different aspects. Nevertheless, the manager should beware of some issues, such as time consuming, conflict, and overburden meetings and reports, caused by inefficient collaboration. Moreover, the key role of customer orientation has been demonstrated in this research. It is quite important for companies to generate a closed relationship with customers. For example, one possible method is to provide online tools to support customer design and then share these collected information with the employees.

Findings of this study should be interpreted in view of their limitations. First, most of the respondents are from the manufacturing sector. More studies of other sectors are needed to assess the proposed model. Second, this study focuses on Japanese companies, so there may be some geographical or cultural specificity, and the findings may not generalize to other settings. It may be interesting to assess the proposed model in other countries, especially those with different culture compared to Japan, such as China, Finland, and Australia, etc. Third, only subjective evaluations of constructs had been used in this research, it needs to carefully consider subjective bias when comprehending and applying the results.

7 Conclusions

Innovation is becoming a typical representative strategy in this information- and knowledge-intensive era. Our study found that cross-functional integration and customer orientation provide important base to innovate. Moreover, business process orientation is a shining way that provides a connection among different knowledge domains and contributes to innovation. Therefore, implementing BPO is a good way for companies to foster the road to innovativeness. By facilitating communications, information sharing, coordination, and collaboration between functional project/business units, the employees can learn more knowledge and accumulate their own innovativeness. Customer orientation aligns diverse goals of different staffs, teams, and functions. In addition, nowadays, innovation cannot be considered as a task for each individual team. It needs a cross-functional integration among project/business units. And it is also possible to extend to the systematic co-innovation with all the shareholders within supply chains, or even cross industries or countries. Companies need to change their vision from only inside to outside.

References

1. Amabile, T.M., Conti, R., Coon, H., Lazenby, J., Herron, M.: Assessing the work environment for creativity. Academy of Management Journal 39(5), 1154–1184 (1996)
2. Barney, J.: Firm Resources and Sustained Competitive Advantage. Journal of Management 17(1), 99–120 (1991)
3. Barron, F., Harrington, D.M.: Creativity, intelligence and personality. Annual Review of Psychology 32, 439–476 (1981)
4. Botzenhardt, A., Meth, H., Maedche, A.: Cross-Functional Integration of Product Management and Product Design in Application Software Development: Exploration of Success Factors. ICIS Proceedings. Paper 10 (2011)
5. De Jong, J.P.J., Den Hartog, D.N.: How leaders influence employees' innovative behavior. European Journal of Innovation Management 10(1), 41–64 (2007)
6. Deshpande, R., Farley, F.U., Webster Jr., F.E.: Corporate Culture, Customer Orientation, and Innovativeness in Japanese Firms: A Quadrad Analysis. Journal of Marketing 57, 23–37 (1992)
7. Desouza, K.C., Awazu, Y., Jha, S., Dombrowski, C., Papagari, S., Baloh, P., Kim, J.Y.: Customer-Driven Innovation. Research-Technology Management 51(3), 35–44 (2008)
8. Enkel, E., Gassmann, O., Chesbrough, H.: Open R&D and open innovation: exploring the phenomenon. R&D Management 39(4), 311–316 (2009)
9. Fishbein, M., Ajzen, I.: Acceptance, yielding, and impact: Cognitive processes in persuasion. In: Petty, R.E., Ostrom, T.M., Brock, T.C. (eds.) Cognitive Responses in Persuasion, pp. 339–359. Erlbaum, Hillsdale (1981)
10. Gassmann, O., Enkel, E.: Towards a theory of open innovation: three core process archetypes. In: Proceedings of the R&D Management Conference, Lisbon, Portugal (2004)
11. Gemmel, P., Vandaile, D., Tambeau, W.: Hospital Process Orientation (HPO): The development of a measurement tool. Total Quality Management & Business Excellence 19(12), 1207–1217 (2008)
12. Hammer, M.: The process audit. Harvard Business Review 82(4), 111–123 (2007)
13. Han, J.K., Kim, N., Srivastava, R.K.: Market Orientation and Organizational Performance: Is Innovation a Missing Link? Journal of Marketing 62(4), 30–45 (1998)
14. Hanawalt, E.S., Rouse, W.B.: Car wars: Factors underlying the success of failure of new car program. Systems Engineering 13(4), 389–404 (2009)
15. Hiranyawipada, T., Beyerlein, M., Blankson, C.: Cross-functional integration as a knowledge transformation mechanism: Implications for new product development. Industrial Marketing Management 39(4), 650–660 (2010)
16. Joshi, K.: Cross-functional integration: the role of information systems. Journal of Information Technology Management 9(3), 21–29 (1998)

17. Kahn, K.B.: Interdepartmental integration: a definition with implications for product development performance. Journal of Product Innovation Management 13(2), 137–151 (1996)
18. Kandampully, J.: Innovation as the core competency of a service organization: the role of technology, knowledge and networks. European Journal of Innovation Management 5(1), 18–26 (2002)
19. Leonard, D.: The role of tacit knowledge in group innovation. California Management Review 40(3), 112–132 (1998)
20. Marques, J.F.: The New Human Resource Department: A Cross-Functional Unit. Human Resource Development Quarterly 17(1), 117–123 (2006)
21. Matsuo, M.: Customer orientation, conflict, and innovativeness in Japanese sales departments. Journal of Business Research 59(2), 242–250 (2006)
22. McCormack, K.: Business Process Maturity: Theory and Application. DRK Research, Releigh (2007)
23. McCormack, K., Johnson, W.C.: Business Process Orientation: Gaining the E-Business Competitive Advantage. CRC Press LLC (2001)
24. Narver, J.C., Slater, S.F.: The Effect of a Market Orientation on Business Profitability. The Journal of Marketing 54(4), 20–35 (1990)
25. Paulus, P.B.: Groups, teams and creativity: the creative potential of idea-generating groups. Applied Psychology: An international Review 49, 237–262 (2000)
26. Pelham, A.M., Wilson, D.T.: A longitudinal study of the impact of market structure, firm structure, strategy, and market orientation culture on dimensions of small-firm performance. Journal of the Academy of Marketing Science 24(1), 27–43 (1996)
27. Reijers, H.A.: Implementing BPM systems: the role of process orientation. Business Process Management 12(4), 389–490 (2006)
28. Rogers, M.: Networks, firm size and innovation. Small Business Economic 22(2), 141–153 (2004)
29. Ruekert, R.: Developing a market orientation: an organizational strategy perspective. International Journal of Marketing 9(3), 225–245 (1992)
30. Santosa, P.I., Wei, K.K., Chan, H.C.: User involvement and user satisfaction with information-seeking activity. European Journal of Information Systems 14(4), 361–370 (2005)
31. Scott, S.G., Bruce, R.A.: Determinants of innovation behavior: a path model of individual innovation in the workplace. The Academy of Management Journal 37(3), 580–607 (1994)
32. Sethi, R., Smith, D.C., Park, W.: Cross-Functional Product Development Teams, Creativity, and the Innovativeness of New Consumer Products. Journal of Marketing Research 38(1), 73–85 (2001)
33. Skrinjar, R., Bosilj-Vuksic, V., Indihar-Stemberger, M.: The impact of business process orientation on financial and non-financial performance. Business Process Management Journal 14(5), 738–754 (2008)
34. Song, X.M., Montoya-Weiss, M.M., Schmidt, J.B.: Antecedents and consequences of cross-functional cooperation: a comparison of R&D, manufacturing, and marketing perspectives. Journal of Product Innovation Management 14(1), 35–47 (1997)
35. Teece, D.J.: Business Models, Business Strategy and Innovation. Long Range Planning 43, 172–194 (2010)
36. Troy, L.C., Hirunyawipada, T., Paswan, A.K.: Cross-Functional Integration and New Product Success: An Empirical Investigation of the Findings. Journal of Marketing 72(6), 132–146 (2008)

37. Van Knippenberg, B., Martin, L., Tyler, T.: Process-orientation versus outcome-orientation during organizational change: The role of organizational identification. Journal of Organizational Behavior 27(6), 685–704 (2006)
38. Xerri, M., Brunetto, Y.: Fostering the Innovative Behavior of SME Employees: A Social Capital Perspective. Research and Practice in Human Resource Management 19(2), 43–59 (2011)

Appendix: List of Questionnaire Items

Business Process Orientation (BPO)

1. The average employee views the business as a series of linked processes.

2. Process terms (input, output, process and process owners) are used in the conversation.

3. Processes are defined and documented by using inputs and outputs, to and from our customers.

4. The business processes are sufficiently defined, so that most people know how they work.

5. Jobs are usually multidimensional and not just simple tasks.

6. Jobs include frequent problem solving.

7. People are constantly learning new things on the job.

8. Process performance (e.g., process outcomes, customer satisfaction) is measured.

9. Process measurements (e.g., output quality, cycle time, process cost and variability) are defined.

10. Resources (e.g., people, expenses, and other capital) are allocated based on process.

11. Specific process performance goals (e.g., target output quality, target cycle time, target process cost and target variability) are in place.

12. Process outcomes (e.g., real output quality, real cycle time, real process cost and real variability) are measured.

Cross-Function Integration (CFI)

1. My company has a formal system for cross-functional human resource development.

2. My company has the process of managing several related projects/business units.

3. My company has formal cross-functional collaborative processes in new products/services development.

Customer Orientation (CO)

1. For continuous innovation, my company keeps a closed communication with customers.

2. My company has information systems to capture and analyze the purchasing behavior of customer.

3. My company collects and shares information about customer's need.

4. My company captures customer's response towards new products/services rapidly and efficiently.

Employees' Innovativeness (EI)

1. In general, employees in my company innovate actively.

2. In general, employees in my company innovate frequently.

3. In general, employees in my company support innovative behavior at work.

4. In general, employees in my company spend significant time innovating at work.

A Visualization Concept for High-Level Comparison of Process Model Versions

Simone Kriglstein[1] and Stefanie Rinderle-Ma[2]

[1] SBA Research, Vienna, Austria
SKriglstein@sba-research.at
[2] University of Vienna, Faculty of Computer Science,
Research Group Workflow Systems and Technology, Vienna, Austria
stefanie.rinderle-ma@univie.ac.at

Abstract. Managing large collections of different process model versions is for many organizations inevitable and results from, e.g., adaption of models to solve different challenges or modifications due to changed or new conditions. One challenge in this context is to make the differences between the versions visible and comparable. Visualizations have the advantage that they can present the relationships between the different process versions in a user-friendly way and therefore support users in their decisions. In this paper we introduce a visualization concept with the goal to provide a simple overview in order to compare complementary or contrasting characteristics between different versions. The design idea is presented on the basis of two use cases. Limitations of the concept are also discussed. The visualization concept should support users to gain a first impression about the characteristics between the versions and can be used as an entry point for a more detailed analysis of the different versions.

Keywords: Visualization, Version management, Business process model collection.

1 Introduction

In the last years, different approaches have been developed to support organizations in adjusting their business processes in order to react flexible on changing environmental conditions (e.g., new or changed requirements) or on unplanned events/exceptions (e.g., to correct design errors) [1]. It is often unavoidable that organizations have large collections of large numbers of different business process versions. Therefore, it is common that organizations have to maintain repositories that can contain hundreds or even thousands of versions usually created by different users with diverse goals and responsibilities [2]. For graphical process notations, process evolution is mainly carried out by applying change operations (e.g., adding, deleting, or moving a process fragment) that are defined over the graph structure of the process model. However, in many cases it is not only sufficient to make the applied change operations comparable between the different versions, but also to consider security-relevant information such as who

M. La Rosa and P. Soffer (Eds.): BPM 2012 Workshops, LNBIP 132, pp. 465–476, 2013.
© Springer-Verlag Berlin Heidelberg 2013

conducted changes or who has permissions to apply change operations. Such kind of information plays an important role, especially for collaborative modeling (e.g., to control inadvertent changes in process models by users who are not designated as editors).

Over the years, approaches (e.g., [2,3,4,5]) have been developed to make the management of versions easier in order to reduce costs and efforts. For example, version management supports companies to re-use processes as reference models and adapt them to their requirements, e.g., by applying pre-defined change operations on the reference process [6]. Further reasons for their increasing popularity are that most users are familiar with version management concepts (e.g., to manage changes of documents, computer programs, and wikis) and that they provide features (e.g., to roll back to any versions at any point in time) to recover process models from mistakes and to see additional security-relevant information (e.g., who changed what and when).

Among other things, visualizations support users to better understand the datasets and to recognize patterns (e.g., detection of data groups) which can be helpful for their further decisions [7]. The potential of visualizations to make things (e.g., patterns, relationships, or anomalies) visible makes them attractive as an additional support for the analysis and management of versions. For example, a graphical representation can help to see which change operations were applied between versions and to compare them with the number of users who conducted these changes. Or a visualization can be used to make the number of users who conducted changes in regard to the assigned permission operations visible.

This paper introduces a visualization concept in order to compare complementary or contrasting characteristics between different process versions. The concept is inspired by Shneiderman's Visual Information-Seeking Mantra *"Overview first, zoom and filter, then details-on-demand"* [8] that describes how data should be presented to make it most effective for users. Based on the Visual Information-Seeking Mantra, the design idea is to develop an approach that provides a simple overview which can be used as starting point in order to move from summary information to detailed information. Furthermore, the ability of human's perception for detection of patterns is taken into account in order to gain a first impression of the visualized characteristics between the different versions.

The remainder of the paper is structured as follows. In Section 2 related work is discussed and Section 3 gives a short overview about the relevant aspects of graphical perception. The visualization concept is introduced in Section 4 and in Section 5 two use cases are presented. Limitations of the visualization concept and future work are discussed in Section 6. Finally, the paper is concluded in Section 7.

2   Related Work

Although version-based visualization approaches are well-known in several fields of computer science (see e.g., [9,10,11,12,13,14,15,16,17,18]), the development of visualization approaches for version management in the business process context has received little attention in the last years [19,20]. Usually the different versions are presented as a list (e.g., Apromore platform [21] or IBM Business Process Manager [22]), as an indented list to highlight the hierarchical structure (e.g., e*Insight Business Process Manager [23]) or as a version graph to visualize the hierarchical and non-hierarchical relationships between versions (e.g., [24,25,26]).

For a comparative analysis of different versions, multiple views are often used (see e.g., [22,23,25,26]). For example, one view gives an overview about the stored versions (e.g., as a list or version graph) and the detail information of the selected version (e.g., change information and/or corresponding process model) is presented in another view. The conducted literature review and survey in [27] shows that change information is usually presented in tables or directly highlighted in the process graph via visual properties, like colors. Although the usage of multiple views allows to simplify the design, users need time to orientate themselves after switching between different views in order to comprehend the context and to compare the different views [28,29]. The focus of our approach is to provide a first overview about version information in order to support a simple comparative analysis among the different versions. Furthermore, it can be integrated into approaches such as the Apromore platform. [4].

3 Background Knowledge: Graphical Perception

In this section, we shortly present relevant aspects of graphical perception which are from interest for our approach. The design considers the ability of human's perception to recognize changes, e.g., in color and length in order to detect simple patterns in categorical datasets. Studies (e.g., [30,31]) show that pre-attentive processing can guide the human's attention toward target objects by visual properties at a glance without effort [32,33,34]. Hence, objects seem to pop out from the rest of the scene provided that the target object is distinguished from the other objects by simple features (e.g., colors) [33,34,35]. For example, it does not take any effort to see the black objects in Figure 1. Furthermore, the example shows well that the black objects can be split into two groups because of their spatial proximity which is one of the Gestalt laws. The Gestalt laws (e.g., proximity, similarity, closure, and symmetry) describe rules how the space has to be organized to see patterns in visual displays [36]. However, the number of visual properties that can be used is limited and pre-attentive processing is not for all tasks sufficient [7]. Typically, pre-attentive processing is combined with attentive processing for the analysis of patterns in order to actively scan serially through the display to find the target object [31,34,35]. For example, to find the target object in Figure 1 (depicted in the thought bubble) the attention is first guided to areas which have the same features (e.g., color, shape, and orientation).

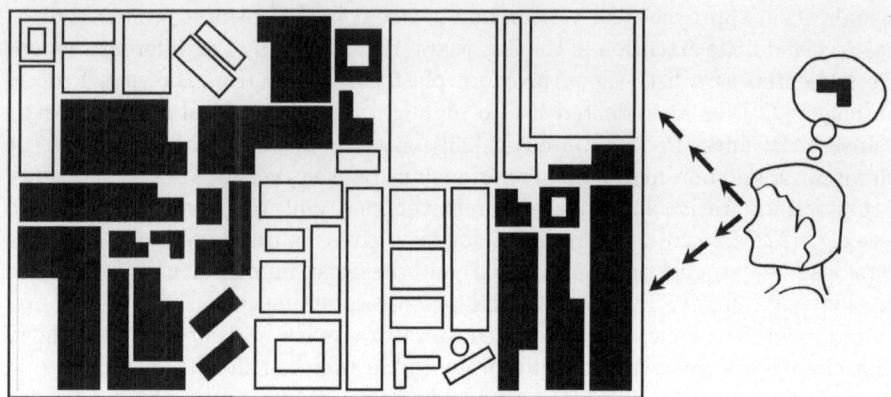

Fig. 1. Example for pre-attentive and attentive processes: The attention is guided to locations that have the same features (e.g., color black) as the target object (shown in the thought bubble) in order to scan these areas serially

4   Design Approach

In this section we present the concept of our visualization approach. The idea is to provide an overview of categorical datasets to help users to compare parts of the data in order to support simple comparative analysis and to provide an entry point that allows users to navigate to areas of interest.

4.1   Basic Concept

The main components are stacked bar charts which are similar to bar charts. Bar charts can be used for various datasets and are one of the most common chart types [37]. In contrast to bar charts, stacked bar charts allow the comparison of numeric values in regard to their corresponding subcategories. Figure 2 shows the concept of our approach. The version numbers are presented chronologically on the y-axis and the subcategories are presented as horizontal bars. The juxta-position of two stacked bar charts makes it possible to compare complementary or contrasting characteristics between different process versions.

4.2   Visual Features

The length of a single bar presents the value of the corresponding subcate-gory. The length of the total stacked bar reflects the sum of the subcategories. Different colors are used to indicate different subcategories. Based on Ware's recommendation [33] it is necessary to consider:

- *Visual Distinctness*: The stacked bars and their subcategories should pop out from the scene to support effective visual search and comparison. In other words the contrast between the background and foreground colors should be as high as possible.

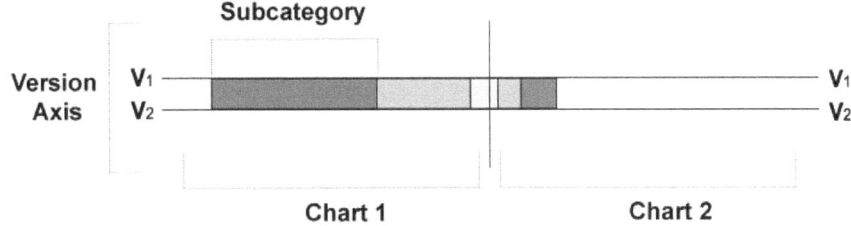

Fig. 2. Basic structure of the concept

- *Learnability*: Colors have to be used consistently in order to be clear that one color presents a specific subcategory.

The number of colors is restricted in order to avoid effects like eyestrain, confusion or disorientation [33,38]. There exist several recommendations (e.g., [33,38]) about how many colors can be used. The recommendations vary from case to case, but often the maximum number is between 6 and 12 colors [33]. Furthermore, it is recommended to use colors that are widely spaced along the color spectrum [39]. For example, in addition to black and white, the following colors are recommended [33,39]: red, yellow, green, blue, brown, pink, orange, grey, and purple.

The different lengths of bars and colors support users to gain a first impression about the distribution of the subcategories and allow users to detect simple patterns between the different versions. For example, to see which versions have high or low differentiation in regard to a specific subcategory or if the values of a specific subcategory increase/decrease over the versions. Furthermore, it can be used to monitor activities between versions and it helps to detect irregularities, unexpected activities or activities which are not allowed (e.g., if more users made changes than users who had the edit permission). Figure 3 shows an example for the interplay between lengths of bars and colors. The colors blue, red, and green are used to present three different subcategories. The different lengths of bars show, e.g., that the subcategory 3 (color green) has the highest value between version 1 (V1) and version 2 (V2) in chart 1. Similarly, subcategory 1 (color blue) has the highest value between version 2 (V2) and version 3 (V3) in chart 2. Moreover, the comparison of chart 1 and chart 2 shows that the value of subcategory 2 (color red) has the biggest differentiation between version 1 (V1) and version 2 (V2).

5   Use Cases

In this section we present two use cases with the aim to show possible applications as an aid to understand the above described design concept better. In the first use case, we juxtapose the change operations with the number of users who conducted the changes. The focus of the second use case is on the number of

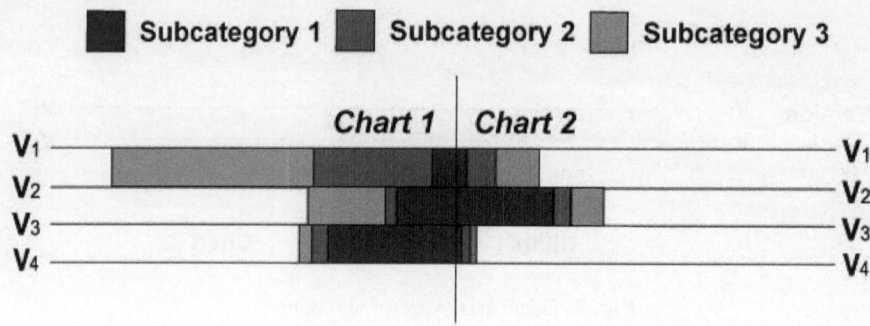

Fig. 3. The example presents the juxtaposition of chart 1 with chart 2 for the analysis of the differences between version 1 (V1), version 2 (V2), version 3 (V3), and version 4 (V4) in regard to three subcategories that are color-coded with blue, red, and green

permission assignments and the number of users who conducted a permission operation between two versions.

5.1   Use Case 1: Change Operations

The results of one of our previous studies [27] confirmed that the comparison between versions in regard to change operations is often from interest. However, it was also mentioned as helpful to see additional information, like, the users who conducted the changes. Such information can be especially from interest for collaboration modeling and shared processes.

Figure 4 shows an example how both information can be presented. The choice of change operations is based on the following six change patterns that are defined by Weber et al. [40]: *Insert, Delete, Move, Replace, Swap,* and *Copy.* These change operations are defined as subcategories. The left chart in Figure 4 presents the distribution of change operations and the right chart shows the distribution of the number of users who performed the change operations between versions. The values of the bars for the corresponding change operations present the number of conducted change operations between the versions (c.f. left chart in Figure 4) and the distinct number of users (c.f. right chart). The representation supports users to answer simple questions such as, which change operations were conducted, which changes were made more/less frequently between which versions, how many users made changes between which versions, or which change operations were executed by more/less users. The juxtaposition of the conducted change operations with the number of users allows to see them not only separately but also in combination. For example, although the sum of change operations are approximately equal between the first stacked bar and the third stacked bar, more users made changes between V1 and V2 than between V3 and V4. Furthermore, each stacked bar between two versions can be analyzed individually, e.g., the change operations *Insert, Delete,* and *Move* were

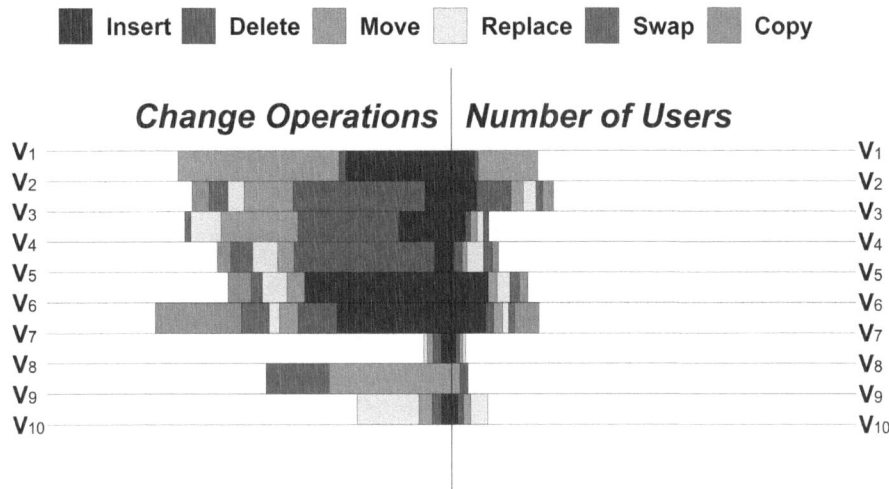

Fig. 4. Example for use case 1: Juxtaposition of change operations with the number of users who conducted the changes between the versions (V1-V10)

conducted between V1 and V2 and between V8 and V9 the change operations *Move* and *Swap* were made. Moreover, the analysis of the overall picture shows, e.g., that the change operation *Delete* builds a cluster between V2 and V5. Such kind of information can introduce further and deeper questions – e.g., Why did more users made changes? or Why were many *Delete* operations conducted? – that can be answered in a detailed view (e.g., after a stacked bar is selected, the process with change information can be presented in another view).

5.2   Use Case 2: Permission Assignments

Over the years, controlling and monitoring of permission assignments become more and more important, especially for shared processes. One research focus is on the comparison between users' activities and permission assignments in order to detect possible discrepancies [41].

The presented approach in Section 4 can be used to provide an overview about the number of permission assignments and the actual number of users who conducted the permission operations between the versions. Figure 5 presents an example with the permission operations as subcategories. The permission operations define users' authorizations and for the example the suggested operations by Leitner et al. [42] are used: *Add*, *Delete*, *Execute*, and *Monitor*. The left chart shows the number of assignments of permission operations to users and the right chart presents the distinct number of users who conducted operations between the versions. The visualization shows that only little differentiations of permission assignments to their users exist between the versions (see left chart in Figure 5). Therefore, changes of permission assignments between versions (e.g..

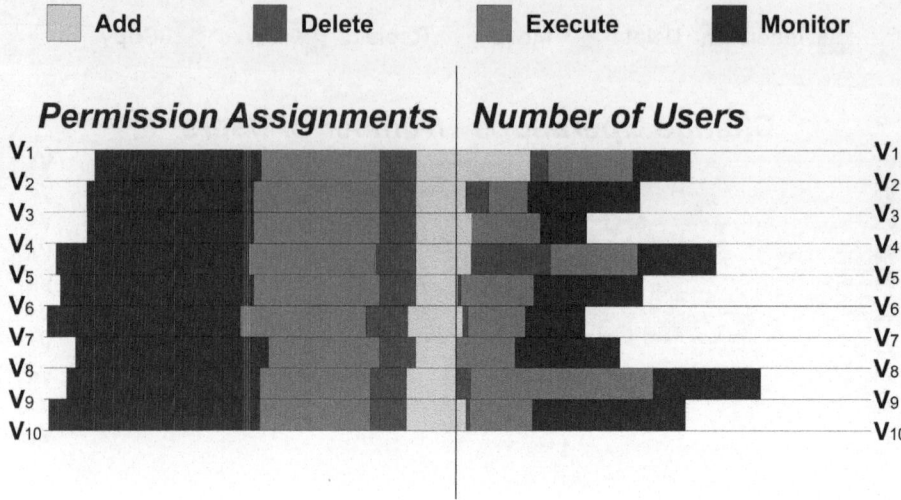

Fig. 5. Example for use case 2: Juxtaposition of the number of permission assignments with the number of users who conducted permission operations between the versions (V1-V10)

between V6 and V8 in Figure 5) stand out from the relative stable representation. The juxtaposition of the number of permissions assignments with the number of users who conducted permission operations allows to see possible discrepancies between the versions. For example, in Figure 5 more users conducted the *Add* operation between V1 and V2 than the number of authorized users who are assigned to this operation. Further possible discrepancies can be found between V4 and V5 for the *Delete* operation as well as between V8 and V9 for the *Execute* operation. Although, further information is necessary for a detailed analysis (e.g., to find out the reasons for these discrepancies), such an overview allows a fast detection of interesting areas. However, detection of discrepancies is only possible if the number of users who conducted permission operations is higher than the number of permission assignments. Therefore, the usage of additional visual hints can be helpful in case a conflict exist between the versions (see Figure 6 for an example). Further limitations are discussed in the next section.

6 Limitations and Future Work

In this section we discuss limitations of the presented design concept and our next steps.

One limitation is that the linear representation of versions in chronological order only allows to analyze versions which are connected directly. For example, a comparison between V2 and V8 in Figure 4 is not possible. Furthermore, it is not possible to compare different branches from one version. Hence it is necessary not only to provide a static visualization but also interactivity. One of our next

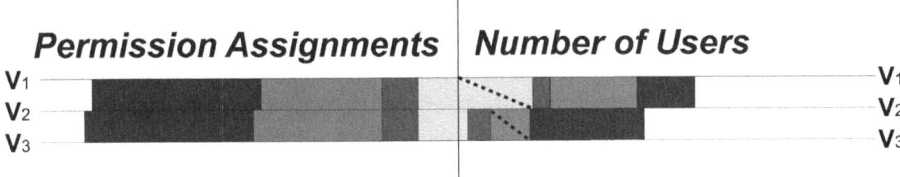

Fig. 6. To highlight subcategories with discrepancies, a dotted line is used as additional visual hint

steps is to find ways to integrate interactivity in our concept, e.g., to select the versions for comparison and the aggregated information is presented in a shared stacked bar.

A further limitation is that only the juxtaposition of two characteristics is possible. For the analysis of more than two characteristics, small multiples [43] can be used as series of paired stacked bar charts to present different juxtapositions of two characteristics between versions. The advantage of small multiples is that multidimensional data can be visualized without packing all information into a single chart.

According to Ware [33,36] the skill to detect complex patterns in visualizations has to be learned by the viewers. Therefore, it is necessary that the visualization is designed in such a way that supports users to easily identify patterns. Ware [36] recommends to consider pattern-finding skills (e.g., based on graphical perceptual capabilities) that are common for the viewers. Therefore, we plan to evaluate our design concept in order to investigate how well viewers can identify patterns and to detect possible improvements.

An increasing number of subcategories and therefore an increasing number of bars makes the comparison – especially for bars which are further away from the midline (y-axis) – more difficult. Hence, we will investigate if the number of bars influence the identification of patterns. Moreover, we want to find out the maximal number of bars which can be used.

The use cases in Section 5 show that visual hints can be helpful to visualize additional information (e.g., to make discrepancies clearly visible). However such additional visual hints can influence the detection of patterns. Therefore we plan to find solutions how we can use such visual hints in order to reduce negative effects on the identification of patterns.

7 Conclusion

In this paper we suggested a visualization concept for a high-level comparison of complementary or contrasting characteristics between different process model versions. The concept based on the Shneiderman's Visual Information-Seeking Mantra to provide an overview in order to detect areas of interest that can be used as starting point for further detailed analysis of the process versions (e.g., with the help of detail-on-demand techniques). Furthermore, the presented approach can be used as add-on feature to the commonly used lists that present the different versions in repositories. This supports users to answer simply questions, like, between which versions more or less change operations were made. We introduced the concept on the basis of two use cases to illustrate the diversity of situations where the approach can be useful. However, the concept also shows several limitations (e.g., only representation of chronological order or limitation of subcategories) that need further investigations. Moreover, we also plan to evaluate the visualization concept with users to improve the concept further.

Acknowledgements. The research was funded by COMET K1, FFG - Austrian Research Promotion Agency.

References

1. Rinderle, S., Reichert, M., Dadam, P.: Correctness criteria for dynamic changes in workflow systems: A survey. Data and Knowledge Engineering 50(1), 9–34 (2004)
2. Ekanayake, C.C., La Rosa, M., ter Hofstede, A.H.M., Fauvet, M.-C.: Fragment-Based Version Management for Repositories of Business Process Models. In: Meersman, R., Dillon, T., Herrero, P., Kumar, A., Reichert, M., Qing, L., Ooi, B.-C., Damiani, E., Schmidt, D.C., White, J., Hauswirth, M., Hitzler, P., Mohania, M. (eds.) OTM 2011, Part I. LNCS, vol. 7044, pp. 20–37. Springer, Heidelberg (2011)
3. Fauvet, M.C., La Rosa, M., Sadegh, M., Alshareef, A., Dijkman, R.M., García-Bañuelos, L., Reijers, H.A., van der Aalst, W.M.P., Dumas, M., Mendling, J.: Managing Process Model Collections with AProMoRe. In: Maglio, P.P., Weske, M., Yang, J., Fantinato, M. (eds.) ICSOC 2010. LNCS, vol. 6470, pp. 699–701. Springer, Heidelberg (2010)
4. La Rosa, M., Reijers, H.A., van der Aalst, W.M.P., Dijkman, R.M., Mendling, J., Dumas, M., García-Bañuelos, L.: APROMORE: an advanced process model repository. Expert Systems with Applications 38(6), 7029–7040 (2011)
5. Yan, Z., Dijkman, R., Grefen, P.: Business process model repositories - framework and survey. Inf. Softw. Technol. 54(4), 380–395 (2012)
6. Hallerbach, A., Bauer, T., Reichert, M.: Capturing variability in business process models: the Provop approach. Journal of Software Maintenance and Evolution: Research and Practice 22(6-7), 519–546 (2010)
7. Fekete, J.-D., van Wijk, J.J., Stasko, J.T., North, C.: The Value of Information Visualization. In: Kerren, A., Stasko, J.T., Fekete, J.-D., North, C. (eds.) Information Visualization. LNCS, vol. 4950, pp. 1–18. Springer, Heidelberg (2008)
8. Shneiderman, B.: The eyes have it: a task by data type taxonomy for information visualizations. In: Proc. of the 1996 IEEE Symposium on Visual Languages. IEEE Computer Society (1996)
9. Collberg, C., Kobourov, S., Nagra, J., Pitts, J., Wampler, K.: A system for graph-based visualization of the evolution of software. In: Proc. of the 2003 ACM Symposium on Software Visualization, pp. 77–86. ACM Press (2003)
10. Diehl, S.: Visualizing the evolution of software systems. In: Software Visualization, pp. 129–147. Springer (2007)
11. Eick, S.G., Graves, T.L., Karr, A.F., Mockus, A., Schuster, P.: Visualizing software changes. IEEE Trans. Softw. Eng. 28, 396–412 (2002)

12. Eick, S.G., Steffen, J.L., Sumner Jr., E.E.: Seesoft - a tool for visualizing line oriented software statistics. IEEE Trans. Softw. Eng. 18, 957–968 (1992)
13. Gracanin, D., Matkovic, K., Eltoweissy, M.: Software visualization. Innovations in Systems and Software Engineering (ISSE) 1(2), 221–230 (2005)
14. Langelier, G., Sahraoui, H., Poulin, P.: Exploring the evolution of software quality with animated visualization. In: Proc. of the IEEE Symposium on Visual Languages and Human-Centric Computing, pp. 13–20. IEEE Computer Society (2008)
15. Maletic, J.I., Marcus, A., Feng, L.: Source viewer 3D (sv3D): a framework for software visualization. In: Proc. of the 25th International Conference on Software Engineering, pp. 812–813. IEEE Computer Society (2003)
16. Ogawa, M., Ma, K.L.: Software evolution storylines. In: Proc. of the 5th International Symposium on Software Visualization, pp. 35–42. ACM Press (2010)
17. Tu, Q., Godfrey, M.: An integrated approach for studying software architectural evolution. In: Proc. of the International Workshop on Program Comprehension (2002)
18. Voinea, L., Telea, A., Chaudron, M.R.V.: Version-centric visualization of code evolution. In: Proc. of the Eurographics/IEEE-VGTC Symposium on Visualization, pp. 223–230. Eurographics Association (2005)
19. Chaâbane, M.A., Andonoff, E., Bouzguenda, L., Bouaziz, R.: Dealing with business process evolution using versions. In: Proc. of the International Conference on e-Business, ICE-B is part of ICETE - The International Joint Conference on e-Business and Telecommunications, pp. 267–278. INSTICC Press (2008)
20. Zhao, X., Liu, C.: Version Management in the Business Process Change Context. In: Alonso, G., Dadam, P., Rosemann, M. (eds.) BPM 2007. LNCS, vol. 4714, pp. 198–213. Springer, Heidelberg (2007)
21. The Apromore Foundation: Apromore platform: v0.2 (August 01, 2011) (2009-2012), http://brahms0.imag.fr:8080/Apromore-portal/ (accessed April 19, 2012)
22. IBM: IBM Business Process Manager, http://www-01.ibm.com/software/integration/business-process-manager/ (accessed April 19, 2012)
23. SeeBeyond Technology Corporation: SeeBeyond eBusiness Integration Suite Primer, Release 4.5.2 (1999-2002), http://docs.oracle.com/cd/E18867_01/4.5.x/4.5.2/Business_Integration_Suite/Primer.pdf (accessed April 19, 2012)
24. Bae, H., Hu, W., Yoo, W.S., Kwak, B.K., Kim, Y., Park, Y.T.: Document configuration control processes captured in a workflow. Computers in Industry 53(2), 117–131 (2004)
25. Cui, D., Feng, G.: Component based design data version management and visualization in IMS-DATE. In: Proc. of the IEEE International Conference on Industrial Engineering and Engineering Management, pp. 1529–1533. IEEE Computer Society (2008)
26. Thomas, O.: Version management for reference models: Design and implementation. In: Becker, J., Delfmann, P. (eds.) Reference Modeling: Efficient Information Systems Design Through Reuse of Information Models, pp. 1–26. Physica-Verlag (2007)
27. Kriglstein, S., Rinderle-Ma, S.: Change visualization in business processes - requirements analysis. In: Proc. of the International Joint Conference on Computer Vision, Imaging and Computer Graphics Theory and Applications (GRAPP/IVAPP). SciTePress (2012)

28. Betz, S., Eichhorn, D., Hickl, S., Klink, S., Koschmider, A., Li, Y., Oberweis, A., Trunko, R.: 3D representation of business process models. In: Proc. of Modellierung betrieblicher Informations Systeme (MobIS). LNI, GI, pp. 73–87 (2008)
29. North, C.: Information visualization. In: Salvendy, G. (ed.) Handbook of Human Factors and Ergonomics, pp. 1222–1246. John Wiley & Sons (2005)
30. Treisman, A.M.: Features and objects in visual processing. Scientific American 255(5), 114–125 (1986)
31. Treisman, A.M., Gelade, G.: A feature-integration theory of attention. Cognitive Psychology 12(1), 97–136 (1980)
32. Fekete, J.D., Plaisant, C.: Interactive information visualization of a million items. In: Proc. of the IEEE Symposium on Information Visualization (InfoVis 2002), pp. 117–124. IEEE Computer Society (2002)
33. Ware, C.: Visual Thinking: for Design. Morgan Kaufmann Publishers Inc. (2008)
34. Williams, E.: Visual search: a novel psychophysics for preattentive vision. Master's thesis, Research Science Institute (1999)
35. Healey, C.G., Booth, K.S., Enns, J.T.: Visualizing real-time multivariate data using preattentive processing. ACM Trans. Model. Comput. Simul. 5(3), 190–221 (1995)
36. Ware, C.: Information Visualization: Perception for Design. Morgan Kaufmann Publishers Inc. (2004)
37. Yau, N.: Visualize This: The FlowingData Guide to Design, Visualization, and Statistics. John Wiley & Sons (2011)
38. Stone, D., Jarrett, C., Woodroffe, M., Minocha, S.: User Interface Design and Evaluation. Morgan Kaufmann (2005)
39. Galitz, W.O.: The Essential Guide to User Interface Design: Introduction to GUI Design Principles and Techniques. Wiley & Sons (2002)
40. Weber, B., Reichert, M., Rinderle-Ma, S.: Change patterns and change support features - enhancing flexibility in process-aware information systems. Data Knowl. Eng. 66(3), 438–466 (2008)
41. Rinderle-Ma, S., Wil, M.: Life-cycle support for staff assignment rules in process-aware information systems. Technical report (2007)
42. Leitner, M., Rinderle-Ma, S., Mangler, J.: AW-RBAC: Access control in adaptive workflow systems. In: Proc. of the 6th International Conference on Availability, Reliability and Security, pp. 25–37. IEEE Computer Society (2011)
43. Tufte, E.R.: Envisioning Information. Graphics Press (1990)

Towards Run-Time Flexibility for Process Families: Open Issues and Research Challenges*

Clara Ayora[1], Victoria Torres[1], Manfred Reichert[2],
Barbara Weber[3], and Vicente Pelechano[1]

[1] Universitat Politècnica de València
{cayora,vtorres,pele}@pros.upv.es
[2] University of Ulm, Germany
manfred.reichert@uni-ulm.de
[3] University of Innsbruck, Austria
barbara.weber@uibk.ac.at

Abstract. The increasing adoption of process-aware information systems and the high variability of business processes in practice have resulted in process model repositories with large collections of related process variants (i.e., process families). Existing approaches for variability management focus on the modeling and configuration of process variants. However, case studies have shown that run-time configuration and re-configuration as well as the evolution of process variants are essential as well. Effectively handling process variants in these lifecycle phases requires deferring certain configuration decisions to the run-time, dynamically re-configuring process variants in response to contextual changes, adapting process variants to emerging needs, and evolving process families over time. In this paper, we characterize these flexibility needs for process families, discuss fundamental challenges to be tackled, and provide an overview of existing proposals made in this context.

Keywords: Run-time Flexibility, Variability, Process Families.

1 Introduction

In recent years, the increasing adoption of *Process-aware Information Systems* (PAISs) has resulted in large process model repositories [4]. Since *Business Process* (BP) models often vary, depending on their application context [6,19], these repositories usually comprise large collections of related *process model variants* (*process variants* for short) [15]. Such process variants pursue the same or similar business objective (e.g., treatment of a patient or maintenance of vehicles in a garage), but may differ in their logic (i.e., process logic) due to varying application context at either design time or run-time (e.g., regulations found in different countries and regions, products or services being delivered, or customer categories) [18,4]. A collection of related process variants is denoted as

---

* This work has been developed with the support of MICINN under the project EV-ERYWARE TIN2010-18011.

M. La Rosa and P. Soffer (Eds.): BPM 2012 Workshops, LNBIP 132, pp. 477–488, 2013.

process family. Examples can be found in almost every domain; e.g., [8] describes a process family for vehicle repair and maintenance with more than 900 process variants with country-, garage-, and vehicle-specific differences.

Properly dealing with process families constitutes a main challenge to reduce development and maintenance efforts in large process repositories. Designing and implementing each process variant from scratch and maintaining it separately would be inefficient and costly for companies. Thus, there is a great interest in capturing common process knowledge only once and re-using it in terms of *reference process models*, e.g., ITIL in IT service management, reference processes in SAP's ERP system, or medical guidelines. Even though respective proposals foster the reuse of common process knowledge, typically, they lack comprehensive support for explicitly describing variations [20]. In addition, they only provide limited support for run-time (re-)configuration and evolution (i.e., run-time flexibility), which inhibits the ability of an organization to respond to changes in an agile way. To deal with exceptions, uncertainty, and evolving processes, however, process families need to provide run-time flexibility as well [29].

In recent years, several proposals have been made to deal with process families. In the BP management field, model-driven techniques provide diverse solutions for managing process variants [23,21,8], i.e., for modeling, configuring, executing, and monitoring a process family. However, run-time flexibility and the evolution of process families have not been sufficiently considered so far. In turn, [9,11] focus on flexibility issues at the execution level. Based on code injection, a process variant can be partially adapted to new environmental needs. However, respective techniques are difficult to apply for non-technical stakeholders and only cover parts of their flexibility needs. In the context of adaptive PAISs, in addition, solutions for enabling process flexibility are proposed [30,31]. Despite the fact that these proposals are well suited for single process models, they cannot face the challenges raised by process model families. Finally, in the field of Software Product Lines, flexibility issues in product families are discussed [10], i.e., feature models allow specifying variations between members of a product family. However, these techniques focus on design time configuration, neglecting run-time configuration support.

In this paper, we characterize run-time flexibility needs of process families using two case studies for illustration purposes. We discuss open issues and research challenges regarding run-time (re-)configuration and evolution of process variants. Further, we provide a review of methods, technologies, and tools for BP variability, and discuss how they address respective run-time flexibility issues.

Section 2 presents two examples of process families used for illustration purpose. In Section 3, we define the main concepts for process families and introduce existing variability proposals. Section 4 analyzes run-time flexibility needs of process families. Finally, Section 5 summarizes the paper.

2   Examples of Process Families

To illustrate run-time flexibility needs of process families, we refer to process families from the healthcare and automotive domains, which we analyzed in two case studies. More precisely, our first family comprises more than 90 process variants for handling medical examinations, either standard (i.e., planned) or emergency (i.e., unplanned), in large hospitals [14]. In turn, our second process family consists of more than 20 variants dealing with product change management in the automotive domain.

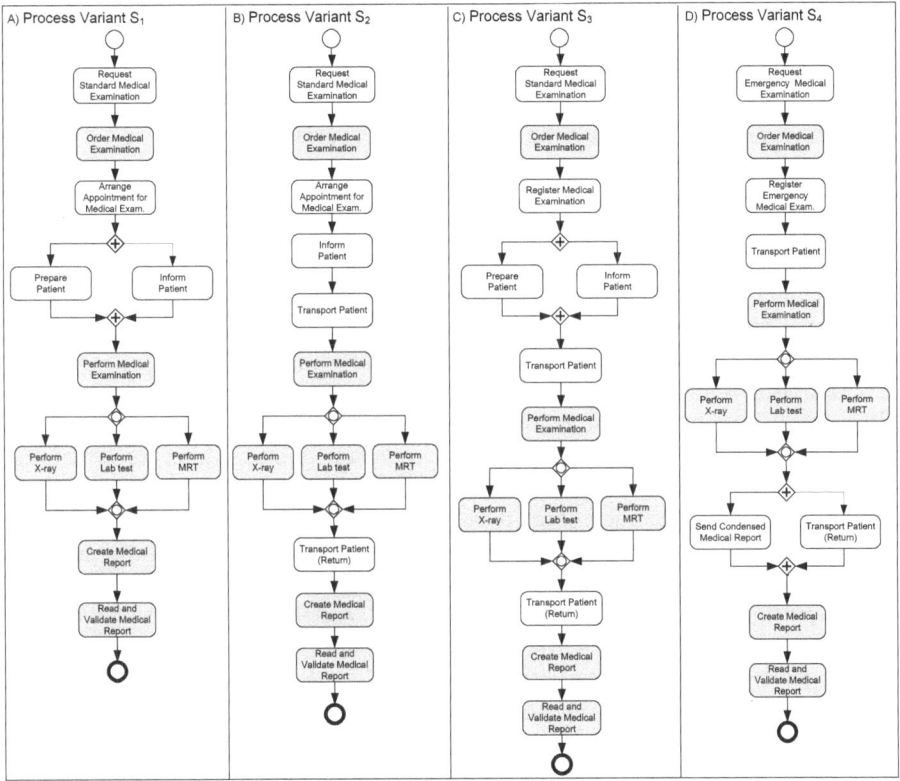

Fig. 1. Process Variants for Handling Medical Examinations

Process Family 1 (Handling Medical Examinations). Fig. 1 exemplifies four simplified process variants of a process family for handling medical examinations. These variants have several activities in common (highlighted in grey), e.g., *Order Medical Examination, Perform Medical Examination, Perform X-ray, Perform Lab Test, Perform MRT*, and *Create Medical Report*. However, the variants also show differences, e.g., in respect to the kind of examination (i.e., standard vs. emergency medical examination), the way the examination is scheduled (e.g., making and appointment or simply registering the examination), or the need for the presence of specific activities depending on the given context and configuration settings (e.g., *Prepare Patient* or *Transport Patient*).

Process Family 2 (Product Change Management). In the automotive domain, product change management constitutes a complex process [6,7] for which different variants exist, depending on the implementation costs and change impact, as well as the product phase during which the change is requested (e.g., development, start-up, or production).

3   Coping with Business Process Variability

This section provides basic notions related to BP variability (cf. Section 3.1) and introduces existing proposals for enabling it (cf. Section 3.2).

3.1   Basic Notions

When dealing with variability, it is important to define (1) what parts of the BP model may vary according to a specific context, (2) what alternatives fit in each of those parts, and (3) which conditions make these alternatives being selected. The first issue refers to the identification of the parts being subject to variation, which are commonly known as *variation points*. The second issue refers to the different alternatives that exist for these variation points, which we denote as *process fragment substitutions*. The third issue refers to the *context* in which these variations occur. Such context is usually represented by a set of variables gathered in a *context model* in which the BP model is used. When combining these variability aspects, we obtain a *configurable process model*, which is capable of representing the complete *process family*, i.e., collection of *process variants*.

Two major approaches are discussed in literature to define a *configurable process model*: behavioral and structural [18]. While a *behavioral approach* is based on a unique artifact integrating the behavior of all family members (i.e., process variants), a *structural approach* results in a set of artifacts, separately representing different aspects of the process family (e.g., commonalities captured in a *base process model* and variations captured in *change artifacts*). Despite these differences, configurable process models—irrespective of the approach used—allow *eliminating redundancies* by representing variant commonalities only once. Further, they allow fostering *model reuse*, i.e., model parts can be shared among multiple variants [26]. After creating the configurable process model, it must be *verified*, i.e., it has to be ensured that all derivable variants are syntactically correct. Additionally, the configurable process model must be *validated*, i.e., it must be ensured that the business requirements are properly reflected by the model. Given a configurable process model and taking the current context conditions into account, an *individualization process* is performed to derive a particular *process variant* [13]. According to the process enactment system chosen, the derived process variant is then transformed such that it can be deployed on this system [5]. Fig. 2 shows how to move from the definition of a process family to the creation and execution of a *process variant instance*. It shows a traditional view when dealing with process families. However, this is not sufficient (as illustrated in Section 4) since run-time (re-)configuration and evolution of process families should be covered along the entire BP lifecycle as well.

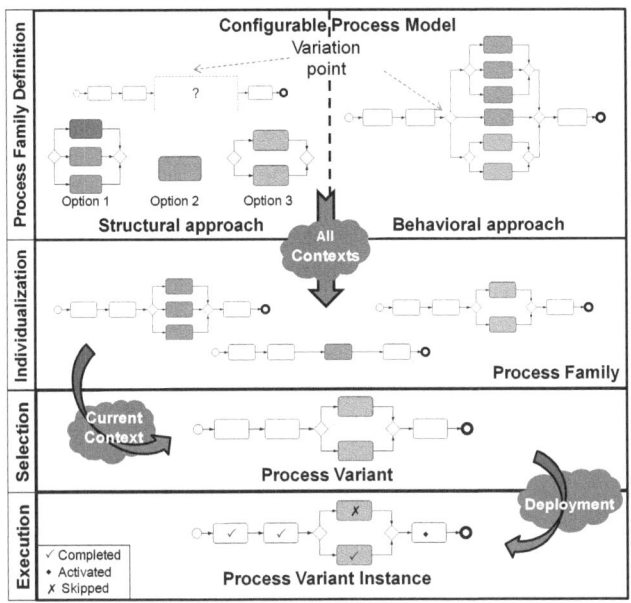

Fig. 2. From Process Family Definition to Process Variant Enactment

3.2   Existing Proposals Dealing with BP Variability

In literature, there are different proposals dealing with BP variability: PESOA [23], C-EPC [21], RULE (Rule representation and processing) [12], Provop [8], PPM (Partial Process Models) [16], and Worklets [1]. **PESOA** and **C-EPC** are both behavioral approaches for capturing variability in process families [23,21]. To identify variation points in the configurable process model, PESOA defines a set of annotations related to the variable activities, while C-EPC makes use of *configurable functions* (i.e., activities) and *connectors* (e.g., OR gateway). The conditions that instantiate the alternatives for such variation points are defined through features or *configuration requirements*. In turn, **Provop** is a structural approach, i.e., a process variant is configured by applying a set of pre-defined *change operations* (i.e., change artifacts) to a base process model [8]. **RULE** is a structural approach that applies *business rules* (i.e., change artifacts) to configure process variants from a *process template* (i.e., base process model) [12]. In turn, **PPM** is a query-based approach where process variants combine their own concrete activities with behavior-inherited from parent processes [16]. Finally, **Worklets** allow handling exceptions at run-time through *dynamic reconfiguration*. A *worklet* is a complete workflow specification which, based on context conditions, handles one specific task in a composite parent process [1].

4   Run-Time Flexibility in Process Model Families

In our context, flexibility represents the ability of a process family to change selected model parts, while keeping other model parts stable [24]. Due to the high dynamics in real-world environments, not all configurations can be made at design time. Thus, run-time flexibility arises as one of the core challenges for managing process families. Specifically, it requires the ability to deal with *pre-planned changes* and *dynamic evolution* (cf. Fig. 3) [30]. While the first issue refers to the *run-time configuration of process variants* (i.e., deferring the resolution of variation points to run-time) as well as their run-time *re-configuration* (i.e., switching between process variant models), the second issue deals with the *evolution of single process variants* (e.g., to copy with non-planned situations in a specific process variants) or the *evolution of the entire process family* (i.e., to deal with the re-design of the configurable process model). For each of these issues, we provide a general description, an illustrative example, a discussion of how existing proposals support them, and challenges to be tackled.

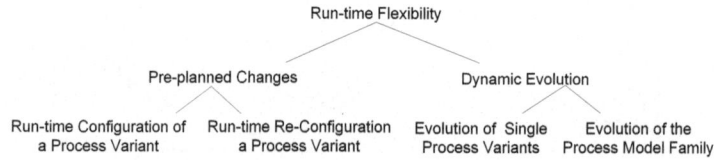

Fig. 3. Run-time Flexibility for Process Model Families

4.1   Run-Time Configuration of Process Variants

General Description. As illustrated in Fig. 2, *process variant instances* are executed according to the schema of the process variant model configured at design time. However, certain configuration decisions (i.e., resolutions of variation points) can only be made during run-time when needed context information becomes available. Thus, techniques are required that allow deferring the resolution of variation points to the run-time. In addition, the subject of run-time configuration may refer to any modeling element (e.g., activities, resources, data, events, or operations); i.e., proper support for dynamically configuring arbitrary model elements during the execution of process variant instances is needed.

Example 3 (Run-time configuration of a process variant). In the medical examination process (cf. Process Family 1), the tests to be performed (i.e., *X-ray*, *MRT*, and *Lab tests*) only become known once the patient has been examined. Hence, their selection can only be done once process variant instances are enacted. In addition, the role in charge of a treatment may change depending on the disease diagnosed. Finally, whether activities related to patient transportation are needed is decided during run-time depending on the status of the patient. As soon as this information becomes available, the process variant model of the respective instance should be configured accordingly, e.g., by removing the activities dealing with transportation.

Existing Support. Current variability proposals do not provide proper support for run-time configuration of process variants. Despite the fact that most proposals provide basic run-time support for process variants (e.g., execution of process variant instances), none of them allows for the inclusion of variation points in process variant models and their run-time configuration by end-users.

Challenges. One challenge is to ensure *soundness* of the (partially) dynamically configured process variant. Even though configuration is partially performed at run-time, soundness should be ensured at design time, i.e., for each process variant models its soundness should be guaranteed at design time even if parts of the model are dynamically configured at run-time. Existing proposals [28,7] mainly focus on control flow, but have neglected other perspectives of process variants so far (e.g., resources, data flow, events). Another challenge is to decide by *whom, when,* and *based on which information* run-time configurations may be made. Sometimes, this might be accomplished automatically based on context information, which can be derived from process data, while in other cases user interactions are required. For the latter, intelligent user support at a high level of abstraction is needed. Finally, techniques for *visualizing dynamic configuration options* are needed.

4.2 Run-Time Re-Configuration of Process Variants

General Description. Application context may dynamically change during run-time [25], making a re-configuration of a running process variant instance necessary to allow it to switch from the current process variant model to another one [27]. Unlike ad-hoc changes (i.e., unplanned changes) known from adaptive PAISs, re-configuration options are usually known at design time and hence can be captured in the configurable process model.

Example 4 (Run-time re-configuration of a process variant). In the context of product change management (cf. Process Family 2), for a particular car model, a change may be requested by a supplier in the *start-up* phase. Assume that during the processing of this change request, which may take several weeks or even longer, the car model switches to phase *production*. Then, the change request must be handled by a process variant model different from the one applied in the start-up phase; e.g., different procedures for estimating the costs of the requested change and for approving it are needed. Therefore, the process variant instance needs to be executed according to a different process variant model, i.e., one must switch to another pre-specified process variant.

Existing Support. Run-time re-configuration of process variants is partially covered by existing proposals. In Provop, it is supported by including *variant branchings* in the configured process variant model and encapsulating the change operations within the variant branches. Worklets allow for run-time re-configuration since their instantiation is performed dynamically based on context changes. In this line, existing proposals for handling exceptions (e.g., exception handling patterns [22]) can be used for enabling run-time re-configurations of process variants. However, neither PESOA, nor C-EPC, nor RULE, nor PPM provide such re-configuration support. Finally, in the area of product families, software system run-time re-configuration is provided by using feature models [3]. By enabling/disabling features, systems dynamically switch from one feature configuration (i.e., a system configuration in terms of functionality) to another.

Challenges. Accurate information about the current context and upcoming context changes must be provided. Thus, *monitoring* as well as *prediction* techniques are needed. For this purpose, existing context monitors (e.g., ASTRO [2]) can be used to gather the required context information. In addition, switching from one process variant to another requires *sophisticated exception handling* beyond already existing techniques (e.g., to abort branches no longer needed [18]). Overall, run-time re-configuration should be supported in a controlled, efficient, and comprehensible manner [7,6]. For example, *consistent process instance states* (including data consistency) must be ensured before continuing executing the process variant instance on the new process variant model.

4.3   Evolution of Single Process Variants

General Description. For many application scenarios, it is unrealistic to assume that all possible situations can be anticipated at design time and thus be incorporated into the configurable process model *a priori*. As a consequence, at run-time situations might emerge in which a process variant model no longer reflects the business case happening in the real world. In such a situation, authorized process participants should be allowed to evolve process variants models to realign their specification to the real-world business case. In addition, such evolution may also require the propagation of the changes to running process variant instances [30].

Example 5 (Evolution of a single process variant). For medical examinations, due to new regulations, every time the patient is transported, an extra physical examination shall be performed. Thus, process variants including patient transportation need to be modified accordingly. For this, the variant model is evolved and changes are propagated to respective instances, if desired.

Existing Support. Existing variability proposals do not provide support for evolving process variants. However, in the area of adaptive PAISs, there are techniques enabling users to evolve process definitions and allowing for propagating changes to process variant instances [18]. Finally, there exist other proposals that allow adapting process variant instances at the execution level. For example, by injecting pieces of code, running process variant instances can be modified according to context changes [9,11]. However, they are not suitable for evolving process variant models since they do not cover changes of the variant model.

Challenges. When evolving a single process variant, proper *change propagation* to running process variant instances is necessary. Note that this might be a complex task in case a process variant contains variation points that may be dynamically configured. In addition, changes in a single process variant model may require checking whether other process variants are affected as well. In the latter, the affected process variants need to be changed accordingly.

4.4 Evolution of the Process Family

General Description. To deal with environmental changes (e.g., changes of legal regulations), a process family must evolve at the schema level, i.e., changes of the configurable process model to address the changing requirements (e.g., by adopting additional variation points), increase its quality, or optimize its use. As a result, a new process family is obtained. In this context, co-existing schema versions of a configurable process model may have to be maintained.

Example 6 (Evolution of the process family). Due to newly emerging legal requirements for medical examinations, every patient needs to sign an extra document before being examined. Hence, the configurable process model must be modified since several process variants are affected by that change, leading to the evolution of the whole process family. In addition, the extra document is also relevant for patients for which the medical examination has already been started. Thus, evolving the process family requires the propagation of the changes to all configured process variants and—if desired—to running process variant instances.

Existing Support. C-EPC, Provop, and Worklets support the evolution of configurable process models, but not the propagation of respective changes to already configured process variants. In turn, in RULE, configurable process models can be evolved by adding new rules: changes are automatically propagated to process variants. Neither PESOA nor PPM support such an evolution. Support for handling different versions is provided by none of the proposals.

Challenges. Schema evolution of process model families may require the *propagation* of the changes to affected configured process variants and—if desired—to their running process variant instances [17]. In addition, this propagation should be performed correctly and efficiently. Furthermore, evolution may include new variation points for which the resolution time is deferred to run-time. Thus, their proper *run-time configuration* is required. Finally, *conflicts* between single process variants which have been individually evolved (cf. in Sect. 4.3), and the evolution of the configurable process model need to be handled. Even though similarities with evolution techniques known from adaptive PAISs exist [18], they cannot be directly applied for evolving configurable process models with their specific modeling elements and their dynamically configured parts. Therefore, different strategies for change propagation are needed.

4.5   Summary and Discussion

As discussed in Sections 4.1-4.4, when dealing with run-time flexibility in process model families, four issues are fundamental: *run-time configuration of process variants* and *re-configuration of process variants, evolution of single process variants*, and *evolution of the entire process model family*. Table 1 summarizes how existing variability proposals support them. For each issue, we differentiate between *no* [-], *partial* [+/-], and *full support* [+].

Table 1. Support for Run-time Flexibility Needs

	PESOA	C-EPC	Provop	RULE	PPM	Worklets
Run-time conf. of process variants	-	-	-	-	-	-
Run-time re-conf. of process variants	-	-	+	-	-	+
Evolution of single process variants	-	-	-	-	-	-
Evolution of the process family	-	+/-	+/-	+/-	-	+/-

An issue partially covered by existing BP variability proposals is run-time re-configuration of process variants. Applying different techniques, Provop and Worklets allow dynamic switches between process variants. However, our analysis has revealed that run-time configuration and evolution of single process variants are not well supported by any of the variability proposals. Regarding the evolution of configurable process models, existing proposals provide basic support, but lack advanced techniques for the controlled propagation of changes of the configurable process model to process variants and related instances. Our analysis has additionally shown that techniques from other areas provide partial solutions for addressing the flexibility needs discussed. For example, in the area of product families, support for the run-time re-configuration of software systems in terms of features is provided [3]. Based on feature models, systems may dynamically switch from one feature configuration to another one. However, this technique cannot be easily transferred to process model families since features cannot be directly mapped to BP specifications. Finally, adaptive PAISs provide techniques enabling users to evolve process schemes [18]. However, support going beyond existing adaptive PAISs is needed for properly handling flexibility issues in process families.

Even though existing proposals have addressed specific aspects partially, holistic support for run-time flexibility (encompassing integrated support for run-time configuration, re-configuration of process variants, evolution of single process variants, and evolution of configurable process models) is still missing. In the context of run-time configuration, correctness of process variants, visualization, and authorization (i.e., who, when, and based on what information changes can be done) constitute, further challenges to be addressed. In addition, sophisticated exception handling techniques (e.g., abort branches or undo already performed activities) are needed to cope with run-time re-configuration of process variants. Finally, regarding the evolution of process families, techniques for propagating changes to already configured process variants are required.

5   Conclusions

In this paper, we describe run-time flexibility needs of process model families and provide an overview regarding the existing support of BP variability. Our research has revealed that holistic support for run-time flexibility in process families is still missing. Although support for modeling, configuring, and executing process variants is provided, dealing with pre-planned changes and evolution at run-time has not been well covered yet. Therefore, in a next step, we plan to introduce run-time flexibility in process families and develop a framework to support the dynamic evolution of configurable process models and process variants.

References

1. Adams, M.J.: Facilitating dynamic flexibility and exception handling for workflows. PhD thesis, Queensland University of Technology (2007)
2. Barbon, F., Traverso, P., Pistore, M., Trainotti, M.: Run-Time Monitoring of Instances and Classes of Web Service Compositions. In: Proc. ICWS, pp. 63–71 (2006)
3. Cetina, C., Giner, P., Fons, J., Pelechano, V.: Autonomic computing through reuse of variability models at runtime: the case of smart homes. Comp. 42(10), 37–43 (2009)
4. Dijkman, R., La Rosa, M., Reijers, H.A.: Managing large collections of business process models - Current techniques and challenges. Comp. in Ind. 63(2), 91–97 (2012)
5. Günther, C.W., Rinderle-Ma, S., Reichert, M., van der Aalst, W.M.P., Recker, J.: Using process mining to learn from process changes in evolutionary systems. Int. Journal of Business Process Integration and Management 3(1), 61–78 (2008)
6. Hallerbach, A., Bauer, T., Reichert, M.: Context-based configuration of process variants. In: Proc. TCoB 2008, pp. 31–40 (2008)
7. Hallerbach, A., Bauer, T., Reichert, M.: Guaranteeing soundness of configurable process variants in Provop. In: Proc. CEC 2009, pp. 98–105 (2009)
8. Hallerbach, A., Bauer, T., Reichert, M.: Capturing variability in business process models: the Provop approach. Soft. Proc. Impro. and Prac. 22(6-7), 519–546 (2010)
9. Hermosillo, G., Seinturier, L., Duchien, L.: Creating Context-Adaptive Business Process. In: Proc. ICSOC 2008, pp. 228–242 (2010)
10. Kang, K.C., Cohen, S.G., Hess, J.A., Novak, W.E., Peterson, A.S.: Feature-oriented domain analysis (FODA) feasibility study. TR, Carniege-Mellon Univ. (1990)

11. Koning, M., Sun, C.-A., Sinnema, M., Avgeriou, P.: VxBPEL: Supporting variability for web services in BPEL. Inf. and Soft. Tech. 51(2), 258–269 (2009)
12. Kumar, A., Wen, Y.: Design and management of flexible process variants using templates and rules. Int. Journal Computers in Industry 63(2), 112–130 (2012)
13. La Rosa, M., Dumas, M., ter Hofstede, A.H.M.: Modelling Business Process Variability for Design-Time Configuration. In: Handbook of Research on Business Process Modeling, pp. 204–228. IGI Publisher (2009)
14. Li, C., Reichert, M., Wombacher, A.: Mining business process variants: challenges, scenarios, algorithms. Data & Knowledge Engineering 70(5), 409–434 (2011)
15. Müller, D., Herbst, J., Hammori, M., Reichert, M.: IT Support for Release Management Processes in the Automotive Industry. In: Dustdar, S., Fiadeiro, J.L., Sheth, A.P. (eds.) BPM 2006. LNCS, vol. 4102, pp. 368–377. Springer, Heidelberg (2006)
16. Pascalau, E., Awad, A., Sakr, S., Weske, M.: On Maintaining Consistency of Process Model Variants. In: Muehlen, M.z., Su, J. (eds.) BPM 2010 Workshops. LNBIP, vol. 66, pp. 289–300. Springer, Heidelberg (2011)
17. Reichert, M., Rinderle, S., Dadam, P.: On the common support of workflow type and instance changes under correctness constraints. In: Proc. CoopIS, pp. 407–425 (2003)
18. Reichert, M., Weber, B.: Enabling flexibility in process-aware information systems: challenges, methods, technologies. Springer (2012)
19. Reinhartz-Berger, I., Soffer, P., Sturm, A.: Organisational reference models: supporting an adequate design of local business processes. IBPIM 4(2), 134–149 (2009)
20. Reinhartz-Berger, I., Soffer, P., Sturm, A.: Extending the adaptability of reference models. IEEE Trans. on Sys., Man, and Cyb. 40(5), 1045–1056 (2010)
21. Rosemann, M., van der Aalst, W.M.P.: A configurable reference modeling language. Information Systems 32(1), 1–23 (2007)
22. Russell, N., van der Aalst, W.M.P., ter Hofstede, A.: Exception Handling Patterns in Process-aware Information Systems. In: Martinez, F.H., Pohl, K. (eds.) CAiSE 2006. LNCS, vol. 4001, pp. 288–302. Springer, Heidelberg (2006)
23. Schnieders, A., Puhlmann, F.: Variability mechanisms in e-business process families. In: Proc. BIS 2006, pp. 583–601 (2006)
24. Soffer, P.: On the notion of flexibility in business processes. In: Proc. CAiSE 2005 Workshops, pp. 35–42 (2005)
25. Soffer, P.: Scope analysis: identifying the impact of changes in business process models. Sof. Process: Impro. and Practice 10(4), 393–402 (2005)
26. Torres, V., Zugal, S., Weber, B., Reichert, M., Ayora, C., Pelechano, V.: A Qualitative Comparison of Appraches Supporting Business Process Variability. In: La Rosa, M., Soffer, P. (eds.) BPM 2012 Workshops. LNBIP, vol. 132, pp. 560–572. Springer, Heidelberg (2013)
27. van der Aalst, W.M.P., Basten, T.: Inheritance of workflows: An approach to tackling problems related to change. Theo. Comp. Science 270(1-2), 125–203 (2002)
28. van der Aalst, W.M.P., Dumas, M., Gottschalk, F., ter Hofstede, A.H.M., La Rosa, M., Mendling, J.: Preserving correctness during business process model configuration. Formal Asp. Comput. 22(3-4), 459–482 (2010)
29. Weber, B., Reichert, M., Rinderle-Ma, S.: Change patterns and change support features - Enhancing flexibility in process-aware information systems. Data & Knoweldge Engineering 66(3), 438–466 (2008)
30. Weber, B., Sadiq, S.W., Reichert, M.: Beyond rigidity - dynamic process lifecycle support. Computer Science - R&D 23(2), 45–65 (2009)
31. Weber, B., Reichert, M., Reijers, H.A., Mendling, J.: Refactoring large process model repositories. Computers in Industry 62(5), 467–486 (2011)

A Runtime Analysis of Graph-Theoretical Algorithms to Detect Patterns in Process Model Collections

Jörg Becker, Dominic Breuker, Patrick Delfmann,
Hanns-Alexander Dietrich, and Matthias Steinhorst

WWU Muenster - ERCIS, Leonardo-Campus 3, 48149 Muenster, Germany
{Becker,Breuker,Delfmann,Dietrich,Steinhorst}
@ercis.uni-muenster.de

Abstract. Pattern detection serves different purposes in managing large collections of process models, ranging from syntax checking to compliance validation. This paper presents a runtime analysis of four graph-theoretical algorithms for (frequent) pattern detection. We apply these algorithms to large collections of process and data models to demonstrate that, despite their theoretical intractability, they are able to return results within (milli-) seconds. We discuss the relative performance of these algorithms and their applicability in practice.

Keywords: Conceptual Model Analysis, Subgraph Isomorphism, Frequent Subgraph Detection, Pattern Matching.

1 Introduction

With the advancement of Business Process Management (BPM) technology, many companies are developing large collections of process models [9, 27]. Pattern detection is a frequently occurring task when managing such collections. For instance, one may wish to identify all syntax errors in the models of a given collection [19]. In this context, a pattern is a subgraph of the overall model graph that represents a particular syntactical error. Another application area of pattern detection is process compliance checking, in which a compliance rule like "activity A has to be executed before activity B" translates to a respective pattern subgraph [1, 31]. When creating new models, one may furthermore wish to reuse fragments that frequently occur in the already existing process models [15, 27]. In all of these scenarios, a pattern is a subgraph that complies with a given pattern query and that needs to be identified within all models of a given collection. With the number and size of process models steadily increasing, detecting such patterns within an entire model collection becomes increasingly complex [15]. It is therefore imperative to use matching algorithms that return results with good performance. In the literature, a huge variety of algorithmic approaches are proposed to accomplish tasks involving pattern detection. These approaches are closely related to graph-theoretical problems. In graph theory, pattern detection is known as the problem of subgraph isomorphism (SGI), which is known to be NP-complete [7]. Yet, despite the theoretical intractability of this problem, considerable research effort has been put into finding solutions with acceptable runtime performance

M. La Rosa and P. Soffer (Eds.): BPM 2012 Workshops, LNBIP 132, pp. 489–500, 2013.
© Springer-Verlag Berlin Heidelberg 2013

(e.g., [28, 7]). While having exponential complexity in the worst case, empirical evaluations demonstrated that these algorithms deliver results within fractions of seconds for many cases encountered in actual application scenarios, even when used on graphs with hundreds of nodes [7, 11]. Thus, even if a problem is theoretically intractable, there may very well be sufficiently fast algorithms for analyzing conceptual models relevant for BPM and Information Systems development. The purpose of this paper is to empirically test this hypothesis. We choose two algorithms for SGI and two algorithms for frequent subgraph detection (FSD) and apply them on large collections of conceptual models. Our runtime analysis suggests that all of these algorithms are able to detect patterns within (milli-) seconds. As there are publicly available implementations for all presented algorithms, the contribution of this paper is to promote incorporating them in standard model analysis approaches discussed in the literature.

The paper proceeds as follows. In section 2, we discuss analysis approaches for conceptual models related to the problem of finding patterns in models. In section 3, we briefly introduce the algorithms that are to be evaluated. Section 4 presents our runtime data. Section 5 provides an outlook on future research.

2   Related Work

There exist numerous analysis techniques that, in some way or another, rely on identifying patterns within conceptual models. Those are the techniques that could benefit from the algorithms evaluated in this work. A non-representative sample of them is sketched in this section to exemplify potential application scenarios.

For instance, consider analysis techniques for business process models. To efficiently estimate process model similarities, one can identify small, characteristic patterns (called features) within models and subsequently match the features of two processes on each other, i.e. check if patterns are isomorphic [35]. Checking if a given business process model satisfies the soundness criterion is possible by searching for a number of error patterns within its corresponding causal footprint. Only if such patterns are not found, the model is sound [29]. Transforming a process model of one modeling notation into a model of another often requires searching for structural patterns in the one notation that are translated to predefined model fragments in the other one. Respective works have been put forth by GARCÍA-BAÑUELOS [12] or OUYANG ET AL. [24]. Searching for patterns representing typical weaknesses in business processes can help business analysts in identifying opportunities for business process improvement [32]. Modularization of business process models is a useful means of reducing its complexity and thereby improving understandability [25]. To facilitate modularization, frequently occurring patterns can be identified within a database of process models in order to extract such patterns into a newly created subprocess [27].

When analyzing models in the area of software engineering, one is interested in the design patterns that have been used in a given piece of software [10]. Naturally, pattern matching algorithms can serve as a tool to accomplish this task [14]. Since models undergo numerous revisions during the process of designing object-oriented software, identifying differences between individual versions is also of interest.

Identifying common patterns is a fundamental step to do this. Similar to the area of BPM, model transformation is also a topic in software engineering. LARA and VANGHELUWE [17] propose a respective metamodel-based technique.

In addition, several algorithms have been developed to search for patterns within BPMN diagrams [2, 4, 20]. Also, metamodel-based search engines for models from software engineering, such as ER diagrams, are subject to research [18].

This selection of literature demonstrates that the IS discipline has put forth a great number of different approaches for the analysis of conceptual models. Each addresses a particular analysis purpose, but all of them are related to identifying certain patterns within models. Graph-theoretical problems such as SGI and FSD can serve as a theoretical basis for such approaches. The purpose of the following runtime analysis is to demonstrate that an algorithm being "inefficient" in general does not necessarily mean it is inefficient on conceptual models (in the sense of actual runtimes). Such an algorithm can thus still be incorporated into existing model analysis approaches. A similar evaluation for detecting maximum common subgraphs was conducted by CONTE, FOGGIA and VENTO [6].

3   Algorithms

3.1   Subgraph Isomorphism

Formally, a graph H is subgraph-isomorphic to a given model graph G if there exists a bijection Φ between the nodes of H and a subset of nodes of G such that for each edge (v,w) between nodes v and w of H there exists a corresponding edge $(\Phi(v), \Phi(w))$ in G and such that Φ complies with the labels of the nodes. The problem of SGI is NP complete in the general case [13]. However, pruning-based techniques have been proposed that cut out parts of the search space to achieve an acceptable runtime performance in practical application scenarios. The most commonly known algorithm of this kind is the one by ULLMANN [28]. The more recent algorithm VF2 has been developed by CORDELLA ET AL. [7]. Empirical studies confirm that VF2 delivers results with acceptable performance [5]. Thus, we use it in our evaluation and compare it to Ullmann's algorithm. Efficient implementations for both algorithms are available.[1]

3.2   Frequent Subgraph Detection

A further problem, closely related to SGI, is detecting frequent subgraphs. Given a set of model graphs and an integer p, called the support, all pattern graphs subgraph-isomorphic to at least p model graphs are supposed to be detected. Depending on the support, both the size of the search trees used by algorithms as well as the number of identified patterns can increase very quickly. Thus, not only runtime performance but also memory requirements are critical. Both factors can be minimized by appropriately traversing the search space [33]. We chose to use gSpan [34] and Gaston [21] for

---

[1] http://www.cs.sunysb.edu/~algorith/implement/vflib/
implement.shtml

our evaluation as studies demonstrate their acceptable performance [33]. Implementations are again publicly available.[2]

4   Evaluation

4.1   Method and Scope

In this section we apply the algorithms introduced above to several collections of models and measure their runtimes as well as memory requirements. We considered two different types of application scenarios. First, we labeled each element of the models with its type (e.g. *function* or *event* in case of EPCs). Secondly, we additionally assigned the actual textual description to it (e.g. *function - check invoice* for a function of an EPC). If no label was given, we only used the type. As all the algorithms can prune the search space with respect to node labels, performance is expected to increase the more specific the labeling is. The two application scenarios thus represent two extreme cases. Using only the types as node labels is more generic and thus expected to be most inefficient, while also using the modeling element labels is more specific and thus expected to be most efficient.

4.2   Model Base

We used ten model collections for our experiments:[3] the SAP reference model [16] (SAP_EPC) containing 604 EPC models, two EPC collections from public administrations (PA1_EPC containing 2200 models and PA2_EPC containing 604 models), two collections of organizational charts (PA1_ORG and PA2_ORG containing 88 and 18 models respectively), a collection of technical term models (PA1_TTM containing 491 models), a collection of process models and a collection of data models from the retail industry (RI_EPC with 54 EPCs and RI_ERM with 33 ER diagrams) [3], a collection of 30 UML class diagrams [23], and a collection of 35 ER meta-models [8]. The average model size of the collections ranges from 40 to 200 elements, which we define as the sum of nodes and edges.

4.3   Patterns

In order to evaluate the Ullmann and VF2 algorithms, we do not only need models but also patterns to be searched for. We used the gSpan algorithm to generate these pattern collections with the minimal possible support subject to memory constraints (between 50 and 0.5% depending on the model collection). Using frequent patterns mined by gSpan we ensure that we search for patterns actually contained in the model collections. We generated two pattern collections; one containing patterns with modeling element types as node labels and a second one containing patterns with the additional textual description as node labels. The first set contains a total of 57592

---

[2] http://www2.informatik.uni-erlangen.de/EN/research/ParSeMiS/
download/index.html
[3] Please note that collections not cited are subject to non-disclosure agreements.

patterns having between one and 41 elements. The second set contains a total of 4063 patterns having between one and 33 elements.

4.4   Technical Setup

We conducted the evaluation with the implementations cited in section 3, run on an Intel® Core™ 2 Duo CPU E8400 3.0 GHZ machine with 3.25 GB RAM and Windows 7 (32 Bit). For gSpan and Gaston, we utilized the Oracle Java Virtual Machine (JVM) 6.0.26 with the maximal heap size under Windows (32 Bit) of 1.2 GB.

The Ullmann and VF2 algorithms were configured to return all pattern occurrences in a given model graph (as opposed to only delivering the first match), as we expect that searching all occurrences of a pattern instead of an arbitrary one is a more realistic use case. Each pattern was searched in all models of the corresponding collection and the total search time was measured. In terms of gSpan and Gaston, the algorithms can be called with a given support as parameter. The support is specified – relative to the size of the model collection – as the percentage of models that contain a particular pattern (70%, 50%, 30%, 20%, 10%, 5%, and 1%).

4.5   Results for Subgraph Isomorphism

Table 1 summarizes runtime results for the two SGI algorithms VF2 and Ullmann with labels containing types and actual labels respectively. For this purpose, a single search is defined as identifying all SGIs between one pattern graph and all models in the corresponding collection. Table 1 provides aggregated information over all search runs executed with a given pattern collection. Furthermore, the data is normalized with respect to collection size (i.e. runtimes have been divided by the number of models in the collection to ensure comparability).

To clarify this, consider the following example. When using VF2, searching all of the 399 patterns created from SAP_EPC labeled by types took 379987.21 milliseconds (ms). As the SAP repository contains 604 EPCs, the normalized runtime amounts to $379987.21/604 = 629.12$ ms. Table 1 reports aggregated information about these normalized runtimes over all patterns. For instance, the average normalized runtime for searching one of the 399 patterns was $629.12 / 399 = 1.58$, as reported in the *Avg* column. Similarly, columns *Std*, *Min* and *Max* report the standard deviation, the minimum and the maximum of normalized pattern search runtimes.

The results demonstrate that both Ullmann and VF2 are able to analyze large model repositories with acceptable performance. All average normalized runtimes lie within a range of 1 to 100 ms, which means that patterns can be searched for in a few seconds even in large collections with several thousand models. For instance, searching a pattern in a process model collection of even 10,000 models would take 6.74 minutes assuming an average runtime of 40.42 ms, which is the maximum average runtime of VF2. VF2 outperforms Ullmann in almost all cases. If the opposite holds, small runtimes for both algorithms have been observed. Thus, a general recommendation can be given to prefer VF2 over the Ullmann algorithm. Nevertheless, runtimes of Ullmann are far from prohibitively high.

In line with our expectations, we found that runtimes are strictly higher when only the types of modeling elements are used to label the nodes of the graphs (left part of Table 1). In case of using entire labels (right part of Table 1), runtime performance decreases significantly. All average runtimes are smaller than 3 ms. Maximum values rarely exceed 10 ms. An exception was searching patterns in the MM_ERM collection with VF2. For this case, we observed a maximum runtime of 13.37 ms.

Table 1. Normalized runtime measurement for subgraph isomorphism

Collection and Algorithm	Type				R^2	Label				R^2
	Runtime [ms/model]					Runtime [ms/model]				
	Avg	Std	Min	Max		Avg	Std	Min	Max	
SAP EPC — VF2	1.58	.91	1.33	19.46	.01	1.28	.10	1.12	2.78	.00
SAP EPC — Ull	1.54	.92	1.32	19.61	.00	1.23	.12	1.10	2.97	.00*
PA1 EPC — VF2	3.13	4.05	2.65	94.37	.00	2.72	.10	2.59	3.26	.00
PA1 EPC — Ull	4.50	7.02	2.66	126.96	.02**	2.74	.15	2.58	3.66	.04**
PA1 TTM — VF2	14.70	28.55	1.11	65.73	.54	.97	.12	.90	1.36	.01
PA1 TTM — Ull	16.11	31.93	1.05	73.18	.53	.98	.14	.90	1.71	.00
PA1 ORG — VF2	33.04	71.80	1.06	179.26	.48	.96	.35	.88	5.10	.00
PA1 ORG — Ull	38.41	83.63	1.07	208.70	.48	.95	.28	.88	4.20	.00
PA2 EPC — VF2	1.69	.11	1.54	11.26	.00**	1.54	.07	1.46	2.15	.02*
PA2 EPC — Ull	69.20	884.46	1.59	35562.25	.02**	1.59	.09	1.47	2.37	.00
PA2 ORG — VF2	40.42	133.21	.94	598.11	.13*	1.10	.34	.94	2.44	.00
PA2 ORG — Ull	53.19	185.70	1.00	875.56	.12*	.99	.08	.94	1.39	.04
RI EPC — VF2	1.62	.36	1.52	10.83	.00	1.40	.05	1.37	2.00	.03
RI EPC — Ull	9.72	27.88	1.54	584.28	.09**	1.42	.20	1.37	4.81	.00
RI ERM — VF2	1.26	.10	.94	2.26	.01	1.16	.16	.94	3.33	.00*
RI ERM — Ull	1.30	.10	.94	1.91	.00	1.17	.16	.96	5.12	.00
CWM CD — VF2	1.17	.05	.50	8.83	.02	1.17	.24	.97	2.00	.20*
CWM CD — Ull	1.25	.06	1.00	9.90	.02	1.04	.09	.97	1.30	.04
MM ERM — VF2	1.73	.09	1.54	5.00	.38	1.65	.23	1.40	13.37	.01
MM ERM — Ull	1.77	.09	1.60	2.26	.66**	1.49	.16	1.40	3.60	.00

In terms of maximum runtimes, one can see that, in general, the maximum values are very low as well, i.e. below 100 ms. However, there are a few exceptions in which higher values have been observed. Most notably, the worst case pattern search using Ullmann on the PA2_EPC collection labeled by element types took 35562.25 ms (~35 seconds). This corresponds to a collection-wide total runtime of almost 6 hours for this pattern search. In contrast to these bad results for Ullmann, worst case results for VF2 are much better. The highest observed runtime was 598.11 ms for one of the patterns searched for in the PA2_ORG collection. We consider this to be acceptable.

To determine if the size of the pattern has an influence on the time required for searching it within a collection, we measured pattern size both in terms of the number of nodes and edges. For each collection we conducted a multiple regression, explaining runtime of the search by two indicators: number of nodes and number of edges in the pattern. The coefficients of determination, which represent the fraction of runtime variance explained by pattern size, are reported in Table 1 in the R^2 columns. Values followed by * indicate that the influence is significant at a p-value of 0.10. Values followed by ** are significant to $p = 0.05$. Most of the R^2 values exhibit very low numerical values smaller than 0.05, which means that the pattern size explains virtually no variance. For some collections, we found higher R^2 values, most of which however are insignificant. This was due to the fact that only a small number of frequently occurring patterns were identified and could be searched for in the respective collections. For instance, for collection PA1_TTM labeled by element types only 5 patterns have been used; hardly enough evidence to get significant results from multiple regressions. Nevertheless, we found evidence for the influence of the pattern size in a few cases. In collection MM_ERM labeled with types, it explains 66% of the variance when using the Ullmann algorithm. Similarly, when using VF2, significant results were found in PA2_ORG labeled with element types, in which 13% of the variance is explained. Despite these few significant results, an influence of the pattern size can in general not be demonstrated by this study. While this conforms to the literature for VF2, our results contradict previous experiments with the Ullmann algorithm [7].

To further analyze this aspect, we examined very long search runs in detail. In particular, we examined all search runs with execution times larger than 1000 ms, of which there are 17. For all of them, the Ullmann algorithm was used. The 17 patterns corresponding to these search runs all are from the PA2_EPC collection labeled with element types. These patterns contained between 13 to 18 nodes and 12 to 17 edges, i.e., they were rather large. This indicates that very long runtimes occur only for large patterns in combination with the Ullmann algorithm, but not necessarily. A visual inspection of models and patterns did not reveal any plausible reasons for these long runtimes. However, we believe that the (arbitrary) choices of permuting the adjacency matrices used by Ullmann could be a reason.

4.6   Results for Frequent Subgraph Detection

Tables 2 and 3 list mean runtime measurements in ms (Avg) as well as the number of frequent patterns found (#p) given a predefined level of support. Table 2 reports results for labeling nodes with element labels. Table 3 contains results for labeling nodes with element types. As explained above, memory requirements are critical in FSD. Out of memory exceptions are indicated by "—".

As the support is specified as a percentage value, certain support levels were inapplicable to small collections. For instance, applying a support of 5% to PA2_ORG, which contains 18 models, would mean that, for a pattern to be returned, it must be found in a minimum of $18 \cdot 0.18 = 0.9$ models. Thus, all possible subgraphs of any model would be returned. We only evaluated cases in which patterns had to be found in a minimum of 2 models and marked all inapplicable cases with "#M<2".

Furthermore, it must be noted that the two algorithms gSpan and Gaston return different numbers of patterns in some cases. This is because the implementation of Gaston treats directed graphs as if they were undirected, while gSpan correctly handles them. Therefore, pattern numbers coincide only for ER and UML class diagrams.

In terms of runtimes, Table 2 demonstrates that both algorithms return results with acceptable performance. Most runtimes are equal or less than one second, with only two exceptions. Applying Gaston (gSpan) to MM_ERM with 5% support took 78 seconds, (26 seconds). If nodes are labeled with their respective element types, runtimes increase significantly (cf. Table 3). This increase was expected as the number of frequent patterns obviously increases. Up to a support of 10%, runtimes still are below 10 seconds, which can be considered acceptable. Smaller supports however, if applicable at all, can result in large runtimes. For instance, applying gSpan to RI_ERM with 5% support took more than 150.000 ms (~2.5 minutes).

Table 2. Runtime Measurement for Frequent Subgraph Detection (actual element labels)

Collection and algorithm		70% Avg	#p	50% Avg.	#p	30% Avg	#p	20% Avg	#p	10% Avg.	#p	5% Avg	#p	1% Avg	#p
SAP EPC	Gaston	31	0	42	2	42	4	41	5	43	6	50	15	1.033	2.042
	gSpan	41	0	41	2	38	3	47	5	51	8	56	14	443	2.023
PA1 PA1 EPC	Gaston	144	2	157	3	188	4	240	7	358	13	691	105	—	—
	gSpan	149	2	152	3	185	4	239	7	350	15	587	87	—	—
PA1 PA1 TTM	Gaston	16	0	24	0	16	0	16	0	16	0	16	0	47	17
	gSpan	16	0	15	0	24	0	16	0	16	0	24	0	31	17
PA1 PA1 ORG	Gaston	16	0	16	0	16	0	15	0	16	0	15	0	#M<2	#M<2
	gSpan	8	0	16	0	16	0	8	0	16	0	8	0	#M<2	#M<2
PA2 PA2 EPC	Gaston	44	1	42	1	48	3	53	5	58	5	75	11	10.375	30.948
	gSpan	45	1	46	1	46	3	55	4	58	5	73	12	5.428	30.337
PA2 PA2 ORG	Gaston	16	0	16	0	8	0	16	2	109	58	#M<2	#M<2	#M<2	#M<2
	gSpan	8	0	15	0	8	0	8	2	16	58	#M<2	#M<2	#M<2	#M<2
RI RI EPC	Gaston	27	2	22	3	26	5	25	6	27	11	102	82	#M<2	#M<2
	gSpan	19	2	20	2	24	5	26	7	27	11	60	76	#M<2	#M<2
RI RI ERM	Gaston	15	0	20	4	29	7	31	14	67	43	188	435	#M<2	#M<2
	gSpan	12	0	16	4	16	7	31	14	24	43	172	470	#M<2	#M<2
MM CWM CD	Gaston	10	0	10	0	11	0	16	2	25	12	53	22	#M<2	#M<2
	gSpan	9	0	9	0	9	0	11	2	12	12	16	22	#M<2	#M<2
MM ERM	Gaston	23	3	23	7	31	17	47	36	219	810	78.391	360.334	#M<2	#M<2
	gSpan	24	3	32	7	40	17	55	36	172	810	26.154	360.334	#M<2	#M<2

Surprising is the fact that gSpan often outperformed Gaston with respect to runtime. This contradicts other empirical studies in which Gaston is found to be faster [33, 22]. This, however, is not caused by the inability of Gaston to work with directed edges. As an example, consider in Table 2 the runtimes of Gaston and gSpan applied to MM_ERM with 5% support. The ER diagrams are undirected and thus both algorithms work on the same graph representation. Nevertheless, gSpan is about three times as fast as Gaston. Similar observations can be made for other applications to undirected models (cf. Tables 2 and 3). The reason why Gaston is supposed to be fast is that it stores certain intermediate results temporarily while gSpan calculates them over and over again. We conclude that this strategy is ineffective for most conceptual models in the IS domain as it adds more computational effort than it saves.

In terms of memory requirements, we observed that both algorithms frequently aborted search runs on the machine we used (indicated by cells containing "—"). Comparing Gaston and gSpan, both Tables 2 and 3 demonstrate that gSpan strictly outperformed Gaston with respect to memory requirements. For all of the collections and regardless of how the nodes were labeled, gSpan either ran out of memory at the same support level as Gaston did or it managed to handle lower values. For this reason, gSpan is clearly preferable with respect to memory requirements.

Table 3. Runtime Measurement for Frequent Subgraph Detection (element types as labels)

Collection and algorithm		70% Avg.	#p	50% Avg.	#p	30% Avg.	#p	20% Avg.	#p	10% Avg.	#p	5% Avg.	#p
SAP EPC	Gaston	58	3	100	13	149	30	303	52	2.027	144	—	—
	gSpan	72	4	75	7	123	30	150	42	1.137	137	11.710	399
PA1 PA1 EPC	Gaston	655	13	1.783	42	—	—	—	—	—	—	—	—
	gSpan	506	8	1.405	40	19.410	275	—	—	—	—	—	—
PA1 PA1 TTM	Gaston	3.534	4	—	—	—	—	—	—	—	—	—	—
	gSpan	2.262	4	61.713	5	—	—	—	—	—	—	—	—
PA1 PA1 ORG	Gaston	63	3	141	4	1.568	5	—	—	—	—	—	—
	gSpan	71	3	125	4	1.139	5	—	—	—	—	—	—
PA2 PA2 EPC	Gaston	245	18	410	36	894	154	2.064	423	6.190	1.945	—	—
	gSpan	160	17	283	41	672	146	1.519	401	4.796	1.733	16.464	8.467
PA2 PA2 ORG	Gaston	23	3	24	4	413	6	—	—	—	—	#M<2	#M<2
	gSpan	16	2	24	4	390	6	5.733	20	—	—	#M<2	#M<2
RI RI EPC	Gaston	55	35	76	79	132	310	210	849	506	4.004	2.795	33.868
	gSpan	67	39	85	93	148	318	242	780	591	3.570	2.479	27.580
RI RI ERM	Gaston	39	12	47	36	125	165	343	555	1.731	4.688	—	—
	gSpan	39	12	55	36	141	168	390	574	1.965	4.816	150.861	315.463
CW M	Gaston	33	3	38	5	76	10	93	15	596	66	1.725	190
	gSpan	26	2	38	5	42	6	98	12	859	107	2.592	364
MM ERM	Gaston	55	14	62	37	125	160	328	462	1.467	3.589	—	—
	gSpan	71	14	55	37	141	160	429	462	1.981	3.589	133.263	402.190

Nevertheless, both algorithms can run out of memory quickly if many frequent patterns are to be found. Looking at Table 2, one can see that if entire element labels are used to name nodes, out of memory exceptions almost never occur. This is due to the fact that there are only few frequent patterns even for low support values. If element types are used as node labels (cf. Table 3), a very large number of frequent patterns is found even for high levels of support. For instance, in the 35 models of the MM_ERM collection, there are more than 400.000 patterns being returned at a support level of 5% (meaning 2 or more models contain the pattern). While for this small collection the algorithms still work, for larger collections, such as PA1_EPC with 2200 models, gSpan and Gaston fail quickly.

The results of applying FSD to organizational charts with nodes labeled by element types are notable (cf. Table 3). Even gSpan ran out of memory at rather high support values of 20% for PA1_ORG and 10% of PA2_ORG, despite the fact that on the last applicable support level only very few patterns were found (a maximum of 20). Also, these collections are rather small (88 and 18 models respectively). Thus, organizational charts appear to be particularly challenging for the algorithms under evaluation.

5   Summary and Outlook

This paper explored the potential of applying algorithms from the field of graph theory to the domain of conceptual model analysis. As a necessary condition for that, we examined if such algorithms can be executed on conceptual models fast and reliably. In particular, we measured runtimes and memory requirements of algorithms for the two problems SGI and FSD when applied to a huge number of conceptual models, created using different modeling languages. Algorithms for the former problem can be expected to deliver results within a few ms and can therefore easily be reused for analysis techniques. Particularly low and stable runtimes have been observed for VF2. Algorithms for the latter problem can also be expected to run in acceptable time, yet problems might occur for low levels of support. Only in few cases runtimes larger than 10 s have been observed. Memory requirements are the bottleneck. As gSpan demands strictly less memory than Gaston, we recommend using it for this problem.

The results of our experiments provide researchers in the IS community with a detailed analysis of how algorithms for the two problems under examination actually behave on conceptual models. When integrating such algorithms into higher level model analysis techniques, the results allow an assessment of the performance the analysis technique will eventually exhibit. In contrast to only considering theoretical complexities, our broad-scale empirical analysis provides insights into the performance in practical applications. Using the algorithms in model analysis techniques may ease their implementation, as large parts of it can be covered by standard software. Moreover, as the algorithms return results with acceptable performance, the runtime of these analysis techniques may even improve.

As for adoption of conceptual model analysis techniques in practical applications, we argue that using standard algorithms as their main components would facilitate the proliferation of these techniques. Software vendors of modeling tools can more easily implement them if only a few graph-theoretical modules have to be wired together in order to incorporate most of the analysis techniques into the software. The algorithms we evaluated have a broad application potential (cf. section 2) and reference implementations are available. Additionally, they do not require building and maintaining complex index structures (unlike approaches from the IS community related to (frequent) subgraph search [15, 27]). This facilitates adoption as it decreases the complexity of the software and eliminates potential sources of errors.

Future research should focus mainly on three interdependent branches. First, it could be fruitful to explore other graph-theoretical problems such as minor containment. This would allow modeling patterns that do only approximately match the actual model, which would in turn provide more flexibility in model analysis. Second, it is necessary to identify exactly how graph-theoretical problems can be used in model analysis techniques, i.e., to establish a formal mapping of the one to the other. Third, correlating standard business process model metrics [30] with performance of search algorithms could help us in developing structural recommendations for business process model design on the one hand, and tailoring algorithms on the other hand.

To conclude, we have demonstrated that bad theoretical worst-case complexity, often put forth as an argument against using graph-theoretical algorithms, is not an argument at all. Given the potential merits we have outlined above, we hope to stimulate more research into the interplay of conceptual model analysis and graph theory.

References

1. Awad, A., Decker, G., Weske, M.: Efficient Compliance Checking Using BPMN-Q and Temporal Logic. In: Dumas, M., Reichert, M., Shan, M.-C. (eds.) BPM 2008. LNCS, vol. 5240, pp. 326–341. Springer, Heidelberg (2008)
2. Awad, A., Sakr, S.: Querying Graph-Based Repositories of Business Process Models. In: Yoshikawa, M., Meng, X., Yumoto, T., Ma, Q., Sun, L., Watanabe, C. (eds.) DASFAA 2010. LNCS, vol. 6193, pp. 33–44. Springer, Heidelberg (2010)
3. Becker, J., Schütte, R.: Handels informations systeme. Redline, Landsberg (2004)
4. Beeri, C., Eyal, A., Kamenkovich, S., Milo, T.: Querying business processes with BP-QL. Information Systems Journal 33(6), 477–507 (2008)
5. Conte, D., Foggia, P., Sansone, C., Vento, M.: Thirty years of graph matching in pattern recognition. International Journal of Pattern Recognition and Artificial Intelligence 18(3), 265–298 (2004)
6. Conte, D., Foggia, P., Vento, M.: Challenging Complexity of Maximum Common Subgraph Detection Algorithms: A Performance Analysis of Three Algorithms on a Wide Database of Graphs. Journal of Graph Algorithms and Appl (JGAA) 11(1), 99–143 (2007)
7. Cordella, L.P., Foggia, P., Sansone, C., Vento, M.: A (sub)graph isomorphism algorithm for matching large graphs. IEEE Transactions on Pattern Analysis and Machine Intelligence 26(10), 1367–1372 (2004)
8. Delfmann, P.: Adaptive Referenzmodellierung. Logos, Berlin (2006)
9. Dijkman, R., Rosa, M.L., Reijers, H.A.: Managing large collections of business process models - Current techniques and challenges. Comp. in Industry 63(2), 91–97 (2012)
10. Dong, J., Zhao, Y., Peng, T.: A review of design pattern mining techniques. International Journal of Software Engineering and Knowledge Engineering 19(6), 823–855 (2009)
11. Ferro, A., Giugno, R., Pigola, G., Pulvirenti, A., Skripin, D., Bader, G.D., Shasha, D.: NetMatch: a Cytoscape plugin for searching biological networks. Bioinformatics 23(7), 910–912 (2007)
12. García-Bañuelos, L.: Pattern Identification and Classification in the Translation from BPMN to BPEL. In: Meersman, R., Tari, Z. (eds.) OTM 2008, Part I. LNCS, vol. 5331, pp. 436–444. Springer, Heidelberg (2008)
13. Garey, M.R., Johnson, D.S.: Computers and Intractability: A Guide to the Theory of NP-Completeness. W. H. Freeman & Co., New York (1979)
14. Gupta, M., Rao, R.S., Pande, A., Tripathi, A.K.: Design Pattern Mining Using State Space Representation of Graph Matching. In: Meghanathan, N., Kaushik, B.K., Nagamalai, D. (eds.) CCSIT 2011, Part I. CCIS, vol. 131, pp. 318–328. Springer, Heidelberg (2011)
15. Jin, T., Wang, J., Wu, N., La Rosa, M., ter Hofstede, A.H.M.: Efficient and Accurate Retrieval of Business Process Models through Indexing. In: Meersman, R., Dillon, T., Herrero, P. (eds.) OTM 2010. LNCS, vol. 6426, pp. 402–409. Springer, Heidelberg (2010)
16. Keller, G., Teufel, T.: SAP R/3 process-oriented implementation: Iterative process prototyping. Addison Wesley Longman, Harlow (1998)
17. Lara, J., Vangheluwe, H.: AToM3: A Tool for Multi-formalism and Meta-modelling. In: Kutsche, R.-D., Weber, H. (eds.) FASE 2002. LNCS, vol. 2306, pp. 174–188. Springer, Heidelberg (2002)

18. Lucrédio, D., de M. Fortes, R.P., Whittle, J.: MOOGLE: A Model Search Engine. In: Czarnecki, K., Ober, I., Bruel, J.-M., Uhl, A., Völter, M. (eds.) MODELS 2008. LNCS, vol. 5301, pp. 296–310. Springer, Heidelberg (2008)
19. Mendling, J., Verbeek, H.M.W., van Dongen, B.F., van der Aalst, W.M.P., Neumann, G.: Detection and Prediction of Errors in EPCs of the SAP reference model. Data & Knowledge Engineering 64(1), 312–329 (2008)
20. Momotko, M., Subieta, K.: Process Query Language: A Way to Make Workflow Processes More Flexible. In: Benczúr, A., Demetrovics, J., Gottlob, G. (eds.) ADBIS 2004. LNCS, vol. 3255, pp. 306–321. Springer, Heidelberg (2004)
21. Nijssen, S., Kok, J.N.: Frequent graph mining and its application to molecular databases. In: Conf. on System, Man and Cybernetics, pp. 4571–4577. IEEE Press, New York (2004)
22. Nijssen, S., Kok, J.N.: Frequent Subgraph Miners: Runtimes Don't Say Everything. In: Proc. of the Int. Works. on Mining and Learning with Graphs, pp. 173–180, Berlin (2006)
23. Object Management Group: Common Warehouse Metamodel 1.1 (2011), http://www.omg.org/spec/CWM/1.1/
24. Ouyang, C., Dumas, M., ter Hofstede, A.H.M., van der Aalst, W.M.P.: Pattern-based Translation of BPMN Process Models to BPEL Web Services. International Journal of Web Services Research 5(1), 1–21 (2007)
25. Reijers, H.A., Mendling, J., Dijkman, R.M.: Human and automatic modularizations of process models to enhance their comprehension. Information Systems Journal 36(5), 881–897 (2011)
26. Smirnov, S., Weidlich, M., Mendling, J., Weske, M.: Action Patterns in Business Process Models. In: Baresi, L., Chi, C.-H., Suzuki, J. (eds.) ICSOC-ServiceWave 2009. LNCS, vol. 5900, pp. 115–129. Springer, Heidelberg (2009)
27. Uba, R., Dumas, M., García-Bañuelos, L., La Rosa, M.: Clone Detection in Repositories of Business Process Models. In: Rinderle-Ma, S., Toumani, F., Wolf, K. (eds.) BPM 2011. LNCS, vol. 6896, pp. 248–264. Springer, Heidelberg (2011)
28. Ullmann, J.R.: An Algorithm for Subgraph Isomorphism. J. of ACM 23(1), 31–42 (1976)
29. Van Dongen, B.F., Mendling, J., van der Aalst, W.M.P.: Structural Patterns for Soundness of Business Process Models. In: 10th IEEE Int. Enterprise Distributed Object Computing Conference, pp. 116–128. IEEE Press, New York (2006)
30. Vanderfeesten, I., Cardoso, J., Mendling, J., Reijers, H.A., van der Aalst, W.: Quality metrics for business process models. In: BPM and Workflow Handbook, pp. 179–190 (2007)
31. Weidlich, M., Polyvyanyy, A., Desai, N., Mendling, J.: Process Compliance Measurement Based on Behavioural Profiles. In: Pernici, B. (ed.) CAiSE 2010. LNCS, vol. 6051, pp. 499–514. Springer, Heidelberg (2010)
32. Winkelmann, A., Weiß, B.: Automatic identification of structural process weaknesses in flow chart diagrams. Business Process Management Journal 17(5), 787–807 (2011)
33. Wörlein, M., Meinl, T., Fischer, I., Philippsen, M.: A Quantitative Comparison of the Subgraph Miners MoFa, gSpan, FFSM, and Gaston. In: Jorge, A.M., Torgo, L., Brazdil, P., Camacho, R., Gama, J. (eds.) PKDD 2005. LNCS (LNAI), vol. 3721, pp. 392–403. Springer, Heidelberg (2005)
34. Yan, X., Han, J.: gSpan: Graph-based substructure pattern mining. In: Proc. of the IEEE Int. Conf. on Data Mining, pp. 721–724. IEEE Press, New York (2002)
35. Yan, Z., Dijkman, R., Grefen, P.: Fast Business Process Similarity Search with Feature-Based Similarity Estimation. In: Meersman, R., Dillon, T., Herrero, P. (eds.) OTM 2010. LNCS, vol. 6426, pp. 60–77. Springer, Heidelberg (2010)

The Process Documentation Cube:
A Model for Process Documentation Assessment

Toomas Saarsen and Marlon Dumas

Institute of Computer Science, University of Tartu, Estonia
{toomas.saarsen,marlon.dumas}@ut.ee

Abstract. This paper presents a model for organizing and assessing business process documentation with the aim of identifying gaps and inconsistencies. The proposed model – namely the Process Documentation Cube (PDC) – has been tested in six public sector organizations in Estonia – three of them with years of process modeling engagement and three others in early stages of process modeling adoption. In the organizations where process modeling is already well established, the PDC allowed the relevant stakeholders to identify gaps in their documentation and directions for improving the integration between process models and other documentation. In the remaining organizations, the PDC was perceived as a useful tool for planning process documentation efforts.

1   Introduction

In contemporary business process management practice, it is common for business process models and associated documentation to be produced in the context of specific projects, be it IT projects, business improvement projects, quality management projects or audits [1]. Often these models are used in the project where they are produced, but not consulted nor systematically maintained past the project, thus creating so-called "pollution" in the organization's process model repositories [1].

Several success factor models are available to measure, explain and predict success of process modeling initiatives [2, 3]. These models shed light into the factors that determine whether or not process models are perceived to be useful by the relevant stakeholders (among other dimensions of process modeling success). Other studies have focused on assessing the quality of process models [4] or improving the syntactic or semantic quality of process model repositories by means of refactoring [5]. However, these studies focus on diagrammatic process models, whereas in practice processes are documented in various ways, ranging from free-text documents, such as manuals of policies and procedures, to structured documents (e.g. legislative documents) and tables [6]. Additionally, process models are captured at different levels of granularity and from different perspectives depending on the intended usage.

In order to reap the full benefits of process modeling beyond individual projects and diagrammatic process models, a more holistic approach to process documentation maintenance is required – one that views process models as integral part of the day-to-day documentation used across the organization.

M. La Rosa and P. Soffer (Eds.): BPM 2012 Workshops, LNBIP 132, pp. 501–512, 2013.
© Springer-Verlag Berlin Heidelberg 2013

In this setting, this paper introduces a process documentation assessment model that is intended to help analysts to holistically map the process documentation of an organization and to assess this documentation with respect to three aspects:

1)   Completeness: the documentation covers all processes and gives a balanced overview of all processes at different levels of granularity via a process hierarchy.

2)   Consistency: different documentation items are consistent with respect to one another. This includes consistency among different types of documents (e.g. textual documents and diagrammatic process models) and across process documentation at different levels of abstraction.

3)   Comprehensibility and updatability: it is possible for all relevant stakeholders to comprehend and to update the process documentation.

The proposed documentation assessment model, namely the Process Documentation Cube (PDC), is validated by means of six case studies in Estonian public sector organizations. Three of the organizations have already collected significant amounts of structured process documentation, including several collections of (diagrammatic) process models, while three others have some process documentation, but mostly unstructured and have not been engaged in any significant process modeling effort. Due to space constraints, we do not present all six case studies in details. Instead we focus on three representative organizations corresponding to the following situations:

- Agricultural Registers and Information Board – processes are not documented in a structured way, but instead unstructured documentation is in active usage;
- Labour Inspectorate – processes are described in a structured way and these structured models are in active usage;
- Estonian Tax and Customs Board – processes are described in a structured way but the structured models are not in active usage; instead other unstructured process documentation is in active usage.

From a methodological perspective, the research presented in this paper follows a Design Science approach [9]. First, an analysis of the problem in light of existing literature was conducted, leading to an initial definition of the PDC. Next, the perceived usability of the PDC was tested by means of six case studies using a three-phased data gathering and hypothesis validation method explained in Section 3. Finally, feedback gathered during these case studies was used to refine the definition of the PDC and to identify directions for extension and improvement.

The paper is structured as follows. Firstly Section 2 introduces the process documentation assessment model and its theoretical foundation. Section 3 presents the selected three case studies. Section 4 reviews related works and finally Section 5 contains the conclusion and gives directions for further research.

2   Process Documentation Assessment Model

The proposed process documentation assessment model takes the form of a cube (cf. Figure 1) consisting of three orthogonal dimensions. The first dimension relates to the type of process being documented (*area*), while the other two refer to the level of detail (*granularity*) and the level of structuredness (*structure*) of the document itself. Each document or group of documents is mapped as a cell in the PDC based on its classification along these dimensions.

The first dimension, namely *area*, is based on Rummler's framework [7], which divides processes into three classes: operational, support and management processes. Operating processes produce outputs directly relevant to external customers. Support processes (e.g. financial and human resource processes) are those required in order to maintain the infrastructure (incl. human and material resources) required to perform the operational processes, while management and those intended to oversee and control other processes and to maximize value to other stakeholders (e.g. shareholders).

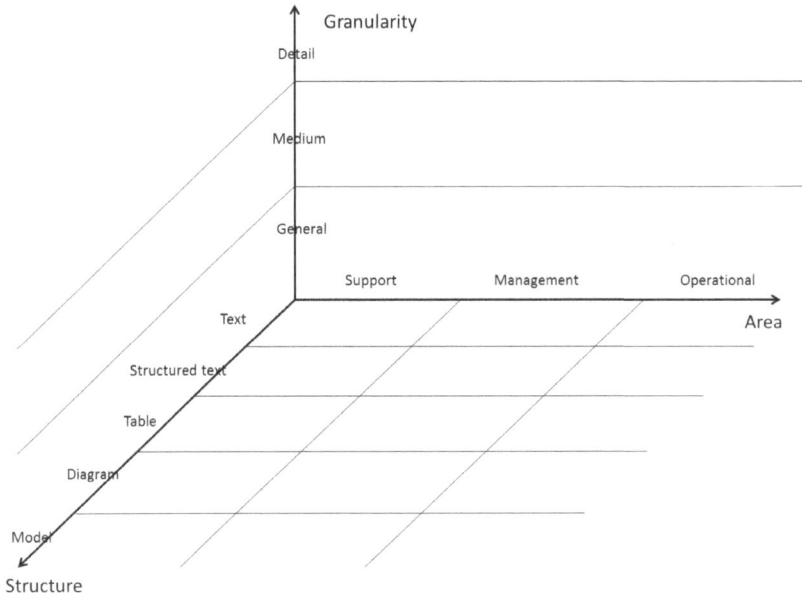

Fig. 1. Documentation cube

The second dimension (*structure*) relates to the level of structural meta-data of the document. Here we distinguish between text (plain text without any prescribed structure), structured text (a text with a strict structure), table (a table with a defined structure), diagram (a simple drawing or diagram that does not follow a prescriptive modeling notation or is not stored in a repository, e.g. a Visio or PowerPoint drawing) and model (a diagram abiding to a prescriptive modeling notation and maintained in a repository). Different types of structure are suitable for different stakeholders. For example, legislative documents (structured text), which are widespread in the public sector, are easy to read for lawyers but hardly accessible for stakeholder without a legal background. These latter stakeholders may prefer simple diagrams or tables.

The third dimension (*granularity*) represents the level of detail (or level of abstraction) of the documentation: general documents, medium-level documents, and detailed documents (cf. process hierarchies [8]). Different granularity levels are suitable for different purposes. For example, for a new employee who has to understand the value chain and their role in the organization – it seems reasonable to have a top down approach. A customer who is interested in getting more information about services should follow the process at the middle or detailed level.

There are many possible ways to define the granularity of process documentation. In order to reduce the scope for subjective interpretation, we rely on the classification provided by the SCOR framework [10], which identifies the following levels:

-   General or Top-level: Process documentation focused on defining the scope of the process (what is done in the process);
-   Medium or Configuration-level: focused on showing how processes are executed with the aim of communicating this information to a wide audience;
-   Detailed or Process element-level: Process documentation that provides details of the process on an element-per-element level (e.g. individual tasks).

In addition to capturing the location of each document along the above dimensions, the PDC includes *consistency links*. A consistency link exists between two documents D1 and D2, if there is a mechanism in place to ensure that an update to D1 leads to an update in D2 and vice-versa. This mechanism can be automated (a document generated from another) or manual. Naturally, consistency links allow us to assess documentation consistency across different dimensions of the cube.

Since a three-dimensional cube is difficult to visualize and comprehend at once, it is convenient to view the PDC through its two-dimensional views. Each view allows one to assess different aspects, as explained below.

2.1   View 1 – Area-Granularity

The first view comprises the area and granularity dimensions. This view gives us the whole picture of the documentation and allows us to assess documentation completeness. Specifically, it allows us to assess if there are documents about different areas (horizontal layout) and covering each level of granularity (vertical layout).

If there is any empty area on the diagram, then it may raise a question – whether we missed a document during documentation gathering or there is a gap in the documentation? For example, in the public sector the main processes are usually described, but not enough attention is paid to the supporting processes and management activities – a gap in the detail documentation.

2.2   View 2 – Structure-Granularity

The combination of structure and granularity form the second view. This view is useful for assessing comprehensibility and updatability. Indeed, different stakeholders need different types of documents and at different levels of granularity. Thus ensuring comprehensibility of process documentation by all stakeholders requires that documents are available in different structures and levels of granularity. Plain text is probably most common format for daily documentation – there are no any restrictions or assumptions – all employees can read text documents. In the public sector several legislative and regulatory documents are used to describe the organization activities, rules, etc. All these documents are described as a structured text. But these voluminous and specialized texts are not easy for employees or clients to comprehend – the latter preferring plain text, simple diagrams or combinations thereof. Business analysts and managers on the other hand may take full benefit from process models, while management and monitoring processes are usually described via different tables. If there is a simple structure (1 or 2 dimensions) and some calculation needed, the table is a good choice as it is easy to define and track later.

2.3   View 3 – Area-Structure

The third view covers area and the structure. This view allows us to assess completeness, comprehensibility and updatability. It gives an opportunity to decide which processes are documented as structured text (e.g. legislative documents), which ones are presented as a table, which documents are generated from a model, etc.

If an organization uses a sophisticated modeling tool, this view is a convenient structure to fit the model outputs onto the documentation map. If most of the facts about the organization (roles and structure, activities and processes, data, etc.) are in the model repository, and different documents are generated (job description, process description, data usage, etc.), documentation update is simplified.

View 3 highlights the parallel layers of documents and gaps that may exist in these layers. For example, legislative documents have to be in place, but additional documents covering the same processes, possibly generated from a business process model also need to be in place for employees performing day-to-day tasks.

3   Case Studies

As a preliminary evaluation, the PDC was applied in six public sector organizations in Estonia. The choice of public sector organizations is motivated by the fact that these organizations are more inclined to disclose their internal documentation – and in many cases this documentation is publicly accessible. This allowed us to freely collect details that would be more difficult to access in some private companies. However, conducting a similar evaluation on private companies is a direction for future work.

3.1   Methodology

In each organization, data collection was performed via three meetings:

1) The first meeting consisted of an interview with a process analysts or the organization's stakeholder who would be closest to playing this role. The aim of the

interview was to make an inventory of all process-related documents in the organization, without restriction on the type of document. For each document we sought to obtain information about three aspects: document creation; maintenance/update; and usage. There were 4 main questions about each phase: who; when; what and how. Copies of the documents were also collected.

2) Based on collected information, the first author prepared three views of the PDC for the organization in question, and highlighted potential gaps and ideas for document integration. The PDC, gaps and integration ideas were discussed during a second meeting with the same stakeholder as in the first interview, plus additional analysts and subject matter experts invited by the first stakeholder. The aim of the second meeting was to gather feedback on the accuracy of the PDC and the pertinence of the gaps and integration ideas.

3) Feedback from the second interview was summarized in a final report that was sent to the participants of the second meeting. Based on this report the last meeting was organized for a wider audience, including management. The aim of the third meeting was to gather feedback about the perceived usefulness of the PDC.

3.2   Case Study 1 – Agricultural Registers and Information Board (ARIB)

This is a typical example of an organization where mainly text is used for a process description. View 1 gives an overview of the documentation (Figure 2). The blue trapeze emphasizes the document hierarchy. Red lines are used to represent consistency links between different documents.

Processes are described through the document "Procedure description". There are ~400 different procedures and the main complaints about these documents were that update is too complicated; documents are not updated properly; quality and usability degrade over time. The update problem is directly related with the size of the document – all descriptions are too voluminous. Instead of a simple diagram with a brief description, there is a bulky text with cross-references inside. These cross-references make the update procedure very complicated and time consuming. Finally, it is very difficult for the reader to grasp general structure of the process and understand all nuances correctly: loops in the process, exceptions, parallel tasks, etc. This case illustrates that if an organization is interested in starting a process modeling project, the PDC provides a structure to design the project outputs and fit these outputs (documents) into the daily documentation and to move toward more structured documents (e.g. Figure 3 → Figure 4). Figure 4 highlights how to bind the process model with the documentation: blue lines indicate documents that are generated from the model; green color highlights new documents; and yellow color highlights old documents in the new format.

In this organization, a process modeling tool would simplify documentation update by generating different outputs (e.g. documents) from models. During the assessment, attention was focused on an upcoming process modeling project – what tools should be used; how to involve and train employees; how to use the process model, etc.

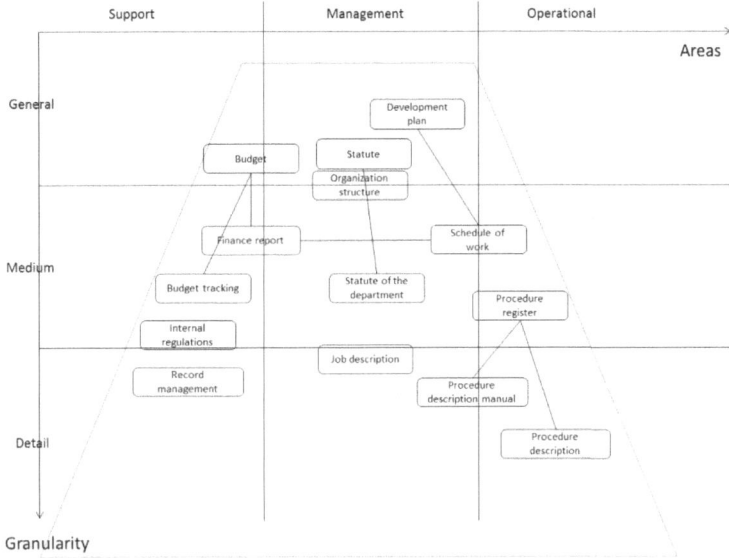

Fig. 2. View 1, ARIB

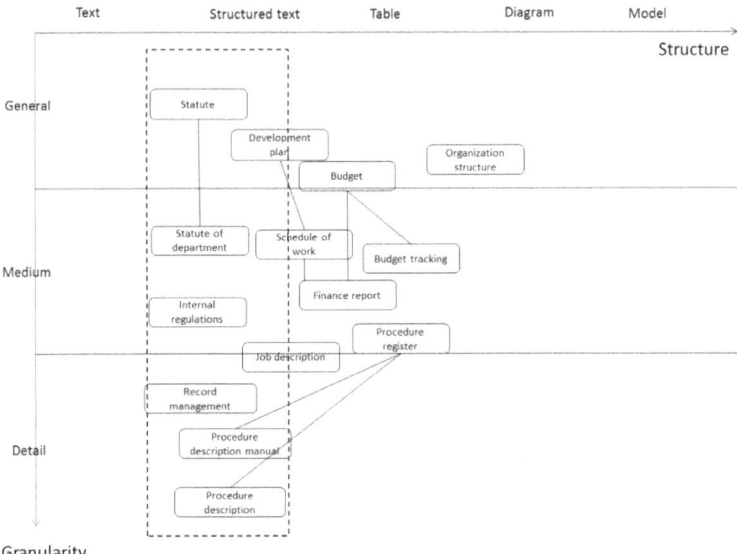

Fig. 3. View 2, ARIB

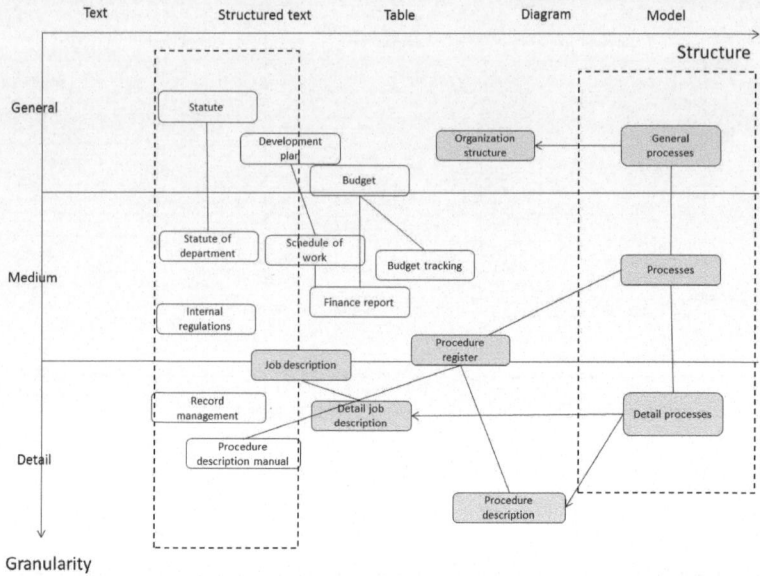

Fig. 4. Proposed "to-be" View 2 for ARIB

3.3   Case Study 2 – Labour Inspectorate

This case study led to a very different picture, as shown in Figure 5. In this organization, there is a sophisticated process modeling tool in use, and number of documents have been generated from the models managed by this tool. In this case, the main gap we discovered was that the process hierarchy was not properly modeled. The green boxes in Figure 5 show where this missing process hierarchy would go in the PDC and how this hierarchy could be bound with other documentation.

An update procedure of detailed documents (job description, daily procedures, data usage etc.) was in place. The process hierarchy gave better understanding about the full processes and a big picture about the whole organization. Upper layers of the process hierarchy give a structured base for general documents like goals and strategy. Additionally, process hierarchy could be used as a table of contents for the process model – flexible entrance into the detail level of the process diagrams.

View 3 gives an interesting result here (Figure 6): there are two layers of duplicated documents: the upper red circle is highlighting legislative documents (that have to be used in theory) and more structured documents (that employees use in practice).

During the assessment process, the main attention was focused on the comprehensibility and usability of the process model outputs. The document cube gave a good structure to design changes

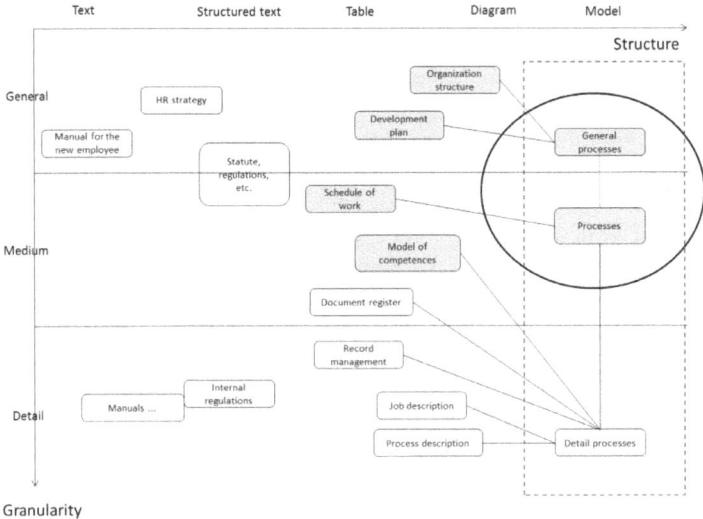

Fig. 5. Proposed "to-be" View 2 for Labour Inspectorate

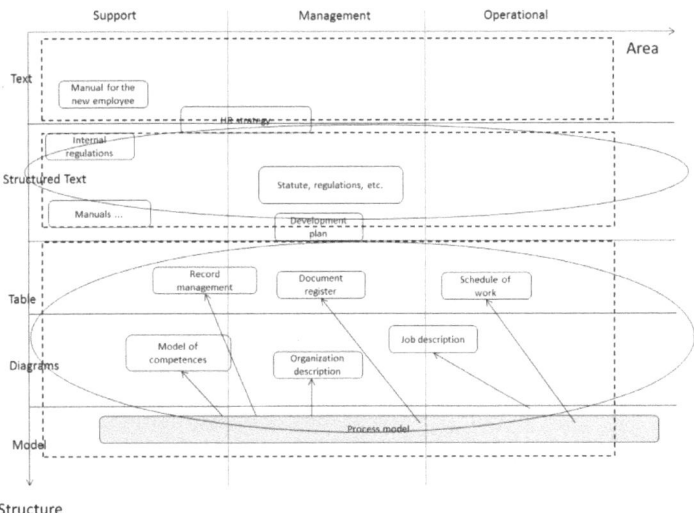

Fig. 6. View 3, Labour Inspectorate

3.4   Case study 3 – Estonian Tax and Customs Board

Case study 3 highlights the problem of lack of integration of process models produced by a modeling project and daily documentation in the organization. The goal of the implemented process modeling project was process optimization and process change. The project produced high-quality process models. The analysis phase of the project highlighted different problems and a To-Be model was produced. If we look at the project from the business process analyses perspective, then result is excellent. Unfortunately, there were not any output to the daily documentation, and for this reason, the model was not used by the employees (Figure 7).

The main problem in the long term here is the process update. After the project, there is not enough time and attention to the process model. The model is not used and updated in daily life. The "death" of the model is just a matter of time.

The PDC was an excellent tool to design changes in the documentation and find suitable outputs from the business process model to support deployment of the model (Figure 8). These changes brought together employees around the process model and made them think about the daily processes, problems, needed changes, etc.

There main issues were identified. First, there was a lack of a proper process hierarchy – table of contents. Second, more documents were needed for daily work of employees. Finally, process modeling tool simplifies documentation update, and even more important, intensive use gives motivation for the model update.

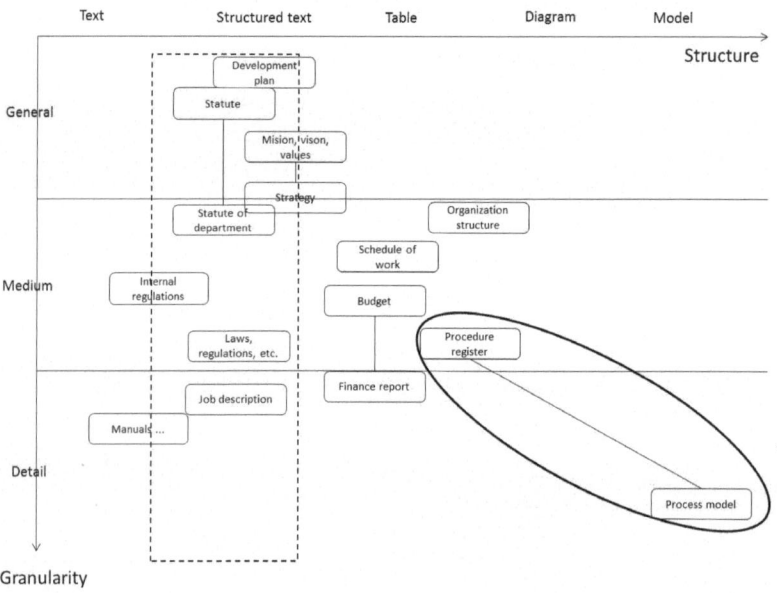

Fig. 7. View 2, Tax and Customs Board

3.5   Discussion

One can distinguish three *patterns of process documentation* from the case studies:

1) Processes described via text (ARIB). The organization used the document cube in process modeling planning phase – design process model outputs and integrate these outputs with daily documentation.

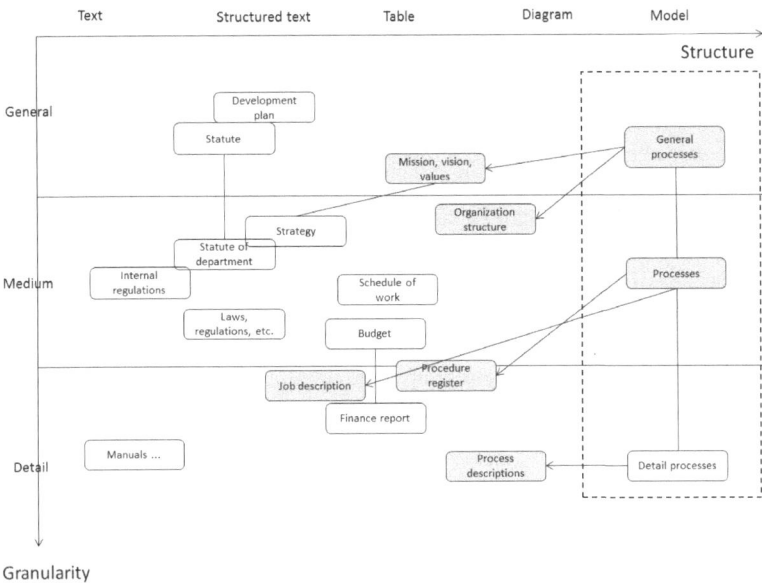

Fig. 8. Proposed "to-be" View 2 for Tax and Customs Board

2) BP tool is used and good integration with daily documentation exists (Labour Inspectorate). The organization in question found several gaps in the documentation and new ideas for the process model integration.

3) BP tool is used but without integration with daily documentation (Tax and Customs Board). The output of the process modeling project was not oriented to employees. The PDC allowed us to identify outputs that could be generated from the process models and thus to integrate the process models with daily documentation.

4   Related Work

We are not aware of previous work that addresses the question of how to visually map organization-wide process documentation (including textual documents) in order to identify gaps and integration opportunities. A recent work [6] proposes a tool for integrated diagrammatic and textual process description, but it does not address the above question. Some related work has addressed the question of what is the perceived value of process modeling and process models [11] or what are the main obstacles and pitfalls of process modeling [1]. Other work has discussed the importance of wider usage of process models – beyond analysts [12]. This latter work argues that participation and involvement of employees in the process modeling project is important and correlates with quality and usability [2, 3]. However, this body of work is orthogonal to the PDC's objective of identifying gaps and integration opportunities.

5   Conclusion

The PDC gives a simple structure for mapping the organization documentation and to assess its completeness, consistency, comprehensibility and updatability. In organization with comprehensive process documentation, the PDC allows one to identify gaps and integration opportunities. Meanwhile, if an organization is starting a new process modeling project, the PDC can be used for planning purposes in order to determine how the process models will fit with other documentation.

In the case of organizations with extensive process documentation, effective visualization of the PDC or its individual views may become a challenge. Accordingly, a possible avenue for future work is to design visualization techniques that can help users to navigate through PDCs covering large amounts of process documentation.

References

1. Rosemann, M.: Potential pitfalls of process modeling: part B. Business Process Management Journal 12(3), 377–384 (2006)
2. Bandara, W., Gable, G.G., Rosemann, M.: Factors and measures of business process modeling: Model building through a multiple case study. European Journal of Information Systems 14, 347–360 (2005)
3. Trkman, P.: The Critical Success Factors of Business Process Management. International Journal of Information Management 30(2), 125–134 (2010)
4. Krogstie, J., Sindre, G., Jørgensen, H.: Process models representing knowledge for action: a revised quality framework. European Journal of Information Systems 15, 91–102 (2006)
5. Weber, B., Reichert, M., Mendling, J., Reijers, H.: Refactoring large process model repositories. Computers in Industry 62(5), 467–486 (2011)
6. Pinggera, J., Porcham, T., Zugal. S., Weber, B.: LiProMo-Literate Process Modeling. In: Proceedings of the CAiSE 2012 Forum, Gdansk, Poland. Springer (to appear, June 2012)
7. Spanyi, A.: Business Process Management Governance. In: Handbook on Business Process Management, vol. 2, pp. 223–238. Springer (2010)
8. Harmon, P.: Business Process Change: A Guide for Business Managers and BPM and Six Sigma Professionals. Morgan Kaufmann (2007)
9. Hevner, A.R., March, S.T., Park, J., Ram, S.: Design Science in Information Systems Research. MIS Quarterly 28(1), 75–105 (2004)
10. Supply-Chain Council. Supply Chain Operations Reference Model Version 10 (2010)
11. Dalberg, V., Jensen, S., Krogstie, J.: Increasing the Value of Process Modelling and Models. In: Proceedings of the Norwegian Conference on the Use of IT in Organizations, NOKOBIT (2005)
12. Eikebrokk, T.R., et al.: Exploring Process-Modelling Practice: Towards a Conceptual Model. In: Proceedings of the 41st Annual Hawaii International Conference on System Sciences (HICSS), pp. 376–376. IEEE (2008)

Event-B Formalisation for Dynamic Composition: A Logistics-Based Process as a Use Case

Lazhar Hamel[1], Mohamed Graiet[1],
Mourad Kmimech[2], and Mohamed Tahar Bhiri[2]

[1] High School of Computer Science and Mathematics, Monastir, Tunisia
lazhar.hamel@gmail.com, mohamed.graiet@imag.fr
[2] MIRACL, ISIMS, Sfax, Tunisia
mkmimech@gmail.com, tahar_bhiri@yahoo.fr

Abstract. The capacity of a composite service to change configuration according to the component services behavior is essential. In particular, this reconfiguration should be done dynamically without disturbing the service execution. To the best of our knowledge, few works were interested in verifying the coherence of this dynamic reconfiguration. By dynamic reconfiguration we mean for example, overcome the failure or the unavailability of a service component by the discovery and the replacement of another service that provides the same functionalities. To do so, we propose an approach based on Event-B for a formal verification of the structural and behavioral properties of the component service before dynamically integrated into the composition during the execution. A logistics-based process is used as use case in order to validate our approach.

Keywords: Web Service, Dynamic reconfiguration, Event-B, formal verification, structural and behavioral properties, logistics-based process.

1 Introduction

Web service is a technology that aims at the implementation of service oriented architecture in the web. A Web service is an independent software component that provides services through an interface. One of the interesting concepts offered by this technology is the ability to create a new value added service by composing existing services, eventually offered by several companies. The resulting composite services can in turn enter into other compositions to provide more complex services to higher value added. Several techniques have been proposed to dynamically compose services. However, they require that users request services in a way that is not intuitive. Basically, we can distinguish the following approaches for dynamic composition of Web services: Dynamic composition with a priori goal [1] [2] : the goal to reach is fixed in advance and then an automatic discovery of services that meets the needs is made. At the end of the discovery and composition process, a composite service that meets the needs of users is

M. La Rosa and P. Soffer (Eds.): BPM 2012 Workshops, LNBIP 132, pp. 513–518, 2013.

provided. Abstract composition, concrete composition [3] : an abstract model of composition at a high level is defined then based on this model the concrete composition of services is induced. This concrete composition has to be conform to the rules defined in the abstract model. The verification of an orchestration before its execution allows to limit any undesired behavior. On the failure of a service component, the composite service has to replace the related service without disrupting its execution. A discovered service that offers the same functionality as the failed service may behave in a way that does not match what is originally verified. It is impossible to claim that what is executed corresponds exactly to what is described. A verification step of the new configuration is necessary to ensure that this new configuration has the same behavior.

This paper is organized as follows. Section 2 presents a motivating example which is a logistics-based process used as use case. Section 3 describes briefly some basic concepts. Section 4 shows our proposed formalization of Web services composition. Finally, Section 5 validates these specifications.

2   Motivating Example: A Logistics-Based Process as a Use Case

In this section, we present a logistics-based scenario to illustrate our approach: a travel agency scenario (Figure 1). The customer specifies its requirement in terms of destinations and hotels via the activity "Specification of Client Needs" (SCN). After SCN termination, the application launches simultaneously two tasks "Flight Booking" (FB) and "Hotel Reservation" (HR) according to customer's choice. Once booked, the "Online Payment" (OP) allows customers to make the payments. Finally travel documents (air ticket and hotel reservations are sent to the client via one of the services "Sending Document by Fedex" (SDF) ,"Sending Document by DHL" (SDD) or " Sending Document by TNT" (SDT). According to our logistics-based process, we suppose that a payment problem is

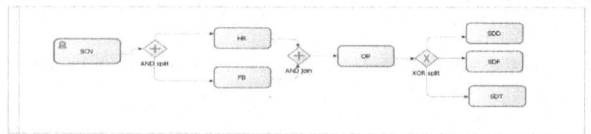

Fig. 1. Motivating example: travel agency Service

observed. The booking service continues to use OP while trying to find another service to replace the failing service at run time. The new service must correct the observed problem and provide the same functionality as OP. Thus the new service must behave like the OP service. Let us consider the payment service represented by the BPMN diagram in Figure 2. P1 is a service that allows the cancellation of its work within 60 minutes. After the task payment authorization two task starts that allows either to wait 60 minutes if there is a cancellation of

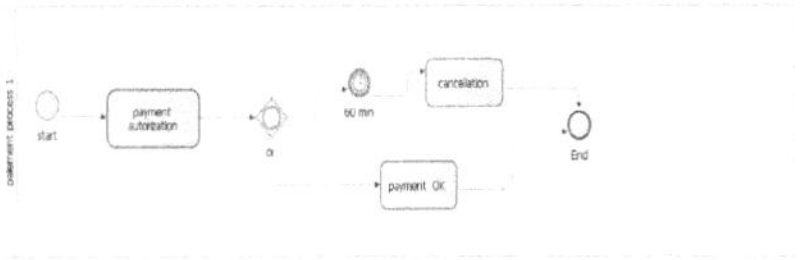

Fig. 2. BPMN diagram of P1 payment service

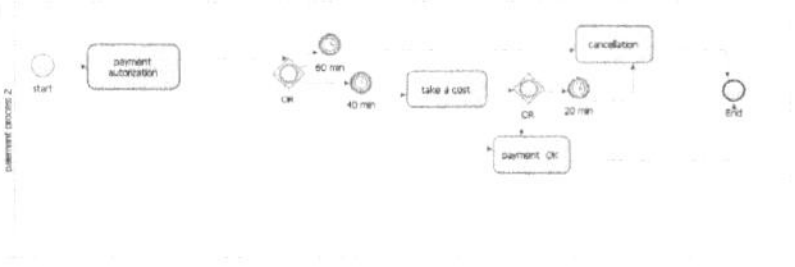

Fig. 3. BPMN diagram of P2 payment service

the service or finalize the payment via the *paiement OK* task. The P2 service represented by its BPMN diagram in Figure 3 can perform the same functionality P1. However it has a different behavior in case of service cancellation . The P2 service informs the client that there is an additional cost to pay after 40 minutes in case of cancellation. In the following section, we show that although a new service does not have the same structure, it can behave as expected in the composition.

3 Basic Concepts

3.1 A Structural Description: WSDL

By Web service we mean a self-contained modular program that can be discovered and invoked across the Internet . WSDL or Web Service Description Language, a W3C recommendation, is a format for describing Web services based on XML. WSDL defines services as a set of operations and messages described abstractly and related to protocols and to concrete network servers.

3.2 Event-B

Event-B [4] is a variant of B method introduced by Abrial to deal with reactive system. An Event-B model contains the complete mathematical development of a discrete system. A model uses two types of entities to describe a system: machines and contexts. A machine represents the dynamic parts of a model. Machine may contain variables, invariants, theorems, variants and events whereas contexts represent the static parts of a model .It may contain carrier sets, constants, axioms and theorems. The refinement concept is the main feature of Event-B. It allows incremental design of systems. Correctness of Event-B machines is ensured by proving proof obligations (POs);

4 Formalizing Web Services with Event-B

4.1 Web Service

This Event-B model is used primarily to fix the vocabulary and definitions on which the general specification is built. We introduce the context "ServiceContext" which presents these carrier sets. The properties considered in this approach are the transactional properties: retriable, pivot and compensatable. The set of states which we consider is *initial, active, aborted, cancelled, failed, compensated, completed. Property* represents the set of properties of a Web service. *OperationOfPT* describe the set of operations of a port types. *TypeOfOperation* represents the type of operation provided by a service. A service receives a message as input (*in*), sends a message (*out*), receives a message as input and returns a message output (*inout*). A service sends a message and receives a correlated message (*outin*). A variable "service_state" defined by total function between "SERVICE" and "STATES" (*service_state* $\in$ *SERVICE* $\to$ *STATES*) and initialised to the empty set, defines the current state of each service.

CONTEXT ServiceContext
SETS *SERVICE STATES PROPERTIES MESSAGE OPERATION TYPE PORT_TYPE*
CONSTANTS *initial active aborted cancelled failed compensated completed Property TypeOfOperation Signature PortTypeOfWS OperationOfPT out in inout*
AXIOMS
Axm1: *STATES* = {*initial, active, aborted, cancelled, failed, compensated, completed*}
Axm2: *PROPERTIES* = {*retriable, compensatable, pivot*}
Axm3: *Property* $\in$ *SERVICE* $\to$ $\mathbb{P}$(*PROPERTIES*)
Axm4: *Signature* $\in$ *OPERATION* $\to$ $\mathbb{P}$(*MESSAGE* $\times$ *MESSAGE*)
Axm5: *OperationOfPT* $\in$ *PORT_TYPE* $\to$ $\mathbb{P}$(*OPERATION*)
Axm6: *PortTypeOfWS* $\in$ *SERVICE* $\to$ $\mathbb{P}$(*PORT_TYPE*)
Axm7: *TypeOfOperation* $\in$ *OPERATION* $\to$ *TYPE*
Axm8: *TYPE* = {*in, inout, outin, out*}
END

4.2   Web Service Properties Verification for a Dynamic Composition

Even though a service s1 has the same properties as another service s2, before replacing s1 by s2 a formal verification step is necessary for s2 additional properties to ensure that the s2 behaves exactly like s1 and to ignore any violation of the global properties of the composite service. The check event allows to check if a service s1 behaves exactly like another service s2 or not. The Substitute event allows to replace a service in the composition by another service. The comparison is made with respect to the features offered by the service. The guards grd1, grd2 express that the new service is not included in the initial configuration of the composition. The guard grd3 can express that the new service has the same properties of the service to substitute. The guard grd4 ensures that the new service offers the features offered by the old service. The guard grd5 allows the verification of the behavior of the new service. If the new service offers additional features, these functions must be an out type. The Out type of an operation indicates that this operation allows to send a simply notification as a display for customers and does not influences the behavior of the service. The guard grd6 ensures that the formal verification of properties is done before the substitution of the service and the integration into the composition. The grd3 guard of the Substitute event ensures that the replacement of s1 is done when it is not in an activated state.

check $\triangleq$ **ANY** $s1$ $s2$ **WHERE**
grd1: $s1 \in SWT$
grd2: $s2 \in SERVICE \setminus SWT$
grd3: $\{s1, s2\} \subseteq dom(Property) \wedge$
$Property(s1) \subseteq Property(s2))$
grd4: $\forall pt.(pt \in portTypeOfWS(s1)$
$\wedge pt \in PortTypeOfWS(s2))$
grd5: $\forall pt, op.(pt \in$
$portTypeOfWS(s2)$
$\wedge op \in operationOfPT(pt)) \Rightarrow$
$TypeOfOperation(op) = out$
grd6: $seq = 0$
THEN act1 : $seq = 1$ **END**

Substitute $\triangleq$ **ANY** $s1$ $s2$ **WHERE**
grd1 : $s1 \in SWT$
grd2 : $s2 \in SERVICE \setminus SWT$
grd3 : $\neg(service\_state(s1) = active)$
grd4 : $seq = 1$
THEN
act1 : $SWT := (SWT \setminus \{s1\}) \cup \{s2\}$
END

5 Validation

In the previous section, we showed how to formally specify a dynamic composition using Event-B. The objective of this section is to show how we verify and validate our model using proof and animation. In an Event-B machine, it is necessary to verify that the initial state (ie initialization) satisfies the invariant. Thus, any event should ensure that a non-deterministic action is feasible. We find many proof obligations (Figure 4) that presents how our approach can help to verify the correct dynamic composition of a our logistics-based process use case. Each of them has got a compound name for example, "evt / inv / INV". A green logo situated on the left of the proof obligation name states that it has been proved (an A means it has been proved automatically). The main advantage of Event-B develop that can repair errors during the development. It allows the backward to correct specification. With refinement, the complexity of the system is distributed; the step by step proofs are more readily.

Proof Obligations
INITIALISATION/inv1/INV
INITIALISATION/inv2/INV
INITIALISATION/inv3/INV
check/grd3/WD
check/grd4/WD
check/grd5/WD
check/inv3/INV
substitute/inv1/INV

Fig. 4. proof obligation

6   Conclusion

In this paper, we were interested in the formalization and the verification of Web service properties for a dynamic composition. The proposed model is an extension of our papers [5] [6]. In this paper, we showed the necessity of a step of formal verification of Web services properties to ensure a dynamic services composition. The proposed model is formalized in event-B. A logistics-based process was used as use case in order to validate our approach. In order to extend this formalization we propose, as a future work, automating the process of extracting properties from a Web service using the tool BPEL2B presented in [7] and to integrate this verification step as a step in the process proposed by this tool.

References

1. Thakkar, S., Knoblock, C.A., Ambite, J.L.: A view integration approach to dynamic composition of web services. In: Proceedings of 2003 ICAPS Workshop on Planning for Web Services (2003)
2. Casati, F., Ilnicki, S., Jin, L., Krishnamoorthy, V., Shan, M.C.: Adaptive and dynamic service composition in eflow (2000)
3. Zhang, D., Chen, M., Zhou, L.: Dynamic and personalized web services composition in e-business. IS Management 22(3), 50–65 (2005)
4. Abrial, J.R.: Modeling in Event-B: System and Software Engineering. Cambridge University Press, Cambridge (2010)
5. Hamel, L., Graiet, M., Kmimech, M., Bhiri, M.T., Gaaloul, W.: A proof-based approach for verifying composite service transactional behavior. In: ICSEA, pp. 386–392 (2011)
6. Hamel, L., Graiet, M., Kmimech, M., Bhiri, M.T., Gaaloul, W.: Verifying Composite Service Transactional Behavior with EVENT-B. In: Crnkovic, I., Gruhn, V., Book, M. (eds.) ECSA 2011. LNCS, vol. 6903, pp. 67–74. Springer, Heidelberg (2011)
7. Ait-Sadoune, I., Ait-Ameur, Y.: From bpel to event-b. In: International Workshop on Integration of Model-based Formal Methods and Tools (IM FMT) at 7th International Conference on Integrated Formal Methods (IFM), Dusseldorf, Germany (2009)

Capability Modelling – Case of Logistics Capabilities

Wassim Derguech and Sami Bhiri

National University of Ireland, Galway
Digital Enterprise Research Institute
firstname.lastname@deri.org
www.deri.org

Abstract. Even though the concept of capability is an important element in service oriented architectures and enterprise information systems, little effort has been put towards modelling it as a first class citizen. Major related contributions were part of other efforts such as modelling business processes, service description and search requests. Current approaches either confuse capabilities with invocation interfaces, do not go beyond the classical IOPEs paradigm, or classify them into categories. Most of these approaches do not allow to determine intuitively what the exact capability is as well as they do not describe it with proper business features. In our work, we are interested in modelling and managing capabilities as stand alone entities, presented via an action verb and a set of domain related attributes/features. Presenting capabilities as such allows us to represent them at different levels of abstraction and make explicit links between them. In this paper, we highlight the benefits of our model and we build on top of it a set of requirements that allow end users to generate more custom capabilities. In order to illustrate our conceptual model benefits, we apply it in describing logistics capabilities.

Keywords: Capability Modelling, Logistics, Use Case.

1   Introduction

The concept of capability defines what an action can do from a functional perspective. An action can range from a simple task to a service or an entire business process. One of the objectives of a capability description is to allow customers to discover services or business processes that perform particular operations that satisfy their needs. In our work we focus on providing a conceptual model for describing capabilities and apply it in the logistics domain. In such context, a "good capability description" is a must either for allowing machine processing or human understandability.

The concept of capability is the glue point between services and business processes. A service gives access to a certain capability which can be achieved by a business process. Despite its importance, this concept has not drawn the research community attention as it deserves. Current approaches for capability modeling were in fact part of efforts for describing related concepts such as business processes, service descriptions and search requests.

We cluster current contributions in capability description into two main classes based on what paradigm is used for modelling capabilities. In the first class, capabilities are

M. La Rosa and P. Soffer (Eds.): BPM 2012 Workshops, LNBIP 132, pp. 519–529, 2013.

described in terms of Inputs, Outputs, Preconditions and Effects [1,2,3,4,5,6]. In such approaches, machine processing is highly privileged and capabilities as described with fine-grained semantics for supporting reasoning to allow for operations like planning, composition, etc. However, user centricity is somehow neglected, in such approaches, end users need search and read the documentation of the service or the business process in order to determine what the capability is (i.e., what a particular service or business process does). In the second class, capabilities are described via a set of attributes. Approaches described in EASY [7] and SoffD [8] are examples of this class. In these approaches, service are described via a set of attributes which allows for organising them respectively as a directed acyclic graph and a tree (i.e., the nodes are service descriptions presented as a set of attributes). However, the attributes used here are not intrinsic business features as they contain even non-functional properties which do not describe the capability from a business perspective.

In our research [9] (briefly discussed in Section 2), we provide a meta model for describing capabilities as first class citizens described via domain specific features and represented at several levels of abstraction. We define explicit links between these levels based on the attributes and attribute values in order to establish a *Capability Description Graph* as it has been done in EASY [7] and SoffD [8]. Unlike these contributions, we represent a capability as an action verb and a set of domain specific properties (i.e., attributes). The action verb as well as these attributes are defined in a domain related ontology that, to some extend, provides the possibles values each attribute can have.

In this paper, we move one step before describing capabilities. It consists of providing some guidelines to end users for creating new capabilities. To do so, we start from a domain ontology that contains fine grained definitions of the action verb, the set of attributes as well as the precondition and effect of a particular capability. Then we give another view of this fine grained description to a coarse grained one that contains some dependency rules between the various attributes associated to an action verb. These rules will be used by the end user when defining new capabilities.

The advantages of our approach are as follows. First, capabilities are described via an action verb a set of business attributes which make the determination of the described action more intuitive. Second, having the domain ontology, we can determine the fine grained semantics of capabilities. Third, the risk of making error when defining new capabilities is reduced.

The remainder of the paper is organized as follows. We start in Section 2 by recalling our method of describing capabilities by presenting our conceptual model. In Section 3, we define the structure of the domain ontology that contains the fine grained semantics of the actions. After this, we define in Section 4 the set of relations that might exist between the capabilities attributes that will serve as guidance mechanism for creating capabilities. Throughout the paper, we use a logistic example of capability, namely delivery capability. Before concluding the paper in Section 6, we review important contributions related to our work in Section 5.

2   A Meta-model for Capability Description

We consider a capability as an attribute featured entity. This entity is defined via an "*action verb*" and a set of "*attribute*"and "*value*" pairs. The *action verb* is not a simple lexical term that gives a natural language indication about what a capability does. It is a concept form a domain related ontology that defines the semantics of the action of the capability and to some extent, it defines the required attributes and their possible values. Definition 1 introduces the concept of capability in our meta-model.

Definition 1. A tuple *Cap = (ActionVerb,Attributes)* is a capability, where:

- *ActionVerb*: This concept has been previously introduced by [2] in order to define, in a natural language, what is the action being described. Different to [2], we consider the action verb as a concept from a domain related ontology that comes form a shared aggreeement on its semantics and it also comes with the required attributes for a particular capability and, to some extent, it defines their possible values.
- *Attributes*: Represents a set of pairs *(Attribute, AttributeValue)* that correspond to the set of characteristics of the capability. An *Attribute* corresponds to a particular property of the capability and *AttributeValue* corresponds either to the value or the possible values that this *Attribute* can have.

Fig. 1 depicts our conceptual model for defining capabilities. The model depicted here (i.e., Fig. 1) shows that a capability has an *ActionVerb* and a set of *Attributes*. Values of these *Attributes* can be of different types such as *EnumerationVlaue, DynamicValue, ConditionalValue*, etc. we refer the reader to a previous work [9] where we have presented in details these attribute types for modelling capabilities.

Defining capabilities as such (i.e., attribute featured entities) has several benefits [9]. First, contrary to the Input, Output, Precondition and Effect paradigm our model features the business and functional characteristics of capabilities which end users are mostly interested in and which are specified in their requests. For example, in logistics systems, users are more familiar in defining capabilities such as "deliver a particular package from a source address to a destination address" rather than a capability defined by a set of inputs, outputs, precondition and effect expressed with complex logical formulas using a particular language.

Second, our meta model can deal with capabilities at different abstraction levels in a uniform way. Levels of abstraction depend on the attributes and their types. We can for example define a delivery capability between any addresses, or a more concrete delivery capability within Europe by defining the range of the source and destination addresses respectively (i.e., any Geographical Location or European Location). In addition, we are able to establish relations between Capabilities at these abstraction levels using the *specify* and *extend* relations (see Fig. 1). For example we explicitly represent that a delivery within Ireland is more specific (specify relation) than a delivery within Europe.

Furthermore, as our meta model defines semantic links between Capabilities (i.e., specify and extend), capability owners can rapidly and easily define new Capabilities by reusing previous definitions. For example if a logistic provider wants to include a new delivery capability to his portfolio that operates within France, he can select the European delivery capability and specify its source and destination addresses. In addition, these relations define a directed acyclic graph of Capabilities where navigation techniques can be developed as an alternative to goal based discovery techniques.

A directed acyclic graph of capabilities description can be easily queried using SPARQL. Actually, we use RDF as a lightweight language for describing and linking

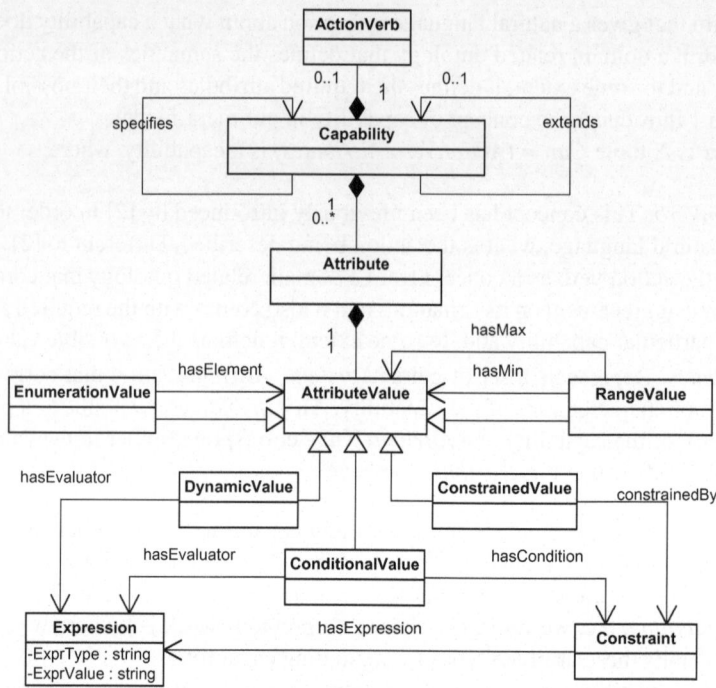

Fig. 1. Capability UML class diagram [9]

capabilities descriptions whereas we can use SPARQL for advanced querying including the usage of SPARQL as a rule language [10].

Finally, since our meta model is RDF based it can be easily extended, while preserving the attribute-featured principle, by considering other types of attributes (such as optional and mandatory attributes) and other types of attribute values.

In a previous work [9], we have presented in details our conceptual model for capability description. In this paper, we build on top of such model some useful guidelines that allow for creating capability descriptions respecting this conceptual model. In the rest of the paper, we will present, having a domain ontology and a set of relations between the attributes, how an end user can define new capabilities.

3 Description of a Domain Ontology for Capabilities

A domain ontology allows for making explicit the knowledge needed in a particular domain. Using a domain ontology for describing capabilities helps to reduce any problems related to the definitions of business terms. In our work, we consider domain ontologies as a key element in modelling capabilities. Indeed, a capability domain ontology defines the action verbs, their related attributes and their possible values as well as the fine grained semantics of describing the corresponding capability in terms of Precondition and Effect. In other words, we use a capability domain ontology as a shared conceptualisation between capability descriptions that expresses the action verb, the attributes, the preconditions and the effects.

Listing 1 shows a fragment of an ontology for physical delivery. In here, the delivery ontology contains attributes such as *ActionVerb, Item, Source*, and *Destination*. This intuitively allows defining capabilities that consist of delivering a physical object from a particular geographical location to another one. We use *vcard*[1] vocabulary for expressing addresses (line 11). We use PDDL 2.1[2] (Planning Domain Definition Language) syntax for describing both the precondition and effect expressions. We use cap[3] to refer to our capability meta-model.

```
1   @prefix dco: <http://vocab.deri.ie/delivery_capability_ontology#>.
2   @prefix vcard: <http://www.w3.org/2006/vcard/ns#>.
3   @prefix cap: <http://vocab.deri.ie/cap#>.
4
5   dco:PhysicalDelivery a rdf:Class.
6
7   dco:Deliver cap:ActionVerb dco:Deliver.
8
9   dco:PhysicalDelivery cap:hasActionVerb dco:Deliver.
10
11  dco:Source a cap:attribute; rdfs:range vcard:Address.
12
13  dco:Destination a cap:attribute; rdfs:range vcard:Address.
14
15  dco:Item a cap:attribute; rdfs:range dco:PhysicalObject.
16
17  dco:Precondition a cap:Expression; cap:exprType "PDDL 2.1";
18       cap:expValue "and PhysicalObject ?Item
19                        GeoLocation ?Source
20                        GeoLocation ?Destination
21                        Location ?Item ?Source".
22
23  dco:PhysicalDelivery cap:hasPrecondition dco:Precondition.
24
25  dco:Effect a cap:Expression; cap:exprType "PDDL 2.1";
26       cap:expValue "Location ?Item ?Destination".
27
28  dco:PhysicalDelivery cap:hasEffect dco:Effect.
```

Listing 1. Snippet of the Ontology for Physical Delivery

It is important to consider that the semantics of the capability related to a particular ActionVerb depend on the set of attributes. If we refer to the example of Listing 1, we can affirm that this capability cannot be possible if the item is not a physical object and the source and destination are not two geographical locations. If we combine other set of attributes, we can define different capability semantics. Consequently, for each action verb and a set of attributes, we end up with a specific precondition and effect:

$$ActionVerb + \{SET\_ATTRIBUTES_1\} \Rightarrow \{Precondition_1, Effect_1\}$$

---

[1] http://www.w3.org/Submission/vcard-rdf/
[2] International Planning Competition,
  http://planning.cis.strath.ac.uk/competition/
[3] http://vocab.deri.ie/cap

$$ActionVerb + \{SET\_ATTRIBUTES_2\} \Rightarrow \{Precondition_2, Effect_2\}$$

$$\dots$$

$$ActionVerb + \{SET\_ATTRIBUTES_N\} \Rightarrow \{Precondition_N, Effect_N\}$$

As a reminder, the *ActionVerb* and the set of *Attributes* constitute the coarse-grained semantics of the capability; adding to them the *Precondition* and the *Effect* we end up with the fine-grained semantics. On the one hand, from an end user perspective, defining capabilities at a coarse-grained semantics is much easier (i.e., no need to define any predicate or logical formula for the precondition and effect). On the other hand, fine-grained semantics is highly needed for machine processing.

In our work, we aim to allow for determining fine grained semantics from a coarse-grained semantics. To do so, we need to have a minimal set of combinations of an *ActionVerb* and *Attributes* with their corresponding *Precondition* and the *Effect*. Using these combinations, we can derive the fine grained semantics of a given set of *ActionVerb* and *Attributes*. This minimal set of combinations constitute our capability domain ontology.

We refer to Table 1 for illustrating an example of delivery capability domain ontology. The first line of this table describes the ontology snippet of Listing 1. (For presentation purposes, we do not use prefixes for the names of attributes.)

Table 1 has four columns each of these columns contains respectively:

1. the action verb which is in our case "Deliver": in this particular example we used this verb because it is somehow the most intuitive term. But, in general this is not a term that has natural language meaning. This is a concept from an ontology that describes a particular action.
2. the related set of attributes: these attributes are specific features that have a particular business meaning in the definition of the capability. Actually, the action "Deliver" consists of moving an item from a source to a destination. Consequently, we can define a delivery capability with the action verb "Deliver" and the attributes "Item", "Source" and "Destination" (see in line 1 of Table 1). Other attributes can also be used for refining more the definition of the capability such as "Vehicle" (see in line 2 of Table 1) that indicates what means of transport has been used to deliver the "Item" or the "Route" (see in line 4 of Table 1) followed for the delivery as well as the number of days "Within" (see in line 3 of Table 1) within which the delivery should be done. Each attribute is described in a one line that contains the name of the attribute followed by its type.
3. the precondition: logical formula that must hold true in order for the capability to be successfully executed.
4. and the effect: logical formula describing the results of the capability execution over the state of the world.

Please note that we use PDDL 2.1[4] (Planning Domain Definition Language) syntax for describing both the precondition and effect expressions. In each line of Table 1, we use

---

[4] International Planning Competition,
http://planning.cis.strath.ac.uk/competition/

either an atomic or a conjunction of atomic formulas (i.e., if the expression starts by "and"). An atomic formula is presented as: PREDICATE_NAME ?ARG1 ... ?ARG_N (e.g., *Location ?Item ?Source* is interpreted as: the location of the item is at the source address).

Table 1. This table shows our domain ontology

Action Verb	Attributes	Precondition	Effect
Deliver	Item= dco:PhysicalObject Source= vcard:Address Destination= vcard:Address	and PhysicalObject ?Item GeoLocation ?Source GeoLocation ?Destination Location ?Item ?Source	Location ?Item ?Destination
Deliver	Item= dco:PhysicalObject Source= vcard:Address Destination= vcard:Address Vehicle= Vehicle	and PhysicalObject ?Item GeoLocation ?Source GeoLocation ?Destination Location ?Item ?Source Vehicle ?Vehicle Available ?Vehicle	Location ?Item ?Destination
Deliver	Item= dco:PhysicalObject Source= vcard:Address Destination= vcard:Address Within= dco:Days	and PhysicalObject ?Item GeoLocation ?Source GeoLocation ?Destination Location ?Item ?Source	and Location ?Item ?Destination DeliveredBefore ?Days
Deliver	Item= dco:PhysicalObject Source= vcard:Address Destination= vcard:Address Route= dco:Route	and PhysicalObject ?Item GeoLocation ?Source GeoLocation ?Destination Location ?Item ?Source Route ?Route Scheduled ?Route	and Location ?Item ?Destination FollowedRoute ?Route
Deliver	EDoc= dco:ElectronicDoc ToEMail= dco:EMail FromEMail= dco:EMail	and ElectronicDoc ?EDoc EMailAdr ?ToEMail EMailAdr ?ToEMail	EMailSent ?EDoc
Deliver	Item= dco:PhysicalObject Prod= dco:Producer Cust= dco:Consumer	and PhysicalObject ?Item Producer ?Prod Consumer ?Cust	HandDelivered ?Item
Deliver	Service= dco:NonPhysicalObject SProd= dco:ServiceProvider SCust= dco:ServiceConsumer	and NonPhysicalObject ?Service ServiceProvider ?SProd ServiceConsumer ?SCust	ServiceDelivered ?Service

From this domain ontology (i.e., Table 1), we can notice that for a particular action verb and a combination of a set of attributes, we can associate specific fine grained semantics (i.e., precondition and effect). In our work, we aim to create another view of this domain ontology such that it helps for creating capabilities without having to define their fine grained semantics. In other words, we want an end user creating capabilities following the conceptual model introduced previously. Eventually, for each capability defined by the end user, we can determine the corresponding fine grained semantics by using this domain ontology.

Recall, we aim to provide a user centric capability modelling method. In our context, the end user has to define for a particular action verb the set of attributes he needs. However, the user needs to be guided for not creating unrealistic capabilities. To this end, we aim to determine some relations that the user has to consider while creating his custom capabilities. These relations define the possible dependencies that exist between attributes. For example, there exist an interdependency between the attributes *dco:Route*, *dco:Source* and *dco:Destination* in the delivery example. This interdependency states for example that we cannot find a capability that has particular *dco:Route* where the *dco:Source* and *dco:Destination* are not taken into account. In the following, we describe the possible relations that we consider.

4   Guidance Relations

As stated previously, we aim to provide a set of guidelines for the end user in order to create capabilities described according to the conceptual model of Section 2. To this end, we defined a set of relations that must hold between the attributes and their types when creating new capabilities. These guidelines can be seen as another view of the domain ontology presented in Section 3.

This is still a work in progress that can be extended. For the moment we have defined a first set of relations that exist between attributes that are clustered under two categories:

– Unary relations: exist between the attribute and the entity it describes (i.e., the capability).
– Multi-party relations: exist between several attributes (as well as sets of attributes).

Unary relations : At this level of our research we have determined only one possible unary relation:

– *Mandatory (Set)*: exactly one of the attributes of *Set* must be available in any capability description.

According to our example, a delivery capability requires one of the attributes *"dco:Item"*, *"dco:EDoc"* and *"dco:Service"*. Consequently, for the delivery capabilities, we have this rule:

– Mandatory (dco:Item, dco:EDoc,dco:Service)

Multi-party relations : At this level of our research we have determined only three possible multi-party relations:

1. *TypeDepend(at,Set)*: the type of *at* depends on the type of the attributes in *Set*. Consequently, if a capability contains the attribute *at*, it must contain also the attributes of *Set*.

   According to our example, in a delivery capability the attribute *"dco:Route"* depends on the attributes *"dco:Source"* and *"dco:Destination"*. Consequently, for the delivery capabilities, we have this rule:

   – TypeDepend(dco:Route,{dco:Source,dco:Destination})

2. *Coexist(Set)*: all the attributes of Set must exist together in each capability description. In other words, if one of the attributes of Set is part of a capability description; the other attributes of Set must also be part of this description. There is no need to have any Value dependency.

According to our example, in a delivery capability the attributes *dco:ToEMAIL* and *dco:FromEMail* must exist together. Consequently, for the delivery capabilities, we have this rule:

- Coexist(dco:ToEMail,dco:dco:From)

3. *Exclusion(Set)*: The attributes in Set cannot exist together in a capability description. They are all mutually exclusive.

    According to our example, we can never have a delivery capability with the attributes *dco:ToEMail* and *dco:Vehicle*. Consequently, for the delivery capabilities, we have this rule:

- Exclusion(dco:Vehicle,dco:ToEMail)

Having the domain ontology described in Section 3 together with these relations between the attributes, end users can create new capabilities according to our meta model of the Section 2. This way, enven with a capability description having only the action verb and a set of attributes, we can determine its semantics by generating the corresponding preconditions and effects. For example, if a user defines a delivery capability with the attributes "dco:Item", "dco:Source", "dco:Destination", "dco:vehiclue" and "dco:Within", we can determine the corresponding preconditions and effects by applying a conjunction operation between the preconditions and effects of line 2 and line 3 of Table 1 (i.e., domain ontology). We refer to Table 2 for a more detailed description of this capability and its corresponding precondition and effect.

Table 2. This table shows a delivery capability using a particular vehicle within a particular number of days with its corresponding Precondition and Effect

Action Verb	Attributes	Precondition	Effect
Deliver	Item= dco:PhysicalObject Source= vcard:Address Destination= vcard:Address Vehicle= Vehicle Within= dco:Days	and PhysicalObject ?Item GeoLocation ?Source GeoLocation ?Destination Location ?Item ?Source Vehicle ?Vehicle Available ?Vehicle	and Location ?Item ?Destination DeliveredBefore ?Days

5   Related Work

The Semantic Web uses ontologies and languages allowing several ways to describe web services. For example WSDL-S[5] and its successor SA-WSDL [11,12] use ontologies to enrich WSDL description and XML Schema of Web services with semantic annotations. Such techniques consider a capability as an invocation interface. However, as explained in this paper a capability is not an interface. It is an entity featured via a set of attributes. In this paper, we share the same vision of OASIS Reference Model[6] and

---

[5] http://www.w3.org/Submission/WSDL-S
[6] OASIS Reference Model for Service Oriented Architecture 1.0,
  http://www.oasis-open.org/committees/download.php/19679/
  soa-rm-cs.pdf

consider a service as an access mechanism to a capability. Within this vision the invocation interface is only one aspect of the whole service description. We believe that our vision and understanding of capability is more accurate. The background of the genesis of SOA, which is distributed method invocation, has influenced these techniques.

In a more refined fashion, languages such as OWL-S [6], WSMO [1], SWSO[7], provide a semantic description of Web services. However, these approaches do not go beyond the classical IOPE paradigm to define services capabilities. They do not feature the business aspects of a capability. In addition, they describe capabilities at an abstract level. They are not able to model concrete capabilities that correspond to specific needs of consumers. However, what clients are interested in are concrete capabilities. The matching of consumer requests has to be against concrete capabilities.

There exist other contributions that were more focusing on extending this IOPE paradigm. For example Oaks et al., [2] proposed a model for describing service capabilities going one step beyond the IOPE paradigm by distinguishing in particular the corresponding action verb and informational attributes (called roles in the paper [2]). Additionally, [3,4,5] have identified the gap between current modeling techniques and real world requirements and initiated the discussions about abstract services and concrete offers descriptions. [4] and [5] rely on and extend the IOPE paradigm without making explicit and clear the business features of services functionalities.

Different from IOPE paradigm, EASY [7] and SoffD [8] propose to describe services via a set of attributes. Using such presentation, services are organised respectively as a directed acyclic graph or a tree. This allows for improved matchmaking techniques that relies on exploring the organizing structure. However, in these approaches, attributes used are not intrinsic business features as they contain even non-functional properties which do not describe the capability from a business perspective. Unlike these contributions, we represent a capability as an action verb and a set of domain specific properties (i.e., attributes). The action verb as well as these attributes are defined in a domain ontology that, to some extend, provides the possibles values each attribute can have.

6   Conclusion

The concept of capability is an important asset either in service computing or process management. Although, this concept has not attracted as much attention as it deserves and it has been marginally modeled as part of other concepts such service description, process modelling or search requests. The notion of capability is a fundamental concept not only for SOA (Service Oriented Architecture) but also for enterprise information systems. The ARIS architecture [13] recognizes the importance of the functional perspective in enterprise information systems and considers it as one of its views. In our work, we are interested in modelling capabilities as stand alone entities described via an action verb and set of domain specific attributes.

Actually, one of the major shortcomings of presenting capabilities as we do is that we do not provide a fine-grained semantics of the actions that is useful for reasoning to do planning or composition operations. To overcome this problem, we have presented in this paper a domain ontology that is detailed enough to allow for generating such fine-grained semantics.

---

[7] http://www.w3.org/Submission/SWSF-SWSO

In this paper, we have shown how using this domain related ontology and some relations between the attributes defining capabilities, we can guide the user to create new capabilities. This also enables moving from the coarse grained semantics of the capabilities to fine grained semantics from the domain ontology.

This work is still in progress, and further investigations over the relations between attributes are still under consideration. Additionally, we have not defined a complete methodology for deriving fine grained semantics from capability descriptions and the domain ontology. The only operation that we consider is the conjuntion between the precondition and effects as presented in Section 4.

Acknowledgment. This work is funded by the Lion II project supported by Science Foundation Ireland under grant number SFI/08/CE/I1380 Lion-2.

References

1. Roman, D., de Bruijn, J., Mocan, A., Lausen, H., Domingue, J., Bussler, C.J., Fensel, D.: WWW: WSMO, WSML, and WSMX in a Nutshell. In: Mizoguchi, R., Shi, Z.-Z., Giunchiglia, F. (eds.) ASWC 2006. LNCS, vol. 4185, pp. 516–522. Springer, Heidelberg (2006)
2. Oaks, P., ter Hofstede, A.H.M., Edmond, D.: Capabilities: Describing What Services Can Do. In: Orlowska, M.E., Weerawarana, S., Papazoglou, M.P., Yang, J. (eds.) ICSOC 2003. LNCS, vol. 2910, pp. 1–16. Springer, Heidelberg (2003)
3. Kopecký, J., Simperl, E.P.B., Fensel, D.: Semantic Web Service Offer Discovery. In: SMRR. CEUR Workshop Proceedings, vol. 243 (2007)
4. Vitvar, T., Zaremba, M., Moran, M.: Dynamic Service Discovery Through Meta-interactions with Service Providers. In: Franconi, E., Kifer, M., May, W. (eds.) ESWC 2007. LNCS, vol. 4519, pp. 84–98. Springer, Heidelberg (2007)
5. Zaremba, M., Vitvar, T., Moran, M., Haselwanter, T.: WSMX Discovery for the SWS Challenge. In: ISWC, Athens, Georgia, USA (November 2006)
6. Martin, D., Paolucci, M., Wagner, M.: Bringing Semantic Annotations to Web Services: OWL-S from the SAWSDL Perspective. In: Aberer, K., Choi, K.-S., Noy, N., Allemang, D., Lee, K.-I., Nixon, L.J.B., Golbeck, J., Mika, P., Maynard, D., Mizoguchi, R., Schreiber, G., Cudré-Mauroux, P. (eds.) ASWC 2007 and ISWC 2007. LNCS, vol. 4825, pp. 340–352. Springer, Heidelberg (2007)
7. Mokhtar, S.B., Preuveneers, D., Georgantas, N., Issarny, V., Berbers, Y.: Easy: Efficient semantic service discovery in pervasive computing environments with qos and context support. Journal of Systems and Software 81(5), 785–808 (2008)
8. Zaremba, M., Vitvar, T., Bhiri, S., Derguech, W., Gao, F.: Service Offer Descriptions and Expressive Search Requests – Key Enablers of Late Service Binding. In: Huemer, C., Lops, P. (eds.) EC-Web 2012. LNBIP, vol. 123, pp. 50–62. Springer, Heidelberg (2012)
9. Bhiri, S., Derguech, W., Zaremba, M.: Web services capability meta model. In: WebIST (2012)
10. Polleres, A.: From sparql to rules (and back). In: WWW, pp. 787–796. ACM (2007)
11. Kopecký, J., Vitvar, T., Bournez, C., Farrell, J.: Sawsdl: Semantic annotations for wsdl and xml schema. IEEE Internet Computing 11(6) (2007)
12. Lathem, J., Gomadam, K., Sheth, A.P.: Sa-rest and (s)mashups: Adding semantics to restful services. In: ICSC. IEEE Computer Society (2007)
13. Scheer, A.W., Schneider, K.: ARIS Architecture of Integrated Information Systems. Bernus Peter Mertins Kai Schmidt Gunter (2006)

Modeling Migration of Mobile Agents

Marzougui Borhen[1], Khaled Hassine[2], and Kamel Barkaoui[3]

[1] Emirates College of Technology -Abu Dhabi, UAE, P.O.BOX 41009
[2] FSG, City Riadh, Zrig, Gabès, 6072, Tunisia
[3] CNAM, 292 Rue Saint-Martin Paris 75 141, Cedex 03 Paris, France

Abstract. In Modeling Multi agent systems (MAS), the mobility of agent is a basic issue to express interactions of flow actions, consequently, modelling migration process is a crucial issue. In this paper, we integrate the Ferber and Müller's Influence/Reaction model in Agent Petri Nets (APN) to model migration mobile agents. This model clarifies the migration process of agent from an environment to another and enhances its capacity for formal verification.

Keywords: Multi Agent Systems. Mobility. Migration. Influence/Reaction. Agent Petri Nets. Verification.

1   Introduction

System modeling is an important task. The complexity is more important if the system is open and dynamic. In such problems it's hard to decide since it involves modeling unbounded dynamic entities. It requires complex techniques of abstraction, creation of discrete and finite models, to approach system. Developers must submit the model to a solid and complete test to achieve desired quality, particularly in terms of robustness and reliability. In this context, the use of formal methods is inevitable. These methods need a rich and varied literature depending on the target system and its scope. Our work is focusing, particularly on the migration process of mobile agents. The main objective is to provide models that describe the behavior of the system in a precise and unambiguous manner while taking into account the complexity introduced by mobility agents that are of various types and can produce unwanted behaviors. This leads to a much more difficult investigation. Indeed, a Mobile Agent has the option to migrate from one site to another looking for information not found or to meet other agents in order to better performing its tasks [1].

Several studies in the literature such as [2], [3], [4] and [5] provide techniques that guide the designer of the Multi-Agent System (MAS) from specification until validation. [6] proposes an algorithm for constructing a predicate/transition model for robotic operations. However, this model considers the interaction between the agents as indirect, which increases exponentially the number of states. The number of states is reduced in the works of [7]. More recently, [8] and [9] model the mobility of the components of a system using Petri Nets (PN). In [10], authors proposed a PN model for the control of a distributed manufacturing system. This model supports

M. La Rosa and P. Soffer (Eds.): BPM 2012 Workshops, LNBIP 132, pp. 530–540, 2012.
© Springer-Verlag Berlin Heidelberg 2012

verification properties related to the operation of each system entity in its own environment, while no tools are introduced to analyze agent's relationship of and other environments.

To achieve this objective, the paper is organized as follows: The second section describes related work. Section 3 presents techniques for modeling the migration of Mobile Agents. Our contribution to a new model of migration is detailed in Section 4. In Section 5, we apply the model already set on a real case. Finally, we conclude the results proved.

2   Related Work

The work already undertaken in the field of MAS does not integrate modeling of agents' migration in the development cycle. Most formal techniques have not addressed the modeling and verification of the Migration Agents Mobile. The work of [11] and [9] describes the communication of agents within the same environment and does not model the migration process explicitly.

In modeling and simulation of [12], model of migration is taken as a predefined task and standard platform for hosting agents. Many platforms like mobile agents OMG, Repast and Mason provide the mechanism for migration but not its politics.

In [2], programming language for autonomous mobile agents is created. This language allows the realization of multi-agent systems for cognitive agents stationary. To represent the mobility of agents, CLAIM [11] defined primitives for mobility. This language is applied as the platform SyMPA. A mobility post is only used by this platform. The only requirement for mobility operations is that the agents involved are the same hierarchical level.

However, [4] proposes a parallel simulation model based on the distribution of conflicts arising between agents, and a dynamic load balancing between processors through policy known as " Dynamic Auto-partition". This leads to insufficient control of the Agent's behavior when changing it during migration. Recently, researchers have relied work on modeling techniques for distributed applications. Indeed, [12] define two levels of modeling: the first is the structural side by examining architecture of Mobile Agents. The second level models the agents hosting environments. However, [9] proposed a model of an agent security policy which visits different sites. Indeed, the transfer of code may undergo undesirable changes during migration. To solve this problem the authors proposed a technique based on modeling site sending code and site hosting the code. [13] indicates that the migration modeling is integrated into the communication model. This creates an ambiguity to distinguish the behavior generated locally (within the same environment) and externally (inter-environment). In [14], the authors express the continuity of the running environment of mobile agents. This does not give "freedom" for an agent to choose his next environment and model cannot build according to current perceptions and actions.

Our work focuses on creation of a model describing the migration in MAS. In fact, the idea is to build an interface called "Migration Interface ", which promotes a model description of the relationship between a mobile agent, its departure environment and its arrival environment. To control the behavior of each agent, each environment, and thus the entire system, we apply theory of Influence / Reaction model [15].

3   Modeling the Migration Agents

Using of mobile agents is now strongly recommended. But, this causes problems of security, privacy, management and monitoring. Many studies of development platforms for mobile agents are marketed, including Aglet, Voyager, Odyssey, NetLogo, Swarm, Repast and Mason. These studies focus on developing an environment of mobile agents. Indeed, they concern the creation of agents, transmission and local communication. Mobility leads to direct implementation of this environment by using multiple tasks (threads). Most of these platforms do not guarantee the transmission of the state vector of agents before and after migration since the resumption of architecture must be made by the designer. On the other platforms of mobile agent, migration is described in a straightforward manner by a code, generally object oriented, such as MADKIT, JADE, ZEUS and JNA. Although the agents share certain characteristics or behavioral level, it is difficult to transform a model from one platform to another. This is due to the lack of a generic model independent of implementation of code.

We propose a "pattern", based on, APN (Agent Petri Nets), which describes in clear and simple components involved in migration (mobile agents, departure environment and arrival environment). These components change dynamically according to the connection between them.

We apply a new model to describe changes of these different behavioral components. Influence / Reaction Model is proposed by [16]. It seeks to separate "what is produced by the agents (influence) from what actually occurs (reaction)" resulting from the coupling influences. In [17], this model was used to check the actions of agents in simulation. Indeed, in the MAS, to verify and to validate certain properties, most research use, in simulation, a dedicated platform. Systems based Mobile Agents is open making, it difficult to simulate different kinds of environments. The degree of certainty according to this validation is insufficient. This therefore, makes a formal validation. Models Petri Nets has often been conducted to verify the competitor aspect as that of [1] and [17] applied in the field of biology. [14] present an operational plan and comprehensive audit of MAS conversation protocol validation of agents. Despite the use of Petri Nets in many modeling of MAS, many of them have not clearly shown aspects of migration agents.

In our study, we focus on the modeling of migration agents. The complex nature of the task dictates the need to use formalism with a great expressive power to model, analyze, verify and validate the changes. Although various formal languages were used in this context, Agents Petri Nets [18] have the advantage to represent the notions of competition, synchronization, modularity and reusability, and an ease of design for MAS. Indeed, agents are presented by tokens.

4   APN Model of Migration

4.1   Presentation of a New Model

The challenge is to construct a formal framework to ensure the accuracy and security of the modeling phase. This model describes and controls the mobility of agents from one environment to another.

A conventional approach in the engineering of PN is to start by creating model, find marking graph, deduce the covering graph (if necessary) and deduce the properties. Although modeling by a Petri nets provides dynamic control systems, a non-expert developer in the engineering of PN faces difficulty in creating the model. So, We simplified the development process by creating a matrix called "Migration Matrix".

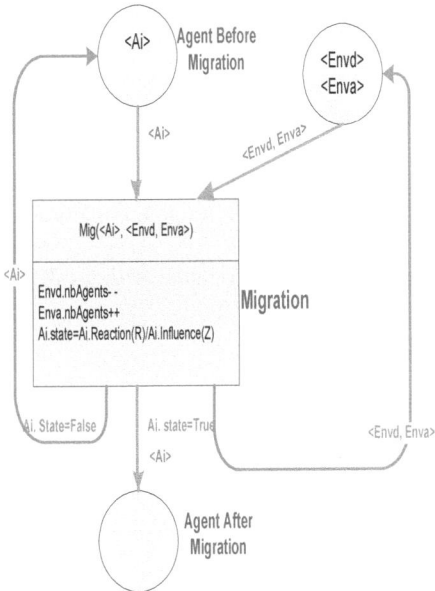

Fig. 1. Model of Migration

We define the migration model of Mobile Agents by a following Petri Nets:
R =< Env, MIG, A, Pre, Post, Z, L, Ei> where:

— Env is a non-empty finished set of places (environment of departure Envd, or of Arrival Enva).
— MIG is a non-empty finished set of Transitions (Migration).
— A is a non-empty finished set of tokens (Mobile Agents); with na=Card (A).
— Pre: Envd x MIG→Enva: an application of front incidence corresponds to environment of departure.

- Post: Enva x MIG →Envd: a back application of incidence environment of Arrival.
- Z: Influence of agent.
- L: Reaction of agent.
- Ei : state variable of environnement.

Consequently, the APN model is presented by Fig.1:

4.2   Model Analysis

In the APN model of Migration, tokens represent agents. Each square symbolizes a state model environments or agents; the transition indicates the initiation of a migration event.

The model we propose is described as follows:

- Env = {Env1, Env2, ..., EnvK}: finite set of non-empty places and each place denotes a state environments or agents.
- Each Envi Environment can be a departure environment (Envd) or arrival (Enva).
- (Mig: non non-empty finished set of transitions, each transition denotes the step of migration. This transition represents an "Interface" between migrant Agent, Envd and Enva.
- Migration of Agent Aj from environment Envd to another results in a crossing token Aj from one place to another through a transition. This is defined by:
- Mig (Ai, <Envd,Enva>).
- For each environment En, Ei is associated with a token that describes its status and any relevant information such as:

  - Ei.Name_Environnement;
  - Ei.Number_Agents_Mobiles, which is incremented when a new agent host environment and decrements if an agent leaves him;
  - Ei.GetInfluence (Aj) returns to the influences Ei of Aj;
  - Ei. GetRéaction (Aj): return the feedback of actions on Ei.

- For each agent, we associate the Boolean function "state" that determines whether an agent will migrate or not Aj.state = (Aj. Reaction (L) / Aj.Influence (Z) <= Threshold (Aj)), with Threshold (Aj) utility function is determined by Enva or Envd Agent can migrate. Uses of Ei can check the status of environmental friendly mobile agents:

  - Initially: Ei. GetInfluence (Aj) = Aj. Influence (Z); with Z is the set of actions to be performed by the agent Aj;
  - After Migration: Ei.GetInfluence (Aj) = Aj. Reaction (L) where L is the set of actions performed by Aj during its migration.
  - The migration of an agent Aj presents a change in 3 levels:
    - Level 1: Departure environment by updating its state variable Ed;
    - Level 2: Mobile Agent for the implementation of actions Aj.Reaction (L) from Aj.Influence(Z);
    - Level 3: Arrival Environment by updating its state variable Ea.

Thus an environment can undergo 3 changes:

- Change 1: When one or more agents leave;
- Change 2: When agents are in the environment;
- Change 3: When one or more agents join him.

Our model is able to distinguish these three levels and these three changes from the bay of places that indicates the level 2 and change 2, by the arcs connected in transitions, indicate level 1.To Indicate a change and lastly, we used the arcs connected downstream transitions for the level 3 and change 3.

Thus, we define a matrix called "Matrix Migration" presented in Fig. 2. This matrix describes a simple departure environment based on those of arrival at the Migration Agents.

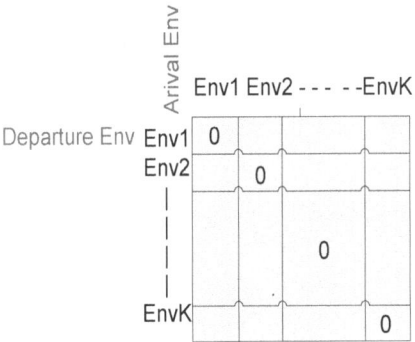

Fig. 2. Migration Matrix

- It is a square matrix that presents the departure environments on line and on column the arrival environments.
- The size of the matrix is k: number of environments.
- The diagonal of the matrix is always filled with zero values (the departure environment is same as the arrival environments: no migration).

5   Example: Study of the Management of the Maritime Transport

5.1   Modeling of System

To validate the proposed approach, we apply the migration model to manage the problem of the Management of the Maritime Transport. Our objective is to model the field of maritime transport by multi agent systems to control the crossing of boats from one port to another.

Table 1. Example of Modeling System

Container	Departure Port	Arrival Port	Boat
C1	Port1	Port2	B1
C2	Port1	Port3	B1
C3	Port1	Port4	B1
C4	Port2	Port4	B1
C5	Port1	Port4	B2

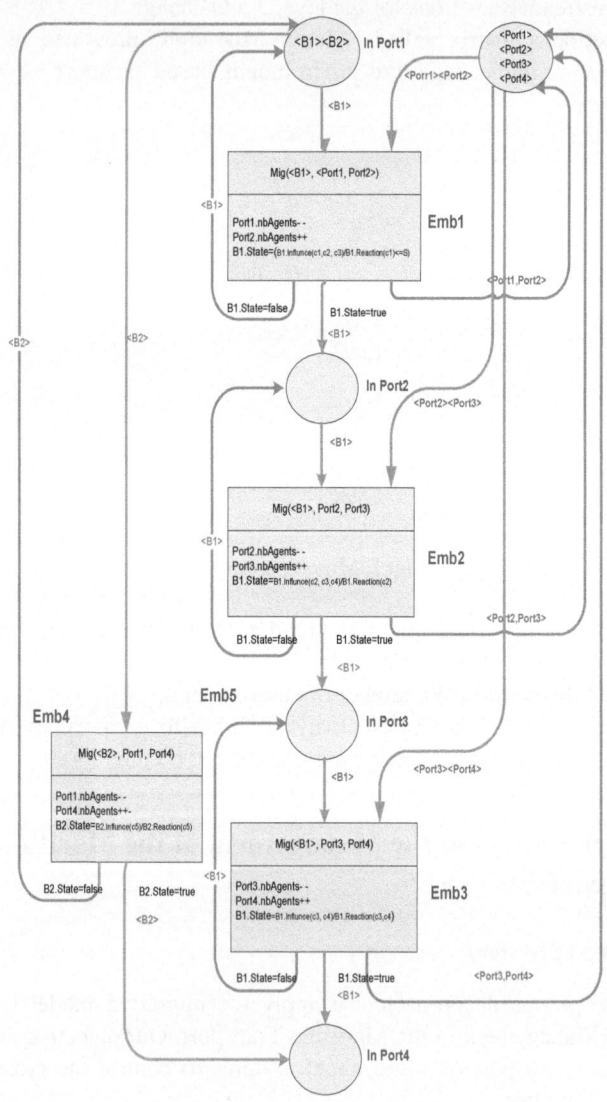

Fig. 3. Migration Model of Boats

We intend to model, verify and validate the operation of the system composed by:

— B1 and B2 are boats embarking from a port to another.
— Port: Port1, Port2, Port 3 and Port4 hosting containers aboard a vessel B1or B2.
— Some containers that should be moved from a port to another depending on the following requests.

In the APN migration model, boats B1 and B2 are two mobile agents. Ports are welcoming the environments of boats.

5.2   Verification with Migration Matrix (cf Fig. 4)

A boat must exist on a single line of migration matrix, this translates to: Verif_Agent (Ports, 4, B1) = true; checks at one point, the boat B1 exists on one of the Port. (Delete 4 and Ports). Similarly for the boat B2 Verif_Agent (Ports, 4, B2) = true for checking all boats, we propose Verif_Mig (Ports, 4) = true; It verifies that each boat is in a single Port. To check the interface of migration for a boat B1, we must know the ports of departure and arrival: Recherche_Env (Ports, 4, B1, Port1, Port2) = (1, 2).

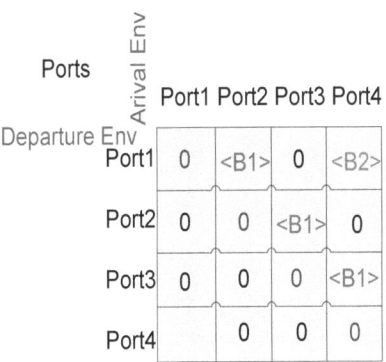

Fig. 4. Migration Matrix

Initially if Mo (<B1> <B2>, 0, 0, 0) then the Ports visited by the vessel B1 and B2 are given respectively by:

• Mig(B1)= Port2, Port3, Port4 and Port1;
• Mig(B2)= Port4 and Port1.

Conversely, attempts ships visiting Ports by:

• Env(Port1)=B1 and B2;
• Env(Port2)=B1;
• Env(Port3)=B1;
• Env(Port4)=B1 and B2.

5.3   Properties Verification of the Boat Model Migration

We construct the Reachability tree of APN migration model (cf Fig. 5)

From the Reachability tree we deduce the following properties:

— The marking shows that a boat at a given time can only exist on one port.
— The model is safe because a port cannot accommodate more than one boat (M0 or M7).
— A change in the number of tokens in places is well controlled. This depends on Migration. This coverage shows the stability of the system.
— The number of mobile agents is constant, therefore the model is bounded.
— The APN is conservative because the set of all places is a conservative component.
— Throughout the migration, the graph of markings never presents a zero weight vector.
— Each transition is quasi - live; hence the whole network is quasi -live.

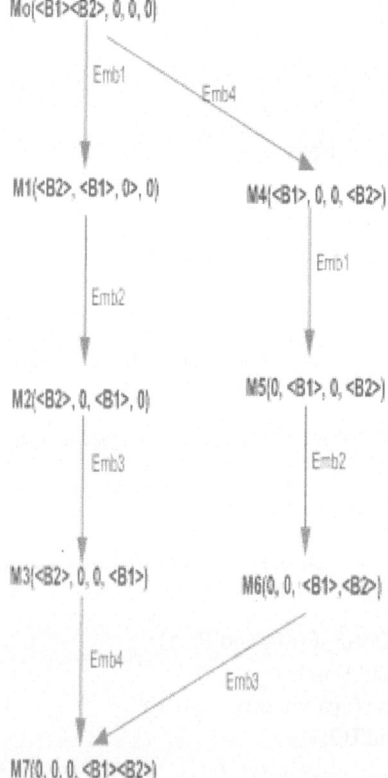

Fig. 5. Reachability tree of APN migration model of Boat

6   Conclusion

Despite the simplicity of the model that we have developed in this work, it offers the possibility to model a migration with a rigorous and efficient manner. Indeed, two levels of modeling are presented. The first is behavioral, where we applied through the model influence / reaction. This ensures reliability for the realization of agents' actions. The second level is structural and provided through the graphical APN model. The migration model developed is bounded, but not live. Its integration is possible with other types of MAS models, especially the communication model. Our approach can be used to create a new property of MAS: environments communicating through a standard interface.

References

1. Harrison, C., Chess, M., Kershen-baum, A.: Mobile agents: Are they a good idea? Technical report, Mars, IBM Research Report, T.J. Watson Research Center, Yorktown Heights, NY (1995)
2. Seghrouchni, A., Suna, A.: CLAIM and SyMPA: A Programming Environment for Intelligent and Mobile Agents. In: 4th Chapter of the book Multi-Agent Programming: Languages, Platforms and Applications, pp. 95–122. Kluwer Academic Publishers, Springer (July 2003)
3. Huget, M.: Engineering interaction protocols for multi-agent systems. PhD thesis, IX-Dauphine University Paris, France, pp. 69–71 (2001)
4. Makram, B., Vincent, C., Stéphane, V., François, C.: Parallel simulation of stochastic agent/environment interaction model. Integrated Computer-Aided Engineering 3, 123–130 (2003)
5. Sibertin, B., Cardoso, J., Hanachi, C.: Specification of interaction protocol with Petri Net. In: actes des JFIADSMA 2001, Montréal, Canada, Hermes, pp. 121 – 147 (November 2001)
6. Murata, T., Nelson, P., Yim, J.: A Predicate-Transition Net Model for Multiple Agents Planning. Information Sciences, 57–58, 361–384 (1991)
7. Xu, D., Volz, R., Loeger, T., Yen, J.: Modeling and verifyning multi agent behaviors Unsing Predicat/Transition Nets. In: SEKE, p. 193 (2002)
8. Hernandez, I.R.: Modeling, formal specification and verification of interaction protocol: approach based in action. PhD thesis, national Institut polytechnique of Grenoble, pp. 84–85 (2004)
9. Celaya, J., Desrochers, A., Robert, J.: Modeling and Analysis of Multi-agents Systems using Petri Nets. Journal of Computers 4(10), 110–118 (2009)
10. Leitão, P., Colombo, A.W., Restivo, F.: An Approach to the Formal Specification of Holonic Control Systems. In: Mařík, V., McFarlane, D.C., Valckenaers, P. (eds.) HoloMAS 2003. LNCS (LNAI), vol. 2744, pp. 59–70. Springer, Heidelberg (2003)
11. Seghrouchni, A., Suna, A.: CLAIM: A Computational Language for Autonomous, Intelligent and Mobile Agents. In: ProMAS, Workshop of AAMAS 2003, Melbourne, Australia, pp. 14–18 (July 2003)
12. Bouali, M.: Contributions to the formal analysis and diagnosis using colored Petri nets with rear access. Thesis of doctorat. Compiegne University of Technologies de, pp. 56–58 (December 2009)
13. Chen, B., David, L., Harry, C.: XML-based Agent Communication, Migration and Computation. Journal of System and Software 81, 1364–1376 (2008)

14. Jiannong, C., Xinyu, F., Jian, L., Sajal, K.: Design of Adaptive and Reliable Mobile Agent Communication Protocols. In: Proceedings of the 22rd International Conference on Distributed Computing Systems, ICDCS 2002 (2002)
15. Ferber, J., Müller, J.P.: Influences and Reactions: a Model of Situated Multi Agent Systems. In: Proc.of ICMAS 2006, pp. 72–79 (1996)
16. Michel, F.: IRM4S Model: uses of Influence/Reaction to simulate MAS. Journal of Artificial Intelligent 21, 5–6 (2007)
17. Pinney, J., Westhead, D., DcConkey, G.: Petri Net representations in systems biology. Biochem. Soc. Trans. 31, 1513–1515 (2003)
18. Marzougui, B., Hassine, K., Barkaoui, K.: A New Formalism for Modeling a Multi Agent Systems: Agent Petri Nets. Journal of Software Engineering and Applications (JSEA) 3(12), 1118–1120 (2010)

A Supply Chain Management with Carbon Offsetting Credits

Ichiro Satoh

National Institute of Informatics
2-1-2 Hitotsubashi, Chiyoda-ku, Tokyo 101-8430 Japan
ichiro@nii.ac.jp

Abstract. This paper presents a novel approach to carbon credit trading with pervasive computing technologies, particularly RFID (or barcode) technology. It introduces RFID tags as certificates for the rights to claim carbon credits in carbon offsetting and trading. It enables buyers, including end-consumers, that buy products with carbon credits to hold and claim these credits unlike existing carbon offsetting schemes. It also supports the simple intuitive trading of carbon credits by trading RFID tags coupled to the credits. The approach was constructed and evaluated with real customers and real carbon credits in a real supply chain. It can also be used to encourage industries and homes to reduce greenhouse gas emissions.

1 Introduction

To build a sustainable world, the reduction of greenhouse gases (GHGs), including carbon dioxide (CO_2), has become one of the most serious issues in the world today. *Carbon credits* provide an economical approach to reducing the amount of GHG emissions, where carbon credits are generated by the reduction of CO_2 emissions in sponsoring projects, which increase CO_2 absorption, such as renewable-energy, energy-efficiency, and reforestation projects. Although carbon credits themselves do not reduce the amount of CO_2 emissions around the world, they are important incentives for GHG reduction projects. Many companies have also sold products with the amount of carbon credits equivalent to the amount of GHGs emitted due to the use or disposal of products so that the credits have been used to offset GHGs emissions. There are a variety of products on the market with carbon credits, e.g., automobiles, disposable diapers, and toys. For example, from September 2007, Lufthansa began offering its customers the opportunity of offsetting carbon emissions through voluntarily donating carbon credits to mitigate the amount of CO_2 emitted due to the actual average fuel consumption per passenger.

However, carbon offsetting poses several serious problems that result from carbon credit trading. Carbon credits are usually acquired through *carbon credit trading* between countries or companies, or in markets via professional traders, called carbon traders or agencies. However, existing trading schemes are too complicated for non-professional traders, individuals, or small and medium-sized

M. La Rosa and P. Soffer (Eds.): BPM 2012 Workshops, LNBIP 132, pp. 541–549, 2013.

enterprises, to participate in. Furthermore, the minimal unit of existing credit trading is usually more than one hundred or one thousand tonnes of CO_2 emissions, whereas the amount of GHGs emitted due to the use or disposal of consumables is less than one kilogram.

This paper aims at enabling a small amount of carbon credits attached to products to be transferred to endconsumers who buy these products and carbon credits to be easily traded. The key idea behind our proposed approach is to use RFID tags (and barcodes) as certificates for the rights to claim carbon credits, because RFID tags are widely used in the management of supply chains. Another idea is to use the return of RFID tags as an authentication mechanism. We designed an architecture for managing RFID-enabled carbon credit offsetting and trading. The architecture was constructed and evaluated with real carbon credits in a real supply-chain system.

2   Related Work

Several researchers have explored computing technology to make a contribution to the environment. For example, Persuasive Appliances [6] was an interface system to provide feedback on energy consumption to users. PowerAgent [1] was a game running on mobile phones to influence everyday activities and minimize the use of electricity in the domestic settings. UbiGreen [3] was an interactive system running on mobile phones and gave users feedback about sensed and self-reported transportation behaviors to reduce CO_2 emissions from the transportation sector.

There have been several projects that have used sensing systems to manage warehouses and logistics to reduce CO_2 emissions. Ilic et al. [4] proposed a system for controlling the temperature of perishable goods to reduce GHG emissions. Dada, et al. [2] proposed a system for accurately quantifying GHG emissions to calculate carbon footprints and communicate the results to consumers through sensing systems. The system also planned to use EPCglobal RFID tags to trace carbon footprint emissions at higher stages of the supply chain. However, as long as our knowledge, there has been no work that supports carbon credits by RFID technology.

3   Basic Approach

This paper aims at proposing an approach for enabling carbon credits attached to products to be transferred to consumers who buy these products. Our approach introduces RFID tags (or barcodes) as carbon credits for the rights to claim credits in carbon offsetting, because RFID tags (or barcodes) are used in supply chains. In fact, our approach can use the RFID tags that have already been attached to products for supply chain management. The approach was designed as a complement to existing supply management systems. It therefore has nothing to do with the commerce of products themselves. It also leave the transfer of carbon credit between companies with existing carbon trading systems, because commerce for carbon credits must be processed by certificated organizations. Instead, the approach is responsible for attaching carbon credits to RFID tags and claims for carbon credits. The approach should support emission credits and caps in a unified manner. It also should not distinguish between products for end-consumer and others, because non-end-consumers may buy products for end-consumers. Some readers may think that our approach is trivial. However, simplicity and clarity are essential to prompt most people and organizations to participate or commit to activities to reduce GHG emission by carbon offsetting.

Our approach satisfies the following main requirements: 1) The approach needs to encourage industries and homes to reduce GHG emissions. It also needs to be compliant with regulations on carbon offsetting. 2) Simplicity must be a key concern in minimizing operation costs, because it tends to be in inverse proportion to cost. This is needed for people and organizations to understand what is required of them. 3) Any commerce scheme provides the potential to advantage some participants at the expense of others. The approach enables organizations or people that reduce more GHG emissions to be rewarded with greater advantages. 4) The values of carbon credits, particular emission credits tend be varied. The amounts, expiration dates, and sources of all carbon credits, which may be attached to products, need to be accessible. 5) When consumers purchase products with carbon credits, they should easily be able to own the credits without any complicated operations to authenticate them. 6) Product commerce in the real world is often done in warehouses and stores, where networks and electronic devices may not be available. Our approach itself should be available offline as much as possible.

4   Design

Our approach introduces RFID tags (or barcodes) as carbon credits for the rights of emitters to claim credits in carbon offsetting and trading, because RFID tags (or barcodes) are used in supply chains. In fact, our approach can use the RFID tags that have already been attached to products to manage supply chains. The approach was designed to complement existing supply management systems. It therefore has nothing to do with the trading of the products themselves. It also leaves the transfer of carbon credits between companies to existing carbon trading systems, because carbon trading must be processed by certificated organizations. Instead, the approach is responsible for attaching carbon credits to RFID tags and claims for carbon credits. The approach should support emission credits and caps in a single manner. It should also not distinguish between products for endconsumers and others, because non-endconsumers may buy products for endconsumers.

4.1   RFID Tags as Certificates to Claim Carbon Credits

One of the most novel and significant ideas behind our approach is to use RFID tags themselves, rather than their identifiers, as certificates for carbon credits.

This is because it is difficult to replicate or counterfeit RFID tags whose identifiers are the same, because their identifiers are unique and embedded into them on the level of semiconductors. That is, we can assume that one identifier will always be held in at most one RFID tag.

To claim carbon credits dominated by RFID tags, we need to return these RFID tags to the stakeholders that assigned carbon credits to the tags. This is because there is at most one RFID tag whose identifier is the same. RFID tags can be used as certificates for carbon credits. For example, when sellers want to attach carbon offsetting credits to products, they place RFID tags on them that represent the credits for the products. Our approach couples carbon credits with RFID tags themselves, instead of the identifiers of the RFID tags. Therefore, purchasers, who buy the products, tear the RFID tags from them and return the tags to the sellers (or the stakeholders of the credits). When the sellers receive the RFID tags from the purchasers, they transfer the credits to any accounts for payments that the purchasers specify.

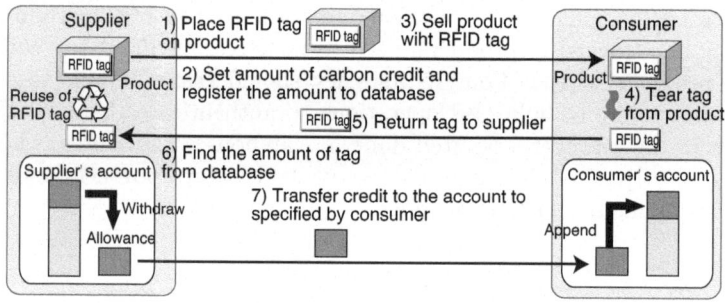

Fig. 1. RFID-based attachment of carbon credits to products

Figure 1 explains our approach to attach carbon credits to products with RFID tags, which involves seven steps

1) A seller places an RFID tag on a product (or a volume of products) if the product has no tag.
2) It sets a certain amount of carbon credits for offsets for a product and registers the amount and the identifier of the tag in a database.
3) It sells the product with the RFID tag to a purchaser.
4) The purchaser tears the tag from the product that it has bought.
5) It only returns the tag with information about the account that the credit should be paid to, to the seller.
6) The seller receives the tag and then finds the amount of carbon credits coupled to the tag in the database.
7) It transfers the amount to the account specified by the purchaser and removes information on the identifier from the database so that the tag can be reused.

4.2   Carbon Credit Trading with RFID Tags

When a purchaser has torn an RFID tag from a product, which might have been attached to a product that he/she purchased, our approach permits the purchaser to resell the tag to others (Figure 2). Instead, the new holder of the tag can claim the carbon credits attached to the tag from the stakeholder of these credits or resell them to someone else. Note that trading RFID tags corresponds to trading carbon credits.

To offset GHG emissions according to the Kyoto protocol, we must donate certified carbon credits to the government via a complicated electronic commerce system. Our approach provides two approaches to carbon offsetting. The first is to simply donate RFID tags coupled to certified carbon credits to the government. For example, people can simply throw RFID (unsigned) tags into mailboxes to contribute to reducing GHG emissions in their home countries. The government then gathers the posted tags. The second is to explicitly specify the certificated cancellation account of the government as the account that the credit should be paid into.

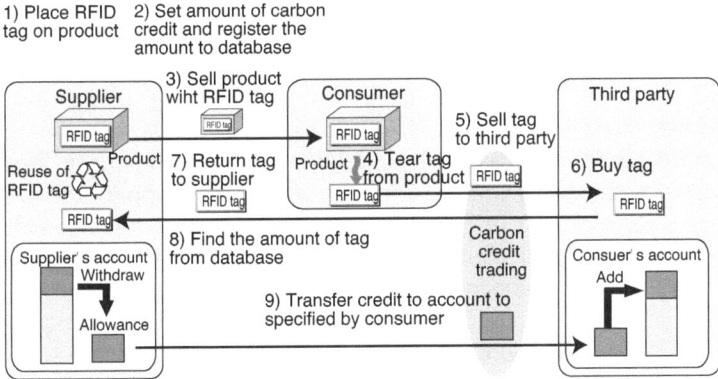

Fig. 2. RFID-enabled trading of carbon credit

5   System

Our approach has been designed so that it can be used in supply chains, where each supply chain consist of sellers, retailers, distributors, transporters, storage facilities, and customers who are involved in moving a product or service from upstream to downstream. Our approach assumes that sellers at steps in a supply chain will sell their products to customers, including raw materials and components, with RFID tags coupled to carbon credits.

- Our approach requires each RFID tag to have its own unique read-only identifier. Most RFID tags used in supply chain management already have such identifiers. For example, we can directly use RFID tags that have been standardized by EPCglobal, because their identifiers, called Electronic Product Code (EPC), consist of the identifiers of the dealers, sellers, manufacturers, or other agents, and the identifiers of the individual products themselves.
- Anyone can access information about the credits attached to the products, because the credits are transferred to purchasers who return the tags themselves to the sellers. The sellers should provide information about the credits, e.g., their amounts, expiration dates, and sources.
- To support carbon offsets, the amount of credits attached to a product need to be equivalent to the total or partial amount of CO_2 emissions resulting from the use or disposal of the products. Nevertheless, the approach itself is intended to leave the amount of credits attached to a product at the stakeholder's discretion, because the credits can be an incentive to sell the product.

Some readers may worry that returning RFID tags to their stakeholders is more costly than returning the identifiers of tags via a network. There are two flows that are opposite to each other between sellers and purchasers at each stage in real supply chains; the flows of products and the flows of receipts or containers for the products. Our approach can directly use the latter flow to return tags from purchasers to sellers. Therefore, our cost and extra CO_2 emissions are small. Actually, returnable containers, which deliver parts or components from sellers and then return them to sellers, are widely used in real supply chains.

To store carbon credits in a certified manner, many companies entrust certified agents to store and transfer their carbon credit accounts just like they entrust their money to banks. Our system assumes that sellers (and purchasers) have such agents. However, existing agents for carbon credit accounts are not concerned with carbon credits that are RFID tag-based. To solve this problem we introduced a new organization, called carbon credit RFID tag agents (simply called RFID agents), which is not included in existing schemes for carbon offsetting and trading. It is responsible for managing RFID tags and carbon credits coupled with the tags. Figure 3 is a minimal set in our system between a seller and a buyer.[1] Each subsystem has four kinds of facilities.

- Each seller has at least one carbon credit account entrusted to agents for carbon credit accounts. It has RFID tag reader systems to read the identifiers of RFID tags. If a seller consigns one or more RFID agents to manage RFID tags for carbon credits, they need a database to maintain which RFID agent will manage each of the RFID tags.
- Each purchaser may have at least one carbon credit account entrusted to agents for carbon credit accounts. It buys products that RFID tags have

---

[1] The proposed approach presented in this paper is described by supports gray rectangular parts in the figure.

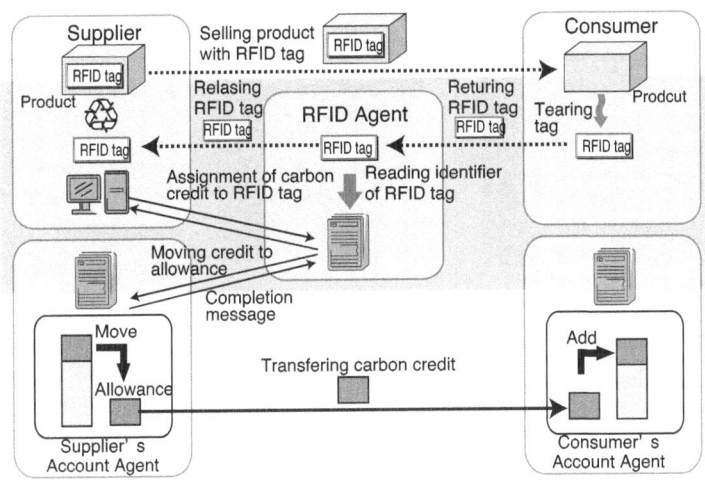

Fig. 3. System architecture

attached to them for carbon credits from sellers or traders. It needs RFID tag
reader systems, when it intends to access information about carbon credits.
- Agents for carbon credit accounts, simply called *account agents*, may be existing certified carbon providers. They have two databases. The first maintains carbon credit accounts and the second maintains information about
  assigned credits. They can only be connected to certain RFID agents and
  other account agents through authenticated and encrypted communications.
- An RFID agent has a database to couple the identifiers of RFID tags and
  information about carbon credits. The agent may lease RFID tags, which
  may already have been assigned a certain amount of credits to sellers.

In the following explanation, we have assumed that RFID tags have been provided to sellers by RFID agents and the identifiers of RFID tags contain the
identifiers of agents in addition to the unique identifiers of products. The system
in Figure 3 is self-contained but it may cascade from upstream to downstream
along a supply chain.

6 Early Experience

The experiment was an early case study on the proposed approach, but was
carried out on a supply chain for beverages it was evaluated at several steps
in the supply chain, including beverage companies (e.g., Pokka and Fujiya), a
supermarket (Kitasuna branch of Ito-yokadou) [2], and a carbon credit agency
(Mitsubishi UFJ Lease). It was carried out for two weeks from 9 am to 10 pm
and more than five thousand goods were sold with carbon offset credits in this

---

[2] The supermarket is one of the biggest in Tokyo area.

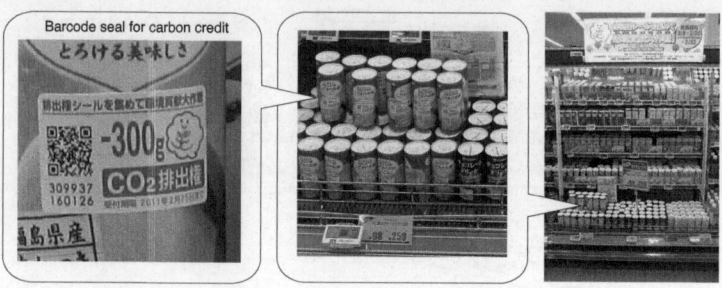

Fig. 4. Beverage with Barcode for carbon credits

experiment. The supermarket opened the returnable containers or cardboard boxes containing the cans. It attached a barcode seal on the cans and sold them to endconsumers, where each barcode seal displayed small amount of J-VER carbon credits, because the price of each RFID tag was relatively more expensive than the price of a can. Each barcode was formatted in a 2D barcode, called QR code, and consisted of its own identifier, the weights of carbon emission credits assigned to it, and the address of the management server. Figure 4 shows beverage cans with barcodes in a showcase at the supermarket.

Endconsumers bought cans and collected barcode seals as their carbon credits. We supported two cases to reclaim credits in the proposed approach.

– The first was for endconsumers to return barcode seals to the supermarket to reclaim credits. Cashiers could distinguish between original or imitation seals, because they received the seals themselves. Therefore, even when someone read the barcodes attached to the cans, the endconsumers who bought the cans could reclaim the credits.
– The second was for endconsumers to read barcodes by using their own scanners, e.g., cellular phones with cameras, and they then sent the information to the server specified in the barcode. As some might peel off the barcode attached on the cans in stores and illegally reclaim carbon credits. The barcodes were concealed by covering them with other seals.[3]

We used the former in our approach. Few endconsumers participated in the latter, because most endconsumers wanted to immediately reclaim their credits. The former also enabled consumers to access information about carbon credits by reading the barcodes with cellular phones before they bought the products attached with the barcodes. The experiment assumed that retailers bought barcode seals that had already been assigned to small amounts of carbon emission credits, like postage stamps. This is because small retailers might not have any terminals.

The sales volumes of cans with carbon credits in two weeks was three times more than usual at the supermarket. Thirty-five percent of barcodes were re-

---

[3] The seals that concealed the barcodes used special adhesive. They could not be attached to the barcode after they had been torn.

turned to the supermarket by customers who claimed the credits. The experiment enabled consumers to offset their CO_2 emissions by using the carbon credits they reclaimed from the barcodes.

7 Conclusion

The approach proposed in this paper can be proposed to solve serious problems with carbon credits, offsetting, and trading. The key idea underlying our approach is to introduce RFID tags (or barcodes) as physical certificates for the rights to claim carbon credits, including carbon emission credits and caps. When purchasers buy products with credits for carbon offsets, they can claim the credits by returning the RFID tags (or barcodes) coupled with the credits to stakeholders, e.g., sellers or agencies, without the need for any complicated authentication. The approach can treat carbon credit trading as the trading of RFID tags. The approach was constructed to complement existing systems of supply chain management and existing systems of carbon credit trading (or barcodes). It can be simply and intuitively provided in real supply chains. Some readers may think that our approach is trivial. However, simplicity and clarity are essential to prompt most people and organizations to participate or commit to activities to reduce GHG emissions by carbon offsetting and trading. Our early experiment proved the feasibility and effectiveness of our approach.

References

1. Bang, M., Gustafsson, A., Katzeff, C.: Promoting New Patterns in Household Energy Consumption with Pervasive Learning Games. In: de Kort, Y.A.W., IJsselsteijn, W.A., Midden, C., Eggen, B., Fogg, B.J. (eds.) PERSUASIVE 2007. LNCS, vol. 4744, pp. 55–63. Springer, Heidelberg (2007)
2. Dada, A., Staake, T., Fleisch, E.: The Potential of UbiComp Technologies to Determine the Carbon Footprints of Products. In: Proceedings of Pervasive Computing 2008 Workshop on Pervasive Persuasive Technology and Environmental Sustainability, pp. 50–53 (2008)
3. Froehlich, J., Dillahunt, T., Klasnja, P., Mankoff, J., Consolvo, S., Harrison, B., Landay, J.A.: UbiGreen: investigating a mobile tool for tracking and supporting green transportation habits. In: Proceedings of the 27th International Conference on Human Factors in Computing Systems (CHI 2009), pp. 1043–1052. ACM (2009)
4. Ilic, A., Staake, T., Fleisch, E.: Using Sensor Information to Reduce the Carbon Footprint of Perishable Goods. IEEE Pervasive Computing 8(1), 22–29 (2009)
5. IPCC fourth assessment report: Climate change 2007. Technical report, IPCC (2007), http://www.ipcc.ch/
6. McCalley, T., Kaiser, F., Midden, C., Keser, M., Teunissen, M.: Persuasive Appliances: Goal Priming and Behavioral Response to Product-Integrated Energy Feedback. In: IJsselsteijn, W.A., de Kort, Y.A.W., Midden, C., Eggen, B., van den Hoven, E. (eds.) PERSUASIVE 2006. LNCS, vol. 3962, pp. 45–49. Springer, Heidelberg (2006)
7. Stern, N.: The Economics of Climate Change: The Stern Review. Cambridge University Press (2007)

Runtime Logistic Process Orchestration Based on Business Transaction Choreography

Wout Hofman

TNO, Brassersplein 2, 2612 CT Delft, the Netherlands
wout.hofman@tno.nl

Abstract. Today logistic systems are business document based, e.g. processing ship manifest, load lists, declarations, and shipping instructions. Business processes are organized in handling these business documents in the context of framework contracts with business partners. Implementations of new requirements like the Entry Summary Declaration 24 hours before the goods are actually loaded on a vessel are therefore difficult to implement in those systems. Furthermore, these systems have difficulties in configuring business processes in a dynamic environment in which processes are configured for one specific business transaction. This paper proposes a high level logistic process modeling environment supporting logistic services according the business document choreography defined for these services.

Keywords: logistic services, logistic processes, business process choreography, process orchestration.

1   Introduction

In a networked economy characterized by dynamic business relationships of a global nature (Heineke J., Davis M., 2007), trade volumes are rapidly growing. A networked economy requires more flexibility of traders and Logistic Service Providers with respect to value exchange (Spohrer & Kwan, 2009) with the possibility to change from hierarchical relations for transaction processing to a market approach (Williamson, 1975). Markets require a clear specification of value propositions (Spohrer & Kwan, 2009) or logistic services. The latter requires a runtime configuration of logistic processes based on services provided and required.

Globalization and increased international trade are the two most important drivers for economic growth, which expose the population to new risks (Hintsa, Ahokas, Zaghbour, Mannisto, Hameri, & Holmstrom, 2010). These new risks impose information requirements on traders and logistic services providers by authorities like customs (Heskhet, 2010). These new requirements are implemented by for instance new procedures and IT systems like the Entry Summary Declaration system (ENS, http://ec.europa.eu/ecip/security_amendment/procedures/index_en.htm). Whereas in the past, a summary declaration was produced when a vessel entered a port, based on Manifest data, currently, a summary declaration needs to be submitted to a port of discharge 24 hours before the goods are actually loaded in a port of loading. Current

M. La Rosa and P. Soffer (Eds.): BPM 2012 Workshops, LNBIP 132, pp. 550–559, 2012.
© Springer-Verlag Berlin Heidelberg 2012

logistic processes and IT systems of traders (e.g. shippers, consignees, forwarders and carriers) need to support these requirements.

This paper proposes runtime logistic process modeling to support logistic services offered by service providers. These logistic processes need to support business transaction choreography of logistic services according to interaction patterns (Dietz, 2006). The methodology used is that of design science (Hevern, March, Park, & Ram, 2004). The choreography is modeled by Business Process Modeling Notation (BPMN) 2.0 (OMG, 2011), which is not explained further in this paper. By formulating new concepts for logistic process modeling, new IT artifacts are proposed that enable business people to model their processes at runtime. This paper is organized as follows. First of all, we present a case as the start for analyzing the issues. Secondly, the choreography to support value exchange for logistics is introduced, and thirdly, runtime process modeling to support the choreography is presented. We conclude by presenting some findings.

2   The Case: A Forwarder

First of all, this section presents a case from logistics. Based on this case, requirements for information sharing are presented. These requirements are modeled by a choreography in the next section.

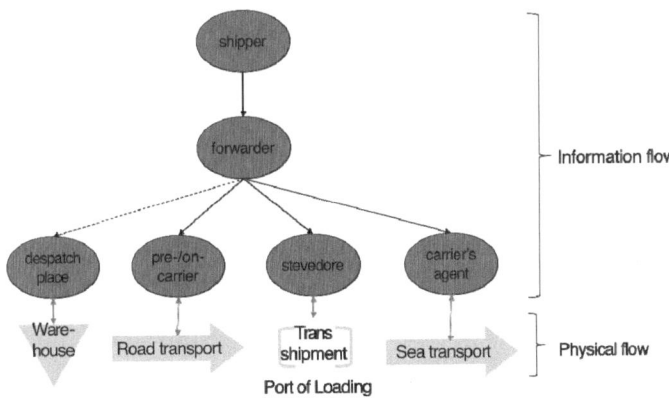

Fig. 1. An example of part of a logistics (export) chain

2.1   Organizing Export of Cargo by a Forwarder

Transportation of cargo via for instance sea consists of many actors (Oosterhout, Baalen, Zuidwijk, & Nunen, 2009). The case is the one of a forwarder as the actor organizing transportation on behalf of a shipper of the cargo. Transport organization depends on the delivery conditions (UNDP, 2012), which are not dealt with in this paper. Figure 1 shows an example in which a forwarder has to arrange transport to a port of loading and sea transport for cargo that has to be shipped from for instance

Holland to the far east. Handling of formalities like customs are not shown, but can also be performed by a forwarder.

The example only shows the export chain. The upper part of the figure shows the information flows where an arrow points from an organization initiating an information flow to the one responding. The dotted arrow indicates only information exchange; there is not a formal outsourcing relation between a forwarder and a dispatch place. The lower part shows the related physical flow by depicting a warehouse from which the goods are dispatched till the sea transport to a port of discharge. During sea transport, a carrier is responsible for the cargo and in a port of discharge, another forwarder can arrange transport and formalities to the final destination. Each organization coordinates its physical task with its information systems; this type of coordination is shown by the lines with two-sided arrows. It implies for instance that a trucker reports its activities to his organization by using a board computer or smart device.

A forwarder receives instructions from a shipper to arrange transport to another country. In this particular case, the forwarder selects transport via sea and an appropriate vessel meeting shipper's requirements in terms of delivery place and time.

By selecting a vessel, the carrier's agent and the stevedore are known, since both act on behalf of the carrier of the selected vessel in a port. Once a stevedore is known, a carrier to the port can be instructed.

The main choice of a forwarder in this particular case is how to organize the so-called main transport: by sea or air. Sea or air have different pricing, can be used for different types of goods, e.g. in terms of volumes and weights (parcels are for instance transported by air), and have different duration (air is faster that sea). Once this choice is made, ports can be selected and transport to the port can be arranged, e.g. by inland waterways, rail or road. A forwarder has to properly align times between different physical activities at the right location, meaning that if a barge operator is selected for transport to a port, a barge has to be at the right time at proper terminal of a stevedore. The vessel should not have left and there is still sufficient time for loading the cargo on the vessel. To be able to align locations and times, a business process of a forwarder has to coordinate all activities by sharing information with all other organizations involved. For this purpose, agreements with respect to information sequencing and syntax have to be made amongst all organizations involved. This paper deals with the information sequencing between two organizations, which is called business transaction choreography.

2.2   Requirements to Information Sharing

This part of the paper specifies requirements for any two organizations in information sharing. First of all, information sharing depends on the type of relationship between two organizations, and secondly, on synchronization between physical tasks in the physical flow as shown in figure 1. Both are discussed.

We distinguish between two types of relations between two organizations, namely a transactional relation in which each individual transaction is negotiated or a long term contract with call off for service delivery (Williamson, 1975). Of course, there are other types of relations in which conditions and prices have been agreed, but still offers are required from more than one organization for service delivery. A transactional relation consists of an offering or booking phase followed by an execution or cancellation phase. The execution phase can be decomposed in a phase in which service delivery planning is coordinated and the actual reporting of service delivery. Service delivery planning consist of an instruction by which a customer commits to the conditions for service delivery agreed in the booking phase and a detailed planning for actual delivering a service. During service delivery planning, the actual cargo or containers to be transported has to be known, whereas in the booking phase only totals could be given. A cancellation is required whilst an organization requesting an offer can still decide to cancel the received offer. The offer or booking phase can be repeated as many times as required to come to agreement on conditions and prices for service delivery. In case a contract exists, only the execution phase for service delivery is performed.

Most typically, organizations have contractual relations in case of scarcity of the supplied service or the dependency of a customer on the quality of the supplied service. In case the dependency is higher, while for instance the customer's service depends on delivery of a logistic service, that customer is willing to have a contractual relation with a logistic service supplier. In case of a buyers' market, e.g. in road transport, a customer can have a transactional relation with a logistic service supplier.

Secondly, requirements for the choreography stem from synchronization of physical tasks. The following situations need to be supported:

- The delivery date of cargo of a previous task is later or earlier than expected or another transport means is used. An update of a previously given instruction needs to be given to inform an organization of these changes.
- The delivery place of cargo of a previous task is different than expected. This may cause cancellation of the succeeding task or an update of a previous issued instruction. The delivery place might also change due to trading of cargo during transport, e.g. which can be the case for oil or grain.
- Reporting of a physical task can be done with one or more reports. Each individual event related to a synchronization with a previous or next task in the physical flow might be reported, e.g. loading the cargo on a vessel and discharging it in a port of destination. After reporting a first or intermediate event, this can lead to an update of the plan, e.g. in terms of the estimated time of arrival of a vessel or truck. An intermediate event might be the transshipment of cargo on another vessel than the one ordered by a forwarder in the port of loading, resulting in an adjustment of the planning in terms of vessel and estimated time of arrival in a port of destination. Reporting of the first or an intermediate event may also lead to an update of an instruction (e.g. rerouting of cargo to another port with the same vessel).
- During transport, the cargo may be destined for another location. It might imply that the cargo has to be discharged in another port of destination and possibly has to be loaded on a different vessel. In such a case, a forwarder receives an update of the instruction, possibly has to cancel the original vessel and book another vessel.

- Incidents or accidents may lead to changes in delivery times and locations. These change may lead to cancellations of the succeeding physical tasks. Whenever an incident takes place, a service provider may cancel the completion of its task since cargo may have been lost.

Cancellation of a logistic service may have financial consequences since a service provider may already have allocated a resource (truck, railway wagon, stowage location in a vessel or barge) to deliver the required service. These consequences need to be agreed upon during the booking phase that might result in a contract.

3   Business Transaction Choreography

This section models the requirements for logistic service delivery by a BPMN choreography for information sharing between any two organizations. First of all, the choreography is discussed, and secondly, an implementation of the choreography by an orchestration process of both a customer and service provider is given. The latter is based on high level tasks of the choreography that can be decomposed according to the requirements of the choreography. These high level tasks are the basis for a forwarder to orchestrate its internal processes for the case identified in section 2. The business process orchestration of a forwarder is given in the next section.

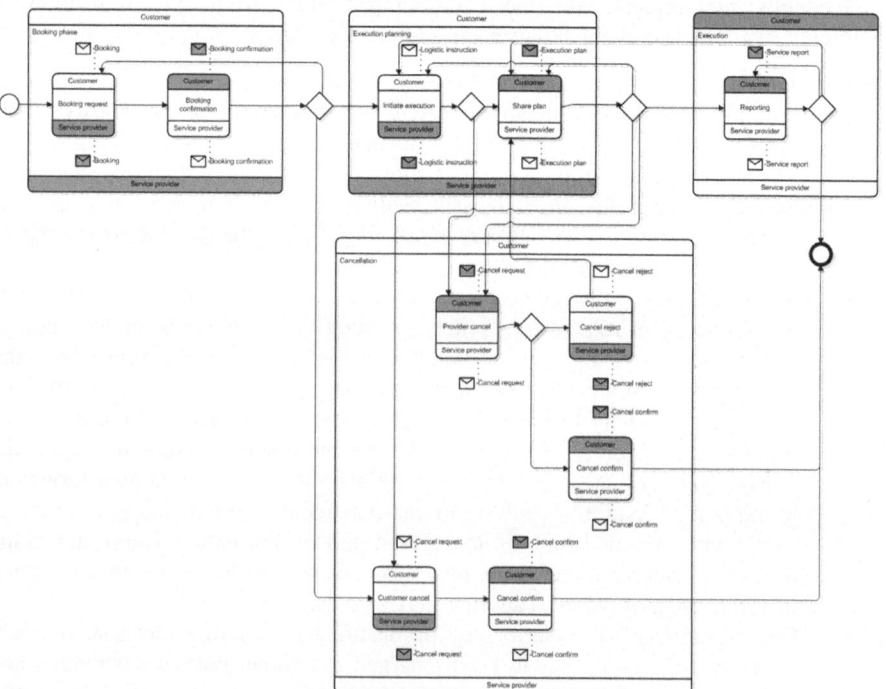

Fig. 2. Choreography for business transactions

3.1   Choreography for Logistic Service Delivery

The objective of information sharing is logistic service delivery, e.g. a transport service is provided by a carrier to a forwarder. In this respect, the actual delivery of a logistic service is called a business transaction. As such, it consists of one or more interactions or business documents (Hofman, 2011). Figure 2 shows the choreography of business transactions for delivery of a logistic service. It consists of a booking phase, execution planning, execution which is the reporting, and a cancellation phase. The booking and execution planning phase is initiated by a customer, the execution phase by a service provider, and the cancellation phase can be initiated by both a customer or service provider as formulated by the requirements.

The choreography still needs to be refined on three aspects to reflect requirements, namely in the execution planning -, the execution and the cancellation phase. In the execution planning phase, a first instruction will not lead to a cancel request by a service provider, whereas an update of an instruction can only lead to a provider initiated cancellation if the execution did not yet start. In the execution phase, the choreography does not yet differ between one report for execution or reports of two or more events that can lead to an update of the planning, e.g. by giving an update on the estimated time of arrival. In the cancellation phase, customer initiated cancellation after the booking phase will not have financial consequences, whereas it may have after completion of the execution planning phase, since a customer and service provider have a contractual agreement after that phase. However, if an update of a planning submitted by a service provider gives deviations from this contract, a customer might be able to cancel the execution. In both cases, a customer is only allowed to initiate cancellation if execution has not yet been started. Additionally, a service provider can initiate a cancellation in case of for instance incidents or accidents or deviations from a contractual agreement caused by an update of the instruction, only if execution did not yet start.

3.2   Orchestration of the Choreography by a Customer and Service Provider

The choreography needs to be implemented by both a customer and a service provider. Figure 3 shows the high level processes of both to support the choreography by showing a lane for each organization. The subprocesses for each lane are the high level processes of the choreography that can be decomposed in tasks, e.g. the booking subprocess of a customer can be decomposed in a task 'compose and submit booking' followed by a task 'receive and process booking confirmation'. Similar tasks can be specified for a service provider. These tasks differ for a customer and a service provider, e.g. a customer has to compose a booking and a service provider has to process that booking, match it with his logistic services, see if there is sufficient capacity available to meet customer requirements, and produce a booking confirmation with prices, conditions, and an initial statement of service delivery based on available resources. These tasks are identical for all customers and service providers cooperating in the choreography.

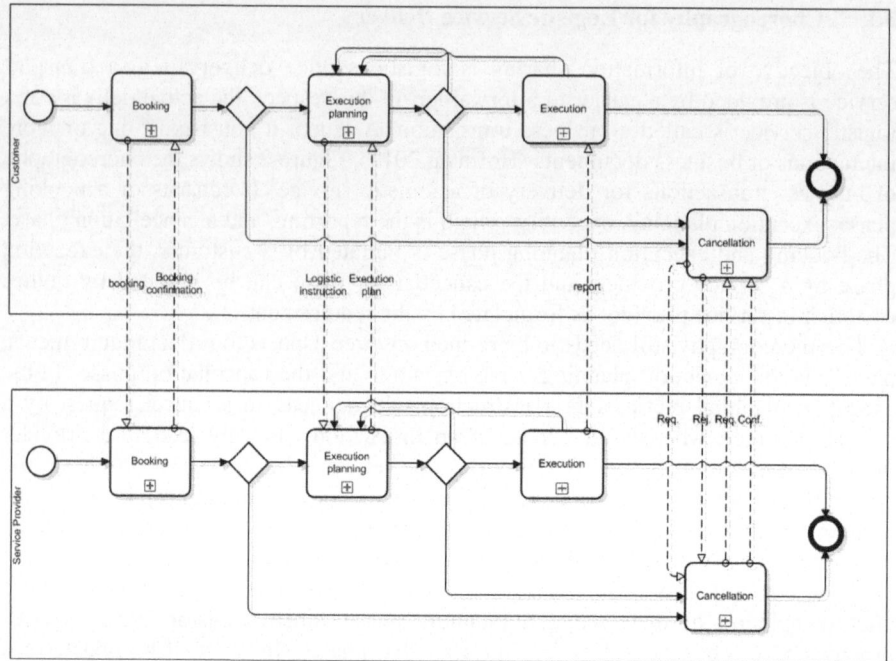

Fig. 3. Orchestration of the choreography by a customer and service provider

Figure 3 shows that a limited set of message types is required. The so-called Common Framework (EURIDICE, 2010) specifies even less message types, namely the Transport Service Description (TSD), the Transport Execution Plan (TEP), and the Transport Execution Status (TES). We will march the functionality of these Common Framework message types to the ones proposed in this paper. The TSD is used by a service provider to publish its services, resulting in a TEP issued by a customer either as a booking or a logistic instruction. A more detailed TSD acts as a booking confirmation. The TEP also acts as an execution plan or an update of a logistic instruction. Cancellation messages are not explicitly specified in the Common Framework, although a TEP could act as such. Additionally, the Common Framework specifies a Goods Item Itinerary (GII) to represent the actual routing of cargo, which is not part of our choreography.

4   Runtime Logistic Process Orchestration by a Forwarder

This section presents a business process orchestration for a forwarder as depicted in the case (section 2). The orchestration is based on the high level tasks shown in the orchestration of the choreography in section 3. In the particular case given in section 2, the forwarder has four business transactions, in the one with the shipper acting as a service provider and as a customer in the other three. Each of these business transactions behaves according to the specified choreography and a forwarder should have the proper tasks implemented for its role as customer or service provider in these business transactions. The business process orchestration of a forwarder has to reflect dependencies between the four business transactions given in section 2.1. Figure 4 shows an example of this business process orchestration for the three transactions in which that forwarder acts as a customer.

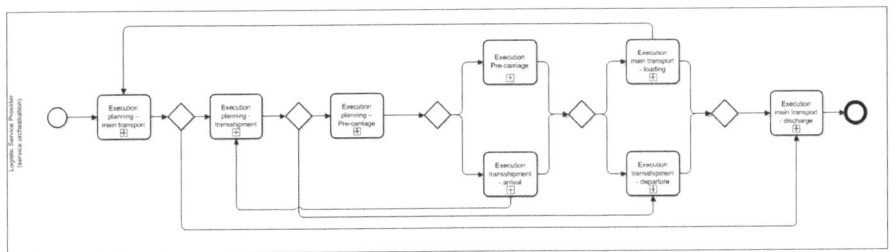

Fig. 4. Business process orchestration by a forwarder acting as customer

The orchestration shown in figure 4 has to be interleaved with the business process orchestration of the forwarder with the shipper. In this case a forwarder has a choice to embed the outsourced services completely in the business transaction with the shipper or are embedded partial. In case of complete embedding, it implies for instance that a booking confirmation or planning can only be given after all booking confirmations or planning messages respectively are received and all reports of subcontractors are passed to the shipper. Partially embedding implies that the forwarder takes a risk by for instance not booking all subcontractors before giving a booking confirmation to a shipper. Furthermore, a forwarder can decide only to report picking up the cargo at the despatch place, the actual loading of the cargo on a vessel, both, or can include delivery of the cargo to the stevedore, which may be required in case the cargo is stored for a longer period on the quay wit financial consequences to te shipper.

These additional choices can be added to the orchestration and will result in different versions of the business process. There are also a number of design issues to be solved, namely:

- Updates of instructions and planning data of a subcontracted service will only affect subcontracted services of tasks succeeding the one producing the updated instruction or planning data. This could be implemented by an overall monitor process with knowledge of the physical flow, but could also be part of the tasks in the subcontracted services. It is also feasible that an update of a next task can give an updated instruction to a previous, e.g. if a vessel arrives later in a port than expected, possibly rail could be used for pre-carriage instead of a truck.
- It is good not to model cancellation at runtime, but have it as a standard subprocess for each business transaction. Again, cancellation can be both upstream and downstream a physical flow, e.g. in case a physical task that acts like a bottleneck is cancelled, all preceding and succeeding physical tasks need to be cancelled. Main transport by sea can be such a bottleneck task. In case of accidents or incidents, all downstream tasks are either cancelled or receive an updated instruction. These types of rules can be implemented as part of some sort of overall monitor (see the previous aspect) or could be part of the tasks in the business processes handling the transactions.

5   Conclusions and Next Steps

This paper proposes the development of a set of composite tasks for runtime logistic process orchestration supporting a business transaction choreography. The proposed approach is illustrated by a forwarder case. The approach allows an end-user to orchestrate a business process based on commercial decisions for service delivery by hiding details of the choreography, especially cancellation rules. The proposed approach requires IT to support a number of standard features for handling updates and cancellations, for instance by an overall monitor. Control flows between different phases of one business transaction can also be hidden, but need to be implemented as part of the business process orchestration.

The proposed approach provides ease of use and ease of orchestration modeling that allows runtime process orchestration based on commercial considerations and standard composite orchestration tasks. Still a lot of work needs to be done by decomposing the composite tasks and relate their processing to a semantic model representing business transactions in logistics.

The standard composite tasks can be represented by a Business Process Execution Language (BPEL) document incorporating Java, that is directly executable in for instance an Enterprise Service Bus (ESB). These software components are provided by several IT solution providers. Further research is require to investigate whether or not an ESB can meet these requirements.

Constructing IT systems that are able to process the standard composite gives flexibility to extend services and incorporate new requirements like the 24 hours ENS declarations quite quickly.

Another issue is the one of globalization of logistics. A migration strategy needs to be developed in which logistic companies can gradually implement the choreography with its semantics and still be interoperable with others implementing different standards. A matching of message type functionality to the choreography as proposed for instance for the Common Framework (see before) needs to be established and data transformations need to be implemented.

Acknowledgments. The work presented in this paper is funded by the EC SEC Cassandra project (www.cassandra-project.eu) and the EC INFSO iCargo project (i-cargo.eu). Tooling to support runtime logistics orchestration and an ontology for logistic business transactions are developed in those projects.

References

1. Dietz, J.: Enterprise Ontology, Theory and Methodology. Springer (2006)
2. Heineke, J., Davis, M.: The emergence of service operations management as an academic discipline. Journal of Operations Management 25, 364–374 (2007)
3. Heskhet, D.: Weakness in the supply chain: who packed the box? World Customs Journal 4(2) (2010)
4. Hevern, A.R., March, S.T., Park, J., Ram, S.: Design Science in Information Systems Research. MIS Quarterly, 75–105 (2004)

5. Hintsa, J., Ahokas, J., Zaghbour, K., Mannisto, T., Hameri, A.-P., Holmstrom, J.: Conceptual model for assessing cost of security in global supply chains. In: 17th International Annual EuroOMA Conference, Porto (2010)
6. Spohrer, J., Kwan, S.K.: Service Science, Management, Engineering, and Design (SSMED): an Emerging Discipline - Outline and References. International Journal of Information Systems in the Service Sector 1(3) (2009)
7. Williamson, O.: Markets and Hierarchies: analysis and antitrust implications. Free Press, New York (1975)

A Qualitative Comparison of Approaches Supporting Business Process Variability*

Victoria Torres[1], Stefan Zugal[2], Barbara Weber[2], Manfred Reichert[3], Clara Ayora[1], and Vicente Pelechano[1]

[1] Universitat Politècnica de València, Spain
{vtorres,cayora,pele}@pros.upv.es
[2] University of Innsbruck, Austria
{stefan.zugal,barbara.weber}@uibk.ac.at
[3] University of Ulm, Germany
manfred.reichert@uni-ulm.de

Abstract. The increasing adoption of Process-Aware Information Systems, together with the *reuse* of process knowledge, has led to the emergence of process model repositories with large process families, i.e., collections of related process model variants. For managing such related model collections two types of approaches exist. While *behavioral* approaches take supersets of variants and derive a process variant by hiding and blocking process elements, *structural* approaches take a base process model as input and derive a process variant by applying a set of change operations to it. However, at the current stage no framework for assessing these approaches exists and it is not yet clear which approach should be better used and under which circumstances. Therefore, to give first insights about this issue, this work compares both approaches in terms of understandability of the produced process model artifacts, which is fundamental for the management of process families and the *reuse* of their contained process fragments. In addition, the comparison can serve as theoretical basis for conducting experiments as well as for fostering the development of tools managing business process variability.

1 Introduction

The increasing adoption of Process-Aware Information Systems (PAISs) by industry has led to large collections of process models in a variety of application domains. Despite the particularities found in specific domains, many of these models share common parts of their definition (e.g., activities). We denote such related process variant models as *process family* in the following.

To properly handle large process families (i.e., avoid redundancies, foster reusability, and reduce modeling efforts) several proposals have been developed in recent years (e.g., [1], [2], [3]), which can be classified as either behavioral or structural approaches. *Behavioral* approaches represent all members of the

---

* This work has been developed with the support of MICINN under the project EVERYWARE TIN2010-18011.

M. La Rosa and P. Soffer (Eds.): BPM 2012 Workshops, LNBIP 132, pp. 560–572, 2013.
© Springer-Verlag Berlin Heidelberg 2013

family within the same model artifact, capturing both, commonalities and particularities of all process variants. In turn, *structural* approaches use different
artifacts to represent the family e.g., by using a base model to which structural
changes such as inserting, deleting, or moving activities may be applied to derive
process variants. To foster reusability of process model families, understandability of the created artifacts is essential. So far, however, no experimental insights
regarding *quality* aspects (e.g., *understandability*) are available and it is not clear
under which circumstances the use of one approach is more appropriate than the
other. Since the results of assessing a process model's understandability significantly depend on the specific understandability tasks [4,5], we have structured
the comparison of both approaches

along a specific comprehension task, i.e., the extraction of a process variant
from a configurable model, elaborating on the process followed by a model reader
to accomplish such task. In addition, we use cognitive psychology as a tool for
explaining the differences between the two approaches. This comparison will provides us the theoretical basis for conducting experiments as well as for fostering
the development of tools for managing variability in business processes.

Sect. 2 presents a process family from the film industry. Sect. 3 provides
basic notions and introduces the behavioral and structural approaches. Sect.
4 describes concepts from cognitive psychology that will be used in Sect. 5 to
assess their understandability. Sect. 6 then presents an overview of related work.
Finally, Sect. 7 concludes the paper and gives an outlook.

2   Example of a Process Family

As running example, we consider a modified version of a process family from the
film industry for editing a screen project, which varies depending on the shooting
media and delivery media used [6]. First, footage is received, either in *tape, film,*
or *tape and film* and *prepared for edition* depending on the shooting medium.
Then *offline edition* is performed. Next, the cut stage is performed through
online edit (if the *shooting medium* is *tape*), through *negmatching* (in the case
of *film*), or through both cuts (when *shooting media* is *tape and film*). After
this point, the finishing on a delivery medium phase starts. For this purpose,
the delivery media (e.g., *tape, film, tape and film, or new medium*) must be
chosen. Now, depending on the delivery medium chosen different variants exist.
For example, when shooting media is *film* or *tape and film* and cutting has been
performed through negmatching, a *finish on film* has to be performed to maintain
the quality of the delivery medium. On the contrary, if the cutting is performed
through *online editing* and *film* or *tape and film* is the delivery medium, *record
digital film master* needs to be mandatorily performed to transfer the editing
results to *film*. Similarly, *telecine transfer* will be performed only if negmatching
is performed previously and the expected delivery format is *tape* or *new medium*.
Finally, if neither *tape* or *film* have been chosen activity *finish on new medium*
must be performed.

3   Approaches for Modeling BP Variability

To properly represent variability in a BP model, it is important to define (1) what parts of the BP model may vary according to a specific context, (2) what alternatives exist in each of those parts, and (3) which conditions make these alternatives being selected. The first issue refers to the precise identification of the parts being subject to variation, which are commonly known as *variation points*. The second issue refers to the different alternatives that exist for all those variation points. In addition, some models may require the definition of *relationships* (e.g., inclusion, exclusion) between alternative process fragment from different variation points. The third issue refers to the *context* of these variations, which is usually represented by a set of variables gathered in a *context model* in which the BP model is used. This subsection presents two different approaches targeted at the representation of such process families, i.e., behavioural and structural.

Behavioural Approach. The behavioral approach represents a process family in a single artifact, known as *configurable process model* capturing both the commonalities and particularities of the *process variants* reflecting all possible behavior.

In the following we take C-EPC [2] as the representative proposal since it constitutes the most well-known and mostly cited proposal. C-EPC extends EPC with configurable elements (i.e., *configurable nodes* and *configuration requirements*) to explicitly model variability. Fig. 1 illustrates the configurable process model representing the postproduction process. On the one hand, *configurable nodes* (i.e., connectors and functions) are represented graphically with thick solid borders and define variations points in the model where different alternatives may exist. Specifically, *configurable functions* (e.g., activity *telecine transfer* in Fig. 1) can be configured as ON (i.e., function is kept in the model), OFF (i.e., function is removed from the model), or OPT (i.e., conditional branching is included in the model deferring the decision to run-time). *Configurable connectors*, in turn, can be configured to an equally or more restrictive connector. For example, a configurable OR can configured as a regular OR (not applying any restrictions), or can restrict its behaviour by configuring it as an XOR (i.e., selecting one of the outgoing/incoming alternatives), AND (i.e., selecting all of the outgoing/incoming alternatives), or SEQ_n (i.e., reducing the alternatives for the configuration of the connector to just one of its outgoing/incoming sequences). On the other hand, *configuration requirements* are graphically represented as tags attached to *configurable nodes* and formalize, by means of logical predicates, domain constraints related to the attached *nodes*. The configuration of the node will the be made based on the evaluation of the attached *configuration requirements* (e.g., *req. 5* requires that activity *edit footage online* is chosen when shooting medium is *tape*). However, *configurable nodes* not always have requirements attached to them (since they are only needed when there is a constraint regarding their configuration). In this case the configurable node is transformed into a regular one, maintaining the behaviour of the original connector and deferring the configuration decision to run-time.

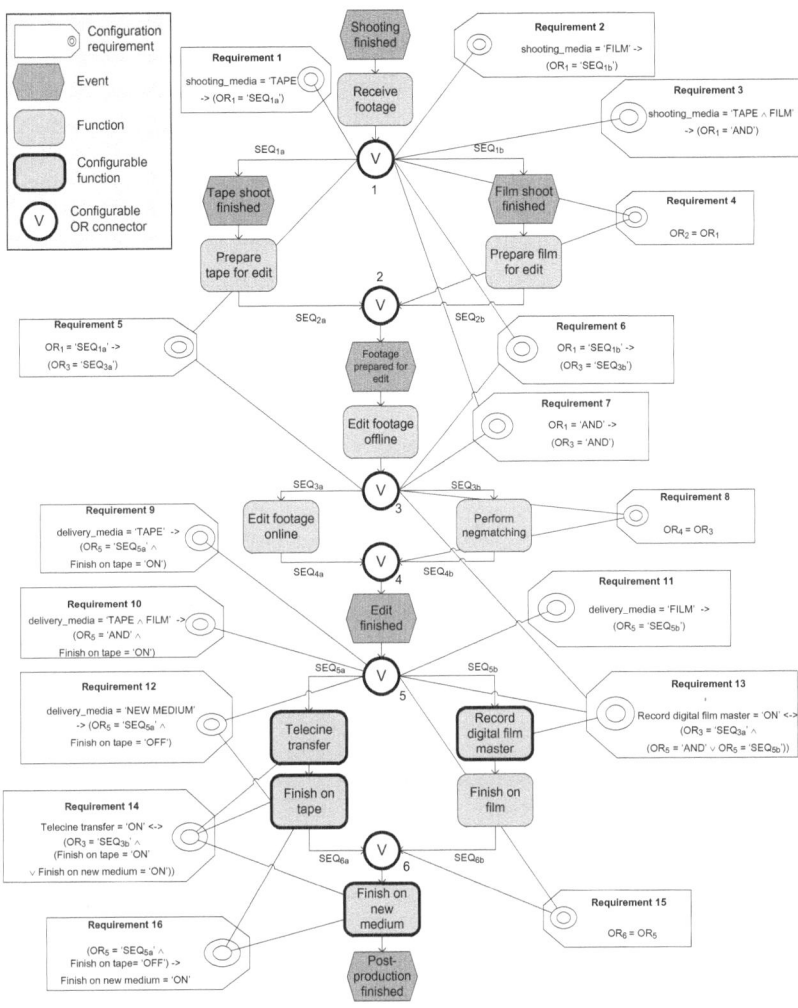

Fig. 1. C-EPC model for the screen postproduction process

Structural Approach. This approach proposes a gradual construction of the process family by modifying the structure of a specific process variant (called *base model*) at specific points (i.e., *variation points*) through *change operations*. Following this approach, we find proposals such as Provop [1] or Rule representation and processing [3]. In the following we use Provop as representative for the structural approach, since it can be considered the most widely used proposal for this approach. Fig. 2 illustrates the process family representing the screen postproduction process using Provop. Provop allows creating process variants by adjusting the *base model* (cf. top part of Fig. 2) by the application of a set of high-level change operations between a couple of *adjustment points*. Furthermore, Provop allows for more complex configuration adjustments by grouping

multiple *change operations* into so-called *change options* (e.g., option 1 combines 2 delete and 2 insert operations). *Change options* are associated with a
context rule, which is used at configuration time to decide, whether a certain
option is applicable for the given context (e.g., regarding option 1 the context
rule states that this option should only be applied if *shooting media* is *tape*). In
addition, Provop allows for an explicit representation of different dimensions of
the context (i.e., *context variables* and allowed *values*) by means of the *context
model*. Finally, to prevent the derivation of semantically invalid variants, Provop
provides the *constraint model* which allows defining *inclusion, exclusion, order
of application, hierarchy,* and *cardinality* relationships between *change options*
(e.g., the application of *option 1* excludes the application of *option 2*).

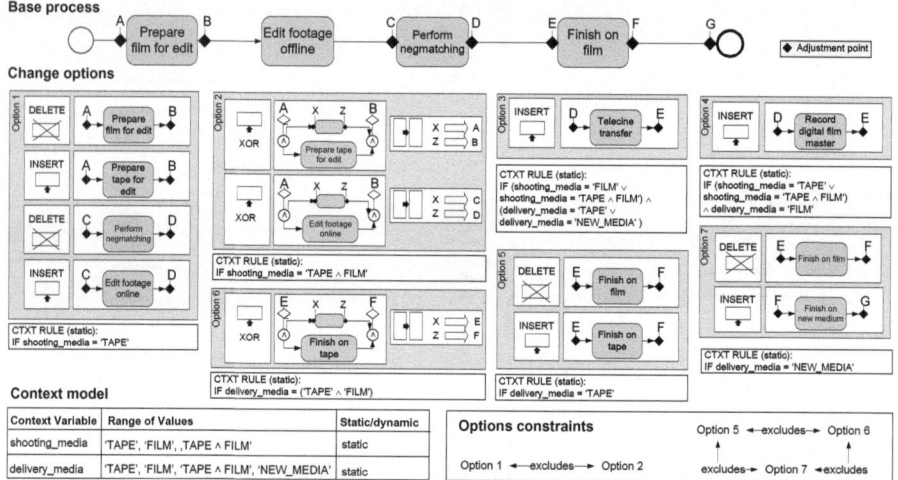

Fig. 2. Provop model for the screen postproduction process

4   Concepts from Cognitive Psychology

In order to discuss differences between C-EPC and Provop, we will make use
the concepts of *external memory, abstraction,* and *split-attention effect* from
cognitive psychology and transfer them to the domain of BP variability.

Basically, three different problem-solving "programs" or "processes" are known
from cognitive psychology: search, recognition, and inference [7]. Search and
recognition allow identifying information of rather low complexity, i.e., locating
an object or recognizing patterns. Most models, however, go well beyond complexity that can be handled by search and recognition. For instance, a Boolean
expression certainly cannot be interpreted just by looking at it and without deliberate thought. Here, the human brain as *"truly generic problem solver"* [8]
comes into play. Thereby, cognitive psychology differentiates between working

memory that contains the information is currently processed, as well as long-term memory in which information can be stored for a long period of time [9]. Most severe, and thus of high interest and relevance, are the limitations of the working memory. As reported in [10], working memory cannot hold more than 7 ± 2 items at the same time. In this context, the concept of mental effort, i.e., the amount of working memory used, is of interest, as it can be used to assess understanding. As discussed in [11], higher mental effort is in general associated with lower understanding, or more generally, errors are more likely to occur when the working memory's limits are exceeded [12]. Instead of only measuring accuracy or time for assessing the understandability of a notation, measuring mental effort allows for a more fine-grained analysis. In particular, when differences with respect to understandability are small, accuracy may not change, even though the mental effort changes significantly (cf. [13]). Subsequently, we will discuss three factors that influence the required mental effort: *external memory, abstraction,* and the *split-attention effect.*

External Memory. First, we would like to introduce a mechanism known for reducing mental effort, i.e., the amount of working memory slots in use. An external memory is referred to any information storage outside the human cognitive system, e.g., pencil and paper or a blackboard [12,8,14,7]. Information taken from the working memory and stored in an external memory is then referred to as cognitive trace. In the context of a diagram, a cognitive trace would be, for instance, to mark, update, and highlight information [14]. Likewise, in the context of process variants, the model itself may serve as external memory. For example, when deriving a process variant in C-EPC for a particular context, the model reader may cross out model elements that have been removed (not requiring her anymore to store them in the working memory). Rather, this information is transferred to the C-EPC model, freeing up working memory capacity.

Abstraction. Basically, the idea of abstraction is to hide information by aggregation. As irrelevant information can be hidden from the reader, it becomes easier to focus on relevant information, i.e., abstraction supports the human mind's attention management [7], leading to decreased mental effort. Unlike in C-EPC, where the process family is represented in a single model, Provop separates the base model from change options and change options are abstracted via variation points. This, in turn, simplifies both the base model and the change options, presumably making both easier to interpret, as attention is not distracted by an abundance of modeling elements.

Split-Attention Effect. Even though abstraction has been attributed to reduce mental effort [11,15,16], it typically co-occurs with the split-attention effect, which is known to increase mental effort [17]. In general, the split-attention effect occurs whenever information from different sources needs to be integrated. As the human mind can only focus on a single aspect at the same time [18], attention needs to be constantly switched between the information sources, leading to increased mental effort. In addition, the task of integrating information is known to further increase mental effort [17]. To illustrate the split-attention effect, consider the change options in the Provop approach. Therein, the model reader has to switch attention between the base model and the change options. When extracting a process variant for a specific context, the model reader has to integrate information from change options, i.e., which model elements to change, with the base model, further increasing mental effort.

5   Qualitative Comparison

So far we have discussed C-EPC and Provop as representatives of approaches for modeling BP variability. In the following, we will use concepts from cognitive psychology to systematically assess differences between these two proposals with respect to understandability. Understandability not only depends on the notation, but also on the type of task to be performed [4,5]. Due to space restrictions we focus in this paper on a specific understandability task, namely the extraction of a process variant from a configurable process model given a certain context. To illustrate the process in both proposals, we assume that a model reader wants to derive the process variant that relates to the production of a low-budget project which implies the use of *tape* as medium for both shooting and delivery tasks. For a description of additional tasks we refer the reader to http://www.pros.upv.es/technicalreports/PROS-TR-2012-03.pdf

In our qualitative comparison, we assume a setting where the model reader has the models available in paper-based form. We are aware that, even though our discussion focuses on cognitive aspects only, tool support is indispensable for working with configurable models. However, to be able to develop effective tool support, it is essential to know what makes configurable process models hard to understand. Without a profound discussion, as provided here, tool development is rather driven by speculation than by systematic consideration.

In the following, we provide a discussion, first for C-EPC and afterwards for Provop, structured along the following points: First, we will describe the steps a model reader has to perform in order to perform the understandability task. This descriptions have been derived in an iterative manner by observing a set of model readers conducting the task. Second, we will perform an analysis to determine the cognitive complexity of the task.

5.1   Extracting a Process Variant Using C-EPC

To obtain the process variant that relates to the low-budget project in C-EPC (i.e., when shooting and delivery medium is tape) the model reader starts with the configuration of *configurable connector 1*. For this purpose, the model reader evaluates all requirements attached to it, i.e., reqs. 1-7. According to the given context (i.e., shooting media is *tape*), *configurable connector 1* is configured as $SEQ1_a$ as stated in req. 1. Next, the configuration of *configurable connector 2* has to be performed. In this case, req. 4 determines that the same configuration performed to *configurable connector 1* should be applied to *configurable connector 2*, i.e., $SEQ2_a$ is chosen. Then, the configuration of *configurable connector 3* has to be done. For such purpose, reqs. 5–8 and 13 are evaluated. After evaluating req. 5 the model reader discovers that $SEQ3_a$ should be chosen. Unlike reqs. 1–3, reqs. 4–8 and 13–16 are entirely expressed in terms of the structure of the model, not providing any information regarding the process variant being configured. This means that the model reader, in order to understand why this configuration is performed, has to either remember the decisions previously taken or go back in the model and revisit the requirements that determined the configuration of related nodes. Similarly to the configuration performed for *configurable connector 2*, req. 8 determines that *configurable connector 4* should be configured equally to connector 3, i.e., as $SEQ4_a$. Regarding *configurable connector 5*, six requirements are attached to it, i.e., reqs. 9-13, and 15. In this case, the model reader discovers by evaluating req. 9 that it should be configured as $SEQ5_a$ and that function *finish on tape* should be switched ON. The fact that these requirements include context variables in it help the model reader to better understand which configuration should be taken. Next, the model reader has to decide about the configuration of function *telecine transfer*. In this case req. 14 states that function *telecine transfer* should be configured as OFF (since connector 3 was configured as $SEQ3_a$). Then, *configurable connector 6* is configured as $SEQ6_a$ according to req. 15. Finally, function *finish on new medium* is switched OFF since function *finish on tape* has been switched ON (req. 16). Considering the **cognitive complexity** the use of C-EPC entails we can identify three basic operations: locating elements, evaluating Boolean expressions, and adapting the model accordingly. As argued in [19], the more distinct properties a visual element has, e.g., shape and color, the easier it is to identify. In C-EPC, requirements are represented by white tags, configurable connectors are represented by white circles with a thick border, whereas configurable functions are represented by green rounded rectangles with a thick border. Hence, the reader can draw on two different properties (i.e., color and shape) for identifying distinct modeling constructs presumably requiring a low mental effort. For identifying whether there are requirements attached to a configurable node, the model reader can rely on pattern recognition [7] to efficiently perform this operation (requirements are connected via dotted lines). The first real challenge occurs when the model reader has to evaluate associated Boolean expressions. As they can be arbitrarily complex and have to be interpreted in the model reader's mind, presumably a high mental effort can be expected. In C-EPC, some requirements are expressed in terms of the structure of the alternatives and not by the semantics of the process variants being described (e.g., reqs. 4-8, 13–16). In addition, the configuration of the configurable node being evaluated can depend on the configuration of previous and/or succeeding related configurable nodes. This requires a bigger cognitive effort by the model reader, since the model reader has to remember decisions taken for already configured nodes and might have to anticipate the configuration of succeeding nodes. For example, when evaluating req. 14 for configuring function *telecine transfer*, the model reader has to go back to the related configurable nodes, i.e., to configurable connector 3, and consider the configuration of functions *finish on tape* and *finish on new medium* to understand the semantics of the configuration. Having evaluated the requirements respective model adaptations have to be performed (e.g., removing model elements). Eventhough these operations are rather simple the model reader has to keep track of all changes made during the configuration. Due to the limited nature of working memory (7±2 slots), it seems essential that the model reader can offload parts of the working memory to an external memory, e.g., by annotating a print-out of the model.

5.2   Extracting a Process Variant Using Provop

To extract a process variant in Provop the model reader first examines all change options including their associated context rules to determine which options are applicable for the given context. Based on this, the model reader then selects *options 1* and *5*, since only these two satisfy the given context and applies them to the based model. For this the model reader checks the constraints between the selected options and concludes that both *option 1* and *option 5* can be applied. The application of *option 1* involves deleting activity *prepare film for edit* between variation points A and B, and inserting activity *prepare tape for edit* instead. In addition, activity *perform negmatching* is replaced by activity *edit footage online*. Moreover, the application of *option 5* implies the replacement of activity *finish on film* by *finish on tape* between adjustment points E and F.

Considering the **cognitive complexity** of Provop we can identify two main operations. First, selecting appropriate change options and second, applying these change options to the model. For the identification of relevant change options the model reader inspects all change options and evaluates whether they are applicable for the current context, i.e., the model reader evaluates the Boolean expression associated with the change option. Similar to C-EPC, it can be expected that the interpretation of such Boolean expressions presumably imposes a high mental effort. However, unlike C-EPC, in Provop Boolean expressions are always expressed in terms of context variables. These variables provide semantics to the change options, helping the model reader to understand the intent of the options. After having identified relevant change options, the model reader has to apply them to the base model. Before applying a change option, it has to be checked whether the change option is conflicting with previously applied change options. This task, however, can easily be accomplished using Provop's *option constraints*, i.e., a set of relationships (e.g., inclusion, exclusion) between *change options* targeted to ensure their proper use based on the semantics of the domain. As these option constraints are visually depicted, the model reader's recognition capabilities will help to efficiently identify conflicting options, hence presumably imposing a low mental effort. Regarding the actual manipulation of the model, the effort for integrating the change options into the base model is determined by the *change distance* [20] between the base model and the variant to be derived. In other words, the more modeling elements are added to / removed from the base model, the more complex the integration task will be. In addition, the type of change operations contained in the change options influences complexity. For example, when deleting an activity, respective parts can be removed from the model by hiding them with a finger on the print-out of the model, or by crossing them out using a pen. In this way, the model reader does no longer have to keep this information in his working memory. Rather, the model serves as external memory, freeing up mental resources. When inserting activities, in turn, this possibility is not available (except this is done through a supporting modeling tool) and has to be done in the reader's mind. Therefore, complexity grows with the number of changes applied to the base model. Therefore, an optimized design of the base model that requires minimum changes to derive different variants presumably requires less effort by the model reader. Altogether it can be said that most mental effort will presumably be required for evaluating Boolean expressions as well as conducting model changes.

5.3   Discussion

After studying both proposals three major differences can be observed. First, in a C-EPC model, modeling elements are mainly removed from the configurable model (with exception of functions when these are configured as optional, which involve the inclusion of some branching condition in the model). By contrast, in Provop model elements can either be added, deleted, or moved during the configuration process. As argued above, the cognitive complexity depends on the type of change operations to be performed (i.e., deletion operations presumably involve less cognitive effort than insertions or movements).

Second, requirements and configurable nodes are integrated in C-EPC, whereas change options and the base model are separated in Provop. Similar to [15,16], we argue that for small models, C-EPC presumably is easier to understand, as all the information is integrated and hence in contrast to Provop no split-attention effect can be expected. However, when model size increases, models may quickly become too complex resulting in an overload for the model reader, especially when there are many relationships between alternative modeling elements. Here, it can be assumed that the abstraction mechanisms provided in Provop (i.e., represented by change operations defined separately from the base model) contributes to retain understandability even for large models.

Third, even though Boolean expressions need to be evaluated in both approaches, the way they are used by the two proposals differs. In C-EPC, one of the biggest challenges faced by the model reader relates to the fact that alternatives are usually expressed at the structural level, neglecting the semantics associated to the different alternatives. This fact involves that, in some cases, the model reader has to evaluate the Boolean expression at hand, but additionally has to keep track of previously made decisions. In contrast, in Provop, Boolean expressions are always expressed in terms of context variables, which contribute to better understand the semantics of the associated change operations. In addition, the concept of options (i.e., grouping of related change operations) as provided by Provop and the explicit specification of constraints between them in the constraint model presumably reduces the mental effort required by the reader for understanding them. Hence, from this point of view, Provop models presumably impose a lower mental effort on average.

6   Related Work

Several proposals have been developed to deal with business process variability (e.g., [1,2,3]). These works take a design-oriented perspective and provide technical solutions for managing variability; the understandability of the artifacts created using such approaches is not in the focus. Recently qualitative evaluations of the C-EPC proposal in form of case studies have been conducted [21,22]. However, to the best of our knowledge no work has addressed understandability of process model families explicitly. Closely related is, however, existing empirical research on the understandability of process models. Most approaches thereby employ the concept of metrics computed on structural aspects of the process model to assess understandability, e.g., [23,24,25]. While metrics seem to be a promising approach to assess model complexity and understandability, in [4,5] it is shown that understandability of a process model significantly depends on the type of question asked. Consequently, a metric will only be able to roughly estimate understandability. In [26,15,16], concepts from cognitive psychology are used as a tool to discuss understandability of process models for specific comprehension tasks. In this paper we build upon this work, and extend it to discuss understandability of configurable process models.

7   Summary and Outlook

The main goal of this paper is to compare the structural and behavioral approaches for modeling process model families in terms of understandability. Instead of looking at understandability from a broad perspective, the discussion is centered around the extraction task of a process variant from the modeling artifacts produced by C-EPC and Provop. The different approaches are discussed in terms of different concepts from cognitive psychology based on which the mental effort required to understand the modeling artifacts produced by the two approaches can be estimated. In turn, this allows us to estimate the understandability of the two approaches for specific comprehension task. The task addressed in this paper constitutes just a first attempt regarding the investigation of understandability of these two approaches. Formal metrics and experiments involving a large number of subjects and different configurable process models are planned as future work to empirically test the discussion. Based on the comprehension tasks presented in this paper, we will conduct a series of experiments to empirically assess the understandability of both approaches and to investigate the factors that impact understandability of process model families improving the modeling of such families and facilitating their reuse.

References

1. Hallerbach, A., Bauer, T., Reichert, M.: Capturing variability in business process models: the Provop approach. J. Soft. Maintenance 22(6-7), 519–546 (2010)

2. Rosemann, M., van der Aalst, W.M.P.: A configurable reference modeling language. Inf. Systems 32(1), 1–23 (2007)
3. Kumar, A., Wen, Y.: Design and management of exible process variants using templates and rules. Int. J. Comput. Ind. 63(2), 112–130 (2012)
4. Figl, K., Laue, R.: Cognitive Complexity in Business Process Modeling. In: Mouratidis, H., Rolland, C. (eds.) CAiSE 2011. LNCS, vol. 6741, pp. 452–466. Springer, Heidelberg (2011)
5. Melcher, J., Detlef, S.: Towards Validating Prediction Systems for Process Understandability: Measuring Process Understandability. In: Proc. SYNASC 2008, pp. 564–571 (2008)
6. La Rosa, M., Lux, J., Seidel, S., Dumas, M., ter Hofstede, A.H.M.: Questionnaire-driven Configuration of Reference Process Models. In: Krogstie, J., Opdahl, A.L., Sindre, G. (eds.) CAiSE 2007 and WES 2007. LNCS, vol. 4495, pp. 424–438. Springer, Heidelberg (2007)
7. Larkin, J.H., Simon, H.A.: Why a Diagram is (Sometimes) Worth Ten Thousand Words. Cognitive Science 11(1), 65–100 (1987)
8. Tracz, W.J.: Computer programming and the human thought process. Software: Practice and Experience 9(2), 127–137 (1979)
9. Paas, F., Tuovinen, J.E., Tabbers, H., Van Gerven, P.W.M.: Cognitive Load Measurement as a Means to Advance Cognitive Load Theory. Educational Psychologist 38(1), 63–71 (2003)
10. Miller, G.: The Magical Number Seven, Plus or Minus Two: Some Limits on Our Capacity for Processing Information. The Psychological Review 63(2), 81–97 (1956)
11. Moody, D.L.: Cognitive Load Effects on End User Understanding of Conceptual Models: An Experimental Analysis. In: Benczúr, A.A., Demetrovics, J., Gottlob, G. (eds.) ADBIS 2004. LNCS, vol. 3255, pp. 129–143. Springer, Heidelberg (2004)
12. Sweller, J.: Cognitive load during problem solving: Effects on learning. Cognitive Science 12(2), 257–285 (1988)
13. Zugal, S., Pinggera, J., Weber, B.: The Impact of Testcases on the Maintainability of Declarative Process Models. In: Halpin, T., Nurcan, S., Krogstie, J., Soffer, P., Proper, E., Schmidt, R., Bider, I. (eds.) BPMDS 2011 and EMMSAD 2011. LNBIP, vol. 81, pp. 163–177. Springer, Heidelberg (2011)
14. Scaife, M., Rogers, Y.: External cognition: how do graphical representations work? Int. J. Human-Computer Studies 45(2), 185–213 (1996)
15. Zugal, S., Pinggera, J., Mendling, J., Reijers, H.A., Weber, B.: Assessing the Impact of Hierarchy on Model Understandability-A Cognitive Perspective. In: EESSMod 2011, pp. 123–133 (2011)
16. Zugal, S., Soffer, P., Pinggera, J., Weber, B.: Expressiveness and Understandability Considerations of Hierarchy in Declarative Business Process Models. In: Bider, I., Halpin, T., Krogstie, J., Nurcan, S., Proper, E., Schmidt, R., Soffer, P., Wrycza, S. (eds.) EMMSAD 2012 and BPMDS 2012. LNBIP, vol. 113, pp. 167–181. Springer, Heidelberg (2012)
17. Sweller, J., Chandler, P.: Why Some Material Is Difficult to Learn. Cognition and Instruction 12(3), 185–233 (1994)
18. Feldmann Barrett, L., Tugade, M.M., Engle, R.W.: Individual Differences in Working Memory Capacity and Dual-Process Theories of the Mind. Psychol. Bull. 130(4), 553–573 (2004)
19. Moody, D.L.: The "Physics" of Notations: Toward a Scientific Basis for Constructing Visual Notations in Software Engineering. IEEE Trans. Soft. Eng. 35(6), 756–779 (2009)

20. Li, C., Reichert, M., Wombacher, A.: On Measuring Process Model Similarity Based on High-Level Change Operations. In: Li, Q., Spaccapietra, S., Yu, E., Olivé, A. (eds.) ER 2008. LNCS, vol. 5231, pp. 248–264. Springer, Heidelberg (2008)

21. Lönn, C.-M., Uppström, E., Wohed, P., Juell-Skielse, G.: Configurable Process Models for the Swedish Public Sector. In: Ralyté, J., Franch, X., Brinkkemper, S., Wrycza, S. (eds.) CAiSE 2012. LNCS, vol. 7328, pp. 190–205. Springer, Heidelberg (2012)

22. Gottschalk, F., Wagemakers, T.A.C., Jansen-Vullers, M.H., van der Aalst, W.M.P., La Rosa, M.: Configurable Process Models: Experiences from a Municipality Case Study. In: van Eck, P., Gordijn, J., Wieringa, R. (eds.) CAiSE 2009. LNCS, vol. 5565, pp. 486–500. Springer, Heidelberg (2009)

23. Mendling, J., Reijers, H.A., Cardoso, J.: What Makes Process Models Understandable? In: Alonso, G., Dadam, P., Rosemann, M. (eds.) BPM 2007. LNCS, vol. 4714, pp. 48–63. Springer, Heidelberg (2007)

24. Vanderfeesten, I., Reijers, H.A., van der Aalst, W.M.P.: Evaluating workflow process designs using cohesion and coupling metrics. Int. J. Comput. Ind. 59(5), 420–437 (2008)

25. Reijers, H.A., Mendling, J.: A Study into the Factors that Influence the Understandability of Business Process Models. SMCA 41(3), 449–462 (2011)

26. Zugal, S., Pinggera, J., Weber, B.: Assessing Process Models with Cognitive Psychology. In: Proc. EMISA 2011, pp. 177–182 (2011)

Querying Process Models Repositories by Aggregated Graph Search

Sherif Sakr[1], Ahmed Awad[2], and Matthias Kunze[3]

[1] National ICT Australia (NICTA) and University of New South Wales, Australia
ssakr@cse.unsw.edu.au
[2] Faculty of Computers and Information, Cairo University, Egypt
a.gaafar@fci-cu.edu.eg
[3] Hasso-Plattner-Institute, University of Potsdam, Germany
matthias.kunze@hpi.uni-potsdam.de

Abstract. Business process modeling is essential in any process improvement project. Yet, it is a time consuming and an error-prone step. With a rapidly increasing number of process models developed by different process designers, it becomes crucial for business process designers to reuse knowledge existing in model repositories, e.g., to find solutions for a recurring situation. Process model querying provides powerful means to address this situation. However, current approaches fail if no single process model satisfies all constraints of a query.

In this paper, we present a novel approach for querying business process models repositories, where a query is decomposed into several subqueries. Each subquery is then used to obtain matching fragments from process models stored in the repository. New process models are constructed from these fragments, which may originate from different process models. By this, several processes are assembled from matching fragments and presented to the process designer as a ranked list. The main advantage of our approach is that the designer does not need to specify the subqueries, as they are derived automatically.

Keywords: Business process design, Reuse, Querying business processes, Process model composition.

1 Introduction

Business Process Management (BPM) aims at the automated support and coordination of business in an integrated manner by capturing, implementing, controlling, and evaluating all activities taking place in an environment that defines the enterprise [1]. Business process modeling is an essential first step in the business process engineering chain, as they enable a better understanding of the organization's operations by facilitating communication between business analysts and IT experts.

In general, designing a new business process model is a tedious and error-prone task that requires identifying the activities that need to be performed, ordering of their execution, handling exceptional cases that can occur, etc. Therefore, in any organization, business process models represent a main source of business knowledge, typically scattered among several IT systems, business documents, and the minds of involved people. This knowledge is usually reused each time a process model is created or updated, however, in an *ad-hoc* and generally uncontrolled fashion. Thus, it is of great value to have

M. La Rosa and P. Soffer (Eds.): BPM 2012 Workshops, LNBIP 132, pp. 573–585, 2013.
© Springer-Verlag Berlin Heidelberg 2013

systematic, flexible, and effective mechanisms to query and reuse the available knowledge of process model repositories to reduce time and effort, and improve the quality newly designed business process model.

Business process repositories have been developed along with techniques to access models, and associate them with metadata [2,3]. While search and retrieval of process models are largely based on keyword and full text search, certain approaches to effectively *query* process models according to their semantics have been proposed recently [4,5,6]. Based on the same notion of a query that is formulated to search a process repositories, these approaches fail, if no single process model satisfies all constraints in the query, i.e., they return no result.

In this paper, we present a novel approach for querying business process models, where the answer of a query graph can be assembled of fragments from different process models, when a single process model can not satisfy all the query constraints. Here, business process designers are enabled to compose new process models by reusing multiple fragments from different process models. The main advantage of our approach is that the designer does not need to specify components of the query, which shall be mapped to fragments in matched process models. Instead, the query is decomposed automatically into subqueries and each subquery is matched against the process model repository to retrieve matching fragments. The retrieved fragments are then combined to provide answers matching the query in form of a ranked list, from which the designer can select.

We implemented a proof of concept of our approach top of existing software, namely the open modeling platform *Oryx* [2] and the *BPMN-Q* query language [4,7,8]. BPMN-Q is a visual query language that closely resembles BPMN and thus, facilitates formulating queries even for non-technical users and novices in a business domain. The benefits of this approach is that it enables designing new process models by reusing fragments from several existing process models, by automatic query decomposition and matching on a fine-granular level of process fragments; hence, effectively reducing time and effort, while improving the quality and maturity of newly designed processes.

The remainder of this paper is organized as follows. We lay out the basics of business process models and BPMN-Q in Section 2 before Section 3 introduces our approach of querying graph-based repositories by aggregated graph search. Section 4 describes the mechanism to decompose the process model query and to aggregate matching process model fragments to form the query answers. An architectural overview of the implementation is provided in Section 5. Related work is discussed in Section 6 before we conclude the paper in Section 7.

2   Preliminaries

This section formally introduces process modeling and querying, which form the groundwork for our approach.

2.1   Business Process Modeling

Currently, there is a number of business process modeling languages, e.g., BPMN, EPC, YAWL, and UML Activity Diagram. Despite the variance in their concrete syntax and expressiveness, they all share the common concepts of tasks, events, gateways (or routing nodes), artifacts, and resources, as well as relations between them, such as control flow. Without loss of generality, we can abstract from particular node types as their execution semantics are not vital to structural query matching, which is rather based on the concept of a process model graph.

Definition 1 (Process Model). *A process model P is a connected graph (N, E), where N is a non-empty set of control flow nodes and $E \subseteq N \times N$ a nonempty set of directed* control flow edges *where $\bullet n$ ($n\bullet$) stands for the set of immediate predecessor (successor) nodes of $n \in N$.*

A process model has exactly one start event $n_{start} \in N$ with no incoming and at least one outgoing control flow edge, i.e., $|\bullet n_{start}| = 0 \wedge |n_{start} \bullet| \geq 1$, and exactly one end event $n_{end} \in N$ with at least one incoming and no outgoing control flow edge, i.e., $|\bullet n_{end}| \geq 1 \wedge |n_{end} \bullet| = 0$. Each other control flow node $n \in N \setminus \{n_{start}, n_{end}\}$ is on a path from n_{start} to n_{end}.

A connected sub-graph of a process model is a *process model fragment*. We refer to a specific type of process model fragments that have a *single entry* node and a *single exit* node [9] as *process model components*.

Definition 2 (Process Model Component). *A connected subgraph (N', E') of a process model (N, E), where $N' \in N, E' \in E$, is a process model component PC iff it has exactly one incoming boundary node $n_{in} \in N'$, i.e., $\bullet n_{in} \subseteq N \setminus N'$ and one outgoing boundary node $n_{out} \in N'$, i.e., $n_{out}\bullet \subseteq N \setminus N'$.*

2.2 Business Process Model Querying

Based on the definition of process models and process model components, we introduce the concept of process model queries as a means to obtain process components from a collection of business processes models by structurally matching a query to each of them. BPMN-Q is a visual process model query language designed to help business process designers access repositories of business process models [4]. The language supports querying the control flow aspects of business process models. Moreover, it introduces new *abstraction* concepts that are useful for various querying scenarios.

Definition 3 (BPMN-Q Query). A BPMN-Q query is a tuple
$Q = (QC, QCF, QP, isAnonymous)$ *where:*

- *QC is a finite set of* control flow nodes *in a query,*
- *$QCF \subseteq QC \times QC$ is the* control flow relation *between control nodes in a query,*
- *$QP \subseteq QC \times QC$ is the* path *relation between control nodes in a query,*
- *isAnonymous : $QC \rightarrow \{true, false\}$ is a function that determines whether control flow nodes of a query are anonymous.*

Matching Queries to Process Models. A BPMN-Q query is matched to a candidate process model via a set of refinements to the query. With each refinement nodes (edges) in a query are replaced with the corresponding nodes (edges) of the matching process model. If one node can have more than one possible replacement within the process model, a new, refined copy of the query is created for each possible replacement. We call the replacement a resolution of an element of the query. Fig. 1 shows a sample BPMN-Q query along with a match to a process model, highlighted in grey. The query represents a path edge which connects two nodes, A and D, and returns the set of nodes that could exist in between these two nodes in the matching process model.

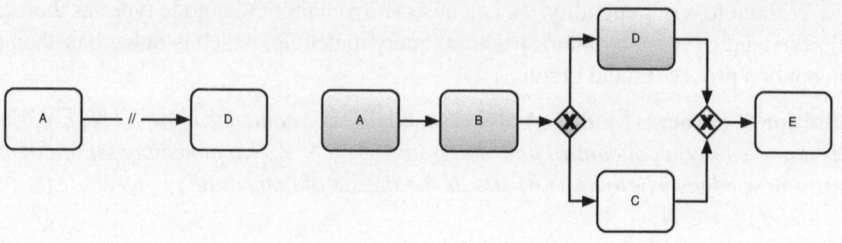

Fig. 1. An example BPMN-Q query with a match to a process model

Basically, the BPMN-Q query processor looks for exact matches of labels of activities in a query with those in the candidate process model. However, in practice, process modelers do not follow a strict naming scheme for activity labels. Thus, the query would find a small set of matching processes. To tackle this problem, we employed information retrieval techniques to automate the discovery of *semantically* similar activities [10]. The BPMN-Q query gets modified by substituting each of its activities with similar ones. With such a substitution step, new BPMN-Q query graphs are generated to constitute an expanded BPMN-Q query set.

Process components matching a query model will have a similarity score assigned ranging from 0 to 1. A similarity score of 1 indicates an exact match between the query and the process. Lower similarity scores indicate that a match was found between a semantically similar query and the process model. For more details about the BPMN-Q query language and its similarity matching mechanism, we refer the reader to [4,10,11].

3   Querying Process Models By Aggregated Search

The approach presented in this paper is based on the notion of *aggregated graph search* [12], where the answer of a process model query can be represented as an aggregation of process model fragments from multiple process models which are stored in the process model repository.

Definition 4 (Process Model Aggregated Search). *Given a process model query q and a process model repository $R = \{M_1, M_2, ..., M_n\}$, the problem of aggregated search of a process model query is to find a set of process models $S \subseteq R$ for which the joining of the matching process model fragments $F_{M_1}, F_{M_2}, ..., F_{M_k}$ from process models $M_1, M_2, ..., M_k \in S$ respectively, $F_{M_1} \bowtie F_{M_2} \bowtie ... \bowtie F_{M_k}$, leads to the answer of the process model query q.*

Fig. 2 shows a BPMN-Q query example which requires containment of an activity "*Check document*" that is immediately followed by an activity "*Verify customer record*" and two path edges from the latter activity to "*Assess risk*" and "*Open savings account*" respectively. Let us assume that the process model repository consists of the two process models which are shown in Fig. 3. Matching the BPMN-Q query to each process model separately fails to find any match. In particular, query evaluation against process model $P1$ fails because there is no path from activity "*Verify customer record*" to the "*Assess risk*" activity. Similarly, the query evaluation against process model $P2$ fails be-

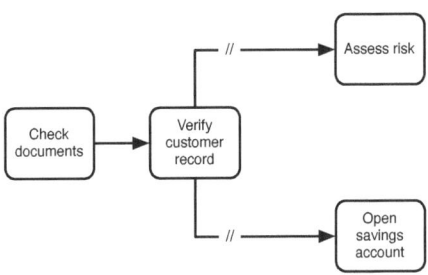

Fig. 2. An example BPMN-Q query

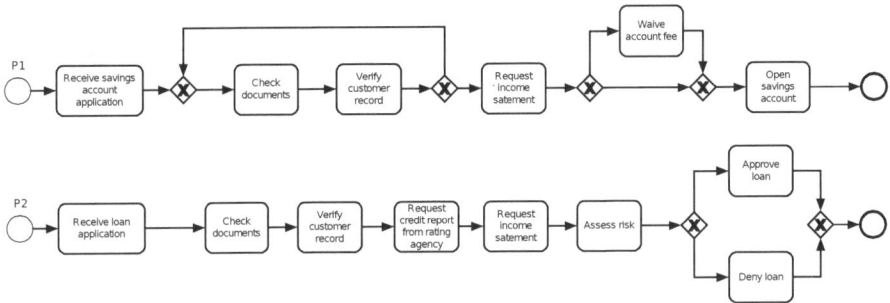

Fig. 3. Two process models to query

cause there is no path from activity "*Verify customer record*" to activity "*Open savings account*".

With our aggregation-based query approach, the query is not only matched collectively to each single process model, but the original BPMN-Q query is decomposed into subqueries which are matched individually against process models and the results of these sub-queries are aggregated to form the query answers.

4   Query Decomposition and Fragments Aggregation

This section introduces our approach towards above scenario, where a query is not met by a single process model, whereas subqueries can successfully be matched and returned fragments are aggregated into a newly designed process model.

4.1   BPMN-Q Query Decomposition

First, we focus on the decomposition of BPMN-Q query graphs. In particular, given an input BPMN-Q query q, we decompose the query graph into two sets of subqueries:

1. A set of static subqueries $StatQ$: where each static query represents a set of query nodes with static labels which are connected with direct flow edges.
2. A set of dynamic subqueries $DynaQ$: where each dynamic query contains at least one dynamic query element, e.g., anonymous node or path edge, in addition to a static join point with another subquery.

Algorithm 1. Decomposition Process of a BPMN-Q Query

Require: BPMN-Q Query: q.
Ensure: A Set of Static Sub-queries: $StatQ$
    A Set of Dynamic Sub-queries: $DynaQ$
    A Set of Join Points: JP
1: $SplitPoints$:= **IdentifyQuerySplitPoints**(q);
2: $StatQ$:= **DetectConnectedStaticNodes**(q);
3: **for all** $P \in SplitPoints$ **do**
4:     **if** $\nexists (Q \in DynaQ \mid P \in Q)$ **then**
5:         **if** P.Type == AnonymousActivity **OR** P.Type == GenericNode **then**
6:             **if** P.HasIncomingEdges **AND** P.HasOutgoingEdges **then**
7:                 $DQ1$:= **TraverseBackwardToFirstStaticPoint**(P);
8:                 $DQ2$:= **TraverseForwardToFirstStaticPoint**(P);
9:                 $DynaQ$.Add($DQ1$);
10:                $DynaQ$.Add($DQ2$);
11:                JP.Add(P);
12:            **else if** P.HasIncomingEdges **AND NOT** P.HasOutgoingEdges **then**
13:                $JoinPoint$:= **GetFirstStaticPointByBackwardTraversal**(P);
14:                DQ:= **TraverseBackwardToFirstStaticPoint**(P);
15:                $DynaQ$.Add(DQ);
16:                JP.Add($JoinPoint$);
17:            **else if** P.HasOutgoingEdges **AND NOT** P.HasIncomingEdges **then**
18:                $JoinPoint$:= **GetFirstStaticPointByForwardTraversal**(P);
19:                DQ:= **TraverseForwardToFirstStaticPoint**(P);
20:                $DynaQ$.Add(DQ);
21:                JP.Add($JoinPoint$);
22:            **end if**
23:         **else if** P.Type == PathEdge **then**
24:            $JoinPoint$:= **GetFirstStaticPointByBackwardTraversal**(P);
25:            $EndPoint$:= **GetFirstStaticPointByForwardTraversal**(P);
26:            DQ:= **SubGraph**($JoinPoint$, $EndPoint$);
27:            JP.Add($JoinPoint$);
28:         **end if**
29:     **end if**
30: **end for**
31: **for all** $Q \in DynaQ$ **do**
32:     **if** Q.HasNoStaticNodes **then**
33:         **ExtendQuerySubgraphToIncludeStaticNode**(Q);
34:         JP.Replace(Q.OriginalJoinPoint,Q.NewStaticNode);
35:     **end if**
36: **end for**
37: **return** $StatQ$, $DynaQ$, JP;

Algorithm 1 describes the steps of our BPMN-Q query decomposition mechanism. We start by identifying the set of *split points* of the input BPMN-Q query (Line 1). In particular, we specify the split points in a BPMN-Q query by the existence of any of the following BPMN-Q language constructs [4].

Anonymous Node. These nodes resemble activity nodes, but are distinguished by the (@) sign at the beginning of the node label. This query construct is used to allow usage of unknown activities in a query.

Path Edge. This query construct states that there must be a path from the source activity A to the destination activity B where the path edge is bound to all nodes and edges between the two nodes.

After determining the set of the split points, the set of decomposed static sub-queries ($StatQ$) is determined by identifying each set of nodes in the input query which have static labels and are connected by direct flow edges (Line 2). It should be noted that static queries cannot contain any of the identified query split points. In addition, a static nodes of the input query cannot be included in more than one decomposed static query. The set of dynamic decomposed queries ($DynaQ$) is specified based on the identified query split points as follows:

- If the split node is of the type *anonymous node*, then the dynamic queries are specified according to the following conditions:
  - If the split node, SN, has *incoming edges and outgoing edges*, then *two* dynamic queries are constructed (Lines 6 to 11).

    The first dynamic query, $DQ1$, is constructed by traversing the query graph *backwardly* starting from the split point to the first node, $ST1$, with a static label or until no further nodes can be reached. The query subgraph that includes the split point SN and $ST1$ represents $DQ1$.

    Similarly, $DQ2$ is constructed by traversing the query graph *forwardly* to the first node, $ST2$, with a static label or until no further nodes can be reached. The query subgraph that includes the split point SN and $ST2$ represents $DQ2$. In this case, the split node (SN) represents the join point between $DQ1$ and $DQ2$.
  - If the split node, SN, has *only incoming edges* but no outgoing edges, then *one* dynamic query is constructed (Lines 12 to 16) by traversing the query graph *backwardly* starting from the split point to the first node, ST, with a static label. The query subgraph that includes the split point, SN, and ST represents DQ. The static node, ST, represents the join point between DQ and the (static or dynamic) query to which ST belongs.
  - If the split node, SN, has *only outgoing edges* but no incoming edges, then also *one* dynamic query is constructed (Lines 17 to 21) by traversing the query graph *forwardly* starting from the split point to the first node, ST, with a static label, to construct DQ. Also in this case, the static node, ST, represents the join point between DQ and the (static or dynamic) query to which ST belongs.
- If the split node is of the type *path edge*, then one dynamic query is specified (Lines 23 to 27) by traversing the query graph backwardly starting from the source node of the path edge to the first node, $ST1$, with a static label and then traversing the query graph forwardly starting from the destination node of the path edge to the first node, $ST2$, with a static label. The dynamic query, DQ, represents the subgraph between $ST1$ and $ST2$, where $ST1$ represents the join point between DQ and the query to which the node $ST1$ belongs.

The last step of our decomposition process is to verify that each dynamic sub-query has at least one node with a static label. It could occur that the dynamic query is generated with no static node if the traversal from the split point backwardly or forwardly stops by reaching a start or end node. If any sub-query fails to satisfy this condition, then it is expanded from its join point forwardly or backwardly until the first reachable static point and the join point is correspondingly adjusted (Lines 30 to 35). There will be no decomposition case if the input query does not have any node with a static label. It should be noted that each split point can be only included in one dynamic sub-query (Line 4).

Query execution starts by matching each query in the set of static sub-queries ($StatQ$) against the process model repository. In principle, the evaluation process of static sub-queries represent the traditional subgraph query matching problem, where exact or approximate means can be applied. The search process terminates if any of the decomposed static sub-queries has no match. Otherwise, query execution continues to evaluate each query in the set of dynamic sub-queries ($DynaQ$).

The results of both, static and dynamic, sub-queries, which may originate from different process models, are then joined to form the aggregated answer of the input query q. Fig. 4(a) illustrates the static and dynamic sub-queries from the decomposed BPMN-Q query of Fig. 2. Fig. 4(b) illustrates an aggregated query answer that combines process model fragments from the two process models which are presented in Fig. 3.

4.2 Aggregating the Process Model Fragments

The main task of a query processor is to evaluate the BPMN-Q queries of the decomposed static or dynamic sub-queries, which are discovered according to the decomposition process of Section 4.1, against the process model repository. For each BPMN-Q sub-query, a result set is returned that comprises *matched* process model components. These matched components could represent exact or similar matches for the query models, cf. Section 2.2. In case of similar matches, each matched process model component is then attached with its similarity score (SS), which is computed during the query evaluation process. In case of an exact match, the value of this similarity score is equal to 1 for each matched component of the result set [10].

From multiple matched components for each sub-query, which usually belong to different process models, follows that we can have several possible aggregation results that originate from distinct process models. Each potentially aggregated result needs to include exactly one component from the answer set of each sub-query. Clearly, it is inconvenient for process designers to go through this potentially very large list of aggregated models to select among them.

Therefore, the set of possible aggregated results are *ranked* according to various criteria, applying a ranking process that starts by initially ranking the matched process model components inside the answer set of each query based on their similarity scores. Then, it computes a ranking score for each possible aggregated model, by a number of

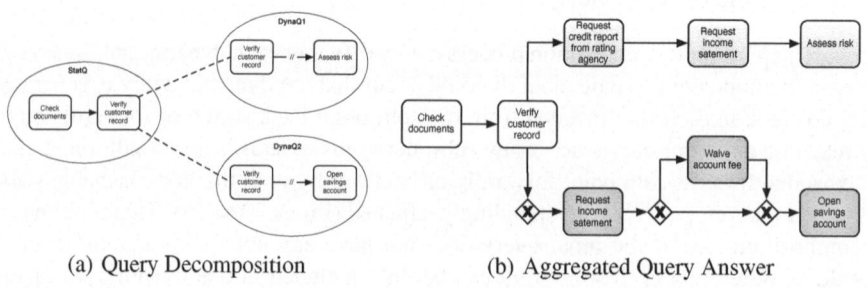

(a) Query Decomposition   (b) Aggregated Query Answer

Fig. 4. BPMN-Q Query Decomposition and Aggregated Search for Business Process Models

elementary aggregation scores. In the following we describe two basic scores, further measures that also incorporate meta data are discussed in [13].

Combined Similarity Matching Score (CS). This score multiplies the respective similarity scores SS of each aggregated model component mc_i with regards to the matched sub-query

$$CS(ccp) = \prod_{i=1}^{n} SS(mc_i)$$

where n represents the number of the model components.

Homogeneity Score (HS). Model components that originate from the same process model shall be preferred over those that stem from different models to increase a result model's homogeneity and consistency. The pair homogeneity score, PHS, computes the homogeneity of each *unique pair* (mc_i, mc_j) of the model components by their origin:

$$PHS(mc_i, mc_j) = \left\{ \begin{array}{l} 0 \text{ if the original models of the pair are different} \\ 1 \text{ if the original models of the pair are the same} \end{array} \right\}$$

In general, the number of unique different pairs n is equal to $\frac{c(c-1)}{2}$ where c is the number of process model components. The homogeneity score of an aggregate model is then computed bị

$$HS(ccp) = \frac{\sum_{i=1}^{n} PHS(udp_i)}{n}$$

where udp represent a unique pair of model components (mc_i, mc_j) and n represent the total number of unique different pairs.

The *final ranking score* of a candidate aggregated model is computed by the weighted sum of the elementary scores above,

$$FinalScore(ccp) = w_1 * CS(ccp) + w_2 * HS(ccp)$$

where w_i represents a weighting factor for a scoring element which can be configured and adjusted by the end-user, while $w_1 + w_2 = 1$. Initially, process designers can rely on a uniform regression parameter where all weighting factors have the same value, i.e., $w_i = 0.5$. With the continuous usage of the system, workload data can be gathered to generate significant training datasets that can be used as an input for a regression analysis process to deduce optimized weighting factors [14].

5 Framework Architecture

In this section, we describe the architecture of our implementation for the *aggregated graph search* framework for querying repositories of business process models, illustrated in Fig. 5, which consists of the following main components.

Process Model Repository. Instead of building our approach on top of a proprietary repository, it shall be connected to several, potentially disparate repositories, obtain and maintain process models stored remotely. Repositories do not only store models [15], but also a set of metadata, which can be used for aggregation and ranking.

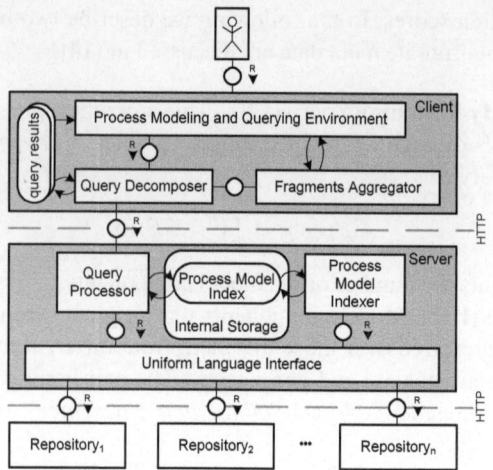

Fig. 5. Framework Architecture

Query Processor & Process Model Indexes. The *query processor* evaluates queries received from the query interface [7]. It provides support for relaxation and refinement of user queries. In case the queries do not return sufficient results, the query processor is able to relax the query according to some similarity notions [10,16]. In order to further improve the searching, process models could be *indexed* upfront to expedite query evaluations [17].

Process Modeling and Querying Environment. provides the process designer with a user-friendly *modeling and querying interface* [2]. Users express their queries using the BPMN-Q language [4]. The *query decomposer* identifies the candidate decomposed sub-queries, cf. Section 4.1, and passes them to the *query processor*. The returned set of process model fragments for each query will then be combined and aggregated by the *fragment aggregator* and return a *ranked* list of aggregated process models as a result of the input query, cf. Section 4.2.

The *process modeling* environment of our framework is the *Oryx* editor, an extensible process modeling platform for research, designed to model and manage process models online [2]. The *Query interface* and *query processor* for BPMN-Q [4,7] components have been implemented as plugins to the Oryx editor and are able to run process model queries against the Oryx online process model repository. The *query decomposer* and *fragment aggregator* components are implemented as plugins to the Oryx editor that uses the BPMN-Q query processor to evaluate the results of each decomposed query and then returns the ranked aggregations to the end-user. Our architecture acknowledges the existence of a multitude of different process model repositories, which is the rationale behind the decoupling of a process modeling, querying, and aggregation components from a particular process model repository.

6   Related Work

Business process model search is a vivid topic among researchers and has attracted many solutions that can generally be distinguished in similarity search and process model querying [18]. An essential aspect of comparing processes is the alignment of process nodes [19]. That is, to discover relationships in one process model and map them to a second one, corresponding nodes must be discovered first. In most cases simple techniques such as string edit distance, n-grams, etc have been used. More complex techniques address one-to-many and many-to-many alignments to compensate for different levels of model granularity [19,20]. While we rely on simple, i.e., one-to-one, mappings to keep the paper concise, also complex mappings could be employed in our case.

With regards to to address process model similarity search, different structural techniques have been applied. For instance, in [16] the graph-edit-distance was used to assess how much two process graphs resemble each other; graph homomorphisms have been used to find models that embrace a given query model [21]. More sophisticated approaches address path resolution in graphs, i.e., if two nodes in a query model are connected by an edge, there must exist a path consisting of edges and nodes that connects correlating nodes in the stored models. Examples are BP-QL [5] which is restricted to BPEL and uses XML to formulate queries, IPM-QL that requires a custom XML representation for models and query, and BPMN-Q [4] where a visual query language that resembles the BPMN notation has been proposed for process model querying. The work presented in this paper, leverages BPMN-Q. Further querying approaches addressed behavior [22,23] or ontological information [6]. In principle, our approach is fully agnostic with respect to integrating and reusing any similarity matching technique for process models into the query processor component.

None of these works addressed decomposing a query into several fragments, querying stored process models with each of these fragments, and constructing of a new model from matches that originate from different models. In earlier work [13], we have presented an approach for reusing process model components based on the notion of a *partial process model* which consists of static and dynamic components. The static components represent the concrete aspects of the process model, while the dynamic components are BPMN-Q queries explicitly defined by a user. Upon search, each dynamic component is matched against models in the repository and returned fragments are to be embedded in the overall process, thus completing the static components.

Here, we develop our approach one step further, such that the specification of static and dynamic components are provided automatically without any user involvement. The idea of *aggregated graph search* has been introduced for the basic exact subgraph matching problem in [12], where the authors present a decomposition of labelled, directed graphs into a relational data schema and means to efficiently query this knowledge by means of SQL. However, the decomposition of a BPMN-Q query is more complex, as the graphs comprise advanced semantics, i.e., different node types must be distinguished during search along with the generic node type that is kind of a wild card; matching of nodes must address the anonymous activity. Further, BPMN-Q provides path-edges that may resolve to a path consisting of several edges in a model to be matched. Hence, more sophisticated means are required to decompose, store, and retrieve models, and aggregate matched fragments.

7 Conclusion

In this paper, we introduced a new approach for querying and reusing knowledge contained in business process model repositories. In this approach, the answer of a process model query can be represented as an assembly of different process model fragments from *multiple* process models, when a single process model can not satisfy all the query constraints. To achieve this, the query is automatically decomposed into several sub-queries and the results of each sub-query—fragments of matched process models in the repository—are aggregated to form a new process model that satisfies the query. A list of possible aggregations is ranked in order to provide the business process designer with the closest answers for his query.

This approach provides several benefits by reusing materialized business knowledge which is available in existing process model repositories. The reuse is not only on the level of a whole process model, but rather on a finer grained level, i.e., process model fragments. The approach *automatically* and *flexibly* collects components from different process models. Therefore, the approach can effectively reduce the time and effort of the business process modeling task. It can also effectively improve the quality and maturity of the newly developed business process models.

References

1. Weske, M.: Business Process Management: Concepts, Languages, Architectures. Springer, Heidelberg (2007)
2. Decker, G., Overdick, H., Weske, M.: Oryx – Sharing Conceptual Models on the Web. In: Li, Q., Spaccapietra, S., Yu, E., Olivé, A. (eds.) ER 2008. LNCS, vol. 5231, pp. 536–537. Springer, Heidelberg (2008)
3. Rosa, M.L., Reijers, H.A., van der Aalst, W.M.P., Dijkman, R.M., Mendling, J., Dumas, M., García-Bañuelos, L.: APROMORE: An advanced process model repository. Expert Syst. Appl. 38(6), 7029–7040 (2011)
4. Awad, A.: BPMN-Q: A Language to Query Business Processes. In: EMISA (2007)
5. Beeri, C., Eyal, A., Kamenkovich, S., Milo, T.: Querying business processes with BP-QL. Inf. Syst. 33(6), 477–507 (2008)
6. Markovic, I.: Advanced querying and reasoning on business process models. In: BIS (2008)
7. Sakr, S., Awad, A.: A framework for querying graph-based business process models. In: WWW (2010)
8. Awad, A., Sakr, S.: Querying Graph-Based Repositories of Business Process Models. In: Yoshikawa, M., Meng, X., Yumoto, T., Ma, Q., Sun, L., Watanabe, C. (eds.) DASFAA 2010. LNCS, vol. 6193, pp. 33–44. Springer, Heidelberg (2010)
9. Vanhatalo, J., Völzer, H., Koehler, J.: The Refined Process Structure Tree. In: Dumas, M., Reichert, M., Shan, M.-C. (eds.) BPM 2008. LNCS, vol. 5240, pp. 100–115. Springer, Heidelberg (2008)
10. Awad, A., Polyvyanyy, A., Weske, M.: Semantic Querying of Business Process Models. In: EDOC (2008)
11. Laue, R., Awad, A.: Visual suggestions for improvements in business process diagrams. J. Vis. Lang. Comput. 22(5), 385–399 (2011)
12. Le, T.-H., Elghazel, H., Hacid, M.-S.: A Relational-Based Approach for Aggregated Search in Graph Databases. In: Lee, S.-g., Peng, Z., Zhou, X., Moon, Y.-S., Unland, R., Yoo, J. (eds.) DASFAA 2012, Part I. LNCS, vol. 7238, pp. 33–47. Springer, Heidelberg (2012)

13. Awad, A., Sakr, S., Kunze, M., Weske, M.: Design by Selection: A Reuse-Based Approach for Business Process Modeling. In: Jeusfeld, M., Delcambre, L., Ling, T.-W. (eds.) ER 2011. LNCS, vol. 6998, pp. 332–345. Springer, Heidelberg (2011)
14. Hwang, C., Hong, D.H., Seok, K.: Support vector interval regression machine for crisp input and output data. Fuzzy Sets and Systems 157(8) (2006)
15. Bernstein, P., Dayal, U.: An overview of repository technology. In: VLDB (1994)
16. Dijkman, R., Dumas, M., García-Bañuelos, L.: Graph Matching Algorithms for Business Process Model Similarity Search. In: Dayal, U., Eder, J., Koehler, J., Reijers, H.A. (eds.) BPM 2009. LNCS, vol. 5701, pp. 48–63. Springer, Heidelberg (2009)
17. Sakr, S.: GraphREL: A Decomposition-Based and Selectivity-Aware Relational Framework for Processing Sub-graph Queries. In: Zhou, X., Yokota, H., Deng, K., Liu, Q. (eds.) DAS-FAA 2009. LNCS, vol. 5463, pp. 123–137. Springer, Heidelberg (2009)
18. Dijkman, R.M., Rosa, M.L., Reijers, H.A.: Managing large collections of business process models - current techniques and challenges. Computers in Industry 63(2), 91–97 (2012)
19. Weidlich, M., Dijkman, R., Mendling, J.: The ICoP Framework: Identification of Correspondences between Process Models. In: Pernici, B. (ed.) CAiSE 2010. LNCS, vol. 6051, pp. 483–498. Springer, Heidelberg (2010)
20. Dijkman, R., Dumas, M., Garcia-Banuelos, L., Kaarik, R.: Aligning Business Process Models. In: EDOC (2009)
21. Grigori, D., Corrales, J.C., Bouzeghoub, M.: Behavioral Matchmaking for Service Retrieval. In: ICWS (2006)
22. Jin, T., Wang, J., Wen, L.: Querying Business Process Models Based on Semantics. In: Yu, J.X., Kim, M.H., Unland, R. (eds.) DASFAA 2011, Part II. LNCS, vol. 6588, pp. 164–178. Springer, Heidelberg (2011)
23. Kunze, M., Weske, M.: Local Behavior Similarity. In: Bider, I., Halpin, T., Krogstie, J., Nurcan, S., Proper, E., Schmidt, R., Soffer, P., Wrycza, S. (eds.) EMMSAD 2012 and BPMDS 2012. LNBIP, vol. 113, pp. 107–120. Springer, Heidelberg (2012)

Enabling Reuse of Process Models through the Detection of Similar Process Parts

Fabian Pittke[1,3], Henrik Leopold[1], Jan Mendling[2], and Gerrit Tamm[3]

[1] Humboldt-Universität zu Berlin, Unter den Linden 6, 10099 Berlin, Germany
henrik.leopold@wiwi.hu-berlin.de
[2] WU Vienna, Augasse 2-6, A-1090 Vienna, Austria
jan.mendling@wu.ac.at
[3] SRH University Berlin, Ernst-Reuter-Platz 10, 10587 Berlin, Germany
fabian.pittke@srh-uni-berlin.de, gerrit.tamm@srh-uni-berlin.de

Abstract. Many companies use business process modeling to support various improvements initiatives leading to an increasing number of process models. Typically, these models are stored in a collection containing several hundreds of process models. In many cases, process models are overlapping, although parts could be easily reused saving costs and efforts. Different labeling styles and evolving process models complicate the detection of reusable model parts. In this paper, we propose a novel approach for the detection of equivalent and similar process model parts that exploits semantic comparison of activity labels and behavioral comparison of control flow. We evaluate our approach on the SAP Reference Model, a collection with 604 process models. The evaluation reveals insights for the thresholds of semantic and behavioral similarity of process models as well as their influence for similar process part detection. Hence, we identify five candidate groups with specific similarity properties that contain reoccurring process parts.

Keywords: Business Process Modeling, Similar Process Part Detection, Semantic Similarity, Behavioral Similarity.

1 Introduction

Due to the increasing popularity of business process modeling many companies face a steadily increasing amount of process models. In some cases, such process model collections range up to thousands of process models [1]. As a result, these companies struggle with the effective maintenance of their process model collections [2].

A corresponding problem of growing model collections is the increasing overlap across process models. Hence, the implementation of consistent changes becomes more and more challenging and cost intensive. Moreover, size and number of overlapping process models is often larger than it necessarily had to be. Reoccurring parts could be easily extracted in form of separate process models that reduce the complexity of the models themselves and of the overall collection. Recent

M. La Rosa and P. Soffer (Eds.): BPM 2012 Workshops, LNBIP 132, pp. 586–597, 2013.

research addressed this problem by detecting clones in process model repositories [3]. Although the detection of clones is undoubtedly a very useful step, it is not complete. Moreover, most approaches only focus on structural aspects and disregard semantic aspects. As a consequence, semantically equal process model parts which are not exact matches remain undetected and impede reuse.

There are at least two issues that complicate non-exact reuse. First, the labeling of process model elements in practice is heterogeneous and modelers use different labeling patterns to express the same semantics [4]. Thus, equivalent process parts with differently labeled elements would not be recognized as the same. Second, minor changes, for instance the insertion of an additional activity or the usage of other words, impede the identification of similar process parts. In this paper, we address this problem by introducing an approach for the identification of semantically equivalent and similar process parts in process model repositories. Our approach exploits the semantic comparison of activity labels and the behavioral comparison of control flow aspects. To demonstrate the applicability of our approach, we conduct an evaluation with the SAP Reference Model. We also provide insights into the sensitivity of the similarity thresholds for semantic and behavioral similarity and their influence for process part detection. While our approach detects clones for high similarity thresholds, it still detects meaningful candidates, when loosen the clone requirement.

The remainder of this paper is structured as follows. Section 2 illustrates the motivation of our work. Section 3 defines our approach for detecting similar process model parts. Section 4 presents the results from our empirical evaluation with the SAP Reference Model. Section 5 discusses related work before Section 6 concludes the paper and gives an outlook on future research.

2   Problem Illustration

The main challenge associated with the identification of similar process parts is given by appropriately covering semantic aspects. While the identification of clones can be accomplished on a structural level [3], this is not possible for process parts deviating in labeling style and behavior.

Figure 1 shows a typical example of two similar process models from the SAP Reference Model. Thereby, functions with a bold line represent activities which are not covered by the other process. Bold font indicates that the function has a corresponding function in the other model, but captures the semantics in a linguistically different way. Considering the models, we observe that both have additional functions and that two functions differ in the label. However, it is also obvious the these models are semantically very close. For instance the label *Processing of Shipping Notifications / Confirmations* gives the same instruction as the label *Shipping Notifications / Confirmation Processing*. In this case the two functions simply make use of different label styles resulting in a different position of the action *to process* [4]. While this is a rather syntactical difference, the labels *Scheduling Agreement Delivery Schedule* and *Schedule Line (Schedule Agreement)* represent a semantically more complex example.

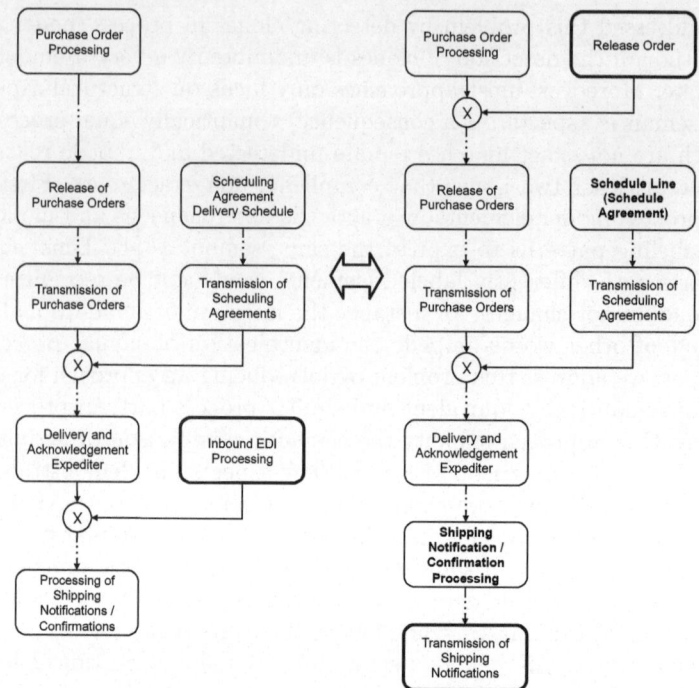

Fig. 1. Almost Completely Similar Process Parts from the SAP Reference Model

The comparison of process models is a widely discussed area and many metrics have been defined. Thereby, many metrics build on the process model structure [5,6] or the execution semantics [7,8]. However, the calculation of a semantic similarity of process model labels which goes beyond the consideration of synonyms has not been addressed so far. However, because of the potential of similar process parts to increase the reuse in process model collections, we consider this to be an important step.

3   Approach for the Detection of Similar Process Parts

This section introduces our three-step approach for the detection of similar process parts. It includes (1) activity label annotation, (2) semantic label similarity calculation, and (3) behavioral similarity calculation.

3.1   Activity Label Annotation

In order to accomplish a comparison which goes beyond a simple string comparison we annotate each activity with its semantic components. As pointed out by [9] each activity can be characterized by three components: an action, a business object, on which the action is performed, and an additional information fragment that provides further details if required. As an example, consider the activity *Send Contract to Customer* which contains the action *to send*, the business object *contract* and the additional information fragment *to customer*. To reliably accomplish the annotation of these components, we employ a technique defined in prior work [4]. The introduced technique builds on the observation that activities follow regular patterns, so called label styles. The most prominent label style is the verb-object style where the action is captured as an infinitive verb at the beginning of the label. Examples are *Notify Customer* or *Print Document*. However, many labels follow actually other styles such as the action-noun style. In these cases the action is not given as a verb but as a noun at the end of the label. Examples are *Order Verification* or *Product Shipment*. The given examples demonstrate that knowledge about label styles can be used to annotate activities. Once the label style is identified, the derivation of the components is a straightforward step.

3.2 Semantic Label Similarity Calculation

The calculation of the semantic process similarity builds on the annotation of the comprised activities. The fundamental idea is to first calculate the semantic similarity between all activities of the input models and then compute an overall similarity score.

The calculation of the semantic similarity between two activities is accomplished as follows. As a result of the annotation, we can use the semantic components of two given activity labels to compute their semantic closeness. Hence, we consider the similarity between the actions, the business objects and the additional fragments. Thereby, the similarity between two components is given by the closeness of the two concepts in the WordNet taxonomy [10]. This closeness can be calculated using a metric defined by Lin [11].

For calculating this semantic similarity between two activity labels l_1 and l_2, we introduce three functions: a component similarity function sim_c, a coverage function cov, and a label similarity function sim_l combining the latter two to an overall result.

The function sim_c calculates the semantic closeness of two label components l_{c_1} and l_{c_2}. In general, the result of the Lin measurement is returned. If only one label includes the considered component, the value is set to zero.

$$sim_c(l_1, l_2) = \begin{cases} 0 & \text{if } l_{1_c} = \emptyset \vee l_{2_c} = \emptyset \\ Lin(l_{1_c}, l_{2_c}) & \text{if } l_{1_c} \neq \emptyset \wedge l_{2_c} \neq \emptyset \end{cases} \tag{1}$$

The coverage function cov is used to determine the number of components in a label l. Assuming that a label always refers to an action, the result of cov ranges from 1 to 3. Note that the index a in the definition denotes the action, bo the business object and add the additional information fragment.

$$cov(l) = \begin{cases} 1 & \text{if } l_a \neq \emptyset \wedge l_{bo} = \emptyset \wedge l_{add} = \emptyset \\ 2 & \text{if } l_a \neq \emptyset \wedge (l_{bo} \neq \emptyset \vee l_{add} \neq \emptyset) \\ 3 & \text{if } l_a \neq \emptyset \wedge l_{bo} \neq \emptyset \wedge l_{add} \neq \emptyset \end{cases} \tag{2}$$

In order to calculate an overall result from the individual similarity results, we introduce the function sim_l. It calculates the arithmetic mean of the similarity values for action, business object and the additional information fragment. This is accomplished by dividing the sum of sim_a, sim_{bo} and sim_{add} by the maximum coverage among l_1 and l_2. As a result, we obtain the overall similarity score for two given labels.

$$sim_l(l_1, l_2) = \frac{sim_a(l_1, l_2) + sim_{bo}(l_1, l_2) + sim_{add}(l_1, l_2)}{\arg\max_{l \in \{l_1, l_2\}} cov(l)} \tag{3}$$

In order to calculate the similarity for the complete process models, we adapt a metric proposed by [5]. By calculating sim_l for all activity pairs which can be derived from the input models we can identify the best activity pairs based on their sim_l value. Accordingly, we use the relation of these pairs and the overall number of activities in both models to yield an overall process similarity score. Let $M_{sim_l}^{opt}$ be an optimal equivalence mapping derived from sim_l. Further A represents the set of activities in a given process models P. As a result, we can define the process model similarity metric sim_p models as follows:

$$sim_p(p_1, p_2) = \frac{2 \cdot \sum_{(l_1, l_2) \in M_{sim_l}^{opt}} sim_l(l_1, l_2)}{|A_1| + |A_2|} \tag{4}$$

3.3 Behavioral Similarity Calculation

Besides containing similarly labeled activities process parts also require these activities to occur in a similar order. To measure such a control-flow oriented similarity of two process models, we use the concept of behavioral profiles [12] and the respective behavioral metric [8].

Behavioral profiles are an abstract representation of control flow aspects. They capture behavioral characteristics by describing the relation between pairs of activities. The possible relations are grounded in the weak order relation between two activities, which holds when there exists a path from activity x to activity y, denoted with $x \succ_P y$. With this background, behavioral profiles can be defined as follows. Let A be the set of all activities of a given process model P. Each pair $(x, y) \in (A \times A)$ has one of the following relations:

- strict order relation $\leadsto_P$, iff $x \succ_P y$ and $y \nsucc_P x$.
- exclusiveness relation $+_P$, iff $x \nsucc_P y$ and $y \nsucc_P x$.
- interleaving order relation $||_P$, iff $x \succ_P y$ and $y \succ_P x$.

Thus, a behavioral profile B_P of a process model P is defined as $B_P = \{\leadsto_P, +_P, ||_P\}$. Also note, that for each pair (x, y) in strict order relation also fulfills the inverse strict order relation for (y, x), i.e. $x \leadsto_P y \Leftrightarrow y \leadsto_P^{-1} x$.

The behavioral profile metric is based upon these basic relations of a behavioral profile. Let B_P and B_Q be two behavioral profiles of the process models P and Q. Hence, the behavioral similarity is defined as,

Algorithm 1. Checking similarity of two process models with given thresholds

```
 1: isSimilar(ProcessModel m1, ProcessModel m2, float thresholdSimP,
    float thresholdSimBP)
 2: similar = false;
 3: sim_p = 0;
 4: List activityPairs = new List();
 5: for i = 1 to m1.getActivities().getLength() do
 6:    currentActivity = m1.getActivities().getItem(i);
 7:    tempActivity = null;
 8:    for j = 1 to m2.getActivities().getLength() do
 9:       maxSim = 0;
10:       sim = sim_l(currentActivity, m2.getActivities().getItem(j));
11:       if sim > maxSim then
12:          maxSim = sim;
13:          tempActivity = m2.getActivities().getItem(j);
14:    if maxSim > 0 then
15:       sim_p = sim_p + maxSim;
16:       activityPairs.add(currentActivity, tempActivity);
17:       cleanLists(currentActivity, tempActivity);
18:    else
19:       cleanLists(currentActivity);
20: sim_p = sim_p/(m1.getActivities().size() + m2.getActivities().size());
21: sim_bp = getBehavioralSimilarity(activityPairs, m1, m2);
22: if sim_p ≥ thresholdSimP then
23:    if sim_bp ≥ thresholdSimBP then
24:       similar = true;
25: return similar;
```

$$sim_{bp}(B_P, B_Q) = 1 - \sum_h w_h \cdot sim_h(B_P, B_Q) \tag{5}$$

with $h \in \{+, \rightsquigarrow, ||, \rightsquigarrow', ||'\}$ and weighting factors $w_h \in \mathbb{R}$, $0 < w_h < 1$ such that $\sum_h w_h = 1$.
sim_h refers to the elementary behavioral similarity metrics introduced in [8].

3.4 Approach for Detecting Similar Process Parts

Our approach builds upon the three steps described above. Activity label annotation is performed for each activity label revealing action, business object and the additional fragment. Afterwards, all available process models are compared with each other resulting in a similarity score of sim_p. In this step, we additionally identify activities that form a semantic pair. Using these activity pairs we can determine the behavioral similarity of the two process models. If the model pair fulfills certain thresholds for sim_p and sim_{bp}, it is considered to be similar. The approach is formalized in Algorithm 1 taking two process models $m1$ and

$m2$ as well as thresholds for sim_p and sim_{bp} as input and returning a boolean score reflecting the similarity and the consistency of the detected process part.

The algorithm starts with some basic initializations (line 2-3). Afterwards, the algorithm processes all possible pairs of activities from $m1$ and $m2$ (line 4, line 7) as follows. The similarity scores between *currentActivity* from $m1$ and the activities from $m2$ are calculated. If the similarity of *currentActivity* and the respective activity from $m2$ is higher than the highest similarity score ($maxSim$) calculated so far, $maxSim$ is updated by the new similarity score and the respective activity from $m2$ temporarily stored (lines 10-13). These steps are repeated for all activities from $m2$. Afterwards, the algorithm checks, whether the maximal calculated similarity is bigger than zero (line 13). If this is the case, the similarity of the input models is increased by the respective similarity (line 15) and the activity pair contributing the similarity score is added to *activityPairs*, a list that contains all pairs of activities with the highest pairwise similarity score (line 16). Additionally, the activity lists of $m1$ and $m2$ are cleaned from the pair activities to prevent one activity occurring in multiple activity pairs (line 17 and line 19). After the calculation of the final model similarity score (line 20), the algorithm proceeds with the calculation of the behavioral similarity using the two process models $m1$ and $m2$ as well as the list *activityPairs* as input (line 21). If sim_p and afterwards sim_{bp} exceed the two thresholds, two boolean variable *similar* is set to *true* (lines 22-24). The algorithm terminates with the output of *similar* indicating a similarity or not (line 25).

4   Evaluation

In this section we evaluate the introduced approach for detecting similar process parts. To this end, we test our technique on the SAP Reference Model, a model collection containing 604 Event-Driven Process Chains [13]. The comprised process models are organized in 29 functional branches, as for instance procurement, sales or financial accounting. In Section 4.1 we present the general results from our test run. In Section 4.2 we discuss the relation between sim_p and sim_{bp} as well as their influence for the detection of process model parts.

4.1   General Results

We conduct a pair-wise comparison of all models in the SAP Reference Model to identify similar processes. Accordingly, we conducted in total $\binom{604}{2} = 182.106$ comparisons and computed sim_p and sim_{bp} for each model pair in the collection. The results are depicted in Figure 2. It illustrates the number of retrieved process model pairs depending on varying thresholds for sim_p. Apparently, the more we decrease the threshold for the sim_p, the more process model pairs are identified by the algorithm.

We also computed the average sim_{bp} values for the respective sim_p as illustrated in Figure 3. We observe a proportional relation between the decrease of sim_p and the average sim_{bp} value, i.e. sim_{bp} is dependent on sim_p. This is the case, because sim_{bp} requires the correspondences between the elements of the two input models that is provided by sim_p [8]. In consequence, weaker correspondences between the model pairs also result in a weaker behavioral similarity.

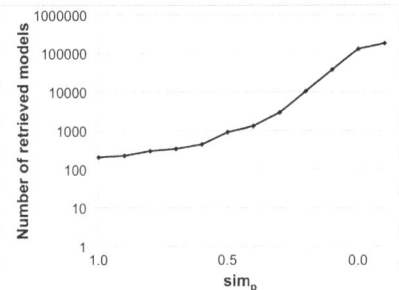
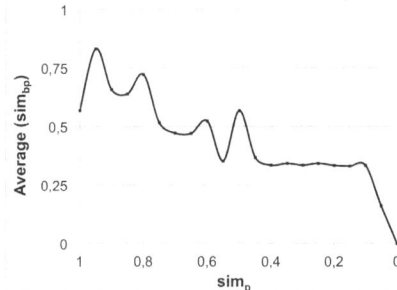

Fig. 2. Retrieved models for sim_p thresholds

Fig. 3. Avg. sim_{bp} for thresholds sim_p

4.2 Similarity Thresholds for Detecting Similar Process Parts

Since different thresholds for the metrics sim_p and sim_{bp} entail completely different results, we investigated how these metrics should be configured in order to obtain the desired outcome. As illustrated in Figure 2, a step-wise decrease of sim_p threshold leads to an increase of the retrieved model pairs, while it reduces the average score of sim_{bp}. Apparently, sim_p has a significantly stronger influence on the detection of similar process parts than sim_{bp}.

Taking the results of Section 4.1 into consideration, we can identify several candidate groups based on a given threshold for sim_p. We summarized all candidate groups in Table 1. The first candidate group amounts to 204 model pairs and contains process models that are perfect clones. Process models of this group have an equal number of activities and equivalent activity labels.

The next candidate group has a sim_p score between 0.6 and 1.0. These models tend to include activity clones as well as semantically similar activities. In general, they differ in the number of activities. The activities themselves are either clones or semantically (very) close activities sharing similar actions and business objects. The example models in Figure 1 represent candidates of this group. For the example sim_p amounts to 0.62.

Candidate group 3 comprises models with an increasing semantic distance. While the semantic closeness of these models is still meaningful for higher scores in this range, models tend to become more and more distant for lower bound thresholds. Hence, the respective activities tend to either share a similar business object or the same action. Figure 4 provides an example of process models that is on the edge of group 3 and 4. The value of sim_p amounts to 0.27 and we note only weak semantic relations between the activities. Consider for instance the activities *Appropriation Request Processing* and *Process Inquiry*. Obviously, both activities share the action *process* that is performed on a business object leading to the correspondence.

As the largest candidate group 4 covers models with small semantic correspondences where activities only share a similar business object or a similar activity. Normally, human perception would ignore these models to be similar. Group 5 consists of all model pairs with no semantic correspondence scoring zero for sim_p.

Table 1. Candidate groups of sim_p

Group Number	Similarity Tendency	Threshold	Group size
1	Perfect Model Clones	$sim_p = 1.0$	204
2	Clone or semantically close models	$0.6 \leq sim_p < 1.0$	237
3	Semantically similar to distant models	$0.3 \leq sim_p < 0.6$	2,481
4	Semantically distant models	$0.0 < sim_p < 0.3$	128,240
5	Semantically dissimilar models	$sim_p = 0.0$	50,944

As already stated above, the decrease of the sim_p threshold corresponds with a decrease of the sim_{bp} value. We observed a high discrepancy between sim_p and $avg(sim_{bp})$ for group 1 (about 43%) and for group 2 (about 22%). In general, most process models only comprise two of the three used behavioral relations for sim_{bp}, which leads to a smaller score of sim_{bp}. The divergence of candidate group 3 is rather small (8%), whereas group 4 shows a high discrepancy again (about 65%). Again, two behavioral relations primarily contribute to sim_{bp} leading to a relatively high sim_{bp} compared to sim_p. Considering the example from Figure 4 sim_{bp} amounts to 0.42, which implies a similar control-flow. There is no discrepancy in group 5, because of the fact that no pair of corresponding activities is found, if $sim_p = 0.0$.

Due to this high discrepancies for higher or smaller thresholds for sim_p we conclude that sim_{bp} is not appropriate for the initial identification of similar process parts. This is supported by the fact that the correspondence of process models which is required for the calculation of sim_{bp} is strongly dependent on sim_p. We conclude that sim_{bp} is more appropriate to verify the correctness of an identified process part, while sim_p is able to identify meaningful candidates in a given collection. In other words, sim_p imposes a necessary and sim_{bp} a sufficient condition for process part detection.

5   Related Work

The work presented in this paper is related to three major streams of research: process model reuse, process model similarity and process model matching.

In disciplines such as software engineering reuse has a long tradition [14,15,16]. Identifying and reusing code fragments and software components does not only save time but also increases the maintainability of the resulting software artifacts. This is line with the Service-Oriented Architecture paradigm, where business

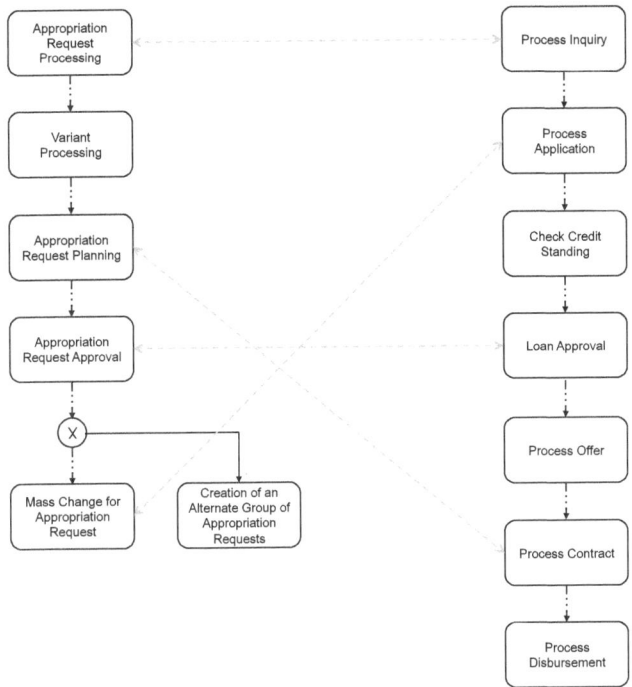

Fig. 4. Semantically distant process models with their corresponding activities

functionality is bundled and centrally provided [17,18]. Recently, this potential was also recognized for business process models. [3] proposed an approach for identifying clones in process model repositories. Our approach deviates from this technique, because it does not aim for detecting clones but explicitly targets the identification of similar process parts. Hence, our approach includes techniques for determining the semantic closeness of models based on their control flow and activity labels. Another technique was introduced by [19]. The authors propose an approach to support to the design and modeling of workflows by introducing a repository, which can be used for adapting workflow cases.

Techniques for determining the overall similarity of process models have been proposed by different authors. An overview is provided by [5]. Some of these works build on an ontology in order to match the labels [20]. Other approaches make use of control-flow based aspects. For instance, [8] use behavioral profiles to determine the similarity of processes. However, this approach assumes that the correspondences between the activities are already given. In general, the vast majority of these approaches focus on structural aspects and do not take semantic aspects into account. As this is crucial for the identification of similar process parts, we use a metric which builds on the semantic comparison of element labels.

The alignment or so-called matching of process models is closely connected with the similarity computation. Usually similarity scores are used to identify potential correspondences between two models which are then used as input for the matching technique [21,22]. However, while matchers try to find the best match for a given pair of models, our approach aims for quantifying the semantic similarity between them. Accordingly, a perfect match is not a prerequisite for our approach. In our context it is more important to identify models which have a certain degree of similarity. As a result, the identification of reuse candidates is automatically accomplished.

6   Conclusion

In this paper, we have proposed an approach that detects similar parts of process models. We exploit semantic and behavioural similarity aspects and challenged our approach against the SAP Reference Model. Our evaluation proved that the approach is applicable to real-world process models. It also revealed five candidate groups and configurable similarity thresholds enabling process part detection. We concluded that semantic similarity represents a necessary requirement for the detection of process parts, while the behavioral similarity formulates a sufficient condition ensuring correctness and consistency of the identified process parts.

There are several directions of our future work. First, we aim at improving our approach. This especially applies for the identification of model correspondences using semantic similarity techniques. Accordingly, we plan to incorporate more sophisticated matching algorithms in order to obtain a more precise sim_p value. Second, we plan to test our approach on further process model collections, as for instance the BIT process library [23] or the process repository of "Nationale Prozessbibliothek"[1]. In addition, we aim for testing our approach in an industrial setting. We think that the resulting feedback will help us to tailor approach to the actual needs of organizations. A third direction for future work is given by combining our approach with other technique facilitating reuse. Particularly, we plan to integrate the approach with automatic identification of services [24].

References

1. Rosemann, M.: Potential Pitfalls of Process Modeling: Part A. Business Process Management Journal 12(2), 249–254 (2006)
2. Reijers, H.A., Mans, R.S., van der Toorn, R.A.: Improved model management with aggregated business process models. Data Knowledge Engineering 68(2), 221–243 (2009)
3. Uba, R., Dumas, M., García-Bañuelos, L., La Rosa, M.: Clone Detection in Repositories of Business Process Models. In: Rinderle-Ma, S., Toumani, F., Wolf, K. (eds.) BPM 2011. LNCS, vol. 6896, pp. 248–264. Springer, Heidelberg (2011)
4. Leopold, H., Smirnov, S., Mendling, J.: On the refactoring of activity labels in business process models. Information Systems 37(5), 443–459 (2012)

---

[1] www.prozessbibliothek.de

5. Dijkman, R.M., Dumas, M., van Dongen, B.F., Käärik, R., Mendling, J.: Similarity of Business Process Models: Metrics and Evaluation. Information Systems 36(2), 498–516 (2011)
6. Grigori, D., Corrales, J., Bouzeghoub, M., Gater, A.: Ranking BPEL Processes for Service Discovery. IEEE Transactions on Services Computing 3(3), 178–192 (2010)
7. Zha, H., Wang, J., Wen, L., Wang, C., Sun, J.: A workflow net similarity measure based on transition adjacency relations. Computers in Industry 61(5), 463–471 (2010)
8. Kunze, M., Weidlich, M., Weske, M.: Behavioral Similarity – A Proper Metric. In: Rinderle-Ma, S., Toumani, F., Wolf, K. (eds.) BPM 2011. LNCS, vol. 6896, pp. 166–181. Springer, Heidelberg (2011)
9. Mendling, J., Reijers, H.A., Recker, J.: Activity Labeling in Process Modeling: Empirical Insights and Recommendations. Information Systems 35(4), 467–482 (2010)
10. Miller, G.A.: WordNet: a Lexical Database for English. Communications of the ACM 38(11), 39–41 (1995)
11. Lin, D.: An information-theoretic definition of similarity. In: Proc. 15th International Conf. on Machine Learning, pp. 296–304. Morgan Kaufmann, San Francisco (1998)
12. Weidlich, M., Mendling, J., Weske, M.: Efficient consistency measurement based on behavioural profiles of process models. IEEE TSE 37(3), 410–429 (2011)
13. Keller, G., Teufel, T.: SAP(R) R/3 Process Oriented Implementation: Iterative Process Prototyping. Addison-Wesley (1998)
14. Bellon, S., Koschke, R., Antoniol, G., Krinke, J., Merlo, E.: Comparison and evaluation of clone detection tools. IEEE TSE 33(9), 577–591 (2007)
15. Jacobson, I., Griss, M., Jonsson, P.: Software Reuse: Architecture, Process and Organization for Business Success, vol. 43. ACM Press (1997)
16. Heineman, G.T., Councill, W.T.: Component-Based Software Engineering: Putting the Pieces Together. Addison-Wesley Professional (2001)
17. Erl, T.: Service-Oriented Architecture: Concepts, Technology, and Design. Prentice Hall PTR, Upper Saddle River (2005)
18. Marks, E.A., Bell, M.: Service-Oriented Architecture: A Planning and Implementation Guide for Business and Techonology. John Willey & Sons Inc. (2006)
19. Madhusudan, T., Zhao, J., Marshall, B.: A case-based reasoning framework for workflow model management. Data and Knowledge Engineering 50(1), 87–115 (2004)
20. Ehrig, M., Koschmider, A., Oberweis, A.: Measuring Similarity between Semantic Business Process Models. In: APCCM 2007, Ballarat, Victoria, Australia, vol. 67, pp. 71–80. Australian Computer Science Communications (2007)
21. Weidlich, M., Dijkman, R., Mendling, J.: The ICoP Framework: Identification of Correspondences between Process Models. In: Pernici, B. (ed.) CAiSE 2010. LNCS, vol. 6051, pp. 483–498. Springer, Heidelberg (2010)
22. La Rosa, M., Dumas, M., Uba, R., Dijkman, R.: Merging Business Process Models. In: Meersman, R., Dillon, T.S., Herrero, P. (eds.) OTM 2010. LNCS, vol. 6426, pp. 96–113. Springer, Heidelberg (2010)
23. Fahland, D., Favre, C., Jobstmann, B., Koehler, J., Lohmann, N., Völzer, H., Wolf, K.: Instantaneous Soundness Checking of Industrial Business Process Models. In: Dayal, U., Eder, J., Koehler, J., Reijers, H.A. (eds.) BPM 2009. LNCS, vol. 5701, pp. 278–293. Springer, Heidelberg (2009)
24. Leopold, H., Mendling, J.: Automatic Derivation of Service Candidates from Business Process Model Repositories. In: Abramowicz, W., Kriksciuniene, D., Sakalauskas, V. (eds.) BIS 2012. LNBIP, vol. 117, pp. 84–95. Springer, Heidelberg (2012)

Systematic Identification of Service-Blueprints for Service-Processes - A Method and Exemplary Application

(Research Paper)

Thomas Kleinert, Silke Balzert, Peter Fettke, and Peter Loos

Institute for Information Systems (IWi) at the German Research Center for Artificial Intelligence (DFKI)
Saarland University, Campus, Bld. D3 2 66123 Saarbrücken, Germany
{Thomas.Kleinert,Silke.Balzert,
Peter.Fettke,Peter.Loos}@iwi.dfki.de

Abstract. Reference modeling research aims at offering exemplary process models, that support business decision makers during the implementation of new or the improvement of existing business processes. The idea of service blueprints is to map the idea of reference modeling onto service processes or business processes with significant service elements. The paper at hand introduces an inductive seven-step method for the creation of service blueprints. By the use of techniques like single-entry single-exit regions in process graphs, we simplify clear partitioning of the business processes into potential service blueprints. To further examine the practical usability of the method we document the usage of the seven-step method in a practical use case that is part of a project work. The result is a set of service blueprints that are derived from prior inquired process models and detailed insights concerning the usability of the proposed method.

Keywords: service blueprint, service process, single-entry single-exit, reference modeling.

1 Motivation and Challenge

To ensure and improve the quality of business performance from an organizational perspective, instruments have established that are summarized under the term of Business Process Management (BPM). BPM is valid for pure product-oriented processes, for hybrid processes containing product and service elements and for pure service processes. Reference modeling in general facilitates the access to a process-oriented organization for deciders, by providing generic exemplary process models for business-scenarios of any kind [1]. Service blueprints transport this idea especially into the area of service related processes

Scientific literature has discussed the specific adaption and modification of reference process models for the use in business processes for several years. Nevertheless there are only few references to the creation of service blueprints.

M. La Rosa and P. Soffer (Eds.): BPM 2012 Workshops, LNBIP 132, pp. 598–610, 2012.

Furthermore there are no references known to the authors of this contribution offering an applicable methodology to generate service blueprints inductively. The paper at hand introduces an inductive seven-step procedure model to derive service blueprints from inquired process models. The model described was developed in the context of a research project with academic and industrial partners. Our method was evaluated in a case study which is presented in this paper.

The presented approach chooses an inductive way of service blueprint creation, leading from inquired business processes as they are seen by the process participants to blueprints usable for process managers and organizational deciders. The generalized results are then transferrable into different process landscapes. This differs from deductive ideas in scientific literature deriving reference models from theoretical analysis and rolling them out to the process execution layer. For the special case of service blueprints, no workable inductive creation methods are described in the literature known to the authors. To contribute to the closing of this research gap, the paper at hand proposes a seven-step method.

To position the paper in the scientific environment, the following section 2 examines the adjoining research fields and gives an overview on the state of research. In section 3 we roll out the model in detail and describe the phases of service blueprint creation. Section 4 describes a case study in order to provide further insights and evaluation of the model described in this paper. In section 5 our approach is discussed, some of its limitations are addressed and an outlook on future research is given.

2   State of Research

2.1   Service Management

In the 1980's and early 1990's, service management research was focused on service development and service design as well as marketing aspects of services (cf. [2],[3]). Accordingly, a customer's perspective and the positioning of services at the market were mainly explored. The different aspects like service development and service realization however were addressed in a very isolated manner.

As a consequence, an integrated perspective or even methodology for service design and development was missing. Since the mid-1990's, this integration of isolated parts of service management is discussed as *Service Engineering*, which comprises procedure models, methodologies and tools for a systematic design and development of services [4].

In the recent past, material and service components are not seen as isolated products any longer but as a bundle of services – a so called product service system - which fulfills very specific customer requirements [5, 6]. In general, Service Engineering and product service system research provides substantial theoretic fundamentals as well as design approaches and IT solutions for the development and provision of services and (hybrid) products. However, what has been neglected in the scientific discussion so far is how to systematically derive reference models for the underlying organizational processes providing such services and products.

2.2 Service Blueprints

The idea of blueprinting dates back to the early 1980's [7]. Service blueprints are specific reference models designed for service processes or business processes with significant service elements. Although the scientific literature has discussed related ideas for several years now, there are no workable models for inductive service blueprint creation known to the authors. The service blueprints created with the method proposed in the paper at hand can be used for the creation of new service processes or hybrid production processes, or can be used in benchmarking scenarios to evaluate existing processes and detect improvement potentials.

While reference models for financial or production process models often attempt to summarize the reference elements into one large reference model applicable for any usage scenario, the service blueprints generally have the character of building stones for service processes or service elements in other processes [7]. These building stones can be used to create new service processes or they can be built into existing production processes via the right process interfaces. Thereby they can embed service elements into existing process structures.

2.3 Single Entry Single Exit

To support the building stone character of the service blueprints in the method at hand and to ease the creation of interfaces with other models or other model fragments, we use single-entry single-exit regions in process graphs for the fraction of the business process models. This approach is inspired by the work of Vanhatalo et al. around the refined process structure tree (see e.g. [8] and [9]). The idea of single-entry single-exit regions is derived from computer science theory. From early ideas in graph theory from the 1960s it evolved into one of the foundations of structured programming. In the method presented here it is used in Event-driven Process Chains (EPCs) to divide graphical representations of business processes into canonic subgraphs.

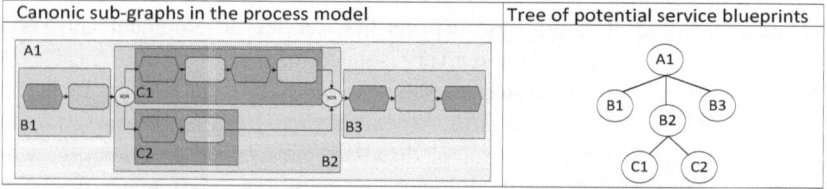

Fig. 1. Exemplary partition of a process model

A subgraph in this understanding, including the single-entry single-exit region theory, is a coherent graph model with exactly one control flow entry and exactly one control flow exit. More exactly following Johnson, Pearson and Pingali [10], a subgraph in this context is a graph with an edge A at the beginning of the graph and an edge B at the end of the graph. If the control flow reaches edge B, it must have passed edge A before and if the control flow reaches A it must reach B before the process ends. At this point we do not introduce a more formal definition as they can be found in literature (e.g. [10]). Once an EPC is divided into canonic subgraphs, it can be represented in a distinct tree. Since all canonic subgraphs in the context of the paper at hand are seen as potential service blueprints, all possible service blueprints derived from the EPC are represented in this tree as leafs or inner knots (cf. Fig 1.).

2.4 Process Mining and Process Analogies

Over the last years scientific literature has discussed several approaches to automate certain tasks of the process model creation. One of these approaches relevant in the scientific environment of the paper at hand is process mining (cf. [11] [12] [13]). It is relevant in this context because it can be seen as a workable approach towards model creation in the first place and reference model creation as well. The basic idea in process mining in business process modeling scenarios is the deduction of process models from the information given in log files of established information systems (IS). This idea is linked to reference models e.g. by Gottschalk, van der Aalst and Jansen-Vullers [14].

The method presented in this paper differs from process mining approaches in two major points. First the process mining approach can only be used in scenarios with broad IS coverage and therefore log file creation. The presence of comprehensive logs of executed processes may be a valid assumption in several special process scenarios but can definitely not be seen as a given fact in any use case. On the contrary, the method presented herein bases on guided process interviews that can be held in any process modeling scenario. Secondly the combination of different perspectives and the merging of process model fragments, which is an element of the method at hand, vary from the procedures in process mining. Furthermore there is no process mining reference known to the authors addressing service blueprints as a special form of reference models.

Nevertheless, another task of the model creation in the method at hand is supported by an automation approach. In the authors' research on process analogies a set of prototypical implementations were developed. These tools give rudimentary support in detection of similar wordings, process structures and are able to support the later division of the inquired process models. For an overview on similarity research in process models based on model repositories see Dijkman et al. [15].

3   Method

3.1   Overview

In this section we propose seven phases for the creation of reference models in general and service blueprints especially. The phases are meant to provide a step-by-step procedure model but do not necessarily have to appear in the order presented here. In general the model will have to satisfy the following needs:

- *Inductive development:* The method has to enable an organizational decider to derive service blueprints based on inquired individual process models.

- *Identification of similarities:* The service blueprint shall contain similarities and parallel elements of the individual process models.
- *Abstraction:* The derived service blueprint has to abstract from the special features of the underlying individual process models.
- *Generalization:* It must be possible to derive the individual service processes from the service blueprints.
- *Managing natural language:* Natural language is an important element in process documentation in general. The method must be able to handle typical aspects like homonyms, synonyms and blurry articulation.

The model described in the following section is based on work in the Refreference Model Mining research project and is now focused on the special needs for service blueprinting. The seven phases addressing the issues named above are:

1. Requirement determination
2. Individual business model inquiry
3. Conditioning (pre-processing) of the individual business models
4. Service blueprint deduction
5. Service blueprint post-processing
6. Evaluation of the deducted service blueprint
7. Maintenance and advancement of the service blueprint

3.2   Phase 1: Requirement Determination

In reference modeling projects and therefore also in service blueprinting projects, the project goal strongly influences the modeling process. Not only does it determine the degree of abstraction and probably elements like wording and formality issues, it also strongly affects the choice of quality measures for the resulting blueprints. The definition of relevant quality attributes related to the usage of the service blueprints is the objective for this first phase. They determine how improvement can be addressed and which dimensions define the quality of a service blueprint.

To define the target of reference modeling activities in general and service blueprinting especially, the following alternatives are chosen typically:

- *Survey:* Interviewing domain experts or potential model users can provide indications which requirements a service blueprint has to meet.
- *Literature review:* Reviewing relevant literature offers insights into requirements a service blueprint necessarily has to fulfill.
- *Analysis of existing reference models:* Examination of existing reference models and service blueprints can provide an overview which requirements are met by other models already.

To clarify what that means for the method proposed, the requirement definition is described exemplary in the following. Taking more then one process into account and then having several interview partners to inquire the different individual processes will provide a broader view for the service blueprint. The results will therefore be more generalizable and in the measure of universal usability of higher quality. By choosing universality as a quality attribute for the resulting service blueprint and deriving the dimensions of number of processes and number of persons in the inquiry, we have set up an environment in which we can compare the overall quality of different service blueprints (cf. Fig. 2). This is necessary to identify possible improvement potential for the service blueprints in later steps.

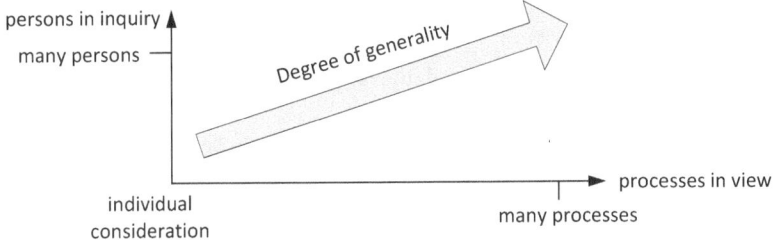

Fig. 2. Quality attribute and derived dimensions

As a result of this phase there is a general decision on the blueprinting project goals, a decision on the quality attribute addressing that goal and derived from that a number of dimensions influencing the quality attribute. The derived dimensions are directly linked to activities in the following inquiry phase. This first phase may be conducted multiple times in large blueprinting projects. In that case the addition of new dimensions or the withdrawal of a dimension may occur.

3.3   Phase 2: Individual Business Model Inquiry

The inductive development of reference models and service blueprints requires a basal insight in the work processes lived in the business considered. The objective of this phase is to create process models that can provide such insight. Prior to the model creation all tasks and events within a process have to be inquired. The goal setting of the first phase (section 3.2) can influence the selection of processes to inquire in this phase.

Inquiries can be performed following different models for process elicitation in scientific literature [16]. Popular methods are e.g. guided interviews in which a process participant is asked to describe the general workflow and an interviewer documents the insights in a protocol. The formal process models are then based on these protocols. Generally a later evaluation of these models with the interviewed process participant significantly increases the quality of the process models.

Since the individual models from this phase serve as a foundation for later consolidation in multi-perspective models some conceptual decisions have to be made before the first inquiries. Defining modeling conventions in advance can significantly facilitate the later joining of models or model fragments. These conventions can address modeling issues like certain structures for certain process circumstances and can also contain rules for wording and phrasing which makes later analogy recognition much easier.

The outcomes of this phase are interview-based models of the working processes as described by the process participants in the interviews. This can be seen as a portrayal of the "AS IS"-processes.

3.4   Phase 3: Conditioning of the Individual Business Models

The objective of this phase is to synchronize and systematically divide the inquired process models for the later phases. As a beginning of this phase, syntactical correctness of the process model and the adherence of the modeling conventions defined in the latter phase have to be ensured.

Theoretically it is possible to create service blueprints based on only one inquired process model, with the method presented in the paper at hand. Since blueprints based on only one process presented by only one person will always have a strong subjectivity in them, the usability of such models is limited to certain special cases. In general we expect the connection of several process models for the creation of high quality blueprints based on the quality attributes and dimensions defined above (cf. section 3.2).

In this coherence, the quality measure can only be addressed relatively. Finding an absolute measure or a number of processes to inquire for generally "high quality" service blueprints would require the definition of a statistically representative choice. This stands against the workability of the method proposed in the paper at hand since it is often very problematic in practice. We therefore blank out the absolute measure of quality for the proposed method.

To prepare the joining of several process models in the later phases, a so called model synset is created in this phase. Following the linguistic understanding of a synset, a model synset is defined as a quantity of one or more elements that can be exchanged within a business process model without the model changing its functionality. In practice these elements can be words in the caption of tasks and events in the process model and also structurally similar process segments.

Furthermore as the last but most important step of this phase, the model is divided into subgraphs with single-entry single-exit virtue (section 2.3). To ensure bijective coherence between the inquired models and the derived single-entry single-exit regions, we propose the division into canonic subgraphs (section 2.3). Based on this definition, all single-entry single-exit segments identified in this phase are handled as potential service blueprints from here on. The results of this phase are models of potential service blueprints derived from the inquired processes and synchronized along the created model synset. Another result is the model synset itself which will be used again in later phases.

3.5   Phase 4: Service Blueprint Deduction

At this point in the procedure model we have the individually inquired process models, the model synset synchronizing the processes by showing equal or similar model elements, canonic subgraphs fulfilling the single-entry single-exit paradigm and quality attributes defined by the goals of the blueprinting project. Like described above it is possible to generate service blueprints from only one inquired process model theoretically, but for the given reasons this opportunity is blanked out in the paper at hand.

The model synset created in phase 3 is used at this point to analyze similarities between potential service blueprints. By finding equal or overlapping process segments and by reuniting the potential service blueprints with respect to the synset and a synchronized wording and structure, we gain a multi-perspective model of the entire process built from potential service blueprints only. The homogenous potential service blueprints serve as building stones for the multi-perspective model. This model is supposed to contain several (if not all) process instances inquired and therefore contains a broad overview of the entire process.

The homogenized potential service blueprints have to be analyzed further to determine their service character. Those that fulfill a preset service character or contain a preset amount of service elements are handled as service blueprints from here on. The decision on the service character of potential service blueprints can e.g. be made on the degree of customer integration in the process fragment.

The result of this phase 4 is a collection of process fragments with strong service character, which are of the highest possible quality regarding the quality attributes defined in phase 1. These process fragments are the service blueprints and they were created inductively.

3.6   Phase 5: Service Blueprint Post Processing

The objective of this phase is to rethink the created service blueprints based on the quality attributes and their transfer into other environments. For example, if generalization is a quality attribute it may be necessary to rethink the wordings of the captions or other elements of the service blueprints to make them usable in other business fields.

If a high service affinity is noticeable in the entire inquired processes it may be possible to reunite the service blueprints into one comprehensive service process containing all service elements of the multi-perspective process model from phase 4. The idea for this phase is based on general thoughts on reference modeling where often one single model is the goal of the inductive model development. Since the service blueprints presented in this paper form a collection of process fragments rather than a unique big service model this phase may be more or less relevant depending on the quality attributes selected in phase 1.

3.7   Phase 6: Evaluation of the Deducted Service Blueprints

The goal of this phase is to find objective measures to proof the practical usability of the service blueprints and their reference character at the same time. As in any modeling project, service blueprints also have to be evaluated to ensure that the needs of the blueprinting project are met. This can address different dimensions of needs.

- *evaluation according to requirements*: The first and most obvious need of a blueprinting project is represented in the quality attributes defined in phase 1. If for example generalization was chosen as a quality attribute, the derived service blueprints have to be transferrable to different process scenarios.
- *comparison to individual process models*: Since the basic idea of service blueprinting is to ease the development or improvement of Service-related business processes (section 1), the deducted service blueprints have to be evaluated regarding the business processes they were derived from. At any time it must be possible to deduct the original business processes by modification of the service blueprints.
- *evaluation based on known reference frames*: If scientific literature offers comparable service blueprints for related business scenarios, these can be used to evaluate the inductively constructed service blueprints by comparison in important attributes. Since the blueprinting of service related processes is rarely discussed currently, this evaluation attempt will need more research and publications in this sector to become relevant.

3.8   Phase 7: Maintenance and Advancement of the Service Blueprint

Maintenance in this coherence means a continuous audit of the usability of the service blueprints. After any new inquiry and deduction of potential service blueprints (cf. phases 2 and 3), the set of derived blueprints will change. The changed service blueprints continuously have to be checked regarding their usability for all instantiated service processes. Only if their objectivity in relation to all concerned service processes remains, they keep the character of service blueprints.

4   Case Studies

4.1   Use Case 1 – Special Machinery Engineering

The first use case addresses a special machinery engineering company producing testing and assembly sections for industrial production lines. The company builds the production line segments and creates own software for testing and quality assurance in the production. The partner proposed one of the recent projects of average monetary and personnel size for the evaluation. In the first set of interviews, the responsible project manager, software engineer and technical engineer were interviewed. To make the process inquired comparable to other project processes, a manager of another special machinery engineering project was interviewed to gain an overview on general project processes of the practical partner.

After these interviews the processes were modeled in the EPC notation. In order to align the process models inquired so far, a model synset was built (phase 3 section 3.4). With some support from a prototypic software tool, this step was done mainly manual. It occurred that certain wording issues were easy to detect and after reviewing all models a common wording was chosen. The resulting process models were then divided into canonic subgraphs as described in phase 3 (section 3.4). This was also supported by a prototypical software solution and was finally decided manually. The so created single-entry single-exit subgraphs were then handled as potential service blueprints.

After the division of the entire graphs inquired into single-entry single-exit regions, the synset created before was used again to reunite the potential service blueprints to one multi-perspective process model of the project process. The degree of generalization met at this point was already higher than it would have been from only one inquiry.

In our exemplary use case the service character was directly linked to customer interaction. Therefore all potential service blueprints with customer interaction were chosen as service blueprints (phase 4 section 3.5). Although this objective choice delivered a valid set of service blueprints derived inductively, it appeared appropriate to manually remove certain process fragments from the collection of service blueprints (phase 5 section 3.6) since they only contained one process step or had obviously no service blueprint character.

As an attempt to evaluate the results achieved so far (phase 6 section 3.7), we decided to use the service blueprints and reconstruct the service processes of the application partner. To make the service blueprints and the original processes comparable, the model synset was used again to detect synonyms in wording and structure. It occurred that the significant service elements of the original processes were represented to a high degree in the collection of service blueprints.

Since a continuous maintenance involves a dimension of aging in the process models and service blueprints, it was decided not to address maintenance in the use case scenario.

4.2   Use Case 2 – Software Development Company

The second application partner involved is a rather small software development company that develops and sells idea management software. The software product is clustered in packets and an implementation project includes the sales elements as well as implementation and modification in the software.

As element of phase 7 of the latter procedure model iteration, advancement of the designed service blueprints was the target of the work described below. Although it was still based on the procedure model presented in this paper, certain phases could be left out (see section 3.8). The goal of the work was set already as mentioned above and so phase 1 was not needed. It was decided to interview project managers of a set of four projects, chosen based on their indifference in monetary and personnel effort. Four different managers had led the four projects and so four perspectives on the project process itself laid within the inquiry group.

The interviews were again documented and recorded to facilitate modeling (phase 2). After the models of the processes had been created in EPC-notation again, another model synset was built for the new process models (phase 3). The new model synset was then synchronized with the synset from the special engineering process models to ensure the transferability of the results and therefore generalization. After synchronizing the four new process models with each other and with the models from the latter iteration afterwards, the new process models were divided into potential service blueprints as well (phase 3). As in the iteration before, the potential service blueprints were then synchronized via the model synset again and combined into a multi-perspective process model for the software development company (phase 4). Phase 5 in this iteration also needed to bring the new service blueprints into relation with the set of blueprints derived before. For this purpose the synchronized model synset was used again to find similarities and overlapping in the two sets of service blueprints. After a manual synchronization process eliminating all obvious overlapping and parallels, a new set of service blueprints related to both application partners was the result.

4.3   Results

Since higher degrees of generalization lead to a higher degree of abstraction it is obvious that only a certain degree of generalization is useful at all. If the service blueprints become too abstract their usability to create new or improve existing service related processes decreases. Nevertheless, the service blueprints created inductively in the use cases described here gained more and more quality, regarding to the chosen quality attribute, as the research project unfolded. Finding the right balance between generalization on the one hand and abstractness of the resulting service blueprints on the other hand seems to be a major issue when generalization is chosen as the quality attribute.

5   Conclusion

The method described in the paper at hand can help organizational deciders to create service blueprints based on the business processes established in their organization. Furthermore, it allows to see the bigger picture when more dimensions of the quality attribute are involved and the service blueprints gain more quality in that matter.

Not all phases of the method discussed can yet be supported technically and a lot of decisions described in the use case were based on common sense rather than on formalisms. This partially originates from the challenge of semantic comparison of data, which forms a research field of its own. Nevertheless prototypic software was tested in the use case described above and valuable insights for the further development of these software systems were gained in the projects. Supporting all phases of the method through smaller or larger software solutions is one of the prospects of the research discussed herein.

Furthermore, the service blueprints presented in this paper are derived from inquiries in two companies, eight people's perspectives and six process instances. With the chosen quality attribute of generalization this appears to be a rather small research frame. Enlarging this frame and further increasing the quality of the set of service blueprints derived from this project will also be part of the future research of the authors.

Despite these limitations, the needs for this research project as formulated in section 3.1 were: inductive development, identification of similarities, abstraction, generalization and managing of natural language. The seven-step procedure model presented in this paper addresses all these needs. By starting with the process inquiry, the inductive development of the service blueprints is ensured. The reunion of the model fragments addresses the identification of similarities. The resulting set of service blueprints abstract the inquired processes and thereby meets a requirement as well. The model creation based on the interviews and the model synset used in several steps finally address the management of natural language. By fulfilling all these needs and by offering a workable inductive way of service blueprint development, the paper at hand contributes into narrowing the research gap between service blueprint theory and practical use of reference models in service related scenarios.

Acknowledgements. Part of the results that inspired the paper at hand were achieved in two funded research projects the authors participate in. "Konzeptionelle, methodische und technische Grundlagen zur induktiven Erstellung von Referenzmodellen (Reference Model Mining)" – support code LO 752/5-1 and „Customizing als kundenoffener B2B-Service für die Entwicklung innovationsorientierter Software- und Maschinenbaulösungen (CustomB2B)" – support code 01 FL 10002.

References

1. Fettke, P., Loos, P.: Referenzmodellierungsforschung. Wirtschaftsinformatik 46, 331–340 (2004)
2. Lovelock, C.H.: Classifying Services to Gain Strategic Marketing Insights. Journal of Marketing 47, 9–20 (1983)
3. Zeithaml, V.A., Parasuraman, A., Berry, L.L.: Problems and Strategies in Services Marketing. The Journal of Marketing 49, 33–46 (1985)
4. Bullinger, H.-J., Schneider, K.: Service Engineering Entwicklung und Gestaltung innovativer Dienstleistungen. 2., vollst. überarb. und erweiterte Aufl. Springer, Berlin (2006)
5. Tukker, A.: Eight types of product–service system: eight ways to sustainability? Experiences from SusProNet. Business Strategy and the Environment 13, 246–260 (2004)
6. Windahl, C., Andersson, P., Berggren, C., Nehler, C.: Manufacturing firms and integrated solutions: characteristics and implications. European Journal of Innovation Management 7, 218–228 (2004)
7. Fließ, S., Kleinaltenkamp, M.: Blueprinting the service company: Managing service processes efficiently. Journal of Business Research 57, 392–404 (2004)
8. Vanhatalo, J.: Process Structure Trees: Decomposing a Business Process Model Into a Hierarchy of Single Entry Single Exit Fragments. Winter Industries (2009)
9. Vanhatalo, J., Völzer, H., Koehler, J.: The refined process structure tree. Data & Knowledge Engineering 68, 793–818 (2009)
10. Johnson, R., Pearson, D., Pingali, K.: The Program Structure Tree - Computing Control Regions in Linear-Time. Sigplan Notices 29, 171–185 (1994)

11. Han, J., Kamber, M.: Data Mining: Concepts and Techniques. Morgan Kaufmann, San Francisco (2006)
12. Aggarwal, C.C., Wang, H.: Managing and Mining Graph Data. Springer (2010)
13. Cook, D.J., Holder, L.B.: Mining Graph Data. John Wiley & Sons (2007)
14. Gottschalk, F., van der Aalst, W.M.P., Jansen-Vullers, M.H.: Mining Reference Process Models and Their Configurations. In: Meersman, R., Tari, Z., Herrero, P. (eds.) OTM-WS 2008. LNCS, vol. 5333, pp. 263–272. Springer, Heidelberg (2008)
15. Dijkman, R., Dumas, M., van Dongen, B., Kaarik, R., Mendling, J.: Similarity of business process models: Metrics and evaluation. Information Systems 36, 498–516 (2011)
16. Balzert, S., Fettke, P., Loos, P.: Plädoyer für eine operationalisierbare Methode der Prozesserhebung in der Beratung. In: Schumann, M., Kolbe, L.M., Breitner, M.H., Frerichs, A. (eds.) Proceedings: Multikonferenz Wirtschaftsinformatik 2010. Multikonferenz Wirtschaftsinformatik (MKWI-2010), Göttingen, Germany, February 23-25, pp. 623–635. Universitätsverlag Göttingen, Göttingen (2010)

Back to Origin: Transformation of Business Process Models to Business Rules

Saleem Malik and Imran Sarwar Bajwa

Department of Computer Science & IT,
The Islamia University of Bahawalpur, Pakistan
saleem@aucklanduni.ac.nz, i.s.bajwa@cs.bham.ac.uk

Abstract. A business process model should be explained to the business stakeholders to validate that it is a correct representation of targeted information of a particular domain. A business process model is typically represented by using a graphical notation such as Business Process Modelling Notation (BPMN). A graphical representation of a business process model can be complex to understand for the business stakeholders. However, a business rule represented in a natural language can be easy to understand for a novel person. Moreover, the extracted business rules can be employed for reuse of information through mapping to other standards such as BPEL, OCL, etc. In this paper, we present a novel approach to automatically generate natural language representation of business process models explained in BPMN. The presented approach employs SBVR (Semantics of Business Vocabulary and Rules) as an intermediate representation to generate natural language expressions those are easy to understand for business stake holders.

Keywords: Business Process Modelling, BPMN, SBVR, Natural Language Representation.

1   Introduction

In modern system engineering, Business Process Modeling [1] (BPM) is a key activity involved in representation of business processes for the continuous analysis and improvement. The modelling of business processes is responsibility of business analysts and managers to attain highly efficient and quality business process in an enterprise. In practice, the business processes are conceptually modeled using various conceptual Business Process Modelling Languages [2] (BPMLs) such as UML 2.0 Activity Diagram (AD) [3], Business Process Definition Metamodel [4] (BPDM), Business Process Modelling Notation [5] (BPMN), Petri Nets [6], etc. A conceptual business process model includes the description of all relevant business rules of the domain. BPMN is a common way of graphically representing business process models. The conceptual business process model is communicated with the external business stakeholders to validate the correctness of the model. However, a graphical representation of a business process model can be complex to understand for the business stakeholders. While, a natural language (NL) representation of a BPMN based model can be easy to understand for external business stakeholders.

M. La Rosa and P. Soffer (Eds.): BPM 2012 Workshops, LNBIP 132, pp. 611–622, 2012.

In this paper, we present a novel approach to automatically generate NL (such as English) representation of a BPMN-based conceptual business process model. In BPMN to NL translation, we have used SBVR (Semantics of Business Vocabulary and Rules) [7] as an intermediate representation. BPMN to NL translation approach works in two phases: SBVR vocabulary is extracted from BPMN model, and SBVR rules are generated from SBVR vocabulary. To make SBVR rules easy to read and understand, various SBVR notations such as SBVR Structured English or RuleSpeak are used. The acquired SBVR rule representation can be presented to the business stakeholders and customers as a list of self-explaining natural language expressions.

As far as we know, the presented approach is the first proposal to provide such translation. However, the automated translations of other formal languages such as UML or OCL to NL [8] have already been proposed but translation of BPMN models to NL is a novel initiative. Moreover, our approach provides a standard format (such as SBVR) for defining the business rules in natural languages.

The rest of the paper is structured as follows. Section 2 presents our preliminary BPMN to SBVR translation. In Section 3, we generate natural language expressions from the resulting SBVR excerpts. Finally, Section 4 presents some conclusions.

2   Preliminaries

2.1   Business Process Modelling Notation (BPMN)

BPMN has emerged into a famous standard used for generating business process diagrams. Typically such diagrams are comprised of a flowcharting technique to generate graphical models of various operations related to a business process. BPMN is used to create the initial drafts of the processes, to the technical developers responsible for implementing the technology that will perform those processes, and finally, to the business people who will manage and monitor those processes. Following are some key type of BPMN diagrams:

Artifacts: In a business process model, artifacts can be used to represent additional information related to the process. Commonly used artifacts in BPMN models are discussed below:

- Data Objects: A data object does not have a direct effect on a process but does provide information relevant to the process. It is represented as a rectangle with the top corner folded over.
- Groups: A group is an informal means for grouping elements of a process. It is represented as a rectangle with a dashed line border.

Annotations: An annotation is a mechanism for the BPMN modeler to provide additional information to the audience of a BPMN diagram. It is represented by an open rectangle containing the annotation text.

Flow Objects: The flow objects are used to define the behavior of a business process. Following three flow objects are commonly used in a BPMN model.

- Activities: An activity is work that is performed within a business process and is represented by a rounded rectangle.
- Events: An event is something that happens during the course of a business process which affects the sequence or timing of activities of a process. Events are represented as small circles with different boundaries to distinguish start events (thin black line) and end events (thick black line).
- Gateways: Gateways are used to control how sequence flows converge and diverge within a process. Gateways can represent decisions, where one or more paths are disallowed, or they can represent concurrent forks.

Flow Object Connectors: The flow objects can be connected to each other by using following three connectors:

- Sequence flows: A sequence flow is used to show the order in which activities are performed within a process. A sequence flow is represented by a line with a solid arrowhead.
- Message flows: A message flow is used to show the flow of messages between two entities, where pools are used to represent entities. A message flow is represented by a dashed line with a light-colored circle at the source and arrowhead at the target.
- Associations: An association is used to associate information and artifacts with flow objects. An association is represented by a dashed line which may or may not have a line arrowhead at the target end.

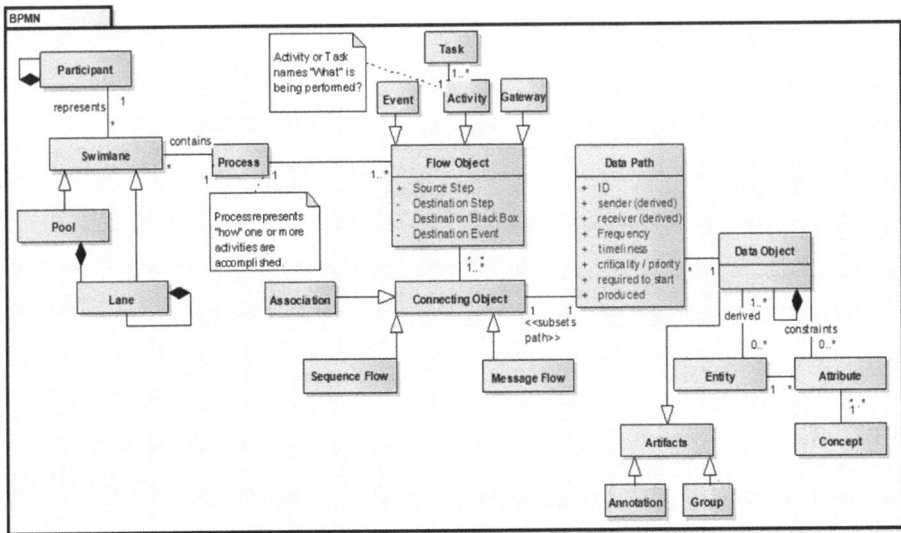

Fig. 1. An extract of the BPMN metamodel: concepts

Swimlanes: The swimlanes or partitions are used to group various objects involved in a process. Two commons types of swimlanes are

- Pools: A pool represents a participant in a process, where a participant may be a business entity or role. It is represented as a partition of the process.
- Lanes: A lane is a sub-division of a pool and is used to organize and categorize activities within the pool.

In our transformations we used the BPMN metamodel given in BPMN [5]. Fig. 1 shows an extract of this metamodel. Activity is used to represent the different process flow objects. Each Activity must be contained in a Pool and possibly a Lane. The ActivityType of an Activity indicates the type of the flow object (Task, Gateway, etc.). Activities are connected to each other through the SequenceEdge element. The Association element is used to relate Activities to Artifacts. DataObject and TextAnnotation are Artifacts that represent the Data Object and Annotation [4], respectively.

2.2   Semantic Business Vocabulary and Rules (SBVR)

Semantics of Business Vocabulary and Rules [7] is an adopted standard used to specify the business rules. Moreover, SBVR can be used as an intermediate representation in translation of formal representations to natural language and vice versa. Examples of such translations are UML/OCL to natural language [8], English to UML models [9], English to OCL constraints [8], etc. A SBVR based representation contains a set of business vocabulary and business rules.

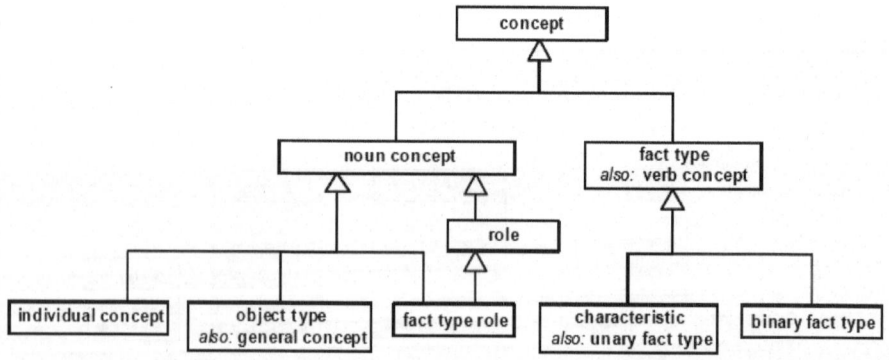

Fig. 2. An extract of the SBVR metamodel: concepts ([7] Figure 8.1)

SBVR Business Vocabulary. A business vocabulary [7] (section: 8.1) consists of all the specific terms and definitions of concepts used by an organization or community in course of business. In SBVR, there are four key elements:

- An *Object Type* is a general concept that exhibits a set of characteristics to distinguishes that object type from all other object types" [7] e.g. bank, account, etc.
- An *Individual Concept* is a qualified noun that corresponds to only one object [4] e.g. 'Lloyds', a famous bank.
- A *Characteristic* is an abstraction of a property of an object [7] e.g. name of bank, here name is characteristic.
- A *Verb Concept* is a verb in English sentences e.g. customer *uses* account.
- A *Fact Type* specifies relationships among noun concepts e.g. car has wheels.

SBVR Business Rules. A SBVR business rule is a formal representation 'Under business jurisdiction' [7]. Each SBVR business rule is based on at least one fact type. The SBVR rules can be a structural rule [ibid] used to define an organization's setup or a behavioural rule [ibid] used to express the conduct of a business entity.

Semantic Formulation. SBVR is typically proposed for business modeling in NL. However, we are using the formal logic based nature of SBVR to semantically formulate the English software requirements statements. A set of logic structures called semantic formulations are provided in SBVR to make English statements controlled such as atomic formulation, instantiate formulation, logical formulation, quantification, and modal formulation. For more details, we recommend user SBVR 1.0 document [7].

3   From BPMN to Natural Language Representation

To generate a natural language representation from a BPMN model, we have developed a framework for mapping all key elements in BPMN metamodel to their respective elements in SBVR metamodel. This process helps in extracting SBVR vocabulary that is finally mapped to Business rules and these Business rules are represented using SBVR Structured English notation to make it easy to read. Following are details of mapping of various types of BPMN elements to natural language:

3.1   Input Acquisition

Primary step in BPMN to NL transition is acquisition of BPMN model. An XML or XMI representation of a BPMN model is used to produce SBVR based English translation of a business process model. The XML representation of a BPMN model can be created by using any CASE tool (such as Enterprise Architect [12]) as most of the CASE tool provides this facility. However, we have used the Enterprise Architect tool to generate a BPMN model shown in Figure 8 and we exported the XML representation of the same BPMN model by using the Enterprise Architect tool. In the following text, we explain the mapping of BPMN elements represented in the form of tags in XML representation to SBVR English by using the example shown in Figure 8. Rest of the details of translation is given in the following sub sections.

3.2 Mapping Flow Objects

Flow objects are the main describing elements within BPMN, and consist of three core elements: events, activities, and gateways. Mapping of all three elements is presented below:

Mapping Events: Start event is mapped with the initiation of the SBVR specification and End event is mapped with the end of the SBVR specification (See Figure 3). To handle Start event, we add a string "The process of" + Model Name + "starts with" to text of the Start event. Here, XML file name is used as Model Name. However, to handle End event, a string "The process of" + Model name + "ends with" is added to the End event text. There can be some other types of Events such as Throwing (use to represent a completion message when a process ends) event or Catching (used to represent an incoming message starts a process) event. However, current implementation only supports Start event and End event.

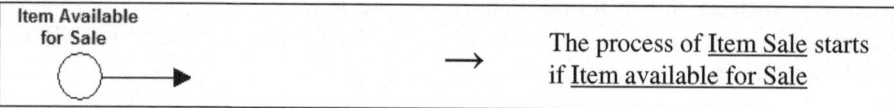

Fig. 3. Mapping BPMN Event to English

Mapping Activity: An Activity is mapped to a Logical Formulation to be used in the *consequent* part of an implication or in Necessity Formulation. Following can be two possible cases for mapping Activity:

- An activity is mapped to the Atomic Formulation in an *ActivityFactType*. In Activity to *ActivityFactType* mapping, the Object Type referred by role1 and the name of the Object Type referred to by role2 is mapped to the actor of the Activity.
- An Activity without any condition is potentially an initial Activity and an initial activity is mapped to a Necessity Formulation in a Logical Formulation of SBVR model (See Figure 4). In SBVR, a Necessity Formulation is represented using the keywords "It is necessary".

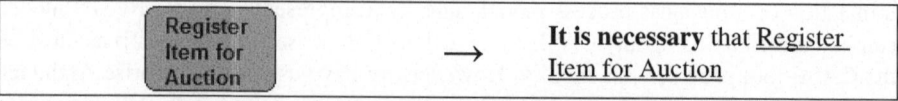

Fig. 4. Mapping BPMN Event to English

Gateway: In a BPMN model, a Gateway represents the conditions such as OR, AND, etc. An example of BPMN gateway to English mapping is shown in Figure 5.

BPMN Element	SBVR Element
XOR	Exclusive Disjunction
OR	Disjunction
AND	Conjunction

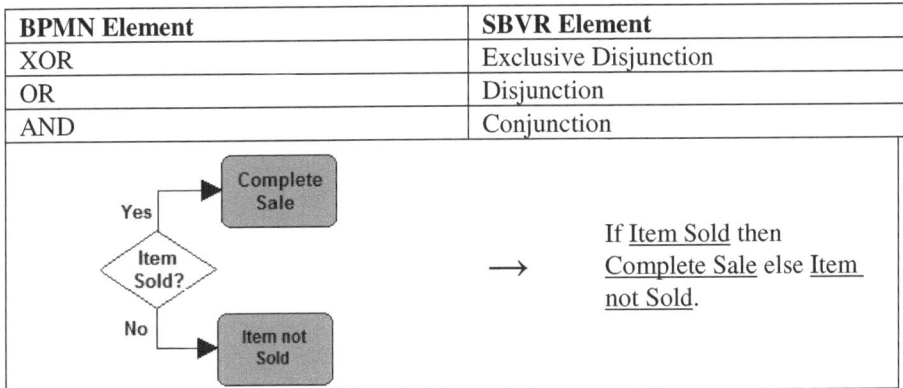

Fig. 5. Mapping BPMN Activity to English

3.3   Mapping Flow Object Connectors

Flow objects are connected to each other using Connecting objects, which are of three types: sequences, messages, and associations. We translate the only connecting objects with captions:

BPMN Element	SBVR Element
Sequence Flow	Activity-A results in Activity-B
Conditional Flow	Activity-B results if condition is True
Message Flow	Pool-A connected with Pool-B
Association	Fact Type (Artifact/Text is connected to Flow Object)

Here, Figure 6 show the mapping of Sequence Flow to SBVR based English while Figure 7 maps a Conditional Flow to SBVR based English.

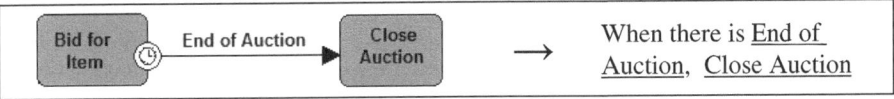

Fig. 6. Mapping BPMN Sequence Flow to English

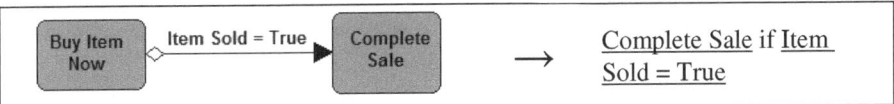

Fig. 7. Mapping BPMN Conditional Flow to English

3.4   Mapping Swim Lanes

As Swim-lanes are used to group activities in a business process model, similarly, we have used Pool and Lane to group the business rules. All activities shown in a single Pool or Lane are grouped together.

3.5   Mapping Artifacts

BPMN was designed to allow modelers and modeling tools some flexibility in extending the basic notation and in providing the ability to additional context appropriate to a specific modeling situation, such as for a vertical market (e.g., insurance or banking). Any number of Artifacts can be added to a diagram as appropriate for the context of the business processes being modeled. The current version of the BPMN specification pre-defines only three types of BPD Artifacts, which are:

BPMN Element	SBVR Element
Data Objects	Source of a information
Group	Activities in a Group are written together.
Annotation	Additional Information

3.6   Process Dependencies

The process dependencies of the BPMN model are mapped to the Logical-Formulations of the SBVR model. For this transformation, we identified two alternative mappings, which depend on where the Logical Formulation is defined: (1) in the condition part of implications, or (2) in the consequent part of implications or in a Necessity Formulation.

Mapping Relation: Here, a Relation is mapped to a Logical Formulation used in the *condition* part such as an And Relation is mapped to conjunction and a Disc Relation is mapped to disjunction and a Single Relation is mapped to other types of a Logical Formulation.

Mapping Variables: In BPMN to NL translation, a variable is mapped to an Atomic Formulation in a *Unary*-Fact Type, *Association*-Fact Type or *IsOfPropertyFactType*. Here, a variable can be of any type; either the Variable that is updated by the Activity or as a Precondition of the Activity.

Mapping Literals: In typical BPMN models, literals are commonly used. We map a literal to a simple Atomic Formulation that is not based on a Fact Type and has only one binding Noun Concept, where the Noun Concept will be represented as an Individual Concept.

3.7 Optimizing the Natural Language Representation

We have shown the way various BPMN elements are mapped to SBVR based natural language representation in Figure 4, 5, 6 and 7,. However, English generated in these examples is difficult to understand. Hence we need to optimize the generated English to make it easy to read and make it understandable. For the sake of optimization we have performed following two steps:

Resolving Phrases: In this phase the unstructured phrases extracted from BPMN elements is structured to make the extracted information sensible. To restructure the phrases following steps were performed:

Process Activity Text: The text in Activity symbol is processed as we append the text "user" at the start of the Activity symbol text. For example, the text "Buy item now" is processed as "User buys item now". Here, we do add 's' with the verb to keep grammar correct. We have used WordNet [6] version 3.1 to identify possible POS tags for each token of the text.

Process Gateway Text: The text in a gateway is handled in various ways.

i. If the Gateway poses a Yes/No question then two copies of the text are generated: one copy with positive sense and second copy with the negative sense. To generate a positive sense we simple add a helping verb in between Noun and Verb. While, for generating the copy with negative sense we also add token "not" with the helping verb. For example the text "Item Sold" is structured to "It is sold" and "Item is not sold".

ii. If the Gateway does not pose Yes/No question then we generate two copies of the Gateway text with by adding the text of respective branch. For example, the text "auction type" is optimized to "auction type is buy now" and "auction type is bid for item".

Applying Structured English Notation: In BPMN to NL translation, the last step is to generate easy to read NL representation by applying the SBVR Structured English notation. In SBVR 1.0 standard, there is another available representation, Rule Speak, as well. However, we have used only SBVR Structured English. Here, we have used WordNet version 3.1 to identify various types of POS types. We have represented common nouns as Object Type and underlined the text e.g. customer; the verbs are represented as Verb Concept and are italicized e.g. *can*; the SBVR keywords are bolded e.g. **It is obligatory**; the proper nouns are represented as Individual Concepts by double underlining e.g. Bible.

4   A Running Example

In this section, we present a running example to demonstrate the working of the presented approach. The presented example is based on a case study that is discussed from the domain of Choreography modeling. In the discussed example, two partners are involved in the example such as a seller and an auctioning service. Here, the choreography in the example describes the interactions needed for creating an auction. The BPMN model for the said example is shown in Figure 8:

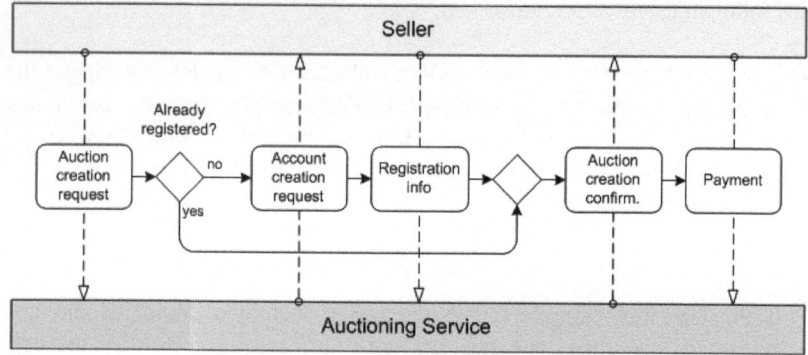

Fig. 8. Auctioning Service Model [11]

To translate BPMN model (shown in Fig. 8) to NL representation, the BPMN model was given as input (XML representation) to our BR-Generator tool. The tool initially parses the XML representation and then extracts the SBVR vocabulary by performing BPMN to SBVR mapping. The complete mapping from BPMN to SBVR for solved case study is shown in Table 1:

Table 1. SBVR vocabulary generated from BPMN XML representation

Details
The <u>Seller</u> *sends* an <u>auction creation request</u> to <u>**Auctioning Service**</u>.
If <u>Seller</u> *is* already *registered*, **it is necessary** that the <u>auction creation</u> *is confirmed*.
If <u>Seller</u> *is* not already *registered*, **it is necessary** that the <u>account creation request</u> *is sent* to <u>Seller</u>.
It is necessary that the <u>Seller</u> *sends* the <u>Registration info</u> to <u>**Auctioning Service**</u> and then the <u>auction creation</u> *is confirmed*.
The <u>Seller</u> *sends* a <u>Payment</u> to <u>**Auctioning Service**</u>.

To evaluate performance of tool that how accurately the BPMN model notation is translated to SBVR based English specification by our tool BR-Generator. There are total 12 BPMN symbols of 3 types in the solved case study problem those were translated to SBVR 1.0 based English sentences. In Table 2, the average recall for

SBVR software requirement specification is calculated 88.46% while average precision is calculated 91.66%.

Table 2. Results of BPMN to SBVR based English Translation

Type/Metrics	N_{sample}	$N_{correct}$	$N_{incorrect}$	$N_{missing}$	Rec%	Prec%
Software Requirements	12	11	0	1	91.66	91.66

Besides measuring accuracy we also conducted a survey to measure the effectiveness of the presented approach. We made two groups with 10 members in each group. First, we gave them three BPMN process models to interpret. Then we told them to interpret those three BPMN models using our tool BR-Generator. Then we gave 1 to 10 score under easy to do and correct understanding categories. The average values calculated for different parameters are clearly showing that the used approach was clearly making an impact. Though the accuracy of the tool is a bit concern but we can overcome this in future work by improving the implementation. The average results we received are shown in Table 3:

Table 3. Usability Survey Results

User	Easy to do		Correct Understanding	
	Manual	By Tool	Manual	By Tool
Novel	30%	90%	36%	87%
Medium	55%	85%	72%	82%
Average	42.50%	87.50%	54.00%	84.50%

5   Conclusion and Future Work

In this paper, we presented automated approach to translate BPMN based business process models to SBVR based natural language representation. The proposed framework was also implemented in Java and the results presented in section 5 depict that the presented approach can be helpful in understanding the complex BPMN models specifically for the novel users that can lead to a better feedback from the Business stakeholders ultimately resulting in better business process models those are more acceptable for Business analysts and Business stakeholders. Additionally, the BPMN models can be analyzed for consistency by translating the output of our approach (such as SBVR) to Alloy that globally accepted language used for model analysis. Moreover, the SBVR based output generated by the tool can be used for automated transformation to other formal specifications such as BPEL, UML, OCL, etc.

References

[1] Korherr, B.: Business Process Modelling. VDM Verlag Saarbrücken, Germany (2008) ISBN:3836487160 9783836487160

[2] Business Process Management Initiative: Business Process Modeling Notation. Specification Version 1.0 (May 3, 2004), http://www.bpmn.org/

[3] OMG. Unified Modelling Language (UML) Standard version 2.1.2. Object Management Group (2007), http://www.omg.org/

[4] Object Management Group. Business Process Definition Metamodel. Version 1.0.2 (January 12, 2004), http://www.bpmn.org/Documents/BPDM/OMG-BPD-2004-01-12-Revision.pdf

[5] WordNet: An Electronic Lexical Database. MIT Press, http://wordnet.princeton.edu/wordnet/publications/

[6] Business Process Management Initiative: Business Process Modeling Notation. Specification Version 1.0 (May 3, 2004), http://www.bpmn.org/

[7] Object Management Group. Semantics of Business vocabulary and Rules (SBVR) Standard v.1.0. Object Management Group (2008), http://www.omg.org/spec/SBVR/1.0/

[8] Pau, R., Cabot, J.: Paraphrasing OCL Expressions with SBVR. In: Kapetanios, E., Sugumaran, V., Spiliopoulou, M. (eds.) NLDB 2008. LNCS, vol. 5039, pp. 311–316. Springer, Heidelberg (2008)

[9] Bajwa, I.S., Naeem, M.A., Ali, A., Ali, S.: A Controlled Natural Language Interface to Class Models. In: 13th International Conference on Enterprise Information Systems (ICEIS 2011), pp. 102–110 (2011)

[10] Bajwa, I.S., Bordbar, B., Lee, M.G.: OCL Constraints Generation from Natural Language Specification. In: 14th IEEE International Enterprise Distributed Object Computing Conference (EDOC 2010), pp. 204–213 (2010)

[11] BPMN.info. BPMN 2.0 takes dancing lessons – do we need choreographies? (2008), http://blog.bpmn.info/2008/10/15/bpmn-20-takes-dancing-lessons-do-we-need-choreographies/

[12] Sparx Systems, Enterprise Architect, http://www.sparxsystems.com.au/

Identifying and Visualising Dependability Concerns – Applications to Business Process Management

Andreas L. Opdahl

Department of Information Science and Media Studies,
University of Bergen, Norway
Andreas.Opdahl@uib.no

Abstract. The project *RecSeq – Requirements for Security* (2008-2012) developed and evaluated techniques that can be used visualise security and other dependability concerns, such as safety, early in the planning of new information systems. A central concern was to allow inclusion of a variety of stakeholders, in particular non-ICT/non-security experts, in the requirements process. This paper reviews the dependability requirements work done in the ReqSec project and highlights its relevance for the dependability of business processes.

1   From Security to Dependability

Dependability of an information system can be defined as its ability to deliver a service that can be justifiably trusted [3]. We can define *dependability requirements engineering* accordingly as the process of eliciting, negotiating specifying and validating the dependability properties required from a new information system or service. Dependability has traditionally covered properties such as availability, reliability and maintainability, but has recently been used more widely to include properties such as safety, security and privacy as well. This paper will focus on two of the latter types of dependability: *security* – or resilience to *intended* threats – and *safety* – or resilience to *unintended* hazards. The two are similar in some respects because they both involve what a new IS should *not* do, i.e., *anti-functional* concerns, whereas existing IS development methods tend to focus on what the system *should* do, i.e., on *functional* ones. Despite many similarities, the two fields have so far evolved independently, each producing their own sets of techniques and tools, and few or no development methods support them both.

Today, *information systems dependability* is becoming more and more important because modern ICT systems and services have become pervasive and tightly integrated with human activities and collaborations in all areas of society. Through ICT support, the activities and collaborations have also become more complex and intertwined and, thus, more vulnerable. For example, safety-critical systems in the aviation and energy sectors that were previously cut-off from the Internet are being re-engineered to become networked – or they are becoming replaced by new inter-networked systems. As a result, more types of dependability concerns are becoming

M. La Rosa and P. Soffer (Eds.): BPM 2012 Workshops, LNBIP 132, pp. 623–629, 2012.

more important more often than before. For many of the same reasons, dependability issues are becoming an important part of *business process management* too. Through ICT, processes are becoming more complex and intertwined, e.g., involving more parallel strands, more interactions, more stakeholders and more inter-organisational and international boundaries. As a result, more types of dependability concerns are again becoming more important more often than before. We can define *process dependability management* as the process of continually defining, realising, monitoring and correcting the dependability properties of business processes. Given the many similarities between defining and evolving a business process and specifying and developing information systems and services to support it, it becomes interesting to explore whether and how methods, techniques and experiences for dependability requirements can be useful also for process dependability management.

2   Results from the ReqSec Project

The project *RecSeq – Requirements for Security* was funded by the Norwegian Research Council form 2008 to 2012 as a collaboration between project leader Professor *Guttorm Sindre* at the Norwegian University of Science and Technology (NTNU) and the author at the University of Bergen (UiB). Other central contributors were *Peter Karpati* and *Vikash Katta* (supervised by Professor *Tor Stålhane*) at NTNU and *Christian Raspotnig* at UiB.

The project developed and evaluated lightweight, integrated techniques that can be used to visualise security and other dependability concerns, such as safety, early in the planning of new information systems. An inspiration were Misuse Cases (MUC) [19-20,11], a technique proposed earlier by the ReqSec collaborators as an extension of regular use cases (UC) to also represent *misusers* and their *misuse cases*. The ReqSec project explored similar extensions to other modelling techniques, with the aim of providing an integrated method of complementary modelling techniques. Drawing on the particular strengths of MUCs, a driving ambition was to include stakeholders with widely different competencies and backgrounds, in particular non-ICT and non-security people, from the start of the requirements work.

Misuse Case Maps (MUCM) [7-9] was proposed by the project to allow architecture considerations to be made when dealing with security requirements. MUCMs adapt Use Case Maps (UCM) [2,4] by introducing security concepts such as *vulnerabilities, exploit paths* and *vulnerable responsibilities*, inspired by MUCs. Regular UCMs depict the *components* in a system as (possibly nested) rectangles and use cases, or *scenario paths*, as lines that originate from users and cut across one the components that take responsibility for its *steps*. MUCMs allow components and their responsibilities to be marked as *vulnerable*, and an *exploit path*, originating from a *misuser*, may cut through one or more vulnerabilities. MUCMs were evaluated by the project using them on practical cases and by experiments involving researchers and students.

Misuse Sequence Diagrams (MUSD) [11] were similarly proposed and evaluated to provide an alternative way of depicting attack sequences, as a supplement to

Mal-Activity Diagrams (MAD) [18]. Regular Sequence Diagrams (SD), e.g., in the Unified Modeling Language (UML), depict how *messages*, originating from *actors* external to the system, are passed on between *objects* or *components* inside it, invoking *actions* along their path. MUSDs allow actors to be *attackers* that originate *exploit messages* that target *vulnerabilities* in the objects or components. MUSDs were compared with MUCMs in a controlled student experiment, among other things suggesting that MUSDs were indeed better for understanding security issues involving attack sequences and MUCMs for architectural concerns.

Failure Sequence Diagrams (FSD) [15-16] were proposed as a safety-variant of SDs, as the project expanded to also include safety requirements. Sindre and Stålhane had already investigated misuse cases for safety purposes [17,22] and Sindre and Opdahl [21] had discussed dependability more broadly in relation to MUCs. FSDs depict *failure scenarios* in which *mishap events* propagate through a system of *vulnerable* objects or components. FSDs were evaluated in combination with the safety technique FMEA (Failure Mode and Effect Analysis) [5] in a series of real live workshops in the aviation sector. In the workshops, FSDs were used in conjunction with *guiding keywords* inspired by safety techniques such as FMEA and Hazard and Operability analysis (HAZOP) [5]. For example, if a component is a physical pipe of some sort, guiding keywords or phrases may be "no flow", "reverse flow", "leak" or "rupture", each suggesting a possible vulnerability to be considered. Although presented as an alternative to MUSDs, there should be no inherent problem with using the two techniques together or combining them, using the safety and security extensions to regular SDs in the same diagrams.

Comparisons of the safety and security requirements fields were initiated when our experiences with using closely related techniques for safety and security concerns suggested that the two – most likely along with other types of dependability issues – were similar in many ways. As mentioned in the introduction, they are all about what a new IS should *not* do, whereas functional requirements focus on what the system *should* do, and both are related to *risk management*. In the final phases of ReqSec and beyond, we are therefore comparing techniques from the two fields systematically to investigate whether and, if so, how, they would benefit from cross-pollination and closer integration [14].

Combined Harm Assessment of Safety and Security for Information Systems (CHASSIS) [13] was proposed as a method for integrated safety and security requirements engineering, comprising three parallel strands of activities. *Eliciting functional requirements* involves creating a UC diagram, writing out its use cases textually using a template and creating sequence diagrams for each of them. *Eliciting safety/security requirements* similarly creates misuse case diagrams from the diagrammatic and textual uses cases using guidewords, writes out the misuse cases textually and details each case using FSDs/MUSDs. *Specifying Safety/Security Requirements* describes the misuse cases in even fuller detail using HAZOP-like tables that are used to specify the final safety and security requirements. CHASSIS is being developed in close cooperation with companies in the aviation sector.

3   Application to Business Process Management

Several of the ideas behind and the results from the ReqSec project might inspire ongoing or new research in the business process area.

Considering Dependability from the Start. In many software development projects, dependability concerns such as security are handled too late, sometimes not until the design and implementation stages or after the system has been put to use and security problems discovered by actual intrusions. This often leads to costly rework of the system to the exclusion of simpler, non-technical ways of solving or avoiding dependability issues at specification or design time. A better approach is to address such concerns already from the start of development, a practice that may also be recommendable for process dependability management.

Involving a Broad Variety of Competencies. Including both process participants, process owners, IT people and safety and security experts was a central idea behind ReqSec. A dependability concern like security is too often considered an expert task that is best left to programmers, network administrators and platform maintainers during late development and operation. But other stakeholders may hold equally vital information about what are the most pressing vulnerabilities of and threats to a new system and about what are the feasible solutions. Were they aware that the proposed functions and architecture would be problematic from a security or other dependability viewpoint, they might have been able to suggest specifications and designs with an equally or more dependable functionality and architecture. In the same way, involving a broad combination of competencies is likely to be beneficial when defining and realising dependable business processes.

Using Visualisations. Visualisations, including multi-perspective ones, have been used by ReqSec to support communication between different types of stakeholders and to assess the dependability of software artefacts before they are implemented. Of course, visualisations of business processes are well known to be useful for similar reasons. The results from ReqSec suggest that, in particular, visualisations of organisation units (*pools*, *lanes*), flows and sequences (spatially ordered *activities* inside *pools* and *lanes*) can be used to investigate dependability concerns.

Broader and More Integrated Handling of Dependability. Business processes should always be defined, realised, monitored and corrected in terms of the properties that matter most from a business perspective. But, as we explained in the introduction, more types of dependability concerns are becoming more important more often than before. These dependability issues are interrelated and can most precisely and completely be investigated together. When similar, or even the same, tools and techniques are used for the different types of concerns, the process becomes easier to master and manage and learning is facilitated across dependability fields that were previously treated separately. In consequence, process dependability could and should be considered more often, more broadly and in a more integrated fashion that what is common today.

Leveraging Integrated Dependability Analysis for Integrated Risk Assessment. A commonality between safety, security and other dependability concerns is that they are closely tied to risk assessment. Using the same or similar techniques to deal with dependability issues in an integrated manner therefore opens also for integrated risk assessment, as an alternative to carrying out independent assessements of safety, security and other dependability risks.

Using Organisational Boundaries. Experiences with MUCMs suggest that security vulnerabilities can be identified by systematically investigating how scenario paths use the responsibilities offered by system components. It is likely that other types of vulnerabilities can be identified in the same way. Although the MUCM notation is not necessarily suitable for modelling processes, organisation units are commonly represented in process models as (possibly nested) *pools* or *lanes* that play roles similar to *components* in UCMs.

Using Guiding Keywords. The guiding keywords used with FSDs for safety purposes might also be usable with other modelling techniques and for driving dependability analyses for purposes other than safety. When multiple stakeholder competencies are represented, systematically identifying dependability vulnerabilities of components and their interconnections offers to reveal a wealth of weaknesses that might otherwise have gone unnoticed. In process settings, guiding words can be associated with types of roles (represented as pools/lanes) or other modelling constructs, such as flows ("lost", "blocked", "eavesdropped", "injected"...) or timers ("early", "late", "shut off", "too frequent", "hi-jacked"...).

Investigating Remedies for Possible Vulnerabilities. An early realisation when exploring MUCs in industrial settings [1] was that remedies (or *security use cases* [6]) introduced to mitigate security threats, could themselves introduce new vulnerabilities. This advocates a recursive investigation strategy in which vulnerabilities and their solutions are, at least sometimes, represented in the same models.

4   Paths for Further Work

Each of these possible applications of ReqSec results to process dependability management are candidates for further research, whether on their own or in combination. While this paper has talked about dependability in general, it has only dealt with two, albeit central, dependability concerns in any depth: those of safety and security. Further work should investigate whether the proposed methods are useful for other dependability concerns as well – such as availability, reliability and maintainability – both in requirements and in process settings.

Privacy is another concern that is growing in importance in both settings. It shares many features – and overlaps – with both safety and security. For example, privacy issues come to the fore in inter-organisational and international business processes that exchange customer information across sectors, such as international air traffic. Hence, further work should explore whether the techniques and methods from ReqSec can be used to deal with privacy issues too, keeping in mind that privacy also involves concerns that may lie outside of dependability.

References

1. Alexander, I.: Misuse cases: Use cases with hostile intent. IEEE Softw. 20(1), 58–66 (2003)
2. Amyot, D.: Use Case Maps Quick Tutorial (1999), http://www.usecasemaps.org/pub/UCMtutorial/UCMtutorial.pdf
3. Avizienis, A., Laprie, J.-C., Randell, B.: Fundamental Concepts of Dependability. CSD Report no. 010028, UCLA Computer Science Dept., Univ. of California, Los Angeles (2001)
4. Buhr, R., Casselman, R.: Use case maps for object-oriented systems. Prentice-Hall (1995)
5. Ericson, C.A.: Hazard Analysis Techniques for System Safety. John Wiley & Sons (2005)
6. Firesmith, D.J.: Security use cases. Journal of Object Technology 2(3) (2003)
7. Karpati, P., Opdahl, A.L., Sindre, G.: Experimental evaluation of misuse case maps for eliciting security requirements. In: Proc. 1st Security Conference – Europe (ISCE), Örebro/Sweden, August 15-17 (2010)
8. Karpati, P., Opdahl, A.L., Sindre, G.: Experimental comparison of Misuse Case Maps with Misuse Cases and System Architecture Diagrams for eliciting security vulnerabilities and Mitigations. In: Proc. 6th Int. Conf. Availability, Reliability and Security, pp. 507–514. IEEE Computer Society (2011) ISBN 978-0-7695-4485-4
9. Karpati, P., Sindre, G., Opdahl, A.L.: Visualizing Cyber Attacks with Misuse Case Maps. In: Wieringa, R., Persson, A. (eds.) REFSQ 2010. LNCS, vol. 6182, pp. 262–275. Springer, Heidelberg (2010)
10. Karpati, P., Sindre, G., Opdahl, A.L.: Characterising and analysing security requirements modelling initiatives. In: Proc. 6th Int. Conf. Availability, Reliability and Security, pp. 710–715. IEEE Computer Society (2011) ISBN 978-0-7695-4485-4
11. Katta, V., Karpati, P., Opdahl, A.L., Raspotnig, C., Sindre, G.: Comparing Two Techniques for Intrusion Visualization. In: van Bommel, P., Hoppenbrouwers, S., Overbeek, S., Proper, E., Barjis, J. (eds.) PoEM 2010. LNBIP, vol. 68, pp. 1–15. Springer, Heidelberg (2010)
12. Opdahl, A.L., Sindre, G.: Experimental comparison of Attack Trees and Misuse Cases for Security Threat Identification. J. Info. and Softw. Tech. 51(5), 916–932 (2009)
13. Raspotnig, C., Karpati, P., Katta, V.: A Combined Process for Elicitation and Analysis of Safety and Security Requirements. In: Bider, I., Halpin, T., Krogstie, J., Nurcan, S., Proper, E., Schmidt, R., Soffer, P., Wrycza, S. (eds.) EMMSAD 2012 and BPMDS 2012. LNBIP, vol. 113, pp. 347–361. Springer, Heidelberg (2012)
14. Raspotnig, C., Opdahl, A.L.: Comparing risk identification techniques for safety and security requirements (submitted manuscript, 2012)
15. Raspotnig, C., Opdahl, A.L.: Improving security and safety modelling with Failure Sequence Diagrams. Int. J. Secure Software Engineering 3(1) (2012)
16. Raspotnig, C., Opdahl, A.: Supporting Failure Mode and Effect Analysis: A Case Study with Failure Sequence Diagrams. In: Regnell, B., Damian, D. (eds.) REFSQ 2011. LNCS, vol. 7195, pp. 117–131. Springer, Heidelberg (2012)
17. Sindre, G.: A Look at Misuse Cases for Safety Concerns. In: Ralyté, J., Brinkkemper, S., Henderson-Sellers, B. (eds.) Situational Method Engineering: Fundamentals and Experiences, vol. 244, pp. 252–266. Springer (2007)

18. Sindre, G.: Mal-Activity Diagrams for Capturing Attacks on Business Processes. In: Sawyer, P., Heymans, P. (eds.) REFSQ 2007. LNCS, vol. 4542, pp. 355–366. Springer, Heidelberg (2007)
19. Sindre, G., Opdahl, A.L.: Eliciting security requirements by Misuse Cases. In: Proc. TOOLS Pacific 2000, Sydney, IEEE CS Press (2000)
20. Sindre, G., Opdahl, A.L.: Eliciting security requirements with Misuse Cases. Requirements Engineering 10(1), 34–44 (2005)
21. Sindre, G., Opdahl, A.L.: Misuse Cases for identifying system dependability threats. J. Information Privacy and Security 4(2) (2008)
22. Stålhane, T., Sindre, G.: A Comparison of Two Approaches to Safety Analysis Based on Use Cases. In: Parent, C., Schewe, K.-D., Storey, V.C., Thalheim, B. (eds.) ER 2007. LNCS, vol. 4801, pp. 423–437. Springer, Heidelberg (2007)

New Technologies for Democratic Elections

Sven Heiberg[1,2]

[1] Cybernetica AS, Ülikooli 2, Tartu, Estonia
[2] Software Technology and Applications Competence Centre,
Ülikooli 2, Tartu, Estonia
sven@cyber.ee

Abstract. Estonia has implemented a specific form of electronic voting – internet voting – as a method to participate in various types of legally binding elections since 2005. The mitigation of security risks in the method has lead to changes in the voting procedures. Those changes might affect the way we think about traditional voting.

1 Electronic Voting in Elections

Elections are process by which citizens in democratic countries elect politicians into office. There are many electoral systems defining the rules of selecting the small set of representatives according to the large set of citizen preferences. Those systems rely on voting methods to gather preferences through the act of voting.

Voting method is a technological, procedural and organizational structure to collect and store voters' votes and to tabulate the voting result. Voting is a process of casting the preference of a voter as a vote and transporting the vote to ballot box hosted by election officials. Voting results are input to the computation of the election result.

Traditional voting methods are paper-based – votes are cast on paper-ballots which are transported to physical ballot box and tabulated by hand. Paper-based methods, their nature and possible threats, are well known. Those methods are strictly regulated by election laws and are applied in accordance to the democratic principles – free, general and uniform elections maintaining ballot secrecy.

Electronic voting methods rely on the help of electronic device(s) in at least some parts of the process. For example – we speak of electronic voting also, when the ballots are cast on paper, but tabulated electronically. Despite the change in technology, the electronic voting methods must adhere to same democratic principles as traditional methods.

Several countries have looked into some form of electronic voting. It is hoped that remote electronic voting improves the availability of elections especially for citizens abroad and increases the voter turnout [10,1,5,16,14]. Electronic tallying is seen as a way to speed up the process to accurate election results [11]. For disabled people, electronic voting is a possibility to vote without assistance [9]. It is even claimed that without online voting, segments of society will stay completely absent from voting [2].

M. La Rosa and P. Soffer (Eds.): BPM 2012 Workshops, LNBIP 132, pp. 630–635, 2013.

2   Internet Voting in Estonia

In Estonia a fully electronic remote voting method has been used in several elections since 2005. The scheme uses internet as a communication channel between individual voters and the digital ballot box [4]. We call this kind of electronic voting internet voting (i-voting).

As of July 2012, i-voting has been used in five Estonian elections. In March 2011 Parliamentary elections, 24.3% of participating voters were internet voters (i-voters). This number indicates that i-voting is accepted by the electorate. It is also evident that the tally of i-voting has potential to significantly influence the election result.

Estonian i-voting uses an election specific voting application to electronically cast a vote. I-voting starts with voter authenticating himself to i-voting system with the National Identity Card (ID-card). I-voting system checks the voter's eligibility to vote and returns the list of candidates upon success. This list is displayed on voter's computer. The voter's choice is encrypted with the public key of the i-voting system and signed with voter's ID-card in a legally binding manner. The signed and encrypted ballot is sent to the i-voting system for storage and tabulation.

The voting scheme resembles the double-envelope scheme used for postal voting. For the tabulation of i-votes the digital signatures are removed from the encrypted ballots. Then the private key of the i-voting system is activated and voting result tabulated.

I-voter, similarly to postal voter, can vote from anywhere. I-voting is allowed during the advance voting period and, unlike the paper voting, is available 24 hours a day. In contrast to official polling booths, voter's environment is uncontrolled. The concept of i-vote revocation is legislated in order to fight the possible coercion. A voter can cast an i-vote several times, only the last one will be counted. I-vote is also revoked if the voter casts a paper-ballot during the advance voting period.

3   Verifiable Voting

Opponents of electronic voting point out, that the application of new technology opens new ways to tamper with elections [8]. The basic threats, such as voter disenfranchisement, are same across all voting methods, but the properties of electronic voting technology allegedly increase the possible impact of the attacks. In case of internet voting, there is no need for the attacker to be physically present in the country holding the election, if the digital ballot box is compromised, a large scale manipulation of ballots might follow.

With traditional voting methods, voter can be relatively sure that the paper captures her will correctly. After the vote is entered into ballot box, voter has to trust election officials to correctly follow procedures. The possibility to observe election adds to this trust. In fully electronic voting systems observability is lost and people rely completely on computers. Voter has to trust that computer encodes her preference correctly and sends this to the voting system as intended. Voter also has to trust that the voting system accepts the votes correctly and takes them into account during tabulation. A mistake in the voting application or a malicious software controlling the voter's computer might change the results without people being able to notice it has happened.

The lack of transparency in straightforward electronic voting has led to a search for electronic voting methods which would help the voter to regain the lost control over the voting process. Individually verifiable voting methods give means to a voter to verify that at least some of certain properties – e.g. cast as intended – hold on the vote cast by the voter [15]. An example of such a voting method is applied in Norway [6,16].

Norwegian method takes advantage of two additional communication channels – pre-channel implemented by postal system and post-channel implemented by cell-phones. Before the election each voter receives a check-list of (*candidate, returncode*) pairs. Although the candidates are the same, return codes differ from voter to voter.

Voter uses voting application to vote in a similar manner to the Estonian method. After the vote has been received by the voting system, a SMS is sent to the voter with the return code calculated from the encrypted vote. If the return code is paired with the voter's actual choice on the check-list, then the voter can be sure that the correct ballot was accepted by the server. If malicious software has modified the voter's choice, the return code shall indicate a different candidate and voter discovers the violation of her rights. Voter still has to trust, that the voting system tabulates her ballot correctly.

Universally verifiable voting methods give means to observers to verify that the voting result was tabulated correctly according to the contents of the ballot box. This often involves the publication of the ballot box contents on a public bulletin board, so that observers can retabulate the votes at their own will. Together with cryptographic techniques to ensure that the ballot-secrecy is maintained and possible coercion avoided, the universal verifiability can give even higher transparency than traditional voting methods.

4   Parliamentary Election 2011

The i-voting conception applied in Estonia acknowledges the risk that the i-voting system can tamper with voting results. It is assumed that this risk can be brought to acceptable level by applying organizational security measures. Secondly it is assumed that although there is a risk of voters computers being infected with election rigging malware, this risk can be accepted as there is a very low probability that a large scale manipulation attack can go unnoticed [3].

During the Parliamentary elections in 2011, those assumptions were set under a serious doubt. There was a student who implemented a proof-of-concept malware demonstrating the possibility to effectively disenfranchise the voter from a right to vote [7]. The malware was screened in the National Television after the election, it initiated several debates over the security of i-voting.

After the end of internet voting period, the student filed a complaint to the NEC demanding the revocation of all i-votes, reasoning that as the voter cannot check whether his vote was accepted by i-voting system or not, the system did not comply with Parliamentary Election Act [13]. The complaint made it to Supreme Court of Estonia and was dismissed on the grounds that person's right to vote was not violated, as the student knowingly put himself into the situation where he was disenfranchised by the malware [17].

OSCE/ODIHR covered the situation in their election assessment mission report and suggested that the use of a verifiable internet voting scheme or an equally reliable mechanism for the voter to check whether or not her vote was changed by malicious software should be considered [12].

In the situation, where there existed an actual piece of election rigging malware, a desire to revoke election results and a suggestion to provide voters with additional instrument of verification, NEC decided to make a new risk analysis to the i-voting conception, before taking any further action.

The analysis points out that the attackers tampering with voting methods are not interested in simply achieving additional votes, but rather achieving something relying on the votes and the implied seats – the actual target of the attacker is increasing his influence in the society. Having this goal in mind and analyzing the events from 2011 three distinct attack categories are described – manipulation, revocation and reputation attacks. A party interested in the voting result may choose to influence the election result either directly by performing a manipulation attack, or indirectly by changing voters' confidence towards i-voting through reputation attack. A trust-based voting model is open to all categories of attacks and therefore not sustainable, whereas verifiability would give tools to voters and election officials to counter those attacks.

5   Change towards Verifiability

In spring 2012, a change in Estonian Election Law was initiated. If the law is accepted, Estonian i-voters shall gain access to mechanisms of individual verifiability, allowing for verification of cast as intended and accepted as cast properties. This is a necessary change, but it comes with a price.

The properties of Norwegian internet voting method are rather characteristic to verifiable voting methods. The setup for voting is complex. There is need for additional communication channels and devices. Voter has to take explicit action in order to verify that certain properties hold which by the traditional voting methods are guaranteed implicitly.

Verifiability introduces new risks. It is feared that malicious voters shall misuse the new tool given to them to disrupt the election by falsely claiming that the verifiability indicates a manipulation with a vote, although there was none. If these voters cooperate, a new threat to trustworthiness of the elections rises. Nevertheless, verifiability is a destination to go to – without verifiability the reputation attacks against voters' confidence are too easy.

The most important implications of verifiability might lie further in the future. We are seeing how the advent of electronic voting methods is slowly shaping our democracies. The new voting methods that were initially meant to automate and mimic the traditional voting methods, have evolved into new forms with properties and possibilities differing significantly from those offered by the traditional voting. If the mechanisms of verifiability are accepted by the society, a demand for even bigger transparency and verifiability could rise. This demand might also affect the traditional voting methods, which currently are trusted due to observability of paper-based processes. Efforts to solve security problems inherent to the new technology, are showing a potential to change the way we think about voting and election.

References

1. The Geneva Internet Voting System (2010),
   http://www.geneve.ch/evoting/english/doc/passport_evoting2010.pdf (last accessed August 16, 2012)
2. BBC News: The world's five biggest cyber threats. An interview with Eugene Kaspersky by technology reporter Katia Moskvitch (April 2012)
3. Ansper, A., Buldas, A., Oruaas, M., Priisalu, J., Veldre, A., Willemson, J., Virunurm, K.: E-voting Concept Security: Analysis and Measures, Estonian National Electoral Commitee, EH-02-01 (2003)
4. Estonian National Electoral Committee. E-Voting System. General Overview (2010)
5. Driza-Maurer, A., Spycher, O., Taglioni, G., Weber, A.: E-voting for Swiss abroad/A Joint Project between the Confederation and the Cantons. In: Kripp, M., Volkamer, M., Grimm, R. (eds.) 5th International Conference on Electronic Voting 2012. Lecture Notes in Informatics, pp. 173–187 (2012)
6. Gjøsteen, K.: Analysis of an internet voting protocol. Cryptology ePrint Archive, Report 2010/380 (2010), http://eprint.iacr.org/
7. Heiberg, S., Laud, P., Willemson, J.: The Application of I-Voting for Estonian Parliamentary Elections of 2011. In: Kiayias, A., Lipmaa, H. (eds.) VoteID 2011. LNCS, vol. 7187, pp. 208–223. Springer, Heidelberg (2012)
8. Jefferson, D., Rubin, A.D., Simons, B., Wagner, D.: A Security Analysis of the Secure Electronic Registration and Voting Experiment, SERVE (2004), http://www.servesecurityreport.org/paper.pdf (last accessed on August 27, 2011)
9. Loide, E., Lepp, Ü.: E-voting - a Key to Independence for All. In: Hersh, M.A., Ohene-Djan, J. (eds.) CVHI. CEUR Workshop Proceedings, vol. 415. CEUR-WS.org (2007)
10. Madise, Ü., Martens, T.: E-voting in Estonia 2005. The first practice of country-wide binding Internet voting in the world. In: Krimmer, R. (ed.) Proceedings of the 2nd International Workshop on Electronic Voting 2006. LNI GI Series, pp. 15–26 (2006)
11. Mirau, G.L., Ovejero, T., Pomares, J.: The Implementation of E-voting in Latin America: The Experience of Salta, Argentina from a Practitioner's Perspective. In: Kripp, M., Volkamer, M., Grimm, R. (eds.) 5th International Conference on Electronic Voting 2012. Lecture Notes in Informatics, pp. 213–224 (2012)
12. OSCE/ODIHR. Estonia. Parliamentary Elections 6 March 2011 OSCE/ODIHR Election Assessment Mission Report (2011)

13. Pihelgas, P.: Complaint no. 14-11/406-2 to NEC. Estonian (March 8, 2011),
    http://www.vvk.ee/valimiste-korraldamine/
    vabariigi-valimiskomisjon-yld/kirjad
14. Pinault, T., Courtade, P.: E-voting in France. In: Kripp, M., Volkamer, M., Grimm,
    R. (eds.) 5th International Conference on Electronic Voting 2012. Lecture Notes
    in Informatics, pp. 189–195 (2012)
15. Popoveniuc, S., Kelsey, J., Regenscheid, A., Vora, P.: Performance requirements
    for end-to-end verifiable elections. In: Proceedings of the 2010 International Con-
    ference on Electronic Voting Technology/Workshop on Trustworthy Elections,
    EVT/WOTE 2010, pp. 1–16. USENIX Association, Berkeley (2010)
16. Stenerud, I.S.G., Bull, C.: When Reality Comes Knocking. Norwegian Experiences
    with Verifiable Electronic Voting. In: Kripp, M., Volkamer, M., Grimm, R. (eds.)
    5th International Conference on Electronic Voting 2012. Lecture Notes in Infor-
    matics, pp. 21–33 (2012)
17. Supreme Court of Estonia. Decision of Supreme Court 3-4-1-4-11. Estonian (March
    21, 2011),
    http://www.vvk.ee/valimiste-korraldamine/
    vabariigi-valimiskomisjon-yld/kirjad

A Language for Multi-Perspective Modelling of IT Security: Objectives and Analysis of Requirements

Anat Goldstein and Ulrich Frank

Institute of Computer Science and Business Information Systems,
University of Duisburg -Essen, Universitaetsstr. 9, 45141 Essen, Germany
{Anat.Goldstein,Ulrich.Frank}@uni-due.de

Abstract. Effectively protecting information systems is a pivotal responsibility of (IT) management, which faces many challenges: technological complexities, business complexities, various stakeholders and conflicting requirements. Yet, there is no holistic modelling approach that comprehensively addresses all these challenges, while accounting for technical, organizational and business aspects. This paper analyzes the requirements of such a comprehensive modelling method for IT security design and management. We argue that enterprise modelling is most suitable to serve as a foundation for such an approach. We apply a method for developing domain specific modelling languages (DSML) that is chiefly based on a structured analysis of use scenarios including prototypical diagrams. It is supplemented by requirements found in literature. Our analysis results in 23 requirements that should be satisfied by the targeted modelling method. These results are intended to serve as a foundation for discussion and discursive evaluation by peers and domain experts.

Keywords: IT security, information security, enterprise modeling, MEMO, DSML.

1   Introduction

The relevance of information technology (IT) security is undisputed in research and practice. It is assumed that the importance of this topic as well as the attention that it experiences in the public will continue to increase mainly as a result of the many threats caused by Internet connectivity and the extensive use of communication and distribution of software services, but also with the increased pressure to follow respective laws and regulations.

Effectively protecting information systems is a pivotal responsibility of (IT) management, which faces many challenges:

- *Increasing technical complexity* as a result of more distributed computing, cloud computing and frequent technological changes. This stresses the need for solutions that are general and not unique for specific technology [1, 2].
- *Increasing risks* by the further upgrading of criminal attackers, who become more sophisticates with time [3, 4]. Apart from criminal attackers, unsatisfied employees as well as careless or insufficiently trained employees may also cause damages intentionally or unintentionally.

M. La Rosa and P. Soffer (Eds.): BPM 2012 Workshops, LNBIP 132, pp. 636–648, 2012.

- *Increasing organizational complexity*: as more business processes as well as financial transactions become automated, a growing number of stakeholders (employees, customers, etc.) receive access to digitized resources and new dangers arise from incorrect use or misuse of systems [5, 1].
- *Increasing pressure to justify the costs* associated with IT security: IT management is required to perform both technical evaluation of alternative solutions and evaluation of their impact on the business competitiveness [6, 7].
- *Communication and cooperation barriers*: language barriers between technical (e.g. IT professionals) and business (e.g. corporate governance) perspectives makes communicating IT security measures more difficult [5, 2, 8].
- *Dealing with conflicting requirements*: high levels of security vs. low levels of costs, high levels of flexibility vs. robust solutions and so forth.

These challenges stress the need for methods and tools for supporting IT management with designing, realizing and managing appropriate IT security systems. According to our conception, an IT security system comprises all technical, organizational and managerial aspects that are required to provide an appropriate level of protection of those resources represented in an information system. Hence, a respective method for protecting information systems does not only need to cover technical aspects of IT security. In addition to that it should also account for behavioral, economic, business and managerial aspects.

An analysis of the state of the art shows that there is a considerable amount of research on various aspects of IT security. However, each one of these streams is isolated from the others and focuses on single aspects only. So far there seems to be no approach which aims at supporting a *holistic view* that integrates the various streams. Also, the majority of respective research is focused on technical aspects. There are only few approaches that consider human factors, e.g. [23] or economic aspects.

Against this background, our research is aimed at a holistic method that integrates the aforementioned technical, organizational, business and behavioral aspects. For this purpose it should provide effective support for mastering the following tasks:

1. Assessing and reducing risks that originate both from within the organization (unsatisfied, careless or untrained employees) and from its outside.
2. Overcoming the increasing technical and organizational complexities, resulting from pervasive distributed computing, frequent technological changes, automation of business processes and growing access to digitized resources.
3. Fostering the participation of non-technical stakeholders (e.g. managers, users)
4. Relating IT security to business, for example, by allowing the analysis of the impact of IT security on business and by allowing cost-benefit analysis.
5. Designing and implementing IS security infrastructures, for example, using automatic creation of security related policies and code fragments.

Each of these tasks is related to one or more perspectives of the enterprise, namely, organization, information systems or strategy perspectives. Accounting for these different perspectives requires a common conceptual framework that covers technical, business and social aspects. Enterprise modelling provides an obvious choice for this purpose: An enterprise model integrates conceptual models of information systems, (e.g. object models) with conceptual models of the surrounding action system (e.g., business process models). However, so far, languages for enterprise modelling [11,14,15] lack specific concepts for modelling security aspects. Thus, we intend to enhance an existing method for enterprise modeling with concepts to represent relevant issues for IT security. Analyzing the requirements for such a method is of crucial importance – and at the same time a remarkable challenge. It might seem as a straightforward approach to ask prospective users for their needs, e.g. for the properties they would want to see with a corresponding DSML. However, due to the novelty of such an artifact, most prospective users will be overburdened with imagining what they can expect from it. This paper is aimed at presenting an elaborate analysis of requirements to be satisfied by DSML for supporting IT security management. It is supplemented by requirements found in literature.

The remainder of this paper is arranged as follows. In the following section we outline how multi-perspective enterprise modelling can be augmented with concepts to represent IS security aspects. In section 3 we discuss related literature. Next, in section 4, we analyze the requirements of the targeted IT security modelling method – based on the literature and based on use-scenarios we derive specific requirements for this method. We present our conclusions in section 5.

2   Outline of the Targeted Approach

Analyzing, developing, using and managing business information systems is a challenging task that requires the active participation of stakeholders with different professional backgrounds. Hence, there is need to effectively reduce complexity, to provide a foundation for implementing software and to coordinate the contributions of different stakeholders. Enterprise modelling has evolved as an approach to address these challenges by enhancing conceptual models of information systems (e.g. an object model) with those of the respective action systems (e.g. business process models or strategy models).

2.1   Multi-Perspective Enterprise Modelling (MEMO)

MEMO includes a high-level conceptual framework that represents a "ball park view" on an enterprise 25]. It is composed of three *generic perspectives* (i.e. strategy, organization, information system) each of which can be further detailed into various *aspects* (e.g. resource, structure, process, goal). The framework serves as a starting point for identifying perspectives that require further attention. To allow for more elaborate analyses, each selected perspective is associated with a set of diagram types. Each diagram type is associated with a domain specific modeling language (DSML). Different from general purpose modelling languages like the ERM or the UML, a DSML includes domain-specific concepts and features a domain-specific graphical notation. Thus, it promises to increase modelling productivity, to improve model integrity and to foster the comprehensibility of models. Currently, MEMO includes DSMLs for resource modelling [9], for modelling IT infrastructures [10] organization modelling [11, 12] and for modelling strategic aspects [13]. So far, security-related aspects have not been addressed explicitly. Nevertheless, various DSML within MEMO include concepts that are relevant for IT security management.

The reason for choosing MEMO over other enterprise modelling methods such as ARIS [14] or ArchiMate [15] is based on the following considerations: First, it is based on a flexible language architecture [16]. The language architecture consists of a meta meta modelling language [11] and an extensible set of DSMLs, the semantics and abstract syntax of which is specified using the meta meta modelling language. All DSML that are part of MEMO are integrated through common concepts. The language architecture allows for extending existing languages or for adding new DSML (for example MEMO has been extended to support Risks, Controls and Indicators). Second, MEMO provides support for method engineering and is supported by corresponding (meta-) modelling tool, MEMO Center [16, 17]. Last, but not least, in contrast to commercial approaches like ARIS, the specifications of MEMO and its meta models are freely available and documented in several publications.

2.2   Enhancing Enterprise Modelling with Security Aspects

A multi-perspective enterprise model covers many aspects that are subject of IT security management, such as IT resources (e.g. application systems, components, networks etc.) or organizational roles and organizational units. In addition to that, models of the organizational strategy and of business processes allow for analyzing costs and benefits related to particular IT security measures. Therefore, our approach is aimed at enriching the existing DSMLs with additional, security-related concepts and – if required – to add a further DSML that focuses solely on specific IT security aspects. Fig. 1 illustrates the extension of enterprise models with IT security aspects. As a consequence, it should enable to model security-related issues on various levels of abstraction, serving different perspectives. For example: A department manager may be especially interested in avoiding negative impact on the performance of business processes he is in charge of. By enriching the representation of a business process with security-related information on an appropriate level of abstraction (e.g. by avoiding too much technical detail), the department manager gets a better idea of what to expect from investments into security management. In addition to that, conceptual models of IT security systems serve as a blueprint for implementing (i.e. at best: generating) corresponding software and for organizational re-design.

3   Related Work

Related work can be grouped into two main categories: work that emphasizes the need for a holistic approach and approaches to model technical aspects of IT security.

3.1   Holistic Security Approaches

There are only few papers that identify the need for a holistic approach for handling IT security in organization. [3] for example, recognizes several dimensions that should not only be considered but also integrated in order to create a secure environment. Among these dimensions are: Strategic/corporate governance, organizational, policy, best practice, ethical, legal, personal/human, technical and auditing. He does not, however, provide any method for identification nor integration of these dimensions. [5] suggests a security management framework for e-commerce that takes into account three dimensions: Society, Technology and Business, throughout all phases of the system lifecycle. However, this framework offers a high-level method, that defines a set of activities for the development of security but it does not provide tools or computer-based support for the implementation and integration of these activities and for their alignment with other aspects of the organization. [6] also recognize a need for a comprehensive approach for information systems security analysis and design (IS-SAD) and suggest incorporating risk analysis and organizational analysis based on business process modelling (BPM). After surveying an extensive list of available BPM techniques they conclude that none of these techniques alone could support IT security analysis and design.

3.2   IT Security Modelling

There is an extensive work that focuses on dedicated modelling approaches to IT security [18,19,1,20,21,22]. SecureUML [8] and SECTET [18] are UML extensions that focus on role-based access control (RBAC). [19] use UML to represent organizational aspects (that is, RBAC) as well. [1] and [2] provide extensions to UML that focus on business process management. [20] develop an extension of BPMN that supports modelling authorization of business processes and allows automatic derivation of authorization policies. [21] introduces UMLSec, an extension of UML that enables developers to formally describe security issues and to identify security errors during the development of information system. [22] present a model based security risk analysis, using CORAS diagrams, which are based on UML. While these approaches are usually aimed at facilitating communication between different stakeholder and providing tools for automatic creation of security-related software, are focused each on a specific aspect of IT security or intended only for supporting software developers.

4   IT Security Modelling: Requirement Analysis

Developing an IT security modelling method requires the specification of corresponding language concepts, either as an extension of existing DSML or as a new DSML. Developing language concepts implies the need for analyzing corresponding requirements. However, analyzing requirements for DSML is a challenging task.

The rest of this section is focused on analyzing the requirements that the IT security modelling language (ML) should satisfy. These requirements will eventually guide the development the DSML.

4.1   General Requirements for IT Security Modelling

A holistic method that will improve the development of comprehensive IT security solutions should account for technological aspects, human/organizational aspects, business aspects and financial aspects. As discussed above, these aspects are (separately) covered by the existing literature and prevalently include topics such as security risk analysis, security policies, security requirements analysis and IT measurements (firewalls, protocols, encryption methods, access control methods). A holistic IT security method should therefore include concepts that are represented by these various security aspects. This is summarized into the first requirement that should be fulfilled by an IT security method,

Requirement 1 - The method should include concepts to describe IT security aspects from various perspectives: technical, human, organizational, business and financial. It should therefore include concepts of other enterprise MLs to support references to respective models that describe aspects of the organization, business processes and IT.

There are many papers that stress the importance of improving the communication and interaction between different stakeholders during the design and management of IT security in organizations (e.g. [22], [2] and [23]). Most of these papers recognize the need for different levels of abstraction when it comes to specifying security requirements, allowing the description of high levels security requirements without getting into technical details. This is important especially because usually managers, who possess a high level perspective of the business processes and functionality, have little knowledge about security issues [2]. Different levels of abstractions can be used not only for differentiating between general and detailed levels of security requirement specifications but can also differentiate between different perspectives of the enterprise: strategic (goals) , organizational (role based access control, security of business processes), technological (vulnerable IT resources, IT measurement) and between different IT security tasks that are under the responsibility of different stakeholders such as security risk management, meeting IT security standards and regulations and cost analysis. This leads us to define the second requirement.

Requirement 2 – facilitating communication and support of different stakeholders: the aimed method should allow for representation of different levels of abstraction and of multiple perspectives specific for the different stakeholders of the IT security design and management. Each perspective should correspond with specific concepts and abstractions from the stakeholder's relevant domain.

Methods for the design of IT security should support the integration of security concerns throughout all the phases of the system lifecycle from requirements analysis to design, implementation, testing and deployment [23, 5, 2, 1, 4]. As indicated by [4], [21] and by [8], most security requirements are added as an afterthought, only after functional requirements analysis has been completed. Thus, we define a third requirement that a method for IT security should fulfill.

Requirement 3 – the aimed method should support all phases of the enterprise's system development lifecycles. IT security issues should be considered already in the initial stages of system requirement analysis. Identified security requirements can be later enriched with technical details in the design phase and eventually used for derivation of security related code fragments.

4.2   Specific Requirements for IT Security Modelling

The three requirements above are high-level or general requirements. While they are Information-security-specific, they are not necessarily intended for MLs.

In order to collect further specific requirements that should be satisfied by IT security MLs, it might seem reasonable to ask prospective users about their needs and expectation from the targeted DSML. However, due to the novelty of such an artifact, it will be difficult for most prospective users to imagine what they can expect from it. To address this challenge, we follow a use scenario development approach, presented in [24], which has evolved from the development of various DSML, e.g. [12]. According to this approach we use modelling scenarios from the past and also create further possible modelling scenarios to identify IT security specific needs. We supplement each scenario with a prototypical diagram type that may build on an existing ML or that has been created for the purpose of analyzing requirements. For each diagram type we develop a list of exemplary questions that the diagram should answer. These questions help us illustrate the purposes a diagram should serve and recognize specific requirements that should be satisfied by our ML. With respect to preparing for a corresponding modelling tool, it is helpful to classify these questions into three types: if these questions can be answered through an automated analysis (in case a corresponding tool is available), they are marked with an $\underline{\mathbf{A}}$; if answering them can be partially supported by an automated analysis, they are marked with a $\underline{\mathbf{P}}$; and if they are subject to human interpretation/analysis only, they are marked with a $\underline{\mathbf{H}}$. These questions are relevant with respect to the targeted level of detail/formalization, the language specification should satisfy and the intended functions of a respective modelling tool.

Due to space limitation we will present only one scenario that focuses on an IT Resource diagram. A full list of scenarios can be found in [26]. The IT Resource diagram allows the representation of the enterprise's IT resources: the software, hardware and network elements composing the organization's information systems. This is a primary diagram of MEMO Information Technology Modelling Language (ITML). Since most security requirements as well as security controls are related to IT resources, this diagram has an important role in describing IT security aspects and in designing IT security infrastructure.

We present an illustration of an augmented IT Resource diagram (Fig. 1) accompanied by illustrative questions it should help answering.

- Which security requirements are related to an IT resource? **A, H**
- Which counter-measure is related to the security requirement? **A, H**
- What is the cost of adding a security measure resource? **A, H**
- How is a security measure implemented? **A, H**
- What is the number of attack attempts on an IT resource? **A**
- What is the number of successful attempts? **A**
- What is the average number of attack attempts per year on a resource? **A**
- Who is allowed to use/access a resource? **A, H**
- What is the justification for purchasing a certain security measure? **A, H**
- Which business processes are affected by attack on the IT resource? **A, H**

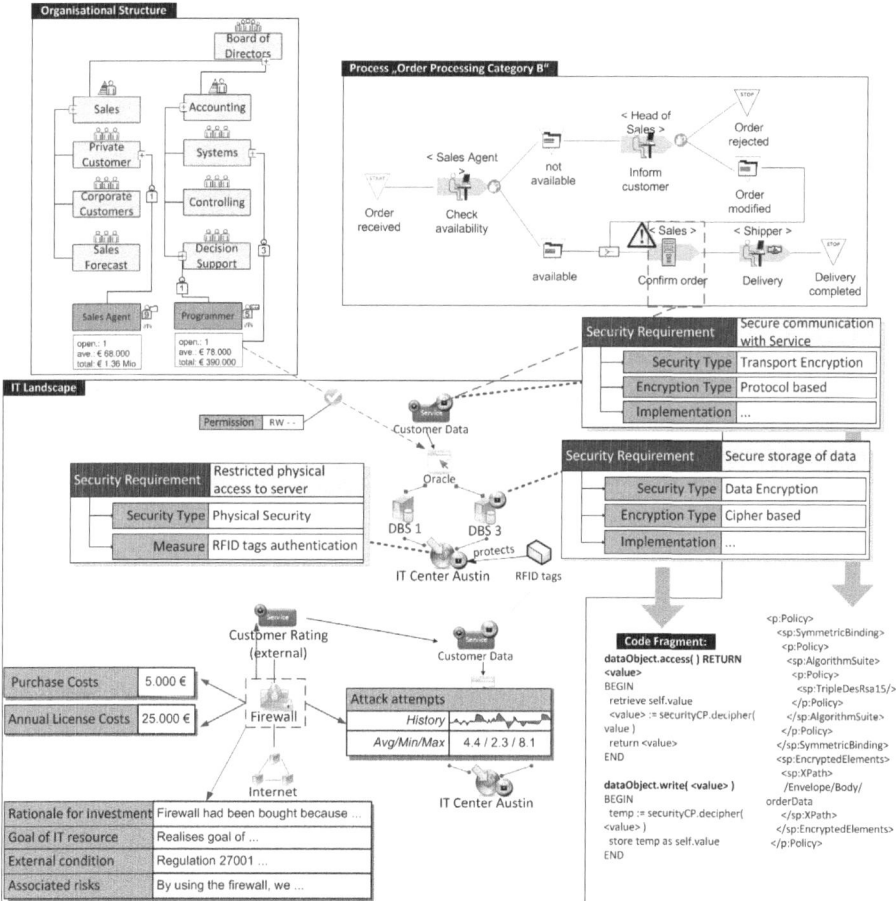

Fig. 1. Illustration of augmented IT resources chart

We derive corresponding requirements that should be satisfied by our ML:

Requirement 4: It should be possible to define security requirements for IT resources (e.g. customer data is confidential and thus should be protected) and to describe the security measures used in detail (e.g. using cipher based encryption). This implies that a *protection* association is required. This association can be used to indicate that one IT resource is intended to protect another IT resource.

Requirement 5:   There should be support for cost-benefit analyses of security measures. For example it should be possible to analyze the effectiveness of a chosen security measure based on the history of attack attempts, to compare the prevented losses against the implementation costs and to justify the acquisition.

Requirement 6: The ML should support different levels of abstraction of security requirements, ranging from high-level, general, definition of security controls to low-level definition of technical details of encryption methods, cipher settings, communication protocols and specific access control policies. Based on the detailed and formal specifications, it should be possible to generate code fragments, web-service descriptors, access control policies, or access tables for databases and applications. This is a specialization of *Requirement 2.*

Requirement 7:   It should be possible to define for each IT resource who is responsible for it, who is allowed to access it and their permissions (read, write, execute, delete).

4.3   Requirements Derived from Other Scenarios

The following requirements were derived from further scenarios, which due to space limitations are not presented here. The scenarios include extensions to existing MEMO diagrams: Business Process diagram, Organizational structure, business process map and object model. An additional scenario is related to security risk analysis and requires the definition of a new type of diagram – security risk analysis diagram.

Security Risk Analysis Related Requirements

Requirement 8: The ML should support activities like risk analysis, risk mitigation and evaluation. Thus, it should include the key concepts of the security risk management domain, namely: *asset, threat, threat-source, vulnerability, counter-measure* and *impact.* The ML should enable to assign vulnerabilities to assets, to define threat-sources and the vulnerabilities they can exploit (threats they create), to assign probabilities to threats and the impact they have, to match counter-measures to vulnerabilities, and to analyze their cost and benefit.

Requirement 9: The assets mentioned above are IT resources such as data, software or hardware, which are the core concepts of the IT perspective, represented by the MEMO ITML. Thus, the IT security ML should be integrated with the ITML. This will enable connecting security concepts with IT resources for example, connecting a vulnerability to an IT resource or connecting a counter-measure to the IT resource which is used to resolve a vulnerability.

Requirement 10: There should be concepts that support comparing different counter-measures against threats and for performing cost-benefit analysis. It should be possible to indicate the selected measures.

Requirement 11: It should be possible to collect information about attack history, i.e. statistics on the occurrence of threats (instance level).

Business Process Related Requirements

Requirement 12: Integration between the business process perspective and the IT perspective is required so that it would be possible to: 1. associate an activity with its vulnerable assets (IT resources); and 2. associate an activity with selected (IT) counter-measures. These associations should allow for cost and impact analysis of the damage/implementation.

Requirement 13: It should be possible to link activities with threats and vulnerabilities. Thus, the ML should be integrated with concepts from the business process diagram (i.e. activities), provided by MEMO OrgML.

Requirement 14: It should be possible to link activities with users who: 1. are authorized to perform them (based on their position, role, belonging to business unit…); 2. might interfere with their execution.

Requirement 15: It should be possible to indicate that two activities should be performed by different users, that is, two different instances of the same role.

Process Map Related Requirements

Requirement 16: It should be possible to assign detailed security requirements to a business process.

Requirement 17: It should be possible to evaluate the total cost of protecting the various activities of a process type.

Requirement 18: It should be possible to analyze the financial impact of the realization of security risks within a process.

Requirement 19: It should be possible to indicate that an association between two process types has security implications. For example, to indicate that two associated business processes, which share information, comply with different security regulations (since they occur in different countries).

Requirement 20: The ML should provide concepts that enable a detailed description of the security needs in order to allow filtering and representation of different types of security requirements. For example to filter only the process types that are affected by a specific regulation.

Requirement 21: It should be possible to add an indication of security requirements on the instance level as well, for example, in a case where the same process is conducted in several countries with different regulations

Organization Structure Related Requirements

Requirement 22: The ML should allow defining access rights for the different positions, roles and business units with respect to data resources. The formal definition of permission sets allows the automatic derivation of access control policies, such as RBAC, which is supported by many software platforms. Thus, the modelling tool should support automatic access control policy generation.

Object Model Related Requirements

Requirement 23: The ML should allow defining that objects of a certain class should be encrypted or that a specific attribute should be encrypted.

5   Conclusions

This paper is creates a foundation for a method for supporting IT management with designing, realizing and managing appropriate IT security. The domain of IT security is interwoven with technical, organizational and managerial aspects. These aspects are required to provide an appropriate level of protection of IT resources. Thus, we argue that a multi-perspective enterprise modelling method such as MEMO provides a suitable foundation for an IT security method. Using an approach that is based on augmented use scenarios, we identified 23 requirements that should be satisfied by the modelling method. This list of requirements builds a foundation for designing language concepts that are suited for multi-perspective modelling of IT security aspects. To the best of our knowledge this is the first comprehensive requirement analysis for such a method. The requirements were reviewed by a number of researchers in the field as well as practitioners, who confirmed their necessity and comprehensiveness. We intend to continue validating these requirements with more prospective users in the near future.

One question that arises from the identified requirements is whether we should define a new, IT security designated DSML or we should enrich the existing DSML supported by MEMO (ITML and OrgML) with concepts to support IT Security. On the one hand, IT security concepts do not have a right to exist on their own – they are always associated with IT resource, business process or with organizational positions/roles. This is also stressed by the above presented diagrams, showing that IT security concepts are closely related to existing diagram types. On the other hand, IT security concepts that are used to describe risk analysis (e.g. vulnerabilities, threats, threat-source, likelihood, impact) are not a natural part of the usual tasks involved in the process of IT resource modelling or in business process modelling. While IT resource diagram might be easily enriched with the concept of 'vulnerability', it is harder to decide which diagram should be enriched with concepts of threat, threat-impact or likelihood. Thus, we intend to follow a twofold approach: extending existing DSMLs as well as defining a new DSML to handle security risk analysis concepts.

An IT security modelling method does not have to address all the requirements which were identified in this document. However, the list of requirements describes the scope of the modelling method. At the same time, this list of requirements is not meant to be complete. The requirements are based on the analysis of use scenarios that seem particularly interesting. There are certainly more use scenarios some of which will result in further requirements.

Our next steps are: 1. validate the requirements with further prospective users, mainly with IT managers; 2. develop language specifications that satisfy the requirements; 3. address a number of use scenarios with respective process models to form specific modelling methods; and 4. develop a corresponding modelling tool based on MEMO Center.

References

1. Rodriguez, A., Fernandez-Medina, E., Piattini, M.: Security Requirements with a UML 2.0 Profile. In: The First International Conference on Availability, Reliability and Security (ARES 2006) (2006)
2. Nakamura, Y., Tatsubori, M., Imamura, T., Ono, K.: Model-driven security based on web services security architecture. In: 2005 IEEE International Conference on Services Computing (SCC 2005), vol. 1, pp. 7–15 (2005)
3. Von Solms, B.: Information Security – A multi-dimensional Discipline. Computers and Security 20, 504–508 (2001)
4. Premkumar, T., Stubblebine, S.: Software engineering for security: a roadmap. In: ICSE 2000, The Future of Software Engineering. ACM, New York (2000)
5. Zuccato, A.: Holistic security management framework applied in electronic commerce. Computer and Security 26, 256–265 (2007)
6. Kokolakis, S.A., Demopoulos, A.J., Kiountouzis, E.A.: The use of business process modelling in information systems security analysis and design. Information Management & Computer Security 8(3), 107–116 (2000)
7. Birch, D.G.W., McEvoy, N.A.: Risk Analysis for Information Systems. Journal of Information Technology 7, 44–53 (1992)
8. Lodderstedt, T., Basin, D.A., Doser, J.: SecureUML: A UML-Based Modeling Language for Model-Driven Security. In: 5th International Conference on the Unified Modeling Language, pp. 426–441 (2002)
9. Jung, J.: Supply Chains in the Context of Resource Modelling. ICB Research Report, Universität Duisburg-Essen, No. 5 (2006)
10. Kirchner, L.: Cost Oriented Modelling of IT-Landscapes: Generic Language Concepts of a Domain Specific Language. In: Desel, J., Frank, U. (eds.) The Workshop on Enterprise Modelling and Information Systems Architectures, pp. 166–179 (2005)
11. Frank, U.: The MEMO Meta Modelling Language (MML) and Language architecture. ICB Research Report No. 43, Universität Duisburg-Essen, Essen (2011)
12. Frank, U.: MEMO Organisation Modelling Language (OrgML): Requirements and Core Diagram Types. ICB Research Report No. 46, Universität Duisburg-Essen, Essen (2011)
13. Frank, U., Lange, C.: A Framework to Support the Analysis of Strategic Options for Electronic Commerce. Arbeitsberichte des Instituts für Wirtschafts- und Verwaltungsinformatik, Universität Koblenz-Landau, No. 41 (2004)
14. Scheer, A.-W.: ARIS—Business Process Modeling, 3rd edn. Springer, Berlin (2000)
15. Lankhorst, M.: Enterprise Architecture at Work: Modelling, Communication and Analysis. Springer, Berlin (2005)
16. Frank, U.: Multi-Perspective Enterprise Modeling: Foundational Concepts, Prospects and Future Research Challenges. Accepted for publication in Software and Systems Modeling
17. Gulden, J., Frank, U.: MEMOCenterNG. A full-featured modeling environment for organisation modeling and model-driven software development. In: 22nd International Conference on Advanced Information Systems Engineering, Hammamet (2010)

18. Alam, M., Hafner, M., Breu, R.: A Constraint based Role Based Access Control in the SECTET A Model-Driven Approach. In: 2006 International Conference on Privacy, Security and Trust: Bridge the Gap Between PST Technologies and Business Services, article 13. ACM, New York (2006)
19. Shin, M.E., Ahn, G.-J.: UML-Based Representation of Role-Based Access Control. In: 9th IEEE International Workshops on Enabling Technologies: Infrastructure for Collaborative Enterprises, pp. 195–200 (2000)
20. Wolter, C., Schaad, A.: Modeling of Task-Based Authorization Constraints in BPMN. In: Alonso, G., Dadam, P., Rosemann, M. (eds.) BPM 2007. LNCS, vol. 4714, pp. 64–79. Springer, Heidelberg (2007)
21. Jürjens, J.: UMLsec: Extending UML for Secure Systems Development. In: Jézéquel, J.-M., Hussmann, H., Cook, S. (eds.) UML 2002. LNCS, vol. 2460, pp. 412–425. Springer, Heidelberg (2002)
22. Braber, F., Hogganvik, I., Lund, M.S., Stolen, K., Vraalsen, F.: Model-based security analysis in seven steps—a guided tour to the CORAS method. BT Technol. J. 25(1), 101–117 (2007)
23. Giorgini, P., Massacci, F., Mylopoulos, J., Zannone, N.: Modeling security requirements through ownership, permission and delegation. In: Proceedings of the 13th ICRE 2005 (2005)
24. Frank, U.: Outline of a Method for Designing Domain-Specific Modelling Languages. ICB Research Report No. 42, Universität Duisburg-Essen, Essen (2010)
25. Frank, U.: Multi-perspective enterprise modeling (MEMO): Conceptual framework and modeling languages. In: 35th Annual Hawaii International Conference on System Sciences (HICSS), Honululu, HI, pp. 72–82 (2002)
26. Open Models - IT Security Scenarios, http://openmodels.wiwinf.uni-due.de/node/204/

Towards Compliance of Cross-Organizational Processes and Their Changes[*]
Research Challenges and State of Research

David Knuplesch[1], Manfred Reichert[1], Jürgen Mangler[2],
Stefanie Rinderle-Ma[2], and Walid Fdhila[2]

[1] Institute of Databases and Information Systems, Ulm University, Germany
[2] Faculty of Computer Science, University of Vienna, Austria
{david.knuplesch,manfred.reichert}@uni-ulm.de,
{juergen.mangler,stefanie.rinderle-ma,walid.fdhila}@univie.ac.at

Abstract. Businesses require the ability to rapidly implement new processes and to quickly adapt existing ones to environmental changes including the optimization of their interactions with partners and customers. However, changes of either intra- or cross-organizational processes must not be done in an uncontrolled manner. In particular, processes are increasingly subject to compliance rules that usually stem from security constraints, corporate guidelines, standards, and laws. These compliance rules have to be considered when modeling business processes and changing existing ones. While change and compliance have been extensively discussed for intra-organizational business processes, albeit only in an isolated manner, their combination in the context of cross-organizational processes remains an open issue. In this paper, we discuss requirements and challenges to be tackled in order to ensure that changes of cross-organizational business processes preserve compliance with imposed regulations, standards and laws.

1 Introduction

Improving the efficiency and quality of their *business processes* and optimizing their interactions with partners, suppliers and customers have become significant success factors for any enterprise. Hence, enterprises increasingly adopt emerging technologies and standards for business process automation [1]. These enable the definition, execution, and monitoring of the operational processes of an enterprise [2,3]. In connection with Web service technology, the benefits of business process automation and optimization from within a single enterprise can be transferred to cross-organizational business processes as well [4,5]. The next step in this evolution will be the emergence of the agile enterprise being able to rapidly implement new processes and to quickly adapt existing ones to

---

[*] This work was done within the research project C³Pro funded by the German Research Foundation (DFG), Project number: RE 1402/2-1, and the Austrian Science Fund (FWF), Project number: I743.

M. La Rosa and P. Soffer (Eds.): BPM 2012 Workshops, LNBIP 132, pp. 649–661, 2013.

environmental changes [3]. While flexibility issues for internal business processes and their implementation (i.e., *process* and *service orchestrations*) are well understood [3,2], the controlled change of the interactions between IT-supported partner processes in a cross-organizational setting (i.e., *process and service choreographies*) has not been adequately addressed so far. If one partner changes its process in an uncontrolled manner, inconsistencies or errors (e.g., deadlocks) regarding these interactions might occur. This is particularly challenging if there exist running instances (i.e., cases) of these process choreographies. As a consequence, adaptations of cross-organizational business processes turn out to be costly and error-prone.

Generally, business processes cannot be defined or changed without considering *business process compliance* with imposed compliance rules (e.g., security guidlines). Due to the increasing importance of regulations like SOX and BASEL, compliance has emerged as one of the most urgent challenges for process-aware information systems. So far, it has been addressed by many approaches, which mostly deal with the automation of audits for verifying compliance rules imposed on internal business processes [6,7,8,9].

Compliance of cross-organizational business processes, however, has not been investigated in connection with process changes or with respect to privacy constraints of partner processes. *Flexibility* on one hand and *compliance* on the other hand are crucial challenges for collaborative settings. However, the picture will be not complete if we do not consider both in interplay as well. Even though a compliance rule might be fulfilled for a collaborative process before a change, it does not automatically remain satisfied afterwards. Thus, it is indispensable to provide adequate mechanisms to control change effects on the compliance of collaborative business processes in a transparent way.

This paper first provides an overview of basic notations related to compliance and (cross-organizational) business processes in Section 2. Section 3 then discusses different layers of correctness that must be considered when modeling and changing business process models. Section 4 discusses the state of the art in related research areas; i.e., cross-organizational processes, process flexibility, and business process compliance. Section 5 elicits novel requirements and challenges for enabling compliance of cross-organizational business processes and their change. Finally, Section 6 closes the paper with summary and conclusion.

2   Basic Notion and Example

We introduce basic notions related to business compliance in the context of cross-organizational processes and discuss their inter-relations. Fig. 1 gives an overview of the terminology we use. Basic to each cross-organizational process is a *collaboration*. In turn, the latter contains abstract *roles* that may be filled by concrete *business partners*. For each role, the set of related *task definitions* describes which tasks a role may perform when a cross-organizational process is executed. The model of a cross-organizational process is denoted as *choreography model* and consists of *public process models* connected through *message exchanges.* In turn, a public process model consist of tasks and refers to a role, whereas a private process model implements a public process model of a business partner enriched with internal (i.e., private) tasks. Both public and private process models may only comprise task definitions related to the role the public process model refers to.

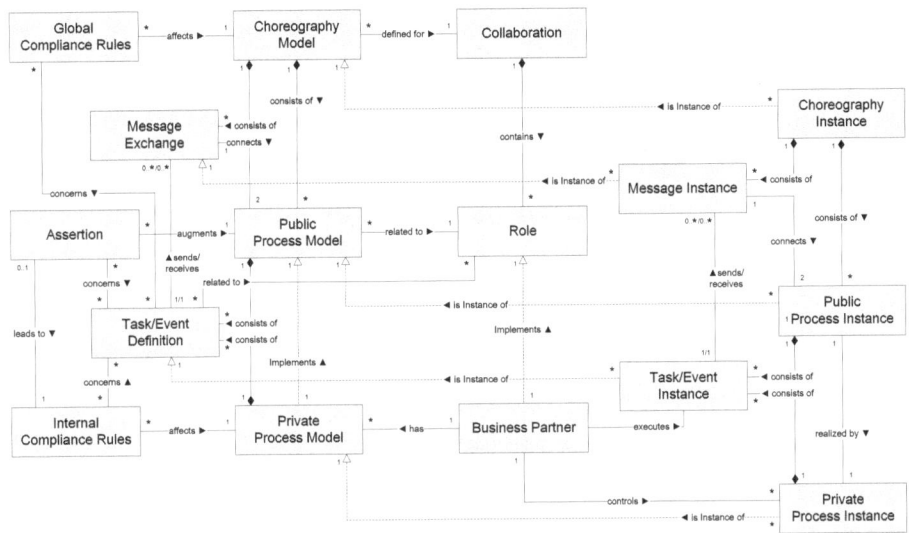

Fig. 1. Terminology Overview

A *choreography instance* reflects the execution of a cross-organizational process defined by a choreography model. Similar to a choreography model, the choreography instance consists of *public process instances*, which are based on the *private process instances* of the related business partner. Such a private process instance is controlled by the respective business partner through executing its *task instances*. The latter send and receive *message instances* connecting the public process instance within the choreography instance.

Both the choreography model and the private process models may be subject to *compliance rules* restricting allowed execution sequences of tasks. In this context, we distinguish between *global compliance rules* referring to a cross-organizational process (i.e., to a choreography model) and *internal compliance rules* restricting private process models. Furthermore, *assertions* can augment public process models. More precisely, they enrich a choreography's specification of a public process model with additional information about its executon behavior. In turn, an assertion constitutes an internal compliance rule restricting the private process model that implements the augmented public process model.

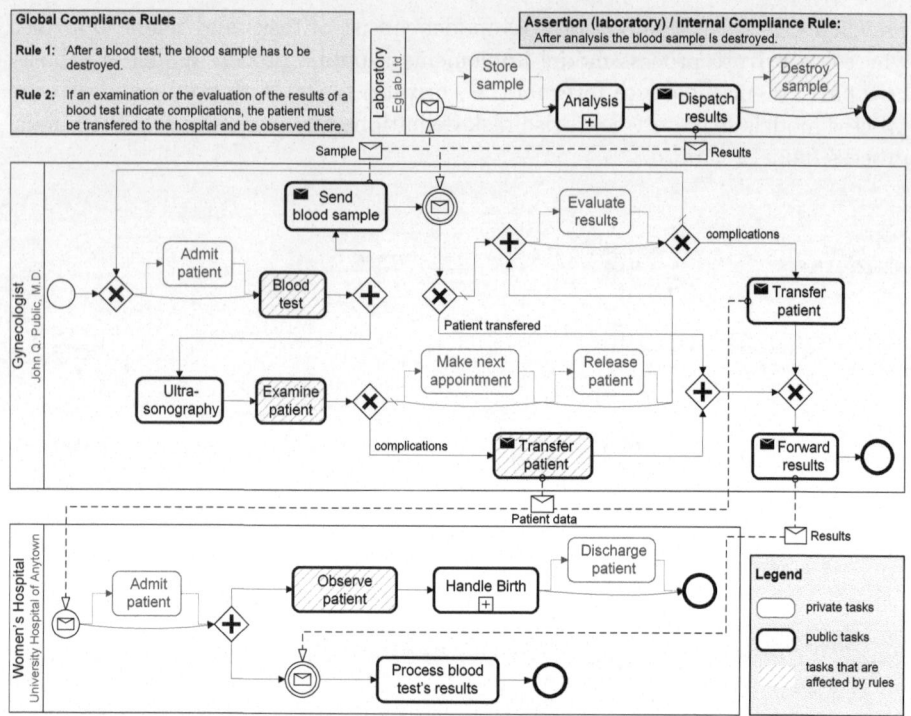

Fig. 2. Example of Cross-organizational Process

Example 1. Fig. 2 shows an example of a cross-organizational process from the healthcare domain. The fundamental collaboration comprises three *roles*: gynecologist, laboratory, and women's hospital. They are filled by the three business partners John Q. Public, M.D., EgLab Ltd., and University Hospital of Anytown. The *choreography model* of this cross-organizational process is based on the *public process models* of the three roles that communicate through *message exchanges*. For example, the *message exchanges* sample and results connect the public process of the gynecologist with the one of the laboratory. In turn, the public process of the gynecologist is connected with the one of the women's hospital based on the two message exchanges patient data and results. The *private process models* of the business partners, in turn, implement the related public processes and additionally enrich them with internal behavior, i.e. private tasks not contained in public processes models. (In Fig. 2 the private tasks are indented and greyed). The logical execution of this *choreography model* results in a *choreography instance* of the cross-organizational healthcare process; it contains related instances of the choreography, i.e. its public as well as private processes, and the messages exchanged. Finally, Fig. 2 shows one assertion and two global compliance rules. Through the assertion, the laboratory ensures the destruction of a blood sample after its analysis. Rule 1 requires a blood sample to be destroyed. In turn, Rule 2 requires the patient to be monitored in the hospital when complications occur.

3 Correctness Levels for Process Models

Business processes models cannot be defined or changed in an arbitrary way. Generally, three correctness levels build on each other and constitute a *pyramid of business process model correctness*. In particular, each level has to be considered and checked for each definition or change of a process model (cf. Fig. 3):

Syntactical Correctness refers to the correct use and composition of the elements of the underlying meta model. Examples of syntactical constraints include the existence of start and end events, as well as the correct use of different kinds of edges; e.g., control flow edges may only connect flow elements (i.e., tasks, gateways, events), while data flow edges connect tasks with data objects. *Syntactical correctness* is a prerequisite for *behavioral correctness*, since the behavior of a syntactical incorrect model is undefined.

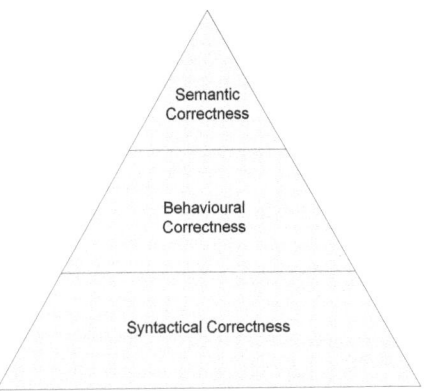

Fig. 3. Pyramid of Business Process Model Correctness

Behavioral Correctness requires from a process model to be executable and includes properties like the absence of deadlocks and lifelocks. Further, it requires a correct flow of data; e.g., data objects must be written before read the first time. In the context of (dynamic) process changes, *state consistency* and *data consistency* respectively, must be preserved; i.e., a running process instance must not face deadlocks, lifelocks, and data-flow errors, when dynamically migrating its execution to a new process model version. In the context of cross-organizational processes, *compatibility* between the public processes of the different partners requires their composition is a behaviorally correct process. *Conformance* requires the private process of a partner to implement the behavior of his public process. Finally, *behavioral correctness* is a prerequisite for *semantic correctness*.

Semantic Correctness (i.e. business process compliance) requires a process model to comply with imposed compliance rules stemming from regulations, standards, and laws. Hence, each possible execution of the process must not violate any compliance rule. For a set of compliance rules, *consistency* requires the conjunction of the rules to be satisfiable; i.e. consistent compliance rules do not conflict with each other.

4 State of the Art

In this section, we outline the state of research. First, we discuss existing approaches in the area of *cross-organizational processes*. Then, we deal with *process flexibility*. Finally, we discuss *business process compliance*.

4.1 Cross-Organizational Processes

Modeling *cross-organizational* processes has been discussed for many years. There are widespread standards such as BPEL4WS, WS-CDL, and RosettaNet, as well as powerful modeling frameworks and notations (e.g. "Let's dance" [10], iBPMN [11], and BPMN 2.0). [12] further identified *interaction patterns*, which describe well-defined patterns for message exchanges between partner processes. For privacy reasons, a choreography definition is usually restricted to those activities relevant for the message exchanges between the partners involved. More precisely, partners publish restricted views on their private processes [13,14]. Several top-down-approaches exist, which, starting from a choreography of public processes, determine whether or not private processes comply with the corresponding public ones [15,16,17]. Furthermore, [18] introduces a set of transformation rules that allow for the inheritance-preserving stepwise enrichment of a public process to obtain the corresponding private one. These rules are also applicable to evolve private processes without changing their public view. To support the opposite direction (i.e., to interconnect existing partner processes), [19] provides a bottom-up-approach for checking whether or not processes can interact with each other successfully. Further, they propose a central as well as distributed architecture, which both allow for the dynamic matching and execution of cross-organizational processes based on a shared registry for public processes. Finally, the scenario of modeling process choreographies and private processes independently is addressed by [20], using the *Formal Contract Language* to check conformance between choreographies and processes.

4.2 Process Flexibility

Issues related to process flexibility have been discussed for more than a decade [21,22,23,5]. However, existing approaches consider flexibility mainly for processes orchestrations; i.e., workflows implementing a private process and being executed by a single process engine. In approaches like Pockets of Flexibility [24] or Worklets [25], for example, processes are executed on the basis of a loosely or partially specified model, which is then fully specified at runtime. Relevant techniques include late modeling and late composition of process fragments as well as declarative modeling styles [26].

Dynamic process adaptations, in turn, represent the ability of the implemented processes to cope with exceptional situations. On one hand, this includes the handling of expected exceptions, which can be anticipated and thus be captured in the process model [27]. On the other hand, it covers non-anticipated exceptions, which are usually handled through structural adaptations of single process instances based on well-defined change patterns (e.g., to add, delete or move activities) [28]. A particular challenge is to ensure the behavioral correctness (i.e., state and data consistency) of a process instance in this context [21]. Approaches like ADEPT [29] guarantee for the behavioral correctness of the modified process model.

Besides this, there exists support for assisting end-users in reusing ad-hoc changes [30] and for restricting changes to authorized users [31]. Another fundamental aspect concerns process schema evolution [32,33]; i.e., the ability of the implemented process to change when the business process evolves. Relevant problems in this context concern the handling of running process instances, which were initiated based on the old model version, but are required to use the new specification from now on [33,32]. Since thousands of active instances may be affected by a given process change the issue of behavioral correctness is rather critical. Traceability of changes and mining of dynamic processes are other relevant issues, closely related to process evolution, which are considered in existing frameworks [34,35].

Only few approaches exist that address changes of distributed processes and choreographies. [36] shows how partitioned workflows can be changed in a controlled way. [37] distinguishes between shallow and deep service changes in the context of a choreography. While the effects of shallow changes (e.g., changes of service versions, interfaces, and operations) are restricted to a service, deep changes have cascading and disseminating effects on the whole choreography. [38] describes how the version of stateful service instances can be changed efficiently, if the behavior of the new service version covers the behavior of the replaced one. Constructing such new service versions is addressed by [39]. However, no comprehensive solution approach is provided.

4.3   Business Process Compliance

In many domains, process execution is subject to compliance rules and restrictions that stem from laws, regulations, and guidelines (e.g. Basel or Sarbanes-Oxley-Act) [40]. Existing approaches that allow ensuring compliance of business processes with imposed compliance rules differ with respect to the lifecycle phase in which compliance is verified as well as the strategy applied. Moreover, different paradigms and formalisms are used to define compliance rules and process models [41]. Compliance rules are often considered as restrictions to the order in which process activities may be executed. In this context, there exist approaches that formalize compliance rules in temporal logic (e.g., LTL [8] and CTL [6]). Other ones emphasize the modalities of compliance rules (e.g., obligations or permissions) by applying deontic logic [42,43]. Since these approaches are not easy to comprehend, [44] suggests a pattern-based approach to encapsulate logic. There also exist graphical notations for modeling compliance rules [7,8,45]. The integration of compliance rules throughout the process lifecycle has been discussed in [46,47,48].

To verify whether compliance rules are fulfilled by process models at design time, many approaches apply model checking techniques [6,7,8,9]. Since these depend on the exploration of the state space of process models, state space explosion constitutes a big obstacle for practical applications. Graph reduction and sequentialization of parallel flows as well as predicate abstraction are proposed to deal with this challenge [8,7,49]. Among those approaches, there exist few that do not only consider the control flow perspective. [50] introduces state-based data objects. [49] enables data-aware compliance checking for larger data-domains and [9] additionally considers temporal constraints. For cycle-free processes, there exist algorithms that allow for more efficient design time compliance verification than model checking [20,51].

Runtime checking and monitoring (i.e. continous auditing [52]) of business process compliance are addressed by several approaches: [53] enriches a process models with a semantic layer of internal controls. Another compliance monitoring framework based on common event standards and middleware is a presented in [54]. [55] discusses the monitoring and enforcement of compliance within process collaborations. [56] uses *Compliance Rule Graphs* and [57] colored automata to enable fine-grain compliance diagnostics at runtime.

To complement design time and runtime compliance checking, backward compliance checking of process logs has been proposed by checking logs for compliance with LTL-formulas [58]. Finally, declarative approaches [26,43,42] ensure compliance in an elegant manner. Since processes are defined by means of a set of rules, imposed compliance rules only have to be added to the process definition to ensure business process compliance.

In summary, there exist many approaches considering aspects of compliance of cross-organizational processes and their changes. However, only few approaches discuss flexibility issues in the context of cross-organizational processes or in the context of business process compliance. Even fewer approches address business process compliance of cross-organizational processes. Finally, Fig. 4 shows that the interplay of change and compliance in the context of cross-organizational processes has not been addressed yet.

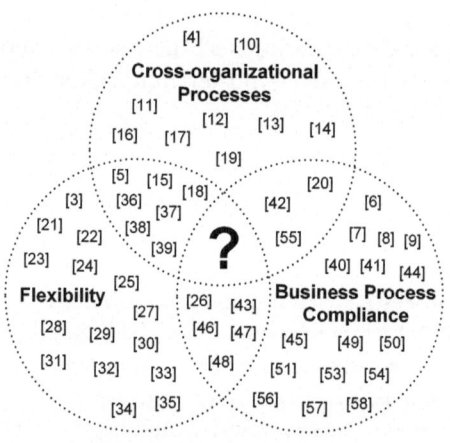

Fig. 4. State of the Art

5   Challenges

As mentioned in Section 4, the interplay of change and compliance in the context of cross-organizational processes has not been addressed yet. In this section we outline challenges arising in the context of this interplay:

Modeling Cross-organizational Compliance Rules. First of all, the (graphical) modeling of assertions and cross-organizational compliance requires proper support. In addition to intra-organizational compliance rules, messages as well as the role executing a task must be considered (cf. Rule 2 of Example 1).

Change Propagation. Before applying a change, all three correctness levels have to be checked as we will illustrate by means of the scenario from Fig. 2: If the message-sending task forward results is deleted in the gynecologist's private process, the corresponding public process will be affected. Furthermore, the message results as well as the public and private process of the women's hospital will be affected by this change. This indicates that a partner must not change his public process in an uncontrolled manner. Otherwise, behavioral correctness of the choreography his public process is involved in cannot be preserved. Thus, the women's hospital should be supported in adapting its public and private processes to the change. Hence, a major research challenge is how to *propagate* changes of a partner's private process to the other partners in order to keep the choreography behaviorally correct.

Efficient Cross-organizational Instance Migration. Changes are particularly challenging if there exist running choreography instances being in different states or partially differing from the original process model (e.g., due to adaptations of single choreographies in the context of exceptions). For any of these hundreds or even thousands of choreography instances it has to be determined whether or not the change or parts of it are applicable, while satisfying all three correctness levels at the same time. Since large numbers of cross-organizational process instances may be affected, efficient algorithms are required.

Ensuring Compliance with Regard to Privacy. Using Example 1 from Fig. 2, we can show that privacy constraints of partner processes aggravate compliance checking at design time. For example, the gynecologist cannot correctly verify Rule 1, since the laboratory hides the relevant task destroy sample from its public process. Nevertheless, when additionally considering the assertion of the laboraty, it becomes clear that Rule 1 is satisfied. Similar difficulties occur when compliance is monitored at runtime. This requires a solution supporting compliance checking with respect to privacy issues. This may become more difficult or even impossible if partners do not publish any parts of their processes.

Efficiently Ensuring Compliance at Change Time. Ensuring compliance of cross-organizational process models and instances at change time is another challenging research issue. Particularly, in the context of compliance, effects of changes cannot be easily traced. For example, assume that task destroy sample is deleted in the laboratory's private process (cf. Fig. 2). Although this task is not part of the laboratory's public process, compliance of the gynecologist's process models with Rule 1 will be affected by this change. However, the task affects the laboratory's assertion that must be withdrawn. Consequently, assertions, internal compliance rules, and global compliance rules should be re-evaluated. Due to the high complexity of current compliance checking approaches and due to the potentially large number of affected process instances, optimization strategies and efficient algorithms are required.

Adequate User Feedback. Users require intelligible feedback on compliance violations. Sources and effects of compliance violations have to be highlighted.

Furthermore, the available courses of action for healing compliance violations should be offered to selected user roles.

6   Summary and Outlook

This paper emphasized that ensuring compliance for cross-organizational processes and their changes raises several challenges. We first provided an overview about the relevant terms in this context, and introduced an example from the medical domain. Next, we introduced three correctness levels, i.e., syntactical correctness, behavioral correctness, and semantic correctness. Then we discussed the state of the art. We came to the viewpoint that the interplay of change and compliance in the context of cross-organizational processes has not been adressed yet. Finally, we provided unanswered challenges that raise from that interplay.

In our future work, we plan to adress the challenges denoted in Section 5, within our research project C³Pro: First, we want to enable graphically modeling of assertions and cross-organizational compliance rules. Second, we will put emphasis on enabling cross-organizational compliance checking and monitoring with respect to privacy issues and assertions. As stated, this requires the checking of syntactical and behavioral correctness before. In addition, we plan to study the efficient application of changes to running choreographies instances first and then look and instances that partially differ from the original process models. Finally, we plan to combine our approaches for ensuring compliance and correct changes to cross-organizational processes and thus enable compliance of cross-organizational changes.

References

1. Mutschler, B., Reichert, M., Bumiller, J.: Unleashing the effectiveness of process-oriented information systems: Problem analysis, critical success factors, and implications. IEEE Trans on Sys. Man and Cybernetics, Part C 38(3), 280–291 (2008)
2. Weske, M.: Workflow management systems: Formal foundation, conceptual design, implementation aspects. Springer (2007)
3. Reichert, M., Weber, B.: Enabling Flexibility in Process-Aware Information Systems. Springer (2012)
4. Alonso, G., et al.: Web Services. Springer (2004)
5. Dustdar, S.: Caramba - a process-aware collaboration system supporting ad hoc and collaborative processes in virtual teams. Dist. & Parall Datab. 15(1), 45–66 (2004)
6. Ghose, A.K., Koliadis, G.: Auditing Business Process Compliance. In: Krämer, B.J., Lin, K.-J., Narasimhan, P. (eds.) ICSOC 2007. LNCS, vol. 4749, pp. 169–180. Springer, Heidelberg (2007)
7. Liu, Y., Müller, S., Xu, K.: A static compliance-checking framework for business process models. IBM Systems Journal 46(2), 261–335 (2007)
8. Awad, A., Decker, G., Weske, M.: Efficient Compliance Checking Using BPMN-Q and Temporal Logic. In: Dumas, M., Reichert, M., Shan, M.-C. (eds.) BPM 2008. LNCS, vol. 5240, pp. 326–341. Springer, Heidelberg (2008)

9. Kokash, N., Krause, C., de Vink, E.: Time and data aware analysis of graphical service models. In: SEFM 2010 (2010)

10. Zaha, J.M., Barros, A., Dumas, M., ter Hofstede, A.: Let's Dance: A Language for Service Behavior Modeling. In: Meersman, R., Tari, Z. (eds.) OTM 2006. LNCS, vol. 4275, pp. 145–162. Springer, Heidelberg (2006)

11. Decker, G., Weske, M.: Interaction-centric modeling of process choreographies. Inf. Sys. 35(8) (2010)

12. Barros, A., Dumas, M., ter Hofstede, A.: Service Interaction Patterns. In: van der Aalst, W.M.P., Benatallah, B., Casati, F., Curbera, F. (eds.) BPM 2005. LNCS, vol. 3649, pp. 302–318. Springer, Heidelberg (2005)

13. Liu, D.R., Shen, M.: Business-to-business workflow interoperation based on process-views. Decision Support Sys. 38(3), 399–419 (2004)

14. Maamar, Z., Benslimane, D., Ghedira, C., Mrissa, M.: Views in composite web services. IEEE Internet Comp. 9(4), 52–57 (2005)

15. van der Aalst, W.M.P.: Inheritance of interorganizational workflows to enable Business-to-Business E-Commerce. Elec. Com. Research 2(3), 195–231 (2002)

16. Martens, A.: Consistency between executable and abstract processes. In: EEE 2005, pp. 60–67 (2005)

17. Decker, G., Weske, M.: Behavioral Consistency for B2B Process Integration. In: Krogstie, J., Opdahl, A.L., Sindre, G. (eds.) CAiSE 2007. LNCS, vol. 4495, pp. 81–95. Springer, Heidelberg (2007)

18. van der Aalst, W.M.P., et al.: Multiparty contracts: Agreeing and implementing interorganizational processes. The Comp. Journal 53(1), 90–106 (2010)

19. Tata, S., et al.: CoopFlow: A Bottom-Up Approach to Workflow Cooperation for Short-Term Virtual Enterprises. IEEE Trans. on Serv. Comp. 1(4), 214–228 (2008)

20. Governatori, G., Milosevic, Z., Sadiq, S.: Compliance checking between business processes and business contracts. In: EDOC 2006, pp. 221–232 (2006)

21. Rinderle, S., Reichert, M., Dadam, P.: Correctness criteria for dynamic changes in workflow systems – a survey. Data & Knowl. Eng. 50(1), 9–34 (2004)

22. Weber, B., Sadiq, S., Reichert, M.: Beyond rigidity–dynamic process lifecycle support. Comp. Science-Research and Dev. 23(2), 47–65 (2009)

23. Reichert, M., Dadam, P.: ADEPT$_{flex}$ – supporting dynamic changes of workflows without losing control. Intelligent Inf. Sys. 10(2), 93–129 (1998)

24. Sadiq, S., Sadiq, W., Orlowska, M.: A framework for constraint specification and validation in flexible workflows. Inf. Sys. 30(5), 349–378 (2005)

25. Adams, M., ter Hofstede, A.H.M., Edmond, D., van der Aalst, W.M.P.: Worklets: A Service-Oriented Implementation of Dynamic Flexibility in Workflows. In: Meersman, R., Tari, Z. (eds.) OTM 2006. LNCS, vol. 4275, pp. 291–308. Springer, Heidelberg (2006)

26. Pesic, M., Schonenberg, H., van der Aalst, W.M.P.: DECLARE: full support for loosely-structured processes. In: EDOC 2007, pp. 287–300 (2007)

27. Reichert, M., Dadam, P., Bauer, T.: Dealing with forward and backward jumps in workflow management systems. Software and Systems Modeling 2(1), 37–58 (2003)

28. Weber, B., Reichert, M., Rinderle-Ma, S.: Change patterns and change support features - Enhancing flexibility in process-aware information systems. Data & Knowl. Eng. 66(3), 438–466 (2008)

29. Reichert, M., Rinderle, S., Kreher, U., Dadam, P.: Adaptive process management with ADEPT2. In: ICDE 2005, pp. 1113–1114 (2005)

30. Weber, B., et al.: Providing integrated life cycle support in process-aware information systems. Int. J. Coop. Inf. Sys. 18(1), 115–165 (2009)

31. Weber, B., Reichert, M., Wild, W., Rinderle, S.: Balancing Flexibility and Security in Adaptive Process Management Systems. In: Meersman, R. (ed.) OTM 2005. LNCS, vol. 3760, pp. 59–76. Springer, Heidelberg (2005)

32. Casati, F., et al.: Workflow evolution. Data & Knowl. Eng. 24(3), 211–238 (1998)

33. Rinderle, S., Reichert, M., Dadam, P.: Flexible support of team processes by adaptive workflow systems. Dist. & Parall. Datab. 16(1), 91–116 (2004)

34. Li, C., et al.: The MinAdept clustering approach for discovering reference process models out of process variants. Coop. Inf. Sys. 19(3) (2010)

35. Günther, C.W., Rinderle, S., Reichert, M., van der Aalst, W.: Change Mining in Adaptive Process Management Systems. In: Meersman, R., Tari, Z. (eds.) OTM 2006. LNCS, vol. 4275, pp. 309–326. Springer, Heidelberg (2006)

36. Reichert, M., Bauer, T.: Supporting Ad-Hoc Changes in Distributed Workflow Management Systems. In: Meersman, R., Tari, Z. (eds.) OTM 2007, Part I. LNCS, vol. 4803, pp. 150–168. Springer, Heidelberg (2007)

37. Papazoglou, M.: The Challenges of Service Evolution. In: Bellahsène, Z., Léonard, M. (eds.) CAiSE 2008. LNCS, vol. 5074, pp. 1–15. Springer, Heidelberg (2008)

38. Liske, N., Lohmann, N., Stahl, C., Wolf, K.: Another approach to service instance migration. Service Oriented Computing, 607–621 (2009)

39. Mooij, A., et al.: Constructing replaceable services using operating guidelines and maximal controllers. In: Web Services and Formal Methods, pp. 116–130 (2011)

40. Sadiq, W., Governatori, G., Namiri, K.: Modeling Control Objectives for Business Process Compliance. In: Alonso, G., Dadam, P., Rosemann, M. (eds.) BPM 2007. LNCS, vol. 4714, pp. 149–164. Springer, Heidelberg (2007)

41. El Kharbili, M., et al.: Business process compliance checking: Current state and future challenges. In: MobIS 2008, pp. 107–113 (2008)

42. Alberti, M., et al.: Expressing and verifying business contracts with abductive logic programming. In: NorMAS 2007, Dagstuhl Seminar Proceedings (2007)

43. Goedertier, S., Vanthienen, J.: Designing Compliant Business Processes with Obligations and Permissions. In: Eder, J., Dustdar, S. (eds.) BPM Workshops 2006. LNCS, vol. 4103, pp. 5–14. Springer, Heidelberg (2006)

44. Dwyer, M.B., Avrunin, G.S., Corbett, J.C.: Property specification patterns for finite-state verification. In: FMSP 1998 (1998)

45. Ly, L.T., Rinderle-Ma, S., Dadam, P.: Design and Verification of Instantiable Compliance Rule Graphs in Process-Aware Information Systems. In: Pernici, B. (ed.) CAiSE 2010. LNCS, vol. 6051, pp. 9–23. Springer, Heidelberg (2010)

46. Ly, L.T., et al.: Integration and verification of semantic constraints in adaptive process management systems. Data & Knowl. Eng. 64(1), 3–23 (2008)

47. Ly, L.T., Rinderle-Ma, S., Göser, K., Dadam, P.: On enabling integrated process compliance with semantic constraints in process management systems - requirements, challenges, solutions. Inf. Sys. Frontiers (2009)

48. Knuplesch, D., Reichert, M.: Ensuring business process compliance along the process life cycle. Technical Report 2011-06, University of Ulm (2011)

49. Knuplesch, D., Ly, L.T., Rinderle-Ma, S., Pfeifer, H., Dadam, P.: On Enabling Data-Aware Compliance Checking of Business Process Models. In: Parsons, J., Saeki, M., Shoval, P., Woo, C., Wand, Y. (eds.) ER 2010. LNCS, vol. 6412, pp. 332–346. Springer, Heidelberg (2010)

50. Awad, A., Weidlich, M., Weske, M.: Specification, Verification and Explanation of Violation for Data Aware Compliance Rules. In: Baresi, L., Chi, C.-H., Suzuki, J. (eds.) ICSOC-ServiceWave 2009. LNCS, vol. 5900, pp. 500–515. Springer, Heidelberg (2009)

51. Weber, I., Hoffmann, J., Mendling, J.: Semantic business process validation. In: SBPM 2008 (2008)
52. Alles, M., Kogan, A., Vasarhelyi, M.: Putting continuous auditing theory into practice: Lessons from two pilot implementations. Inf. Sys. 22(2), 195–214 (2008)
53. Namiri, K., Stojanovic, N.: Pattern-Based Design and Validation of Business Process Compliance. In: Meersman, R., Tari, Z. (eds.) OTM 2007, Part I. LNCS, vol. 4803, pp. 59–76. Springer, Heidelberg (2007)
54. Giblin, C., et al.: From regulatory policies to event monitoring rules: Towards model-driven compliance automation. Technical Report RZ-3662, IBM (2006)
55. Berry, A., Milosevic, Z.: Extending choreography with business contract constraints. Coop. Inf. Sys. 14(2-3), 131–179 (2005)
56. Ly, L.T., Rinderle-Ma, S., Knuplesch, D., Dadam, P.: Monitoring business process compliance using compliance rule graphs. In: CoopIS 2011, pp. 82–99 (2011)
57. Maggi, F.M., Montali, M., Westergaard, M., van der Aalst, W.M.P.: Monitoring Business Constraints with Linear Temporal Logic: An Approach Based on Colored Automata. In: Rinderle-Ma, S., Toumani, F., Wolf, K. (eds.) BPM 2011. LNCS, vol. 6896, pp. 132–147. Springer, Heidelberg (2011)
58. van der Aalst, W.M.P., de Beer, H.T., van Dongen, B.F.: Process Mining and Verification of Properties: An Approach Based on Temporal Logic. In: Meersman, R. (ed.) OTM 2005. LNCS, vol. 3760, pp. 130–147. Springer, Heidelberg (2005)

Secure and Compliant Implementation
of Business Process-Driven Systems

Achim D. Brucker and Isabelle Hang

SAP AG, SAP Research, Vincenz-Priessnitz-Str. 1, 76131 Karlsruhe, Germany
{achim.brucker,isabelle.hang}@sap.com

Abstract. Today's businesses are inherently process-driven. Consequently, the use of business-process driven systems, usually implemented on top of *service-oriented* or *cloud-based* infrastructures, is increasing. At the same time, the demand on the security, privacy, and compliance of such systems is increasing as well. As a result, the costs—with respect to computational effort at runtime as well as financial costs—for operating business-process driven systems increase steadily.

In this paper, we present a method for statically checking the security and conformance of the system implementation, e. g., on the source code level, to requirements specified on the business process level. As the compliance is statically guaranteed—already at design-time—this method reduces the number of run-time checks for ensuring the security and compliance and, thus, improves the runtime performances. Moreover, it reduces the costs of system audits, as there is no need for analyzing the generated log files for validating the compliance to the properties that are already statically guaranteed.

Keywords: business process security, secure service tasks, BPMN, static program analysis.

1 Introduction

Business-process driven systems form the backbone of most modern enterprises. As a consequence, process-models as such and Business Process Modeling (BPM) as a methodology are becoming more and more important, not only as a documentation artifact but also for controlling and steering the execution of business processes. Moreover, the number of businesses that operate in regulated markets, i. e., that need to comply to regulations such as Health Insurance Portability and Accountability Act (HIPAA) [15] in the health care sector or Basel II [6] in the financial sector, is increasing. Such compliance regulations along with the increased awareness of IT security result in the need for modeling, analyzing, and execution techniques for business processes that treat security, privacy, and compliance properties in business processes as first class citizen.

To meet these requirements, several approaches, e. g., [12, 20, 23, 27], have been suggested to integrate the security specification into process models. Only a few of these approaches use the security models for more than documentation

M. La Rosa and P. Soffer (Eds.): BPM 2012 Workshops, LNBIP 132, pp. 662–674, 2013.
© Springer-Verlag Berlin Heidelberg 2013

purposes. Usually, the approaches that use the security models besides documentations only provide means for generating access control configurations for monolithic workflow management systems and, therefore, are not adequate for modern service-oriented or cloud-based infrastructures.

Modern service-oriented or cloud-based infrastructures are usually operated by multiple parties and, moreover, comprise many technical layers (see Fig. 1):

- The *User Interface Layer* managing the interaction with end users, i. e., allowing them to claim new tasks, querying input, or displaying results.
- The *Business Object Layer* or *Service Layer* comprises all backend systems as well as (external) services providing the functionality required for implementing the service tasks.
- The *Business Process Layer* comprising a business process execution engine that links the user interface

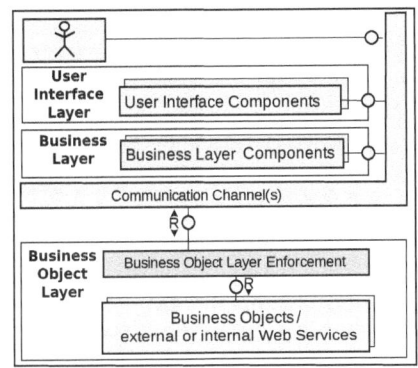

Fig. 1. System architecture or, potentially distributed or cloud-based, workflow management systems

layer and the business object layer, i. e., for human tasks, the necessary interaction with users is triggered and for automated tasks, the calls to backend systems or, e. g., services.

Each of these layers has to comply to the various compliance and security requirements to ensure that the overall systems complies to the security and compliance properties expressed at the business process level. Most works on integrating security aspects into business process models concentrate on the modeling as well as the process execution in the business process layer. In contrast, we concentrate on ensuring that the accompanying implementations (and system configurations) in the user interface layer as well as the business process layer comply to the process level security and compliance requirements.

In this paper, we present a novel approach that allows for statically checking the conformance of service implementations, i. e., on the source code level, to requirements specified on the business process level. As the compliance is statically guaranteed—already at design-time—this method reduces the number of run-time checks necessary and, thus, improves the runtime performances. Moreover, it reduces the costs of system audits, as there is no need for analyzing the generated log files for validating the compliance to the properties that are already statically guaranteed.

The rest of the paper is structured as follows: After introducing secure business process models using SecureBPMN in Sect. 2, we present a mapping from process level security and compliance requirements to the implementation level in Sect. 3. In Sect. 4 we describe our prototype and in Sect. 5 we discuss related work and draw our conclusions.

2   Secure Business Processes: An Example

Modeling security properties, as a first class citizen of business processes, requires an integrated language for both security and business requirements. One option is the extension of a process modeling language with security concepts. In our work, we follow the meta-modeling approach for extending the meta-model of BPMN [22] with a security language, called SecureBPMN, that allows for specifying hierarchical role-based access control (RBAC) [1] as well as further security and compliance properties. The decision for a meta-model based approach is based on our previous experience in extending UML with RBAC [10].

Overall, SecureBPMN [12] enables the specification of security properties at a fine granular level. For example, separation of duty and binding of duty can restrict individual permissions (e.g., completing a task requires two *clerks* or one *manager*) rather than restricting the whole task.

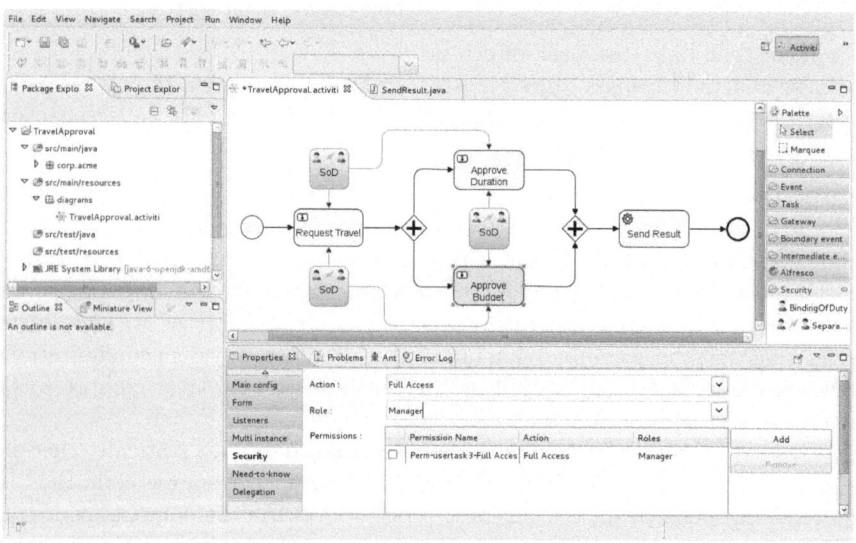

Fig. 2. The SecureBPMN modeling environment allows for specifying security requirements diagrammatically as well as using specialized user interfaces

For example, consider a travel approval process in which the budget and the travel duration need to be approved by different managers. The main window in Fig. 2 illustrates such a process. This simple process requires already the following compliance and security requirements for a more detailed discussion of security requirements for process models):

```
<userTask id="Approve Duration">
  <extensionElements>
    <activiti:formProperty id="user_lastname" writable="false"/>
    <activiti:formProperty id="user_firstname" writeable="false"/>
    <activiti:formProperty id="travel_destination" writeable="false"/>
    <activiti:formProperty id="travel_duration" writeable="false"/>
    <activiti:formProperty id="travel_budget" writeable="false"/>
  </extensionElements>
</userTask>
```

Listing 1. User interface implementation for Request Travel using form properties

- *Access Control:* Access to resources as well as actions need to be restricted to certain roles (e. g., clerks, managers) or subjects.
  In our example, we assume a simple role hierarchy containing the roles staff and manager where every member of the role manager is also a member or role staff. Moreover, the role staff has *full access* (e. g., is allowed to claim, execute, or cancel) for task Request Travel; members of the role manager have full access for the tasks Approve Duration and Approve Budget.
- *Separation of Duty:* More than one subject is required to successfully complete the process. Similarly, one can define *Binding of Duty* as the requirement that certain tasks need to be handled by the same subject.
  In our example, we use separation of duty to ensure that the subject requesting a travel is not allowed to approve the absence or the budget–even though he or she might be a member of the role manager.

While, in this example, most likely not necessary, we also assume the strict application of the need to know principle. In more detail:

- *Need to Know:* User should only be able to access the information that is required for their work.
  In our example, we apply the need to know principle to ensure that the manager approving the absence has only access to the duration of the travel and the manager approving the budget has only access to the travel costs.

Executing this process in the context of an enterprise system requires more than deploying the process model in a business process execution engine (recall Fig. 1): among others, user interfaces for the manual or human tasks, e. g., Request Travel or Approve Duration, need to be implemented. Listing 1 shows such an implementation of the user interface for Request Travel using an HTML like formalism, called *form properties*. Moreover, the internal flow of the service tasks, e. g., Send Result, needs to be implemented. Listing 2 shows such an implementation in Java that, e. g., can be used as the business logic of a web service.

These examples show that the implementation of business process-driven systems requires much more than only the business process model itself. Moreover, these artifacts are, compared to the high-level process models, quite low-level. Consequently, specifying security and compliance properties on the process level is not enough to ensure the secure and compliant operation of business process-driven enterprise systems.

```
package corp.acme;

import java.util.ArrayList;
import java.util.Date;
import java.util.List;
import org.activiti.engine.delegate.JavaDelegate;
import org.activiti.engine.delegate.DelegateExecution;

public class SendResult implements JavaDelegate {
    @Override
    public void execute(DelegateExecution execution) throws Exception {
        String lastname    = (String) execution.getVariable("user_lastname");
        String firstname   = (String) execution.getVariable("user_firstname");
        String email       = (String) execution.getVariable("user_email");
        String destination = (String) execution.getVariable("travel_destination");
        String duration    = (String) execution.getVariable("travel_duration");

        if (firstname.equals("eve"))
          execution.setVariable("travel_budget",
              (new Integer(execution.getVariable("travel_budget")*2)).toString());

        sendEmail(firstname, lastname, email, destination, duration);

    }
}
```

Listing 2. Excerpt of the Java implementation of Send Result

While there are works, e.g., [12, 28], that use process level security specifications for generating configurations for access control infrastructures such as XACML [21], we are not aware of any works that allow for checking process level security and compliance properties on the actual implementations of user interfaces or services. In the following, we present an approach that allows for checking the conformance of source code artifacts to process level requirement specifications. For many properties, such a conformance check can be done statically at implementation time. Thus, such checks help to improve the overall runtime of business process-driven systems as they reduce the number of runtime security checks required.

3 Mapping Secure Business Processes to Implementations

Checking process-level security and compliance specifications on the implementation level requires to link the implementation artifacts to process-level concepts such as tasks, data objects or process variables as well as the translation of the high-level to security and compliance requirements to low level concepts on the implementation level.

Tab. 1 summarizes the mapping from process-level security concepts to checks on the implementation level for three different implementations aspects. Namely, the implementation of service tasks and the two forms of implementing user interfaces: using domain specific languages such as the form properties provided by the Activiti BPM Platform as well as user interfaces implemented in generic programming languages such as Java or JavaScript. In more detail:

Table 1. Mapping process level requirements to the implementation level

	Service Impl.	UI (Form Prop.)	UI (Java)
Access Control	AC check impl.	–	AC check impl.
Separation of Duty	AC check impl.	–	AC check impl.
Binding of Duty	AC check impl.	–	AC check impl.
Need to Know	proc. var. access	proc. var. access	proc. var. access
Confidentiality	dataflow	proc. var. access	dataflow

- For service task implementations, e. g., in Java, we can statically ensure that *access control* checks for enforcing access control in general and *separation of duty* (*binding of duty*) in particular are implemented. If we assume that the actual enforcement is based on a standard architecture for distributed systems, e. g., using an XACML policy decision point, we can only that the policy enforcement point is implemented correctly, but we still need to rely on a correctly implemented or generated policy.
  To ensure the conformance to the *need to know principle*, we can check the (read or write) access to process variables representing data objects. Similarly, we can check if a task implementation accesses confidential information. Still, checking *confidentiality* requirements requires a data flow analysis on the source code level. This allows, for example, also to ensure the compliance in situation in which a confidential information can be processed locally but it is not allowed to persist the data or transmit it to a third party. Even fine-grained requirements such as "this data object needs to be encrypted with a specific encryption algorithm and key length" can be checked on the implementation level.
- For user interface implementations using form properties, only a very limited set of properties can be checked. Namely, we can check if such a form accesses certain process variables (either read-only, write-only, or read and write) which allows us to detect violations against the *need to know* principle or data *confidentiality*. For all other requirements, in particular the access control, we need to rely either on checks by the business layer components or on the business object layer enforcement.
- For user interfaces written in a generic programming language (e. g., Java, JavaScript), we can apply the same checks as for service task implementation. Note that from a security perspective, one cannot rely on security checks in the user interface layer. Thus, these checks are only an addition to the checks in the other layers.

Note that this mapping is, in most cases, not complete, i. e., while the checks on the implementation level can detect violations to process level security policies, they do not, in general, guarantee the conformance to all aspects of the process-level security requirements.

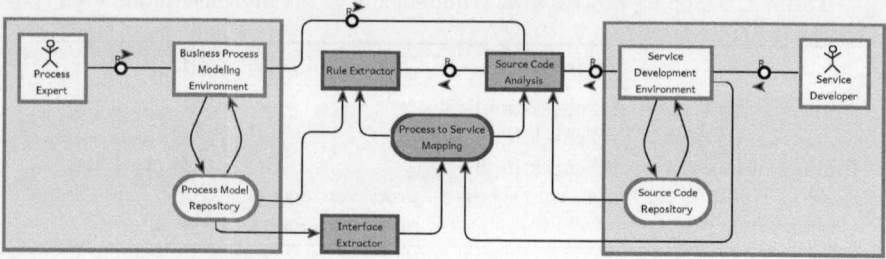

Fig. 3. Architecture of the Analysis Engine for Checking Process level Requirements on the (Service-) Implementation-level

4   Design and Implementation

We implemented our method in a prototype using the Activiti BPM Platform (http://www.activiti.org). Fig. 3 illustrated the overall architecture including the environments for modeling business processes (e. g., Activiti Designer) and for developing services and user interfaces (e. g., Eclipse). The architecture comprises in particular:

- *Interface extractor:* This components extracts the (initial) interfaces of service implementations and user interface implementations from the process models (stored in the process model repository). These interfaces are used for managing the mapping between the business process layer and the implementation layer. The actual mapping is stored in the Process to Service Mapping Database.
- *Rule extractor:* This component extracts the business-process level security and compliance specification from the process model repository and translates them to the implementation level. This includes a de-composition of high-level requirements into a set of technical requirements that can be checked on the implementation level.
- *Process to Service Mapping (Database):* This database stores the mapping between the business process layer and the implementation layer.
- *Source Code Analyzer:* The source code analyzer checks the service implementations as well as the user interface implementations based on the extracted rules. The results of the analysis are displayed to the developer in the service/user-interface development environment. If required, the results can be displayed to the process expert as well.

This system interacts, on the one hand, with one or more business process modeling environments (left hand side of Fig. 3) that stores the process model in a dedicated Process Model Repository. This component allows for modeling business processes and is also used for documenting the business-process level security and compliance requirements. On the other hand, the system interacts with one or more software or user interface development environments (right hand

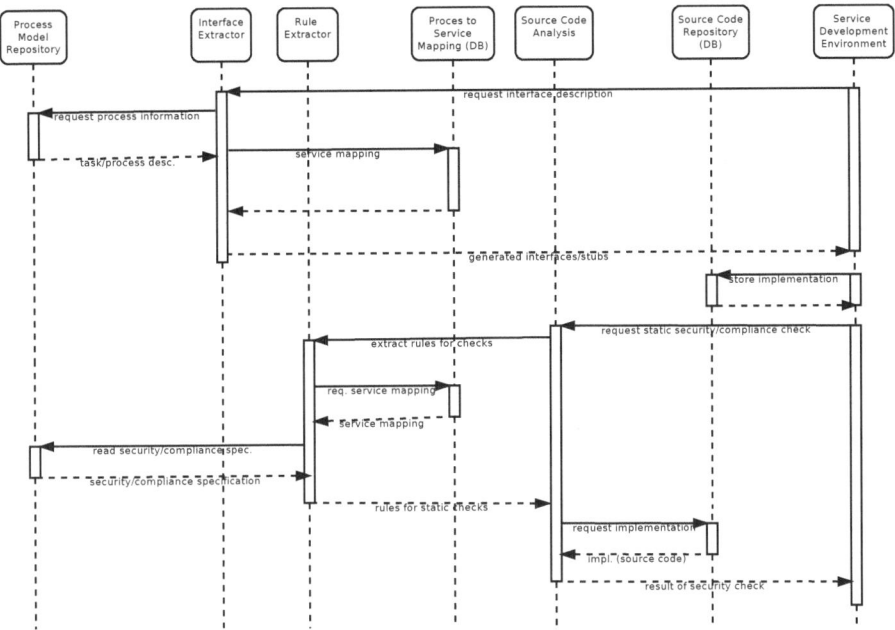

Fig. 4. Sequence diagram illustrating the use of our approach

side of Fig. 3). Fig. 4 illustrates the interaction of the different components in more detail:

1. Generating the mapping from business processes to (service) implementations, i. e., the service developer initiates the creation of the service interfaces based on the process model.
   (a) The developer initiates, via the Service Development Environment, the interface generation using the Interface Extractor.
   (b) The Interface Extractor queries the Process Model Repository and generates the mapping from tasks and processes to interfaces (e. g., implemented in Java). This mapping is stored in the Process to Service Mapping database.
2. Service development:
   (a) Using the infrastructure provided by Service Development Environment, interfaces stubs are generated and stored in the source code repository.
   (b) The service developer creates or modifies the source of the services and stores the result in the source code repository.
3. Checking the correctness, security, and compliance on the implementation level:
   (a) From the Service Development Environment, the developer can check that her/his implementation fulfills the specified requirements. For this she/he uses the Source Code Analysis Module.
   (b) The Source Code Analysis module uses the Rule Extractor for generating a process specific (i. e., based on the information stored in the Process to

Service Mapping database as well as the Process Model Repository) setup for the analysis of the service implementations.

(c) The Source Code Analysis module executes a static source code analysis and reports the results (e. g., service fulfills the requirements, required property violated in module x on line y to the service developer.

Recall our example from Sect. 2: from the high-level specification of our example (see Fig. 2), we derive automatically requirements that need to be fulfilled on the source code level, i. e., by the programs implementing the user-interfaces for human tasks (e. g., Approve Budget) as well as for the service implementation that implement the automated tasks (e. g., Send Result). Here, for example, our method can ensure, at design-time, and, thus, without additional costs at run-time or during the audit, that

- the user interface for Approve Duration does not show/access the budget information,
- the user interface for Approve Budget does not show/access travel details (duration, destination, etc.),
- the necessary runtime-checks for enforcing the access control for all tasks are actually implemented,
- neither a service nor an user interface implementation accesses information in the back-end that is not needed for executing this process.

In particular, we detected the following two violations in our toy example:

- The user interface of task Request Travel access both the travel budget and the travel destination which violates the need to know principle.
- The service implementation contains a backdoor granting users with first name eve twice the amount of travel budget that was visible to the manager executing the task Approve Budget.

To review and fix the detected violation in the source code, we offer a direct jump to the line of the implementation where the violations occur.

Our prototype extends the Activiti BPM Platform and its modeling component, called Activiti Designer, which is based on Eclipse. For the static code analysis, we use our own analysis tool based on Wala (http://wala.sf.net). As an alternative, we are also experimenting with generating configurations for a commercially available static code analysis tools.

5   Related Work and Conclusion

5.1   Related Work

We see three areas of related work: modeling of security requirements for business processes, analyzing security properties of business processes, and runtime enforcement of security properties for business-process driven systems.

There is a large body of literature extending graphical modeling languages with means for specifying security or privacy requirements. One of the first approaches is SecureUML [18], which is conceptually very close to your BPMN extension. SecureUML is a meta-model-based extension of UML that allows for specifying RBAC-requirements for UML class models and state charts. There are also various techniques for analyzing SecureUML models, e. g., [7, 11]. While based on the same motivation, UMLsec [16] is not defined using a meta-model. Instead, the security specifications are written, in an ad-hoc manner, in UML profiles. In contrast, integrating security properties in to business processes is a quite recent development, e. g., motivated by Wolter and Schaad [27]. In the same year, Rodríguez et al. [23] presented a meta-model based approach introduction a secure business process type supporting global security goals. In contrast, our approach allows the fine-grained specification of security requirements for single tasks or data objects. Similar to UMLsec, Mülle et al. [20] present an attribute-based approach (i. e., the conceptual equivalent of UML profiles) of specifying security constraints in BPMN models without actually extending BPMN.

With respect to the validation of security requirements on the business process level, the closed related work is the work of Wolter and Meinel [25] and Arsac et al. [5] both support the checking if an access control specification enforces binary static of duty and binding of duty constraints. Besides security properties, there is also the strong need for checking the consistency of business processes itself, e. g., the absence of deadlocks. There are several works that concentrate on these kind of process internal consistency validation, e. g., [3, 14]. Moreover, there are several approaches for analyzing access control constraints over UML models, e. g., [11, 16, 24]. These approaches are limited to simple access control modes, as it UML models are usually quite distant from business process descriptions comprising high level security and compliance goals.

Wolter et al. [26] present an approach for generating XACML policies for RBAC models in the context of process models as well as generating configurations for Apache Rampart (http://axis.apache.org/axis2/java/rampart/). Moreover, model-based security approaches for UML, e. g., [8, 13, 16], support, usually, the generation of security configurations as well.

5.2 Conclusion and Future Work

We presented an approach for checking process level security and conformance requirements on the implementation level. Our approach is integrated framework for modeling, analyzing, and enforcing security, privacy, and trust requirements in business process-driven systems. Checking process-level security and compliance requirements on the implementation level has several advantages. For example, all security requirements that can be guaranteed based on a static checked not need to be checked (or enforced) and runtime. As the conformance to those requirements is guaranteed "by design," these requirements are not subject to manual audits. Thus, our approach helps to improve the overall system performance as well as reduce costs for manual compliance audits.

There are several lines of related work, among them the development of support for system audits, e. g., by integrating analysis techniques such as [2, 4]. In particular, process mining approaches appear to be particularly interesting:

combing process mining with our business process animation, i. e., the visualization of attack traces, allows for interactively investigation deviations of the actual process execution with the intended one. Moreover, we see the integration analysis techniques checking the internal consistency of processes, e. g., [14], as well as their reconfiguration, e. g., [3]. To improve the run-time of the enforcement architecture, the generation of security artifacts can extended with support for advanced caching architectures, e. g., [17] or optimization techniques, e. g., [19]. Finally, we intend to integrate security testing approaches, e. g., [9], for validating the compliance of services and (legacy) back-end systems in a black-box scenario.

Acknowledgments. The research leading to these results has received funding from the European Union Seventh Framework Programme (FP7/2007-2013) under grant no. 257930. We thank Jan Alexander and Matthias Klink for valuable discussions on earlier versions of this paper.

References

[1] American National Standard for Information Technology – Role Based Access Control. ANSI, New York (2004) ANSI INCITS 359-2004

[2] van der Aalst, W., de Medeiros, A.: Process mining and security: Detecting anomalous process executions and checking process conformance. ENTCS 121, 3–21 (2005), doi:10.1016/j.entcs.2004.10.013

[3] van der Aalst, W.M.P., Dumas, M., Gottschalk, F., ter Hofstede, A.H.M., La Rosa, M., Mendling, J.: Correctness-Preserving Configuration of Business Process Models. In: Fiadeiro, J.L., Inverardi, P. (eds.) FASE 2008. LNCS, vol. 4961, pp. 46–61. Springer, Heidelberg (2008)

[4] Accorsi, R., Wonnemann, C.: InDico: Information Flow Analysis of Business Processes for Confidentiality Requirements. In: Cuellar, J., Lopez, J., Barthe, G., Pretschner, A. (eds.) STM 2010. LNCS, vol. 6710, pp. 194–209. Springer, Heidelberg (2011)

[5] Arsac, W., Compagna, L., Pellegrino, G., Ponta, S.E.: Security Validation of Business Processes via Model-Checking. In: Erlingsson, Ú., Wieringa, R., Zannone, N. (eds.) ESSoS 2011. LNCS, vol. 6542, pp. 29–42. Springer, Heidelberg (2011)

[6] Basel Committee on Banking Supervision: Basel III: A global regulatory framework for more resilient banks and banking systems. Tech. rep., Bank for International Settlements, Basel, Switzerland (2010),
http://www.bis.org/publ/bcbs189.pdf

[7] Basin, D., Clavel, M., Doser, J., Egea, M.: Automated analysis of security-design models. Information and Software Technology 51(5), 815–831 (2009), doi:10.1016/j.infsof.2008.05.011; Special Issue on Model-Driven Development for Secure Information Systems

[8] Basin, D.A., Doser, J., Lodderstedt, T.: Model driven security: From UML models to access control infrastructures. ACM Transactions on Software Engineering and Methodology 15(1), 39–91 (2006), doi:10.1145/1125808.1125810

[9] Brucker, A.D., Brügger, L., Kearney, P., Wolff, B.: An approach to modular and testable security models of real-world health-care applications. In: ACM SACMAT, pp. 133–142. ACM Press, New York (2011), doi:10.1145/1998441.1998461

[10] Brucker, A.D., Doser, J.: Metamodel-based UML notations for domain-specific languages. In: Favre, J.M., Gasevic, D., Lämmel, R., Winter, A. (eds.) 4th International Workshop on Software Language Engineering (ATEM 2007) (2007)

[11] Brucker, A.D., Doser, J., Wolff, B.: A Model Transformation Semantics and Analysis Methodology for SecureUML. In: Wang, J., Whittle, J., Harel, D., Reggio, G. (eds.) MoDELS 2006. LNCS, vol. 4199, pp. 306–320. Springer, Heidelberg (2006)

[12] Brucker, A.D., Hang, I., Lückemeyer, G., Ruparel, R.: SecureBPMN: Modeling and enforcing access control requirements in business processes. In: ACM SACMAT. ACM Press (2012), doi:10.1145/2295136.2295160

[13] Brucker, A.D., Petritsch, H.: Extending access control models with break-glass. In: Carminati, B., Joshi, J. (eds.) ACM SACMAT, pp. 197–206. ACM Press (2009), doi:10.1145/1542207.1542239

[14] Dijkman, R.M., Dumas, M., Ouyang, C.: Semantics and analysis of business process models in BPMN. Information & Software Technology 50(12), 1281–1294 (2008), doi:10.1016/j.infsof.2008.02.006

[15] HIPAA: Health Insurance Portability and Accountability Act of 1996 (1996), http://www.cms.hhs.gov/HIPAAGenInfo/

[16] Jürjens, J., Rumm, R.: Model-based security analysis of the german health card architecture. Methods Inf. Med. 47(5), 409–416 (2008)

[17] Kohler, M., Brucker, A.D., Schaad, A.: Proactive Caching: Generating caching heuristics for business process environments. In: International Conference on Computational Science and Engineering (CSE), vol. 3, pp. 207–304. IEEE Computer Society (2009), doi:10.1109/CSE.2009.177

[18] Lodderstedt, T., Basin, D.A., Doser, J.: SecureUML: A UML-Based Modeling Language for Model-Driven Security. In: Jézéquel, J.M., Hussmann, H., Cook, S. (eds.) UML 2002. LNCS, vol. 2460, pp. 426–441. Springer, Heidelberg (2002)

[19] Miseldine, P.: Automated XACML policy reconfiguration for evaluation optimisation. In: Win, B.D., Lee, S.W., Monga, M. (eds.) SESS, pp. 1–8. ACM (2008), doi:10.1145/1370905.1370906

[20] Mülle, J., von Stackelberg, S., Böhm, K.: A security language for BPMN process models. Tech. rep., University Karlsruhe, KIT (2011)

[21] OASIS: eXtensible Access Control Markup Language (XACML), version 2.0 (2005), http://docs.oasis-open.org/xacml/2.0/XACML-2.0-OS-NORMATIVE.zip

[22] Object Management Group: Business process model and notation (BPMN), version 2.0 (2011), Available as OMG document formal/2011-01-03

[23] Rodríguez, A., Fernández-Medina, E., Piattini, M.: A BPMN extension for the modeling of security requirements in business processes. IEICE - Trans. Inf. Syst. E90-D, 745–752 (2007), doi:10.1093/ietisy/e90-d.4.745

[24] Sohr, K., Ahn, G.J., Gogolla, M., Migge, L.: Specification and Validation of Authorisation Constraints Using UML and OCL. In: De Capitani di Vimercati, S., Syverson, P.F., Gollmann, D. (eds.) ESORICS 2005. LNCS, vol. 3679, pp. 64–79. Springer, Heidelberg (2005)

[25] Wolter, C., Meinel, C.: An approach to capture authorisation requirements in business processes. Requir. Eng. 15(4), 359–373 (2010), doi:10.1007/s00766-010-0103-y

[26] Wolter, C., Menzel, M., Schaad, A., Miseldine, P., Meinel, C.: Model-driven business process security requirement specification. Journal of Systems Architecture 55(4), 211–223 (2009), doi:10.1016/j.sysarc.2008.10.002; Secure Service-Oriented Architectures (Special Issue on Secure SOA)

[27] Wolter, C., Schaad, A.: Modeling of Task-Based Authorization Constraints in BPMN. In: Alonso, G., Dadam, P., Rosemann, M. (eds.) BPM 2007. LNCS, vol. 4714, pp. 64–79. Springer, Heidelberg (2007)
[28] Wolter, C., Schaad, A., Meinel, C.: Deriving XACML Policies from Business Process Models. In: Weske, M., Hacid, M.-S., Godart, C. (eds.) WISE 2007 Workshops. LNCS, vol. 4832, pp. 142–153. Springer, Heidelberg (2007)

Modeling Wizard for Confidential Business Processes

Andreas Lehmann and Niels Lohmann

Universität Rostock, Institut für Informatik, 18051 Rostock, Germany
{andreas.lehmann,niels.lohmann}@uni-rostock.de

Abstract. One driver of business process management is the opportunity to reduce costs by outsourcing certain tasks to third-party organizations. At the same
time, it is undesirable that delicate information (e. g., trade secrets) "leak" to the
involved third parties, be it for legal or economic reasons. The absence of such
leaks — called *noninterference* — can be checked automatically. Such a check requires an assignment of each task of the business process as either confidential
or public. Drawbacks of this method are that (1) this assignment of every task
is cumbersome, (2) an unsuccessful check requires a corrected confidentiality
assignment although (3) the diagnosis and correction of information leaks is a
nontrivial task. This paper presents a modeling prototype that integrates the noninterference check into the early design phase of an interorganizational business
process. It not only allows for instant feedback on confidentiality assignments,
but also for an automated completion of partial assignments toward guaranteed
noninterference.

1   Introduction

One advantage of systematic business process management is the ability to outsource
individual tasks or whole subprocesses to third parties. Beside cost reduction, this allows the business owner to concentrate on the core business (specialization), to ensure
that certain regulations are met (standardization), or to exclude liability. This trend has
led to the cloud computing paradigms such as SaaS, IaaS, or PaaS.

The distributed execution of a business process adds new challenges, as a business
process is usually a very sensitive asset of a company. In this setting, *confidentiality*
of sensible information is paramount. Though the interplay with third parties can be
regulated by contracts, a business owner should never entirely trust other agents. This
paper focuses on confidentiality and studies *noninterference* (i. e., the absence of information leaks) as central correctness criterion. Noninterference guarantees that third
parties cannot deduce information on the execution of confidential tasks by observing
the execution of outsourced tasks. It is important to note that *this problem cannot be
tackled by security instruments such as encryption or access control*. Noninterference
needs to be checked at design time using a suitable business process model, because
detecting information leaks at runtime would be too late.

Recent literature [1,2,3] introduced noninterference checks and reported promising
numbers on the required resources for those checks. The prerequisite of the checks is
a fully annotated model; that is, each task is annotated whether it is confidential. This
has two major drawbacks. First, it is a tedious job for the modeler to make this decision

M. La Rosa and P. Soffer (Eds.): BPM 2012 Workshops, LNBIP 132, pp. 675–688, 2013.
© Springer-Verlag Berlin Heidelberg 2013

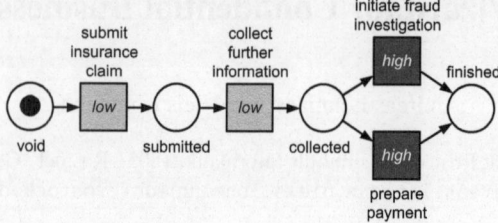

Fig. 1. Running example: Petri net model with a secure outsource strategy

for every task. Though it may be obvious for a few tasks (e. g., business decisions), it is rather arbitrary for a lot of other tasks (e. g., pure routing constructs). At the same time, the modeler has to face the dilemma that outsourcing too many tasks brings the danger of information leaks while outsourcing too few tasks raises the overall costs. Second, if the check is unsuccessful, the detected information leakage must be understood, fixed, and rechecked. This introduces another loop to the modeling process. Hence, an integrated, continuous check similar to a wizard or a spell checker with instant error detection and correction proposals would be desirable to support the modeler.

This paper makes three contributions toward this goal. First, we support the modeling of confidential business processes by instant feedback with respect to noninterference. Second, we reduce the modeling effort by completing partial confidentiality assignments while guaranteeing noninterference. We achieve this by presenting a compact representation of all valid assignments. Third, we sketch the applicability of these techniques in the early design phase of business process modeling.

The rest of this paper is organized as follows. The next section provides an overview of modeling and analyzing noninterference using business process models. Section 3 discusses how all valid assignments of a business process model can be characterized efficiently in terms of runtime and memory. We also provide experimental results. The completion of partial assignments and the integration into a business process modeling tool is presented in Sect. 4. Section 5 is dedicated to related work before Sect. 6 concludes the paper.

2   Background

2.1   Informal Introduction

Figure 1 depicts a business process, expressed as a Petri net, we shall use as running example for the rest of the paper. In this process, an insurance claim is handled in the following way: After the claim is submitted to the insurance company, further details are collected. Based on these collected facts, a decision is made to either initiate a fraud investigation due to suspicious information or to prepare the payment. In either case, the process is completed. Of course, this is only a toy example, but it can be seen as a high level view on a larger business process in which the fraud investigation itself consist of several subprocesses. Considering outsourcing within this process, basically any task is a possible candidate to reduce the insurance company's costs — in particular as this process will be executed very often. A budget analyst may therefore suggest to outsource all tasks in order to keep the process as cheap as possible, but due to the impact of a fraud investigation (despite the question whether it is justified), the insurance company may consider especially this task to be *confidential*. In contrast to the fraud investigation the submit task is supposed to be outsourced to a call center. Confidential tasks must not be outsourced. A different approach would be to perform all tasks within the company, which is indeed secure according to confidentiality, but at the same time very expensive. So neither idea (outsource everything or outsource nothing) is suitable for the management. Considering our running example with four tasks, there exist theoretically $2^4 = 16$ possible outsourcing strategies. Hence, the question raises, which one to choose with respect to costs and confidentiality.

Not all of the possible outsourcing strategies are secure with respect to confidentiality. Examples such as outsourcing everything may be obviously insecure, but let us consider a tradeoff where only the fraud investigation is performed in-house, whereas all remaining tasks are outsourced. Outsourcing the mutually exclusive tasks prepare payment while keeping the task initiate fraud investigation confidential is also not secure: Assume that all participants know the whole process (due a service agreement) and are aware of all outsourced tasks. Note that the second assumption is not unrealistic, because also outsourcing each task to a different company cannot ensure that those companies do not reallocate their tasks to another (for instance the same) company or collaborate together. So in case a participant can observe the occurrence of the task prepare payment, he can deduce that the task initiate fraud investigation was not performed, and vice versa. Therefore, it is not sufficient to only keep initiate fraud investigation confidential, but the task prepare payment needs to be confidential as well to obtain a secure outsourcing strategy. This type of example can be called a *conflict relation* between two tasks (cf. the red colored tasks in Fig. 1).

Another example of such a dependency is a *causal relation* between two tasks. Consider the task submit insurance claim to be confidential in an outsourcing strategy where all other tasks are outsourced. A participant can deduce that the task submit insurance claim has been executed after he observes the execution of task collect information.

Note that *both conclusions can be deduced from the fact that information flow between third parties and the insurance company — regardless of the use of a perfect encryption and a perfect access control*. Therefore, traditionally security mechanism are not suitable to express and ensure the mentioned confidentiality. To reason about those dependencies of confidential and public tasks, noninterference is a suitable property. In the rest of this section, we shall provide the formal background of our formalisms and sketch the verification of noninterference for business processes.

2.2 Noninterference

Noninterference is a property in terms of *information flow control*, which provides a powerful abstraction to certify confidentiality and integrity properties [4]. In the context of this paper, we concentrate on confidentiality, but integrity can be seen as a dual problem to confidentiality. Therefore a business process model is divided into two security domains (*high* for confidential, *low* for public). In the previous section, we used the term outsourcing as use case for the public domain. A flow happens whenever information meant to remain in the confidential domain *leaks* to the public domain. A business process model is assumed secure if it enforces noninterference; that is, the actions in the *high* domain do not produce an observable effect (*interference*) in the *low* domain. Interferences thus open up the possibility to deduce information about confidential behavior. If exploited, these *covert channels* violate the security requirements [5].

We shall first present how noninterference can be formalized using Petri nets. Based on this, we shall sketch the noninterference analysis in terms of Petri nets. We employ Petri nets as they combine a graphical notation with a formal semantics. Furthermore, mappings from common modeling languages, such as WS-BPEL, BPMN, and EPC, exist [6]. Finally, Petri nets are extensively used to reason about the correctness of business processes which yield to the availability of mature tool support. We consider *safe* Petri nets for the rest of the paper; that is, each place holds at most one token on all reachable markings. This eases our definitions, but introduces no restriction, because in the domain of business processes we focus on sound process models, which by definition are bounded and therefore can be expressed by safe Petri nets as well.

Definition 1 (Petri net). *A Petri net $N = [P, T, F, m_0]$ consists of two finite and disjoint sets P of* places *and T of* transitions, *a* flow relation *$F \subseteq (P \times T) \cup (T \times P)$, and an* initial marking m_0. *A* marking *$m \subseteq P$ represents a state of the Petri net and is visualized as a distribution of tokens on the places. Let $x \in (P \cup T)$. The* preset *of x is the set $^\bullet x = \{y \mid [y, x] \in F\}$, the* postset *of x is $x^\bullet = \{y \mid [x, y] \in F\}$. Transition t is* enabled *in marking m iff, $^\bullet t \subseteq m$. An enabled transition t can* fire, *transforming m into the new marking m' with $m' = (m \setminus {}^\bullet t) \cup t^\bullet$. The firing of one transition is denoted as $m \xrightarrow{t} m'$ and a sequence $\sigma \in T^*$ of transitions transforming m to m' is denoted as $m \xrightarrow{\sigma} m'$. A marking m' is* reachable *from m, if $m \xrightarrow{*} m'$ (with $*$ for an arbitrary sequence).*

To reason about noninterference, we need an extension to the Petri net definition. Therefore, transitions are partitioned into the two security domains *high* and *low* necessary for the noninterference property. We call such an extended Petri net a *labeled Petri net*, because transitions are *labeled* with a security domain. We shall use the term "Petri net" from now on as short form for "labeled Petri net".

Definition 2 (Labeled Petri net). *A* labeled Petri net *$N = [P, L, H, F, m_0]$ is a Petri net $[P, L \cup H, F, m_0]$ with $L \cap H = \emptyset$.*

Running example. In Fig. 1 the *high* security domain represents tasks that should remain confidential (red colored) and the *low* security domain represents tasks that are supposed to be outsourced (green colored).

Earlier, we gave an intuition of noninterference in our setting and mentioned already two possible kinds of problems: the conflict case and the causal case. In the conflict case, there is a mutual exclusion between two tasks which different security domains. As tasks are represented by transitions and mutually exclusion is expressed as a common preplace, this case can be straightforwardly expressed in terms of Petri nets. The causal case can be expressed similarly: a transition with security domain *high* produces a token on a place which is the preset of another task in the *low* security domain. Busi and Gorrieri [2] defined those two types as follows:

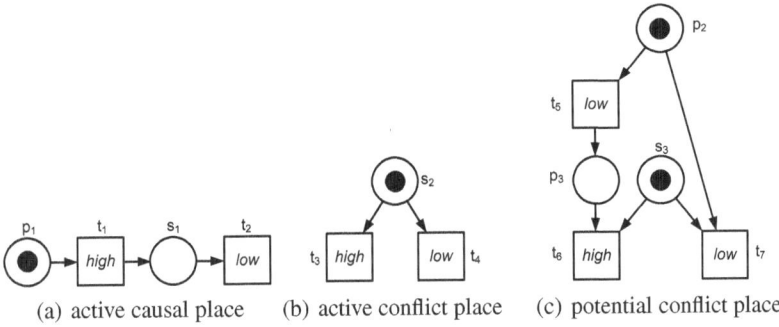

(a) active causal place   (b) active conflict place   (c) potential conflict place

Fig. 2. Patterns for potential causal and conflict places *s*

Definition 3 (Causal and conflict places s). *Let* $N = [P, L, H, F, m_0]$ *be a labeled Petri net. The place* s *is a* potential causal place *if there exists a transition* $l \in s^\bullet \cap L$ *and a transition* $h \in {}^\bullet s \cap H$. *A potential causal place* s *is an* active causal place *if, additionally, a marking* m *is reachable such that a transition sequence* σ *exists with* $m \xrightarrow{h\sigma l} m'$ *and* $s \notin t^\bullet$ *for all* $t \in \sigma$.

The place s *is a* potential conflict place *there exists a transition* $l \in s^\bullet \cap L$ *and a transition* $h \in s^\bullet \cap H$. *A potential conflict place is an* active conflict place *if, additionally, a marking* m *is reachable such that a transition sequence* σ *exists with* $m \xrightarrow{h} m'$, $m \xrightarrow{\sigma l} m''$ *and* $s \notin t^\bullet$ *for all* $t \in \sigma$.

Figure 2 illustrates the two types of possible interference places, the causal case (a) and the conflict case (b). In the causal case, the *low* labeled transition t_2 can only fire after the *high* labeled transition t_1 has fired, so the fact that t_1 (and its corresponding confidential task) has fired is leaked. In the conflict case, the two transitions t_3 and t_4 are mutually exclusive, which means that from firing of the *low* labeled transition t_4 one may deduce that the *high* labeled transition t_3 has not fired.

Based on Defs. 2 and 3 the analysis of noninterference is carried out with *Positive place-based noninterference* (PBNI+) [2]. The idea is that causal and conflict places encode the two possible leaks from the *high* to the *low* domain. A Petri net is called *secure* in terms of noninterference if each of its places is neither an active causal nor an active conflict place. One may think PBNI+ is a structural property which can be decided on the net structure. Whereas potential places are indeed identified by the net *structure*, the decision whether a potential place is an active place depends on the *behavior* of the net (viz. the presence of a transition sequence σ) [2]. Figure 2(c) depicts an example in which the place s_3 is a potential but not an active conflict place; that is, the structural conflict between t_6 and t_7 is not decided by s_3, but by p_2. How active places can be identified is part of the following section.

2.3 Verification of Noninterference

According to Def. 3, each active place can be described as a triple $[s, h, l]$ of a place s, a *high* labeled transition h and a *low* labeled transition l. More than one *high* or *low* labeled transition in the preset or postset of s yield to more triples with s. A place s is active if at least one triple is active according to Def. 3. In earlier work [1], we showed that active triples can be identified by reachability checks.

Running example (cont.). Considering the business process of our running example without any given confidentiality requirements, one would identify two potential places. The place collected is a potential causal and a potential conflict one, whereas place submitted is only a potential causal one. The corresponding triples are: (1) [collected, initiate, prepare], (2) [collected, prepare, initiate] (both with potential conflict place collected), (3) [collected, collect, initiate], (4) [collected, collect, prepare] (both with potential causal place collected), and (5) [submitted, submit, collect] (with potential causal place submitted). The introduced order is used in the continuations of the running exmaple.

3   Characterization of All Valid Assignments

3.1   Motivation

As mentioned in the introduction, even a quick PBNI+ check has several drawbacks: First, it requires a complete confidentiality assignment; that is, each transition has to be labeled with either *high* or *low*. This means that the modeler needs to make a manual decision for each transition whether the modeled task is confidential or public. Such choices can be very arbitrary, yet still affect overall noninterference. That said, if an information leak was detected, the assignment has to be manually corrected and re-checked. This results in a constant interruption of the design workflow of a business process.

To this end, we present in this section the first contribution of this paper: a characterization of all valid confidentiality assignments given a partial (or even empty) assignment. This allows to apply our approach in the very early stage of modeling and also supports the assignment of existing, but not labeled, business process models. Such a characterization has several benefits:

1. In case the set of valid assignments is empty, we can provide *immediate feedback* to the modeler. This immediate feedback is important as it can be correlated to the most recent action of the modeler, whereas later feedback would require a search for the transition whose labeling introduced an information leak.
2. If in turn the set of valid assignments is not empty, it can be used to *efficiently check* refined assignments, because any further assignment of transitions only restricts the set and a complete recalculation is not required.
3. Finally, a complete characterization allows to reason about *implicit information*. If, for instance, a certain transition is assigned to *high* in all valid assignments, then this should be immediately presented to the modeler.

Whereas previous work [1] showed that a noninterference check is typically very fast, a naive enumeration of all possible assignment has two major downsides:

1. The number of assignments grows exponentially in the number of transitions. Even with an average checking time of 24 milliseconds [1] the exponential blowup makes this enumeration not applicable to industrial models with hundreds of transitions.

2. Even if we can determine the valid assignments, an explicit representation is infeasible due to the same exponential blowup. However, only a complete set of all valid assignments gives the modeler maximal freedom to come up with an optimal outsourcing plan.

The rest of this section is dedicated to reduce the complexity required to calculate the characterization. Thereby, we first tackle the runtime by reducing the number of required checks. Then, we present a compact representation to store all valid assignments. We conclude the section with experimental results conducted with industrial business process models. The mentioned applications of the characterization and the integration into a modeling tool is subject of Sect. 4.

3.2   Reducing the Number of Checks

A given business process model with T tasks (transitions) has $2^{|T|}$ possible outsourcing strategies (assignments) in case no confidentiality assignment is given. For each assignment, one has to decide whether it is secure using PBNI+. Typically more than one potential place with at least one triple exists for each assignment. The number of all triples can be estimated by $O(|P| \cdot |T| \cdot (|T| - 1))$, following from the structure of the triples. Together with $2^{|T|}$ possible assignments one would end up with $O(2^{|T|} \cdot |P| \cdot |T| \cdot (|T| - 1))$ checks to investigate all possible assignments. This makes the approach infeasible for industrial business process models with hundreds of tasks. This section will show how this number of checks can be decreased dramatically.

Based on the definition of PBNI+, one active place is enough to violate the noninterference property. Consequently, one active triple (one active place may be detected by more than one triple) is also enough to violate PBNI+. For each assignment, it is therefore sufficient to find one active triple to convict it invalid.

Previously, we showed that triple checks can be performed independently [1] for a given assignment. In fact, this does not reduce the number of triples, but all potential critical assignments follow from the structure of the Petri net. Thus, for PBNI+ only potential causal and conflict places are relevant, which can be expressed as triples. For instance, four assignments from the process in Fig. 1 have no potential triple and are hence valid without the need of a check. For all other assignments only specific parts (the triples) of the net are interesting and necessary to decide PBNI+. Those triples follow from the net structure (one place and two connected transitions) and the labeled security domains, therefore it is sufficient to check every possible triple only once. Each triple reasons about two transitions and especially their labeling and therefore influences $2^{|T|-2}$ assignments. The number of checks is so decreased from $O(2^{|T|} \cdot |P| \cdot |T| \cdot (|T| - 1))$ to $O(|P| \cdot |T| \cdot (|T| - 1))$.

Running example (cont.). Considering the running example with the initial confidentiality requirements, where the task initiate fraud investigation shall be confidential and the task submit insurance claim is supposed to be outsourced, further checks can be ruled out. As the labeling for two tasks is fixed, the triples (1) and (4) are left to be checked for all assignments.

3.3   Compact Representation

The previous subsection showed how a few checks are sufficient to verify noninterference in all possible assignments. As motivated earlier, a characterization of all valid assignments allows for various applications, ranging from immediate feedback to the completion of incomplete assignments. Thereby, an explicit naive enumeration of all valid assignments is infeasible due to exponential blowup.

Each failed check can be understood as a constraint that needs to be satisfied by all assignments to be valid. As discussed earlier, each triple consists of a place s, a *high*-labeled transition h and a *low*-labeled transition l. If the respective check fails, the constraint $\neg(label(h) = high \wedge label(l) = low)$ expresses that this assignment is invalid. Our particular domain allows to use Boolean formulae to encode the constraints. Thereby, we use transition names as variables, the value *true* and *false* for the label *high* and *low*, respectively. The above constraint can be expressed as $\neg(h \wedge \neg l)$. The conjunction of such constraints provides an implicit description of all valid assignments, and its length is polynomial in the size of the business process model.

Given the formula φ for the whole process, any truth assignment of the variables (i. e., any assignment of *high* or *low* to the transitions) that satisfies φ characterizes a valid assignment. Given a complete assignment, this check is linear in the number of transitions. The satisfiability check (i. e., does there exist an assignment that satisfies φ?) is known to be $\mathcal{NP}$-complete for arbitrary Boolean formulae. However, the special structure of our constraints makes this a 2-SAT instance for which linear satisfiability checks are known. To check whether the assignment of certain variables can be deduced by the formula, we proceed as follows. Given a transition t, it must be assigned *true* in all satisfying assignments iff $(\varphi \implies t)$ is a tautology. Likewise, t must be assigned *false* iff $(\varphi \implies \neg t)$ is a tautology. As tautology checks can be reduced to satisfiability, checking for implicit assignment has the same linear complexity.

However, extensions of the noninterference check (e. g., intransitive noninterference [7] which additionally considers downgrading transitions with a new *downgrade* security domain) may allow for more than two security domains which would leave the 2-SAT structure and make these problems $\mathcal{NP}$-complete. To make our approach applicable in the future, we decide to represent the satisfying assignments symbolically using *binary decision diagrams* (BDDs) [8]. For our approach, BDDs offer three advantages: (1) they can represent large sets of bit vectors very compactly, (2) operations such as conjunction or deducing implicit variable assignments are very efficient, and (3) they allow for *typically* very efficient algorithms to check for satisfiability (though they can, of course, not rule out the exponential worst case).

To calculate a BDD that characterizes all valid assignments, we begin with a BDD that models a tautology; that is, allows any assignment. Then, we check for each potential causal and conflict triple whether it is an actual violation of noninterference (i.e., active places). In case a violation is found, the respective (partial) assignment is excluded by adding a constraint to the BDD. At any time, implicit or "static" assignments can be derived from the BDD using the tautology approaches described earlier. Alternatively, BDDs offer more efficient structural methods to check whether the value of a single variable is determined. Such implicit assignments can then be passed to the modeler as a support to avoid redundant manual assignments.

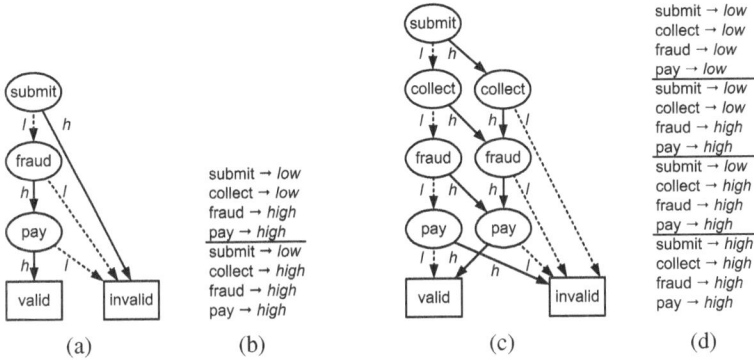

Fig. 3. Running example: BDDs

Running example (cont.). Figure 3(a) depicts the BDD that represents all valid assignments of the running example. The oval nodes are labeled with transition names and represent decisions whether to label the transition as *high* (continuous outgoing arrow) or *low* (dashed outgoing arrow). After a sequence of decisions, either the node "valid" or "invalid" is reached which describes the status of the resulting assignment. Note that Fig. 3(a) does not mention the "collect" transition: This means that either label is valid for this transition, resulting in two valid assignment (cf. Fig. 3(b)). We can further derive that the prepare payment task must be confidential in any case. In case no initial assignment is given, the resulting BDD (cf. Fig. 3(c)) characterizes two additional valid assignments: setting all transitions to *high* or all transitions to *low* (cf. Fig. 3(d)).

3.4 Experimental Results

For experimental evaluation, we used a library of 559 industrial business process models from different business branches, including financial services, ERP, supply-chain, and online sales. Details on the benchmark set and the translation into Petri nets are provided by Fahland et al. [9]. All of these nets are sound and safe. Based on their origins, the transitions are not labeled for security analysis. To this end, this is a good start for our approach, because we want to characterize all valid assignments.

As summarized in Tab. 1, a characterization for an average process is calculated in 90 milliseconds consuming 8.62 MB of memory and contains 107 nodes. The results of our experiments with industrial business processes are very promising. Even for the biggest process only 282 checks in contrast to more than 2^{100} checks are performed in less than 3 seconds. Thereby the current implementation consumes less than 10 MB of memory and also the biggest characterization can be presented with 1,314 nodes. In all cases no transition was labeled; that is, the numbers reflect the worst case. If a user labels some transitions the problem size decreases noticeable, therefore model support for industrial business processes is feasible.

4   Tool Integration and Modeling Wizard

As mentioned earlier, the complete characterization of all valid assignments is just a means to an end: In this section, we report on the prototypic integration of the discussed

Table 1. Experimental results of the 559 industrial business processes

	min	avg	max	running ex.
transitions (exponent of problem size)	1	20	100	4
causal triples (cf. Fig. 2(a))	3	34	242	3
conflict triples (cf. Fig. 2(b))	0	4	90	2
possible assignments (main factor for checks)	2	$> 10^6$	$> 10^{30}$	16
total number of triples (necessary checks)	3	38	282	5
nodes in BDD representation (cf. Fig. 3(c))	7	107	1,317	7
computation time (sec)	0.01	0.09	2.26	0.01
memory consumption (MB)	8.54	8.62	9.45	8.54

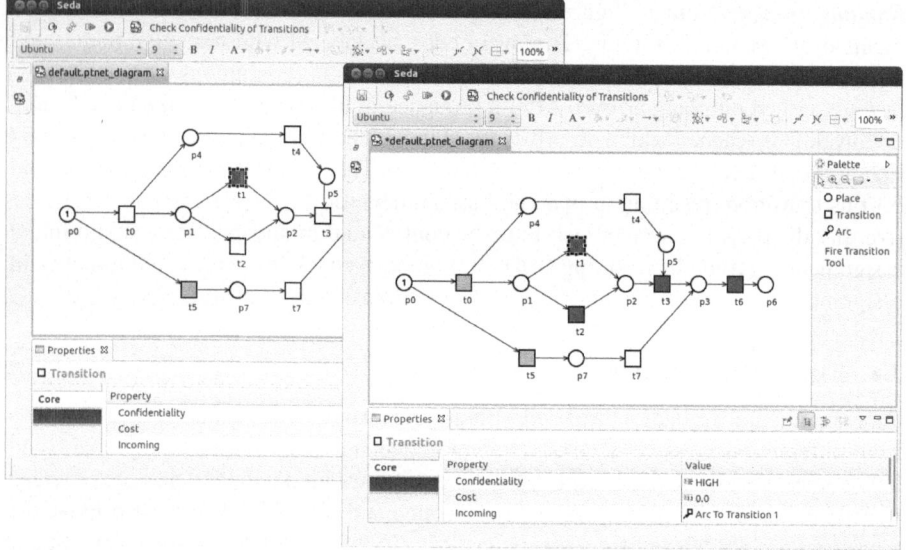

Fig. 4. Screen shots of the editor prototype. After assigning a few transitions (left), implied assignments are calculated automatically (right).

techniques into an Eclipse-based business process modeling tool and sketch several supported use cases.

To show the basic applicability of our approach, we implemented a proof of concept prototype[1] that is basically a reasoner between a verification library and a modeling tool. As editor, we extended Seda[2], an open source Eclipse-based Petri net modeling tool. Seda offers the usual functionality to model and simulate Petri nets, and was extended to label the transitions with the confidentiality levels *high* and *low*, cf. Fig.4 (left).

---

[1] Freely available at http://service-technology.org/anica.
[2] Freely available at http://service-technology.org/seda.

By pressing a button "Check Confidentiality of Transitions", the modeler can check the current assignment for noninterference[3]. In case a leak is detected, a respective error message is displayed. As our experiments showed in Sect. 3.4, the worst case check took about 2 seconds, so a frequent or continuous background check is possible. In fact, a complete verification is only necessary in case the net structure is changed. If only the assignment of transitions is changed, the validity of the assignments can be quickly checked using the calculated BDD. As a consequence, a failed check can be immediately correlated to the last edit actions and avoids a tedious search within the model for the "scapegoat" transitions.

In case the current assignment is valid, the reasoner evaluates the refined BDD and returns all implicit assignments of transitions; that is, transitions where only one possible labeling allows for a completion toward a complete valid assignment. By automatically labeling such transitions, the modeler gets an immediate feedback on his choices and does not need to make these redundant assignments manually. Of course, unwanted choices can be undone.

Figure 4 (right) depicts the automated completion of the assignment on the left. This small example shows the impact on the whole net after assigning only two transitions. As a result, only two transitions remain unlabeled. For these transitions, any labeling is still free to choose. For further details on the tool the interested is referred to [10].

5   Related Work

Security has received a lot of attention in the business process management community. In the huge area of security we focus on information flow security. Contributions related to information flow security in the business process management community can be classified as follows.

Explicit information flow. Former research clearly focus on explicit information flow and due the extensive use of Petri nets as formalism for business processes, Petri nets are also often used to reason about security. Atluri et al. [11] proposed a Chinese wall security model for decentralized workflows. Kang et al. [12] used a separation strategy for a similar purpose and provide tool support. Yildiz and Godart [13] focused on information flow policies of different principals. Barletta et al. [14] and Shafiq et al. [15] used colored Petri nets (CPN) and concentrate on role based access control to express separation of duty. Juszczyszyn [16] used CPN for mandatory access control in distributed systems. Zhang and Xiao [17] also used CPN to express and reason about the strict integrity policy, comparable with the approach of Knorr [18]. Huang and Kirchner [19] used CPN for the specification and composition of security policies. Barkaoui et al. [20] are concerned of the data consistency in a multilevel security policy according to information flow rules of the Bell-LaPadula model. In contrast to our work different properties are considered and model support is not in their scope.

Other formalism are used as well to reason about information flow security in business processes [21,22,23,24], but for almost all approaches an automated translation from existing business process modeling languages to used formalisms is missing.

---

[3] A screen cast is available at http://youtu.be/L7mbIHkGb7A.

Implicit information flow. Implicit information flow analysis of business processes is a young research strand in the business process management community. In 2009, Busi and Gorrieri [2] defined noninterference properties for Petri nets, which inspired the community of business process management.

Atluri and Huang [25] presented a kind of CPNs which can be used to automatically detect and prevent violating task dependencies. Beside explicit data flows they also consider implicit data flows. Frau et al. [3] proposed the Petri Net Security Checker, which implements PBNI+ checks for Petri nets. Accorsi et al. [26] introduced information flow nets to capture business process transformations to automatically label the model with classes to consider other properties, including data flow-based properties, separation of duties and declassification. This is indeed another kind of model support. Similar to Frau et al. [3] and Accorsi et al. [26] we presented a verification technique [1] based on reachability and implemented it in the tool Anica.

All realizations so far focus clearly on the verification of a completely assigned business process whereas we provide here a support for this necessary assignment. Only Accorsi and Wonnemann offer some kind of support in the Security Workflow Analysis Toolkit [26], but their support is based on the expression of properties and not on the business process itself. The paper [27] is an unreviewed extended abstract of this paper where we proposed first ideas. In this paper we added the concrete implementation and provided the formal details for the whole approach.

6   Conclusion and Future Work

Noninterference is an important correctness criterion for business processes that is orthogonal to classical security properties such as encryption or access control. As runtime checks do not make much sense, it has to be considered at the early design phase of a business process. So far, only the verification of noninterference was considered, whereas the design of confidential business processes was neglected. In this paper, we aimed at filling this gap by providing modeler support. We investigated how confidentiality assignments can be efficiently checked and automatically completed and integrated this "modeling wizard" into a prototypic business process modeling tool to demonstrate principal applicability.

So far, we only considered qualitative checks, but made no differentiation between assignments as long as they are valid. Consequently, the consideration of quantitative properties such as costs is an interesting direction of future research. This could allow for the completion of an assignment toward an optimum such as a cheapest outsourcing plan.

Acknowledgement. The authors cordially thank Dirk Fahland for the integration of the reasoner into Seda. This work was partially funded by the German Research Foundation in the project WS4Dsec in the priority program Reliably Secure Software Systems (SPP 1496).

References

1. Accorsi, R., Lehmann, A.: Automatic Information Flow Analysis of Business Process Models. In: Barros, A., Gal, A., Kindler, E. (eds.) BPM 2012. LNCS, vol. 7481, pp. 172–187. Springer, Heidelberg (2012)
2. Busi, N., Gorrieri, R.: Structural non-interference in elementary and trace nets. Mathematical Structures in Computer Science 19(6), 1065–1090 (2009)
3. Frau, S., Gorrieri, R., Ferigato, C.: Petri Net Security Checker: Structural Non-interference at Work. In: Degano, P., Guttman, J., Martinelli, F. (eds.) FAST 2008. LNCS, vol. 5491, pp. 210–225. Springer, Heidelberg (2009)
4. Denning, D.E., Denning, P.J.: Certification of programs for secure information flow. Commun. ACM 20(7), 504–513 (1977)
5. Lampson, B.W.: A note on the confinement problem. Commun. ACM 16(10), 613–615 (1973)
6. Lohmann, N., Verbeek, E., Dijkman, R.: Petri Net Transformations for Business Processes – A Survey. In: Jensen, K., van der Aalst, W.M.P. (eds.) ToPNoC II. LNCS, vol. 5460, pp. 46–63. Springer, Heidelberg (2009)
7. Gorrieri, R., Vernali, M.: Foundations of security analysis and design vi, pp. 125–151. Springer (2011)
8. Bryant, R.E.: Graph-based algorithms for Boolean function manipulation. IEEE Trans. Computers C-35(8), 677–691 (1986)
9. Fahland, D., Favre, C., Koehler, J., Lohmann, N., Völzer, H., Wolf, K.: Analysis on demand: Instantaneous soundness checking of industrial business process models. Data Knowl. Eng. 70(5), 448–466 (2011)
10. Lehmann, A., Fahland, D.: Information flow security for business process models - just one click away. In: BPM Demo 2012 (2012)
11. Atluri, V., Chun, S.A., Mazzoleni, P.: A chinese wall security model for decentralized workflow systems. In: ACM CCS 2001, pp. 48–57. ACM (2001)
12. Kang, M.H., Froscher, J.N., Sheth, A.P., Kochut, K., Miller, J.A.: A Multilevel Secure Workflow Management System. In: Jarke, M., Oberweis, A. (eds.) CAiSE 1999. LNCS, vol. 1626, pp. 271–285. Springer, Heidelberg (1999)
13. Yildiz, U., Godart, C.: Design and implementation of information flow-sensitive business processes. In: ECOWS 2008, pp. 177–186. IEEE Computer Society (2008)
14. Barletta, M., Ranise, S., Viganò, L.: A declarative two-level framework to specify and verify workflow and authorization policies in service-oriented architectures. Serv. Oriented Comput. Appl. 5(2), 105–137 (2001)
15. Shafiq, B., Masood, A., Joshi, J., Ghafoor, A.: A role-based access control policy verification framework for real-time systems. In: WORDS 2005, pp. 13–20. IEEE Computer Society (2005)
16. Juszczyszyn, K.: Verifying enterprise 's mandatory access control policies with coloured Petri nets. In: WETICE 2003, pp. 184. IEEE Computer Society (2003)
17. Zhang, Z.L., Hong, F., Xiao, H.J.: Verification of strict integrity policy via Petri nets. In: ICSNC 2006, p. 23. IEEE Computer Society (2006)
18. Knorr, K.: Multilevel security and information flow in Petri net workflows. Technical report, Proceedings of the 9th International Conference on Telecommunication Systems - Modeling and Analysis (2001)
19. Huang, H., Kirchner, H.: Formal specification and verification of modular security policy based on colored Petri nets. IEEE Trans. Dependable Secur. Comput. 8(6), 852–865 (2011)
20. Barkaoui, K., Ayed, R.B., Boucheneb, H., Hicheur, A.: Verification of workflow processes under multilevel security considerations. In: CRiSIS, pp. 77–84. IEEE (2008)

21. Attali, I., Caromel, D., Henrio, L., Del Aguila, F.L.: Secured information flow for asynchronous sequential processes. Electron. Notes Theor. Comput. Sci. 180(1), 17–34 (2007)
22. Bossi, A., Focardi, R., Piazza, C., Rossi, S.: Transforming Processes to Check and Ensure Information Flow Security. In: Kirchner, H., Ringeissen, C. (eds.) AMAST 2002. LNCS, vol. 2422, pp. 271–286. Springer, Heidelberg (2002)
23. Harris, W.R., Kidd, N., Chaki, S., Jha, S., Reps, T.W.: Verifying Information Flow Control over Unbounded Processes. In: Cavalcanti, A., Dams, D.R. (eds.) FM 2009. LNCS, vol. 5850, pp. 773–789. Springer, Heidelberg (2009)
24. Kovács, M., Seidl, H.: Runtime Enforcement of Information Flow Security in Tree Manipulating Processes. In: Barthe, G., Livshits, B., Scandariato, R. (eds.) ESSoS 2012. LNCS, vol. 7159, pp. 46–59. Springer, Heidelberg (2012)
25. Atluri, V., Huang, W.K.: An extended Petri net model for supporting workflow in a multi-level secure environment. In: DBSec 1996. IFIP Conference Proceedings 79, pp. 240–258. Chapman & Hall (1997)
26. Accorsi, R., Wonnemann, C., Dochow, S.: SWAT: A security workflow toolkit for reliably secure process-aware information systems. In: ARES 2011, pp. 692–697. IEEE (2011)
27. Lehmann, A., Lohmann, N.: Model support for confidential service-oriented business processes. In: ZEUS 2012, Bamberg, Germany (2012)

Towards Security Risk-Oriented Misuse Cases

Inam Soomro and Naved Ahmed

Institute of Computer Science, University of Tartu
J. Liivi 2, 50409 Tartu, Estonia
{inam,naved}@ut.ee

Abstract. Security has turn out to be a necessity of information systems (ISs) and information *per se*. Nevertheless, existing practices report on numerous cases when security aspects were considered only at the end of the development process, thus, missing the systematic security analysis. Misuse case diagrams help identify security concerns at early stages of the IS development. Despite this fundamental advantage, misuse cases tend to be rather imprecise; they do not comply with security risk management strategies, and, thus, could lead to misinterpretation of the security-related concepts. Such limitations could potentially result in poor security solutions. This paper applies a systematic approach to understand how misuse case diagrams could help model organisational assets, potential risks, and security countermeasures to mitigate these risks. The contribution helps understand how misuse cases could deal with security risk management and support reasoning for security requirements and their implementation in the software system.

Keywords: Security risk management, Misuse cases, Security engineering, Information system security.

1 Introduction

During the last two decades, line between digital and social life is diminishing, leading that modern society is mainly dependent on information system (IS) and its security. The demand for IS security is constantly growing. Also developing and maintaining system security is increasingly gaining attention. Consideration of IS security at the early stages of software development is also acknowledged in [18]. The security breaches in IS can lead to the negative consequences. The practitioners of IS security must inspect security threats with a negative perspective from the very beginning of IS development process. Consideration of security at early development stages assists to analyse and estimate security measures of the IS to be developed.

This paper discusses the security risk management at requirement elicitation and analysis stage. We will consider the question *"how security risk management could be addressed using misuse case diagrams?"*. To answer this question we analyse misuse cases proposed by Sindre and Opdahl [18]. The misuse case diagrams [17, 18] are one of the possible techniques to relate security analysis and functional requirements of software systems. The main goal is to model negative scenarios with respect to functional requirements. The misuse cases are already proved to be useful in industry [15].

M. La Rosa and P. Soffer (Eds.): BPM 2012 Workshops, LNBIP 132, pp. 689–700, 2013.
© Springer-Verlag Berlin Heidelberg 2013

Existing misuse cases is relatively a simple language, since it contains few constructs to model security concerns. However the previous analysis [9] showed several limitations of misuse cases; for example, misuse cases do not comply with security risk management strategies, because they lack several concrete constructs to address secure assets, security risks and their countermeasures; misuse cases lack distinct constructs for representing security risk concepts. These limitations could result in misinterpretation of the security-related concepts leading to poor security solutions. In this paper we tend to propose few improvement to the misuse cases diagrams.

We apply a systematic approach to understand how misuse case diagrams could help to model organisational assets, potential system risks, and security requirements to mitigate these risks. More specifically we introduce new constructs to extend the misuse cases in order to align their constructs with the concepts of Information Systems Security Risk Management (ISSRM) domain model [11,12]. The benefit of syntactical and semantic extensions is that they introduce the missing semantics in to the language. The domain model is a touchstone to verify if the concepts presented are acceptable and appropriate for the security risk management.

The structure of the paper is organised as follows: in Section 2 we provide background knowledge needed for our study. In Section 3, we describe our research method and introduce Security Risk-oriented Misuse Cases (SROMUC) through an online banking example [1,8]. Next we discuss alignment of SROMUC to ISSRM. In Section 4 we review the related work, discuss our results and conclude our study.

2   Background

2.1   Information System Security Risk Management (ISSRM)

Information System Security Risk Management (ISSRM) [11,12] is a systematic approach, which addresses the security related issues in an IS domain. The model is defined after a survey of risk management and security related standards, security risk management methods and software engineering frameworks [12]. The domain model (see Fig. 1) supports the alignment of security modelling languages. It improves the IS security and security modelling languages as it conforms to the security risk management of organizations. The model describes three different conceptual categories:

Asset-related concepts describe the organization's assets grouped as *business asset* and *IS asset*. It also defines the *security criterion* as a constraint of a business asset expressed as *integrity, confidentiality* and *availability*.

Risk-related concepts define *risk*, potential harm to business, it is composed of a threat that contains one or more vulnerabilities, if executed successfully, harms the system assets which has negative consequences on assets defined as an *impact*. They negate the security criterion imposed by the business asset. An *event* is an abstraction aggregated as a threat and vulnerability where *vulnerability* is a weakness in a system that can be exploited by threat agent. A *threat* is a way to inflict an attack. It harms IS and business asset carried out by a threat agent and an attack method to target IS assets. *Threat Agent* is an attacker that initiates a threat to harm the IS asset. *Attack Method* is a mean through which a threat agent executes a threat.

Risk treatment related concepts define a risk treatment *decision* to avoid, reduce, retain, or transfer the potential risks. It is refined by the *security requirement.* A *control* implements the security requirement.

The ISSRM process [11,12] is a 6-step process, based on existing risk analysis methodologies and standards. It starts with *context and asset identification* of the organization, proceeding to *determine the security objectives* for identified assets. Next, *risk analysis and assessment* to examine and estimate potential risks and its impacts. In next step, *risk treatment decisions* are taken to identify the security requirements. Finally, *security control* is implemented as security requirement. The process is iterative which may identify new risks and security controls.

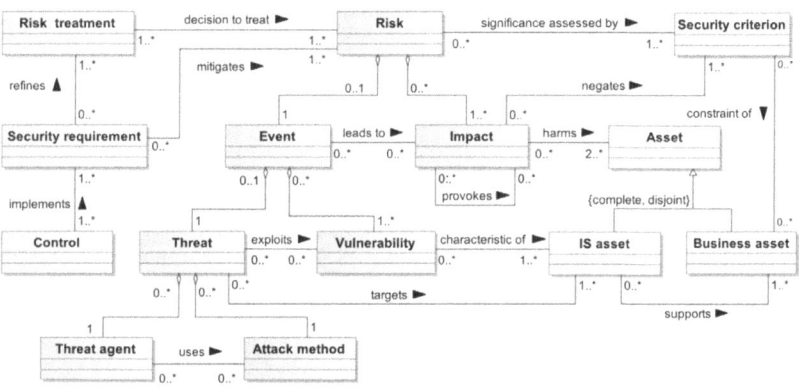

Fig. 1. ISSRM Domain Model [11]

2.2   Misuse Cases

Misuse cases are proposed by Sindre and Opdhal in [18]. They have extended the standard UML use cases to model security concerns at the early stages of software system development. The misuse cases include both the graphical notation and textual representation. Sindre and Opdahl define *misuse case* as a list or sequence of steps, if performed by an agent successfully, cause harm to the stakeholder and/or to the system. They define *misuser* as an actor that is willing to use the system with unfavourable intents. Initially, only threats were modelled as misuse cases. Later on, Sindre and Opdahl adapted the concept of security use case discussed by Firesmith [6] where security use cases are defined as a function to protect the system assets from the identified risks. In [16] Røstad has extended the misuse cases with a concept of vulnerability as weakness of the system (see a grey-filled use case in Fig. 3).

3   Security Risk-Oriented Misuse Cases (SROMUC)

This section describes the research method used to develop SROMUC. We illustrate SROMUC using three different security scenarios on asset *integrity* (see Fig. 2, 3, and 4), *confidentiality* (see Fig. 5), and *availability* (see Fig. 6) in an example of online banking. This section results in a conceptual alignment between SROMUC and ISSRM domain model.

3.1   Research Method

The main research objective of this study is to enable misuse cases to support the security risk management during the IS development. We followed a 3-step research method: firstly, we conduct literature review of security in IS and the ISSRM domain model to identify the security risk concepts. Secondly, we investigate how the misuse case diagrams express the security risk concepts. Hence, we observed the limitations of misuse cases in modelling the ISSRM concepts and executing the risk management process. Lastly, we define misuse case extensions, thus resulting in the Security Risk-oriented Misuse Cases (SROMUC). The extensions are done on all three components of the modelling language, namely concrete syntax, meta-model and semantics.

3.2   Scenario 1: SROMUC Modelling for Integrity

We illustrate the application of SROMUC using the online banking example [1, 8]. This scenario is particularly focussed on the IS integrity. To achieve better under-standability, we split the scenario to 3 models[1]: one for assets (see Fig. 2), one for security threats (see Fig. 3), and one for security requirements (see Fig. 4).

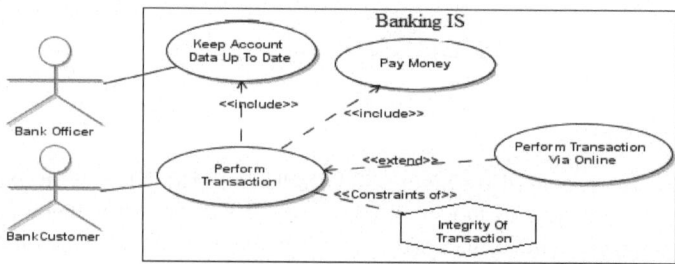

Fig. 2. Asset Modelling

Asset Model. In Fig. 2, we illustrate the context of an online banking IS in a use case diagram. A *security criterion* is a security constraint imposed on *business use case* (i.e., business asset). The example focusses on the bank customer and bank officer who both communicate with Banking IS. The Bank Customer and Bank Officer are the assets characterising the users of the system in reference to ISSRM domain model. The bank customer seeks to Perform Transaction and bank officer seeks to Keep Account Data Up To Date. The Perform Transaction *includes* two use cases Pay Money and Keep Account Data Up To Date and *extends* Perform Transaction Via Online. Perform Transaction has a *security criterion* Integrity of Transaction represented as a *hexagon* (see Fig. 2) as it characterises a security constraint of a

---

[1] To create these models we use the Microsoft Visio tool.

business use case (i.e., Perform Transaction). In Fig. 2, a dotted line with stereo type *constraints of* is linked from *business use case* (i.e., Perform Transaction) to *security criterion* (i.e., Integrity of Transaction) shows the relationship between the two. According to ISSRM domain model we identified Perform Transaction as the business asset that has some business value. Hence Perform Transaction Via Online supports the business asset and is considered as an IS asset.

   Risk Model. In Fig. 3, we model the potential security threat scenario. A *misuser* (i.e., Attacker) initiates a *misuse case* (i.e., Intercept Money *includes* Transfer money to another account and Change details of transaction) by exploiting the *vulnerability* (i.e., Unsecure Network Channel) in a *use case* (i.e., IS asset). Following [10] in Fig. 3, this *vulnerability* is represented by filled grey use case. The *misuse case* Intercept Payment *threatens* the *use case* Perform Transaction Via Online (i.e., IS Asset). The threat Intercept Money *leads to* an *impact* (i.e., Money Transferred to Unintended Account) which *harms* the *business use case* (i.e., Perform Transaction) and disaffirms the *security criterion* (i.e., Integrity of Transaction). An *impact* is a state of system that is represented as *rounded rectangle* (see Fig. 3). A *misuse case* is linked to impact using *leads to* relationship. On one hand, an *impact* disaffirms the *security criterion* linked with *negates* relationship. On another hand *impact harms* a *business use case* (i.e., Perform Transaction).

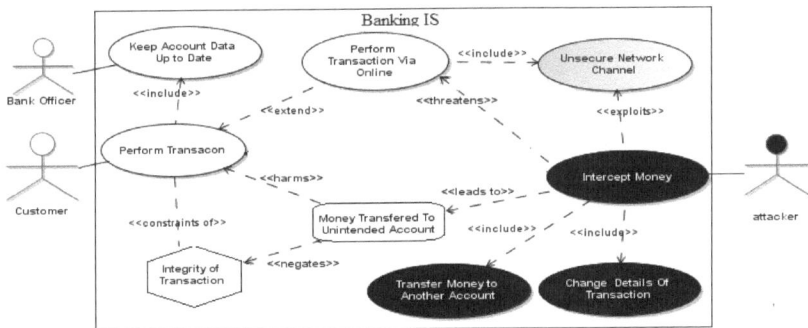

Fig. 3. Threat Modelling

   Risk Treatment Model. The ISSRM domain model defines the risk treatment, control and its implementation. However, SROMUC does not support the modelling of these concepts but security requirement is modelled as a *security use case*. The *security use case* is represented as a *use case with a lock inside* (see Fig. 4). In Fig. 4, we present the security requirement for identified threats. The *use case* Perform Transaction Via Online (i.e., IS Asset) *includes* a *security use cases* (i.e., Apply Cryptographic Procedures and Use Secure Communication Protocol). The *security use case mitigates* the *misuse case* (i.e., Intercept Money). It ensures *security criterion* (i.e., Integrity of Payment) imposed by *business use case* (i.e., Perform Transaction).

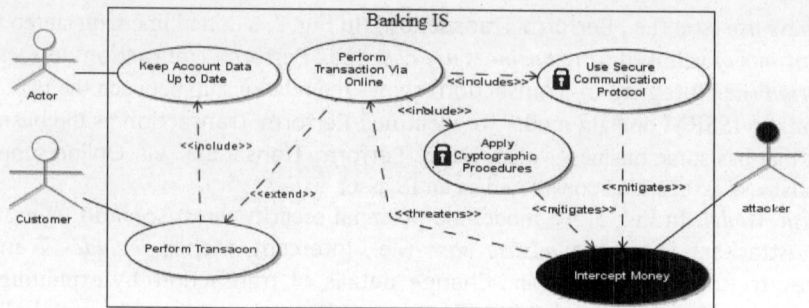

Fig. 4. Security Requirement Modelling

3.3   Scenario 2: SROMUC Modelling for Availability

In Fig. 5, we model an online banking IS [1, 8] for Availability of Service. In our example, the *business use case* (i.e., Perform Transaction) has a constraint of *security criterion* (i.e., Availability Of Online Service). The *misuser* (i.e., Attacker) initiates a *misuse case* (i.e., Make Online Service Unavailable *includes* Initiate Half Opened Connections To Server). It exploits the *vulnerability* (i.e., Allow Unlimited Number Of Connections) included in a *use case* Perform Transaction Via Online (i.e., IS Asset). The *misuse case* Make Online Service Unavailable *threatens use case* Perform Transaction Via Online (i.e., IS asset) and *leads to* an *impact* (i.e., Availability Of Service Is Compromised), moreover, it *harms* the business use case Perform Transaction. The *impact* of the *misuse case negates* the *security criterion*.

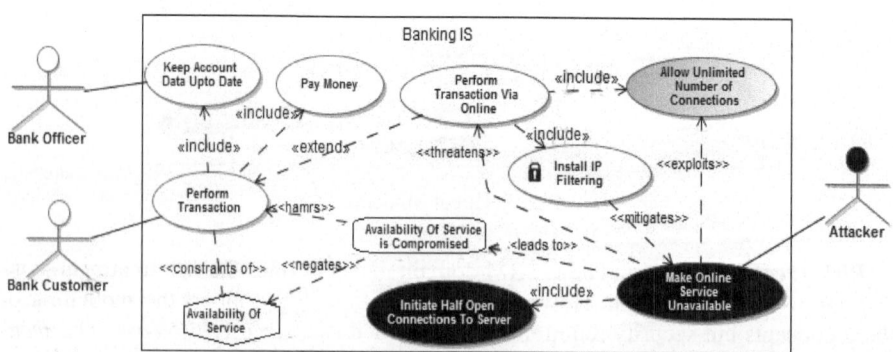

Fig. 5. Modelling for Availability of Service

3.4   Scenario 3: SROMUC Modelling for Confidentiality

In Fig. 6, we model the example of an online banking IS [1, 8] for the Confidentiality Of Data. In this example, the *business use case* (i.e., Perform Transaction) has a constraint of *security criterion* (i.e., Confidentiality Of Transaction). The *use case*

Perform Transaction Via Online (i.e., IS asset) *includes* another *use case* (i.e., Ensure Account privacy *includes* Enter PIN Code) for securing an online transaction. The *misuser* (i.e., Attacker) initiates a *misuse case* (i.e., Steal Account Data *includes* Retrieve Transaction Data *includes* Disclose Transaction Data) by exploiting the *vulnerability* (i.e., Data Is Not Encrypted and Accept Malicious Data). The *misuse case* (i.e., Steal Account Data) *threatens* the *use case* Perform Transaction Via Online (i.e., IS asset) and *leads to* an *impact* (i.e., Confidentiality Of Data Is Compromised), moreover, It also *harms* the *business use case* (i.e., Perform Transaction). The *impact* of the *misuse case negates* the *security criterion*.

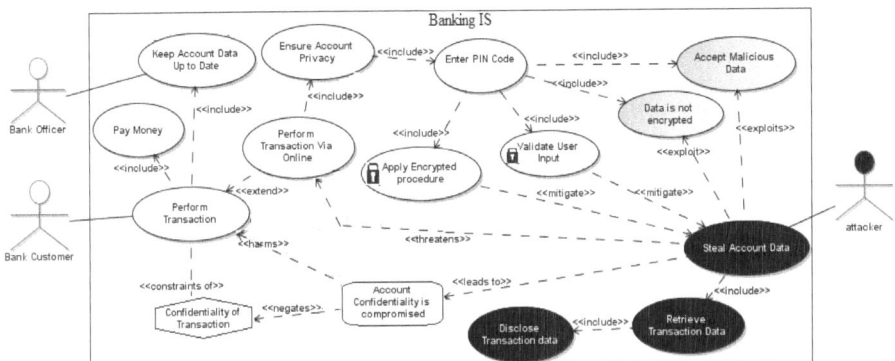

Fig. 6. Modelling for Confidentiality of Data

3.5   Concept Alignment of SROMUC and ISSRM

In [9] authors discuss the alignment between the misuse cases and the ISSRM domain model. However it presents only the correspondences, overlaps or/and similarities. In this section we describe the alignment of SROMUC with the concepts found in ISSRM domain model. In Table 1, 2 and 3, first column outlines the ISSRM concepts. The second column expresses their synonyms found in the literature. The third column distinguishes the concepts and relationship. The last column defines the SROMUC visual constructs.

Alignment of Asset-Related Concepts. In Table 1, we introduce SROMUC syntax to represent the ISSRM asset-related concepts. In ISSRM domain model, assets correspond to *Actor* and *Use case* in SROMUC. The business asset and the IS asset are modelled as a *use case*. The *supports relationship* in ISSRM between IS asset and business assets is expressed using *extends* and *includes relationships*. We introduce *hexagon* construct in SROMUC to represent the ISSRM *security criterion*. A *security criterion* is the constraint on business asset therefore the *hexagon* is linked to *business use case* through dotted line with *constraint of relationship*.

Alignment of Risk-Related Concepts. In Table 2, we introduce the SROMUC syntax to represent the ISSRM risk-related concepts. In SROMUC, a *threat agent* is represented as *misuser, attack method* as *misuse case* and *vulnerability* as a *use case* filled in grey. A *threat* is modelled as a combination of *misuser* and *misuse case*

Table 1. Asset Related Concepts (C – Concept, R – Relationships)

ISSRM Concepts	Synonyms	Type	SROMUC Syntax
Assets		C	actor
Business Asset	Business Use Case	C	
IS Asset	IS Use Case	C	
Security Criterion	Security Constraint	C	
Supports	-	R	_<<extends>>_> _ _<<includes>>_>
Constraints of	Restriction	R	<<constraints of>>

(i.e., misuser communicates with misuse case). The ISSRM *targets relationship* is represented as an SROMUC *threatens relationship*. We introduced a *rounded rectangle* to model the *impact* concept of ISSRM.

In order to be compliant with ISSRM domain model, we also introduce the *exploits*, *leads to*, *harms* and *negates* relationships. *Exploits* relationship defines a link between *misuse case* and the *vulnerability* whereas the *leads to* relationship defines a link between the *misuse case* and the *impact*. The *harms* relationship defines the link between an *impact* and a *business use case* whereas a *negates* relationship defines a link between an *impact* and the *security criterion* (see Table 2). We combine the concepts of *threat agent, attack method, vulnerability,* and *impact* all together to represent an *event*, where a *risk* is understood as a combination of *event* and the *impact*.

Alignment of Risk Treatment-Related Concepts. In risk treatment-related concepts, we update the visual syntax of *security use case* by adding a padlock to *security use case*, which represents *security requirement* (see Table 3). The ISSRM *mitigates relationship* is modelled with *mitigates relationship* from *security use cases* (i.e., security requirement) to *misuse case* in SROMUC.

Table 2. Alignment of Risk related Concepts(C – Concepts, R – Relationships)

ISSRM Concepts	Synonyms	Type	SROMUC Syntax
Risk	Hazard	C	Misuser <<includes>> Vulnerability <<include>> Misuse Case <<threatens>> Asset <<leads to>> Impact
Impact	Effect	C	Impact
Event	Incident	C	Misuser Misuse Case <<exploit>> Vulnerability <<include>> <<threatens>> Asset
Attack Method	Violence	C	Misuse Case
Vulnerability	Weakness	C	Vulnerability

Table 2. *(Continued)*

Threat Agent	Attacker	C	
Threat	Hazard	C	
Exploits	-	R	----<<exploits>>---->
Negates	Denies,	R	-----<<negates>>---->
Harms	-	R	<<harms>> --------------->
Leads to	-	R	----<<leads to>>--->
Characteristics of	-	R	<<includes>> ----------> <<extends>> ---------->
Uses	-	R	————————————

Table 3. Risk Treatment related Concepts (C – Concepts, R – Relationships)

ISSRM Concepts	Synonyms	Type	SROMUC Syntax
Risk Treatment		C	
Security Requirement	Countermeasure	C	
Control		C	-
Refines		R	-
Mitigates	Diminishes	R	--<<mitigates>>-->
Implements			-

3.6   Abstract Syntax of Security Risk-oriented Misuse Cases

In Section 3.1, we presented the SROMUC before abstract syntax due to the simple introduction of the language. However, to illustrate the application of proposed SROMUC, we need to introduce its abstract syntax in Fig. 7. The major elements in the meta-model are an *Actor OR Misuser* and *Use OR Misuse Case*. *Actor OR Misuser* initiates the *communication* to interact with *Use OR Misuse Case*. Their cardinality shows that an *Actor or Misuser* can communicate with one or more *Use or Misuse Case*. *Actor* and *misuser* are the specialisations of an *Actor OR Misuser*. *Use Or Misuse case* can *includes* or *extends* another *Use OR Misuse Case*. The *Use Case, Vulnerability* and *Misuse Case* are the specialization of *Use OR Misuse Case*. The *Use Case* includes one or more Vulnerabilities that can be exploited by one or more misuse cases. A *Misuse Case* threatens (i.e., *threatening*) one or more use cases. A *Misuse Case Leads To* one or more *Impact*. An *Impact Harms* one or more use cases (see Fig. 3) by negating one or more *Security Criterion* define as *Constraint Of* on that *use case*. A *Security Use Case* is a specialised *Use Case* that *Mitigates* one or more *Misuse Cases*.

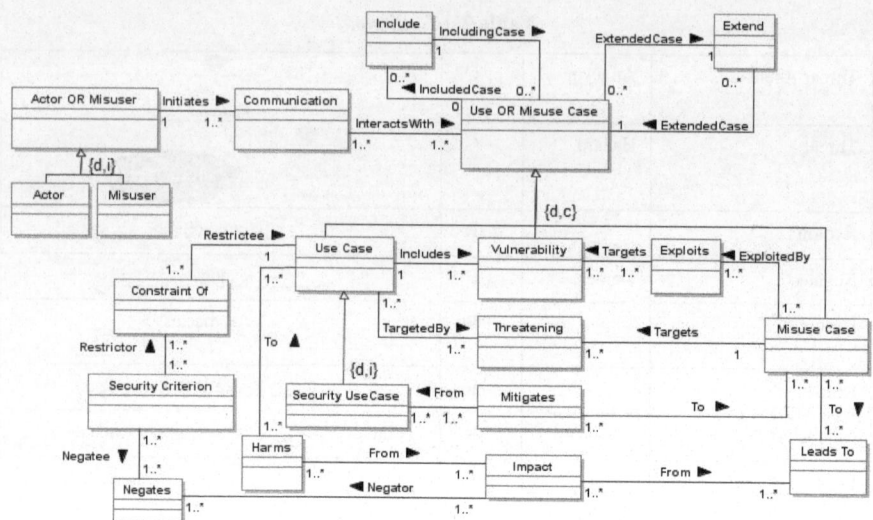

Fig. 7. Meta-model of SROMUC

4   Discussion and Conclusion

In this paper, we have analysed how misuse cases can be used to manage security risks at the early stages of the IS development. Firstly, we identified the limitations in existing misuse cases with respect to the ISSRM domain model. Secondly, we extend the language syntax and semantics to respect the ISSRM domain model (see, Tables 1, 2 and 3). This work is a part of the larger effort to align several modelling languages to the ISSRM model that define the semantics at full extend and develop a systematic model transformation-based approach for secure IS development.

4.1   Related Work

Security Risk Management. The ISSRM covers the identification and specification of security risks, and also supports the risk management process, which focusses on the whole IS, instead of defining security requirements for one or more IS components. The ISSRM approach could potentially be applicable during the IS development while other approaches (see details in [11]) are mainly focused on an existing IS (not its development) and also lacks the Requirement Engineering (RE) activities [11]. In Automated Risk and Utility Management (AURUM) framework [5], when the controls are selected, the decision makers are informed along with the consequences. Whereas, ISSRM integrate the risk management tasks throughout all the stages of IS development. Hence, the risk management tasks and IS development go parallel. Herrmann et al. [7] present a Risk-based Security Requirement, Elicitation and Prioritization (RiskREP) method for managing IT security risks. It defines a set of security requirements, which outline how security as the quality goal can be achieved. It performs Business-IT-alignment and prioritises the IT requirement. Similarly,

ISSRM align these concepts by supporting the definition of security for the key IS constituents and addresses the IS security risk management process at three different conceptual levels (see Section 2.1).

Misuse Cases. There have been few studies carried out on misuse cases and its extension. In [13, 14] McDermott and Fox have proposed abuse cases to explore how threats and countermeasures could be modelled using standard UML use case but keeping abuse cases in a separate model. Abuse case focusses on security requirements whereas our approach is aligned with ISSRM and focusses on the overall security risk management. It identifies vulnerabilities and threats, and analyses potential risks and their impacts. Therefore, the elicited security requirements are aligned with the functional system requirements. In [2] Alexander has considered how security use cases can be threatened by misuse cases. Matulevičius *et al.* [9] have aligned misuse cases with ISSRM however they leave the misuse case extensions for the future development. In this paper the extensions of the misuse cases are built on the previous work of Matulevičius *et al.* [9] and covers the complete security risk management strategy of an organisation at the early development stage.

4.2   Discussion

SROMUC is an approach to elicit security requirements at the early stages of the system development. It will potentially help designers, architects and analysts to understand the potential threats and security attacks. At both the architecture and design stages, risk analysis is a necessity. The SROMUC approach enables the security analysts to discover the architectural flaws so that their mitigation could begin early in the system development. Otherwise disregarding the risk analysis at this level leads to costly problems later. In practice, system stakeholders are not motivated to invest on security concerns, as it does not add direct value to the systems' functionality. The proposed SROMUC strengthens the misuse case diagrams by extending their syntax and semantics. The proposed graphical extensions are not intuitive and they related to the security concerns supported by the ISSRM domain model. However the primary idea is to keep it comprehensible and to compliable with the original definition of (mis)use cases. We differentiate the construct for impact and security criterion from the standard UML use case constructs. The security use case construct has been enhanced to differentiate security requirements from the functional requirements. In [9] Matulevičius *et al.* have suggested to differentiate the concepts of the IS asset and the business asset. But here, we did not differentiate the assets as it changes the definition of original use case construct. We make an exception regarding the security use because it addresses the system functionality in terms of security countermeasures. Regarding the completeness of alignment between SROMUC and ISSRM domain model, SROMUC does not address the risk treatment and control implementation.

SROMUC is not the only approach that has been aligned to ISSRM domain model. Currently ISSRM is becoming a common model [11] to understand security risk modelling using different modelling languages, like BPMN [3], Secure Tropos [10], KAOS extensions to security [11], and Mal-activities [4]. Finally, this may lead to interoperability between different security languages.

Although in the online banking example we have illustrated the applicability and performance of our proposal, we acknowledge the importance of the industrial case study to validate the SROMUC in the practice. As a future work, we also plan to experiment the language in a case study to validate its usefulness and effectiveness.

Acknowledgement. We would like to express our gratitude to Dr. Raimundas Matulevičius for his invaluable contributions in completing this research.

References

1. Ahmed, N., Matulevičius, R., Mouratidis, H.: A Model Transformation from Misuse Cases to Secure Tropos. In: Proc of the CAiSE 2012 Forum at the 24th Int. Conf. (CAiSE), pp. 7–14. CEUR-WS (2012)
2. Alexander, I.: Misuse cases: Use cases with Hostile Intent. IEEE Soft. 20(1), 58–66 (2003)
3. Altuhhova, O., Matulevičius, R., Ahmed, N.: Towards Definition of Secure Business Processes. In: Bajec, M., Eder, J. (eds.) CAiSE Workshops 2012. LNBIP, vol. 112, pp. 1–15. Springer, Heidelberg (2012)
4. Chowdhury, M.J.M., Matulevičius, R., Sindre, G., Karpati, P.: Aligning Mal-activity Diagrams and Security Risk Management for Security Requirements Definitions. In: Regnell, B., Damian, D. (eds.) REFSQ 2011. LNCS, vol. 7195, pp. 132–139. Springer, Heidelberg (2012)
5. Ekelhart, A., Fenz, S., Neubauer, T.: AURUM: A Framework for Information Security Risk Management. In: HICSS 2009, pp. 1–10. IEEE Computer Society (2009)
6. Firesmith, D.: Security Use Cases. Journal of Object Technology 2(3), 53–64 (2003)
7. Herrmann, A., Morali, A., Etalle, S., Wieringa, R.J.: RiskREP: Risk-based Security Requirements Elicitation and Prioritization. In: Perspectives in Business Informatics Research, Riga, pp. 155–162. Riga Technical University (2011)
8. van Lamsweerde, A.: Elaborating Security Requirements by Construction of Intentional Anti-Models. In: Proceedings of the 26th International Conference on Software Engineering, ICSE 2004, pp. 148–157. IEEE Computer Society (2004)
9. Matulevičius, R., Mayer, N., Heymans, P.: Alignment of Misuse Cases with Security Risk Management. In: Proceedings of 3rd International Conf. on Availability, Reliability and Security, pp. 1397–1404. IEEE Computer Society (2008)
10. Matulevičius, R., Mouratidis, H., Mayer, N., Dubois, E., Heymans, P.: Syntactic and Semantic Extensions to Secure Tropos to Support Security Risk Management. J. UCS 18(6), 816–844 (2012)
11. Mayer, N.: Model-based Management of Information System Security Risk. Ph.D. thesis, University of Namur (2009)
12. Mayer, N., Heymans, P., Matulevičius, R.: Design of a Modelling Language for Information System Security Risk Management. In: Proceedings of the First International Conference on Research Challenges in Information Science, RCIS 2007, pp. 121–132 (2007)
13. McDermott, J.: Abuse-Case-Based Assurance Arguments. In: Proc. of the 17th Annual Comp. Security Applications Conf., ACSAC 2001, pp. 366. IEEE Computer Society (2001)
14. McDermott, J., Fox, C.: Using Abuse Case Models for Security Requirements Analysis. In: Proceedings of ACSAC 1999, pp. 55–66. IEEE Computer Society (1999)
15. Pauli, J.J., Xu, D.: Trade-off Analysis of Misuse Case-based Secure Software Architectures: A Case Study. In: Proc. of MSVVEIS Workshop, pp. 89–95. INSTICC Press (2005)
16. Røstad, L.: An Extended Misuse Case Notation: Including Vulnerabilities and The Insider Threat. In: Proc. 12th Working Conf. REFSQ 2006 (2006)
17. Sindre, G., Opdahl, A.L.: Templates for Misuse Case Description. In: Proc. of the 7th International Workshop on REFSQ 2001 (2001)
18. Sindre, G., Opdahl, A.L.: Eliciting Security Requirements with Misuse Cases. Requir. Eng. 10(1), 34–44 (2005)

A Process Deviation Analysis Framework

Benoît Depaire[1,2,*], Jo Swinnen[1], Mieke Jans[1], and Koen Vanhoof[1]

[1] Hasselt University, Agoralaan Building D, 3590 Diepenbeek, Belgium
{jo.swinnen,benoit.depaire,mieke.jans,koen.vanhoof}@uhasselt.be
[2] Research Foundation Flanders (FWO), Egmontstraat 5, 1000 Brussels, Belgium

Abstract. Process deviation analysis is becoming increasingly important for companies. This paper presents a framework which structures the field of process deviation analysis and identifies new research opportunities. Application of the framework starts from managerial questions which relate to specific deviation categories and methodological steps. Finally a general outline to detect high-level process deviations is formulated.

Keywords: Conformance checking, Deviation Detection, High-level Deviations, Deviation Diagnosis, Process Mining.

1 Introduction

In order to understand and control business processes, reliable normative process models are crucial. However, studies [7, 8] show that real process executions often deviate from their designed model. Some deviations are desirable and provide process flexibility, while others are errors or indications of fraud. Monitoring process deviations is needed for internal control purposes and has become increasingly important (cfr. Sarbanes-Oxley Act (2002),Basel II (2004) and HIPAA (1996)).

The current state of conformance checking research reveals a strong focus on questions such as "Does a case deviate?" and "Where does the process deviates?". More important questions from a managerial perspective, such as "How does the process deviate?" and "What is causing these deviations?" received much less attention. Neither does the current literature make a clear distinction between different natures of process deviations and the possible consequences.

This paper provides a managerial framework which guides and structures process deviation analysis. The remainder of this paper is organized as follows: section 2 describes the process deviation analysis framework; section 3 suggests a formal approach to detect high-level process deviations; section 4 covers related work; and section 5 concludes the work.

---

* The authors wish it to be known that, in their opinion, both first two authors should be regarded as joint First Authors.

M. La Rosa and P. Soffer (Eds.): BPM 2012 Workshops, LNBIP 132, pp. 701–706, 2013.
© Springer-Verlag Berlin Heidelberg 2013

2   Process Deviation Analysis Framework (PDA-framework)

Figure 1 presents the Process Deviation Analysis framework (PDA-framework). This framework structures process deviation research and identifies three important dimensions, i.e. the deviation category, the methodological research steps and the managerial questions to be addressed. Note that this framework starts from a business perspective rather than focussing on the technical aspects.

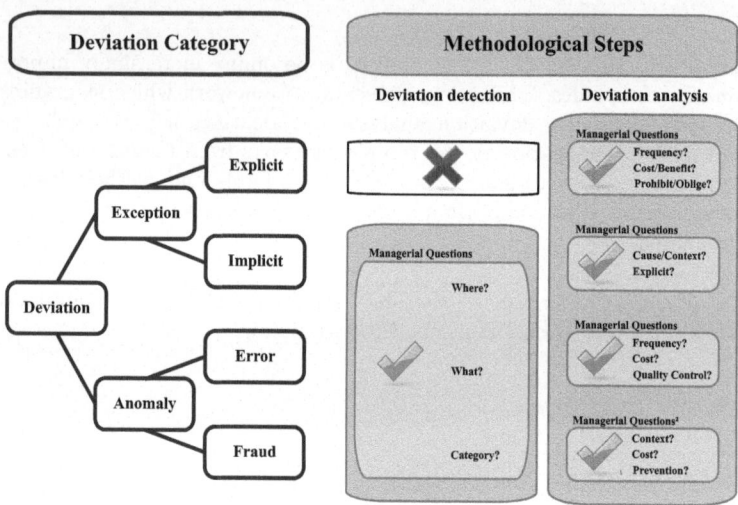

Fig. 1. The PDA-framework

2.1   Process Deviation Categories

Deviation denotes the fact that a process execution is not conform to the normative process model. A first distinction must be made between *exceptions* and *anomalies*. Exceptions are acceptable and guarantee necessary flexibility to operate effectively. *Anomalies* are deviations that provoke undesirable business results.

Explicit and Implicit Exceptions. Exceptions can be divided into *Explicit Exceptions* and *Implicit Exceptions*. Explicit exceptions are widely accepted and are either explicitly depicted in the process model or described by a set of business rules. Implicit exceptions are not formalized and are more ad-hoc, e.g. when an employee asks his supervisor to skip a less relevant activity to operate more quickly.

Errors and Fraud. Among anomalies, a distinction can be made between (operational) errors and fraud. *(Operational) Errors* refer to mistakes in the process execution caused by information systems, human mistakes or a combination of both. *Fraud* is the worst kind of process deviation and refers to deliberate actions by employees to work around the system for personal gains at the expense of the company.

2.2 Methodological Steps and Managerial Questions

The second and third part of the PDA-framework identify respectively two methodological steps and several managerial questions in process deviation analysis. The PDA-framework is a managerial framework and its application should always start from a specific managerial question regarding process deviations. Based on this question, the PDA-framework identifies the deviation type of interest and the appropriate methodological step.

Process Deviation Detection. For all deviations, except explicit exceptions, analysis always starts with a set of three managerial questions: "Where do deviations occur?", "What kind of deviations do occur?" and "To which deviation category do they belong?". All three questions deal with the first methodological step of detecting process deviations. For explicit exceptions, the deviations are known and this step can be skipped.

The 'where' question is typically asked first. It deals with identifying deviating cases as well as locations within the process where something deviates. A large part of conformance research deals with this particular question. LTL can be used for identifying non-compliant cases and the 'token game' can be played to find deviating locations in a process [10]. Once process deviations are discovered, managers typically want to know how the process deviates. The current literature only partially answers this important question by indicating where activities are skipped or inserted [2]. However, managers are more interested in high-level process deviations, such as delayed or swapped activities. Section 3 presents a general approach to detect high-level deviations. Finally, a manager is often interested in a particular deviation category. Either he identifies a specific category in advance or the detected deviations are classified afterwards. To our knowledge, the work of Swinnen et al. [9] is the only research that deals with this managerial question. They summarize the detected deviations in terms of business rules to allow fast determination of the deviation category.

Process Deviation Diagnosis. The second methodological step of the framework diagnoses the detected process deviations. Each deviation category relates to a different set of managerial questions. For explicit exceptions, it is important to determine their frequency and perform a cost-benefit analysis. This can lead to the integration of the exception in the main process execution, changing the preconditions of the exception or prohibiting the exception. For implicit exceptions, the cause or context should be determined and the desirability of the deviation has to be assessed. This can result in making the implicit exception explicit. For operational errors, their frequency and cost should be determined and their analysis should be part of quality control programs. Corrective actions should be taken to prevent these errors. As for fraud, the frequency and cost should be determined to assess the consequences, but the process should also be redesigned or controls should be implemented to prevent fraud in the future. To our knowledge, the issue of process deviation diagnosis has not yet been addressed in the academic literature.

3   Detecting High-Level Deviations

While research predominantly focusses on where the process deviates, managers are more interested in how the process deviates. This question has only been addressed in [2], where low-level deviations of skipped and inserted activities are discovered. However, to be truly useful to management, higher level deviations need to be identified. Examples of such higher level deviations are delayed activities, activities replaced by other activities, two activities which swapped places, a set of activities which is repeated and many others. Given the space limitations, only a general approach for detecting higher level deviations is provided.

3.1   Basic Concepts

To detect process deviations, a normative model M is compared with each trace τ from an event log L. A trace can be represented as an ordered set of executed activities[1], $\tau = \langle a_1, \ldots, a_n \rangle$. A process model M corresponds to a directed graph, which comprises activities and control connectors (e.g. XOR-split, AND-join). Concurrency and choice constructs in the model allow multiple ways to execute the process from start to end. An execution path $p_i = \langle a_1, \ldots, a_n \rangle$ is any sequence of activities that represent a valid execution of M.

3.2   Algorithm Structure

The identification of higher-level process deviations comes down to the comparison of a trace $\tau = \langle a_1, \ldots, a_n \rangle_t$ with the correct execution path $p_i = \langle a_1, \ldots, a_m \rangle_p$. Therefore, the first step in the deviation detection algorithm is **finding the appropriate execution path** p_i for a specific trace $\tau \in L$. A first approach matches case information with decision rules in the process model to determine the correct execution path. A second approach, applied in [2], minimizes the cost of a case execution in terms of inserted and deleted activities. Note that the alignment stage of the algorithm deals with loops, i.e. it needs to determine how many times the trace should have repeated a specific loop.

Instead of searching for high-level deviations straight away, the second step in the deviation detection algorithm **searches** for low-level deviations, i.e. **inserted and deleted activities**. Since any high-level deviation can be constructed from these two low-level deviations, it suffices to detect the low-level deviations in order to combine them into high-level deviations. This decomposition of the

---

[1] More precisely, a trace is an ordered set of events where each event relates to a specific activity type.

problem also prevents the algorithm from having to pass the event log multiple times to find all possible combinations of high-level deviations.

The third step of the algorithm is an optimization problem and combines the set of low-level deviations into high-level deviations. Note that there are multiple ways to **combine low-level deviations into high-level deviations**. For example, assume $\tau = \langle a_1, a_4, a_3, a_2, a_5 \rangle_t$ and $p_i = \langle a_1, a_2, a_3, a_4, a_5 \rangle_p$. The deviation between τ and its matching execution path p_i can be explained by a switch between activities a_2 and a_4, but also by a delay of activity a_2 and activity a_3.

4   Related Work

Various terms have been given to express non-conform patterns, i.e. *anomalies, outliers, discordant observations, exceptions, aberrations, surprises, peculiarities* or *contaminants*. In [5], a survey provides a structured and comprehensive overview of the research on anomaly detection in general.

With regard to anomaly detection in process aware information systems, various research has already been done [3, 4, 6, 11]. All this research is limited to the determination of whether a trace is anomalous or not and only addresses the 'Where' question in the deviation detection stage. It does not determine in which way and how severe these deviations are. Adriansyah et al. address these limitations [1, 2]. They defined the low-level deviations of 'skipped' and 'inserted' activities and identify their exact occurrence in a trace. The severity of these deviations is expressed by assigning a cost to skipping or inserting a certain activity. Their research focusses on the questions "Where in the process does it go wrong?" and to some extent "How does the process deviate?", albeit at a low level of deviations.

The PDA-framework suggests that the existing research only covers a small part of process deviation analysis from a managerial point of view and one of the issues that should be addressed is the identification of high-level deviations. To define interesting high-level deviations, the work of Weber et al. [12] on change patterns in process aware information systems provides an interesting starting point.

5   Conclusions

The PDA framework decomposes process deviation analysis into three dimensions, i.e. deviation categories, methodological steps and managerial questions. The framework acts as a guidance to managers and allows them to quickly identify the type of deviation analysis they require. However, the PDA framework also reveals that there are still many managerial questions that lack a sound scientific methodology and a set of appropriate algorithms.

The authors hope that the PDA framework will inspire other researchers to further develop the field of process deviation analysis. To this end, a general three step approach to identify high-level deviations have been suggested in this paper.

References

[1] Adriansyah, A., Sidorova, N., van Dongen, B.: Cost-based fitness in conformance checking. In: ACSD, pp. 57–66 (2011)

[2] Adriansyah, A., van Dongen, B., Van der Aalst, W.M.P.: Conformance checking using cost-based fitness analysis. In: EDOC, pp. 55–64. IEEE Computer Society (2011)

[3] Bezerra, F., Wainer, J.: Anomaly detection algorithms in logs of process aware systems. In: Applied Computing 2008, VOLS 1-3, pp. 951–952 (2008)

[4] Bezerra, F., Wainer, J., van der Aalst, W.M.P.: Anomaly Detection Using Process Mining. In: Halpin, T., Krogstie, J., Nurcan, S., Proper, E., Schmidt, R., Soffer, P., Ukor, R. (eds.) BPMDS 2009 and EMMSAD 2009. LNBIP, vol. 29, pp. 149–161. Springer, Heidelberg (2009)

[5] Chandola, V., Banerjee, A., Kumar, V.: Anomaly detection - a survey. Technical report, University of Minnesota (2007)

[6] Jalali, H., Baraani, A.: Genetic-based anomaly detection in logs of process aware systems. World Academy of Science Engineering and Technology 64, 304–309 (2010)

[7] Rozinat, A., de Jong, I.S.M., Günther, C.W.: Process mining applied to the test process of wafer steppers in asml. IEEE Transactions on Systems, Mand and Cybernetics - Part C Applications and Reviews, 1–6 (2010)

[8] Rozinat, A., van der Aalst, W.M.P.: Conformance checking of processes based on monitoring real behavior. Inf. Syst. 33, 64–95 (2008)

[9] Swinnen, J., Depaire, B., Jans, M.J., Vanhoof, K.: A Process Deviation Analysis - A Case Study. In: Daniel, F., Barkaoui, K., Dustdar, S. (eds.) BPM 2011 Workshops, Part I. LNBIP, vol. 99, pp. 87–98. Springer, Heidelberg (2012)

[10] van der Aalst, W.M.P.: Business alignment: using process mining as a tool for delta analysis and conformance testing. Requirements Engineering 10, 198–211 (2005)

[11] Van der Aalst, W.M.P., de Medeiros, A.K.A.: Process mining and security: Detecting anomalous process executions and checking process conformance. Electronic Notes in Theoretical Computer Science 121(4), 3–21 (2005)

[12] Weber, B., Reichert, M., Rinderle-Ma, S.: Change patterns and change support features - enhancing flexibility in process-aware information systems. Data & Knowledge Engineering 66, 438–466 (2008)

Securely Storing and Executing Business Processes in the Cloud

David Martinho and Diogo R. Ferreira

IST – Technical University of Lisbon
{davidmartinho,diogo.ferreira}@ist.utl.pt

Abstract. This paper proposes an architectural solution that allows organizations to rely on cloud-based services to securely operate their business processes. The solution is built upon a thick client and thin server architectural pattern, where security constructs such as public-key and symmetric cryptographic systems are used to maintain confidentiality between the participants while keeping the server unaware of their participations and business process instances.

Keywords: Cloud Computing, Security, BPM, Cryptography Systems.

1 Introduction

Given the latest advances in IT, the envisioning of computing as an essential utility for the general community led to the proposal of novel computing paradigms such as cloud computing. Cloud computing [1] is presented as being able to transform the IT industry by introducing a delivery model of Software as a Service (SaaS), and shaping the way infrastructural hardware is designed and adopted. Rather than acquiring expensive Business Process Management System (BPMS) software licenses, and install and manage the software within a local hardware infrastructure, an organization signs up to use the application hosted by the company that develops and sells the software as a service.

However, cloud computing means entrusting data to information systems managed by external parties on remote servers "in the cloud". This raises privacy and confidentiality concerns given that the service provider can access all data, and accidentally or deliberately leak it or use it for unauthorized purposes [7]. These threats hinder the adoption of cloud-based solutions by organizations.

This paper proposes an architectural solution that enables organizations to securely store their business processes within cloud-based services, while preserving zero-knowledge of the service provider concerning their business processes. To validate such solution, the following requirements must be preserved: (R1) a process instance must be shared among its participants, allowing concurrent executions to take place; (R2) the service provider must never have access to the business process instance content, and (R3) never know which process instances are associated to which participants; (R4) communication must never be compromised by potential eavesdropping; and (R5) a malicious party cannot deprive authorized process participants to access their business processes.

M. La Rosa and P. Soffer (Eds.): BPM 2012 Workshops, LNBIP 132, pp. 707–712, 2013.
© Springer-Verlag Berlin Heidelberg 2013

2   Architectural Solution

The use of cloud-based services is associated with the client-server architectural pattern. This architectural pattern allows to centralize the data manipulated by an application within a server, and distribute the interaction with end-users through a set of multiple clients that communicate with the centralized server. The use of this architectural pattern contributes to the fulfillment of the first requirement (R1) where the process instance must be shared among the process participants, allowing concurrent executions to take place.

However, this client-server architectural pattern creates problems when security requirements are introduced. To ensure that (R4) communication is not compromised by potential eavesdropping, two possible solutions exist: either the client communicates with the server through Secure Socket Layer (SSL) protocols, ensuring the communication is encrypted, or the client encrypts the business process before sending it to the server. Considering also that (R2) the service provider must never have access to the content of business process instances, we must adopt the latter strategy.

By encrypting data beforehand, it becomes impossible for the server to actually make domain-specific computations (e.g. execute the process model, compute work allocation, etc...). Hence, we must adopt a particular variant of the client-server architectural pattern: a thick client and a thin server. With this variant, all the business logic is essentially present in the client, where the business process instance is decrypted and executed, while the server takes the role of a centralized repository, providing access to encrypted process instances.

Now that we justified the decisions on the main architectural pattern, we will focus on the security layer that empowers the communication workflow occurring between the client and server applications. When integrating a cross-cutting concern such as security into our solution, we must consider the following security qualities [6]: *confidentiality* to ensure that the content of a business process instance is only available to authorized parties; *integrity* to ensure that the content of a business process instance has not been tampered and modified by unauthorized parties; and *availability* to ensure that authorized parties cannot be deprived from accessing their business process instances.

In this proposal, we are interested in supporting all three security qualities. However, in what concerns availability, we will not focus on tackling denial-of-service attacks, which can be avoided by using generic infrastructure-based strategies that are outside the scope of this paper. Instead, we are concerned to ensure (R5) that a malicious party cannot deprive authorized process participants to access their business processes, in situations that the service is still available (e.g. data corruption).

To ensure (R2) that a service provider can never access the business process instance's content, and (R3) never know which process instances are associated to which participants, public-key and symmetric cryptography systems are used.

Depending on whether the encryption or decryption key is publicly shared, the public-key cryptography system can be used to address either confidentiality or integrity qualities respectively. In order to achieve both confidentiality and integrity security requirements, our solution assigns two distinct pairs of asymmetric keys to each user for each purpose. However, in public-key cryptographic systems, the security is handled peer-to-peer, meaning that it is not well-suited for sharing confidential business process instances with more than one participating party at a time, hindering (R1) the sharing of business process instances among the process participants, and for concurrent executions to take place.

The symmetric cryptography system works upon a shared secret strategy, where two or more parties may exchange confidential (i.e. encrypted) business process instances because they secretly share the same symmetric key. This means that a symmetric cryptography system is only valid to support the confidentiality security requirement, since there is no concept of public key with which other users can verify the authorship and integrity of a message.

Our solution makes use of both these public-key and symmetric cryptographic systems within a communication workflow between a thick client where business processes are executed, and a thin server that allows process participants to share encrypted business process instances while keeping the server, and consequently the service provider completely unaware of the business processes' content.

2.1   Client-Server Communication Workflow

Let us assume that we have a participant named Alice, who creates a new business process instance and executes the first activity. To do so, she logs in into the workflow client using her credentials (i.e. username and password). Using her credentials, the workflow computes her respective symmetric key P_K, and uses her username to retrieve her encrypted passport (see Definition 1) from the server provider, and decrypts it using the computed symmetric key P_K.

Definition 1 (Passport). *Given a particular user U working for organization O, let O_i be the organization identity containing information necessary to communicate with the service provider. Let (E_{K^c}, D_{K^c}) be her pair of asymmetric keys respecting to confidentiality, and (E_{K^i}, D_{K^i}) her pair of asymmetric keys concerning integrity. Let P_L be her list of available process instances containing tuples (process-title, ID_R, p_k) which refer to the process title, the server's remote ID of the encrypted process instance, and the symmetric key used to encrypt the process instance. Finally, let S_K be a symmetric key that is shared with all organization members. A passport is defined by the 5-tuple $(O_i, D_{K^c}, E_{K^i}, P_L, S_K)$.*

After Alice logs in, and the workflow client application retrieves her passport from the server, it uses the first element of her passport tuple, the organization identity O_i, to fetch the shared organization's information repository from the server, which is encrypted with S_K. The organization's information repository contains the organization's business process models that can be executed within the thick workflow client, and the list of employees with their respective public confidentiality and integrity keys, as well as their organizational roles to allow the workflow engine to perform work allocation. Then, Alice selects one process model P from the list of available business processes available according to her organizational roles, and begins the workflow depicted in Figure 1.

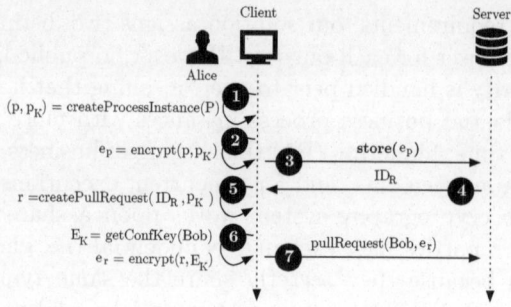

Fig. 1. Alice's Communication Workflow with the Server

First, (1) Alice creates a new business process instance p from the business process model P, also generating a new symmetric process key p_K to encrypt that process instance. Then, after executing her workflow task, the workflow client application decides, based on the model for organizational roles contained in the organization repository fetched earlier, the process participant that will execute the next task, which is Bob in this case. Afterwards, (2) the workflow client, before sending the process to the server, encrypts it using the generated symmetric key p_K, originating an encrypted process instance e_p. Then, (3) the workflow client sends a new storage request to the server so that it stores the encrypted process instance and (4) respond with the remote identifier ID_R that will be used for future retrievals and re-storages. After the server replies with the remote identifier, the workflow client application can (5) create a pull request (see Definition 2) containing the remote identifier ID_R and the symmetric key p_K that will be needed to decrypt the process instance. In this step, the workflow client also adds the process instance information in Alice's process list P_L. The workflow client application then (6) confidentially addresses the pull request to Bob by encrypting it with his public encryption key E_{K^c}, listed in the previously fetched organization repository, and signing the content with Alice's private integrity key. Finally, the workflow client sends that signed and encrypted pull request to the server (7).

Definition 2 (Pull Request). *Let (ID_R, S_K) be a tuple containing a remote identifier ID_R that identifies a business process instance encrypted with a symmetric key S_K. Sending a pull request to user U, consists on encrypting such tuple with the user's confidentiality public key E_{K^c} and store it in the server, associating it to the respective user U.*

The pull request is encrypted so that (R3) the service provider must never know which process instances are associated to which process participants. Omitted for the sake of space, the pull request is signed by Alice so that Bob can verify the authorship of the request and avoid malicious parties outside his organization to send him pull requests. The communication workflow between Bob's client and the server is depicted in Figure 2.

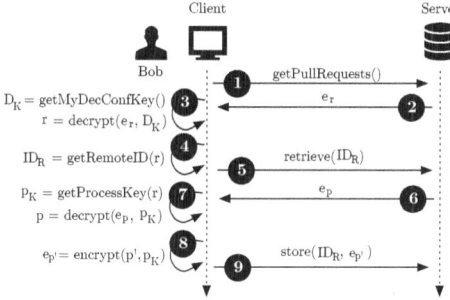

Fig. 2. Bob's Communication Workflow with the Server

After Bob logs in into the system, (1) the client also fetches the server for any new pull requests addressed to Bob. The server will then (2) reply to the client with the encrypted pull request e_r earlier originated from Alice's task execution. Then, (3) the client decrypts the request using Bob's private confidentiality decryption key D_{K^c} available in his passport, obtaining the decrypted pull request r. With the pull request decrypted, (4) the client may use the remote id ID_R to (5) retrieve the encrypted process e_p from the server. After the server replies with the encrypted process (6), the client can (7) use the process symmetric key p_k, also contained in the pull request r, to decrypt the encrypted process e_p into p. Finally, after Bob executes his task, the workflow client application repeats all the steps, storing the process instance information in Bob's process list P_L, and (8) re-encrypting the new version of the process instance p' with the same encryption key p_K , but with the particularity of (9) re-storing it within the same ID_R: this allows previous participants to continually access the business process instance.

In fact, the server does not overwrite the process instance, it rather creates a new version of it. We consider versioning for the situation where a malicious party discovers the remote id ID_R, and attempts to overwrite the currently stored business process instance with the intention of depriving authorized process participants to access their business processes. As the server versions the encrypted business process instances stored under the same ID_R, if the workflow client fails to decrypt the business process instance using the process symmetric key present in the pull request, the server flags that version and responds with the previous version, repeating the process until a version is accepted or there are no versions left. This strategy contributes directly to ensure the delivery of requirement R5.

The solution proposed can be easily extended to support choreographies among organizations. Nevertheless, such extensibility presumes that the choreography actors, i.e. the organizations, would have compatible business process models [8], and their workflow clients implementing the same architectural solution proposed here.

3   Related Work

There is previous work [2, 4] focusing on adapting access control and authorization techniques used in database and operating systems to the business process management scope. Nevertheless, such fields envision security within relatively narrow applications. Security is often integrated into business process management systems in an ad-hoc manner, during the implementation process [3], disregarding the specificities of its domain.

In [5], a novel architecture of cloud-based BPM is proposed and analyzed, supporting end-user distribution of non-compute-intensive activities and sensitive data. Nevertheless, they do not approach aspects concerning privacy and confidentiality of business processes in the cloud as proposed in this paper.

4   Conclusions

In this paper, we introduced an architectural solution that establishes a workflow of interactions between a thick client that executes the business process and a thin server, subscribed on a cloud-based delivery model, that is confined to simple services of data storage and retrieval. The solution is based on a client application that manages both the execution of business process instances and the participant's access control lists while leveraging on untrusted data storage and retrieval cloud services through a well-defined layer of security based on symmetric and asymmetric cryptographic constructs.

References

[1] Armbrust, M., Fox, A., Griffith, R., Joseph, A.D., Katz, R., Konwinski, A., Lee, G., Patterson, D., Rabkin, A., Stoica, I., et al.: A view of cloud computing. Communications of the ACM 53(4), 50–58 (2010)
[2] Atluri, V., Huang, W., Bertino, E.: An execution model for multilevel secure workflows. Database Security 11, 151–165 (1998)
[3] Backes, M., Pfitzmann, B., Waidner, M.: Security in Business Process Engineering. In: van der Aalst, W.M.P., ter Hofstede, A.H.M., Weske, M. (eds.) BPM 2003. LNCS, vol. 2678, pp. 168–183. Springer, Heidelberg (2003)
[4] Bertino, E., Ferrari, E., Atluri, V.: A flexible model supporting the specification and enforcement of role-based authorization in workflow management systems. In: 2nd ACM Workshop on RBAC, pp. 1–12 (1997)
[5] Han, Y.B., Sun, J.Y., Wang, G.L., Li, H.F.: A cloud-based bpm architecture with user-end distribution of non-compute-intensive activities and sensitive data. JCST 25(6), 1157–1167 (2010)
[6] Herrmann, P., Herrmann, G.: Security requirement analysis of business processes. Electronic Commerce Research 6(3), 305–335 (2006)
[7] Ryan, M.D.: Cloud computing privacy concerns on our doorstep. Communications of the ACM 54(1) (2011)
[8] Weske, M.: Business process management: concepts, languages, architectures. Springer (2010)

Advanced Protection of Workflow Sessions with SEWebSession

Maxime Fonda[1,2], Stéphane Moinard[1], and Christian Toinard[2]

[1] Qualnet, 24 route de Creton F-18110 Vasselay, France
{fonda,moinard}@qualnet.fr,
http://www.qualnet.fr
[2] ENSI - LIFO, 88 Bld Lahitolle, F-18020 Bourges Cedex, France
christian.toinard@ensi-bourges.fr

Abstract. This paper presents Secure Enhanced Web Session providing an advanced protection of the Web sessions required in the Workflow environments. SEWebSession provides mandatory access control to the session state since the proposed policy is outside the scope of the Workflow developers and participants. Our MAC approach authorises various confidentiality and integrity properties for the session state. SEWebSession controls a session state whether it is maintained in the memory of the Web server, a dedicated server or a SQL Database. The protection rules can be reused from one platform to another one. SEWebSession has been successfully integrated within an industrial Workflow environment running on Windows platforms. The experimentations show the efficiency of SEWebSession for protecting Microsoft Windows/IIS platforms. However, SEWebSession can be easily ported within Linux/ Apache platforms.

Keywords: Workflow, Web sessions, Mandatory Protection.

1 Introduction

The problem of enforcing the security of a Web session for supporting a workflow is poorly addressed. On one hand, authors like [1] propose formal models of protection but do not show how to integrate the proposed models into the Web platforms. On the other hand, solutions like [2] prevent against the replay of session identifiers but do not provide mandatory access control for the session state. However, controlling the accesses to the session state must enable to guarantee various confidentiality and integrity properties for the session state. The objective is thus to prevent the security violations associated with malicious accesses to the session state. SEWebSession eases the formalization of the required protection properties in order to minimize the flows between a Web application and the session state. SEWebSession enables to enforce the protection of the session state whether it is located into a Web, a SQL or a persistent server. One can say that the protection is mandatory since the rules are outside the scope of the programmers of the workflow, the participants and even the administrator of the various servers.

M. La Rosa and P. Soffer (Eds.): BPM 2012 Workshops, LNBIP 132, pp. 713--718, 2013.

Section 2 describes the motivations of our work dealing with the protection of shared sessions and the enforcement of the protection for covering the different servers. Section 3 presents SEWebSession including the proposed language and the enforcement of the protection for the considered distributed system. Section 4 covers the work related to the protection of the Web based workflow platforms. Finally, a conclusion summarises the novelty of SEWebSession and describes the promising improvements of our future works.

2 Motivations

The first objective is to provide a satisfying protection system for controlling the accesses of the workflow applications to the Web session state. Indeed, controling the accesses to the session state enables to guarantee different security properties. For example, the figure 1 shows a workflow where the ordinary participant named *Fonda* asks for a vacation to *Moinard* acting as his supervisor. Let us consider two properties for the sake of demonstration. First, the protection system must allow *Moinard* to act as supervisor in order to garantee the integrity of that status. Second, *Moinard* must be able to read and write the vacation days allocated to *Fonda*. Thus, all the other users can neither violate the confidentiality nor the integrity of the vacations of *Fonda*. The supervisor status and vacations days are two examples of information available into the session state. So, SEWebSession must minimise the accesses to those information. Thus, our solution aims at easing the definition of the rules required to protect the session and enforcing the requested rules outside the programmer, participant and administrator scope.

The second objective is to enforce the requested protection rules in the context of the heteregeneous distributed system enabling to store the session state. Indeed, the session state is usually maintained into the address space of the Web server, a persistency server or a SQL server. The state must be consistent into those different servers. For this purpose, a single point of access control must be available as a unique reference monitor [3] for the whole distributed system.

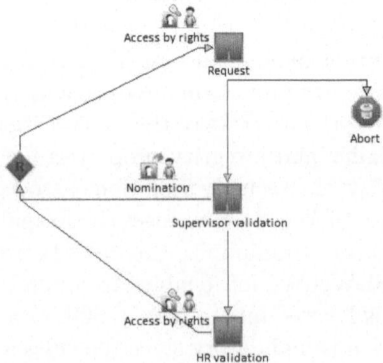

Fig. 1. Vacation request workflow

3   SEWebSession

3.1   Protection Language

The idea is to have a protection language dedicated to the control of the session data. A protection rule *allow(Subject, Action, Object)* allows a Subject the Action for the considered Object. If a rule is not expressed then SEWebSession denies the access (default-deny setup). Security contexts must designate the Subject and the Object and Actions must express precisely the requested operations:

- A security context is an extensible string including an unbounded number of elements in order to designate safely the considered entity i.e. either the Web application or a data of the session state.
- An action is an unbounded number of elements defining the considered access to the target object.

The security context of the subject, i.e. the Web application, is derived from different information of the incoming Web request including the session identifier, the user identifier, the application domain, the application identifier plus any other additional information.

The security context of the object, i.e. a data of the session state, includes the session identifier, the data identifier plus any other additional attribute characterising the data.

An action includes a type of access (read/write/create/delete) plus any additional constraint for the action, e.g. a logic expression between the session data, in order to express a constraint between the data.

Let us consider two rules associated to the vacation workflow of the figure 1. A first rule grants the user *Moinard* to use the *vacationRequest* application into the *intranet* context in order to write the *supervisor* status:

$$allow\ (*: moinard: intranet: vacationRequest, write, \$1: supervisor)$$

A second rule enables *moinard* to read and write the value of the vacation Days available for *Fonda*:

$$allow\ (*: moinard: intranet: vacationRequest, read\|write, \$1: vacationDays\ [user == Fonda])$$

The first rule corresponds to an integrity property for the *supervisor* status while the second rule enforces both the confidentiality and the integrity of the *vacationDays* of *Fonda*.

3.2   Protection of the Different Servers

Let us describe the implementation of SEWebSession for Intraqual Dynamic i.e. the workflow system provided by Qual'Net. Intraqual Dynamic is a full-web workflow system based on Microsoft softwares. Since SEWebSession provides secure session state for the Windows/IIS/.Net environment, Intraqual Dynamic takes advantages of the proposed security enforcement.

During the processing of an HTTP request, the ASP.Net framework provides a serie of events such as *BeginRequest, AcquireRequestState,etc.* Our own handlers, available in an HttpModule, hook those events. Each handler can extract information from the request and/or modify the context of the request. Currently, the parsing of each SEWebSession rule produces a dedicated piece of code for the different handlers.

The handler *AcquireRequestState* accesses to the live session object including the session data according to the session identifier of the incoming request. This handler enables the control of the live session state. In case of a deny, the handler sends an error message such as *violation detected for session 05ados3sjhm3jkmpb4rcw1iv:login=fonda writing the supervisor data.* This error shows that SEWebSession blocks the writing of the *supervisor* status for *Fonda*.

When the live session satisfies the requested SEWebSession rules, the processing of the Web request continues. In this case, *ReleaseRequestState* enables to have a copy of the updated session object before ASP.Net stores that session object into the session server (SQL or ASP.NET state).

When IIS is configured to store the session state into a SQL Server database, the *EndRequest* handler recovers the global session state directly from the SQL Server using an SQL *SELECT* statement in order to perform the comparison with the copy of the updated session object. Thus, the handler compares the database session state with the live session state in order to guarantee the consistency. Our handler sends an error in case of inconsistency. It can correct the SQL session state coming from illegal activities or faults using an *UPDATE/INSERT/DELETE* request.

With these four SQL statements, SEWebSession implements the protection language proposed in section 3.1 for the SQL Server in order to support the four types of action (read/write/create/delete).

When IIS is configured to store the session state in the ASP.Net State server (aspnet_state.exe service), the *EndRequest* handler recovers the global session state directly from the ASP.Net session state server to ensure the consistency with the live session state as previously described for the SQL server.

Using the *GET* and *PUT* statements of the HTTP protocol, the handler implements the four types of action. In the same manner than the SQL Server, SEWebSession can thus update the ASP.NETState server to correct wrong sessions.

4   Related Works

The field of access control policy is very large. Works like [4] provide a formal approach for modeling access control policies. But these language have never been implemented. Role Based Access Control such as [5] aims at factorising the access control rules. They do not extend the expressiveness of the control.

Discretionary Access Control is known to be fragile [6]. Only Mandatory Access Control, such as proposed in SELinux [7], is able to guarantee security properties.

However, MAC solutions are generally complex. For example, [8] proposes an architecture to provide an end-to-end access control over web applications. They use SELinux and XSM policies to enforce a mandatory access control inside and between Virtual Machines. So, multiple MAC policies are requested using millions of rules. Moreover, they cannot express high level security properties and do not cover the protection of Web Sessions.

Flow analysis [9] between Web pages can control the information flows between the Web resources. But they do not control the flows between the applications and the session state. Role-based approaches [10] enable to control the accesses to the database tables and web pages.

Testing approaches [11] can detect SQL and PHP injections. However, they fail to detect illegal accesses to the session state.

[12] proposes a language to ease the control of the information flows within a distributed architecture. However, this language does not support the control of Web applications accessing session states.

Thus, current approaches poorly address the control of Web application accessing to the session state. Moreover, they are complex and do not fit well with the workflow systems. Moreover, a better detection and prevention of attacks, associated to the session state, could provide inputs to improve the vulnerability typing and classification [13].

5   Conclusion and Future Works

SEWebSession is a novel approach aiming at protecting the session state whether it is located. A dedicated language eases the formalization of the security requirements. Various confidentiality and integrity properties can thus be easily expressed. A unique reference monitor controls the accesses to the session state that can be located into the Web, SQL or State servers. SEWebSession guarantees that the different copies of the session state satisfy the requested protection rules. The experimentation on a real workflow environment shows the efficiency of SEWebSession to prevent threats associated with illegal accesses to the Microsoft IIS, SQL and ASP.NETState servers.

Future works deal with the improvement of the parsing of our language to avoid the production of code for the control of the protection rules. Moreover, the usage of the PIGA approach [12] will enable to enforce the protection of the SEWebSession reference monitor in order to prevent attacks on the SEWebSession monitor. Thus, a safe SEWebSession reference monitor will be proposed. Finally, the SEWebSession policies can be reused by the PIGA advanced reference monitor. In contrast with SEWebSession that only controls the direct access of the Web application to the session state, the PIGA language enables to control transitive information flows crossing different Web applications and session state ressources. PIGA supports advanced properties i.e. a property that controls a combination of multiple direct/indirect information flows. Thus, advanced properties such as separation of duties or conflict of interest will be supported.

References

1. Wainer, J., Kumar, A., Barthelmess, P.: DW-RBAC: A formal security model of delegation and revocation in workflow systems. Inf. Syst. 3(32), 365--384 (2007)
2. Adida, B.: Sessionlock: securing web sessions against eavesdropping. In: Proceedings of the 17th International Conference on World Wide Web, pp. 517--524. ACM (2008)
3. Anderson, J.: Computer Security Technology Planning Study, ESD-TR-73-51, Section 4.1.1, US Air Force Electronic Systems Division (1973), http://csrc.nist.gov/publications/history/ande72.pdf
4. Li, N., Mitchell, J.C.: DATALOG with Constraints: A Foundation for Trust Management Languages. In: Dahl, V. (ed.) PADL 2003. LNCS, vol. 2562, pp. 58--73. Springer, Heidelberg (2002)
5. Finin, T., Joshi, A., Kagal, L., Niu, J., Sandhu, R., Winsborough, W.H., Thuraisingham, B.: ROWLBAC - Representing Role Based Access Control in OWL. In: Proceedings of 13th Symposium on Access Control Models and Technologies, pp. 58--73. ACM Press (2008)
6. Harrison, M.A., Ruzzo, W.L., Ullman, J.D.: Protection in operating systems. Communications of the ACM 19(8), 461--471 (1976)
7. Loscocco, P., Smalley, S.: Integrating flexible support for security policies into the linux operating system. In: 2001 USENIX Annual Technical Conference (FREENIX 2001). USENIX Association, Boston (2001)
8. Hicks, B., Rueda, S., King, D., Moyer, T., Schiffman, J., Sreenivasan, Y., McDaniel, P., Jaeger, T.: An architecture for enforcing end-to-end access control over web applications. In: Proceedings of the 15th ACM Symposium on Access Control Models and Technologies, SACMAT 2010, pp. 163--172. ACM, New York (2010)
9. Wu, Y., Offutt, Y.: Modeling and testing web-based applications, Technical Report, Department of Information and Software Engineering, George Mason University, Fairfax, VA (2009)
10. Fard, R.E., Nezhad, R.K.: Dynamic Workflow Management Based On Policy-Enabled Authorization. Journal of Information Technology Management XX(4), 57--68 (2009)
11. Wassermann, G., Yu, D., Chander, A., Dhurjati, D., Inamura, H., Su, Z.: Dynamic test input generation for web applications. In: Proceedings of the 2008 International Symposium on Software Testing and Analysis, ISSTA 2008, Seattle, WA, USA, pp. 249--260. ACM, New York (2008)
12. Afoulki, Z., Bousquet, A., Briffaut, J., Rouzaud-Cornabas, J., Toinard, C.: MAC Protection of the OpenNebula Cloud Environment. In: Proceeding of the Second International Workshop on Security and Performance in Cloud Computing, SP-CLOUD 2012, Madrid, Spain (to appear, June 2012)
13. Lowis, L., Accorsi, R.: Vulnerability Analysis in SOA-Based Business Processes. IEEE T. Services Computing 4(3), 230--242 (2011)

A Case Study on the Suitability of Process Mining to Produce Current-State RBAC Models

Maria Leitner[1], Anne Baumgrass[2], Sigrid Schefer-Wenzl[2],
Stefanie Rinderle-Ma[1], and Mark Strembeck[2]

[1] University of Vienna, Austria
Faculty of Computer Science
{maria.leitner,stefanie.rinderle-ma}@univie.ac.at
[2] Vienna University of Economics and Business (WU Vienna), Austria
Institute for Information Systems, New Media Lab
firstname.lastname@wu.ac.at

Abstract. Role-based access control (RBAC) is commonly used to implement authorization procedures in Process-aware information systems (PAIS). Process mining refers to a bundle of algorithms that typically discover process models from event log data produced during the execution of real-world processes. Beyond pure control flow mining, some techniques focus on the discovery of organizational information from event logs. However, a systematic analysis and comparison of these approaches with respect to their suitability for mining RBAC models is still missing. This paper works towards filling this gap and provides a first guidance for applying mining techniques for deriving RBAC models.

Keywords: Process Mining, RBAC, Security in Business Processes.

1 Introduction

Process-aware information systems (PAIS) support the execution of tasks in business processes and store so called "event log" files (e.g., [10]). In this context, process mining techniques are used to analyze and extract process-related information from event logs. In general, process mining techniques do not directly focus on the derivation of access control models. However, such models are an important means to define which subject is permitted to execute certain tasks (e.g., [3,9]).

In recent years, role-based access control (RBAC) (e.g., [3]) has developed into a de facto standard for access control in both, research and industry. In RBAC, roles correspond to different job-positions and scopes of duty within a particular organization or information system. Access permissions are assigned to roles according to the duties this role has to accomplish, and subjects (e.g., human users) are assigned to roles. In the business process context, RBAC has been extended to consider access permissions for tasks included in a business process (e.g., [9]).

This paper investigates into the applicability of three different process mining approaches and one role derivation approach to extract RBAC information from

M. La Rosa and P. Soffer (Eds.): BPM 2012 Workshops, LNBIP 132, pp. 719–724, 2013.
© Springer-Verlag Berlin Heidelberg 2013

event logs. In particular, we aim to provide an initial decision guidance on which of these approaches can be applied in a particular context and which prerequisites are necessary to retrieve proper results. For this purpose, we conducted a case study where we analyzed an event log of a real-life business process from the university context.

The remainder of this paper is structured as follows. Section 2 presents an overview of the four different approaches used in our case study, our running example, and the results of the four approaches. Next, these results are discussed and evaluated in Section 3. Finally, Section 4 concludes the paper.

2   Case Study

In the context of PAIS, event logs store information that can be used to produce so called *current-state RBAC models* (see, e.g, [1,2,4,6,7]). In particular, **role derivation** approaches automatically derive a current-state RBAC model from event logs and precisely reflect how subjects performed tasks in PAIS (see, e.g., [1]). In [1], we developed a derivation component that is able to produce a current-state RBAC model. Based on the results of this derivation, we can conduct a refinement via the role engineering tool xoRET which detects and combines roles with (partially) identical permissions [8].

Furthermore, process mining approaches can also be applied to derive current-state RBAC models (see, e.g, [4,6,7]). The resulting RBAC models provide an abstraction of the information contained in an event log. Using ProM 5.2 [11] and its plugin for **organizational mining**, we are able to extract and represent organizational structures via organizational models (e.g., [7]). In organizational models, subjects with a similar frequency of performed tasks are grouped into organizational entities. Thereby, these models provide information on the relationship between the organizational entities and the tasks assigned to the subjects of these entities. Thus, they can be used to build a current-state RBAC model. Similar, a **role hierarchy miner** [6] is able to identify groups of subjects performing similar tasks and, in addition, to identify hierarchical structures between the groups of subjects. In this case, these hierarchical structures can be used to build a current-state RBAC model including a role hierarchy. Moreover, **staff assignment mining** aims to discover assignment rules from event log files (e.g., [4]). We apply staff assignment mining using corresponding organizational information (see Section 2.1). As a result, the staff assignment rules identify the set of subjects who are allowed to perform certain tasks based on a combination of properties (e.g., roles, organizational units, or abilities of a subject).

In summary, we use the prototypical derivation component introduced in [1] and xoRET [8] to apply role derivation, while ProM 5.2 [11] is used to apply mining techniques in this case study.

2.1   Running Example

For our case study, we selected a typical teaching process from the higher education system. The process is divided into two subprocesses. As shown in Fig. 1,

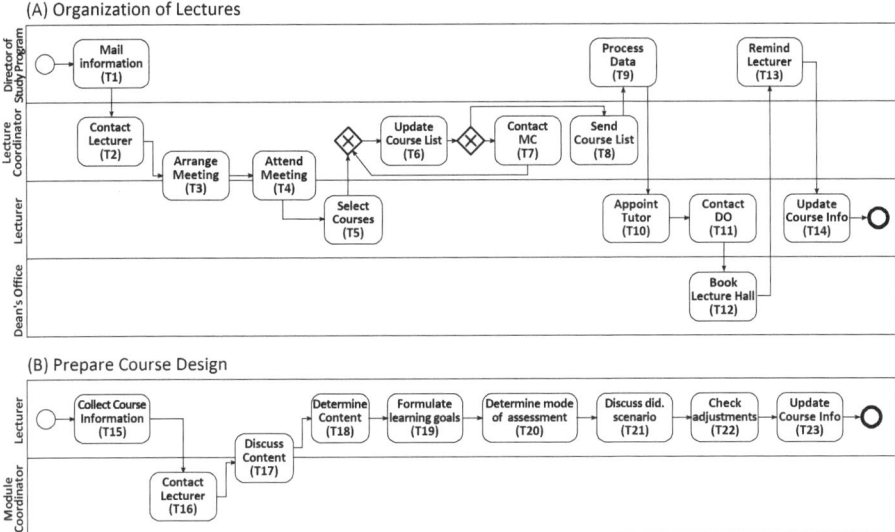

Fig. 1. Process *Prepare Lectures*

the first subprocess models the organization and assignment of lectures to the faculty. The second subprocess shown in Fig. 1 contains the preparation and course design of the lectures. As illustrated in Fig. 1, the roles *Director of the Study Program* (DSP), *Lecturer* (L), *Lecture Coordinator* (LC), *Module Coordinator* (MC), and *Dean's Office* (DO) are involved in the teaching process. In the context of RBAC, each role has a set of permissions. Thus, a permission defines that a subject having a particular role is authorized to execute a specific task. For example, a *DSP* has the permission to execute the task `Mail Information` (`T1`) (see Fig. 1).

Based on this running example, we used CPN Tools [5] to generate an event log including 100 cases. Furthermore, this log contains 11 subjects performing these tasks. In Section 3, we use this event log to assess the suitability of selected approaches to produce RBAC models from event logs.

2.2 Results

Fig. 2 shows the original role model on the left hand side surrounded by a gray rectangle. The other models from Fig. 2 show the results of the role derivation, role hierarchy mining, organizational mining, and staff assignment mining approaches applied in our case study, respectively. For each approach, the differences compared to the original model are displayed in grey-shaded areas. In the following section, these outcomes serve as basis to evaluate the suitability of each approach to produce a current-state RBAC model.

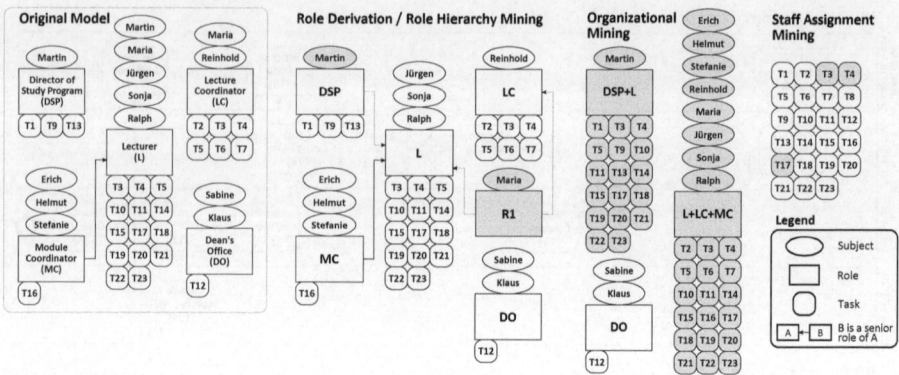

Fig. 2. Overview of Results: Role Models

3   Evaluation and Discussion

In this section, we compare the results from the four approaches with the original
model (see Fig. 2). In fact, we investigate if all techniques can identify the same
roles compared to the running example, reveal differences or similarities, and examine how the results of the approaches are suitable to generate RBAC models.

For the first step in our evaluation, we identified three essential issues within
the results that we discuss in the following:

- **Discovering original roles:** In our case study, most of the roles were identified by all approaches. In addition, role derivation and role hierarchy mining
  provide a role hierarchy that covers all task-to-role assignments using less
  role-to-subject assignments than in the original model. Furthermore, these
  two approaches generated an additional role *R1* which is the accumulation
  of the roles *L* and *LC*. This role is assigned to its tasks via inheritance relations in the role hierarchy. As a customization towards the original model,
  the role *R1* may be removed and the related subject can be assigned to the
  other two roles.
- **Unidentified roles:** Mostly, we were able to obtain all roles that are required to perform the teaching process of our case study (see Section 2.1).
  Yet, domain knowledge is required to define reasonable threshold levels for
  organizational mining. Depending on these threshold values certain roles
  may not be identified (*L*, *LC*, and *MC*). Other approaches (e.g., [12]) propose that in systems with existing organizational and role models, those roles
  which were unidentified by mining techniques can potentially be eliminated
  from the model; this can apply to roles which are scarcely used and do not
  provide enough administrative benefits.
- **Frequency of executions:** Results may vary if the techniques consider the
  frequency of task executions. For example, role hierarchy mining techniques
  can be applied considering different frequencies of executions. In contrast,
  role derivation excludes the frequency and also establishes roles with rarely
  used task sets. However, these roles can be customized and further evaluated.

Table 1. *Quantitative Measures of Results*

	Original Model	Role Derivation	Role Hierarchy	Staff Assignment	Organizational Mining
Characteristics					
Roles	10 (5 relevant)	6	6	-	3
Organizational Units	11 (2 relevant)	-	-	-	-
Role-to-Subject Assignments	13	11	11	-	11
Task-to-Role Assignments	25	25	25	23	36
Comparison to Original Model					
Roles exactly identified	-	5	5	-	1
Role-to-Subject Assignments	-	11	11	-	11
Task-to-Role Assignments*	-	25	25	20**	1
Accuracy (acc)	-	100%	100%	-	20%
Coverage (cov)	-	100%	100%	80%	4%

* covered by discovered (exactly identified) roles
** staff assignment rules matched by (exactly identified) task-to-role assignments

In a next step, we compare the results from the techniques used in this paper. Table 1 documents the discovered roles, organizational units, role-to-subject assignments, and task-to-role assignments for each technique. Furthermore, it shows that role derivation and role hierarchy mining were able to identify most of the original roles. For all techniques, there is a similar number of role-to-subject and task-to-role assignment relations.

Further, we examine the roles which were exactly identified, the role-to-subject assignments, the tasks of subjects covered by the exactly identified roles, the accuracy (acc), and the coverage (cov) of each technique. Therefore, we adapted the quantitative measures for accuracy and role coverage from [12]:

$$acc = \frac{\text{no. of roles identified exactly}}{\text{no. of roles in original model}}$$

$$cov = \frac{\text{no. task-to-role assignments covered by discovered roles}}{\text{no. task-to-role assignments in original model}}$$

In our case study, Table 1 shows that role derivation and role hierarchy mining have the highest accuracy and coverage of all tested techniques for our running example. Hence, the two methods are the most suitable techniques and their results can be used as basis to build RBAC models. With a few additional customizations, these two models can be tailored to the original model. In case role and organizational models exist, staff assignment mining is the most suitable technique to establish task-to-role assignment relations. Furthermore, we revealed that domain knowledge is essential to generate suitable roles via organizational mining. Without the knowledge and definition of thresholds it was difficult to obtain roles and assignment relations similar to the original model.

4   Conclusion

In this paper, we evaluated four approaches, namely role derivation, role hierarchy mining, organizational mining, and staff assignment mining, in order to obtain access control information from event logs. We applied these four techniques in a case study on a typical teaching process from the higher education system. First, we compared the models derived via the four techniques to the original model. Most of these techniques were able to identify the roles and tasks from the original model. Then, we evaluated the results with respect to similarities and differences and further examined if the results are suitable candidates for RBAC models. In future work, we will examine mining techniques for deriving RBAC models using more enhanced processes and corresponding event logs to determinate if we can obtain similar results.

Acknowledgements. The authors cordially thank Alexander Brandl for modeling the use case in CPN tools.

References

1. Baumgrass, A.: Deriving Current-State RBAC Models from Event Logs. In: Proc. of the 6th International Conference on Availability, Reliability and Security (ARES). IEEE Computer Society (2011)
2. Baumgrass, A., Schefer-Wenzl, S., Strembeck, M.: Deriving Process-Related RBAC Models from Process Execution Histories. In: Proc. of the 2012 IEEE 36th Int. Conference on Computer Software and Applications Workshops. IEEE Computer Society (2012)
3. Ferraiolo, D.F., Kuhn, R.D., Chandramouli, R.: Role-Based Access Control, 2nd edn. Artech House, Inc., Norwood (2007)
4. Ly, L., Rinderle, S., Dadam, P., Reichert, M.: Mining Staff Assignment Rules from Event-Based Data. In: Bussler, C., Haller, A. (eds.) BPM 2005. LNCS, vol. 3812, pp. 177–190. Springer, Heidelberg (2006)
5. de Medeiros, A.K.A., Günther, C.W.: Process Mining: Using CPN Tools to Create Test Logs for Mining Algorithms. In: Proc. of the 6th Workshop and Tutorial on Practical Use of Coloured Petri Nets and the CPN Tools (2005)
6. de Medeiros, A.K.A., van den Brand, P., van der Aalst, W.M.P., Weijters, T., Gaaloul, W., Pedrinaci, C.: Semantic Process Mining Tool - Final Implementation, Deliverable 6.11, Project IST 026850 SUPER (September 2008)
7. Song, M., van der Aalst, W.M.P.: Towards comprehensive support for organizational mining. Decision Support Systems 46(1) (2008)
8. Strembeck, M.: A Role Engineering Tool for Role-Based Access Control. In: Proc. of the 3rd Symposium on Requirements Engineering for Information Security (SREIS) (August 2005)
9. Strembeck, M., Mendling, J.: Modeling process-related RBAC models with extended UML activity models. Information and Software Technology 53(5) (2011)
10. van der Aalst, W.M.P.: Process Mining - Discovery, Conformance and Enhancement of Business Processes. Springer (2011)
11. van der Aalst, W.M.P., van Dongen, B.F., Günther, C., Rozinat, A., Verbeek, H.M.W., Weijters, A.J.M.M.: ProM: The Process Mining Toolkit. In: Proc. of the BPM 2009 Demonstration Track. vol. 489. CEUR-WS.org (September 2009)
12. Zhang, D., Ramamohanarao, K., Ebringer, T., Yann, T.: Permission Set Mining: Discovering Practical and Useful Roles. In: Proc. of the 2008 Annual Computer Security Applications Conference. IEEE Computer Society (2008)

Visualizing Large Business Process Models: Challenges, Techniques, Applications

Manfred Reichert

Institute of Databases and Information Systems, Ulm University, Germany
manfred.reichert@uni-ulm.de

Abstract. Large process models may comprise hundreds or thousands of process elements, like activities, gateways, and data objects. Presenting such process models to users and enabling them to interact with these models constitute crucial tasks of any process-aware information systems (PAISs). Existing PAISs, however, neither provide adequate techniques for visualizing and abstracting process models nor for interacting with them. In particular, PAISs do not provide tailored process visualizations as needed in complex application environments. This paper presents examples of large process models and discusses some of the challenges to be tackled when visualizing and abstracting respective models. Further, it presents a comprehensive framework that allows for personalized process model visualizations, which can be tailored to the specific needs of the different user groups. First, process model complexity can be reduced by abstracting the models, i.e., by eliminating or aggregating process elements not relevant in the given visualization context. Second, the appearance of process elements can be customized independent of the process modeling language used. Third, different visualization formats (e.g., process diagrams, process forms, and process trees) are supported. Finally, it will be discussed how tailored visualizations of process models may serve as basis for changing and evolving process models at a high level of abstraction.

Keywords: process visualization, process model abstraction, large process models.

1 Introduction

Many companies have to deal with a large number of business processes involving numerous tasks, data objects, organizational entities, and resources. Usually, these processes are captured in process models, which are stored in large process repositories comprising hundreds or even thousands of process models [1]. In turn, each of these process models may comprise a large number of activities and involve a multitude of stakeholders. In practice, each stakeholder may require a different perspective on the processes he or she is involved in, providing a customized visualization and information granularity. For example, managers rather prefer an abstract overview, whereas process actors need a detailed view of those process parts they are involved in. Hence, a personalized process visualization is

M. La Rosa and P. Soffer (Eds.): BPM 2012 Workshops, LNBIP 132, pp. 725–736, 2013.
© Springer-Verlag Berlin Heidelberg 2013

a much needed feature to be provided by any process-aware information system (PAIS).

Despite its practical importance, current PAISs do not offer adequate process visualization support. Usually, process models are displayed to the user in the same way as drawn by the process designer. However, these process models are often too complex (see Fig. 1 for an example) and, hence, are not comprehensible to end-users (e.g., when containing data transformation steps or other kinds of technical activities). Some tools allow altering the graphical appearance of a process and hiding selected process aspects (e.g., data flow). However, more sophisticated and flexible process visualization concepts are still missing in most PAISs.

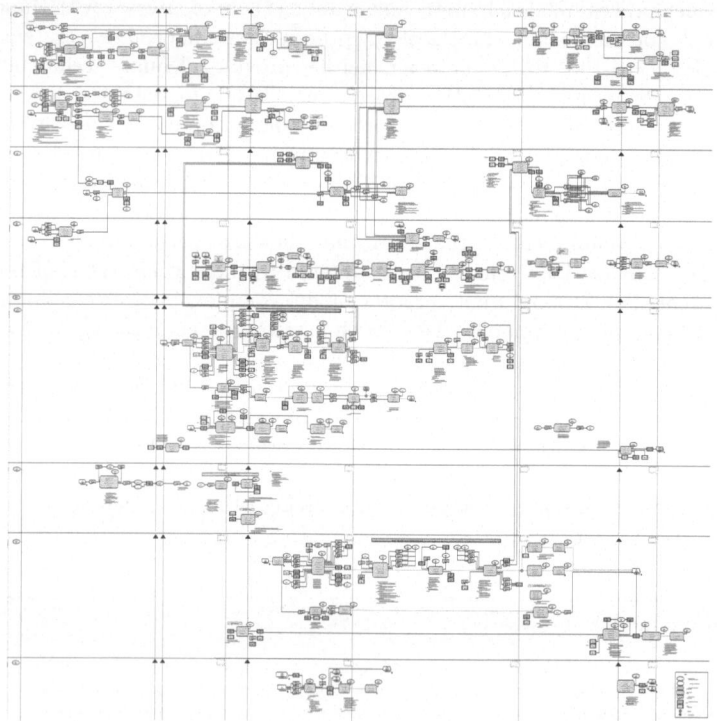

Fig. 1. Example of an engineering process model (partial view)

To elaborate basic visualization requirements we conducted several case studies [2], in which we identified three fundamental process visualization dimensions. First, it must be possible to reduce complexity by hiding or aggregating process information not relevant in the given context. Second, the notation and appearance of process nodes (e.g., activities and data objects) shall be customizable. Third, different visualization formats (e.g., process graph, table) need to be supported. This paper summarizes the Proviado framework that addresses all three visualization dimensions. Section 2 summarizes basic considerations required for understanding this paper. Section 3 presents the Proviado visualization framework, while Section 4 illustrates its use by means of an example. Finally, next steps in our research are discussed in Section 5.

2   Basic Considerations

Generally, any process visualization tool should distinguish between the model and instance level (cf Fig. 2). The former gathers various enterprise models, including organization, function, data, IT system, and process models. Thereby, a process model refers to elements of the other models and comprises a set of inter-connected activities, collectively realizing a certain business objective [3]; i.e., the activities are executed in a coordinated manner by different entities (e.g., humans and software agents) to reach process goals such as changing the design of a product, delivering merchandise, or treating a patient [4]. Furthermore, user- as well as pre-defined attributes may be associated with process models or activities (e.g. costs, needed resources), and hence become relevant in the context of process visualizations [5]. Examples of frameworks supporting the integrated modeling of the different enterprise aspects include ArchiMate [6], ADONIS [7], and ARIS [8].

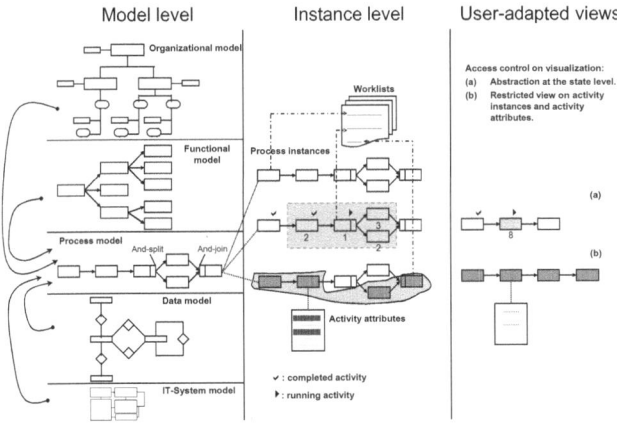

Fig. 2. Basic considerations

At the *model level*, a secure visualization of data related to a particular process model is required. An example of such a process model is depicted in Fig. 3. It shows a simplified model of a *change request process* as it can be found in the automotive domain. More precisely, this process model comprises five phases with 20 different activities in total. Furthermore, the control and data flow between activities, exceptional paths, role assignments, and IT system resources

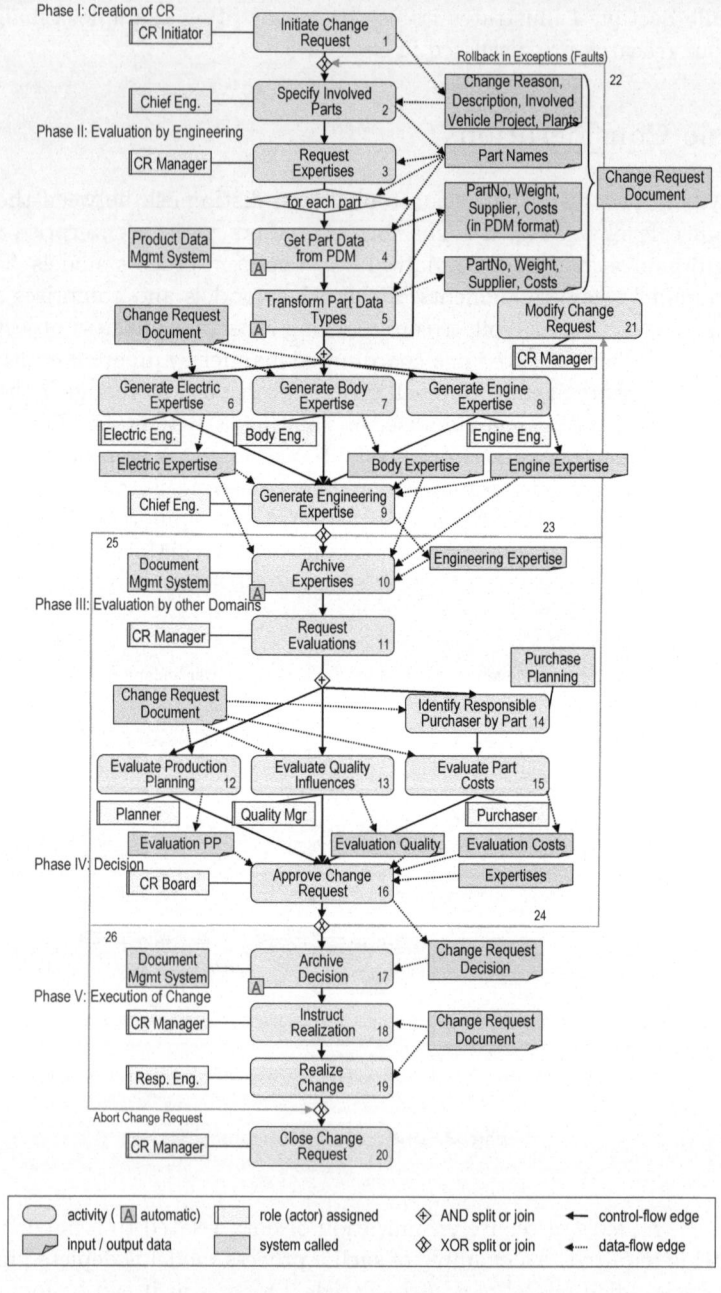

Fig. 3. Process model of a change request (CR)

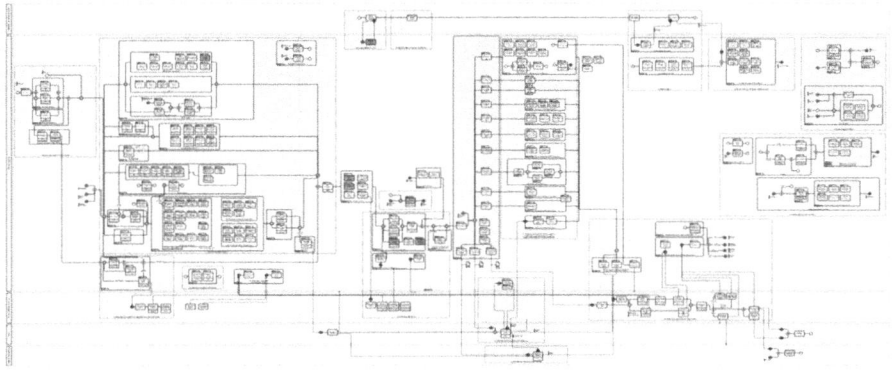

Fig. 4. A more complex variant of a change request process

are shown.—Note that more complex variants of this change request process exist in practice (see Fig. 4 for an example from the automotive domain).

In this paper, we will use the process model from Fig. 3 to illustrate basic process visualization concepts. Furthermore, we will show how a process model may be enriched with run-time data and then be displayed to authorized users [9]. Overall, flexible *configuration* and *personalization* of large process models are fundamental for the user-friendly visualization of these models.

At the *instance level*, a secure monitoring of running process instances is needed. More precisely, a process instance represents a particular enactment of a business process model (i.e., a single business case). Artifacts such as user work lists, activity execution states (e.g. `Running`), and invoked application services are characteristic for the instance level and hence need to be considered [3].

3   The Proviado Framework

The Proviado framework targets at a flexible and configurable visualization of large business process models and related process instances [2,10,11,9]. In particular, respective process visualizations must be customizable to the specific needs of the different stakeholders involved the process [2]. In this context, three dimensions need to be considered: First, it must be possible to reduce process model complexity by eliminating or aggregating information not relevant in the given context or for which the user does not have sufficient access rights. Second, the appearance of process elements (e.g., activities, data objects, control and data edges) should be customizable to user preferences, independent from the way the source process model is represented. Third, different visualization formats (e.g., process diagrams, Gantt charts, tables, or forms) need to be supported to cope with different user preferences.

For realizing a particular visualization of a process model and process instance, respectively, Proviado allows specifying related visualization models separately from the given process model. Such a visualization model comprises a number of configuration settings, which determine the process elements to be displayed and the graphical notation to be used. In particular, respective configuration settings can be specified at a high level of abstraction based on a sophisticated process view concept as well as on a flexible template mechanism.

3.1 Process View Concept

The view generation approach provided by Proviado [11,12] allows reducing the complexity of business process models through abstracting them. This model abstraction, in turn, is accomplished by applying well-defined transformation rules, which rely on model reduction as well as model aggregation techniques. As a result one obtains an abstracted *process view* of the original process model. *Model reduction operations* may be applied in order to hide (i.e., delete) selected elements of a process model. For example, consider Fig. 5: activities E, F and G are removed from the process model and a new control edge is inserted instead. Further, Fig. 5 illustrates the use of *aggregation operations*. For example, Aggregate(B,C,H,K) aggregates four activities and replaces them by one abstract node in the process model. Depending on the concrete structure of the sub-graph, induced by the set of activities to be aggregated, different model transformations become necessary. While in some cases simple model transformations are sufficient, in other scenarios a more complex restructuring of the process model to be visualized is required. Generally, realizing model abstractions based on aggregation operations is more difficult compared to the use of reduction operations. In particular, the relations the activities show in respect to their satellite objects (e.g., data elements, organizational entities) need to be preserved (cf. Fig. 5). Furthermore, for an abstracted node, its attribute values must be determined based on the attributes of all activities aggregated. Finally, aggregation operations are provided for all process aspects including data flow and actor assignments [12].

It is noteworthy that the Proviado view-building operations maintain the soundness of a process model if required. However, to introduce additional flexibility for process visualization, operations may violate certain structural model constraints if favorable (see [12] for a detailed discussion on this). Furthermore, complex view-building operations based on elementary aggregation and reduction operations are provided; e.g., "Show a process view containing all activities performed by a particular user role." Overall, these high-level view-building operations ease the definition and creation of meaningful process views significantly [12]).

3.2 Proviado Template Mechanism

While the described view-building approach allows us to define which process elements shall be displayed, the *Proviado Template Mechanism* [10] enables a flexible configuration of the graphical appearance of the different elements of a process model. For this purpose, Proviado provides a sophisticated template

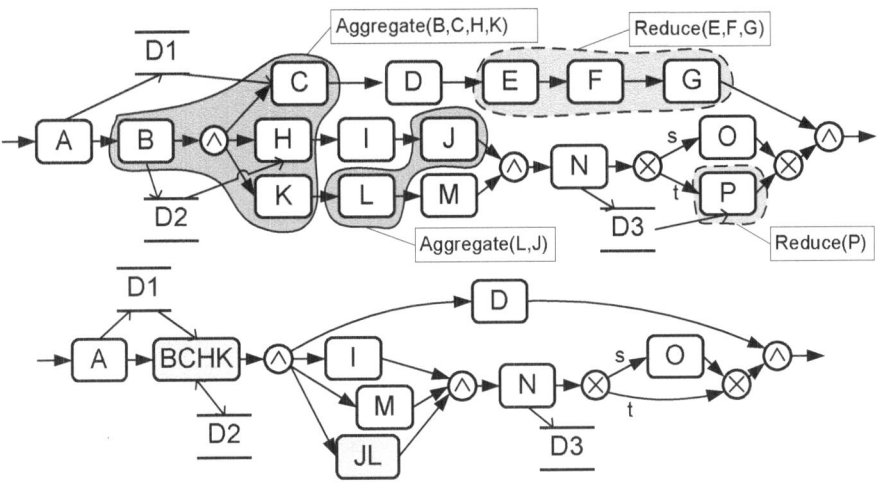

Fig. 5. Proviado view concept

mechanisms. More precisely, a *visualization template* describes the concrete notation (i.e. the symbols) to be used for visualizing a particular process element (e.g. an activity or a data object). Its graphical appearance (e.g. shape, arrow), in turn, is described using SVG (Scalable Vector Graphics). Based on this XML format, to a large degree, templates may be graphically defined using a standard SVG Editor.

Each template comprises a set of data fields (i.e. parameters) that may be filled with concrete process attribute values (e.g. activity name or activity state) at visualization time. Proviado uses XPath expressions to establish the relationship between symbol definition and data fields. Required data transformations (e.g. date format conversion) can be realized via ECMA-Script expressions. Altogether, a complete notation for process visualization comprises a set of templates. More precisely, each process element must be linked to a template. This link can be established statically (i.e. remain unchanged) or dynamically based on selected process data (e.g. depending on the runtime status of the process element). For example, the latter enables the use of different symbols for activities, e.g. depending on their state or the actor working on them. Finally, *Cascading Style Sheets* are used to vary the look of process drawings. Fig. 6 shows an example of a respective template.

Overall, the Proviado template mechanism allows for the use of a tailored process notation in a non-ambiguous and easy to maintain manner. In combination with the view concept described above, personalized process visualizations become possible. While non-relevant process elements can be removed or aggregated with other objects, the visualization of relevant process elements can be customized to specific user or application needs.

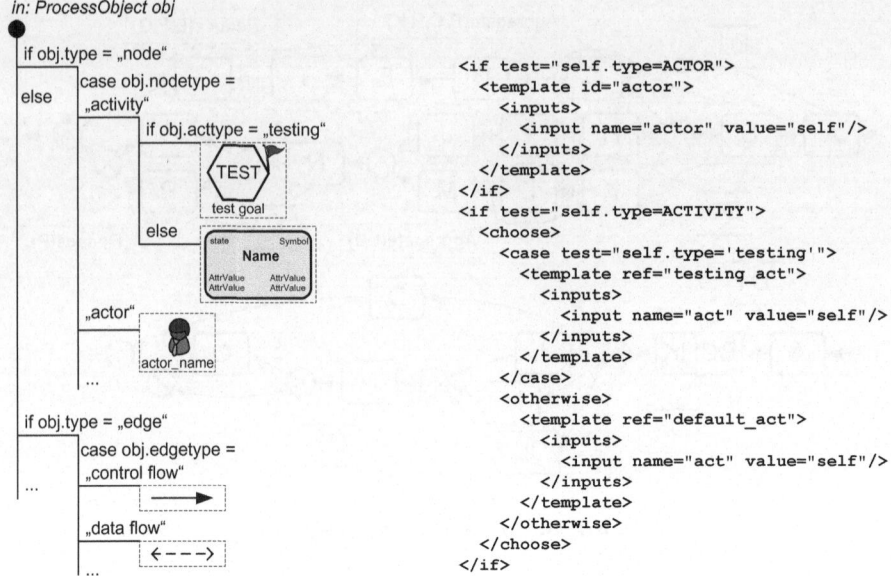

Fig. 6. Example of a Proviado template

3.3   Proviado Visualization Formats

In addition to the two visualization dimensions presented so far, Proviado enables different visualization formats for one and the same business process and further allows users to dynamically switch between these different visualizations. Examples include process diagrams, Gantt charts, trees (see [13] for a concrete approach), tables, and form-based visualizations (cf. Fig. 7).

3.4   Configuring a Process Visualization

Fig. 8 summarizes the basic steps required to automatically generate a particular process visualization. The starting point is an integrated process model, which correlates fragmented process data from different source information systems in a harmonized way. First, we restrict the visualization to that information needed by a particular user (S0). This is realized by a view component, which applies the sketched aggregation and reduction techniques to the given process model. Step S0 is followed by formatting steps S1, S2, and S3: S1 fixes the graphical symbols designed for the different process elements. For this purpose, Proviado considers information from a *visualization model*; S2 fills graphical symbols with real attribute values related to the process model or process instance that shall be displayed. Finally, in step S3 formatting parameters are customized to user preferences, e.g. by coloring the process visualization in accordance to cooperate identity guidelines.

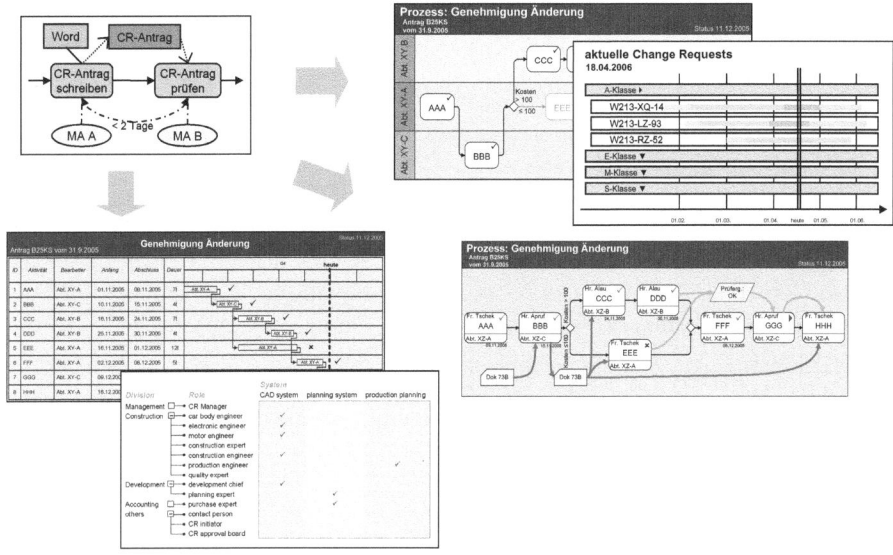

Fig. 7. Examples of different visualization formats

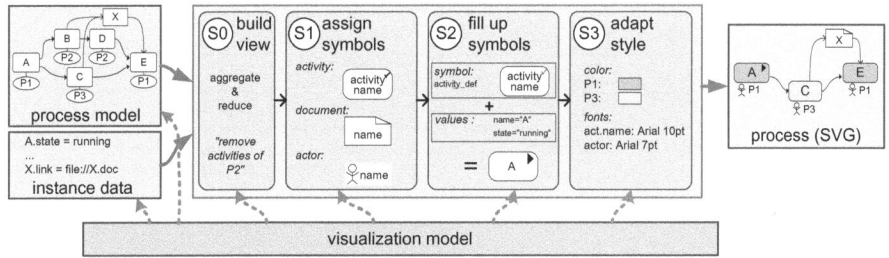

Fig. 8. Generating a process visualization in Proviado

4   Application Example

Consider again the process model from Fig. 3. Assume that an instance of this process shall be visualized for an actor from the engineering domain. For this purpose, non-relevant process elements have to be discarded. Automated steps for transforming and exchanging data (e.g. Steps 4 and 5), for example, shall not be displayed. The same applies to selected interactive steps (e.g. Steps 2 and 3). Finally, control edges capturing forward and backward jumps shall be removed. Altogether this process view can be realized by applying the following view-building operations (listed in brackets for each operation):

Aggregation:[1]. {1, 2}, {11, 12, 13, 14, 15}
Reduction: {3}, {4, 5}, {10}, {17, 18}, {20}, {21}
DeleteEdge: {22, 23, 24}, {25, 26}

The resulting process view would still contain a large number of satellite nodes (representing actors, systems, etc.) which usually shall not be displayed. Proviado visualization models allow omitting such nodes and assigning their data values to other visualization objects, e.g. activity boxes (cf. Fig. 9). Furthermore, with the *Proviado Template Mechanism* any desired appearance of the process view to be displayed can be realized. For example, the visualization from Fig. 9 contains information like change reason, change description, and involved product parts. Furthermore, a header has been added. Other data like a detailed change request (CR) description can be accessed via a tool tip. Finally, activities being of particular importance for engineers are highlighted.

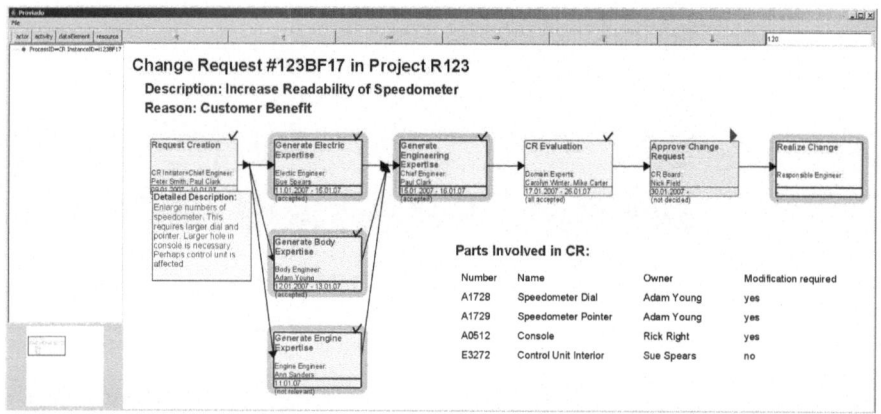

Fig. 9. Visualization of a CR process instance for engineers

Note that the created process drawing (cf. Fig. 9) constitutes one possible abstracted visualization of the process model from Fig. 3. Depending on specific user requirements, for example, Proviado allows providing different visualizations of the same process view, e.g. using a standardized notation like BPMN. Basic to this exchangeability of visual representations is the *Proviado Template Mechanism*. Generally, different information and layouts can be presented. Furthermore, new process views (with same or different appearance) can be easily realized. For example, for managers each of the five phases of the CR process could be aggregated to one single activity and only information about deadlines, delays, resources, and the final decision be visualized (cf. Fig. 10)

---

[1] Each operation is listed in brackets. The aggregations result in activities "Request Creation" and "CR Evaluation".

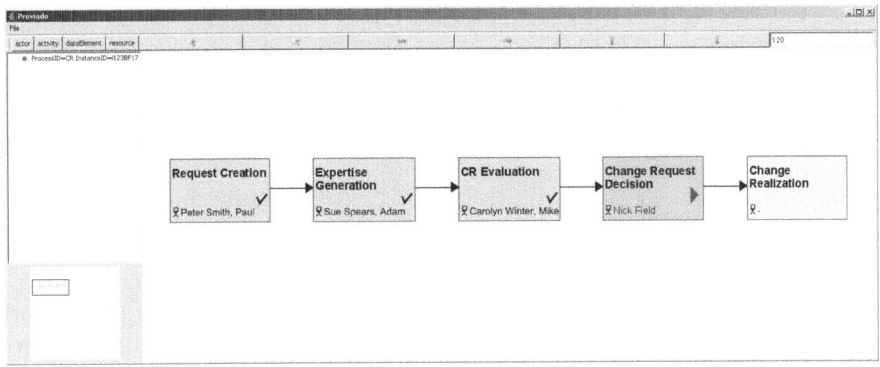

Fig. 10. Visualization of a CR process instance for managers

5   What are the Next Steps?

In the meantime, several other approaches for creating process model abstractions based on process views have been proposed (e.g., [14,15,16]). Like Proviado, these proposals focus on creating and visualizing abstracted process views, but do not consider another fundamental aspect of PAISs: change and evolution [3,17]. More precisely, they do not allow changing a large process model through editing or updating any of its view-based abstractions. As a consequence, process changes still must be directly applied to the original process model, which constitutes a complex as well as error-prone task for domain experts, particularly when confronted with large process models. To overcome this limitation, in addition to view-based process abstractions, users should be allowed to change large process models through updating respective process views. However, this must not be accomplished in an uncontrolled manner to avoid inconsistencies or errors.

In the proView project we address these and other challenges by providing powerful view-creation operations similar to the ones suggested in the context of Proviado; i.e., the operations allow abstracting process models through the reduction and aggregation of process elements as well as through changes of the process model notation. In addition, view-update operations allow adapting process views and propagating the respective changes to the underlying process model as well as to other related process views [18,19]. A series of user experiments is planned to evaluate whether process model abstractions and tailored process visualizations contribute to ease the change and evolution of complex process models.

References

1. Weber, B., Reichert, M., Mendling, J., Reijers, H.A.: Refactoring Large Process Model Repositories. Computers in Industry 62(5), 467–486 (2011)
2. Bobrik, R., Reichert, M., Bauer, T.: Requirements for the visualization of system-spanning business processes. In: Proc. DEXA 2005 Workshops, Copenhagen, pp. 948–954 (2005)

3. Reichert, M., Weber, B.: Enabling Flexibility in Process-aware Information Systems - Challenges, Methods, Technologies. Springer (2012)
4. Mutschler, B., Reichert, M., Bumiller, J.: Unleashing the effectiveness of process-oriented information systems: Problem analysis, critical success factors and implications. IEEE Transactions on Systems, Man, and Cybernetics 38(3), 280–291 (2008)
5. Michelberger, B., Mutschler, B., Reichert, M.: Process-oriented information logistics: Aligning enterprise information with business processes. In: 16th IEEE International EDOC Conference (EDOC 2012). IEEE Computer Society Press (2012)
6. Groenewegen, J., Hoppenbrouwers, S., Proper, E.: Playing ArchiMate Models. In: Bider, I., Halpin, T., Krogstie, J., Nurcan, S., Proper, E., Schmidt, R., Ukor, R. (eds.) BPMDS 2010 and EMMSAD 2010. LNBIP, vol. 50, pp. 182–194. Springer, Heidelberg (2010)
7. Kühn, H., Bayer, F., Junginger, S., Karagiannis, D.: Enterprise Model Integration. In: Bauknecht, K., Tjoa, A.M., Quirchmayr, G. (eds.) EC-Web 2003. LNCS, vol. 2738, pp. 379–392. Springer, Heidelberg (2003)
8. Davis, R.: ARIS Design Platform: Advanced Process Modelling and Administration. Springer (2008)
9. Reichert, M., Bassil, S., Bobrik, R., Bauer, T.: The Proviado access control model for business process monitoring components. Enterprise Modelling and Information Systems Architectures - An International Journal 5(3), 64–88 (2010)
10. Bobrik, R., Bauer, T., Reichert, M.: Proviado – Personalized and Configurable Visualizations of Business Processes. In: Bauknecht, K., Pröll, B., Werthner, H. (eds.) EC-Web 2006. LNCS, vol. 4082, pp. 61–71. Springer, Heidelberg (2006)
11. Bobrik, R., Reichert, M., Bauer, T.: View-Based Process Visualization. In: Alonso, G., Dadam, P., Rosemann, M. (eds.) BPM 2007. LNCS, vol. 4714, pp. 88–95. Springer, Heidelberg (2007)
12. Reichert, M., Kolb, J., Bobrik, R., Bauer, T.: Enabling Personalized Visualization of Large Business Processes through Parameterizable Views. In: Proc. ACM SAC 2012, Riva del Garda (Trento), Italy (2012)
13. Kolb, J., Reichert, M., Weber, B.: Using Concurrent Task Trees for Stakeholder-centered Modeling and Visualization of Business Processes. In: Oppl, S., Fleischmann, A. (eds.) S-BPM ONE 2012. CCIS, vol. 284, pp. 237–251. Springer, Heidelberg (2012)
14. Tran, H.: View-Based and Model-Driven Approach for Process-Driven, Service-Oriented Architectures. TU Wien, PhD thesis (2009)
15. Chiu, D.K.W., Cheung, S.C., Till, S., Karlapalem, K., Li, Q., Kafeza, E.: Workflow view driven cross-organizational interoperability in a web service environment. Inf. Techn. and Mgmt. 5(3-4), 221–250 (2004)
16. Smirnov, S., Reijers, H.A., Weske, M., Nugteren, T.: Business process model abstraction: a definition, catalog, and survey. Distributed and Parallel Databases 30(1), 63–99 (2012)
17. Reichert, M., Rinderle-Ma, S., Dadam, P.: Flexibility in Process-Aware Information Systems. In: Jensen, K., van der Aalst, W.M.P. (eds.) ToPNoc II. LNCS, vol. 5460, pp. 115–135. Springer, Heidelberg (2009)
18. Kolb, J., Kammerer, K., Reichert, M.: Updatable Process Views for Adapting Large Process Models: The proView Demonstrator. In: Proc. of the Business Process Management 2012 Demonstration Track, Tallinn, Estonia (2012)
19. Kolb, J., Kammerer, K., Reichert, M.: Updatable Process Views for User-Centered Adaption of Large Process Models. In: Liu, C., Ludwig, H., Toumani, F., Yu, Q. (eds.) ICSOC 2012. LNCS, vol. 7636, pp. 484–498. Springer, Heidelberg (2012)

A 3D-Navigator for Business Process Models

Philip Effinger

Wilhelm-Schickard-Institut für Informatik,
Eberhard Karls Universität Tübingen, Germany
effinger@informatik.uni-tuebingen.de

Abstract. In this tool report, we present an approach to inspect and present business process models in *3D*. We show our interactive *3D*-software *Flight Navigator*. Flight Navigator supports numerous interaction paradigms that enable the user to easily present, inspect and analyse a process model in a *3D*-environment. A major feature, that is part of our contribution, is the support of interactively browsing through a process (performing 'flights'). The tool provides navigational help for the user by displaying possible directions for further browsing using a head-up-display (HUD). The goal of Flight Navigator is to present, inspect and analyse business process models exploiting *3D*-navigation features. At the same time, the tool is aiming to provide ease of use without cognitively overburdening the user faced with a *3D*-environment.

1 Introduction

There are countless tools for modeling business processes. They serve the purpose of creating models from new or existing business processes. However, in many cases, a model might already exist but has to be understood and/or analysed. For instance, the wide field of 'Process Optimisation' is targeted on the improvement of (existing) business processes.

The understanding of a business process model depends on the preferred method of presentation. In this tool report, we present an alternative method *'Flight Navigator'* for presenting and analysing models.

We exploit the freedom of an additional dimension for displaying models (*3D*) and offer keyboard/mouse interaction methods to the user for simple navigation in *3D*.

For sequential analysis/presentation of models, we support 'flights' through the process model using smooth animations. Since we aim at supporting the user to keep his/her mental model while browsing in *3D*, the amount of information perceived by the user is higher than compared to *2D*-diagrams [1]. For preservation of a user's mental model, we keep the number of animation motions per flight step steady and set the orientation in the *3D*-environment as fixed, e.g. the up-direction in *3D* is set to a constant.

In the following, we specify the method that Flight Navigator uses for projection of an input model to its *3D*-environment and describe the navigation and flight features of our tool.

M. La Rosa and P. Soffer (Eds.): BPM 2012 Workshops, LNBIP 132, pp. 737–743, 2013.
© Springer-Verlag Berlin Heidelberg 2013

2   Related Work

Results from related fields can be divided into contributions to the field of *3D*-visualization or (*3D*-) process modeling:

3D (Process) visualization: Information visualization is a huge field even if restricted to *3D*, a good overview can be found in [2]. Early approaches on visualization in *3D* stem from the graph drawing community presenting interactive graph visualization [3] and program information [4] in *3D*. The rise of new modeling languages allowed more fields of information visualization, e.g. for class template diagrams [5] or UML diagrams [6]. In previous work [7], business process models are projected in a so-called *2.5D*-environment which projects model elements on fixed hyperplanes in *3D*-space. We will also use this projection in the following. A framework for *2.5D*-visualizations is presented in [8] and is extended to three dimensions in [9]. Other works made use of the *3D* hyperbolic space for the investigation of methods for visualizations of larger graphs [10].

For our *3D*-navigation tool, we adopted conventions for navigation and interaction from [11], a comprehensive survey on navigation and interaction techniques.

Process Modeling in 3D: A representation of business process models that allows for modeling in *3D* is developed in [12] and [13]. A dedicated environment for modeling in *3D* with support of various types of (workflow) diagrams is presented in [14]. The approach also offers integration into the powerful Eclipse editing framework GEF[1]. A case study on business processes in the *3D*–space is performed in [15]. Modeling environments in *3D* that use, for instance, Second Life®[2] are presented in [16]; an extended version for collaborative modeling in *3D* is shown in [17].

3   Presentation of Flight Navigator

In this section, we will present our Flight Navigator, a software with features providing interactive browsing in a *3D*-environment. The goal is to support presentation, inspection and analysis of business process models, also with the help of Business Process Flights (BPFs).

For modeling the process models, we use the de facto standard modeling language *Business Process Model and Notation (BPMN)* [3]. More specifically, we use the part of *collaboration diagrams* of BPMN which represent interactions between roles and responsibilities and their corresponding tasks.

In the following, we describe used techniques for projection of process models into *2.5D*, supported navigation features and flight planning of Flight Navigator.

---

[1] http://www.eclipse.org/gef/, last accessed: 12-07-20.

[2] http://secondlife.com/, last accessed: 12-07-20.

[3] http://www.bpmn.org, last accessed: 12-07-20.

3.1 Perspectives and Projection onto *2.5D*

For the creation of our BPMN-models in *3D*, we use two techniques: organizational perspective and *2.5D*-projection. In [18], the following set of perspectives on a general business process is presented:

- Functional perspective: describes single process steps and their purpose.
- Data (flow) perspective: describes data used in the process and the flow of data including external data flow. Thus, data flow and sequence flow can be treated separately.
- Operational perspective: specifies which operation (service) is invoked in order to execute a process step. It relates to services derived from (external) service libraries.
- Organizational perspective: defines agents, e.g. users or roles in general, that are responsible for specific process steps.
- Behavioural perspective: defines causal dependencies, also called control flow, between modeling elements.

For our purpose, we employ the organizational perspective. We derive the roles and responsibilities from the structure of swimlanes/pools in the original BPMN model. For instance, swimlanes and pools represent departments or single executives in companies which are assigned specific tasks in a process. If not given by the input model, we compute element positions in layers (without overlaps) by applying techniques of automatic layout algorithms, see [19].

After having derived the view from the organizational perspective of a model, we project the view into *3D*, using the concept of two-and-a-half dimensions (*2.5D*) [7]. In *2.5D*, elements of the model are assigned to layers. Layers are hyperplanes in *3D*, with a individual but fixed value in z-axis direction (z defines the depth values of layers). The layers can be considered as a stack of hyperplanes with equal size in *3D*. The final view of a process model after projection is depicted in Figure 1.

3.2 Navigation Support

For navigating in Flight Navigator, we aimed to support high user interactivity and smooth transitions when moving in the *2.5D*-model. Flight Navigator offers mouse-actuated navigation on the viewing plane and rotation of that plane, as well as changing the viewing height to accommodate viewing of different layers. For easier use, we implemented keyboard shortcuts for rotation, tilt and change of viewing height of the display. Moreover, distances between layers and zoom scale can be changed dynamically using keyboard shortcuts (or scroll wheel). These features are designed to enable the user to navigate freely in the *2.5D*-visualization and adapt the display to individual preferences. All transitions between different viewpoints are animated with soft movements (using smooth camera animations). Thus, the mental model of the viewer remains present and we achieve a persistent process model with convenient navigation handling. With Flight Navigator, users should be able to survey large and complicated processes.

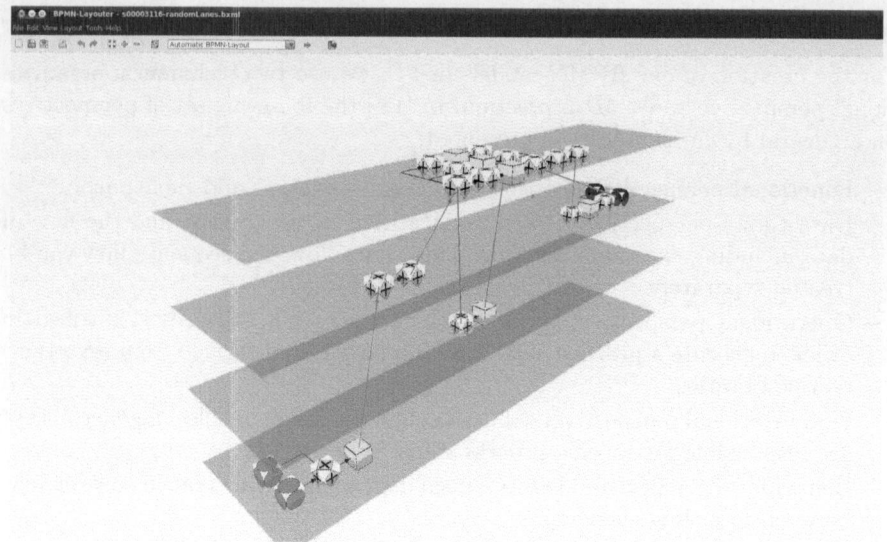

Fig. 1. Overview of a complete process model in the *3D*-navigator. The layout of the model considers the flow orientation (left to right) of the process.

3.3   Navigating Flights

The idea of flights in process models is the following: (a) start at an element that represents an entry point of the process; (b) then, follow the process by considering the predetermined directed sequence flow; (c) analyse/present the sequence flow, e.g., check if the order of tasks in this flight was correct and as expected. A jump (a step in the flight) from an element a to an element b is allowed only if b is a successor of a in the process' sequence flow, or if b is a predecessor of a. A jump is performed by a smooth animated transition of the view perspective in Flight Navigator.

Since an element a may have several predecessors and/or successors, we use a head-up-display (HUD) to preview miniature images of the possible destination elements. The destination elements are updated after every jump since the destination candidates (the sets of predecessors and successors) depend on the current element. In Figure 2, the HUD is depicted for a node with two predecessors and one successor. The placing of the HUD miniature preview images is derived from the keyboard shortcut for the destination node, e.g. Key '8' represents the top center of HUD, Key '1' for the left bottom position of the HUD, see Figure 2 for an example. The keyboard shortcuts are chosen for good support of a intuitive user interface: going 'forward' is assigned to keys '7' to '9' on the numerical pad for successors; going 'backwards' is assigned to keys '1' to '3' for predecessors while '2' (backwards) is also used to keep a history of the last visited nodes. Keys '4' to '6' are dynamically assigned if the set of neighbours of either direction (forward, backward) grows larger than 3. However, this is a rare case. The maximum size of predecessors/successors in our test set, taken from [20], was 5.

Also, in activated flight mode, the user can simply select a random node from the model to start a flight. The HUD is then updated immediately. Also, we implemented to switch to start/end nodes using keys 'HOME' / 'END'.

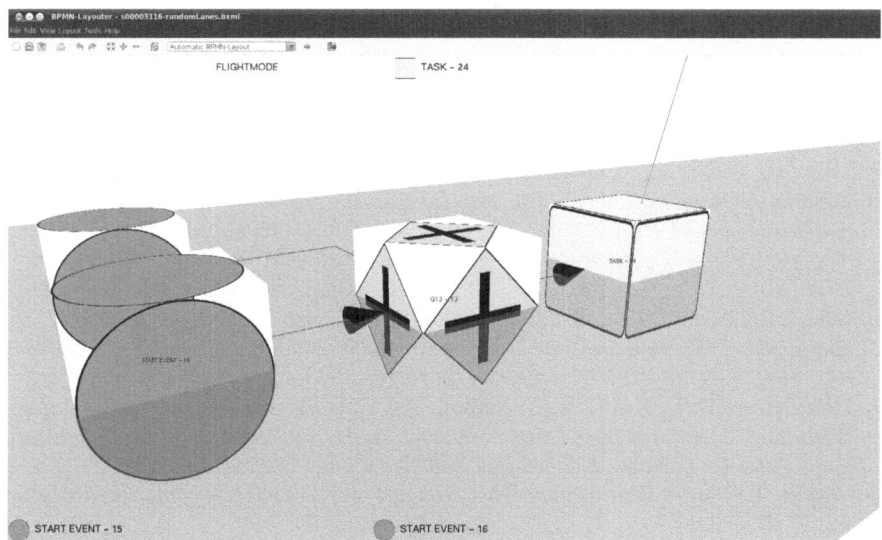

Fig. 2. Display of the HUD (head-up-display) in the *3D*-navigator. From the current node (Gateway 'G13'), a single successor ('TASK - 24') is reachable by pressing keyboard shortcut '8', see top center HUD position; the two predecessors ('START EVENT - 15','START EVENT - 16') are reachable by pressing '1', or '2' respectively, see bottom HUD positions.

3.4   Implementation

The Flight Navigator is implemented using standard technology. We use JAVA™ 1.5 and JOGL [4], an open-source interface for binding OpenGL® into a JAVA program. For graph analysis and basic data structures, we employ the graph library yFiles developed by yWorks [5]. Flight Navigator is also integrated into our academic BPMN modeling tool *BPMN-Layouter* [6].

---

[4] http://download.java.net/media/jogl/www/, last accessed: 12-07-20.

[5] http:///www.yworks.de, last accessed: 12-07-20.

[6] http://algo.inf.uni-tuebingen.de/?site=forschung/graphenzeichnen/ bpmn-layouter, a video demonstrating interactivity and animations in Flight Navigator is available here, last accessed: 12-07-20.

4   Summary

We presented our software tool 'Flight Navigator', a *3D*-navigator for analysing and presenting business process models. It supports strong interactivity with the user using keyboard/mouse input and real-time *3D*-presentation. For the presentation, we use the concept of *2.5D* for projection of business process models into *3D*.

Future development might comprehend adding more features: The Flight Navigator software is ready to be extended, e.g. for editing business process models in *3D* or for activating an 'autopilot' for automatic process presentations.

References

1. Ware, C., Franck, G.: Viewing a graph in a virtual reality display is three times as good as 2D diagram. In: VL, pp. 182–183 (1994)
2. Teyseyre, A.R., Campo, M.R.: An overview of 3D software visualization. IEEE Transactions on Visualization and Computer Graphics 15, 87–105 (2009)
3. Bruß, I., Frick, A.: Fast Interactive 3-D Graph Visualization. In: Brandenburg, F.J. (ed.) GD 1995. LNCS, vol. 1027, pp. 99–110. Springer, Heidelberg (1996)
4. Reiss, S.P.: 3-D Visualization of Program Information. In: Tamassia, R., Tollis, I.G. (eds.) GD 1994. LNCS, vol. 894, Springer, Heidelberg (1995)
5. Hoipkemier, B.N., Kraft, N.A., Malloy, B.A.: 3D visualization of class template diagrams for deployed open source applications. In: Proceedings of the 18th Intern. Conference on Software Engineering and Knowledge Engineering (2006)
6. Dwyer, T.: Three Dimensional UML Using Force Directed Layout. In: InVis.au, pp. 77–85 (2001)
7. Effinger, P., Spielmann, J.: Lifting business process diagrams to 2.5 dimensions. In: IS&T/SPIE Electronic Imaging, Visualization and Data Analysis, San Jose. Proc. SPIE, vol. 7530 (2010)
8. Hong, S.-H., Murtagh, T.: Visualisation of Large and Complex Networks Using PolyPlane. In: Pach, J. (ed.) GD 2004. LNCS, vol. 3383, pp. 471–481. Springer, Heidelberg (2005)
9. Hong, S.-H.: MultiPlane: A New Framework for Drawing Graphs in Three Dimensions. In: Healy, P., Nikolov, N.S. (eds.) GD 2005. LNCS, vol. 3843, pp. 514–515. Springer, Heidelberg (2006)
10. Munzner, T.: H3: laying out large directed graphs in 3D hyperbolic space. In: INFOVIS, pp. 2–10 (1997)
11. Herman, I., Melançon, G., Marshall, M.S.: Graph visualization and navigation in information visualization: A survey. IEEE Trans. Vis. Comput. Graph. 6(1), 24–43 (2000)
12. Betz, S., Eichhorn, D., Hickl, S., Klink, S., Koschmider, A., Li, Y., Oberweis, A., Trunko, R.: 3D representation of business process models. In: MobIS, pp. 73–87 (2008)
13. Brown, R.A., Recker, J.C.: Improving the traversal of large hierarchical process repositories. In: 20th Australasian Conference on Information Systems, Monash University, Melbourne (2009)
14. von Pilgrim, J., Duske, K.: GEF3D: a framework for two-, two-and-a-half-, and three-dimensional graphical editors. In: SOFTVIS, pp. 95–104 (2008)

15. Schönhage, B., van Ballegooij, A., Eliëns, A.: 3D gadgets for business process visualization - a case study. In: Web3D, pp. 131–138 (2000)
16. Brown, R.: Conceptual modelling in 3D virtual worlds for process communication. In: 7th Asia-Pacific Conference on Conceptual Modelling, APCCM 2010, pp. 25–32 (2010)
17. West, S., Brown, R.A., Recker, J.C.: Collaborative business process modeling using 3D virtual environments. In: 16th Americas Conference on Information Systems, Association for Information Systems (AIS) (2010)
18. Jablonski, S., Goetz, M.: Perspective Oriented Business Process Visualization. In: ter Hofstede, A.H.M., Benatallah, B., Paik, H.-Y. (eds.) BPM 2007 Workshops. LNCS, vol. 4928, pp. 144–155. Springer, Heidelberg (2008)
19. Effinger, P., Krug, R.: 2.5D Layout Approaches for Process Models (submitted, 2012)
20. Fahland, D., Favre, C., Jobstmann, B., Koehler, J., Lohmann, N., Völzer, H., Wolf, K.: Instantaneous Soundness Checking of Industrial Business Process Models. In: Dayal, U., Eder, J., Koehler, J., Reijers, H.A. (eds.) BPM 2009. LNCS, vol. 5701, pp. 278–293. Springer, Heidelberg (2009)

Visualizing the Process of Process Modeling
with PPMCharts

Jan Claes[1], Irene Vanderfeesten[2], Jakob Pinggera[3], Hajo A. Reijers[2],
Barbara Weber[3], and Geert Poels[1]

[1] Ghent University, Belgium
{jan.claes,geert.poels}@ugent.be
[2] Eindhoven University of Technology, The Netherlands
{i.t.p.vanderfeesten,h.a.reijers}@tue.nl
[3] University of Innsbruck, Austria
{jakob.pinggera,barbara.weber}@uibk.ac.at

Abstract. In the quest for knowledge about how to make good process models, recent research focus is shifting from studying the quality of process models to studying the process of process modeling (often abbreviated as *PPM*) itself. This paper reports on our efforts to visualize this specific process in such a way that relevant characteristics of the modeling process can be observed graphically. By recording each modeling operation in a modeling process, one can build an event log that can be used as input for the *PPMChart Analysis* plug-in we implemented in ProM. The graphical representation this plug-in generates allows for the discovery of different patterns of the process of process modeling. It also provides different views on the process of process modeling (by configuring and filtering the charts).

Keywords: Analysis Techniques and Visualization for Processes, Visualization Techniques for Processes, Change Visualization for Processes.

1   Introduction

"A picture is worth a thousand words." This phrase is believed to originate from an Asian verb and advocates the use of visualization. The actual value of the graphical representation of models, however, is heavily influenced by its understandability [1, 2]. In our research we look for determinants of the modeling process that influence the understandability of the process modeling result (i.e., a process model) [3]. The visualization presented in this paper is developed to support our research to the process of process modeling. The *process of process modeling* is the course of action taken by the modeler to create/design/construct a (business) process model consisting of start and end event(s), activities, gateways, edges, etc. Such a process model artifact is created by a stepwise design process, e.g., first putting a start event on the canvas, then an activity, then an arc connecting the start event and the activity, etc.

To get insights into how process models are constructed, we searched for a technique to visualize the process of process modeling based on a log of recorded

M. La Rosa and P. Soffer (Eds.): BPM 2012 Workshops, LNBIP 132, pp. 744–755, 2013.

modeling actions, such that one can *quickly* obtain *in-depth* insights in the visualized process. In earlier research we used Modeling Phase Diagrams [4] to focus on high-level, less detailed process characteristics: i.e., modeling phases. A modeling phase (e.g., reconciliation phase) summarizes a set of 'equivalent' events in the process (e.g., move_node, create_edge_bendpoint) as one phase of which a modeling phase diagram shows only the duration and number of constructed model elements. For the more extensive representation described in this paper, we drew inspiration from the *Dotted Chart Analysis* plug-in of the process mining framework ProM [5]. This technique provides much detail and at the same time lets the user take a helicopter view on the visualized process. We extended the existing plug-in to solve three concrete issues when representing an instance of the process of process modeling:

(i)   the process of process modeling has a fixed set of possible events and therefore we mapped these events on *fixed colors* used in the visualization, which allows for visually comparing different charts,

(ii) to establish a clear link between the visualization of the process and the constructed process model, we provided *two extra sort options* that are based on the execution order of the modeling elements in the process model,

(iii) we added the possibility to *filter* certain modeling operations in order to be able to take different, more abstract views on the same modeling process.

The visualization technique presented in this paper allows us to zoom in on the separate operations of the construction of the model. At the same time, it provides an overview of the entire modeling process. In this way it enables to obtain graphically a fast but detailed impression of how a process modeling effort was conducted. The acquired insights facilitate the study of the process of process modeling.

The structure of the paper is as follows. Section 2 presents related research. Section 3 describes the necessary data for our visualization, the visualization itself, and the implemented tool support. Section 4 illustrates the use of the tool by describing how it was used to discover patterns in process model construction. Finally, Section 5 concludes with a discussion and an overview of future research plans.

2   Related Research

There is a wide body of literature that focuses on the *quality* of process models [6–10]. Mostly, the process model is considered in these papers as a given, complete, and finished artifact. Other literature reports on research on *methods* for business process modeling (e.g., [11] provides a comparative analysis between different techniques for business process modeling and contains an extensive list of related papers on process model notations). Recently, approaches are emerging that aim to connect the previous two topics: In what way does the used (in)formal modeling method relate to the properties (e.g., quality) of the outcome: a process model? In this context, various authors refer to the construction of a process model as *the process of process modeling* [12–15], a term often abbreviated as *PPM*.

Crapo et al., report on research about the process of modeling in terms of visualization (i.e., they focus on graphical modeling) [16]. However, we are not aware of other research about the visualization *of* the process of process modeling. In [4] the possibilities of representing different phases of process modeling in Modeling Phase Diagrams were examined. Three specific phases are distinguished: comprehension, modeling and reconciliation. The visualization described in [4] differs from the one presented in this paper by the level of abstraction: While a Modeling Phase Diagram abstracts from individual modeling operations, our representation shows all recorded operations and all present information about the operations (e.g., timing aspects, model element type, and order in the model).

The ultimate goal of our research is to improve knowledge about how to make correct and more understandable process models. Other research that provides guidelines or techniques for improved business process modeling includes Seven process modeling guidelines (7PMG) [17] and Guidelines of Modeling (GoM) [18].

3   Visualizing the Process of Process Modeling with PPMCharts

We called our visualization of the process of process modeling a *PPMChart*. Section 3.1 explains which data is used for construction of the charts, Section 3.2 describes the properties of PPMCharts, and Section 3.3 centers on the developed tool support for generating PPMCharts.

3.1   Data Collection

In order to visualize the process of process modeling, we use a record of modeling operations done by the modeler, and recorded by our experimentation tool, during the modeling process. The list of possible operations we consider is given in Table 1. For instance, the operation of creating an activity in the process model is logged by an event "CREATE_ACTIVITY". In our analysis and experiments we build on a subset of the BPMN notation that can be used for the modeling. This subset was selected to correspond with the supported notation of our experimentation tool (see Section 4.1) and consists of six of the ten most used elements of BPMN according to [19]: *start* and *end event, activities, XOR* and *AND gateways*, and *edges*.

Besides *creation* of these model elements, the visualization also includes changes in the model. Activities, events and gateways can be *moved* over the canvas or *deleted*. Edges can be *deleted* or *reconnected* (which we categorized as a deletion and creation), an edge can be rerouted through *creation, movement* and *deletion* of bendpoints, and the label of an edge can be *moved*. Finally, activities and edges can be *named* or *renamed*. Note, that for the rest of the paper we assume only these modeling operations as part of the modeling process (according to the recorded operations of the experimentation tool), but our approach can easily be adapted for other modeling operation sets.

Table 1. Operations in the construction of a process model

Create	Move	Delete
CREATE_START_EVENT	MOVE_START_EVENT	DELETE_START_EVENT
CREATE_END_EVENT	MOVE_END_EVENT	DELETE_END_EVENT
CREATE_ACTIVITY	MOVE_ACTIVITY	DELETE_ACTIVITY
CREATE_XOR	MOVE_XOR	DELETE_XOR
CREATE_AND	MOVE_AND	DELETE_AND
CREATE_EDGE	MOVE_EDGE_LABEL	DELETE_EDGE
RECONNECT_EDGE (**)	CREATE_EDGE_BENDPOINT (*)	RECONNECT_EDGE (**)
	MOVE_EDGE_BENDPOINT (*)	
	DELETE_EDGE_BENDBPOINT (*)	

Other : NAME_ACTIVITY, RENAME_ACITIVTY, NAME_EDGE, RENAME_EDGE

(*) create, move and delete edge bendpoint were considered as moving an edge

(**) reconnect edge was considered as deleting and creating an edge

3.2   Visualization with PPMChart

The collected data about consecutive operations in the process of process modeling for one modeler are used to construct a PPMChart (see Fig. 1). The horizontal axis represents a time interval of one hour. Vertically, each line represents one element of the model as it was present during modeling. Each dot represents one operation performed on the element; the color of the dot represents the type of operation: create (green), move (blue), delete (red) and (re)name (pink). The elements are vertically sorted by the time of their first operation; the first operation performed on each model element is its creation. The dots are aligned to the right such that the last operation performed by the modeler is shown to occur at the end of the one hour interval. Fig. 2 shows the process model resulting from the process model construction process that is visualized in Fig. 1.

3.3   Tool Support

We implemented a plug-in for the popular process mining framework ProM[1]. The input for most plug-ins in this tool is an event log. The file format for event logs for ProM is xml based and follows a certain hierarchical structure: A *process* consists of *traces* and each trace is a collection of *events*. The process, traces and events can have attributes (e.g., a time stamp). In our case *modeling operations* correspond with events and the operations on the same model element are bundled in one trace. We expect the *names* of events to correspond with the operations in Table 1. Further, each event has an attribute *id* that corresponds with the name of its trace. It can be seen as the unique identifier of the modeling element.

---

[1] For information and download we refer to http://www.promtools.org

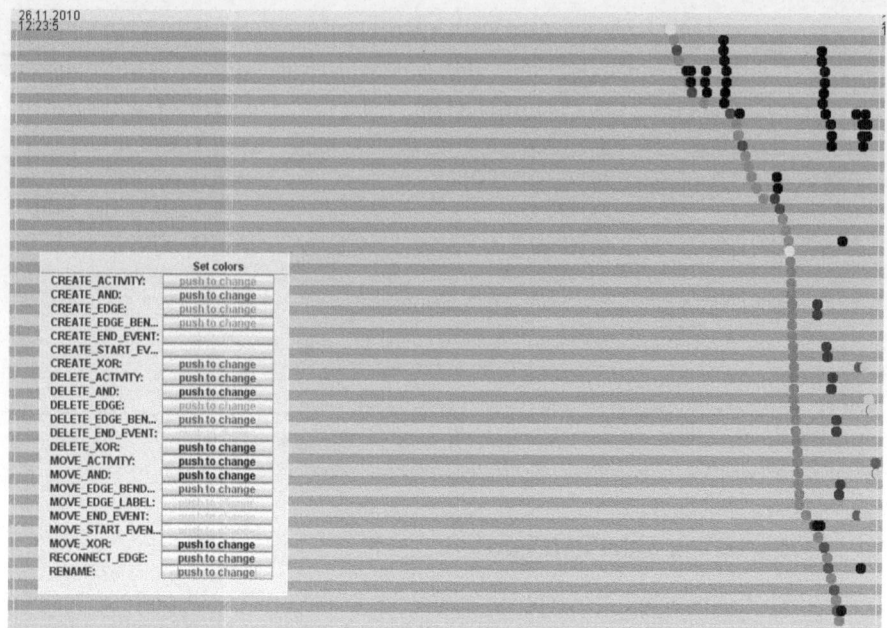

Fig. 1. Visualization of the operations in the creation of one model by one modeler.[2] The operations creating nodes (activities and gateways) are depicted as green dots; the creation of edges is depicted in light green/blue, the moving of model elements in darker blue, the deletion in reddish colors and the reconnect or renaming in pink/purple. The first line for instance shows the creation of the start event, followed by a move of the start event on a later time.

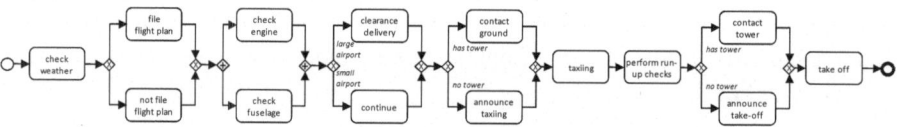

Fig. 2. Process model as result of the modeling process in Fig. 1[2]

Our *PPMChart Analysis* plug-in (see Fig. 3) is an adapted version of the existing *Dotted Chart Analysis* plug-in [5]. In the middle, the PPMChart is presented. At the right-hand side the user can customize the view by filtering on specific operations or elements: The top part represents a small view on the unfiltered PPMChart. Below, one can choose to hide specific element types (e.g., hide edges), hide specific operations (e.g., hide (re)name operations), or hide elements with a specific operation (e.g., hide deleted elements). For users that are familiar with the features of the Dotted Chart Analysis plug-in, we have chosen to keep the options of that plug-in in our implementation at the left-hand side of the window (see [5] for more information).

---

[2] High resolution graphs are available from
http://www.janclaes.info/papers/PPMViz

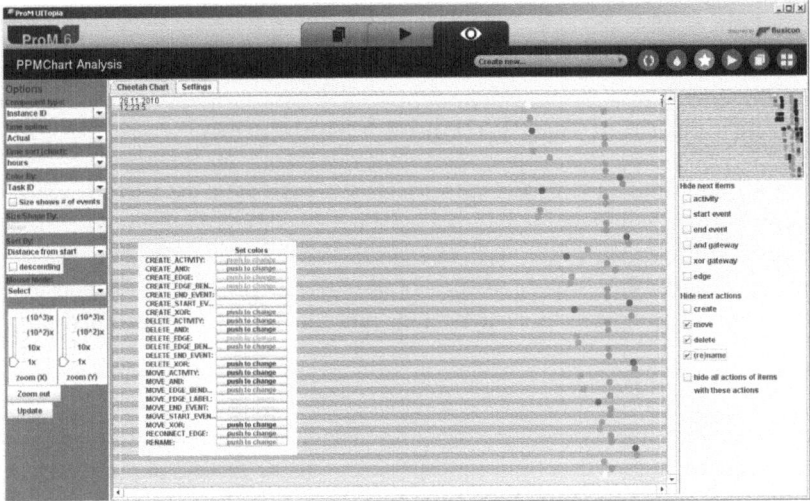

Fig. 3. Screenshot of the PPMChart window in ProM[2]

To facilitate relating the different lines of the chart to the proper model elements in the process model, we also provided an additional *sort* option. This option sorts the lines of the chart from top to bottom according to the execution order of the model elements in the process model from start to end. Fig. 3 shows an example for the same case as for Fig. 1 and Fig. 2 but sorted in a different way. The green dots from top to bottom in the chart correspond to the model elements in the execution order in the process model (in Fig. 2 graphically from left to right). There are two variants of the additional sort option:

- The *Distance from start* sort option focuses on *execution* order. The value for nodes, events and gateways is defined as the sum of the lengths of the edges in the model, for the longest non-iterative path from that model element to the start event. The value for an edge is the average of the values for the source and target node of that edge.

- The *Create order from start* sort option centers on the *creation* of model elements from start to end and therefore it sorts an edge not between the nodes it connects, but after these nodes (an edge can only be created after both nodes exist). We use the same value for nodes, events and gateways, but for edges the value is one more than the maximum of values of source and target node.

Note that these calculations are highly influenced by the layout of the process model. This means that we adopt the modeler's view on the process in the visualizations.

For the example shown in Fig. 3, we selected 'Sort by Distance from start' and show only create operations (*start/end event* creation operations are colored light green, *activity* creations are bright green, *gateways* are dark green, *edges* are blue-green). It can be observed that the modeler first creates events, nodes and gateways in an order from start to end. Next, edges were created to connect the model elements.

Finally, some extra nodes and edges were added. In the top right panel, all operations are displayed: Many intermediate move operations (blue dots) can be noticed.

4   Application of the PPMChart Visualization

Section 4.1 describes an experiment to which we applied our visualization technique to discover underlying patterns in process model construction. Section 4.2 describes how we used the experimental data to evaluate the correctness of our visualization technique. Section 4.3 lists a number of discovered patterns to demonstrate the usefulness of our technique for analyzing the process of process modeling data.

4.1   Experiment Design

In order to test the correctness and usefulness of our visualization and the implementation, we used data from our experiments on the process of process modeling, supported by Cheetah Experimental Platform (CEP)[3]. This platform instruments a basic process modeling editor to record each user's modeling operations along with the corresponding time stamps in an event log. Table 1 summarizes all recorded operations.

The experiment was conducted in November 2010 with 103 students following a graduate course on Business Process Management at Eindhoven University of Technology. Their task was to create a process model in BPMN from an informal description[4] while their process of process modeling was recorded in CEP. In the development of CEP, the developers decided to use a subset of BPMN (that we adopted for our research) without providing sophisticated tool features. The reasoning behind this was to not get the modelers confused or overwhelmed with tool aspects [16].

4.2   Evaluation of Correctness: Replay the Modeling Process

By capturing all of the described interactions with the modeling tool, we are able to replay a recorded modeling process at any point in time, without interfering with the modeler. This allows for observing how the process model unfolds on the modeling canvas [4]. The evaluation of correctness was done by means of comparing the properties of the dots in the visualization with the observed properties of the steps in the replay. The test data concerned the process modeling efforts of the 103 students.

4.3   Demonstration of Usefulness: Discovered Properties and Variations of the Process of Process Modeling

This section demonstrates the usefulness of the visualization by providing five concrete examples of properties of the process of process modeling that were derived from an analysis of the PPMCharts.

---

[3] For detailed information and download we refer to
http://www.cheetahplatform.org

[4] The case description is available at http://www.janclaes.info/papers/PPMViz

4.3.1 General Dimensions: Number of Created Model Elements and Duration of the Modeling Process

First, as one would expect from a visualization of the process of process modeling, the size and modeling time dimensions of the process can easily be compared between charts. Fig. 4a shows a variant where more modeling elements (91 elements) were created than the one in Fig. 4b (32 elements). Because operations for deleting or moving elements are included too, this provides more information than what can be obtained by comparing the resulting process models. Comparison of Fig. 4b and Fig. 4c reveals the difference in modeling time between two sessions (distances in the charts can be compared because the width of a PPMChart is always set to one hour).

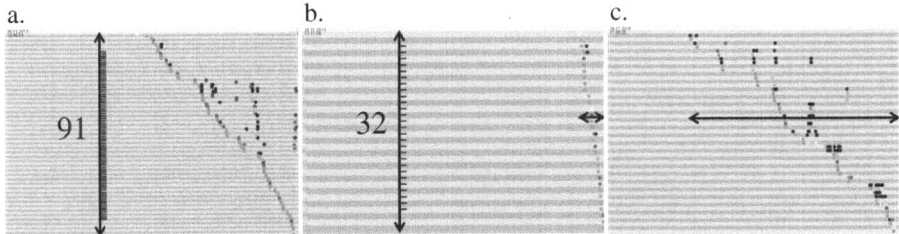

Fig. 4. Number of created model elements and duration of the modeling process[2]

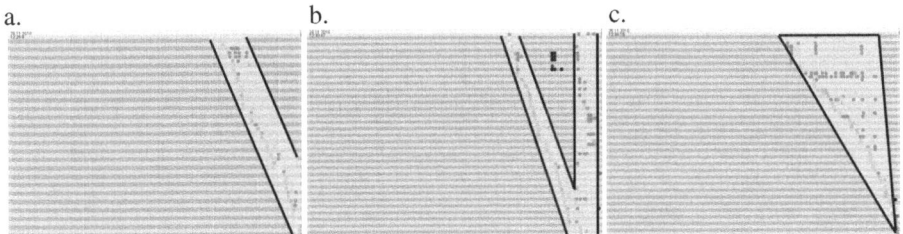

Fig. 5. Order of creating and changing model elements (sorted by First event)[2]

4.3.2 Order of Modeling Operations (Create, Move, Delete, (Re)name)

Besides the general dimensions of the modeling process, one can also zoom in on the relative positions of the dots in the chart. Fig. 5 shows, for example, the modeling process of three modelers that moved some model elements after creation. Fig. 5a shows an example where elements were moved not long after their creation, the modeler of Fig. 5b performed most moves after *all* elements were created, while Fig. 5c shows a session in which move operations occurred during the whole modeling process.

Instead of using complex data mining techniques (e.g., Activity Clustering) to reveal these differences, the PPMChart allows for a quick visual detection of graphical patterns that provide the same information. The discovered modeling patterns can, for example, be used to identify different modeling styles.

4.3.3   Order of Creation of Elements (Events, Nodes, Gateways, Edges)

The filtering option enables to take different views on the process. By filtering the operations, one can, for example, focus on the order of creation of elements. Fig. 6 shows two extreme examples. The modeler of Fig. 6a first created the events, nodes and gateways and only afterwards the model elements were connected by edges. The modeler of Fig. 6b first created only events and nodes and afterwards the gateways and edges were created.

Even if the process would consist of hundreds of modeling operations, this could be quickly observed in our visualization. Arguably, it would take much longer to discover this from the pure data or by replaying individual models. The discovered patterns can, for example, be used to identify different modeler profiles.

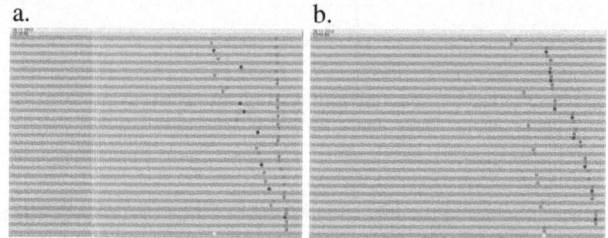

Fig. 6. Order of creation of elements (view: only create operations; move / delete filtered out)[2]

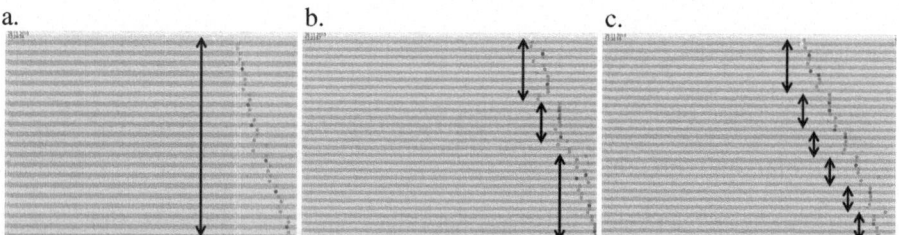

Fig. 7. Chunked process modeling (sorted by Distance from start, only create operations)[2]

4.3.4   Chunked Process Modeling

Because of the limited capacity of the human working memory [20], most modelers work in chunks, i.e., they work on calculable pieces of the model, one at a time. In the charts this can be observed in the form of clear pauses between the operations. In Fig. 7a the modeler seems to construct the whole model in a continuous way: We only observe a quite large pause after the creation of the start event. In Fig. 7b one could distinct three clear chunks of modeling operations. The modeler of Fig. 7c pauses after completion of each block (i.e., all elements between a set of matching split and join gateways, see Section 4.3.5).

The length of a period without operations that should be defined as a pause might differ between modelers because of the difference between slower and quicker modelers. However, the decision of which gaps are clear pauses seems to be easy when based on the graphical representation at hand.

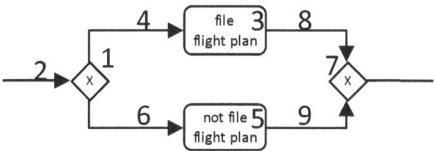

Fig. 8. Example of a 'block' in a model[2]

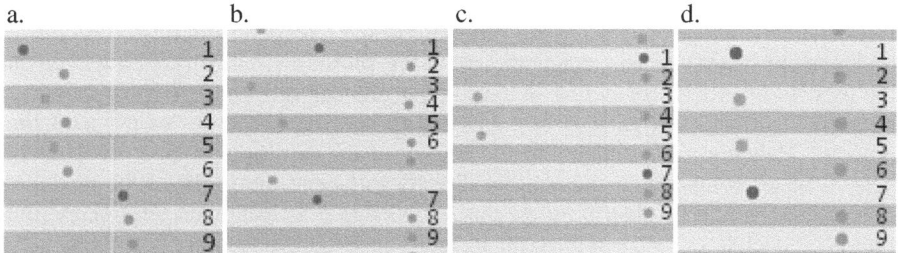

Fig. 9. Order of constructing blocks. The numbers correspond with the numbers in Fig. 8. (sorted by Create order from start, only create operations).[2]

4.3.5   Working in Blocks: Order of Constructing Blocks

The notion of a 'block' appears to be very relevant in the study of the process of process modeling. In [3] we discovered a relation between the order modelers construct blocks in the modeling process (structuredness) and the understandability of the resulting process model (perspicuity). Fig. 8 shows an example of a block in a model: it is a unit of alternative (OR split/join) or parallel (AND split/join) paths consisting of the split and join gateway and all elements in between. The order of creating the elements in a block can tell us more about the modeler's general modeling style. Fig. 9 shows four alternative ways of constructing a block. In Fig. 9a one can observe the modeling operations for creating the block, where the modeler created the elements from left to right. Fig. 9b shows an example where first the involved activities were created, then the gateways, and finally the edges. In the modeling process of Fig. 9c first the two activities were created, then the gateways and edges. In Fig. 9d both gateways and both nodes were created before all the edges. The option to sort by Create order from start and the filtering of create operations enables the user to focus on this particular part of the modeling process (see Fig. 9).

5   Discussion and Conclusion

This paper proposes a technique for visualizing a very specific process: i.e., the process of process modeling. Supported by a modeling tool that records all modeling operations, one should be able to construct an event log that can be used as input for our technique. It graphically represents the recorded modeling operations in a so called PPMChart, which consists of time lines per modeling element and dots on these lines that represent the different operations on each modeling element in time.

The visualization technique and its implementation as a tool are based on the Dotted Chart Analysis plug-in in ProM [5]. However, we extended the functionality of this plug-in with three new features. First, we used a fixed mapping of the recorded events in the creation of a process model and the colors of the dots in the charts. This makes it easier to visually compare different charts. Second, we provided two extra sort options to match the order of the lines of a PPMChart with the order of the corresponding elements in the process model. Third, we provided filter options to hide certain model elements or modeling operations which allows a user to take different views on the data. We applied the visualization technique to the process of process modeling data of 103 students. To demonstrate its usefulness, we presented five concrete observed characteristic variations of the recorded modeling processes.

The main benefit of our technique is that we show raw, uninterpreted data about the process of process modeling in a way that one can quickly discover (graphical) *patterns* in the charts (that can be translated to specific properties of the modeling process). Relating these patterns to the quality of the resulting process model could help to better comprehend factors that directly influence the result of the modeling process. We would be able to utilize this knowledge in training and tools supporting process modeling, which could result in more understandable process models and a more efficient modeling process as well. At the opposite side, one must be careful to draw conclusions from the analysis of the charts, because of a lack of information about the *intentions* of the modeler. A pause in the modeling activity can indicate, for example, that the modeler was thinking about next operations or also that the modeler was distracted.

In other current research we are exploring the relation between the properties of the modeler, the way a modeler constructs process models and the quality of the resulting process model. For instance, in [3] we used the PPMChart visualization to derive three concrete conjectures about the relation of structuring, movement and speed of the modeling process to the understandability of the modeling result, which we then further tested statistically. Future research will include a search for causes and consequences of the patterns that can be discovered with PPMCharts. This will probably lead to further improvement of the visualization and its usefulness. In addition to that, we will investigate other visualization techniques that may enhance the analysis of the process of process modeling data. Currently, our visualization builds heavily on the Dotted Chart Analysis that was already available in ProM. This has given us many insights, but is not guaranteed to be the best technique. Therefore, we will investigate alternative graphical representations (such as time line trees).

Acknowledgements. Our research builds upon the work of the development team of CEP and the researchers involved in the experiments. Therefore, we wish to express our extensive gratitude to Stefan Zugal, Jan Mendling and Dirk Fahland. This research was funded by the Austrian Science Fund (FWF): P23699-N23.

References

1. Mendling, J., Reijers, H.A., Cardoso, J.: What Makes Process Models Understandable? In: Alonso, G., Dadam, P., Rosemann, M. (eds.) BPM 2007. LNCS, vol. 4714, pp. 48–63. Springer, Heidelberg (2007)

2. Genero, M., Poels, G., Piattini, M.: Defining and validating metrics for assessing the understandability of entity-relationship diagrams. Data & Knowledge Engineering 64(3), 534–557 (2008)
3. Claes, J., Vanderfeesten, I., Reijers, H.A., Pinggera, J., Weidlich, M., Zugal, S., Fahland, D., Weber, B., Mendling, J., Poels, G.: Tying Process Model Quality to the Modeling Process: The Impact of Structuring, Movement, and Speed. In: Barros, A., Gal, A., Kindler, E. (eds.) BPM 2012. LNCS, vol. 7481, pp. 33–48. Springer, Heidelberg (2012)
4. Pinggera, J., Zugal, S., Weidlich, M., Fahland, D., Weber, B., Mendling, J., Reijers, H.A.: Tracing the Process of Process Modeling with Modeling Phase Diagrams. In: Daniel, F., Barkaoui, K., Dustdar, S. (eds.) BPM Workshops 2011, Part I. LNBIP, vol. 99, pp. 370–382. Springer, Heidelberg (2012)
5. Song, M., Van der Aalst, W.M.P.: Supporting process mining by showing events at a glance. In: Proc. WITS 2007, pp. 139–145 (2007)
6. Krogstie, J., Sindre, G., Jørgensen, H.: Process models representing knowledge for action: a revised quality framework. Eur. Journal of Information Systems 15(1), 91–102 (2006)
7. Reijers, H.A., Mendling, J., Recker, J.C.: Business process quality management. In: Handbook on Business Process Management 1, pp. 167–185. Springer (2010)
8. Gruhn, V., Laue, R.: Complexity metrics for business process models. In: Proc. ICBIS 2006, pp. 1–12 (2006)
9. Vanderfeesten, I., Cardoso, J., Mendling, J., Reijers, H.A., Van der Aalst, W.M.P.: Quality metrics for business process models. In: BPM and Workflow Handbook, pp. 179–190 (2007)
10. Rittgen, P.: Quality and perceived usefulness of process models. In: Proc. SAC 2010, pp. 65–72. ACM (2010)
11. Recker, J., Rosemann, M., Indulska, M., Green, P.: Business process modeling: a comparative analysis. Journal of the Association for Information Systems 10(4), 333–363 (2009)
12. Pinggera, J., Zugal, S., Weber, B.: Investigating the process of process modeling with cheetah experimental platform. In: Proc. ER-POIS 2010, pp. 13–18 (2010)
13. Indulska, M., Recker, J., Rosemann, M., Green, P.: Business Process Modeling: Current Issues and Future Challenges. In: van Eck, P., Gordijn, J., Wieringa, R. (eds.) CAiSE 2009. LNCS, vol. 5565, pp. 501–514. Springer, Heidelberg (2009)
14. Soffer, P., Kaner, M., Wand, Y.: Towards Understanding the Process of Process Modeling: Theoretical and Empirical Considerations. In: Daniel, F., Barkaoui, K., Dustdar, S. (eds.) BPM Workshops 2011, Part I. LNBIP, vol. 99, pp. 357–369. Springer, Heidelberg (2012)
15. Pinggera, J., Soffer, P., Zugal, S., Weber, B., Weidlich, M., Fahland, D., Reijers, H.A., Mendling, J.: Modeling Styles in Business Process Modeling. In: Bider, I., Halpin, T., Krogstie, J., Nurcan, S., Proper, E., Schmidt, R., Soffer, P., Wrycza, S. (eds.) EMMSAD 2012 and BPMDS 2012. LNBIP, vol. 113, pp. 151–166. Springer, Heidelberg (2012)
16. Crapo, A.W., Waisel, L.B., Wallace, W.A., Willemain, T.R.: Visualization and the process of modeling: a cognitive-theoretic view. In: Proc. ACM SIGKDD 2000, pp. 218–226 (2000)
17. Mendling, J., Reijers, H.A., Van der Aalst, W.M.P.: Seven process modeling guidelines (7PMG). Information and Software Technology 52(2), 127–136 (2010)
18. Becker, J., Rosemann, M., von Uthmann, C.: Guidelines of Business Process Modeling. In: van der Aalst, W.M.P., Desel, J., Oberweis, A. (eds.) Business Process Management. LNCS, vol. 1806, pp. 30–49. Springer, Heidelberg (2000)
19. zur Muehlen, M., Recker, J.: How Much Language Is Enough? Theoretical and Practical Use of the Business Process Modeling Notation. In: Bellahsène, Z., Léonard, M. (eds.) CAiSE 2008. LNCS, vol. 5074, pp. 465–479. Springer, Heidelberg (2008)
20. Miller, G.: The magical number seven, plus or minus two: some limits on our capacity for processing information. Psychological Review 63(2), 81–97 (1956)

Panoramic View for Visual Analysis of Large-Scale Activity Data

Kazuo Misue and Seiya Yazaki

University of Tsukuba, Tsukuba, Japan
misue@cs.tsukuba.ac.jp

Abstract. Understanding the activities in large-scale organizations such as big companies is very important. A challenge in the information visualization field is how to combine a representation of the global structure of an organization with representations of each activity. We developed a representation technique to provide a panoramic view of such activities. The representation embeds charts expressing activities into cells of a treemap. By using this representation, both quantitative and temporal aspects of activities can be seen simultaneously. We also developed an analysis tool called "Series at a Glance," which provides functions to manipulate the representation. The tool helps in the analysis of tens of thousands of activities by providing useful visual information.

Keywords: panoramic view, visualization of activity data, treemap, Gantt chart, issue tracking system.

1 Introduction

In a big company, more than several thousand projects are being run every year. The progress of each project is often managed by referring numeric data such as its costs and profit. For the management of projects, there is a lot of detail data as important as such the summarized numerical one. While upper management should take responsibility for more projects, it is difficult for them to pay attention to detail of every project. Therefore, it is useful if they can grasp the progress of a lot of projects simultaneously.

Our challenge is to help to understand the activities in a large-scale organization such as a big company. Many existing management tools and analysis tools can help in determining particular characteristics of these activities. However, these tools have been designed for well-known characteristics, so we cannot apply them for revealing unfamiliar characteristics in many activities. To determine unknown characteristics, a wide-ranging observation of activities is essential, and therefore the panoramic view of activities should be useful. Our technical challenge is to develop a panoramic view of activities to help users to fully understand them.

We adapted tickets of the issue tracking system as activity target data. We developed a visualization technique for the tickets. The technique gives a panoramic

M. La Rosa and P. Soffer (Eds.): BPM 2012 Workshops, LNBIP 132, pp. 756–767, 2013.

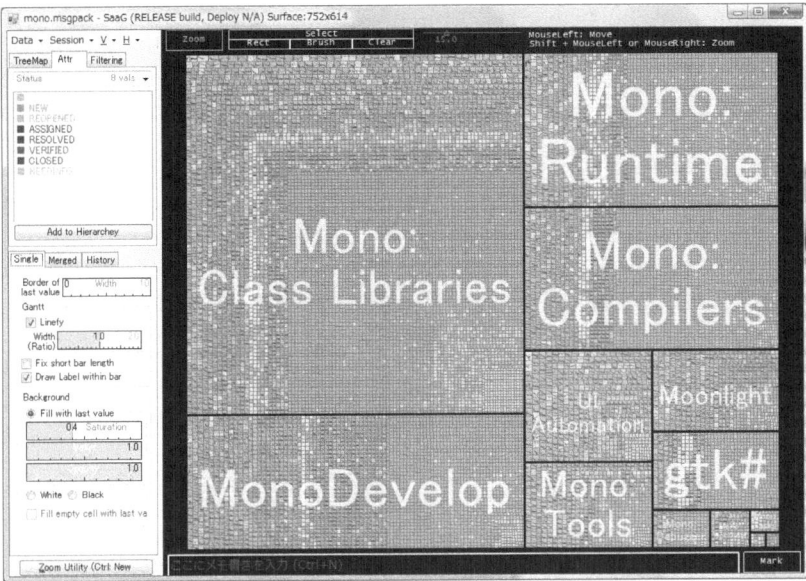

Fig. 1. Screen shot of Series at a Glance, in which about 20,000 tickets are displayed as a treemap. All tickets are categorized by Product and are drawn as polyline charts (see Section 4.2) in Tiling mode (see Section 4.3).

view of the progress of information from many tickets at the same time. Our contributions are as follows:

Hierarchical Representation + Time-line Representation. The visual representation we developed expresses the hierarchical structures of ticket groups and the temporal information of each ticket. The representation enables us to observe temporal information of a ticket and ticket groups while being aware of the global structure of tickets.

Visual Analysis Tool for Many Activities. We developed a tool that shows tens of thousands of tickets in a window (see Figure 1). The tool provides functions that are required to perform visual analysis processes. Users may change the hierarchical structure of the ticket group, attributes to be displayed, etc.

2   Activities and Their Analysis

We roughly formulated a unit of activity in an organization as follows: A unit has some attributes, and the values of the attributes may change with time. For example, a project can be a unit and the section, products, costs, profits, and status of the project can be attributes. Attributes and the values of the attributes are varied depending on companies.

2.1   Tickets in the Issue Tracking System

Tickets are activity data managed by the issue tracking system (ITS). Although it is difficult to get actual data for specific companies, it is relatively easy to get tickets for open-source software (OSS) projects. A ticket corresponds to a task within the project and records the history of the task. Tickets have attributes such as *Status*, *Assigned to*, *Product*, etc. Attribute values are updated through a project management tool when the task corresponding to the ticket has progressed. For example, the attribute Status may have values of *New*, *Assigned*, *Resolved*, *Verified*, *Closed*, etc. Attributes, the values of the attributes, and meanings of the values are also varied according to projects and organizations. The total number of tickets may exceed 10,000. This is similar to activities in a big company.

2.2   Analysis of Tickets

One goal of our analysis is to find unknown but useful characteristics of some groups of activities. We should observe tickets from various angles to find some useful knowledge in situations in which our interest has never fixed on some specific aspects. One popular approach to achieving this goal is to perform analytical processes along visual information-seeking mantra[1].

Overview. First, we should get an overview of all tickets or an entire group of tickets, that is, a panoramic view of the activities. The following two aspects are essential in the overview:

1. the number of tickets and
2. time changes of the attribute values of the tickets.

We can divide tickets into groups according to their attributes. Iteratively dividing tickets into groups can allow construction of various hierarchical structures by the order of attributes of interest. It is useful if the overview of the tickets is based on the hierarchical structure. We can look at the entire group of tickets with interesting attributes as clues.

Zoom. Only the tickets in some groups should be enlarged in the window. A group is a set of one or more tickets with specific attribute values. Focusing on a group of tickets means paying our attention to tickets with some specific attribute values.

Filter. Tickets with specific attribute values should be excluded. Excluding completed tickets or tickets we are not interested in makes it easy to concentrate on valid tickets that may include some useful characteristics.

Detail on Demand. One or several tickets are displayed in detail. About a specified attribute, it is desirable that we can understand changes of the values.

3   Related Work

When we look at our research from the viewpoint of objectives of our ticket analysis, its purpose has something in common with the analysis of software development projects. Therefore, we see our challenge as part of a visualization of the activities in such projects. If a group of tickets is regarded as time-series data, our technique can be considered as one of the visualization techniques of large-scale time-series data.

3.1   Visualization of Software Development

There is a considerable amount of research on visualization of the activities of software development projects that support users to obtain knowledge from them[2]. Ball et al. and Froehlich et al. present visual representations of the history of source programs extracted from a repository[3,4]. We suppose that we should analyze human activities as well as the history of source programs.

MDS-Views[5] applies multidimensional scaling to data extracted from CVS[1] and Bugzilla[2] and shows relationships among elements in a project as a node-link diagram. Social Health Overview[6] is a tool for evaluating the soundness of activities of a project. It expresses tickets and their attributes extracted from Bugzilla as dots with colors.

Software evolution storylines[7] and code_swarm[8] support observation of changes within a development community. They show the time change of individual contributions or a contribution portion to a project.

Most of the existing tools are unsuitable for observing activity data from varied viewpoints because they only cover some limited viewpoints of analysis and use special measures and simplification based on these viewpoints.

3.2   Visualization of Time-Series Data

A lot of research has been conducted on visualization of time-series data. Aigner et al. have developed a systematic view on the diversity of methods for visualizing time-oriented data[9].

To show a large amount of data in a view, it is necessary to increase space efficiency. As examples of techniques considering space efficiency, Reijner developed Horizon Graph[10], Heer et al. improved it[11], and Krstajić et al. proposed CloudLines[12]. Chromograms by Wattenberg et al. [13] can be regarded as one of these techniques. They have devised color mapping to acquire information from series data efficiently.

Although these techniques are equipped with some outstanding feature, we need some more effort to embed tens of thousands of activities to a limited screen area.

---

[1] http://www.nongnu.org/cvs/
[2] http://www.bugzilla.org/

4   Visual Representation for Large-Scale Activities

Our requirements to realize an overview of all tickets are (a) the number of tickets and (b) time changes of the attribute values of the tickets. The number of tickets can be tens of thousands. The area for each ticket should be small to get an overview of all tickets. The set of tickets comprises a hierarchical structure as a global structure and every ticket has a temporal structure as a local structure. Our problem is how to combine a representation of the global structure with a representation of the local structures.

4.1   Representation of Global Structure

We adapted Treemap[14,15] to express the global structure of tickets. A rectangular area is assigned to a ticket or a group of tickets. Treemap can represent quantitative data by the sizes of the rectangles. When we assign the same weight to all tickets, we can understand the number of tickets in a group by seeing the size of the corresponding rectangle. When we regard a quantitative attribute as their weight, we see the size of the rectangle as the sum of the attribute values. For example, we can express a different work load (in other words, the number of update times) by the size of the rectangles.

OSS project tickets do not necessarily follow a moneylike concept. Therefore, we describe the number of update times as an example of quantitative data. However, when we treat activities in a company, we are certainly expected to express the budget scales of every activity.

4.2   Representation of Local Structures

To express the time change of attribute values of tickets, we developed two types of charts: Gantt charts and polyline charts.

(i) Gantt Chart. A Gantt chart is a widely used chart to express the progress of projects. By placing values of an attribute vertically and time horizontally, the attribute value in a time interval is expressed as a horizontal bar. Our charts can occupy only a very narrow area. Therefore, we assign a different color to every attribute value to be able to read information simply from a bar without labels (see Figure 2). Moreover, we paint the background of the area with a lighter color of the current status.

(ii) Polyline Chart. A polyline chart is a variation of a Gantt chart. It uses polygonal lines instead of horizontal bars. On a Gantt chart drawn on a narrow area, short bars sometimes become dots. To increase the visibility of the charts, we replaced the horizontal bars with polygonal lines. On a polyline chart, each point expresses an attribute value and a time the value was updated, and line segments connect such points (see Figure 3).

When the interval to the next update is short, a line segment with a steep gradient is drawn, and when the interval is long, a line segment with a gentle gradient is drawn. Although it is not so appropriate to have change of the attribute value on a nominal scale connected by a polygonal line, in consideration of the visibility of changes, we adopted this representation on the assumption that they are drawn on narrow areas.

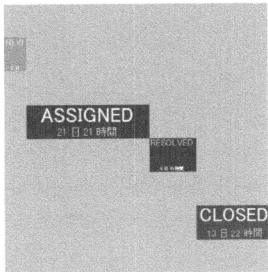

Fig. 2. Gantt chart

Fig. 3. Polyline chart

4.3   Representation of a Group of Tickets

We developed three types of modes for groups of tickets: tiling, overlapping, and stacking.

(i) Tiling Mode. In the tiling mode, a rectangle is assigned to each ticket. A ticket chart is drawn in the rectangular area. The background color of each small chart contributes in this mode. When many tickets are displayed simultaneously, a ticket can occupy only a narrow area. Even in such a case, the observer can roughly grasp the overall situation first by observing the distribution of background colors.

(ii) Overlapping Mode. We designed an overlapping mode for a polyline chart. In this mode, all charts for tickets in a group are drawn in piles in an area assigned to the group. All charts for tickets share the same time axis. We can easily grasp the tendency of time change of tickets in a group. When many polygonal lines are drawn in piles, visual confusion becomes possible. To cope with this problem, we give reverse gradation to line segments. We can read where a line segment comes from and where it goes simply by looking near both end points of the line segment.

(iii) Stacking Mode. By using the overlapping mode, we can grasp the density distribution of the attribute value in a certain time to some extent. However, spatial size is more suitable than the density of line segments to express how many tickets exist in a certain time. In the stacking mode, tickets with the same attribute value are collectively drawn like ThemeRiver[16]. We can get an idea of the number of tickets with each attribute value in a certain time by looking at the vertical length of the stacked bands.

Fig. 4. Tickets categorized by Product, drawn as polyline charts in the overlapping mode. The time axis is relative.

Fig. 5. Tickets categorized by Product, drawn in the stacking mode. The time axis is absolute.

4.4   Time Axis of a Group of Tickets

Whereas each ticket occupies an area in the tiling mode, two or more tickets share the same area in the overlapping and stacking modes. We prepared two types of time axis modes: an absolute time mode and a relative time mode.

(i) Absolute Time Mode. The horizontal axis expresses absolute time. We can get an idea of the situation of the project during a certain period and at a specific time. For example, we can read what type of ticket existed on October 1, 2011, and how the tickets changed for three months from October 1 to December 31.

(ii) Relative Time Mode. The horizontal axis expresses a relative time beginning with the start time of each ticket. We can follow how the status of tickets changed with elapsed time from the start. If the change of status has a particular pattern, it is expected that the pattern will actually be visible as well. Examples of such patterns are cases in which most tickets in a category were completed in a week or tickets in another category were neglected for one month or more.

5   Series at a Glance

We developed a tool named "Series at a Grance (SaaG)" to manipulate the visual representation explained in the previous section (see Figure 1). This section explains functions offered by SaaG.

Setup of the Global Structure. SaaG shows tickets based on their hierarchical structures. For that, it is necessary to determine a hierarchical structure of tickets. A hierarchical structure can be constructed by repeating categorization based on attributes. However, since the attributes that can be used for the categorization varied according to projects, we cannot determine them beforehand. SaaG constitutes a menu of attributes used for the categorization according to ticket data. Users can specify the attribute of the first layer, the attribute of the second layer, and the attribute of the third layer with a pull down menu, respectively.

Representation of Local Structures. By specifying an attribute to be expressed visually, time change of the value of the attribute is displayed in the cell of Treemap. Expression of one ticket and expression of a ticket group can be changed at any time by choosing from a menu. The option of the time-axis in the overlapping mode or the stacking mode can also be changed at any time with a menu. In the overlapping mode and the stacking mode, a group of tickets that shares an area is chosen depending on the global structure. At the stage of construction of a hierarchical structure, if only attribute for the first layer was specified, tickets would be collected in the groups of the first layer. If two attributes for the first and second layers were specified, tickets would be collected in the groups of the second layer.

Zooming. Zooming function expands a specified area in the Treemap. By using this function, users can pay their attention to a group of tickets collected into a certain area on Treemap. When a user chooses an area to pay one's attention to in the rubber band by mouse dragging, the selected area is expanded to the limit of a display window. The user can repeat this operation any number of steps. One ticket can also be displayed to the limit of a display window. Cancel of the zoom operation is easy. Single click cancels last zoom operation. By this, users can easily pay their temporal attention to a part of the visualization.

Filtering. Filtering function hides or shows only tickets that match some condition on attributes. By using this function, users can get some selective display, for example, users can hide expired tickets, display only tickets assigned to a certain person, and so on. Attribute values used for the conditions of filtering can be chosen from a drop-down menu. Or by clicking a specific ticket or a ticket group, all attribute values of the ticket or all common attribute values of tickets in the group are used as conditions of filtering.

Detailed View of Each Ticket. When each ticket is displayed in a separated area in the tiling mode, detailed view of ticket can be shown in a new window by double-clicking on the area for the ticket. The users can update values of the ticket through the window.

Recording Logs. SaaG records all user operations. Users may add comments to the operation logs and get screenshots with the comments after a series of operations. Exploratory analysis is accompanied by trial and error. Even if an analyst found some useful knowledge, it would be difficult to remember the process to the knowledge. Recording all operations with annotated comments makes analytical tasks more efficient and valuable. Furthermore, screenshots with comments help to review the processes.

6   Case Study

To verify the feasibility of the representation technique and SaaG, we performed a ticket analysis. The objective of the analysis is the Mono project [3]. The analyst is a person outside the project who explores features of the project.

The Mono project is an open-source software (OSS) project in which software for realizing an environment compatible with .Net Framework is developed according to the Ecma standard. The project is divided into several subteams for products.

The analyst observed about 20,000 tickets in search of getting to know the background of the project, particularly by seeing what type of subteams comprise the project. The analyst selected the attribute Product as the first layer of the hierarchical structure and then drew a polyline chart in overlapping mode (see Figure 4).

---

[3] http://www.mono-project.com/Main_Page

In the Class Libraries group, there are many line segments with steep gradients from green to purple. These segments express tickets changed from *New* (green) to *Resolved* (purple) in a short period. There are also many line segments going to and from yellow at the bottom. These segments express tickets becoming *Needinfo* (yellow) for a while. That is, although many tickets were processed quickly, many other tickets stopped processing for a while owing to lack of information. In the Mono Develop and Runtime groups, we can see a similar tendency.

Groups with smaller areas on the screen, such as UI Automation, differ in form from the others. In a group with a small area, most segments are not far stretched toward the right. That is, it turned out that work periods were generally short. Moreover, although there are many blue segments and red segments, there are relatively few purple segments. We can interpret this to mean that many tickets became *Closed* (red) instead of *Resolved* (purple), and many of them also became *Reopened* (light blue). From these, the analyst guessed that the pace of work is generally quick, but resolved judgments were rarely received and there is much rework involved.

The analyst thought that this was a tendency found in new products, and then selected the absolute time axis in the stacking mode. It became apparent that UI Automation was a new product.

Fig. 6. Zoomed-in view of the UI Automation group. Tickets are drawn as polyline charts in the tiling mode.

To investigate UI Automation in detail, the analyst expanded the group with the zoom function and selected a polyline chart in the tiling mode (see Figure 6). The current status of most tickets is *Closed* (red) and many tickets have downward-sloping, favorable patterns. From these observations, although there are a few *Reopened* tickets, the analyst guessed that progress in this product is generally favorable. However, a few tickets exhibit a pattern of vertical vibration. These ticket tasks did not progress smoothly.

The following information about the Mono project was acquired:

1. Many Class Library tasks were solved in a short time.
2. Many Class Library tasks failed owing to a dearth of information.
3. Many UI Automation tasks were completed in a comparatively short time.
4. For a small-scale product, the resolved judgment was not necessarily received and there was much rework involved.

7   Conclusions

We developed a representation technique for visualizing numerous activities. The developed technique embeds charts showing activities in rectangles of nodes on the basis of Treemap. Both quantitative and temporal aspects of activities can be simultaneously seen with this representation technique. We also developed an analytical tool, SaaG, which can manipulate the representation. To our knowledge, there are no tools based on the combination of treemap views and project charts like Gantt chart. The tool targets tickets as activity data. Analysts are allowed to construct and modify the global structure of tickets by specifying their attributes. They can easily observe activity data from various viewpoints. To show simultaneously tens of thousands of tickets, each ticket is allowed to occupy only a small area. We designed representations of local structures to cope with the problem. In the tiling mode, their background colors show most important values even in a few pixels' area. In the overlapping and stacking mode, tickets in a group share an area and unveil major trends of the local structures. With the tool, a visual analysis can be performed more flexibly for tens of thousands of tickets.

Acknowledgement. This work was partially supported by JSPS KAKENHI Grant Number 22500081.

References

1. Shneiderman, B.: The eyes have it: a task by data type taxonomy for information visualizations. In: Proceedings of IEEE Symposium on Visual Languages, pp. 336–343 (1996)
2. Storey, M.A.D., Čubranić, D., German, D.M.: On the use of visualization to support awareness of human activities in software development: a survey and a framework. In: Proceedings of the 2005 ACM Symposium on Software Visualization (SoftVis 2005), pp. 193–202. ACM, New York (2005)

3. Ball, T., Eick, S.G.: Software visualization in the large. Computer 29(4), 33–43 (1996)
4. Froehlich, J., Dourish, P.: Unifying artifacts and activities in a visual tool for distributed software development teams. In: Proceedings of the 26th International Conference on Software Engineering (ICSE 2004), pp. 387–396 (2004)
5. Fischer, M., Gall, H.: MDS-views: Visualizing problem report data of large scale software using multidimensional scaling. In: Proceedings of the International Workshop on Evolution of Large-scale Industrial Software Applications (ELISA), pp. 110–121 (2003)
6. Ellis, J.B., Wahid, S., Danis, C., Kellogg, W.A.: Task and social visualization in software development: evaluation of a prototype. In: Proceedings of the SIGCHI Conference on Human Factors in Computing Systems (CHI 2007), pp. 577–586. ACM, New York (2007)
7. Ogawa, M., Ma, K.L.: Software evolution storylines. In: Proceedings of the 5th International Symposium on Software Visualization (SoftVis 2010), pp. 35–42. ACM, New York (2010)
8. Ogawa, M., Ma, K.L.: code_swarm: A design study in organic software visualization. IEEE Transactions on Visualization and Computer Graphics 15(6), 1097–1104 (2009)
9. Aigner, W., Miksch, S., Müller, W., Schumann, H., Tominski, C.: Visualizing time-oriented data — a systematic view. Computer & Graphics 31(3), 401–409 (2007)
10. Reijner, H.: The development of the horizon graph. In: Electronic Proceedings of the VisWeek Workshop From Theory to Practice: Design, Vison and Visualization (2008)
11. Heer, J., Kong, N., Agrawala, M.: Sizing the horizon: the effects of chart size and layering on the graphical perception of time series visualizations. In: Proceedings of the 27th International Conference on Human Factors in Computing Systems (CHI 2009), pp. 1303–1312. ACM, New York (2009)
12. Krstajić, M., Bertini, E., Keim, D.A.: CloudLines: Compact display of event episodes in multiple time-series. IEEE Transactions on Visualization and Computer Graphics 17(12), 2432–2439 (2011)
13. Wattenberg, M., Viégas, F.B., Hollenbach, K.: Visualizing Activity on Wikipedia with Chromograms. In: Baranauskas, C., Abascal, J., Barbosa, S.D.J. (eds.) INTERACT 2007. LNCS, vol. 4663, pp. 272–287. Springer, Heidelberg (2007)
14. Shneiderman, B.: Tree visualization with tree-maps: 2-d space-filling approach. ACM Trans. Graph. 11, 92–99 (1992)
15. Bruls, M., Huizing, K., van Wijk, J.: Squarified treemaps. In: Proceedings of the Joint Eurographics and IEEE TCVG Symposium on Visualization, pp. 33–42 (2000)
16. Havre, S., Hetzler, E., Whitney, P., Nowell, L.: ThemeRiver: visualizing thematic changes in large document collections. IEEE Transactions on Visualization and Computer Graphics 8(1), 9–20 (2002)

Visualizing Complex Process Hierarchies during the Modeling Process

Andreas Seyfang, Katharina Kaiser, Theresia Gschwandtner, and Silvia Miksch

Institute of Software Technology & Interactive Systems
Vienna University of Technology, Vienna, Austria
{seyfang,kaiser,gschwandtner,miksch}@ifs.tuwien.ac.at

Abstract. Clinical practice guidelines are documents that include recommendations describing appropriate care for the management of patients with a specific clinical condition, such as diabetes or chronic heart failure. Several representation languages exist to model these documents in a computer-interpretable and -executable form with the intention of integrating them into clinical information systems. *Asbru* is one of these representation languages that is able to model the complex hierarchies of these medical processes (called *plans* in Asbru). To allow their efficient evaluation and manipulation, they must be visualized in a compact and still clear form. This visualization must be integrated into an editing environment which makes changes to the process hierarchy easy and gives immediate feedback on the changes.

In this paper, we present a novel visualization, Plan Strips, which represents the hierarchy of plans, i.e., processes, as a set of nested strips. It represents the synchronization of the plans by colour-coding the strips and by the ordering of the strips. This saves considerable space compared to graph representations. The visualization is integrated into an editing environment which allows the immediate modification of the plan hierarchy, but also changes to all other aspects of the plan.

Keywords: Process modeling, block-oriented process hierarchies.

1 Introduction

Clinical Guidelines and Protocols (CGPs) are established means of improving health care quality and limiting cost. Modeling them in a computer-executable form is a prerequisite to integrating them into the electronic data flow at the place of care, which again improves adherence to guidelines and which reduces the workload of care staff by showing only relevant recommendations for the case at hand.

Several languages for executable or computer-interpretable CGPs have been developed (see [1] for an overview and comparison). They are tailored to the medical domain and share many features with process modeling and workflow languages. One of them is *Asbru* [2], a language using the block-oriented paradigm. Each block of actions, called plan, has child blocks, called sub-plans, which are ordered in one of the following fashions: sequential, parallel (manadory simultaneous start), unordered (no timing constraints), or any-order (only one sub-plan is active at any time, the order of execution is not defined). In addition, there is the cyclical plan to implement loops. Besides

M. La Rosa and P. Soffer (Eds.): BPM 2012 Workshops, LNBIP 132, pp. 768–779, 2013.

these modes of ordering, conditions to start and finish each plan influence the course of performed actions.

Due to the block-oriented paradigm the hierarchy can become quite complex containing a high number of hierarchy levels. Thus, for the knowledge engineer it is important to maintain an overview over the whole hierarchy, even when it is big and deeply nested. The example guideline model used in this paper comes from the field of breast cancer treatment.

CPG modeling, in general, remains a practical knowledge modelling challenge to this day, requiring the collaboration of a knowledge engineer and domain experts (physicians, guideline developers), because expertise from both computer sciences and medicine must be combined. In the modeling process, it is crucial for the knowledge engineer to present the resulting model in an easily comprehensible form to the domain experts, who are not at all familiar with complex representations of graphs such as hierarchies of treatment steps.

In the context of modeling CGPs in Asbru, we used various representations in the past which all satisfied to some degree (compare Section 2), but still there was a gap left defined by the following requirements.

- *Dense presentation.* Many graph-like presentation use arcs between boxes, which consume considerable space. Also decorations on boxes and arcs tend to increase the space consumed because they need to be printed at a certain size to be readable while they only occupy a small part of the box border or area, or the arc, preventing the utilization of considerable areas along them.
- *Intuitively arrange parallel plans and sequences.* Declaring one axis the time axis and arranging alternatives and parallel plans along the other axis is a well-accepted and immediately comprehensible organization of content.
- *Qualitative presentation of the temporal dimension.* In contrast to other approaches which focus on scale representation of duration and temporal uncertainty, we focus on the mere sequence of plans here. This is attractive if one or more of the following is given: a) The duration holds no interest for the editing task at hand. b) The duration is unknown. c) The durations of different plans are very dissimilar (weeks versus years).
- *Easy to explain to a non-IT person.* Domain experts such as physicians have limited time and little motivation for dealing with IT concepts. For a presentation to be well-received, it is crucial to demonstrate from the start that it is simple. At the same time, we do not see physicians as those modeling CGPs themselves. Therefore, it is not required that they understand our visualisation without an aide, it is only important that it does not appear overly complex or technical.

Since the ultimate aim is to support the knowledge engineering task, such a presentation must be tightly integrated with an editing tool, in which the user modifies the relevant parts of the plans, and which immediately updates the graphical presentation.

In the following, we first discuss related work (Section 2), then present our new representation, Plan Strips, in Section 3, together with the editing tool built around them, and conclude the paper in Section 5.

2   Related Work

The complex nature of clinical practice guidelines demands for a plain and compact vi-sualization of the underlying information to facilitate the generation of a formal guide-line model. This includes the temporal ordering of plans and the mode of operation of their sub-plans. Dealing with logical sequences, hierarchical data, as well as time-oriented data, the visualization of clinical treatment plans relates to several specific fields of Information Visualization.

According to [3] two tasks are mentioned which address the visualization of clin-ical guidelines explicitly: (1) plan visualization during design time, and (2) plan and data visualization during execution time. The first refers to authoring of computer-interpretable clinical guidelines, where the main focus lies on the communication of the different clinical guideline components to domain experts. The second one handles the visual representation of clinical guidelines in connection with patient data.

We are here focusing on the first task where a variety of techniques exists aimed at vi-sualizing logical sequences, such as Flow Charts [4], Clinical Algorithm Maps [5], and Petri Nets [6]. On one hand, tree diagrams and Treemaps [7] are well known techniques to visualize the specific characteristics of hierarchical data, using both dimensions of the plane to spread out the hierarchy. In our case, we need to limit the hierarchy to a single dimension only, in order to show temporal ordering on the second dimension.

On the other hand, several visualization methods have been developed to depict time and time-oriented data (e.g., Time Lines, GANTT Charts, Pert Charts, and Temporal Objects [8]) and clinical time-oriented data in particular (e.g., LifeLines [9] and Life-Lines2 [10], Paint Strips [11], and Interactive Parallel Bar Charts (IPBC) [12]).

However, communicating the logics of clinical treatment plans in order to facilitate the modeling of clinical practice guidelines require a visualization method with respect to all of these specific data characteristics. In recent years sophisticated approaches to support the modeling and handling of the complex underlying information were introduced.

VisiGuide, part of the DeGeL (Digital electronic Guideline Library) project [13], is a web-based architecture aimed at facilitating the transformation of a textual guideline into a formal model. The VisiGuide tool is used to browse guidelines and to visualize their structure. It supports the presentation of large amounts of guidelines organized by indexing semantic axes as well as the exploration of the different components of a single guideline.

Protégé [14] is an extensible Java tool for the development of customized knowledge-based systems. The flexible development environment allows for ontology development and knowledge acquisition in order to facilitate the authoring of clinical guidelines in various guideline representation languages. The graphical user interface illustrates the clinical algorithm in a way similar to Flow Charts by using different shapes for plans, decisions, actions, enquiries, and root tasks which are connected by arrows. The Tallis Toolset [15] and the domain-independent GLARE system [16] represent the flow of clinical guidelines in a similar way.

GUIDE [17] was developed at the University of Pavia as part of a guideline mod-eling and execution framework. It serves a three-fold purpose, i.e., integrating a mod-elled guideline into clinical workflow, using decision trees and influence diagrams to visualize complex relations, and using extended Petri Nets for the simulation of guideline implementation. Additionally, the GUIDE tool allows for graphically authoring the workflow of guidelines.

AsbruView [18], part of the Asgaard/Asbru project [2], is a graphical user interface to visualize the logical and temporal information of treatment plans expressed in the Asbru modeling language. It uses visual metaphors such as traffic signs and running tracks to communicate complex information, i.e., the hierarchical composition of plans, temporal order of plans, conditions, precise temporal constraints, temporal uncertainties, etc. AsbruFlow (part of the CareVis prototype [19]) is based on Clinical Algorithm Maps [5] extended by Focus+Context techniques to avoid an overcrowded appearance and elaborated symbols indicating the execution order of plans.

None of these approaches deals with compressing the representation to show large plan hierarchies on limited space while maintaining the greatest possible overview. In particular, graph-based representations need space for the arcs in addition to the space used for the boxes. Also, most of the above approaches only show two of the following three aspects in a single diagram: plan decomposition, temporal dimension, and parallel or alternative plans.

There are several fields related to our domain. Extensive research goes into the display of hierarchies much larger than the model of a clinical guideline, e.g., phylogenetic trees. See [20] for an overview. These approaches do not deal with a time dimension but promise to complement our approach. E.g., the magnifying glass effect of hyperbolic trees [21] could be added to our representation of the hierarchy.

The phonetically related field of process modelling guidelines [22,23] provides guidelines to model processes, rather than visualisations. However, applying the principles of business process modelling to guideline development does fertilize the field of guideline modelling in general, albeit beyond the scope of this paper.

The traditional representation of business process models uses node-arc diagrams. The representation of nested sub-diagrams is very limited under such schemes. Also, arranging the nodes in such a way that arcs do not cross more than necessary is an important challenge. See [24] for further reading.

3 Plan Strips

During the modelling process of a CGP in a formal representation such as Asbru, users often lose the overview on the hierarchy of plans, what plans have already been modelled and how plans are synchronized altogether.

With Plan Strips we want to provide a simple and intuitive as well as space-saving means to allow users to get an overview on the hierarchy of plans during the editing process. To keep it small and simple the visualization has to represent the following information:

– The timely order of the plans has to be represented.
– The hierarchy of plans has to be shown.
– The kind of synchronization with other plans has to be displayed: serial, parallel, or cyclical order, alternative plans as well as plans where no synchronization is assigned at all.

3.1   The General Concept

In order to display all the information mentioned above, we use the following methods:

Representing Plans and Their Temporal Order. Plans are represented by rectangles or strips (see Figure 1). Time is presented along the X axis in a qualitative way. This means that sequences of plans are arranged horizontally from left to right. The length of the strips representing them does not relate to the duration, but is optimized for presentation. Thereby, Plan Strips are also applicable with uncertain and undefined timely information. Plans executed in parallel are arranged along the Y axis.

Representing the Hierarchy of Plans. Child plans are stacked on top of their parent plans, with a certain inset. Therefore, the colour of the parent forms a frame around and a link between the children.

Representing the Kind of Synchronization among Plans. We use colour for representing the kind of synchronization of the plans. colour is a well accepted and powerful means to encode different data attributes. In Plan Strips it is used to show the order of plans:

- *Parallel* plans are defined – in Asbru – to start together.
- For *any-order* plans the relative order is not known, but it is known that only one of them can be active at any time, as defined by the Asbru syntax.
- For *unordered* plans nothing is known about the timing of the children.
- For *sequential* plans only one can be active at any time; the order of execution is predefined.
- *Cyclical* plans are repeated several times.

3.2   Finding the Right Colours

In our (western) or any other culture there is no colour-coding that refers to the ordering of plans or processes.

Our initial idea was to map the semantics of plan ordering to colours using the traffic light analogy. Under this scheme, the parallel plan, where everything is clear, was associated with green; the unordered one, where nothing is known, with red; and the any-order plan, which lies inbetween, with yellow. However, initial feedback showed that this scheme was not found intuitive by the target audience.

Next, we use a perception-based colour scheme as suggested in [25] and [26], which have proven to be effective. From a collection of such schemes we choose the most appropriate one with respect to the users' visualization goal, which consists of five different qualitative values of plan ordering. The second dimension to visualise is whether a plan was selected or not. Thus, we need five colour pairs. We used the ColorBrewer2 tool[1] [27,28] with ten different qualitative classes and chose the *Paired* colour system, which consists of five pairs of colours in shades of green, blue, red, orange, and violet. Each colour pair has a very similar hue and differs in saturation and brightness. With these colours the less saturated versions were clearly to distinguish from each other and all the fully saturated colours (compare Figure 1).

---

[1] http://www.colourbrewer2.org, last accessed: June 3rd, 2012

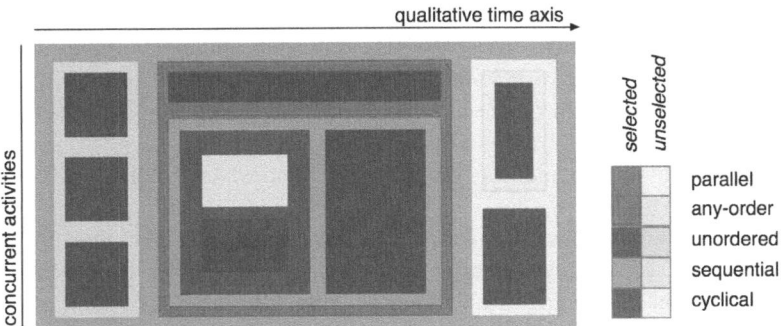

Fig. 1. Explanatory sample of Plan Strips. The light gray box in the center is the currently selected user-performed plan. Its ancestors are shown with normal bright colours. All other plans are shown by colours with less saturation and brightness. The example shows a sequential plan which consists of an unordered plan, an any-order plan, and a parallel plan. The *unordered plan to the left* consists of three user-performed plans. The *any-order plan in the center* consists of a user-performed plan and a sequential plan. This nested sequential plan consists of a cyclical plan and a user-performed plan. The cyclical plan contains a second unordered plan containing two user-performed plans (one of which is the currently selected one). The *parallel plan to the right* contains a cyclical plan containing a user-performed plan, and a user-performed plan.

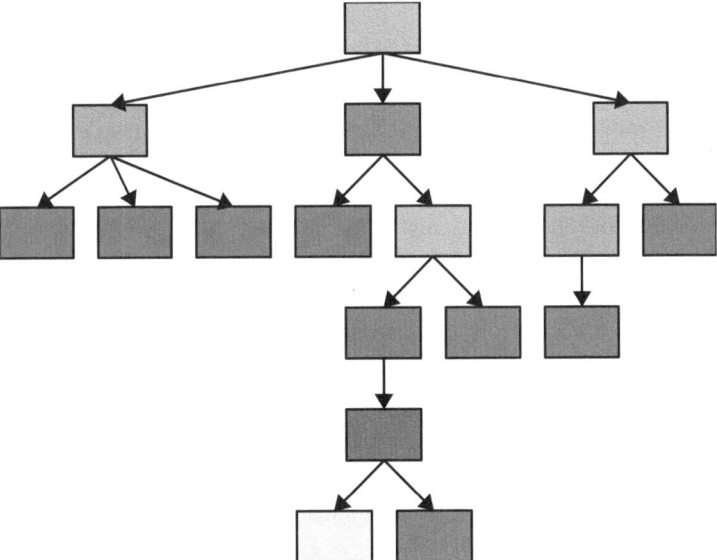

Fig. 2. The same hierarchy as shown in Figure 1, displayed as a conventional tree. The information regarding the ordering of sub-plans and the current plan in focus is represented by colours similar to those in the previous figure.

3.3   Integration with Plan Editing

In order to support productive knowledge acquisition session, our tool not only visualizes the plan hierarchy. It is integrated into an editing environment which permits changes to the hierarchy on the fly, with immediate feedback in the presentation of the Plan Strips.

Figure 3 shows the window of the editing tool into which the Plan Strips visualization is integrated.

When the user clicks on a plan, it is shown in bright colours together with all its ancestors. In contrast, plans currently not selected are shown in colours with lower saturation and higher brightness. After clicking the button "Show all instances", all instances of this plan in the plan hierarchy are shown in bright colours in the Plan Strips display.

When the user moves over a plan with the cursor, tooltips are shown that display the plan type (parallel, any-order, unordered, sequential, cyclical, user-performed), the name of the plan, or a combination of both. These tooltips assist the users especially in the beginning of their handling with the editor in memorizing the colours that refer to a certain plan type. A legend of the colour palette is also permanently displayed at the bottom of the Plan Strips.

Beside the Plan Strip, the list of ancestors of this plan is shown (including the name of the selected plan itself). Clicking on one of the "Select" buttons in this list selects the corresponding ancestor plan, thereby truncating the ancestor list below the corresponding line. This relieves the user from clicking on the rather small margins between user performed plans to select a plan higher in the hierarchy.

Editing the plan properties takes place on three levels of sophistication.

1. Some plan properties are directly manipulated using the controls in the dialog windows. This comprises adding a child plan, removing the selected plan (via the corresponding buttons), changing the plan ordering (via the combo box showing "user-performed" in Figure 3, and editing the comment attached to the top-level plan element in Asbru in the text area at the bottom.
2. Selected knowledge roles are displayed as abstractions generated by XSL scripts, to the right of the "Select" buttons. This gives them a much more compact presentation compared to the XML code. For each of them, there is a dedicated "Edit" button, which brings up a window showing the XML code of this knowledge role in a tree notation, and allowing the modification of the content.
3. The whole plan can be edited in a similar manner without limits after clicking the "Edit whole plan" button. This allows for more complex modification of the plan body, and of those knowledge roles which are not in the focus of this tool, such as intentions and resources.

The knowledge roles in the second group are the filter precondition, setup precondition, suspend condition, reactivate condition, abort condition, complete condition, continuation specification, and propagation specification. They are displayed for the whole list of ancestors of the selected plan. This is necessary because of their effect. E.g., the activation of a plan only becomes possible if the filter preconditions of all its ancestors are fulfilled. Without a list as shown in Figure 3, it is easy to introduce redundant conditions

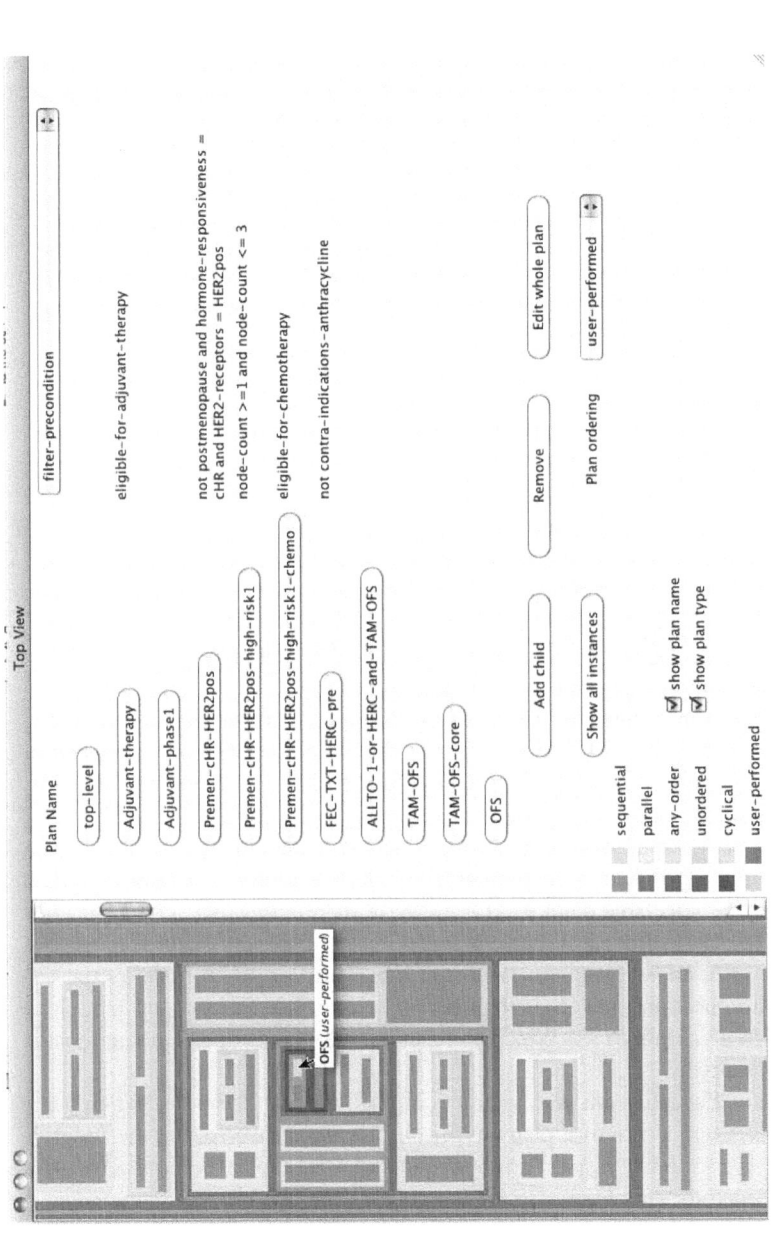

Fig. 3. Plan editing tool featuring Plan Strips to the left, with the selected plan in light gray inside orange; the list of ancestors of the selected plan in the middle; and a selected knowledge role (here, the filter-precondition) for each of them to the right. Below the list of plans there is the legend of the colour palette showing both the colours for selected and unselected plans according to their plan type. Next to the legend there are two check boxes where the user can select the content of the tooltips. As in Figure 1, the time axis runs from left to right. See Section 3.3 for further details.

into a plan hierarchy, or to omit one by mistake, assuming that it is present in another layer of the hierarchy.

The "Settings" menu takes the user to various configurable aspects of the presentation, such as zoom factor of the Plan Strips.

A range of a user-supplied XSL scripts can be invoked from entries in the "XSL" menu, producing custom excepts of various aspects of the plan library, such as lists of plan names, parameter names, cross-reference tables, and similar.

4   Evaluation

We conducted a qualitative user evaluation with four users (computer scientists with and without experience in guideline modelling) to gain insight how well Plan Strips are suited to explore the logic of a guideline's plan hierarchy.

We presented the Plan Strips editor to the users using a protocol for the medical treatment of breast cancer. The modelled protocol consists of 247 distinct plans which are invoked in 440 different places. In the adjuvant therapy part, which constitutes the largest part of the plan library, nesting depth is around 10. The users used Plan Strips to interactively explore the guideline's plan hierarchy and to analyse the dependencies among the plans. The evaluation was carried out separately with each user; in all cases, the interaction with Plan Strips took about half an hour. Users not familiar with guideline modelling were introduced in CPGs and guideline modelling. After a short introduction of the visualization and its features, all users used the Plan Strips editor autonomously to investigate the plan hierarchy. After the interaction phase, the users were interviewed using a mix of open and closed questions.

All users reacted in a positive way to using Plan Strips. It took all of them very little time to learn how to use Plan Strips. When being asked about shortcomings of the visualization, they suggested the following additions and changes: adding the ability for zooming the Plan Strips pane horizontally; adding boundaries between plans and sub-plans of the same type; short term highlighting of the plan in the Plan Strips pane that is selected in the plan list on the right side; adding the ability for collapsing plans; and providing more selectable details to be shown in the tooltips (e.g., conditions of a plan).

The interviews consisted of eight questions, which can be summed up in the following two main questions: (1) Does Plan Strips help to faster assess and model the plan hierarchy of a guideline? (2) Which concepts of the Plan Strips help you most in identifying a plans type?

All users gave affirmative answers to practically all of these questions. When being asked what makes one aware of a plan's type, all of them answered that the ordering on the time axis was the first issue. Further details (whether a plan's type is any-order, parallel, or unordered) were then seen by the colour. Tooltips were also appreciated, although only for seeing the plan's name and not the plan's type, as the colour-coding was quickly memorised and therefore sufficient for identifying the type of ordering.

5   Conclusion

Plan Strips are designed for visualizing process hierarchies in block-oriented process modeling languages, such as Asbru. Plan Strips provide a dense and translucent presentation of plan (or process) hierarchies, omitting quantitative aspects of the temporal dimension. Their usage is advised under the following conditions:

- The hierarchy is highly nested and large.
- There is no interest in the metrics of the temporal dimension, nor in displaying the temporal uncertainty.
- The distinction between parallel or alternative tasks on the one hand and sequential ones on the other hand is crucial.
- The user of the visualization has a basic understanding of the five types of plan ordering in Asbru, but does not want to delve into further details.

Graphical presentations like AsbruView and CareVis are not dense enough for such a high amount of information. Likewise, standard graph representations proved to be too space-consuming (compare Figures 1 and 2). While the amount of space-saving is hard to quantify in a general way, it is obvious that the arcs between the boxes need space to be legible, and this space is wider than the frame formed by the parent plan in Plan Strips.

Initially, we created text-based representations of the call graph, using different types of frames to represent the different plan orderings, but this was less intuitive. It also consumed considerable space – too much to be integrated into the side bar of an editing window.

Clearly, to promote productivity in knowledge acquisition, any visualization must be integrated with a tool that allows the immediate modification of the content presented. In the case of the Plan Strips, we achieved this by showing them side by side with the editing window.

To offer a more versatile solution to knowledge engineers facing the task of creating and maintaining plan hierarchies, the integration of the Plan Strips visualization with other approaches like CareVis and AsbruView is desirable, as well as the implementation on a client-server based architecture which allows the remote collaboration of different users.

Future extensions to Plan Strips include the integration of fish eye perspective, where the mouse acts as a magnifying glass when moved over the Plan Strips; and adding a list of plan names with fish eye perspective, where all the plan names are given beside the Plan Strips, but only those under focus are zoomed sufficiently to be read easily, with the plan under focus clearly standing out.

For the swift modification of plan hierarchies, a drag-and-drop feature would be useful, preferably utilizing a range of clipboards to which parts of the hierarchy can be moved temporarily. Also, the right mouse button could bring up a pop-up menu allowing the user to change the plan ordering of the plan at the mouse pointer, and to remove or add child plans.

We have also evaluated the usefulness in the modelling process. The outcome of the evaluation was very positive; apart from some minor deficiencies that can and will easily be corrected in the near future, the overall outcome of the evaluation showed that

Plan Strips is a valuable enhancement of editing environments for such complex tasks like guideline modelling.

Acknowledgements. The research leading to these results has received funding from the "Fonds zur Förderung der wissenschaftlichen Forschung FWF" (Austrian Science Fund), grant TRP71-N23, and from the Centre for Visual Analytics Science and Technology CVAST (funded by the Austrian Ministry of Economy, Family and Youth in the exceptional Laura Bassi Centres of Excellence initiative, project number 822746).

The plan library shown in the figures was developed during the OncoCure project, which was partly funded by Fondazione Caritro of Trento.

References

1. Peleg, M., Tu, S.W., Bury, J., Ciccarese, P., Fox, J., Greenes, R.A., Hall, R., Johnson, P.D., Jones, N., Kumar, A., Miksch, S., Quaglini, S., Seyfang, A., Shortliffe, E.H., Stefanelli, M.: Comparing computer-interpretable guideline models: A case-study approach. JAMIA 10(1), 52–68 (2003)
2. Shahar, Y., Miksch, S., Johnson, P.: The Asgaard Project: A task-specific framework for the application and critiquing of time-oriented clinical guidelines. Artificial Intelligence in Medicine 14, 29–51 (1998)
3. Aigner, W., Kaiser, K., Miksch, S.: Visualization techniques to support authoring, execution, and maintenance of clinical guidelines. In: ten Teije, A., Lucas, P., Miksch, S. (eds.) Computer-Based Medical Guidelines and Protocols: A Primer and Current Trends, Health Technology and Informatics, pp. 140–159. IOS Press (2008)
4. Goldstine, H.H., von Neumann, J.: Planning and coding problems for an electronic computing instrument, part II, vol. 1, U.S. Ordinance Department (1947); Reprinted in von Neumann, J.: Collected Works, vol. 5, pp. 80–151. McMillian, New York (1963)
5. Hadorn, D.C.: Use of algorithms in clinical practice guideline development: Methodology perspectives. Clinical Practice Guideline Development: Methodology Perspectives 9(95), 93–104 (1995)
6. Petri, C.A.: Fundamentals of a theory of asynchronous information flow. In: Proceedings of IFIP Congress, vol. 62, pp. 386–390. North Holland Publ. Comp., Amsterdam (1963)
7. Shneiderman, B.: Tree visualization with tree-maps: 2-d space-filling approach. ACM Trans. Graph. 11(1), 92–99 (1992)
8. Combi, C., Portoni, L., Pinciroli, F.: Visualizing Temporal Clinical Data on the WWW. In: Horn, W., Shahar, Y., Lindberg, G., Andreassen, S., Wyatt, J.C. (eds.) AIMDM 1999. LNCS (LNAI), vol. 1620, pp. 301–314. Springer, Heidelberg (1999)
9. Plaisant, C., Mushlin, R., Snyder, A., Li, J., Heller, D., Shneiderman, B.: Lifelines: Using visualization to enhance navigation and analysis of patient records. In: Proceedings of the American Medical Informatics Association Fall Symposium (AMIA 1998), pp. 76–80 (1998)
10. Wang, T.D., Plaisant, C., Quinn, A., Stanchak, R., Shneiderman, B., Murphy, S.: Aligning temporal data by sentinel events: Discovering patterns in electronic health records. In: Proceedings of the ACM Conference on Human Factors in Computing Systems (CHI 2008), pp. 457–466 (2008)
11. Chittaro, L., Combi, C.: Visual Definition of Temporal Clinical Abstractions: A User Interface based on Novel Metaphors. In: Quaglini, S., Barahona, P., Andreassen, S. (eds.) AIME 2001. LNCS (LNAI), vol. 2101, pp. 227–230. Springer, Heidelberg (2001)

12. Chittaro, L., Combi, C., Trapasso, G.: Visual data mining of clinical databases: an application to the hemodialytic treatment based on 3d interactive bar charts. In: Proceedings of VDM 2002: 2nd International Workshop on Visual Data Mining, pp. 97–111 (2002)
13. Shahar, Y., Young, O., Shalom, E., Mayaffit, A., Moskovitch, R., Hessing, A., Galperin, M.: DEGEL: A Hybrid, Multiple-Ontology Framework for Specification and Retrieval of Clinical Guidelines. In: Dojat, M., Keravnou, E., Barahona, P. (eds.) AIME 2003. LNCS (LNAI), vol. 2780, pp. 122–131. Springer, Heidelberg (2003)
14. Gennari, J.H., Musen, M.A., Fergerson, R.W., Grosso, W.E., Crubézy, M., Eriksson, H., Noy, N.F., Tu, S.W.: The evolution of Protégé: An environment for knowledge-based systems development. International Journal of Human-Computer Studies 58, 89–123 (2002)
15. Steele, R., Fox, J.: Tallis PROforma Primer – introduction to PROforma language and software with worked examples. Technical report, Advanced Computation Laboratory, Cancer Research, London, UK (2002)
16. Terenziani, P., Montani, S., Bottrighi, A., Torchio, M., Molino, G., Correndo, G.: The GLARE approach to clinical guidelines: Main features. In: Kaiser, K., Miksch, S., Tu, S.W. (eds.) Computer-based Support for Clinical Guidelines and Protocols. Proceedings of the Symposium on Computerized Guidelines and Protocols (CGP 2004). Studies in Health Technology and Informatics, vol. 101, pp. 162–166. IOS Press, Prague (2004)
17. Quaglini, S., Stefanelli, M., Lanzola, G., Caporusso, V., Panzarasa, S.: Flexible guideline-based patient careflow systems. Artificial Intelligence in Medicine 22(1), 65–80 (2001)
18. Kosara, R., Miksch, S.: Metaphors of movement: A visualization and user interface for time-oriented, skeletal plans. Artificial Intelligence in Medicine, Special Issue: Information Visualization in Medicine 22(2), 111–131 (2001)
19. Aigner, W., Miksch, S.: Carevis: Integrated visualization of computerized protocols and temporal patient data. Artificial Intelligence in Medicine 37(3), 203–218 (2006)
20. Pavlopoulos, G., Soldatos, T., Barbosa-Silva, A., Schneider, R.: A reference guide for tree analysis and visualization. BioData Mining 3(1), 1 (2010)
21. Lamping, J., Rao, R., Pirolli, P.: A focus+context technique based on hyperbolic geometry for visualizing large hierarchies. In: Proceedings of the ACM Conference on Human Factors in Computing Systems, pp. 401–408 (1995)
22. Mendling, J., Reijers, H., van der Aalst, W.: Seven process modeling guidelines (7pmg). Information and Software Technology (IST) 52(2), 127–136 (2010)
23. Becker, J., Rosemann, M., von Uthmann, C.: Guidelines of Business Process Modeling. In: van der Aalst, W.M.P., Desel, J., Oberweis, A. (eds.) Business Process Management. LNCS, vol. 1806, pp. 30–49. Springer, Heidelberg (2000)
24. Reichert, M., Kolb, J., Bobrik, R., Bauer, T.: Enabling personalized visualization of large business processes through parameterizable views. In: Proceedings of the 27th Annual ACM Symposium on Applied Computing, SAC 2012, pp. 1653–1660. ACM, New York (2012)
25. Brewer, C.A.: Color Use Guidelines for Mapping and Visualization. In: MacEachren, A.M., Taylor, D.R.F. (eds.) Visualization in Modern Cartography, ch. 7, pp. 123–147. Elsevier Science, Tarrytown (1994)
26. Bergman, L., Rogowitz, B., Treinish, L.: A rule-based tool for assisting colormap selection. In: Proceedings of IEEE Visualization 1995, pp. 118–125 (1995)
27. Brewer, C.A.: Color use guidelines for data representation. In: Proceedings of the Section on Statistical Graphics, pp. 55–60. American Statistical Association, Baltimore (1999)
28. Harrower, M.A., Brewer, C.A.: Colorbrewer.org: An online tool for selecting color schemes for maps. The Cartographic Journal 40(1), 27–37 (2003)

Author Index